TWELFTH EDITION

Social Problems

Census Update

D. Stanley Eitzen
Colorado State University

Maxine Baca Zinn
Michigan State University

Kelly Eitzen Smith

Allyn & Bacon

Boston ▪ Columbus ▪ Indianapolis ▪ New York ▪ San Francisco ▪ Upper Saddle River
Amsterdam ▪ Cape Town ▪ Dubai ▪ London ▪ Madrid ▪ Milan ▪ Munich ▪ Paris ▪ Montreal ▪ Toronto
Delhi ▪ Mexico City ▪ Sao Paulo ▪ Sydney ▪ Hong Kong ▪ Seoul ▪ Singapore ▪ Taipei ▪ Tokyo

Publisher: Karen Hanson
Associate Editor: Mayda Bosco
Editorial Assistant: Christine Dore
Development Editor: Maggie Barbieri
Executive Marketing Manager: Kelly May
Marketing Assistant: Janeli Bitor
Media Editor: Thomas Scalzo
Production Editor: Pat Torelli
Manufacturing Buyer: Megan Cochran
Editorial Production and Composition Service: PreMediaGlobal
Photo Researcher: Katharine S. Cebik
Cover Designer: Kristina Mose-Libon

Credits appear on page 635, which constitutes an extension of the copyright page.

Cataloging-in-Publication Data unavailable at press time.

10 9 8 7 6 5 4 3 2 1 RRD-W 15 14 13 12 11

Allyn & Bacon
is an imprint of

www.pearsonhighered.com

ISBN 10: 0-205-17907-X
ISBN 13: 978-0-205-17907-7

BRIEF CONTENTS

CONTENTS

PART 5 INSTITUTIONAL PROBLEMS 392

CHAPTER 14 THE ECONOMY AND WORK 392

CHAPTER 15 FAMILIES 426

CHAPTER 16 EDUCATION 458

PART 6 SOLUTIONS 554

BOX FEATURES

Social Problems in Global Perspective

Social Policy

A Closer Look

Voices

Looking Toward the Future

Speaking to Students

PREFACE

Social Problems, twelfth edition, examines subjects such as corporate crime, racism, sexism, urban decay, poverty, health care, the changing economy, the politics of drugs, antigovernment movements, and terrorism. These topics are inherently interesting. The typical book on social problems describes these phenomena separately, using a variety of explanations. Students exposed to such a mélange of approaches might retain their interest in these problems, but they probably would complete the book with little grasp of how social problems are interrelated and of society's role in their creation and perpetuation. This book is different. The approach is consistently sociological. There is a coherent framework from which to analyze and understand society's social problems.

Our overarching goal in *Social Problems,* twelfth edition, is to capture the imaginations of our readers. We want them not only to be interested in the topics but also to become enthusiastic about exploring the intricacies and mysteries of social life. We want them, moreover, to incorporate the sociological perspective (imagination) into their explanatory repertoire. The sociological perspective requires, at a minimum, acceptance of two fundamental assumptions. The first is that individuals are products of their social environment. Who they are, what they believe, what they strive for, and how they feel about themselves are all dependent on other people and on the society in which they live. The incorporation of the sociological perspective requires that we examine the structure of society to understand such social problems as racism, poverty, and crime. This method, however, runs counter to the typical explanations people offer for social ills. The choice is seen in an example supplied by Thomas Szasz:

> *Suppose that a person wishes to study slavery. How would he go about doing so? First, he might study slaves. He would then find that such persons are generally brutish, poor, and uneducated, and he might conclude that slavery is their "natural" or appropriate social status. . . . Another student "biased" by contempt for the institution of slavery might proceed differently. He would maintain that there can be no slave without a master holding him in bondage; and he would accordingly consider slavery a type of human relationship and, more generally, a social institution supported by custom, law, religion, and force. From this point of view, the study of masters is at least as relevant to the study of slavery as is the study of slaves.* (Szasz 1970:123–124)

Most of us, intuitively, would make the first type of study and reach a conclusion. This book, however, emphasizes the second type of study: looking at "masters" as well as "slaves." An observer cannot gain an adequate understanding of racism, crime, poverty, or other social problems by studying only bigots, criminals, and the affluent. Therefore, we focus on the social structure to determine the underlying features of the social world in an effort to understand social problems.

Because our emphasis is on social structure, the reader is required to accept another fundamental assumption of the sociological perspective (see Eitzen, Baca Zinn, and Smith 2010). We refer to the adoption of a critical stance toward all social forms. Sociologists must ask these questions: How does the social system really work? Who has the power? Who benefits under the existing social arrangements, and who does not? We should also ask questions such as, Is the law neutral? Why are some drugs illegal and others, known to be harmful, legal? Why are so few organizations in the United States—which is characterized as a democracy—democratic? Is U.S. society a meritocratic one in which talent and effort combine to stratify people fairly? Questions such as these call into question existing myths, stereotypes, and official dogma. The critical examination of society demystifies and demythologizes. It sensitizes the individual to the inconsistencies present in society. But, most important, a critical stance toward social arrangements allows us to see their role in perpetuating social problems. In conclusion, the reader should be aware that we are not dispassionate observers of social problems.

Let us, then, briefly make our values more explicit. We oppose social arrangements that prevent people from developing to their full potential. That is, we reject political and social repression, educational elitism, institutional barriers to racial and sexual equality, economic exploitation, and official indifference to human suffering. Stating these feelings positively, we favor equality of opportunity, the right to dissent, social justice, an economic system that minimizes inequality, and a political system that maximizes citizen input in decisions and provides for an adequate health care system and acceptable living conditions for all people. Obviously, we believe that U.S. society as currently organized falls short of what we consider to be a good society. The problem areas of U.S. society are the subjects of *Social Problems,* twelfth edition. So, too, are structural arrangements around the globe that harm people.

In 2001, the Colorado Commission on Higher Education (a state oversight commission appointed by the governor) commissioned a conservative watchdog group to evaluate teacher education programs in the state universities of Colorado. The report criticized the University of Colorado's school of education for pushing an agenda that "indoctrinates" students in issues of race, class, gender, and sexual orientation. David Saxe, the principal investigator of the report, said, "More than any other reviewed institution, CU's teacher education programs are the most politically correct and stridently committed to the social justice model" (quoted in Curtin 2001:1B). Suffice it to say that our approach to social problems would also be castigated by Mr. Saxe, for we are absolutely committed to social justice; and this means, among other things, understanding how many social problems of U.S. society are rooted in the hierarchical arrangements based on class, race, gender, and sexuality.

New to This Edition

Since the eleventh edition of *Social Problems* was published, certain events have shaken U.S. society, and important trends have become even more significant, making a major revision necessary. For example,

- The Iraq war is winding down while the Afghanistan war escalates. The U.S. budget for the military continues to rise. The terrorist threat remains with us, both from external and internal sources.

- World population continues to increase by about 76 million a year, almost all of the increase in poor countries. Put another way, 157 new people join the world's population every minute, 153 of them in developing countries.
- The U.S. population has moved past 300 million and will add another 120 million by 2050. At about 5 percent of the world's population, the United States has an enormous environmental footprint—emitting one-fourth of the world's greenhouse gases and using one-fourth of the world's resources.
- Non-Whites will be the numerical majority in the United States by 2042. Immigration increases racial/ethnic tensions in some parts of the nation.
- The election of Barack Obama in 2008, the first African American president, created a stir among certain groups, some because of his racial heritage, and some because of their fears of where the new president was leading the country.
- We are reminded daily of the cozy relationship between money and politics. The cost of the presidential and congressional elections in 2008 was $5.3 billion. Money pours into these campaigns from special interests, making democracy all the more tenuous. The Supreme Court decision in 2010 giving special interests the right to use unrestricted funds to influence elections exacerbates the undemocratic drift.
- Although some large cities in the United States are showing signs of vigor, most are troubled with growing dependent populations, shrinking job markets, increasing racial tensions, and declining economic resources to meet their problems.
- The economy continues its massive transformation from a manufacturing economy to one based on service/knowledge. This causes disruptions as some companies fail while others succeed. Globalization, with jobs and tasks moving outside the country, adds to the unemployment woes accompanying the economic transformation.
- The Great Recession hit in 2007 and caused havoc on Wall Street, Main Street, and in families. Unemployment rose precipitously. Wall Street tumbled. The value of housing dropped, causing bankruptcies and foreclosures.
- Government bailouts of the banks and recovery efforts such as an economic stimulus, plus the cost of conducting two wars, raised the national debt dramatically to $12.8 trillion by April 2010. This huge debt provided a rationale to limit government by reducing or eliminating social welfare programs.
- Responding to two major problems in the U.S. health delivery system: 47 million people are left out of it, and those included find it very expensive and inefficient, Congress passed health care reform with no Republican support and a divided citizenry.

This twelfth edition of *Social Problems* considers each of these important trends and events as well as others. The chapters on the economy and work, health care, and national security have been completely rewritten. Some of the topics new to this edition are:

- A section on sociological methods
- The Supreme Court decision giving corporations the right to unlimited spending to influence elections
- The use and misuse of the filibuster in the Senate
- The effects of the Great Recession on families
- The new homelessness

- The politics of health reform
- The strengths and weaknesses of the health reform legislation of 2010
- The Tea Party movement
- The threat of domestic terrorism
- The gridlock in Congress
- Race relations after the election of President Obama
- What it means to be White
- The gender shift in the U.S. workforce
- The debate over global warming and "climategate"
- Don't Ask, Don't Tell: Gays in the military
- The drug war on the U.S.–Mexico border
- The persistent problem of not enough jobs

Six types of panels are included:

- Voices panels provide the personal views of those affected by a social problem.
- A Closer Look elaborates on a topic in detail.
- Social Problems in Global Perspective panels illustrate how other societies deal with a particular social problem. This global emphasis is also evident in panels and tables that compare the United States with other nations on such topics as crime/incarceration, medical care, and education.
- Social Policy panels look at policy issues and highlight social policies that work to alleviate particular social problems.
- Looking Toward the Future panels examine the trends concerning the social problems under consideration at the beginning of a new millennium.
- Speaking to Students panels address issues especially pertinent to college students.

End-of-chapter pedagogy includes Chapter Reviews, Key Terms, and assignments for MySocLab.

In summary, this twelfth edition of *Social Problems* improves on the earlier editions by focusing more deliberately on five themes: (1) the structural sources of social problems; (2) the role of the United States in global social problems; (3) the centrality of class, race, gender, sexuality, and disability as sources of division, inequality, and injustice; (4) the critical examination of society; and (5) solutions to social problems.

Note on Language Usage

In writing this book, we have been especially sensitive to our use of language. Language is used to reflect and maintain the secondary status of social groups by defining them, diminishing them, trivializing them, or excluding them. For example, traditional English uses masculine words (*man, mankind, he*) to refer to people in general. Even in the ordering of *masculine* and *feminine* or of *Whites* and *Blacks* within the discussion, one category consistently preceding its counterpart subtly conveys the message that the one listed first is superior to the other. In short, our goal is to use language so that it does not create the impression that one social class, race, or gender is superior to any other.

The terms of reference for racial and ethnic categories are changing. Blacks increasingly use the term *African American,* and Hispanics often refer to themselves as *Latinos*. In *Social Problems,* Twelfth Edition, we use both of these terms for each social category because they often are used interchangeably in popular and scholarly discourse.

Also, we try to avoid the use of *America* or *American* society when referring to the United States. America should be used only in reference to the entire Western Hemisphere: North, Central, and South America (and then, in the plural, Americas). Its use as a reference to only the United States implies that the other nations of the Western Hemisphere have no place in our frame of reference.

Census Update

2010 Census Update Edition– Features fully updated data throughout the text–including all charts and graphs–to reflect the results of the 2010 Census.

A Short Introduction to the U.S. Census– A brief seven-chapter overview of the Census, including important information about the Constitutional mandate, research methods, who is affected by the Census, and how data is used. Additionally, the primer explores key contemporary topics such as race and ethnicity, the family, and poverty. The primer can be packaged at no additional cost, and is also available online in MySeachLab, as a part of MySocLab.

A Short Introduction to the U.S. Census Instructor's Manual with Test Bank– Includes explanations of what has been updated, in-class activities, homework activities, discussion questions for the primer, and test questions related to the primer.

MySocLab 2010 Census Update gives students the opportunity to explore 2010 Census methods and data and apply Census results in a dynamic interactive online environment. It includes a series of activities using 2010 Census results , video clips explaining and exploring the Census , primary source readings relevant to the Census, and an online version of the 2010 Census Update Primer

Supplements

Instructor's Manual and Test Bank (ISBN 0205842445): Each chapter in the Instructor's Manual includes the following resources: Chapter Summary, New to This Chapter, Chapter Outline, Learning Objectives, Critical Thinking Questions, Activities for Classroom Participation, and Suggested Films. Designed to make your lectures more effective and to save preparation time, this extensive resource gathers together useful activities and strategies for teaching your Social Problems course.

Also included in this manual is a test bank of over 1,500 multiple-choice, true/false, and essay questions. The Instructor's Manual and Test Bank is available to adopters at www.pearsonhighered.com.

MyTest (ISBN 0205842437): This computerized software allows instructors to create their own personalized exams, to edit any or all of the existing test questions, and to add new questions. Other special features of this program include random generation of test questions, creation of alternate versions of the same test, scrambling question sequence, and test preview before printing. For easy access, this software is available within the instructor section of the MySocLab for *Social Problems,* Twelfth Edition, or at www.pearsonhighered.com.

TestGen (ISBN 0205085059): This computerized software allows instructors to create their own personalized exams, to edit any or all test questions, and to add new questions. Other special features of this program include random generation of an item set, creation of alternate versions of the same test, scrambling question sequence, and test preview before printing.

PowerPoint Presentations (ISBN 0205842402): The PowerPoint presentations for *Social Problems,* Twelfth Edition, are informed by instructional and design theory. You have the option in every chapter of choosing from any of the following types of slides: Lecture & Line Art, Clicker Response System, and/or Special Topics PowerPoints. The Lecture PowerPoint slides follow the chapter outline and feature images from the textbook integrated with the text. The Clicker Response System allows you to get immediate feedback from your students regardless of class size. The Special Topics PowerPoint slides allow you to integrate rich supplementary material into your course with minimal preparation time. Additionally, all of the PowerPoints are uniquely designed to present concepts in a clear and succinct way. They are available to adopters at www.pearsonhighered.com.

MySocLab (ISBN with eBook 0205013791, without eBook 0205016359)

MySocLab is a state-of-the-art interactive and instructive solution for the Social Problems course, designed to be used as a supplement to a traditional lecture course, or to completely administer an online course. MySocLab provides access to a wealth of resources all geared to meet the individual teaching and learning needs of every instructor and every student.

Combining an eBook, streaming audio files of the chapters, video and audio-based activities, interactive flash cards, practice tests and exams, research support, and a guide for improving writing skills, and more, MySocLab engages students by giving them the opportunity to explore important sociological concepts, and enhance their performance in this course.

Three of the exciting new features of MySocLab are Social Explorer, MySocLibrary, and Core Concepts in Sociology Videos. Social Explorer provides easy access to U.S. Census data from 1790 to the present, and allows for exploration of Census data visually through interactive data maps. MySocLibrary includes over 100 classic and contemporary readings, all with assessments, and linked to the specific text in use. Core Concepts in Sociology videos feature sociologists in action, exploring important concepts in Sociology. Each video is accompanied by a short quiz.

MySocLab is available at no additional cost to the student when an access code card is packaged with a new text. It can also be purchased separately. Visit www.mysoclab.com for more information.

Acknowledgments

We want to thank the following reviewers for their helpful comments:

Payton Andrews, Cape Fear Community College
Ernestine Avila, California State University, San Bernardino
Leonard Beeghley, University of Florida
Moshe ben Asher, California State University, Northridge
Deva Chopyak, Cosmunes River College
Jesse Goldstein, Baruch College
Jeanne Humble, Bluegrass Community & Technical College

Gary Hytrek, California State University, Long Beach
Dana Mayhew, Bristol Community College
Adrienne Trier-Bieniek, Western Michigan University

Special thanks to our friend and longtime user of *Social Problems,* Laurel Davis-Delano, Springfield College, for her careful and helpful critiques of previous editions. Maxine Baca Zinn thanks Paula Miller in the Department of Sociology, Michigan State University, for research assistance.

It is the glory and the greatness of our tradition to speak for those who have no voice, to remember those who are forgotten, to respond to the frustrations and fulfill the aspirations of all Americans seeking a better life in a better land. We dare not forsake that tradition. . . . For all those whose cares have been our concern, the work goes on, the cause endures, the hope still lives, and the dream shall never die.

—Senator Edward Kennedy

PART 1 The Political Economy of Social Problems

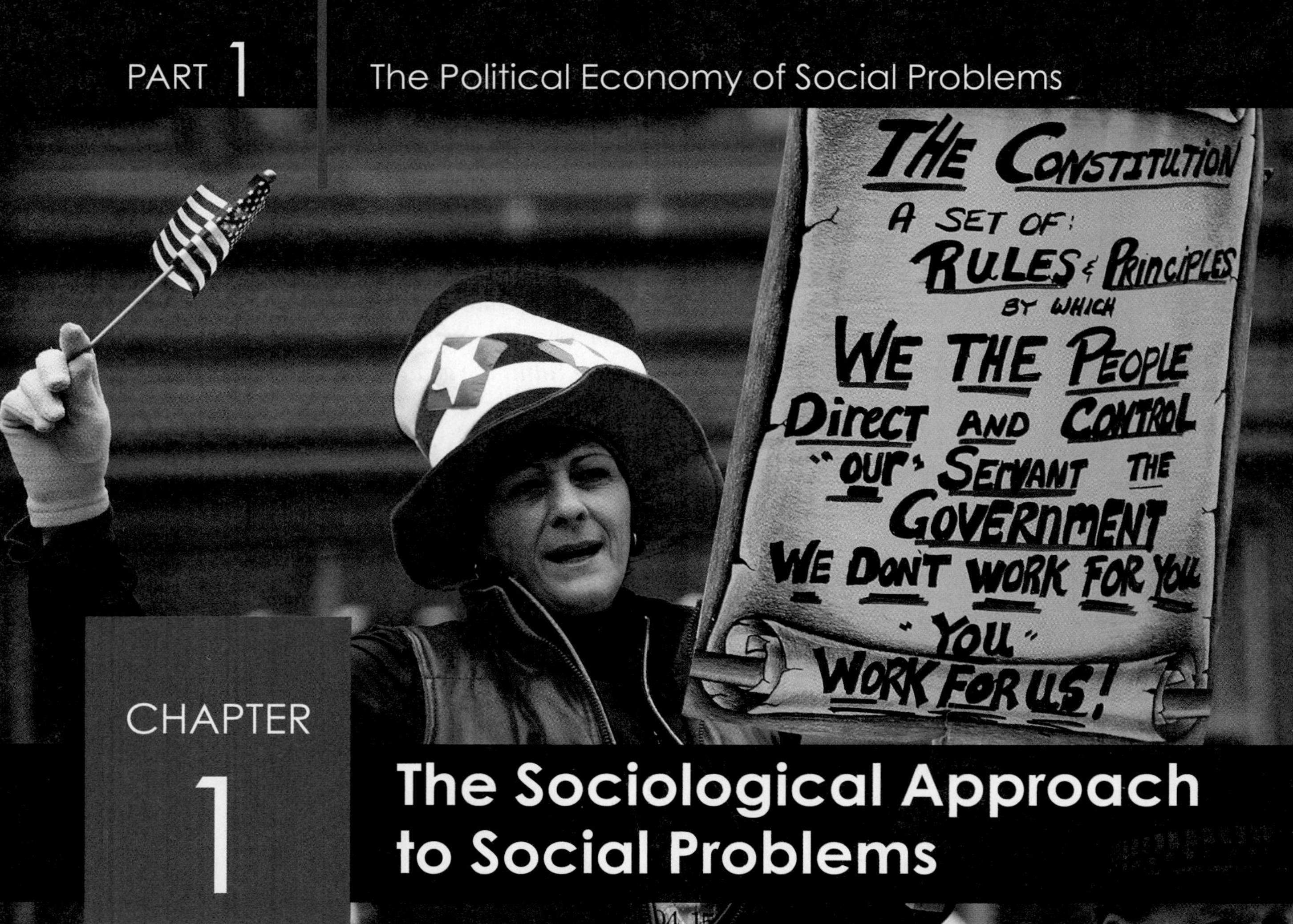

CHAPTER 1

The Sociological Approach to Social Problems

Our most serious problems are social problems for which there are no technical solutions, only human solutions.

—George E. Brown, Jr.

Time magazine declared the first decade of this century "the decade from Hell." "This decade was as awful as any peacetime decade in the nation's entire history" (Serwer, 2009:31). It was a decade defined by terror, war, natural disaster, economic boom and bust, fear, insecurity, division, the decline of the middle class, and the dimming of the American Dream. Here are some indicators of the increasing magnitude of social problems during this tumultuous decade (Serwer 2009; Meyerson, 2009; Hampson, 2009):

- The 2000 presidential election was the most divisive and confusing in American history, with George W. Bush elected, although he had 500,000 fewer votes than Al Gore.

- Islamic terrorists flew hijacked jets into the World Trade Center and the Pentagon, killing nearly 3,000.
- The United States invaded Afghanistan in 2001, and in 2002 Congress authorized military action against Iraq. These wars cost an estimated $2 trillion, the lives of over 5,000 Americans and unknown hundreds of thousands of Iraqis and Afghans, and further destabilized the Middle East.
- Hurricane Katrina ravaged the Gulf Coast in 2005, the largest natural disaster in United States history, causing 1,500 deaths, $100 billion in damages, and the displacement of hundreds of thousands of people. The levees protecting New Orleans were known to be inadequate before the hurricane, and they did not hold. The responses by the federal and state governments were woefully inadequate following the disaster.
- The stock market lost 26 percent during this decade (in 2008 alone, the Dow dropped 34 percent and the S & P 500 declined 38.5 percent, the worst declines since the 1930s).
- Unemployment more than doubled to 10 percent by the end of the decade. The net job creation for the decade was zero (in past decades the average job creation gain was 20 percent; Herbert 2010).
- The median household income dropped from $52,500 in 2000 to $50,303 in 2008 (the most recent available data).
- In 2000, 11.3 percent of Americans were living below the poverty line. By 2008, the rate was 13.2 percent.
- The percentage of Americans without health insurance rose from 13.7 percent to 15.4 percent.
- The housing bubble burst, leaving 23 percent of homeowners owing more than their mortgages were worth. Individual bankruptcies and foreclosures rose sharply.
- Many major corporations such as Kmart, United Airlines, Circuit City, Lehman Brothers, General Motors, and Chrysler went bankrupt.
- During the decade, the price of a barrel of oil went from $25 to $150 and ended 2009 above $70, straining the economy.

In sum, this was a decade of dramatic change, much of it negative. The United States experienced its worst attack by foreigners, its worst natural disaster, its most divisive election, and its worst economic downturn since the Great Depression, and it initiated two wars, both lasting longer than World War II.

This book explores the social problems brought to the fore in the last decade. Among other problems we will explore are the consequences of population growth and change.

The official population of the United States surpassed the 300 million mark at 7:46 a.m. EDT on October 17, 2006. In 2043, when the typical reader of this text is about 52 years old, it is estimated that the United States will have added another 100 million people, reaching 400 million. What will life in the United States be like when you reach middle age with that added 100 million? Will the problems of today be eliminated or reduced, or will they have worsened? Consider these issues:

Immigration and the browning of America. Immigration from Latin America and Asia is fueling the population growth. About half of the last 100 million Americans are immigrants and their U.S.-born children. Half of the next 100 million will be immigrants or their children. Without them, the

Immigration, especially illegal immigration, is fueling ethnic animosity in some areas of the United States.

Latino population would total 16 million instead of 44 million today, and Asian Americans would number 2 million, not 13 million (Samuelson 2006). By 2043, the race/ethnicity mix will be such that non-Whites will surpass Whites as the numerical majority. The increasing numbers of non-Whites will likely fuel racial/ethnic unrest among them as they experience discrimination and low-paying, demeaning jobs and among the native-born, who fear that the low wages of recent immigrants either take away their jobs or keep their wages low. With the additional millions of immigrants added in the coming decades, previously White rural areas and small towns will begin to deal with the challenges of new ethnic and racial residents.

The graying of America. After 2030, one of five U.S. residents will be at least 65 (similar to the proportion in Florida today). The increase in the number of elderly will cause problems with funding Social Security and Medicare, placing a greater burden on the young to support the elderly through these programs. This divide between workers who support the old with payroll taxes will have a racial, as well as a generational, dimension because the workers will be increasingly people of color and the elderly overwhelmingly White (Harden, 2006).

The inequality gap. Today the wealth and income of the affluent increases while the income of workers languishes. The inequality gap now is at record levels, resulting in a diminished middle class. In the words of Bill Moyers,

> *As great wealth is accumulated at the top, the rest of society has not been benefiting proportionately. In 1960 the gap between the top 20 percent and the bottom 20 percent was 30-fold. Now it is 75-fold. Thirty years ago the average annual compensation of the top 100 chief executives in the country was 30 times the pay of the average worker. Today it is 1,000 times the pay of the average worker. A recent article in* The Financial Times *reports on a study by the American economist Robert J. Gordon, who finds "little long-term change in workers' share of U.S. income over the past half century." Middle-ranking Americans are being squeezed, he says,*

"Where did we go wrong?"

because the top 10 percent of earners have captured almost half the total income gains in the past four decades and the top 1 percent have gained the most of all— "more in fact, than all the bottom 50 percent." (Moyers 2006:2)

Globalization and the transformation of the economy. The U.S. economy has undergone a dramatic shift from one dominated by manufacturing to one now characterized by service occupations and the collection, storage, and dissemination of information. As a result of this transformation, relatively well-paid employment in manufacturing products such as automobiles has dwindled and been replaced with jobs in lower-paying service industries. Most of the manufacturing is now done in foreign countries where U.S. corporations produce the same products but with cheaper labor, lower taxes, and fewer governmental controls. Some services, such as research, accounting, and call centers, have also been transferred to overseas companies to increase profits. Currently, these trends have negatively affected U.S. workers by making their jobs more insecure and reducing or eliminating their benefits.

In the coming decades, as 100 million people are added and new technologies enhancing globalization are developed, will the working conditions and standard of living of U.S. workers decline or be enhanced?

The plight of the poor. One of eight Americans is poor. Some 35.9 million Americans received food stamps in 2009, up from 29.1 million a year earlier. Emergency food requests and people seeking emergency shelter are increasing. Some 46.3 million Americans in 2008 were without health insurance, including one in five workers and 7.3 million children. The government considers those with incomes at or below 50 percent of the poverty level to be "severely poor." In 2008, 17.1 million Americans were in this category. Two factors lead to the speculation that the needs of the poor will not be met satisfactorily in the future. First, the trend is for the federal government to reduce "safety net" programs to help the poor,

A CLOSER LOOK

THE HEALTH OF WOMEN AND THEIR CHILDREN

International Comparisons

A few days before Mother's Day 2009, a global relief and development organization, Save the Children, published its "State of the World's Mothers," ranking twenty-six developed nations and ninety-nine countries in the developing world on ten measures related to the health of women and their children, their education, and their political status. Sweden ranked number one as the best place to be a mother, and the United States ranked twenty-seventh. The six indicators of mothers' well-being are lifetime risk of maternal mortality, percentage of women using modern contraception, percentage of births attended by skilled personnel, percentage of pregnant women with anemia, adult female literacy rate, and participation of women in national government. Among the factors affecting the placement of the United States were the following:

- The U.S. rate of lifetime maternal mortality was 1 in 4,800, compared to 1 in 17,400 for Sweden.
- The United States ranked eighth in under 5 mortality rate per 1,000 live births.
- The United States also lags in the political status of women. Only 17 percent of seats in the U.S. national government were held by women, compared to 47 percent in Sweden, 42 percent in Finland, 41 percent in the Netherlands, 38 percent in Denmark, 37 percent in Finland, and 36 percent in Norway and Spain.
- The United States has a female life expectancy of 81 years. Eighteen nations have a higher life expectancy for women, led by Japan with 86 years.

Source: State of the World's Mothers. 2009. Save the Children, London, UK (May).

such as welfare to single mothers, nutrition programs, Head Start, and the like. Moreover, the national minimum wage was only $7.25 an hour in 2009.

The environmental impact. Currently, the United States, at about 4.5 percent of the world's population, consumes one-fourth of the world's energy, most particularly oil, and is the world's greatest producer of greenhouse gases that result in global warming. More people means more traffic congestion, more suburban sprawl, and more landfills. Population growth means greater demand for food, water, fossil fuels, timber, and other resources. At present, land is being converted for development (housing, schools, shopping centers, roads) at about twice the rate of population growth: about 3,000 acres of farmland are converted to nonagricultural uses daily, up 20 percent from 20 years ago (Knickerbocker 2006). Pollution has made more than 40 percent of the rivers and lakes unsuitable for fishing or swimming (Markham 2006). Adding another 100 million people with today's habits (large houses, gas-guzzling transportation, suburban sprawl, and the consumption of products designed to be obsolete) will lead to an ecological wasteland. But perhaps recognition of the negative environmental impacts of current usage patterns will lead to our reducing waste, finding alternative energy sources, making greater use of mass transit, increasing housing density, and finding other ways to sustain and even enhance the environment. Richard Stengel, managing editor of *Time* put it this way:

> *In America, we have always done Big well—big cars, big screens, Big Macs; we're the supersize nation. But now we are being challenged to trade Big for Smart.*

Developers are building greener buildings, scientists talk of a 100-m.p.g. car, Wal-Mart is testing the use of solar panels. We need to continue growing but in smarter and more sustainable ways. (Stengel 2006:8)

At the global level, the earth is warming because of human activities, most prominently the use of oil and other carbons. Global warming will have disastrous effects during this century—coastal flooding, shifting agricultural patterns, violent weather, spread of tropical diseases, and loss of biodiversity, to name a few. The United States is the primary user of petrochemicals, and China will surpass it around 2025.

The growing global inequality. While the United States' population increases by 100 million before midcentury, the world will grow by 50 percent, adding 3 billion (for a total of 9 billion) people. Almost all this growth (the United States is the exception) will occur among the poorest nations. Today, an estimated 1.1 billion people are undernourished. Most do not have clean water and adequate sanitation. Half of the world's people live on less than $2 a day, one-sixth on less than $1 a day. Hundreds of millions are ravaged by diseases such as malaria, chronic diarrhea, Ebola, dengue, and parasites. At the other extreme, the richest nations live lavish lifestyles, consuming and wasting most of the world's resources. Multinational corporations profit from exploiting the resources and labor of the poorest countries. This gap between the fortunate few and the impoverished, desperate masses continues to widen.

The underdeveloped world, already in dire straits, will face enormous obstacles in providing the minimum of food, water, housing, and medical attention for their peoples as they add billions in population. The result will be ever-greater numbers of desperate people on this planet, making the world less safe. Unless the affluent nations and international organizations make structural changes to aid the underdeveloped countries, conflicts over scarce resources will increase, as will sectarian and tribal violence and acts of terrorism.

An increasingly dangerous world. September 11, 2001, unleashed a chain of negative events. Those terrorist acts on the World Trade Center and the Pentagon caused death and destruction and redirected government policies. The United States responded with a war on Al-Qaeda in Afghanistan and a preemptive war on Iraq, presumably to squelch terrorism and spread democracy throughout the Middle East. To fight the war on terror, the United States suspended the civil rights of prisoners, including their protection from the use of techniques that many would define as torture, and spied on American citizens. Suicide bombers (the "guided missiles" of the militarily weak) have destabilized the Middle East and threaten terror worldwide. There is the growing threat of nuclear proliferation, with North Korea joining the nuclear club in 2006 and Iran threatening to join the club soon. As the world's population soars, with its consequent poverty, hunger, disease, and political chaos, the United States will be increasingly unsafe. Will we face these incredible problems and find solutions? That is the ultimate question.

These issues highlight the social problems addressed in this book. Although the focus is on the dark side of social life, our hope is that readers will find this exploration intriguing, insightful, and useful.

HISTORY OF SOCIAL PROBLEMS THEORY

Typically, social problems have been thought of as social situations that a large number of observers felt were inappropriate and needed remedying. Early U.S. sociologists applied a medical model to the analysis of society to assess whether some pathology was present. Using what were presumed to be universal criteria of normality, sociologists commonly assumed that social problems resulted from "bad" people—maladjusted people who were abnormal because of mental deficiency, mental disorder, lack of education, or incomplete socialization. These social pathologists, because they assumed that the basic norms of society are universally held, viewed social problems as behaviors or social arrangements that disturb the moral order. For them, the moral order of U.S. society defined such behaviors as alcoholism, suicide, theft, and murder as social problems. But this approach did not take into account the complexity inherent in a diverse society.

In a variation of the absolutist approach, sociologists in the 1920s and 1930s focused on the conditions of society that fostered problems. Societies undergoing rapid change from the processes of migration, urbanization, and industrialization were thought to have pockets of social disorganization. Certain areas of the cities undergoing the most rapid change, for example, were found to have disproportionately high rates of vice, crime, family breakdowns, and mental disorders.

In the past few decades, many sociologists have returned to a study of problem individuals—deviants who violate the expectations of society. The modern study of deviance developed in two directions. The first sought the sources of deviation within the social structure. Sociologists saw deviance as the result of conflict between the culturally prescribed goals of society (such as material success) and the obstacles to obtaining them that some groups of people face. The other, of relatively recent origin, has focused on the role of society in creating and sustaining deviance through labeling those people viewed as abnormal. Societal reactions are viewed as the key in determining what a social problem is and who is deviant.

Most recently, some sociologists have tried to alert others to the problematic nature of social problems themselves (see Spector and Kitsuse 1987). These theorists emphasize the **subjective nature of social problems**. They say that what is defined as a social problem differs by audience and by time. Pollution, for example, has not always been considered a social problem. This perspective also examines how particular phenomena come to be defined as social problems, focusing on how groups of people actively influence those definitions.

This brief description reveals several issues that must be addressed in looking at social problems. First, sociologists have difficulty agreeing on an adequate definition of social problems. Second, there is continuing debate over the unit of analysis: Is the focus of inquiry individuals or social systems? Related to the latter is the issue of numbers: How many people have to be affected before something is a social problem? In this regard, C. Wright Mills (1962) made an important distinction: If a situation such as unemployment is a problem for an individual or for scattered individuals, it is a "private trouble." But if unemployment is widespread, affecting large numbers of people in a region or the society, it is a "public issue" or a "social problem."

TOWARD A DEFINITION OF SOCIAL PROBLEMS

There is an **objective reality of social problems**: there are conditions in society (such as poverty and institutional racism) that induce material or psychic suffering for certain segments of the population; there are sociocultural phenomena that prevent a significant number of societal participants from developing and using their full potential; there are discrepancies between what a country such as the United States is supposed to stand for (equality of opportunity, justice, democracy) and the actual conditions in which many of its people live; and people are fouling their own nest through pollution and the indiscriminate use of natural resources (Eitzen 1984). This normative approach assumes that some kinds of actions are likely to be judged deleterious in any context. Therefore, one goal of this book is to identify, describe, and explain situations that are objective social problems.

There are several dangers, however, in defining social problems objectively. The most obvious is that subjectivity is always present. To identify a phenomenon as a problem implies that it falls short of some standard. But what standards are to be used? Will the standards of society suffice? In a pluralistic society such as the United States, there is no uniform set of guidelines. People from different social strata and other social locations (such as region, occupation, race, and age) differ in their perceptions of what a social problem is and, once defined, how it should be solved. Is marijuana use a social problem? Is pornography? Is the relatively high rate of military spending a social problem? Is abortion a social problem? There is little consensus in U.S. society on these and other issues. All social observers, then, must be aware of differing viewpoints and respect the perspectives of the social actors involved.

In looking for objective social problems, we must also guard against the tendency to accept the definitions of social problems provided by those in power. Because the powerful—the agencies of government, business, and the media—provide the statistical data (such as crime rates), they may define social reality in a way that manipulates public opinion, thereby controlling behaviors that threaten the status quo (and their power). The congruence of official biases and public opinion can be seen in several historical examples. Slavery, for instance, was not considered a social problem by the powerful in the South, but slave revolts were. In colonial New England, the persecution of witches was not a social problem, but the witches were (Szasz 1970). Likewise, racism was not a social problem of the Jim Crow South, but "pushy" Blacks were. From the standpoint of U.S. public opinion, dispossessing Native Americans of their lands was not a social problem, but the Native Americans who resisted were.

Thus, to consider as social problems only those occurrences so defined by the public is fraught with several related dangers. First, to do so may mean overlooking conditions that are detrimental to a relatively powerless segment of the society. In other words, deplorable conditions heaped on minority groups tend to be ignored as social problems by the people at large. If sociologists accept this definition of social problems as their sole criterion, they have clearly taken a position that supports existing inequities for minority groups.

Second, defining social problems exclusively through public opinion diverts attention from what may constitute the most important social problem: the existing social order (Liazos 1972). If defined only through public opinion, social problems are limited to behaviors and actions that disrupt the existing social order. From this perspective, social problems are manifestations of the behaviors of abnormal people, not of society; the inadequacies and inequalities perpetuated by the existing system are not questioned. The distribution of power, the system of justice, how children are educated—to name but a few aspects of the existing social order—are assumed to be proper by most of the public, when they may be social problems themselves. As Skolnick and Currie noted,

> *Conventional social problems writing invariably returns to the symptoms of social ills, rather than the source; to criminals, rather than the law; to the mentally ill, rather than the quality of life; to the culture of the poor, rather than the predations of the rich; to the "pathology" of students, rather than the crisis of education. (Skolnick and Currie 1973:13)*

By overlooking institutions as a source of social problems (and as problems themselves), observers disregard the role of the powerful in society. To focus exclusively on those who deviate—the prostitute, the delinquent, the drug addict, the criminal—excludes the unethical, illegal, and destructive actions of powerful individuals, groups, and institutions in U.S. society and ignores the covert institutional violence brought about by racist and sexist policies, unjust tax laws, inequitable systems of health care and justice, and exploitation by the corporate world (Liazos 1972).

TYPES OF SOCIAL PROBLEMS

This book examines two main types of social problems: (1) acts and conditions that violate the norms and values present in society and (2) societally induced conditions that cause psychic and material suffering for any segment of the population.

Norm Violations

Sociologists are interested in the discrepancy between social standards and reality for several reasons. First, this traditional approach directs attention to society's failures: the criminals, the mentally ill, the school dropouts, and the poor. Sociologists have many insights that explain the processes by which individuals experience differing pressures to engage in certain forms of deviant behavior because of their location in the social structure (social class, occupation, age, race, and role) and in space (region, size of community, and type of neighborhood). A guiding assumption of our inquiry here, however, is that norm violators are symptoms of social problems, not the disease itself. In other words, most deviants are victims and should not be blamed entirely by society for their deviance; rather, the system they live in should be blamed. A description of the situations affecting deviants (such as the barriers to success faced by minority group members) helps explain why some categories of persons participate disproportionately in deviant behavior.

Another reason for the traditional focus on norm violation is that deviance is culturally defined and socially labeled. The sociologist is vitally interested in the social and cultural processes that label some acts and persons as deviant and others as normal. Because by definition some social problems are whatever the public determines, social problems are inherently relative. Certain behaviors are labeled as social problems, whereas other activities (which by some other criteria would be a social problem) are not. People on welfare, for example, are generally considered to constitute a social problem, but slumlords are not; people who hear God talking to them are considered schizophrenic, but people who talk to God are believed perfectly sane; murder is a social problem, but killing the enemy during wartime is rewarded with medals; a prostitute is punished, but the client is not; aliens entering the country illegally constitute a social problem and are punished, but their U.S. employers are not. The important insight here is that "deviance is not a property *inherent* in certain forms of behavior; it is a property *conferred upon* these forms by the audiences which directly or indirectly witness them" (Schur 1971:12). The members of society, especially the most powerful members, determine what is a social problem and what is not.

Powerful people play an important role in determining who gets the negative label and who does not. Because there is no absolute standard that informs citizens of what is deviant and what is not, our definition of deviance depends on what behaviors the law singles out for punishment. Because the law is an instrument of those in power, acts that are labeled deviant are so labeled because they conflict with the interests of those in power. Thus, to comprehend the labeling process, we must understand not only the norms and values of the society but also what interest groups hold the power (Quinney 1970).

Social Conditions

The second type of social problem emphasized in this text involves conditions that cause psychic and material suffering for some category of people in the United States. Here, the focus is on how the society operates and who benefits and who does not under existing arrangements. In other words, what is the bias of the system? How are societal rewards distributed? Do some categories of persons suffer or profit because of how schools are organized or juries selected, because of the seniority system used by industries, or because of how health care is delivered? These questions direct attention away from individuals who violate norms and toward society's institutions as the generators of social problems.

Social problems of this type generate individual psychic and material suffering. Thus, societal arrangements can be organized in a way that is unresponsive to many human needs. As a benchmark, let us assume, with Abraham Maslow, that all human beings have a set of basic needs in common: the fundamental needs for shelter and sustenance, security, group support, esteem, respect, and **self-actualization** (the need for creative and constructive involvement in productive, significant activity; Maslow 1954). When these needs are thwarted,

> *individuals will be hostile to society and its norms. Their frustration will be expressed in withdrawal, alcohol or other drugs, or in the violence of crime, terrorism, and aggression. People will take up lives outside of the pale of social control and normative structure; in so doing they will destroy themselves and others. They will rightly be condemned as "bad" people, but* this is so because they have lived in bad societies. *(Doyle and Schindler 1974:6; emphasis added)*

When health care is maldistributed, when poverty persists for millions, when tax laws permit a business to write off 50 percent of a $100 luncheon but prohibit a truck driver from writing off a bologna sandwich, when government is run by the few for the benefit of the few, when businesses supposedly in competition fix prices to gouge the consumer, when the criminal justice system is biased against the poor and people of color, then society is permitting what is called **institutionalized deviance** (Doyle and Schindler 1974:13). Such a condition exists when the society and its formal organizations are not meeting the needs of individuals. But these conditions often escape criticism and are rarely identified as social problems. Instead, the focus has often been on individuals who vent their frustration in socially unacceptable ways. A major intent of this book is to view individual deviance as a consequence of institutionalized deviance.

In summary, here we consider **social problems** to be (1) societally induced conditions that cause psychic and material suffering for any segment of the population and (2) acts and conditions that violate the norms and values found in society. The distribution of power in society is the key to understanding these social problems. The powerless, because they are dominated by the powerful, are likely to be thwarted in achieving their basic needs (sustenance, security, self-esteem, and productivity). In contrast, the interests of the powerful are served because they control the mechanisms and institutions by which the perceptions of the public are shaped. By affecting public policy through reaffirming customs and through shaping the law and its enforcement, powerful interest groups are instrumental in designating (labeling) who is a problem (deviant) and who must be controlled. Our focus, then, is on the structure of society—especially on how power is distributed—rather than on "problem" individuals. Individual deviants are a manifestation of society's failure to meet their needs; the sources of crime, poverty, drug addiction, and racism are found in the laws and customs, the quality of life, the distribution of wealth and power, and the accepted practices of schools, governmental units, and corporations. As the primary source of social problems, society, not the individual deviant, must be restructured if social problems are to be solved. (See the panel titled "Social Problems in Global Perspective," which compares the United States with other nations on social problems, and the panel titled "Social Policy," which shows how societies can be designed to minimize social problems.)

THE SOCIOLOGICAL IMAGINATION

Sociology is the discipline that guides this inquiry into the sources and consequences of social problems. This scholarly discipline is the study of society and other social organizations, how they affect human behavior, and how these organizations are changed by human endeavors. C. Wright Mills (1916–1962), in his classic *The Sociological Imagination* (1959), wrote that the task of sociology is to realize that individual circumstances are inextricably linked to the structure of society. The **sociological imagination** involves several related components (Eitzen and Smith 2003:8):

- The sociological imagination is stimulated by a willingness to view the social world from the perspective of others.
- It involves moving away from thinking in terms of the individual and her or his problem and focusing rather on the social, economic, and historical circumstances that produce the problem. Put another way, the sociological imagination is the ability to see the societal patterns that influence individuals, families, groups, and organizations.
- Possessing a sociological imagination, one can shift from the examination of a single family to national budgets, from a poor person to national welfare

SOCIAL PROBLEMS IN GLOBAL PERSPECTIVE

SOCIAL WELFARE STATES: A MIXTURE OF CAPITALISM AND SOCIALISM

The nations of Western Europe, Scandinavia, and Canada have generous welfare policies for their citizens, certainly much more generous than those available in the United States (the description here is general, characterizing all the nations to a degree, although there are variations among them). These nations are capitalistic, permitting private property and privately owned businesses. To a much greater degree than in the United States, these nations have publicly owned enterprises and some nationalization of industry, typically transportation, mineral resources, and utilities.

Most important, these nations provide an array of social services to meet the needs of their citizens that is much greater than in the United States. These services include a greater subsidy to the arts (symphony orchestras, art exhibitions, artists, auditoriums), more public spaces (parks, public squares, recreation facilities), more resources for public libraries, universal preschool education, free public education through college, universal health insurance, housing subsidies to help low-income families, paid leave for new parents (mother and father), the provision of safe government child care facilities, extended unemployment benefits, paid vacations, and excellent retirement benefits, including paid long-term care if necessary.

These services are expensive, resulting in relatively high taxes, almost double the rate in the United States. But as Joe R. Feagin and Clairece Booher Feagin point out in their discussion of Sweden,

> If we were to add to the taxes Americans pay, the cost of the private medical insurance carried by many Americans . . . as well as the cost of medical care not covered by insurance and the cost of private social services such as day care centers, [the taxes of the social welfare states] and U.S. "taxes" are much more nearly equal. Much of what [they] pay for through the tax system, Americans buy, if they can get it at all, from private enterprise—and they often get less adequate health care, child care, and other services as a result. Indeed, Americans probably pay more per capita for all such support services than do [those in the social welfare states]—and Americans receive less. (Feagin, Feagin, and Baker 2006:483)

As a result of these extensive social services, the people in the social welfare states have several advantages over those living in the United States: longer life expectancy, lower infant and maternal mortality, greater literacy, less poverty and homelessness, lower rates of violent crime, a lower proportion of single-parent households, and a proportionately larger middle class.

Are the people in these countries less free than Americans? There is freedom of speech and freedom of the press in each of the nations. The governments in these countries, for the most part, permit greater individual freedom than is found in the United States for personal behaviors (greater acceptance of homosexuality, legalization of prostitution, few restrictions on abortion, and the like).

Is there a downside? These countries are not immune to economic problems such as recessions, high unemployment, and citizen unrest over high taxes. In the past few years, the governments in these countries have reduced some of their social programs, but they are still much more generous than the United States (which has also curbed its more meager welfare programs). Typically, government leaders in each of these countries have argued that more austere programs are needed to stimulate the economy and permit the government to pay its bills. These measures have been met with citizen protest, particularly from the labor unions, which are much stronger than in the United States. It will be interesting to see how reduction in the welfare state plays out. If the austerity measures hold, will the countries follow the U.S. example and become more unequal, experience increased social unrest, see a rise in social problems? Or, as conservatives argue, will more capitalism and less socialism make these nations more efficient and more prosperous?

SOCIAL POLICY

SOCIAL PROBLEMS AND SOCIAL POLICY

The political-social-economic system of a society does not simply evolve from random events and aimless choices. The powerful in societies craft policies to accomplish certain ends, within the context of historical events, budgetary constraints, and the like. Addressing the issue of inequality, Claude Fischer and his colleagues from the sociology department at the University of California–Berkeley say,

> The answer to the question of why societies vary in their structure of rewards is more political. In significant measure, societies choose the height and breadth of their "ladders." By loosening markets or regulating them, by providing services to all citizens or rationing them according to income, by subsidizing some groups more than others, societies, through their politics, build their ladders. To be sure, historical and external constraints deny full freedom of action, but a substantial freedom of action remains. . . . In a democracy, this means that the inequality Americans have is, in significant measure, the historical result of policy choices of Americans—or, at least, Americans' representatives. In the United States, the result is a society that is distinctly unequal. Our ladder is, by the standards of affluent democracies and even by the standards of recent American history, unusually extended and narrow—and becoming more so. (Fischer et al., 1996:8)

In other words, America's level of inequality is by design (Fischer et al., 1996:125).

Social policy is about design, about setting goals and determining the means to achieve them. Do we want to regulate and protect more, as the well-developed welfare states do, or should we do less? Should we create and invest in policies and programs that protect citizens from poverty, unemployment, and the high cost of health care, or should the market economy sort people into winners, players, and losers based on their abilities and efforts? Decision makers in the United States have opted to reduce the welfare state. Are they on the right track? Can those policies that the generous welfare states have adopted be modified to reduce the United States' social problems? If societies are designed, should the United States change its design?

Source: D. Stanley Eitzen. 2007. "U.S. Social Problems in Comparative Perspective." In D. Stanley Eitzen (Ed.), *Solutions to Social Problems: Lessons from Other Societies,* 4th ed. Boston: Allyn & Bacon, pp. 9–10.

policies, from an unemployed person to the societal shift from manufacturing to a service/knowledge economy, from a single mother with a sick child to the high cost of health care for the uninsured, and from a homeless family to the lack of affordable housing.

- To develop a sociological imagination requires a detachment from the taken-for-granted assumptions about social life, and establishing a critical distance (Andersen and Taylor 2000:10–11). In other words, one must be willing to question the structural arrangements that shape social behavior.

When we have this imagination, we begin to see the solutions to social problems not in terms of changing problem people but in changing the structure of society.

SOCIAL STRUCTURE AS THE BASIC UNIT OF ANALYSIS

There is a very strong tendency for individuals—laypeople, police officers, judges, lawmakers, and social scientists alike—to perceive social problems and prescribe remedies from an individualistic perspective. For example, they blame the individual for being poor, with no reference to the maldistribution of wealth and other

Are families to blame for their poverty or are the institutions of society to blame for their plight by not providing jobs, adequate wages, and health care?

socially perpetuated disadvantages that blight many families generation after generation; they blame African Americans for their aggressive behavior, with no understanding of the limits placed on social mobility for African Americans by the social system; they blame dropouts for leaving school prematurely, with no understanding that the educational system fails to meet their needs. This type of thinking helps explain the reluctance of people in authority to provide adequate welfare, health care, and compensatory programs to help the disadvantaged.

The fundamental issue is whether social problems emanate from the pathologies of individuals (**person-blame**) or from the situations in which deviants are involved (**system-blame**), that is, whether deviants are the problem itself or only victims of it. The answer no doubt lies somewhere between the two extremes, but because the individual- or victim-blamers have held sway, we should examine their reasoning (Ryan 1976).

Person-Blame Approach versus System-Blame Approach

Let us begin by considering some victims, such as the children in a slum school who constantly fail. Why do they fail? The victim-blamer points to their **cultural deprivation.*** They do not do well in school because their families speak different dialects, because their parents are uneducated, because they have not been exposed to the educational benefits available to middle-class children (such as visits to the zoo, computers in the home, extensive travel, attendance at cultural events, exposure to books). In other words, the defect is in the children and their families. System-blamers look elsewhere for the sources of failure. They ask, What is there about the schools that make slum children more likely to fail? The answer is found in the irrelevant curriculum, class-biased IQ

*Cultural deprivation is a loaded ethnocentric term applied by members of the majority to the culture of the minority group. It implies that the culture of the group in question is not only inferior but also deficient. The concept does remind us, however, that people can and do make invidious distinctions about cultures and subcultures. Furthermore, people act on these distinctions as if they were valid.

tests, the tracking system, overcrowded classrooms, differential allocation of resources within the school district, and insensitive teachers, whose low expectations for poor children create a self-fulfilling prophecy.

Ex-convicts constitute another set of victims. Why is their **recidivism** rate (reinvolvement in crime) so high? The victim-blamer points to the faults of individual criminals: their greed, their feelings of aggression, their weak control of impulse, their lack of conscience. The system-blamer directs attention to very different sources: the penal system, the scarcity of employment for ex-criminals, and even the schools. For example, 20 to 30 percent of inmates are functionally illiterate; that is, they cannot meet minimum reading and writing demands in U.S. society, such as filling out job applications. Yet these people are expected to leave prison, find a job, and stay out of trouble. Illiterate ex-criminals face unemployment or at best the most menial jobs, with low wages, no job security, and no fringe benefits. System-blamers argue that first the schools and later the penal institutions have failed to provide these people with the minimum requirements for full participation in society. Moreover, lack of employment and the unwillingness of potential employers to train functional illiterates force many to return to crime to survive.

The inner-city poor are another set of victims. The conditions of the ghetto poor, especially African Americans, have deteriorated since the mid-1960s. Some observers believe that this deterioration is the result of the transplantation of a southern sharecropper culture (Lemann, 1986), welfare programs (Murray, 1984), and laziness. The more compelling system-blame argument, however, is made by William J. Wilson (1987). He claims that the ghetto poor endure because of the disappearance of hundreds of thousands of low-skill jobs, those mainly involving physical labor, in the past 40 years or so. Wilson's contention, supported by research, is that the pathologies of the ghetto (such as teenage pregnancy, illegitimacy, welfare dependency, and crime) are fundamentally the consequence of too few jobs.

The strong tendency to blame social problems on individuals rather than on the social system lies in how people tend to look at social problems. Most people define a social problem as behavior that deviates from the norms and standards of society. Because people do not ordinarily examine critically the way things are done in society, they tend to question the exceptions. The system not only is taken for granted but also has, for most people, an aura of sacredness because of the traditions and customs with which they associate it. Logically, then, those who deviate are the source of trouble. The obvious question observers ask is, Why do these people deviate from norms? Because most people view themselves as law-abiding, they feel that those who deviate do so because of some kind of unusual circumstance, such as accident, illness, personal defect, character flaw, or maladjustment (Ryan 1976:10–18). The flaw, then, is a function of the deviant, not of societal arrangements.

Interpreting social problems solely within a person-blame framework has serious consequences. First, because societal causes are not addressed, social problems remain in place (Davis-Delano 2009). Second, it frees the government, the economy, the system of stratification, the system of justice, and the educational system from any blame:

> *[B]laming the poor [for example] is still easier than fixing what's really wrong with America: segregated schools, unjust wages, inadequate health care, and other such complicated matters. (Vogel 1994:31)*

This protection of the established order against criticism increases the difficulty of trying to change the dominant economic, social, and political institutions. A good example is the strategy social scientists use in studying the origins of poverty. Because the person-blamer studies the poor rather than the nonpoor, the system of inequality (buttressed by tax laws, welfare rules, and employment practices) goes unchallenged. A related consequence of the person-blame approach, then, is that the relatively well-off segments of society retain their advantages.

A social-control function of the person-blame approach is that troublesome individuals and groups are controlled in a publicly acceptable manner. Deviants—whether they are criminals, mentally ill, or social protesters—are incarcerated in prisons or mental hospitals and administered drugs or other forms of therapy. This approach not only directs blame at individuals and away from the system, but it also eliminates the problems (individuals).

A related consequence is how the problem is treated. A person-blame approach demands a person-change treatment program. If the cause of delinquency, for example, is defined as the result of personal pathology, then the solution must clearly lie in counseling, behavior modification, psychotherapy, drugs, or some other technique aimed at changing the individual deviant. The person-blame interpretation of social problems provides and legitimates the right to initiate person-change rather than system-change treatment programs. Under such a scheme, norms that are racist, sexist, or homophobic, for example, go unchallenged.

The person-blame ideology invites not only person-change treatment programs but also programs for person-control. The system-blamer would argue that this emphasis, too, treats the symptom rather than the disease.

A final consequence of a person-blame interpretation is that it reinforces social myths about the degree of control individuals have over their fate. It provides justification for a form of **social Darwinism**: that the placement of people in the stratification system is a function of their ability and effort. By this logic, the poor are poor because they are the dregs of society. In short, they deserve their fate, as do the successful in society. Thus, in this viewpoint, little sympathy exists for government programs to increase welfare to the poor. (See the insert on William Graham Sumner for an example of this ideology.)

Reasons for Focusing on the System-Blame Approach

We emphasize the system-blame approach in this book. We should recognize, however, that the system-blame orientation has dangers. First, it is only part of the truth. Social problems are highly complex phenomena that have both individual and systemic origins. Individuals, obviously, can be malicious and aggressive for purely psychological reasons. Clearly, society needs to be protected from some individuals. Moreover, some people require particular forms of therapy, remedial help, or special programs on an individual basis if they are to function normally. But much behavior that is labeled deviant is the end product of social conditions.

A second danger of a dogmatic system-blame orientation is that it presents a rigidly deterministic explanation of social problems. Taken too far, this position views individuals as robots controlled totally by their social environment. A balanced view acknowledges that human beings may choose between alternative courses of action. This issue raises the related question of the degree to

William Graham Sumner and Social Darwinism

William Graham Sumner (1840–1910), the sociologist who originated the concepts of folkways and mores, was a proponent of social Darwinism. This doctrine, widely accepted among elites during the late nineteenth and early twentieth centuries, was a distorted version of Charles Darwin's theory of natural selection. From this viewpoint, success is the result of being superior. The rich are rich because they deserve to be. By this logic, the poor also deserve their fate because they are biological and social failures and therefore unable to succeed in the competitive struggle.

Social Darwinism justified not only ruthless competition but also the perpetuation of the status quo. Superior classes, it was believed, should dominate because their members were unusually intelligent and moral. The lower classes, on the other hand, were considered inferior and defective. Their pathology was manifested in suicide, madness, crime, and various forms of vice.

On the basis of this philosophy, Sumner opposed social reforms such as welfare to the poor because they rewarded the unfit and penalized the competent. Such reforms, he argued, would interfere with the normal workings of society, halting progress and perhaps even contributing to a regression to an earlier evolutionary stage.

which people are responsible for their behavior. An extreme system-blame approach absolves individuals from responsibility for their actions. To take such a stance would be to argue that society should never restrict deviants; this view invites anarchy.

Despite these problems with the system-blame approach, it is the guiding perspective of this book for three reasons. First, because average citizens, police officers, legislators, social scientists, and judges tend to interpret social problems from an individualistic perspective, a balance is needed. Moreover, as noted earlier, a strict person-blame perspective has many negative consequences, and citizens must recognize these negative effects of their ideology.

A second reason for using the system-blaming perspective is that the subject matter of sociology is not the individual—who is the special province of psychology—but society. Because sociologists focus on the social determinants of behavior, they must make a critical analysis of the social structure. An important ingredient of the sociological perspective is the development of a critical stance toward social arrangements. Thus, the sociologist looks behind the facades to determine the positive and negative consequences of social arrangements. The sociologist's persistent questions must be, Who benefits under these arrangements? Who does not? For this reason, there should be a close fit between the sociological approach and the system-blaming perspective.

A final reason for the use of the system-blame approach is that the institutional framework of society is the source of many social problems (such as racism, pollution, unequal distribution of health care, poverty, and war). An exclusive focus on the individual ignores the strains caused by the inequities of the system and its fundamental intransigence to change. A guiding assumption of this book is that because institutions are made by human beings (and therefore are not sacred), they should be changed whenever they do not meet the needs of the people they were created to serve. As Skolnick and Currie stated,

Democratic conceptions of society have always held that institutions exist to serve people, and not vice versa. Institutions therefore are to be accountable to the people whose lives they affect. Where an institution—any institution, even the most "socially valued"—is found to conflict with human needs, democratic thought holds that it ought to be changed or abolished. (Skolnick and Currie 1973:15)

SOCIOLOGICAL METHODS: THE CRAFT OF SOCIOLOGY

The analysis of social problems depends on reliable data and logical reasoning. These necessities are possible, but some problems must be acknowledged. Before we describe how sociologists gather reliable data and make valid conclusions, let us examine the kinds of questions sociologists ask and the two major obstacles sociologists face in obtaining answers to these questions.

Sociological Questions

To begin, sociologists try to ascertain the facts. For example, let's assume that we want to assess the degree to which the public education system provides equal educational opportunities for all youngsters. To determine this, we need to conduct an empirical investigation to find the facts concerning such items as the amount spent per pupil by school districts within each state and by each state. Within school districts we need to know the facts concerning the distribution of monies by neighborhood schools. Are these monies appropriated equally, regardless of the social class or racial composition of the school? Are curriculum offerings the same for girls and boys within a school? Are extra fees charged for participation in extracurricular activities, and does this affect the participation of children by social class?

Sociologists also may ask comparative questions—that is, how does the situation in one social context compare with that in another? Most commonly, these questions involve the comparison of one society with another. Examples here might be the comparisons among industrialized nations on infant mortality, poverty, murder, leisure time, or the mathematics scores of sixteen-year-olds.

A third type of question that a sociologist may ask is historical. Sociologists are interested in trends. What are the facts now concerning divorce, crime, and political participation, for example, and how have these patterns changed over time? Figure 1.1 provides an example of a trend over time by examining the divorce rate in the United States from 1860 to 2005.

The three types of sociological questions considered so far determine the way things are. But these types of questions are not enough. Sociologists go beyond the factual to ask why. Why have real wages (controlling for inflation) declined since 1973 in the United States? Why are the poor, poor? Why do birthrates decline with industrialization? Why is the United States the most violent (as measured by murder, rape, and assault rates) industrialized society?

A **sociological theory** is a set of ideas that explains a range of human behavior and a variety of social and societal events. "A sociological theory designates those parts of the social world that are especially important, and offers ideas about how the social world works" (Kammeyer, Ritzer, and Yetman 1997:21). The late Michael Harrington said this regarding the necessity of theory: "The data of society are, for all practical purposes, infinite. You need criteria that will provisionally permit you to bring some order into that chaos of data and to distinguish

FIGURE 1.1
Annual Divorce Rates, United States, 1860–2005 (Divorces per Thousand Married Women Age 15 and Over)

Sources: Cherlin, Andrew J. *Marriage, Divorce, Remarriage.* Cambridge, MA: Harvard University Press, 1981, p. 22; Levitan, Sar A., Richard S. Belous, and Frank Gallo, *What's Happening to the American Family?* Rev. ed. Baltimore: Johns Hopkins University Press, 1988, p. 27; and current U.S. Census Bureau douments.

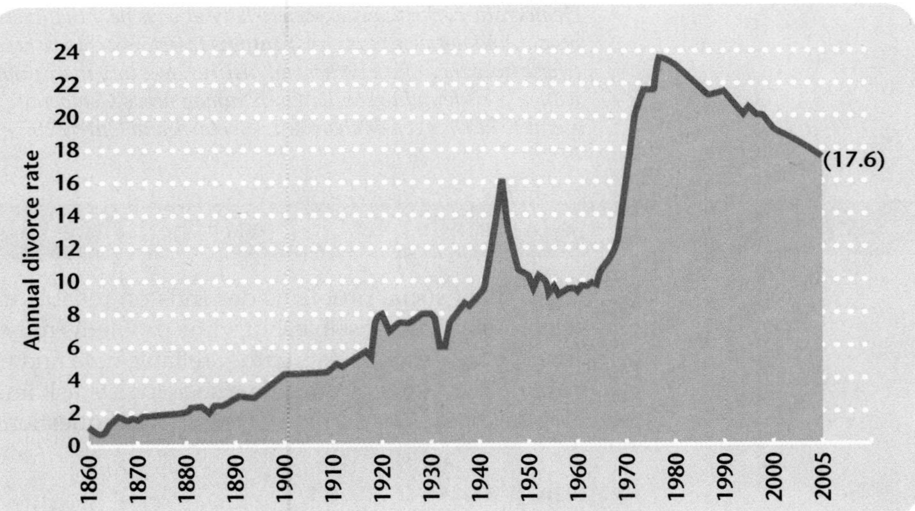

between relevant and irrelevant factors" (Harrington 1985:1). Thus, theory not only helps us to explain social phenomena, but it also guides research.

Problems in Collecting Data

A fundamental problem with the sociological perspective is that bane of the social sciences—objectivity. We are all guilty of harboring stereotyped conceptions of such social categories as Muslims, hard hats, professors, gays and lesbians, fundamentalists, business tycoons, socialists, the rich, the poor, and jocks. Moreover, we interpret events, material objects, and people's behavior through the perceptual filter of our religious and political beliefs. When fundamentalists oppose the use of certain books in school, when abortion is approved by a legislature, when the president advocates cutting billions from the federal budget by eliminating social services, or when the Supreme Court denies private schools the right to exclude certain racial groups, most of us rather easily take a position in the ensuing debate.

Sociologists are caught in a dilemma. On the one hand, they are members of society with beliefs, feelings, and biases. On the other hand, though, their professional task is to study society in a disciplined (scientific) way. This latter requirement is that scientist–scholars be dispassionate, objective observers. In short, if they take sides, they lose their status as scientists.

This ideal of value neutrality (to be absolutely free of bias in research) can be attacked from three positions. The first is that scientists should not be morally indifferent to the implications of their research. Alvin Gouldner has argued this in the following statement:

> *It would seem that social science's affinity for modeling itself after physical science might lead to instruction in matters other than research alone. Before Hiroshima, physicists also talked of a value-free science; they, too, vowed to make no value judgments. Today many of them are not so sure. If we today concern ourselves exclusively with the technical proficiency of our students and reject all responsibility for their moral sense, or lack of it, then we may someday be compelled to accept responsibility for having trained a generation willing to serve in a future Auschwitz.*

> *Granted that science always has inherent in it both constructive and destructive potentialities. It does not follow from this that we should encourage our students to be oblivious to the difference (Gouldner 1962:212).*

Or, put another way, this time by historian Howard Zinn, explaining his style of classroom teaching:

> *I would start off my classes explaining to my students—because I didn't want to deceive them—that I would be taking stands on everything. They would hear my point of view in this course, that this would not be a neutral course. My point to them was that in fact it was impossible to be neutral.* You Can't Be Neutral on a Moving Train *[the title of Zinn's memoir] means that the world is already moving in certain directions. Things are already happening. Wars are taking place. Children are going hungry. In a world like this—already moving in certain, often terrible directions—to be neutral or to stand by is to collaborate with what is happening (quoted in Barsamian 1997:37–38).*

The second argument against the purely neutral position is that such a stance is impossible. Howard Becker, among others, has argued that there is no dilemma—because it is impossible to do research that is uncontaminated by personal and political sympathies (Becker 1967; see also Gould 1998:19). This argument is based on several related assumptions. One is that the values of the scholar–researcher enter into the choices of what questions will be asked. For example, in the study of poverty, a critical decision involves the object of the study—the poor or the system that tends to perpetuate poverty among a certain segment of society. Or, in the study of the problems of youth, we can ask either of these questions: Why are some youths troublesome for adults? Or, Why do adults make so much trouble for youths? In both illustrations, quite different questions will yield very different results.

Similarly, our values lead us to decide from which vantage point we will gain access to information about a particular social organization. If researchers want to understand how a prison operates, they must determine whether they want a description from the inmates, from the guards, from the prison administrators, or from the state board of corrections. Each view provides useful insights about a prison, but obviously a biased one. If they obtain data from more than one of these levels, researchers are faced with making assessments of which is the more accurate view, clearly another place in the research process where the values of the observers have an impact.

Perhaps the most important reason why the study of social phenomena cannot be value free is that the type of problems researched and the strategies used tend either to support the existing societal arrangements or to undermine them. Seen in this way, social research of both types is political. Ironically, however, there is a strong tendency to label only the research aimed at changing the system as political. By the same token, whenever the research sides with the powerless, the implication is that the hierarchical system is being questioned—thus, the charge that this type of research is biased. Becker has provided us with the logic of this viewpoint:

> *When do we accuse ourselves and our fellow sociologists of bias? I think an inspection of representative instances would show that the accusation arises, in one important class of cases, when the research gives credence, in any serious way, to the perspective of the subordinate group in some hierarchical relationship. In the case of deviance, the hierarchical relationship is a moral one. The superordinate parties in the relationships are those who represent the forces of approved and official morality; the subordinate parties are those who, it is alleged, have violated that morality. . . . It is odd that, when*

> *we perceive bias, we usually see it in these circumstances. It is odd because it is easily ascertained that a great many more studies are biased in the direction of the interests of responsible officials than the other way around.* (Becker 1967:240, 242)

In summary, bias is inevitable in the study and analysis of social problems. The choice of a research problem, the perspective from which one analyzes the problems, and the solutions proposed all reflect a bias that either supports the existing social arrangements or does not. Moreover, unlike biologists, who can dispassionately observe the behavior of sperm and the egg at conception, sociologists are participants in the social life they seek to study and understand. As they study homelessness, poor children, or urban blight, sociologists cannot escape from their own feelings and values. They must, however, not let their feelings and values render their analysis invalid. In other words, research and reports of research must reflect reality, not as the researcher might want it to be. Sociologists must display scientific integrity, which requires recognizing biases in such a way that these biases do not invalidate the findings (Berger 1963:5). When research is properly done in this spirit, an atheist can study a religious sect, a pacifist can study the military-industrial complex, a divorced person can study marriage, and a person who abhors the beliefs of the Ku Klux Klan can study that organization and its members.

In addition to bias, people gather data and make generalizations about social phenomena in a number of faulty ways. In a sense, everyone is a scientist seeking to find valid generalizations to guide behavior and make sense of the world. But most people are, in fact, very unscientific about the social world. The first problem, as we have noted, is the problem of bias. The second is that people tend to generalize from their experience. Not only is one's interpretation of things that happen to him or her subjective, but there also is a basic problem of sampling. The chances are that one's experience will be too idiosyncratic to allow for an accurate generalization. For example, if you and your friends agree that abortion is appropriate, that does not mean that other people in the society, even those of your age, will agree with you. Very likely, your friends are quite similar to you on such dimensions as socioeconomic status, race, religion, and geographic location.

Another instance of faulty sampling leading to faulty generalizations is when we make assumptions from a single case. An individual may argue that African Americans can succeed economically in this country as easily as Whites because she or he knows a wealthy African American. Similarly, you might argue that all Latinos are dumb because the one you know is in the slowest track in high school. This type of reasoning is especially fallacious because it blames the victim (Ryan, 1976). The cause of poverty or crime or dropping out of school or scoring low on an IQ test is seen as a result of the flaw in the individual, ignoring the substantial impact of the economy or school.

Another typical way that we explain social behavior is to use some authority other than our senses. The Bible, for example, has been used by many people to support or condemn activities such as slavery, capital punishment, war, homosexuality, or monogamy. The media provide other sources of authority for individuals. The media, however, are not always reliable sources of facts. Stories are often selected because they are unusually dramatic, giving the faulty impression of, for example, a crime wave or questionable air safety.

Our judgments and interpretations are also affected by prevailing myths and stereotypes. We just "know" certain things to be true, when they actually may be contradicted by scientific evidence. As examples, six common beliefs about the poor and racial minorities are presented and discussed.

1. *Most homeless people are disabled by drugs, mental disease, or physical afflictions.* The facts show, however, that the homeless, for the most part, are not "deficient and defective" but rather not much different than the nonhomeless. Most people are not homeless because of their individual flaws but because of structural arrangements and trends that result in extreme impoverishment and a shortage of affordable housing (Timmer, Eitzen, and Talley 1994).
2. *African American and Latino youth are more likely than White youth to smoke tobacco and be heavy binge drinkers of alcohol.* The facts belie this myth (Centers for Disease Control study, report in McClam 2000).
3. *Welfare makes people dependent, lazy, and unmotivated.* Contrary to this image, however, the evidence is that most daughters of welfare recipients do not become welfare recipients as adults (Sklar 1993). Put another way, most women on welfare did not receive welfare as children (Center on Social Welfare and Law 1996).
4. *Welfare is given more generously to the poor than to the nonpoor.* Farm subsidies, tax deductibility for taxes and interest on homes, low-interest loans to students and victims of disasters, and pork-barrel projects are examples of government welfare and even the dependency of nonpoor people on government largesse. Most important, these government handouts to the nonpoor are significantly greater than the amounts given to the poor.
5. *African Americans are similar in their behaviors.* Blacks are not a monolithic group, with members acting more or less alike. A study by the Rand Corporation, for example, found that about 1 in 100 young, high-ability, affluent Black women from homes with two parents become single, teenage mothers (for White women in this category, the chances were 1 in 1,000, explained, in part, by the much greater willingness to use abortion). In contrast, a poor Black teenager from a female-headed household who scores low on standardized tests has a 1 in 4 probability of becoming an unwed teenage mother (for White women in this category, the odds were 1 in 12) (cited in Luker 1991:76–77). In the words of Kristin Luker, "Unwed motherhood thus reflects the intersecting influences of race, class, and gender; race and class each has a distinct impact on the life histories of young women" (Luker 1991:77).
6. *Unmarried women have babies to increase their welfare payments.* Three facts show that this belief of political conservatives is a myth (Males 1996): (a) From 1972 to 1996, the value of the average Aid to Families with Dependent Children (AFDC) check declined by 40 percent, yet the ratio of out-of-wedlock births rose in the same period by 140 percent; (b) states that have lower welfare benefits usually have more out-of-wedlock births than states with higher benefits; and (c) the teen out-of-wedlock birthrate in the United States is much higher than the rate in countries where welfare benefits are much more generous.

Conventional wisdom is not always wrong, but when it is, it can lead to faulty generalizations and bad public policy. Therefore, it is imperative to know the facts, rather than accept myths as real.

A similar problem occurs when we use aphorisms to explain social occurrences. The problem with this common tactic is that society supplies us with ready explanations that fit contradictory situations and are therefore useless. For instance, if we know a couple who are alike in religion, race, socioeconomic status, and political attitudes, that makes sense to us because "birds of a feather flock together." But the opposite situation also makes sense. If partners in a relationship are very different on a number of dimensions, we can explain this by the obvious explanation: "opposites attract." We use a number of other proverbs to explain behavior. The problem is that there is often a proverb or aphorism to explain the other extreme. These contradictory explanations are commonly used and, of course, explain nothing. The job of the sociologist is to specify under what conditions certain rates of social behaviors occur.

Sources of Data

Sociologists do not use aphorisms to explain behavior, nor do they speculate based on faulty samples or authorities. Because we are part of the world that is to be explained, sociologists must obtain evidence that is beyond reproach. In addition to observing scrupulously the canons of science, four basic sources of data yield valid results for sociologists: survey research, experiments, observation, and existing data. We describe these techniques only briefly here.

- **Survey Research.** Sociologists are interested in obtaining information about people with certain social attributes. They may want to know how political beliefs and behaviors are influenced by differences in sex, race, ethnicity, religion, and social class. Or sociologists may wish to know whether religious attitudes are related to racial antipathy. They may want to determine whether poor people have different values from other people in society, the answer to which will have a tremendous impact on the ultimate solution to poverty. Or they may want to know whether voting patterns, work behaviors, or marital relationships vary by income level, educational attainment, or religious affiliation.

To answer these and similar questions, the sociologist may use personal interviews or written questionnaires to gather the data. The researcher may obtain information from all possible subjects or from a selected **sample** (a representative part of a population). Because the former method is often impractical, a random sample of subjects is selected from the larger population. If the sample is selected scientifically, a relatively small proportion can yield satisfactory results—that is, the inferences made from the sample will be reliable about the entire population. For example, a probability sample of only 2,000 from a total population of 1 million can provide data very close to what would be discovered if a survey were taken of the entire 1 million.

Typically with survey research, sociologists use sophisticated statistical techniques to control the contaminating effects of confounding **variables** to determine whether the findings could have occurred by chance, to determine whether variables are related, and to see whether such a relationship is a causal one. A variable is an attitude, behavior, or condition that can vary in magnitude and significance from case to case.

A special type of survey research, **longitudinal surveys**, has special promise. This type of research collects information about the same persons over many years and in doing so has "given the social sciences their Hubble telescope. Both allow the observing researcher to look back in time and record the antecedents of current events and transitions" (Butz and Torrey 2006:1898). For example, the Panel Study of Income Dynamics at the University of Michigan has followed the same people for 40 years, "documenting the importance of accumulated life experience in causing transitions from health to infirmity; from work to unemployment or retirement; and across the states of marriage, family structure, and wealth" (Butz and Torrey 2006:1898).

- **Experiments.** To understand the cause-and-effect relationship among a few variables, sociologists use controlled experiments. Let us assume, for example, that we want to test whether White students in interracial classrooms have more positive attitudes toward African Americans than Whites in segregated classrooms have toward them. Using the experimental method, the researcher would take a number of White students previously unexposed to Blacks in school and randomly assign a subset to an integrated classroom situation. Before actual contact with the Blacks, however, all the White students would be given a test of their racial attitudes. This pretest establishes a benchmark from which to measure any changes in attitudes. One group, the **control group**, continues school in segregated classrooms. (The control group is a group of subjects not exposed to the independent variable.) The other group, the **experimental group**, now has Blacks as classmates. (The experimental group is a group of subjects who are exposed to the independent variable.) Otherwise, the two groups are the same. Following a suitable period of time, the Whites in both groups are tested again for their racial attitudes. If this post-test reveals that the experimental group differs from the control group in racial attitudes (the dependent variable), then it is assumed that interracial contact (the independent variable) is the source of the change. (The **dependent variable** is a variable that is influenced by the effect of another variable. The **independent variable** is a variable that affects another variable.) As an example of a less-contrived experiment, a researcher can test the results of two different treatments on the subsequent behavior of juvenile delinquents. Delinquent boys who had been adjudicated by the courts can be randomly assigned to a boys' industrial school or a group home facility in the community. After release from incarceration, records are kept on the boys' subsequent behavior in school (grades, truancy, formal reprimands) and in the community (police contacts, work behavior). If the boys from the two groups differ appreciably, then we can say with assurance, because the boys were randomly assigned to each group, that the difference in treatment (the independent variable) was the source of the difference in behavior (the dependent variable).

- **Observation.** Famed baseball great Yogi Berra once said in his unique way: "You can observe a lot by just watching." The researcher, without intervention, can observe as accurately as possible what occurs in a community, group, or social event. This type of procedure is especially helpful in understanding such social phenomena as the decision-making process, the stages of a riot, the attraction of cults for their members, or the depersonalization of patients in a mental hospital. Case studies of entire communities have been very instrumental in the understanding of power structures and the complex interaction patterns in cities. Longtime participant observation studies of slum neighborhoods and gangs have been insightful in showing the social organization present in what the casual observer might think of as disorganized activity.

- **Existing Data.** The sociologist can also use existing data to test theories. The most common sources of information are the various agencies of the government.

Data are provided for the nation, regions, states, communities, and census tracts on births, deaths, income, education, unemployment, business activity, health delivery systems, prison populations, military spending, poverty, migration, and the like. Important information can also be obtained from such sources as business firms, athletic teams and leagues, unions, and professional associations. Statistical techniques can be used with these data to describe populations and the effects of social variables on various dependent variables.

One goal of this book is to help the reader understand the social nature of social problems. Accepting the system-blame perspective is a necessary first step in efforts to restructure society along more humane lines. The job of social scientists in this endeavor should be to provide alternative social structures (based on theory and research) for those about which we complain. To do this job, social scientists must ask very different research questions from those posed in the past, and they must study not only the powerless but also the powerful.

ORGANIZATION OF THE BOOK

The organizing theme of this book is that many aspects of social problems are conditions resulting from cultural and social arrangements. It therefore begins by examining the fundamental organization of U.S. society. The remainder of Part One elaborates on the political economy of social problems, emphasizing the political and economic organization of society and its impact on social problems. The focus is on power because the powerful, by making and enforcing the laws, create and define deviance. They determine which behaviors will be rewarded and which ones punished. The powerful influence public opinion, and they can attempt to solve social problems or ignore them. Through policies for taxation and subsidies, the powerful determine the degree to which wealth is distributed in society. They also determine which group interests will be advanced and at whose expense.

The economy is equally important. The particular form of the economy establishes a distribution process not only for wealth but also for goods and services. In many important ways, Karl Marx was correct: The economy is the force that determines the form and substance of all other institutions—the church, school, family, and polity.

Critical scrutiny of the polity and the economy provides clues for the bias of society. It helps explain the upside-down qualities of society whereby the few benefit at the expense of the many; how reality gets defined in contested issues; how political and economic processes affect what is currently being done about social problems; and thus, why so many social policies fail.

Part Two focuses on the context of social problems in the United States. Chapter 3 examines world population and global inequality. Chapter 4 looks at environmental degradation globally and domestically. Chapter 5 focuses on two major population changes in the United States: the browning and the graying of America. The final chapter in Part Two provides a useful overview to social problems by focusing on the problems of location: urban, suburban, and rural. Part Three examines a crucial element of U.S. social structure: the various manifestations of social inequality. It describes inequality based on wealth, race/ethnicity, gender, sexual orientation, and disability.

Part Four examines the impact of social structure on individuals. **Deviant behavior** is activity that violates the norms of an organization, community, or society. Consequently, deviance is culturally defined and socially labeled. Certain behaviors are also labeled as deviant because they conflict with the interests of the powerful in society. Public policy, then, reflects the values and interests of those in power and is codified into law. Members of society are also taught how to respond to deviants. The law and these structured responses to deviants are societal reactions that establish deviance in social roles; paradoxically, the degraded status that results from societal reactions reinforces the deviance that society seeks to control. Deviance, then, is fundamentally the result of social structure. We examine these processes in relation to two types of deviance: crime and drug use.

Part Five describes problems found within five representative institutions. Chapter 14 addresses the allocation and remuneration of jobs. The number and types of jobs are undergoing a major shift with globalization and as society deindustrializes and moves toward a service economy. Although the resulting changes bring many opportunities, they also bring many problems, such as the widening gap between the haves and the have-nots and the emergence of a new form of poverty. Chapter 15 looks at the family-related problems of child care, violence, and divorce. Chapter 16 illustrates how education, although necessary as the source for transmitting the necessary skills and shared understandings to each generation, is also a generator of social problems. Thus, it shows once again how social problems (in this case, inequality) originate in the basic structure of society. Chapter 17 focuses on the reasons for the high cost of health care in the United States and the effort to reform the health care system. National security, especially the threat of terrorism, is the final topic of Part Five.

The book concludes with a chapter that answers the question, What do we do about social problems? The solutions come from the bottom up—that is, people organize through human agency to change social structures (Eitzen and Stewart 2007). Solutions also come from the top down—social policies determined by the powerful (Eitzen and Sage 2007). Both of these forces and the interaction between the top and the bottom are the topics of the concluding chapter.

■ CHAPTER REVIEW

1. Historically, U.S. sociologists have viewed social problems in terms of social pathology: "bad" people were assumed to be the sources of social problems because they disturbed the prevailing moral order in society.
2. In the 1920s and 1930s, sociologists focused on the conditions of society, such as the rapid changes accompanying urbanization and industrialization, as the sources of social problems.
3. More recently, many sociologists have returned to a study of problem individuals—deviants who violate the expectations of society. The modern study of deviance has developed in two directions. The first sought the sources of deviation within the social structure. The other, of relatively recent origin, has focused on the role of society in creating and sustaining deviance through labeling those viewed as abnormal. In this view, societal reactions are assumed to determine what a social problem is and who is deviant.
4. There is an objective reality to social problems; some conditions or situations do induce material and psychic suffering. There are several dangers, however, in defining social problems objectively. Subjectivity cannot be removed from the process. A standard must be selected, but in a pluralistic society, there are many standards. Moreover, social scientists not only disagree on what a social

problem is but also cannot escape their own values in the study of social problems. Most important, the objective approach to social problems entails acceptance of the definitions provided by the powerful. The acceptance of these definitions diverts attention away from the powerful and toward those the powerful wish to label negatively, thus deflecting observations away from what may constitute the most important social problem—the existing social order.

5. This book examines two types of social problems: (a) acts and conditions that violate the norms and values of society and (b) societally induced conditions that cause psychic and material suffering for any segment of the population. The key to understanding both types of social problems is the distribution of power.
6. The sociological imagination involves (a) a willingness to view the social world from the perspective of others; (b) focusing on the social, economic, and historical circumstances that influence families, groups, and organizations; (c) questioning the structural arrangements that shape social behavior; and (d) seeing the solutions to social problems in terms not of changing problem people but of changing the structure of society.
7. The focus is on the structure of society rather than on "problem" individuals. A guiding assumption of our inquiry is that norm violators are symptoms of social problems. These deviants are, for the most part, victims and should not be blamed entirely for their deviance; the system in which they live should also be blamed.
8. The person-blame approach, which we do not use, has serious consequences: (a) The social sources of social problems are ignored. (b) It frees the institutions of society from any blame and efforts to change them. (c) It controls "problem" people in ways that reinforce negative stereotypes. (d) It legitimates person-control programs. (e) It justifies the logic of social Darwinism, which holds that people are rich or poor because of their ability and effort or lack thereof.
9. The system-blame orientation also has dangers. Taken dogmatically, it presents a rigidly deterministic explanation for social problems, suggesting that people are merely robots controlled by their social environment.
10. Sociology depends on reliable data and logical reason. Although value neutrality is impossible in the social sciences, bias is minimized by the norms of science.
11. Sociologists use a variety of methods: surveys, experiments, observation, and the use of existing data sources.

■ KEY TERMS

Subjective nature of social problems. What is and what is not a social problem is a matter of definition. Thus, social problems vary by time and place.

Objective reality of social problems. Some societal conditions harm certain segments of the population and therefore are social problems.

Self-actualization. The assumed need (by Maslow) of individuals for creative and constructive involvement in productive, significant activity.

Institutionalized deviance. When a society is organized in such a way as to disadvantage some of its members.

Social problems. Societally induced conditions that harm any segment of the population, and acts and conditions that violate the norms and values found in society.

Sociological imagination. C. Wright Mills's term emphasizing that individual troubles are inextricably linked to social forces.

Person-blame. The assumption that social problems result from the pathologies of individuals.

System-blame. The assumption that social problems result from social conditions.

Cultural deprivation. The assumption by the members of a group that the culture of some other group is not only inferior but also deficient. This term is usually applied by members of the majority to the culture of a minority group.

Recidivism. Reinvolvement in crime.

Social Darwinism. The belief that the place of people in the stratification system is a function of their ability and effort.

Deviant behavior. Activity that violates the norms of a social organization.

Sociological theory. A set of ideas that explains a range of human behavior and a variety of social and societal events.

Sample. A representative part of a population.

Variable. An attitude, behavior, or condition that can vary in magnitude and significance from case to case.

Longitudinal surveys. The collection of information about the same persons over many years.

Control group. The subjects not exposed to the independent variable.

Experimental group. The subjects exposed to the independent variable.

Dependent variable. The variable that is influenced by the effect of another variable.

Independent variable. A variable that affects another variable.

■ SUCCEED WITH PEARSON mysoclab www.mysoclab.com

Experience, Discover, Observe, Evaluate

MySocLab is designed just for you. Each chapter features a pre-test and post-test to help you learn and review key concepts and terms.

Experience sociology in action with dynamic visual activities, videos, and readings to enhance your learning experience. Complete the following activities at www.mysoclab.com.

Social Explorer is an interactive application that allows you to explore Census data through interactive maps.

- Explore the Social Explorer Map: *Create Your Own "Hypothetical Subway Ride"*

The Core Concepts in Sociology video clips offer a real-world perspective on sociological concepts.

- Watch *Anti-Abortion March*

MySocLibrary includes primary source readings from classic and contemporary sociologists.

- Read Babbie, *The Importance of Social Research;* Adler & Adler, *The Promise and Pitfalls of Going into the Field;* Coontz, *How History and Sociology Can Help Today's Families*

CHAPTER 2 Wealth and Power: The Bias of the System

We can have a democratic society or we can have the concentration of great wealth in the hands of a few. We cannot have both.

—Justice Louis Brandeis

The thesis of this book is that the problems of U.S. society result from the distribution of power and the form of the economy. This chapter begins the analysis of U.S. social problems by looking at the political and economic realities of interest groups and also at power, powerlessness, and domination. As we discuss, the state is not a neutral agent of the people but is biased in favor of those with wealth—the upper social classes and the largest corporations. As we analyze the bias of the system, we begin to see that, contrary to popular belief, the U.S. system does not produce a society that is democratic, just, and equal in opportunity. Rather, we find that the United States is an upside-down society, with the few benefiting at the expense of the many. Finally, we see how our society itself is the source of social problems.

The study of social problems requires the critical examination of the structure of society. Some readers will find this approach uncomfortable, even unpatriotic. In this regard, introducing his critical analysis of the United States, Michael Parenti said,

> *If the picture that emerges in the pages ahead is not pretty, this should not be taken as an attack on the United States, for this country and the American people are greater than the abuses perpetrated upon them by those who live for power and profit. To expose these abuses is not to denigrate the nation that is a victim of them. The greatness of a country is to be measured by something more than its rulers, its military budget, its instruments of dominance and destruction, and its profiteering giant corporations. A nation's greatness can be measured by its ability to create a society free of poverty, racism, sexism, imperialism, and social and environmental devastation, and by the democratic nature of its institutions. Albert Camus once said, "I would like to love my country and justice too." In fact, there is no better way to love one's country, no better way to strive for the fulfillment of its greatness, than to entertain critical ideas and engage in the pursuit of social justice at home and abroad. (Parenti 1995b:6)*

This chapter is divided into three sections. The first describes the U.S. economy, with its concentration of corporate and private wealth. The second examines the political system and its links to the economic elites. The final section shows how the politicoeconomic system is biased in favor of those who are already advantaged.

U.S. ECONOMY: CONCENTRATION OF CORPORATE WEALTH

The U.S. economy has always been based on the principles of **capitalism**; however, the present economy is far removed from a free enterprise system. The major discrepancy between the ideal system and the real one is that the U.S. economy is no longer based on competition among more-or-less equal private capitalists. It is now dominated by huge corporations that, contrary to classical economic theory, control demand rather than respond to the demands of the market. However well the economic system might once have worked, the increasing size and power of corporations disrupt it. This development calls into question what the appropriate economic form is for a modern industrialized society.

Monopolistic Capitalism

Karl Marx, more than 125 years ago, when bigness was the exception, predicted that capitalism was doomed by several inherent contradictions that would produce a class of people bent on destroying it (see the insert on Karl Marx and "self-destruct" capitalism). The most significant of these contradictions for our purposes is the inevitability of monopolies. Marx hypothesized that free enterprise would result in some firms becoming bigger and bigger as they eliminate their opposition or absorb smaller competing firms. The ultimate result of this process is the existence of a monopoly in each of the various sectors of the economy. Monopolies, of course, are antithetical to the free enterprise system because they, not supply and demand, determine the price and the quality of the product.

Karl Marx and Self-Destruct Capitalism

Karl Marx (1818–1883) was one of history's greatest social theorists. His ideas have fueled revolutionaries and revolutions. His writings have had an enormous impact on each of the social sciences. His intellectual contributions to sociology include (1) elaboration of the conflict model of society, (2) the theory of social change based on antagonisms between the social classes, (3) the insight that power originates primarily in economic production, and (4) concern with the social origins of alienation.

Marx believed that the basis of social order in every society is the production of economic goods. What is produced, how it is produced, and how it is exchanged determine the differences in people's wealth, power, and social status. Marx argued that because human beings must organize their activities to clothe, feed, and house themselves, every society is built on an economic base. The exact form this organization takes varies among societies and across time. The form that people chose to solve their basic economic problems would, according to Marx, eventually determine virtually everything in the social structure, including polity, family structure, education, and religion. In Marx's view, all these social institutions depend on the basic economy, and an analysis of society will always reveal its underlying economic arrangements.

Because it owns the means of production, the social class in power uses the noneconomic institutions to uphold its position. Thus, Marx believed that religion, the government, and the educational system are used by the powerful to maintain the status quo.

Marx argued that every economic system except **socialism** produces forces that eventually lead to a new economic form. In the feudal system, for example, the market and factory emerged but were incompatible with the feudal way of life. The market created a professional merchant class, and the factory created a proletariat. Thus, new inventions create a tension with the old institutions, and new social classes threaten to displace old ones. Conflict results, and society is rearranged with a new class structure and an alteration in the division of wealth and power based on a new economic form. Feudalism was replaced by capitalism; land ownership was replaced by factories and the ownership of capital.

Capitalism, Marx maintained, also carries the seeds of its own destruction. Capitalism will produce a class of oppressed people (the proletariat) bent on destroying it. The contradictions inherent in capitalism are (1) the inevitability of monopolies, which eliminate competition and gouge consumers and workers; (2) lack of centralized planning, which results in overproduction of some goods and underproduction of others, encouraging economic crises such as inflation, slumps, and depressions; (3) demands for labor-saving machinery, which force unemployment and a more hostile proletariat; (4) employers will tend to maximize profits by reducing labor expenses, thus creating a situation where workers will not have enough income to buy products, thus the contradiction of causing profits to fall; and (5) control of the state by the wealthy, the effect of which is passage of laws favoring themselves and thereby incurring more wrath from the proletariat. All these factors increase the probability that the proletariat will build class consciousness, which is the condition necessary to class conflict and the ushering in of a new economic system.

Sources: Robert J. Werlin. 1972. "Marxist Political Analysis." *Sociological Inquiry* 42 (Nos. 3–4):157–181; Karl Marx. 1976. *Karl Marx: Selected Writings in Sociology and Social Philosophy* (T. B. Bottomore, Trans.). New York: McGraw-Hill, pp. 127–212. See also Michael Harrington. 1976. *The Twilight of Capitalism.* New York: Simon & Schuster.

For the most part, the evidence in U.S. society upholds Marx's prediction. Less than 1 percent of all corporations produce over 80 percent of the private-sector output. Most sectors of the U.S. economy are dominated by a few corporations. Instead of one corporation controlling an industry, the typical situation is domination by a small number of large firms. When four or fewer firms supply 50 percent or more of a particular market, a **shared monopoly** results, which performs much as a monopoly or cartel would. Most economists agree that above this level of concentration—a four-firm ratio of 50 percent—the economic costs of shared monopoly are most manifest. Government data show that a number of industries are highly concentrated (e.g., each of the following industries has four or fewer firms controlling at least 60 percent: light bulbs, breakfast cereals, milk supply, turbines/generators, aluminum, cigarettes, beer, chocolate/cocoa, photography equipment, trucks, cosmetics, film distribution, soft drinks, snack foods, guided missiles, and roasted coffee; Mokhiber 2010).

This trend toward ever-greater concentration among the largest U.S. business concerns has accelerated because of two activities—mergers and interlocking directorates.

- **Megamergers.** There are thousands of mergers each year as giant corporations become even larger. In 2006, $1.45 trillion worth of mergers and acquisitions occurred in the United States, and in 2007, there were $1.21 trillion worth. The ten largest mergers in U.S. history have occurred in the past 15 years (i.e., Time, Inc., and AOL joining with Warner Communications; Disney merging with Capital Cities/ABC; the combining of Wells Fargo and First Interstate Banks; the merger of NationsBank and BankAmerica; Philip Morris taking over Miller Brewing; the AT&T buyout of Tele-Communications, Inc.; Citicorp merging with Travelers Group; Texaco buying out Getty Oil; Exxon merging with Mobil Oil; Exxon merging with XTO, and MCI World.Com's acquisition of Sprint). In the first three months of 2009, major mergers took place in the pharmaceutical industry as Pfizer bought Wyeth, Merck merged with Schering-Plough, Roche purchased Genentech, and Gilead Sciences merged with CV Therapeutics. There have also been megamergers combining U.S. and foreign firms (e.g., Daimler and Chrysler, British Petroleum and Amoco, and Deutsche Bank and Bankers Trust). The federal government encouraged these mergers by relaxing antitrust law enforcement on the grounds that efficient firms should not be hobbled.

  This trend toward megamergers has at least five negative consequences: (1) it increases the centralization of capital, which reduces competition and raises prices for consumers; (2) it increases the power of huge corporations over workers, unions, politicians, and governments; (3) it reduces the number of jobs (for example, when Qwest combined with US West, 11,000 jobs were eliminated); (4) it increases corporate debt; and (5) it is nonproductive. Elaborating on this last point, mergers and takeovers do not create new plants, products, or jobs. Rather, they create profits for chief executive officers, lawyers, accountants, brokers, bankers, and big investors.

- **Interlocking Directorates.** Another mechanism for the ever-greater concentration of the size and power of the largest corporations is **interlocking directorates**, the linkage between corporations that results when an individual serves on the board of directors of two companies (a **direct interlock**) or when two companies each have a director on the board of a third company (an **indirect interlock**). These arrangements have great potential to benefit the interlocked companies by reducing competition through the sharing of information and the coordination of policies.

In 1914, the Clayton Act made it illegal for a person to serve simultaneously on corporate boards of two companies that were in direct competition with each other. Financial institutions and indirect interlocks, however, were exempt. Moreover, the government has had difficulty determining what constitutes "direct competition." The result is that, despite the prohibition, over 90 percent of large U.S. corporations have some interlocking directors with other corporations. When directors are linked directly or indirectly, the potential exists for cohesiveness, common action, and unified power. Clearly, the principles of capitalism are compromised when this phenomenon occurs.

Despite the relative noncompetitiveness among the large corporations, many of them devote considerable efforts to convincing the public that the U.S. economy is competitive. Many advertisements depict the economy as an Adam Smith–style free market with competition among innumerable small competitors. This, however, is a myth. Competition does exist among the mom-and-pop stores, but they control only a minute portion of the nation's assets. The largest assets are located among the very large corporations, and competition there is minimal.

CASE STUDY Media Monopolies

The media, through movies, television, radio, books, magazines, newspapers, and advertising, are major players in the creation of the culture, shaping what we think and do. The media play an influential role in a democracy because a democracy hinges on whether there is an informed electorate. The people need unbiased information and the push-and-pull of public debate if they are to be truly informed. These conditions become problematic, however, when the sources of information are increasingly concentrated in a few huge conglomerates guided only by commercial and bottom-line values. In 1983, fifty corporations controlled media in the United States. Now there are five—News Corporation, General Electric, Disney, Time Warner, and Viacom. Consider the range and scope of their media holdings (*The Nation* 2006:23–26):

- Viacom owns CBS, UPN, Simon & Schuster, Pocket Books, Scribner, Free Press, Paramount Pictures, DreamWorks, MTV, Nickelodeon, Nick at Night, *The Daily Show with Jon Stewart,* TV Land, CMT, VH1, Showtime, Movie Channel, Sundance Channel, Flick, Black Entertainment, and Comedy Central, to name a few of their holdings.
- Some of Time Warner's holdings include *Time, People, Sports Illustrated, Fortune, Entertainment Weekly, Popular Science,* AOL, CompuServe, Netscape, CNN, Cinemax, NASCAR.com, Warner Brothers Pictures, Warner Brothers Cable, TBS, TNT, Cartoon Network, HBO, The Movie Channel, and Court TV.
- A sample of News Corporation's media holdings includes Fox News, Fox Sports, Fox Business Network, National Geographic Channel, 175 newspapers worldwide, Speed, Twentieth Century Fox, 28 television stations in the United States, *New York Post, The Wall Street Journal, Weekly Standard, TV Guide, Barron's,* HarperCollins, ReganBooks, Zondervan Publishing, FX, and My Space.
- Disney's media affiliates are ABC, ESPN, The Disney Channel, E! Entertainment, The History Channel, Disney Publishing, Hyperion Books, ABC Radio (73 stations), Walt Disney Pictures, Miramax Films, Buena Vista Productions, and Pixar.
- Some of General Electric's media holdings are NBC, 14 television stations in major markets, Telemundo, Universal Pictures, Universal Studios, CNBC, MSNBC, Bravo,

In addition to amusement parks, Disney has media holdings including ABC, ESPN, The Disney Channel, Hyperion Books, ABC radio, Walt Disney Pictures, Miramax Films, Buena Vista Productions, and Pixar.

USA Network, and A & E. Late in 2009, Comcast attempted a merger with NBC Universal, "marrying" the largest cable company and the biggest residential Internet server provider. Should this merger be approved, the resulting Comcast/NBC would own 52 cable channels including the Golf channel, PBS Kids, E!, and the NBC channels listed earlier, 27 local TV stations, and the NBC network.

In addition to these media giants, ten companies broadcast to two-thirds of the nation's radio audience. One of these, Clear Channel Communications, owns more than 1,200 radio stations, each day reaching 54 percent of all people in the United States ages 18 to 49. Clear Channel also owns 42 television stations and a substantial number of billboards and other outdoor advertising.

Three-quarters of cable channels are owned by six corporate entities, four of which are the major TV networks

Pearson Higher Education is the world's largest publisher of college textbooks. Included among its subsidiaries are Addison-Wesley (Allyn and Bacon, the publisher of this text, is part of that organization), Prentice Hall, Scott Foresman, and Penguin. College textbook publishing in the United States is dominated by Pearson, Thomson, and McGraw-Hill.

In 1965, there were 860 owners of daily newspapers. Today there are fewer than 300. Many cities now have only one major newspaper. The most important newspapers are (1) the *New York Times,* which also owns the *Boston Globe* and 15 other daily newspapers, as well as television and radio stations, and (2) the *Washington Post,* owner of *Newsweek,* as well as other newspapers and TV and cable stations.

These examples show the extent to which a few major corporations control what we see, hear, and read. What does it mean when the information and entertainment we receive are increasingly under monopolized control? First, the media help to define reality by determining what is important and, conversely, what is not. This shapes our understanding of what is a social problem. For instance, the evening news focuses much more on street crime, using a disproportionate number of images of people of color as perpetrators, than it does on white-collar and corporate crime.

Second, diverse opinions are rarely heard. Because a few media giants control the content and distribution of programming, smaller companies with distinctive viewpoints are increasing rare. The content of talk radio, for example, leans heavily to the political right, as evidenced by the views of Rush Limbaugh, Glenn Beck, G. Gordon Liddy, Oliver North, Sean Hannity, Armstrong Williams, Michael Savage, Bob Grant, and Laura Ingraham. In a nation that is divided more or less equally politically, there are few, if any, progressive voices on the radio.

Third, reporting is sometimes compromised by conflict of interest. For example, did NBC, when it was owned by General Electric, report extensively on the long-term contamination of the Hudson River by a GE plant? Similarly, media corporations might shy away from news that is too critical of the government because of the corporation's political leanings, they do not want to offend customers, or they depend on government subsidies and favorable legislation.

Fourth, a media giant may, through its subsidiaries, push a political stance. For example, Clear Channel Communications, with more than 1,200 radio stations, used its considerable market power to drum up support for the war in Iraq. Following the 9/11 terrorist attacks, songs such as Cat Stevens's "Peace Train" and John Lennon's "Imagine" were blacklisted in the corporation's stations. The network sponsored prowar rallies and a continuous barrage of uncritical comment (Marshall 2003). When one of the Dixie Chicks said that she was ashamed that President Bush came from Texas, Clear Channel Communications banned the Dixie Chicks' music from its country music stations (as did Cumulus Media).

Fifth, big stories (war, corruption, the economy, legislation) are often pushed aside in favor of "hot" stories, such as kidnappings and murders, and salacious stories about celebrities, such as the philandering behavior of Tiger Woods, that entice audiences with their sensationalism.

Finally, the messages we hear and see tend to focus on problem individuals rather than on problems with structural origins. Thus, the media pull us away from sociological interpretations—with critical consequences for social policy as we will see throughout this book.

Transnational Corporations

The thesis of the previous section is that there is a trend for corporations to increase in size, resulting eventually in huge enterprises that join with other large companies to form effective monopolies. This process of economic concentration provides the largest companies with enormous economic and political power. If, for example, we compare government budgets with gross corporate revenues, in 2003, the total sales of Wal-Mart, British Petroleum, and ExxonMobil each exceeded the gross domestic product of Indonesia (the fourth most populous country in the world). Combining these three transnational corporations, their sales revenues were more than the combined economies of the world's poorest 118 countries (Teller-Elsberg, Folbre, and Heintz 2006:15).

Another trend—the globalization of the largest U.S. corporations—makes their power all the greater. This fact of international economic life has very important implications for social problems, both at home and abroad.

A number of U.S. corporations have substantial assets overseas, with the trend to increase these investments rapidly. In 2008, five of the top ten multinationals in sales were U.S.-based corporations (*Forbes* 2009a:130). Why are U.S. corporations shifting more and more of their total assets outside the United States? The obvious answer is that the rate of profit tends to be higher abroad. Resources necessary for manufacture and production tend to be cheaper in many other nations. Most significant, U.S. corporations increase their profits by moving their production facilities from high-wage situations to low-wage nonunion countries. Moreover, foreign production costs are lower because labor safety laws and environmental protection laws are much more lax than in the United States.

The consequences of this shift in production from the United States to other countries are significant. Most important is the reduction or even drying up of many semiskilled and unskilled jobs in the United States. The effects of increased unemployment are twofold: increased welfare costs and increased discontent among people in the working class. (This problem of domestic job losses through overseas capital investments is discussed in detail in Chapter 14, where globalization, deindustrialization, capital flight, and outsourcing are considered.)

Another result of the twin processes of concentration and internationalization of corporations is the enormous power wielded by gigantic transnational corporations. In essence, the largest corporations control the world economy. Their decisions to build or not to build, to relocate a plant, or to start a new product or scrap an old one have tremendous impacts on the lives of ordinary citizens in the countries they operate from and invest in and on their disinvestment in U.S.-based operations.

Finally, transnational corporations tend to meddle in the internal affairs of other nations to protect their investments and maximize profits. These activities include attempts to overthrow governments considered unfriendly to corporate interests and payment of millions of dollars in bribes and political contributions to reactionary governments and conservative leaders in various countries.

Concentration of Wealth

The other discrepancy between free enterprise in its real and ideal states is the undue concentration of wealth among a few individuals and corporations. This imbalance makes a mockery of claims that capitalism rewards the efforts of all enterprising individuals.

- **Concentration of Corporate Wealth.** Wealth in the business community is centralized in a relatively few major corporations, and this concentration is increasing. In 2008, for example, the U.S. corporation with the most assets ($2.175 trillion) was JPMorgan Chase; the top corporation in sales—Wal-Mart—had $405.6 billion in revenues; and the greatest producer of profits was ExxonMobil at $45.22 billion (*Forbes* 2009a:128-133). The following examples show just how concentrated wealth is among the major U.S. corporations:

  - Less than 1 percent of all corporations account for over 80 percent of the total output of the private sector.
  - Of the 15,000 commercial U.S. banks, the largest 50 hold more than one-third of all assets.
  - One percent of all food corporations control 80 percent of all the industry's assets and about 90 percent of the profits.
  - Six transnational corporations ship 90 percent of the grain in the world market.

- **Concentration of Private Wealth and Income.** Capitalism generates inequality. Wealth is concentrated not only in the largest corporations but also among individuals and families. For example, in 2009, according to *Forbes* (2009b), the two wealthiest were Bill Gates, head of software giant Microsoft, with an estimated fortune of $50 billion, and Warren Buffett of Berkshire Hathaway, with

"Hold it! We almost forgot your backdated stock options."

$40 billion. Each of the four heirs to the Wal-Mart fortune was worth from $19.0 billion to $21.5 billion.

The concentration of wealth is greatly skewed. Consider the following facts:

- The combined net worth of the 400 richest Americans in 2009 was more wealth than the total for the bottom 155 million Americans (DeGraw, 2010).
- In 2007, the latest year for data from the Federal Reserve Board, the richest 1 percent of U.S. households owned 33.8 percent of the nation's private wealth. That is more than the combined wealth of the bottom 90 percent (Kennickell, 2009).
- From 1980 to 2006 the richest 1 percent of Americans tripled their after-tax percentage of the nation's total income, while the income of the bottom 90 percent dropped by over 20 percent (DeGraw, 2010).

The data on wealth always show more concentration than do income statistics, but the convergence of money among the few is still very dramatic when considering income. The share of the national income of the richest 20 percent of households was 50.3 percent, while the bottom 20 percent received only 3.4 percent of the nation's income in 2009. The data in Table 2.1 show that income inequality is increasing in U.S. society. Especially noteworthy is the sharp gain in the Gini index, which measures the magnitude of income concentration from 1970 to 2009. (See Table 2.1.)

Another measure of this increasing gap is the difference in earnings between the heads of corporations and the workers in those corporations. In 1960, the average chief executive officer (CEO) of a *Fortune* 500 corporation was paid 40 times more than the average worker. By 2007, it had risen dramatically to 344 times more. The top 50 hedge fund and private equity managers received more than 19,000 times as much as typical workers earned.

The inequality gap has risen dramatically for a number of reasons. The gain at the top reflects the increased tax benefits received by the affluent from changing tax laws. Another factor explaining this inequality gap is the changing

TABLE 2.1

Share of Aggregate Income by Each Fifth of Households, 1970, 1980, 1990, 2009

	Percentage Distribution of Aggregate Income					
Year	*Lowest Fifth*	*Second Fifth*	*Third Fifth*	*Fourth Fifth*	*Highest Fifth*	*Gini* Index*
2009	3.4	8.6	14.6	23.2	50.3	.468
1990	3.9	9.6	15.9	24.0	46.6	.428
1980	4.3	10.3	16.9	24.9	44.7	.403
1970	4.1	10.8	17.4	24.5	43.3	.394

*The income inequality of a population group is commonly measured using the Gini index. The Gini index ranges from 0, indicating perfect equality (i.e., all persons having equal shares of the aggregate income), to 1, indicating perfect inequality (i.e., where all of the income is received by only one recipient or one group of recipients and the rest have none). The increase in the Gini index for household income between 1970 and 2009 indicates a significant increase in income inequality.

Sources: U.S. Bureau of the Census, Current Population Surveys. Online. Available: http://www.census.gov/hhes/www/incineq.html. U.S. Census Bureau, Current Population Survey, 2009 and 2010 Annual Social and Economic Supplements.

SOCIAL POLICY

GOVERNMENT POLICIES EXACERBATE WEALTH INEQUALITY

Government policies have the power to expand or reduce the gap between the haves and the have-nots. Consider what we could do to lift up the underserved:

> We could truly address the disgraceful truth that in this rich nation one in six children is raised in poverty and deprived of the healthy, fair start vital to equal opportunity. Now we have the resources to rebuild an aging and overburdened infrastructure—witnessed daily in power blackouts, collapsing sewers and aged water systems, overburdened airports, deferred toxic waste cleanups. Now we can redress the growing shortage of affordable housing and insure that every American has access to healthcare. (Borosage 2001:5).

All these actions are within our reach, but the decision makers have ruled them out, making the reduction of taxes paramount, which increases the inequality gap, already the most unequal by far among the industrialized nations. Economist Paul Krugman argued that current government policies entrench the advantages of the haves. Examples (Krugman, 2004:17):

- Getting rid of the estate tax so that large fortunes can be passed on to the next generation.
- Reducing tax rates both on corporate profits and on unearned income such as dividends and capital gains so that the wealthy can more easily accumulate even more.
- Reducing tax rates on people with high incomes, shifting the burden to the payroll tax and other revenue sources that bear most heavily on people with lower incomes.
- On the spending side, cutting back on health care for the poor, on the quality of public education, and on state aid for higher education. This makes it more difficult for people with low incomes to achieve upward mobility.

The affluent, by paying less in taxes, will, in effect, withdraw their support from programs that help those who are poor, those who do not have health insurance, and those who cannot afford decent housing. Former secretary of labor Robert Reich argues that what is really at issue here is the sorting of America, where our society is becoming more rigidly stratified. Reich says,

> There's only one way to reverse the sorting mechanism. . . . We have to rededicate ourselves to strong public institutions that are indubitably public because they work well for everyone. Of course this means more money and higher performance standards. But it also requires a renewed public spiritedness—a we're-all-in-this-together patriotism that says it's good for Americans to transcend class, race, education, health, and fortune, and to participate together. (Reich 2000b:64)

© 2005 Matt Wuerker. Used with the permission of Matt Wuerker and the Cartoonist Group.

job structure as the economy shifts from manufacturing to service and as U.S. jobs are exported. At the upper end, corporate executives added handsomely to their incomes while downsizing their domestic workforces. Congress has increased this upper-class feast by reducing taxes on capital gains (taxes on the profits from the sale of property) and by allowing the affluent to place as much of their income as they wish in special tax-deferred pay plans not available to the less well-to-do. Most significant were the tax cuts in 2001 and 2003. Since 2001, they resulted in $491 billion going to the richest 1 percent (Drucker 2008). To illustrate, in the 2008 tax year, households in the bottom 20 percent received $26 from these tax cuts while households in the top 1 percent received $50,495, and households in the top 0.1 percent received $266,151 in tax savings. See the "Social Policy" panel for more government policies that increase the inequality gap.

The recent tax policies have four major consequences. First, they exacerbate the unequal distribution of wealth in the United States, which is already the most unequal in the Western world. Second, the huge tax cuts are in place at the very time that the U.S. is conducting two costly wars in Iraq and Afghanistan and spending huge amounts to get the country out of the greatest economic disaster since the Great Depression. The result is a dramatic increase in the national debt. This leads to the third consequence: the ever-increasing debt will have the effect of reducing government spending for programs that help the less fortunate, and it will weaken public institutions that benefit society. As the late political observer Molly Ivins has put it,

> *The . . . reason it's dumb to cut taxes for the rich is the problem of social justice. We're already in trouble because the income gap between the rich and the rest of us keeps getting worse and worse. The rich buy their way out of our public*

institutions—schools, hospitals, parks—and then contribute money to politicians who let the public infrastructure go to hell. It doesn't work. (Ivins 2003:39A)

Ivins points to the fourth negative consequence of the widening gap between the haves and the have-nots—the increasing political influence of the wealthy, which is the topic of the next section.

POLITICAL SYSTEM: LINKS BETWEEN WEALTH AND POWER

In many ways, the U.S. government represents the privileged few rather than the majority. Although the government appears democratic, with elections, political parties, and the right to dissent, the influence of wealth prevails. This influence is seen in the disproportionate rewards the few receive from the politicoeconomic system and in government decisions that consistently benefit them. Senator Bernie Sanders argues that the United States is, increasingly, an oligarchy. An **oligarchy** is a government ruled by the few. In Sanders's words, "Oligarchy refers . . . to the fact that the decisions that shape our consciousness and affect our lives are made by a very small and powerful group of people" (Sanders 1994:B1). Other critics have taken this a step further, suggesting that the United States is a **plutocracy** (a government by or in the interest of the rich; e.g., Parenti 2008: 27–39). In the words of Kevin Phillips, a conservative scholar,

> *By 2000 the United States could be said to have a plutocracy. . . . Compared with 1990, America's top millennial fortunes were three or four times bigger, reflecting the high-powered convergence of innovation, speculation, and mania in finance and technology. Moreover, the essence of plutocracy, fulfilled by 2000,* has been the determination and ability of wealth to reach beyond its own realm of money and control politics and government as well. *(Phillips 2002:xv; emphasis added)*

Government by Interest Groups

Democracy may be defined as a political system that is of, by, and for the people. It is a system under which the will of the majority prevails, there is equality before the law, and decisions are made to maximize the common good. The principles that define a democracy are violated by the rules of the Senate (see "A Closer Look," The Structure of the Senate as a Barrier to Democracy), special-interest groups, which by deals, propaganda, and the financial support of political candidates attempt to deflect the political process for their own benefit. Individuals, families, corporations, unions, professional associations, and various other organizations use a variety of means to obtain tax breaks, favors, subsidies, favorable rulings, and the like from Congress and its committees, regulatory agencies, and executive bureaucracies. Among the means used to accomplish their goals are the following:

> *[A]long with the slick brochures and expert testimony corporate, lobbyists offer the succulent campaign contributions, the "volunteer" campaign workers to help members of Congress get reelected, the fat lecture fees, easy-term loans, prepaid vacation jaunts, luxury resorts, four-star restaurants, lush buffets, lavish parties with attractive escorts, stadium suites at major sporting events, and the many other hustling enticements of money. (Parenti 2008:213).*

A CLOSER LOOK

THE STRUCTURE OF THE SENATE AS A BARRIER TO DEMOCRACY

The U.S. Senate is designed to thwart popular will in at least two ways: the filibuster and the disproportionate power of small states.

The filibuster is a self-imposed rule not found in the Constitution. It is the practice of holding the Senate floor to prevent a vote on a bill. In 1917 the Senate adopted a rule that allowed the Senate to end a debate with a two-thirds majority vote for "cloture." For the next 50 years, the Senate tried to invoke cloture but usually failed to gain the necessary two-thirds votes. Filibusters were used primarily by segregationists seeking to derail civil rights legislation. South Carolina's Strom Thurmond, for example, filibustered for 24 hours and 18 minutes (the all-time record) against the Civil Rights Act of 1957. The southern senators tried to stymie antilynching legislation in the Civil Rights Act of 1964, but failed when cloture was invoked after a fifty-seven-day filibuster. In 1975, the Senate reduced the number of votes required for cloture from two-thirds (67) to three-fifths (60). That is the rule now in place.

The political composition of the Senate in 2010 was 57 Democrats, 2 Independents who caucus with the Democrats, and 39 Republicans. Despite the public's election of a Democratic president in 2008 and adding enough Democrats to have large majorities in Congress, the Democrats have not been able to get legislation passed for two reasons: the Republicans vote as a bloc to block the agenda of the Democrats and the difficulty in garnering 60 votes to defeat a filibuster. The use of the filibuster or the threat of a filibuster, once a relatively rare parliamentary move, has become commonplace. Political scientist Barbara Sinclair has found that in the 1960s, extended-debate-related problems affected only 8 percent of major legislation. By the '80s this had risen to 27 percent. Since 2006, when Republicans became a minority, it was 70 percent (reported in Krugman, 2009b). As a result, the health reform package was watered down and a few wavering centrist Democrats were allowed to shape the bill to their liking.

The majority, which won so conclusively in 2008 should be able to make major changes. As Paul Krugman has said:

> We need to deal with climate change. We need to deal with our long-run budget deficit. What are the chances that we can do all that . . . if doing anything requires 60 votes in a deeply polarized Senate? . . . . Our current situation is unprecedented: America is caught between severe problems that must be addressed and a minority party determined to block action on every front. Doing nothing is not an option—not unless you want the nation to sit motionless, with an effectively paralyzed government, waiting for financial, environmental and fiscal crises to strike. (Krugman 2009b, para 12)

Added to the filibuster is that the Senate is designed to thwart popular will by giving extraordinary power to small states (the following is from MacGillis 2009). For example, the key senators drafting health reform legislation, the so-called "Gang of Six" (three Democrats and three Republicans) came from the least-populous states, states with few voters who swept Obama to victory and with so few uninsured people. In total these states hold 8.4 million people—less than New Jersey—and represent only 3 percent of the U.S. population. Climate change legislation, which passed the House, faces tough odds in the Senate because the states dominated by agriculture, coal, and oil, which are typically underpopulated states, are opposed. The coal state of Wyoming has a single vote in the House, compared to New York's 29 and California's 53. In the Senate, each state has two. North and South Dakota with a combined population of 1.4 million has twice as many in the Senate as Florida (18.3 million) or Texas (24.3 million) or Illinois (12.9 million). A few additional inequities with each state having two senators, regardless of population size:

- California is 70 times as large as the smallest state, Wyoming.
- The 10 largest states have more than half the people in the United States, yet have only a fifth of the votes in the Senate.
- The 21 smallest states combined have fewer people than California, yet they have 42 senators, while California has only two.

Although three small states (Vermont, Delaware, and Rhode Island) favor the Democrats, most of the states with small populations and large land areas are staunchly Republican. Thus, the Senate structure is not only unequal, it has a built-in bias. Is this what the founders of the United States had in mind when they wrote the Constitution?

Special interests (e.g., National Rifle Association [NRA], the pharmaceutical industry, labor unions, dairy farmers) hire lobbyists to persuade legislators to vote their way. At the national level, lobbying in 2008 was a $3.3 billion business. There were twenty-three lobbyists for each member of Congress in 2008 (Eggen 2009b). Lobbyists for the health industry alone, for example, outnumbered the members of Congress by 3,300 to 535 and spent more than $1 million a day trying to influence legislation on health-related issues (Kroll 2009).

Interested parties lobby because there can be a significant payoff. In 2003 and 2004, for example, 840 U.S. corporations lobbied Congress to change the tax laws enabling transnational companies to bring home their overseas earnings at a tax rate of 5.25 percent instead of 35 percent (the following is from Belsie 2009). They succeeded, accruing benefits through the new law—the American Jobs Creation Act of 2004. These benefits were stunning. For every dollar spent on lobbying for the tax break, corporations reaped a $220 benefit on their U.S. taxes—*a 22,000 percent return on their investment*. For those corporations spending more than $1 million on tax lobbying did even better—a 24,300 percent return. For example, Eli Lilly & Co. spent $8.52 million lobbying for this bill. It reaped more than $2 billion in return.

The argument supporting lobbying is that on various issues, there are lobbyists on both sides. Thus, it is argued, there is a balance of viewpoints that legislators weigh in their decision making. The evidence, however, does not support such a cheerful view (Parenti 2008:215). The existence of lobbyists does not ensure that the national interest will be served but only that the interests of the powerful typically get their way. For instance, from 1998 to 2008 the financial sector spent more than $5 billion on campaign contributions (Nader 2010). With these contributions, along with the efforts of as many as 3,000 lobbyists, the business community was able to get Congress and executive agencies to reduce or eliminate regulatory restraints and to not enforce rules that were in place. Combined, these deregulatory moves helped pave the way for the current financial meltdown (Weissman 2009), and the massive oil leakage along the Gulf coast. Moreover, the interests of the powerless are not heard. Who, for example, speaks for the interests of minority groups, the poor, the mentally retarded, children, renters, migrant workers—in short, who speaks for the relatively powerless? And if there is a voice for these people, does it match the clout of lobbyists backed by immense financial resources?

Financing of Political Campaigns

Perhaps one of the most undemocratic features (at least in its consequences) of the U.S. political system is how political campaigns are financed. (See A Closer Look for the other undemocratic features.) Campaigns are becoming increasingly expensive, with money needed to pay for staff, direct-mail operations, phone banks, computers, consultants, and media advertising. The cost of the presidential and congressional election in 2008 was $5.3 billion (up from $2.2 billion in 1996), including monies from the federal government, individuals, political parties, and organizations outside political parties. Candidate Barack Obama raised $750 million for his presidential campaign in 2008, a record amount. Compare this with the $650 million that President Bush and Senator John Kerry collected together for their campaigns in 2004.

The cost of winning a seat in Congress is enormous. In 2008, the average winning House race cost $1.1 million, and the average winning Senate race

A CLOSER LOOK

UNDEMOCRATIC ELECTIONS IN A DEMOCRACY?

A democracy is a political system that is of, by, and for the people. Democratic principles include (1) fair and open elections; (2) access by the people to accurate information; (3) accountability of the governors to the governed; (4) political equality among all citizens; and (5) due process of law. The United States claims to be a democracy. Is it?

The short answer is that the United States is a democracy in theory but not always in practice. We focus here on elections. Indian novelist Arundhati Roy has said this about elections: "I think it is dangerous to confuse the idea of democracy with elections. Just because you have elections doesn't mean you're a democratic country" (cited in Mickey Z 2006:7). Consider the following undemocratic practices in U.S. elections.

First, the writers of the Constitution framed what they considered a democracy, but they allowed voting only for White male property owners, which, of course, excluded women, Native Americans, Blacks, and renters. Senators were not popularly elected. Clearly, most of the governed had no power. The framers also set up the Electoral College, a device that gave the ultimate power of electing the president to the elite in each state and gave extraordinary power to the least populous states. Now most of these undemocratic principles have been overturned by amendments to the Constitution. But the Electoral College remains, allowing for a president to be elected with fewer votes than his or her opponent (e.g., George W. Bush was elected in 2000 with 539,893 *fewer* votes than Al Gore). The Electoral College gives *all* electoral votes from a state to the winner in that state (e.g., in 2000 with nearly 3 million votes cast in Florida, George W. Bush won by a disputed margin of 537 votes and received *all* of Florida's electoral votes, giving Bush a majority in the Electoral College). And, to top it all, an electoral vote in Wyoming (in 2004) corresponded to 167,081 persons, while an electoral vote in California represented 645,172 persons (because the number of electors is determined by the number of senators and representatives in that state, giving states with small populations disproportionate votes). In short, the Electoral College may or may not reflect the popular will. Clearly, "the democratic faith in majority rule sustains and validates every other form of American election, but the election of the president takes place in an

cost \$6.5 million. Obviously, candidates must either be wealthy or accept money from various sources to finance their expensive campaigns. These costly campaigns favor incumbents, who have an easier time raising money.

In 2002, Congress passed the Bipartisan Campaign Reform Act (also known as the McCain-Feingold law). This law limited the use of "soft money" in federal elections. Before this act was passed, individuals, corporations, unions, and other organizations were allowed to give unlimited amounts of money to political parties at the national, state, and local levels or to other private organizations that are technically independent of the candidates. Because this tactic was not covered by the election laws, the amounts raised were unlimited. This loophole was used by wealthy persons to contribute to the Republican and Democratic national parties (and indirectly to the presidential candidates).

McCain-Feingold did eliminate soft money in federal elections (buttressed by a favorable Supreme Court decision in 2003), but it did not limit the giving of large sums to affect election outcomes. A number of ways were employed to navigate the system and give large donations to build support among Democrat or Republican voters. The loophole used is called 527s, which are advocacy groups, tax exempt under Section 527 of the Internal Revenue Code, that finance political advertisements while not directly calling for the election or alternative universe" (Lapham 2004:8).

The winner-take-all system means that minorities may not be represented. Assume that a state has five districts, each electing a representative to the House of Representatives. If this state is predominantly Republican, it could have all five Republican representatives even though 40 percent (in this hypothetical case) are Democrats. Also, what if 30 percent of the state is Latino? It is possible that their voice will not be heard in Washington. Similarly, a city may have a seven-member city council elected at large by majority vote. The usual result is that not one council member represents a poor section of the city.

Disenfranchisement also occurs when state legislatures under partisan control deliberately shape congressional districts (called *gerrymandering*) to increase their advantage. By moving the district boundaries (made all the easier these days with computers), the party in power can take an area that is overwhelmingly composed of their party members and move some of them to a neighboring area that is more evenly split. In this way, they can make both districts *their* districts. This rigging of the system means, in effect, that the public is denied a choice. "By trying to fix the outcomes of House races before Election Day, professional partisans are effectively disenfranchising voters" (*USA Today* 2002b:13A).

The two-party system that has emerged in the United States (political parties are not mentioned in the Constitution) is a major impediment to democracy. Corporations, special interests, and wealthy individuals sponsor both parties. The federal government subsidizes the two major parties, which keeps the strong parties strong and the weak parties weak. Third-party candidates are often excluded from political debates because, it is argued, they have no chance of winning. The election laws also make it difficult for third parties to get on the ballot. "How can U.S. elections be deemed truly democratic when only 'major' candidates are allowed to participate in televised debates and only those accepting inordinate amounts of cash from wealthy/corporate donors are considered 'major' candidates?" (Mickey Z 2006:7).

Finally, as shown in this chapter, money makes the difference in politics. The people get to vote between candidates selected by the wealthy (corporations, interest groups, or individuals), which means that voting does not always express the public will. As Mark Green says: "Because average voters pull levers but big donors pull strings, often public sentiment wants one thing while political elites deliver something else" (Green 2006:6). Thus, when public sentiment is at odds with the moneyed interests, the public often loses.

defeat of specific candidates (Dwyer 2004). Democrats, for example, created such organizations as the Media Fund and America Coming Together. Working through these organizations, billionaires George Soros and Peter Lewis pledged a total of $15 million, creating among other strategies the liberal Internet organization MoveOn.org. Republicans have set up comparable groups, such as the Leadership Forum, a fund-raising group headed by Washington lobbyists.

McCain-Feingold also limited maximum contributions to $2,300 per election cycle. While technically adhering to this limitation, corporate executives, lobbyists, and other insiders could maximize their political influence by a sophisticated system of bundling—the pooling of a large number of contributions. This tactic is used by both political parties.

Another method to raise money is through contributions to a "foundation" or to the favorite charity. Through this loophole, donors could give unlimited contributions to a candidate. For example, during the 2008 campaign, four major defense contractors—Northrop Grumman, General Dynamics, Boeing, and Lockheed Martin—donated hundreds of thousands of dollars to the symphony orchestra in Johnstown, Pennsylvania. Why? Well, the orchestra is a favorite charity of Representative John Murtha, the chairman of the congressional committee that gives out lucrative defense contracts (Hernandez and

Used with permission of Clay Bennett and the Washington Post Writers Group in conjunction with the Cartoonist Group. All rights reserved.

Chen 2008). Similarly lobbyists can donate to favorite causes of the legislator, such as $336,224 that Representative James Clyburn received for his James E. Clyburn Research and Scholarship Foundation (Schouten and Overberg 2009). A fourth way to funnel special interest money legally is to honor members of Congress. In 2008 special interests donated $35.8 million to honor legislators. A fifth source of money is the contributions to the political conventions. In 2008, for example, the cost of the Democratic convention in Denver was underwritten by such entities as Quest Communications ($3 million), Molson Coors Brewing ($1 million), the American Federation of Teachers ($750,000), and the American Federation of State, County and Municipal Employees $500,000 (Schouten and O'Driscoll 2007; Schouten 2008). The Republican convention in Minneapolis received many millions as well from special interests. Similarly, corporations and wealthy individuals spent millions to fund Obama's inauguration in 2009. Although technically not a political contribution, the parties and candidates are beholden to the contributing corporations.

- **The Supreme Court Decision (*Citizens United v. Federal Election Commission*) in 2010.** As noted, while McCain-Feingold attempted to control spending, it was not always successful because of various ways to evade the law. With a Supreme Court decision in 2010, however, these efforts to get around McCain-Feingold were no longer necessary. By a landmark 5–4 decision the Supreme Court struck down the laws of 22 states and the federal government. It invalidated part of the McCain-Feingold campaign finance reform law that sought to limit corporate influence by ruling that the constitutional guarantee of free speech means that corporations, labor unions, and other organizations can spend unlimited sums to help elect or defeat political candidates.* These organizations

*It is important to point out that although labor unions have the same right as corporations to spend freely in elections, they are no match to the corporations. The Center for Responsive Politics provides the data from the 2007–2008 election cycle: (1) corporations gave $1.964 billion in federal campaign contributions, compared to labor, which spent $74.8 million—a 15–1 disadvantage for labor (cited in Bybee, 2010); and (2) business and corporate interests accounted for 70.8 percent of the total political contributions, while only 2.7 percent came from labor (cited in Chapin 2010).

In 2010 by a 5–4 vote, the Supreme Court gave organizations the right to use unlimited funds to sway prospective voters.

are still barred from making direct contributions to politicians but they can now legally give unlimited amounts for ads to sway voters, as long as the ads are produced independently and not coordinated with a candidate's campaign. In effect, Exxon can spend millions to defeat an environmentalist candidate or Goldman Sachs could fund the entire cost of every congressional campaign in the United States (Alter 2010). As the *New York Times* editorialized: "The court's conservative majority has paved the way for corporations to use their vast treasuries to overwhelm elections and intimidate elected officials into doing their bidding" (*New York Times* 2010a, para 1).

This ruling has changed the political landscape. Small donors, who played a major role in the 2008 presidential election, have become irrelevant, being unable to match corporate treasuries. Somehow money has been interpreted by a majority of the Supreme Court to be a form of speech, and big money trumps small money. So the "speech" of the well-heeled is more important than the "speech" of ordinary citizens. Future elections will likely be inundated by a flood of corporate spending. What will be the effects of this newly unleashed torrent of attack advertisements? Will the United States be a functioning democracy with this triumph of corporate power?

Candidate Selection Process

Closely related to the financing of campaigns is the process by which political candidates are nominated. Being wealthy or having access to wealth is essential for victory because of the enormous cost of the race. Consider the cost for a run at the presidency. In the first three months of 2006, 18 months before the 2008 presidential election, three candidates had each raised more than $20 million—Democrats Hillary Clinton ($26 million), Barack Obama ($25 million), and Republican Mitt Romney ($23 million). And that was only the beginning. By the end of the 2008 presidential campaign, Obama had raised $750 million. Thus, the candidates tend to represent a limited constituency—the wealthy.

The two-party system also works to limit choices among candidates to a rather narrow range. Each party is financed by the special interests—especially business. As William Domhoff puts it,

> *Campaign donations from members of the corporate community and upper class are a central element in determining who enters politics with any hope of winning a nomination. . . . It is the need for a large amount of start-up money—to travel around the district or the country, to send out large mailings, to schedule radio and television time in advance—that gives members of the power elite a very direct role in the process right from the beginning and thereby provides them with personal access to politicians of both parties. (Domhoff 1978:225)*

Affluent individuals and the largest corporations influence candidate selection by giving financial aid to those candidates sympathetic with their views and withholding support from those whose views differ. The parties, then, are constrained to choose candidates with views congruent with the monied interests.

BIAS OF THE POLITICAL SYSTEM

Most people think of the machinery of government as a beneficial force promoting the common good, and it often is. But although the government can be organized for the benefit of the majority, it is not always neutral (Parenti 1978). The state regulates; it stifles opposition; it makes and enforces the law; it funnels information; it makes war on enemies (foreign and domestic); and its policies determine how resources are apportioned. In all these areas, the government is generally biased toward policies that benefit the business community. In short, power in the United States is concentrated in a **power elite**, and this elite uses its power for its own advantage.

Power in the United States is concentrated among people who control the government and the largest corporations. This assertion is based on the assumption that power is not an attribute of individuals but rather of social organizations. The elite in U.S. society are those people who occupy the power roles in society. The great political decisions are made by the president, the president's advisers, cabinet members, members of regulatory agencies, the Federal Reserve Board, key members of Congress, and the Supreme Court. Individuals in these government command posts have the authority to make war, raise or lower interest rates, levy taxes, dam rivers, and institute or withhold national health insurance.

Formerly, economic activity was the result of many decisions made by individual entrepreneurs and the heads of small businesses. Now, a handful of companies have virtual control over the marketplace. Decisions made by the boards of directors and the managers of these huge corporations determine employment and production, consumption patterns, wages and prices, the extent of foreign trade, the rate at which natural resources are depleted, and the like.

The few thousand people who form this power elite tend to come from backgrounds of privilege and wealth. It would be a mistake, however, to equate personal wealth with power. Great power is manifested only through decision making in the very large corporations or in government. We have seen that this elite exercises great power. Decisions are made by the powerful, and these decisions tend to benefit the wealthy disproportionately. But the power elite is not formally organized; there is no conspiracy per se.

The interests of the powerful (and the wealthy) are served, nevertheless, through the way in which society is structured. This bias occurs in three ways: by the elite's influence over elected and appointed government officials at all levels, by the structure of the system, and by ideological control of the masses.

As noted earlier, the wealthy receive favorable treatment either by actually occupying positions of power or by exerting direct influence over those who do. Laws, court decisions, and administrative decisions tend to give them the advantage over middle-income earners and the poor.

More subtly, the power elite can get its way without actually being mobilized at all. The choices of decision makers are often limited by what are called **systemic imperatives**; that is, the institutions of society are patterned to produce prearranged results, regardless of the personalities of the decision makers. In other words, a bias pressures the government to do certain things and not to do other things. Inevitably, this bias favors the status quo, allowing people with power to continue to exercise it. No change is easier than change. The current political and economic systems have worked and generally are not subject to questions, let alone change. In this way, the laws, customs, and institutions of society resist change. Thus, the propertied and the wealthy benefit, while the propertyless and the poor remain disadvantaged. As Parenti has argued,

> *The law does not exist as an abstraction. It gathers shape and substance from a context of power, within a real-life social structure. Like other institutions, the legal system is class-bound. The question is not whether the law should or should not be neutral, for as a product of its society, it cannot be neutral in purpose or effect.* (Parenti 1978:188)

In addition to the inertia of institutions, other systemic imperatives benefit the power elite and the wealthy. One such imperative is for the government to strive to provide an adequate defense against our enemies, which stifles any external threat to the status quo. Thus, Congress, the president, and the general public tend to support large appropriations for defense and homeland security, which in turn provide extraordinary profit to many corporations. In addition, the government protects U.S. transnational companies in their overseas operations so that they enjoy a healthy and profitable business climate. Domestic government policy also is shaped by the systemic imperative for stability. The government promotes domestic tranquility by squelching dissidents.

Power is the ability to get what one wants from someone else, by force, authority, manipulation, or persuasion. In Parenti's words, "The ability to control the definition of interests is the ability to define the agenda of issues, a capacity tantamount to winning battles without having to fight them" (Parenti 1978:41). U.S. schools, churches, and families possess this power. The schools, for instance, consciously teach youth that capitalism is the only correct economic system. This indoctrination to conservative values achieves a consensus among the citizenry concerning the status quo. Each of us comes to accept the present arrangements in society because they seem to be the only options that make sense. Thus, there is general agreement on what is right and wrong. In sum, the dominance of the wealthy is legitimized. Parenti observes, "The interests of an economically dominant class never stand naked. They are enshrouded in the flag, fortified by the law, protected by the police, nurtured by the media, taught by the schools, and blessed by the church" (Parenti 1978:84).

Finally, popular belief in democracy works to the advantage of the power elite, as Parenti has noted:

> *As now constituted, elections serve as a great asset in consolidating the existing social order by propagating the appearances of popular rule. History demonstrates that the people might be moved to overthrow a tyrant who shows himself provocatively indifferent to their woes, but they are far less inclined to make war upon a state, even one dominated by the propertied class, if it preserves what Madison called "the spirit and form of popular government." Elections legitimate the rule of the propertied class by investing it with the moral authority of popular consent. By the magic of the ballot, class dominance becomes "democratic" governance. (Parenti 1978:201)*

Consequences of Concentrated Power

Who benefits from how power is concentrated in U.S. society? At times, almost everyone does; but often the decisions made tend to benefit the wealthy. Whenever the interests of the wealthy clash with those of other groups or even of the public at large, the interests of the former are served. Consider how the president and Congress deal with the problems of energy shortages, inflation, or deflation. Who is asked to make the sacrifices? Where is the budget cut—are military expenditures reduced or are funds for food stamps slashed? When Congress considers tax reform, after the clouds of rhetoric recede, which groups benefit from the new legislation or from the laws that are left unchanged? When the economy was on the verge of collapse in 2008, who was bailed out by the government—the unemployed? The newly bankrupt? Those who lost their homes through foreclosure? No, the government spent many hundreds of billions of dollars to lift up the banks and insurance companies. When a corporation is found guilty of fraud, violation of antitrust laws, or bribery, what are the penalties? How do they compare with the penalties for crimes committed by poor individuals? When there is an oil spill or other ecological disaster caused by a huge enterprise, what are the penalties? Who pays for the cleanup and the restoration of the environment? The answers to these questions are obvious: the wealthy benefit at the expense of the less well-to-do. In short, the government is an institution run by people—the rich and powerful or their agents—who seek to maintain their advantageous positions in society.

Two journalists, Donald Bartlett and Steele, argue that there are two ways to get favorable treatment by Congress and the White House: contribute generously to the right people and spend lavishly on lobbying (Barlett and Steele, 2000:40-42). If you do you will get, for example, favorable tax rates, immunity from certain laws, government subsidies, and even a government bail out if needed. If you do not make generous political contributions and have lobbyists to make your case, then you will, according to Barlett and Steele, pay a disproportionate share of taxes, pay higher prices for a range of products, be compelled to pay all of your debts, and you will see legislation for the social good weakened or killed. In essence, we have a political system where spending money for political purposes makes a huge difference, dividing Americans into the fortunate few and second-class citizens.

The bias of the system today is nothing new. Since the nation's founding, the government's policy has primarily favored the needs of the corporate system. The founding fathers were upper-class holders of wealth. The Constitution they wrote gave the power to people like themselves—White, male property owners.

This bias continued throughout the nineteenth century as bankers, railroad entrepreneurs, and manufacturers joined the landed gentry as the power elite. The shift from local business to large-scale manufacturing during the last half of the nineteenth century saw a concomitant increase in governmental activity in the economy. Business was protected from competition by tariffs, public subsidies, price regulation, patents, and trademarks. When there was unrest by troubled miners, farmers, and laborers, the government invariably sided with the strong against the weak. Militia and federal troops were used to crush railroad strikes. Antitrust laws, though not used to stop the monopolistic practices of business, were invoked against labor unions.

During this time, approximately one billion acres of land in the public domain (almost half the present size of the United States) were given to private individuals and corporations. The railroads in particular were given huge tracts of land as a subsidy. These lands were and continue to be very rich in timber and natural resources. This active intervention by the government in the nation's economy during the nineteenth century was almost solely on the behalf of business. Parenti noted, "The government remained laissez-faire affording little attention to poverty, unemployment, unsafe work conditions, child labor, and the spoliation of natural resources" (Parenti 2008:56).

The early twentieth century was a time of great government activity in the economy, which gave the appearance of restraining big business. However, the actual result of federal regulation of business was to increase the power of the largest corporations. The Interstate Commerce Commission, for instance, helped the railroads by establishing common rates instead of ruinous competition. Federal regulations in meat packing, drug manufacturing, banking, and mining weeded out the weaker cost-cutting competitors, leaving a few to control the markets at higher prices and higher profits. Even the actions of that great trustbuster, Teddy Roosevelt, were largely ceremonial. His major legislative proposals reflected the desires of corporation interests. Like other presidents before and since, he enjoyed close relations with big businessmen and invited them into his administration (Parenti 2008:57).

World War II intensified the government bias on behalf of business. Industry was converted to war production. Corporate interests became more actively involved in the councils of government. Government actions clearly favored business in labor disputes. The police and military were used against rebellious workers; strikes were treated as efforts to weaken the war effort and therefore as treasonous.

The New Deal is typically assumed to be a time when the needs of people impoverished by the Great Depression were paramount in government policies. But as Parenti has argued, "The central dedication of the Franklin Roosevelt administration was to business recovery rather than social reform" (Parenti 1980:74). Business was subsidized by credits, price supports, bank guarantees, stimulation of the housing industry, and the like. Welfare programs were instituted to prevent widespread starvation, but even these humanitarian programs also worked to the benefit of the big business community. The government's provision of jobs, minimum wages, unemployment compensation, and retirement benefits obviously aided people in dire economic straits. But these programs were actually promoted by the business community because of the benefits to them. The government and business favored social programs not because millions were in misery but because violent political and social unrest posed a real threat.

Two social scientists, Frances Fox Piven and Richard A. Cloward, in a historical assessment of government welfare programs, determined that the government institutes massive aid to the poor only when the poor constitute a threat (Piven and Cloward 1971). When large numbers of people are suddenly barred from their traditional occupations, they may begin to question the legitimacy of the system itself. Crime, riots, looting, and social movements aimed at changing existing social, political, and economic arrangements become more widespread. Under this threat, the government initiates or expands relief programs to defuse the social unrest. During the Great Depression, Piven and Cloward contend, the government remained aloof from the needs of the unemployed until there was a surge of political disorder. Added proof for Piven and Cloward's thesis is the contraction or even abolition of public assistance programs when stability is restored.

The historical trend for government to favor business over less powerful interests continues in current public policy. This bias is perhaps best seen in the aphorism enunciated by President Calvin Coolidge and repeated by subsequent presidents: "The business of America is business."

Subsidies to Big Business

A general principle applies to the government's relationship to big business: Business can conduct its affairs either undisturbed by or encouraged by government, whichever is of greater benefit to the business community. The government benefits the business community with $125 billion in subsidies annually. Corporations receive a wide range of favors, tax breaks, direct government subsidies to pay for advertising, research and training costs, and incentives to pursue overseas production and sales (Gillespie 2003). The following are examples of governmental decisions that were beneficial to business.

- State and local governments woo corporations with various subsidies, including tax breaks, low-interest loans, infrastructure improvements, and relatively cheap land. In 2006, for example, Mississippi offered Kia, the Korean automaker, $1 billion in incentives to build a plant (Georgia offered Kia $400 million). Similarly, to keep the New York Stock Exchange in New York City, the city and state of New York offered an incentive package worth more than $1 billion. To which Ralph Nader replied: "It would be hard to script a more brazen and shameless corporate giveaway from a city where nearly one in three children lives in poverty, and public investment necessities go begging" (Nader 2001:26). Citizens for Tax Justice argued that when these subsidies occur, corporations manage to shield as much as two-thirds of their profits from state corporate income taxes. "The result: Money that could be spent on real economic development opportunities flows instead into the pockets of executives and the bill gets passed along to small taxpayers—local businesses and workers" (Singer 2006:6).
- The government installs price supports on certain commodities, increasing the profits of those engaged in those industries and simultaneously costing consumers. For example, sugar price supports cost consumers $3 billion a

year; dairy and milk price supports increase the annual cost to consumers by $9 million (Green 2002:161).

- Eleven days after the terrorist attacks of September 2001, Congress rushed through a $15 billion bailout of the airlines. Congress did not provide any relief to the 140,000 fired airline workers or to the 2 million people employed by the hotel industry whose jobs were imperiled (Hightower 2002a).
- In 1996, instead of auctioning off leasing or auctioning off the rights, Congress *gave* broadcasters spectrum rights to broadcast one channel of superhigh-resolution digital programs or several channels that could be used for digital interactive services or TV programs of high, but not superhigh, resolution—to which the *New York Times* editorialized, "By giving the new spectrum away instead of auctioning it off to the highest bidders, Congress deprived the treasury, and thus taxpayers, of tens of billions of dollars" (*New York Times* 2000c:1).
- The government often funds research and develops new technologies at public expense and turns them over to private corporations for their profit. This transfer occurs routinely with nuclear energy, synthetics, space communications, and pharmaceuticals. Although the pharmaceutical industry, for example, argues that it must charge high prices on drugs to recoup its costly research, the Joint Economic Committee of Congress found that public research led to 15 of the 21 drugs considered to have the highest therapeutic value introduced between 1965 and 1992 (reported in Goozner 2000). Three of those drugs—Capoten, Prozac, and Zovirax—have sales of more than $1 billion each.
- Congress subsidizes the timber industry by building roads for logging at an annual cost of $173 million (Zepezauer 2004). Under an 1872 law, mining companies need not pay for the $2 billion worth of minerals they extract from public lands (Scher 2000). The government subsidizes corn growers and its processors by mandating the use of ethanol (a corn-based fuel product) in gasoline.
- Transnational corporations are permitted to set up tax havens overseas to make various intracompany transactions from a unit in one foreign country to another, thus legally sheltering them from U.S. taxes.
- In 2003, Congress passed the Medicare Prescription Bill. The pharmaceutical industry, using 675 lobbyists from 138 firms, nearly 7 lobbyists for each senator, was successful in achieving favorable treatment in the legislation, including (1) a prohibition on the Medicare program from using its bargaining clout to directly negotiate deep drug-price discounts (one estimate is that prohibition will increase profits by $139 billion over 8 years) and (2) a ban on the reimportation of prescription drugs from Canada, which cost about 50 percent less than in the United States (*Public Citizen* 2003).
- Perhaps the best illustration of how business benefits from government policies are the benefits provided by the tax code. The 2001 and 2003 tax cuts slashed an estimated $175 billion in corporate taxes through 2004. Moreover, the tax code provides corporations with numerous ways to avoid taxes through generous exemptions, credits, and deductions. Corporations legally escape much of the tax burden through such devices as the investment tax credit, accelerated depreciation, capital gains, and locating in tax havens overseas. The key point is that Congress has allowed the tax burden to shift from corporations to individuals—in 1940, companies and

individuals each paid about half the federal income tax collected; in 2003 the companies paid 13.7 percent and individuals 86.3 percent (Byrnes and Lavelle 2003).

- The more than $700 billion in government bailouts to the banks and financial firms in 2008 actually rewarded them for their reckless behavior (see Chapter 14).

Trickle-Down Solutions

Periodically, the government is faced with finding a way to stimulate the economy during an economic downturn. One solution is to spend federal monies through unemployment insurance, government jobs, and housing subsidies. In this way, the funds go directly to the people most hurt by shortages, unemployment, inadequate housing, and the like. Opponents of such plans contend that the subsidies should go directly to business, which would help the economy by encouraging companies to hire more workers, add to their inventories, and build new plants. Subsidizing business in this way, the advocates argue, benefits everyone. To provide subsidies to businesses rather than directly to needy individuals is based on the assumption that private profit maximizes the public good. In effect, proponents argue, because the government provides direct benefits to businesses and investors, the economic benefits indirectly trickle down to all.

Opponents of "trickle-down" economics argue that this is an inefficient way to help the less-than-affluent.

> *One way to understand "trickle-down" economics is to use a more graphic metaphor: horse-and-sparrow economics—that is, if you feed the horse well, some will pass on through and be there on the ground for the sparrow. There is no doubt that sparrows can be nourished in this manner; and the more the horses get fed, the more there will be on the ground for the sparrows to pick through. It is, however, probably not a very pleasant way for sparrows to get their sustenance, and if one's primary goal is to feed the sparrows, it is a pretty silly—and inefficient—way to do the job. . . . Why waste the money on the horses when it might go directly to the sparrows? (MacEwan 2001:40)*

There are at least two reasons government officials tend to opt for these trickle-down solutions. First, because they tend to come from the business class, government officials believe in the conservative ideology that says that what is good for business is good for the United States. The second reason for the probusiness choice is that government officials are more likely to hear arguments from the powerful. Because the weak, by definition, are not organized, their voice is not heard or, if heard, not taken seriously in decision-making circles.

Although the government most often opts for trickle-down solutions, such plans are not very effective in fulfilling the promise that benefits will trickle down to the poor. The higher corporate profits generated by tax credits and other tax incentives do not necessarily mean that companies will increase wages or hire more workers. What is more likely is that corporations will increase dividends to the stockholders, which further increases the inequality gap. Job creation is also not guaranteed because companies may use their newly acquired wealth to purchase labor-saving devices. If so, then the government programs will actually have widened the gulf between the haves and the have-nots.

The Powerless Bear the Burden

Robert Hutchins, in his critique of U.S. governmental policy, characterized the basic principle guiding internal affairs as follows: "Domestic policy is conducted according to one infallible rule: the costs and burdens of whatever is done must be borne by those least able to bear them" (Hutchins 1976:4). Let us review several examples of this statement.

When threatened by war, the government sometimes institutes a military draft. A careful analysis of the draft reveals that it is really a tax on the poor. During the height of the Vietnam War, for instance, only 10 percent of men in college were drafted, although 40 percent of draft-age men were in college. Even for those educated young men who ended up in the armed services, there was a greater likelihood of their serving in noncombat jobs than for the non-college-educated. Thus, the chances of getting killed while in the service were about three times greater for the less educated than for the college educated (Zeitlin, Lutterman, and Russell 1977). Even more blatant was the practice that occurred legally during the Civil War. The law at that time allowed the affluent who were drafted to hire someone to take their place in the service. In the Afghanistan and Iraq wars beginning in 2003, the government decided not to have a draft. Instead, the forces were made up of volunteers. This meant, in effect, that the battles were fought overwhelmingly by young men and women from the working and lower classes. As one critic put it: "If this war is truly worth fighting, then the burdens of doing so should fall on all Americans. . . . If it's not worth your family fighting it, then it's not worth it, period" (Broyles 2004:A25).

The poor, being powerless, can be made to absorb the costs of societal changes. In the nineteenth century, the poor did the backbreaking work that built the railroads and the cities. Today, they are the ones pushed out of their homes by urban renewal and the building of expressways, parks, and stadiums.

Following the devastation from Hurricane Katrina in Louisiana and Mississippi in 2005, priorities were set by decision makers as to where rebuilding should be initiated and where it should be delayed or ignored. In New Orleans, the bulk of the money spent first went to the business community and for repairing the Superdome (home field for the New Orleans Saints). Left behind were low-income families. Although Congress required that half of federal grant money help low-income people, some 90 percent of $1.7 billion in federal money spent in Mississippi went to repair condominiums for the affluent, rebuild casinos and hotels, and expand the Port of Gulfport (Eaton 2007).

The government's attempts to solve economic problems generally obey the principle that the poor must bear the burden. A common solution for runaway inflation, for example, is to increase the amount of unemployment. Of course, the poor, especially minorities (whose rate of unemployment is consistently twice the rate for Whites), are the ones who make the sacrifice for the economy. This solution, aside from being socially cruel, is economically ineffective because it ignores the real sources of inflation—excessive military spending, excessive profits by energy companies (foreign and domestic), and administered prices set by shared monopolies, which, contrary to classical economic theory, do not decline during economic downturns (Harrington 1979).

More fundamentally, a certain level of unemployment is maintained continuously, not just during economic downturns. Genuine full employment for all job seekers is a myth. But why is it a myth, since all political candidates extol the work ethic and it is declared national policy to have full employment? Economist Robert Lekachman (1979) has argued that it is no accident that we tolerate millions of unemployed persons. The reason is that a "moderate" unemployment rate is beneficial to the affluent. These benefits include the following: (1) people are willing to work at humble tasks for low wages; (2) the children of the middle and upper classes avoid military service as the unemployed disproportionately join the volunteer army; (3) the unions are less demanding; (4) workers are less likely to demand costly safety equipment; (5) corporations do not have to pay their share of taxes because local and state governments give them concessions to lure them to their area; and (6) the existing wide differentials between White males and the various powerless categories such as females, Latinos, and African Americans are retained.

Foreign Policy for Corporate Benefit

The operant principle here is that "foreign policy seems to be carried on in the light of the needs of the munitions makers, the Pentagon, the CIA, and the multinational corporations" (Hutchins 1976:4). For example, military goods are sold overseas for the profit of the arms merchants. Sometimes, arms are sold to both sides in a potential conflict, the argument being that if we did not sell them the arms, then someone else would, so we might as well make the profits.

The government has supported foreign governments that are supportive of U.S. multinational companies, regardless of how tyrannical these governments might be.

U.S. rulers mainly have been interested in defending the capitalist world from social change—even when the change has been peaceful and democratic. They overthrew reformist governments in Iran, Guatemala, the Congo, the Dominican Republic, Brazil, Chile, and Uruguay. Similarly, in Greece, the Philippines, Indonesia, and at least ten Latin American nations, military oligarchs—largely trained and financed by the Pentagon and the CIA—overthrew popular governments that pursued egalitarian policies for the benefit of the destitute classes. And in each instance, the United States was instrumental in instituting right-wing regimes that were unresponsive to popular needs and wholly accommodating to U.S. investors (Parenti 2008:85).

The U.S. government has directly intervened in the domestic affairs of foreign governments to protect U.S. corporate interests. As Parenti has characterized it,

> *Sometimes the sword has rushed in to protect the dollar, and sometimes the dollar has rushed in to enjoy the advantages won by the sword. To make the world safe for capitalism, the United States government has embarked on a global counter-revolutionary strategy, suppressing insurgent peasant and worker movements throughout Asia, Africa, and Latin America. But the interests of the corporate elites never stand naked; rather they are wrapped in the flag and coated with patriotic appearances. (Parenti 1988:94)*

Reprise: The Best Democracy Money Can Buy

Billions are spent on each federal election campaign. The consequence of this flood of money in elections is that it sabotages democracy in several ways. First, it makes it harder for government to solve social problems.

> *How can we produce smart defense, environmental, and health policies if arms contractors, oil firms, and HMOs have a hammerlock over the committees charged with considering reforms? How can we adequately fund education and child care if special interests win special tax breaks that deplete public resources? (Green 2002:4)*

Second, and related to the first, the have-nots of society are not represented among the decision makers. Moreover, because the successful candidate must either be wealthy or be beholden to the wealthy, they are a different class of people from a different social world than most Americans. Thus, the money–politics connection is undemocratic because "democracy requires diversity in its legislatures in order to reflect the popular will" (Green 2002:18).

> *Since cash is the currency of elections, candidates troll for money where it is concentrated: in largely white, wealthy neighborhoods. . . . When a small, wealthy group in effect decides which candidates will have enough money to run a viable campaign, it is no great surprise that the agenda of policymakers is skewed toward its interests and not those of people of color and other underserved communities. (Gonzalez and Moore 2003:23A)*

Third, the money chase creates part-time elected officials and full-time fund-raisers. It now takes an average of $1.1 million to win a seat in the House of Representatives and $6.5 million to become or remain a senator. Senators have to raise an average of $20,833 a week every week of their 6-year term to raise the necessary capital.

Fourth, money diminishes the gap between the two major political parties because the candidates and parties seek and receive funds from the same corporate sources and wealthy individuals. Democrats in need of funds, even though they are more inclined than Republicans to support social programs and raising taxes, must temper these tendencies or lose their monetary support from wealthy interests. As Robert Reich has observed, "It is difficult to represent the little fellow when the big fellow pays the tab" (Reich 1989:A29).

Fifth, the money chase in politics discourages voting and civic participation (of the twenty-four Western democracies, the United States ranks twenty-third in voting turnout). In the 2000 presidential election, 49 percent of those who could have voted did not vote. This meant in effect that George W. Bush was elected by 24 percent of the electorate.

Sixth, big money in politics means than special interests get special access to the decision makers and receive special treatment from them.

> *The pay-to-play mentality has so seeped into our system that there now exist two classes of citizens. There are those for whom tax breaks, bailouts, and subsidies are granted; for whom running for and winning office is plausible; and with whom elected officials take time to meet. And then there are the rest of us—the non-donors for whom taxes go up, consumer prices rise, and influence evaporates. (Green 2002:148)*

In sum, the current politicoeconomic system is biased. It works for the benefit of the few at the expense of the many. Because the distribution of power and the organization of the economy give shape and impetus to the persistent social problems of U.S. society, the analysis of these problems requires a politicoeconomic approach.

■ CHAPTER REVIEW

1. The state is not a neutral agent of the people but is biased in favor of the upper social classes and the largest corporations.
2. Marx's prediction that capitalism will result in an economy dominated by monopolies has been fulfilled in the United States. But rather than a single corporation dominating a sector of the economy, the United States has shared monopolies, whereby four or fewer corporations supply 50 percent or more of a particular market.

3. Economic power is concentrated in a few major corporations and banks. This concentration has been accomplished through mergers and interlocking directorates.
4. Private wealth is also highly concentrated. Poverty, on the other hand, is officially dispersed among 39.8 million people (2008); many more millions are not so designated by the government but are poor nonetheless.
5. The inequality gap in the United States is the widest of all the industrialized nations. The gap continues to grow especially because of tax benefits for the affluent.
6. These tax policies, in addition to increasing the unequal distribution of wealth, increase the national debt, reduce government spending for programs to help the less fortunate, and weaken public institutions that benefit society. The widening gap increases the political influence of the wealthy.
7. The government tends to serve the interests of the wealthy because of the influence of interest groups and how political campaigns are financed.
8. Democracy is a political system that is of, by, and for the people. Democracy is undermined by special interests, which use money to deflect the political process for their own benefit.
9. The powerful in society (those who control the government and the largest corporations) tend to come from backgrounds of privilege and wealth. Their decisions tend to benefit the wealthy disproportionately. The power elite is not organized and conspiratorial, but the interests of the wealthy are served, nevertheless, by the way in which society is organized. This bias occurs through influence over elected and appointed officials, systemic imperatives, and ideological control of the masses.
10. The government supports the bias of the system through its strategies to solve economic problems. The typical two-pronged approach is, on the one hand, to use trickle-down solutions, which give the business community and the wealthy extraordinary advantages; and, on the other hand, to make the powerless bear the burden and consequently become even more disadvantaged.
11. Business benefits from governmental actions through foreign policy decisions, which typically are used to protect and promote U.S. economic interests abroad.
12. The flood of money to support political parties and candidates sabotages democracy in several ways: (a) it makes it more difficult to solve social problems; (b) the interests of the have-nots are not served; (c) the money chase creates part-time legislators and full-time fund-raisers; (d) money diminishes the gap between the two major parties because both seek and receive funds from the same corporate and individual sources; (e) it discourages voting and civic participation; and (f) big money in politics leads to a bias in the laws passed and the subsidies provided.

■ KEY TERMS

Shared monopoly. When four or fewer companies control 50 percent or more of an industry.

Interlocking directorate. The linkage between corporations that results when an individual serves on the board of directors of two companies (a direct interlock) or when two companies each have a director on the board of a third company (an indirect interlock).

Oligarchy. A political system that is ruled by a few.

Plutocracy. A government by or in the interest of the rich.

Democracy. A political system that is of, by, and for the people.

Power elite. People who occupy the power roles in society. They either are wealthy or represent the wealthy.

Systemic imperatives. The economic and social constraints on political decision makers that promote the status quo.

Power. The ability to get what one wants from someone else.

■ SUCCEED WITH mysoclab www.mysoclab.com

Experience, Discover, Observe, Evaluate

MySocLab is designed just for you. Each chapter features a pre-test and post-test to help you learn and review key concepts and terms.

Experience sociology in action with dynamic visual activities, videos, and readings to enhance your learning experience. Complete the following activities at www.mysoclab.com.

Social Explorer is an interactive application that allows you to explore Census data through interactive maps.

- Explore the Social Explorer Map: *Max Weber: Property, Power, and Prestige*

The Core Concepts in Sociology video clips offer a real-world perspective on sociological concepts.

- Watch *Democracy: Those Who Don't Participate*

MySocLibrary includes primary source readings from classic and contemporary sociologists.

- Read Clawson & Weller, *Dollars and Votes: How Business Campaign Contributions Subvert Democracy*; William, *Who Rules America? The Corporate Community and the Upper Class*; Weber, *The Characteristics of Bureaucracy*

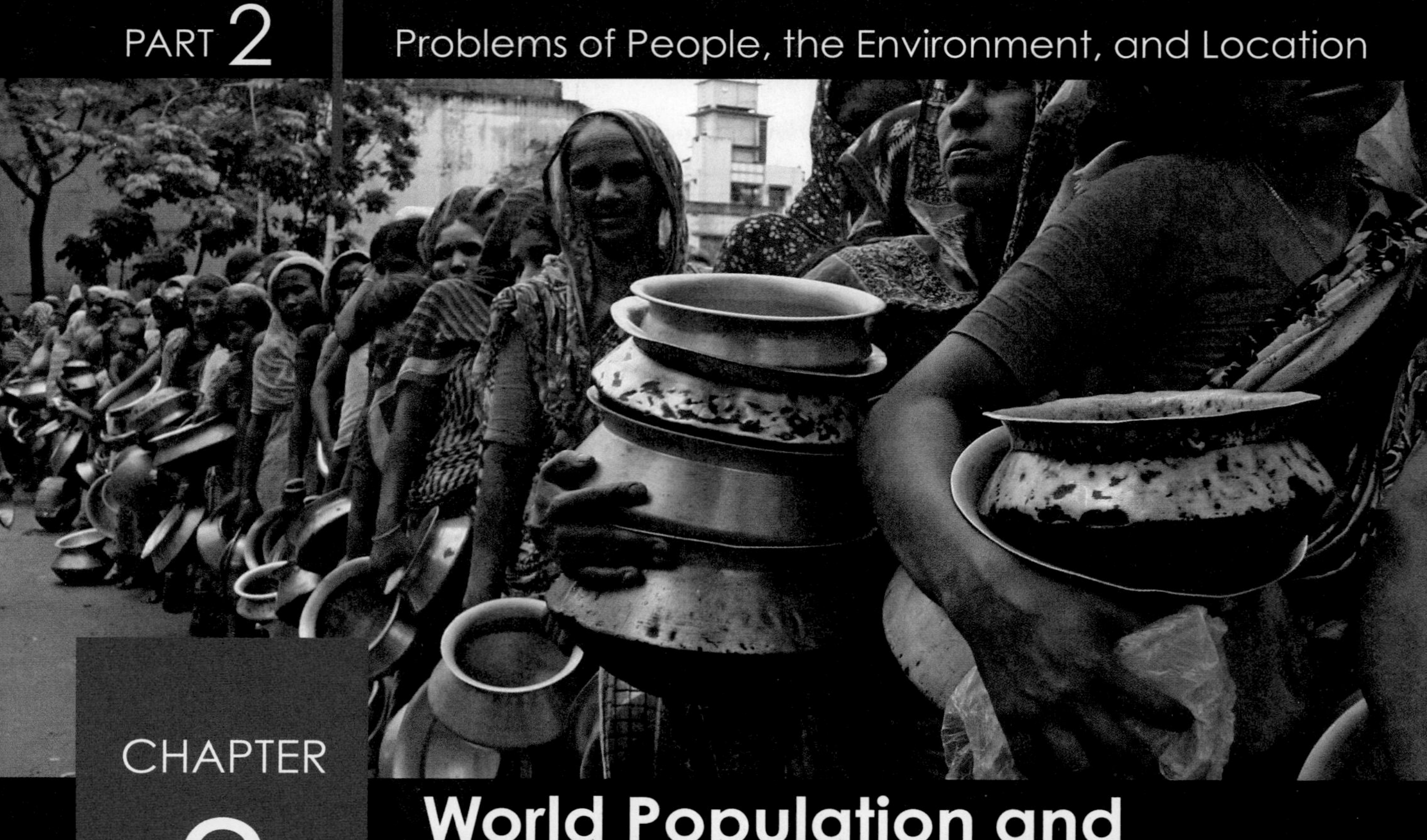

CHAPTER 3 World Population and Global Inequality

If the global village were reduced to 1,000 who proportionately represent the world's population, 584 would be Asians, 124 Africans, 84 Latin Americans, 95 eastern/western Europeans, 55 from the former Soviet Union, 52 North Americans, four Australians and two would be from New Zealand. . . . Rich folks call the shots in the global village. One-fifth of the people control three-quarters of the wealth. Another fifth of the population receive only 2 percent of the wealth. Only 70 people own automobiles. Only one-third of the population have access to clean drinking water. Fewer than 20 have a college education.

—Brigada

The countries of the world vary widely in levels of material conditions. Some nations are disproportionately poor with rampant hunger, disease, and illiteracy. Other nations are exceptionally well off, with ample resources. Table 3.1, using an index based on life expectancy, educational attainment, and real income, ranks the world's nations on "livability." Notice that the bottom twenty

TABLE 3.1

Most and Least Livable Countries: UN Human Development Index, 2007

"Most Livable" Countries, 2007	
1. Iceland	11. Finland
2. Norway	12. United States
3. Australia	13. Spain
4. Canada	14. Denmark
5. Ireland	15. Austria
6. Sweden	16. United Kingdom
7. Switzerland	17. Belgium
8. Japan	18. Luxembourg
9. Netherlands	19. New Zealand
10. France	20. Italy

"Least Livable" Countries, 2007	
1. Sierra Leone	11. Burundi
2. Burkina Faso	12. Côte d'Ivoire
3. Guinea-Bissau	13. Zambia
4. Niger	14. Malawi
5. Mali	15. Benin
6. Mozambique	16. Angola
7. Central African Republic	17. Rwanda
8. Chad	18. Guinea
9. Ethiopia	19. Tanzania
10. Congo	20. Nigeria

Source: United Nations Human Development Index, 2007. Online: http://www.hdr.undp.org

countries are all in sub-Saharan Africa, a region where 50 percent of the people live below the poverty line.

Here are some facts concerning the uneven distribution of the world's wealth:

- The richest 2 percent of adults own more than half of the world's household wealth.
- The poorest half of the world's adult population own barely 1 percent of global wealth.
- The top ranks in wealth are dominated by the Americans, Japanese, and Europeans.

The reasons for such global inequality include, as one might suspect, the degree of geographic isolation, climate, overpopulation, and natural resources. Another key determinant is the effect of power. The poor are poor, as we discuss, because they have been and continue to be dominated and exploited by powerful nations and corporations that have extracted their wealth and labor. This continuing domination of the weak by the powerful has resulted in an ever-widening gap between the rich and poor nations.

This chapter examines the plight of the poorest countries and the role of the richest—especially the United States—in maintaining global inequality. The first section focuses on world population growth, examining in particular the variables affecting why some nations have high growth and others do not.

The second part examines poverty throughout the world and the social problems generated by impoverishment, such as hunger, unhealthy living conditions, and economic/social chaos. The third part explores the relationship of the United States with the poor nations, historically through colonialism and currently through the impact of multinational corporations and official government policies.

WORLD POPULATION GROWTH

The number of people on this planet constitutes both a major problem and potential future calamity. The world population in mid-2009 was estimated to be 6.8089 billion, and at its current rate of growth, the net addition annually is 75 to 80 million people (the equivalent of adding a city the size of San Francisco every three days, or a New York City every month, or the combined populations of France, Greece, and Sweden every year). According to the latest projections, the world's population will increase to 7 billion in the latter half of 2011 and reach 9 billion in 2050 (Population Reference Bureau 2009).

> *The jump from six billion to nine billion is the equivalent of the impact of adding 33 more Mexicos to the world. And 33 additional Mexicos is the appropriate metaphor, because essentially all of the projected increase will occur in developing nations, the very places that strain to accommodate those already present. (Easterbrook 1999:23)*

To put the population growth curve in perspective: it took all of human history until about 1830 to reach the first billion. The next billion took 100 years (1930); the third billion, 30 years (1960); the fourth billion, 15 years (1995); the fifth billion, 12 years (1987); the sixth billion, 12 years (1999); and the next billion will also take about 12 years.

Most significant, 99 percent of the current population growth occurs in the less-developed nations, where poverty, hunger, and infectious disease are already rampant. There is a strong inverse relationship between per capita GNP and population growth rates—the lower the per capita GNP, the higher the population growth. For example, the less-developed nations are expected to increase in population from 5.6 billion in 2009 to 8.2 billion in 2050, whereas the more developed countries are projected to grow from 1.2 billion to just 1.3 billion (Bremer et al., 2009). This is a consequence of **differential fertility** (differences in the average number of children born to a woman by social category). To illustrate, the **fertility rate** in the more developed countries in 2009 was 1.7, compared to 4.6 in the least developed countries. These differences in fertility rate (the average number of births per woman) reveal a future world population that will be overwhelmingly from the developing countries (see Figure 3.1).

The population growth rates in the poor countries make it difficult to provide the bare necessities of housing, fuel, food, and medical attention. Ironically, there is a relationship between poverty and fertility: the greater the proportion of a given population living in poverty, the higher is the fertility of that population. This relationship is not as irrational as it first appears. Poor parents want many children so that the children will help them economically and take care of them in their old age. Because so many children die, the parents must have a large number to ensure several surviving children. Large families make good economic sense to the poor because children are a major source of labor and income.

FIGURE 3.1

World Population Growth Is Now Almost Entirely Concentrated in the World's Poorer Countries

Source: UN Population Division, *World Population Prospects: The 2008 Revision*, medium variant (2009).

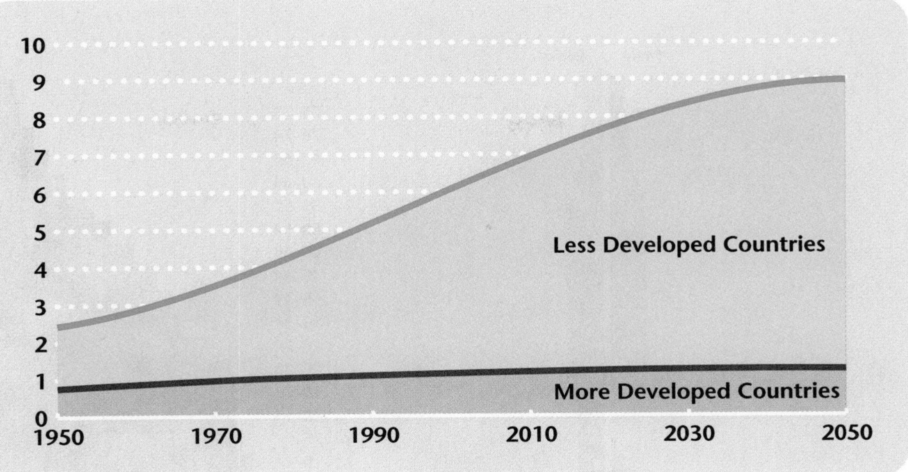

How can the nations of the world deal with the problems of expanding population? Basically, there are three ways to reduce fertility—through economic development, family-planning programs, and social change.

Demographic Transition

Historically, as nations have become more urban, industrialized, and modernized, their population growth has slowed appreciably. Countries appear to go through three stages in this process, which is known as the **modern demographic transition**. In the agricultural stage, both birth and death rates are high, resulting in a low population growth rate. In the transition stage, birthrates remain high, but the death rates decrease markedly because of access to more effective medicines, improved hygiene, safer water, and better diets. Many nations are presently in this stage, and the result for them is a population explosion. Much later in the process, as societies become more urban and traditional customs have less of a hold, birthrates decline, slowing the population growth and eventually stopping it altogether (as is now occurring in many nations of Europe and Japan). Figure 3.2 shows the population pyramids for less-developed countries where population growth is booming, and the more developed, where population growth is slow. Especially important to population growth is the "critical cohort" of those under age 20. There are more than 2 billion in this category in the developing countries. These young people will soon become parents (400 million are already between 15 and 19). What will be the fertility of this critical cohort? If the growth rate is to continue to slow, the demographic transition with its accompanying urbanization, medical advances, and the liberation of women from traditional gender roles will have worked.

The concept of a demographic transition is supported empirically. For example, birthrates in the developed world are down dramatically. Peter Drucker summarizes the situation:

> *In the developed countries the dominant factor in [the near future] will be something to which most people are only just beginning to pay attention: the rapid growth in the older population and the rapid shrinking of the younger generation. . . . In every single*

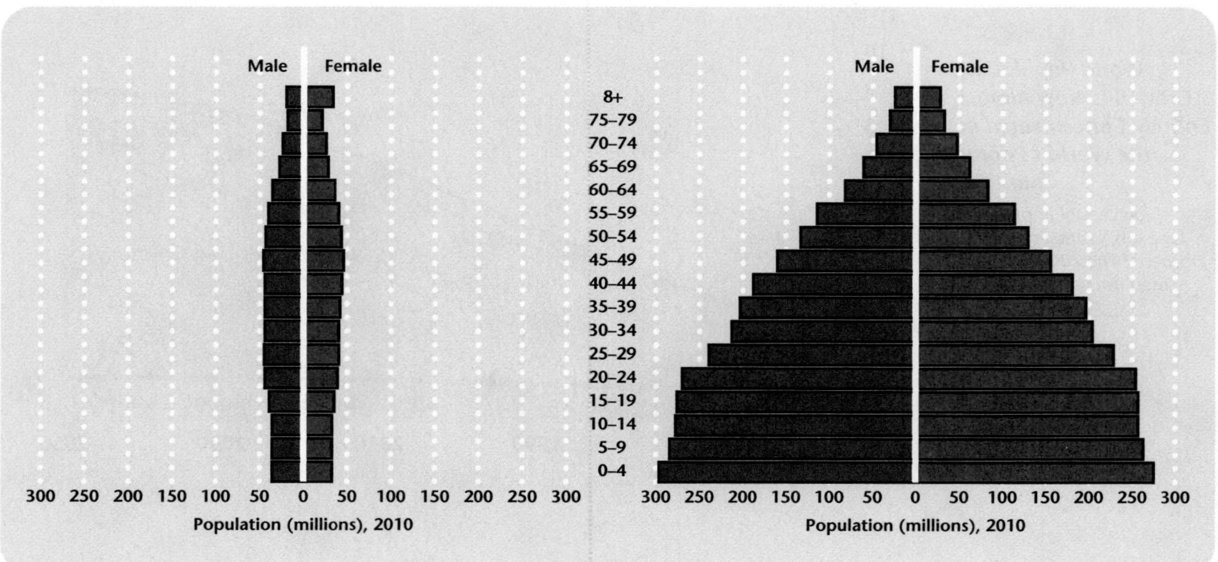

FIGURE 3.2

(a) More Developed Countries Have Fewer Young People

(b) Less Developed Countries Have More Young People

Source: UN Population Division, *World Population Prospects: The 2008 Revision* (2009).

> *developed country, but also China and Brazil, the birth rate is now well below the replacement rate of 2.2 live births per woman of reproductive age. (Drucker 2001:3)*

For example, not a single country in Europe is producing enough children to replace itself. According to the United Nations, approximately 43 percent of the world's peoples live in countries at or below the replacement rate of 2.1.

The problem, of course, is that the modern demographic transition experienced in Europe took about 200 years. With relatively high growth rates in the less-developed world plus a huge cohort in, or soon to be in, the child bearing category, this length of time is unacceptable because the planet cannot sustain the massive growth that will occur while the demographic transition runs its course. But the fertility rate is dropping more quickly than expected, even in the less-developed countries. For example, in sub-Saharan Africa, where the fertility rate is the highest, it has fallen from 6.7 children per woman in 1950 to 5.3 now. Worldwide, the use of contraception has risen from 10 percent of married women in the 1960s to 62 percent in 2009 (Bremer et al., 2009). The global fertility rate (2.6 in 2009) will continue to decline, but with so many women of childbearing age in the less-developed countries, the world's population is projected to increase by 2.4 million over the next 40 years to about 9.2 billion in 2050, at which it will stabilize.

Family Planning

Beginning in the 1960s, international organizations such as the World Health Organization and UNICEF incorporated reproductive health into their missions. National governments, beginning with India in 1951, began to adopt

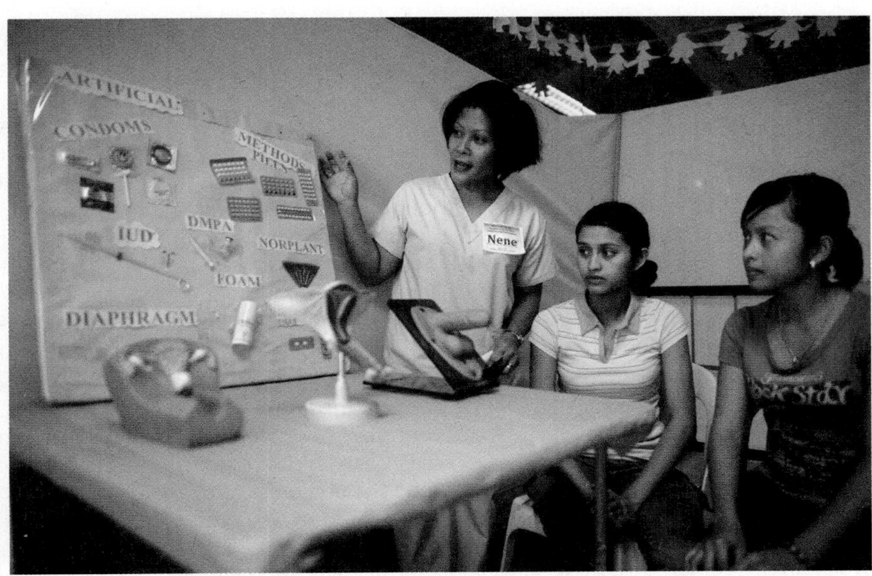

The World Bank estimates that it would take $8 billion to make birth control readily available globally.

family-planning policies (see the "Social Problems in Global Perspective" panel for a description of the mildly successful family-planning effort in India). As a result, fertility rates have fallen. Worldwide, the average number of children per woman fell from 5.0 in 1950 to 2.6 in 2009. Declines were most significant in Asia, Latin America, and the Caribbean. Only in sub-Saharan Africa did the average remain well above 5. The nations with the least use of modern contraceptives are largely rural and agricultural with very low per capita incomes. But with the continuing migration of the poor to the cities, there is less incentive to have large families.

The United Nations estimates that about 200 million worldwide would like to prevent pregnancy, but are not using effective contraception either because they cannot afford it or are not knowledgeable about it (cited in Francis 2009). The World Bank estimates that it would take $8 billion to make birth control readily available on a global basis. Such availability would reduce the projected world population from 10 billion to 8 billion during the next 60 years. The important point is that family-planning programs do work. Beginning in the late 1960s, the United States and the United Nations began funding such programs.

Formal policies by the United States, beginning with the Reagan and Bush administrations (1980–1992), have not supported the efforts of international organizations to promote contraceptive use. Because of popular opposition to abortion and the use of the drug RU-486 (a pill that induces a relatively safe miscarriage in the early stages of pregnancy), the United States withdrew aid from the United Nations Population Fund and the International Planned Parenthood Federation. President Clinton reversed these policies. President George W. Bush cut off U.S. contributions to the fund and defunded a British charity focusing on AIDS programs because it cooperated with the U.N. Population Fund (*Los Angeles Times* 2004). President Obama, however, restored U.S. funding for the United Nations Population Fund and rescinded the antifamily policy of the Bush administration (going back to President Reagan) that required all nongovernmental organizations that receive federal funds to refrain from performing abortions or citing abortion services offered by others.

SOCIAL PROBLEMS IN GLOBAL PERSPECTIVE

POPULATION GROWTH IN INDIA

More than one-third of the world's population live in either China or India. In mid-2009, China's population was 1.331 billion and India's was 1.171 billion (Population Reference Bureau 2009). If current growth rates continue, India will surpass China as the country with the world's largest population before 2030. China has reduced its population growth significantly by placing limits on family size (one child per urban couple while rural residents may have two children). India's population policy is to encourage small family size through family planning (53 percent of married women use contraceptives), female literacy programs, and sterilization, which has reduced the birthrate over the past 50 years from six births for each woman of childbearing age to 2.9. Still India grows by 48,000 every day.

Although India has had birth control programs since the early 1950s and public education at virtually no cost, the population continues to grow, especially in poor rural areas.

In poor rural areas—such as Bihar state, where women's literacy rates are lowest and family sizes are largest—girls are often married by the age of 15 and pressured to produce children quickly—especially sons who will one day provide for their elders and light their fathers' funeral pyres, a ritual central to Hinduism.

"Many women do not want large families any more, but this is still a patriarchal society, where men make the decisions on reproduction," says Saroj Pachauri, who heads the local branch of the Population Council, an international nonprofit group. "Ask a woman in Bihar if she wants more children, and she will say no. Ask her if she is using [birth control], and she will also say no."

Another obstacle is the popular notion, especially in the countryside, that more children mean more hands to work—rather than mouths to feed—and that larger clans mean mightier defenses (Constable 1999:16).

India, roughly one-third the geographical size of the United States, has more than four times as many people. The national literacy rate is 65 percent (75 percent for males and 54 percent for females). More than 260 million survive on less than one dollar a day. Nearly half of India's children below age six are undernourished. Resources such as arable land and water are strained to the limit. That is the situation now. What will it be like when they add another 500,000 million people in the next half century?

Societal Changes

The third strategy to reduce population growth involves societal changes. Ingrained cultural values about the familial role of women and about children as evidence of the father's virility or as a hedge against poverty in old age must be changed.

Religious beliefs, such as the resistance of the Roman Catholic hierarchy and of fundamentalist Muslim regimes such as in Saudi Arabia to the use of contraceptives, are a great obstacle to population control. However, religion is not an insurmountable barrier. Despite the Catholic hierarchy's resistance to family planning, some nations with overwhelming Catholic majorities have extremely low birthrates. As examples, Italy had a fertility rate of 1.4 in 2009, Spain a rate of 1.5, and Chile had a 1.9 rate, each below the average of 2.11 needed to sustain a stable population. And some Muslim countries have instituted successful family planning. For example, Iran and the United Arab Emirates each had a 2.0 fertility rate in 2009. Perhaps the most significant social change needed to reduce fertility is to change the role of women. When women are isolated from activities outside the home, their worth depends largely on their ability to bear and rear children. Conversely, fertility rates drop when women gain opportunities and a voice in society (Sen 2000). Women need to be included in the formal education process. Research has shown that increasing education is one of the most effective ways to reduce birthrates. Educated women are more likely than uneducated women to use effective methods of family planning (*New York Times* 2002a).

Unplanned social change, such as economic hard times, also affects birthrates. Recent data show that economic difficulties for individual families in less-developed countries can cause couples to delay marriage and to be more likely to use contraceptives. When enough families are affected negatively by an economic downturn, the fertility rate can fall for a nation. This is opposite the usual relationship of declining birthrates accompanying long-term economic success (the demographic transition).

Thus, in the long run, the population problem may abate, perhaps even reducing economic inequality and altering the balance of power among nations. However, for those living now, their lives will be negatively affected by the current population growth in developing nations, environmental degradation, and the overwhelming poverty of billions.

> *Chaos is the increasingly real result of trying to support more than 6 billion people on this planet, spawning desperate mass migrations, wars over rights to fresh water, medical epidemics, bloody riots and crime waves nurtured in teeming shantytowns.*
>
> *The war on terrorism, too, cannot logically be divorced from the struggle for population sanity. Refugee camps and hopeless slums steadily churn out alienated, landless young men and women who are perfect cannon fodder for ambitious religious and political zealots. (Scheer 2002:1)*

POVERTY

According to the World Bank, 1.4 billion people are living below the poverty line, defined as living on less than $1.25 a day. More than one-fourth of the developing world's population are living in this extreme poverty, with 50 percent in sub-Saharan Africa, and 42 percent Indian people found below this poverty marker (reported in the *New York Times* 2008). The global inequality gap is enormous. Consider, for example, that the global Gini index of inequality is 0.892. Recall from the previous chapter that the Gini coefficient in the United States is 0.451 and that the closer the coefficient is to 1.00, the greater the inequality gap).

The underdeveloped and developing nations are not only characterized by poverty, hunger, and misery but also by relative powerlessness because most of them were colonies and remain economically dependent on developed nations and transnational corporations, especially those of North America and Europe. These nations are also characterized by rapid population growth, high infant mortality, unsanitary living conditions, high rates of infectious diseases, low life expectancy, and high illiteracy. This section documents hunger, squalor, and marginality of life in these countries.

There is a striking maldistribution in **life chances** (the chances throughout one's life cycle to live and experience the good things in life) between the developed and developing nations. The significance of worldwide poverty and its concentration in the developing-world nations cannot be overstated. The gap between the rich and poor countries is increasing, and the gap between the rich and poor in the poor countries is increasing. Those in **absolute poverty** suffer from disease, malnutrition, squalor, stigma, illiteracy, unemployment, and hopelessness. These deplorable conditions will likely lead to extreme solutions such as terrorist movements and government policies of military expansion.

Food and Hunger

The Food and Agricultural Organization maintains that the world's agriculture produces enough food to provide every person with at least 2,720 kilocalories every day for the world's population (cited in Cain 2004). Actually, if everyone adopted a vegetarian diet and no food was wasted, current production would feed 10 billion people, more than the projected population for 2050 (Bender and Smith 1997:5). Food production, however, is unevenly distributed, resulting in about 1 billion being malnourished (one in six people), about one in every three of the world's inhabitants being food insecure, and around 9 million people dying of malnutrition each year. How can we explain these chilling figures?

An obvious source of the problem is rapid population growth, which distorts the distribution system and strains the productive capacity of the various nations. The annual increase of 75 to 80 million people requires an enormous increase in grain production just to stay even. A number of factors are shrinking the productive land throughout the world, in rich and poor countries alike. The earth loses 24 billion tons of topsoil each year. Irrigation systems that tap underground reserves are dropping water tables to dangerously low levels in many areas, causing the land to revert to dry-land farming. Air pollution and toxic chemicals have damaged some crops and water sources. The rising concentration of greenhouse gases (see Chapter 4) is changing the climates negatively. Each year millions of acres of productive land are converted to housing and roads. A growing number of people in developing countries are affluent enough to eat like Westerners; that is, they are eating more meat (Krugman 2008). The result is that a good deal of grain is diverted to feed livestock (it takes about 8 pounds of grain to produce a pound of beef; 6 pounds of grain to produce a pound of pork). Another important diversion of grains away from the food chain is the government subsidized conversion of crops into fuel (e.g., corn into ethanol)

Most significant, of course, is that almost all the population increase is occurring in regions and countries that are already poor. Because of low levels of economic development, the various levels of government, farmers, and others in these countries lack adequate money and credit for the machinery, fertilizer, pesticides, and technology necessary to increase crop production to meet the always increasing demand. The high cost of oil has an especially devastating effect on food production in poor nations. Food production in developing-world nations is also more adversely affected by natural disasters (floods and droughts) than it is in more affluent nations because these countries are less likely to have adequate flood control, irrigation systems, and storage facilities. As a result,

> *most of the world's hungry [are] concentrated in two regions: the Indian subcontinent and sub-Saharan Africa. In India, with more than a billion people, 53 percent of all children are undernourished. In Bangladesh, the share is 56 percent. And in Pakistan, it is 38 percent. . . . In Ethiopia, 48 percent of all children are underweight. In Nigeria, the most populous country in Africa, the figure is 39 percent. (Brown 2001:44)*

Another way to explain the food problem is to view it as a poverty problem. Food supplies are adequate, but people must have the resources to afford them.

Because the poor cannot afford the available food, they go hungry. Although this view of poverty is correct, it has the effect of blaming the victims for their plight. To do so ignores the political and economic conditions that keep prices too high, make jobs difficult to obtain and poorly paid, and force too many people to compete for too few resources.

The major problem with food shortages is not food production, although that is exceedingly important, but the political economy of the world and of the individual nations. Economic and political structures thwart and distort the production and distribution of agricultural resources. (The following discussion is adapted from Lappe and Collins, 1979, 1986; and Murdoch, 1980.) The primary problem is inequality of control over productive resources. In each country in which hunger is a basic problem, most of the land is controlled by a small elite, and the rest of the population is squeezed onto small plots or marginal land or is landless. For example, although colonial rule ended in southern Africa decades ago, the small White minority still controls most of the arable land. The evidence is that when the few control most of the agriculture, production is less effective than when land is more equally apportioned among farmers. Yields per acre are less, land is underused, wealth produced is not reinvested but drained off for conspicuous consumption by the wealthy, and credit is monopolized. Most important, monopoly control of agricultural land is typically put into cash crops that have value as exports but neglect basic local needs.

Agriculture controlled by a few landowners and agribusiness interests results in investment decisions made on the basis of current profitability. If prices are good, producers breed livestock or plant crops to take advantage of the prices. This approach results in cycles of shortages and gluts. Small farmers, on the other hand, plant crops on the basis of local needs, not world prices.

The way food surpluses are handled in a world in which more than a billion people are chronically hungry is especially instructive. The grain surplus is handled by feeding more than a third of the world's production to animals. Crops are allowed to rot or are plowed under to keep prices high. Surplus milk is fed to pigs or even dumped to keep the price high. The notion of food scarcity is an obvious distortion when the major headaches of many agricultural experts around the world are how to reduce mountains of surplus and keep prices high.

From this point of view, then, the problem of food scarcity lies in the social organization of food production and distribution. The solution to hunger is to construct new forms of social organization capable of meeting the needs of the masses. The problem, though, goes beyond the boundaries of individual countries. The policies of the rich nations and multinational corporations are also responsible for the conditions that perpetuate poverty in the developing world. The United States, for example, supports the very conditions that promote hunger and poverty. The last section of this chapter documents this role.

Sickness and Disease

Chronic malnutrition, an obvious correlate of greater numbers of people and poverty, results in high infant mortality rates, shorter life expectancies, and a stunting of physical and mental capacities.

> *Malnutrition takes its heaviest toll on children, and the health damage can begin before birth. Pregnant women who receive inadequate nourishment are likely to have underweight babies, who are especially vulnerable to infections and parasites that can*

lead to early death. Children who survive but receive inadequate food in the first five years of life are susceptible to the permanent stunting of their physical growth. (Bender and Smith 1999:6)

We know that protein deficiency in infancy results in permanent brain damage. "When protein is not available in the diet to supply the amino acids from which brain proteins are synthesized, the brain stops growing. Apparently it can never regain the lost time. Not only is head size reduced in a malnourished youngster, but the brain does not fill the cranium" (Ehrlich and Ehrlich 1972:92).

Vitamin deficiencies, of course, cause a number of diseases such as rickets, goiter, and anemia. Iron deficiency is a special problem for hungry children: some 25 percent of men and 45 percent of women (60 percent for pregnant women) in developing countries are anemic, a condition of iron deficiency (Gardner and Halweil 2000). Almost one-third of the world's people do not get enough iodine from food and water, causing goiters, dwarfism, and mental slowness (Kristof 2008).

Vitamin deficiencies make the individual more susceptible to influenza and other infectious diseases. Health in overpopulated areas is also affected by such problems as polluted water and air and inadequate sewage treatment.

Malnourishment also causes a low level of energy. Not only lack of food but also intestinal disorders commonly associated with poverty cause general lassitude in the afflicted.*

The United Nations estimates that 1.1 million people do not have access to safe water and that 2.6 billion live in unsanitary squalor. This lack of a safe water supply and sanitation results in millions of cases of water-related diseases and more than 5 million deaths every year (DeSouza, Williams, and Meyerson 2003). Polluted water, contaminated food, exposure to disease-carrying insects and animals, and unsanitary living conditions make the world's poor highly vulnerable to, among other diseases, chronic diarrhea, tuberculosis, malaria, Ebola, dengue, hepatitis, cholera, and parasites (see A Closer Look). More than half of the annual deaths in sub-Saharan Africa are caused by infectious and parasitic diseases. In addition to these diseases, one has emerged in the last 30 years or so with devastating effects—HIV.

HIV, the virus that causes AIDS, is transmitted through the exchange of bodily fluids, usually through sex, but also from contaminated needles, contact with tainted blood, or during birth for an infant born of an infected mother. Since the start of the AIDS **pandemic** (a worldwide epidemic) some three decades ago, some 60 million people have been stricken with AIDS worldwide, and 25 million have died. By the end of 2008, in addition to the deaths, 33.4 million were infected with HIV, two-thirds of them in sub-Saharan Africa, where 5.2 percent of the population were living with HIV/AIDS (Avert 2009).

HIV/AIDS is the worst epidemic in human history. The Black Death that ravaged Europe in 1348 killed approximately 25 million, and the United Nations Programme on HIV/AIDS predicts that AIDS will claim 68 million lives by 2020 (cited in Sternberg 2002). Two-thirds of those infected with HIV worldwide live in sub-Saharan Africa, where AIDS is the leading cause of

---

*Although low energy levels are a result of poverty, many persons have blamed poverty on an inherent lack of energy, or "drive" in the poor—a classic example of blaming the victim.

A CLOSER LOOK

THE BILL AND MELINDA GATES FOUNDATION'S WAR AGAINST MALARIA

Bill Gates, the cofounder of Microsoft, and his wife, Melinda, founded the Bill and Melinda Gates Foundation. The foundation is richly endowed with money from Bill Gates, the richest person in the United States, plus the bulk of the fortune of the second wealthiest person in the United States, Warren Buffett. In October 2008, the foundation had an endowment of $35.1 billion. The amount it donates each year more than doubles the annual budget of the United Nations Educational, Scientific, and Cultural Organization (UNESCO; O'Brien and Saul 2006).

The efforts of the foundation are directed at three main problems: global health, global development, and programs in the United States to improve education. We focus here on one part—the eradication of malaria, which the foundation, working with other organizations, hopes to eradicate by 2015.

Malaria is a disease of the developing world, mostly in sub-Saharan Africa and Asia. The disease is caused by a parasite transmitted by certain types of mosquitoes. As many as 2.7 million people a year die from malaria annually, 75 percent of them African children. Bill Gates feels that the corporate world is not working on the problem because the potential profits are few. "More money is being spent finding a cure for baldness than developing drugs to combat malaria. The market does not drive scientists, thinkers, and governments to do the right things" (quoted in Gardner 2009). The Bill and Melinda Gates Foundation seeks to fill the void. It funds research to discover, develop, and clinically test malaria vaccines; it develops new malaria drugs that are more effective and affordable; it develops improved methods for malaria control (effective pesticides, insecticide-treated bed nets that protect against mosquitoes); it distributes insect nets and other protective gear; and it works to develop greater public awareness about malaria and advocate for effective research and control (Bill and Melinda Gates Foundation n.d.).

death. The high death rate is the result of poor people in these regions not being able to afford the costly drugs to fight the disease.

> *More than 2 million children in Africa under age 15 are living with HIV. . . . Of these youngsters, perhaps 660,000 are sick enough to require medical intervention. Yet only 1 in 20 children who need ARVs [antiretroviral drugs] get them. In addition, fewer than 1 in 10 HIV-positive mothers receive the drugs they need to keep from transmitting the virus to newborns.* (Gorman 2006:96)

The New Slavery

"In almost every culture and society there has been, at one time or another, slavery" (Bales 2000:xiii; this section is dependent largely on Bales [1999, 2000], Re [2002], and Cockburn, [2009]). Typically, slaves were captured by the powerful to work the rest of their lives for the benefit of their captors. Often slavery was legalized with people bought and sold as property to work at the whim of their owners. Slavery was outlawed in the United States with the ratification of the Thirteenth Amendment in 1865.

By conservative estimate, there are 27 million slaves in the world today, and the number is growing. Slavery today (the **new slavery**), just as slavery in other times, means the loss of freedom, the exploitation of people for profit, and the control of slaves through violence or its threat. But today's forms of slavery also differ from the past. First, slavery is no longer a lifelong condition, as the slave typically is freed after he or she is no longer useful (e.g., a prostitute who has AIDS). Second, sometimes individuals and families become slaves by choice—a choice forced by extreme poverty. The population explosion in the poorest nations has created a vast supply of potential workers who are desperate and vulnerable, conditions that sometimes translate into enslavement. Often the poor must place themselves in bondage to pay off a debt. Faced with a crisis (crop failure, illness), an individual borrows money, but having no other possessions uses his or her family's lives as collateral. The slave must work for the slaveholder until the slaveholder decides the debt is repaid. This situation is problematic because many slaveholders use false accounting or charge very high interest, making repayment forever out of reach. Sometimes the debt can be passed to subsequent generations, thus enslaving offspring. Debt bondage is most common in South Asia.

Impoverishment may also lead desperate parents to sell their children (often told that the children will have good jobs) to brokers who in turn sell them to slaveholders. This practice is common in Thailand as the conduit for young girls to end up as prostitutes in brothels against their will. The United Nations Children's Fund estimates that 200,000 children in West and Central Africa are sold into slavery annually by their parents. Most come from the poorest countries, such as Benin, Burkina Faso, or Mali, where up to 70 percent of the people live on less than $1 a day. Faced with grinding poverty, parents may sell their children to traders for as little as $15, in the hope that the children will find a better life. Girls end up as domestic workers or prostitutes while boys are forced to work on coffee or cocoa plantations or as fishermen. Sometimes poor young people with little prospect for success may deal directly with a broker who promises legitimate jobs, but once they are away from their homes, violence is used to take control of their lives.

There is an international traffic in slavery, involving forced migration, the smuggling of illegal immigrants, and criminal networks. The Central Intelligence Agency (CIA) estimates that 900,000 people are sold across international borders each year, yielding an annual income to the perpetrators of $7 billion (Hardy 2004). These migrants who end up as slaves come from Asia, Africa, Latin America, Eastern Europe, and the nations of the former Soviet Union, where as many as two-thirds of women live in poverty. The antitrafficking program at Johns Hopkins University estimates that 1 million undocumented immigrants are trapped in the United States in slavelike conditions (Bowe 2007). The State Department estimates that as many as 50,000 women and children (and a smaller number of men) are smuggled into the United States each year to be forced into prostitution (about 40,000), domestic service, or as bonded labor in factories and sweatshops. Immigrants pay as much as $50,000 (in debt bondage) to get smuggled into the United States with false promises of decent jobs. Once in this country, most find their passports are stolen, and they are forced to work as prostitutes or maids, on farms, or in sweatshops. They may be locked up, but even if not, they are trapped because they fear violence by the slaveholders, and they fear the police because they are illegals and because they are strangers in a strange land.

Concentration of Misery in Cities

In 1800, just 3 percent of the world's population lived in cities. In 2007, for the first time, more people were city dwellers than rural dwellers. And, by 2050,

Often the poor must place themselves in debt bondage, using one's family as collateral, thus enslaving their children.

when the planet's population reaches 9 billion, two-thirds will likely live in cities, some of them huge cities.

In 1950, only one city in the developing countries, Shanghai, had a population of more than 5 million. By 2009, there were five cities in the developing world with populations exceeding 20 million.

A major problem is that the infrastructure of these cities are overwhelmed by the exploding population growth. A second problem is providing employment for their citizens. The special problem is to find employment for new immigrants to the cities—the farmers pushed off the land because of high rural density and the resulting poverty. The people who migrate to the cities are, for the most part, unprepared for life and work there. They do not possess mechanical skills; they are illiterate; they are steeped in tradition. The cities, too, are unprepared for them. Aside from the obvious problems of housing, schools, and sanitation, the cities of the developing nations do not have the industries that employ many workers. Because their citizens are usually poor, these countries are not good markets for products, so there is little internal demand for manufactured goods.

Another massive problem of the cities in the developing world is the mushrooming of squatter settlements ("shantytowns"), where 1 billion struggle to survive without clean water, sanitation, schools, and other infrastructure.

The immediate question for these immigrants is where to live. They have little choice but to create houses out of scraps (tin, plywood, paper) on land that does not belong to them (in streets, alleys, or ravines or on hillsides). Often they literally "live in shit" because the lack of sanitation forces excrement to pile up, creating serious health dangers (Montgomery 2009). Shantytowns are the fastest-growing sections of cities of the developing countries.

How do squatters react to their deplorable situation? They are unemployed or work at the most menial of tasks. They are hungry. Their children remain illiterate. They suffer the indignities of being social outcasts. Will their alienation lead to terrorism and/or revolutionary activity? Some observers believe that those experiencing abject poverty, the struggle is for the next meal, not for a redistribution of power. Others see the growing squatter settlements as breeding grounds for riots, terrorism, and radical political movements. Thomas Friedman says that "the growth of third world cities occurs in the countries least able to sustain it, and that will create a situation that will likely fuel instability and extremism—not just in those areas, but beyond them as well" (Friedman 2008:29).

The prospects for the cities of the developing countries are bleak. Their growth continues unabated. Unbelievable poverty and hunger are common. The inequality gap between the rich and poor is staggering. Jobs are scarce. Resources are limited and becoming more scarce as the number of inhabitants increases. The capital necessary for extensive economic development or for providing needed services is difficult to raise.

In sum, the high growth rates of cities, combined with the high concentration of people who are poor, unemployed, angry, hungry, and miserable, magnifies and intensifies other problems (such as racial and religious animosities, resource shortages, and pollution).

U.S. RELATIONS WITH THE DEVELOPING WORLD

There is a huge gap between the rich and poor nations of the world. About 75 percent of the world's people live in the overpopulated and poverty-afflicted developing world, yet these nations produce only one-tenth of the world's industrial output and one-twelfth of its electric power output.

The nations of the developing world are underdeveloped for a number of reasons, including geography, climate, lack of arable land and minerals, and a history of continuous warfare; but the rich nations are also responsible. The developing world economies are largely the result of a history of colonialism and of economic domination by the developed nations in the postcolonial era.

As recently as 1914, approximately 70 percent of the world's population lived in **colonies** (in those areas now designated as the developing world). As colonies of superpowers, their resources and labors were exploited. Leadership was imposed from outside. The local people were treated as primitive and backward. Crops were planted for the colonizer's benefit, not for the needs of the indigenous population. Raw materials were extracted for exports. The wealth thus created was concentrated in the hands of local elites and the colonizers. Population growth was encouraged because the colonizer needed a continuous supply of low-cost labor. Colonialism destroyed the cultural patterns of production and exchange by which these societies once met the needs of their peoples. Thriving industries that once served indigenous markets were destroyed. The capital generated by the natural wealth in these countries was not used to develop local factories, schools, sanitation systems, agricultural processing plants, or irrigation systems. Colonialism also promoted a two-class society by increasing land holdings among the few and landlessness among the many.

Although the process began centuries ago and ended, for the most part, in the 1960s and 1990s, the legacy of colonialism continues to promote poverty today. In short, the heritage of colonialism that systematically promoted the self-interest of the colonizers and robbed and degraded the resources and the lives of the colonized continues. Vestigial attitudes, both within and outside these countries, and the continued dependency of developing nations on the industrialized superpowers, exacerbate their problems. As a result, the gap between the developing world and the industrial nations continues to widen.

This section explores the relationship of the United States to the developing world, focusing on the economic mechanisms that maintain dependency and the political policies that promote problems within these countries.

Transnational Corporations

Gigantic **transnational corporations**, most of which are U.S.-based, control the world economy. Their decisions to build or not to build, to relocate a plant, to begin marketing a new product, or to scrap an old one have a tremendous impact on the lives of ordinary citizens in the countries in which they operate and in which they invest.

In their desire to tap low-wage workers, the multinational corporations have tended to locate in poor countries. Although the poor countries should have benefited from this new industry (by, say, gaining a higher standard of living and access to modern technology), they have not for the most part. One reason is that the profits generated in these countries are mostly channeled back to the United States. Second, global companies do not have a great impact in easing the unemployment of the poor nations because they use advanced technology whenever feasible, which reduces the demand for jobs. Also, the corporations typically hire workers from a narrow segment of the population—young women.

The global corporations have enormous advantages over local competition when they move into an underdeveloped country. Foremost, they have access to the latest technology in information technology, machinery, or genetic engineering. Second, they receive better terms than local businesses when they borrow money. They are preferred customers because their credit is backed by their worldwide financial resources. Moreover, global banks and global corporations are, as noted in Chapter 2, closely tied through interlocking directorates and shared ownership. Thus, it is in the interest of these banks to give credit under favorable conditions to their corporate friends. Finally, the global corporations have an enormous advantage over local companies through their manipulation of the market, influence over local government officials, and their control of workers.

An important source of the developing countries' current dependency on the United States and on other industrialized countries is their growing public and private debt. This debt, which is more than half the collective GNP of these countries, is so large for some nations that they cannot spend for needed public works, education, and other social services. Available monies must be spent, rather, on servicing the debt. Thus, the debt treadmill stifles progress. This situation is further exacerbated by the toll on the natural resources of the developing countries as they overexploit their resources to pay foreign creditors.

The United States, as a lender nation, is also negatively influenced. First, the United States is encouraged to buy imports and reduce exports, which eliminates domestic jobs. Second, to the degree that foreign governments default on their loans, the U.S. banks that made the bad loans are subsidized by American taxpayers, ensuring the banks' profit. This occurred, for example, in Mexico's 1995 financial crisis and in the 1998 financial crises in a number of Asian nations. Although this money shored up a teetering economy, in reality it protected the assets of U.S. banks that were in danger of losing their investments in Mexico and Asia.

Two activities by transnationals are highly controversial because they have negative costs worldwide, especially to the inhabitants of developing nations—arms sales and the sale of products known to be harmful.

- **Arms Sales.** The wealthy nations sell or give armaments to the poorer nations. Since the end of the Cold War, the United States has sold well over $100 billion worth of weapons abroad. In 2008, global arms sales by the United States totaled $37.8 billion. In 2008, for the sixteenth straight year, the United States was the number one seller of arms abroad, accounting for 68.4 percent of all weapons sales (followed in order by Italy, Russia, and France). The United States was not only the leader worldwide but also in sales to the developing world (76 percent of its sales went to nations in the developing world) (Shanker 2009).

The United States is actively engaged in promoting and financing weapons exports through 6,500 full-time government employees in the Defense, Commerce, and State Departments. These sales efforts are motivated by what was deemed to be in the national interests of the countries involved and by the profit to the manufacturers (in the United States, the multinationals most involved are Lockheed Martin, General Motors/Hughes, Northrop Grumman, General Electric, and Boeing). Not incidentally, the top ten arms-exporting companies give millions in political contributions (political action committees and soft money) during federal election campaigns.

There are several important negative consequences of these arms sales. First, they fan the flames of war. The United States sells weapons to countries actively engaged in military conflict. So rather than working to promote stability in already tense regions, the search for profits exacerbates the situation. Second, the United States has become an informal global shopping center for terrorists, mercenaries, and international criminals of all stripes (Bergman and Reynolds 2002). These gun sales are made through retail stores (not corporations), as the United States has such a lax system of controls over gun dealers and transactions at gun shows. September 11 and the subsequent war on terrorism have not changed U.S. gun control policies.

A third consequence is that arms sales can boomerang; that is, they can come back to haunt the seller—for example, the United States has sold armaments to Iraq to aid in their fight with Iran, only to have those weapons used against its forces in the Gulf War in 1990 and the Iraq War of 2003 and beyond. Similarly, the United States aided the freedom fighters in Afghanistan as they fought the Soviets, only to have those weapons used later by Al-Qaeda and the Taliban against the United States after the terrorist attacks of September 11, 2001.

Fourth, the United States, in its zeal to contain or defeat regimes unfriendly to its interests, has sold arms to countries that are undemocratic and that violate human rights.

- **Corporate Sales That Endanger Life.** **Corporate dumping**, the exporting of goods that have either been banned or not approved for sale in the United States because they are dangerous, is a relatively common practice. Most often the greatest market for such unsafe products is among the poor in the developing world. These countries often do not bar hazardous products, and many of their poor citizens are illiterate and therefore tend to be unaware of the hazards involved with the use of such products.

The United States and other industrialized nations continue to use the nations of the developing world as sources of profits as nations purchase these unhealthy products. For example, the Dalkon Shield intrauterine device was sold overseas in forty-two nations after the manufacturer, A. H. Robins, withdrew it from the U.S. market because of its danger to women. Similarly, after the Consumer Product Safety Commission forced children's garments with the fire retardant called tris phosphate off the domestic market because it was found to be carcinogenic, the manufacturer shipped several million garments overseas for sale.

Chemical pesticides pollute water, degrade the soil, and destroy native wildlife and vegetation. The use of the most potent pesticides is banned in the United States. This ban, however, does not pertain to foreign sales: 25 percent of the pesticides exported by the United States are restricted or banned by the Environmental Protection Agency for domestic use.

Another form of corporate dumping, in the literal sense of the word, is the practice of shipping toxic wastes produced in the United States to the developing world for disposal. This practice is attractive to U.S. corporations because the Environmental Protection Agency requires expensive disposal facilities, whereas the materials can be dumped in developing-world nations for a fraction of the cost. The host nations engage in such potentially dangerous transactions because they need the money.

Some companies dump workplace hazards as well as hazardous products and waste materials in poor nations. Governmental regulations often require U.S. corporations to provide a reasonably safe environment for their workers. These requirements, such as not exposing workers to asbestos, lead, or other toxic substances, are often expensive to meet. Thus, many corporations move their manufacture (and unsafe working conditions) to a country with few or no restrictions. This move saves the companies money and increases their profits, but it disregards the health and safety of workers outside the United States.

Corporate dumping is undesirable for three reasons. First, and most obvious, it poses serious health hazards to the poor and uninformed consumers of the developing world. Second, the disregard of U.S. multinational corporations for their workers and their consumers in foreign lands contributes to anti-U.S. feelings in the host countries. Third, many types of corporate dumping have a boomerang effect; that is, some of the hazardous products sold abroad by U.S. companies are often returned to the United States and other developed nations, negatively affecting the health of the people in those countries. For example, the United States imports about one-fourth of its fruits and vegetables, and some of this produce is tainted with toxic chemical residues.

UNITED STATES IN THE GLOBAL VILLAGE

In the global economy, the fate of the world's poorest nations and the poor within these nations are of crucial importance to all nations and the people within them. Huge gaps in income, education, and other measures of the quality of life make the world less safe. And, as the population growth surges in the developing world, the inequality gap will widen and the world will become less stable. Unless wealthy nations do more to help the poor nations catch up, the twenty-first century will witness Earth split into two very different planets, one inhabited by the fortunate few, and the other by poverty-stricken, desperate masses.

What can the wealthy nations do to help the impoverished nations? First, the affluent nations can pledge more resources targeted for development aid. The United Nations set a goal for the rich nations to give 0.7 percent of Gross National Income (GNI) to alleviate poverty in the poor nations. There are two major problems with this. First, the rich nations have failed to meet this obligation, giving instead around 0.2 to 0.4 percent, falling more than $100 billion short each year. Second, the type of aid often is not helpful. Rather than targeted to meet the needs of the poor, it is sometimes designed to meet the strategic and economic interests of the donor countries (for a nongovernmental approach to solving poverty, see the Social Policy panel); the aid benefits powerful domestic interest groups; and too little aid reaches those who most desperately need it (Shah 2009). For example, in 2008, the U.S. government spent $26 billion in foreign aid to address the plight of the world's poor. Much of this aid, however, was for armaments not humanitarian aid. In the case of Egypt, the United States

SOCIAL POLICY

ARE MICROLOANS THE ANSWER FOR THE WORLD'S POOR?

The 2006 Nobel Peace Prize was awarded to Muhammad Yunus, an economics professor from Bangladesh. Since the 1970s, Yunnis, through his Grameen Bank, has been offering very small loans (usually under $100) to the impoverished to start activities such as buying a dairy cow or a mobile phone that villagers can pay to use. Since then, the Bank has disbursed more than $5.3 billion to nearly 7 million borrowers who have no collateral. They pay a high interest rate (as much as 20 percent) to service these small loans, but 98 percent of the loans are paid off. Ninety-six percent of these loans are to women because traditionally, banks in the developing world lend only to men.

This model for helping the world's poorest has attracted funds from various foundations (e.g., Michael and Susan Dell Foundation, Google.org, Bill and Melinda Gates Foundation) and from the World Bank, which grants loans of as little as $1,000 for enterprises such as brick making. Through these foundations, 113 million borrowers received microloans in 2005. The goal of the Microcredit Summit Campaign is to reach 175 million of the world's poorest families by 2015.

Without question, this microcredit movement has helped many poor women and their families. The trouble, as Alexander Cockburn has put it, "is that microloans don't make any sort of macrodifference" (2009:9). In other words, "Loans to the poor have not yet had a demonstrable effect on aggregate poverty levels" (Bruck 2006:67). Bangladesh and Bolivia, for example, have two of the most successful microcredit programs in the world, but they also remain two of the poorest countries of the world.

Two plans should be added to the microcredit program. At the microlevel, lending should be combined with other initiatives, such as education and health care. And foremost, the structural causes of poverty in these impoverished nations must be addressed. Economist Robert Pollin says that poor countries need publicly subsidized macrocredit programs to support "manufacturing, land reform, marketing cooperatives, a functioning infrastructure, and, most of all, decent jobs" (quoted in Cockburn 2009:9). "What poor countries need most, then, is not more microbusinesses. They need more small-to-medium sized enterprises . . . companies that are relatively rare in the developing world" (Surowieki 2008:35).

"Governments like microloans because they allow them to abdicate their most basic responsibilities to poor citizens. Microloans make the market a god" (Cockburn 2009:9). The market, however, is a major source for the abject poverty in the world. Although microloans do help many individuals, they must be combined with structural societal reforms necessary to reduce overall poverty.

gave $1.3 billion in 2008 to buy weapons; only $103 million for education, and $74 million for health care (O'Brien 2008).

According to the chief economist of the World Bank, Nicholas Stern, "If the rich nations increased aid to 0.7 percent of their economic output, it would add $100 billion a year in assistance" (quoted in Memmott 2001:3B). What could be accomplished with an additional $100 billion?

- The global relief agency Oxfam argues that about $8 billion more each year is needed in spending for education in the world's poorest countries to fulfill a pledge by 155 nations that every child on earth have a basic level of literacy by 2015 (Briscoe 1999).
- The world's poor countries owe the rich ones trillions of dollars. The annual interest owed on this debt exceeds the amount spent on health and education in the poor countries. Some poor countries spend 40 percent of their income for interest on a foreign debt that will never be repaid (much like the contract debt that enslaves poor individuals). The rich countries must provide debt relief to the poor countries. Currently, there is a partial debt relief plan whereby the United States pays 4 percent of the wealthy nation's total, or $920 million over 4 years. Each dollar contributed to this plan produces $20 in debt relief.
- There could be a frontal assault by the World Health Organization and the developed countries to reduce the incidence and spread of infectious diseases such as tuberculosis, malaria, and meningitis. Eradication of diseases for which the technology is already available (poliomyelitis, leprosy, tetanus, Chagas' disease, and dracunculiasis) and the disorder of iodine deficiency could be reached. Education programs need to be instituted to warn about sexually transmitted diseases and how to protect against them.
- Meeting the basic nutrition and health needs of the world's poorest people would cost $13 billion a year (Cain, 2004).
- When Kofi Annan was secretary-general of the United Nations, he argued that an annual expenditure of $7 billion to $10 billion (five times the current expenditure) sustained for many years is needed to defeat AIDS in the developing world. Other estimates are that a comprehensive AIDS program would exceed $20 billion annually. Specifically, the money would be used for prevention through education, providing medicines to prevent the transmission from mother to child, care and treatment of those infected, and protection of those left most vulnerable (widows and orphans; Annan, 2006).

The wealthy nations can provide humanitarian aid to the developing nations with three provisos: (1) that it is truly humanitarian (such as technology, medical supplies, food, inoculation programs, family planning, agricultural equipment, sewage treatment systems, water treatment) and not military aid; (2) that the aid reaches the intended targets (those in need), not the well-off elites; and (3) that the governments in the impoverished nations have sensible plans for using the new resources, such as spending on health (e.g., the vaccination of children) and education, especially for women (Sen 1999).

How much commitment should the United States make to bringing poor nations up to a minimum standard? Many citizens, corporations, and politicians are indifferent to the plight of the poor, hungry, and sick far away. Many have misgivings about helping corrupt governments. Others are opposed to our support of family planning and the funding of abortion.

The ultimate interest of the United States is best served if there is peace and stability in the developing world. These goals can be accomplished only if population growth is slowed significantly, hunger and poverty alleviated, and the extremes of inequality reduced.

If the United States and other developed nations do not take appropriate steps, human misery, acts of terrorism against affluent nations, tensions among neighbors, and wars—even nuclear war—will increase. The last factor becomes especially relevant given that a number of developing nations have nuclear bomb capabilities. Moreover, a number of developing-world countries have been alleged to have used chemical weapons. The ultimate question is whether the way these steps are implemented will help the developing world reduce its dependence on the more developed nations, the hunger and misery within their countries, and in the process, international tensions. We ignore the poor of the developing world at our peril.

■ CHAPTER REVIEW

1. The term *developing world* refers to the underdeveloped and developing nations where poverty, hunger, and misery are found disproportionately. These nations also are characterized by relative powerlessness, rapid population growth, high infant mortality, unsanitary living conditions, and high rates of illiteracy.
2. In mid-2009, the world population exceeded 6.8089 billion and was increasing by 75 to 80 million annually. About 99 percent of the population growth occurs in the developing world, where food, housing, health care, and employment are inadequate to meet present needs.
3. While world population is growing rapidly, the amount of productive land is shrinking in rich and poor countries alike because of the loss of topsoil, the lowering of water tables from irrigation and overgrazing, and pollution.
4. Within the nations experiencing the most rapid population growth, cities are growing much faster than are rural areas. The problems of survival for individuals and families are increased dramatically in cities: food is too expensive, jobs are scarce and poorly paid, and sanitation problems increase the likelihood of disease. The concentration of the poor in the limited space of cities increases tensions and the probability of hostility.
5. There are three ways to reduce high fertility in the developing world: (a) economic development (modern demographic transition), (b) family-planning programs, and (c) social change, especially through the changing of traditional women's roles.
6. Poverty is a special problem of the developing world: 1.3 billion people have inadequate diets, high infant mortality, low life expectancy, and high rates of illiteracy. Poverty also contributes to high fertility.
7. Hunger is a worldwide problem, especially in the developing world, but even there food production is adequate to meet the needs of all of the people. The problem of hunger results from high prices, unequal distribution of food, overreliance on cash crops, and concentration of land ownership among very few people—all the consequences of the political economy in these nations and the world.
8. The developing world is underdeveloped for a number of reasons, the most important of which is a heritage of colonialism. Colonialism destroyed local industries and self-sufficient crop-growing patterns, drained off resources for the benefit of the colonizers, and promoted local elites through concentration of land ownership among the few. In the postcolonial era, the dependency of the developing world and its control by outside forces continue.
9. A huge worldwide problem, especially among the poor in the developing world, is HIV/AIDS. Since 1980 some 60 million people have contracted this disease worldwide, with 25 million deaths.
10. It is estimated that there are 27 million slaves in the world. The new slavery is a consequence of extreme poverty, resulting in debt bondage and the sale of people to slaveholders.
11. The world economy is controlled by transnational corporations, the majority of which are based in the United States. Their power in the

underdeveloped nations perpetuates the dependency of many developing-world nations on the United States.

12. Transnationals add to the tensions in developing-world countries through arms sales, corporate dumping of products known to be dangerous, and intervention in the domestic affairs of host countries.
13. The developed nations must work to alleviate the problems faced by the developing nations by increasing their financial commitment, by providing debt relief, and by working with international agencies to promote education and health programs. To do so is in our national interest.

KEY TERMS

Differential fertility. Differences in the average number of children born to a woman by social category.

Fertility rate. The average number of children born to each woman.

Modern demographic transition. A three-stage pattern of population change occurring as societies industrialize and urbanize, resulting ultimately in a low and stable population growth rate.

Absolute poverty. A condition of life so degraded by disease, illiteracy, malnutrition, and squalor as to deny its victims the basic necessities. Statistically, those making less than $1 a day are in this category.

Life chances. The chances throughout one's life cycle to live and experience the good things in life.

Pandemic. A worldwide epidemic.

New slavery. The new slavery differs from traditional slavery in that it is, for the most part, not a lifelong condition and sometimes individuals and families become slaves by choice—a choice forced by extreme poverty.

Colony. A territory controlled by a powerful country that exploits the land and the people for its own benefit.

Transnational corporation. A profit-oriented company engaged in business activities in more than one nation.

Corporate dumping. The exporting of goods that have either been banned or not approved for sale in the United States because they are dangerous.

SUCCEED WITH PEARSON mysoclab www.mysoclab.com

Experience, Discover, Observe, Evaluate
MySocLab is designed just for you. Each chapter features a pre-test and post-test to help you learn and review key concepts and terms.

Experience sociology in action with dynamic visual activities, videos, and readings to enhance your learning experience. Complete the following activities at www.mysoclab.com.

Social Explorer is an interactive application that allows you to explore Census data through interactive maps.

- Explore the Social Explorer Map: *Burgess' Concentric Zone Model*

The Core Concepts in Sociology video clips offer a real-world perspective on sociological concepts.

- Watch *Population Growth and Decline*

MySocLibrary includes primary source readings from classic and contemporary sociologists.

- Read Ehrenreich & Hochschild, *Global Woman*; Eglitis, *The Uses of Global Poverty: How Economic Inequality Benefits the West*

CHAPTER 4

Threats to the Environment

The threat from climate change is serious, it is urgent, and it is growing. Our generation's response to this challenge will be judged by history, for if we fail to meet it—boldly, swiftly, and together—we risk consigning future generations to an irreversible catastrophe.

—President Barack Obama (2009)

Human societies have always altered their physical environments. They have used fire, cleared forests, tilled the soil, terraced hillsides, mined for mineral deposits, dammed rivers, polluted streams, and overgrazed grasslands. Since 1950 the pace and magnitude of the negative environmental impacts of human activities have increased and intensified. Especially significant are the extraordinary use of fossil fuels, the deforestation of the rain forests, the pumping of billions of tons of greenhouse gases into the air, the pollution of water by fertilizers, pesticides, and animal wastes, emission of toxic chemicals, and the rapid erosion of topsoil. In effect, we human beings are fundamentally changing the planet in ways that are diminishing the planet's ability to sustain life.

The Worldwatch Institute concluded its annual State of the World report in 2000 saying: Species are disappearing, temperatures are rising, reefs are dying, forests are shrinking, storms are raging, water tables are falling: Almost every ecological indicator shows a world in decline. And with the global population expected to hit 9 billion in the next 50 years, those indicators are likely to worsen. (quoted in Braile 2000:16a)

As environmental problems are examined in this chapter, the discussion is guided by three facts. First, while some environmental problems are beyond human control (volcanoes, earthquakes, solar flares), *most are social in origin*. As Paul and Anne Ehrlich summarize it,

Our species' negative impact on our own life-support systems can be approximated by the equation I = PAT. In that equation, the size of the population (P) is multiplied by the average affluence or consumption per individual (A), and that in turn is multiplied by some measure of the technology (T) that services and drives the consumption. Thus commuting in automobiles powered by subsidized fossil fuels on proliferating freeways creates a much greater T factor than commuting on bikes using simple paths or working at home on a computer network. The product of P, A, and T is Impact (I), a rough estimate of how much humanity is degrading the ecosystem services it depends upon. (2008:1)

Second, the magnitude of environmental problems has become so great that the ultimate survival of the human species is in question (see the "Looking Toward the Future" panel). Third, although environmental problems may originate within a nation's borders, they usually have global consequences. Thus, this chapter examines human-made environmental problems at both the domestic and international levels. The first section describes the nature of these problems and their consequences. The second focuses on the United States. The third section examines the social sources of these problems and alternative solutions. The final section describes the long-range international implications of environmental problems.

WORLDWIDE ENVIRONMENTAL PROBLEMS

Earth's **biosphere** (the surface layer of the planet and the surrounding atmosphere) provides the land, air, water, and energy necessary to sustain life. This life-support system is a complex, interdependent one in which energy from the sun is converted into food:

The goods and services that ecosystems provide us with form the foundation of our economies. Agriculture, forestry, and fishing are responsible for 50% of all jobs worldwide and 70% of the jobs in sub-Saharan Africa, East Asia, and the Pacific. In 25% of the world's nations, crops, timber, and fish still contribute more to the economy than do industrial goods. Ecosystems also purify our air and water, help to control our climate, and produce soil-services that can't be replaced at any reasonable cost. (PBS 2010:1)

Three social forces are disturbing these **ecosystems** profoundly. First, the tremendous increase in population increases the demand for food, energy, minerals, and other products. With the world's population (approximately 6.8 billion in 2009) increasing by 76 million a year (in effect, adding the population of Sweden every month), the stresses on the environment mount (see Figure 4.1: World Population Estimates).

LOOKING TOWARD THE FUTURE

ENVIRONMENTAL COLLAPSES

Geographer Jared Diamond, in his book *Collapse: How Societies Choose to Fail or Succeed,* describes a number of past civilizations (e.g., Easter Island, the Anasazi of the Southwest United States, the Maya, and the Norse in Greenland) that disappeared, leaving behind great ruins and a mystery as to why they collapsed. Diamond argues that the mystery is explained, at least in part, by "ecological suicide." That theory has obvious implications for humanity today.

> It has long been suspected that many of those mysterious abandonments were at least partly triggered by ecological problems: people inadvertently destroying the environmental resources on which their societies depended. This suspicion of unintended ecological suicide—ecocide—has been confirmed by discoveries made in recent decades by archaeologists, climatologists, historians, paleontologists, and palynologists (pollen scientists). The processes through which past societies have undermined themselves by damaging their environments fall into eight categories, whose relative importance differs from case to case: deforestation and habitat destruction, soil problems (erosion, salinization, and soil fertility losses), water management problems, overhunting, overfishing, effects of introduced species on native species, human population growth, and increased per capita impact of people.
>
> Those past collapses tended to follow somewhat similar courses constituting variations on a theme. Population growth forced people to adopt intensified means of agricultural production (such as irrigation, double-cropping, or terracing), and to expand farming from the prime lands first chosen onto more marginal land, in order to feed the growing number of hungry mouths. Unsustainable practices led to environmental damage of one or more of the eight types just listed, resulting in agriculturally marginal lands having to be abandoned again. Consequences for society included food shortages, starvation, wars among too many people fighting for too few resources, and overthrows of governing elites by disillusioned masses. Eventually, population decreased through starvation, war, or disease, and society lost some of the political, economic, and cultural complexity that it had developed at its peak.

FIGURE 4.1

World Population Estimates 1950–2050

Source: U.S. Census Bureau, International Data Base, December 2010 update.

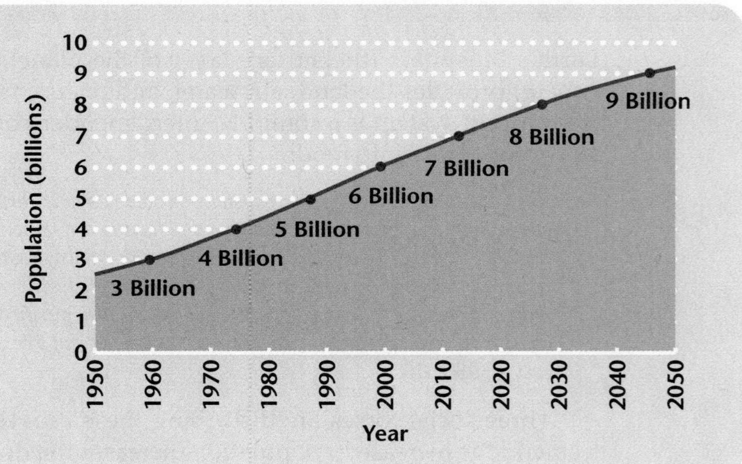

Writers find it tempting to draw analogies between those trajectories of human societies and the trajectories of individual human lives—to talk of a society's birth, growth, peak, senescence, and death—and to assume that the long period of senescence that most of us traverse between our peak years and our deaths also applies to societies. But that metaphor proves erroneous for many past societies (and for the modern Soviet Union): they declined rapidly after reaching peak numbers and power, and those rapid declines must have come as a surprise and shock to their citizens. In the worst cases of complete collapse, everybody in the society emigrated or died. Obviously, though, this grim trajectory is not one that all past societies followed unvaryingly to completion: different societies collapsed to different degrees and in somewhat different ways, whereas many societies didn't collapse at all.

The risk of such collapses today is now a matter of increasing concern; indeed, collapses have already materialized for Somalia, Rwanda, and some other Third World countries. Many people fear that ecocide has now come to overshadow nuclear war and emerging diseases as a threat to global civilization. The environmental problems facing us today include the same eight that undermined past societies, plus four new ones: human-caused climate change, buildup of toxic chemicals in the environment, energy shortages, and full human utilization of the Earth's photosynthetic capacity. Most of these 12 threats, it is claimed, will become globally critical within the next few decades: either we solve the problems by then, or the problems will undermine not just Somalia but also First World societies. Much more likely than a doomsday scenario involving human extinction or an apocalyptic collapse of industrial civilization would be "just" a future of significantly lower living standards, chronically higher risks, and the undermining of what we now consider some of our key values. Such a collapse could assume various forms, such as the worldwide spread of diseases or else of wars, triggered ultimately by scarcity of environmental resources. If this reasoning is correct, then our efforts today will determine the state of the world in which the current generation of children and young adults lives out their middle and late years.

Source: From *Collapse: How Societies Choose to Fail or Succeed* by Jared Diamond, copyright © 2005 by Jared Diamond. Used by permission of Viking Penguin, a division of Penguin Group (USA) Inc.

The second driving force contributing to the pressures on Earth's natural systems is growing inequality in income between the rich and poor (as discussed in Chapter 3). In 2005, the richest 20 percent of the world's population accounted for 76.6 percent of total private consumption, whereas the poorest 20 percent accounted for just 1.5 percent (Shah, 2008). This inequality is a major source of environmental decline. Those at the top overconsume energy, raw materials, and manufactured goods, and for survival the poor must cut down trees, grow crops, fish, or graze livestock, often in ways that are harmful to the planet.

These consumption patterns apply to nations as well. Consider the consumption patterns in the United States, with but 4.5 percent of the world's population:

- The United States consumes 25 percent of the world's fossil fuel, 20 percent of its metals, and 33 percent of its paper, and produces about three-fourths of the world's hazardous waste.
- Americans waste more food than most people eat in sub-Saharan Africa. Forty-eight million tons of food suitable for human consumption is wasted each year in the United States (*Harper's* 2001).
- There are three automobiles for every four people in the United States. These cars guzzle about 11 percent of the world's daily oil output (Zuckerman 2006a).

- On average, a person in India uses only 5 percent of the primary energy (e.g., oil, coal) that an American does, and a person in China uses 10 percent of that used by the average American (Zuckerman 2006a).
- The United States produces 30.3 percent of the greenhouse gases that cause global warming (more than the combined contributions of South America, Africa, the Middle East, Australia, Japan, and all of Asia) (Gore 2006:250).
- For every dollar's worth of goods and services the United States produces, it consumes 40 percent more energy than other industrialized nations (Walter 2001:1).

Although the U.S. population increases by roughly 3 million a year compared to India's nearly 16 million, the additional Americans have greater environmental impact. They are responsible for 15.7 million tons of additional carbon to the atmosphere, compared with only 4.9 million tons in India (Gardner, Assadourian, and Sarin 2004:5).

The third driving force behind the environmental degradation of the planet is economic growth. Since 1950, the global economy has expanded fivefold. This expansion, although important for the jobs created and the products produced, has an environmental downside. Economic growth is powered by the accelerated extraction and consumption of fossil fuels, minerals, water, and timber. In turn, environmental damage increases proportionately.

Degradation of the Land

Across the planet, a thin, three-foot layer of topsoil provides food crops for 6.8 billion people and grazing for about 4 billion domesticated animals. This nutrient-rich topsoil, the source of food, fiber, and wood, is eroding at a faster rate than it can form. In fact, researchers estimate that we are losing about 1 percent of our topsoil every year (Paulson 2008). This topsoil is being depleted or lost because of careless husbandry and urbanization. Farmland is lost because of plowing marginal lands, leading to wind and water erosion. The fertility of farmland is lost because it is exhausted by overuse. It is also lost because of irrigation practices that poison the land with salt, a process called salinization. The overuse of irrigation also drains rivers and depletes aquifers faster than they can be replenished. The use of chemical fertilizers and pesticides kills helpful creatures, taints groundwater, and creates dead zones in the oceans (e.g., where the Mississippi River drains into the Gulf of Mexico). In a special issue on the "State of the Planet," *Time* summarized the United Nations' assessment of Earth's ecosystems. With respect to the situation for agricultural lands:

> *One-third of global land has been converted to food production, but three-quarters of this area has poor soil. So far, harvests outpace population growth, but the future is clouded by the loss of land to urban development, soil degradation, and water scarcity. . . . More than 40 percent of agricultural land has been badly degraded [through] erosion, nutrient depletion and water stress.* (Linden 2000:20)

In addition to the degradation and loss of topsoil, productive land is lost through the growth of cities and urban sprawl, the building of roads, and the damming of rivers. Consider these facts for the United States (Knickerbocker 2006):

- More area than the entire state of Georgia is now under pavement.
- Nearly 3,000 acres of farmland are converted to nonagricultural uses daily.

- Land is being converted for development at about twice the rate of population growth.
- When housing, shopping, schools, roads, and other uses are added up, each American occupies 20 percent more developed land than he or she did 20 years ago.

Environmental Pollution and Degradation

The following description of the various forms of pollution present in industrial societies, especially the United States, presents a glimpse of how humanity is fouling its nest.

Chemical Pollution. More than 75,000 chemicals have been released into the environment. These chemicals are found in food. They are used in detergents, fertilizers, pesticides, plastics, clothing, insulation, and almost everything else. People are exposed to the often toxic substances in the products they use and to the chemicals that seep into ground water, are carried in the air, and contaminate food. Some 202 of these chemicals, such as lead and mercury, harm children's brains and may be responsible for many developmental disabilities such as autism and attention deficit disorder (Laurance 2006).

More than 20,000 pesticide products are used in the United States. Agricultural workers use about 1.2 billion pounds of pesticides annually, adversely affecting themselves and their families with disproportionate levels of leukemia and stomach, uterine, and brain cancer (Feagin, Feagin, and Baker 2006:411).

The manufacture of chemicals requires disposing of the waste. Waste disposal, especially safe disposal of toxic chemicals, is a huge problem. These toxic chemicals are released into the air, water, land, underground, and public sewage either by accident or deliberately. Over 4 billion pounds of toxic chemicals are released by industry in the United States each year, including 72 million pounds of recognized carcinogens (*Scorecard* 2010). Typically, corporations choose the cheapest means of disposal, which is to release the waste products into the air

A crop duster sprays pesticides on a local farm. This is one source of chemical food contamination.

and waterways and to bury the materials in dump sites. In one infamous instance, the Hooker Chemical and Plastics Corporation over a number of years dumped 43.6 million pounds of 82 different chemical substances into Love Canal, New York, near Niagara Falls. Among the chemicals dumped were 200 tons of trichlorophenol, which contained an estimated 130 pounds of one of the most toxic and carcinogenic substances known—dioxin. Three ounces of this substance can kill more than a million people. (A variant of dioxin—Agent Orange—was used in the Vietnam War with extremely adverse results to vegetation and human life.) As a result of exposure to the various chemicals dumped at Love Canal, nearby residents had an unusual number of serious illnesses, a high incidence of miscarriages, and an unusual number of children born with birth defects.

The Love Canal dump site is only one of many dangerous locations in the United States. The federal government estimates there are over 400,000 hazardous waste sites. The Environmental Protection Agency (EPA) places sites that pose the greatest risk to public health and the environment on the Superfund National Priorities List. Hurricane Katrina flooded three Superfund toxic waste sites in and around New Orleans, and this poses serious threats if any of their protective shields have been degraded (Eilperin 2005).

A movement known as **environmental justice** works to improve environments for communities and is especially alert to the injustices that occur when a particular segment of the population, such as the poor or minority groups, bears a disproportionate share of exposure to environmental hazards (Pellow 2000). This movement is a reaction against the overwhelming likelihood that toxic-producing plants and toxic waste dumps are located where poor people, especially people of color, live (when this pattern occurs, it is called **environmental racism**). In Mississippi, for example, people of color represent 64 percent of residents near toxic facilities—but just 37 percent of the state population (Dervarics 2000). "In Los Angeles more than 71 percent of African Americans live in highly polluted areas, compared to 24 percent of whites. Across the United States, black children are three times more likely to have hazardous levels of lead in their blood as a result of living near hazardous waste sites" (Oliver 2008:2). Robert Bullard, an expert on environmental racism, says that "Blacks and other economically disadvantaged groups are often concentrated in areas that expose them to high levels of toxic pollution: namely, urban industrial communities with elevated air and water pollution problems or rural areas with high levels of exposure to farm pesticides" (Bullard 2000:6–7). For example, the toxic pesticide methyl bromide is permitted on agricultural fields because the growers say that there are no affordable alternatives. As a result, workers in the fields, mostly poor and Latino, risk being poisoned (Lewis 2004).

U.S. corporations are also involved in global chemical pollution. They not only dump wastes into the oceans and the air, which of course can affect the people in other countries, but they also sell to other countries chemicals (such as pesticides) that are illegal to sell here because they are toxic. In addition, U.S. corporations have used other countries as dump sites for their hazardous substances because the U.S. government outlawed indiscriminate dumping of toxic wastes in this country in 1975.

The nations of Western Europe and North America have relatively strict environmental laws, which is good for their inhabitants. These countries, however, transport roughly 2 million tons of toxic waste annually to poor nations that desperately need the cash.

Toxic wastes are also exported when U.S. multinational corporations move operations to countries with less stringent environmental laws. For example, the 2,000 foreign-owned (mostly by the United States) factories along the United States–Mexico border in Mexico (*maquiladoras*) have created environmental hazards on both sides of the border.

Another problem with toxic wastes is accidental spills from tankers, trucks, and trains as the wastes are transported. These spills number about 400 a year in the United States alone. When these incidents occur, the air is polluted, as is the groundwater and the oceans. Fires sometimes occur along with explosions. The result is that people, animals, and plant life are endangered.

- **Solid Waste Pollution.** The United States discards 30 percent of the world's resources (Rogers 2005). As such, it is the largest producer of solid waste among the industrialized nations, both in absolute and per capita terms. Americans throw away approximately 250 million tons of old food, glass, clothing, electronics, plastics, metals, textiles, rubber, wood, and paper. On average, each American produces 4.5 pounds of solid trash a day (up from 2.7 pounds in 1960). Approximately 33 percent of this trash is recycled, and the rest is incinerated or buried in landfills (see Figure 4.2).

The problem of what to do with solid waste is compounded by the increased amounts of waste that are contaminated with compounds and chemicals that do not appear in nature. These wastes pose new and unknown threats to human, animal, and plant life. One such health hazard is toxic sludge, a mix of human and industrial waste produced by wastewater treatment plants. About 4 million tons of sludge are dumped on farmland, golf courses, and parks as a form of fertilizer. Unless sludge is carefully treated and monitored, it can be tainted with *E. coli*, bacteria, viruses, heavy metals, solvents, and any combination of the thousands of chemicals used in U.S. industries (Orlando 2001). Exposure to tainted sludge increases the risk of serious infections, illness, and death (Fackelmann 2002).

All landfills leak seeping toxic residues into the groundwater. Many communities have contaminated drinking water and crops as a result. With the problem clearly becoming serious, some experimentation is now being

FIGURE 4.2

Municipal Solid Waste Disposal in the United States

Source: U.S. Environmental Protection Agency, "Municipal Solid Waste Generation, Recycling, and Disposal in the U.S.: Facts and Figures for 2008." http://www.epa.gov/waste/nonhaz/municipal/pubs/msw2008rpt.pdf

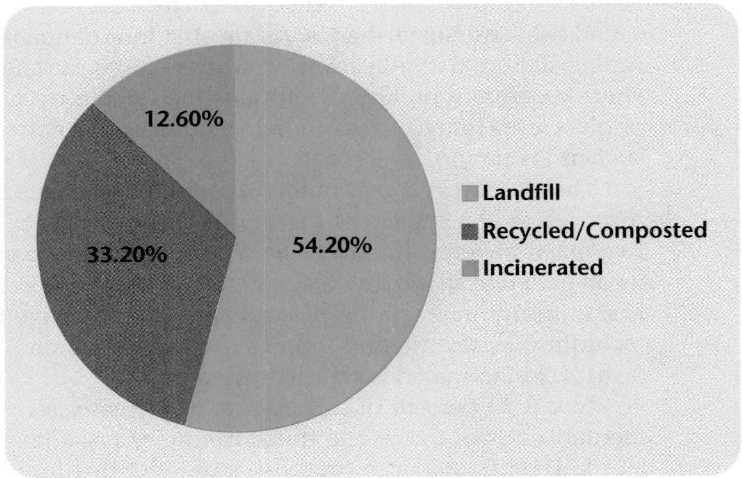

A CLOSER LOOK

THE NEW TECHNOLOGY AND TOXIC WASTE

The new technology found in most households in the developed world—personal computers, cell phones, televisions, and other electronic equipment—is laden with toxins that when thrown away will leach into groundwater or produce dioxins and other carcinogens when burned. Let us consider computers.

The computer revolution changes quickly, with each new generation having much more memory and being infinitely faster, yet available at a cheaper price than the original. As a result, millions of computers become obsolete every year. Thus, personal computers and consumer electronics ("e-waste") "compose one of the fastest growing and highly toxic waste streams in the industrialized world" (Grassroots Recycling Network [GRRN] 2005). Following are some facts regarding computers:

- On average, U.S. consumers toss an estimated 2.6 million tons of e-waste each year (Green 2007).
- Printed circuit boards and semiconductors contain cadmium. In 2005, more than 2 million pounds of cadmium were discarded along with computers.
- The batteries and switches contain mercury; 400,000 pounds of mercury were discarded nationwide in 2005.
- Chromium is used as corrosion protection in computers. In 2005, there were an estimated 1.2 million pounds of chromium in landfills.
- PVC (polyvinyl chloride) plastics are used on cables and housings, creating a potential waste of 250 million pounds per year.
- With the increased use of flat-panel monitors, it is estimated that 500 million defunct monitors were discarded by 2007, each of which contains phosphorous and 4 to 8 pounds of lead.
- Santa Clara County, California, the home of the semiconductor industry, contains more toxic waste sites than any other county in the United States (Worldwatch Institute n.d.).

The problem is that only 10 percent of computers are recycled. The rest threaten the environment—here and abroad. Chances are that most of the obsolete computers will end up in the developing world—Africa, India, and China—where the poor, with little or no protection, are hired to extract items of value (*USA Today* 2002a).

conducted with landfills that have impermeable linings to prevent such pollution. (See "A Closer Look" panel on personal computers and toxic waste.)

There are several alternatives to dumping trash in landfills. One option has been to dump rubbish in the ocean. This practice has polluted beaches, poisoned fish, and hurt fisheries. As a result, international agreements and domestic legislation within various countries have curtailed this alternative. The environmentally preferred solutions are for the trash to be reprocessed to its original uses (paper, glass containers, metals) or converted into new products such as insulation.

The alternative most commonly selected is to incinerate the garbage (which disposes of 12.6 percent of the country's total waste). The burning of trash has two major benefits. It reduces the volume of garbage by almost 90 percent, and it can generate steam and electricity. The downside of burning trash, however, is significant. Incinerating plastics and other garbage releases toxic chemicals, including deadly dioxins and heavy-metal emissions, into the air. The residue (ash) is contaminated with lead and cadmium.

About 33 percent of solid waste is currently recycled, a positive environmental step. So, too, is the transforming of organic waste-paper, food scraps, and lawn clippings into compost, a product that invigorates agricultural soils.

European countries are leading the way with composting. If we could sort trash into recyclables, compostables, and disposables, we could "keep 60 to 70 percent of what was trash out of our landfills and incinerators" (Gavzer 1999:6).

- **Water Pollution.** The major sources of water pollution are: (1) industries, which pour into rivers, lakes, and oceans a vast array of contaminants such as lead, asbestos, detergents, solvents, acid, and ammonia; (2) farmers, whose pesticides, herbicides, fertilizers, and animal wastes drain into streams and lakes; (3) cities, which dispose of their wastes, including sewage, into rivers to end up downstream in another city's drinking water; and (4) oil spills, caused by tanker accidents and leaks in offshore drilling. These are problems throughout the world.

Water pollution is a most immediate problem in the less developed countries. Contaminated water in poor countries results in high death rates from cholera, typhoid, dysentery, and diarrhea. About 1.2 billion people do not have enough safe drinking water. Nearly 3 billion people are at risk of contaminated water because of improper sanitation. More than 5 million die each year of easily preventable waterborne diseases such as diarrhea, dysentery, and cholera (Leslie 2000).

> *The world is facing a water crisis due to pollution, climate change, and surging population growth of unprecedented magnitude. Unless we change our ways, by the year 2025 two-thirds of the world's population will face water scarcity. The global population tripled in the 20th century, but water consumption went up sevenfold. By 2050, after we add another 3 billion to the population, humans will need an 80 percent increase in water supplies just to feed ourselves. No one knows where this water is going to come from. (Barlow 2008:A3)*

In the United States, the Mississippi River provides an example of the seriousness of water pollution. Greenpeace USA, an environmental organization, surveyed pollution in the Mississippi River and found that industries and municipalities along the river discharged billions of pounds of heavy metals and toxic chemicals into it. This dumping occurs along the 2,300 miles of the river; the worst pollution is concentrated along 150 miles in Louisiana, where 25 percent of the nation's chemical industry is located. More than a hundred heavy industrial facilities there release poison into the air, land, and water at a rate of almost half a billion pounds per year (*Witness to the Future* n.d.).

A serious threat to drinking water comes from the chemicals that farmers put on their fields to increase yields (fertilizers), kill pests (pesticides), and destroy weeds (herbicides). The chemicals applied seep into wells and drain into streams and rivers. As a result, about 40 percent of U.S. rivers and lakes are too polluted for fishing or swimming (Kelly 2004).

The EPA has a list of large toxic sites to be cleaned up with funds supplied by Congress. The largest of these Superfund sites is a 200-mile stretch of the upper Hudson River, where General Electric dumped 1.3 million pounds of polychlorinated biphenyls (PCBs) into the river over a 30-year period. PCBs cause cancer in laboratory animals, and they are linked to premature births and developmental disorders. General Electric stopped the practice in 1977 when the federal government banned PCB use. More than three decades later, the New York State Health Department continues to advise women of childbearing age and children under age 15 not to eat any fish from the Hudson River and urges that no one eat any fish from the upper Hudson, where the cancer risk from such consumption is 700 times the EPA protection level. Between May and

October of 2009, Phase 1 of the Hudson River Dredging Project was completed, and 10 percent of the contaminated sediment was removed. The problem is that thousands of pounds of PCBs remain in the sediment of the Hudson and continue to poison fish, wildlife, and humans.

The ocean, the cornerstone of the Earth's life-support system, is also in serious danger because of human activity.

> *We are altering the nature of the ocean by what we put in and by what we take out. Tons of toxic substances flowing from the land have altered the ocean's chemistry. More than 50 "dead zones" blight coastal areas. Gigantic swaths of toxic algae are fueled by high levels of nitrates and phosphates in runoff from over-fertilized fields, farms, and lawns. Coral reefs, the "rain forests of the sea," have declined about 30 percent in 30 years, largely because of overfishing, coastal development, and global warming. Mercury levels are so high in some top-of-the-food-chain predators such as swordfish, sharks, and tuna that people are advised to strictly limit their consumption. Swimmers, surfers, and sunbathers are finding many of their favorite beaches contaminated—and closed. (Earle 2003:1)*

- **Radiation Pollution.** Human beings cannot escape radiation from natural sources such as cosmic rays and radioactive substances in Earth's crust. Technology has added greatly to these natural sources through the extensive use of x-rays for medical and dental uses, fallout from nuclear weapons testing and from nuclear accidents, and the use of nuclear energy as a source of energy.

  The dangers of radiation are evidenced to the extreme in the physical effects on the survivors of the atomic bombs at the end of World War II. These victims experienced physical disfigurement, stillbirths, infertility, and extremely high rates of cancer. A government study estimated that the radioactive fallout from Cold War nuclear weapons tests across the Earth probably caused at least 15,000 cancer deaths and 20,000 nonfatal cancers in U.S. residents born after 1951 (reported in Eisler 2002). In 1986, the most serious nuclear accident to date occurred at Chernobyl in the Soviet Union. The full consequences of this accident will not be known for years, but so far there have been numerous deaths in Russia, a large-scale increase in cancers and other illnesses, and widespread contamination of food and livestock as far away as Scandinavia and Western Europe. The most serious nuclear accident in the United States occurred with the near meltdown in Pennsylvania at Three Mile Island in 1979.

  Less dramatic than nuclear accidents but lethal just the same have been the exposures to radiation by workers in nuclear plants and those living nearby. The Hanford nuclear weapons plant in Washington State provides an example. For more than 40 years, the U.S. government ran this facility, monitoring nuclear emissions but not notifying the workers or the 270,000 residents in the surrounding area of the dangers:

  > *From 1944 to 1947 alone, the Hanford plant spewed 400,000 curies of radioactive iodine into the atmosphere. The bodily absorption of 50 millionths of a single curie is sufficient to raise the risk of thyroid cancer. For years thereafter, Hanford poured radioactive water into the Columbia River and leaked millions of gallons of radioactive waste from damaged tanks into the groundwater. . . . Some 13,700 persons absorbed an estimated dose of 33 rads to their thyroid glands [equivalent to about 1,650 chest x-rays] some time during the last 40 years. . . . There was no diagnostic or therapeutic purpose. No one told them; there was no informed consent. Some have called this situation a "creeping Chernobyl" but there is a difference. Chernobyl was an accident. Hanford was deliberate. Chernobyl was a singular event, the product of faulty reactor*

Hanford was the world's first full-scale nuclear reactor, built to produce plutonium for an atomic bomb during World War II.

design and human error. Hanford was a chronic event, the product of obsessive secrecy and callous indifference to public health. (Geiger 1990:E19)

Similar situations occurred at the weapons factories at Rocky Flats near Denver, Fernald near Cincinnati, and Savannah River in South Carolina, and at the testing sites for weapons in Nevada and other areas in the Southwest.

Utility companies in thirty-one states operate 103 commercial nuclear reactors, providing about 20 percent of the nation's electricity (second only to coal). Unlike coal, the electricity generated by nuclear energy does not produce carbon dioxide and other greenhouse gases. The problem involves the safe storage of nuclear waste. The generation of nuclear power creates radioactive by-products such as uranium mill tailings, used reactors, and the atomic waste itself. The safe storage of these materials is an enormous and perhaps impossible task because some remain radioactive for as long as 250,000 years. Neither the nuclear industry nor the government has a long-term technology for safe nuclear waste disposal.

- **Air Pollution.** According to the World Health Organization, air pollution causes 70,000 premature deaths a year in the United States (cited in Kelly 2004). It is a major source of health problems such as respiratory ailments (asthma, bronchitis, and emphysema), cancer, impaired central nervous functioning, and cirrhosis of the liver. These problems are especially acute among people who work in or live near industrial plants in which waste chemicals are released into the air and among people who live in metropolitan areas where conditions such as temperature and topography tend to trap the pollutants near the ground (e.g., cities such as Mexico City, Los Angeles, and Denver). The EPA estimates that more than 133 million Americans live in areas where air quality is unhealthy at times because of high levels of at least one pollutant (cited in Kelly 2004). The pollutants emitted into the air have extremely serious consequences for the environment; the greenhouse effect and the loss of ozone protection are topics discussed later in this chapter.

The two major sources of air pollution are emissions from automobiles and from industrial plants (lesser but nonetheless serious sources are toxic waste dumps, burning trash, wood burning, and aerosols). Automobiles emit five gases implicated in global warming: carbon monoxide, carbon dioxide, nitrous oxide, chlorofluorocarbons, and ozone smog. Currently, automobile-generated air pollution is a problem of the wealthier nations.

Simply put, "cars have bad breath," as one environmental biologist observed. The airborne emissions are deadly. Charles Levy of Boston University goes on to say, "The agencies looking at studies of toxins, many on animals, cite acute toxicities—lungs, respiratory, eyes, nasal passages." Such chronic poisons ingested through the lungs and penetrating into the body through the respiratory system, or even through the skin, hit the stomach and bloodstream. Together, they interact, increasing the probability of disease years down the road—cancer, lung diseases like asthma and bronchitis, and possible cardiovascular conditions (Kay 1997:111).

Industrial emissions are the second major source of air pollution in the United States. Industrial plants and factories release several billion pounds of poisonous chemicals annually, and the EPA cites hundreds of industrial plants annually as posing the greatest risks to human health.

GLOBAL ENVIRONMENTAL CRISES

Each form of pollution just described threatens human life. This section focuses on environmental threats to Earth itself. The discussion is limited to three interrelated threats: dependence on fossil fuels for energy, destruction of the tropical rain forests, and global warming.

Fossil Fuel Dependence, Waste, and Environmental Degradation

The Industrial Revolution involved, most fundamentally, the replacement of human and animal muscle by engines driven by fossil fuels. These fuels (coal, oil, natural gas) are also used for heating, cooking, and lighting. Considering just oil, the world consumes 85 million barrels of oil a day. The United States is the greatest consumer of oil products, using approximately 21 million barrels of oil a day (25 percent of the world's daily consumption). China is second at 7.6 million barrels, followed by Japan, Russia, and India (NationMaster 2010). Carbon dioxide emissions from fossil fuels, the main villain among the greenhouse gases, have gone from almost nothing a hundred years ago to more than a ton of carbon per person each year. Each person in the United States, by the way, produces twenty times that much. The United States, for example, with 4.5 percent of the world's population, has one-third of the world's cars and drives 50 percent of the total world mileage. To provide for this extravagance, the United States imports 60 percent of the 21 million barrels used daily. (See the "Social Policy" panel on automobiles and fossil fuels.)

The worldwide demand for energy will rise sharply as the developing nations, where 99 percent of the world's population growth is taking place, industrialize and urbanize. In China, for example, car sales are increasing rapidly (from a private vehicle fleet of 5 million in 2000 to about 20 million in 2005). By 2020, China could have 120 million (Samuelson 2005). In 2000, 71 percent of

The United States is the world's greatest consumer of oil products, using 25 percent of the world's daily consumption.

motor vehicles were in the more developed countries. In 2020, it is projected that this proportion will be reduced to 55 percent (De Souza, Williams, and Meyerson 2003:18). People in the developing countries will be replacing traditional fuels such as wood and other organic wastes with electricity, coal, and oil. This likely trend has important consequences for the world and its inhabitants. First, the demand for fossil fuels has given extraordinary wealth to the elites in the nations of the Persian Gulf area, where two-thirds of the world's estimated petroleum reserves are located. Stability in this region is vital to U.S. interests because interruption in the flow of Persian Gulf oil (primarily Saudi oil, which supplies 15 percent of the world's total oil) would cause shortages and the price of other oil imports to rise dramatically, devastating the U.S. economy (Tepperman 2004)—thus, our involvement in the 1991 Gulf War to stop Iraq's attempts to control Kuwait and other oil-rich nations, as well as the 2003 invasion and control of Iraq. In short, the maldistribution of the world's energy supply heightens world tensions.

Second, because most nations need to import oil, vast amounts are carried across the world's oceans in about 2,600 tankers. Along with offshore drilling, these voyages increase the probability of accidents that damage aquatic life, birds, and coastal habitats. Four examples of large-scale spills are the wreck of the *Amoco Cadiz* off the coast of France in 1978, spilling 68 million gallons of crude oil; the blowout of the Ixtoc I oil well, which poured 140 million gallons of oil into the Gulf of Mexico in 1979; the grounding of the *Exxon Valdez* in Alaska's Prince William Sound in 1989, which released 11 million gallons of crude oil into an ecologically sensitive region, contaminating 1,000 miles of coastline and destroying extraordinary amounts of fish and wildlife; and the April 2010 explosion of the Deepwater Horizon oil rig, operated by British Petroleum [BP]. The BP oil spill killed eleven workers, and at the time of this writing, had leaked 5,000 barrels (i.e., millions of gallons) of oil into the Gulf of Mexico per day. The oil slick is as big as Maryland and Delaware combined, and threatens marine life, the coastal lands of Louisiana, and the livelihoods of people who fish and shrimp in the Gulf.

SOCIAL POLICY

U.S. DEPENDENCE ON THE AUTOMOBILE AND FOSSIL FUELS

Our nation's fleet of automobiles (230 million) smother communities in pollution and contribute 30 percent of the emissions that cause climate change through global warming (Gore 2006). Other forms of environmental degradation from automobiles are the 20 million cars and the 250 million tires discarded each year, the millions of tons of corrosive salt and other chemicals spread on highways to combat icy road conditions, and the almost 40 million acres of roads and parking lots that are covered with asphalt or concrete. The United States in 2006 used about 21 million barrels of oil a day to provide fuel for its cars (and other uses such as heating oil and natural gas), about 60 percent of which is imported (12 million barrels a day). Most of our oil imports go to

> finance both sides of the war on terrorism. We are financing the U.S. armed forces with our tax dollars, and, through our profligate use of energy, we are generating huge windfall profits for Saudi Arabia, Iran and Sudan, where the cash is used to insulate regimes from any pressure to open up their economies, liberate their women or modernize their schools, and where it ends up instead financing madrassas, mosques and militants fundamentally opposed to the progressive, pluralistic agenda America is trying to promote. (Friedman 2005:15)

Moreover, the United States spends hundreds of billions of dollars on a military presence to protect this Middle East energy source (Zuckerman 2005b).

Our insatiable appetite for oil has other negative consequences: degrading local environments by drilling for oil, oozings from pipelines, leaking underground tanks, oil spills from shipping accidents, the routine flushing of tankers, and leaks and accidents from deep-sea drilling.

What can be done to reduce oil consumption? There are several strategies, none of which is currently in political favor: (1) High taxes, such as a tax that would keep prices at $4 a gallon (the average in Europe is about $6 a gallon), could reduce usage. (2) The automobile industry could increase the fuel efficiency of vehicles. Existing technology could bring automobile fuel economy to an average of 45 miles per gallon, but under current federal laws, a passenger car must average 27.5 miles per gallon (the automobile industry lobbies against the higher gas mileage because it would add $2,000 or so to the cost of a vehicle). Moreover, the automobile manufacturers were successful in achieving legislation that creates a loophole for sport utility vehicles (SUVs) and light trucks (52 percent of new vehicles purchased in the United States are SUVs and light trucks), which are held to a lower miles-per-gallon standard (originally 20.7, and increased to 22.2 miles per gallon in 2007). (3) The automobile industry and the government could make a greater effort to produce and market electric and hybrid-electric automobiles. (4) Instead of subsidizing federal highways, which led to the development of urban sprawl and suburbs where people must drive to work, play, and shop, mass transit in urban areas and train travel between cities could be subsidized to a much greater degree. West Europeans use public transit for 10 percent of all urban trips compared with Americans at only 2 percent. "This is significant because for every kilometer people drive by private vehicle, they consume two to three times as much fuel as they would by public transit" (Sawin 2004:30). (5) Alternative and affordable sources of energy need to be developed for transportation, heating, cooling, and the like. Included among these possibilities are fuel cell, solar, wind, tidal, and geothermal sources. There is a huge roadblock to these needed changes, however, in the form of powerful corporations who profit from the current technologies.

Ultimately, transforming transportation to meet twenty-first-century environmental goals means moving beyond the internal combustion engine and beyond petroleum. Doing so requires major changes in the country's largest business; half of the top ten *Fortune* 500 companies are either automobile or oil companies. Such concentrated economic power leads to great political clout.

Meanwhile, the number of cars grows. Worldwide, there are about 800 million automobiles. It is estimated that by 2050 there will be 3.25 billion—"an unimaginable threat to our environment and a surefire guarantee of global warming" (Zuckerman 2005:72).

Finally, and most important, the combustion of fossil fuels results in the emission of carbon dioxide, which appears to be related to climate change. The consequences of the present level of carbon dioxide emissions, plus the expected increase in the near future, may have disastrous consequences for Earth in the form of global warming, as discussed later in this section.

Destruction of the Tropical Rain Forests and Other Forms of Deforestation

Tropical rain forests cover about 7 percent of Earth's dry land surface (about the same area as the 48 contiguous United States) and house about half of all species on Earth. About 1.9 billion acres of these forests remain in equatorial countries in the Caribbean, West Africa, Southeast Asia, and Latin America. These rich forests are losing an area about half the size of Florida each year (Wilson 2000). For example, it is estimated that the island nation of Comoros (north of Madagascar) lost nearly 60 percent of its forests between 1990 and 2005. In this same period, Brazil led the world in losing 163,543 square miles of forest, which is roughly the size of California (Lindsey 2007). This massive destruction continues to occur because of economics, from the greed of developers to the desperation of poor peasants.

Lumber, petroleum, and mining companies build roads into the jungles to extract their products and transport them to markets. Governments encourage the poor people to settle in these regions by building roads and offering land to settlers, who must clear it for farming. Cattle ranchers require vast expanses for their herds (five acres of pasture for each head). Land speculators clear huge areas for expected profits. The recovered land, however, is fragile, which leads to a cycle of further deforestation.

The sources of deforestation are not just local. The poverty of these nations (often the result of their colonial heritage), their indebtedness to wealthy nations, and the products needed by the wealthy nations are also responsible for the destruction of the tropical forests.

The world's tropical rain forest is losing an area about half the size of Florida each year.

U.S. corporations are directly and indirectly involved in various aspects of rain forest destruction. These involve the timber companies such as Georgia-Pacific and Weyerhaeuser; mining companies such as Alcoa and Freeport McMoRan; oil companies such as Amoco, Arco, Chevron, Exxon-Mobil, Occidental, Conoco Phillips, and Unocal; paper companies such as Kimberly-Clark; and agricultural companies such as Castle & Cooke and Chiquita.

The two major environmental consequences of this deforestation are climate change and the vanishing of species. The climate is affected in several related ways. As hundreds of thousands of forest acres are destroyed, rain patterns change. Huge areas once covered with plants, which give off moisture, are replaced by exposed, sandy soils. Also, the massive burning required to clear the land creates clouds of smoke that block the sun and lead to weather change. Thus, lush, green areas often become near deserts. The tropical forest in Brazil (the world's largest) has so much rainfall that it provides 20 percent of Earth's freshwater supply. What will be the long-range effects as this water supply dwindles? Just as important, forests absorb huge quantities of carbon dioxide through photosynthesis. Consequently, as forests are diminished so, too, is Earth's capacity to absorb the gas most responsible for global warming. This diminished capacity to process carbon dioxide, changing it into oxygen, leads to changes in the climate and to desertification.

The second critical environmental consequence of deforestation is the loss of animal and plant species. The eminent expert on biodiversity, E. O. Wilson, describes the contemporary threat:

> *[Biologists] generally agree that the rate of species extinction is now 100 to 1,000 times as great as it was before the coming of humanity. Throughout most of geological time, individual species and their immediate descendants lived an average of about 1 million years. They disappeared naturally at the rate of about one species per million per year, and newly evolved species replaced them at the same rate, maintaining a rough equilibrium. No longer. Not only has the extinction rate soared, but also the birthrate of new species has declined as the natural environment is destroyed. (Wilson 2000:30)*

Wherever humans destroy their habitat, species are eliminated. Although these tropical forests cover only 7 percent of Earth's dry land surface, they are Earth's richest factory of life, containing more than half of the world's species of plants, insects, birds, and other animals. As the forests are cleared and burned, species become extinct.

Humanity benefits from nature's diversity in many ways. One important aspect is that exotic plants and animals are major sources of pharmaceuticals. For example, Squibb used the venom of the Brazilian pit viper to develop Capoten, a drug to lower high blood pressure. The yew, which grows in the Pacific Northwest, produces a potent chemical, taxol, which shows promise for curing certain forms of lung, breast, and ovarian cancer. Biotechnology provides the potential to improve agricultural crops by transferring genes from wild plants to domestic crops so that they can be drought resistant, repel insects, or create their own fertilizers naturally. By destroying the forests, we may be eliminating future solutions to disease and famine.

Global Warming

As noted, the burning of fossil fuels and the destruction of the tropical forests contribute to the greenhouse effect. The **greenhouse effect** occurs when harmful

"Is this a bad time to talk about global warming?"

gases (carbon dioxide, nitrous oxide, chlorofluorocarbons, and methane)—all products of diverse human activities—accumulate in the atmosphere and act like the glass roof of a greenhouse. Sunlight reaches Earth's surface, and the gases trap the heat radiating from the ground. The results, according to the theory, are a warming of Earth, the melting of the polar ice caps, a significant changing of climate, droughts and megastorms, and the rapid spread of tropical diseases such as malaria, dengue fever, cholera, and encephalitis.

Before the Industrial Revolution, forest fires, plant decomposition, and ordinary evaporation released carbon dioxide into the atmosphere, but in small enough amounts to be absorbed by growing plants and by the oceans without noticeable environmental effect. But in the past century or so, human activities—especially the reliance on fossil fuels for internal combustion engines and in smokestack industries, and the use of chlorofluorocarbons to make plastic foam and as coolants in refrigerators and air conditioners, coupled with the destruction of the tropical rain forests—have increased the prevalence of dangerous gases beyond Earth's capacity to absorb them; hence, a gradual warming. The preindustrial concentration of carbon dioxide was 280 parts per million. In 2005, that level was 381 parts per million (Gore 2006:37). This level is expected to rise to 560 parts per million by 2050 (Dybas 2005). This potential doubling (from 280 to 560 parts per million) will increase global temperatures from three and a half to seven degrees. "A global temperature rise of just three degrees would render the earth hotter than it has been at any point in the past two million years" (Kolbert 2006:34).

China and the United States currently emit almost 40 percent of the world's greenhouse gases. China's emissions are the highest in the world, but the United States still leads in carbon dioxide emissions per person. The average American is responsible for 19.4 tons, while the average Chinese is responsible for 5.1 tons (Rosenthal 2008).

Earth is now the warmest it has been in the past 6,000 years or so. The decade of the 1990s was very likely the hottest of the last millennium. The first nine years of the twentieth century have been hotter still. The average global temperature rose 2 degrees over the past 50 years. As a result, mountain glaciers are retreating, polar ice is melting, ocean levels are rising and becoming more acidic, ocean currents are altered, storms are more intense, weather patterns are shifting, pests and diseases are spreading, and the future prospects for the Earth and its inhabitants are grim.

Scientists do not debate that Earth is warmer or that carbon dioxide is emitted into the air in ever-increasing amounts, but they do differ on the relationship between the two facts. Some scientists are cautious, arguing that recent warming and dramatic climatic events are random and part of the natural year-to-year variations in weather. Their skepticism is fueled by a recent scandal in the scientific community. In late 2009, an anonymous computer hacker made public e-mails sent between climate scientists that seemed to indicate that data regarding global warming had been fabricated. Dubbed "Climategate" by the media, it fueled the debate over the extent and cause of global warming. See "A Closer Look" panel for more information on Climategate.

On the other side of the debate, the majority of scientists are convinced that the magnitude of the greenhouse effect is great and accelerating and the cause is human behavior.

> *Global warming has become perhaps the most complicated issue facing world leaders. On the one hand, warnings from the scientific community are becoming louder, as an increasing body of science points to rising dangers from the ongoing buildup of human-related greenhouse gases—produced mainly by the burning of fossil fuels and forests. On the other, the technological, economic and political issues that have to be resolved before a concerted worldwide effort to reduce emissions can begin to have gotten no simpler, particularly in the face of a global economic slowdown.* (Revkin 2009:1)

SOURCES OF U.S. ENVIRONMENTAL PROBLEMS

The United States has been blessed with an abundance of rich and varied resources (land, minerals, and water). Until recently, people in the United States were unconcerned with conservation because there seemed to be so vast a storehouse of resources that waste was not considered a problem. And as a result, Americans have disproportionately consumed the world's resources. For example, although they constitute 4.5 percent of the world's population, people in the United States use 25 percent of the world's oil output each year. This is because we own 230 million cars and trucks (29 percent of the world's supply) and drive some 1.7 trillion miles annually, almost as much as all the rest of the world.

Although the perception of abundance may explain a tendency to be wasteful, it is only a partial and superficial answer. The underlying sources of our present environmental problems can be located in the culture and structure of U.S. society.

Cultural Sources

Culture refers to the knowledge that the members of a social organization—in this case, a society—share. Shared ideas, values, beliefs, and understandings

A CLOSER LOOK

Climategate

In 2007, the Intergovernmental Panel on Climate Change produced a report that claimed:

- Eleven of the previous twelve years (1995–2006) rank among the twelve warmest years on record since 1850.
- Sea levels are rising.
- Snow and ice are decreasing.
- Over the past 50 years, cold days, cold nights, and frosts have become less frequent.

Using data from a number of sources, the IPCC concluded that warming of the climate system is "unequivocal."

The issue of global warming has many critics, however. For example, meteorologist Mark Johnson writes, "I talk about the fallacy of man-made global warming to whomever will listen. I talk to many groups, large and small about how AGW [Anthropogenic Global Warming] is just bad science. I tell them that study results are hand-picked and modified to fit a pre-determined conclusion" (2009:1). Critics of global warming theory have become even more outspoken since the incident in October 2009 dubbed "Climategate." A computer hacker posted more than a thousand e-mails from scientists at the Hadley Climatic Research Unit at Britain's University of East Anglia. The e-mails contain details regarding data gathering, and sceptics claim they are evidence of scientific fraud and misconduct. One particular e-mail cited most often refers to using a statistical "trick" to "hide the decline" in global temperatures. Although all of this is currently under investigation, a few items are clear. According to Jess Henig at Factcheck.org (2009:1):

- The messages, which span 13 years, show a few scientists in a bad light, being rude or dismissive. An investigation is underway, but there is still plenty of evidence that the earth is getting warmer and that humans are largely responsible.
- Some critics say the e-mails negate the conclusions of the 2007 report by the Intergovernmental Panel on Climate Change, but the IPCC report relied on data from a large number of sources, of which CRU was only one.
- E-mails being cited as "smoking guns" have been misrepresented. For instance, one e-mail that refers to "hiding the decline" isn't talking about a decline in actual temperature as measured at weather stations. These have continued to rise, and 2009 may turn out to be the fifth warmest year ever recorded. The "decline" actually refers to a problem with recent data from tree rings.

Climategate seems to have had little influence on the world's understanding of global warming, as the U.N. Climate Change Conference proceeded as planned in December 2009. In advance of the conference "the national academies of 13 nations issued a joint statement of their recommendations for combating climate change, in which they discussed the 'human forcing' of global warming and said that the need for action was 'indisputable'" (Henig 2009:4).

shape the behaviors, perceptions, and interpretations of the members of society. Although the United States is a multicultural society filled with diversity, some of the dominant ideologies of U.S. society have tended to legitimize or at least account for the wastefulness of Americans and their acceptance of pollution.

- **Cornucopia View of Nature.** Many Americans conceive of nature as a vast storehouse waiting only to be used by people. They regard the natural world as a bountiful preserve available to serve human needs. In this view, nature is something to be conquered and used; it is free and inexhaustible. This **cornucopia view of nature** is widespread and will likely persist as a justification for continuing abuse of the environment, even in an age of ecological consciousness. This view is complemented by an abundant faith in science and technology.

- **Faith in Technology.** There are three basic ways in which human beings can relate to nature. They can view it as a controlling force and thereby submit to the environment in a fatalistic manner. They can strive to attain harmony with it: people need nature and nature needs people. Finally, they can try to attain mastery over nature.

  Many Americans regard human beings as having mastery over nature. Rather than accepting the environment as given, they have sought to change and conquer it. Damming rivers, cutting down timber, digging tunnels, plowing prairie land, conquering space, and seeding clouds with silver nitrate are a few examples of this orientation to overcoming nature's obstacles rather than acquiescing to them.

  From this logic proceeds a faith in technology; a proper application of scientific knowledge can meet any challenge. If the air and water are polluted and if we are rapidly running out of petroleum, science will save us. We will find a substitute for the internal combustion engine, create plants that will "scrub" the air by using carbon dioxide as food, find new sources of energy, develop new methods of extracting minerals, or create new synthetics. Although this faith may yet be vindicated, we are beginning to realize that technology may not be the solution and may even be the source of the problem.

  Scientific breakthroughs and new technology have solved some problems and do aid in saving labor. But often, new technology creates unanticipated problems. Automobiles, for example, provide numerous benefits but they also pollute the air and kill about 50,000 Americans each year. It is difficult to imagine life without electricity, but the generation of electricity pollutes the air (over half of the carbon emissions in the United States come from coal-burning electrical plants) and causes the thermal pollution of rivers. Air-conditioning accounts for 16 percent of the average U.S. household's electricity consumption, and it adds 3,400 pounds of global-warming carbon dioxide annually for each household (Cox 2006). Insecticides and chemical fertilizers have performed miracles in agriculture but have polluted food and streams (and even "killed" some lakes). Obviously, the slogan of the DuPont Corporation—"Better living through chemistry"—is not entirely correct. Jet planes, while helping us in many ways, cause air pollution (one jet taking off emits the same amount of hydrocarbon as the exhausts from 10,000 automobiles) and noise pollution near busy airports.

- **Growth Ethic.** Many Americans place a premium on progress and believe that something better is always attainable. This desire (which is encouraged by corporations and their advertisers) causes people to discard items that are still usable and to purchase new things. Thus, industry continues to turn out more products and to use up natural resources.

  The presumed value of progress has had a negative effect on contemporary U.S. life. Progress is typically defined to mean either growth or new technology. Community leaders typically want their cities to grow. Chambers of commerce want more industry and more people (and, incidentally, more consumers). The logic of capitalism is that every company needs to increase its profits from year to year. Thus, we all benefit if the gross national product increases each year. For all these things to grow as people wish, there must be a concomitant increase in population, products (and use of natural resources), electricity, highways, and waste. Continued growth will inevitably throw the tight ecological system out of balance, for there are limited supplies of air, water, and places to dump waste materials, and these supplies diminish as the population increases.

- **Materialism.** The U.S. belief in progress is translated at the individual level into consumption of material things as evidence of one's success. The U.S. economic system is predicated on the growth of private enterprises, which depend on increased demand for their products. If the population is more or less stable, then individuals can accomplish growth only through increased consumption. The function of the advertising industry is to create a need in individuals to buy a product that they would not buy otherwise. Consumption is also increased if products must be thrown away (such as nonreturnable bottles) or if they do not last very long. The policy of **planned obsolescence** (manufacturing and selling goods designed to wear out or to become out of fashion) by many U.S. companies accomplishes this goal of consumption very well, but it overlooks the problems of disposal as well as the unnecessary waste of materials.

- **Belief in Individualism.** Most people in the United States place great stress on personal achievement. They believe that hard work and initiative will bring success. There is a tendency to sacrifice present gains for future rewards (*deferred gratification*). Many people sacrifice by working days and going to school at night to get a better job. Parents may make great sacrifices so that their children have the opportunity for a college education or other advantages the parents never received. In this manner, success is accomplished vicariously through the achievements of one's children.

  This self-orientation (as opposed to a collective orientation) forms the basis for a number of the value configurations of work, activity, and success mentioned previously. The individual is successful through his or her own initiative and hard work. The stress on individualism is, of course, related to capitalism. Through personal efforts, business acumen, and luck, the individual can (if successful) own property and see multiplying profits. Most Americans share this goal of great monetary success—the "American dream"—and believe that anyone can make it if he or she works hard enough. Curiously, people who are not successful commonly do not reject capitalism. Instead, they wait in the hope that their lot will improve or that their children will prosper under the system.

  The belief that private property and capitalism should not be restricted has led to several social problems: (1) unfair competition (monopolies, interlocking directorates, price fixing); (2) an entrepreneurial philosophy of caveat emptor ("let the buyer beware"), whose aim is profit with total disregard for the welfare of the consumer; and (3) the current environmental crisis, which is due in great measure to the standard policy of many people and most corporations to do whatever is profitable while ignoring conservation of natural resources. Industrial pollution of air and water with refuse and agricultural spraying with pesticides that harm animal and human life are two examples of how individuals and corporations look out for themselves with little or no regard for the short- and long-range effects of their actions on life.

  As long as people hold a narrow self-orientation rather than a group orientation, this crisis will steadily worsen. The use people make of their land, the water running through it, and the air above it has traditionally been theirs to decide because of the belief in the sanctity of private property. This belief has meant, in effect, that individuals have had the right to pave a pasture for a parking lot, to tear up a lemon grove for a housing development, to put down artificial turf for a football field, and to dump waste products into the ground, air, and water. Consequently, individual decisions have had the collective effect of taking millions of acres of arable land out of production permanently, polluting the air and water, and covering land where vegetation once grew with asphalt, concrete buildings, and Astroturf, even though green plants are the only source of oxygen.

In summary, traditional values of U.S. citizens lie at the heart of environmental problems. Americans want to conquer nature. They want to use nature for the good life, and this endeavor is never satisfied. Moreover, they want the freedom to do as they please.

Our individualistic and acquisitive values lead us to resist group-centered programs and humanitarian concerns. Will an energy crisis or continued global warming change our values? Will we vote for politicians who argue for societal planning and sacrifice to reduce environmental perils, or will we opt for politicians who favor the traditional values?

Structural Sources

The structural arrangements in U.S. society buttress the belief system that reinforces the misuse of resources and abuses the ecosystem.

- **Capitalist Economy.** The U.S. economic system of capitalism depends on profits. The quest for profits is never satisfied: companies must grow; more assets and more sales translate into more profits. To maximize profits, owners must minimize costs. Among other things, this search for profits results in abusing the environment (such as strip mining and the disposal of harmful wastes into the air or waterways), resisting government efforts to curb such abuse, and using corporate and advertising skills to increase the consumption of products, including built-in obsolescence, and to even denigrate the notion of global warming. For instance, the Union of Concerned Scientists asserted that ExxonMobil, the world's largest oil company, funded forty-three ideological organizations between 1998 and 2005 in an effort to mislead the public by discrediting the science behind global warming (reported in the *Hutchinson News* 2007; see also Mooney 2006).

This last point needs elaboration. Profits require consumers; growing profits require overconsumption. Corporations use several mechanisms to generate the desire to purchase unnecessary products. Advertising generates hyperconsumerism by creating demand for products that potential consumers did not know they needed. Innovative packaging designs also help to sell products; the size, shape, and colors of the package and its display affect choices. Another common tactic is product differentiation whereby existing products (such as an automobile) are given cosmetic changes and presented to consumers as new. This planned obsolescence creates consumer demand as purchasers trade or throw away the "old" product for the "new."

The increased production that results from greater levels of consumption has three detrimental consequences for the environment: more pollution of air and water, depletion of resources, and a swelling of waste products (sewage, scrap, and junk).

Because the profit motive supersedes the concern for the environment, corporations are unwilling to comply with government regulations and to pay damages for ecological disasters such as oil spills. In addition, the possibility of solving environmental problems is further minimized under a capitalist system because jobs depend on business profits. Economic prosperity and growth mean jobs. Thus, most observers see only a narrow alternative between a safe environment and relatively full employment. The fate of many workers depends on whether companies are profitable. Solving environmental problems appears to be incompatible with capitalism unless ecological disasters occur.

- **Polity.** As discussed in Chapter 2, powerful interest groups fundamentally influence political decisions. This bias of the political system is readily seen in what has been government's relatively cozy relationship with large polluters: corporations. Typically, government intervention has had the effect of administering a symbolic slap on the wrist, and pollution of the environment has continued virtually unabated. The government has been ineffective in pushing the largest and most powerful corporations to do something unprofitable. Not only are these corporations the largest polluters, but they also have a vested interest in the status quo. General Motors and Ford, for example, resist congressional attempts to legislate stricter standards for reducing pollution because the necessary devices add to the cost of automobiles and might curb sales. The government has achieved gradual change, but the powerful automobile industry has consistently responded more slowly than the environmental lobby wanted.

  Since Barack Obama became president, there has been a shift toward greater regulation. For example, in October 2009 the Environmental Protection Agency (EPA) proposed a groundbreaking rule that would hold big polluters accountable for their greenhouse gas emissions. In the proposal, large emitters would have to obtain construction and operating permits and prove that they are using the best control technologies and energy efficient measures available. Under the Bush White House, the EPA was loath to regulate greenhouse gas emissions (Bradbury 2009). While a step in the right direction, it remains to be seen whether the rule will be followed and enforced.

- **Demographic Patterns.** The population of the United States is generally concentrated in large metropolitan areas. Wherever people are concentrated, the problems of pollution are increased through the concentration of wastes. Where people are centralized, so too will be the emission of automobile exhausts, the effluence of factories, and the dumps for garbage and other human refuse.

  The location of cities is another source of environmental problems. Typically, cities have evolved where commerce would benefit the most. Because industry needs plentiful water for production and waste disposal, cities tend to be located along lakes, rivers, and ocean bays. Industry's long-established pattern of using available water to dispose of its waste materials has caused rivers, such as the Missouri, Mississippi, and Ohio; lakes, such as Erie and Michigan; and bays like Chesapeake and New York to be badly polluted.

  The ready availability of the automobile and the interstate highway system resulted in the development of suburbs. The growth of suburbs not only strained already burdened sewage facilities but also increased air pollution through increased use of the automobile. The greater the urban sprawl, the greater the smog is.

- **System of Stratification.** One major focus of this book (and of Chapter 7, in particular) is how U.S. society victimizes the poor. Because of where they live and work, poor people and racial minorities are more susceptible than are the

The polluted condition of a section of the Hudson River in New York before sewage treatment plants were built to serve towns along the river. Raw sewage had starved the river of dissolved oxygen, harmed fish and rendered the water unsightly and malodorous.

well-to-do to the dangers of pollution, whether it takes the form of excessive noise, foul air, or toxic chemicals such as lead poisoning. These probabilities are called **environmental classism** and environmental racism. Another inequity is that the poor will have to pay disproportionately for efforts to eliminate pollution. That is, their jobs may be eliminated, their neighborhoods abandoned, and a greater proportion of their taxes required (through regressive taxes) to pay for environmental cleanups.

The bitter irony of the poor having to sacrifice the most to abate environmental problems is that it is the affluent that drive excessively, travel in jet planes, have air-conditioned, large homes, consume large quantities of resources (conspicuous consumption), and have the most waste to dispose. Their demand increases economic demand and, concomitantly, industrial pollution.

This system of stratification extends globally to the differences between countries, with the world's poorest people having the lowest carbon footprint, but suffering the most from climate change.

> *Comparing the average annual per capita carbon footprints of the rich and poor certainly makes for unsettling reading: The average American's annual carbon footprint—20.4 tons—is around 2,000 times that of someone living in the African nation of Chad. And the average Briton will emit as much carbon dioxide in one day as a Kenyan will in an entire year. Overall, the United Nations estimates that the carbon footprint of the world's 1 billion poorest people (those living on less than $1 a day) represents just 3 percent of the global total. (Oliver 2008)*

In summary, the United States is a wasteful, inefficient, and vulnerable energy-centered economy. The natural environment is being destroyed by pollution and waste, for several reasons. First, the economic system exploits people and resources. The emphasis on profit requires growth and consumption.

Thus, meeting short-term goals supersedes planning to prevent detrimental long-term consequences. Second, we depend on technology that is wasteful. Third, most people believe in capitalism, growth, and consumption. Finally, population growth increases the demand for products, energy, and other resources.

SOLUTIONS TO THE ENVIRONMENTAL CRISES

Probusiness Voluntaristic Approach

The solution advocated by conservatives is based on the premise that if left alone, mechanisms in the marketplace will operate to solve environmental problems. When cleaning up pollution becomes profitable enough, entrepreneurs will provide the services to clean the air, treat the water, and recycle waste. There is a contradiction here, though: the free market approach will not eliminate pollution; pollution controls reduce profits, and the goal of companies is to maximize profits. A possible compromise is for the government to provide incentives to industries to curb their polluting activities. These incentives could take the form of tax breaks for the purchase and use of pollution controls or outright grants for the use of effective controls.

The probusiness approach, exemplified by the George W. Bush administration, sought to unleash the energy industry to produce more by drilling aggressively for more oil and gas, even in marginal areas (Alaska, offshore), burning more coal (of which there is an abundance), and building more nuclear plants. At the same time, efforts at conservation, to quote Vice President Cheney, "may be a sign of personal virtue but not the basis for a sound, comprehensive energy policy" (quoted in Moberg 2001:14). The oil and gas industry during the 2000 and 2004 election cycles gave Bush and Republican politicians considerably more in contributions than it did to Democratic candidates. Moreover, former President Bush and former Vice President Cheney were both executives in the oil industry before their stint in politics.

Egalitarian/Authoritarian Plan

According to its opponents, the business-oriented plan just described has a basic flaw: it lacks overall provision for the whole society. To allow individuals and companies free choice in what to consume, how much to consume, what to produce, and in what quantities is a luxury that society cannot afford in a time of scarcity and ecological crises. Let us look at the two main authoritarian alternatives to solving the problem of pollution.

The current Obama administration has pledged to crack down on polluters and close the "carbon loophole." This approach entails the enactment of comprehensive laws carrying severe criminal and civil penalties for harming the environment. At the corporate level, it means rigorous inspections of companies and prosecution of violators. Moreover, if penalized, these companies must not be allowed to pass the fines on to consumers through higher prices. At the individual level, it means inspection of vehicles and homes to enforce compliance with accepted standards.

One obstacle to a comprehensive plan to curb pollution is our federal system of government, in which states and communities are free to set their own standards. In principle, this system makes sense because the people in an area should be the most knowledgeable about their situation. However, mining operations along Lake Superior cannot be allowed to dump tailings in the lake on the rationale that having to pay for recycling would reduce local employment levels. Similarly, air pollution is never limited to one locality; wind currents carry the pollutants beyond local borders and add to the cumulative effect on an entire region. Therefore, it seems imperative that the federal government establish and enforce minimum standards for the entire country. Localities could make the standards stricter if they wish. For example, because of its high altitude, Denver has special problems with air pollution. Denver is susceptible to temperature inversions that trap pollutants near the land surface, and automobiles at high altitude emit more pollutants than they do at lower elevations. The city of Denver may therefore want to impose very strict automobile emission standards, just as California has to meet the unusual conditions of its geography.

But although it is easy to list what the government should do, it is also easy to see that the implementation of a centralized, authoritarian plan will meet many obstacles and considerable opposition. Industries, corporations, and communities will resist what will be commonly interpreted as arbitrary and heavy-handed tactics by bureaucrats who do not understand the necessity of profits for maintaining employment and a good local tax base. More fundamentally, the concept of free enterprise means, for many, the freedom to use one's property as one wishes. Will Congress, faced with these pressures, institute a national antipollution program with the necessary clout to be effective? Unless people and their representatives take a more realistic view of the ecological dangers that now exist, Congress will not act.

Control of Resource Use

To start any effective system of resource use, the government must begin by gathering correct information about the extent of natural resource reserves. Currently, government data depend largely on information provided by private firms. Data must also be gathered about the use of the various resources. How much actual waste is there? Can the waste be recycled? What is the turnaround time for renewable resources? Are there alternatives to existing resources? Once authoritative answers to these questions are determined, the government can plan rationally to eliminate waste, develop alternatives, and limit use to appropriate levels.

A rational plan to conserve energy, for example, could include government insistence on new-car fuel economy averaging 40 miles per gallon (which would reduce U.S. oil consumption by 2.8 million barrels a day); universal daylight saving time (it could even be extended to a 2-hour difference, rather than one); strict enforcement of a relatively low speed limit (the 55 mph speed limit in 1983 saved an estimated 2.5 billion gallons of gasoline and diesel fuel [Mouawad and Romero 2005]); the use of governors on automobiles and thermostats; banning neon signs and other energy used in advertising; minimal use of outdoor lighting; and a reversal of the current policy that reduces rates for electricity and natural gas as the volume increases. These steps are important, but the key ingredient to conservation is mandatory rationing, which would reduce consumption in an equitable fashion.

Regardless of the plan that is eventually chosen, most people would agree that the waste of energy must be curtailed. Conserving energy will require not only individual alterations of lifestyles but also changes in the economic system.

Under the current private enterprise system based on profits, corporations seek the profitable alternative rather than the conserving one. In the search for greater profits, we have shifted from railroads and mass transit (the most energy-efficient means of moving people and freight on land) to energy-inefficient cars, trucks, and planes. Instead of using energy-sparing and renewable resources such as wood, cotton, wool, and soap, companies have switched to synthetic fibers, plastics, and detergents made from petroleum.

On the positive side, some U.S. corporations are leading the way in promoting conservation efforts. Thanks to "green" ideology becoming mainstream in the media (Davis Guggenheim's documentary of Al Gore's *An Inconvenient Truth* won an Academy Award and was one of the highest grossing documentaries of all time), numerous companies are making a concentrated effort to "go green." In 2009, *Newsweek* magazine ranked the 500 largest U.S. companies based on their environmental impact, their green policies, and their reputation among their peers and environmental experts. Hewlett-Packard earned the title of the "greenest company in America" thanks to its strong program to reduce greenhouse gas emissions and its efforts to use renewable energy (McGinn 2009).

Can the United States continue to operate on an economic system that allows decisions about what to produce and how to produce it to be governed by profit rather than the common good? The heart of the capitalists' argument, going back to Adam Smith more than 200 years ago, is that decisions made on the basis of the entrepreneur's self-interest will also accomplish the needs of society most efficiently. This fundamental precept of capitalism is now challenged by the environmental crisis, the energy crisis, and the problems related to them. Can capitalism be amended to incorporate central planning regarding societal needs of a safe environment and plentiful resources? Perhaps it can. In the case of Hewlett-Packard, the company's recycling program has allowed HP to reclaim 1.7 billion pounds of e-waste over the past decade, including gold and copper, which it resells. In addition, reducing packaging material has paid off in reduced shipping costs (McGinn 2009). This shows that going green can result in company benefits.

The exact form that the economy should take in an energy-short and polluted world is a source of controversy. At one extreme are people who believe that capitalism is the solution, not the problem. Others would demand a socialistic system with its emphasis on the common good as the only answer. At a minimum, it would seem that (1) there must be central planning; (2) pollution must be controlled and such control tightly enforced; (3) the monopoly structure of the energy industry must be broken up (currently, the largest oil companies control the production, refining, transportation, and retail distribution of oil and are the largest owners of coal, uranium, and geothermal energy); (4) there must be mandatory conservation measures; and (5) the government must subsidize efforts to obtain alternative, nonpolluting sources of energy, and the resulting structures should be publicly owned so that the public good, not profit, is the primary aim.

A final problem is that an energy-short world will not continue to tolerate America's disproportionate use of energy and other resources. The possibility of war increases with the growing resentment of have-not nations toward the haves.

At the international level, the United States along with other developed nations must seek solutions to the environmental crises facing the planet. This means mandating that the developed countries reduce the production of materials that pollute the air, water, and land. The United States must also develop for itself and for other countries environmentally appropriate technologies that will sustain economic progress and be substituted for the ecologically destructive technologies currently in use. As the United States makes trade agreements such as the ones encouraging free trade with Mexico and Canada, agreements must include standard environmental protections. Similarly, loan agreements must contain environmental protections as a condition to receive monies. Finally, the wealthy nations can help themselves and help the debtor nations by engaging in "debt-for-nature" exchanges. Many of the poor nations are hopelessly in debt to the rich nations. Presently, many pay the interest (rarely the principal) by cutting down their forests or by farming marginal lands. The creditor nations could reduce debt in exchange for enforceable agreements by the debtor nation to protect vulnerable parts of their environment.

INTERNATIONAL IMPLICATIONS OF ENVIRONMENTAL PROBLEMS

Environmental problems are not confined within political borders. The world's inhabitants share the oceans, rivers, lakes, and air. If a corporation or a nation pollutes, the world's citizens are the victims. If the tropical forests are destroyed, we are all affected. If a country wastes finite resources or uses more than its proportionate share, the other nations are short-changed.

What will the world be like in 50 years or so? In all likelihood, its population will have levelled off at about 9 billion. The planet will be crowded; the production of enough food and its fair distribution will be extremely problematic. Fresh water will be scarce. Oil will have been replaced by some other energy source. Unless dramatic changes are instituted, the quality of air and water, especially in the less developed, rapidly growing nations, will have deteriorated greatly, and the climate will have been altered. Global warming will have altered climates and flooded low-lying regions.

What should the nations of the world do about environmental crises? In December 2009, world leaders met in Copenhagen, Denmark, for the United Nations Climate Change Conference (called COP 15). Eleven days of heated debates ensued, with a dominant theme of rich countries versus poor countries. In the end, leaders from the United States, China, Brazil, India, and South Africa met and drafted what is known as the Copenhagen Accord. The Accord, which lays the foundation for international action to combat climate change, asks for countries to pledge to reduce their greenhouse gas emissions and to work to hold the increase in global temperature below 2 degrees Celsius. (See the Looking Toward the Future panel for some selections from the Accord). It remains to be seen how many countries will agree to sign it.

The safe prediction about the future is that nations that are now affluent will undergo dramatic changes. Expanding technology will have to be limited because of its demands on precious resources, its generation of harmful heat, and other negative ecological effects. People's freedom to order life as they please—to pave a vacant lot, to irrigate land, to have as many children as they want, to acquire things, to consume fuel on a pleasure trip—will be controlled. The needs of the group, community, society, and perhaps even the world will take precedence over those of the individual. Other values people in the United States hold dear—such as growth and progress, capitalism, individualism, and

LOOKING TOWARD THE FUTURE

SELECTIONS FROM THE COPENHAGEN ACCORD

1. We underline that climate change is one of the greatest challenges of our time. We emphasize our strong political will to urgently combat climate change in accordance with the principle of common but differentiated responsibilities and respective capabilities. To achieve the ultimate objective of the Convention to stabilize greenhouse gas concentration in the atmosphere at a level that would prevent dangerous anthropogenic interference with the climate system, we shall, recognizing the scientific view that the increase in global temperature should be below 2 degrees Celsius, on the basis of equity and in the context of sustainable development, enhance our long-term cooperative action to combat climate change. We recognize the critical impacts of climate change and the potential impacts of response measures on countries particularly vulnerable to its adverse effects and stress the need to establish a comprehensive adaptation programme including international support.

2. We agree that deep cuts in global emissions are required according to science, and as documented by the IPCC Fourth Assessment Report with a view to reduce global emissions so as to hold the increase in global temperature below 2 degrees Celsius, and take action to meet this objective consistent with science and on the basis of equity. We should cooperate in achieving the peaking of global and national emissions as soon as possible, recognizing that the time frame for peaking will be longer in developing countries and bearing in mind that social and economic development and poverty eradication are the first and overriding priorities of developing countries and that a low-emission development strategy is indispensable to sustainable development.

3. Adaptation to the adverse effects of climate change and the potential impacts of response measures is a challenge faced by all countries. Enhanced action and international cooperation on adaptation is urgently required to ensure the implementation of the Convention by enabling and supporting the implementation of adaptation actions aimed at reducing vulnerability and building resilience in developing countries, especially in those that are particularly vulnerable, especially least developed countries, small island developing states and Africa. We agree that developed countries shall provide adequate, predictable and sustainable financial resources, technology and capacity building to support the implementation of adaptation action in developing countries.

4. We recognize the crucial role of reducing emission from deforestation and forest degradation and the need to enhance removals of greenhouse gas emission by forests and agree on the need to provide positive incentives to such actions through the immediate establishment of a mechanism including REDD-plus, to enable the mobilization of financial resources from developed countries.

5. We call for an assessment of the implementation of this Accord to be completed by 2015, including in light of the Convention's ultimate objective. This would include consideration of strengthening the long-term goal referencing various matters presented by the science, including in relation to temperature rises of 1.5 degrees Celsius.

Source: http://www.denmark.dk/NR/rdonlyres/C41B62AB-4688-4ACE-BB7B-F6D2C8AAEC20/0/copenhagen_accord.pdf

Note: There are twelve total points in the Accord.

the conquest of nature—will no longer be salient in a world of less space, endangered ecology, energy shortages, and hunger. These values will die hard, especially the choice of individual freedom. No doubt there will be a great deal of social upheaval during the period of transition from growth to stability, from affluence to subsistence. But these changes must occur or we will perish.

The dangers posed by the future require solutions at two levels. At the physical level, efforts must be directed to finding, for instance, new sources of energy (e.g., fuel cells, solar, wind, biomass), methods to increase the amount of arable land, new types of food, better contraceptives, and relatively inexpensive ways to desalt seawater. At the social level, there must be changes in the structural conditions responsible for poverty, wasted resources, pollution, and the like. One such target would be to determine ways of overcoming the cultural habits (customs, values, beliefs) that reinforce high fertility, people's refusal to eat certain foods or to accept central planning, and the dependence on growth and technology. New forms of social organization, such as regional councils and world bodies, may be required to deal with social upheavals, economic dislocations, resource allocation, and pollution on a global scale. These new organizations will require great innovative thinking, for it is likely that the dominant modes of the present age not only are unworkable for the demands of an overpopulated planet but also are in large measure responsible for many of our present and future difficulties.

One complicating factor is that, currently, nations tend to focus on national problems rather than on transnational cooperative efforts. Moreover, they direct their efforts to physical rather than social solutions. They seek answers in technological and developmental wizardry. These solutions are important and should not be neglected, but massive efforts should also be directed to finding ethical, legal, religious, and social solutions.

■ CHAPTER REVIEW

1. Three social forces disturb Earth's biosphere profoundly: population growth, the concentration of people in urban areas, and modern technology.
2. Although population growth (which occurs mostly in the developing countries) has adverse effects on the environment, the populations of rich countries are much more wasteful of Earth's resources and generate much more pollution.
3. Chemicals, solid waste disposal, and radiation pollute the land, water, and air.
4. The Earth faces three major interrelated environmental crises: the burning of fossil fuels, the destruction of the tropical forests, and global warming.
5. The United States, although only 4.5 percent of the world's population, consumes roughly one-fourth of the world's resources. China and the United States emit more greenhouses gases than any other countries.
6. The cultural bases of the wasteful and environmentally destructive U.S. society are the dominant ideologies of (a) the cornucopia view of nature, (b) faith in technology, (c) the growth ethic, (d) materialism, and (e) the belief in individualism.
7. The structural bases for the misuse and abuse of the U.S. environment and resources are (a) urbanization, (b) the system of stratification, (c) capitalism, and (d) the bias of the political system.
8. The probusiness voluntaristic solution to the environmental crisis is based on the premise that if left alone, mechanisms in the marketplace will operate to solve environmental problems. When cleaning up pollution becomes profitable enough, entrepreneurs will provide the services to clean the air, treat the water, and recycle waste.
9. The egalitarian/authoritarian solution is based on government planning and control to reduce problems and promote conservation. This solution shares the burdens throughout the social strata. Moreover, it controls consumption to meet societal goals.
10. If world leaders cannot come to an agreement regarding climate change, the worldwide problems of pollution and resource depletion will become more acute in the future because of population growth, urbanization, expanding technology, and the lack of planning by nations individually and collectively.
11. The dangers posed by these critical problems require solutions at two levels: (a) at the physical level, we need discoveries and inventions of nonpolluting technologies and renewable resources; and (b) at the social level, we need changes in the structural conditions responsible for these problems and the creation of new forms of transnational social organizations.

KEY TERMS

Biosphere. The surface layer of the planet and the surrounding atmosphere.

Ecosystems. The mechanisms (plants, animals, and microorganisms) that supply people with the essentials of life.

Environmental justice. A movement to improve community environments by eliminating toxic hazards.

Environmental racism. The overwhelming likelihood that toxic-producing plants and toxic waste dumps are located where poor people, especially people of color, live.

Greenhouse effect. When gases accumulate in Earth's atmosphere and act like the glass roof of a greenhouse, allowing sunlight in but trapping the heat that is generated.

Culture. The knowledge (ideas, values, beliefs) that the members of a social organization share.

Cornucopia view of nature. The belief that nature is a vast and bountiful storehouse to be used by human beings.

Planned obsolescence. The manufacture of consumer goods designed to wear out. Or existing products are given superficial changes and marketed as new, making the previous products out of date.

Environmental classism. The poor, because of dangerous jobs and residential segregation, are more exposed than the more well-to-do to environmental dangers.

SUCCEED WITH PEARSON mysoclab www.mysoclab.com

Experience, Discover, Observe, Evaluate
MySocLab is designed just for you. Each chapter features a pre-test and post-test to help you learn and review key concepts and terms.

Experience sociology in action with dynamic visual activities, videos, and readings to enhance your learning experience. Complete the following activities at www.mysoclab.com.

Social Explorer is an interactive application that allows you to explore Census data through interactive maps.

- Explore the Social Explorer Map: *Carbon Emissions and the Effects of Global Warming on the Environment*

The Core Concepts in Sociology video clips offer a real-world perspective on sociological concepts.

- Watch *World Climate Change*

MySocLibrary includes primary source readings from classic and contemporary sociologists.

- Read Scanlan, Jenkins, & Peterson, *The Scarcity Fallacy*; Krauss, *Women of Color on the Front Line*; Brown, *Sixteen Impacts of Population Growth*

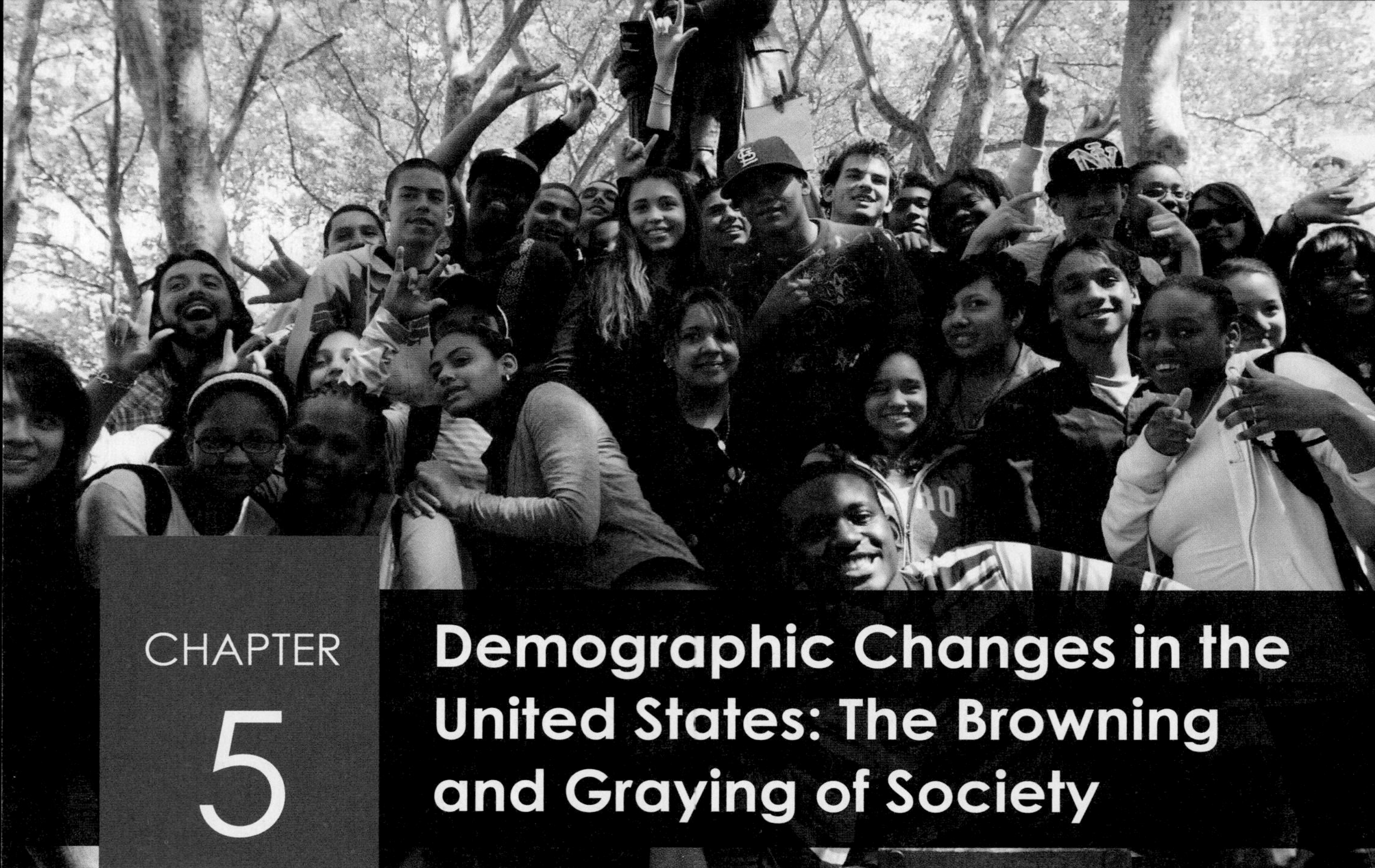

CHAPTER 5

Demographic Changes in the United States: The Browning and Graying of Society

Nothing that happened in the United States over the last third of the twentieth century—not terrorism, the explosion of new technology, or the transformation of politics or the end of the Cold War, not even the profound changes in the status and expectations and role of American women—will have more long-term consequences for the future of the United States than the new immigration.

—Godfrey Hodgson

Two population shifts are transforming U.S. society—one with external sources and the other internal. The first is the "new immigration." The racial landscape and rate of population growth are greatly affected as approximately 1 million immigrants annually, mostly Latino and Asian, set up permanent residence in the United States. The second population change is internal—the age of the population is rising rapidly. Both of these demographic transitions have profound implications for social problems, creating some and exacerbating others. The facts, myths, and consequences of these two demographic changes are the subjects of this chapter. We begin, though, with a brief demographic overview of the United States.

PROFILE OF THE U.S. POPULATION

At mid-2009, the population of the United States was approximately 306,800,000, the third highest in the world (behind China at 1.331 billion and India at 1.171 billion, and above Indonesia and Brazil). Unlike other developed nations, the population of United States continues to increase (at a rate of 1 percent per year) primarily because of the large influx of immigrants. The U.S. Census Bureau projects that the United States will have a population of 439 million by 2050 (Population Reference Bureau 2009). Following are some additional facts:

- In 2009, the average life expectancy at birth was 78 years (75.65 for males and 80.69 for females).
- Over four-fifths (83.7 percent) of Americans live in cities. Nine cities exceed 1 million residents: New York, Los Angeles, Chicago, Houston, Philadelphia, Phoenix, San Antonio, San Diego, and Dallas.
- The total **fertility** rate (the number of children a woman bears in her child-bearing years) is 2.1, exactly at the replacement rate. This rate varies by race/ethnicity: Whites (1.8), Asian Americans (1.9), African Americans (1.9), and Latinos (2.9).
- One out of eight (12.5 percent) in the U.S. population is foreign born.
- The baby boom generation, roughly 76 million Americans born between 1946 and 1964, is the largest generation in U.S. history (at the crest of the boom, the total fertility rate was 3.8 children per woman). In 2006, they were 42 to 60 years old, and as they have done from the beginning, they are having an enormous impact on U.S. society. In 2011, the leading edge of the baby boomers will be 65. This means that beginning in that year, and for the next 20 years, an average of 10,000 additional people will become eligible for Medicare *each day.*
- Non-Whites are the majority in four states—California, Texas, New Mexico, and Hawaii—and the District of Columbia.
- Almost one in three Americans is non-White, compared to one in five in 1980.
- The number of Latinos in the United States is greater than the population of Canada.
- One in five U.S. doctors is foreign born, as are two in five medical scientists (Knickerbocker and Jonsson 2006).
- Google, Sun Microsystems, eBay, and Yahoo! are all companies that were founded or cofounded by immigrants.
- The boundary between Mexico and the United States has become perhaps the most militarized frontier between two nations at peace anywhere in the world (Massey 2006:2).
- There are approximately 6 million Muslims and 1.1 million Hindus in the United States.
- One in five householders is age 65 or older.

NEW IMMIGRATION AND THE CHANGING RACIAL LANDSCAPE

A societal upheaval is shaking up society: massive immigration. This demographic force—the new immigration—is challenging the cultural hegemony of the White European tradition, creating incredible diversity in race, ethnicity, language, and culture; rapidly changing the racial landscape; and leading, often, to division and hostility.

Historically, immigration has been a major source of population growth and ethnic diversity in the United States. Immigration waves from northern and southern Europe, especially from 1850 to 1920, brought many millions of people, mostly Europeans, to America. In the 1920s, the United States placed limits on the number of immigrants it would accept, the operating principle being that the new immigrants should resemble the old ones. The "national origins" rules were designed to limit severely the immigration of Eastern Europeans and to deny the entry of Asians.

The Immigration Act amendments of 1965 abandoned the quota system that had preserved the European character of the United States for nearly half a century. The new law encouraged a new wave of immigrants, only this time the migrants arrived not from northern Europe but from the Third World, especially Asia and Latin America. Put another way, 100 years ago Europeans were 90 percent of immigrants to the United States; now 90 percent of immigrants are from non-European countries. The result, obviously, is a dramatic alteration of the ethnic composition of the U.S. population (see Figure 5.1). And the size of the contemporary immigrant wave has resulted in a visible and significant

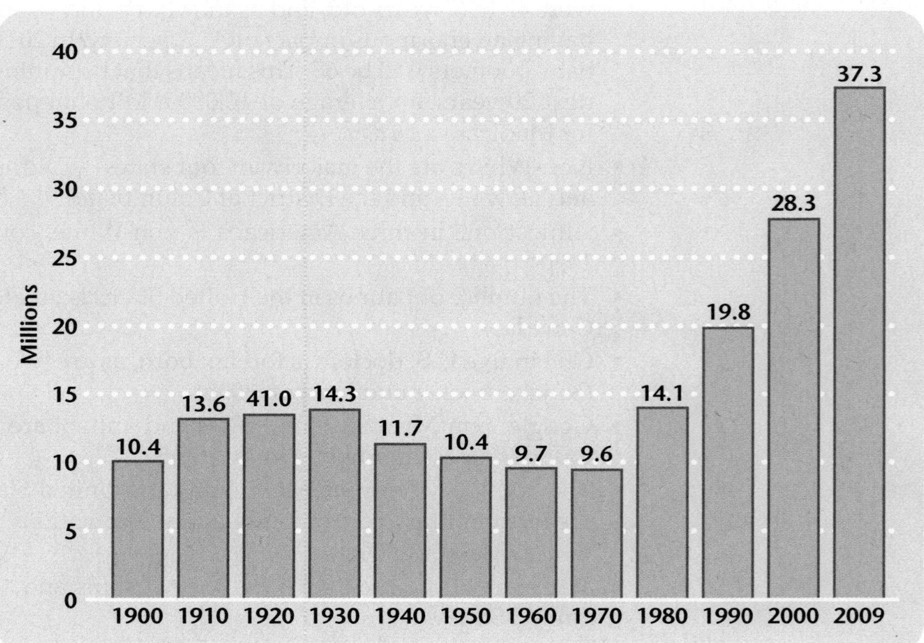

FIGURE 5.1 ***Foreign-born population: 1900–2009***

Source: U.S. Census Bureau, 2005–2009 American Community Survey.

number of U.S. residents who are foreign born—12.4 percent of the total population, in 2009, up from 8 percent in 1990 (U.S. Census Bureau, 2005–2009 American Community Survey).

About 1 million immigrants enter the United States legally each year. Another 1.5 million to 2.5 million people enter the United States illegally each year, but many return to their native countries either voluntarily or by force if caught by the Immigration and Naturalization Service. (See the "Social Policy" panel.) Although the number that enters clandestinely is impossible to determine, the best estimate is that about 11 million unauthorized foreign nationals resided in the United States in 2006. Roughly 80 percent of these undocumented immigrants are Latino (and two-thirds of them are Mexicans). The number of unauthorized immigrants declined in 2008 and 2009 because of tougher enforcement and border control and the Great Recession, which made jobs more uncertain.

The settlement patterns of this new migration differ from previous flows into the United States. Whereas previous immigrants settled primarily in the industrial states of the Northeast and Middle Atlantic regions or in the farming areas of the Midwest, recent immigrants have tended to locate on the two coasts and in the Southwest. Asians have tended to settle on the West Coast; Mexicans, although predominantly in the Southwest, are also scattered across the country,

SOCIAL POLICY

THE UNINTENDED CONSEQUENCES OF RIGID POLICING OF THE BORDER

The U.S.–Mexican border is 1,989 miles in length. U.S. policy has been to increase the policing of this border, apprehending those who crossed illegally and sending them back to Mexico. Now Congress has authorized the building of a fence along this border. The cost to build and maintain this fence is an estimated $49 billion over the expected 25-year life span of the fence.

Until the 1990s, the border was patrolled but passage was relatively easy. In the early 1980s, there were about 2,500 Border Patrol officers; now there are 12,000. The agency's annual budget rose during that period from $200 million to $1.6 billion today (Massey 2006). The Border Patrol, in the last decade, has directed its efforts especially to areas where border crossings were the easiest (around San Diego, California, and El Paso, Texas). As a result, the likelihood of successfully crossing the border has decreased dramatically. In 2005, the Border Patrol stopped 1.19 million people from entering the United States illegally. These arrests are filmed and shown to the public, promoting ever-greater fears about the waves of Mexican workers flooding into the United States.

The increased emphasis on sealing the border has had two unintended consequences. First, it shifted the crossing routes to more remote but more dangerous areas. Using alternative routes has tripled the cost of getting across the border illegally and resulted in many people dying of thirst and exposure in long foot marches across the desert. Second, and related to the first, those successful in crossing now tend to stay in the United States rather than move back and forth between the two countries.

In the past, many undocumented workers came to the United States, usually without their families, to follow the harvest or do other jobs for brief periods, and then returned to their families in Mexico. Now, with better policing, the migrants know that if they go back to Mexico, the odds are greater that they will not be able to return. This "seawall effect" keeps them here, and for that reason, they now arrive with their families and tend to stay. In other words, the increased militancy by the Border Patrol has had the effect of building a "wall" that, rather than keeping migrants out, actually keeps them in.

from urban Chicago to rural Kansas, as are other Latinos (e.g., Cubans in Florida and Puerto Ricans and Dominicans in New York).*

California is a harbinger of the demographic future of the United States. As recently as 1970, California was 80 percent White, but since then, it has been uniquely affected by immigration. The result is that Whites now are a numerical minority (41 percent in 2007, with 37 percent Latino, 12 percent Asian, and 6 percent African American; Schrag 2007). One-fourth of California's schoolchildren are studying English as a foreign language. "In another generation Latinos will be an absolute majority, and there will be 2 million fewer non-Hispanic Whites than there are now" (Schrag 2007:18). For example, Los Angeles has the largest population of Koreans outside Korea, the biggest concentration of Iranians in the Western world, and a huge Mexican population. The diverse population of southern California speaks 88 languages and dialects. Greater Los Angeles has more than 50 foreign-language newspapers and television shows that broadcast in Spanish, Mandarin, Armenian, Japanese, Korean, and Vietnamese. For example, in one ZIP code—90706—lies Bellflower, where 38 languages are spoken (Mohan and Simmons 2004).

For all this diversity, though, California, especially southern California, is becoming more and more Latino. California holds nearly half the U.S. Latino population and well over half the Mexican-origin population. Latinos are expected to surpass Whites in total California population by 2025 and become an absolute majority by 2040 (Purdum 2000).

Similar concentrations of Latinos are found in Arizona and Texas. Historian David Kennedy argues that there is no precedent in U.S. history of one immigrant group having the size and concentration that the Mexican immigrant group has in the Southwest today:

> *If we seek historical guidance, the closest example we have in hand is the diagonally opposite corner of the North American continent, in Quebec. The possibility looms that*

*Note well that there is a wide diversity among immigrant groups. For example, although there are over three million Latinos living in Florida, they come from several ethnic backgrounds: Cubans, Puerto Ricans, South Americans, Central Americans, Mexicans, and Dominicans (*USA Today*, 2008).

> *in the next generation or so we will see a kind of Chicano Quebec take shape in the American Southwest, as a group emerges with strong cultural cohesiveness and sufficient economic and political strength to insist on changes in the overall society's ways of organizing itself and conducting its affairs.* (Kennedy 1996:68)

Immigration and Increasing Diversity

The United States is shifting from an Anglo-White society rooted in Western culture to a society with three large racial/ethnic minorities, each of them growing in size while the proportion of Whites declines. Five facts show the contours and magnitude of this demographic transformation.

- *About one-third of the people in the United States are African American, Latino, Asian, or Native American.* The non-White population is numerically significant, comprising more than one-third of the population (up from 15 percent in 1960). Four states have non-White majorities (California, Texas, New Mexico, and Hawaii). Minorities make up the majority in six of the eight U.S. cities with more than a million people—New York, Los Angeles, Chicago, Houston, Detroit, and Dallas.
- *Racial minorities are increasing faster than the majority population.* Although non-Whites are now one-third of the population, by 2023 a majority of children (under 18) will be from a minority background (U.S. Census estimate, reported in Yen 2009). They will surpass Whites among working-age Americans by 2039, and by 2042 non-White minorities will exceed the White population in size (Roberts 2008; see Figure 5.2).
- *African Americans have lost their position as the most numerous racial minority.* In 1990, for the first time, African Americans were less than half of all

FIGURE 5.2

U.S. Population by Race and Ethnic Group, 1970–2050

Sources: U.S. Census Bureau, "Table 1: United States. Race and Hispanic Origin, 1970 to 1990" (www.census.gov/population, accessed May 5, 2003); and J. S. Passel, Projections of the U.S. Population and Labor Force by Generation and Educational Attainment: 2000–2005" (2003). Reprinted from Philip Martin and Elizabeth Midgley, "Immigration: Shaping and Reshaping America," Revised and updated 2nd Edition. *Population Bulletin* 61 (December 2006): p. 17, Figure 5. Reprinted with permission from the Population Reference Bureau.

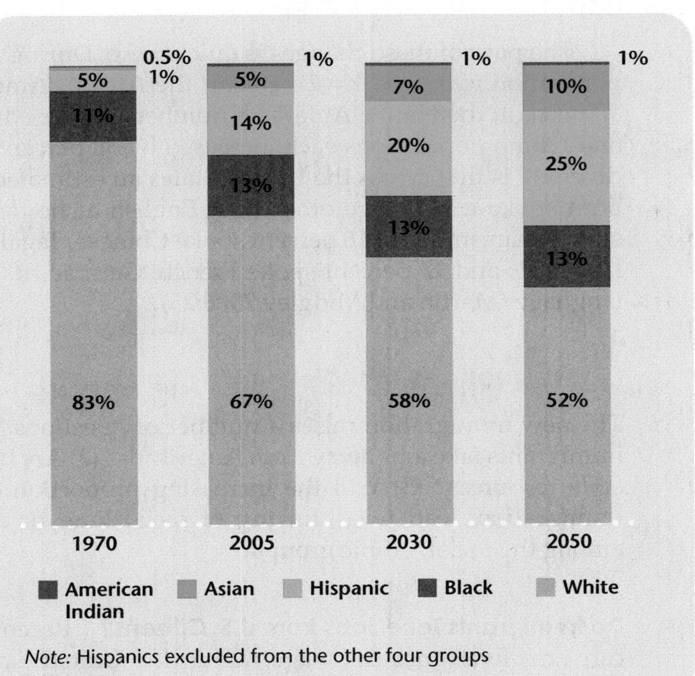

minorities. By 2000, Latinos outnumbered African Americans 42.7 million to 39.7 million. By 2050, Latinos will comprise a projected 29 percent of the U.S. population, with African Americans at about 13 percent. This demographic transformation will make two common assumptions about race obsolete: that "race" is a "Black-and-White" issue, and that the United States is a "White" society (Chideya 1999).

- *Immigration now accounts for a large share of the nation's population growth.* Today 12.5 percent of current U.S. residents are foreign born. The U.S. Census Bureau estimates that Latinos and Asians are growing more than ten times the pace of Whites (reported in El Nasser and Grant 2005). Immigration accounts for over a third of the current population growth directly and adds more indirectly, as first- (those foreign born) and second-generation (children of the foreign born) Americans have more children on average than the rest of the population.
- *New patterns of immigration are changing the racial composition of society.* Among the expanded population of first-generation immigrants, the Asian born now outnumber the European born, and those from Latin America, especially Mexicans, outnumber both. This contrasts sharply with what occurred as recently as the 1950s, when two-thirds of legal immigrants were from Europe and Canada.

These trends signal a transformation from a White majority to a multiracial/multicultural society:

> *[Sometime after the year 2042], Whites will become a "minority." This is uncharted territory in this country, and this demographic change will affect everything. Alliances between the races are bound to shift. Political and social power will be reapportioned. Our neighborhoods, our schools and workplaces, even racial categories themselves will be altered. (Chideya 1999:35)*

The pace of these changes is quickening. During the 1990s, while the White population increased by 2 percent, the African American population rose by 12 percent, the Native American numbers increased by 15 percent, the Asians and Latino populations each increased by 58 percent. One consequence of this diversity is that across the United States an estimated 84 percent of the foreign born spoke a language other than English at home. Slightly fewer than half spoke Spanish; about 18 percent spoke Chinese, Tagalog, Korean, or other Asian language; and 17 percent spoke French, German, Italian, or another European language (Martin and Midgley 2006:25).

Consequences of the New Immigration

The new immigration raises a number of questions. We consider three: (1) Do immigrants take jobs away from Americans? (2) Are immigrants a drain on society's resources? (3) Will the increasing proportion of non-Whites, fueled by immigration, lead to a blurring of racial lines or a heightening of tensions among the racial/ethnic groups?

- **Do Immigrants Take Jobs from U.S. Citizens?** Recent immigrants from Mexico can earn five times the wage rate in the United States that they can earn in

Mexico. This is the lure. Because most do not speak English and their skills are limited, they tend to work at low-wage occupations, such as gardeners, roofers, assemblers, custodians, restaurant help, maids, and migrant farm workers. The evidence is that immigrants do not have negative effects on the wages of most Americans, but they do on the low-wage/poorly skilled/poorly educated segment of workers. Harvard economist George J. Borjas, a long-time researcher of immigration, says that "the primary losers in this country are workers who do not have high school diplomas, particularly Blacks and native-born Hispanics" (cited in Henderson 2006). The wages of the lowest 15 percent of the workforce (typically, those with less than a high school degree) receive about 5 percent less in their paychecks because of competition from a large number of immigrants who are relatively uneducated, unskilled, and eager to work. See the "A Closer Look" box for some positive benefits from undocumented workers.

This problem will increase in the future as the federal and state governments no longer provide welfare benefits to legal immigrants and most nonimmigrant welfare recipients are required to leave welfare and find work, adding several million workers to compete for relatively few jobs at the low end of the occupational scale.

A CLOSER LOOK

SOME SOCIETAL BENEFITS FROM UNDOCUMENTED WORKERS

The presence of 11 million illegal immigrants is a contentious issue in the United States. Most folks assume that these workers have negative consequences for society. Although there are some negative costs from undocumented workers (e.g., some native borns are hurt by the competition from illegal immigrants who are willing to work cheaply, the cost of educating their children, and the cost of emergency room care for uninsured migrants), they also bring major benefits to the overall economy (Streitland 2006).

- If there were no undocumented workers, a variety of industries would be disrupted. Employers in construction, hospitality, child care, factories, food preparation, building maintenance, landscaping, and agriculture would have to attract new workers with higher wages. Wages for undereducated workers, retail prices at restaurants, and costs of food, housing, and many other goods and services would soar.
- Most undocumented immigrants contribute to Social Security but do not receive benefits, either because they used false papers to get payroll jobs or they returned to their native country. Through 2002, illegals paid an estimated $463 billion into Social Security and very few received any benefits (Cullen and Fonda 2006).
- As society ages, there will be a continuous need for more workers, especially service workers. The Department of Labor estimates that in the next decade we will need 7.7 million more workers. Much of this demand will be for unskilled labor that has been met by undocumented workers (Zuckerman 2006b).
- The 11 million undocumented immigrants are consumers, and although their household income is relatively low, collectively, they have considerable buying power. They pay rent, buy groceries and clothing, and take out loans for furniture, automobiles, and houses (Grow 2005). The estimated annual gross income of all U.S. workers born in Latin America, of both legal and illegal immigration status, was $450 billion in 2004. Approximately 93 percent of that amount is spent in the United States (from the Inter-American Development Bank, reported in Thornburgh 2006).

Immigration is only partly responsible for this relationship between somewhat lower wages and undereducated workers. Also pushing wages lower are the shrinking manufacturing sector, the decline in union membership, the outsourcing of jobs, and the Great Recession, which has especially brought unemployment to the construction industry, where so many new immigrants have worked.

On the positive side, immigrants are more likely than the rest of the population to be self-employed and to start their own businesses, which in turn creates jobs and adds strength to local economies. For example, 5 years after the 1992 Los Angeles riots, there was an unexpected rebirth in some of the riot-torn areas, led largely by Asian and Latino entrepreneurs, many of whom were first-generation immigrants. These people invested locally and hired locals, who spent much of their wages locally. Similar patterns of a migrant-based economy have been led by entrepreneurs from Jamaica, Mexico, Korea, Taiwan, and India.

To the extent that cheap, low-skilled labor helps hold down prices, there is more demand for some services, leading to more economic growth and jobs. "Lower menu prices encourage consumers to dine out more, leading to the opening of more restaurants. Lower construction costs make home-building more profitable and home remodeling more affordable" (Henderson 2006).

Are Immigrants a Drain on Society's Resources? In the short run, immigrants consume more in public services and benefits than they pay in taxes. There are two reasons immigrants require more resources from the state than do nonimmigrant families. First, they have relatively large families, and these children go to public schools. Second, they pay less in taxes because they tend to earn low wages and have relatively little discretionary income.

In the long run, however, immigrants are a good investment for society. The Academy of Sciences study (Cassidy 1997) found that by the time a typical immigrant with a family dies, that immigrant and his or her children will have paid $80,000 more in taxes than they received in government benefits. The evidence is that immigrants are a fiscal burden for two decades or so, mainly because of educational costs. After that, the society benefits monetarily.

This conclusion fits at the national level: that is, most taxes paid by immigrants and income taxes withheld by the federal government are used in part to provide Social Security and health care benefits to the elderly. However, the state and local taxes paid by immigrants are relatively low, yet the services they consume (in particular, education) are disproportionately funded by state and local taxes. Immigration is a national problem, but one borne by the states. This unbalance is a source of growing hostility as evidenced by the anti-immigrant legislation in 2010 passed by the Arizona legislature.

Research also shows that legal and illegal immigration add $1 billion to $10 billion per year to the U.S. gross domestic product, "largely because immigration holds down wages for some jobs, and thus prices, and increases the efficiency of the economy" (Martin and Midgley 1999:24).

There is also a global dimension to the economic benefits derived from immigrants. Most undocumented immigrants (i.e., those who entered the country illegally) are young, male, and Mexican. They leave their families in Mexico and work for months at a time as manual laborers in the United States. Typically, they send some of their earnings back to their families in Mexico—an aggregate $25 billion annually, according to the World Bank. As a source of foreign capital to Mexico, migrant remittances trail only oil, tourism, and illegal drugs.

- **Will the Increasing Proportion of Non-Whites Fueled by Immigration Lead to a Blurring of Racial Lines or a Heightening of Tensions among the Racial/Ethnic Groups?** The latest wave of immigration has taken place in a historical context that includes the restructuring of the U.S. economy (see Chapter 14) and an increasingly conservative political climate. New immigrants have always been seen as a threat to those already in place. The typical belief is that immigrants, because they will work for lower wages, drive down wages and take jobs away from those already settled here. These fears increase during economic hard times, when businesses downsize or when they outsource jobs, pay lower wages, and replace workers with technology as they adapt to the economic transformation. The hostility toward immigrants is also the result of the common belief that the new immigrants increase taxes because they require services (education, health care, and welfare) that cost much more than the taxes they produce. Former U.S. Labor Secretary Robert Reich sums up the rationale for hostility toward immigrants.

> *Many Americans feel themselves overtaxed. . . . They worry about schools, they are concerned about jobs, they worry about the state of social services, and they're concerned about crime. An influx of immigrants serves as a focal point of those concerns. (cited in Olinger and Florio 2002:1A)*

Previous immigration waves were White, coming mostly from Ireland, England, Germany, Italy, and Eastern Europe. Today's immigrants, in sharp contrast, are coming from Latin America and Asia. They are non-White and have distinctly non-European cultures. When these racial and ethnic differences are added to economic fears, the mix is very volatile.

The situation is worsened further by where the new immigrants locate. Typically, they move where immigrants like themselves are already established. For example, 20 percent of the 90,000 Hmong in the United States live in Minnesota, mostly around Minneapolis–St. Paul. One in twelve Asian Indians lives in Illinois, primarily in the Chicago area. Approximately 40 percent of all Asian Americans live in California. This tendency of migrants to cluster geographically by race/ethnicity provides them with a network of friends and relatives who provide them with support. This pattern of clustering in certain areas also tends to increase the fear of nonimmigrants toward them. They fear that wages will be depressed and taxes will be greater because their new neighbors are relatively poor, tend to have children with special needs in school, and likely do not have health insurance.

A second tendency is for new immigrants to locate where other poor people live for the obvious advantage of cheaper housing. A problem often arises when poor Whites live side by side with one or more racial minorities. Despite their common condition, tensions in such situations are heightened as groups disadvantaged by society often fight each other for relative advantage. The tensions between African Americans and Asian immigrants were evidenced, for example, during the South Los Angeles riots in 1992, when roughly 2,000 Korean-owned business were looted or damaged by fire.

The result of these factors is commonly an anti-immigrant backlash. Opinion polls taken over the past 50 years report consistently that Americans want to reduce immigration. Typically, these polls report that Americans believe that immigration in the past was a good thing for the country but that it no longer is.

The states with the most immigrants have the highest levels of anti-immigrant feeling. Several states have filed suit against the federal government, seeking reimbursement for the services provided to immigrants. Some twenty-two states have made English the official state language. The voters in California have passed two propositions that indicate anti-immigrant feelings. In 1994, they denied public welfare such as nonemergency medical care, prenatal clinics, and public schools to undocumented immigrants. In-state college tuition has been denied to noncitizens in some states. At the federal level, Congress passed a bill in late 2006 that authorized fencing a third of the 2,100-mile border between the United States and Mexico.

If present immigration patterns continue, by 2042 some one-third of the U.S. population will be post-1970 immigrants and their descendants and non-Whites will outnumber Whites. Under these circumstances of racial diversity, will the social meaning of ethnic and racial lines become increasingly blurred or more starkly defined? Will the people be pulling together or pulling apart? Will the gulf between affluent Whites and the disproportionately poor non-Whites be narrowed or widened? Will there be a de facto segregation as Whites who once lived and worked together with non-Whites move to White enclaves? Demographer William Frey has noted a "White flight" from high-immigration areas, a trend he fears may lead to the Balkanization of America (cited in Cassidy 1997:43). Is this our future?

Anti-immigration activists are becoming more numerous and vocal. The Southern Poverty Law Center says that tension over illegal immigration is contributing to a rise in hate groups and hate crimes across the nation (cited in Johnson 2006). White supremacy groups are growing. Vigilante groups have organized to watch the borders. What brings the anti-immigration activists together is a generalized belief "that a brown-skinned, Spanish-speaking tidal wave is about to swamp the white-skinned population of the United States" (Zeskind 2005:A15). Former Congressman Tom Tancredo sums up this fear: "If we don't control immigration, legal and illegal, we will eventually reach the point where it won't be what kind of a nation we are, Balkanized or united; we will have to face the fact that we are no longer a nation at all . . ." (quoted in Zeskind 2005:A15).

There are unofficial groups at the border organized to prevent entry by illegal immigrants into the United States.

Immigration and Agency

Immigration can be forced (e.g., the slave trade) or freely chosen. Immigration in this latter sense is clearly an act of **human agency** (rather than passively accepting structural constraints, people cope with, adapt to, and change their social situations to meet their needs). Most people in developing countries do not move. Others move, breaking with their extended family and leaving neighborhood and community ties, mostly to improve their economic situations or to flee repression.

Typically, new immigrants face hostility from their hosts, who, as we have seen, fear them as competitors or hate them because they are "different" or because they fear that they may be terrorists. In this latter instance, immigrants from Muslim countries have had to confront considerable hostility and suspicion since the terrorist acts of September 11, 2001. Recent immigrants also face language barriers as they seek jobs. Often, most especially for undocumented immigrants, their initial jobs are demeaning, poorly paid, and without benefits. How do they adapt to these often very difficult circumstances? Most commonly, immigrants move to a destination area where there is already a network of friends and relatives. These networks connect new immigrants with housing (often doubling up in very crowded but inexpensive conditions), jobs, and an informal welfare system (health care, pooling resources in difficult times). These mutual-aid efforts by immigrant communities have been used by immigrant networks throughout U.S. history, whether by Swedish settlers in Minnesota, Mennonite settlers in Kansas, Irish settlers in Boston, or Mexican or Vietnamese settlers now (Martin and Midgley 1999).

To overcome low wages, all able family members may work in the family enterprise or at different jobs and combine family resources. To overcome various manifestations of hostility by others, the immigrant community may become closer (the pejorative word is "clannish"), having as little interaction with outsiders as possible. Some may become involved in gangs for protection. Still others may move to assimilate as quickly as possible.

Effects of Immigration on Immigrants: Ethnic Identity or Assimilation?

Martin and Midgley sum up the universal dilemma for immigrants:

> *There is always a tension between the newcomers' desires to keep alive the culture and language of the community they left behind, and their need and wish to adapt to new surroundings and a different society. (Martin and Midgley 1999:35–36)*

Assimilation is the process by which individuals or groups adopt the culture of another group, losing their original identity. A principal indicator of assimilation is language. In 2000, slightly less than one in five Americans age 5 and older spoke a language other than English at home. Assuming the experience of earlier immigrants to the United States, it is likely that the shift to English usage will take three generations—from almost exclusive use by newcomers of their traditional language, to their children being bilingual, to their children's children (third-generation immigrants) being monolingual English speakers (Martin and Midgley 1999). According to the Pew Hispanic Center, in 2007, for example, 23 percent of adult first-generation Latinos said they could carry on a conversation very well in English, compared to 88 percent in the second generation and 94 percent in the third (reported in Gorman 2007).

If the past is a guide, the new immigrants will assimilate. "Our society exerts tremendous pressure to conform, and cultural separatism rarely survives more than a generation" (Cole 1994:412). But conditions now are different.

An argument countering the assumption that the new immigrants will assimilate as did previous generations of immigrants is that the new immigrants are members of racial/ethnic groups, not Whites. The early waves of immigrants (post-1965) were mostly White Europeans. Over time these groups were absorbed into the "melting pot" of society's mainstream because jobs were relatively plentiful and they did not face racial antipathy. Today's immigrants, however, face a different reality. A commonly held assumption (the reasoning of the culture of poverty—see Chapter 7) is that when new immigrants do not assimilate easily or if they continue to be poor, it is their fault. Thus, blame for many social problems and resistance to assimilation is placed on the immigrants, thereby "ignoring the impact of larger forces, such as racism and the economic order, that limit opportunities for success and present barriers to assimilation" (Pyke 2008:212).

The current political mood is to eliminate affirmative action (as California did in 1997) and to reduce or eliminate social programs that help level the playing field so that minorities would have a fair chance to succeed. Some legislation is especially punitive toward recent immigrants, particularly the undocumented. Such public policies make it more difficult for new immigrants to assimilate than did their predecessors, should they wish to do so.

Another factor facing this generation of immigrants is that they enter the United States during a critical economic transformation and, since 2007, an economic crisis in which the middle class is shrinking and the working class faces difficult economic hurdles (see Chapter 14). A possible result is that the new immigrants, different in physical characteristics, language, and culture, will become scapegoats for the difficulties that so many face (Powers 2007). Moreover, their opportunities for advancement will be limited by the new economic realities.

The issue of immigrant adaptation to the host society is complex, depending on a number of variables. Zhou (1997) described a number of these critical variables, including the immigrant generation (i.e., first or second), their level in the ethnic hierarchy at the point of arrival, what stratum of U.S. society absorbs them, and the degree to which they are part of a family network.

Immigrants who move to the United States permanently have four options regarding assimilation. Many try to blend into the United States as quickly as possible. Others resist the new ways by either developing an adversarial stance toward the dominant society or resisting acculturation by focusing more intensely on the social capital (i.e., social networks) created through ethnic ties (Portes and Zhou 1993). The fourth alternative is to move toward a bicultural pattern (Buriel and De Ment 1997). That is, immigrants adopt some patterns similar to those found in the host society and retain some from their heritage. Although this concept of a bicultural pattern appears to focus on culture, the retention or abandonment of the ethnic ways depends on structural variables (Kibria 1997:207). These variables include the socioeconomic resources of the ethnic community, the extent of continued immigration from the sending society, the linkages between the ethnic community and the sending society, and the obstacles to obtaining equal opportunity in the new society.

In sum, the new immigration, occurring at a time of economic uncertainty and reduced governmental services, is having three pronounced effects that will accelerate in the foreseeable future: (1) an increased bifurcation between the haves and the have-nots, (2) increased racial diversity, and (3) a heightened tension among the racial and ethnic groups.

THE AGING SOCIETY

The population of the United States is experiencing a pronounced change in its age structure—it has become older and is on the verge of becoming much older. In 1900, about one in twenty-five residents of the United States was 65 years and older. By 1950, it was about one in twelve. In 2000, one in eight was 65 and older, and by 2030, it will likely be around one in five, with more people over 65 than under age 18. In effect, by 2030, when most of today's college students will be around 50, there will be more grandparents than grandchildren. "The Senior Boom is coming, and it will transform our homes, our schools, our politics, our lives and our deaths. And not just for older people. For everybody" (Peyser 1999:50).

This section is divided into two parts: (1) a demographic (**demography** is the study of population) description of the aged category now and in the future and (2) the implications of an aging society for social problems.

Demographic Trends

Until the twentieth century high **fertility** (birthrate) and high **mortality** (death rate) kept the United States a youthful nation. During the last century, however, the birthrate fell (except for during the post–World War II period, which was an anomaly), resulting in fewer children as a proportion of the total population. Most important, greater longevity because of advances in medical technology (everything from beta-blockers for reducing hypertension to organ transplants) has increased the life expectancy of Americans. The average life expectancy in 1900 was 49 years, and in 2009 it was 78.

So, essentially in 130 years (from 1900 to 2030), people age 65 and older will have shifted from one out of twenty Americans to one in five. The surge in the number of elderly during the next few decades is the consequence of three demographic forces: a continued low fertility rate, ever-greater life expectancy rates, and the **baby boom generation** (the 75 million born between 1946 and 1964, representing 70 percent more people than were born during the preceding two decades) reaching old age, beginning in 2011 and ending in 2030. (See Figure 5.3 showing the population pyramids for 1900 [characteristic of a young population], 1980, 2000, and 2020. The latter three show the changing age structure as the baby boom group moves toward old age.)

Hidden within these statistics is another important fact about the old—they are getting older: the relatively vigorous "young old" (ages 65 to 74) will continue to make up the majority of older Americans until about 2030. After that time, people age 85 or older (the "old-old") will account for more than half of all elderly. By the middle of the twenty-first century, most of the projected growth of older Americans will occur because of increases in the population age 85 and older. In 1950, there were 600,000 in this category of 85 and older compared to 4,300,000 in 2000, a sevenfold increase. In 2030, there will be 8,500,000 age 85 and over (see Figure 5.4). In 2000, some 72,000 Americans were at least 100 years old. Because of the continued advances in medicine and nutrition, it is expected that the number of centenarians will increase to about 1 million by the middle of the twenty-first century. Children born today have a fifty-fifty chance of reaching 100 years of age.

Demographic Portrait of the Current Elderly Population

- **Sex Ratio.** Older women outnumber older men by a ratio of 3 to 2. As age increases, the disparity becomes greater—for those age 85 and older, there are about five women to every two men. By age 100 and older, four in five are women.

  A combination of biological advantages for women and social reasons explains this difference. The secondary status of women in U.S. society has provided them with extra longevity. Traditional gender roles have demanded that men be engaged in the more stressful, demanding, and dangerous occupations. It will be interesting to note whether there are any effects on female longevity as women receive a more equal share of all types of jobs. Meanwhile, though, the current situation creates problems for the majority of elderly women, who are often widows and have low incomes.

  Elderly women are more likely than men to live alone as widows. This is the result of two factors: the greater longevity of women and the social norm for men to marry younger women. Thus, to the extent that isolation is a problem of the aged, it is overwhelmingly a problem of elderly women. Because of pensions through work and the traditional bias of Social Security toward women who had not worked outside the home, elderly women are much more likely than elderly men to be poor (a 13 percent poverty rate compared with 7 percent for men). African American and Latino elderly women have an even higher probability than their male counterparts of being poor.

- **Racial Composition.** Because racial minorities have a lower life expectancy than do Whites (African Americans, e.g., live about six fewer years), they form a smaller proportion of the elderly category than of other age groups. Whites are overrepresented among the elderly population (e.g., in 2000, about 84 percent of the elderly population was White, compared with only 5 percent of the Latino population and 8 percent of the Black population). The trend is for the

FIGURE 5.3

U.S. Population by Age and Sex, 1900, 1980, and 2000, and projections for 2020

Source: Martha Farnsworth Riche. 2000. "America's Diversity and Growth: Signposts for the 21st Century." *Population Bulletin* 54 (June): 20–21.

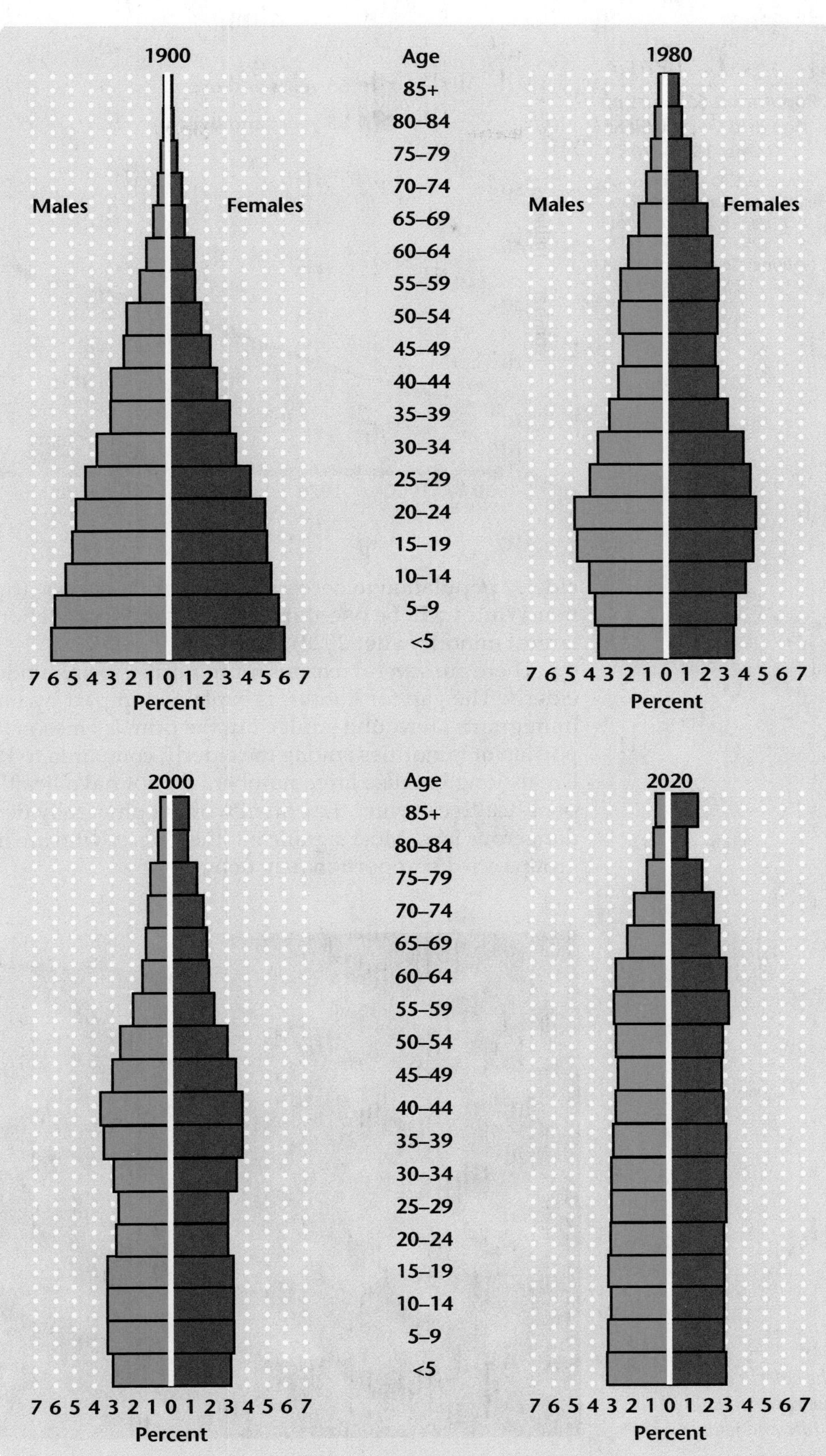

FIGURE 5.4

Population 65 Years of Age and Over: United States, 1950–2030

Source: U.S. Department of Health and Human Services. 1999. *Health, United States, 1999*. Hyattsville, MD: National Center for Health Statistics, p. 23.

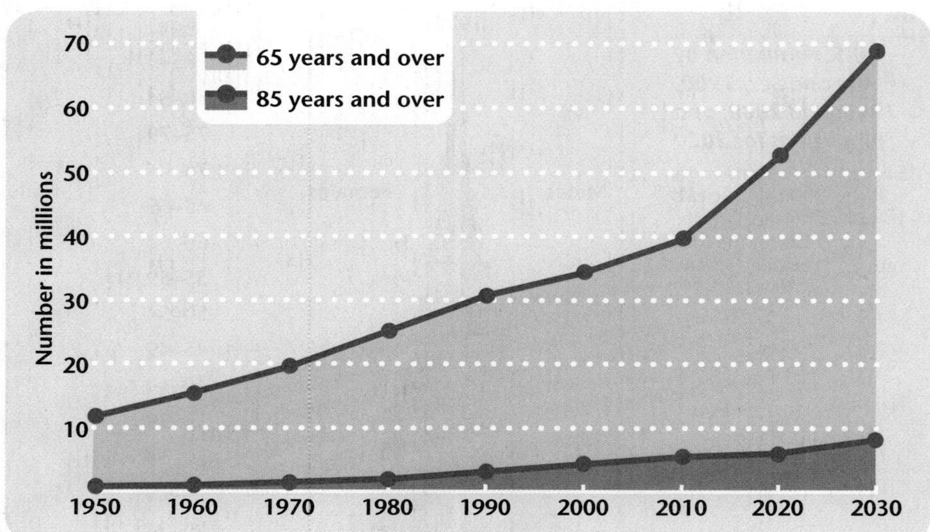

elderly population to become more racially diverse (by 2050, it is expected that non-Whites will be one-third of the elderly population, with Latinos being the largest minority after 2020).

There are several reasons for minorities being underrepresented among the elderly. The gap for Latinos is explained in part by immigration because most immigrants are young adults. But the primary reason for the relatively low proportion of minorities among the elderly, compared to Whites, is that they do not live as long because large numbers do not have health insurance, they receive poor health care, and they often work at physically demanding and sometimes dangerous jobs. Most significant, the elderly who are members of racial/ethnic groups are disproportionately poor.

The elderly are disproportionately White and female.

- **Longevity.** At the founding of the United States, life expectancy at birth was about 35 years. By 1900, life expectancy had increased to 47 years. Now it is about 78 years. This average masks some differences: (1) women live longer than men (their life expectancy is 79, compared to 74 for men), and (2) there are racial gaps that show little sign of closing. For instance, the life expectancy for White females is 80 and for White males it is 73 years; for Black females it is 74 and for Black males it is 65.

- **Geographic Distribution.** Some states and communities have disproportionately more older residents. One-fourth of all elderly Americans live in three states (California, Florida, and New York). Many rural states have a relatively high proportion of elderly, as these states experience a large outmigration of young people. Most elderly remain in their communities after retirement ("aging in place"), but those who move tend to migrate to the favorable climate found in the Sun Belt states (Florida, California, Arizona, Nevada, and Texas). Those who migrate are not representative of the elderly. They tend to be younger and more affluent than those who stay in their home communities. Thus, they benefit their new communities by broadening the tax base through home ownership, strong purchasing power, and not burdening the local job market. The communities they left in the Snow Belt are negatively affected. The elderly who remain are disproportionately older and poorer and require more public assistance from a lower community tax base.

- **Wealth, Income, and Cumulative Advantage or Disadvantage.** For obvious reasons, the wealth accrued over a lifetime of work affects the quality of life during retirement. The economically challenged will continue to struggle with the exigencies of life after retirement, whereas those with economic advantage retain it in their later years. This changed for the relatively affluent, however, with the bursting of the economic bubble in 2007. Prior to the Great Recession, recent retirees, in general, had personal resources—education, income, and assets—unknown to previous cohorts. They benefited from a sharp rise in the stock market during the 1990s and extraordinary gains in real estate markets in the previous three decades, which ultimately they passed on to their fortunate heirs. Yet, many elderly missed out on the boom. They did not own a home or have enough assets to invest. But the boom did not last, which is discussed in greater detail in Chapter 14, presenting difficulties for many of the previously affluent.

  Home equity is most significant in having a reasonable net worth. In this regard, those who are currently in the old category had an advantage because their home purchases in the 1950s and 1960s were much cheaper in interest and mortgage payments relative to wages than were homes bought in the 1970s, 1980s, and 1990s. However, in the three years after the housing bubble burst, homes had lost $11 trillion in value. Moreover, the stock market lost over $7 trillion in value, with mutual funds dropping 38 percent. Investments in retirement savings (401(k)s) lost more than $1 trillion, and over an 18-month period, the investments in public pension plans lost a combined $1.3 trillion (Byrnes and Palmeri 2009). As a result, many who thought they had more than enough saved for retirement found that they did not. Many had to postpone retirement, remaining in the labor force indefinitely. Of course, although losing money, many of the affluent old, remained comfortable affluent.

  The elderly who are members of a racial or ethnic minority are disproportionately poor. This relative lack of resources for racial minorities translates into a reduced likelihood, compared to Whites, of their receiving adequate health care and, when needed, living in nursing homes with full-time skilled nursing care under a physician's supervision.

Elderly married couples tend to have greater net worth than elderly singles. Households maintained by unmarried elderly males have a greater net worth than households maintained by unmarried elderly women. Similarly, White married-couple households with a householder age 65 or older will likely have higher family incomes than racial minority married couples.

Personal income is usually reduced by one-third to one-half after retirement. The important point is that those groups with advantage before becoming old maintain their economic advantage in old age—and the poor get poorer.

Typically, we assume that economic inequality narrows after age 65, when benefit programs replace work as principal income sources. This is not the case as the inequalities from income and privilege tend to be magnified among elderly people. People who are initially advantaged, for example, are more likely than their less fortunate counterparts to receive good educations and obtain good jobs with better health and pension benefits, which lead to higher savings and better postretirement benefit incomes.

Most noteworthy, the government is partly responsible for these skewed advantages to the affluent. The relatively affluent are encouraged by the government, because of tax incentives, to invest in retirement income programs such as IRAs (individual retirement accounts), Keogh plans, or other tax-deferred programs. Thus, the already advantaged are given preferential tax treatment, which amounts to tax subsidization, thereby increasing their economic advantage over the disadvantaged after age 65.

About 10 percent of people age 65 and older are poor. This proportion is lower than the overall poverty rate because Social Security benefits are indexed for inflation. This poverty rate, slightly below the poverty rate for the nation as a whole, is perceived typically as a success. However, over 3 million elderly are poor, and another 30 percent of them are in the "economically vulnerable" category—that is, they have incomes above the poverty line but below 150 percent of the official poverty rate.

The elderly spend about 20 percent of their incomes on health care, with the poor elderly spending about 35 percent of their incomes on health care. Roughly half of the incomes of the poor elderly goes for food. Thus, they are especially affected by inflation at the grocery store. The only recourse for the poor in inflationary times, when their incomes do not increase with spiraling costs, is either to eat less or to eat cheaper, less nutritious food.

The elderly poor spend about 20 percent of their incomes on energy for heat and electricity, both of which increase with inflation. Those on fixed incomes are likewise negatively affected by inflationary increases in the cost of rents, taxes, and health care. The last is a special burden for the old who are poor. Health costs for the elderly are almost four times those for people under age 65. The result is that the elderly poor tend to live in substandard housing, receive inadequate medical care, and have improper diets.

If the poor and the old are doubly cursed, then the elderly poor who are members of a racial or ethnic minority group experience a triple disadvantage. Individual and institutional sources of discrimination coalesce to make these people's lives especially miserable and problematic. The higher probability of older African Americans being poor is a direct consequence of their relatively low status throughout life. With average incomes only about 60 percent those of

Whites, they have little chance to build a nest egg to supplement their pension incomes. African Americans are also more likely than Whites to have worked at jobs that did not provide retirement benefits and that did not qualify for Social Security (prior to 1974, e.g., only 80 percent of elderly Blacks received some Social Security benefits, compared with 90 percent of older Whites). If they have worked at jobs qualifying for Social Security, minority members usually are eligible only for lower benefits because of their lower wages.

These related problems reflect the discrimination in the job market and unfair legislation. Clearly, equity in Social Security benefits will not occur until racial minorities and Whites experience similar work careers and compensation.

After a lifetime of lower earnings and receiving small or no pensions, elderly minorities must live in substandard housing. They are much more likely than elderly Whites to live in deteriorated housing with inadequate plumbing, heating, and sewage disposal. Similarly, the minority elderly suffer more health problems than do the majority elderly. For instance, among all minority elderly the prevalence of chronic disabilities is twice as high as among the White elderly.

PROBLEMS OF AN AGING SOCIETY

We focus on three problems inherent in our aging society: (1) inadequate income from pensions or Social Security, (2) the high cost of elderly health care, and (3) abuse of the elderly.

Social Security

"One out of three seniors depends on Social Security for 90 to 100 percent of their income. Two out of three seniors depend on it for more than half their income" (Sklar 2004a). Since the introduction of Social Security in the 1930s, this program has been a significant aid to the elderly. Social Security has reduced poverty significantly among the elderly—from 35.2 percent in 1959 to 9.7 percent in 2008. "Without Social Security income, 54 percent of America's elderly would live in poverty" (Wellstone 1998a:5). Social Security also provides life insurance benefits to the survivors in cases of the death of a breadwinner and disability payments when a wage earner is unable to work. Most fundamentally, Social Security expresses the belief in society taking responsibility for the welfare of all its citizens. In the words of economist Robert Kuttner,

> *Social Security serves, and reinforces, a kind of collective solidarity rarely articulated explicitly in the ordinary idiom of American politics. But it has precisely expressed the modern liberal view of social entitlement—the collectivity taking responsibility for unearned misfortune, not by singling out (and thus stigmatizing) the certifiably needy, but within a universal system. This approach offers a logic that is both moral and political, both redistributive and inclusive. It cultivates a politics of social empathy and, in turn, an astonishing level of political support for a surprisingly social concept in a fiercely capitalistic society. (Kuttner 1998:30)*

Despite its considerable strengths, the Social Security program has several serious problems that place a disproportionate burden on certain categories of the elderly and on some portions of the workers paying into the program.

An immediate problem is that not all workers are covered by Social Security. Some groups of workers are unable to participate because they work for states with alternative retirement programs. Also, legislation has specifically exempted certain occupations (such as agricultural workers) from the Social Security program.

For workers who are eligible for Social Security, there are wide disparities in the benefits received. The amount of benefits depends on the length of time workers have paid into the Social Security program and the amount of wages on which they paid a Social Security tax. In other words, low-paid workers receive low benefits at retirement. Thus, 30 percent of the elderly who depend almost exclusively on Social Security benefits are still below the poverty line despite these benefits. These elderly typically are people who have been relatively poor during their working years or are widows.

On the surface, the Social Security system is gender neutral. Benefits are based purely on employment history, earnings, and family composition. "However, gender-related differences in the American work culture mean that, in reality, Social Security provides different levels of retirement security for women and men" (American Academy of Actuaries, 2007). Some of the disadvantages for women are

- Social Security recognizes only paid work. The benefits for spouses (typically wives) who did not work in the labor force are 50 percent of the working spouse's benefits.
- Social Security benefits are based on the number of years worked and the amount earned from wages. Because women are in the workforce fewer years than men (mostly because they take time off to bear and care for children, 11 years on average) and because women generally earn less than men, women will receive smaller retirement benefits than men (Cawthorne and Gross 2008).
- A divorced woman receives half of her former husband's benefit if the couple was married at least 10 years. If the divorce occurs before being married 10 years, then she receives nothing.
- Where wife and husband are both employed, the wife will receive Social Security benefits for her work only if her benefits exceed those earned by her husband. If she collects a benefit based on her own wages, she loses the 50 percent spouse's payment for which her husband's payroll taxes paid.
- A woman who is widowed will not receive any Social Security benefits until age 60 unless she has a child under 16 or an older disabled child or she herself is disabled.

The Social Security system is financed through taxes on wages and salaries. From a payroll tax of 2 percent on the first $3,000 of earnings when it began in the 1930s, the rate has increased substantially over the years. The 2009 rate was 12.4 percent on the first $106,800 (the cap rises with inflation) of earnings, with the cost being split between the worker and the employer, but most economists agree that the burden of the tax is on the employee because employers finance their share by paying their employees that much less.

The method of financing Social Security is not equitable because it disproportionately disadvantages lower-income wage earners. In other words, it is a **regressive tax**: it takes a larger percentage from people with the lowest incomes. The Social Security tax has the following negative features:

- It is levied at a constant rate (everyone, rich and poor, pays the same rate).
- It starts with the first dollar of earned income, offering no allowances or exemptions for the very poor.

- It applies only to wages and salaries, thus exempting income typical for the wealthy, such as interest, dividends, rents, and capital gains from the sale of property.
- It is imposed up to a ceiling ($106,800 in 2009). Thus, in effect, in 2009 a worker making $106,800 and an executive or a professional athlete making a $5 million salary paid exactly the same Social Security tax.

An overarching problem is facing Social Security—how to finance it in the future. Three demographic factors make financing the program problematic. The first is that more people are living to age 65, and the second is that people live much longer after reaching 65 than in earlier generations. Average life spans are 14 years longer than they were when Social Security was created in 1935. The obvious consequence of this greater longevity is that the Social Security system pays out more and more to an ever-expanding pool of elderly who live longer and longer.

The third demographic factor working against the system is a skewed **dependency ratio** (the proportion of the population who are workers compared to the proportion not working). Social Security is financed by a tax on workers and their employers. In 1950, there were 16 workers for each person on Social Security; in 1970 there were 3.7 workers; in 2000, there were 3.2; and in 2030, there will be 2.1 workers for each person receiving benefits. At present, the Social Security Administration collects more in taxes than it pays out, with the surplus going into a trust fund. But as people live longer and the baby boomers reach retirement, this system will no longer support itself. Estimates vary, but sometime around 2018 the system will begin paying out more than it collects, and after 2042 it will be able to pay out only about 70 cents of each dollar of promised benefits (Zuckerman 2000). See the "Social Problems in Global Perspective" panel for the problems facing the developed nations as they become disproportionately old.

To deal with this pending crisis in funding Social Security, Congress will have to either raise Social Security taxes, use other revenues, or cut benefits. Other options include raising the age of eligibility (starting in 2000 and continuing to 2022, the age for receiving full benefits will gradually rise from 65 to 67). Raising the eligibility age is unfair to certain groups: African American males, for example, live nearly 8 years less than White males, meaning that relatively few would receive benefits if the retirement age were raised to 70. Blue-collar workers also die earlier than professionals. A lifelong mine worker, for example, has only a fifty-fifty chance of reaching age 65. Another plan is the reduction or elimination of the cost of living adjustment (COLA), which allows the payments to keep pace with inflation. This proposal hurts the poor most because it is regressive. Another strategy is to tax Social Security benefits as income, which would protect the poor because they pay little, if any, federal income tax. Another solution that is popular with the Republican Party is to privatize Social Security. Generally, this would allow each individual to invest part of his or her Social Security taxes in the stock market. This plan would be beneficial when the stock market goes up, but it also makes retirement savings vulnerable to stock market declines. Imagine the consequences if Social Security had been privatized prior to the Great Recession.

> *Social Security is far more than a pension system, and its payouts are government guaranteed. It is also deliberately redistributive. More than three-fifths of retired Americans derive at least half their income from Social Security; without it, half would live in poverty. Dedicating some of the payroll tax to a private account system would divert that much revenue into a system that is neither redistributive nor government guaranteed. (Kuttner 1998:34)*

SOCIAL PROBLEMS IN GLOBAL PERSPECTIVE

THE DEVELOPED WORLD TURNS GRAY

Over the next several decades, the nations in the developed world will experience an unprecedented growth in the number of their elderly and an unprecedented decline in the number of their youths. Peter Peterson, author of *Gray Dawn: How the Coming Age Wave Will Transform America and the World,* calls this demographic transformation the "Floridization of the Developed World" (Peterson 1999). In effect, today's Florida with its concentration of seniors (about one in five) is a demographic benchmark that every developed nation will reach and exceed, as did Italy in 2003, Japan in 2005, and Germany in 2006. France and Britain will exceed it in 2016, the United States in 2021, and Canada in 2023. In today's developed world, the elderly population is 14 percent, but by the year 2030, it will reach 25 percent.

This demographic shift has several consequences. First, as the proportion of the elderly population grows beyond 20 percent in a society, coupled with a corresponding fertility rate that does not replace itself (below 2.11), the working-age population will shrink. Japan, for example, suffered a 25 percent decline from 2000 to 2010.

Second, the shrinking of the working-age population means that productivity will decline and taxes and/or debts will rise to pay for the enormous burden of pensions and health care for the elderly. Or, alternatively, governments will have to reduce benefits to the elderly significantly, causing political upheavals.

Third, unless their fertility rates turn up, the total populations of Western Europe and Japan will shrink to about one-half of their current size by the end of the twenty-first century. The developing nations will continue to grow rapidly until leveling off around 2050, resulting in an ever-enlarging population gap between the developed and developing worlds and increasing resentment by the latter over the disproportionate resource use by an ever-smaller developed world.

Fourth, worker shortages will increase the demand for immigrant laborers, bringing diversity in religion, language, and customs. This diversity increases the possibility of racial and ethnic conflicts. Moreover, the increasing inequality gap between the new immigrants who arrive at the bottom of society's stratification system and those who are privileged will increase the possibility of clashes between the haves and the have-nots.

Paying for Health Care

Most older people are in reasonably good health. Of all age groups, however, the elderly are the most affected by ill health. Health problems escalate especially from age 75 onward, as the degenerative processes of aging accelerate. Consider the following facts:

- Although the elderly comprise only about 13 percent of the population presently, they consume more than one-third of all health care in the United States.
- The elderly are four times as likely as the nonelderly to be hospitalized. When hospitalized, they stay an average of about three days longer than the nonelderly.
- The medical expenses of the elderly are three times greater than those of middle-aged adults, yet their incomes are typically much less.
- The elderly account for more than one-third of all spending for prescription drugs.
- One in eight who are at least 65 years old has Alzheimer's disease. By 2030 the number will have doubled to one in four due to the aging of the population (Hyman 2008). The incidence of Alzheimer's disease, the leading cause

of dementia in old age, rises sharply with advancing age—from one in ten people over the age of 65 to a fifty-fifty chance of getting the disease after age 85.
- Osteoarthritis, the degeneration of protective tissues around the body's joints, afflicts about half of those age 65 and older.
- The cost of long-term care is prohibitive. The average cost of a year in a nursing home in 2008 was $213 a day or $77,745 annually (*SmartMoney*.com 2008), and in some cities it is much higher.

Fidelity Investments estimates that a 65-year-old couple retiring in 2006 will need about $200,000 to cover health costs that are not covered by Medicare. That estimate does not include the cost of over-the-counter drugs, dental services, or long-term care (cited in Block 2006). Because Medicare does not pay for most long-term care, long-term care insurance is expensive, and Medicaid will help only after the patient's resources are exhausted, resulting in many elderly spending their last years impoverished.

Medicare, begun in 1965, is the federal health insurance program begun in 1965 for those 65 and older. Everyone is automatically entitled to hospital insurance, home health care, and hospice care through this program (known as Medicare Part A). The supplemental medical insurance program (known as Medicare Part B) helps pay for doctor bills, outpatient services, diagnostic tests, physical therapy, and medical supplies. People may enroll in this program by paying a relatively modest monthly fee. Overall, Medicare is financed by payroll taxes, premiums paid by recipients, and a government subsidy.

There are three major problems with Medicare. First, it is insufficiently financed by the government. Second, from the perspective of the elderly, only about half of their health care bills are paid through the program, leaving many with substantial costs. The affluent elderly are not hurt because they can purchase supplemental health insurance. The poor are not hurt because they are also covered by Medicaid, a separate program financed by federal and state taxes that pays for the health care of indigent persons. The near poor, however, do not qualify for Medicaid, and they cannot afford additional health insurance.

A third problem with Medicare is that physicians feel the program pays them too little for their services. As a result, many physicians limit the number of Medicare patients they will serve, some even refusing to serve any Medicare patients. Thus, some elderly have difficulty finding a physician.

Elderly Abuse

- **Problems of the Institutionalized Elderly.** About 3.5 million people will live in a nursing home over the course of a year (Schmitt 2002). By 2020, it will be almost a million more. The data indicate that at any one time, between 4 and 5 percent of people age 65 and older are confined to nursing homes and other extended-care facilities. This low figure is misleading, however. It does not mean that only 4 to 5 percent of the aged ever will be confined to a nursing home. At age 65, a person may have no need for such a facility, but at 85 it may be a necessity.

The residents of nursing homes are typically age 75 and older (87 percent), female (75 percent), and White (89 percent; Curran and Renzetti 2000:287). Conspicuously absent are racial minorities, as Curran and Renzetti noted:

> *The small number of elderly people of color in nursing homes is the result of several factors. First, the states with the highest numbers of people of color are in areas of the*

country—the South and the Southwest, for example—that have low overall nursing care institutionalization rates. Second, many racial and ethnic minority groups have cultural norms that include respect and veneration of the elderly, so members of these groups often care for their elderly themselves rather [than] using institutional care. However, a third reason for the small number of people of color in nursing homes is discrimination in nursing home admissions. Research indicates that African American and other minority elderly are sometimes channeled into other types of institutions, such as state mental hospitals, or they are admitted to nursing homes that have low quality-of-care ratings. (Curran and Renzetti 2000:287)

The economically advantaged elderly are not as likely as their less wealthy age cohorts to be institutionalized, and if institutionalized, they are apt to be in private nursing homes and to receive better care. Kosberg (1976) compared nursing homes for private residents with those for welfare recipients and found the former decidedly superior in staffing, freedom, pleasantness of surroundings, cleanliness, patient communication, and meals. Kosberg found that homes for the affluent old tend to provide **therapeutic care** (the approach that focuses on meeting the needs of patients and on treatment), whereas homes housing welfare recipients tend to provide **custodial care** (the approach in a health facility that focuses on meeting the needs of the institution rather than those of the residents). This distinction is an important attitudinal difference; custodial "residents are conceived of in stereotyped terms as categorically different from 'normal' people, as totally irrational, insensitive to others, unpredictable, and dangerous. . . . Custodialism is saturated with pessimism, impersonalness, and watchful mistrust" (Kosberg 1976:427–428). This finding has implications for the federal law stating that nursing home residents must use all their savings before receiving Medicaid. Because nursing home care costs are very high, and less than 8 percent of Americans have private insurance for lengthy care, long-term care results in many residents' spending themselves into poverty, at which time Medicaid will take over the financial payments. Previous research indicates that the shift to Medicaid results in a change from therapeutic care to custodial care.

There are two extreme points of view concerning the functions of nursing homes. One view is that such homes are necessary places for the elderly who need extensive health care. Obviously, such facilities are needed for people who have Alzheimer's disease and for people who have been paralyzed by strokes or are bedridden. The opposing view sees nursing homes as dumping grounds or repositories for getting rid of people who represent what we do not want to be or see. Whatever one's views on these institutions, one fact is pertinent: although many nursing homes provide good environments for their residents, there are serious problems in others. There are no federal standards that nursing homes must meet for the health and safety of their residents. The standards are left to the individual states, and they vary in their standards and rigor in enforcing them.

Government studies of nursing homes (reported in Pear 2002; McQueen 2001b) found the following:

- Nearly one in three of the nation's nursing homes has been cited by state inspectors for abusing patients.
- Problems will likely increase as the rapidly increasing elderly population puts even greater pressure on the nation's nursing homes.
- Nursing homes have become dangerous places largely because they are understaffed and underregulated (nine of ten nursing homes lack adequate staff).

- A review of nursing home deaths in California suggests that if the same percentages hold elsewhere, as many as 20,000 U.S. nursing home residents die prematurely or are in unnecessary pain, or both.

Common problems in nursing homes with a custodial style are the overuse and misuse of drugs. Drugs can be used for a host of therapeutic reasons, but one common use is not healthful—drugging an individual to control behavior. The use of tranquilizers, for example, keeps people from complaining and from asking for service. This procedure minimizes disturbances, thereby requiring fewer personnel and thus increasing profits. Of course, the quality of life for the residents is diminished, and even their lives may be broken:

> *The scenario is all too familiar. An elderly woman goes into a nursing home suffering from a broken hip, but is otherwise alert and continent. A few months later, she is depressed, drooling, incontinent, unable to remember things or follow simple conversation. When her children ask what happened, they discover their mother has been placed on psychoactive drugs. They ask why and are told that she was "agitated." She withdraws still further and spends her remaining months of life effectively warehoused, an empty, broken shell of a person. (Beck 1990:77)*

The nursing home business is big business. Two factors make the profit potential especially great: (1) the elderly population is growing at a 2 percent annual rate, and (2) the federal and state governments pay for much of the care (63 percent). One consequence of these factors is the proliferation of private nursing homes (about 75 percent are private) organized to generate profits. Many of these facilities provide excellent care for their clients, but others have shown that their interest in profit exceeds their interest in clients.

Not all nursing homes are unnecessary, and not all owners and personnel are greedy and uncaring. Many older people benefit from a sheltered environment, and doubtless many of the 17,000 nursing homes in the United States are resident oriented and provide adequate—perhaps even superior—services to their clients. But we must also acknowledge that there are widespread abuses in U.S. nursing homes. The danger, of course, is the profit motive—the less money that nursing homes spend on care such as living space, staff, food, heat in the winter and air conditioning in the summer, and recreational equipment, the more profit for the company and its shareholders.

What is the effect of institutionalization on the residents? Obviously, it will vary according to the facilities and treatment philosophy of a particular nursing home. But all care institutions (including prisons, mental hospitals, and nursing homes) must be wary of depersonalizing individual clients. In the name of efficiency, people eat the same food at the same time, wear the same type of clothing, perform the same chores in the prescribed manner, watch the movies provided them, and live in rooms with identical dimensions and decor. The widespread use of tranquilizers compounds this depersonalization. The result is that docility and similarity abound, which makes management happy but obviously overlooks the individual needs of the elderly residents.

- **Noninstitutionalized Care of the Elderly by Their Children.** Two demographic trends mentioned earlier—the decline in fertility and an increased life expectancy—increase the likelihood of elderly parents living with their adult children. These trends result in a **beanpole family structure**—a vertical, four-generation family structure.

> *In the decades to come, individuals will grow older having more vertical than horizontal linkages in the family. For example, vertically, a four-generation family structure has three tiers of parent–child relationships, two sets of grandparent–grandchild ties, and one great-grandparent–great-grandchild linkage. Within generations of this same family, horizontally, aging individuals will have fewer brothers and sisters. In addition, at the level of extended kin, family members will have fewer cousins, aunts, uncles, nieces, and nephews. (Bengtson, Rosenthal, and Burton 1990:264)*

A variation of the beanpole family structure is the three-generation household, called the **sandwich family structure**, where parents care for their parents and their children.

Families make the decision for the elderly to live with their children for a variety of reasons. Regardless of the reason, the new living arrangement may be satisfactory or it may be difficult because the elderly or their children or both may resent the lack of privacy and the erosion of independence, or there may be disagreement over disparate lifestyles.

With this trend for more and more children assuming a caretaker role of their elderly parents, there is an increased likelihood of elder abuse. This abuse can take the following forms:

- *Physical abuse:* hitting, slapping, shoving, and use of physical restraints, as well as the withholding of personal care, food, medicine, adequate medical attention, and the like.
- *Psychological abuse:* verbal assaults, threats, fear, and isolation.
- *Drug abuse:* encouragement by doctors and families to take too many drugs, which serves the families by keeping the elderly manageable.
- *Financial exploitation:* theft or misuse of money and other personal property owned by the elderly.
- *Violation of rights:* forcing a parent into a nursing home, for instance.

For the most part, accurate information on how many elderly people are subjected to these abusive acts is impossible to obtain. The elderly victims are in a double-bind situation that traps them in an abusive situation in which they feel that they cannot notify the authorities.

> *[T]he abuser is providing financial and other resources necessary for the victim's survival. Thus, the [elderly victim recognizes his or her dependency on the] abusing caretaker. These battered parents, whose attacks cover an even wider range of abuse than that perpetrated upon children, often refuse to report the abuse for fear of retaliation, lack of alternative shelter, and the shame and stigma of having to admit that they reared such a child. Paralleling the battered wife, these abused old people prefer the known, even when it includes physical abuse, to the unknown, if they seek to leave the situation. (Steinmetz 1978:55)*

As a result, as many as five out of six cases of elder abuse go unreported (National Center on Elder Abuse 1998). Contributing to underreported elder abuse, many mistreated elders are homebound and isolated, and thus are unlikely to be seen at banks, senior centers, hospitals, health programs, and police stations (Wolf 2000:8).

Despite these problems with underreporting, Rosalie Wolf (2000), summarizing the findings from community surveys, found that 4 to 6 percent of older adults report experiencing incidents of domestic elder abuse, neglect, and financial exploitation. With about 35 million Americans 65 and older, a middle estimate of 5 percent yields an estimated 1,750,000 who are victims of some form of abuse.

The problem seems to occur in situations in which adult children are overwhelmed by the role of taking care of their parent or parents. The emotional, physical, and financial costs of caregiving can be enormous. Hospital and other medical costs are extremely expensive for the elderly because they are more prone to illness. There are obvious additional food and housekeeping costs. Furthermore, the timing of the additional financial burdens may be especially difficult for caretakers because it is likely to coincide with higher expenses for their children (college, wedding, helping them buy their first home).

Parents living with their adult children cause stress and resentment in a number of other ways as well. The household is more crowded, causing, for example, different sleeping arrangements, overcrowded bathrooms, and shortages of hot water. The caretaking responsibility is likely to be assumed by the wife, and she may resent the elders' presence because of the extra work, the intrusion into her privacy, and the excessive demands on her time. Of course, as parents age and disabilities become more pronounced, the care they need can become overwhelming. The wife may be especially hostile to the parents because she is losing the freedom she expected to have once her children were gone—freedom to travel, go back to school, or take a job. But with elderly parents to restrain her, she is back to the parental role.

Parents living with an adult child can cause special problems when they have not resolved their problems from an earlier time. The parents may continue to treat their adult child as a child, taking over or trying to take over the decision-making role. Or the hostile feelings generated when the child was an adolescent return to haunt both parties. Clearly, there is tension when the behaviors and values of the adult child do not coincide with those of the elderly parent. They may differ on political issues, religious issues, how the grandchildren should be raised, and what television programs to watch.

The adult child may also resent parents living in his or her home because the adult child feels forced into the situation. Perhaps the other siblings live in different communities, and so the parents, no longer able to live alone, move in with the child living in their community. The hostile feelings increase if the adult child feels that other relatives are not sharing the burden, at least financially.

This emphasis on the elderly causing stress among caregivers blames the victim. In the words of Karl Pillemer, a major researcher in the field,

> *In the same way that some writers held that "spoiled" children were more likely to be abused, or that nagging, demanding wives were more likely to be battered, the elderly themselves have been cited as the cause of abuse. Focusing on caregiver stress normalizes the problem: it relieves the abuser of much of the blame because, after all, the elderly are demanding, hard to care for, and sometimes even downright unpleasant. (Pillemer 1993:246–247)*

Despite this disclaimer, the stress generated between the elderly and their caregivers is a major source of abuse. Stresses and tensions between the generations are inevitable. For some families, such a situation results in actual physical and mental abuse of the elderly. The psychological and social factors related to child and spouse abuse are also pertinent for the abuse of the elderly. One additional catalyst that must be considered is the **ageism** prevalent in society. Ageism promotes an atmosphere in which the elderly are devalued, negatively stereotyped, and discriminated against. To the extent that older people accept these negative definitions of the aged, they may view abusive treatment as deserved or at least unavoidable. Similarly, if their children accept tenets of ageism, they are likely to assume that the elderly deserve their mistreatment.

RESPONSES BY THE ELDERLY

People at age 65 today have 20, 30, or 40 years more of life ahead of them. Some are financially secure, and many will be relatively healthy throughout their remaining years. Elderly people who are healthy and financially secure have opportunities to enjoy travel, leisure activities, social involvement, and other pursuits that make their lives full and meaningful.

But being old is a difficult stage in life for many. People who were once attractive, active, and powerful may no longer be so. They no longer are "tethered to society through a series of institutions—school, work, family, church, community—that structured [their] lives, defined [their] place in the world, and gave shape to [their] identity" (Rubin 2006:93). Their lives, once organized around pursuing goals, seem empty and meaningless. Some experience debilitating diseases that cause constant pain, restrict their freedom, and rob them of their vitality. Others are isolated in nursing homes or because they lost a spouse and their children live at a distance. Some elderly are poor and live lives of desperation and hopelessness, with inflation eating away their meager resources.

The elderly possess a devalued status in U.S. society. Being considered old by society and by oneself is a catalyst that provokes the individual to respond in characteristic ways. But—and this is the crucial sociological point—the elderly are reacting to socially structured inequalities and socially constructed definitions, not to age as such. In a different cultural setting in which status increases with age, observers might find different personality types and responses.

Some researchers have argued that senior citizens respond to the aging process by retreating from relationships, organizations, and society (called **disengagement**). This behavior is considered normal and even satisfying for the individual because withdrawal brings a release from societal pressures to compete, perform, and conform. Other researchers have quarreled with disengagement theory, arguing that many elderly people are involved in a wide range of activities.

Most elderly people do remain active until health problems curtail their mobility. Some 60 percent of people over 80 continue to live independently (Rubin 2006:90). A striking number of them are becoming more politically active in an attempt to change some of the social conditions especially harmful for them. Senior citizens are more politically active (voting, volunteering) than other age groups in society. Faced with common problems, many join in a collective effort to make a difference. Several national organizations are dedicated to political action that will benefit the elderly, including the American Association for Retired Persons (AARP), which, having over 40 million members, is the nation's largest special-interest organization; the National Committee to Preserve Social Security and Medicare; the National Council of Senior Citizens; the National Council on Aging (a confederation of some 1,400 public and private social welfare agencies); the National Caucus on Black Aged; and the Gerontological Society. Collectively, these organizations have many millions of members. They work through lobbyists, mailing campaigns, phone banks, advertising, and other processes to improve the lot of the elderly in U.S. society.

Just how effective these organizations are or will be is unknown. But as the elderly continue to increase in proportion, their sphere of influence is likely to increase as well. Currently, the elderly account for around 20 percent of the voting public. By 2038, they are projected to make up more than one-third of the electorate. Elderly citizens could be a significant voting bloc if they developed an age consciousness and voted alike. Politicians from states with a high concentration of elderly people are increasingly aware of their potential voting power, and legislation more sympathetic to the needs of the elderly may be forthcoming. It is probably only a matter of time before the elderly focus their concerns and become an effective pressure group that demands equity.

CHAPTER REVIEW

1. A major demographic force in U.S. society is massive immigration. This immigration (adding about 1 million immigrants annually) differs from previous waves because the immigrants come primarily from Latin America and Asia rather than Europe.
2. Racial and ethnic diversity ("the browning of America") is increasing with the influx of immigrants and differential fertility (i.e., immigrant groups having a higher fertility rate than other groups).
3. The two fastest growing minorities are Latinos and Asian Americans.
4. The reaction of Americans to the new immigrants is typically negative. This reaction is based on two myths: (a) immigrants take jobs away from those already here, and (b) immigrants are a drain on society's resources.
5. Immigrants face a dilemma: Do they fit into their new society, or do they retain the traditions of the society they left? Immigrants in the past, for the most part, assimilated. But conditions are different for the new immigrants: (a) they are members of racial/ethnic groups, not Whites; (b) the current political mood is to eliminate affirmative action programs and welfare programs; and (c) they have entered during difficult economic times brought about by the economic transformation.
6. The second major demographic shift is toward an aging society ("the graying of America").
7. The proportion of the U.S. population age 65 and older is growing. In this category, women outnumber men, and minorities are underrepresented. Although the elderly as a category are not disproportionately poor, the elderly who are women, minorities, or who live alone are disproportionately poor.
8. The Social Security program is the only source of income for about one-half of retired people and a major source of income for 80 percent of the elderly. The key problem is how this program will be financed in the future.
9. The Social Security program is biased in several ways: (a) some workers are not included, (b) people with low career earnings receive fewer benefits, (c) women (homemakers, divorced, and widowed) are disadvantaged, and (d) the tax is regressive.
10. Medicare is the health insurance program for almost everyone age 65 and older. The program is insufficiently financed: (a) from the perspective of the elderly, the program does not pay enough of the medical expenses, and (b) the program is too expensive for the government to finance adequately.
11. At any one time, only about 5 percent of people age 65 and older are confined in nursing homes. These homes have important functions for those needing their services, but abuses are associated with some of these operations: Residents are given custodial care, drugged, and provided with inadequate nutrition.
12. As many as 1.5 million elderly people in the United States are physically abused by relatives annually. Most commonly, abuse occurs when adult children are overwhelmed by the role of taking care of their parents. Elder abuse also occurs in about one-third of the nation's nursing homes, according to government studies.
13. The elderly may respond to their devalued status in several characteristic ways. They may withdraw from social relationships; they may continue to act as they have throughout their adult lives; or they may become politically active to change the laws, customs, and social structures that disadvantage them.
14. The numbers and proportion of the elderly in the U.S. population will increase. This aging population will create a difficult burden for the

young, who, through taxes, will be required to finance pension plans and other assistance for the elderly. If the gap between the needs of the elderly and the benefits they receive widens, political activity and age consciousness among older people are likely to increase.

KEY TERMS

Human agency. People are agents and actors who cope with, adapt to, and change social structures to meet their needs.

Assimilation. The process by which individuals or groups adopt the culture of another group, losing their original identity.

Demography. The study of population.

Fertility. Birthrate.

Mortality. Death rate.

Baby boom generation. The people born in the 15-year period following World War II, when an extraordinary number of babies were born in the United States.

Regressive tax. Taxing at a set percentage, which takes a larger proportion of the wealth from the poor than from the nonpoor.

Dependency ratio. The proportion of the population who work compared to the proportion who do not work.

Therapeutic care. The approach in a health facility that focuses on meeting the needs of residents.

Custodial care. The approach in a health facility that focuses on meeting the needs of the institution, resulting in poor-quality care for the patients.

Beanpole family structure. A family structure in which the number of living generations within linkages increases, but there is an intragenerational contraction in the number of members within each generation.

Sandwich generation. Where parents care for both their parents and their children simultaneously.

Ageism. The devaluation of and the discrimination against the elderly.

Disengagement. The response by some people to the aging process of retreating from relationships, organizations, and society.

SUCCEED WITH PEARSON mysoclab www.mysoclab.com

Experience, Discover, Observe, Evaluate

MySocLab is designed just for you. Each chapter features a pre-test and post-test to help you learn and review key concepts and terms.

Experience sociology in action with dynamic visual activities, videos, and readings to enhance your learning experience. Complete the following activities at www.mysoclab.com.

Social Explorer is an interactive application that allows you to explore Census data through interactive maps.

- Explore the Social Explorer Map: *The "Graying of the United States"*

The Core Concepts in Sociology video clips offer a real-world perspective on sociological concepts.

- Watch *The Longevity Revolution*

MySocLibrary includes primary source readings from classic and contemporary sociologists.

- Read Macarthur Foundation Research Network on an Aging Society, *Facts and Fictions About an Aging America*; Telles, *Mexican Americans and Immigrant Incorporation*; The Economist, *A Gradual Goodbye: If People Are Living Longer, They Will Have to Work Longer Too*

CHAPTER 6 Problems of Place: Urban, Suburban, and Rural

In most nations, cities are a big deal. . . . But in America, cities are the neglected stepchildren, exploited and abused when not simply ignored.

—Joel Rogers

The United States is an urban nation, with 30 percent of its people living in central cities, surrounded by half of the population living in suburbs—that is four out of five Americans live in metropolitan areas. The remaining fifth reside in rural communities and in open areas. This chapter examines the social problems of place: the problems unique to cities, to suburbs, and to rural areas.

URBAN PROBLEMS

Some observers argue that although American cities in the past had problems, they are on the rebound as neighborhoods are revitalized, formerly abandoned downtowns are rebuilt with financial services and other businesses moving back, and it is becoming fashionable to live in the urban core. But although there are successes, many cities of the United States are in trouble. And, these troubles have been magnified by the Great Recession.

> *Cities are facing quadruple indemnity: falling real estate values, declining sales tax revenue, shrinking pension funds and skyrocketing social costs. The Feds and the states pay most of the freight for health care and unemployment benefits, but everything else—from schools to street repair to fighting crime—is mostly a local responsibility. (Fineman 2009:29)*

The focus of this section is on the grim reality for many, if not most, cities in the United States.

No other industrial nation has allowed the kind of decline and deterioration facing U.S. urban centers. Most of the social and economic problems discussed in this book are primarily concentrated and have their severest consequences in the city, particularly the largest cities (three out of ten Americans live in eight metropolitan areas with populations of 5 million or more). It is in this locale, more than any other, that many of these problems are expanding and intensifying. In this sense, place is crucial to understanding U.S. social problems.

Urban poverty is especially acute and contributes to and is associated with a host of other city problems. These problems include a decaying infrastructure, a shortage of affordable housing, homelessness, inadequate public transit, pollution, lack of health care, failing public school systems, drugs, gangs, and crime.

Urban Job Loss

About one-third of the jobs in major U.S. metropolitan areas are with corporations that export goods and services outside the metro area. These are the highest paying jobs with the best benefit packages, in such industries as aerospace, defense, international trade, oil refining, computer software and hardware development, pharmaceuticals, and entertainment. These export jobs create a second type of employment in metropolitan areas—regional-serving jobs. About a quarter of jobs in most metropolitan areas are regional serving—in finance, real estate, utilities, media, and other professional services. These jobs generally pay less than export jobs but still represent good employment opportunities. The remainder of jobs in metropolitan areas serve the local area. The best of these include schoolteachers, police officers, firefighters, other municipal employees, and neighborhood doctors and lawyers. The worst include low-wage, insecure, temporary, part-time, dead-end work with few or no benefits in retail, clerical, custodial, food service, and private security work. The "good" jobs are leaving or, in the case of business expansion and new jobs, not locating in the central city or in the older, closer suburbs; thus they are farther and farther away from the growing proportion of poor and minority people in the city.

Race and class, as well as the fear of crime, play into the corporate motivation to move to the fringes of urban areas. The perception of many corporations and their employees is that the central city is now unsafe and has a large minority workforce. Sears's relocation from the Sears Tower in downtown Chicago to Hoffman Estates, 37 miles to the northwest, is a prime example of this perception. The move allows Sears to hire more highly educated workers, mostly White, who live near the 1.9-million-square-foot campus-style complex. The state of Illinois used taxpayer dollars to subsidize Sears's relocation with lowered land costs, infrastructure and expressway improvements, and tax abatements.

In addition to the jobs that cities have lost to the suburbs, there has been a net loss of good-paying and well-benefited jobs in the wider U.S. economy. These economic changes and their impact on U.S. society are discussed in detail in Chapter 14.

Particularly as the business of the old industrial cities of the Northeastern and Midwestern United States shifted from manufacturing to legal, financial, real estate, and other service work discussed earlier, the worst of the local-serving jobs, the jobs of low-skill workers, were hit hard. Especially affected were people of color in the inner city. As a result of the exodus of jobs away from the city and the deindustrialization of the economy, unemployment is high in the central cities.

According to the U.S. Census Bureau, nearly one-fifth of all full-time jobs in the U.S. economy are low-wage jobs, not making enough to lift an urban family of four above the government's poverty line. As low-wage employment proliferates throughout the U.S. economy, it is increasingly the only kind of employment available to less-skilled central-city workers.

But often, not even low-wage employment is available. For growing numbers of people in the city, there are no jobs. Microchip technology and the electronics revolution have fueled the development of a global economy in which large corporations have little or no loyalty to any particular locale or country; they are footloose multinational corporations. Since the early 1970s, many high-wage industries have fled U.S. cities to relocate in places with a more advantageous business climate—lower wages, weak or nonexistent unions, and lax environmental regulations. Sometimes these places have been suburbs, the urban fringe, or sprawling new metropolitan areas in the Sun Belt states; often they have been nations in the developing world. This corporate flight has been promoted in the United States by tax policies that encourage businesses to relocate to new sites rather than to modernize and expand their old plants in the cities. And with the U.S. government involved in international agreements that eliminate tariffs and other protections against free and unfettered trade—agreements such as GATT (General Agreement on Tariffs and Trade) and NAFTA (North American Free Trade Agreement)—American business will only find more reasons to relocate outside the United States.

Add to the loss of urban jobs from the transformation of the economy and through capital flight (companies moving to low-wage locales either within or outside the United States) the economic ravages of the Great Recession, where companies cut payrolls and consumers spent less. As a result, urban areas were especially hard hit. According to the Bureau of Labor Statistics, at the end of 2009 when the official U.S. unemployment rate was 10 percent, seventeen urban areas recorded jobless rates of at least 15 percent. Of the cities with 1 million or more, Detroit had the highest rate at 15.4 percent (U.S. Department of Labor 2010).

Disinvestment

Systematic patterns of investment and disinvestment have hurt U.S. cities. Banks, savings and loans, and insurance companies have redlined cities and metropolitan areas—literally drawing red lines on the map and making loans and providing insurance on one side of the line and not on the other. **Redlining** refers to the practice of not providing loans or insurance in what are deemed undesirable areas. These areas are almost always made up of high concentrations of poor

Central cities were especially hard hit by job losses in the Great Recession.

minorities and located in the central cities. They are the communities that suffer the consequences of the disinvestment that denies loans to home buyers, small-business entrepreneurs, and neighborhood real estate developers.

The patterns of disinvestment and investment that have resulted from redlining in U.S. metropolitan areas have discriminated by both race and place.

- **Race.** The most significant factor determining the flow of mortgage credit in U.S. cities is the racial composition of a neighborhood. In fourteen metropolitan areas nationwide, in a 1-year period, banks and savings and loans made on the average three times more loans in White census tracts than in minority census tracts. In a recent 7-year period in Atlanta, five times as many mortgages in predominantly White areas of the city were approved by local banks and savings and loans as were mortgages in Black neighborhoods with the same income level. Another study found that the lending ratio in Detroit, a city that is three-fourths Black, was three to one in favor of White neighborhoods. Nationwide, Black home mortgage applicants are rejected at savings and loan institutions twice as often as Whites, even when their income level and other indicators of credit are similar. In fact, a study of Atlanta indicated that the home lending rate disparity between Blacks and Whites was greatest in areas where Blacks had the highest incomes. A study conducted by ACORN (the Association of Community Organizations for Reform Now), using statistics available from the Home Mortgage Disclosure Act, found that African Americans in the Denver metropolitan area were 1.86 times as likely to be denied for conventional loans and Latinos 2.06 times as likely to be rejected as White applicants. Moreover, Latinos and African Americans earning more than $74,259 a year were more likely to be turned down than Whites who made between $49,000 and $62,100 (Arellano 2000). Another ACORN study, this time for Chicago, found that 30.2 percent of all first mortgage applications by African Americans were made by subprime lenders, whereas only 3.1 percent of such applications by Whites were from subprime lenders. To be assigned a subprime loan rather than a conventional loan means paying interest rates as much as 4 percentage points higher (Theresa Williamson 2000). Similar problems have occurred with securing car loans, insurance (*Consumer Reports* 2004), bank loans (Malveaux 2003a), and predatory lending (Squires 2005). Automobile insurance redlining, for example, charges higher premiums in low-income, minority neighborhoods, which are located near the downtown, than in middle-income, White neighborhoods away from the central core. Insurance rates are based on accident rates, and these rates are higher downtown than elsewhere—hence, the higher rates for those living nearby. Most downtown traffic, however, is not by residents but by people who live outside the city but shop or work downtown. The consequence is that the poor pay more. A study of this phenomenon in Los Angeles concluded:

> *One of the societal consequences . . . is that disadvantaged people bear a disproportionate share of the economic burden generated by the region's traffic. . . . Insurance premiums are tied to actuary rates, but our analysis reveals that the high accident and claim rates in these neighborhoods are associated with externally generated traffic. These inequalities are embedded in the city's spatial structure and in institutionalized practices. (Ong 2004:41)*

- **Place.** Patterns of lending also discriminate with regard to location. Suburbs receive a much greater and disproportionate share of loans compared to the central city. This discrimination, of course, is clearly related to the patterns of disinvestment and investment based on race described previously because suburban areas are predominantly White, but inner-city neighborhoods are often African American or Latino. Moreover, research on 4,600 small businesses found that Black-owned businesses were twice as likely to be denied a loan from a bank or financial institution as similar White-owned businesses (Koretz 1998).

City dollars, central city capital, regularly go to the suburbs. Bank deposits made by inner-city residents in city banks are more likely to be used for home and business loans in the suburbs than in the cities, where the need for capital is so apparent.

This sort of redlining, discrimination, and disinvestment ultimately leads to a self-fulfilling prophecy of decline in inner-city neighborhoods. When banks disinvest in a neighborhood, residents and small businesses cannot maintain their homes and property. Without loans, small businesses often fail, and the jobs, goods, and services they provide are lost to the neighborhood. Indeed, often the banks themselves are among the businesses that physically leave the community. Disinvestment by banks, savings and loans, and insurance companies also discourages other private investors and government agencies from investing in poor and minority neighborhoods.

The racist myth in the United States is that Black inner-city neighborhoods are run-down because Blacks lack pride and other middle-class values. In reality, they lack capital, not pride and good values. This capital is denied to them and to their communities by primarily White-controlled financial institutions.

Federal Abandonment

Over the past three decades, the federal government has also made huge cuts in dollars and services for the central cities. Federal aid to cities has been systematically cut since the Reagan administration. Cuts have been made in the federal revenue sharing program, welfare, medical aid, subsidized housing, and essential social services. Successful urban programs—for public works, economic development, job training, housing, schools, and health and nutrition—have been systematically cut. In addition, most states, because of federal cutbacks, have reduced various forms of public assistance to the poor. Facing their fiscal crisis alone and with a shrinking tax base (because businesses have left), cities have had to cut services or raise taxes, with most doing both. Raising taxes while closing schools, hospitals, and police and fire stations, laying off municipal employees, neglecting health and housing codes, cutting public transit, and postponing infrastructure maintenance and improvements had the effect of encouraging more businesses, industry, jobs, and middle-class residents to leave the city. This movement, of course, only deepens the budgetary crisis of the downward-spiraling cities. And as urban government downsizes, the poor and working-class residents of the city are left to compete for the dwindling resources and services still available.

As the central cities lose population, jobs, and businesses, they also lose political clout in state legislatures. As the suburbs gain these things, they also gain power. With half of the U.S. population now living in the suburbs, politicians are more likely to make policies favorable to the suburbs than to the central cities where only 30 percent of Americans live and relatively few of them vote. Moreover, politics is involved. Central cities, with their relatively high concentrations of racial and ethnic minorities tend to favor Democrats, whereas people in the suburbs are more likely to be Republicans. Thus, Republicans are not motivated to fund the cities' needs, whereas Democrats are.

Urban Poverty

Poverty is a problem in many central cities, especially in the nation's largest cities. Within cities, poverty and especially child poverty is concentrated in particular urban neighborhoods. There has been not only an increase in poverty in central cities but also an increase in poverty in central city **poverty areas** (neighborhoods in which at least one in five households live below the poverty line are designated by the federal government as poverty areas). There has also been an increase in the poverty concentrated in **high-poverty areas** in U.S. cities—areas where at least two in five households, or 40 percent of households, fall below the official poverty line. Urban public housing developments are most likely to fall into this category.

People of color are also more likely to be concentrated in poverty areas in the city and much more likely to be among the poorest of the poor. Matching the high rates of Black and Latino central-city poverty are high rates of residential segregation. Actually, even the extremely high levels of segregation reflected in census-tract data underestimate racial separation and isolation. Racial segregation is even more severe when smaller units, such as immediate neighborhoods and blocks, are analyzed. High levels of segregation in housing also lead to segregation in schools, churches, and other neighborhood institutions.

This means that not only are the urban poor a growing proportion of all poor people in the United States but also that a growing proportion of the urban poor are racially segregated in poverty and high-poverty areas in the central city. Racial segregation contributes to and perpetuates poverty because it isolates poor people from the educational and economic opportunities they need. The schools in racially segregated, poor Black communities in the inner city are separate but not equal. The poor people living in the poorest, racially segregated, central-city neighborhoods are disconnected—both socially and physically—from urban labor markets. As a consequence of this "American apartheid," urban African Americans and Latinos are disproportionately unemployed and uneducated. Also, as poverty is more concentrated in inner cities, crime and violence proliferate. The poor may adopt violence as a survival strategy, which escalates violence even further. The structural analysis employed in our analysis focuses on social conditions, not immoral people. This focus allows us to understand that social conditions and policies of abandonment create racial impoverishment in U.S. inner cities.

Urban Housing Crisis

There are two sources of the current urban housing crisis—the lack of decent, affordable housing for the poor and the bursting of the housing bubble—leading to the Great Recession.

- **The lack of affordable housing.** The government defines housing as "unaffordable" if it costs more than 30 percent of a family's monthly income. The demand for low-income and affordable housing in U.S. cities far exceeds the supply. For example, in 2007 some 9 million households in search of affordable rental housing were competing for only 6.2 million affordable units, a shortfall of 2.8 million. Moreover, 70 percent of low-income renter households were spending more than half their income on rent, and this *was before the current economic crisis* (Wardrip 2009:1). The sources of this gap include trends in the urban housing market that affect both the affordability of existing housing and the number of low-income units.

One factor reducing housing affordability and the supply of low-income housing units in urban areas is that private developers and builders tend to invest only in middle-class and luxury housing, where the market provides the highest margins. This private real estate investment includes both condo conversion and gentrification.

The housing squeeze on low-income people is exacerbated by gentrification—the redevelopment of cheap apartments into upscale condominiums.

Condominium conversion involves taking rental units and turning them into apartments for sale. This process often displaces people who cannot afford a down payment and do not qualify for a home mortgage, which more affluent residents who can and do. **Gentrification** is the redevelopment of poor neighborhoods (run-down properties, warehouses, cheap apartments) into middle-class and upscale condominiums, townhouses, single-family dwellings, lofts, and apartments. Often, the original residents are displaced because they are unable to afford the increased rents, purchase prices, and property taxes based on the neighborhoods' rising property values.

The redevelopment of the downtown areas in many U.S. cities during the past two decades has also led to the loss of significant numbers of low-income housing units. As the economy moved from manufacturing to services, many big-city downtowns were remade as financial, real estate, legal, and retail centers. Building often boomed on the fringes of the old downtown areas and in the process destroyed most of the SROs (single-room occupancy hotels) in many cities. SROs had historically provided housing for economically marginal single persons in the city. Although apartments were small, and occupants often had to share a bathroom or a kitchen or both, the units were affordable and available for this part of the urban population. Now the SRO has become a thing of the past.

Slumlords have also contributed to the housing shortage in the inner city. **Slumlording** occurs when landlords buy properties in poor neighborhoods and have no intention of investing in their upkeep and maintenance. While neglecting these properties, slumlords collect as much rent as they can from their poor tenants. Or, with gentrification, the slumlords sell their deteriorated dwellings at a profit.

Another urban housing market phenomenon that adds to the housing crisis in some cities is **warehousing**. Here urban real estate speculators withhold apartments from the housing market. Speculators purchase buildings and gradually empty them by not renewing the rents. They hold the property until developers on the edges of gentrifying areas become interested and purchase them for considerably more than their original cost. Developers are especially attracted to warehoused apartments, which spare them the trouble of getting rid of poor and working-class tenants who will not be able to afford the newly gentrified property.

All the forces in the urban housing market that have led to the shrinking supply of affordable and low-income housing have been met with, or encouraged by, failing government housing policies.

As early as the 1960s, federally financed urban renewal projects were bulldozing low-income housing in poor and working-class neighborhoods. In theory, federal urban renewal funds were meant for the rehabilitation and redevelopment of decaying urban neighborhoods. In practice, what usually happened was quite different. Cities applied for the federal funds and, when they received them, used their legal powers of eminent domain and other powers granted them under both federal and state urban renewal legislation to declare an area to be blighted. Once so designated, all structures in the area were eliminated. Often, this was done to facilitate the development of large public projects such as airports, colleges or universities, medical centers, or even private commercial projects on the now available land. The second phase of federal urban renewal was to include replacement housing for people who lost their homes or apartments and neighborhood. For the most part, however, funds were never appropriated for this phase, and urban renewal projects reduced the supply of low-income housing. Much of the housing stock lost was in fact blighted, but for many people, it was at least an affordable place to live.

The budget cutbacks during the Reagan and Bush administrations slashed federal housing funds by 70 percent. New construction of low-income housing by the Department of Housing and Urban Development (HUD), the federal agency responsible for the creation and maintenance of low-income housing in American cities, decreased by 90 percent. Congress and the Clinton administration decreased the HUD budget again in 1995—this time by 25 percent. For the first time in 20 years, funding for the construction of new public housing units was cut. For the first time, there was no increase in the number of available Section 8 certificates (certificates that subsidize tenants who live at or below the poverty line and who pay 30 percent of their incomes toward rent). Congress and the president also slashed funds for the maintenance and rehabilitation of existing public housing, thereby ensuring its further deterioration. They also repealed the long-standing federal one-for-one replacement rule, which required that a new unit of public housing be built before any old unit could be demolished. The Republican Congress and President Clinton endorsed these changes in public and subsidized housing at a time when the housing needs of the poorest households in U.S. cities were at an all-time high. Under President George W. Bush, HUD reduced the rent subsidies under Section 8. This affected 1.9 million of the most vulnerable urban residents.

These recent cutbacks in public housing in the United States come on top of an already meager public housing sector. When compared to the industrial democracies of Europe, for example, U.S. public housing makes up a small share of the total housing stock. In Germany, France, the Netherlands, and the Scandinavian countries, urban public housing often accounts for as much as 40 percent or more of all housing. In the United States, only 1.3 percent of the housing stock is publicly owned. Throughout Europe there has been a more widespread recognition that the private housing market—housing for profit—will not adequately house all parts of the population. Therefore, a larger share of the housing stock, as compared to the United States, has been provided by the not-for-profit or public sector. In European social democracies, public housing has been for middle-class as well as for poor and working-class residents. In U.S. cities, public housing has been the housing of last resort for the poorest of the poor only. And only one-fifth of the poor live in government-subsidized housing of any kind, be it public housing run by local government, privately owned developments subsidized by HUD, or private apartments where tenants pay rent with government vouchers.

U.S. housing policies have also contributed to the **jobs/housing mismatch**. What little affordable low-income housing there is in U.S. metropolitan areas is kept out of the suburbs and urban fringe. The suburbs and edge cities have used legal, political, and economic means to prevent this kind of housing from being built in their communities. The problem with this is that job growth occurs on the remotest edges of metropolitan areas. Thus, people who need the jobs the most, the poor in the central city, are the farthest from them. The jobs are located where the inner-city poor cannot afford to live, or discrimination prevents their living there. The poor are also the least likely to be able to afford to own a car, and public transit systems rarely extend to the urban fringe.

The jobs/housing mismatch is a form of **spatial apartheid**. Jobs and job growth occur in one place, populated by relatively affluent Whites, whereas poor African Americans and Latinos are restricted to another place.

Trends in the urban housing market together with failed housing policies have had, and continue to have, predictable consequences for a growing number of urban households. One consequence is that more and more households are experiencing a rent squeeze. More than half of all tenants pay rents that exceed the federal government's definition of affordable housing—not more than 30 percent of household income. More than one-quarter of all renters now devote more than half their income to rent. When the demand for low-cost housing exceeds the supply, the cost of low-cost rents rises, as it also does when gentrification upscales areas that once housed the poor and the near poor. When urban residents, particularly poor urban residents, have to pay more for housing, they have less money available for food, transportation, education, and health care.

When so much of an economically marginal family's budget is devoted to housing, a crisis such as a medical emergency or sudden unemployment often means that they are evicted from their homes, resulting in homelessness. Homelessness is most concentrated in big cities, with families with children as the fastest-growing segment of the nation's homeless people (Koch 2006).

- **The bursting of the housing bubble.** The decade prior to 2007 was characterized by a housing frenzy—a housing boom with a surge in home/condominium buying, escalating housing values, and "flipping" (buying a home to be sold quickly for a profit). In the process, people took on mortgages that were too large, making them vulnerable to a downturn in housing values (Timmer and Eitzen forthcoming). People on the economic margins wanted in on the action and because of their questionable credit were given subprime loans, which on the surface offered no-money down loans with what appeared to be low interest rates. These "low" rates were low for a brief time, after which the "adjustable rate clause" (found in the fine print of the loan contract) was enforced. The resulting mortgage payments were beyond the reach for many.

  Add to this mix the reckless and irresponsible deal making on Wall Street involving an intricate, intertwined system of loan brokers, mortgage lenders, hedge funds, and other predators. Typically, subprime loans were bundled and sold to third parties. This allowed banks and insurance firms to leverage their assets by as much as 40 times the value of the underlying asset. In the case of subprime mortgages, this was "financial alchemy that turned low-quality mortgages into trillions of dollars of high-priced derivatives" (Karabell 2009:35).

  These forces converged in late 2007, creating a "perfect storm" of economic devastation. It began when subprime borrowers began defaulting on their mortgages, sending housing prices tumbling (Gandel and Lim 2008). Banks and brokerages that had borrowed money to increase their leverage failed or were sold for bargain rates. Credit dried up. Business slowed, causing companies to lay off workers by the tens of thousands. The newly unemployed had difficulty meeting their mortgage payments, causing the rate of foreclosures and bankruptcies to soar. By 2009 some 1.5 million homes owned through subprime loans were lost through foreclosures. Many home owners found that they owed more on their mortgages than what their homes were worth. In 2009 alone, there were 3.5 million foreclosure-related filings, up from 2.3 million in 2008.

Decaying Infrastructure

The fiscal crisis of the cities has also affected them physically. The urban infrastructure is crumbling. Old water mains regularly erupt in the winter. Streets are marred with potholes. Clogged and overburdened expressways deteriorate. Sewer systems are decaying and overstressed. Public transit stations, subway tunnels, and rail and trolley tracks all make mass transportation less efficient as years go by without needed maintenance. The U.S. Department of Transportation has rated 40 percent of all U.S. bridges, many in the oldest cities, as structurally deficient or functionally obsolete.

Spending on infrastructure is only about 2.5 percent of the federal budget. Governments in countries such as Germany, Japan, and the Netherlands invest public dollars in the urban infrastructure at a rate three to four times that of the United States. As a result of the U.S. government's failure to spend adequately on the infrastructure of the nation's cities, people are increasing endangered because of inadequate waste treatment, tainted water, leaking gas lines, structurally unsound bridges, and the like.

Many economists now believe that investing public dollars in a job creation program to rebuild the nation's infrastructure and a much needed and expanded mass transit system are the best way to spur economic growth and productivity.

Transportation, Pollution, and the Environment

The urban transportation system in the United States, again in contrast to most European cities, is dominated by the private automobile. Since 1970, the number of vehicles has increased more than twice as fast as population growth. Meanwhile, the road capacity has increased only by 6 percent (Seabrook 2002:121). The consequences of this attachment to the automobile are enormous:

- Traffic jams are getting much worse. The annual amount of time the average commuter spent in traffic delays was 47 hours in 2003 (Copeland 2005).
- Cars contribute 25 percent of global-warming emissions (Kay 2004). The United States produces twice as much carbon dioxide per capita as Germany, Japan, and Great Britain; eight times as much as China; and twenty-three times as much as India (Lazare 2001:264).
- The development of the auto-dependent urban transportation system contributes to the suburbanization and deconcentration of metropolitan areas. Highways, interstates, expressways, and cars helped to gut the central cities, taking away middle-class taxpayers, jobs, business, and retail and commercial activity.

Between 1945 and 1970, cities, states, and the federal government spent \$156 billion constructing hundreds of thousands of miles of roads, but only 16 miles of subway were built in the entire country during the same time period (Liazos 1982). This subsidization of the automobile by the government continues, as more than 80 percent of federal transportation funds go to highways. Similarly, the federal government has subsidized air travel, with the building and expansion of airports, air traffic control, and security. Meanwhile, Amtrak and energy-efficient, city-friendly public transit systems are left behind (Kay 2002).

The reliance on the private automobile at the expense of mass public transportation also further disadvantages the urban poor. Unable to afford owning and operating a car, they must rely on an underfunded and often undependable public transit system with limited service. Because most jobs are amid the malls, office parks, and construction in the suburbs, inner-city residents have difficulty finding the transportation to work there. "Instead of springing up where they are needed, jobs are being created where they are not" (Lazare 2001:x). Unlike the suburbs, compact and walkable cities are efficient.

> *It is estimated . . . that a nickel trolley fare in turn-of-the-century Chicago brought a typical worker within reach of an estimated forty-eight thousand jobs. A century or so later, that same worker would have to invest thousands of dollars in a car, drive through endless miles of suburban sprawl, consume hundreds of gallons of gasoline, and generate dangerous levels of pollution and carbon dioxide in order to gain access to a fraction of that number. (Lazare 2001:203)*

- **Other Environmental Threats in the Central City.** The air is not the only source of the environmental pollution concentrated in urban areas. Illegal dumping, lead paint poisoning, and abandoned hazardous waste sites also plague the central city. Research shows that communities that are low-income neighborhoods, especially those populated by people of color, bear a disproportionate burden of environmental hazards (Pellow 2000; Bullard 2000). For example, according to the Centers for Disease Control, 12 percent of U.S. children have been diagnosed with asthma at some point in their lives, but the rate is 34 percent for Puerto Rican children and 25 percent for African American children. This asthma epidemic is connected to air pollution from diesel engines and power plants, both of which tend to be concentrated in lower-income urban neighborhoods (Kehrl 2004).

  Evidence of **environmental racism** abounds in U.S. metropolitan areas. For example, the Center for Policy Alternatives analyzed toxic release information by ZIP code and found that people of color were 47 percent more likely than Whites to live near toxic waste sites (reported in Dervarics 2000).

  As poor minority communities are illegally dumped on and find themselves on top of more and more toxic and hazardous wastes, waste management corporations scramble to locate their incinerators and disposal facilities in these neighborhoods. This often places these impoverished communities in the position of choosing between at least some kind of economic development and their collective health.

Health and Health Care

Health and health care problems in U.S. society are discussed at length in Chapter 17. But here, these problems in urban locations deserve special attention because some health and health care problems are more concentrated in large cities.

Because poverty is concentrated in the central city, so are the diseases associated with it. Poor people in the city get tuberculosis and other diseases almost unheard of among the suburban middle class. Poor city dwellers are much more likely to die of cancer. Chronic conditions such as diabetes often go untreated. Many of the urban poor, without health insurance of any kind, cannot afford to burden their families with the huge debt that lifesaving technologies would bring.

Infant mortality rates are highest in poor minority neighborhoods in the inner city and are as high as or higher than in many developing world countries. African American infants are four times more likely to die from low birth weight than White infants. Many poor inner-city children who survive their first year are then threatened by such diseases as measles, tetanus, polio, tuberculosis, diphtheria, and whooping cough because they have not received adequate inoculations.

Another health problem adding to the burden of public hospitals is AIDS. The Centers for Disease Control and Prevention (CDC) confirms that the incidence of AIDS and the costs of caring for people with AIDS are highest and most concentrated in central cities, where gay men and intravenous drug users are overrepresented.

Many poor and working-class central-city residents have seen their small neighborhood or community hospitals close under the pressure of rising costs. For many of these hospitals, the number of indigent nonpaying patients became too high a proportion of their total number. Some city hospitals have begun to turn away patients who are uninsured and/or cannot pay the prevailing charge for medical treatment they require (Cousineau 2006). More than one in ten U.S. hospitals are now routinely refusing to treat these people.

This means that more and more central-city residents are unable to find any medical care in private for-profit or private not-for-profit hospitals and clinics. Increasingly, they have only one alternative—the large, underfunded, understaffed, underequipped public hospital that cannot legally deny them care. The problem is threefold (Orenstein 2001). First, the number of patient visits is rising. Second, the number of emergency departments is declining, increasing the load for those remaining emergency rooms, as the average annual patient volume is rising. Third, and related to the second, the number of hospital beds is declining while the nation's population is rising. One obvious reason for the decline in hospital beds is the closing of public hospitals in cities, which leaves the poor in increasing jeopardy.

Thus, facilities are being overwhelmed by the number of patients and the cost of treating them. Because they are unable to afford doctor visits or are unable to find doctors who will accept the lower fees of Medicaid (the state and federal government's insurance program for the poor), patients are coming to the emergency room sicker and in need of more costly care. But the urban public hospitals are less and less able to provide adequate care. As a result, urban public hospitals are forced to practice **triage**—treating the most urgent emergencies first. Other patients must wait for treatment, sometimes for days.

Many private hospitals that have remained open have done so by cutting high-cost services for the indigent. Many have closed emergency rooms and trauma units. High-risk obstetrical care, as well as drug and alcohol abuse treatment programs, also have been shut down. As private hospitals in the city abdicate these high-cost services, more of them must be taken over by public hospitals, increasing their burden with more patients and higher costs.

In short, the increasing number of uninsured and underinsured people seeking health care in the emergency rooms of public hospitals, the lack of federal government support for these hospitals, and the inability of city governments caught in a budgetary crisis to fund them, all ensure that without major reforms, urban health and health care can only deteriorate further.

Urban Schools

Public schools in the United States are separate and unequal. The more affluent middle class has moved to the suburbs, where their children attend virtually all-White schools; or if they have remained in the city and can afford it, they send their children to private schools. The less affluent and racial minorities are left in the city's public schools.

Urban schools are class segregated. With poverty becoming more geographically concentrated, poor children typically go to school with other poor children. Most significant, the amount of money spent on the education of the children attending city schools pales in comparison to what is spent on each student in the more affluent suburbs. This imbalance results from the heavy reliance on local property taxes to finance public schooling in the United States.

As suburbanization robs the city's tax base, the city becomes less able to adequately fund public education. Consequently, suburban schools, when compared to inner-city schools, are more likely to have smaller class sizes, more computers, a better library, special programs for the gifted and the disabled, and state-of-the-art equipment and facilities. Chapter 16 provides the details and the consequences of these severe inequities. As a preview, we note that the results of all of this inequity are predictable: lower standardized test scores and high dropout rates in many urban school districts. Already disadvantaged inner-city students are further disadvantaged.

Crime, Drugs, and Gangs

The problems of crime and drugs in the United States are discussed in Chapters 12 and 13. These problems also have a special relation to urban areas. In the United States, crime has become a euphemism for cities. More specifically, there is a media and popular identification of crime, and the drugs and gangs assumed to be related to it, with the inner city. And because crime is also a code word for race, it comes to be associated in both media and popular accounts primarily with young African American males in the inner city.

Admittedly, the FBI's *Uniform Crime Report* and the U.S. Justice Department's *National Crime Survey* have shown for some time that poor minority males in the inner city have the highest arrest rates for serious felony offenses and are, along with other members of poor minority inner-city communities, the most likely to be victims of street crimes.

As we have seen, the cities have been gutted by job loss, disinvestment by corporations and banks, and a declining tax base that negatively affects schools and hospitals. Cities have increasing concentrations of poverty, rising unemployment and low-wage employment, and a dwindling supply of decent and affordable housing. All these conditions are related to street crime (F. Hagan 1994). And because the inner cities, mostly populated by racial and ethnic minorities, are especially vulnerable to these conditions, street crime is concentrated there, especially among inner-city youth and young adults.

In late 2009 the jobless rate for 16- to 24-year-old Black men was 34.5 percent, more than three times the rate for the entire population. Moreover, research finds evidence of discrimination (summarized in Haynes 2009):

- Lower-income White teens are more likely to find work than upper-income Black teens.
- Black men are less likely to receive a call back or job offer than equally qualified White men.
- Black men with a clean record fare no better than White men just released from prison in finding a job.

These young people are "disconnected youth" with nothing constructive to do. Many turn to hustling, "doing what they can—much of it illegal—to get along" (Herbert 2003b:2). They engage in an alternate or informal economy (alternative economic activities) to ensure their survival. An important part of this **informal economy** is criminal, much of it involving drugs. In effect, street crime becomes their work (Hagedorn 1998). Participation in drug rings can spell money, status, and survival. That the socioeconomic conditions in the inner city make it an ideal location for the illegal drug economy has not been lost on the people who control international drug trafficking. The gangs that provide members with meaningful social relationships and status in the barren, isolated inner city and with protection from other sources of violence in their communities can also ensure survival with specialized stolen property, drug, and weapons sales (Hagedorn 1998).

Official U.S. drug policy has deleterious effects on inner-city communities as well. By criminalizing them, the official strategy is to eliminate drugs and their negative consequences by arresting, prosecuting, convicting, and imprisoning drug users, buyers, and sellers. This "war on drugs" actually escalates drug selling, use, and addiction and magnifies the negative consequences that go with them (see Chapter 13). Criminalization increases drug prices and profits, thus making the drug trade more attractive. Sellers thus work to recruit more users and addicts. Because their drugs are illegal and expensive, users and addicts may have to steal or sell drugs themselves to afford their own habits.

Besides failing as a drug-control strategy, the war on drugs is not being waged fairly. Although the official claim is one of zero tolerance, pursuing all users, buyers, and sellers no matter who or where they are, the war is racist and focused on young African American males in poor inner-city neighborhoods (see Chapter 12). One in three Black males is now under the supervision of the criminal justice system—on probation or parole, in jail or prison, or under pretrial release (a rate eight times higher than for White men). In many cities, and in many inner-city neighborhoods, this proportion is much higher. This only serves to marginalize further the already highly marginal poor Black inner-city residents, with ripple effects throughout Black families, schools, and communities.

- **Fear of Crime in the City.** Fear of crime is often exaggerated in comparison to the reality of, or actual potential for, criminal victimization. Often the fear is not of crime at all. What people identify as a fear of crime is often a fear of people of cultural and racial groups different than their own. Nonetheless, such misdirected fear of crime is often a significant factor in central-city decline. If people, corporations, retailers, and small businesses will not stay in or move to the city because they believe it is not safe, then the process of urban decline cannot be turned around. A self-fulfilling prophecy of central-city decline sets in. Because of the belief that the city is crime-ridden and unsafe, people, businesses, and jobs leave the city, thereby helping make it more crime prone and unsafe and further removing the possibility that the businesses and jobs that could begin to change the socioeconomic conditions that produce crime will go there in the future.

SUBURBAN PROBLEMS

For over 50 years, there has been a dramatic population shift in the United States—people moving from cities to the suburbs. Although this shift had begun in some metropolitan areas at the turn of the century or even earlier, it accelerated and became the dominant demographic trend in almost every major U.S. metropolitan area after 1950. As a result of this exodus, more Americans now live in the suburbs than in cities, rural areas, and small towns combined.

Although some middle-class Blacks have moved to the suburbs, those who move to the suburbs are predominantly upper-middle-class, middle-class, and, to a lesser extent, working-class Whites. This process of **White flight** has increased and continues to increase both class and race segregation. As suburbs grow and become essentially middle class and White, shrinking central cities are left with a greater proportion of their remaining population who are poor and minority, a trend heightened by the huge number of immigrants, mostly Latino and Asian, moving to U.S. cities. The suburbanization of the United States has meant the geographic separation of classes and races, particularly of middle-class Whites from poor African Americans. Today, very high levels of racial segregation persist in most major U.S. metropolitan areas. Even when Blacks leave the city, they are often resegregated in Black suburbs or in Black neighborhoods in White suburbs.

Middle-class Whites move to the suburbs for a better place to raise their children, better schools, and less crime, or as Eric Klinenberg has put it, moving to the suburbs was and is motivated often by the "search for sanctuary, security and class segregation" (Klinenberg 2004:40). Race plays a part in these motives. "A better place to raise children" often meant a neighborhood with few or no African Americans or Latinos. "Better schools" often meant virtually all-White schools not under court order to desegregate. And "crime" was synonymous with inner-city Blacks for many suburbanites. Those people moving to the suburbs were also attracted to the open space and the prospect of an unattached, single-family dwelling with a yard. This prospect was made more attainable by generally lower real estate costs and lower property tax rates outside the city.

Suburban Sprawl

Suburbanization is not a naturally occurring phenomenon. The suburbs were encouraged, supported, and directly subsidized by the federal government, and they profited large developers and corporations. The history of suburbanization in the United States, as Kenneth Jackson (1985), Peter Dreier (2000), and Daniel Lazare (2001) make clear, shows that federal government policies and spending shaped consumer choices that pushed people out of the cities and pulled them into the suburbs. The federal government financed the construction of the interstate highway and expressway system, which opened the suburbs to speculation and development and connected them to the city, where many suburbanites still worked. Housing policies implemented by the FHA (Federal Housing Authority) and VA (Veterans Administration), offering low-cost government-insured mortgages—reserved, for the most part, for Whites and the suburbs—facilitated the population shift. The government subsidizes home ownership by permitting taxes and mortgage interest to be tax deductible (a savings to homeowners of about $80.1 billion in 2009). Homeowners can also deduct local property taxes and receive a lower tax rate on profits from home sales (capital gains) than on regular income. When all the tax breaks for homeowners are totaled, the amount saved in 2008 was $145 billion (Timmer and Eitzen forthcoming). Housing policies that allow local suburban governments to refuse public and subsidized housing in their communities have also encouraged the White middle class to reside where there is less affordable housing and few poor and minority residents. Cheap fossil fuels and low fuel taxes (such taxes are five to ten times higher in Europe than in the United States) have supported both suburbanization and the extreme dependency of American metropolitan areas on automobiles (discussed later). Also, policies set by Congress earmark these taxes to be spent on road building rather than mass transit. And, local governments have set more favorable property tax rates to lure people, businesses, and jobs to the suburbs. Suburban municipalities added to their growth by providing commercial property tax waivers and other inducements to entice business to move there.

More than one-fourth of all cities with a population of between 100,000 and 400,000 are suburbs. The rapid growth of the suburbs has led to a new city form called "boomburgs." A **boomburg** is defined as a suburban city that has at least 100,000 people and has experienced double-digit growth every decade since it became defined by the Census Bureau as urban (2,500 or more). The 2000 Census found that there are fifty-three boomburgs, eighteen of which are in the Los Angeles area. Four boomburgs exceed 300,000, a population size bigger than Miami or St. Louis.

> *These cities, built in the late 20th century, feature all the elements of sprawl: office parks, "big-box" retailers such as Home Depot, strip developments and subdivisions of large, single-family homes. They have now coalesced into suburban super cities that have all the functions of a traditional city but are built for a drive-through society.* (El Nasser 2001)

The kind of dispersal and sprawl of population, retail business, and jobs that suburbanization brings continues unabated. The population of the Los Angeles metropolitan area increased more than fourfold during the past 50 years, but its geographic size increased twenty times. Metropolitan Chicago's population increased only 4 percent over the past two decades, but its geographic area grew by 46 percent. But now the spreading out and deconcentration of metropolitan areas over more land are becoming more extreme. The city of Phoenix, for example, covers 517 square miles. Surrounding it is 14,000 square miles (twice the size of New Jersey) of desert with scattered suburban developments (El Nasser 2008a, 2008b).

The deconcentration of U.S. metropolitan areas is proceeding beyond the suburbs to what are being called "urban villages" or "edge cities" even more remote from the central cities, sometimes as far as 40 miles from the central business district.

The addition of new highways and beltways around and through metropolitan areas typically opens up new land for development of tract homes and strip malls at a rate about twice that of population growth. Such **urban sprawl** (low-density, automobile-dependent development) absorbs nearly 3,000 acres of farmland every day. It also results in slow commutes, traffic congestion, polluted air, overcrowded schools, automobile dependency, and visual blight (a similar look, whether on the outskirts of Phoenix, Omaha, or Detroit, composed of fast-food franchises, Wal-Marts, drive-through banks, tract housing architecture, and the like), which one observer has called a new kind of "postindustrial ugliness that has overspread the landscape" (Lazare 2001:276–277).

Following are some facts associated with sprawl:

- Farmland around Denver is falling to sprawl at a rate of 90,000 acres a year.
- About 3.3 million Americans commute more than 50 miles each way to work.
- The greater Los Angeles metropolitan area continues to spread, especially 60 to 70 miles east toward the desert.
- Grass (most of it in suburban lawns) is the largest irrigated crop in the United States (Weiss 2005).
- There are more cars than people in Seattle, Washington, with the number of automobile trips each day per household twice the number in 1990.

The effects of suburbanization and sprawl are enormous. First, there are environmental effects such as the disruption of wildlife habitats, the altering of rivers and streams, and pollution.

A second consequence of suburbanization is "the draining of the center while flooding the edges" (Katz and Bradley 1999:30). As mentioned earlier, as the more affluent leave cities for the suburbs, they take their spending and their taxes with them, leaving businesses less profitable and city governments strapped for the funds to provide adequate services. This stress on the city is exacerbated by concentrating poverty in the cities—the homeless, new immigrants, the working poor, the elderly, and people with disabilities. This is further compounded by the movement of jobs from the cities to the suburbs.

Third, the economic costs of all this suburbanization, deconcentration, and sprawl are extremely high. Each time metropolitan areas spread out, new highways, streets, bridges, sewers, police and fire stations, and schools must be built. Much of this cost is covered by government with the public's tax dollars. Meanwhile, taxpayers in the cities and older suburbs watch their infrastructures, public transit, and schools deteriorate, even though it is almost always less costly to repair and maintain old infrastructure than to build new. See the "Social Policy" panel.

Finally, there are some health concerns. People who live in sprawling suburbs are much more likely to drive to school, to work, or to the store than are people living in densely populated cities and neighborhoods. As a result of less exercise, suburbanites have higher blood pressure and weigh an average of six pounds more than their counterparts in more walkable locales. "In Europe, people make 33 percent of their trips by foot or bicycle, compared with 9.4 percent of Americans' trips . . . the life expectancy in the Netherlands and in Germany is about two years longer than in the United States, and . . . obesity rates were lower" (*New York Times* 2003b:15). Research also shows that people making long commutes are at a higher risk for high blood pressure, sleep deprivation, and depression (Longman 2001). They have more frequent disputes with their coworkers and families. They suffer more frequent and more serious illnesses, and they are more likely to experience premature deaths (Frank 2001).

Automobile Dependency

As auto dependency causes sprawls and decentralizes urban areas, a vicious cycle of more cars and highways sets in. More automobiles traveling greater distances to the suburbs increases traffic congestion. This, in turn, leads to the construction of more and bigger highways, which encourages even more cars, further decentralizing metropolitan areas.

The decentralization that comes with auto transportation has destroyed the landscape and encouraged the spread of commercial strips, shopping malls, and multilane roads and streets. The shopping areas are spread out so that suburban residents cannot walk to a store, as is possible in high-density cities. Instead they must use an automobile.

Urban sprawl, with its reliance on the automobile, has also led to environmental pollution and a waste of natural resources. Writing more than 10 years ago, Jane Holtz Kay said,

> *"One one-thousand," environmentalist David Burwell counted, clocking an instant in the polluting life of the automobile. In that single second America's cars and trucks traveled another 60,000 miles, used up 3,000 gallons of petroleum products, and added 60,000 pounds of carbon dioxide to the atmosphere. . . . Our fossil fuel vehicles . . . not only consume more than one-third of all U.S. energy but [they also exhale] two-thirds of its carbon dioxide emissions, one-quarter of its chlorofluorocarbons (CFCs), more*

SOCIAL POLICY

RIGHTING THE URBAN–SUBURBAN IMBALANCE

Typically, there are huge disparities between cities and their suburbs. Businesses (and their property taxes) have left cities for the suburbs. People, usually relatively prosperous, have moved their residences (and their property taxes) from the city to the suburbs. Shopping areas have been built in the suburbs, taking customers and their sales taxes from the cities and causing many central-city businesses to close, with the subsequent loss of jobs.

Thus, with a few exceptions, the central cities of the United States have struggled financially, resulting in a decaying infrastructure, a decline in services, and inadequately financed schools. City residents, especially racial/ethnic minorities, have declining job opportunities and deal face-to-face with crime and drugs. But as the central cities decline, the suburbs prosper. The suburbs have incorporated into separate municipalities and school districts. The enlarged tax bases have provided for state-of-the-art schools, fire and police protection, parks, and other amenities. The result is a decaying central city, ringed by a series of growing, prosperous governmental entities separate from the city. In effect, the cities "remain woebegone, in part because so much of their potential taxable wealth lies in the suburbs, beyond their reach" (Traub 2003:17).

Do the suburbs and their residents owe anything to the central cities and, if so, should there be any redress for the inequities? Many suburbanites work in the central cities, thus depending on the city for adequate streets, subway systems, police protection, sanitation, and the like, but at no cost to them in taxes. Moreover, suburbanites are free riders when they use the amenities of the cities such as parks, zoos, symphony orchestras, museums, professional sports teams, and urban universities. One solution is a commuter tax of, say, 3 percent of income generated in the city. The mayor of New York City, for example, could say "to all those doctors and bankers in Westchester, 'we've given you a beautifully refurbished Grand Central Terminal, and we've given you Broadway and Central Park and subways without graffiti, and we're paying to protect you from terrorists; give us a mite out of your adjusted gross, for God's sake'" (Traub 2003:18). This idea seems fair enough, but it is almost universally rejected (an exception is Kansas City, Missouri, which taxes workers who commute from Kansas suburbs to work there).

Better yet would be the political integration of cities with their suburbs. Such integration is the only fair way for central cities to have their share of the wealth in metropolitan areas. Moreover, regional governments could better manage regional problems such as pollution control, safe water, police and fire protection, equality of educational opportunity, and efficient public transportation. Will these changes happen? Will the advantaged give up some of their advantages to achieve fairness, or will they continue to abuse this unequal but symbiotic relationship?

than 50 percent of its methane, and 40 percent of its nitrogen oxides, plus most of the carbon monoxide. (Kay 1997:80–81).

Social Isolation in the Suburbs

Moving to the suburbs is a move away from diversity and toward homogenization (Eitzen 2004). The suburbs are disproportionately White and relatively affluent. Suburbanites leave immigrants, racial minorities, poor people, and the homeless for life near people like themselves. More than 6 million households are situated in gated communities where the residents are walled off physically and socially from "others."

The physical arrangements of suburbs are especially socially isolating. Rather than walking to the corner grocery or nearby shop and visiting with the clerks and their neighbors, suburbanites drive somewhere away from their immediate neighborhood to shop among strangers. Or they may not leave their home at all, working, shopping, banking, and paying bills by computer. For suburban teenagers and children, almost everything is away—friends, practice fields, music lessons, jobs, schools, and the malls, resulting in a disconnect from those nearby. Suburban neighborhoods in particular are devoid of meeting places. In effect, the suburbs often suffer from a lack of community—and connection.

Transforming the Suburbs: The End of Sprawl?

The collapse of the housing market and relatively high gasoline prices have resulted in some changes in the suburbs. More and more people are reconsidering the wisdom of living so far from work.

> *Soaring energy costs and the foreclosure epidemic have jolted many Americans into realizing that their lifestyles are at risk. For many, ever-lengthening commutes in the search for affordable homes no longer makes financial sense. (El Nasser 2008a:1A)*

With housing values plummeting in the suburbs while neighborhoods close to downtown have held the value, there is a move back closer to the urban core. Homes close to urban centers or that have convenient access to mass transit are especially desirable (Penalver 2008).

Builders/developers of new suburban areas are changing their philosophy. Instead of isolated bedroom communities, with no core, they are building whole communities. Instead of strip malls and big box stores (Home Depot, Sam's Club) that people drive to, there will be community centers with shops, schools, and services nearby. These neighborhoods promote walking. Instead of building single-family homes exclusively, builders are providing a mix of residential styles.

These trends reflect "the priorities of the times: saving energy, reducing traffic congestion, saving land, and promoting walking and mass transit" (El Nasser 2008b:3A).

RURAL PROBLEMS

By **rural**, we refer to the nonmetropolitan population that resides in small towns and the open countryside. The nonmetropolitan population in 2008 was 50.1 million (out of a total U.S. population approaching 304 million).

Some 1,346 (43 percent of all counties) counties lost population from 2000 to 2007, nearly twice the number of counties that lost population during the 1990s (Mather 2008). The largest population losers were counties in the Great Plains and Appalachia. Nearly 500 rural counties lost population from both outmigration (people leaving) and deaths outnumbering births. Counties growing in population did so because of in-migration: 60 percent from international migrants (mostly Latino) and 40 percent from people moving to rural and small-town places from metropolitan areas (U.S. Department of Agriculture 2006a).

This section examines a variety of social problems faced by rural communities. But first, let's demythologize rural communities. To begin, contrary to common stereotypes, rural areas are not always alike. Typically, the image of rural areas is of family farms in farming communities in the Midwest.

> *In fact, rural areas embrace ski slopes, mines, farms, retirement communities, Native American reservations, bedroom communities next to large cities, and much, much*

more. Today, rural communities probably differ more among themselves than they do, on average, from urban areas. (Flora et al. 1992:4)

Second, rural communities have changed dramatically in the last 50 years or so. In the past, rural areas were relatively homogeneous and self-sufficient, with a strong sense of common identity.

There was a time when rural people turned to their communities for nearly everything. People lived, worked, worshiped, shopped, banked, sent their children to school, and socialized all in the same place. When the community's economy rested on a single resource, such as mining, people even had a shared sense of what it took to make a living. (Flora et al. 1992:14)

But times have changed and, with them, so too the essence of rural life. Automobiles have made it possible to live in one town, work in another, and shop in a third. Schools have consolidated, with children from a wider area and even more than one town attending, lessening the attachment to one's community. Work, once centered on a single activity such as farming, ranching, mining, or lumbering, has broadened to, for example, making furniture, producing mobile homes, factory farming (replacing family farming), and massive food processing. Thus, work roles, once similar throughout the community, have become very different. Many of these communities, once comprising people similar in ethnicity, religion, and culture, have faced the influx of new neighbors, many of whom were recent immigrants with different customs and religious beliefs. The effect of these changes has been to lessen the bonds and common identity among rural residents in most contemporary rural communities.

Third, poverty is a greater problem in rural America than in the cities.

The human faces of poverty for many Americans are the inner-city homeless who sleep on grates, beg on corners and line up, mornings and afternoons, at local parks for a cup of soup and a sandwich. But of the 50 counties with the highest child-poverty rates, 48 are in rural America. Compared with urban areas, unemployment is typically higher, education poorer and services severely limited because people are so spread out. (Pierre 2004:30)

Poverty

The poverty rate is highest in central cities, followed in order by rural and suburban (see Table 6.1). There are important differences between the rural and urban poor. The rural poor have some advantages over the urban poor (low-cost housing, raising their own food) and many disadvantages (low-paid work, higher prices for most products, lack of public transportation, fewer social services, and fewer welfare benefits).

TABLE 6.1
Poverty Rates by Place 2008

	Poverty Rate
Central Cities	17.7%
Suburbs	9.8%
Nonmetropolitan areas	15.1%

Source: De Kavan-Walt, Carmea, Bernadette D. Proctor, and Jessica C. Smith, 2009. "Income, Poverty, and Health Insurance Coverage in the United States: 2008. *Current Population Reports*, P60–236 (September), p. 14.

Poverty rates in rural America are higher for racial and ethnic groups than for Whites, reflecting a historical legacy that has left rural areas with concentrated minority populations in certain areas. The highest concentration of U.S. poverty exists in four nonmetropolitan pockets: the Appalachian mountain region, where the poor are predominantly White; the old Southern cotton belt from the Carolinas to the Louisiana Delta, where the poor are mostly African American; the Rio Grande Valley/Texas Gulf Coast, where the poor are largely Latino; and the Southwest and upper Plains states, where Native Americans are concentrated in and around reservations. Indicating these patterns, thirteen states in 2007 had child poverty rates above 20 percent, and four (Mississippi, Louisiana, Arkansas, and New Mexico) were above 25 percent. Eighteen states had 10 percent or more of their children living in extreme poverty (household income below half the official poverty rate (Children's Defense Fund 2008). (See "A Closer Look" panel for a description of the poorest place in the United States.)

Rural minorities are especially vulnerable to poverty. To a large extent, poverty among rural minorities is rooted in societal-level forces that work against those of lower-class origins and non-Whites. For example, drawing on intensive ethnographic research, Cynthia Duncan (1999) finds that the dire circumstances of Blacks in the Mississippi Delta can be traced to a rigid class system—itself an echo of slave plantation economy—that denies employment and other opportunities to rural Blacks in the region (Jensen, McLaughlin, and Slack 2003:124).

The extent of poverty in a region is directly related to structural factors. "Structural explanations for poverty stress the importance of local opportunities rather than individual characteristics [see Chapter 7] as central to understanding poverty. . . . Poverty is clearly associated with the quality and quantity of jobs available" (Jensen et al. 2003:125).

Jobs in Rural Areas

Historically, the work of rural people has centered on the resources of the land, whether through farming, mining, or forestry. These industries experience boom and bust cycles as the costs go up and down, depending on foreign competition, decline in prices because of too much production and discoveries of new deposits, or high prices because of scarcity. New technologies reduce the number of workers required for production. Employment in these activities peaked in the early 1900s. Since then, farm employment has dropped by 70 percent and employment in the other resource industries by half (McGranahan 2003).

Income in rural areas is lower than in metropolitan areas. In 2007, for example, the per capita income in rural America was $28,781, compared to the per capita income in urban areas of $40,570 (U.S. Department of Agriculture 2009).

- **Farming.** Around 1800, 95 percent of Americans made their full-time living from agriculture. A hundred years ago it was 45 percent, and by the turn of the twenty-first century, it was less than 2 percent. The United States still has agriculture, but it is mostly large-scale agribusiness, as 1 percent of farmers account for more than half of all farm income. The demise of the family farm is the result of market forces. Competition from global markets required producing more per acre. The demands of national retail chains such as Wal-Mart and McDonald's (Schlosser 2001) require standardization and huge outputs. This is accomplished with the latest and very expensive machinery, the cost of which is justified by farming huge areas, squeezing out the smaller farmers. Large-scale,

A CLOSER LOOK

THE POOREST COMMUNITY IN THE UNITED STATES

There are about 1,450 **colonias** (shantytown settlements of Latino immigrants), home to an estimated 500,000, located along the Texas–Mexico border in South Texas (Hockstader 2002; Brezosky 2002; Texas Health and Human Services Commission 2003; South Texas Colonia Initiative 2010). As described by the Attorney General of Texas, Greg Abbott: "Colonias are substandard housing developments, often found along the Texas–Mexico border, where residents lack basic services such as drinking water, sewage treatment, and paved roads" (Abbott 2009, para 1). Moreover, "these areas have become a geographic, social and economic state of isolation for thousands of families. Theirs is a daily reminder of the debilitating effects of poverty, lack of education, social isolation and critical need for essential health and human services" (Texas Health and Human Services Commission 2003).

Among places with 1,000 households or more, a colonia called Cameron Park is the poorest spot in the United States. Cameron Park, an unincorporated community of 6,000, is near Brownsville, Texas. It has the lowest per capita income of any location in the United States, $4,103 a year, and only about 20 percent of its residents are high school graduates. Like other colonias, its housing is composed of shacks, trailers, campers, and run-down houses. Along with the decrepit housing, there are inadequate sewers, filthy conditions (roaches, rats, stagnant water), and terrible roads.

> According to local officials and scholars, colonias were condemned to poverty at birth. Starting in the 1950s, developers snapped up low-lying, agriculturally worthless land along the border. They divided it into plots and sold it to the growing population of migrant workers allowed into the United States during and after World War II. . . . Lots were sold without access to water, sewers or electricity. Immigrant purchasers could buy land cheaply, but they did not receive title until it had been paid off. If they missed a payment, the developer could repossess the land, evict the buyer and sell it anew. For years the colonias grew, unfettered by state laws or local ordinances. They were filthy, frequently flooded and forgotten. Some were on the edge of cities, but the cities wanted no part of them, seeing them as a potential financial drain. . . . That left Texas colonias in the hands of county governments, which, lacking the power to enact ordinances, were outgunned by Texas developers and real estate agents. (Hockstader 2002:29)

The economy has made the situation worse for the inhabitants of Cameron Park and the other colonias. The drought has meant fewer agricultural jobs. The textile industry that employed many (at relatively low wages) disintegrated as Levi's, Haggar, and Horace Small factories closed. Meanwhile the North American Free Trade Agreement (NAFTA) triggered a population boom, outpacing the supply of affordable housing.

Recently, there have been governmental efforts to fix substandard living conditions. The Texas Legislature has passed laws intended to remedy the conditions in existing colonias and to prevent new colonias (Abbott 2009). Moreover the legislature has authorized up to $175 million in state bonds to build or improve roads and drainage. And the U.S. Department of Housing and Urban Development now offers low-cost financing to build homes. Moreover, developers must provide basic infrastructure (water, sewer, roads, and drainage). Despite the laudable attempts, colonias still remain wretched places.

homogenized production is profitable. In addition to harvesting crops (corn, soybeans, wheat, potatoes, vegetables, fruit), factory farms produce pigs, cattle, turkeys, chickens, and even catfish. Work is mechanized as much as possible, reducing the number of workers required.

> *Since the end of World War II, farmers in the United States have been persuaded to adopt one new technology after another, hoping to improve their yields, reduce their costs, and*

> *outsell their neighbors. By embracing this industrial model of agriculture—one that focuses narrowly on the level of inputs and outputs, that encourages specialization in just one crop, that relies heavily on chemical fertilizers, pesticides, fungicides, herbicides, advanced harvesting and irrigation equipment—American farmers have become the most productive farmers on earth. Every increase in productivity, however, has driven more American farmers off the land. (Schlosser 2001:119–120)*

The implications of the demise of small-scale farms are several. The first and obvious consequence is that former farmers must find a new occupation, and the opportunities are few in rural America. Second, many, especially young people, are forced to leave the community for nonagricultural jobs (the average age of farmers was 57.1 in 2007, up from 54.0 in 1997; U.S. Department of Agriculture 2009). Third, with the loss of people and their resources, many local communities decline in importance and function. This decline is exacerbated when the factory farms in a region are owned by outside corporations because the profits leave the area. Fourth, rural communities have become increasingly stratified with a few large-scale farmers at the top, small farmers barely getting by, and farm workers at the bottom making very meager wages without benefits.

- **Manufacturing.** Contrary to the common assumption, manufacturing employs nearly twice as many nonmetropolitan workers as does farming (U.S. Department of Agriculture 2006b). Some rural areas have industries tied to their agricultural base, such as textile mills and apparel manufacturing near the cotton growing in the South. But these industries have faded dramatically because of global competition. So mills have closed and manufacturers such as Levi's have moved their operations outside the United States to countries where labor and supplies are cheaper.

Other industries have been attracted to rural areas, where land is relatively cheap and because of the supply of nonunionized labor willing to work for wages lower than in urban/suburban areas. So, for example, production of agricultural machinery, recreational vehicles, and parts supplies for the automotive industry has moved into rural areas. The problem is that these industries may leave at any moment. These

> *communities [are] characterized by relative isolation, specialization in one or two industries with relatively well-paying, low-skill jobs for men, and outside ownership [making them] extremely vulnerable to economic misfortune and decline. If the main industry becomes unprofitable in that location, capital moves on, leaving the community with few alternatives, as most investment has gone to support the given industry and profits have gone to outside owners. (McGranahan 2003:144)*

A particular industrial form—meatpacking—has transformed some rural areas. Corporations such as Tyson, ConAgra, and Cargill have built slaughterhouses in remote towns across the rural Great Plains. In southwestern Kansas, for example, meatpacking operations in places such as Garden City, Dodge City, and Liberal have made these towns rural boomtowns and Kansas the biggest beef-packing state in the United States. The slaughterhouses in these three areas have a daily slaughter capacity of 20,000 cattle, producing 20 percent of the beef consumed in the United States (Frank 2004). The work in these plants is routinized, deskilled, and dangerous. The workers are primarily immigrants from Southeast Asia, Mexico, and Central America, thus transforming the racial/ethnic composition and cultural life of once homogeneous areas.

> *Confronted with some of the most advanced union-avoidance strategies ever conceived by the mind of business men, these people receive mediocre wages for doing what is statistically the most dangerous work in industrial America. Thanks to the rapid turnover at the slaughterhouses, few of them receive health or retirement benefits. The "social costs" of supporting them—education, health care, law enforcement—are "externalized," as the scholar types put it, pushed off onto the towns themselves, or onto church groups and welfare agencies, or onto the countries from which the workers come. . . . [These towns] despite their best efforts, [are] at the mercy of the meat industry's insatiable appetite for cheap labor and the social turmoil that follows from it. (Frank 2004:54)*

- **Recreation/Leisure.** Rural areas with natural amenities—mountains, lakes, pleasant climates—have encouraged development and jobs, while the conditions best suited for agriculture—flat terrain and humid summers—have been left out. In some of these areas, mining or timber industries once flourished, then experienced economic decline. But with the coming of tourism, winter and summer resorts, and the building of vacation homes, these areas have been reborn. Jobs have been created in the building trades and in service areas. The jobs in the service sector tend to be lower wage, sometimes part time, with little opportunity for advancement and few benefits. These jobs are highly volatile because of the seasonality of tourism and second-home residency. When amenity-based development occurs, there tends to be a significant change in the cost of living. "Property value inflation can lead to windfall profits for those who choose to sell or develop their land and other properties; however, such inflation can also contribute to residential displacement of persons who have limited or fixed incomes" (Krannich and Petrazelka 2003:193). Moreover, many low-paid workers cannot afford to live in the amenity-based communities and must commute from more affordable locations, sometimes at considerable distance. Similar to the situation in the slaughterhouse towns, the influx of newcomers and massive development into these once pristine areas often create a culture clash as traditional and newcomer values collide (Smith and Krannich 2000).

Environment

At least four environmental problems involve rural America. First, there is the continued reduction in the land devoted to farming and ranching. This lost land is covered subsequently with concrete, asphalt, and buildings. Covering the land, and consequently destroying its flora, intensifies global warming.

Second, there are several problems involving water. Most significant, massive irrigation takes water from the underground aquifers much faster than it can be replenished. For example, the Ogallala aquifer provides 30 percent of groundwater used for irrigation in the United States. This aquifer, which stretches 800 miles north to south and 400 miles east to west under the Great Plains, was first tapped in 1912. Its early use was from wells 50 feet deep or less with windmills as the primary mechanism for drawing the water. Now wells are sometimes 500 feet deep with pumps that allow a flow rate of 1,000 gallons a minute. Consequently, the Ogallala aquifer is now only one-third its original capacity. The common estimate of experts is that the Ogallala aquifer will be dry in 30 years (Cook 2002). The overuse of water from the Ogallala and other aquifers will result in the loss of land for farming and increased desertification of the land (Rothschild 2003).

Related to the draining of the aquifers by farmers is another problem with the water supply: entrepreneurs buying agricultural land not for farming or ranching but primarily for the water beneath it (Cook 2002; Hightower 2002b). For example, Cadiz, Inc., owns 20,000 acres in the Mojave Desert. It proposes to pump some 20 billion gallons of water to cities in Southern California. Similarly, land owned by T. Boone Pickens is above the Ogallala aquifer in the Texas Panhandle. He has been authorized by Texas to pump and sell up to 65 billion gallons of water a year, sending it by pipeline to San Antonio and Dallas. This privatization of water for profit—substituting private interest for public interest—will hasten the loss of water, this most precious of resources, for all of us.

A third environmental problem is a consequence of the use of pesticides, herbicides, and chemical fertilizers to maximize crop production. These chemicals are a serious health danger to workers in the fields.

> *In 1939 there were thirty-two pesticide products registered in the United States; there are now more than 20,000, and farmers use an estimated 1.2 billion pounds of pesticides annually. . . . As many as 300,000 farm workers are injured annually by pesticides, and of these as many as 1,000 die, according to an estimate from the Bureau of Labor Statistics. (cited in Clarren 2003:23)*

These chemicals drain from the fields into streams, rivers, and lakes, raising the levels of nitrates and other poisons to dangerous levels. So, too, with the chemicals that seep into private and municipal wells destined for human consumption.

Factory farms present serious air and water pollution. A single hog operation may involve as many as 20,000 pigs, which produce an awful stench and problems with waste products from these animals (Johnson and Kuppig 2004). So, too, with cattle.

There is some evidence that the location of large-scale factory farms involves *environmental racism*. For example, a study found that "reductions in community quality of life attributed to large-scale hog operations are more like to be found in counties that are disproportionately Black than White and located in states that are expanding the number of large-scale hog operations" (Stretesky, Johnston, and Arney 2003:231).

Health Care and Delivery

This section is divided into two parts: disparities in health status comparing rural with metropolitan areas and the relatively inadequate medical infrastructure in rural America.

Residents in rural areas have greater health difficulties than those in metropolitan areas (Morton 2003):

- Death rates for children and young adults (ages 1 to 24 years) are higher.
- Death rates from unintentional injuries are higher.
- Death rates from motor vehicle traffic-related injuries are higher.
- Suicide rates for males are higher.
- Age-adjusted death rates for heart diseases, strokes, diabetes, nutritional deficiencies, and digestive organ cancers are higher.

Among the reasons for these disparities are the relatively old population in nonmetropolitan areas, the more dangerous nature of work, the relatively high rate of uninsured, and exposure to pesticides, herbicides, and other dangerous chemicals. Most significant is the lack of medical help available in rural areas.

The medical infrastructure includes hospitals, public health departments, and emergency medical services. In each instance, the medical infrastructure is inadequate or sometimes nonexistent in rural America. Many rural hospitals have closed for financial reasons due to a low tax base and due to the relatively high proportion of Medicare and Medicaid patients that are underfinanced by federal and state governments. As hospitals close, patients must seek help but must travel greater distances for care. With fewer emergency rooms, more accident victims will die for lack of timely treatment.

Added to the weak health care infrastructure in rural areas is the difficulty in recruiting physicians and dentists. With low patient volume, relatively low income, and poor access to hospitals and the latest diagnostic tools, most physicians locate in the more lucrative metropolitan areas. The U.S. Office of Rural Health Policy estimates that people in rural areas are almost four times more likely than residents of metropolitan areas to live where there is a shortage of health professionals (cited in Morton 2003).

Small-Town Decline

Traditionally, social life in rural America centered on three local institutions—the town, the school, and the church. Of these, only the church remains. Schools have consolidated into much larger districts with schools located between towns they represent.

Rural towns once were the commercial and social hubs for the people living in the region. People shopped and banked there. They went there to have their hair cut or styled. They ate at the family-owned restaurants. They went to town on Saturday nights to shop, visit with friends, or engage in some form of recreation. The town gave the people its identity and sense of community. But this dynamic has changed. Local banks have been acquired by large corporations. Many local residents now work outside the community. They and others now eat in restaurants owned by corporations and do their shopping at the Wal-Marts, Home Depots, and supermarkets in larger towns many miles away. Combined with shopping on the Internet, the competition from these low-cost businesses caused many local businesses to shut down, in effect bringing about the closing of "Main Street" and the sense of community that binds residents in a rural area together.

Crime and Illicit Drugs

Statistically, rural areas are safer places than metropolitan areas. The data show consistently that rural crime rates are lower than in the central cities and their suburbs (see Table 6.2 for a comparison of victimization crime rates in cities, suburbs, and rural areas).

Rural dwellers are involved in illicit drugs (consumption, production, and transshipment), just as are their counterparts in central cities and suburbs (the following is from a study funded by the Drug Enforcement Administration, reported in Hazelden Foundation 2003):

- Eighth-graders in rural America are 83 percent more likely than those in urban areas to use crack cocaine, 43 percent more likely to smoke marijuana, and 29 percent more likely to drink alcohol.

TABLE 6.2
Crimes by Location 2005

	Violent Crime per 1000 Persons age 12 or older	*Property Crime per 1000 Households*
Urban	29.4	200.0
Suburban	18.3	141.4
Rural	18.1	125.1

Source: Catalano, Shannon M. 2006. "Criminal Victimization, 2005," Bureau of Justice Statistics, NCJ 214644 (September).

- Tenth-graders in rural areas use drugs, except for Ecstasy and marijuana, at higher rates than tenth-graders in urban areas.
- Twelfth-graders in rural America use cocaine, amphetamines, inhalants, alcohol, cigarettes, and smokeless tobacco at higher rates than their urban counterparts.
- Adults in rural areas and large urban areas abuse alcohol and other drugs at about the same rates.

Also, most of the marijuana is grown in rural areas. By some measures it is the number 1 cash crop in the United States. Methamphetamine, in particular, is a rural drug phenomenon in production (clandestine laboratories) and consumption.

> *Meth is making its way to the East Coast, but the problem "has exploded" in the middle of the country, says Rusty Payne, a spokesman for the Drug Enforcement Administration. "Meth is now the No. 1 drug in rural America—absolutely, positively, end of question." In Tennessee, Missouri and Arkansas—among the states with the worst problems—meth is overwhelming law-enforcement efforts to combat the homemade drug. (D. Johnson 2004:41)*

The arrest rate for drug offenses in rural America is lower than found in metropolitan areas by a factor of four (Mann, Pittiway, and Weisheit n.d.). There are several reasons for this anomaly. Rural law enforcement agencies have fewer resources and relatively large areas to patrol. It is easier to hide clandestine activities in remote residences than in high-density areas of the city where neighbors are more likely to detect unusual odors and irregular activities. Covert operations, a common device to break urban drug rings, are difficult in rural areas because everyone knows the local police and is wary of strangers. Finally, because rural inhabitants, including police personnel, know everyone, there is a tendency to handle first offenses informally rather than in the criminal justice system.

The focus of this chapter has been on the social significance of geographical location and the social problems found there, whether in urban centers, bordering these centers in suburbs, or in rural areas. In effect, where one lives is a social location because the immediate environment affects social behavior—patterns of social interaction, population density, services available, employment opportunities, tax base, public transportation, and the like. The next five chapters center on other forms of social location as they influence social behavior and as they are the bases for social problems: poverty, race/ethnicity, gender, sexual orientation, and physical ability/disability.

■ CHAPTER REVIEW

1. Many social problems in the United States, including poverty, homelessness, decaying infrastructure, inadequate public transit, pollution, failure to deliver health services to all social classes, failing public schools, drugs, gangs, racism, and crime, are concentrated in large cities.
2. Through the process of suburbanization and metropolitan deconcentration, the central cities have lost people, jobs, industry, business, and their tax base. Central cities have also lost jobs in the transformation from a manufacturing to a service economy.
3. Beginning in the 1950s, U.S. business and financial and lending institutions have tended to (a) disinvest in cities and invest in suburbs and (b) disinvest in Black and Latino neighborhoods and invest in White communities. This pattern of disinvestment is directly responsible for urban neighborhood and central city decline.
4. The declining quality of life in U.S. big cities is reflected in increasing and intensifying poverty, the lack of affordable housing, homelessness, decaying infrastructure, inadequate public transit, pollution, health problems and the lack of access to adequate health care, underfunded and failing schools, crime, drugs, and gangs.
5. Urban poverty has been increasing and becoming more concentrated in particular areas in the central city. The poor have also been getting poorer, especially the minority poor. African Americans and Latinos are more likely than Whites in the city to be poor, and Blacks are much more likely to live in highly segregated neighborhoods that are also high-poverty areas.
6. Both the urban housing market and government-subsidized and public housing have failed to provide enough decent and affordable shelter in U.S. cities. The results are a dwindling supply of low-income housing and increasing urban homelessness.
7. The lack of public investment in the urban infrastructure has begun to significantly limit growth and productivity in the U.S. economy.
8. An automobile-dependent transportation system has polluted U.S. cities and promoted urban sprawl.
9. Poor and minority communities in the inner city are the site of a disproportionate amount of illegal dumping and toxic and hazardous waste (environmental classism and environmental racism).
10. Residents of poor and minority inner-city neighborhoods suffer most from lack of access to adequate health care as private hospitals in cities close their doors to under- and uninsured patients.
11. Because U.S. public education is funded primarily with local property taxes, gross inequalities exist between suburban and city schools.
12. When opportunities in the formal and legal economy are not forthcoming, young minority males turn to the informal economy for survival. Much of the informal economy is illegal, involving property crime, drug trafficking, and certain gang activities.
13. More Americans live in the suburbs than in cities and rural areas (including small towns) combined.
14. The suburbanization of the United States has meant the geographic separation of classes and races, particularly of middle-class Whites from poor African Americans.
15. Suburbs have been encouraged, supported, and directly subsidized by the federal government. Among these federal policies: the interstate highway system with beltways around cities, low-cost mortgages, tax breaks for homeowners, and low fuel taxes.
16. The physical arrangements of the suburbs are socially isolating. There are gated communities, fences between neighbors, and the necessity of driving away from the neighborhood to shop, work, and engage in leisure activities.
17. Rural poverty is higher and more persistent in rural areas than in metropolitan areas.
18. Employment in rural areas was once centered on resources of the land—farming, mining, and forestry. This situation has changed with the demise of small farms, replaced by large enterprises, the shift to factory farm operations. Manufacturing enterprises now employ many rural dwellers but at low pay and with few benefits, and workers live with the fear that businesses might move to other localities where wages are lower.
19. There are four environmental problems in rural America: (a) arable land is being lost to the suburbs; (b) irrigation is depleting aquifers faster than they can be recharged; (c) there is massive use of chemicals in farming; and (d) factory farms create serious pollution of the air, land, and water.
20. Rural residents have greater health difficulties than their urban counterparts. Two of the

reasons for this disparity are a lack of medical personnel and inadequate health facilities.

21. Small towns are declining as commercial and social hubs. Many residents now work outside the community. They shop and seek entertainment elsewhere. The cumulative effects are the closing of local businesses and a loss of a sense of community.

22. Rural areas are safer than metropolitan areas, but rural crime rates are trending up. Comparing rural and urban residents on drug use, rural teenagers are more likely than urban teenagers to consume illicit drugs. Adults in both rural and urban settings use drugs at about the same rate.

KEY TERMS

Redlining. When banks, savings and loans, government agencies, and insurance companies refuse to make home and small-business loans and insure property in poor and minority neighborhoods.

Poverty areas. Neighborhoods in which at least one in five households live below the poverty line.

High-poverty areas. Neighborhoods where at least two in five households live below the poverty line.

Gentrification. The redevelopment of poor and working-class urban neighborhoods into middle- and upper-middle-class enclaves; often involves displacement of original residents.

Slumlording. Landlords buy properties in poor neighborhoods for rent income. They do not maintain these properties because to do so would lower their profits.

Warehousing. The withholding of apartments from the housing market by speculators who hope to sell them at a profit to developers.

Jobs/housing mismatch. The inability of central-city residents most in need of decent jobs to reach them on the urban fringe because (1) they cannot afford to operate a private automobile, and (2) the public transportation system is inadequate; moving to the urban fringe is not an option because of housing costs and racial segregation. To the extent that jobs and job growth occur in one place—affluent and White areas—and poor Blacks or Latinos are restricted to another, this "mismatch" is a form of spatial apartheid.

Spatial apartheid. The physical separation of Whites and nonwhites with Whites located where jobs and job growth are found and nonwhites located where they are not.

Environmental racism. The tendency for poor and minority areas in cities and metropolitan areas to be the targets of a disproportionate share of illegal dumping and the sites where most toxic and hazardous waste is disposed; these communities also suffer, as compared to more affluent White communities, from lax enforcement of environmental regulations and laws.

Triage. The practice in understaffed and underfinanced public hospitals of treating the most urgent emergencies first, thereby delaying the treatment of other cases.

Informal economy. When opportunities are not present in the regular legal economy, people in poor inner-city neighborhoods often turn to this alternate economic exchange and activity for survival; much of the informal economy is illegal activity involving crime and drug trafficking.

White flight. The movement of predominantly upper-middle-class, middle-class, and working-class Whites from the central cities to the suburbs.

Boomburg. A suburban city of at least 100,000 that has experienced double-digit growth each decade since it became urban.

Urban sprawl. Low-density, automobile-dependent development outside the central city.

Rural. The nonmetropolitan population that resides in small cities and the open countryside.

Colonias. Shantytown settlements of Latino immigrants.

■ SUCCEED WITH PEARSON mysoclab www.mysoclab.com

Experience, Discover, Observe, Evaluate

MySocLab is designed just for you. Each chapter features a pre-test and post-test to help you learn and review key concepts and terms.

Experience sociology in action with dynamic visual activities, videos, and readings to enhance your learning experience. Complete the following activities at www.mysoclab.com.

Social Explorer is an interactive application that allows you to explore Census data through interactive maps.

- Explore the Social Explorer Map: *Residential Stability*

The Core Concepts in Sociology video clips offer a real-world perspective on sociological concepts.

- Watch *Challenges Facing Cities*

MySocLibrary includes primary source readings from classic and contemporary sociologists.

- Read Logan, *Life and Death in the City: Neighborhoods in Context*; Kubrin, *Gangstas, Thugs, and Hustlas: The Code of the Street in Rap Music*; Gurwitt, *Death of a Neighborhood*

PART 3 Problems of Inequality

CHAPTER 7 Poverty

Any city, however small, is in fact divided into two, one the city of the poor, the other of the rich; these are at war with one another.

—Plato

Many people in the world envy the United States. It is blessed with great natural resources, the most advanced technology known, and a very high standard of living. Despite these advantages, a significant portion of U.S. residents live in a condition of **poverty** (with a standard of living below the minimum needed for the maintenance of adequate diet, health, and shelter). Many millions are ill-fed, ill-clothed, and ill-housed. These same millions are discriminated against in the schools, in the courts, in the job market, and in the marketplace, and discrimination has the effect of trapping many of the poor in that condition. The so-called American dream is just that for millions of people—a dream that will not be realized.

This chapter is descriptive, theoretical, and practical. On the descriptive level, we examine the facts of poverty—how many poor there are in the United

States, where the poor are located, and what it means to be poor. Theoretically, we look at the various explanations for poverty—individual, cultural, and structural. On the practical level, we explore what might be done to eliminate extreme poverty.

There are two underlying themes in this chapter. The first theme is that most of the poor are impoverished for structural reasons, not personal ones, as is commonly believed. That is, the essence of poverty is inequality—in money and in opportunity. The second theme is important when we take up the possible solutions to this social problem: The United States has the resources to eliminate poverty if it would give that problem a high enough priority.

EXTENT OF POVERTY

What separates the poor from the nonpoor? In a continuum, there is no absolute standard for poverty. The line separating the poor from the nonpoor is necessarily arbitrary. Originally developed by the Social Security Administration (SSA), the **official poverty line, or poverty threshold**, is based on the minimal amount of money required for a subsistence level of life. To determine the poverty line, the SSA computed the cost of a basic, nutritionally adequate diet and multiplied that figure by three. This multiplier is based on a government research finding that in 1955, poor people spent one-third of their income on food. Since then, the poverty level has been readjusted annually by the Consumer Price Index to account for inflation. Using this official standard (the weighted average poverty thresholds are $11,369 for one person under age 65, $17,590 for a family of three, and $22,162 for a family of four), 14.3 percent of Americans (43.6 million) were poor in 2009 (the statistics for this section are taken in part from DeNavas-Walt, Proctor, and Smith 2010). This is the highest poverty rate the United States has seen in twelve years, with an increase of 6.3 million people living in poverty from 2007. See Figure 7.1 for the poverty rate data over time.

In this chapter, we consider the poor as people who fall below this arbitrary line. However, not only is the government procedure arbitrary, but it also minimizes the extent of poverty in the United States. Critics of the measure point out that the government measure does not keep up with inflation, that housing costs now take up a much larger portion of the family budget than food, and that the poverty line ignores differences in health insurance coverage and the medical care needs of individual families (Shipler 2004; Rodgers 2006).

Critics of the poverty thresholds also argue that a "one size fits all" standard is not an adequate measure of poverty because there is a wide variation in the cost of living by locality. A 2004 study found that for a family to be able to afford rent and utilities on a typical two-bedroom apartment, they would need an hourly wage of $22.83 in the District of Columbia, $20.93 in Massachusetts, $14.93 in Arizona, and $9.63 in Arkansas (Associated Press 2004d). Obviously, these figures are far above the federal minimum hourly wage of $7.25.

In October 2009, the Census Bureau released poverty estimates using a revised formula based on recommendations by experts at the National Academy of Sciences. The revised formula factors in expenses such as housing and medical costs and shows the poverty rate to be closer to 15.8 percent (nearly one in six Americans, or 47 million people; Llanos 2009). Current government policies are still based on the previous formula, and it remains to be seen

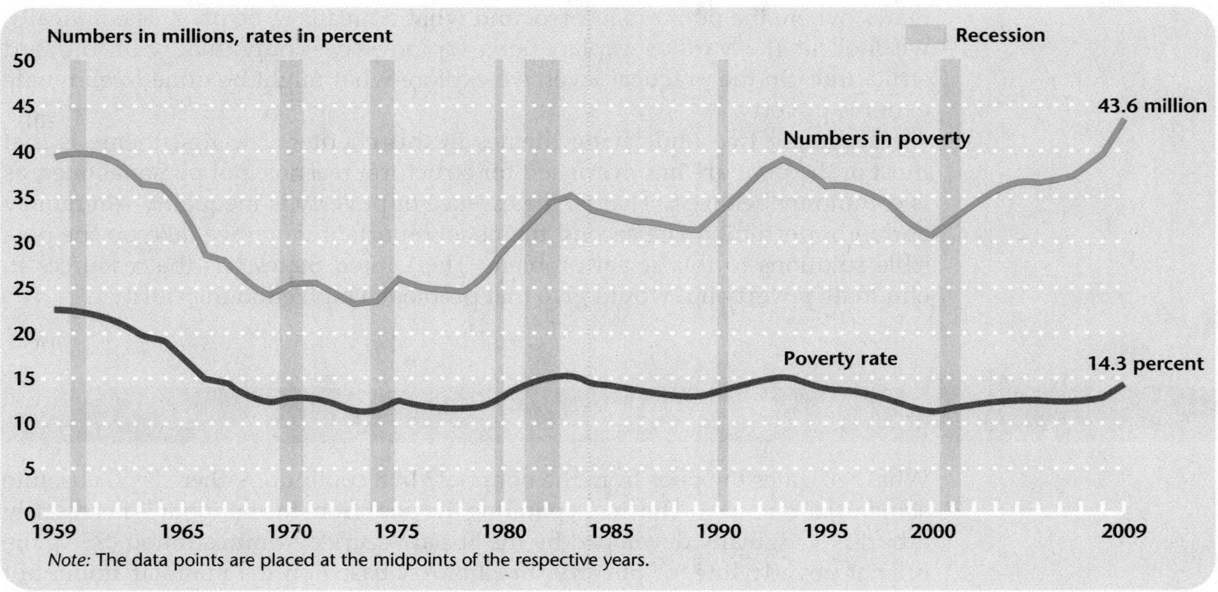

FIGURE 7.1

Number in Poverty and Poverty Rate, 1959 to 2009

Source: Carmen DeNavas-Walt, Bernadette D. Proctor, and Jessica C. Smith. U.S. Census Bureau, Current Population Reports, *Income, Poverty, and Health Insurance Coverage in the United States, 2009*. U.S. Government Printing Office, Washington, D.C., 2010.

whether lawmakers will move to adopt the revised formula and the higher poverty estimates.

Exact figures on the number of poor are difficult to determine. A major difficulty is that the poor are most likely to be missed by the U.S. Census. People most likely overlooked in the census live in high-density urban areas where several families may be crowded into one apartment or in rural areas where some homes are inaccessible and where some workers follow the harvest from place to place and therefore have no permanent home. Transients of any kind may be missed by the census. Also, there are several million immigrants in this country illegally who avoid the census. The inescapable conclusion is that the proportion of the poor in the United States is underestimated because the poor tend to be invisible, even to the government. The Census Bureau estimated, for example, that it missed 3.4 million people, largely members of minority groups and the homeless, in the 2000 census. This underestimate of the poor has important consequences because U.S. census data are the basis for political representation in Congress and for the allocation of $185 billion a year in federal funds to states and cities (El Nasser 2001a).

Despite these difficulties and underestimates of the poverty population, the official government data are the best available to provide information about the poor. In the following sections we examine the facts of poverty using these government statistics. In December 2007, the United States experienced a collapse in the housing market that marked the beginning of an economic recession. As a result, many of the statistics demonstrate a worsening of economic conditions from 2007 to 2008 (the latest government census figures). See Chapter 14 for more on the Great Recession.

TABLE 7.1

Demographics of the Poverty Population, 1980, 2001, 2009

	Percentage of the Poor		
	1980	*2000*	*2009*
All People	13.0%	11.3%	14.3%
Race/Ethnicity			
White	9.1	7.4	12.3
African American	32.5	22.5	25.8
Latino	25.7	21.5	25.3
Asian/Pacific Islander	17.2	9.9	12.5
Nativity			
Native	*	10.8	13.7
Foreign born	*	15.4	2.1
Family Structure			
In all families	11.5	9.6	11.1
In families, female householder, no spouse present	36.7	28.5	29.9
Age			
Children under 18	18.3	16.2	20.7
Adults age 65 and older	15.7	9.9	8.9
Residence			
Central cities	17.2	16.3	18.7
Suburbs	8.2	7.8	11.0
Outside metropolitan areas	15.4	13.4	16.6

Sources: U.S. Census Bureau, Current Population Survey, 2009 and 2010 Annual Social and Economic Supplements.

Racial/Ethnic Minorities

Income in the United States is unequally distributed by race (for data on race and other social characteristics, see Table 7.1). In 2009, the U.S. Census Bureau found that the median family income for Asian American households was $78,330, compared with $69,530 for non-Hispanic White households, $42,445 for Latino households, and $40,698 for African American households. Not surprisingly, then, 12.3 percent of Whites were officially poor, compared with 12.5 percent of Asian Americans, 25.3 percent of Latinos, and 25.8 percent of African Americans.

Due to the economic recession, for every racial category real median income declined between 2007 and 2008. Statistics indicate that Hispanic households experienced the largest decline in income (5.6 percent) compared to a 2.6 percent decline for Whites, a 2.8 percent decline for Blacks, and a 4.4 percent decline for Asian Americans.

These summary statistics mask the differences within each racial/ethnic category. For example, Americans of Cuban descent, many of whom were middle-class professionals in Cuba, have relatively low poverty rates, whereas Puerto Ricans, Mexicans, and Central Americans have disproportionately high poverty rates. Similarly, Japanese Americans are much less likely to be poor than Asians from Cambodia, Laos, and Vietnam.

Native Americans have a slightly higher poverty rate than African Americans and Latinos (25.9 percent). Similar to other racial categories, there is a wide variation among Native Americans, with some in the middle class, some poor, and some extremely poor. According to Native American Aid (2006), approximately half of the 2.5 million Native Americans live on reservations. There, poverty rates and unemployment tend to be very high, health problems rampant, and educational attainment comparatively low. According to the Housing Assistance Council, one in three Native Americans living on reservations is poor (2004).

In 2009, 7.2 million of the foreign-born individuals in the United States (19.0 percent of the foreign born) were poor. Of these poor foreign born, 24.4 percent were naturalized citizens and the remaining were noncitizens. Their poverty rates of 10.8 and 25.1 percent, respectively, indicate that those individuals who became citizens had significantly lower rates of poverty. These official statistics do not include the 6 to 10 million undocumented workers and their families who enter the United States illegally.

Gender

Women are more likely than men to be poor. This is a consequence of the prevailing institutional sexism in society. There is a dual labor market, with women found disproportionately in lower-paying jobs with fewer benefits. Thus, the female-to-male earnings ratio was 0.78 in 2009 (i.e., women earned 78 cents for every dollar earned by men). The relatively high frequency of divorce and the large number of never-married women with children, coupled with the cost of child care, housing, and medical care, have resulted in high numbers of female-headed families (with no husband present) being poor (29.9 percent, compared to 5.8 percent for married-couple families and 16.9 percent for male-headed families with no wife present). This trend has been called the **feminization of poverty**, a term that implies that the large proportion of poor women is a relatively new phenomenon in U.S. society. However, this obscures the fact that women have always been more economically vulnerable than men, especially older women and women of color. But when women's poverty was mainly limited to these groups, their economic deprivation was mostly invisible. The plight of women's poverty became a visible problem when the numbers of White women in poverty increased rapidly in the past decade or so with rising marital disruption. Even with the growing numbers of poor White women, the term *feminization of poverty* implies that all women are at risk, when actually the probability of economic deprivation is much greater for certain categories of women. The issue, then, is not only gender by itself but class and race as well.

Age

The nation's poverty rate was 14.3 percent in 2009, but the rate was 20.7 percent for children under age 18 (see Table 7.1). The younger the child is, the greater the probability of living in poverty, with the rate being 23.8 percent for children under age 6. Related children under age 6 living in families with a female head of household, no husband present, had a poverty rate of 54.3 percent, a rate more than four times that for their counterparts in married-couple families (13.4 percent).

To put a finer point on the magnitude of children's poverty in the United States, one out of every six American children was poor in 2009. Children in poverty are more likely to suffer from stunted growth, score lower on tests and be held back in school, suffer from lead poisoning, and suffer a host of other problems. In addition, 7.5 million children did not have health insurance in 2009.

In terms of the elderly (age 65+), 8.9 percent of the elderly population lived below the poverty line in 2009. The number of poor elderly varies greatly by state, from a high of 24 percent in Mississippi to a low of 7 percent in Utah and Vermont (Kaiser Family Foundation 2005). It is also important to note that a higher proportion of the elderly than nonelderly hover just above the poverty line. In other words, the elderly are overrepresented among the near poor. Moreover, elderly women are much more likely than elderly men to be living in poverty (for example, in 2009 the rate was 11.1 percent for women, 6.4 percent for men).

Place

Poverty is not randomly distributed geographically; it tends to cluster in certain places. Regionally, the area with the highest poverty in 2009 was the South (15.7 percent), compared to 14.8 percent in the West, 12.2 percent in the Northeast, and 13.3 percent in the Midwest. The higher poverty rate in the South and West reflects their large minority populations and the relatively large number of recent immigrants. The three places with the highest average poverty rates in 2009 were Mississippi (21.9 percent), Kentucky (18.6 percent), and the District of Columbia (18.4 percent). The states with the lowest poverty rates were New Hampshire (8.5 percent), Maryland (9.1 percent), and Connecticut (9.4 percent).

There are 382 counties in the United States where more than 20 percent of the people live below the poverty line, called *persistent poverty counties* (Miller and Weber 2004). These counties are overwhelmingly rural, with especially high numbers in counties such as Shannon in South Dakota, where the Pine Ridge reservation is located (52.3 percent live in poverty), and Starr in Texas, which is predominantly Latino (50.9 percent live in poverty). See Figure 7.2 for a closer look at where the extremely poor live.

FIGURE 7.2

Where the Extremely Poor Live

U.S. states with the highest rates, the highest number and the fastest growth of extremely poor people:

National rate 5.7% | National total 15.9

Highest rates Percent of population		**Largest totals** In millions		**Fastest growth** From 2000 to 2005	
Washington, D.C	10.8%	Calif.	1.9	Minn.	62%
Miss.	9.3%	Texas	1.6	N.H.	59%
La.	8.3%	N.Y.	1.2	Idaho	58%
N.M.	7.8%	Fla.	0.9	Alaska	47%
Ala.	7.3%	Ill.	0.7	Kan.	43%
Ark.	7.3%	Ohio	0.7	Maine	43%
Texas	7.3%	Pa.	0.6	Mich.	41%
W.Va.	7.2%	Mich.	0.6	Colo.	41%
Ky.	7.1%	Ga.	0.6	Nev.	40%
Okla.	6.9%	N.C.	0.5	Wis.	40%

Note: People in extreme poverty earn half the U.S. Census thresholds for poverty.

In metropolitan areas, the poverty rate in 2009 was higher in the central cities (18.7 percent) than in suburban areas (11.0 percent). For those living outside metropolitan areas, the poverty rate was 16.6 percent. Two trends are significant: The proportion who are poor is increasing in the central cities, and increasingly, the poverty is more concentrated (i.e., the poor are increasingly likely to be living in already poor neighborhoods). This spatial concentration of poverty means that the poor have poor neighbors, the area has a low tax base to finance public schools, and the number of businesses dwindles as they tend to move to areas where the local residents have more discretionary income. As businesses close or relocate, the central city experiences a reduction in services and the elimination of local jobs.

Poverty is greatest among those who do not have an established residence. People in this classification are typically the homeless and migrant workers. In 2005, the Department of Housing and Urban Development reported that there were 754,000 homeless people across the country, approximately 300,000 more people than available beds in shelters and transitional housing (Associated Press 2007b). Nearly half the homeless population were single adult men, and about 59 percent were members of minority groups. Although the exact numbers are impossible to calculate, since the 2007 recession many cities are reporting a significant increase in the number of homeless families seeking shelter and food assistance (U.S. Conference of Mayors 2009).

The other category, migrant workers, is believed to comprise about 3 million adults and children who are seasonal farm laborers working for low wages and no benefits. It is estimated that over half of all farm workers live below the official poverty line and that this percentage has not changed since the 1960s. Latinos are overrepresented in this occupation.

Finally, the United States, when compared to other major industrialized democracies, has more poverty, has more severe poverty, and supports its poor people least. See the "Social Problems in Global Perspective" panel.

The New Poor

In the past two decades, millions of blue-collar workers have lost their jobs as plants have closed and companies have moved in search of cheaper labor, or as workers have been replaced by robots or other forms of automation (see Chapter 14). Almost half of these newly unemployed were longtime workers (workers who had held their previous jobs at least 3 years). In January 2010, the United States hit an all-time high unemployment rate of 10 percent (Bureau of Labor Statistics 2010). Hardest hit was the state of Michigan (14.6 percent), as a result of the collapse of the auto industry, and Nevada (13 percent), as a result of the housing and construction bust.

These **new poor** are quite different from the **old poor**. The old poor—that is, the poor of other generations—had hopes of breaking out of poverty; if they did not break out themselves, at least they believed their children would. This hope was based on a rapidly expanding economy. There were jobs for immigrants, farmers, and high school dropouts because of the needs of mass production. The new poor, however, are much more trapped in poverty. A generation ago, those who were unskilled and uneducated could usually find work and could even do quite well financially if the workplace was unionized. But now these workers are displaced or misplaced. Hard physical labor is rarely needed in a high-tech society. This phenomenon undercuts the efforts of the working class, especially African Americans, Latinos, and other minorities who face the additional burden of institutional racism.

SOCIAL PROBLEMS IN GLOBAL PERSPECTIVE

POVERTY IN THE UNITED STATES RELATIVE TO OTHER WESTERN DEMOCRACIES

The United States does not fare well when compared to other Western democracies on various dimensions of poverty. Consider these facts:

- According to the United Nations' Human Development Reports, out of seventeen high-income countries, the United States scores the worst on the Human Poverty Index. This index measures early mortality rates, illiteracy rates, poverty, and long-term unemployment. Sweden, Norway, and the Netherlands received the best (lowest) scores on the index (2003).
- The probability of living in poverty is more than twice as high for a child born in the United States than for children in Belgium, Germany, or the Netherlands (Block et al. 2006).
- The poverty thresholds as defined by the United States are much higher than international standards. If the United States used the most common international measure, which counts people who live on less than half of a country's median income as poor, than almost 55 million people would be counted as poor (rather than 39.8 million; Block et al. 2006).
- Among the industrialized nations, the United States ranks first in military spending, first in gross domestic product, first in the number of billionaires, first in the number of persons incarcerated, twenty-fifth in infant mortality rates, last in the gap between the rich and poor, and last in relative child poverty (Children's Defense Fund 2008).
- According to the Economic Policy Institute (2004), out of sixteen industrialized countries, the United States stands out as spending the lowest amount on social welfare and having the highest child poverty rate. At the other end of the spectrum are countries like Sweden, Norway, and Finland, who spend the most on social welfare and have the lowest child poverty rates.
- The average exit rate from poverty is lower in the United States (where 28.6 percent move above the poverty line annually) than in Sweden (36 percent), Germany (37 percent), Canada (42 percent), and the Netherlands (where 44 percent leave poverty status; Economic Policy Institute 2001).

The Working Poor

Having a job is not necessarily a path out of poverty. U.S. census data show that over 2.6 million full-time workers were below the poverty line in 2009, as were another 8.0 million workers who worked at least part of the year. Despite working, these people remain poor because they hold menial, dead-end jobs that have no benefits and pay the minimum wage or below. In 2008, 1.9 million workers were paid less than the federal minimum wage (Bureau of Labor Statistics 2010). In July 2009 the federal minimum wage was increased to $7.25 an hour. This adds up to only $13,920 (before taxes) for full-time work (falling over $3,000 short of the poverty threshold for a family of three). In 2008, the majority of all low-wage workers were concentrated in service occupations, mostly food service.

The majority of the working poor are white (58 percent), female (58 percent), and high school educated (37 percent; Conlin and Bernstein 2004). For Whites and Latinos, women are twice as likely to be low wage earners as men (Bureau of Labor Statistics 2004a). Compounding the economic woes of the poor is a lack of health insurance coverage. In 2009, 50.7 million people were without health insurance (14.6 million of these were full-time workers).

The lot of the **working poor** is similar to that of the nonworking poor on some dimensions and worse on others. They do society's dirty work for low pay and few if any benefits. They live in substandard housing, and their children go to underfinanced public schools. They are poor, but unlike the nonworking

Since December 2007, the number of foreclosures in the United States has skyrocketed.

poor, they are not eligible for many government supports such as subsidized housing, medical care (Medicaid), and food stamps.

The Near Poor

The **near poor** are people with family incomes at or above the poverty threshold but below 125 percent of the threshold (e.g., with the official poverty line at $17,163 for a family of three, 125 percent of that number is $21,454). In 2009, 18.7 percent of the population was near poor, a significant portion of those being under the age of 18. The 2007 recession brought into focus the vulnerability of the near poor. The near poor are one accident, one illness, one job loss away from severe poverty, as indicated by the number of home foreclosures in 2008. Home foreclosure filings topped three million in 2008, up 81 percent from 2007 and 225 percent from 2006 (Armour 2009).

The Severely Poor

Use of the official poverty line designates all people below it as poor, whether they are a few dollars short or far below that threshold. In reality, most impoverished individuals and families have incomes considerably below the poverty threshold. In 2008, for example, the average dollar amount needed to raise a poor family out of poverty was $9,102 (i.e., the average family needed $9,102 *additional* income just to reach the poverty threshold). For poor individuals not in families, the average income deficit was $5,912, and for poor women in female-headed households, the average income deficit was $9,638.

In 2009, 6.3 percent of the population (19 million Americans) was **severely poor** (i.e., living at or below half the poverty line). Some facts about these people who are the poorest of the poor are as follows:

- Of these 17 million, 6.9 million are children under 18.
- Of these 17 million, 4.6 million are African American.
- Typically, the severely poor must use at least 50 percent or more of their income for housing.

This number of severely poor has significantly increased since 1979. This upsurge in the truly destitute occurred because (1) many of the severely poor live in rural areas that have prospered less than other regions, (2) a decline in marriage resulted in a substantial increase in single mothers and unattached men, and (3) public assistance benefits, especially in the South, have steadily declined since 1980. We return to the explanations for poverty later in this chapter.

MYTHS ABOUT POVERTY

What should be the government's role in caring for its less-fortunate citizens? Much of the debate on this important issue among politicians and citizens is based on erroneous assumptions and misperceptions. Those myths and misperceptions are refuted in this section.

Refusal to Work

Several facts belie the faulty assumption that poor people refuse to work. First, 10.7 million poor people worked in 2009, and 2.6 million of them worked full time but were still under the poverty threshold. They hold menial, dead-end jobs that have no benefits and pay the minimum wage (many actually less than the minimum wage). Today a full-time minimum-wage worker earns only 81 percent of the poverty level for a family of three (in 1968 a family of three with one minimum-wage earner had a standard of living 17 percent above the poverty line). Second, many of the poor who do not work are too young (under age 18), too old (age 65 and older), or have a work disability. Third, the main increase in the number of poor since 1979 has been among the working poor. This increase is the result of declining wages, higher numbers of working women who head households, a low federal minimum hourly wage, and an increase in housing costs.

According to a 2004 report, in only four of the nation's 3,066 counties could someone working full time and earning the federal minimum wage afford to pay rent and utilities on a one-bedroom apartment. "Least affordable was the San Francisco metropolitan area; rent and utilities for a one-bedroom apartment in Marin, San Francisco, or San Mateo counties in California required a wage of at least $22.63 an hour, tops in the nation" (Associated Press 2004d:1).

The misconception that the poor refuse to work ignores all those "invisible poor," those who are working but not making it and those who work in the informal economy, not captured by the Census Bureau statistics. Many work (either for money or for the exchange of goods or services) in the informal economy by cleaning, painting, providing child care, repairing automobiles or appliances, or other activities. These people are workers; they just are not in the official economy. Clearly the statistics contradict the myth that the poor refuse to work.

Welfare Dependency

In 1996 Congress passed the **Personal Responsibility and Work Opportunity Reconciliation Act (PRWORA)** that reformed the welfare system. This new law encompassed the following:

- It shifted welfare programs from the federal government to the states.
- It mandated that welfare recipients find work within 2 years.
- It limited welfare assistance to 5 years.
- It cut various federal assistance programs targeted for the poor by $54.5 billion over 6 years.

Thus, this law made assistance to the poor temporary and cut monies to supplemental programs such as food assistance and child nutrition. The assumption by policy makers was that welfare was too generous, making it easier to stay on welfare than to work, and welfare was believed to encourage unmarried women to have children.

We should recognize some facts about government welfare before the 1996 welfare reform (O'Hare 1996:11). First, welfare accounted for about one-fourth of the income of poor adults; nearly half of the income received by poor adults came from some form of work activity. Second, about three-fourths of the poor received some form of noncash benefit (Medicaid, food stamps, or housing assistance), but only about 40 percent received cash welfare payments. Third, the welfare population changes—that is, people move in and out of poverty every year (Rodgers 2006). Around 70 percent of welfare recipients are on welfare for less than 2 years (Welfare Rights Organizing Coalition 2000). Fourth, although the prereform welfare system was much more generous than now, it was inadequate to meet the needs of the poor. The average poor family of three on welfare had an annual income much below the poverty line. For example, in 1995, the *maximum* monthly cash benefit for a family of three under the old welfare system ranged from $120 in Mississippi to $712 in Hawaii, a level far below the poverty threshold (Rodgers 2006).

Fifth, contrary to the common assertion that welfare mothers keep having babies to get more welfare benefits and thereby escape working, research from a number of studies shows that most welfare recipients bring in extra money

"I would share my cookies, but I'm afraid I'll set up a cycle of dependency."

from various activities such as house cleaning, laundry, repairing clothing, child care, and selling items they have made. For example, sociologist Kathleen Harris, summarizing her findings from a nationally representative sample of single mothers who received welfare under the old system, says:

> *I found exclusive dependence on welfare to be rare. More than half of the single mothers whom I studied worked while they were on welfare, and two-thirds left the welfare rolls when they could support themselves with jobs. However, more than half (57 percent) of the women who worked their way off public assistance later returned because their jobs ended or they still could not make ends meet. (Harris 1996:B7)*

Concerning the larger picture about government welfare programs, there is a fundamental misunderstanding by the U.S. public about where most governmental benefits are directed. We tend to assume that government monies and services go mostly to the poor (**welfare**), when in fact the greatest amount of government aid goes to the nonpoor (**wealthfare**). Most (about three-fourths) of the federal outlays for human resources go to the nonpoor, such as to all children in public education programs and to most of the elderly through Social Security Retirement and Medicare.

The upside-down welfare system, with aid mainly helping the already affluent, is also accomplished by two hidden welfare systems. The first is through tax loopholes (called **tax expenditures**). Through these legal mechanisms, the government officially permits certain individuals and corporations to pay lower taxes or no taxes at all. For illustration, one of the biggest tax expenditure programs is the money that homeowners deduct from their taxes for real estate taxes and interest on their mortgages, a total of approximately $76 billion in 2006 (mortgage interest is deductible on mortgages up to $1 million). Ironically, although less than one-fourth of low-income Americans receive federal housing subsidies, more than three-quarters of Americans, many living in mansions, get housing aid from Washington. According to Roger Lowenstein,

> *More than 70 percent of tax filers don't get any benefit from the deduction at all. . . . But cumulatively, the deduction is a big deal. This year, it is expected to cost the U.S. Treasury $76 billion. And the rewards are greatly skewed in favor of the moderately to the conspicuously rich. On a million-dollar mortgage (the people with those really need help, right?) the tax benefit is worth approximately $21,000 a year. And according to the Joint Committee on Taxation, a little over half of the benefit is taken by just 12 percent of taxpayers—or those with incomes of $100,000 or more. (2006:1)*

The second hidden welfare system to the nonpoor is in the form of direct subsidies and credit to assist corporations, banks, agribusiness, and defense industries. Some examples (from Goodgame 1993; Zepezauer and Naiman 1996; Glassman 1997; *Multinational Monitor* 1997) are the following:

- The savings and loan bailout ($37 billion every year for 30 years)
- Agribusiness subsidies ($18 billion a year)
- Media subsidies ($8 billion a year; in 1997, the Federal Communications Commission [FCC] gave broadcast licenses for digital television to existing broadcasters at no cost. The FCC itself estimated the value of these licenses to be worth $20 billion to $70 billion)
- Timber subsidies ($427 million a year, not counting tax breaks)
- Aviation subsidies ($5.5 billion a year)
- Mining subsidies ($3.5 billion a year)
- Tax avoidance by transnational corporations ($12 billion annually)

These subsidy programs to wealthy and corporate interests amount to many times more than welfare assistance to the poor. Ironically, when Congress passed the sweeping welfare reforms of 1996, it did not consider the welfare programs for the nonpoor. See Chapter 19 for an in-depth assessment of the 1996 welfare reform.

The Poor Get Special Advantages

The common belief is that the poor get a number of handouts for which other Americans have to work—food stamps, Medicaid, and housing subsidies. As we have seen, these subsidies amount to much less than the more affluent receive, and recent legislation has reduced them even more. Most significant, the *poor pay more than the nonpoor for many services*. This, along with earning low wages and paying a large proportion of their income for housing, helps to explain why some have such difficulty getting out of poverty.

The urban poor find that their money does not go as far in the inner city. Food and commodities, for example, cost more because supermarkets, discount stores, outlet malls, and warehouse clubs have bypassed inner-city neighborhoods. Because many inner-city residents do not have transportation to get to the supermarkets and warehouse stores, they must buy from nearby stores, giving those businesses monopoly powers (a similar situation to those poor in rural communities). In this and other ways, the poor pay more. Consider the following:

- Hospitals routinely charge more (sometimes twice as much or more) for services to patients without health insurance compared to those covered by a health plan (Ehrenreich 2004; S.E.I.U. 2005).
- Check-cashing centers, largely located in poor neighborhoods, prey on customers without bank accounts. They often charge 10 percent of the check's value, so a person cashing a $300 check will leave with only $270 (Curtis 2000; Ehrenreich 2006).
- There is a new trend in WIC (women, infants, and children)-only grocery stores that cater to low-income families. These stores are for participants of the Special Supplemental Nutrition Program for Women, Infants, and Children, and they accept only WIC vouchers as payment, not cash. State officials show prices are 10 to 20 percent higher in the WIC-only stores (Pear 2004).
- The "payday loan" industry offers an advance on a person's paycheck. With interest rates averaging more than 400 percent (costing borrowers $3.4 billion per year), this is a devastating financial obligation for those strapped for cash (Jeffery 2006; Lydersen 2002). Nationwide, the number of payday lending outlets has risen 11,000 percent since 1990 (Jeffery 2006). Some states have begun taking legal action to limit the interest rates on this thriving industry.
- Women, minorities, and lower-income borrowers are more likely than others to take out high-cost, subprime mortgages (Kirchhoff 2005).
- A 2002 study by the National Bureau of Economic Research found that in 1999–2000, African Americans, Hispanics, and women paid more for new cars than other buyers (reported in Koretz 2002).

The conclusion is obvious: rather than receiving special advantages, the poor pay more for commodities and services in absolute terms, and they pay a much larger proportion of their incomes than the nonpoor for comparable items. Similarly, when the poor pay sales taxes on the items they purchase, the tax takes more of their resources than it does from the nonpoor, making it a **regressive tax**. Thus, efforts to move federal programs to the states will cost the poor more because state and local taxes tend to be regressive. Barbara Ehrenreich sums it up this way:

> *So let's have a little less talk about how the poor should learn to manage their money, and a little more attention to all the ways that money is being systematically siphoned off. Yes, certain kinds of advice would be helpful: skip the pay-day loans and rent-to-pay furniture, for example. But we need laws in more states to stop predatory practices like $50 charges for check cashing. Also, think what some microcredit could do to move families from motels and shelters to apartments. And did I mention a living wage?*
> *If you're rich, you might want to stay that way. It's a whole lot cheaper than being poor.* (2006;2)

Welfare Is an African American and Latino Program

The myth is that most welfare monies go primarily to African Americans and Latinos. Although poverty rates are higher for African Americans and Latinos than for other racial/ethnic groups, they do not make up a majority of the poor. Although the poverty rate is 9.4 percent for non-Hispanic Whites, 25.8 percent for African Americans, and 25.3 percent for Hispanics, over 29 million Whites are poor compared to 9.9 million African Americans and 12.4 million Hispanics. Thus, although minorities are overrepresented in the poverty population given their numbers in the general population, non-Hispanic Whites account for 42.5 percent of those in poverty and take up a large share of the welfare budget.

CAUSES OF POVERTY

Everyone in the United States has heard of the "American dream," the dream of upward mobility and economic success that is available to all. Yet, the statistics reveal that for the majority, upward mobility really is just a dream. According to The Century Foundation, "Studies show that life chances differ profoundly depending on the circumstances into which a child is born. . . . Only a small share of the children of the poor end up earning high incomes—most remain in or near poverty" (Wasow 2004). In fact, only 7 percent of those born in the bottom fifth income tier end up in the top tier (see Figure 7.3). Who or what is to blame for poverty and lack of upward mobility? There are two very different answers to this question. One is that the poor are in that condition because of some deficiency: either they are biologically inferior or their culture fails them by promoting character traits that impede their progress in society. The other response places the blame on the structure of society: some people are poor because society has failed to provide equality in educational opportunity, because institutions discriminate against minorities, because private industry has failed to provide enough jobs, because automation has made some jobs obsolete, and so forth. In this view, society has worked in such a way as to trap certain people and their offspring in a condition of poverty.

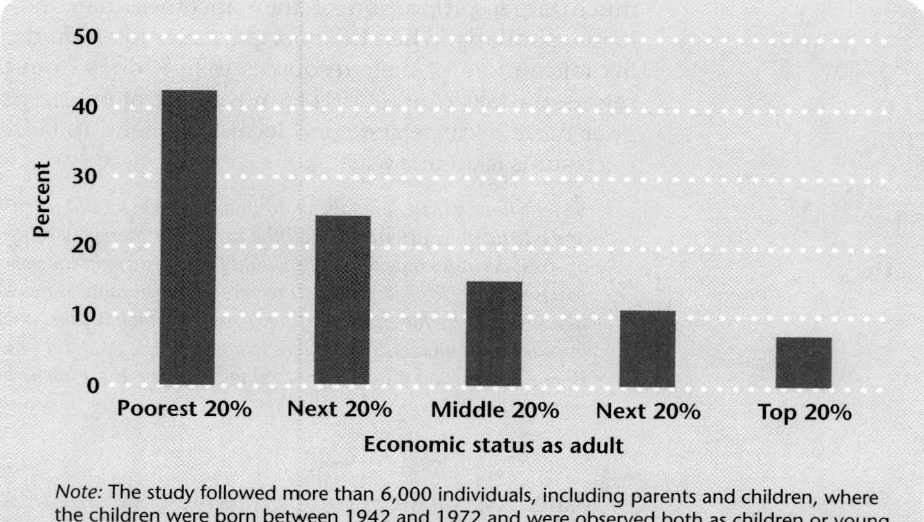

Note: The study followed more than 6,000 individuals, including parents and children, where the children were born between 1942 and 1972 and were observed both as children or young adults in a household they did not head and then later as adult heads of households or adult spouses.

FIGURE 7.3

Where Those Born into the Poorest 20 Percent of the Population End Up as Adults

Source: Figure found in Wasow (2004) "Rags to Riches? The American Dream Is Less Common in the United States than Elsewhere" The Century Foundation. http://www.tcf.org. Accessed 1/14/05. Reprinted with permission.

Source: Reproduced by permission from Bernard Wasow, "Rags to Riches: The American Dream Is Less Common in the United States than Elsewhere" (New York: The Century Foundation, March 19, 2004).

Deficiency Theories

Innate Inferiority. In 1882, the British philosopher and sociologist Herbert Spencer came to the United States to promote a theory later known as social **Darwinism** (see Chapter 1). He argued that the poor were poor because they were unfit. Spencer believed that as societies evolve, the strong will flourish and the weak will eventually die out. He felt that the government should stay out of the way of this progression and even went so far as to say that the government should not help the poor in any way, as that would impede the natural progression of evolution. Any type of government aid would just encourage laziness and slow down the elimination process.

Social Darwinism has generally lacked support in the scientific community for 50 years, although it has continued to provide a rationale for the thinking of many individuals. In the last 40 years, the concept has resurfaced in the work of three scientists. They suggest that the poor are in that condition because they do not measure up to the more well-to-do in intellectual endowment.

Arthur Jensen, professor emeritus of educational psychology at the University of California, has argued that there is a strong possibility that African Americans are less well endowed mentally than Whites. From his review of the research on IQ, he found that approximately 80 percent of IQ is inherited, and the remaining 20 percent is attributable to environment. Because African Americans differ significantly from Whites in achievement on IQ tests and in school, Jensen claimed that it is reasonable to hypothesize that the sources of these differences are genetic as well as environmental (Jensen 1969, 1980).

The late Richard Herrnstein, a Harvard psychologist, agreed with Jensen that intelligence is largely inherited. He went one step further, positing the formation of hereditary castes based on intelligence (Herrnstein 1971, 1973). For Herrnstein, social stratification by inborn differences occurs because (1) mental ability is inherited and (2) success (prestige of job and earnings) depends on mental ability. Thus, a **meritocracy** (social classification by ability) develops through the sorting process. This reasoning assumes that people who are close in mental ability are more likely to marry and reproduce, thereby ensuring castes by level of intelligence. According to this thesis, "in times to come, as technology advances, the tendency to be unemployed may run in the genes of a family about as certainly as bad teeth do now" (Herrnstein 1971:63). This is another way of saying that the bright people are in the upper classes and the dregs are at the bottom. The social Darwinists justify inequality just as it was years ago.

Charles Murray, along with Herrnstein, wrote *The Bell Curve* (Herrnstein and Murray 1994), the latest major revival of social Darwinism. Using data from the National Longitudinal Study of Youth, they argued that wealth and other positive social outcomes are increasingly distributed across society according to intelligence (as measured by IQ tests), rather than social background. Although their work has come under fire in the scientific community, arguments regarding the role of biological inferiority continue to surface. For example, in 2005 Lawrence Summers (president of Harvard University at the time) made a speech regarding the underrepresentation of women in science. In his speech, he claimed that girls are less likely than boys to get the highest scores on standardized math and science tests and that a possible explanation for that is genetic differences between the sexes (Davidson 2005). Notwithstanding the flaws in the logic and in the evidence used by biological deficiency theorists (for excellent critiques of the Herrnstein and Murray work, see Gould 1994; Herman 1994; Reed 1994; and *Contemporary Sociology* 1995), we must consider the implications of their biological determinism for dealing with the problem of poverty.

First, biological determinism is a classic example of **blaming the victim**. The individual poor person is blamed instead of inferior schools, culturally biased IQ tests, low wages, corporate downsizing, or social barriers of race, religion, or nationality. By blaming the victim, this thesis claims a relationship between lack of success and lack of intelligence. This relationship is spurious because it ignores the advantages and disadvantages of ascribed status.

The Jensen-Herrnstein-Murray thesis divides people in the United States by appealing to bigots. It provides "scientific justification" for their beliefs in the racial superiority of some groups and the inferiority of others. By implication, it legitimates segregation and unequal treatment of so-called inferiors. The goal of integration and the fragile principle of egalitarianism are seriously threatened to the degree that members of the scientific community give this thesis credence or prominence.

Another serious implication of the biological determinism argument is the explicit validation of the IQ test as a legitimate measure of intelligence. The IQ test attempts to measure innate potential, but this measurement is impossible because the testing process must inevitably reflect some of the skills that develop during the individual's lifetime. For the most part, intelligence tests measure educability—that is, the prediction of conventional school achievement. Achievement in school is, of course, also associated with a cluster of other factors, most notably socioeconomic status.

Thus, the Jensen-Herrnstein-Murray thesis overlooks the important contribution of social class to achievement on IQ tests. This oversight is crucial because most social scientists feel that these tests are biased in favor of those who have had a middle- and upper-class environment and experience. IQ tests discriminate against the poor in many ways. They discriminate obviously in the language that is used, in the instructions that are given, and in the experiences they assume the subjects have had. The discrimination can also be more subtle. For minorities, the race of the person administering the test influences the results. Another less well-known fact about IQ tests is that in many cases they provide a **self-fulfilling prophecy**. IQ scores on the low or high end of the spectrum can influence the way a child is treated from that moment on. If a child is seen as "bright" or "slow," the child will be treated as such by his or her teachers. The kind of education the child receives as a result of that testing thus influences his or her future IQ.

Another implication is the belief that poverty is inevitable. The survival-of-the-fittest capitalist ideology is reinforced, justifying discrimination against the poor and continued privilege for the advantaged. Inequality is rationalized so that little will be done to aid its victims. Herrnstein and Murray in *The Bell Curve* argue that public policies to ameliorate poverty are a waste of time and resources. "Programs designed to alter the natural dominance of the 'cognitive elite' are useless, the book argues, because the genes of the subordinate castes invariably doom them to failure" (Muwakkil 1994:22). The acceptance of this thesis, then, has obvious consequences for what policy decisions will be made or not made in dealing with poverty. If their view prevails, then welfare programs will be abolished, as will programs such as Head Start.

This raises the serious question: Is intelligence immutable, or is there the possibility of boosting cognitive development? A number of studies have shown that programs such as Head Start raise scores among poor children by as much as 9 points. These results, however, fade out entirely by the sixth grade. Heckman (2006) argued that critics of Head Start are missing the larger picture. In other studies of early preschool intervention programs (similar to Head Start), participants have other successful outcomes, such as higher high school graduation rates, higher percentages of home ownership, lower rates of receipt of welfare assistance as adults, and fewer out-of-wedlock births. Consider the following examples:

- The Abecedarian Project conducted at the University of North Carolina studied high-risk children from 111 families. The study followed these families and children up to age 21 and found that those high-risk children who received high-quality, intense preschooling earned significantly higher scores on intellectual and academic measures as young adults, attained more years of total education, were more likely to attend a four-year college, and showed a reduction in teen pregnancy. They conclude that "the positive findings from this study have important policy implications. They show that a high-quality child care program can have a lasting impact on the academic performance of children from poverty backgrounds" (Campbell et al. 2002:55).
- In Ypsilanti, Michigan, high-risk African American children were randomly divided into two groups. Similar to the Abecedarian Project, one group received a high-quality, active-learning program as 3- and 4-year-olds. The other group received no preschool education. The two groups were compared when they were age 27, with these results:

  By age 27, those who had received the preschool education had half as many arrests as the comparison group. Four times as many were earning $2,000 or more a

> *month. Three times as many owned their own homes. One-third more had graduated from high school on schedule. One-fourth fewer of them needed welfare as adults. And they had one-third fewer children born out of wedlock.* (Beck 1995:7B)

- Researchers at the University of Wisconsin studied 989 poor children, all born in 1980, who enrolled in the Chicago Child Parent Center Program no later than age 4 and were taught an average of 2.5 hours a day for 18 months (reported in Steinberg 2001). The students were tracked until age 20. Comparing these students with 550 other poor children from the same neighborhoods, few of whom attended any preschool, researchers found that (1) fewer graduates of the Chicago program had been arrested for juvenile crimes, (2) more graduates of the program also graduated from high school, and (3) the Chicago program children were much less likely to be assigned to special education classes or to repeat a grade.

Recall that Herrnstein and Murray in *The Bell Curve* (1994) argued that public policies to ameliorate poverty are a waste of time and resources because of the biological inferiority of the poor. These examples indicate otherwise.

- **Cultural Inferiority.** One prominent explanation of poverty, called the **culture-of-poverty hypothesis**, contends that the poor are qualitatively different in values and lifestyles from the rest of society and that these cultural differences explain continued poverty. In other words, the poor, in adapting to their deprived condition, are found to be more permissive in raising their children, less verbal, more fatalistic, less likely to defer gratification, and less likely to be interested in formal education than the well-to-do. Most important is the contention that this deviant cultural pattern is transmitted from generation to generation. Thus, there is a strong implication that poverty is perpetuated by defects in the lifestyle of the poor. These ideas were behind the welfare reform of 1996. Welfare recipients were seen as individuals who needed to learn to value work, stop being "dependent," and stop transmitting deviant values to their children. From this view, the poor have a subculture with values that differ radically from values of the other social classes.

Edward Banfield, an eminent political scientist, has argued that the difference between the poor and the nonpoor is cultural—the poor have a present-time orientation, whereas the nonpoor have a future-time orientation (Banfield 1977). He does not see the present-time orientation of the poor as an adaptation to the hopelessness of their situation. If poverty itself was to be eliminated, the former poor would probably continue to prefer instant gratification, be immoral by middle-class standards, and so on.

A modern example of the culture-of-poverty position can be found in comments made by Lieutenant Governor Andre Bauer, who was running for governor of South Carolina in 2010. In a town hall meeting with state lawmakers and residents, he compared government assistance to feeding stray animals. He said:

> *My grandmother was not a highly educated woman but she told me as a small child to quit feeding stray animals. You know why? Because they breed. You're facilitating the problem if you give an animal or a person ample food supply. They will reproduce, especially ones that don't think too much further than that. And so what you've got to do is you've got to curtail that type of behavior. They don't know any better.* (Quoted in Cary 2010:1)

Bauer went on to say that the government is rewarding bad behavior by giving money to people who don't have to do anything for it (as previously mentioned, opinions similar to this were the driving force behind the welfare reform of 1996).

Critics of the culture-of-poverty hypothesis argue that the poor are an integral part of U.S. society; they do not abandon the dominant values of the society but, rather, retain them while simultaneously holding an alternative set of values focused on day-to-day survival. This alternative set is a result of *adaptation* to the conditions of their environment.

Most Americans believe that poverty is a combination of biological and cultural factors. Judith Chafel reviewed a number of studies on the beliefs of Americans and found that they "view economic privation as a self-inflicted condition, emanating more from personal factors (e.g., effort, ability) than external-structural ones (e.g., an unfavorable labor market, racism). Poverty is seen as inevitable, necessary, and just" (Chafel 1997:434). A 2005 study by Adeola confirms these findings: Even though Americans seem to perceive that the government spends too little on the poor, they also tend to blame poverty on the poor themselves. However, the economic downturn of 2007 may have an effect on people's attitudes toward poverty as more and more people find themselves vulnerable in a struggling economy. In this case, individuals might turn to structural theories to explain poverty.

Structural Theories

In contrast to blaming the biological or cultural deficiencies of the poor, the structural theory states that how society is organized creates poverty and makes certain kinds of people especially vulnerable to being poor.

- **Institutional Discrimination.** Michael Harrington, whose book *The Other America* was instrumental in sparking the federal government's war on poverty, has said, "The real explanation of why the poor are where they are is that they made the mistake of being born to the wrong parents, in the wrong section of the country, in the wrong industry, or in the wrong racial or ethnic groups" (Harrington 1963:21). This is another way of saying that the structural conditions of society are to blame for poverty, not the poor. When the customary ways of doing things, prevailing attitudes and expectations, and accepted structural arrangements work to the disadvantage of the poor, it is called **institutional discrimination**. Let us look at several examples of how the poor are trapped by this type of discrimination.

Most good jobs require a college degree, but the poor cannot afford to send their children to college. Scholarships go to the best-performing students. Children of the poor often do not perform well in school. This underperformance by poor children results from the lack of enriched preschool programs for them and low expectations for them among teachers and administrators. This attitude is reflected in the system of tracking by ability as measured on class-biased examinations. Problems in learning and test taking may also arise because English is their second language. Because poverty is often concentrated geographically and schools are funded primarily by the wealth of their district, children of the poor typically attend inadequately financed schools. All these acts result in a self-fulfilling prophecy—the poor are not expected to do well in school, and they do not. Because they are failures as measured by objective indicators (such as the disproportionately high number of dropouts and discipline problems and the small proportion who desire to go to college), the school feels justified in its discrimination toward the children of the poor.

Another job-related trap for the poor is the way low-end jobs are paid. Peter Edelman argued,

> *The basic problem is the way our economy is structured. There are too many jobs that don't pay enough to let workers get by. Everybody knows that many high-paying manufacturing jobs have disappeared to automation, to other countries, and that those opportunities have been replaced by lower-paying service jobs. But not everybody seems to know what that has done to the income of millions of Americans. They do the best they can every day but don't earn enough to make ends meet.* (Edelman 2001:1–2)

The poor are also trapped because they get sick more often and stay sick longer than the well-to-do. The reasons, of course, are that they cannot afford preventive medicine, proper diets, and proper medical attention when ill. The high incidence of sickness among the poor means either that they will be fired from their jobs or that they will not receive money for the days missed from work (unlike the well-to-do, who usually have jobs with such fringe benefits as sick leave and paid medical insurance). Not receiving a paycheck for extended periods means that the poor will have even less money for proper health care, thereby ensuring an even higher incidence of sickness. Thus, there is a vicious cycle of poverty. The poor tend to remain poor, and their children tend to perpetuate the cycle.

The traditional organization of schools and jobs in U.S. society has limited the opportunities of racial minorities and women. The next two chapters describe at length how these two groups are systematically disadvantaged by the prevailing laws, customs, and expectations of society, so we will only summarize the structural barriers that they face. Racial minorities are deprived of equal opportunities for education, jobs, and income. As a result, African Americans, for example, are half as likely to be wealthy and twice as likely to be poor as Whites. They are also twice as likely as Whites to be unemployed. Structuralists argue that these differences are not the result of flaws in African Americans but rather of historical and current discrimination in communities, schools, banks, and the work world. Similarly, women typically work at less prestigious jobs than do men and, when working at equal-status jobs, receive less pay and have fewer chances for advancement. These differences are not the result of innate gender differences but of personal, social, and societal barriers to equality based on gender.

• **Political Economy of Society.** The basic tenet of capitalism—who gets what is determined by private profit rather than collective need—explains the persistence of poverty. The primacy of maximizing profit works to promote poverty in several ways. First, employers are constrained to pay their workers the least amount possible in wages and benefits. Only a portion of the wealth created by the laborers is distributed to them; the rest goes to the owners for investment and profit. Therefore, employers must keep wages low. That they are successful is demonstrated by the millions of people *who worked full-time but were below the poverty line.*

A second way that the primacy of profit promotes poverty is by maintaining a surplus of undereducated and desperate laborers who will work for very low wages. A large supply of these marginal people (such as minorities, women, and undocumented workers) aids the ownership class by depressing the wages

Angered that political leaders were meeting to discuss ways to protect corporations and bank profits, more than 1,000 protesters marched through the streets of Pittsburgh on September 20, 2009, demanding a real jobs program.

for all workers in good times and provides the obvious category of people to be laid off from work in economic downturns.

A third impact of the primacy of profits in capitalism is that employers make investment decisions without regard for their employees (potential or actual). If costs can be reduced, employers will purchase new technologies to replace workers (such as robots to replace assembly line workers and word processors to replace secretaries). Similarly, owners may shut down a plant and shift their operations to a foreign country where wages are significantly lower.

In sum, the fundamental assumption of capitalism is individual gain without regard for what the resulting behaviors may mean for other people. The capitalist system, then, should not be accepted as a neutral framework within which goods are produced and distributed but rather as an economic system that perpetuates inequality.

A number of political factors complement the workings of the economy to perpetuate poverty. Political decisions made to fight inflation with high interest rates, for example, hurt several industries, particularly automobiles and home construction, causing high unemployment.

The powerful in society also use their political clout to keep society unequal. For example, they resist efforts to raise the minimum wage, and they seek to reduce or eliminate government programs to help the poor. Clearly, the affluent in a capitalist society will resist efforts to redistribute their wealth to the disadvantaged. Their political efforts are, rather, to increase their benefits at the expense of the poor and the powerless.

In summary, the structural explanation of poverty rests on the assumption that the way society is organized perpetuates poverty, not the characteristics of poor people. The reality is that the causes of poverty are very complicated, as is evident by the diversity of the poverty population. In his ethnography of the working poor, David Shipler noted,

> *In reality, people do not fit easily into myths or anti-myths, of course. The working individuals in this book are neither helpless nor omnipotent, but stand on various points along the spectrum between polar opposites of personal and societal responsibility. Each person's life is the mixed product of bad choices and bad fortune, of roads not taken and roads cut off by the accident of birth or circumstance. It is difficult to find someone whose poverty is not somehow related to his or her unwise behavior—to drop out of school, to have a baby out of wedlock, to do drugs, to be chronically late to work. And it is difficult to find behavior that is not somehow related to the inherited conditions of being poorly parented, poorly educated, poorly housed in neighborhoods from which no distant horizon of possibility can be seen.* (2004:6–7)

Whether the causes of poverty are personal, structural, or a combination of both, 39.8 million individuals live below the federal poverty threshold, and the costs to society are enormous.

COSTS OF POVERTY

Almost 43.6 million people in the United States were officially poor in 2009. These people and those just above the poverty line generally receive inferior educations, live in substandard housing, are disproportionately exposed to toxic chemicals, are malnourished, and have health problems (see "A Closer Look: It's a Disaster for the Poor"). Let's further examine some of the consequences and economic costs of poverty.

Crime

The United States, by far, has the highest rate of violent crimes of any industrialized nation. The reasons for this high rate are complex, with many sources, but two stand out—the extraordinarily high rate of poverty in the United States and the very high degree of inequality in the United States (i.e., the gap between the rich and the poor).

A high unemployment rate, for example, leads to higher rates of property crimes, homicide rates, and drug/alcohol abuse (Currie 1998). In fact, half of male prisoners are unemployed when arrested (Oppenheim and MacGregor 2006). The poor and especially minority poor are disproportionately in prison (Reiman 2004).

Family Problems

Poverty damages families. Poor couples are twice as likely to divorce as more affluent couples. Jobless people are three to four times less likely to marry than those with jobs. Two-thirds of teenagers who give birth come from poor or low-income families, and their children are more likely to be poor (Zimmerman 2008).

Health Problems

According to the U.S. Census Bureau, in 2009, 50.7 million people (7.2 million children) had no private or public health insurance. About 15.8 million Hispanics, 8.1 million African Americans, and 23.7 million non-Hispanic Whites were uninsured. "When uninsured people get sick, they are less likely to seek medical attention until they are really sick and it is more expensive to treat them. Then, if they were not poor already, medical bills can push them into poverty. So poverty helps make people sick, and being sick helps make people poor" (Oppenheim and MacGregor 2006:2). Further, the uninsured may use emergency medical

A CLOSER LOOK

IT'S A DISASTER FOR THE POOR

Poverty and Vulnerability

Most people are aware of some of the effects of poverty, like the poor are less likely to have health care and more likely to suffer from illness. What is less obvious are the other vulnerabilities that result from being poor. The following examples demonstrate that socioeconomic status can make a real life-and-death difference:

- When the *Titanic* was rammed by an iceberg in 1912, 3 percent of female first-class passengers were killed; 16 percent of female second-class passengers were killed; and 45 percent of female third-class passengers were killed. In this case, the higher the economic status of the individual, the greater the probability of survival.
- The United Nations has determined a "disaster risk index" for countries that shows a direct correlation between vulnerability and poverty. Being poor greatly affects the risk of being a victim in an earthquake, a tropical cyclone, and a flood (United Nations 2004). This relationship appears to be largely the effect of the quality and structural soundness of housing. Obviously, housing that is the least expensive may also be the least structurally sound and most vulnerable.
- In August 2005, Hurricane Katrina devastated the city of New Orleans. A close look at the numbers indicates that New Orleans was in trouble long before the hurricane. The Lower Ninth Ward of New Orleans was one of the most heavily damaged areas of the city. The residents of the Ninth Ward were 99 percent Black with a median household income of $19,918. Most important, 32 percent of residents in the Lower Ninth Ward had no vehicle in which to evacuate (Wagner and Edwards 2007).
- An Associated Press analysis of government data on industrial air pollution shows that Black Americans are 79 percent more likely than Whites to live in neighborhoods where industrial pollution is suspected of posing the greatest health danger. Residents in neighborhoods with the highest pollution scores also tend to be poorer, less educated, and more often unemployed (Pace 2005).
- Research has shown that lower socioeconomic status is correlated with unsafe conditions that make the poor vulnerable to death by fire. These conditions may include absent or defective smoke detectors, use of space heaters, overcrowding, less fire-resistant housing, and electrical or heating malfunctions in poor households. Analyzing data from all large U.S. metropolitan counties, Hannon and Shai (2003) found that a high proportion of African Americans combined with low income appears to be associated with extremely high fire-death rates. They concluded: "It appears that the disadvantages associated with institutional racism (physical segregation and social isolation) exacerbate the problems of low income in relation to fire deaths" (2003:134).
- In July 1995, Chicago suffered a weeklong heat wave; temperatures soared, and 739 people died. In *Heat Wave,* sociologist Eric Klinenberg demonstrated how the patterns of mortality from this disaster reflect the inequalities that divide Chicago. Most of those who died were elderly, and most lived alone. He states,

  > The conditions that proved most consequential in the heat wave include the literal social isolation of poor senior citizens, particularly in the city's most violent areas. . . . [Most of the Blacks who died were] segregated and ghettoized in community areas with high levels of abandoned housing stock, empty lots, depleted commercial infrastructure, population decline, degraded sidewalks, parks and streets, and impoverished institutions. (quoted in Yardley 2002:32)

services in place of a regular doctor, as hospitals are required to render treatment regardless of insurance or ability to pay.

The infant mortality rate in some poor urban neighborhoods exceeds the rate in developing countries. The United States has a higher infant mortality rate than most other industrialized countries. Reflecting the disproportionate number of African Americans in poverty, infants born to African American mothers are twice as likely to die before their first birthday than infants of White mothers (Children's Defense Fund 2004a). In Mississippi, for example, the infant mortality rate for non-White babies was 17.0 in 2005, compared to a rate of 6.6 for White babies (*Time* 2007b).

Problems in School

In addition to health problems, children in the poorest families are six times as likely as their affluent counterparts to drop out of high school. Marian Wright Edelman, president and founder of the Children's Defense Fund, aptly stated,

> *Forty years after President Johnson declared a War on Poverty and signed the Civil Rights Act of 1964 into law, 50 years after* Brown v. Board of Education, *108 years after* Plessy v. Ferguson, *and 141 years after President Lincoln's Emancipation Proclamation, a Black child still lacks a fair chance to live, learn, thrive, and contribute in America. Our nation's doors of economic and educational opportunity still have not opened to all of God's children who are Black, Brown, White, Native and Asian American, and poor. (Children's Defense Fund 2004a:1)*

Economic Costs

What are the consequences for society if a significant proportion of the populace is poor? In economic terms, the cost is very high. Holzer and colleagues (2007) examined these economic costs in detail and estimated that the costs to the United States associated with childhood poverty total about $500 billion per year. These costs are the inevitable consequence of reduced productivity and economic output by the poor, increased criminal behavior, and poor health.

> *Most arguments for reducing poverty in the U.S., especially among children, rest on a moral case for doing so—one that emphasizes the unfairness of child poverty, and how it runs counter to our national creed of equal opportunity for all. But there is also an economic case for reducing child poverty. When children grow up in poverty, they are somewhat more likely than non-poor children to have low earnings as adults, which in turn reflects lower workforce productivity. They are also somewhat more likely to engage in crime (though that's not the case for the vast majority) and to have poor health later in life. Their reduced productive activity generates a direct loss of goods and services to the U.S. economy. (Holzer et al. 2007:1)*

If poverty were eliminated through jobs that pay a living wage and adequate monetary assistance to the permanently disabled or elderly, the entire society would prosper from the increased purchasing power and the larger tax base. But economic considerations, though important, are not as crucial as humanitarian ones. A nation that can afford it must, if it calls itself civilized, eliminate the physical and psychological misery associated with poverty.

ELIMINATION OF POVERTY

Must some portion of U.S. society live in poverty? Is there a way to get everyone above the poverty level to a level at which they are not deprived of the basics of adequate nutrition, health care, and housing? The remainder of this chapter enumerates some assumptions that appear basic to achieving such a goal.

Assumption 1: Poverty is a social problem and the source of other social problems; therefore, it must be eliminated. As presented in the previous section, poverty is correlated with crime, teenage pregnancy, divorce, poor health, and a host of societal problems. The costs to society are too extensive to ignore.

Assumption 2: Poverty can be eliminated in the United States. "There is no justification for ignoring the millions of people who live in poverty; no longer should they be invisible to our public policy makers. To propose tenable solutions for poverty, the general population must become aware of the persistent poverty problems" (Trent, Caputo, and Baker 2004:20).

The United States could reduce its defense budget ($654.7 billion for fiscal year 2009), by many billions of dollars without threatening national security. The United States spends more than the next ten biggest defense spenders combined (see Chapter 18). In fact, the U.S. accounts for 41.5 percent of the world's total military spending, followed distantly by China (5.8 percent of the world's spending). We could spend $100 billion less a year and still be number one militarily. The resulting savings, called the Peace Dividend, could be committed to bringing all people in the United States above the poverty line.

Similarly, we could make a commitment to help children living in poverty, with a commitment like the one we make to meet a national emergency. In the words of the late Albert Shanker, president of the American Federation of Teachers,

> *When a great disaster, like a hurricane or an earthquake, strikes people in our country, the president often declares a state of emergency. This mobilizes resources; it cuts through red tape; and it focuses attention on the people who are in danger so they get the help they need—and get it right away. . . . Victims of floods and earthquakes didn't bring their misfortunes on themselves, and we give them help in rebuilding their lives. How can we deny poor children the chance to build theirs? (Shanker 1992a:E9)*

Or sometimes the government makes a huge financial commitment to bolster a sagging part of the economy. If, for example, the government can agree to bail out the deregulated, imprudent, and sometimes fraudulent savings and loan industry then surely the government is able to spend a fraction of that amount to lift 39.8 million people out of poverty.

Assumption 3: Poverty is caused by a lack of resources, not a deviant value system. Basic to a program designed to eliminate poverty is the identification of what keeps some people in a condition of poverty. Is it lack of money and power or the maintenance of deviant values and lifestyles? This question is fundamental because the answer determines the method for eliminating poverty. The culture-of-poverty proponents would address non-middle-class traits. The target would be the poor themselves, and the goal would be to make them more socially acceptable. Developing the social competence of the poor—not changing the system—would bring an end to poverty. This approach treats the symptom, not the disease. The disease can be cured only by attacking its sources within the society—the structural arrangements that maintain inequality. Thus, the attack must be directed at the structural changes that will enable lower-class people to earn a living wage to support their families adequately and to help their children succeed in school.

Assumption 4: Poverty is not simply a matter of deficient income; it results from other inequities in the society as well. Poverty involves a reinforcing pattern of restricted opportunities, deficient community services, powerful predators who profit from the poor, institutional racism and sexism (see Chapters 8 and 9), and unequal distribution of resources. These problems can be eliminated through structural changes, including (1) the enforcement of the laws regarding equal opportunity for jobs, advancement, and schooling, and (2) the redistribution of power on the local and national levels. The present system works to keep the poor powerless. What is needed, rather, is the organization of the poor into groups with power to determine, or at least to shape, policy in local communities. The poor need to have some power over school policies. They need to have a voice in the decisions about the distribution of resources within the community (such as money for parks and recreation, fire protection, street maintenance, and refuse collection). The U.S. system of representative democracy is one of "winner take all" and is therefore to blame for the powerlessness of all minorities. A system of proportional representation would guarantee a degree of power. A third structural change involves an increasing reliance on planning and action at the national level to alleviate the causes of poverty.

Assumption 5: Poverty cannot be eliminated by the efforts of the poor themselves. The poor have neither the power nor the resources to bring about the structural changes necessary to eliminate poverty. Some poor people escape poverty by their own efforts, but most will remain poor unless the people and groups with the power and the resources change the system. This is not to say that the poor cannot have some effect. They can, but usually only indirectly through influential people or groups who become concerned about their plight.

Assumption 6: Poverty cannot be eliminated by the private sector of the economy. Assuming that private enterprises will not engage in unprofitable activities, we can assume also that private enterprise efforts will never by themselves eliminate poverty. In other words, private profit will tend to subvert the human needs that are of public concern; businesses will not provide jobs that they consider unnecessary or not immediately profitable, nor will they voluntarily stop activities that are profitable (e.g., renting deteriorated housing because the unimproved land may increase in value, or charging exorbitant interest rates to the poor, or lobbying to keep certain occupational categories outside minimum-wage restrictions, or moving their operations to another state or nation where wages are lower).

Conventional wisdom, however, suggests that private business is the answer because it will generate new and better-paying jobs. This solution simply will not work because the new poor, as noted earlier, differ dramatically from the old poor. Some of the new poor are workers who have been displaced by robots, computers, and other labor-saving devices. The jobs of others have moved—from the urban core to the suburbs, to other regions of the country, or to other countries, or have been lost due to the recession. The jobs were lost because of rational business decisions. In short, the private sector, with its emphasis on profit (and therefore efficiency), will not generate the new jobs needed to eliminate poverty.

Assumption 7: Poverty will not be eliminated by a rising economy. A common assumption is that a growing economy will help everyone—"a rising tide lifts all boats." This assumption has some validity, as evidenced by the very robust economy of the late 1990s, when unemployment dipped to 4 percent, jobs were plentiful, and wages for the bottom segment of the population shifted upward. But even in this untroubled economic time period, the lot of the poor did not improve much. Actually, affordable housing became even more of a problem because much low-cost housing was gentrified (refurbished for upscale renters) or demolished for office buildings or other uses irrelevant to the poor. Even in the best of times, the conditions of poverty limit and deny. Cities with low tax bases do not provide the needed social services such as pre- and postnatal health care and good schools. During the boom times of the 1990s, the federal government cut programs for the poor such as Head Start, Food Stamps, and Aid to Families with Dependent Children (AFDC). Employers do not have jobs with decent wages and benefits, even in good times, for those with inadequate education and training.

Assumption 8: Volunteer help from well-meaning individuals, groups, and organizations will not eliminate poverty. In 1988, presidential candidate George H. W. Bush called for "a thousand points of light" as the solution to social problems such as poverty. Bush meant that charities and volunteers are the answers, not big government. At one level, this makes good sense. That is, churches and private organizations can and do provide food for the hungry, shelters for the homeless, and emergency care for the victims of natural disasters. In Fort Collins, Colorado, for example, a retired physician began a health clinic for indigent children. With volunteer help and donations, this clinic provides free medical and dental care for thousands of poor youth each year. This wonderful program provides services not provided by the city, county, state, and federal governments. It is also rarely found in other localities.

There are two problems with leaving poverty to charities. The first is that since 1980, the money received by charities and the number of adults volunteering their services to charities has declined. These declines occurred at a time of increasing need by the poor. The second problem is that because this plan is voluntary, the poor in many communities will be denied adequate food, clothing, health care, and shelter. Only a national program will ensure that the needs of every poor person are met.

In 2001, President George W. Bush proposed a variation on his father's "thousand points of light." This was for the federal government to provide funds to religious organizations that help the needy ("faith-based initiative"). In effect, the plan proposed to allow religious charities that serve the poor to compete for $8 billion annually in government funds (Benedetto 2001). Although laudable in many respects, given the important contributions by religious charities such as Catholic Charities and the Salvation Army, there are several problems with the plan. First, there is the danger that the churches will use federal resources to try to win converts to their religion, clearly an unconstitutional activity. Second, the government may bypass religious organizations that are not Christian or otherwise mainstream (e.g., Moslems, Buddhists, Scientologists), thereby missing important clusters of poor people. A third objection is that the White House might funnel funds on a political basis rather than according to need, such as to Catholic organizations to win the Catholic vote. Finally, this plan misses the essence of a federal plan to solve the poverty crisis across the United States (J. Jackson 2001).

In 2001, former President George W. Bush proposed a faith-based initiative, where religious charities could compete for federal money to serve the poor.

Assumption 9: Poverty will not be eliminated by the efforts of state and local governments. A basic tenet of political conservatism is decentralization of government. Indeed, that was the cornerstone of the 1996 welfare reform. Relatively small and locally based governmental units are believed to be best suited for understanding and meeting the needs of the people. This theory, though logical, has not always worked in practice. In fact, it has increased the problems of some localities.

A good deal of money is gathered and dispensed at the city, county, and state levels for the purpose of alleviating the misery associated with poverty. Some federal programs function only through local units of government. The basic problem is that these local units differ dramatically in their willingness and resources to attack poverty. There are vast differences among states in levels of welfare assistance. Social welfare expenditures encompass three different types: (1) medical assistance (payments to health care providers on behalf of low-income persons); (2) social services (for example, homeless shelters and other programs); and (3) cash assistance for the poor. Overall, states have greatly reduced their welfare spending on cash assistance since the 1996 welfare reform. In 1996, states spent 76 percent of their welfare monies on cash assistance. In 2007, cash assistance to the poor was only 5.2 percent of all social welfare spending (see Figure 7.4) (Gais, Dadayan, and Bae 2009). This percentage also greatly differs by state, with some states spending much less of their funds on cash assistance.

Because many politicians believe that relatively high welfare benefits attract poor people from other states and because many states are in a fiscal crisis, there is a current trend to reduce welfare benefits at the state level. Many state legislatures also reflect the current mood to reduce government, beginning with taxes and welfare.

Assumption 10: Poverty is a national problem and must be attacked with massive, nationwide programs financed largely and organized by the federal government. Poverty must be addressed at the federal level to ensure that the poor throughout the nation will receive equal benefits and services. Poverty must be attacked nationally to deal with the structural problems that cause poverty (e.g., the changing economy that results in too few jobs, declining real wages for all but the top 20 percent, uneven resources for education, and a health care delivery system that misses or overlooks so many). Poverty must be handled at the national level to ensure that the programs are funded uniformly.

FIGURE 7.4

State and Local Social Welfare Spending, 2007

Source: U.S. Bureau of the Census, 2009. "Federal, State, and Local Governments: State and Local Government Finances," http://www.census.gov/govs/estimate

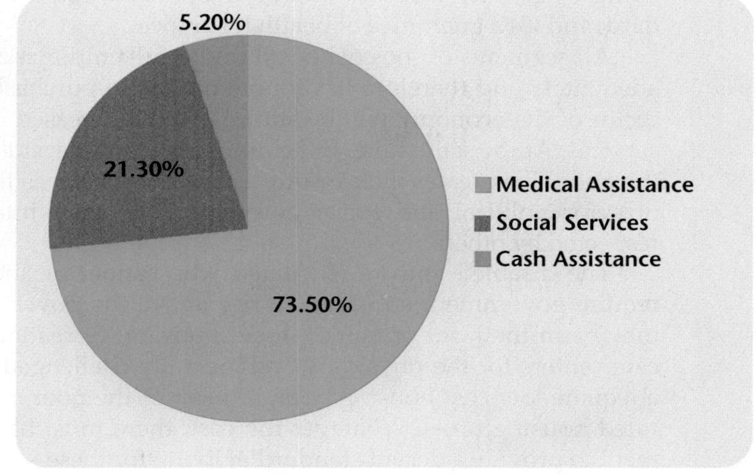

Poverty can be eliminated through the massive infusion of money and compensatory programs, coupled with federal mandates and state cooperation. A federal program funded by taxes (which, by definition, will mean some states will underpay and others will overpay) is a form of socialism because it redistributes resources and therefore is suspect to many. Government control and government subsidies are not new phenomena in the United States, yet it is a curious fact that subsidies for the poor are generally decried while other subsidies go unnoticed or even praised. The federal government has subsidized, for example, defense industries (loans), the oil industry (oil depletion allowance), all corporations (tax write-offs), students (government scholarships and interest-free loans), professors (research grants), homeowners (the interest on mortgages and home taxes is deductible), churches (no property tax or income tax), and farmers (farm subsidies).

What can the federal government do to achieve the goal of getting all people permanently above the poverty line? Three quite different programs are needed because there are three kinds of poor people: (1) those who are unemployed (or employed at low-wage jobs); (2) those who cannot work because they are too old, are physically or mentally handicapped, or are mothers with dependent children; and (3) the children of the poor.

The able-bodied poor need three things: (1) adequate training, (2) guaranteed employment, and (3) a guaranteed minimum income that provides the necessities of food, clothing, shelter, and medical care. New jobs and even new occupational categories must be created. These new jobs may involve working as "indigenous" neighborhood social workers, teachers' aides, child care providers, community organizers, or research assistants. These new opportunities would be in the service sector of the economy rather than in the goods-producing sector, where automation occurs. Other jobs could be in such public works areas as highway construction, mass transit, improving the nation's infrastructure, recycling waste materials, and park maintenance. An important component of such jobs is social usefulness. Jobs with high social productivity would also have some beneficial by-products (latent consequences) in the form of less estrangement of workers from their jobs and overall improvements for the society itself.

For poor parents in the workforce, at least three things are needed: (1) subsidized child care that is safe and nurturing; (2) if their employer does not pay a living wage, then a subsidy that brings their wages up to the minimum standard; and (3) a guarantee of health insurance.

All segments of society benefit under full employment. If the poor are paid adequately and therefore have more money to purchase products, the private sector of the economy will be stimulated by increased demand for goods and services. At the same time, full employment and decent pay will give power to the poor. The greater their resources are, the greater is their likelihood to organize for political and social power, to vote their interests, and to become respected by others.

The disabled and incapacitated who cannot or should not be employed require government subsidies to rise above the poverty line. These subsidies may be in the form of money, food, housing, recreational facilities, or special care centers for the physically and mentally challenged. An important need is adequate low-cost housing because most of the poor currently live in deteriorated housing units. Whatever the cost, there must be a nationwide commitment to provide a decent standard of living for these people.

About 35 percent of the poor in the United States are children. Their economic disadvantage translates into educational disadvantages. Many drop out of school for dead-end jobs or even criminal activities. How can this cycle of disadvantage be broken? One clear need is for compensatory programs. Head Start is one federally funded program that has documented positive effects for economically disadvantaged children such as improved cognitive, language, and social-emotional development. The problem with Head Start is that it is underfunded, with only four in ten eligible children able to be included.

Although education is critical, the problem with this emphasis on education (and with alleviating poverty in general) is the difficulty of providing enough socially useful jobs with a decent U.S. standard of pay. The creation of jobs, then, is the key to eliminating poverty. Because most of these jobs will no doubt be in the public sector of the economy, the government must divert its best minds to tackling this immense problem.

Universal programs such as these are necessary if the United States is to get everyone above the absolute minimum level of economic security. This goal is attainable because the productive capacity of the United States is great enough to make it possible without too much sacrifice. If implemented, they will eliminate the human suffering associated with extreme deprivation.

CHAPTER REVIEW

1. According to the government's arbitrary dividing line, (which minimizes the actual extent of poverty) 13.2 percent of the U.S. population (2008) is officially poor. Disproportionately represented in this category are African Americans, Latinos, Native Americans, children, and women (especially female heads of families; DeNavas-Walt, Proctor, and Smith 2009).
2. December 2007 marked the beginning of an economic recession in the United States, which resulted in the highest rates of poverty since 1996.
3. The poor are not poor because they refuse to work. Most adult poor work at low wages, cannot find work, work part time, are ill or disabled, or work in the informal economy. A full-time minimum wage worker earns only 81 percent of the poverty level for a family of three.
4. In 1996, the federal welfare program was reformed. Assistance programs to the poor were drastically cut, and time limits were set for welfare recipients.
5. Most governmental assistance is targeted to the affluent rather than the poor. Tax expenditures and other subsidies provide enormous benefits to the already affluent, which further redistributes the nation's wealth upward.
6. Rather than the poor receiving special advantages, research shows that the poor pay more than the nonpoor for many services.
7. One explanation for poverty is that the poor themselves are in some way deficient. The innate inferiority hypothesis, for example, is a variant of social Darwinism promoted by Arthur Jensen and Richard Herrnstein. This hypothesis states that certain categories of people are disadvantaged because they are less well endowed mentally.
8. Another position that blames the poor for their condition is the culture of poverty hypothesis. This hypothesis contends that the poor are qualitatively different in values and lifestyles from the affluent and that these differences explain their poverty and the poverty of their children.
9. Critics of the culture-of-poverty and the innate inferiority hypotheses charge that in blaming the victim, both theories ignore how social conditions trap individuals and groups in poverty.
10. In contrast to blaming biological or cultural deficiencies of the poor, structural theories focus on how society is organized in a way that creates poverty and makes certain people vulnerable to being poor.

11. Poverty is correlated with crime, teenage pregnancy, divorce, poor health, and a host of societal problems.
12. The elimination of poverty requires (a) a commitment to accomplish that goal; (b) a program based on the assumption that poverty results from a lack of resources rather than from a deviant value system; (c) a program based on the assumption that poverty results from inequities in society; (d) recognition that poverty cannot be eliminated by the efforts of the poor themselves, by the private sector of the economy, by charitable individuals or groups, or by the efforts of state and local governments alone; and (e) recognition that poverty is a national problem and must be attacked by massive, nationwide programs largely financed and organized by the federal government.
13. Three quite different programs are needed because there are three kinds of poverty. The unemployed or underpaid need adequate training, guaranteed employment, and a guaranteed minimal income that is adequate to provide necessities. The disabled and incapacitated require government subsidies to meet their needs. Finally, the children of the poor need education and opportunities to break the poverty cycle.

■ KEY TERMS

Poverty. Standard of living below the minimum needed for the maintenance of adequate diet, health, and shelter.

Official poverty line, or poverty threshold. Arbitrary line computed by multiplying the cost of a basic nutritionally adequate diet by three.

Feminization of poverty. Viewed erroneously as a trend for contemporary women to be more economically vulnerable than men. This view obscures the fact that women have always been poorer than men, especially older women and women of color.

New poor. Poor who are displaced by new technologies or whose jobs have moved away to the suburbs, to other regions of the country, or out of the country. They have less hope of escaping poverty than did the old poor.

Old poor. Poor of an earlier generation, who had hopes of breaking out of poverty because unskilled and semiskilled jobs were plentiful.

Working poor. People who work but remain below the poverty threshold.

Near poor. People whose incomes are above the poverty threshold but below 125 percent of that threshold.

Severely poor. People whose cash incomes are at half the poverty line or less.

Personal Responsibility and Work Opportunity Reconciliation Act (PRWORA). In 1996, Congress passed this act, which reformed the welfare system. PRWORA shifted welfare programs from the federal government to the states; mandated that welfare recipients find work within 2 years; limited welfare assistance to 5 years; and cut various federal assistance programs targeted for the poor by $54.5 billion over 6 years.

Welfare. Government monies and services provided to the poor.

Wealthfare. Government subsidies to the nonpoor.

Tax expenditures. Legal tax loopholes that allow the affluent to escape paying certain taxes and therefore to receive a subsidy (e.g., the tax deduction to homeowners).

Regressive tax. Tax rate that remains the same for all people, rich or poor. The result is that poor people pay a larger proportion of their wealth than do affluent people.

Social Darwinism. Belief that the place of people in the social stratification system is a function of their ability and effort.

Meritocracy. Social classification based on ability.

Blaming the victim. Belief that some individuals are poor, criminals, or school dropouts because they have a flaw within them, which ignores the social factors affecting their behaviors.

Self-fulfilling prophecy. Event that occurs because it is predicted. That is, the prophecy is fulfilled because people alter their behavior to conform to the prediction.

Culture-of-poverty hypothesis. View that the poor are qualitatively different in values and lifestyles from the rest of society and that these cultural differences explain continued poverty.

Institutional discrimination. When the social arrangements and accepted ways of doing things in society disadvantage minority groups.

■ SUCCEED WITH PEARSON mysoclab www.mysoclab.com

Experience, Discover, Observe, Evaluate

MySocLab is designed just for you. Each chapter features a pre-test and post-test to help you learn and review key concepts and terms.

Experience sociology in action with dynamic visual activities, videos, and readings to enhance your learning experience. Complete the following activities at www.mysoclab.com.

Social Explorer is an interactive application that allows you to explore Census data through interactive maps.

- Explore the Social Explorer Map: *Change in Poverty Levels in the U.S. from 1970 to 2000*

The Core Concepts in Sociology video clips offer a real-world perspective on sociological concepts.

- Watch *Consequences of Poverty*

MySocLibrary includes primary source readings from classic and contemporary sociologists.

- Read Block, Korteweg, & Woodward with Schiller & Mazid, *The Compassion Gap in American Poverty Policy*; Marchevsky & Theoharis, *The End of Welfare As We Know It: An Overview of the PRWORA*; Rice, *The Threat of Global Poverty*

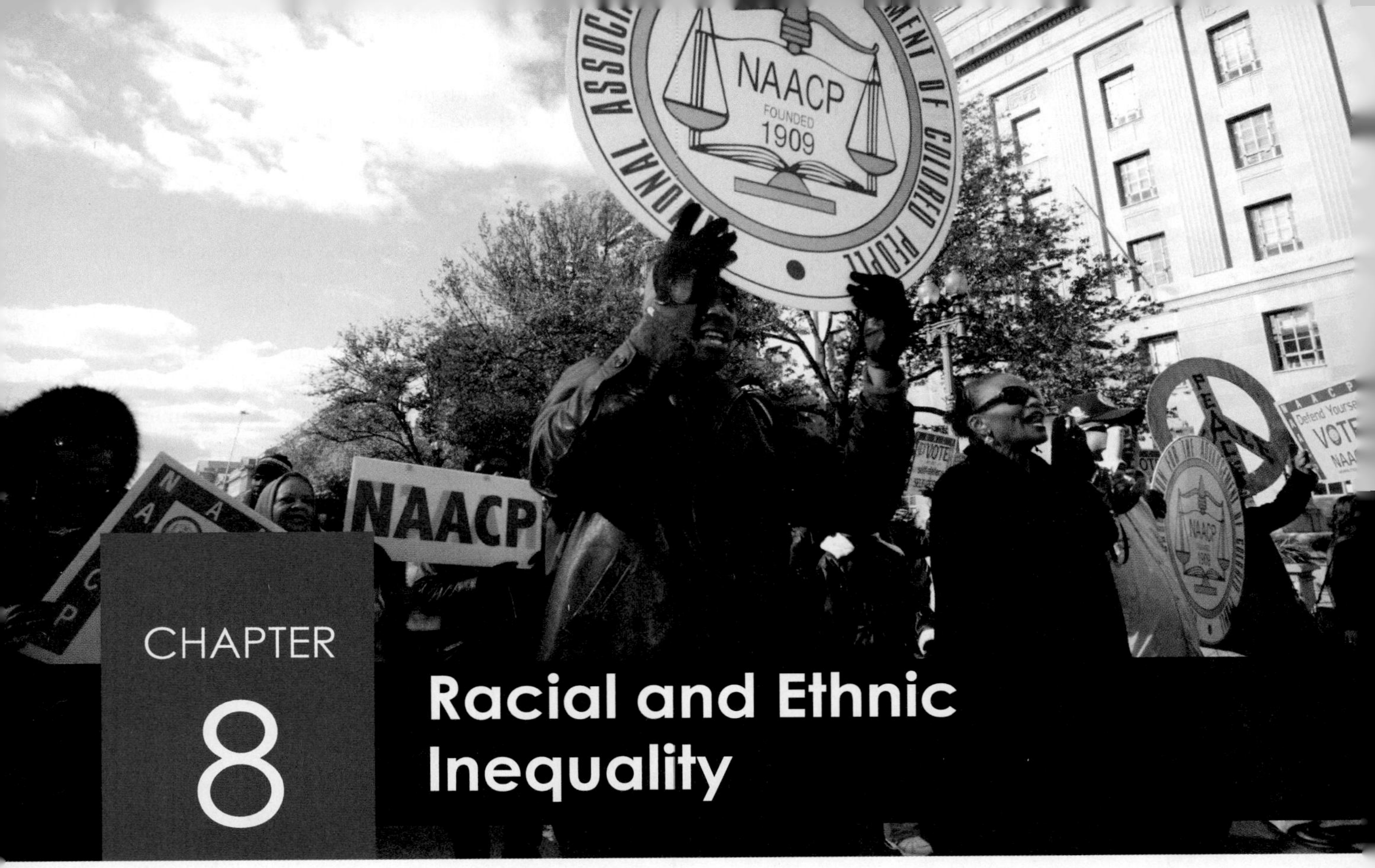

CHAPTER 8

Racial and Ethnic Inequality

Racial oppression makes the United States very distinctive, for it is the only major Western country that was explicitly founded on racial oppression. Today, as in the past, this oppression is not a minor addition to U.S. society's structure but rather is systemic across all major institutions. Oppression of non-European groups is part of the deep social structure.

—Joe R. Feagin

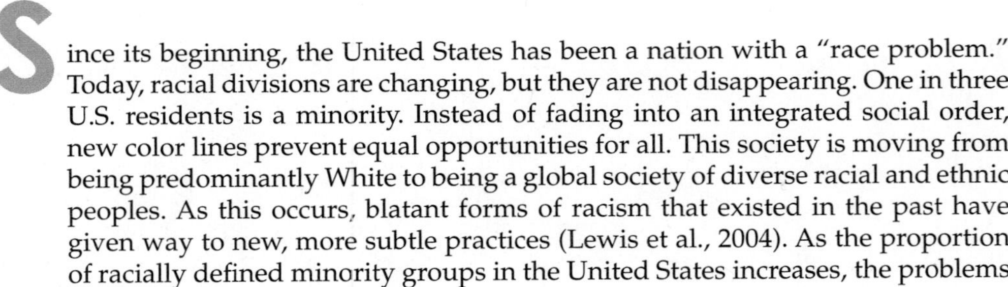

Since its beginning, the United States has been a nation with a "race problem." Today, racial divisions are changing, but they are not disappearing. One in three U.S. residents is a minority. Instead of fading into an integrated social order, new color lines prevent equal opportunities for all. This society is moving from being predominantly White to being a global society of diverse racial and ethnic peoples. As this occurs, blatant forms of racism that existed in the past have given way to new, more subtle practices (Lewis et al., 2004). As the proportion of racially defined minority groups in the United States increases, the problems they face become more and more the problems of the entire society. This chapter focuses on how structured racial inequality produces social problems.

HOW TO THINK ABOUT RACIAL AND ETHNIC INEQUALITY

Why are some groups dominant and others subordinate? The basic reason is power—power derived from superior numbers, technology, weapons, property, or economic resources. Those holding superior power in a society—the **dominant group**—establish a system of inequality by dominating less powerful groups. This system of inequality is then maintained by power. The terms *dominant group* and *minority group* describe power differences regardless of the size of the groups.

Racial inequalities produce opportunities for some and oppression for others. The word *oppression* comes from a Latin word meaning "to crush," and thus racial oppression means keeping people of color down—that is, crushing them physically and in many other ways (Feagin 2006:8). Racial oppression reaches far back into the past of the United States. The racial hierarchy with White groups of European origin at the top and people of color at the bottom serves important functions for society and for certain categories of people. It ensures, for example, that some people are available to do society's dirty work at low wages. The racial hierarchy reinforces the status quo. It enables the powerful to retain their control and their advantages.

Racial stratification offers better occupational opportunities, income, and education to White people. These patterns are found throughout the world even as societies become more racially and ethnically diverse. Today, many racially defined people are becoming even more marginalized by global restructuring (discussed in Chapter 14), which includes sweatshops that employ people of color, new fiscal policies imposed on developing countries, and disruptions of national and local economies that force people to migrate in search of better jobs and better lives. Racial inequalities shape social relations around the world.

This chapter examines racial inequality from several vantage points. First, we outline the important features of racial and ethnic groups. We then profile four racial minority groups: African Americans, Latinos, Asian Americans, and Native Americans. Next, we examine explanations of racial inequality, followed by a look at its effect on Blacks and Hispanics in terms of income, jobs, education, and health. Finally, the chapter turns to contemporary trends in racial and ethnic relations.

The theme of the chapter is that racial problems have structural foundations. This framework challenges myths about race and "the race problem." Many people think that the United States is now a "color blind" society where race no longer matters. They claim that the election of the first African American president in U.S. history reflects a postracial society. But despite the tremendous significance of President Obama's electoral victory, and despite the changing character of racism, our society remains structured by racial inequality. In this chapter we show that racial divides persist and that minority groups lack the same opportunities as everyone else. Keep in mind that minorities are not to blame for the race problem. Instead, the cause lies in our race-based system of social rights and resources. Keep in mind that our emphasis on persistent racial domination does not mean that minorities are passive victims of oppression. Their histories are filled with human agency and for centuries, racial minorities in the United States have fought against oppression, both as individuals and in groups.

RACIAL AND ETHNIC MINORITIES

Racial categories are a basis of power relations and group position. Because race relations are power relations, conflict (or at least the potential for conflict) is always present. Overt conflict is most likely when minority groups attempt to change the distribution of power. Size is not crucial in determining whether a group is the most powerful. A numerical minority may in fact have more political representation than the majority, as is the case in South Africa. Thus, the most important characteristic of a **minority group** is that it is dominated by a more powerful group.

Determining who is a minority is largely a matter of history, politics, and judgment—both social and political. Population characteristics other than race and ethnicity—such as age, gender, or religious preference—are sometimes used to designate minority status. However, race and ethnicity are the characteristics used most often to define the minority and majority populations in contemporary U.S. society (O'Hare 1992:5).

Sociologists agree that race is socially constructed. This means that some groups are racially defined, even though races per se, do not exist. What does exist is the *idea* that races are distinct biological categories. Races are thought to be physically distinguishable populations that share a common ancestry. But despite the common belief, social scientists now reject the biological concept of race. Scientific examination of the human genome finds no genetic differences between the so-called races. Fossil and DNA evidence show that humans are all one race, evolved in the last 100,000 years from the same small number of tribes that migrated from Africa and colonized the world (Angier 2000; American Sociological Association 2003; Mukhopadhyay and Henze 2003; Bean, et al., 2004). Although there is no such thing as biological race, races are real insofar as they are *socially defined*. In other words, racial categories *operate* as if they are real. Racial categories are a mechanism for sorting people in society. They structure and segregate our neighborhoods, our schools, our churches, and our relationships (Higginbotham and Andersen 2009).

Racial classification in the United States is based on a Black–White dichotomy—that is, the construction of two opposing categories into which all people fit. However, social definitions of race have changed throughout the nation's history. At different points in the past, "race has taken on different meanings. Many of the people considered White and thought of as the majority group are descendants of immigrants who at one time were believed to be racially distinct from native-born White Americans, the majority of whom were Protestants" (Higginbotham and Andersen 2009:41). Racial categories vary in different parts of the country and around the world. Someone classified as "Black" in the United States might be considered "White" in Brazil and "Colored" (a category distinguished from both Black and White) in South Africa (Bamshad and Olson 2003:80). In the United States, a Black–White color line has always been complicated by regional racial divides. Today, the rapidly growing presence of Latino and Asian immigrants and the resurgence of Native American identification have changed the meaning and boundaries of racial categories (Lewis, Kryson, and Harris 2004:5). Their non-White racial status marks them as "other" and denies them many opportunities (Pyke 2004:55). Global events also complicate the color lines. Since the terrorist attacks on the World Trade Center and the Pentagon, Arab Americans, Muslims, and people of Middle-Eastern descent (viewed by many as a single entity) are stereotyped as different and possibly dangerous.

Racial Categories

In Chapter 5, we discussed current immigration patterns that are reshaping the U.S. racial landscape. Immigration from Asia, Latin America, and the Caribbean is also changing the character of race and ethnic relations. Sociologists Michael Omi and Howard Winant use the term **racial formation** to mean that society is continually creating and transforming racial categories (1994:55). For example, groups once self-defined by their ethnic backgrounds such as Mexican Americans and Japanese Americans are racialized as "Hispanics" and "Asian Americans." Middle Easterners coming from such countries as Syria, Lebanon, Egypt, and Iran are commonly grouped together and called "Arabs."

The U.S. government has changed its racial categories over time. The U.S. Census Bureau, which measures race on the basis of self-identification, revised its racial categories for the 2000 Census. In 2000, for the first time, people were allowed to record themselves in two or more racial categories. Of the U.S. population, 2.4 percent, or 7 million people, identified themselves as multiracial, reporting that they were of two races. The option of choosing more than one race provides a more accurate and visible portrait of the multiracial population in the United States. The 2010 Census provides, for the first time, a glimpse at the evolution of racial identification. Of all racial categories, the Two or More Races population was one of the fastest-growing, increasing approximately one-third between 2000 and 2010 Census. "Those who were children in 2000 and were identified as one race by their parents may respond differently as adults today, and select more than one race" (El Nasser 2010:1A–2A). In addition, marrying across racial lines is on the increase, as attitudes toward interracial unions become more tolerant. Already, children are much more likely than adults to identify themselves as multiracial. Four percent of the population under age 18 were identified in more than one racial category in the 2000 Census, twice the percentage for adults (Kent et al., 2001:6; Prewitt 2003:39).

Although the 2000 Census began to capture the complex mix of racial groups present in the United States, it used a confusing classification for Hispanics. According to the 2000 U.S. Census guidelines, Hispanics were considered to be an ethnic group, not a race. People who identified their ethnicity as Hispanic could also indicate a racial background by choosing "some other race." The Census Bureau acknowledged that the distinction between race and ethnicity is flawed and even tested options for adding "Hispanic" to the list of racial categories for the 2010 Census (Lewis 2006). In reality, Hispanics *are racialized* in the United States. Although classified as an ethnic group, "Hispanic" encompasses a range of ethnic groups. At the same time, although Hispanics are not officially defined as a race, they are *socially defined* in racial terms. In other words, the dominant society treats them as racially inferior. When any

Speaking to Students

Got Privilege? Studying What It Means to Be White

What does it mean to be "white"? Surprisingly, the answer to this question is not as simple as it may seem. Whiteness is not biological, nor is it determined solely by skin color or other physical attributes. Instead, whiteness is socially constructed, a product of micro and macro social forces and interactions across time. These forces work together to create the boundaries for the unique racial location we call white. Although all of those who identify or are identified as white live within the boundaries of this racial location, the concept of whiteness does not imply that everyone who is white will have identical experiences. Historical and demographic location, class, gender and sexuality amongst other things shape what it means to be white.

Over the past thirty years, a new field has begun to emerge that studies the social constructions and boundaries of whiteness, which is called "Critical Whiteness Studies (CWS)." This field has begun to piece together historical and contemporary data and narratives to determine who was considered to be "white" at different historical periods and why. In addition, CWS examines how these racial determinations granted individuals privilege based on whether or not they were perceived to be white.

One of clearest texts in showing how white privilege operates is Peggy McIntosh's "Unpacking the Invisible Knapsack" (1988). By privilege, she means "an invisible package of unearned assets that [whites] can count on cashing in each day, but about which [whites were] "meant," to remain oblivious. White privilege is like an invisible weightless knapsack."*

At the heart of her argument is a focus on whiteness as a system, not an individual identification. What this means is that white people reap certain benefits based on the fact that the system is set up to accommodate them, whether or not they themselves directly support racist practices or ideologies. These privileges allow whites as a whole greater access to society's resources than people of color and leave less than an equal share of resources for those who are not similarly privileged.

As a student, you may be asking yourself "What, if anything does this have to do with me?" If you are white, you may feel that you did not receive any special treatment just because of your skin color. You may have had to overcome obstacles that were placed in your path due to your class, gender or sexuality. It may be especially difficult for you to accept your privilege in comparison with other people of color who you perceive as not having had to overcome such obstacles. Recognizing white privilege does not mean that across the board, in every

group comes to be thought of as a race, this means the group has become racialized (Taylor 2009:4). Hispanics are treated as a racial group, and many identify themselves as belonging to a distinctive racial category.

Despite the past and present racialization of people of color, common thinking about race is flawed. We tend to see race through a Black and White lens, thereby neglecting other rapidly growing racial groups. At the same time, we think of Whites, the dominant group, as raceless, or having no race at all (McIntosh 1992:79). In this view, Whiteness is the natural or normal condition. It is racially unmarked and immune to investigation. This is a false picture of race. In reality, the racial order shapes the lives of all people, even Whites who are advantaged by the system. (See the Speaking to the Students Panel titled "Got Privilege? Studying What It Means to Be White.") Just as social classes exist in relation to each other, "races" are labeled and judged *in relation to other races*. The categories "Black" and "Hispanic" are meaningful only insofar as they are scenario, whites always have it better than people of color. Just as there is white privilege, there are also privileges that come with being from the upper class, or possessing masculinity and/or heterosexuality. What it does mean is that you have been privileged in the area of race.

David Roediger's *Wages of Whiteness: Race and the Making of the American Working Class* (1991) is a great example of how white working class men, although not having access to the privileges of the upper class, utilized white privilege to their benefit. In this work, Roediger argues that constructions of whiteness were at the heart of the establishment of the working class. White workers used race to separate themselves from workers of color and to rally other white workers, including white ethnics. This gave them enough power to receive certain benefits as a group, including higher wages and better jobs that were not accessible to other workers.

Another book that highlights the interplay between different categories of social location is Ruth Frankenburg's *White Women, Race Matters: The Social Construction of Whiteness* (1993). The primary focus of this book is to show how whiteness is constructed via gender and sexuality. Frankenburg provides numerous examples to detail how white women's experience of race differs from white men's, especially within sexual relationships. For example, she shows how white women who were in relationships with men of color were often seen as "supersexual" beings in ways they would not have been if they were a white man choosing to date a woman of color. Although white women have to overcome barriers created by their gender and sexuality, Frankenburg notes it is still important to recognize the fact that they are at the same time able to maintain their racial privilege.

Fortunately, there is a growing movement to examine white privilege. There are small steps we all can take to assist in this process. Becoming aware of the different ways "whiteness" affects you and those around you is the first step toward fighting against white privilege and for racial equality. If you are white, another step you can take is to attempt to forego the benefits reaped upon you by whiteness. This will be difficult, especially in the beginning since you may be unaware of many of these benefits. Tim Wise, in his book *White Like Me: Reflections on Race from a Privileged Son,* outlines a number of practical strategies that can be used to help tear down white privilege. These include "refus[ing] to shop at institutions with a pattern or history of discrimination," and "refer[ing] to white people with a racial designation when discussing them so as to stop normalizing whites as synonymous with human beings, people, or Americans."**

*Working Paper 189, "White Privilege and Male Privilege: A Personal Account of Coming to See Correspondences through Work in Women's Studies" (1988), by Peggy McIntosh.
**Wise, Tim (2008). *White Like Me: Reflections on Race from a Privileged Son.* Soft Skull Press. Brooklyn, NY. Page 118.

Source: Paula Miller, Department of Sociology, Michigan State University, 2010. This essay was written expressly for *Social Problems, 12th Edition.*

set apart from, and in distinction to, "White." This point is particularly obvious when people are referred to as "non-White," a word that ignores the differences in experiences among people of color (Lucal 1996:246). Race is not simply a matter of two opposite categories but of power relations between dominant and subordinate groups (Weber 2010).

How is race different from ethnicity? Whereas race is used for socially marking groups on the basis of presumed physical differences, ethnicity allows for a broader range of affiliation. **Ethnic groups** are distinctive on the basis of national origin, language, religion, and culture. Today's world is replete with examples of socially constructed ethnicities. At the same time that the world is becoming thoroughly globalized, it is also becoming transformed by new ethnic diversities. As European countries struggle with political and economic integration, people may no longer identify as Italian, but as Lombardians, Sicilians, or Romans (Wali 1992:6). "The arrival of large numbers of people from the Middle

East, East Asia, and Africa—many European countries now have minority ethnic populations of around 10 percent—is pushing aside old concepts of what it means to be French, or German, or Swedish" (Richburg 2004:17). Expanding communications networks and the increased social interaction that has resulted from immigration have not suppressed ethnic conflicts. In the last decade of the twentieth century, ethnic and religious differences led to massacres of ethnic Tutsis by Hutus in Rwanda; full-scale war involving Serb, Bosnian, Albanian, and other ethnic groups in the Balkans; and violence against ethnic Chinese in Indonesia (Pollard and O'Hare 1999:5). Across Europe today, anti-immigrant racism is on the rise. Growing fears of a mounting foreign influx are fueling political movements to stop immigration.

In the United States, race and ethnicity both serve to mark groups as different. Groups *labeled as races* by the wider society are bound together by their common social and economic conditions. As a result, they develop distinctive cultural or ethnic characteristics. Today, we often refer to them as **racial-ethnic groups** (or racially defined ethnic groups). The term *racial-ethnic group* refers to groups that are socially subordinated and remain culturally distinct within U.S. society. It is meant to include (1) the systematic discrimination of socially constructed racial groups and (2) their distinctive cultural arrangements. The categories of *African American, Latino, Asian American,* and *Native American* have been constructed as both racially and culturally distinct. Each group has a distinctive culture, shares a common heritage, and has developed a common identity within a larger society that subordinates it. The racial characteristics of these groups have become meaningful in a society that continues to change (Baca Zinn and Dill 1994).

Terms of reference are also changing, and the changes are contested both within groups as well as between them. For example, *Blacks* continue to debate the merits of the term *African American,* whereas *Latinos* disagree on the label *Hispanic*. In this chapter, we use such terms interchangeably because they are currently used in both popular and scholarly discourse.

Differences among Ethnic Groups

Both race and ethnicity are historical bases for inequality in that they are constructed in a hierarchy from "superior" to "inferior." In the United States, some immigrants were viewed as belonging to an inferior race. For example, Jews were once racialized and later reconstructed as White (Brodkin 2009). Nevertheless, race and ethnicity have differed in how they incorporated groups into society. Race was the social construction setting people of color apart from European immigrant groups (Takaki 1993:10). Groups identified as races came into contact with the dominant majority through force and state-sanctioned discrimination in work that was unfree and offered little opportunity for upward mobility. In contrast, European ethnics migrated to the United States voluntarily to enhance their status or to market their skills in a land of opportunity. They came with hope and sometimes with resources to provide a foundation for their upward mobility. Unlike racial groups, most had the option of returning if they found the conditions here unsatisfactory. The voluntary immigrants came to the United States and suffered discrimination in employment, housing, and other areas. Clashes between Germans, Irish, Italians, Poles, and other European groups during the nineteenth and early twentieth centuries are well documented. But most European immigrants and their descendants—who accounted for four-fifths of the U.S. population in 1900—eventually achieved full participation in U.S. society (Pollard and O'Hare 1999:5).

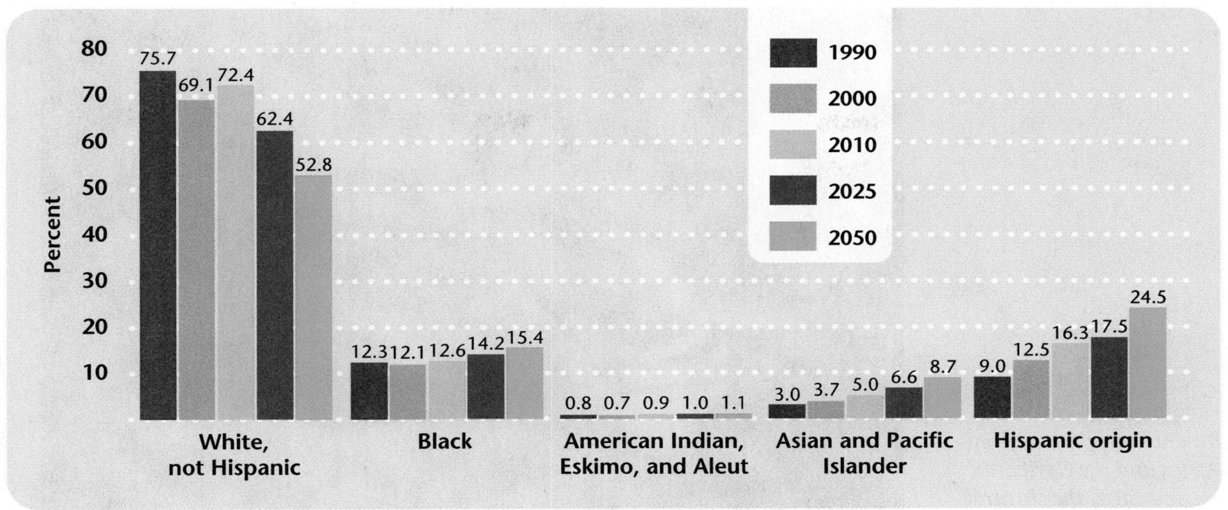

FIGURE 8.1

Percent of the Population, by Race and Hispanic Origin, 1990, 2000, 2025, and 2050 (middle-series projection)

Sources: U.S. Bureau of the Census, 1997. "Population of the United States: 1997." *Current Population Reports*. Series P23-194. Washington, DC: U.S. Government Printing Office, p. 9. U.S. Bureau of the Census accessed online: www.census.govb/population/www/cen2000; U.S. Census Bureau, *Census 2000 Redistricting Data (Public Law 94-171) Summary File*, Tables PL1 and PL2; and *2010 Census Redistricting Data (Public Law 94-171) Summary File*, Tables P1 and P2.

Although European ethnics have moved into the mainstream of society, racially defined peoples have remained in a subordinate status. Native Americans, African Americans, Latinos, and Asians have not been assimilated. Continuing racial discrimination sets them apart from others. (See Figure 8.1 for the percentage of the U.S. population by race in selected years.)

- **African Americans.** By 2010, African Americans (38.9 million) were 12.6 percent of the total population (U.S. Census Bureau, Census *2000 Redistricting Data (Public Law 94-171) Summary File*, Tables PL1 and PL2; and *2010 Census Redistricting Data (Public Law 94-171) Summary File*, Tables P1 and P2). Before 1990, virtually all African Americans descended from people who were brought involuntarily to the United States before the slave trade ended in the nineteenth century. They entered the southern states to provide free labor to plantations, and as late as 1890, 90 percent of all Blacks lived in the South, 80 percent as rural dwellers. In the South, they endured harsh and violent conditions under slavery, an institution that would have consequences for centuries to come. During the nineteenth century, the political storm over slavery almost destroyed the nation. Although Blacks left the South in large numbers after 1890, within northern cities they also encountered prejudice, discrimination, and segregation that exposed them to unusually high concentrations of poverty and other social problems (Massey 1993:7; Takaki 1993:7). African Americans have a distinctive history of slavery and oppression.

In the past two decades, the Black population in the United States has changed due to immigration from Africa and the Caribbean. In fact, more Blacks are coming from Africa than during the slave trade. About 50,000 legal immigrants arrive annually, and more have migrated here than in nearly the entire preceding centuries (Roberts 2005:A1). The increase in Black immigration from Africa and the Caribbean is making the population more diverse and posing unique challenges to today's Black immigrants (Shaw-Taylor 2009). The

Recent immigration from Africa and the Caribbean has increased the cultural diversity of "African Americans."

demographic shift is also changing what it means to be Black. It has sparked a new debate about the "African American." It ignores the enormous linguistic, physical, and cultural diversity of the peoples of Africa. The term *Black* is also problematic in that it risks conflating people of African descent who were brought here as slaves with recent immigrants from Africa and the Caribbean (Mukhopadhyay and Henze 2003:675). In fact, the experiences of today's immigrants are markedly different from those who have descended as slaves.

- **Latinos.** As we saw in Chapter 5, the U.S. Latino population has now surpassed the African American population to become the nation's largest minority. In many respects, the Latino population is the driving force of this society's racial and ethnic transformation (Saenz 2004:29). In 2010, Hispanics or Latinos numbered 50.5 million, or 16.3 percent of the total U.S. population (U.S. Census Bureau, Overview of Race and Hispanic Origin: 2010, 2010 Census Briefs, March 2011). Although Hispanics are the largest minority, they are a varied collection of ethnic groups. Two-thirds (65 percent) of all Hispanic Americans are Chicanos or Mexican Americans, 9.2 percent are Puerto Ricans, 3.5 percent are Cubans, and 6.6 percent are "other Hispanic or Latino" (Social Explorer Tables: ACS 2005 to 2009 (5-Year Estimates) (SE), ACS 2005–2009 (5-Year Estimates), Social Explorer; U.S. Census Bureau).

  The *Hispanic* category was created by federal statisticians to provide data on people of Mexican, Cuban, Puerto Rican, and other Hispanic origins in the United States. The term was chosen as a label that could be applied to all people from the Spanish-speaking countries of Latin America and from Spain. Because the population is so heterogeneous, there is no precise definition of group membership. Even the term *Latino,* which many prefer, is a new invention.

  Immigration is a thread that unifies much of the Latino experience in the United States. The vast majority of Latinos are immigrants or children of immigrants (Suarez-Orozco and Paez 2002). However, the national origins of Latinos are diverse, and so is the timing of their arrival in the United States. As a result, Mexicans, Puerto Ricans, Cubans, and other Latino groups have distinctive histories that set them apart from each other. Cubans arrived largely in the period between 1960 and 1980; Mexicans indigenous to the Southwest were forcibly annexed into the United States in 1848, whereas others have been migrating continuously since 1890. Puerto Ricans came under U.S. control in 1898 and obtained citizenship in 1917; Salvadorans and Guatemalans have been migrating to the United States in substantial numbers during the past two decades.

As a result of these different histories, Hispanics are found in many legal and social statuses—from fifth-generation Americans to new immigrants, from affluent and well-educated to poor and unschooled. Such diversity means that there is no "Hispanic" population in the sense that there is a Black population. Hispanics neither have a common history nor compose a single, coherent community. Rather, they are a collection of national-origin groups with heterogeneous experiences of settlement, immigration, political participation, and economic incorporation into the United States. Saying that someone is Hispanic or Latino reveals little about attitudes, behaviors, beliefs, race, religion, class, or legal situation in the United States (Massey 1993).

Despite these differences, Latinos in the United States have a long history of discrimination by governments controlled by non-Hispanic Whites. Mexican Americans in the Southwest lost property and political rights as Anglos moved into the region in the 1800s. As late as the 1940s, local ordinances in some Texas cities blocked Mexican Americans from owning real estate or voting. Also, Mexican Americans were required to attend segregated public schools in many jurisdictions before 1950 (Pollard and O'Hare 1999:6).

- **Asian Americans.** Asian Americans are another rapidly growing minority group in the country. In 2010, Asian Americans numbered 14.7 million, or about 4.8 percent of the U.S. population (Humes, Karen R., Nicholas A. Jones, and Roberto R. Ramirez. 2011. "Overview of Race and Hispanic Origin: 2010." *U.S. Census Briefs*, U.S. Census Bureau and the U.S. Department of Commerce.).

Like the Latino population, the Asian population in the United States is extremely diverse, giving rise to the term *Pan-Asian*, which encompasses immigrants from Asian and Pacific Island countries and native-born citizens descended from those ethnic groups (Lott and Felt 1991:6). Until recently, immigrants who arrived in the United States from Asian countries did not think of themselves as Asians, or even as Chinese, Japanese, Korean, and so forth, but rather as people from Toisan, Hoeping, or some other district in Guangdong Province in China or from Hiroshima, Yamaguchik, or some other locale. It was not until the late 1960s, with the advent of the Asian American movement, that a Pan-Asian consciousness was formed (Espiritu 1996:51).

The largest Asian American groups in the United States are Chinese (23 percent), Filipinos (18 percent), Japanese (6.1 percent), Vietnamese (11 percent), Koreans (10 percent), and Asian Indians (19 percent) (Social Explorer Tables: ACS 2005 to 2009 (5-Year Estimates) (SE), ACS 2005–2009 (5-Year Estimates), Social Explorer; U.S. Census Bureau). There also are Laotians, Kampucheans, Thais, Pakistanis, Indonesians, Hmong, and Samoans (Lee 1998:15).

The characteristics of Asians vary according to their national origins and time of entry into the United States. Most come from recent immigrant families, but many Asian Americans can trace their family's American history back more than 150 years. Much of this period was marked by anti-Asian laws and discrimination. The 1879 California Constitution barred the hiring of Chinese workers, and the federal Chinese Exclusion Act of 1882 halted the entry of most Chinese immigrants until 1943. Americans of Japanese ancestry were interned in camps during

World War II by an executive order signed by President Franklin D. Roosevelt. Not until 1952 were Japanese immigrants granted the right to become naturalized U.S. citizens (Pollard and O'Hare 1999:6–7).

Whereas most of the pre–World War II Asian immigrants were peasants, recent immigrants vary considerably by education and social class. On the one hand, many arrived as educated middle-class professionals with highly valued skills and some knowledge of English. Others, such as the Indochinese, arrived as uneducated, impoverished refugees. These differences are reflected in the differences in income and poverty level by ethnic category. Asian Americans taken together have higher average incomes than do other groups in the United States. Although a large segment of this population is financially well off, many are poor. Asian Americans are commonly seen as "the model minority," a well-educated and upwardly mobile group. But this stereotype is misleading. Not only is it used to blame other racial minorities for their own inequality, but it also ignores both the history of discrimination against Asians and their wide differences. Even the term *Asian American* masks great diversity.

- **Native Americans.** Once thought to be destined for extinction, today the Native American or American Indian population is comprised of 2.9 million individuals (U.S. Census Bureau, 2010 Census Redistricting Data (Public Law 97-171) Summary File, Table P1). Native Americans have more autonomy and are more self-sufficient than at any time since the last century (Snipp 1996:390). Nevertheless, the population remains barred from full participation in U.S. society.

The tribes located in North America were and are extremely heterogeneous, with major differences in physical characteristics, language, and social organization. As many as 7 million indigenous people lived in North America when the Europeans arrived. The conquest made them "Indians." By 1890, they were reduced to less than 250,000 by disease, warfare, and in some cases, genocide. In the first half of the nineteenth century, the U.S. government forced Indians from their homelands. Those forced migrations accelerated after President Andrew Jackson signed the Indian Removal Act of 1830. Many tribes then lived on marginal land that was reserved for them.

The current political and economic status of Native Americans is the result of the process that forced them into U.S. society. Many factors led to the disparities we now observe between Native Americans and others, including the appropriation of Indian land for the gain of White Settlers, the mismanagement by the Bureau of Indian Affairs of resources found on native lands, and the underinvestment of land by the general government in Native American education and health care (Adamson 2009).

Important changes have occurred in the social and economic well-being of the Native American population from 1960 to the present. At the time of the 1970 Census, Native Americans were the poorest group in the United States, with incomes well below those of the Black population. By 1980, despite poverty rates as high as 60 percent on many Indian reservations, poverty among Native Americans had declined. At the end of the twentieth century, Native Americans were better off than they were in the 1900s. Over the past few decades, Native Americans have made important gains in cutting poverty rates and increasing their educational levels. Yet even with these gains, Native Americans are nowhere near parity with White Americans. Today, Native Americans have a poverty rate of almost 24 percent, twice the White poverty rate (Muhammad 2009). Native peoples rank at the bottom of most U.S. socioeconomic indicators, with the lowest levels of life expectancy, per capita income, employment, and education (Harjo 1996; Thornton 1996; Pollard and O'Hare 1999; Muhammad 2009).

Although the conditions prevailing on many reservations resemble conditions in the developing world, a renaissance has occurred in Native American communities. In cities, modern pan-Indian organizations have been successful in making the presence of Native Americans known to the larger community and have mobilized to meet the needs of their people (Snipp 1996:390). A college-educated Native American middle class has emerged, Native American business ownership has increased, and some tribes are creating good jobs for their members (Fost 1991:26).

To summarize this section, the combined population of the four racial minority groups now accounts for 30 percent of the total U.S. population. New waves of immigration from non-European countries, high birthrates among these groups, and a relatively young age structure account for the rapid increase in minorities. By the middle of the twenty-first century, today's minorities will comprise nearly one-half of the U.S. population. (See Figure 8.1 for population projections through 2050.) African Americans, Latinos, Asian Americans, and Native Americans are different in many respects. Each group encounters different forms of exclusion. Nevertheless, as racial minorities, they remain at the lowest rungs of society.

EXPLANATIONS OF RACIAL AND ETHNIC INEQUALITY

Why have some racial and ethnic groups been consistently disadvantaged? Some ethnic groups, such as the Irish and the Jews, have experienced discrimination but managed to overcome their initial disadvantages. However, African Americans, Latinos, Asian Americans, and Native Americans have not been able to cast off their secondary status. Three types of theories have been used to explain why some groups are treated differently: deficiency theories, bias theories, and structural discrimination theories.

Deficiency Theories

A number of analysts have argued that some groups are disadvantaged because they *are* inferior. That is, when compared with the majority, they are deficient in some important way. There are two variations of **deficiency theories**.

- **Biological Deficiency.** This classical explanation for racial inferiority maintains that group inferiority is the result of flawed genetic—and therefore hereditary—traits. This is the position of Arthur Jensen, Richard Herrnstein, and Charles Murray (as discussed in Chapter 7). *The Bell Curve* (Herrnstein and Murray 1994) is the latest in a long series of works claiming that Blacks are genetically inferior to Whites and that this inferiority explains differences in the social success of racial groups. Despite the media attention given the work of these and other theorists, there is no definitive evidence for the thesis that racial groups differ in intelligence. Biological deficiency theories are generally not accepted in the scientific community (see *Contemporary Sociology* 1995).

- **Cultural Deficiency.** Many explanations of racial subordination center on group-specific cultural traits handed down from generation to generation. According to this explanation, the cultures and behaviors of minority groups are dysfunctional when compared to those of the dominant group. In addition, these groups remain at the bottom because they fail to take advantage of the opportunities in society (Brown and Wellman 2005:188). From this perspective, minorities are disadvantaged because of their group-specific heritage and customs. Cultural deficiency was the basis of Daniel Patrick Moynihan's famous 1967 report, which charged that the "tangle of pathology" within Black ghettos was rooted in the deterioration of the Negro family (U.S. Department of Labor 1965). High rates of divorce, female-headed households, out-of-wedlock births, and welfare dependency were said to be the residues of slavery and discrimination, a complex web of pathological patterns passed down through the generations. The Moynihan report was widely criticized for being a classic case of "blaming the victim." It finds the problem within Blacks, not in the structure of society.

Cultural deficiency theorists ignore the social opportunities that affect groups in different ways. Many social scientists have long opposed cultural explanations. Nevertheless, this approach is still found in scholarship and popular thought. Today, much of the public discussion about race and poverty rests on false assumptions about deficient minorities (Reed 1990; di Leonardo 1992; Bonilla-Silva 2003). Family "breakdown" is still used to explain African American problems, whereas a backward culture is said to produce Latino problems. Today's immigrant debates use culture to generate fear. For example, in his book, *Who Are We? The Challenges to American Identity* (2004), Samuel, P. Huntington argues that a culture alien to Anglo-Saxon ways makes unchecked Latino immigration a threat to U.S. society.

Bias Theories

The deficiency theories blame minorities for their plight. **Bias theories**, on the other hand, blame the members of the dominant group. They blame individuals who hold *prejudiced attitudes* toward minorities. Gunnar Myrdal, for example, argued in his classic book, *An American Dilemma,* that prejudiced attitudes toward an entire group of people are the problem (Myrdal 1944). This argument reduces racism to the "prejudiced" acts of individual White Americans (Brown and Wellman 2005:189).

Many sociologists have argued that prejudiced attitudes are not the essence of racism. For example, David Wellman (1977) has challenged the notion that the hostile attitudes of White Americans, especially lower-class Whites, are the major cause of racism. Instead, he shows that many unprejudiced White people defend the traditional social arrangements that negatively affect minorities. Research by Lawrence Bobo (2009) shows that although prejudice has declined, most White Americans are still unwilling to support social practices and policies to address racial inequalities. Unbiased people fight to preserve the status quo by favoring, for example, the seniority system in occupations, or they oppose affirmative action, quota systems, busing to achieve racial balance, and open enrollment in higher education.

Today, we live in an era when laws to protect citizens from racial discrimination are firmly in place. The new conventional wisdom views racism as a remnant of the past, the result of individual White bigotry, which is diminishing (Brown and Wellman 2005). The focus strictly on prejudice is inaccurate because it concentrates on the bigots and ignores the structural foundation of racism. The determining feature of dominant-minority relations is not prejudice but differential systems of privilege and disadvantage. "The subordination of people of color is functional to the operation of American society as we know it and the color of one's skin is a primary determinant of people's position in the social structure" (Wellman 1977:35). Even if active dislike of minorities ceases, "persistent social patterns can endure over time, affecting whom we marry, where we live, what we believe and do, and so forth" (Elliot and Pais 2006:300).

Thus, institutional and individual racism generate privilege for Whites. Discrimination provides the privileged with disproportionate advantages in the social, economic, and political spheres. Racist acts, in this view, not only are based on hatred, stereotyped conceptions, or prejudgment but also are rational responses to the struggle over scarce resources by individuals acting to preserve their own advantage.

Structural Discrimination Theories

Deficiency and bias theories focus, incorrectly, on individuals: the first on minority flaws and the second on the flawed attitudes of the majority. Both kinds of theory ignore the social system that oppresses minorities. Michael Parenti has criticized those who ignore the system as victim blamers: "Focusing on the poor and ignoring the system of power, privilege, and profit which makes them poor is a little like blaming the corpse for the murder" (1978:24). The alternative view is that racial inequality is not fundamentally a matter of what is in people's heads, not a matter of their private individual intentions, but rather a matter of public institutions and practices that create racism or keep it alive. **Structural discrimination theories** move away from thinking about "racism-in-the-head" toward understanding "racism-in-the-world" (Lichtenberg 1992:5).

Many sociologists have examined race as a structural force that permeates every aspect of life. Those who use this framework make a distinction between individual racism and institutional racism (Carmichael and Hamilton 1967). **Individual racism** is related to prejudice. It consists of individual behavior that harms other individuals or their property. **Institutional racism** is structural. It comprises more than attitudes or behavior. It is structural, that is, *a complex pattern of racial advantage built into the structure of society*—a system of power and privilege that advantages some groups over others (Higginbotham and Andersen 2009:78). Because institutional racism views inequality as part of society's structure, individuals and groups discriminate whether they are bigots or not. These individuals and groups operate within a social milieu that ensures racial dominance. The social milieu includes laws, customs, religious beliefs, and the stable arrangements and practices through which things get done in society.

Institutional or structural racism is not about beliefs. It is not only about actions directed at those considered racially different (meaning those not considered White). According to Howard Winant:

> *. . . structural racism is about the accretion of inequality and injustice in practice; it's about the way things work, regardless of the reasons why, it's about outcomes, not intentions or beliefs. So, if vast inequalities in wealth persist across racial lines, for example, they may persist not because White people presently intend to impoverish Black or Brown people; they may persist because of years and years of some people doing better than others do. Inequality accumulates; injustice becomes normal; they come to be taken for granted. (Winant 2009:58).*

Structural racism operates through social institutions in three ways. First is the importance of history in determining present conditions and affecting resistance to change. Historically, institutions defined and enforced norms and role relationships that were racially distinct. The United States was founded and its institutions established when Blacks were slaves, uneducated, and different culturally from the dominant Whites (Patterson 2007:58). From the beginning, Blacks were considered inferior (the original Constitution, for example, counted a slave as three-fifths of a person). Religious beliefs buttressed this notion of the inferiority of Blacks and justified the differential allocation of privileges and sanctions in society.

Second, discrimination can occur without conscious bigotry. Everyday practices reinforce racial discrimination and deprivation. Although the actions of individual bigots are unmistakably racist, many other actions (choosing to live in a suburban neighborhood, sending one's children to a private school, or opposing government intervention in hiring policies) also maintain racial dominance (Bonilla-Silva 1996:475). With or without malicious intent, racial discrimination is the "normal" outcome of the system. Even if racism-in-the-head disappeared, racism-in-the-world would not, because it is the *system* that disadvantages (Lichtenberg 1992).

Finally, institutional discrimination is reinforced because institutions are interrelated. The exclusion of minorities from the upper levels of education, for example, is likely to affect their opportunities in other institutions (type of job, level of remuneration). Similarly, poor children will probably receive an inferior education, be propertyless, suffer from bad health, and be treated unjustly by the criminal justice system. These inequities are cumulative.

Institutional derogation occurs when minority groups and their members are made to seem inferior or to possess negative stereotypes through legitimate means by the powerful in society. The portrayal of minority group members in the media (movies, television, newspapers, and magazines) is often derogatory. For example, many studies depict Black men disproportionately as drug users, criminals, lower class, and "pathological" (Muwakkil 1998b:18). Such stereotypes are "controlling images" that define perceptions of minorities (Collins 1990). If we based our perceptions of minority populations on media images, we would have considerably skewed views. The media also provide us with explanations and interpretations intended to help us make sense of our society, including its multiracial composition. The ideas that pervade today's mass media obscure pervasive racial inequality. Instead we are bombarded by depictions of race relations that suggest discriminatory racial barriers have been dismantled and that the United States has become a truly color-blind nation (Gallagher 2010; Weber 2010).

Why is U.S. society organized along racial lines? Sociologists have a long-standing debate over the relative importance of race and class in shaping systems of racial inequality. Those emphasizing class contend that the economy and class system are what produce racial inequality (see the discussion of the underclass later in the chapter). Some scholars argue that modern race relations are produced by world capitalism. Using the labor of non-White peoples began as a means for White owners to accumulate profits. This perspective contends that capitalism as a system of class exploitation has shaped race and racism in the United States and the world (Bonacich 1992).

Other structural theories point to race itself as a primary shaper of inequality. For example, racial-formation theory explains the sociohistorical process by which racial categories are created. This theory proposes that the United States is organized along racial lines from top to bottom—a racial state composed of institutions and policies to support and justify racial stratification (Omi and Winant 1986, 1994). Another theory, called *systemic racism,* also argues that race itself explains racial inequality. Systemic racism includes a diverse assortment of racism practices: the unjustly gained economic and political power of Whites, the continuing resource inequalities, and the White-racism ideologies, attitudes, and institutions created to preserve White advantages and power. Systemic racism is both structural and interpersonal. "At the macrolevel, large-scale institutions . . . routinely perpetuate racial subordination and inequalities. These institutions are created and re-created by routine actions at the microlevel by individuals" (Feagin 2000:16) Systemic racism is far more than a matter of individual bigotry, for it has been from the beginning a mental, social, and ideological reality (Feagin 2006: xiii).

Why does the United States have this tremendous degree of racial equality even though most White people are not "racist"? According to sociologist Eduardo Bonilla-Silva (2009:176), racial inequality exists because it benefits members of the dominant race.

DISCRIMINATION AGAINST AFRICAN AMERICANS AND LATINOS: CONTINUITY AND CHANGE

The treatment of Blacks and Hispanics has been disgraceful throughout American history. Through public policies and everyday practices, they have been denied the opportunities that should be open to all people. Since World War II, however, under pressure from civil rights advocates, the government has led the way in breaking down many discriminatory practices. Community organizing, civil rights legislation, landmark court decisions, and rising education have advanced the cause of racial equality. By the close of the twentieth century, many well-educated people of color had climbed into the middle class.

In 2009, 41 percent of African Americans and 42 percent of Latino families had incomes of $50,000 or more (compared with 64.5 percent of White families; U.S. Census Bureau, 2005–2009 American Community Survey (5-Year Estimates). They have taken advantage of fair-housing legislation and moved to the suburbs looking for better schools, safer streets, and better services. Yet having "made it" in the United States does not shield people of color from discrimination. Studies of public accommodation have found that in stores, bars, restaurants, and theaters, middle-class Blacks are ignored or treated with hostility (Feagin and Sikes 1994). No matter how affluent or influential, Blacks and other dark-skinned people are vulnerable to "microinsults" such as being followed around in stores (Muwakkil 1998a; Bonilla-Silva 2003; Feagin 2006).

Substantial growth of the minority middle class has not erased the problem of segregation. A class divide now characterizes minority communities across the country. As some successful people of color have become richer, many more unsuccessful ones have been marginalized. To be sure, much progress is evident in some areas. But in others, "there are clear signs of retrenchment, if not outright worsening. Across a range of institutions, the most consistent pattern is one of both persistence and change" (Lewis et al., 2004:104).

Racism was clearly present in the aftermath of Hurricane Katrina, the costliest natural disaster ever to hit the United States. For days, the world watched as federal officials moved slowly to assist those stranded and dying in flooded houses and overcrowded shelters in New Orleans and the Gulf Coast areas. What was exposed was not just a broken levee but race and class divides both familiar and yet new. Even media commentators raised the reasonable question of whether the fact that a majority of those hardest hit in New Orleans were low-income Black residents had affected the slowness of the federal government response (Feagin 2006:xv; DeParle 2007:163). The most comprehensive survey of Hurricane Katrina survivors found that both race and class played important roles in shaping response to the disaster (Elliot and Pais 2006). The evacuation plan was based on people driving out, yet 35 percent of Black households did not have a car, compared to 15 percent of White households. The Lower Ninth Ward, very poor and almost entirely Black, was one of the most heavily damaged areas of the city, while Whites disproportionately lived in more affluent higher areas less likely to suffer flooding (Feagin 2006:xv; DeParle 2007).

The present segregation of African Americans cannot be dismissed as wrongs committed in the past. U.S. neighborhoods were sharply segregated in the 1990s (Massey and Denton 1993). Today, they are just as segregated. Whites and African Americans tend to live in substantially homogeneous neighborhoods as do many Asians and Hispanics. In recent years, the segregation rates of Blacks have declined slightly while the rates of Asians and Hispanics have increased (Higginbotham and Andersen 2009:34).

Income

The average income for White families and households is greater than the average income for those of Blacks and Hispanics. Racial income disparities have remained unchanged over time. In 2008, the median income of Black households was about $34,000, the median income of White households was about $55,000, and the median income of Hispanic households was about $37,000 (DeNavas-Walt et al., 2009:5). Even though the median household income for Blacks is still below that of Hispanics, per-person income for Hispanics is actually lower because Hispanics tend to have larger households (see Figure 8.2).

Although the racial income gap is wide, the racial *wealth gap* is even wider. White families are generally wealthier than Black or Latino families (Collins, Leondar-Wright, and Sklar 1999). *Wealth* is the sum of important assets a family owns. It includes home ownership, pension funds, savings accounts, and investments. Many of these resources are inherited across generations. White families generally have greater resources for their children and bequeath them as assets at death. Sociologists call this "the cost of being Black" (Oliver and Shapiro 1995). According to this line of thought, African American disadvantage will persist until the wealth divide is closed (Shapiro 2004).

One important indicator of a family's wealth is home ownership. Paying off a home mortgage is the way most people build net worth over their lifetimes. But because racial minorities encounter discrimination in their efforts to buy, finance, or insure a home, a great race gap remains (Farley and Squires 2009:360). Fewer than half of Blacks and Latinos and fewer than 60 percent of Asian Americans and Native Americans own their own homes, compared to three-quarters of Whites. Rampant racial discrimination prevails in the housing market, even after 40 years of federal housing laws (Crowley 2002:25; Briggs 2005; Leondar-Wright et al., 2005:11).

Poverty rates for all minority groups are higher than for Whites. The percentage of Blacks, Hispanics, and Native Americans in poverty is about three

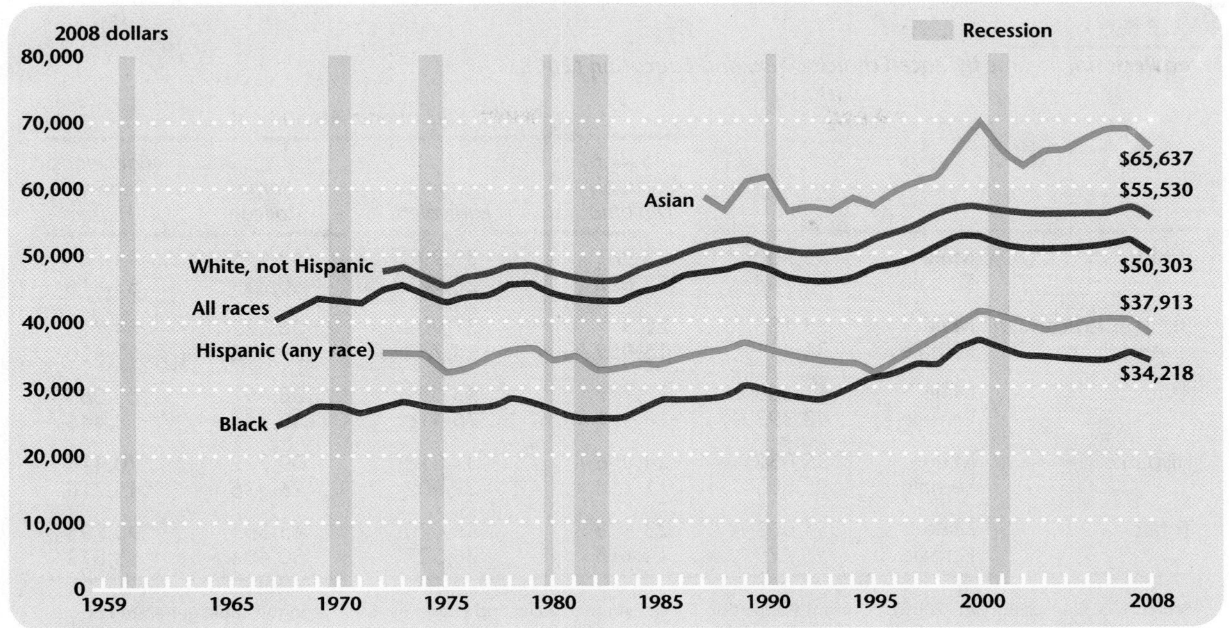

FIGURE 8.2

Real Median Household Income by Race and Hispanic Origin: 1967–2008

Source: Carmen DeNavas Walt, Bernadette D. Proctor, and Jessica C. Smith, 2009 U.S. Census Bureau, Current Population Reports, P60-236, *Income, Poverty, and Health Insurance Coverage in the United States: 2008*. Washington, DC: U.S. Government Printing Office, p. 7.

times that of Whites. Even Asian Americans, who have a higher average income than Whites, are more likely to live in families with incomes below the poverty line (O'Hare 1992:37). Although most poor people are White, Blacks and Hispanics are disproportionately poor. In 2008, 11 percent of Whites were poor, compared with 11 percent of Asian Americans, 23 percent of Hispanics, and 24 percent of Blacks (DeNavas-Walt et al., 2008:15). Although this is an advance for African Americans in recent decades brought about by the growth of the Black middle class, it is still a shamefully high number. By contrast, immigration has increased poverty among Hispanics (Alter 2007:37).

Many factors explain the difference in White and minority incomes. Racial-ethnic groups are concentrated in the South and Southwest, where incomes are lower for everyone. Another part of the explanation is the differing age structure of minorities. They are younger, on average, than the White population. A group with a higher proportion of young people of working age will have a lower average earning level, higher rates of unemployment, and lower rates of labor force participation.

Looking at racial inequalities by age reveals another disturbing pattern. The degree of inequality increases after the teenage years. Racial disparities become greater in peak earning years. This fact suggests that another part of the explanation for racial inequalities in earnings lies in the lack of education and the skill levels required to move out of poor-paying jobs. All these explanations leave a substantial amount of inequality unexplained. Minorities at all levels of employment and education still earn less than do Whites, as we see in Chapter 14. (See Table 8.1 for average earnings by race, sex, and Hispanic origin.)

TABLE 8.1

Mean Personal Income by Race-Ethnicity, Sex, and Education (2008)

			Educational Attainment			
		All	*No High School Diploma*	*High School or Equivalent*	*Some College*	*Bachelor's Degree or Higher*
White	Male	55,900	23,961	39,996	47,175	93,765
	Female	35,748	13,676	26,978	30,759	53,816
Black or African American	Male	38,185	20,517	31,909	36,277	64,717
	Female	31,591	15,059	24,752	29,456	51,450
Asian	Male	61,369	22,777	33,699	38,597	83,084
	Female	43,393	18,597	25,416	30,344	58,446
Hispanic	Male	35,032	24,056	31,818	39,772	70,416
	Female	25,805	15,358	22,902	26,936	45,716
Totals	Male	54,063	23,398	38,670	45,561	90,795
	Female	35,429	14,118	26,527	30,484	53,873

Source: U.S. Census Bureau (2009). "Current Population Survey, Annual Social and Economic Supplement," Table generated at url: http://www.census.gov/hhes/www/cpstc/cps_table_creator.html.

Education

In 1954, the Supreme Court outlawed segregation in the schools. Yet the landmark *Brown v. Board of Education* ruling did not end segregation. By 2004, on the fiftieth anniversary of the historic ruling, U.S. racial gaps in education were on the rise, and schools had become increasingly segregated. Today, schools are nearly as segregated as they were fifty years ago. Almost half of Latino and Black students attend school where students of color make up more than 90 percent of the students body. In contrast, the average White student goes to a school that is 80 percent White (Williams 2007; Orfield 2009). Latino students are the most segregated group in today's public schools (Tienda and Simonelli 2001).

Among young adults, Hispanics have the lowest levels of educational completion, whereas Whites and Asians have the highest. The 2009 high school graduation rate for Whites was 87 percent compared with 88 percent for Asian Americans, 84 percent for African Americans, and 62 percent for Hispanics (U.S. Census Bureau, Statistical Abstract of the United States: 2011, Table 225. Educational Attainment by Race and Hispanic Origin: 1970 to 2009). This is a growing problem because most new jobs in the twentieth century require education beyond high school (Pollard and O'Hare 1999c:30).

What explains the minority education gap? Although some educators point to a "culture of opposition" that causes underperformance among Black and Latino students, recent research suggests that school practices and personnel is a better explanation for racial differences. The minority education gap is caused by several factors, including a difference in their social class characteristics, which produce different educational opportunities (Lewis et al., 2004; Rothstein 2007:120).

TABLE 8.2

Percentage distribution of students enrolled in degree-granting institutions, by race/ethnicity: Selected years, fall 1976 through fall 2007

	Institutions of Higher Education			*Degree-Granting Institutions*						
Race/ethnicity	*1976*	*1980*	*1990*	*2000*	*2002*	*2003*	*2004*	*2005*	*2006*	*2007*
Total	**100.0**	**100.0**	**100.0**	**100.0**	**100.0**	**100.0**	**100.0**	**100.0**	**100.0**	**100.0**
White	82.6	81.4	77.6	68.3	67.1	66.7	66.1	65.7	65.2	64.4
Total minority	15.4	16.1	19.6	28.2	29.4	29.8	30.4	30.9	31.5	32.2
Black	9.4	9.2	9.0	11.3	11.9	12.2	12.5	12.7	12.8	13.1
Hispanic	3.5	3.9	5.7	9.5	10.0	10.1	10.5	10.8	11.1	11.4
Asian or Pacific Islander	1.8	2.4	4.1	6.4	6.5	6.4	6.4	6.5	6.6	6.7
American Indian/ Alaskan Native	0.7	0.7	0.7	1.0	1.0	1.0	1.0	1.0	1.0	1.0
Nonresident alien	2.0	2.5	2.8	3.5	3.6	3.5	3.4	3.3	3.4	3.4

Source: U.S. Department of Education, National Center for Education Statistics. (2009). *Digest of Education Statistics, 2008* (NCES 2009-020), Table 226.

Several additional trends are creating problems for minority students. The general movement against increased taxes hurts public schools. Inner-city schools, where minorities are concentrated and which are already understaffed and underfinanced, face even greater financial pressures because of current reduction in federal programs.

Minority participation in high education has risen since the 1960s. College campuses are far more diverse than they were a century ago (Rothstein 2007:129). Nevertheless, there are large racial gaps in college enrollment. Of the total campus population in 2007, 64 percent were White, 13 percent were African American, 11 percent were Latino and 6 percent were Asian (U.S. Department of Education 2008). (See Table 8.2.) Although many colleges actively recruit students of color, many factors contribute to low retention rates. Even when they reach college, students of color often confront a range of discriminatory barriers. Studies have consistently found that they are more alienated than White students and drop out more often than White students. Discrimination by Whites on and off campus is a recurring problem (Feagin 2000:170).

All these disparities translate into economic inequalities. Yet education alone is not the answer. Even with a college degree, African Americans and Latinos have higher unemployment rates than their White counterparts. This is compounded by the reality that education does not pay equally. Minority membership, regardless of the level of education, is underpaid compared with Whites of similar education. A highly educated White man still makes more money than anyone else (U.S. Bureau of the Census 2009c). (See Table 8.3.)

TABLE 8.3

Selected Labor Force Characteristics by Sex, Race, and Ethnicity (2008)

		Total %	*Black %*	*Hispanic %*	*Asian %*	*White %*
In civilian labor force	Men	73	66.7	80.2	75.3	73.7
	Women	59.5	61.3	56.2	59.4	59.5
Unemployed	Men	6.1	11.4	7.6	4.1	5.5
	Women	5.4	8.9	7.7	3.7	4.9
Occupations						
Management and profession	Men	33.5	23	14.8	50.1	34
	Women	39.5	31.3	23.5	46	40.6
Sales and Service	Men	30.4	38.3	33.5	31.1	29.3
	Women	53.7	60.1	64.2	45.5	53
Skilled and unskilled manual	Men	36.1	38.7	51.7	18.8	36.7
	Women	6.8	8.6	12.3	8.4	6.3

Source: Bureau of Labor Statistics (2009). "Current Population Survey, Household Data Annual Averages," Tables 4, 5, 10. Can be accessed from http://www.bls.gov/cps/tables.htm.

Unemployment

African Americans and Latinos are more likely than Whites to be unemployed. For the last three decades, unemployment among Black workers has been twice that of White workers, with Latinos in between. In 2009, the unemployment rate for Latinos was 5.2 percent, compared with 8.9 percent for African Americans and 4.0 percent for Whites (Bureau of Labor Statistics 2009a). Minority teenagers had an even harder time. The unemployment rate among Black teens was 48 percent; for Latinos, it was 34 percent; and for Whites, it was 23 percent (Bureau of Labor Statistics 2009a).

These government rates are misleading because they count as employed the almost 6 million people who work part time because they cannot find full-time jobs, and these rates also do not count as unemployed the discouraged workers, numbering more than 1 million, who have given up their search for work.

Type of Employment

African Americans and Latinos have always been an important component of the U.S. labor force. However, their job prospects are different from those of other people in the United States. Not only are they twice as likely as Whites to be unemployed, but they are also more likely to work in low-skilled occupations and less likely to work in managerial or professional occupations (see Table 8.3). Black and Latino workers are more likely to be in jobs with pay too low to lift a family of four above the poverty line (Leondar-Wright et al., 2005:9). Sociological research shows that race is related to workplace recruitment, hiring, firing, job levels, pay scales, promotion, and degree of autonomy on the job. Seemingly neutral practices can advantage some groups and adversely affect others (American Sociological Association 2003; Shulman 2007).

Immigrants generally work in the lowest rungs of the low-wage workforce. They are more likely than natives to be food-preparation workers, sewing machine operators, parking lot attendants, housekeepers, waiters, private household cleaners, food-processing workers, agricultural workers, elevator operators and janitors, operators, fabricators, and laborers (Shulman 2007:101). Although Blacks, Hispanics, and Native Americans are in the least rewarding jobs, and many face discrimination in hiring and promotion, the occupational status of minorities improved slowly during the last decade. Between 1990 and 2009, the percentage of Blacks in managerial and professional occupations increased from 17 to 27 percent, while the percentage increased from 13 to 18 percent for Hispanics (Pollard and O'Hare 1999:33; Bureau of Labor Statistics 2009a). Despite these gains, however, a huge gap remains. As more minorities enter high-status work, they are confronting new discrimination practices in the form of "job ceilings" that keep them out of executive suites and boardrooms (Higginbotham 1994).

Seismic shifts in the U.S. economy have diminished work opportunities across the land (see Chapter 14). The job crisis in minority communities is linked to globalization and the structural transformation of the economy. This transformation is eliminating jobs for unskilled, poorly educated workers. The Great Recession has affected minority communities much like a depression and has threatened the viability of many Black communities. In 2009, joblessness for 16- to 24-year-old Black men reached Great Depression proportions with a rate of 34 percent—more than three times the rate for the general U.S. population (Ehrenreich and Muhammad 2009; Haynes 2009).

Because African Americans and Latinos established successful niches in civil service, they are also being replaced by government downsizing (American Sociological Association 2003). The new economy will be increasingly made up of people of color. If they continue to be denied equal access to higher-paying jobs, the entire society will be at risk for poverty and other problems associated with economic inequality.

Health

The health of the U.S. population is distributed unevenly across race. Hispanics are the most likely to be without health coverage. Thirty percent of Hispanics, 19 percent of African Americans, 17 percent of Asian Americans, and 12 percent of Whites were not covered by private or government medical insurance in 2007 (DeNavas-Walt et al., 2008; see Figure 8.3). Hispanics born outside the United States were almost twice as likely to lack health insurance as their U.S.-born counterparts. Many are unfamiliar with the U.S. health care system, and a few are illegal immigrants who are afraid to seek medical assistance (del Pinal and Singer 1997:37; Folbre and Center for Popular Economics 2000).

Racial discrimination affects health in other ways as well. **Environmental racism** is the disproportionate exposure of some racial groups to environmental toxic substances. Race is the strongest predictor of hazardous waste facility location in the country, even after adjustment for social class. Even before Hurricane Katrina struck in 2005, New Orleans was already struggling with environmental assaults that ranged from floodwaters to toxic debris. People of color were most vulnerable to these assaults. Katrina was among the deadliest and most devastating disasters in U.S. history. Although public attention has

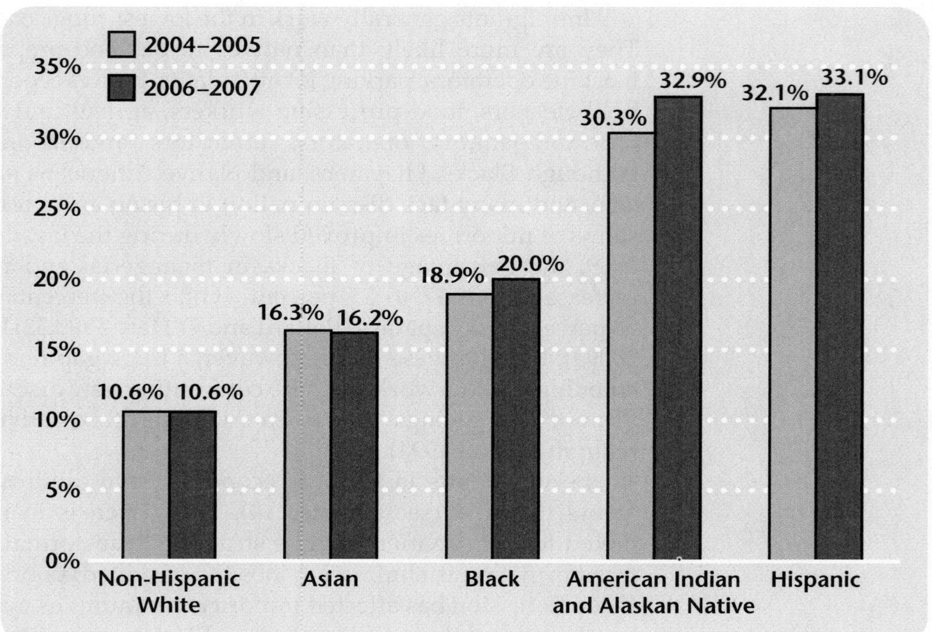

FIGURE 8.3
Percentage without Health Insurance Based on Two-Year Averages
Source: Dedrick Muhammad. 2009. *Challenges to Native American Advancement: The Recession and Native America*. New York: Institute for Policy Studies, p. 16.

focused on rebuilding the Gulf Coast, a lesser known crisis of lethal debris lingers, left over from hurricane damage (Bullard and Wright 2009). Nationally, three out of five African Americans and Latinos live in communities with abandoned toxic waste sites because of land use, housing patterns, and infrastructure development (Bullard 2007:87).

There are significant racial disparities between racial minorities and Whites in access to health care and in treatment of serious diseases. Minorities receive lower-quality health care than Whites, even when their insurance and income are the same, because of racial prejudice and difference in the quality of health plans (Stolberg 2002; Brown and Wellman 2005:191). On virtually every measure of health, African Americans and Latinos are disadvantaged, as revealed in the following selected facts:

- Compared to the general population, Blacks and Hispanics are less likely to have a consistent source of medical care and more likely to use emergency rooms as a primary source of care. Compared to Whites, Hispanics had a 700 percent higher rate of visits to community health centers but a 35 percent lower rate of visits to physicians' offices. Compared to Whites, Blacks had a 550 percent higher rate of visits to community health centers but a 48 percent lower rate of visits to physicians' offices (Forrest and Whelan 2000).
- Black Medicare patients are more likely than White women to reside in areas where medical procedure rates and the quality of care is low. In addition, a small group of physicians, who are more likely to practice in low-income areas, provide most of the care to Black patients. These providers are less likely than other physicians to be board certified and less able to provide high-quality care and referrals to specialty care (Bach 2004; Baicker

Perceptions that immigrants are taking jobs from Anglos increase racial tensions.

2004). Also, pharmacies in segregated neighborhoods are less likely to have adequate medication supplies, and hospitals in these neighborhoods are more likely to close (Williams and Jackson 2005).

- In 2009, American Indian women were 1.9 times as likely to die from cervical cancer compared to White women, and African Americans were 1.5 times as likely as Whites to have high blood pressure (National Conference of State Legislatures 2009).
- Black babies are nearly twice as likely as White babies to die within their first year. Although the infant mortality rate for Hispanic infants is less than the rate for White infants, within the Puerto Rican subgroup, the rate of infant deaths from sudden infant death syndrome is 1.5 times higher than for Whites (U.S. Department of Health and Human Services 2004b).
- HIV/AIDS has had a devastating impact on minorities in the United States. In 2007, racial-ethnic minorities accounted for almost 68 percent of newly diagnosed cases of AIDS. In 2007, 88 percent of babies born with HIV/AIDS belonged to minority groups (U.S. Department of Health and Human Services 2009b).

CONTEMPORARY TRENDS AND ISSUES IN U.S. RACIAL AND ETHNIC RELATIONS

Racial diversity presents new social conditions that reflect differences in group power and access to social resources. Three major trends reveal old and new forms of racial inequality: racial strife, economic polarization of minorities, and a national shift in U.S. racial policies. These trends are occurring in a global context, closely associated with macrosocial forces around the world.

Ongoing Racial Strife

Although the social dynamics of race are changing, the United States has not transcended racial divisions. The growing immigrant and minority presence together with the economic crisis gripping the nation are adding *new* tensions in society. In the United States and other countries, racial and ethnic diversity is marked by growing conflicts. Some cities are divided societies where minorities seldom meet Whites as neighbors, as classmates in public schools, in church, or in the new ethnic shopping centers now springing up across the country (Harris and Bennett 1995:158).

Racial conflict is often associated with uncertain economic conditions. Lack of jobs, housing, and other resources can add to fear and minority scapegoating on the part of Whites. In Florida and many parts of the West and Southwest, perceptions that Cubans, Mexicans, and other Hispanics are taking jobs from Anglos have touched off racial tensions. Racial tensions often erupt in violence between Whites and minorities and among minorities themselves as individuals compete for a shrinking number of jobs and other opportunities.

We now see new expressions of anti-Muslim/anti-Arab racism. Like old-fashioned forms of bigotry and hate crimes, this racism is also fueled by misbeliefs about minorities (Blauner 2001:191). Anti-Hispanic incidents have increased steadily during the past two decades. Crimes against Hispanics are on the rise. Anti-immigration movements often translate into hate-related activities. One effect of the increasing anti-immigrant sentiment in the nation is the surge in incidents of vigilantism—unauthorized attempts by ordinary citizens to enforce immigration laws. Some private citizens are increasingly taking the law into their own hands to stem the perceived "flood" of illegal immigrants into the country (National Council of La Raza 1999; Southern Poverty Law Center [SPLC] 2006b, 2007, 2009b).

Instead of moving society "beyond race," the historic election of the first African American president has thrust some incidents of racial conflict onto center stage. In 2009, President Obama hosted a "beer summit" at the White House to try to smooth over a controversy he helped fuel with comments at a press conference regarding the arrest of a Black Harvard professor by a White Cambridge policeman. Prominent Democrats such as former President Carter have publicly speculated that race—and by implication racism—is behind some of the attacks on President Obama at venues ranging from town hall meetings to the floor of Congress. And Republicans accuse Democrats of playing the race card to deflect legitimate criticisms of the president's policies (Morin 2009).

More Racially Based Groups and Activities

The Southern Poverty Law Center (SPLC) documented 888 hate groups in forty-eight states and the District of Columbia in 2008, a number that has swelled by 48 percent since 2000 (SPLC 2008). Hate groups include White supremacist groups with such diverse elements as the Ku Klux Klan, neo-Confederate groups (those describing Southern culture as fundamentally White), Nazi-identified parties, and skinheads. Many groups use the Internet to spread their literature to young people. As a result, more than half of all hate crimes are now committed by young people ages 15 to 24. In addition to racist websites, cyber extremism flourishes in e-mail and in discussion groups and chat rooms (*Intelligence Report* 2001:47). Racism is also fueled by the proliferation of cable TV hosts, who

Inner cities are beset with a disproportionate share of social problems.

spread and legitimize extremist propaganda. In 2009, the SPLC reported a rise in right-wing racial extremism reinvigorated by fears of immigration, the election of President Obama, and the nation's economic woes (SPLC 2009a, 2009b).

- **Profiling and Maltreatment.** Racial discrimination in the criminal justice system has drawn scrutiny in recent years. The past three decades have seen "numerous cases of race-related police brutality and misconduct, and official acknowledgements of systematic racial profiling" (Lewis et al., 2004:95). Blacks and dark-skinned Latinos are disproportionately targeted by police officers. Lower-class communities where minorities reside are often subjected to higher levels of police suspicion, stops, interrogations, and searches (Bonilla-Silva 2003; Warren et al., 2006). *Racial profiling* is the use of race and ethnicity as clues to criminality and potential terrorism. According to the Federal Bureau of Justice Statistics, in 2005 Black drivers were twice as likely to be arrested during traffic stops, whereas Latino drivers were more likely than Black or White drivers to receive a ticket (Robinson 2007). Racial profiling on the highways has become so prevalent that a term has emerged to explain it: "driving while Black" (Bonilla-Silva 2003). Prior to the September 11 terrorist attacks, racial profiling was a state and local law enforcement practice that unfairly targeted Blacks, Native Americans, Asian Americans, and Latinos. Since September 11, Arab Americans, Muslims, and other Middle Easterners have been the targets of threats, gunshots, firebombs, and other forms of vigilante violence (Fahim 2003). Fear of terrorism has provoked a rash of hate crimes and a national debate about the official use of profiling—that is, the use of race and ethnicity as clues to criminality and potential terrorism.

- **Campus Racial Tensions.** Recent headlines about racism on college campuses have surprised many people because educational institutions are formally integrated. Yet campus racism is widespread. Over the past few years, students of color have reported a dramatic increase in acts of racial discrimination, intolerance, hate crimes, and insensitivity among different cultures at institutions of higher education. Hateful and racially insensitive incidents have occurred on some of the most prestigious campuses in the country (NAACP 2009). According to the U.S. Department of Education and watchdog and advocacy groups, every year more than half a million college students are targets of bias-driven slurs or physical assaults. Every day, at least one hate crime occurs on a college campus, and every minute, a college student somewhere sees or hears racist, sexist, homophobic, or otherwise biased words or images. Of all hate crime incidents motivated by racial bias in 2008, 12.5 percent happened at schools or colleges (Federal Bureau of Investigation [FBI] 2008). These problems are not isolated or unusual events. Instead, they reflect what is occurring in the wider society (Sidel 1994; Feagin 2000).

Social and Economic Isolation in U.S. Inner Cities

The notion of a troubled "underclass," locked in U.S. inner cities by a deficient culture, is commonly used to explain racial poverty. According to this reasoning, broken families and bad lifestyles prevent minorities from taking advantage of the opportunities created by antidiscrimination laws. However, like the older cultural deficiency models we discussed earlier, this explanation is wrong on many counts. It relies heavily on behavioral traits to explain poverty. It blames the victims for conditions that are actually rooted in social structure. Social and economic changes have removed jobs and resources from inner-city residents. This reality is a better explanation of poverty among African Americans.

Hurricane Katrina exposed stark levels of racial impoverishment in the northern Gulf Coast. But disparities between Blacks and Whites are not unique to New Orleans. In large cities across the nation, African Americans are much more likely than Whites to live in communities that are geographically and economically isolated from the economic opportunities, services, and institutions that families need to succeed. Of the fifteen U.S. metropolitan areas with the most African Americans in absolute numbers in 2000, New Orleans had the highest Black poverty rate at 33 percent. But racial differences in poverty were stark in each of these metropolitan areas except New York. In Chicago, Newark, Memphis, and St. Louis, African Americans were about five times more likely than Whites to be impoverished. High poverty rates for African Americans are linked to lower levels of education and employment. In 2000, Blacks in these large cities were also far less likely to own a car or a phone (Saenz 2005:1).

Without jobs, cars, or phones, inner-city residents are utterly vulnerable to urban disaster. (See the "Social Policy" panel on reducing the risk of future disasters for African Americans.) This social entrapment can be explained *structurally*. In his classic studies of African American poverty at the end of the twentieth century, sociologist William J. Wilson found that the problems of the inner city are due to transformations of the larger economy and to the class structure of ghetto neighborhoods (1987, 1996). The movement of middle-class Black professionals from the inner city has left behind a concentration of the most disadvantaged segments of the Black urban population. Wilson's research reveals how crime, family dissolution, and welfare are connected to the structural removal of work from the inner city. The Black inner city is not destroying itself by its own culture; rather, it is being destroyed by economic forces.

SOCIAL POLICY

REDUCING THE RISK OF FUTURE DISASTERS FOR URBAN AFRICAN AMERICANS

African Americans not only have the highest levels of poverty in the country, but they are also the group that is most residentially segregated from and least likely to intermarry with Whites. Surveys also continue to reveal that many non-Black Americans express high levels of social distance (the degree to which people desire close or remote social relations with members of other groups) from African Americans. Given their limited social and economic resources, along with their geographic isolation, poor urban African Americans—especially children and the elderly—are disproportionately vulnerable to being left behind during a crisis situation.

What measures need to be taken to improve the social and economic position of African Americans and to avoid future disasters such as the recent one in New Orleans?

- Skills-development, employment, and health-maintenance programs need to be targeted to and strengthened for African Americans.
- Funding and access to education—including Head Start—should be increased for African Americans to bolster their social and economic well-being and competitiveness in the labor market.
- Additional policies, resources, and investment are needed to promote the development and relocation of businesses (and thus jobs) to African American urban neighborhoods.
- Government agencies responsible for responding to natural disasters need to factor into their planning the economic and geographic isolation of African Americans—especially the African American urban poor.

Aggressive actions are needed to erase the marginalization of African Americans that Hurricane Katrina exposed. The failure to take such actions will have enormous economic and social costs—not just for African Americans, but for a society living with a disjuncture between its ideals and the reality of continued stratification along the color line.

Source: Rogelio Saenz, "The Social and Economic Isolation of Urban African Americans." Population Reference Bureau (2007):3–4. Reprinted with permission from the Population Reference Bureau.

Rising poverty rates among Latinos have led many policy makers and media analysts to conclude that Latinos have joined inner-city African Americans to form a hopeless underclass. This view of minority impoverishment is inaccurate. Although changes in the U.S. economy have hit Latinos hard because of their low educational attainment and their labor market position, structural unemployment has different effects on the many diverse Latino barrios across the nation (Moore and Pinderhughes 1994). The loss of jobs in Rust Belt cities has left many Puerto Ricans living in a bleak ghetto economy. Mexicans living in the Southwest, where low-paying jobs remain, have not suffered the same degree of economic dislocation. Despite high levels of poverty, Latino communities do not fit the conventional portrait of the underclass.

A structural analysis of concentrated poverty does not deny that inner cities are beset with a disproportionate share of social problems. As poverty is more concentrated in inner cities, crime and violence proliferate. The poor may adopt violence as a survival strategy, which escalates violence even further (Massey 1996a). A structural analysis, however, focuses on social conditions, not immoral people. Vanishing jobs and many forms of unemployment are related to the worldwide realignment of work that accompanies corporate globalization. According to national Urban League president Hugh Price, "The manufacturing jobs that once enabled blue-collar workers to purchase their own homes and occasional new cars have all but vanished from the inner city"; and although racism is still widespread, "the global realignment of work and wealth is also a culprit" (cited in Brecher, Costello, and Smith 2000).

Racial Policies in the New Century

The 1960s civil rights movement legalized race-specific remedies to end racial bias. Government policies based on race overturned segregation laws, opened voting booths, created new job opportunities, and brought hopes of racial justice for people of color. As long as it appeared that conditions were improving, government policies to end racial injustice remained in place.

But by the 1980s, the United States had become a very different society from the one in which civil rights legislation was enacted. Economic restructuring brought new dislocations to both Whites and minorities. As racial minorities became an ever larger share of the U.S. population, racial matters grew more politicized. Many Whites began to feel uncomfortable with race-conscious policies in schools and the workplace. The social climate fostered an imaginary White disadvantage, said to be caused by affirmative action and multiculturalism. Although there is no empirical evidence for White disadvantage, a powerful conservative movement is producing new debates about the fairness of racial policies.

The United States is becoming a multiracial society. Barack Obama's rise to the presidency galvanized debates about race in the United States. His election marked a transformative moment in U.S. history. But despite these changes, new forms of racism support White privilege. Claims of **color blindness** only obscure twenty-first-century racism in all arenas of public life. Higginbotham and Andersen (2009) describe race as a building block of society: Race . . . "segregates our neighborhoods, our schools, our churches, and our relationships. Race . . . is often a matter of heated political debate, and the dynamics of race lie at the heart of the systems of justice and social welfare" (7–8).

Despite claims about color blindness, contemporary forms of racism continue in all arenas of public life. Racial equality is being downsized through policies related to affirmative action, school desegregation, and voting rights. Growing racial populations are controlled through many different forms of discrimination, including employment practices, neighborhood and school segregation, and other inequalities discussed in this chapter. In addition, the demise of the welfare state and the retreat from health care and other forms of social responsibility have caused minorities to lose ground. Finally, international systems of dominance (global capitalism and geopolitical relations) are producing still more racial inequalities in the United States (Allen and Chung 2000:802; Barlow 2003).

Dominant groups use their power to marginalize minorities, but racial inequalities are not simply accepted. Although racism is a tool for exclusion, it is also the basis for political mobilization. Since the country was founded, people of color have struggled for social change. All racially defined groups have rich histories of resistance, community building, and social protest. Racial projects, according to Omi and Winant (1994), are organized efforts to distribute social and economic resources along racial lines. Through social movements, groups organize and act to bring about social change (Higginbotham and Andersen 2009:431). Despite the new racial climate, the struggle against racism continues. Multiracial organizations composed of racial ethnic *and* White antiracist activists continue to work at national and local levels to fight and eradicate racist prejudices and institutional racism.

CHAPTER REVIEW

1. Racial and ethnic stratification are basic features of U.S. society. They are also found throughout the world and are an important feature of globalization. Patterns of inequality are built into normal practices. They exclude people from full and equal participation in society's institutions. Racial and ethnic stratification exist because they benefit certain segments of society.
2. The concept of race is a social invention. It is not biologically significant. Racial groups are set apart and singled out for unequal treatment.
3. An ethnic group is culturally distinct in race, religion, or national origin. The group has a distinctive culture. Some ethnic groups such as Jews, Poles, and Italians have distinguishing cultural characteristics that stem from religion and national origin. Because racial groups also have distinctive cultural characteristics, they are referred to as *racial-ethnic* groups.
4. Minority racial and ethnic groups are systematically disadvantaged by society's institutions. Both race and ethnicity are traditional bases for social inequality, although there are historical and contemporary differences in the societal placement of racial-ethnic groups and White ethnic groups in this society.
5. Racial-ethnic groups are socially subordinated and remain culturally distinct within U.S. society. African Americans, Latinos, Asian Americans, and Native Americans are constructed as both racially and culturally distinct. Each group has a distinctive culture, shares a common history, and has developed a common identity within a larger society that subordinates it.
6. Deficiency theories view minority group members as unequal because they lack some important feature common among the majority. These deficiencies may be biological (such as low intelligence) or cultural (such as the culture of poverty).
7. Bias theories place the blame for inequality on the prejudiced attitudes of the members of the dominant group. These theories, however, do not explain the discriminatory acts of the unprejudiced, which are aimed at preserving privilege.
8. Structural theories argue that inequality is the result of external constraints in society rather than cultural features of minority groups. There are four main features of institutional discrimination: (a) forces of history shape present conditions; (b) discrimination can occur without conscious bigotry; and (c) institutional discrimination is less visible than are individual acts of discrimination; and (d) discrimination is reinforced by the interrelationships among the institutions of society.
9. Civil rights legislation improved the status of some racial-ethnic groups, yet the overall position of Blacks and Latinos relative to Whites has not improved. Large gaps remain in work, earnings, and education. Global and economic transformations have contributed to the persistent poverty in U.S. urban centers.
10. The racial demography of the United States is changing dramatically. Immigration and high birthrates among minorities are making the United States a multiracial, multicultural society. These trends are also creating racial anxiety and racial conflict.
11. Public policy has shifted from race-conscious remedies to a color-blind climate that is dismantling historic civil rights reforms.

KEY TERMS

Dominant group. Group assigning subordinate status to minority groups.

Racial stratification. System of inequality in which race is the major criterion for rank and rewards.

Minority group. Subordinate group in society.

Racial formation. Sociohistorical process by which races are continually being shaped and transformed.

Ethnic groups. Culturally distinctive characteristics based on race, religion, or national origin.

Racial-ethnic group. Group labeled as a "race" by the wider society and bound together by their common social and economic conditions, resulting in distinctive cultural and ethnic characteristics.

Deficiency theories. Explanations that view the secondary status of minorities as the result of their own behaviors and cultural traits.

Bias theories. Explanations that blame the prejudiced attitudes of majority members for the secondary status of minorities.

Structural discrimination theories. Explanations that focus on the institutionalized patterns of discrimination as the sources of the secondary status of minorities.

Individual racism. Overt acts by individuals that harm members of another race.

Institutional racism. Established and customary social arrangements that exclude on the basis of race.

Environmental racism. The disproportionate exposure of some racial groups to toxic substances.

Color blindness. Idea that race no longer matters in explaining inequality or in policymaking because racism has been overcome.

■ SUCCEED WITH PEARSON mysoclab www.mysoclab.com

Experience, Discover, Observe, Evaluate

MySocLab is designed just for you. Each chapter features a pre-test and post-test to help you learn and review key concepts and terms.

Experience sociology in action with dynamic visual activities, videos, and readings to enhance your learning experience. Complete the following activities at www.mysoclab.com.

Social Explorer is an interactive application that allows you to explore Census data through interactive maps.

- Explore the Social Explorer Map: *Racial Income Extremes*

The Core Concepts in Sociology video clips offer a real-world perspective on sociological concepts.

- Watch *Discrimination at Swim Club*

MySocLibrary includes primary source readings from classic and contemporary sociologists.

- Read Lui, *Doubly Divided: The Racial Wealth Gap*; McArdle, *Sociologists on the Color Blind Question*; Ogbu, *Racial Stratification and Education in the United States: Why Inequality Persists*

CHAPTER 9

Gender Inequality

More than ever, it is time to take stock of current experiences with and perceptions of sexism. We are living at a particularly crucial historical moment for examining the problem of sexism.

—Carol Rambo Ronai, Barbara A. Zsembik, and Joe R. Feagin

Every society treats women and men differently. Today, there is no nation where women and men are equals. Worldwide, women perform an estimated 60 percent of the work, yet they earn only 10 percent of the income and own only 10 percent of the land. Two-thirds of the world's illiterate are women. Despite massive political changes and economic progress in countries throughout the world, women continue to be the victims of abuse and discrimination. Even where women have made important strides in politics and the professions, women's overall progress remains uneven.

This chapter examines the social basis of gender inequality. We show how gender disparity and its problems are built into the larger world we inhabit. From the macrolevel of the global economy, through the institutions of society, to interpersonal relations, gender is the basis for dividing labor, assigning roles, and allocating social rewards. Until recently, this kind of differentiation seemed natural. However, new research shows that gender is not natural at all. Instead, "women" and "men" are social creations. To emphasize this point, sociologists distinguish between *sex* and *gender*. **Sex** refers to the biological differences between females and males. **Gender** refers to the social and cultural patterns attached to women and men. Both sex and gender organize social life throughout the world.

Gender is not only about women. Men often think of themselves as "genderless," as if gender did not matter in the daily experience of their lives. Yet, from birth through old age, men are also **gendered**. This "gendering process, the transformation of biological males into socially interacting men, is a central experience for men" (Kimmel and Messner 2007:xvi). In the big picture, gender divisions make women and men unequal. But, we cannot understand the gender system, or women's and men's experiences, by looking at gender alone; gender operates together with other power systems such as race, class, and sexual orientation. These overlapping categories produce different gender experiences for women and men of different races and classes. Nevertheless, the gender system denies women and men the full range of human and social possibilities. Gender inequalities produce social problems. This chapter examines gender stratification in U.S. society at both structural and interpersonal levels of social organization. Taking a **feminist approach** (one in support of women's equality), the theme of this chapter is that social factors make women unequal to men.

WOMEN AND MEN ARE DIFFERENTIATED AND RANKED

Gender stratification refers to the hierarchical placement of the sexes that gives women unequal power, opportunities, and resources. Although there is worldwide variation in women's and men's roles, gender inequality exists in most parts of the world. Every society has certain ideas about what women and men should be like as well as ways of producing people who are much like these expectations.

Scientists have competing explanations for gender differences. Biological models argue that innate biological differences between males and females program different social behaviors. Anthropological models look at masculinity and femininity cross-culturally, stressing the variations in women's and men's roles. Sociologists treat gender as a feature of social structure.

Is Gender Biological or Social?

We know that there *are* biological differences between the two sexes. Debates about gender differences often fall back on "nature vs. nurture" arguments. The nurture camp argues that most differences are socially constructed. The opposing camp claims that differences between women and men are rooted in evolution. In 2005, Larry Summers, then president of Harvard University, caused a storm by suggesting that innate ability could be a reason there were so few women in the top positions in mathematics, engineering, and the physical sciences. Biological explanations have also become a favorite theme in the media

(Barnett and Rivers 2004). Is the popular biological explanation correct? Are men "hardwired" to dominate women? To answer this question, let us first review the evidence for each position.

- **Biological Bases for Gender Roles.** Males and females are different from the moment of conception. Chromosomal and reproductive differences make males and females physically different. Hormonal differences in the sexes are also significant. The male hormones (androgens) and female hormones (estrogens) direct the process of sex differentiation from about six weeks after conception throughout life. They make males taller, heavier, and more muscular. At puberty, they trigger the production of secondary sexual characteristics. In males, these include body and facial hair, a deeper voice, broader shoulders, and a muscular body. In females, puberty brings pubic hair, menstruation, the ability to lactate, prominent breasts, and relatively broad hips. Actually, males and females have both sets of hormones. The relative proportion of androgens and estrogens gives a person masculine or feminine physical traits.

These hormonal differences may explain in part why males tend to be more active, aggressive, and dominant than females. However, there are only slight differences in the levels of hormones between girls and boys in childhood. Yet, researchers find differences in aggression between young girls and boys (Fausto-Sterling 1992).

Biological differences between women and men are only averages. They are often influenced by other factors. For example, although men are on the average larger than women, body size is influenced by diet and physical activity, which in turn may be influenced by culture, class, and race. The all-or-none categorizing of gender traits is misleading because there is considerable overlap in the distribution of traits possessed by women and men. Although most men are stronger than most women, many women are stronger than many men. And although males are on the average more aggressive than females, the differences among males and among females are greater than the differences between males and females (Basow 1996:81; Barnett and Rivers 2004). Furthermore, gender is constantly changing. Femininity and masculinity are not uniformly shaped from genetic makeup. Instead, they are molded differently (1) from one culture to another, (2) within any one culture over time, (3) over the course of all women's and men's lives, and (4) between and among different groups of women and men, depending on class, race, ethnicity, and sexuality (Kimmel 1992:166).

- **The Social Bases for Gender Roles.** Cross-cultural evidence shows a wide variation of behaviors for the sexes. Table 9.1 provides some interesting cross-cultural data from 224 societies on the division of labor by sex. This table shows that for the majority of activities, societies are not uniform in their gendered division of labor. Even activities requiring strength, presumably a male trait, are not strictly apportioned to males. In fact, activities such as burden bearing and water carrying are done by females more than by males. Even an activity such as house building is not exclusively male. Although there is a wide variety in the social roles assigned to women and men, their roles seldom vary "randomly" (O'Kelly 1980:41). Despite the widespread cultural variation in women's and men's activities, every known society makes gender a major category for organizing social life. This is the social construction of gender. It is a sociological perspective that calls on social rather than biological differences to show how

TABLE 9.1

Gender Allocation in Selected Technological Activities in 224 Societies

	Number of Societies in Which the Activitiy Is Performed by:					
Activity	*Males Exclusively*	*Males Usually*	*Both Sexes Equally*	*Females Usually*	*Females Exclusively*	*Percent Male*
Smelting of ores	37	0	0	0	0	100.0
Hunting	139	5	0	0	0	99.3
Boat building	84	3	3	0	1	96.6
Mining and quarrying	31	1	2	0	1	93.7
Land clearing	95	34	6	3	1	90.5
Fishing	83	45	8	5	2	86.7
Herding	54	24	14	3	3	82.4
House building	105	30	14	9	20	77.4
Generation of fire	40	6	16	4	20	62.3
Preparation of skins	39	4	2	5	31	54.6
Crop planting	27	35	33	26	20	54.4
Manufacture of leather products	35	3	2	5	29	53.2
Crop tending	22	23	24	30	32	44.6
Milking	15	2	8	2	21	43.8
Carrying	18	12	46	34	36	39.3
Loom weaving	24	0	6	8	50	32.5
Fuel gathering	25	12	12	23	94	27.2
Manufacture of clothing	16	4	11	13	78	22.4
Pottery making	14	5	6	6	74	21.1
Dairy production	4	0	0	0	24	14.3
Cooking	0	2	2	63	117	8.3
Preparation of vegetables	3	1	4	21	145	5.7

Source: Adapted from George P. Murdock and Caterina Provist. 1973. "Factors in the Division of Labor by Sex. A Cross-cultural Analysis." *Ethnology* 12 (April) 2007. Reprinted by permission from *Ethnology*.

all societies transform biological females and males into socially interacting women and men (Andersen 2009).

Gender and Power

Gender differences are social creations that are embedded in society. The term **gendered institutions** means that entire institutions are patterned by gender (Acker 1992; Lorber 2005). Everywhere we look—the global economy, politics, corporate life, family life—men are in power. But men are not uniformly dominant. Some men have great power over other men. In fact, most men do not feel powerful; most feel powerless, trapped in stifling old roles and unable to changes their lives in ways they want (Kimmel 1992:171). Nevertheless, socially defined differences between women and men legitimate **male dominance**, which refers to the beliefs, meanings, and placement that value men over women and that institutionalize male control of socially valued resources. **Patriarchy** is the term used for forms of social organization in which men are dominant over women.

Like race and class, "gender is a multilevel system of differences and disadvantages that includes socioeconomic arrangements and widely held cultural beliefs at the macrolevel, ways of behaving in relation to others and the interactional level, and acquired traits and identities at the individual level" (Ridgeway 1997:219). Gender inequality is tied to other inequalities such as race, class, and sexuality to sort women and men differently. These inequalities also work together to produce differences *among women* and differences *among men*. Some women derive benefits from their race, their class, or their sexuality while they are simultaneously restricted by gender. Such women are subordinated by patriarchy, yet race, class, and sexuality intersect to create for them privileged opportunities and ways of living (Baca Zinn, Hondagneu-Sotelo, and Messner 2005). For example, men are encouraged to behave in "masculine" fashion to prove that they are not gay (Connell 1992). In defining masculinity as the negation of homosexuality, **compulsory heterosexuality** is an important component of the gender system. Compulsory heterosexuality inflicts negative sanctions on those who are homosexual or bisexual. This system of sexuality shapes the gender system by discouraging attachment with members of the same sex. This enforces the dichotomy of "opposite" sexes. **Sexuality** is also a form of inequality in its own right because it grants privileges to those in heterosexual relationships. Like race, class, and gender, sexual identities are socially constructed categories. Sexuality is a way of organizing the social world on the basis of sexual identity and is a key linking process in the matrix of domination structured along the lines of race, class, and gender (Messner 1996:223).

Gender scholars have debated the question of universal male dominance, that is, whether it is found in all societies across time and space. Many scholars once claimed that all societies exhibit some forms of patriarchy in marriage and family forms, in division of labor, and in society at large (Ortner 1974; Rosaldo 1974). Other scholars have challenged universal patriarchy with cases that serve as counterexamples (Shapiro 1981). Current thought follows the latter course. Sexual differentiation, it seems, is found in all societies, but it does not always indicate low female status (Rogers 1978). Male dominance is not homogeneous. Instead, it varies from society to society.

We should keep in mind that although gender stratification makes women subordinate to men, they are not simply the passive victims of patriarchy. Like other oppressed groups, women find ways to resist domination. Through personal and political struggles, they act in their own behalf, often changing the social conditions that subordinate them.

What Causes Gender Inequality?

To explain gender and power, sociologists turn to social conditions. Structural thinking treats gender inequality as the outcome of male control over socially valued resources and opportunities. There are several models of gender inequality. Most of them focus on the divisions of labor and power between women and men and the different value placed on their work. This idea originated in the work of Friedrich Engels and Karl Marx. They wrote that industrialism and the shift to a capitalist economy widened the gap between the power and value of men and women. As production moved out of the home, the gendered division of labor left men with the greater share of economic and other forms of power (Chafetz 1997; Sapiro 1999:67).

Macrostructural theories explain gender inequality as an outcome of how women and men are tied to the economic structure of society (Neilson 1990:215).

These theories say that women's economic role in society is a primary determinant of their overall status (Dunn 1996). The division between domestic and public spheres of activity gives men and women different positions of advantage and disadvantage. Their roles in the labor force and in the family are interdependent. Whether or not they work outside the home, women do the vast majority of child care and household labor. Men are freed from these responsibilities. Women's reproductive roles and their responsibilities for domestic labor limit their association with the resources that are highly valued (Rosaldo 1980; Ridgeway 1997). Men's economic obligations in the public sphere ensure them control of highly valued resources and give rise to male privilege.

In capitalist societies, the domestic–public split is even more significant because highly valued goods and services are exchanged in the public, not the domestic, sphere. Women's domestic labor, although important for survival, ranks low in prestige and power because it does not produce exchangeable commodities (Sacks 1974). Because of the connections between the class relations of production (capitalism) and the hierarchical gender relations of its society (patriarchy; Eisenstein 1979), the United States is a **capitalist patriarchy** where male supremacy keeps women in subordinate roles at work and in the home.

Socialization versus Structure: Two Approaches to Gender Inequality

To understand gender inequality, we must distinguish between (1) a gender roles approach and (2) a gender structure approach. The **gender roles approach** emphasizes traits that individuals acquire during the course of socialization, such as independent or dependent behaviors and ways of relating. The **gender structure approach** emphasizes factors that are external to individuals, such as the social structures and social interactions that reward women and men differently. These approaches differ in how they view the sexes, in how they explain the causes and effects of sexism, and in the solutions they suggest for ending inequality. Understanding sexism requires both the individual and the structural approaches. Although gender roles are learned by individuals, and produce differences in the personalities, behaviors, and motivations of women and men, gender stratification is essentially maintained by societal forces. This chapter places primary emphasis on social structure as the cause of inequality.

LEARNING GENDER

The most complex, demanding, and all-involving role that a member of society must learn to play is that of female or male. "Casting" for one's gender role takes place immediately at birth, after a quick biological inspection; and the role of "female" or "male" is assigned. It is an assignment that will last one's entire lifetime and affect virtually everything one ever does. A large part of the next 20 years or so will be spent gradually learning and perfecting one's assigned sex role (David and Brannon 1980:117).

Sociologists use the term *gender socialization* to describe how gender is learned. Understanding socialization is important not only to explaining gender, but to the construction of gender inequality (Martin 2005:457). From infancy through early childhood and beyond, children learn what is expected of boys and girls, and they learn to behave according to those expectations.

The traits associated with conventional gender roles are those valued by the dominant society. Keep in mind that gender is not the same in all classes and races. However, most research on gender socialization reflects primarily the experience of White middle-class people—those who are most often the research subjects of these studies. How gender is learned depends on a variety of social conditions affecting the socialization practices of girls and boys. Still, society molds boys and girls along different lines.

Children at Home

Girls and boys are perceived and treated differently from the moment of birth. Their access to clothes, toys, books, playmates, and expressions of emotion are severely limited by gender (Martin 2005:457). Parents' and "congratulations" greeting cards describe newborn daughters as "sweet," whereas boys are immediately described as "strong" and "hardy." Cards sent to parents depict ribbons, hearts, and flowers for girls, but mobiles, sports equipment, and vehicles for boys. Newborn greeting cards thus project an early gender scheme that introduces two "classes" of babies: one decorative, the other physically active and bringing greater joy (Valian 1998:19–20).

Children learn at a very early age what it means to be a boy or girl in our society. One of the strongest influences on gender role development in children occurs within the family setting, with parents passing on both overtly and covertly their own beliefs about gender (Witt 1997:254). From the time their children are babies, parents treat sons and daughters differently, dressing infants in gender-specific colors and giving them gender-differentiated toys. Color-coded differences reveal a relentless gender segregation with "little girls becoming adamantly attached to pink" (Sandler 2009). Parents expect different behaviors from boys and girls (Thorne 1993; Witt 1997). Although both mothers and fathers contribute to the gender stereotyping of their children, fathers have been found to reinforce gender stereotyping more often than mothers (Idle, Wood, and Desmarias 1993; Witt 1997; Valian 1998; Campenni 1999).

In addition to the parents' active role in reinforcing society's gender demands, a subtler message is emitted from picture books for preschool children. A classic sociological study of award-winning children's books conducted 40 years ago found the following characteristics (Weitzman et al., 1972):

- Females were virtually invisible. The ratio of male pictures to female pictures was 11:1. The ratio of male to female animals was 95:1.
- The activities of boys and girls varied greatly. Boys were active in outdoor activities, whereas girls were passive and most often found indoors. The activity of the girls typically was that of some service for boys.
- Adult men and women (role models) were very different. Men led, women followed. Females were passive and males active. Not one woman in these books had a job or profession; they were always mothers and wives.

We have seen improvements in how girls and women are portrayed. Females are no longer invisible, they are as likely as males to be included in the books, and they have roles beyond their family roles. In many respects, however, gendered messages in children's books still exist (Crabb and Bielawski 1994). An update of the classic Weitzman study found that although the majority of female characters were portrayed as dependent and submissive, male characters were commonly portrayed as being independent and creative (Oskamp, Kaufman, and Wolterbeek 1996). A subsequent study, which focused on the representation of gender and physical activity level in award-winning books from 1940 through 1999, found that female characters are much less likely than male characters to be depicted in active roles and that this depiction has not changed significantly over this vast time period (Nilges and Spencer 2002).

Gendered socialization is found even where gender roles are changing and socialization is becoming more flexible or androgynous. **Androgyny** refers to the combination of feminine and masculine characteristics in the same individual. Are girls more androgynous than boys? If so, what explains the difference? And what difference does androgyny make in an individual's overall well-being? Research has found that fathers who display the most traditional attitudes about gender transmit their ideas onto their sons more so than onto their daughters, whereas mothers who tend to have more liberal attitudes do not transmit their attitudes onto their daughters more than their sons. Consequently, "when the sons establish their own families, they will be more likely than the daughters to transmit traditional attitudes to their own sons" (Kulik 2002:456). Other researchers have also found that whereas adolescent girls tend to be more supportive of egalitarian gender roles than their parents (especially their fathers), adolescent boys follow their fathers' resistance to changes in traditional male roles. Therefore, it is predictable that males would be less likely than females to develop androgynous characteristics (Burt and Scott 2002). In a study of child care books and parenting websites, sociologist Karen Martin found some evidence of gender-neutral child rearing. But she also found that children's nonconformity to gender roles is still viewed as problematic because it is linked with homosexuality (Martin 2005).

Gender identities affect individuals' well-being in various ways. Witt (1997) found that parents who foster androgynous attitudes and behaviors in their children ultimately cause their girls and boys to have high self-esteem and self-worth. Androgynous individuals appear to be able to more effectively manage stress and practice good health (Edwards and Hamilton 2004), and androgynous college students report having better relationships with their parents (Guastello and Guastello 2003:664).

Children at Play

Children teach each other to behave according to cultural expectations. Same-sex peers exert a profound influence on how gender is learned. In a classic study of children's play groups, Janet Lever (1976) discovered how children stress particular social skills and capabilities for boys and others for girls. Her research among fifth-graders (most of whom were White and middle class) found that boys, more than girls, (1) played outdoors, (2) played in larger groups, (3) played in age-heterogeneous groups, (4) were less likely to play in games dominated by the opposite sex, (5) played more competitive games, and (6) played in games that lasted longer.

Barrie Thorne's (1993) study of gender play in multiracial school settings found that boys control more space, more often violate girls' activities, and treat girls as contaminating. According to Thorne, these common ritualized interactions reflect larger structures of male dominance. In reality, the fun and games of everyday schoolchildren are *power play,* a complex social process involving both gender separation and togetherness. Children's power play changes with age, ethnicity, race, class, and social context. In her analysis of how children themselves construct gender in their daily play, Thorne shifted the focus from individual to *social relations*:

> *The social construction of gender is an active and ongoing process. . . . Gender categories, gender identities, gender divisions, and gender-based groups, gender meanings—all are produced actively and collaboratively, in everyday life. When kids maneuver to form same-gender groups on the playground or organize a kickball game as "boys-against-the-girls," they produce a sense of gender as dichotomy and opposition. And when girls and boys work cooperatively on a classroom project, they actively undermine a sense of gender as opposition. This emphasis on action and activity, and on everyday social interactions that are sometimes contradictory, provides an antidote to the view of children as passively socialized. Gender is not something one passively "is" or "has." (Thorne 1993:4–5)*

New research on fourth-grade children in schoolyards supports Thorne's conclusions about gendered interaction in schoolyards. Boyle and her colleagues (Boyle, Marshall, and Robeson 2003) found a great deal of intragender variation in the schoolyard, with girls in particular engaging in many different activities. They also found that boys are more easily accepted into play with girls than is the case when girls try to play with a group of boys, and that boys tend to use more space in the schoolyard and are more likely to violate girls' space and games than the reverse.

Toys play a major part in gender socialization. Toys entertain children; they also teach them particular skills and encourage them to explore a variety of roles they may one day occupy as adults. Like clothing, kids' toy stores and departments are sharply divided into girls' and boys' sections. Toys for boys tend to encourage exploration, manipulation, invention, construction, competition, and aggression. In contrast, girls' toys typically rate high on manipulability, creativity, nurturance, and attractiveness. Playing with gendered toys may encourage different skills in girls and boys (Renzetti and Curran 2003:89–92).

In a study of parents and children in a day care setting, children eagerly accepted most of the toys presented to them by their parents and discarded other available toys in favor of their parents' choices (Idle et al., 1993). When parents discouraged their sons from playing with cross-gender toys, their sons learned and adopted this behavior. Campenni (1999) found that adults were most likely to choose gender-specific toys for their children. Toys that adults deemed most appropriate for girls included items pertaining to domestic tasks (such as a vacuum cleaner or kitchen center), child rearing (dollhouse, cradle stroller), or beauty enhancement (makeup kits, jewelry items). Toys rated "appropriate" for boys included sports gear, male action figures, building items, plastic bugs, and attire for traditional male occupations. Like other researchers, the Campenni study found that girls are often involved in cross-gender or neutral toy behavior. Girls are encouraged by both parents to branch out and play with neutral toys some of the time, but boys tend not to be given this same encouragement (Campenni 1999). Although we may be seeing some breakdown of traditional play patterns and socialization of girls, the same does not appear true for boys. Studies have also found that messages transmitted to children from advertisements affect their toy use and that the effects are different for boys and girls. Research finds that the messages in commercials have stronger effects on boys than on girls (Pike and Jennings 2005).

Although girls are now encouraged to engage in activities such as playing video games, traditional gender stereotypes still underlie this pastime. Research finds that girls tend to become less stereotypical in their play as they age—choosing more neutral toys, sports, and computer games (while boys remain masculine in their play) (Orenstein 2008).

Dichotomous gender experiences may be more characteristic of White middle-class children than of children of other races. An important study on Black adolescent girls by Joyce Ladner has shown that Black girls develop in a more independent fashion (Ladner 1971). Other research has also found that among African Americans, both girls and boys are expected to be nurturant and expressive emotionally as well as independent, confident, and assertive (McAdoo 1988; Stack 1990). Recent studies examining whether or not the socialization of Black children is more gender-neutral than that in other groups is inconsistent. Most scholars now say there is too much variation in any group to make generalizations (Hill and Sprague 1999; M. Smith 2001).

Formal Education

In 1972, Congress outlawed gender discrimination in public schools through Title IX of the Educational Amendments Act. More than three decades later, girls and boys in the United States are still not receiving the same education. Reports by the American Association of University Women (AAUW 1992, 1999) have offered compelling evidence that two decades after the passage of Title IX, discrimination remained pervasive.

Research contradicts the media myth of the "boy crisis," which portrays young men as marginalized, while girls are taking over the schools. Studies find that "over the past three decades, boys' test scores are mostly up, more boys are going to college, and more are getting bachelor's degrees" (Matthews 2006:A01; Von Drehle 2007). Although males do drop out of school more often than females, the trend is most pronounced among minorities and boys from low-income homes (Barnett and Rivers 2004; Matthews 2006). The "boy crisis" is an issue of race and class disadvantage, not one of gender difference.

Schools shortchange girls in every dimension of education. Let us examine the following areas: course offerings, textbooks, teacher–student interactions, sports, female role models, and counseling.

- **Curriculum.** Schools are charged with the responsibility of equipping students to study subjects (e.g., reading, writing, mathematics, and history) known collectively as the formal curriculum. But schools also teach students particular social, political, and economic values that constitute the so-called hidden curriculum operating alongside the more formal one. Both formal and informal curricula are powerful shapers of gender (Renzetti and Curran 2003:109, Booher-Jennings 2008).

The courses that high school girls enroll in are increasingly similar to those of boys. Still, there are noticeable gaps. Female enrollment in science and mathematics courses increased dramatically in recent years. Girls are more likely to take biology and chemistry as well as trigonometry and algebra II. But in general, girls are more oriented toward the life sciences and boys toward preparation in the physical sciences (Adamuti-Trache and Andres 2007; Sadker 2002:238).

Although girls on the average receive higher grades in high school than boys, they tend to score lower on some standardized tests, which are particularly important because such tests scores are used to make decisions on the awarding of scholarships and admissions. Schools ignore topics that matter in students' lives. The "evaded curriculum" is a term coined in the AAUW Report to refer to matters central to the lives of students that are touched on only briefly, if at all, in most schools. Students receive inadequate education on sexuality, teen pregnancy, the AIDS crisis, and the increase of sexually transmitted diseases among adolescents. According to the AAUW report, gender bias also affects males. Three out of four boys currently report that they were the targets of sexual harassment in schools—usually of taunts challenging their masculinity. In addition, although girls receive lower test grades, boys often receive lower overall course grades.

- **Textbooks.** The content of textbooks transmits messages to readers about society, about children, and about what adults are supposed to do. For this reason, individuals and groups concerned about gender bias in schools have looked carefully at how males and females are portrayed in textbooks assigned to students. Their findings provide a consistent message: Textbooks commonly used in U.S. schools are both overtly and covertly sexist. Sexism has become a recent concern of publishers, and a number have instituted guidelines for creating inclusive images in educational materials.

  No doubt these efforts have produced better textbooks. Reading lists are more inclusive and textbooks are more balanced than they used to be. But notable disparities still exist. Girls, for instance, tend to be in needy positions, whereas males are more likely to be portrayed as offering help. Furthermore, girls are pictured less often, but if included, they typically maintain supportive rather than lead roles in the stories or pictures. Also, girls are more likely to be the spectators rather than the participants in textbook pictures (Bauer 2000:23). "Males are more likely to be discussed in the context of their occupational roles, whereas when females are discussed, it is their personality characteristics that get the most attention" (Renzetti and Curan 2003:109).

- **Teacher–Student Interactions.** Even when girls and boys are in the same classrooms, boys are given preferential treatment. Girls receive less attention and different types of attention from classroom teachers.

  Teachers are now advised to encourage cooperative cross-sex learning, to monitor their own (teacher) behavior, to be sure that they reward male and female students equally, and to actively familiarize students with gender-atypical roles by assigning them specific duties as leaders, recording secretary, and so on (Lockheed 1985; cited in Giele 1988).

  Despite the fact that many teachers are trying to interact with their students in nongendered ways, they nonetheless continue to do so. In her study of third-grade classes, Garrahy (2001) found that although the teachers were claiming to be gender neutral, they often interacted differently with boys in the classroom. Spencer and Toleman (2003) found that the teachers spent more time with the male students when they were working independently and in small groups; perhaps most troubling, the students normalized and naturalized these gender differences. Unfortunately, despite the increasing awareness of gender inequality within schools, new teachers are not adequately being taught about gender equity issues.

Many forms of gender bias exist in education. For example, girls receive less attention and different types of attention from classroom teachers.

- **Sports.** Sports in U.S. high schools and colleges have historically been almost exclusively a male preserve (this section is dependent on Eitzen and Sage 2010). The truth of this observation is clearly evident if one compares by sex the number of participants, facilities, support of school administrations, and financial support.

  Such disparities have been based on the traditional assumptions that competitive sport is basically a masculine activity and that the proper roles of girls and women are as spectators and cheerleaders. What is the impact on a society that encourages its boys and young men to participate in sports while expecting its girls and young women to be spectators and cheerleaders? Sports reinforce societal expectations for males and females. Males are to be dominant and aggressive—the doers—while females are expected to be passive supporters of men, attaining status through the efforts of their menfolk.

  An important consequence of this traditional view is that approximately half of the population has been denied access to all that sport has to offer (physical conditioning, enjoyment, teamwork, goal attainment, ego enhancement, social status, and competitiveness). School administrators, school boards, and citizens of local communities have long assumed that sports participation has general educational value. If so, then girls and women should also be allowed to receive the benefits.

  In 1972, passage of Title IX of the Educational Amendments Act required that schools receiving federal funds must provide equal opportunities for males and females. Despite considerable opposition by school administrators, athletic directors, and school boards, major changes occurred over time because of this federal legislation. More monies were spent on women's sports; better facilities and equipment were provided; and women were gradually accepted as athletes. The most significant result was an increase in female participation. The number of high school girls participating in interscholastic sports increased from 300,000 in 1971 to 3.11 million in 2008. By the 2008 school year, 41.3 percent of all high school participants were female, and the number of sports available to them was more than twice the number available in 1970. Similar growth patterns occurred in colleges and universities.

At the intercollegiate level, on the positive side, budgets for women's sports improved dramatically, from less than 1 percent of the men's budgets and no athletic scholarships in 1970 to 38 percent of the men's budgets and 33 percent of the scholarship budgets in 2008. Despite this marked improvement, women athletes remain underfunded. Although women account for 57 percent of the college student population, female athletes receive only 43 percent of participation opportunities. And male athletes receive $179 million more in athletic scholarships than their female counterparts (Lopiano 2008). This inequality is reinforced by unequal media attention, the scheduling of games (men's games are always the featured games), and the increasing lack of women in positions of power. One ironic consequence of Title IX has been that as opportunities for female athletes increased and programs expanded, the opportunities for women as coaches and administrators diminished. In the early 1970s, most coaches of women's intercollegiate teams were women. By 2008, 46 percent of women's team coaches were women (Lopiano 2008). Females who aspire to coaching and athletic administration have fewer opportunities than males; girls and women see fewer women as role models in such positions. Thus, even with federal legislation mandating gender equality, male dominance is maintained.

- **Female Role Models.** The work that women and men do in the schools supports gender inequality. The pattern is the familiar one found in hospitals, business offices, and throughout the work world: Women occupy the bottom rungs while men have the more powerful positions. Women make up a large percentage of the nation's classroom teachers but a much smaller percentage of school district superintendents. In 2008, women comprised 81 percent of all elementary school teachers, more than half of all secondary school teachers (56 percent), and 65 percent of all school administrators (Bureau of Labor Statistics 2009b).

  As the level of education increases, the proportion of women teachers declines. In the 2007–2008 academic year (more than 20 years after the Office of Civil Rights issued guidelines spelling out the obligations of colleges and universities in the development of affirmative action programs), women represented only 45 percent of full-time faculty. Furthermore, they remained overwhelmingly in the lower faculty ranks, where faculty are much less likely to hold tenure. In 2009, women comprised 26 percent of full professors, 39 percent of associate professors, 47 percent of assistant professors, and 53 percent of instructors/lecturers. Since 1986, the percentage of college presidents has doubled—from 10 percent to 23 percent of the total in 2009 (National Center for Education Statistics 2008). Although women now hold a greater percentage of the top positions at colleges and universities than ever before, women presidents remain underrepresented in comparison to their share of all faculty and senior staff positions (American Council on Education 2000).

- **Counseling.** A fundamental task of school guidance personnel is to aid students in their choice of a career. The guidance that students receive on career choice tends to be biased. High school guidance counselors may channel male and female students into different (i.e., gender-stereotyped) fields and activities. There is evidence that gender stereotyping is common among counselors and that they often steer females away from certain college preparatory courses, especially in mathematics and the sciences (Renzetti and Curran 2003:116).

In the past, aptitude tests have themselves been sex-biased, listing occupations as either female or male. Despite changes in testing, counselors may inadvertently channel students into traditional gendered choices.

Socialization as Blaming the Victim

The discussion so far demonstrates that gender differences are learned. This does not mean that socialization alone explains women's place in society. In fact, a socialization approach can be misused in such a way that it blames women themselves for sex inequality. This is the critique offered by Linda Peterson and Elaine Enarson (1974). Many years ago, they developed the argument that socialization diverts attention from structured inequality: "Misuse of the concept of socialization plays directly into the Blaming the Victim ideology; by focusing on the victim, responsibility for 'the woman problem' rests not in the social system with its sex-structured distribution of inequality, but in socialized sex differences and sex roles" (1974:8).

Not only is the cause of the problem displaced, but also so are the solutions. "Rather than directing efforts toward radical social change, the solution seems to be to change women themselves, perhaps through exhortation ('If we want to be liberated, we'll have to act more aggressive'). . . . Or, for example, changing children's literature and mothers' child-rearing practice" (8).

This issue raises a critical question: If the socialization perspective is limited and perhaps biased, what is a better way of analyzing gender inequality? To answer this question, let us look at how male dominance affects our society.

REINFORCING MALE DOMINANCE

Male dominance is both a force that socializes and a force that structures the social world. It exists at all levels of society, from interpersonal relations to outside institutions. This section describes the interpersonal and institutional reinforcement of gender inequality.

Language

Language perpetuates male dominance by ignoring, trivializing, and sexualizing women. Use of the pronoun *he* when the sex of the person is unspecified and of the generic term *mankind* to refer to humanity in general are obvious examples of how the English language ignores women. Common sayings such as "that's women's work" (as opposed to "that's men's work!"), jokes about female drivers, and phrases such as *women and children first* or *wine, women, and song* are trivializing. Women, more than men, are commonly referred to in terms that have sexual connotations. Terms referring to men (*studs, jocks*) that do have sexual meanings imply power and success, whereas terms applied to women (*broads, bimbos, hos*) imply promiscuity or subordination. In fact, the term *promiscuous* is usually applied only to women, although its literal meaning applies to either sex (Richmond-Abbott 1992:93). Research shows that there are many derogatory terms for women, but there are few for men generically (Sapiro 1999:329). Not only are there fewer derogatory terms that refer to men, but often such terms are considered derogatory because they invoke the images of women.

"Some of the more common derogatory terms applied to men such as *bastard, motherfucker,* and *son of a bitch* actually degrade women in their role as mothers" (Romaine 1999:99). (See "A Closer Look" on the use of animal terms to denigrate women.)

Interpersonal Behavior

Gender inequality is different than other forms of inequality because individuals on both sides of the power divide (that is women and men) interact very frequently (in the home, in the workplace, and in other role relations). Consequently, gender inequalities can be reproduced and resisted in everyday interactions (Ridgeway and Smith-Lovin 1999:191).

Sociologists have done extensive research on the ways in which women and men interact, with particular attention being paid to communication styles. This research has found that in mixed-sex groups, men talk more, show more visual dominance, and interrupt more, whereas women display more tentative and polite speech patterns (Ridgeway and Smith-Lovin 1999).

Various forms of nonverbal communication also sustain male dominance. Men take up more space than do women and also touch women without permission more than women touch men. Women, on the other hand, engage in more eye contact, smile more, and generally exhibit behavior associated with low status. These behaviors show how gender is continually being created in various kinds of social interaction. Candace West and Don Zimmerman (1987) call this "doing gender." It involves following the rules and behaviors expected of us as males or females. We "do gender" because if we do not, we are judged incompetent as men and women. Gender is something we create in interaction, not something we are (Risman 1998:6).

Producing gender through interaction is becoming a lively sociological topic. Instead of treating gender only as identity, or a socialization, or stratification, this perspective emphasizes gender as dynamic *practices*—what people say and do as they engage in social interaction (Ridgeway 1997; Martin 2003). In this view, gender is a system of action:

> *Gendered practices are learned and enacted in childhood and in every major site of social behavior over the life course, including in school, intimate relationships, families, workplaces, houses of worship, and social movements. In time, like riding a bicycle, gendering practices become almost automatic.* (Martin 2003:352)

Mass Communications Media

Much of the information we receive about the world around us comes not from direct experience but from the mass media—radio, television, newspapers, magazines, and the Internet. Although media are often blamed for the problems of modern society, they are not monolithic and do not present us with a simple message. The media have tremendous power. They can distort women's images and they can bring about change as well (Sapiro 1999:224). Women are still underrepresented on op-ed pages, on Sunday chat shows, and as experts in news stories (Pollit 2010). Studies show that women journalists' role in newsrooms is shrinking even though women predominate in undergraduate and graduate journalism programs and have for decades (Lauer 2002). In magazines, women's portrayal has become less monolithic since the 1980s. With the

A CLOSER LOOK

"Bitches," "Bunnies," and "Biddies"

How Animal Metaphors Degrade, Sexualize, and Denigrate Women

Many of the most derogatory words used to refer to women in our society share something in common: they use animal imagery to degrade women. For instance, women are frequently ridiculed as "bitches" and "shrews." Examining the definitions of these words makes their deeper meanings clear: in *Webster's New World Dictionary*, the word *bitch* is defined as "the female of the dog, wolf, fox, etc." and second as "a lewd, or promiscuous woman" (1991:143), and a *shrew* is defined as "a scolding, nagging, evil-tempered woman" (1991:1243).

Why have such words that originally referred to animals come to be used as common slurs against women? To answer this question, we must address the positioning of animals in our society. In brief, humans are perceived as being distinct from and superior to other animals. This belief has left animals vulnerable to widespread abuse at human hands. This widespread abuse is possible because animals are considered property and are generally treated as commodities. Equating women (and other marginalized groups) with animals through language simultaneously degrades them as "less-than-human" (read as "less-than-men") and reinforces our society's devaluation of their lives.

Animal metaphors are also used to refer to privileged groups of men, but such references are certainly fewer in number (as are derogatory terms toward men in general) and tend to invoke the image of strong, virile, and more revered animals, such as tigers and bulls. In contrast, women are compared to smaller, domesticated/dominated animals (such as cats or "chicks"), or to animals that are hunted as prey (such as foxes; Romaine 1999:101; Weatherall 2002:26). The use of specific animal metaphors therefore both illustrates and reinforces the power differentials between men and women in society. As Lakoff explained,

> English (like other languages) has many words describing women who are interested in power, presupposing the inappropriateness of that attitude. *Shrew* and *bitch* are among the more polite. There are no equivalents for men. There are words presupposing negative connotations for men who do not dominate "their" women, *henpecked* and *pussy-whipped* among them. There is no female equivalent. (2003:162; emphasis in original)

rise of feminism, many magazines devoted attention to women's achievements. Alongside these new magazines, many "ladies" magazines continue to define the lives of women in terms of men—husbands or lovers.

Two of the network news programs are now anchored by women (Katie Couric and Diane Sawyer), while "Rachel Maddow rules on cable" (Pollitt 2010). Still, women are underrepresented in television newsrooms. In 2008, women made up 40 percent of the television news workforce, whereas the percentage of women news directors in television was at 28 (Radio-Television News Directors Association [RTNDA 2008).

Studies have continually demonstrated that highly stereotyped behavior characterizes both children's and adult programming as well as commercials. Male role models are provided in greater numbers than are female, with the exception of daytime soap operas, in which men and women are equally represented. Prime-time television is distorted. Although men represent 49 percent of the U.S. population, they represented 60 percent of prime-time television characters in 2007 (Media Report to Women 2007).

Images of women on entertainment television have changed greatly in recent decades. A report by the National Commission on Working Women found increasing diversity of characters portraying working women as television's most significant improvement. In many serials, women do play strong

Not only are women who seek power commonly vilified as animals, but also the terms used to refer to men who fail to invoke their power against women likewise appeal to images of women as animals. Women are said to "henpeck," "pussywhip," and consequently emasculate and thus dehumanize men.

These animal metaphors not only serve to degrade individuals, but some also objectify and sexualize women: referring to a woman as a "pussy" or a "piece of tail" are clear illustrations. Often this sexualization is intertwined with the imagery of the hunt, whereby the (heterosexual) man is viewed as the predator and the woman/animal his prey. Is it a coincidence that the most infamous corporate symbol of the sexualization of women—the Playboy bunny—is an animal, and a popularly hunted animal at that? The reverse is also true: hunted animals are frequently referred to in ways that conjure up sexualized images of women. For instance, a study of sport hunting magazines details instances where bird decoys were referred to as "Barbie hens," deer antlers were referred to as "big 'uns," and the use of the feminine pronoun "she" to refer to hunted animals was commonplace (Kalof, Fitzgerald, and Baralt forthcoming).

In addition to the use of animal metaphors to degrade and sexualize women, animals and women who do not conform to society's demands and standards are also referred to using the same terms. For instance, the term *maiden* refers to a horse who has not won a race, but it is also used to refer to an unmarried woman (Romaine 1999:92). Animals and women who are perceived as being "past their prime" and whose bodies no longer neatly conform to the needs of society are referred to using the same terms, such as "biddy": "The hen ('biddy') who offers neither desirable flesh nor continued profitable egg production is regarded as 'spent'—and discarded. No longer sexually attractive or able to reproduce, the human 'old biddy' too has outlived her usefulness" (Dunayer 1995:13).

At first glance these linguistic metaphors may appear to be harmless. However, they not only reflect the current place of women and animals in society relative to men, but they also serve to subtly reinforce it. Therefore, these metaphors, and what they represent, warrant further examination and critique.

Source: Amy Fitzgerald, Department of Sociology, Michigan State University, 2004. This essay was written expressly for *Social Problems,* 10th edition.

and intelligent roles, but in just as many shows, men are still the major characters and women are cast as glamorous objects, scheming villains, or servants. And for every contemporary show that includes positive images of women, there are numerous other shows in which women are sidekicks to men, sexual objects, or helpless imbeciles (Andersen 2009:62). In response to the imbalances in prime-time television, the National Organization for Women states, "If you are a middle-aged woman, a lesbian, a Latina, a woman with a disability, a woman of size, a low-income mom struggling to get by . . . good luck finding programming that even pretends to reflect your life" (National Organization for Women 2002).

Television commercials have long presented the sexes in stereotyped ways. Women appear less frequently in ads than men, are much more likely to be seen in the home than in work settings, and are much more likely to appear in ads for food, home, and beauty/clothing products (Andersen 2009:61). In the past decade, however, the potential buying power of working women has caused the advertising industry to modify women's image. Working women have become targets of advertising campaigns. But most advertising aimed at career women sends the message that they should be superwomen—managing multiple roles of wife, mother, and career woman, and being glamorous as well. Such multifarious expectations are not imposed on men.

The advertising aimed at "the new woman" places additional stresses on women and at the same time upholds male privilege. Television commercials that show women breezing in from their jobs to sort the laundry or pop dinner in the oven reinforce the notion that it is all right for a woman to pursue a career as long as she can still handle the housework.

Religion

Most U.S. religions follow a typical pattern. The clergy is male, while the vast majority of worshipers are women (Paulson 2000). Despite important differences in religious doctrines, there are common views about gender. Among these are the beliefs that (1) women and men have different missions and different standards of behavior, and (2) although women and men are equal in the eyes of the deity, women are to some degree subordinated to men (Sapiro 1999:219; Thomas, 2007). Limiting discussion to the Judeo-Christian heritage, let us examine some teachings from the Old and New Testaments regarding the place of women. The Old Testament established male supremacy in many ways. Images of God are male. Females were second to males because Eve was created from Adam's rib. According to the scriptures, only a male could divorce a spouse. A woman who was not a virgin at marriage could be stoned to death. Girls could be purchased for marriage. Employers were enjoined to pay women only three-fifths the wages of men: "If a male from 20 to 60 years of age, the equivalent is 50 shekels of silver by the sanctuary weight; if it is a female, the equivalent is 30 shekels" (Leviticus 27:3–4). As Gilman (1971) notes:

> *The Old Testament devotes inordinate space to the listing of long lines of male descent to the point where it would seem that for centuries women "begat" nothing but male offspring. Although there are heroines in the Old Testament—Judith, Esther and the like—it's clear that they functioned like the heroines of Greek drama and later of French: as counterweights in the imaginations of certain sensitive men to the degraded position of women in actual life. The true spirit of the tradition was unabashedly revealed in the prayer men recited every day in the synagogue: "Blessed art Thou, O Lord . . . for not making me a woman."* (51)

The New Testament retained the tradition of male dominance. Jesus was the son of a male God, not of Mary, who remained a virgin. All the disciples were male. The great leader of the early church, the Apostle Paul, was especially adamant in arguing for the primacy of males over females. According to Paul, "the husband is supreme over his wife," "woman was created for man's sake," and "women should not teach nor usurp authority over the man, but to be silent." Contemporary religious thought reflects this heritage. In 1998, the Southern Baptist Convention, the nation's biggest Protestant denomination, amended its statement of beliefs to include a declaration that "a woman shall submit herself graciously to her husband's leadership and a husband should provide for, protect and lead his family." Some denominations limit or even forbid women from decision making. Others allow women to vote but limit their participation in leadership roles.

There are, however, many indications of change. Throughout the West, women are more involved in churches and religious life (Paulson 2000; Van Biema 2004; Thomas 2007). The National Council of Churches seeks to end sexist language and to use "inclusive language" in the Revised Standard Version of the Bible. Terms such as *man, mankind, brothers, sons, churchmen,* and *laymen* would be replaced by neutral terms that include reference to female gender. But these terms, although helpful, do not address a fundamental theological cause: "When God is perceived as a male, then expecting a male voice interpreting the word of God naturally follows" (Zelizer 2004:11A).

The percentage of female seminary students has exploded in the past few decades. Yet women made up only 14.8 percent of the nation's clergy in 2008 (Bureau of Labor Statistics 2009b). Across the United States, women clergy are struggling for equal rights, bumping up against what many call a "stained glass ceiling." Today, half of all religious denominations in the United States ordain women. At the same time, the formal rules and practices discriminate against women. In denominations that ordain women and those that do not, women often fill the same jobs: leading small churches, directing special church programs, preaching, and evangelizing (Van Biema 2004). Despite the opposition of organized religion, many women are making advances within established churches and leaving their mark on the ministerial profession.

The Law

That the law has been discriminatory against women is beyond dispute. We need only recall that women were denied the right to vote prior to the passage of the Nineteenth Amendment.

During the past four decades, legal reforms and public policy changes have attempted to place women and men on more equal footing. Some laws that focus on employment include the 1963 Equal Pay Act, Title VII of the 1964 Civil Rights Act, and the 1978 Pregnancy Discrimination Act. The 1972 Educational Amendments Act calls for gender equality in education. Other reforms have provided the framework for important institutional changes. For example, sexist discrimination in the granting of credit has been ruled illegal, and discrimination against pregnant women in the workforce is now prohibited by the law. Affirmative action (which is now under assault) remedied some kinds of gender discrimination in employment. Sexist discrimination in housing is prohibited, and the gendered requirements in the airline industry have been eliminated. Such laws now provide a basis for the equal treatment of women and men. But the force of these new laws depends on how well they are enforced and how they are interpreted in the courts when they are disputed.

Legal discrimination remains in a number of areas. There are still hundreds of sections of the U.S. legal code and of state laws that are riddled with sex bias or sex-based terminology, in conflict with the ideal of equal rights for women (Benokraitis and Feagin 1995:24). State laws vary considerably concerning property ownership by spouses, welfare benefits, and the legal status of homemakers.

Today, many legal reforms are threatened by recent Supreme Court decisions in the areas of abortion and affirmative action. In 1989 and 1992, the Supreme Court narrowed its 1973 landmark *Roe v. Wade* decision, which established the right to abortion. *Roe v. Wade* was a major breakthrough for women, giving them the choice to control their bodies. The 1989 and 1992 decisions made it easier for the states to restrict women's reproductive freedoms at any stage of pregnancy, including the first three months. These decisions have steadily chipped away at a woman's right to abortion.

Roe v. Wade is still on the books, but the Supreme Court has returned the nation to a pre-Roe patchwork of laws and conditions by moving the battleground to state legislatures. State restrictions that now make it more difficult for women to obtain abortions include parental notification rules and mandatory waiting periods. In 2005, the House passed a teen endangerment bill, restricting the ability of young women to obtain an abortion outside their home state. The bill makes no exception for a medical emergency unless the young woman has complied with her home state's parental involvement laws (National Organization for Women 2005). Since 1995, more than 4,000 antichoice measures have been enacted. In the congressional heath care reform debate of 2010, antichoice legislators removed abortion coverage from the health care bill (National Organization of Women 2010).

Politics

Women's political participation has always been different from that of men. Women received the right to vote in 1920, when the Nineteenth Amendment was ratified. Although women make up a very small percentage of officeholders, 1992 was a turning point for women in politics. Controversies such as Anita Hill's harassment allegations, the abortion rights battle, and the lack of representation at all levels of politics propelled women into the political arena. In 1992, Congress experienced its biggest influx of women (and minorities) in history. Subsequent elections have increased the number of women in our national legislature. As of 2009, 17 U.S. senators are women, and 73 women are in the House of Representatives (Center for American Women and Politics 2009). (See Table 9.2 for the percentages of U.S. women in elective office.) If Congress were representative of the nation, the Senate would have 51 women and the House 222 (Sklar 2004c).

The gender gap in our nation's capital is scandalous. In Washington, D.C.'s less visible workforce of professional staff employees, women hold 60 percent of the jobs, but they are nowhere equal to men. Congress has two classes of personal staff employees: highly paid men who hold most of the power and lower-paid women who are relegated to clerical and support staff. Many answer the phones and write letters to constituents—invisible labor that is crucial to their boss's reelection.

The United States lags behind other countries in the number of women elected officials. (Pictured is Nancy Pelosi, Speaker of the U.S. House of Representatives)

TABLE 9.2

Percentages of Women in Elective Offices

Year	U.S. Congress	Statewide Elective	State Legislatures	Year	U.S. Congress	Statewide Elective	State Legislatures
1979	3%	11%	10%	**1999**	12.1%	27.6%	22.4%
1981	4%	11%	12%	**2001**	13.6%	27.6%	22.4%
1983	4%	11%	13%	**2003**	13.6%	26.0%	22.4%
1985	5%	14%	15%	**2004**	13.8%	26.0%	22.5%
1987	5%	14%	16%	**2005**	15.0%	25.7%	22.7%
1989	5%	14%	17%	**2006**	15.0%	25.1%	22.8%
1991	6%	18%	18%	**2007**	16.1%	24.1%	23.5%
1993	10.1%	22.2%	20.5%	**2008**	16.5%	23.2%	23.7%
1995	10.3%	25.9%	20.6%	**2009**	16.8%	22.6%	24.3%
1997	11.0%	25.4%	21.6%				

[1] According to data from the U.S. Bureau of the Census.

[2] Information was compiled using the United States Conference of Mayors' 2009 website directory, www.usmayors.org/uscm/meet_mayors, as the primary reference

Source: Center for Women in Politics (CWAP). "Women in Elective Office 2009." Eagleton Institute of Politics, Rutgers. The State University of New Jersey. p. 2. http://www.rci.rutgers.edu/~cwap/Officeholders/elective.pdf; "Women Officeholders Fact Sheets and Summaries, 2008."

Women had a major place in the 2008 presidential election, with Hillary Clinton in the Democratic primary and Sarah Palin as the Republican nominee for vice president. Although neither candidate was elected to office, their campaigns sparked a national debate about women's access to political power. Globally, women are making substantial gains in politics. The United States has just over 16 percent female lawmakers in Congress. Although many facets of the gender gap appear to be narrowing, as Nancy Pelosi was sworn in as the first female speaker of the House of Representatives, sixty-five countries do better than the United States when it comes to women serving in national legislatures. For example, in Norway, 37 percent of lawmakers are women. In Sweden it is 45 percent (Wheatcroft 2007). Furthermore, women have served as heads of state in nations such as Canada, France, Germany, United Kingdom, Turkey, Pakistan, Chile, South Korea, and Liberia (Falk 2008). In the 200-year history of the United States, there has never been a female president or vice president. With the appointment of Justice Sonia Sotomayor to the highest court in the land, there are now two female justices on the U.S. Supreme Court.

The gender gap refers to measurable differences in the way women and men vote and view political issues. Voting studies of national elections since 1980 demonstrate that women often vote differently from men, especially on issues of economics, social welfare, and war and peace (Renzetti and Curran 2003:229).

STRUCTURED GENDER INEQUALITY

In this section of the chapter, we focus on the contemporary workplace because its patterns of segregation are among "the most tenacious problems in U.S. society" (Williams 1992:235). In fact, the United States has one of the highest levels of workplace gender inequality in the industrial world (Kimmel 2004:186). The workplace distributes women and men in different settings, assigns them different duties, and rewards them unequally.

Occupational Distribution

The new economy, discussed in Chapter 14, has changed both women's and men's employment rates. Increasingly, it is viewed as "normal" for adult women and men, regardless of parental status, to be employed (Bianchi 1995:110). The increase in women's participation in the U.S. labor force is one of the most important social, economic, and cultural trends of the past century. Yet men's labor force participation rates have decreased slightly while women's have increased dramatically. (See the labor force participation rates for men and women, 1950 through 2009, in Figure 9.1.)

Women's labor force participation has grown at a faster pace than men's in recent decades. Between 1970 and the early 1990s, women's number in the labor force increased twice as fast as those of men. At present, women's rate of labor force participation is holding steadily, while men's is declining slightly. Today, as in the past, the proportions of employed women vary by race. African American women have had a long history of high workforce participation rates. In 2004, they edged ahead of other women. By 2008, they participated in the labor force at a rate of 61 percent; 59 percent of White women were in the labor force in 2008, compared with 56 percent of Hispanic women (Bureau of Labor Statistics 2008). (See the projected labor force participation rates for women by race in Table 9.3.)

Today's working woman may be any age. She may be any race. She may be a nurse or a secretary or a factory worker or a department store clerk or a public school teacher. Or she may be—though it is much less common—a physician or the president of a corporation or the head of a school system. Hers may be the familiar face seen daily behind the counter at the neighborhood coffee shop, or she may work virtually unseen, mopping floors at midnight in an empty office building. The typical female worker is a wage earner in clerical, service, manufacturing, or some technical jobs that pay poorly, give her little possibility for advancement, and often little control over her work. More women work as sales workers, secretaries, and cashiers than in any other line of work. The largest share of women (54 percent), however, works in "service" and "sales and office" jobs (Bureau of Labor Statistics 2006c).

FIGURE 9.1 ***Labor Force Participation Rate by Sex, 1950–2009, and Projected, 2009–2016***

Sources: Occupational Outlook Quarterly, Winter 2001–2002. Washington DC: U.S. Department of Labor, Bureau of Labor Statistics, p. 39; "Employment Projections." U.S. Department of Labor, 2007. Online: http://www.bls.gov/emp/emplab05.htm

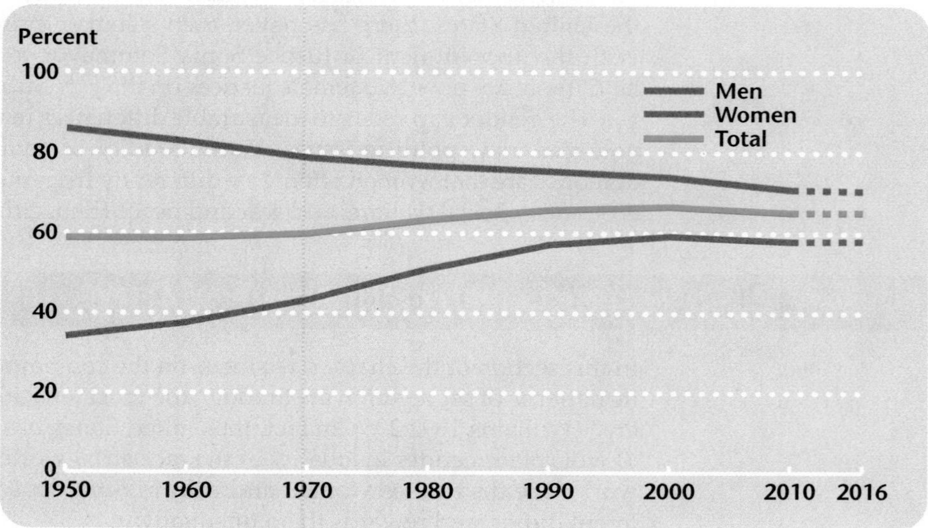

TABLE 9.3

Labor Force Participation Rates for Women, by Race, Selected Years and Projected 2016

Year	*Black*	*White*	*Hispanic*	*Asian*
1975	48.8	45.9	n.a.	n.a.
1986	56.9	55.4	50.1	57.0
1996	60.4	59.8	53.4	58.8
2006	61.5	59.3	56.1	57.6
2016	63.1	58.8	57.8	58.7

Source: "Employment Projections," U.S. Department of Labor, 2007, Table 3. Online http://www.bls.gov/emp/emplab05.htm

Economic restructuring has fundamentally altered the gender distribution of the labor force. Since 1980, women have taken 80 percent of the new jobs created in the economy. This gender shift in the U.S. workforce has accelerated in the current economic downturn, which has affected men and women differently. The current recession has disproportionately laid off men, who are more likely to work in cyclically sensitive industries like manufacturing and construction. Women, on the other hand, are overrepresented in economic sectors that are growing, like education and health care. As a result, for the first time in history, women are coming close to representing the majority of the national workforce. As of June 2009, women held 49.83 percent of jobs, compared to men, who held 50.17 percent of jobs (Cauchon 2009; Rampell 2009). Although this marks a historic shift in the national workforce, it does not mean that women have achieved equality in the workforce. Women still lag behind on many measures. In this chapter we examine gender segregation and earnings.

Gender segregation refers to the pattern whereby women and men are situated in different jobs throughout the labor force (Andersen 2009:124). The overall degree of gender stratification has not changed much since 1900. Women and men are still concentrated in different occupations (Dubeck and Dunn 2002). Overall, just 15 percent of women work in jobs typically held by men (engineer, stockbroker, judge), whereas fewer than 8 percent of men hold female-dominated jobs such as nurse, teacher, or sales clerk (Bernstein 2004).

In 2009, the six most prevalent occupations for women in order of magnitude were: (1) secretary and administrative assistant, (2) registered nurse, (3) elementary and middle school teacher, (4) cashier, (5) retail sales, and (6) nursing, psychiatric, and home health aide (Bureau of Labor Statistics 2009b; see Table 9.4).

Media reports of women's gains in traditionally male jobs are often misleading. In blue-collar work, for example, gains look dramatic at first glance, with the number of women in blue-collar jobs rising by 80 percent in the 1970s. But the increase was so high because women had been virtually excluded from these occupations until then. Women's entry into skilled blue-collar work such as construction and automaking was limited by the very slow growth in those jobs (Amott 1993:76). In 2008, only 1.6 percent of automotive service technicians and mechanics, 3 percent of construction workers, and 1 percent of tool and die makers were women (Bureau of Labor Statistics 2009b). The years from 1970 to

TABLE 9.4

Twenty Leading Occupations of Employed Women 2008 Annual Averages (employment in thousands)

Occupation	*Total Employed Women*	*Total Employed (Men and Women)*	*Percent Women*	*Women's Median Weekly Earnings*
Total, 16 years and older (all employed women)	67,876	145,362	46.7	$638
Secretaries and administrative assistants	3,168	3,296	96.1	614
Registered nurses	2,548	2,778	91.7	1,011
Elementary and middle school teachers	2,403	2,958	81.2	871
Cashiers	2,287	3,031	75.5	349
Retail salespersons	1,783	3,416	52.2	440
Nursing, psychiatric, and home health aides	1,675	1,889	88.7	424
First-line supervisors/managers of retail sales workers	1,505	3,471	43.3	556
Waiters and waitresses	1,471	2,010	73.2	367
Receptionists and information clerks	1,323	1,413	93.6	502
Bookkeeping, accounting, and auditing clerks	1,311	1,434	91.4	603
Customer service representatives	1,302	1,908	68.3	568
Maids and housekeeping cleaners	1,287	1,434	89.7	371
Child care workers	1,256	1,314	95.6	393
Managers, all others	1,244	3,473	35.8	1,010
First-line supervisors/managers of office and administrative support	1,169	1,641	71.2	688
Accountants and auditors	1,077	1,762	61.1	908
Office clerks, general	993	1,176	84.4	582
Teacher assistants	936	1,020	91.8	413
Cooks	801	1,997	40.1	363
Personal and home care aides	744	871	85.4	404

Source: U.S. Department of Labor, Bureau of Labor Statistics, Women's Bureau, 2008. "20 Leading Occupations of Employed Women 2008 Annual Averages (employment in thousands)," http://www.dol.gov/wb/factsheets/20lead2008.htm

1990 found more women in the fields of law, medicine, journalism, and higher education. Today, women fill 37 percent of all management positions (up from 19 percent in 1972). Still, there are fewer women than men in prestige jobs. In 2008, only 30 percent of lawyers, and 35 percent of physicians and surgeons were women (Bureau of Labor Statistics 2009b).

Although women have made inroads in the high-paying and high-prestige professions, not all have fared equally. White women were the major beneficiaries of the new opportunities. There has been an occupational "trickle down" effect, as White women improved their occupational status by moving into male-dominated professions such as law and medicine, and African American women moved into the female-dominated jobs, such as social work and teaching, vacated by White women. This improvement for White women was related to federal civil rights legislation, particularly the requirement that firms receiving federal contracts comply with affirmative action guidelines (Amott 1993:76).

The Earnings Gap

Although women's labor force participation rates have risen, the gap between women's and men's earnings has remained relatively constant for three decades. Women workers earn less than men even when they work in similar occupations and have the same levels of education.

The pay gap between women and men has narrowed. It hovered between 70 and 74 percent throughout the 1990s. In 2009, women earned 78.2 cents for every dollar men earned. Closing the wage gap has been slow, amounting to less than half a cent per year! "At this rate, 87 more years could go by before women and men reach parity" (Sklar 2004c).

For women of color, earning discrimination is even greater. Women's incomes are lower than men's in every racial group. Among women and men working year-round and full-time in 2008, White women earned 80 percent of White men's earnings; Black women earned 89 percent of Black men's earnings; Hispanic women earned 89 percent of Hispanic men's earnings (Bureau of Labor Statistics, 2009b; see Figure 9.2). The earnings gap affects the well-being of women and their families. If women earned the same as men, their annual family incomes would rise by $4,000. and poverty rates would be cut in half. Their lost earnings could have bought a home, educated their children, and been set aside for retirement (Greim 1998; Love 1998; The Wage Gap 2003).

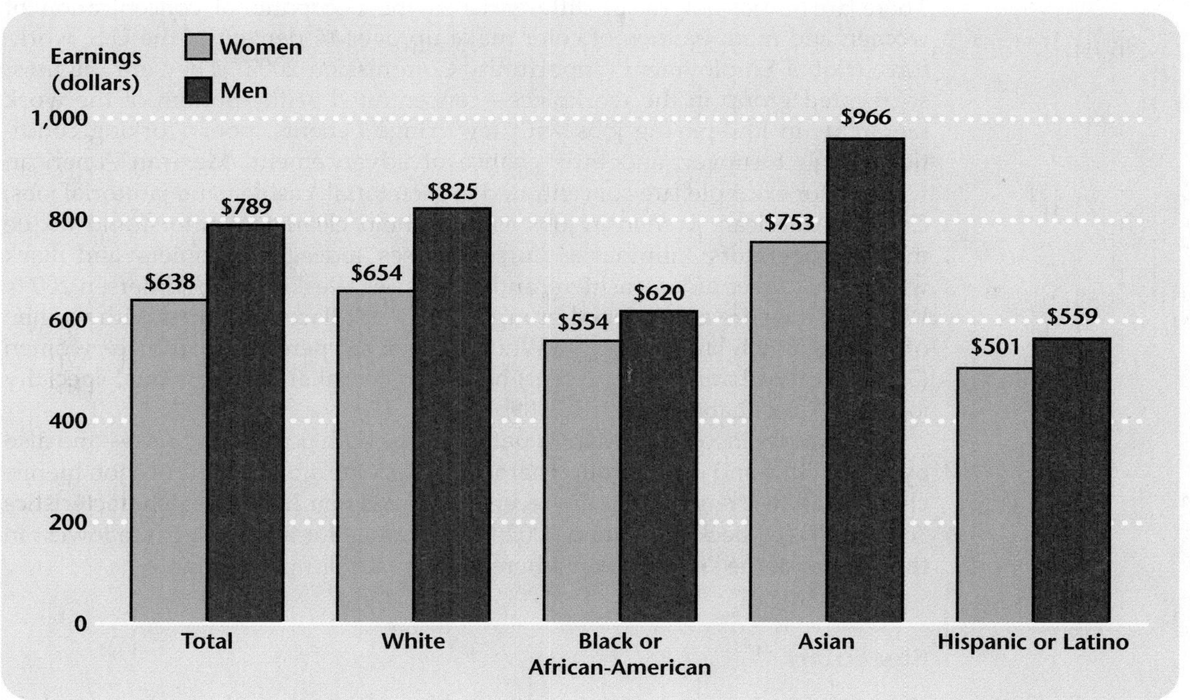

FIGURE 9.2

Median Weekly Earnings of Full-Time Wage and Salary Workers, by Sex, Race, and Hispanic or Latino Ethnicity, 2008 Annual Averages

Source: U.S. Department of Labor, Bureau of Labor Statistics, "Highlights of Women's Earnings in 2008" (July 2009), p. 4. http://www.dol.gov/wbls.gov/opub

The earnings gap persists for several reasons:

- Women are concentrated in lower-paying occupations.
- Women enter the labor force at different and lower-paying levels than men.
- Women as a group have less education and experience than men; therefore, they are paid less than men.
- Women tend to work less overtime than men.

These conditions explain only part of the earnings gap between women and men. They do not explain why female workers earn less than male workers with the same educational level, work histories, skills, and work experience. Men with professional degrees may expect to earn almost $2 million more than their female counterparts (Sklar 2004c). Study after study finds that if women were men with the same credentials, they would earn substantially more. Research on the income gap has found that women's and men's credentials explain some differences, but experience accounts for only one-third of the wage gap. The largest part of the wage gap is caused by sex discrimination in the labor market that blocks women's access to the better-paying jobs through hiring, promotion, and simply paying women less than men in any job (*ISR Newsletter* 1982; Dunn 1996; Leinwand 1999).

Intersection of Race and Gender in the Workplace

There are important racial differences in the occupational concentration of women and men. Women of color make up over 16 percent of the U.S. workforce (Equal Employment Opportunity Commission 2007). They are the most segregated group in the workplace—concentrated at the bottom of the work hierarchy, in low-paying jobs with few fringe benefits, poor working conditions, high turnover, and little chance of advancement. Mexican American women, for example, are concentrated in secretarial, cashier, and janitorial jobs; Central American women in jobs as household cleaners, janitors, and textile machine operators; Filipinas as nurses, nurses' aides, and cashiers; and Black women as nurses aides, cashiers, and secretaries (Reskin 1999; Andersen 2009). White women are a privileged group in the workplace compared with women of color. A much larger share of White women (38 percent) than Black women (31 percent) or Latinas (23 percent) held managerial and professional specialty jobs (Bureau of Labor Statistics 2009b).

Workplace inequality, then, is patterned by both gender and race—and also by social class and other group characteristics. One's placement in a job hierarchy as well as the rewards one receives depends on how these characteristics "combine" (Dubeck and Dunn 2002:48). Earnings for all workers are lowest in those areas of the labor market where women of color predominate.

Pay Equity

Women's low earnings create serious problems for women themselves, for their families, and for their children. Increasingly, families need the incomes of both spouses, and many working women are the sole providers for their children. Given these trends, equal pay is a top social concern.

The Equal Pay Act, passed in 1963, made it illegal to pay women less for doing the same work as men. However, the law is difficult to enforce because women and men are located in different occupations. For example, to be a secretary (usually a woman) requires as much education and takes as much responsibility as being a carpenter (usually a man), but the secretarial job pays far less (Folbre, Heintz, and Center for Popular Economics 2000). Pay equity in jobs that are dominated by women (where women comprise 70 percent or more of the workforce) would result in an 18 percent increase in wages for women (National Organization for Women 2005).

In the early 1980s, a number of state and local governments began addressing the pay-gap issue by instituting policies for pay equity in the public sector. Pay-equity policies are a means to eliminating sex and race discrimination in the wage-setting system. **Pay equity** means that the criteria employers use to set wages must be gender and race neutral. Today, the National Committee on Pay Equity supports legislation in the U.S. Senate aimed at curbing wage discrimination (National Committee on Pay Equity 2007a). In 2009, the Lilly Ledbetter Fair Pay Act became a crucial step forward in the battle to close the wage gap. The law reverses a 2007 Supreme Court ruling and restores the right of workers to go to court to hold their employers accountable for pay discrimination (National Committee on Pay Equity 2009; Samuels 2009).

Since 1980, more than twenty states have implemented pay-equity programs that reduced the gender wage gap. Minnesota, Oregon, and Washington were among the most successful (Folbre et al., 2000). Pay-equity struggles are difficult. Yet, in recent years, women willing to fight for their rights have won multimillion-dollar pay-equity settlements from corporations such as Home Depot, Eastman Kodak, Merrill Lynch, and Texaco.

How Workplace Inequality Operates

Why are women unequal in the workplace? Several theories are used to explain job segregation and ongoing wage inequality. Some focus on individuals, others focus on structural conditions, and others call on interactional processes to explain women's disadvantages in the workplace.

Popular explanations for gender differentials point to women themselves. They claim that women's socialization, their education, and the "choices" they make to take time out of the workforce to have children produce different work experiences for men and women. *Human capital theory,* for example, rests on the individual characteristics that workers bring to their jobs. Of course, time in the workplace, education, and experience all play a part. But the reality is far more complex. Research finds that woman's individual characteristics, or their human capital, explains only a small part of employment inequality (Ridgeway 1997:224). Research shows that ideas and practices about gender are embedded in workplace structures. This means that the workplace itself produces gender disparities (Acker 1990; Williams 1995; Martin 2003). Let us examine the organization of the labor force that disadvantage women and advantage men.

Dual labor market theory centers on the labor market itself. The labor market is divided into two separate segments, with different characteristics, different roles, and different rewards. The primary segment is characterized by stability, high wages, promotion ladders, opportunities for advancement, good working conditions, and provisions for job security. The secondary market is characterized by low wages, fewer or no promotion ladders, poor working conditions, and little provision for job security. Women's work tends to fall in the secondary segment. For example, clerical work, the largest single occupation for women, has many of the characteristics associated with the secondary segment.

To understand women's disadvantages, we must look at structural arrangements that women confront in the workplace. A classic study by Rosabeth Kanter (1977), *Men and Women of the Corporation*, found that organizational location is more important than gender in shaping workers' behavior. Although women and men behave differently at work, Kanter demonstrated that the differences were created by organizational locations. Workers in low-mobility or blocked situations (regardless of their sex) tended to limit their aspirations, seek satisfaction in activities outside work, dream of escape, and create sociable peer groups in which interpersonal relationships take over other aspects of work. Kanter argued that "when women seem to be less motivated or committed, it is probably because their jobs carry less opportunity" (Kanter 1977:159).

Many features of work itself block women's advancement. For example, some structural explanations call on gender segregation, per se, in which women and men are concentrated in occupational categories based on gender. Much research in this tradition has explained why job segregation and wage inequality persist even as women have flooded the workforce and moved into "male" jobs. Sociologists Barbara Reskin and Patricia Roos (1990) studied eleven once-male-dominated fields that had become integrated between 1979 and 1988: book editing, pharmacy, public relations, bank management, systems analysis, insurance sales, real-estate sales, insurance adjusting and examining, bartending, baking, and typesetting and composition. Reskin and Roos found that women gained entry into these fields only *after* earnings and upward mobility in each of these fields declined; that is, salaries had gone down, prestige had diminished, or the work had become more like "women's work" (Kroeger 1994:50). Furthermore, in each of these occupations, women specialized in lower-status specialties, in different and less desirable work settings, and in lower-paid industries. Reskin and Roos call this process *ghettoization*. Some occupations changed their sex-typing completely, whereas some became resegregated by race as well as gender (Reskin and Roos 1990; Amott 1993:80).

Many fields that have opened up to women no longer have the economic or social status they once possessed. Their structures now have two tiers: (1) higher-paying, higher-ranking jobs with more authority and (2) lower-paying, more routinized jobs with less authority. Women are concentrated in the new, more routinized sectors of professional employment, but the upper tier of relatively autonomous work continues to be male dominated, with only token increases in female employment (Carter and Carter 1981). For example, women's entry into three prestige professions—medicine, college teaching, and law—has been accompanied by organizational changes. In medicine, hospital-based practice has grown as more women have entered the profession. Women doctors are more likely than men to be found in hospital-based practice, which provides less autonomy than the more traditional office-based practice. In college teaching, many women are employed in two-year colleges, where heavy teaching loads leave little time or energy for writing and publishing—the keys to academic career advancement. And in law, women's advancement to prestigious positions is being eroded by the growth of the legal clinic, where much legal work is routinized.

Many organizational features block women's advancement. In the white-collar workforce, the well-documented phenomenon of women going just so far—and no further—in their occupations and professions is called the

glass ceiling. This refers to the invisible barriers that limit women's mobility despite their motivation and capacity for positions of power and prestige (Lorber 1994:227). In contrast, men who enter female-dominated professions generally encounter *structural advantages*, a "glass escalator," which tends to enhance their careers (Williams 1992).

Many of the old discriminatory patterns are difficult to change. In the professions, for example, sponsor–protégé systems and informal interactions among colleagues limit women's mobility. Sponsorship is important in training personnel and ensuring leadership continuity. Women are less likely to be acceptable as protégés. Furthermore, their sex status limits or excludes their involvement in the buddy system or the old-boy network (Epstein 1970). Such informal interactions continually re-create gender inequality. *Interactional theories* also explain why gender is such a major force in the labor process. Taken-for-granted interactions block women's progress:

> *Interactional processes contribute to the sex-labeling of jobs, to the devaluation of women's jobs, to forms of sex-discrimination, . . . to differences between men's and women's reward expectations, and to the processes by which women's entrance into male occupations sometimes leads to feminization or resegregation by specialty. (Ridgeway 1997:231)*

Individual, structural, and interactional explanations of women's workplace inequality rest on *social processes* rather than outright discrimination. But it is important to recognize that outright discrimination can be found in the workplace. For example, sexual harassment affects women in all types of jobs. Sexual harassment can include unwanted leers, comments, suggestions, or physical contact of a sexual nature as well as unwelcome requests for sexual favors. Some research finds that sexual harassment is prevalent in male-dominated jobs in which women are new hires because it is a way for male workers to dominate and control women who should be their equals. The problem is one outcome of gender segregation, with serious and harmful consequences for many women (Renzetti and Curan 2003:226–227).

Gender in the Global Economy

Gender relations in the United States and the world reflect the larger changes of economic globalization. Private businesses make investment decisions that have a major impact on the work, community, and family lives of women and men all around the world. In their search for profit, transnational corporations have turned to developing nations and the work of women and children. The demand for less expensive labor has produced a global system of production with a strong gendered component. The international division of labor affects both men and women. As manufacturing jobs switch to low-wage economies, men are often displaced. The global assembly line uses the labor of women, many of them young, single, and from poor rural areas. Women workers of particular classes/castes and races from poor countries provide a cheap labor supply for the manufacture of commodities distributed in the richer industrial nations.

Economic globalization is altering gender relations around the world by bringing women into the public sphere (Walby 2000). Although this development presents new opportunities for women, the disruption of male dominance can also result in the reaffirmation of local gender hierarchies through right-wing militia movements, religious revivalism, and other forms of masculine fundamentalism (Connell 1998). In addition, old forms of women's exploitation and abuse are being remade on a massive scale. For example, the commodification of women in the sex industry is now seen as an important part of globalization. The worldwide expansion of the sex club industry is closely linked to organized crime and the trafficking of women and girls across national boundaries (Jeffries 2008).

THE COSTS AND CONSEQUENCES OF SEXISM

Who Benefits?

Clearly, gender inequality enters all aspects of social life in the United States and globally. This inequality is profitable to certain segments of the economy, and it also gives privileges to individual men.

Transnational corporations derive extra profits from paying women less than men. Women's segregation in low-paying jobs produces higher profits for some economic sectors—namely, those where most workers are women. Women who are sole breadwinners and those who are in the workforce on a temporary basis have always been a source of exploitable labor. These women provide a significant proportion of the marginal labor force capitalists need to draw on during upswings in the business cycle and to release during downswings (Edwards, Reich, and Weisskopf 1978:333).

Gender inequality is suited to the needs of the economy in other ways as well. The U.S. economy must accumulate capital and maintain labor power. This requires that all workers be physically and emotionally maintained. Who provides the daily maintenance that enable workers to be a part of the labor force? Women! They maintain workers through the unpaid work they do caring for home, children, and elders. Their caregiving keeps the economy going, and it also provides privileges for individual men at women's expense.

The Social and Individual Costs

Gender inequality benefits certain segments of society. Nevertheless, society at large and individual women and men pay a high price for inequality. Sexism diminishes the quality of life for all people. Our society is deprived of half of its resources when women are denied full and equal participation in its institutions. If women are systematically kept from jobs requiring leadership, creativity, and productivity, the economy suffers. The pool of talent consisting of half the population will continue to be underutilized.

Women's inequality also produces suffering for millions. We have seen that individual women pay a heavy price for economic discrimination. Their children pay as well. The poverty caused by gender inequality is one of the most pressing social problems facing the United States in the new century. Adult women's chances of living in poverty are still higher than men's at every age. As we saw in Chapter 7, this phenomenon is called the *feminization of poverty* (Pearce 1978). Economist Nancy Folbre points out that the highest risk of poverty comes from being female and having children—which helps explain the high rates of both female and child poverty in the United States. Folbre calls this trend the "pauperization of motherhood" (Folbre 1985; cited in Albelda and

Tilly 1997:23). Of course, sexism produces suffering around the world. Some women are persecuted simply because they are women.

Sexism also denies *men* the potential for full human development because gender segregation denies employment opportunities to men who wish to enter such fields as nursing, grade-school teaching, or secretarial work. Eradicating sexism would benefit such males. It would benefit all males who have been forced into stereotypic male behaviors. In learning to be men, boys express their masculinity through physical courage, toughness, competitiveness, and aggression. Expressions typically associated with femininity, such as gentleness, expressiveness, and responsiveness, are seen as undesirable for males. Rigid gender norms make men pay a price for their masculinity.

Male inexpressiveness can hinder communication between husbands and wives, between fathers and children; it has been called "a tragedy of American society" (Balswick and Peck 1971). Certainly, it is a tragedy for the man himself, crippled by an inability to show the best part of a human being—his warm and tender feelings for other people (Balswick and Collier 1976:59).

FIGHTING THE SYSTEM

Feminist Movements in the United States

Gender inequality in this society has led to feminist social movements. Three stages of feminism have been aimed at overcoming sex discrimination. The first stage grew from the abolition movement of the 1830s. Working to abolish slavery, women found that they could not function as equals with their male abolitionist friends. They became convinced that women's freedom was as important as freedom from slavery. In July 1848, the first convention in history devoted to issues of women's position and rights was held at Seneca Falls, New York. Participants in the Seneca Falls convention approved a declaration of independence, asserting that men and women are created equal and that they are endowed with certain inalienable rights.

During the Civil War, feminists for the most part turned their attention to the emancipation of Blacks. After the war and the ratification of the Thirteenth Amendment abolishing slavery, feminists were divided between those seeking far-ranging economic, religious, and social reforms and those seeking voting rights for women. The second stage of feminism gave priority to women's suffrage. The women's suffrage amendment, introduced into every session of Congress from 1878 on, was ratified on August 26, 1920—nearly three-quarters of a century after the demand for women's suffrage had been made at the Seneca Falls convention. From 1920 until the 1960s, feminism was dormant. "So much energy had been expended in achieving the right to vote that the women's movement virtually collapsed from exhaustion" (Hole and Levine 1979:554).

Feminism was reawakened in the 1960s. Social movements aimed at inequalities gave rise to an important branch of contemporary feminism. The civil rights movement and other protest movements of the 1960s spread the ideology of equality. But like the early feminists, women involved in political protest movements found that male dominance characterized even movements seeking social equality. Finding injustice in freedom movements, they broadened their protest to such far-reaching concerns as health care, family life, and relationships between the sexes. Another strand of contemporary feminism emerged among

Surrounded by members of Congress, President Barack Obama signs the Lilly Ledbetter bill with Lilly Ledbetter, at center, behind Obama.

professional women who discovered sex discrimination in earnings and advancement. Formal organizations such as the National Organization for Women evolved, seeking legislation to overcome sex discrimination (Freeman 1979).

These two branches of contemporary feminism gave rise to a feminist consciousness among millions of U.S. women. As a consequence, during the 1960s and early 1970s, many changes occurred in the roles of women and men. However, periods of recession, high unemployment, and inflation in the late 1970s fed a backlash against feminism. The contemporary women's movement may be the first in U.S. history to face the opposition of an organized antifeminist social movement. From the mid-1970s, a coalition of groups calling themselves profamily and prolife emerged. These groups, drawn from right-wing political organizations and religious organizations, oppose feminist gains in reproductive, family, and antidiscrimination policies. In addition, many gains have been set back by opposition to affirmative action programs and other equal rights policies. Political, legal, and media opposition to feminism continues to undermine women's equality (Faludi 1991).

Women's Struggles in the Twenty-First Century

The women's movement is not over. Quite the contrary, the women's movement remains one of the most influential sources of social change, even though there is not a unified organization that represents feminism (Andersen 2009:351). Not only do mainstream feminist organizations persist, but also the struggles for women's rights continue. Today, many feminist activities occur at the grassroots level, where issues of race, class, and sexuality are important. In communities across the country women and men fight

> *against the abuse of women, against corporate poisoning of their neighborhoods, against homophobia and racism, and for people-centered economic development, immigrants' rights, educational equity, and adequate wages. Many have been engaged in such struggles for most of their lives and continue despite the decline in the wider society's support for a progressive social agenda.* (Naples 1998:1)

Whether or not they call themselves feminists, activists across the country and around the world are using their community-based organizing to fight for social justice. Instead of responding passively to the outside world, women are forging new agendas and strategies to benefit women.

■ CHAPTER REVIEW

1. U.S. society, like other societies, ranks and rewards women and men unequally.
2. Gender differences are not natural. They are social inventions. Although gender divisions make women unequal to men, different groups of men exhibit varying degrees of power, and different groups of women exhibit varying levels of inequality.
3. Men as well as women are gendered beings.
4. Gender works with the inequalities of race, class, and sexuality to produce different experiences for all women and men.
5. Many sociologists have viewed gender inequality as the consequences of learned behavior. More recently, sociologists have moved from studying gender as the individual traits of women and men to studying gender as social structure and social interaction.
6. Gender inequality is reinforced through language, interpersonal behavior, mass communication, religion, the law, and politics.
7. The segregation of women in a few gendered occupations contrasts with that of men, who are distributed throughout the occupational hierarchy; and women, even with the same amount of education and when doing the same work, earn less than men in all occupations.
8. Gender segregation is the basic source of women's inequality in the workforce. Work opportunities for women tend to concentrate in a secondary market that has few advancement opportunities, fewer job benefits, and lower pay.
9. The combined effects of gender and racial segregation in the labor force keep women of color at the bottom of the work hierarchy, where working conditions are harsh and earnings are low.
10. The global economy is strongly gendered. Around the world, women's labor is the key to global development strategies.
11. Gender inequality deprives society of the potential contributions of half its members, creates poverty among families headed by women, and limits the capacities of all women and men.
12. Feminist movements aimed at eliminating inequality have created significant changes at all levels of society. Despite a backlash against feminism, women and men across the country and around the world continue to work for women's rights.

■ KEY TERMS

Sex. Biological fact of femaleness and maleness.

Gender. Cultural and social definition of feminine and masculine.

Gendered. Differentiation of women's and men's behaviors, activities, and worth.

Feminist approach. View that supports equal relations between women and men.

Gender stratification. Differential ranking and rewarding of women's and men's roles.

Gendered institutions. All social institutions are organized by gender.

Male dominance. Beliefs, meanings, and placement that value men over women and that institutionalize male control of socially valued resources.

Patriarchy. Forms of social organization in which men are dominant over women.

Compulsory heterosexuality. The system of sexuality that imposes negative sanctions on those who are homosexual or bisexual.

Sexuality. A way of organizing the social world on the basis of sexual identity.

Capitalist patriarchy. Condition of capitalism in which male supremacy keeps women in subordinate roles at work and in the home.

Gender roles approach. Males and females differ because of socialization. The assumption is that males and females learn to be different.

Gender structure approach. Males and females differ because of factors external to them.

Androgyny. The integration of traditional feminine and masculine characteristics.

Gender segregation. Pattern whereby women and men are situated in different jobs throughout the labor force.

Pay equity. Raising pay scales according to the worth of the job instead of the personal characteristics of the workers.

Glass ceiling. An invisible barrier that limits women's upward occupational mobility.

SUCCEED WITH mysoclab www.mysoclab.com

Experience, Discover, Observe, Evaluate

MySocLab is designed just for you. Each chapter features a pre-test and post-test to help you learn and review key concepts and terms.

Experience sociology in action with dynamic visual activities, videos, and readings to enhance your learning experience. Complete the following activities at www.mysoclab.com.

Social Explorer is an interactive application that allows you to explore Census data through interactive maps.

- Explore the Social Explorer Map: *Gender Stratification in Wealth, Power, and Privilege*

The Core Concepts in Sociology video clips offer a real-world perspective on sociological concepts.

- Watch *Gender Socialization*

MySocLibrary includes primary source readings from classic and contemporary sociologists.

- Read Jacobs, *Detours on the Road to Equality: Women, Work and Higher Education*; Espiritu, *All Men Are Not Created Equal: Asian Men in U.S. History*; Lorber, *Night to His Day: The Social Construction of Gender*

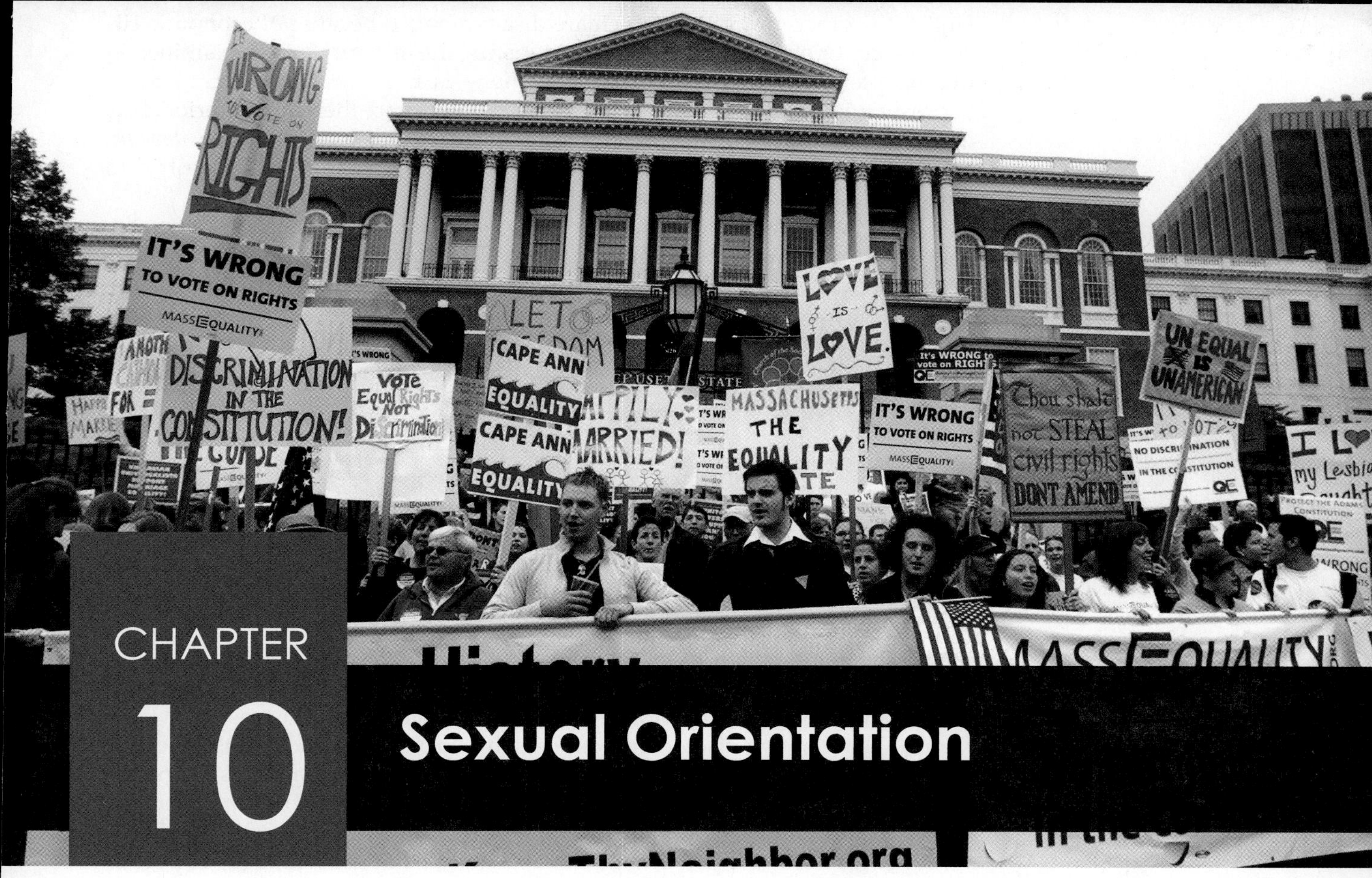

CHAPTER 10 Sexual Orientation

For more than forty years, the homosexual movement has sought to implement a master plan that has had as its centerpiece the utter destruction of the family. Barring a miracle, the family as it has been known for more than five millennia will crumble, presaging the fall of Western civilization itself.

—James Dobson, Focus on the Family

The strength or weakness of traditional families depends on how those families act: Staying faithful to one's spouse and caring for one's children, or failing to do those things. It's hard to see how the legal status of homosexual behavior affects anyone else's ability to maintain a strong family.

—Paul Schrag, *Mennonite Weekly Review*

The previous three chapters examined categories of people designated as minorities in society because of their impoverishment, race/ethnicity, or gender. The members of these social categories suffer from powerlessness, negative stereotypes, and discrimination. This chapter looks at another type of minority group.

Unlike the other minorities, which are disadvantaged because of economic circumstances or obvious ascribed characteristics, the minority group examined in this chapter—gay men and lesbian women—is the object of discrimination because it is defined by the majority as deviant and therefore inferior. It is important to underscore a crucial point—*homosexuality is not inherently deviant, but it is defined and labeled as deviant.* In other words, the deviance ascribed to gays and lesbians is a social construction.

This chapter is divided into four sections. The first section examines the concept of deviance and its implications. The next section presents what is known about homosexuals. The third section describes the various forms of discrimination faced by gay men and lesbian women in the United States. The final section describes the coping strategies of gays and lesbians and their political activities aimed at changing the societal structures that are unfair to them.

SOCIAL DEVIANCE

Most of us conform to the norms of society most of the time. Similarly, most of us on occasion violate minor social norms, and these violations are usually tolerated or even ignored. An occasional breach of etiquette, participation in a riotous celebration after an important sports victory, or loud chatter in a theater may bring some minor social disapproval to the violators but no serious punishment. Sociologists are most interested in social deviance that is disapproved of by many people and therefore evokes serious social consequences for the violators. The following discussion examines five important principles that help us understand social deviance in general and a sexual orientation that is defined as deviant in particular: (1) Deviance is socially constructed. (2) Deviance is a relative, not an absolute, notion. (3) Deviance is an integral part of all societies. (4) Whoever holds the power determines who or what is deviant. (5) The violators of important social norms are often stigmatized.

Because **deviance** is behavior that does not conform to social expectations, *it is socially constructed*. Societies create right and wrong by originating norms and saying that failure to follow the rules constitutes deviance. Whether an act is deviant depends on how other people react to it.

Even though sexuality has a biological base, it is also a social construction. Society impinges on this intensely private form of intimacy to shape our ideas about what is erotic, to define what is taboo, and to determine appropriate sexual partners and appropriate sexual behaviors. For example, during the 2004 Superbowl game halftime show, pop star Janet Jackson exposed her breast on national television. This act caused an outcry from the public, even though it is commonplace for women's breasts to be exposed in movies, on cable television, and in other forms of media. This reaction shows how behavior in one context is labeled as acceptable and in another context is labeled deviant. In contemporary U.S. society, **heterosexuality** (opposite-sex eroticism) is the expected—actually, demanded—sexual orientation. Thus, the term **compulsory heterosexuality** applies; that is, within U.S. society, the beliefs and practices of the majority enforce heterosexual behavior as normal while stigmatizing other forms of sexual expression. In fact, some people in the United States believe that **homosexuality** (sexual preference for someone of the same sex) or **bisexuality** (attraction to both sexes) is evidence of moral weakness or pathology. Thus, society has created homosexuality as deviance. For a closer look into the social construction of female and male sexuality, see "The Sexual Double Standard."

Because deviance is not a property inherent in any particular kind of behavior, *deviance is a relative, not an absolute, notion*. Evidence for its relative nature is found in the wide variation in definitions of deviance among societies and across history. For example, "On the streets of New York at the turn of the nineteenth century, men engaged in sexual acts with other men without any bearing on their identity as heterosexual, as long as they took what they thought of as the 'male part.' Women embraced their women friends, pledged their undying love, and slept with each other without necessarily interfering with their married lives" (Rupp 2007:55). In ancient Greece, homosexual relationships between men were expected. Men in ancient Greece and Rome were regarded as naturally bisexual, and one's sexual partner was not considered important. More importance was placed on how that sexual behavior was practiced. As Joan Roughgarden notes,

> *Ancient Greeks had a right way and wrong way of participating in male–male sexuality. In ancient Greece, male same-sex relationships were almost always between an older partner and a younger one. . . . The code for how a proper young man was to have male–male sex as the passive partner of an older man dictated that he never accept payment, that he refuse any unworthy active partner, that he avoid enjoyment, that he insist on an upright position, that he not meet the active partner's eye during orgasm, and that he avoid positions with penetration. The passive partner was understood to grant a favor to the active partner. (Roughgarden 2004:367–368)*

Historical and cross-cultural data support strongly that sexuality is a social construction, and that societal norms dictate appropriate and inappropriate sexual behavior in any given time period. In her essay on the social construction of heterosexuality, Pepper Schwartz argues,

> *Whatever the culture, its norms about masculinity and femininity are supposed to co-vary with heterosexual enactment, and gender itself is expected to be unambiguous and performed according to the cultural outlines of the moment. Even today, after the sexual and gender revolutions of the late 1960s and 70s, heterosexual dress codes, mannerisms, and body language are all strictly mandated. Although our culture has antiheroes who disdain these conventions . . . the majority culture creates cultural icons in its magazines, TV shows, movies, featuring models that tell us what exact gender displays portray heterosexual correctness. (2007:81)*

Deviance is an integral part of all societies. According to Emile Durkheim, deviant behavior actually has positive consequences for society because it gives the nondeviants a sense of solidarity. By punishing the deviant, the group expresses its collective indignation and reaffirms its commitment to the rules. Indeed, it is the very process of defining deviance that gives the majority a firm sense of what those rules are in the first place. Rupp explains,

> *We know that, without the concept of homosexuality, there would be no heterosexuality. Without knowing which sexual desires and acts are deemed deviant, we would not know which ones passed muster. Knowing how identities are created, institutions established, communities built, and movements mobilized, we learn from the margins what the center looks like. (2007:56)*

Thus, when individuals in an organization condemn a homosexual colleague, they are reaffirming that their sexuality—heterosexuality—is the only legitimate option. The negative sanctions applied to the deviant (gossip,

A CLOSER LOOK

THE SEXUAL DOUBLE STANDARD

In contemporary society, a prime example of the social construction of deviance and sexual behavior can be seen in the differential treatment of female same-sex sexuality versus male same-sex sexuality. Case in point, the well-publicized onstage kiss between pop icons Madonna and Britney Spears at the 2003 MTV Video Music Awards. It has received over 2,000,000 hits on Google and was voted the "best kiss of the decade" based on a poll by Selfridges. Now contrast that to the 2009 American Music Awards, where another pop star, Adam Lambert, kissed a male keyboard player. ABC received numerous complaints, and *Good Morning America* cancelled his subsequent appearance on their show. In an interview with CBS, Lambert refused to apologize and said that, as a gay man, he was being held to a different standard than female performers (for example, Janet Jackson groped one of her male dancers that same night, and no one complained.) CBS then came under fire for replaying the footage of Lambert's performance and blurring out the infamous kiss, but then showing unedited the 2003 Madonna–Spears kiss. Why the double standard? Pepper Schwartz argues that lesbianism has been eroticized through heterosexual pornography.

> As long as female performers in porno eventually show they are sexually available to men, their homosexual sex is seen as kinky rather than deviant. (2007:86).

Female same-sex sexuality is seen as erotic as long as the women engaging in it are defined as attractive, feminine, and still available to men. Schwartz argues that our culture tends to confuse heterosexuality with gender performance. Indeed, in interviews with gay youth in middle school, Benoit Denizet-Lewis found this to be clear.

> In particular, openly gay youth who are perceived as conforming to adolescent gender norms are often fully integrated into their peer and school social circles. Girls who come out as bisexual but are still considered "feminine" are often immune from harassment, as are some gay boys, like Laddie, who come out but are still considered "masculine." "Bisexual girls have it the easiest," Austin told me in Oklahoma. "Most of the straight guys at school think that's hot, so that can make the girl even more popular." (2009:39)

The sexual double standard illustrated by the Madonna–Spears kiss versus Adam Lambert's kiss clearly demonstrates how the same sexual behavior can be constructed in different ways. If Madonna and Britney Spears did not conform to societal standards of beauty and femininity, the societal reaction to their kiss would have undoubtedly been very different.

Madonna and Britney Spears at the 2003 MTV Video Music Awards.

Adam Lambert at the 2009 American Music Awards.

avoidance, exclusion) serve to enforce conformity in the group by restraining other people from deviating and thus reaffirming compulsory heterosexuality.

Whoever holds the power determines who or what is deviant. Power is a crucial element in deciding who or what is deviant. Certain social groups have relatively greater power and resources than others in getting their definitions of deviance to prevail. The major religious bodies in the United States, for example, have taken strong positions against homosexuality, and their opposition has influenced the laws and community norms. And occasionally, even deviants can mobilize power to change a discriminatory situation. As discussed later in this chapter, homosexual activists were able to mobilize enough political power to persuade the psychiatric community to no longer consider homosexuality a mental disorder.

The violators of important social norms are often **stigmatized**. That is, deviants are not only believed to be different from the majority, but they are also set apart by being socially disgraced. The society—through the church, the medical community, and the law—stigmatizes gays as sick, sinful, and criminal. In the community, they are pejoratively labeled as "queers," "dykes," and "faggots." From verbal harassment to physical violence, the consequences of deviating from the norm can be severe. This societal/community reaction to gays and lesbians has several consequences for them that are considered later in this chapter. The extremely negative reaction may keep many gays and lesbians invisible, will drive those open about their sexuality into gay ghettos, and may cause extreme personal distress. In the latter instance, gays experiencing the disgust that some heterosexuals have toward them may accept society's negative label and consider themselves sinners, criminals, sick, and therefore in need of help. The opposite may also occur: people labeled outsiders may reject the dominant rules and regard those who judge them as the problem.

GAY AND LESBIAN COMMUNITY: AN OVERVIEW

Defining Homosexuality

Homosexuality has become more visible in U.S. society in the past 25 years or so. This emergence of homosexuality into the mainstream of society has generated new questions about how homosexuality should be labeled and defined. The terms *sexual preference* and *sexual orientation* are both used to denote one's sexuality. The implications of each are important. **Sexual preference** implies a sense of choice regarding the sex of people to whom one is attracted, whereas **sexual orientation** implies a deterministic view of sexual proclivities. Heterosexuals tend to assume that homosexuality is a matter of sexual preference, whereas gays and lesbians tend to define their sexuality in terms of sexual orientation.

Roots of Homosexuality

Central to the issue just considered is the debate on whether homosexuality has genetic or social origins. Homosexuality is fairly common in the animal world. It has been found that male sheep exhibit homosexuality at least as often as humans: roughly 8 percent of rams turn out to have sex exclusively with other rams (Cloud 2007). At Oregon Health and Science University, researchers have been able to study the sheep's brains to examine the neurological basis of sexual attraction.

The Oregon group's work has shown that gay rams have different brain structures from heterosexual ones, news that should cheer those who see homosexuality and heterosexuality as mere biological variations. (Cloud 2007: 54)

A growing scientific literature provides evidence for a biological basis for homosexuality in humans (Thompson 1995; Pillard and Bailey 1998; Johnson 2003; Kristof 2003; Associated Press 2005; Hamer and Rosbash 2010). So far, however, the scientific evidence is inconclusive. Most studies are based on very small, nonrandom samples. Some researchers are convinced that an area of the brain, the hypothalamus, is responsible. Others find that the size of the anterior commissure of the brain makes the difference, although these brain differences seem to be true for gay men but not for lesbians. According to a 2008 study, Swedish researchers found that gay men have brains that are strikingly similar to straight women in terms of symmetry, and lesbians have brains that are similar to straight men. The researchers analyzed the brains of ninety subjects using magnetic resonance imaging and found some interesting differences in the amygdala, the portion of the brain responsible for the complex interplay of thoughts and emotions (*Science Daily* 2008b). In these types of studies, there is always a question of causation. In other words, were the brains different to begin with (at birth), or did the brains change in response to environment?

The most convincing evidence in the field comes from twin studies. The chance that identical twins will both be gay ranges from about 25 percent to 50 percent, depending on the study (Kristof 2003; Roughgarden 2004). Recent findings also point to a possible "sibling factor," where men who have several older brothers—whether they were raised together or not—have an increased chance of being gay (Schmid 2006). Other researchers remain unconvinced, given the complexity of biology and environmental factors on individual behavior (Byne 1999). John D'Emilio, a historian of sexuality, expresses this ambiguity:

There's a tremendous amount of evidence in history and cross-cultural studies to suggest that human sexual behavior and desire are enormously malleable, not just from culture to culture or from time period to time period, but in an individual's life. I'm not willing to say that there isn't a biological component, but there's too much else we haven't explored. (Quoted in Wheeler 1992:A9)

If biology is indeed destiny and homosexuality is genetic, then it is natural, not an aberration that results from selection, socialization, or seduction. Such a finding has profound implications. As Nicholas Kristof states,

A basic principle of our social covenant is that we do not discriminate against people on the basis of circumstances that they cannot choose, like race, sex, and disability. If sexual orientation belongs on that list (with the caveat that the evidence is still murky), then should we still prohibit gay marriage and bar gays from serving openly in the armed forces? Can we countenance discrimination against people for something so basic as how they blink—or whom they love? (2003:A19)

Indeed, "recent studies in college classrooms show that exposure of students to information on the causes of homosexuality has a direct influence on opinions about gay rights. This fits with polling data showing that people who believe that gays are 'born that way' are generally supportive of full equality, whereas those who believe it is 'a choice' are opposed" (Hamer and Rosbash 2010).

Although many gays and lesbians assume that the biological argument is conclusive, there are negative implications to consider. If homosexuality is largely a biological phenomenon, it will be seen by some as a physical illness in need of a cure. Brain surgery, gene splicing, or some other technique might be used to change the "deviant." Or prenatal testing might be used to identify homosexual fetuses for abortion.

Whatever its origins, there are two important sociological points. The first is that sexualities are malleable, shaped differently across time and location and even within a person's life span. Second, the issue of whether homosexuality has biological roots, social roots, or a combination of both is immaterial. The real issue is one of social justice, not origins (Davis-Delano 2000). As long as the majority defines homosexuality as deviant, prejudice, discrimination, and homophobia will continue.

Numbers: How Many Gays and Lesbians?

The numbers of gay men and lesbian women are unknown and probably unknowable because many never reveal their sexual orientation, living lives that appear heterosexually oriented. Moreover, the number of gays and lesbians willing to identify themselves as homosexuals to survey researchers is probably less than the real number. There are also problems of definition. Some people may be attracted to persons of the same sex but they do not act on it or identify as homosexual. Others may have had same-sex sexual encounters, but do not identify as homosexual. How is homosexuality to be defined?

Alfred Kinsey's research in the late 1940s and early 1950s stunned society with his findings on sexuality. First, Kinsey argued that there should be a scale of sexuality, where individuals are rated from 100 percent homosexual to 100 percent heterosexual, with lots of combinations in between. He further astonished Americans by placing the percent of homosexuals at around 10 percent for men. In the 1990s, a study found that the incidence rate of homosexual *desire* was 7.7 percent for men and 7.5 percent for women, whereas the rate at which men *identify* themselves as gay was 2.8 percent, and the rate for which women *identify* themselves as lesbians was 1.4 percent (Laumann, Gagnon, and Michaels 1994).

Using 2000 census data, Gates and Ost demonstrated that same-sex unmarried partners were present in 99.3 percent of all counties in the United States. The census indicates that about 2 percent of all adults are gay or lesbian (2004). The most recent census data come from the American Community Survey 2008. Consider the following facts (taken from Gates 2009 unless noted otherwise):

- In 2008, there was an estimated 565,000 same-sex couples living in the United States.
- More than 1 in 4 (nearly 150,000) identified themselves as "spouses." Same-sex spouses were identified in every state.
- Same-sex unmarried partners differ from their different-sex counterparts. In general they are older, more educated, wealthier, more likely to own a home, more likely to have both partners employed, and less likely to be raising children. (See Table 10.1.)
- In 2005, there were an estimated 8.8 million gay, lesbian, and bisexual people (single and coupled) living in the United States (Romero et al., 2007).

Gays and lesbians, like other minorities, tend to cluster in certain cities and neighborhoods within those cities (e.g., the Castro district in San Francisco and Greenwich Village in New York City). Research by Gates and Ost (2004) found several patterns concerning the geographic concentration of gays:

1. Vermont has the highest concentration of gay and lesbian couples in the nation.

TABLE 10.1

Demographic Characteristics by Couple Type, 2008 American Community Survey

	Married Different-Sex Couples	*Unmarried Different-Sex Couples*	*Same-Sex Couples (spouses and unmarried partners)*
Total	55,692,136	5,648,999	564,743
Average age	49.7	37.0	46.2
Both partners have at least a college degree	21.1%	9.8%	30.6%
Both partners are employed	51.6%	61.6%	63.5%
Average household income	$95,075	$65,685	$107,277
Own home	82.5%	45.2%	72.8%
Interracial couple	5.9%	12.0%	11.2%
Raising children	43.2%	43.1%	20.5%

Source: Gary Gates. (2009). "Same-sex Spouses and Unmarried Partners in the American Community Survey, 2008." The Williams Institute, October 2009. Retrieved February 16, 2010, from http://www.law.ucla.edu/williamsinstitute/pdf/ACS2008_Final(2).pdf

2. San Francisco, Fort Lauderdale, Santa Rosa, Seattle, and New York top the list of metropolitan areas for gay male couples to live, and the top cities for lesbian couples are Santa Rosa, Santa Cruz, Santa Fe, San Francisco, and Oakland.
3. Gay and lesbian couples are most likely to live in college towns, resort communities, and state capitals.

The numbers debate has repercussions. Gay activists accept the higher numbers because it makes violence and discrimination against them more of an outrage, politicians will have to take them seriously, and there is a greater chance for public acceptance. The census numbers indicating that same-sex unmarried partners were present in 99.3 percent of all counties in the United States helped gay activists back up the claim that gays and lesbians are indeed "everywhere." The antigay right, on the other hand, argues for the lower numbers because it undercuts the gay movement for equality. Perhaps Congressman Henry Waxman gave the best response to the numbers issue: "One percent, 10 percent, discrimination is discrimination" (Cole and Gorman 1993:29).

Interpersonal Relationships and Domestic Arrangements among Gays and Lesbians

With the ever-growing controversy surrounding the issue of same-sex marriage, some social scientists have turned to empirical investigations of gay couples. Their conclusions about sexual relationships point to a number of similarities and differences between homosexuals and heterosexuals and between gay men and lesbian women, some of which contradict the prevailing stereotypes.

Gays are similar to heterosexuals in their desire for an intimate relationship with one special person. Because most homosexuals are denied marriage in most states, homosexual couples must turn to cohabitation relationships. Research has found that long-lived partnerships between gay men are not uncommon, but neither are they typical. Lesbians, on the other hand, tend to attach a high priority to domestic partnerships. Lawrence Kurdek has studied gay and lesbian couples over time and found that overall they are more similar than different; however, lesbians reported more trust and more equality in their relationships (2003). In another study, Kurdek found that lesbian couples reported higher levels of cohesion and higher levels of satisfaction than the heterosexual couples studied, whereas gay male couples reported lower levels of commitment compared to heterosexual couples (2001).

The issue of sexual exclusivity is often a major source of tension in male homosexual relationships. Solomon and colleagues (2005) found that over 40 percent of the gay men in their study had an agreement that sex outside their relationship was permissible in some circumstances, whereas 5 percent or fewer of the lesbian and heterosexual couples in their study had such an agreement. They also noted that gay men were significantly more likely to have conflict about nonmonogamy than lesbian or heterosexual couples (2005:574). The tendency for gay men to be less sexually exclusive than lesbian women parallels the difference in heterosexual males and females and the socialization process whereby males learn they are expected to have more sexual partners than women, and women learn to place an emphasis on relationships.

In contrast to many heterosexual relationships, research shows that homosexual couples tend to be more egalitarian. Heterosexual couples, whether in cohabitation or marriage relationships, tend to accept the traditional gender roles for men and women. Solomon, Rothblum, and Balsam (2005) are some of the first researchers to study same-sex couples in legal relationships (947 couples who had civil unions in Vermont) and compare them to heterosexual married couples. Their findings indicate that gay and lesbian couples are more egalitarian in terms of the division of housework and household finances. Married heterosexuals in their study had a more traditional division of labor in the household.

There are three likely reasons for this difference from the heterosexual pattern. One is the conscious effort by homosexuals to reject the dominant marriage model that prescribes specific and unequal roles. Another reason is that in same-sex relationships, the partners have received the same gender-role socialization. Another source of equality in gay relationships is that there tends to be little income difference between the partners, a condition rare in heterosexual relationships in which most women have less earning potential than their male partners. Most gay and lesbian couples are dual-income units. And because both partners in a homosexual relationship are of the same sex, they are often subject to the same degree of sex discrimination in jobs and income. Whatever the reason, same-sex couples do not typically adopt "husband" and "wife" roles in their relationships but are more flexible in sharing housework (Peplau, Veniegas, and Campbell 2004).

Although there are many similarities between homosexual couples and heterosexual couples, homosexual couples face additional problems. Gay men and lesbian women are not encouraged to be open about their sexual orientation and their relationships; hence they may feel restricted in showing public affection toward their lovers. They are seldom extended such commonplace courtesies as having a partner invited to an office party or to a retirement banquet. Sometimes, this lack of social support comes from family members. Solomon and colleagues (2005) found that same-sex couples were less likely than heterosexual couples to have contact with their family of origin. Similarly, Kurdek (2004) compared gay and lesbian couples to heterosexual couples and concluded,

> *When differences were found, 78 percent of these differences indicated that gay partners and lesbian partners functioned better than heterosexual partners did, although most effects were small in size. The only area in which gay partners and lesbian partners faired less well than heterosexual partners was in perceived levels of social support from family members. (Kurdek, 2004:891)*

In summary, lesbian and gay couples are similar to heterosexual couples in their quest for love and relationships. Research shows that they tend to be more egalitarian than heterosexual couples in their division of household work and finances and that gay male couples tend to be less monogamous than lesbian and heterosexual couples. This sometimes becomes a source of conflict for gay male couples. Another source of conflict for gay and lesbian couples resides in the lack of support received from the dominant society and, in many cases, from their own families.

DISCRIMINATION

Variance from the societal norm of heterosexuality is not a social problem; the societal response to it is. Society has defined what is appropriate sexual behavior and orientation. Consequently, people who differ from the approved orientation are objects of derision and contempt by members of society and are discriminated against by individuals and by the normal way that the institutions of society operate. In short, their different sexual orientation makes homosexuals a minority group. Gays confront three types of oppression: (1) ideological, in which their behaviors are defined and stigmatized as immoral; (2) legal, where their activities are defined as illegal or they are treated unfairly by the courts; and (3) occupational, where jobs, advancement, and income are restricted or denied. This section examines each of these manifestations of institutional discrimination that homosexuals experience.

Ideological Oppression

Homophobia is fear and loathing of homosexuality and homosexuals. It shares many of the same roots with other prejudices. Like racism and anti-Semitism, homophobia includes "an intolerance toward otherness; a fear of lives, perspectives, and practices that one doesn't understand; and a visceral desire for a social hierarchy that puts some people on the rungs below you" (Angier 1993:4E). There is a long tradition of homophobia in Western society. Even though it is now politically incorrect to make racial, ethnic, and gay slurs, gay slurs such as "fag" and "dyke" are still heard in the movies, on television, and in schools. Homosexuals are often targets of ridicule, restricted from social interaction, and stigmatized. The Pew Research Center National poll (2009) found:

- Forty-nine percent of Americans feel that homosexual behavior is morally wrong.
- Blacks are much more likely to think homosexuality is morally wrong (64 percent) than Whites (48 percent).
- Fifty-three percent oppose same-sex marriage.
- Fifty-six percent opposed allowing gays and lesbians to serve as priests, ministers, or rabbis (Kaiser Family Foundation 2004).

For many people, the homosexual individual is an outcast. Gays are seen as an aberration, perhaps even a dangerous deviation, from so-called normal sexuality. When people believe that gays are immoral, they belittle their lifestyle; tell jokes about them; deny their rights to housing, jobs, and memberships in organizations; and even engage in hostile acts (verbal and physical assaults) such as gay bashing by adolescent males (see the Speaking to Students panel entitled "Homophobia in Schools and Its Consequences"). In June 2004, the U.S. Senate voted to expand hate crime legislation to cover crimes that target people because of their sexual orientation, gender, or disability. According to the Uniform Crime Reports collected by the Federal Bureau of Investigation, in 2008 hate crimes involving sexual orientation ranked number three (17.6 percent of all hate crimes), just behind religion hate crimes (17.9 percent) and racial hate crimes (51.0 percent).These homophobic attitudes and behaviors cause many homosexuals to have personal problems with self-concept and other adjustment problems. The way that society views homosexuality is shaped significantly by our religious heritage and the views of the medical community.

- **Religion.** The Judeo-Christian tradition considers homosexual behavior to be a sin. The Old Testament approves of sexual intercourse only within marriage and for the purpose of procreation. Homosexuality has therefore been expressly forbidden.

> *The rejection of homosexual behavior that is found in the Old Testament is well known. In Genesis 19, two angels in disguise visit the city of Sodom and are offered hospitality and shelter by Lot. During the night, the men of Sodom demand that Lot hand over his guests for homosexual intercourse. Lot refuses, and the angels blind the men of Sodom. (Catholic.com 2004:1)*

In all, roughly twenty Bible passages have been interpreted as involving homosexual behavior. Most fundamentalists and other Evangelical Christians believe that God hates homosexual behavior and that sexually active homosexuals will end up in Hell, not Heaven (Religious Tolerance.org 2009).

The New Testament continues the tradition of the Old Testament. The early Christians strived for human perfection unencumbered by the desires of the flesh—celibate religious leaders, sexual intercourse only within marriage, and condemnation of homosexuality. Speaking of homosexuality, the apostle Paul, for example, considered lustful behavior between men and between women as "vile passions . . . against nature" (Romans 1:26). Paul in Corinthians also wrote that homosexuals, along with fornicators, idolaters, adulterers, and thieves, would never inherit the kingdom of God.

Like all passages in the Bible, those pertaining to sexual behavior are hotly debated. Many scholars have contested the traditional interpretations of the

Speaking to Students

Homophobia in Schools and Its Consequences

Adolescence is a difficult time of emotional, physical, and sexual changes. It is also a stage when peer approval is especially crucial for a positive sense of self. Today, many schools across the country have gay–straight alliance clubs, teens can watch mainstream media that include gays and lesbians in the programming, some novels and magazines are written for a gay and lesbian teen audience, and websites offer support and information for gay and lesbian teenagers. Despite such resources, the American Academy of Pediatrics worries about gay and lesbian youths because they are subjected to abuse and isolation at this critical time in their lives. Homosexual youths "are severely hindered by societal stigmatization and prejudice, limited knowledge of human sexuality, a need for secrecy, a lack of opportunities for open socialization. . . . Peers may engage in cruel name-calling [and] ostracize or even physically abuse the identified individual. School and other community figures may resort to ridicule or open taunting, or they may fail to provide support" (quoted in Carman 2001:1B). Thus, for the 2 million or so school-age children who are lesbian, gay, bisexual, or transgendered, school can be an extremely difficult place. According to the 2007 National School Climate Survey (Gay, Lesbian and Straight Education Network 2008):

- 86.2 percent of LGBT students reported being verbally harassed in school.
- 44.1 percent of LGBT students reported being physically harassed, and 22.1 percent reported being physically assaulted because of their sexual orientation.
- 73.6 percent hear derogatory remarks such as "faggot" or "dyke" frequently or often at school.
- 60.8 percent reported that they felt unsafe in school.

These statistics are the reason that the Harvey Milk School opened in the fall of 2003 to provide a "practical, safe solution for certain at-risk students subject to extreme levels of violence and harassment" (Harvey Milk High School mission statement). Those opposed to the Harvey Milk School argue that the segregation of gay and lesbian students is not the answer and that more resources should be put into making existing schools safer for students. However, studies

Religion fuels much of the protest against same-sex marriage.

show that the attacks and abuse are extremely pervasive. Here are some comments from lesbian or gay students surveyed by Human Rights Watch in 2001:

- "Relentless verbal abuse and other forms of harassment are all part of the normal daily routine" (Dylan N.).
- One of Ron T.'s classmates vandalized the school theater, scrawling messages such as "[Ron] is a faggot" and "All gays must die."
- Alex M. said that he missed fifty-six days of school the previous semester. "I'm not proud of that. I know I should've done better. I just couldn't deal with it anymore."
- "People will start rumors about me because I'm the only gay person who's out in the whole school. The worst was when people were saying I had AIDS" (Miguel S.).

These attacks on lesbian, gay, and bisexual students create a hostile climate that can be unbearable for them. It can undermine their confidence and lead to feelings of isolation. At the very worst, teens can experience serious physical assault. In 1995, a 17-year-old student, Bill Clayton, committed suicide after being beaten and assaulted for being bisexual. In 1998, Matthew Shepherd, a gay student at the University of Wyoming, was beaten and killed because of his sexual orientation. In 2004, 18-year-old Scotty Joe Weaver was beaten, strangled, and stabbed. The authorities believe the killing was motivated by his sexual orientation. In 2008, Lawrence Fobes King, a 15-year-old student, was shot and killed by another 14-year-old male after asking him to be his valentine. Unfortunately, these are just a few of many examples of violence.

Sometimes, the intolerance, harassment, and homophobia come from the authority figures that teenagers are supposed to trust. For example, in 2002, the ACLU filed a lawsuit on behalf of an eighth-grader who was forced to sit in the principal's office during physical education class (for a week and a half) after the gym teacher heard that she was a lesbian (American Civil Liberties Union 2002). In 2003, the ACLU took action again, this time on behalf of a 14-year-old student. The ACLU claimed that school officials "outed" the gay student to his parents against his wishes, told him he must not discuss being gay while at school, forced him to read from the Bible, and disciplined him for being open about his sexual orientation (American Civil Liberties Union 2003).

To summarize, there are numerous support groups for gay and lesbian teens, growing numbers of gay–straight alliances in schools, more gay characters on television, and attitude polls show growing support among youth for things such as gay marriage and gays in the military. Despite these positive signs, on a day-to-day individual basis gay youth continue to face pervasive harassment and threats of violence.

Bible, whereas others feel the passages are unambiguously clear. Contemporary Christian churches and denominations are currently struggling between traditional views that are consistent with Christian history and a more modern approach of tolerance and acceptance.

For centuries, the Christian church ostracized homosexual people and gave its blessing to civil persecutions. The current expression of this position continues the heritage of moral condemnation toward gays. The Reverend Jerry Falwell, fundamentalist preacher and founder of the Moral Majority, for example, called the outbreak of AIDS among homosexuals a "form of judgment of God upon a society" (Crooks and Baur 1987:312). The Reverend Pat Robertson, television evangelist, said in 1998 that the widespread practice of homosexuality will bring God's wrath: "[It] will bring about terrorist bombs, it'll bring earthquakes, tornadoes and possibly a meteor" (Wharton 1998:14A). In another extreme example of fundamentalist thinking on homosexuality, Pastor Peter J. Peters asserts, "The truth is, the Bible advocates discrimination against, intolerance of, and the death penalty for homosexuals" (Peters 1992:1).

The Roman Catholic Church has consistently reaffirmed its opposition to same-sex relationships, same-sex marriages, and same-sex adoptions. For example, in 1999, the Vatican ordered a Maryland-based priest and a nun to end their 22-year ministry to lesbians and gays because they refused to condemn homosexuality as intrinsically evil (Associated Press 1999). More recently, Roman Catholic bishops drafted new guidelines that encourage parishes to reach out to gay Catholics who feel alienated by the Catholic Church, but at the same time, the guidelines reaffirm the Church's stance against homosexuality (Associated Press 2006b).

It is important to realize how much power is in the hands of different religious denominations, power to shape both thoughts and behavior. For example, a 2001 poll found that born-again Christians were twice as likely as non-born-again adults to state that homosexuality should not be considered an acceptable alternative lifestyle. Furthermore, eight out of ten born-again adults disapprove of clergy performing marriage ceremonies and blessing marriage unions between two gay people (Barna 2001). Similarly, Olson, Cadge, and Harrison found in their nationally representative survey that non-Protestants were much more likely than Protestants to support same-sex unions (2006).

The power of the church goes further than simply influencing beliefs, however. For example, in 1996 the Southern Baptist Convention voted to boycott Disney parks, movies, and products, for Disney's "promotion of homosexuality" because it provides the same health care benefits for the live-in mates of gay employees as it does for the spouses of straight workers and it allowed gay groups to organize an event at Disney World (Means 1996).

More recently, the American Family Association, a nonprofit Christian organization claiming the support of over 3 million people, called for boycotts of both Sears and Ford Motor Company for advertising during television programming that supports the "homosexual agenda" (Wildmon 2007).

Many congregations and denominations are more accepting of homosexuality. Some maintain that homosexuality must be condemned but, because of God's grace, homosexuals must *not* be condemned. Others are even more accepting, ranging from the acceptance of gay Christians as members to the ordination of gays as ministers. "Currently, a mere handful of the nation's 375,000 religious congregations call themselves 'welcoming and affirming' or 'reconciling.' Such phrases signify that gay, lesbian, bisexual and transgendered people are accepted in the church with the same rights, responsibilities and opportunities as heterosexuals" (Grossman 2001:D2). Although it is not a totally comprehensive list, Gaychurch.org has a listing of 5,940 "affirming" churches from all over the world.

The acceptance of gays and lesbians within religious denominations has reached a critical point in our history. The two most pressing and divisive issues concern (1) whether qualified gays and lesbians should be eligible to be priests, bishops, and ministers; and (2) whether the church should engage in rituals that recognize and bless same-sex unions. Conservative factions within these churches are threatening to break away if full acceptance of homosexuals becomes a reality. For example, the U.S. Episcopal Church confirmed an openly gay priest as bishop of New Hampshire in 2003, and as a result more than a dozen churches have defected in protest (Moore 2006). In February 2010, the Episcopal Church was on the verge of consecrating a second openly homosexual bishop (although her confirmation was not yet complete at the time of this writing).

The United Church of Christ is one of the first Christian denominations to approve a resolution endorsing same-sex marriage, and in 2009 the Evangelical Lutheran Church in America voted in favor of allowing practicing homosexuals in committed relationships to hold positions of authority within the sect. Strongly opposed to this decision were Lutheran members of CORE (Coalition for Reform), representing over 400 conservative Lutheran congregations.

Perhaps the most telling example of this paradox regarding gays and lesbians is the December 2006 ruling by the Committee on Jewish Law and Standards. The leaders of the Conservative Jewish movement passed guidelines that opened the door for the ordination of gay rabbis and the recognition of gay marriage. However, in a separate vote, the group also upheld a 1992 statement that advises against gay ordinations and the recognition of same-sex marriages. The result is a mixed approach that will allow both liberals and the more orthodox in the movement to pursue whichever policies they prefer (Nichols 2006).

As the issue of same-sex marriage becomes more and more imminent, thorny theological questions surround the church's definition and treatment of homosexuals. Churches face an uncertain future and the possibility of alienating members as they vote on these important issues. There is an ideological divide between generations (with younger Americans being more in favor of same-sex marriage), between conservative and liberal factions within religious groups, and between individuals over the interpretations of scripture.

> *The Bible endorses slavery, a practice that Americans now universally consider shameful and barbaric. It recommends the death penalty for adulterers (and in Leviticus, for men who have sex with men, for that matter). It provides conceptual shelter for anti-Semites. A mature view of scriptural authority requires us, as we have in the past, to move beyond literalism. The Bible was written for a world so unlike our own, it's impossible to apply its rules, at face value, to ours. . . . We cannot look to the Bible as a marriage manual, but we can read it for universal truths as we struggle toward a more just future. (Miller 2008:30-31)*

- **Medicine.** The beliefs that people in the United States have about homosexuals have been shaped by religion, as we have seen, and also by the prevailing views of the medical community. Whereas religious ideology tends to view homosexuality as a sin, psychiatric theory, until 1973, considered homosexuality as an illness. As an illness, it was assumed to be curable, and many techniques were tried, including prefrontal lobotomies, crude forms of conditioning (such as drugs that induce a sensation of suffocation or emetics to induce vomiting), and even castration. These and more moderate strategies of psychoanalysis were singularly unsuccessful in treating this so-called malady.

The American Psychiatric Association publishes the *Diagnostic and Statistical Manual,* which defines officially the conditions considered mental illnesses. In the first edition, homosexuality was labeled a mental illness. Some mental health professionals held the minority view that this label was wrong. Dr. Robert Spitzer, for example, said,

> *With the exception of homosexuality, all other disorders were associated with impairment in general, occupational or social functioning, or inherently caused some distress. . . . The argument the gay activists were making was that any distress was a reaction to social pressure. (Mach 1987:44)*

In 1973, after years of lobbying by gay activists and the efforts of other people, the American Psychiatric Association by a majority vote of its membership declassified homosexuality as a mental disorder; homosexual behavior was henceforth to be regarded simply as a manifestation of a preference, not as sick or bad. The Association recommends that treatment focus on the problems that may result from being part of a stigmatized group, problems such as guilt, anger, and low self-esteem.

> *There is no published scientific evidence supporting the efficacy of "reparative therapy" as a treatment to change one's sexual orientation, nor is it included in the APA's Task Force Report,* Treatments of Psychiatric Disorders. *More importantly, altering sexual orientation is not an appropriate goal of psychiatric treatment. Some may seek conversion to heterosexuality because of the difficulties that they encounter as a member of a stigmatized group. Clinical experience indicates that those who have integrated their sexual orientation into a positive sense of self function at a healthier psychological level than those who have not. "Gay affirmative psychotherapy" may be helpful in the coming out process, fostering a positive psychological development and overcoming the effects of stigmatization. (American Psychiatric Association 2007)*

In August 2009, the American Psychiatric Association's governing council formally adopted a resolution declaring that mental health professionals should not tell gay clients they can become straight through therapy or other treatments (Associated Press 2009).

Legal Oppression: The Law and the Courts

In fourteenth-century Europe, the common punishment for homosexuality was burning at the stake. The Puritans in the colonies continued the death penalty for this "crime." Around the time of the American Revolution, Thomas Jefferson and some liberal reformers of the day proposed changing Virginia law, replacing the death penalty for homosexuality with castration (Tivnan 1987).

The legal status of homosexuals has progressed considerably since the days of death and castration, but they are still not treated equally. According to the Human Rights Campaign, legally a person can be fired from his or her job in twenty-nine states just for being homosexual (2009). Furthermore, the marriage of homosexuals is recognized in just five states. In addition to losing the symbolic importance of having a union legitimated by the state, same-sex couples and their families are denied access to more than 1,138 federal rights, protections, and responsibilities automatically granted to married heterosexual couples (Human Rights Campaign 2009).

This section begins by surveying the major historical developments in the law in three areas of great concern to the gay community: sodomy laws, discrimination against gays by the military, and family rights for homosexuals.

• **The History of Sodomy Laws.** Prohibitions against **sodomy** (oral or anal sex) were universal in the United States until 1961, when Illinois became the first state to repeal its sodomy law. Other states followed, but others kept their sodomy laws intact. In 1986, there was a constitutional challenge to sodomy laws. The argument in this challenge was that sexual activity between consenting adults in private is not questioned, let alone regulated, even in states with laws prohibiting sodomy, provided the adults are heterosexual. In short, sodomy laws are used to harass homosexuals, especially gay men.

In *Bowers v. Hardwick* (1986), the Supreme Court reversed the U.S. Court of Appeals decision, ruling by a five-to-four vote that states had the right to prohibit sodomy. Justice Byron White's opinion "characterized as 'facetious' the argument that gay people have a 'fundamental right' to engage in consensual sex" (Leonard, 1990:12).

In 1998, Texas police mistakenly entered an apartment looking for a gunman and instead found John Lawrence and Tyrone Garner engaged in a sexual act. Lawrence and Garner were taken to jail and ordered to pay a fine for breaking the "Homosexual Conduct Law" banning oral and anal sex between two men or two women. In 2002, the U.S. Supreme Court agreed to hear the case, which would prove to be a watershed ruling for gay rights. On June 27, 2003, in *Lawrence v. Texas,* the Supreme Court overruled by six-to-three the Texas sodomy law. After the ruling, Justice Anthony Kennedy said, "Gay people are entitled to respect for their private lives. The state cannot demean their existence or control their destiny by outlawing private sexual conduct" (Greenhouse 2003:4A). The 2003 decision brought the United States in line with Europe and other developed countries in stating that what consenting adults do in the privacy of their own homes is none of the government's business. Although it is a big step forward for gay rights, this ruling does not affect one prominent institution that still formally forbids sodomy—the U.S. military.

- **The Military.** The U.S. armed forces have always discriminated against gays and lesbians. From 1982 to 1992, about 14,000 people were dishonorably discharged from the military as homosexuals. These discharges have led to many lawsuits. The decisions consistently reaffirm the military's right to purge homosexuals from its ranks. In 1990, the Supreme Court refused to hear two challenges to the Pentagon regulation that homosexuality is incompatible with military service. In doing so, the Supreme Court upheld this rule, although by not hearing the case, the court did not set a precedent affecting future cases.

In 1993, newly elected President Clinton vowed to change the regulations so that homosexuals would not be discriminated against in the military. Many citizens, politicians, military leaders, and military personnel resisted this proposal. The result was a compromise—the "Don't Ask, Don't Tell, Don't Pursue" rule. This policy meant that the military was not to ask its personnel about their sexuality and was to prosecute only if gay and lesbian service members were blatant about their sexual orientation. In short, as long as homosexual service members "stayed in the closet," they were allowed to be in the military.

Since the "Don't Ask, Don't Tell" policy was adopted in 1994, more than 12,000 military personnel have been discharged due to their sexual orientation (see Figure 10.1; Servicemembers Legal Defense Network 2009). Analysts have noted that when America went to war after September 11, 2001, the numbers of discharges dropped dramatically, as more military personnel were needed. "As fighting in Afghanistan and Iraq continues, the Pentagon has discharged the fewest lesbian, gay, and bisexual service members since 1995. The Pentagon expelled 787 service members for being gay in FY2003, down 17% from FY2002, and 39% from FY2001. Gay discharge numbers have dropped every time America has entered a war, from Korea to Vietnam to the Persian Gulf to the present conflicts" (Servicemembers Legal Defense Network 2006:1). According to an editorial in the *Washington Post,* "'Don't ask, don't tell' wastes federal resources while impugning the patriotism and wrecking the careers—at the convenience of the brass—of Americans who want to serve their country. It is past time to repeal the policy" (April 5, 2004:24A).

In 1995, President Clinton ended 50 years of official federal discrimination against homosexuals by ordering that gays and lesbians are no longer considered

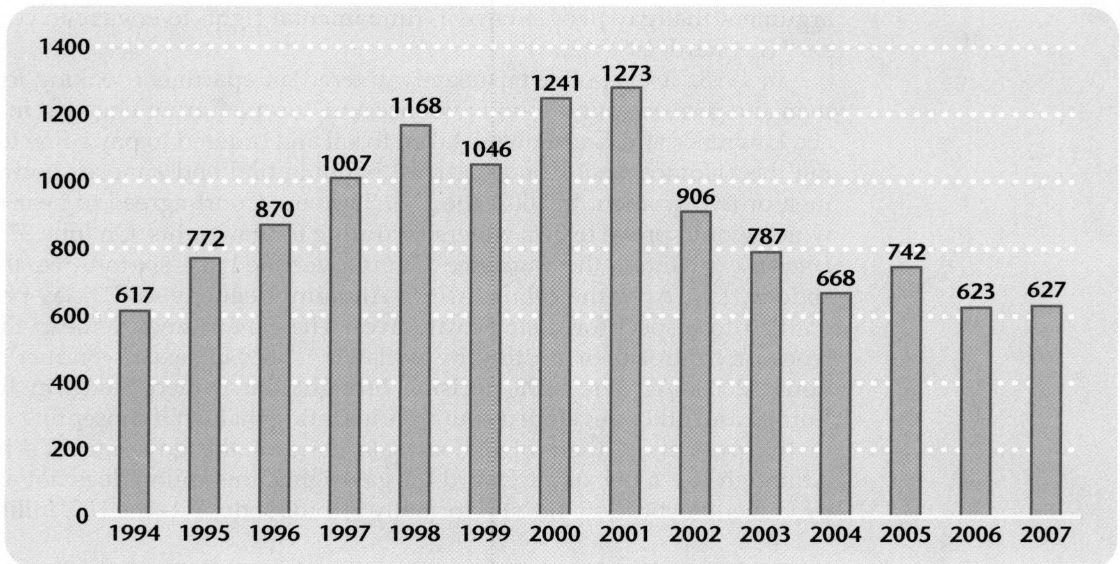

FIGURE 10.1

Number of Military Personnel Discharged Under Don't Ask, Don't Tell: 1994–2007

Source: Servicemembers Legal Defense Network, 2009. Retrieved from http://www.sldn.org/pages/about-dadt

security risks. This ruling meant that gays and lesbians in government would be granted access to classified government documents on the same basis as other federal employees. Although a small step forward, gays and lesbians in the military continue to face not only antigay harassment from their fellow military personnel and those in authority, but also the constant threat of being discharged.

In February 2000, Pentagon officials changed the name of the policy to reflect the problem of antigay harassment. In the wake of the murder of Private First Class Barry Winchell, the policy became "Don't Ask, Don't Tell, Don't Pursue, Don't Harass." A fellow service member murdered Winchell, believed to be gay, with a baseball bat in his barracks in 1999.

Despite legislation in a more favorable direction, as late as July 2006, the military's disability policy still classified homosexuality as a mental illness. In July 2006, the Pentagon reclassified homosexuality, this time grouping it under "conditions, circumstances, and defects." This grouping also includes such characteristics as repeated bed-wetting, dyslexia, stammering or stuttering, and obesity (Rosenberg 2006). According to Congressman Marty Meehan (D-MA, member of the House Armed Services Committee), "More than 30 years after the mental health community declassified homosexuality as a mental disorder, it is disappointing that the Pentagon still continues to mischaracterize it as a 'defect' " (quoted in Baldor 2006:1).

How many service members are affected by these policies? A 2010 report issued by the Williams Institute at the UCLA School of Law indicates that an estimated 66,000 lesbians, gay men, and bisexuals are currently serving in the U.S. military (Gates 2010). Furthermore, the study author, Dr. Gary Gates, argues that lifting "Don't Ask, Don't Tell" restrictions could attract an estimated

36,700 men and women to active duty service and 12,000 more to the guard and reserves. According to Gates, the "Don't Ask Don't Tell" policy has cost the military between $290 million and more than half a billion dollars since 1994 (Gates 2010). In his 2008 presidential campaign, Barack Obama pledged to repeal "Don't Ask, Don't Tell," but in his first year of office he did not address it. Pressure from interest groups and increasing support from the public has pushed the issue to the forefront. In President Obama's 2010 State of the Union address, he vowed once again to repeal the policy.

- **Family Rights.** The United States has a history of regulating the sexual behavior of its citizens through laws regarding marriage. For example, African Americans were not allowed to legally marry until after the Civil War. Mixed-race couples were not allowed to legally marry until 1967. And until recently, same-sex marriages were forbidden in all states.

Because same-sex couples are not allowed to marry, they are denied of the Family and Medical Leave Act, which permits individuals to take leave from work to care for ill spouses; the right to inherit property from a partner in the absence of a will; and the right to family-related Social Security benefits, disability benefits, and military and veterans benefits (Human Rights Campaign 2009).

Bernard and Lieber set out to examine this issue from a monetary standpoint. They created a hypothetical gay couple, gave them two children and assumed that one partner would stay home for five years to care for the children. They gave their couple an income of $140,000 and considered the taxes in the three states that have the highest estimated gay population. They concluded,

> *In our worst case, the couple's lifetime cost of being gay was $467,562. But the number fell to $41,196 in the best case for a couple with significantly better health insurance, plus lower taxes and other costs. These numbers will vary, depending on a couple's income and circumstance. Gay couples earning, say $80,000, could have health insurance costs similar to our hypothetical higher-earning couple, but they might well owe more in income taxes than their heterosexual counterparts. For wealthy couples with a lot of assets, on the other hand, the cost of being gay could easily spiral into the millions. Nearly all the costs that gay couples face would be erased if the federal government legalized same-sex marriage.* (2009:1)

Currently, five states have adopted same-sex marriage laws. In a landmark case in 2003, the Supreme Court ruled that the Massachusetts Constitution allowed for same-sex marriages, and the state began to issue marriage licenses to same-sex couples in May 2004. Connecticut, then Iowa and Vermont, and finally New Hampshire followed Massachusetts. At the time of this writing, Washington, D.C., is poised to follow as well. These five states join Belgium, Canada, the Netherlands, South Africa, Norway, Sweden, and Spain in allowing same-sex marriage.

As an alternative to same-sex marriage, some states offer civil unions for same-sex couples. Civil unions fall something short of marriage, but the couples have the same rights and responsibilities as heterosexual couples in the matters of insurance, inheritance, child custody, and taxes. Like married couples, couples can apply for a divorce to dissolve their union. Unlike married couples, civil union couples are denied over 1,000 *federal* rights and are unable to transfer their civil union to another state should they wish to move.

Other states have passed laws granting some statewide benefits to unmarried couples without granting civil unions. These domestic partnerships range from granting broad benefits and responsibilities to same-sex partners (for example in

Same-sex marriage is legal in just five states across the United States.

California and Nevada) to more limited benefits and protections known as reciprocal or designated beneficiaries (for example in Colorado and Hawaii). See Table 10.2 for a detailed look at the different states.

In a resulting backlash to these changes, many states have adopted various forms of the federal Defense of Marriage Act (DOMA), which defines marriage as the exclusive union of a man and a woman and refuses to recognize same-sex marriage licenses issued in other states. Seven of these states passed marriage amendments in the 2006 election, some with a very high pass rate. For example, the amendment in Tennessee passed by 81 percent of the voters (Alliance Defense Fund 2006). According to Pinello (2009), ten states have amended their constitutions to include "mini-DOMAs" limiting marriage to a man and a woman; another 10 states have statutory (but not constitutionally based) mini-DOMAs; and another 19 state constitutions have been amended to include "super DOMAs," which deny all forms of relationship recognition to same-sex couples.

The fight for same-sex marriage has been one of two-steps-forward, two-steps-back. In June 2006, gays and lesbians experienced a victory in the defeat of a proposed constitutional amendment. The Federal Marriage Amendment would have amended the U.S. Constitution to bar any recognition of marriage or its legal incidents for same-sex couples. Then, just a month later, a step back occurred when high courts in New York, Georgia, Nebraska, and Washington all upheld their states' bans on marriage for same-sex couples.

This step-forward, step-back process is clearly demonstrated in the case of California. Same-sex marriage was legal there for five-and-a-half months, and from June through November 2008, approximately 18,000 same-sex couples were married. Then, a step back came in November, when California voters

TABLE 10.2

Same-Sex Marriage, Civil Unions, and Domestic Partnerships in the United States

Partnership Recognition Type	*State*	*Enacted*
Same-Sex Marriage Equality	Massachusetts	2004
	Connecticut	2008
	Iowa	2009
	Vermont	2009
	New Hampshire	2010
Civil Unions/Domestic Partnerships (Broad benefits and protections)	California	2000
	Washington, DC	2002
	New Jersey	2006
	Washington	2007
	Oregon	2007
	Nevada	2009
Domestic Partnerships/Reciprocal or Designated Beneficiary (Limited benefits and protections)	Hawaii	1997
	Maine	2004
	Maryland	2008
	Wisconsin	2009
	Colorado	2009

passed Proposition 8, effectively banning same-sex marriage. The California Supreme Court voted that Proposition 8 is valid so no further same-sex marriages will be allowed; however, they agreed to uphold the existing same-sex marriages as valid. The state will also recognize same-sex couples that are married in other states.

Public opinion polls regarding same-sex marriage and civil unions demonstrate that this is a divisive issue that will be very important in political elections. In a 2009 Gallup Poll, 57 percent of respondents felt that same-sex marriages should *not* be recognized by law as valid and come with the same rights as traditional marriages (Gallup 2009). On the other hand, the majority (60 percent) of the younger generation (aged 18–29) is more in favor of same-sex marriage than the older generation, signifying a shift in societal attitudes and the potential for social change in years to come.

Barriers to marriage are just one form of legal oppression; parenthood is another battleground for lesbian and gay rights. The legality of homosexual parenthood varies from state to state, and the interpretation of the law often varies from judge to judge. Florida, Mississippi, and Utah have laws that explicitly prohibit homosexual individuals and/or couples from adopting children, and Michigan has prohibited same-sex couples from adopting but does not prohibit single homosexual individuals from adopting. Other states may not explicitly prohibit same-sex adoption but may have requirements that only *married* couples may adopt, which thus prohibits same-sex couples from adopting. Despite restrictions, an estimated 65,500 adopted children are living with a lesbian or gay parent (Gates et al., 2007).

Another situation is custody of children following a heterosexual marriage. In such a situation, judges routinely give custody to the heterosexual parent, assuming that this arrangement is better for the child. According to the American Civil Liberties Union, some states, primarily in the South, continue to discriminate against gay parents. "There is no guarantee that family court judges will treat gay parents fairly—no matter where you live or how fair the laws appear. Because the 'best interest of the child' standard that governs custody and visitation is so flexible, homophobic judges often can rule against a gay parent without acknowledging that it was based on the parent's sexual orientation" (American Civil Liberties Union 2007:1).

Some lesbians achieve parenthood through artificial insemination. The trick with this arrangement is for the partner of the biological mother to achieve legal status through adoption. Presently, nine states and the District of Columbia permit second-parent or stepparent adoption by same-sex couples. Four states have a court ruling that does not allow second-parent or stepparent adoption by same-sex couples (Colorado, Nebraska, Ohio, and Wisconsin; Human Rights Campaign 2007).

A final extreme example shows the negative feelings that some have about gay parents. In Pensacola, Florida, a judge ruled that custody of a young girl should go to the father and not the mother. He made this ruling despite the father's failure to make child support payments and his history of having served 8 years in prison for murdering his first wife. The judge ruled that this father could provide a better environment for the child because the child's mother is a lesbian and single:

> *Notwithstanding the studies proving that people don't "become" homosexual because of their parent's orientation, and despite incontrovertible evidence that gay and lesbian*

parents can provide love and nurturance, and despite dozens of studies showing that it is heterosexual men who commit 97 percent of the child molesting in this country, "family values" means heterosexuality at all costs. (Townsend 1996:12)

Occupational Discrimination

The exact amount of job discrimination against homosexuals is unknown, primarily because the government does not provide gay employment discrimination statistics, as it does for women, African Americans, and other minorities. Statistics on employer discrimination are also impossible to calculate because an employer can use other excuses for the termination or nonhiring of a gay employee or job applicant. Based on stories and surveys of gays and lesbians, however, employer discrimination is fairly common. For example, a 2004 survey in Topeka, Kansas, found that 16 percent of gay and lesbian respondents reported that they were denied employment because of their sexual orientation, 15 percent were fired because of their sexual orientation, and 35 percent had received harassing letters, e-mails, or faxes at work because of their sexual orientation (Colvin 2004). In another example, in 2005, a photographer named Laurel Scherer lost her photography contract with a ski resort in North Carolina after she and her partner were married in Massachusetts and ran their wedding announcement in their local newspaper (Gunther 2006). Many homosexuals fear that they will lose their jobs if their sexual orientation is revealed. Or, if not fired, they may experience other forms of discrimination, such as being passed over for deserved promotions, being given relatively low salary raises, and being harassed.

These fears are based on reality. Legally, a person can be fired from his or her job in twenty-nine states just for being homosexual (Human Rights Campaign 2009). The New York State Health Code includes a section, for example, that states that employees can be fired for moral turpitude (which includes homosexuality as such a case). Because few legal protections are available to homosexuals, especially in the private sector, and because homophobic attitudes are common, many homosexuals have little choice but to hide their sexual orientation.

A few employers are taking the lead in breaking down discrimination in the workplace. Corporate nondiscrimination clauses are being added to protect gay workers from harassment, and some companies are now offering domestic partner benefits. "To date, 357, or 71 percent, of *Fortune* magazine's 500 largest U.S. corporations have added nondiscrimination clauses that include the words 'sexual orientation' to their policies" (Schepp 2004b:A3). In addition, more than half (293 of the *Fortune* 500) offer health benefits for domestic partners (Human Rights Campaign 2009). Coors Brewing Company, for example, offers all family benefits to gay and lesbian employees and their partners. Thus, gay employees of Coors and their partners receive medical and dental care, vision and hearing coverage, bereavement leave, and coverage for natural or adopted children or children of whom one partner has legal custody. Other large corporations that provide same-sex partner benefits include Microsoft, Walt Disney Company, Boeing, General Motors, Ford, DaimlerChrysler, Prudential, Motorola, General Mills, Honeywell, and Xerox. Some progressive corporations (e.g., Microsoft, AT&T, Xerox, Apple Computer, and Pacific Gas and Electric) provide diversity training to demystify homosexuality and to encourage gay and lesbian groups within the organizations. IBM is on the cutting edge as the number-one financial supporter of gay rights groups in the United States, and other corporations are following suit. "So it's clear where big business is going. What's interesting is to watch it pull the rest of the country along. It turns out that the most important factor shaping people's feelings about gay issues is not their age or even their religion—although those do matter—but whether they have relatives, friends, or coworkers who are gay" (Gunther 2006:5).

In 2002 President Bush signed a bill allowing death benefits to be paid to the domestic partners of firefighters and police officers who die in the line of duty, permanently extending a federal death benefit to same-sex couples (Allen 2002:31). Despite these positive steps and progressive companies, a 2003 survey found that overall, just 23 percent of employers offer benefits to domestic partners (Armour 2004).

FIGHTING THE SYSTEM: HUMAN AGENCY

The chapter to this point has documented the hostility, anger, and discrimination aimed at homosexuals in U.S. society. These reactions occur at the societal level through court actions that discriminate and through punitive religious ideology that condemns homosexuals' immorality. At the personal level, hostility occurs with looks, taunts, ostracism, and even violence. The objects of this assault—individual lesbian women and gay men—experience great personal stress as a result. Studies routinely show that gay and lesbian youth attempt suicide at a rate two to three times higher than that of their heterosexual peers (Cody 2002).

Gays use two basic strategies for living in a society hostile to their sexual orientation. One is to conceal their sexual orientation to avoid stigmatization, harassment, and discrimination. These closeted gays segregate their lives into gay and straight activities. When in the straight world, they conceal their sexual orientation from family, friends, co-workers, and other associates. Those most likely to stay in the closet are from the working class. The structural and personal pressures against coming out are much greater for them than for those from the middle and upper classes.

Gay activists, on the other hand, identify themselves openly as homosexuals. Rather than evade the efforts of straights to stigmatize them, they challenge society in an effort to transform it. The gay men and lesbian women who confront society are the focus of this section.

The negative sanctions from society, employers, friends, and family have kept lesbians and gays for most periods of U.S. history from organizing to change a repressive situation. Political activist Emma Goldman in 1915 became the first person to speak publicly in favor of gay and lesbian rights. A few homosexual organizations were formed (the first, the Chicago Society for Human Rights in 1924, and the first modern gay rights organization, the Mattachine Society in 1950) for mutual support, but only a relatively few homosexuals were willing at the time to publicly declare their deviance from the norm of heterosexuality.

The 1960s provided a better climate for change when youths, African Americans, women, pacifists, and other groups questioned the norms and ideologies of the dominant society. This decade clearly was one of heightened awareness among the oppressed of their oppression and of the possibility that through collective efforts they could change what had seemed to be unchangeable.

The precipitating event for gay and lesbian unity occurred at 3 A.M. on June 28, 1969, when police raided the Stonewall Inn of New York's Greenwich Village. Instead of dispersing, as gays had always done in similar situations, the 200 patrons threw objects at the police and set fire to the bar. The riot lasted only 45 minutes, but it gave impetus to a number of collective efforts by gays to publicize police harassment of the gay community, job discrimination, and other indignities they faced. In effect, the Stonewall resistance came to symbolize the birth of the modern gay rights movement.

Following Stonewall, gay liberation groups emerged in many cities and on university campuses. Many neighborhoods in major cities became openly homosexual—most notably the Castro district in San Francisco, New Town in Chicago, and Greenwich Village in New York City. These communities included gay churches, associations of professionals, health clinics, and networks of gay-owned businesses to supply the gay community's needs. The proliferation of these organizations for lesbians and gays provided a supportive climate, allowing many of them to come out of the closet.

The increased numbers of public gays and lesbians have provided the political base for changing the various forms of oppression that homosexuals routinely experience. The Gay and Lesbian Alliance Against Defamation (GLAAD) promotes accurate and positive images of gays in television, films, and advertising; the Human Rights Campaign and Lambda Legal promote favorable legislation; the Gay Men's Health Crisis helps gays deal with the reality of AIDS; and the National Gay and Lesbian Task Force furthers gay interests by attacking the minority-group status of homosexuals in a variety of political and ideological arenas.

Two countervailing forces in the 1980s affected the gay rights movement. The election of Ronald Reagan and his conservative agenda, along with the surge of Christian fundamentalism, inhibited the movement's momentum in the first part of the decade. The AIDS epidemic propelled the movement in the late 1980s. As it became clear that AIDS endangered the lives of more and more gay males, the sense of a shared danger and the realization that they needed to push the government into action quickly inspired unity. More organizations formed, some directed specifically at the health needs of people with AIDS and others aimed at lobbying Congress and state governments for legislation important to gays.

On October 11, 1987, the largest gay rights demonstration occurred when approximately 250,000 lesbians, gay men, and their supporters marched in Washington, D.C. They held a parade, had a huge marriage ceremony to protest the laws forbidding the marriage of gays, mourned their comrades who had died of AIDS, staged a mass civil disobedience action at the U.S. Supreme Court to protest the 1986 decision upholding state sodomy laws (840 people were arrested), and joined with other activist groups. The Reverend Jesse Jackson spoke at the rally:

> *We are together today to say we insist on legal protection under the law of every American . . . for workers' rights, for civil rights, for the rights of religious freedom, the rights of individual privacy, for the rights of sexual preference. We come together for the rights of the American people. (quoted in Freiberg 1987:15)*

By 2010, 41 years after Stonewall, many positive changes have occurred for the gay community:

- At the time of Stonewall, forty-eight states had sodomy laws meant to outlaw homosexual sex. In 2003, those laws were overturned.
- In 1969, no state or local government had a law protecting the civil rights of homosexuals. In 1996, the Supreme Court in *Romer v. Evans* ruled that states and municipalities had the duty to protect gays from discrimination. Many observers feel that this ruling marked a turning point in the generation-long battle for gay rights. The majority opinion stated that gay people are a distinct class who do not receive the same protections as other people without specific legal protections. This ruling struck down a constitutional amendment passed by Colorado voters that denied civil rights protections to homosexuals. In doing so, the Supreme Court overturned efforts by states to treat gays as second-class citizens.
- In another groundbreaking decision, the Supreme Court in 1998 ruled unanimously that sexual discrimination in the workplace applies to harassment between workers of the same sex. This ruling gives civil rights protections to all employees, male or female, homosexual or heterosexual, something unheard of in 1969.
- In 1994, more than 11,000 athletes from forty-four countries competed in Gay Games IV in New York City, an event beyond imagination in 1969; in 2006, Chicago hosted the games with approximately 12,000 participants.
- In 1997, there were approximately 100 gay–straight alliances (GSAs)—clubs for gay and gay-friendly kids—on U.S. high school campuses. Today there are at least 3,000 GSAs. In the 2004–2005 academic year, GSAs were established at the rate of three per day (Cloud 2005).
- Prominent athletes have come out and announced to the world that they are gay—for example, former Olympic champion diver Greg Louganis, former NFL player Esera Tuaolo, former NBA player John Amaechi, and three-time MVP WNBA player Sheryl Swoops. Although the number of professional athletes who have come out is very small, these individuals are paving the way for a new generation of athletes.
- According to the Gay and Lesbian Leadership Institute, there are 755 openly LGBT appointed and elected officials across the United States. There are only four states with no gay or lesbian officials (2010).
- Public opinion polls show a gradual acceptance of gays and lesbians, especially among the younger generation. The mainstream media is slowly incorporating more gays and lesbians into prime-time television shows, and MTV Network has even introduced a cable channel specifically for a lesbian, gay, bisexual, and transgender audience (LOGO). Perhaps the most prominent signs of progress are found in the movies *Brokeback Mountain* and *Milk*. *Brokeback Mountain* (a love story featuring two men) grossed more than $178 million worldwide and won four Golden Globe awards, including Best Motion Picture Drama in 2005. *Milk* was based on the life story of Harvey Milk, the first openly gay man elected to public office. It was nominated for Best Motion Picture of the

More television shows are featuring gay characters, such as ABC's sitcom Modern Family, *where gay couple Mitchell and Cameron adopt a baby.*

year and received Oscars for Best Actor (Sean Penn) and Best Screenplay (Dustin Lance Black) in 2008.

Homosexuals have also made some modest gains through court decisions, laws by progressive legislatures and city commissions, and acceptance of gays and lesbians by some religious leaders and a few congregations. But huge obstacles remain. The religious right (e.g., James Dobson's Focus on the Family, Gary Bauer's Family Research Council, Donald Wildmon's American Family Association, and Pat Robertson's Christian Coalition) refuses to yield on gay rights, making opposition to gay rights a defining issue. Gay issues such as the ordination of gay pastors and priests and the sanctification of same-sex unions continue to divide religious denominations and local churches.

This chapter began with the idea that whoever holds power in society has the power to define and label deviance. When examining sexual orientation, it is clear that powerful groups in society are currently in flux and disagreement over these definitions. On one hand, some progress has been made in certain areas of the law, the media, and the workplace. On the other hand, major religious groups and politicians continue to disagree over issues such as same-sex marriage, and homophobia is still a problem in our schools. Judy Shepard summarizes this paradox on the fifth anniversary of the death of her son Matthew Shepard, murdered for being gay:

> *Recently, I've been thinking about what really has changed—and more importantly, what has not—to make our communities safe from hatred against gays. It's clear that in some ways our nation has become a more accepting place. We have witnessed the progress of gay and lesbian rights with the recent U.S. Supreme Court decision,* Lawrence v. Texas, *striking down the state's sodomy law. . . . We have seen growing visibility, understanding, and acceptance of lesbian, gay, bisexual, and transgender people in our families, in society and in the corporate world. However, there has been scant progress in other areas, particularly in terms of legislation and securing rights for the gay community. . . . It is as if we are living in two Americas—one that tunes in to* Queer Eye for the Straight Guy *but turns a blind eye to the injustices gay and lesbian people still face. (Shepard 2003)*

■ CHAPTER REVIEW

1. Homosexuals are a minority group in U.S. society. They are the objects of negative stereotypes and discrimination.
2. Unlike the status of most minorities, the minority status of homosexuals is based on deviance from society's norms rather than on ascribed characteristics. There are several important characteristics of social deviance: (a) it is socially created; (b) it is a relative, not an absolute, concept; (c) it is an integral part of all societies; (d) the powerful determine who or what is deviant; and (e) it creates an atmosphere in which deviants can be stigmatized for their behavior.
3. The response to homosexuals varies by society and historical period. Although homosexuality is considered deviant behavior in contemporary U.S. society, it was not so considered in ancient Greece and Rome, nor was it deviant among some Native American tribes.
4. Although there have been some studies pointing to biological origins of homosexuality, given the complex relationship between biology and environment there are no definitive conclusions. It is important to remember that (a) sexualities are shaped differently across time and location; and (b) the real issue is one of social justice, not origins.
5. Although the proportion of the population that is homosexual is not known and is probably unknowable, the best estimate from the 2000 U.S. Census is about 2 percent of all adults. In 2008, there were an estimated 565,000 same-sex couples living in the United States.
6. Lesbian and gay couples are similar to heterosexual couples in their quest for love and

relationships. Gay men are more likely than lesbian women to have sex with someone other than their steady partners, a similarity shared with heterosexual males. Homosexual couples are much more likely than heterosexual couples to be egalitarian in sharing housework.

7. Variance from the societal norm of heterosexuality is not a social problem; the societal response to it is. Gays confront three types of oppression: (a) ideological, stemming from traditional homophobic beliefs, especially religious; (b) legal, stemming from the law and court decisions; and (c) occupational, where jobs, advancement, and income are restricted or denied.
8. Homosexuals use two basic strategies to cope with living in a society hostile to their sexual orientation. One is to conceal their homosexuality from heterosexuals. The other is to identify openly as a homosexual. Gay activists, of course, are in this latter category as they challenge society in an effort to transform it.
9. The challenge to change society's oppression of homosexuals began with the Stonewall Inn riot in 1969. Since then, homosexuals have organized communities, organized protests, and formed self-help and political lobbying organizations.

■ KEY TERMS

Deviance. Behavior that does not conform to social expectations.

Heterosexuality. Sexual orientation toward someone of the other sex.

Compulsory heterosexuality. Beliefs and practices that enforce heterosexual behavior as normal while stigmatizing other forms of sexual expression.

Homosexuality. Sexual orientation toward someone of the same sex.

Bisexuality. Sexual orientation toward or attraction to both sexes.

Stigma/stigmatized. Powerful negative social label that affects a person's social identity and self-concept.

Sexual preference. Person's choice regarding the sex of people to whom he or she is attracted.

Sexual orientation. Sexual attraction to the same or opposite sex is not a matter of choice but is determined by genetic or environmental factors.

Homophobia. Fear or loathing of homosexuality and homosexuals.

Sodomy. Oral or anal sex.

Gay activists. Homosexuals who openly identify themselves as such and challenge society in an effort to eliminate the stigma and discrimination they face.

■ SUCCEED WITH PEARSON mysoclab www.mysoclab.com

Experience, Discover, Observe, Evaluate
MySocLab is designed just for you. Each chapter features a pre-test and post-test to help you learn and review key concepts and terms.

Experience sociology in action with dynamic visual activities, videos, and readings to enhance your learning experience. Complete the following activities at www.mysoclab.com.

Social Explorer is an interactive application that allows you to explore Census data through interactive maps.

- Explore the Social Explorer Map: *Cohabitation Among Unmarried Same-Sex Couples*

The Core Concepts in Sociology video clips offer a real-world perspective on sociological concepts.

- Watch *Alternative Sexual Orientation*

MySocLibrary includes primary source readings from classic and contemporary sociologists.

- Read Kinsey, Pomeroy, & Martin, *Understanding Sexual Orientation*; Stacey, *Gay Parenthood and the Decline of Paternity as We Knew It*; Fausto-Sterling, *The Five Sexes: Why Male and Female Are Not Enough*

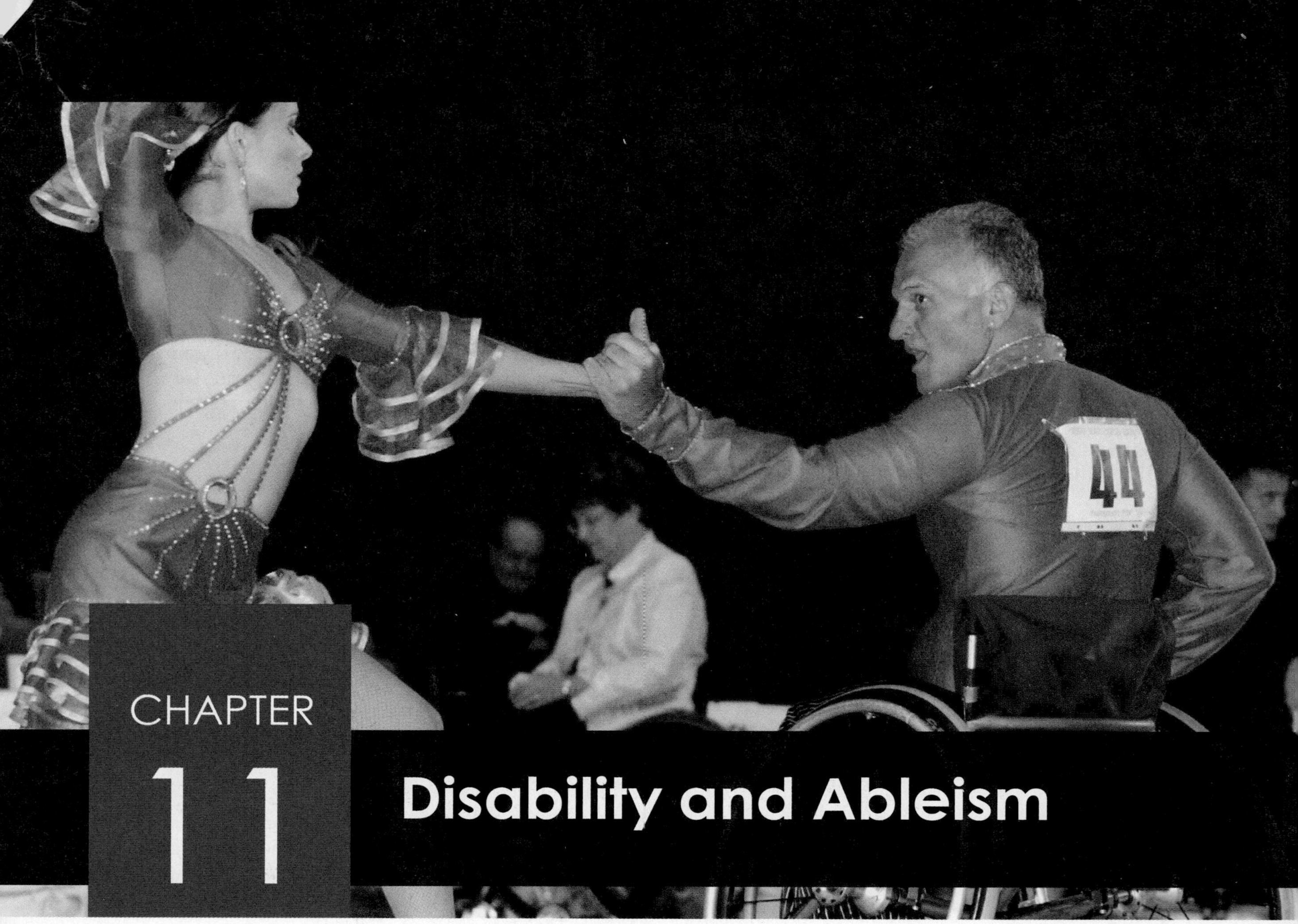

CHAPTER 11 Disability and Ableism

The salience of disability resides not in a medical condition or in statistically verified shortcomings in individual ability. . . . The key lies not in the individual but in the way various aspects of society respond to that individual. In this light, disability is an imminently social and political phenomenon.

—Scot Danforth

This part of the book is devoted to various forms of inequality, examining categories of people experiencing discrimination, negative stereotypes, and powerlessness because of their being different from the dominant category in economic resources (the impoverished), racial classification (people of color), gender (females), and sexual orientation (gays and lesbians). This chapter turns our attention to another category of people defined as different and who constitute a minority group—those with physical, sensory, or cognitive impairments. This category is the largest minority group in the United States. People with disabilities, however, although sharing the characteristics of a minority group in most ways, differ in one significant way—it is a category in which most of us will eventually be included.

> *It is a category whose constituency is contingency itself. Any of us who identify as "nondisabled" must know that our self-designation is inevitably temporary, and that a car crash, a virus, a degenerative genetic disease, or a precedent-setting legal decision could change our status in ways over which we have no control whatsoever.*
> *(Berube 1998:iii)*

The facts are these, according to a 2005 survey by the U.S. Census Bureau (Brault 2008):

- About one in five U.S. residents (20 percent) had some form of impairment (54.4 million in 2005, up from 51.2 million in 2002), 35 million of them had a severe disability).
- The probability of disability increases with age. People aged 55 to 64 were nearly three times as likely to have a disability as people aged 15 to 24. Some 52 percent of people 65 and older had a disability. Of this number, 37 percent had a severe disability. For people 80 and older, the disability rate was 71 percent, with 56 percent having a severe disability (see Figure 11.1).

FIGURE 11.1

Disability Prevalence and the Need for Assistance by Age: 2005

Note: The need for assistance with activities of daily living was not asked of children under 6 years.

Source: U.S. Census Bureau. Survey of Income and Program Participation, June–September 2005.

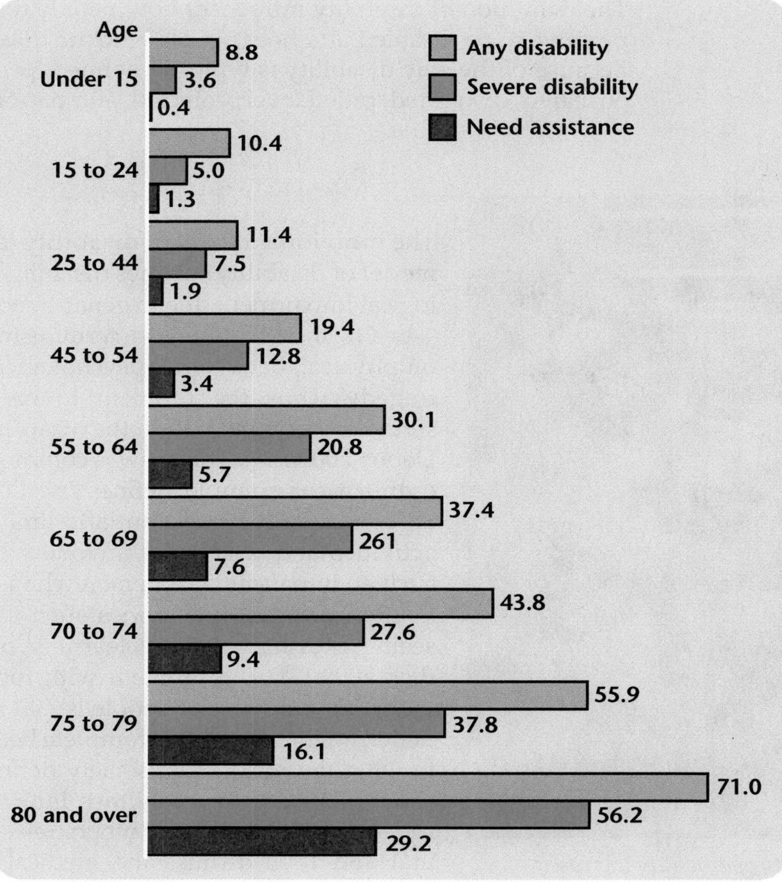

- There were 4.7 million children ages 6 to 14 (13 percent) with a disability.
- Among the population age 15 and older, 3.3 million used a wheelchair and 10.2 million an ambulatory aid such as a cane, crutches, or a walker.
- More than 16 million people had difficulty with cognitive, mental, or emotional functioning. This included 8.4 million with one or more problems that interfered with daily activities.
- About 15 percent of people with a disability were born with it; 85 percent will experience a disabling condition in the course of their lives, usually from accidents, disease, environmental hazards, or criminal victimization (Russell 2000).

Social scientists, until recently, have largely ignored people with disabilities because their impairments were considered physical and psychic shortcomings, having little to do with the social. That assumption is false. The very definition of who is able and who is disabled is a social construction; the stereotypes and fears about people who are disabled are social constructions; and society creates financial, physical, and discriminatory barriers for people who are disabled.

DEFINITIONS

The definition of disability influences how people relate to people whom they perceive to be disabled and how people who are disabled think of themselves. Because of the way disability is typically defined, people with disabilities may be feared, distrusted, pitied, overprotected, and patronized (Barton 1996:8).

The probability of disability increases with age.

Individual Model of Disability

The **individual model of disability** (also known as the medical model of disability) defines disability in terms of some physiological impairment due to genetic heritage, accident, or disease. "As a form of biological determinism, the focus of disability is on physical, behavioral, psychological, cognitive, and sensory tragedy. Thus the problem to be addressed by disability services is situated within the disabled individual" (Gilson and Depoy 2000:208). This view is commonly held. The federal government, for example, defines *disability* as any physical or mental condition that substantially limits one or more major life activities and *disabled* as anyone who is regarded as having such an impairment. A person who is disabled might have difficulty performing activities such as personal care, walking, seeing, hearing, speaking, learning, or working (Taub and Fanflick 2000:13). The problem with focusing on the physical or mental impairment of people is that individuals are defined as deficient, inferior, and incomplete because they do not conform to what the majority in society define as "normal." Although some people with disabilities internalize these negative attitudes about themselves, others reject being defined as abnormal and thus dismiss the medical model as the dominant model of disability (Llewellyn and Hogan 2000).

Because the focus is on the individual, the goal of rehabilitation is for health practitioners to overcome, or at least minimize, the negative consequences of an individual's disability by addressing the person's special needs and personal difficulties. If possible, these health professionals would like to return disabled individuals to the "normal" condition of being able bodied. Although these goals seem appropriate, they make people with disabilities dependent on a vast army of allied professionals who dominate their lives (Barnes, Mercer, and Shakespeare 1999:25). Moreover, adaptation to the environment—rather than changing the social arrangements that make life difficult for people with disabilities—is stressed during rehabilitation. Because of the emphasis on the individual, "courage, independence, will-power are all lauded when a disabled person proves that overcoming disability is a matter of individual effort" (Llewellyn and Hogan 2000:158). The concentration on the biology of disability also defines people by only one dimension, ignoring their other qualities. To counteract this problem, we use the phrase "person with a disability" rather than "a disabled person," thereby reorienting our social construction so that it puts the human being first and the impairment second, rather than making the impairment the defining characteristic (Linton 1998:13).*

Finally, a note of caution. People with disabilities are a heterogeneous category. Although most have visible impairments, others have invisible disabilities such as chronic pain or dyslexia. Those who cannot hear face different societally induced problems than those who cannot see or those people who must use wheelchairs. Thus, as we discuss people with disabilities, we must remember that the people involved are complex, varying by type of disability and their other social locations (e.g., gender, race, social class, sexual orientation).

Social Model of Disability

The **social model of disability**, while acknowledging the biological conditions of disability, challenges the notion that disability is primarily a medical category. From this perspective, the real problem with physical and mental impairment is not physical but social: It is the way people with able bodies view people with disabilities and the institutionalization of these views that are the genuine handicaps (Oliver 1996b; Duncan 2001). For adherents of the social model, the consequence of the power to define the identity of the disabled by professionals results in the disempowerment, marginalization, and dependency of people with disabilities (Barton 1996:9). The limited physical access, limited access to resources, and negative attitudes create barriers that interfere with the potential of people with disabilities to actualize their desired roles (Gilson and Depoy 2000). Furthermore, it is the way that people with disabilities are oppressed by societal views of normality. In effect, then, society disables people. Consider, for example, the argument by a man with a disability:

> *[We] are disabled by buildings that are not designed to admit us, and this in turn leads to a whole range of further disablements, regarding our education, our chances for*

---

*The naming of people with disabilities is a complicated issue. On the one hand, many people with disabilities have wanted to keep disability as a characteristic of the individual as opposed to the defining characteristic. Yet beginning in the early 1990s, the term "disabled people" became popular among disability rights activists. Rather than keeping disability as a secondary characteristic, *disabled* became a marker of identity that they wanted to highlight as they protested for social change (Linton 1998:13).

> *gaining employment, our social lives and so on. However, this argument is usually rejected, precisely because to accept it involves recognizing the extent to which we are not merely unfortunate, but are directly oppressed by a hostile social environment. (Brisenden 1986:176)*

With the incredible medical, technological, and manufacturing advances available, many people made dysfunctional by infection, injury, or deleterious genes "need not remain so if appropriate social arrangements are in place to address these deficits. . . . In this sense, then, when disadvantage attendant on disability goes unremedied, its persistence is a social rather than a biological phenomenon" (Silvers 1998:16).

Congruent with this perspective, the Union of Physically Impaired against Segregation (UPIAS) in the United Kingdom promotes this definition of disability: "Disability is the disadvantage or restriction of activity caused by a contemporary social organization which takes no or little account of people who have physical impairments and thus excludes them from participation in the mainstream of social activities" (UPIAS 1976:3–4). The social model of disability redirects attention away from the individual and places the problem back on the collective responsibility of society (Llewellyn and Hogan 2000:159). The social model focuses on the experience of disability. It considers a wide range of social, economic, and political factors and conditions such as family circumstances, financial support, education, employment, housing, transportation, the built environment, disabling barriers and attitudes in society, and the impact of government policies and welfare support systems (Barnes et al., 1999:31).

Adherents of the social model see the goal of rehabilitation as being much different from the individual model:

> *A social model of disability is socially constructed. This lens views the locus of the "problem" to be addressed by services and supports within the social context in which individuals interact. Rather than attempting to change or fix the person with the disability, a social model of disability sets service goals as removal of social and environmental barriers to full social, physical, career and spiritual participation. (Gilson and Depoy 2000:208)*

But it is more than the removal of architectural or other physical barriers:

> *The social model is not about showing that every dysfunction in our bodies can be compensated for by a gadget, or good design, so that everybody can work an 8-hour day and play badminton in the evenings. It's a way of demonstrating that everyone—even someone who has no movement, no sensory function and who is going to die tomorrow—has the right to a certain standard of living and to be treated with respect. (Vasey 1992:44).*

Toward a More Complete Definition of Disability

The focus of the medical model is on **impairment** (the state of being mentally or physically challenged) and **disability**.

> *Disability, in contrast, is the political and social repression of impaired people. This is accomplished by making them economically and socially isolated. . . . Disablement is a political state and not a personal one and thus needs to be addressed as a civil rights issue. (Taylor 2004:35).*

The assumptions of both the medical and social models of disability are contradictory. Taken alone, each of these perspectives fosters a one-sided and therefore incomplete and faulty perception and interpretation of disability and people with disabilities (Shakespeare 2006). A synthesis that combines the best of each model will aid our understanding and allow for an acceptable definition.

The individual (medical) model is correct in that there is an **ontological truth** (a universal and undeniable reality) to the claim that disabilities result from some physiological or mental impairment. It follows, then, that disabled people do need medical support at specific points in their lives (Barton 1996:9). But this emphasis on locating problems and solutions within the disabled person is only half of the equation because it overlooks the role of society in defining and creating barriers for people with disabilities. The social model points to the very real (ontological) social barriers for most people with disabilities.

The definition of disability that we use combines the insights of the individual and social models: Disability, then, refers to a reduced ability to perform tasks one would normally do at a given stage of life that are exacerbated by the individual and institutional discrimination that people with disabilities encounter.

PEOPLE WITH DISABILITIES AS A MINORITY GROUP

Disability shares a number of characteristics common to the social constructions of race, sex and gender, and sexual orientation, thus making it a minority group as they are.* These characteristics are (1) being defined as different; (2) derogatory names; (3) their "differentness" is a master status; (4) categorization, stigma, and stereotypes; (5) exclusion and segregations; (6) the matrix of domination; and (7) discrimination.

Defined as Different

Minority groups are socially constructed categories. Which categories have minority status varies among societies and over time within a society. Society assigns some categories of people—in the United States, these categories are races other than Caucasian, certain ethnic groups, women, homosexuals, and people with disabilities—to minority status. The minority is composed of people with similar characteristics that are defined as significantly different from the dominant group. These characteristics are salient: They are visible, though not necessarily physical, and they make a difference. Whites dominate Blacks, Whites dominate Latinos, men dominate women, heterosexuals dominate homosexuals, and the able bodied dominate people with disabilities.

Derogatory Naming

Naming is not a neutral process; the names given to the members of minority groups by the majority have enormous symbolic significance that contributes to and perpetuates the dominance of the majority (Hall 1985; Eitzen and Baca Zinn 1989b). These pejorative names belittle, trivialize, exclude, diminish, deprecate, and demean. In essence, pejorative names not only put the minority "down" but also separate and segregate. Just as "boy" can be blatantly offensive to minority

---

*There are several ways to view people with disabilities. We use the minority groups model because of its (1) emphasis on social and economic discrimination; (2) consistency with our structural emphasis that explains systematic exclusion on the basis of gender, class, race, and sexual orientation; and (3) emphasis on social factors rather than biological and cultural ones (Block, Balcazar, and Keys 2001).

men, so "girl" can have comparable patronizing and demeaning implications for women (Miller and Swift 1980:71). Gays and lesbians are called "queers" and "faggots," terms that clearly separate them from the heterosexual majority.

Consider the implications of names for people with disabilities, such as "invalid," "cripple," "freak," "gimp," "vegetable," "dumb," "deformed," "handicapped," and "retard." These labels imply not only impairment but also a lack of worth, marginality, and their dependence on the "able" (Barton 1996; Swain, French, and Cameron 2003:11–19). The images that these names evoke are opposite the notion that "disability stems from the failure of a structured social environment to adjust to the needs and aspirations of citizens with disabilities rather than from the inability of a disabled individual to adapt to the demands of society" (Hahn 1986:128).

Minority as a Master Status

Although people have many statuses simultaneously, typically, one status is dominant. This is known as a **master status**. The master status may be imposed by others, or it may be internalized by the individual, with exceptional significance for social identity. The master status of minority group members is the characteristic (or set of characteristics) that distinguish them from the majority. That is, African Americans or gays or homeless families are known and identified by others foremost by their race, sexual orientation, or impoverishment. Disability can be and often is a master status, as people frequently perceive those with disabilities first in terms of their disability and only second as individuals. That is, an impairment such as blindness or using a wheelchair is seen as the most salient part of a person's identity and therefore trumps all other statuses, such as occupation, educational attainment, and income level.

Categorization, Stigma, and Stereotypes

Not only are minority members singled out by their master status, but they also encounter the negative stereotypes and beliefs that accompany their defining characteristics. In other words, being a minority is not only a master status, but it is also a master status with a stigma. The stigma originates in the portrayals of people with disabilities in literature, movies, and television.

> *A summary audit of media's preference for "crippling images" includes a fondness for "wonder cure" stories, the role of charity appeals, the invisibility of disabled people on television, the stereotyped portrayal of disabled characters, and the under-employment of disabled people in TV and radio. The most frequently documented cultural stereotypes represent the disabled person as pitiable and pathetic, an object of violence, as sinister and evil, as atmosphere or curio, as "super-cripple," as an object of ridicule, as their own worst enemy, as burden, as sexually abnormal, as incapable of participating fully in community life. . . . (Barnes and Mercer 2003:95)*

A **stigma** is an attribute that is socially devalued and disgraced. Sociologist Erving Goffman described it this way:

> *While the stranger is present before us, evidence can arise of his possessing an attribute that makes him different from others in the category of persons available for him to be, and of a less desirable kind—in the extreme, a person who is quite thoroughly bad, or dangerous, or weak. He is thus reduced in our minds from a whole and usual person to a tainted, discounted one. Such an attribute is a stigma, especially when its*

> *discrediting effect is very extensive; sometimes it is also called a failing, a shortcoming, a handicap. (Goffman 1963:3)*

People with stigmas have what Goffman called a spoiled identity, and this spoiled identity has negative consequences.

> *By definition, of course, we believe the person with a stigma is not quite human. On this assumption we exercise varieties of discrimination, through which we effectively, if often unthinkingly, reduce his life chances. We construct a stigma-theory, an ideology to explain his inferiority and account for the danger he represents, sometimes rationalizing an animosity based on other differences such as those of social class. We use specific stigma terms such as cripple, bastard, moron in our daily discourse as a source of metaphor and imagery, typically without giving thought to the original meaning. We tend to impute a wide range of imperfections on the basis of the original one, and at the same time to impute some desirable but undesired attributes, often of a supernatural cast, such as "sixth sense," or "understanding." (Goffman 1963:5)*

Minority group members are stigmatized. The majority defines certain characteristics as different and abnormal and then discriminates against those in the category defined as inferior. Thus, some people are "in," whereas others are defined as "out," or they are either "us" or "them." In effect, the minority is defined as "other" because the members have characteristics that differ from the majority. The definition is simplified by making the distinctions binary. "'Race' becomes Black or White, 'gender' becomes male or female, 'sexual orientation' becomes gay or straight, and people are either disabled or normal" (Gordon and Rosenblum 2001:12). In each instance, the side defined as "other" is considered not only different but also deficient. Their characteristics are stigmatized. For example, people with disabilities face the negative evaluations given their identity by society.

> *Whatever the physically impaired person may think of [himself or herself, the individual is] given a negative identity by society, and much of social life is a struggle against this imposed image. It is for this reason that we can say that stigmatization is less a by-product of disability than its substance. The greatest impediment to a [person with a disability] taking full part in society is . . . the tissue of myths, fears, and misunderstandings that society attaches to them. (Murphy 1995:140)*

The disabled confront the dichotomous comparison with the able bodied, where they always come up short in one of two ways. Many internalize the inadequacy society regularly ascribes to them, thinking of themselves as incomplete or broken. Others reject the dichotomy dictated by society. "Although they certainly have greater physical challenges to overcome, they discover authenticity in them, not embarrassment or shame" (Tingus 2000:10B).

The dominant members of society perceive disability as a medical matter, associating disability with physiological, anatomical, or mental "defects." Viewed in this way, those with physical and mental impairments seem not only different but also lacking the "normal" interests and concerns that occupy others of their social class, race, gender, age, and gender orientation. In short, their "otherness" moves them to the margins of society as "inferiors."

The disabled, therefore, confront not only the challenges of living with their conditions but also the challenges of inequality characterized by ableism. The short definition of **ableism** is discrimination in favor of the able bodied (Tullock 1993). Similar to racism and sexism, ableism also includes "the idea that a person's abilities or characteristics are determined by disability or that people with disabilities as a group are inferior to nondisabled people" (Linton 1998:9). As an example, research shows that those who murder children with disabilities are punished less severely by the criminal justice system than those who murder able children (Unnithan 1994).

A longer and more inclusive definition illuminates further:

> *Ableism is that set of often contradictory stereotypes about people with disabilities that acts as a barrier to keep them from achieving their full potential as equal citizens of society. Among these are the beliefs that people with disabilities are inherently unable to manage their own lives, that they are embittered and malevolent, and that they are, by reason of their disability, morally, intellectually, and spiritually inferior to temporarily able-bodied people, or, conversely, that people with disabilities are saintlike, ever cheerful, asexual, childlike, and unusually heroic. Ultimately, it is the belief that people with disabilities are different from normal people, and that their lives are inherently less worthwhile than those of people without disabilities. It is the "ism" at the root of discrimination against people with disabilities on the job, in school, and in the community. (Pelka 1997:3)*

Implicit in the ideology of ableism that permeates U.S. society is the belief that disability is an individual problem, susceptible to individual solutions. This frees the nondisabled to ignore or minimize social issues of accessibility, accommodation, and personhood (Duncan 2001).

Exclusion and Segregation

Stigmatized race, sex/gender, and sexual orientation categories have traditionally been excluded from full participation in society by institutional barriers or custom. Historically, racial minorities have been excluded through Jim Crow segregation, Supreme Court rulings (e.g., *Plessy v. Ferguson,* which gave "separate but equal" facilities legal authority), and legislation that denied voting and other civil rights. Although recent laws have outlawed blatant discrimination by race, de facto segregation still exists in residential housing, in schools, and in private clubs. Women were once property of their husbands. Their "imputed physical and mental frailty . . . became the grounds for refusing her any civil or legal rights" (Miles 1988:187). Women today are underrepresented in the professions and in leadership positions in government, business, and religious organizations. Gays are not allowed as leaders in the Boy Scouts. Same-sex marriages are illegal, and the right of gays and lesbians to adopt is difficult and in some states impossible because of legal barriers.

Historically, people with disabilities were often separated by segregated housing, sheltered workshops, and occasionally, in attics and basements to hide a family's shame. They have also been separated in nursing homes, asylums, and hospitals for "incurables." In the past, children with disabilities were separated from their "able" classmates in separate "special education" classrooms. However, the Individuals with Disabilities Education Act (IDEA), originally passed as the Education for All Handicapped Children Act in 1975, now requires that children be educated in the "least restrictive environment." This requirement generally has been interpreted to mean that children with disabilities should be included in classrooms with typically developing children. Although inclusion is required by law, many children continue to be segregated in special education classes. Sometimes, of course, "special education" is reasonable, allowing educators to be more responsive to the "special" needs of children who cannot see, hear, think, or move as well as others. There are drawbacks, however, as those segregated as "different" are sometimes objects of abuse by other students. "Special education" teachers may be either more attentive to the conditions of their students than to their scholarship and/or they may have reduced expectations for these students, resulting in a negative self-fulfilling prophecy. The evidence is that children with disabilities who have been in segregated schooling are, in general, less well prepared than other children to exercise the skills and knowledge in the basic subjects of English, math, and science (Silvers 1998:24).

Despite the Americans with Disabilities Act, which requires the elimination of architectural barriers, many still remain, and thus people with disabilities are often separated from mainstream society by the lack of access to public transportation or by architectural barriers.

> *The present forms of architectural structures and social institutions exist because statutes, ordinances, and codes either required or permitted them to be constructed in that manner. These public policies imply values, expectations and assumptions about the physical and behavioral attributes that people ought to possess in order to survive or to participate in community life. Many everyday activities, such as the distance people walk, the steps they climb, the materials they read, and the messages they receive impose stringent requirements on persons with different levels of functional skills. (Hahn 1988:40)*

It does not matter if policy makers intend their policies to discriminate—what matters are the consequences of their actions. "Stairs, curbs, or small-print signs hung over doorways make admission nearly impossible. They may lack discriminatory intent, but they have the effect nonetheless" (Gordon and Rosenblum 2001:12).

Matrix of Domination

The hierarchies of stratification—class, race, gender, and sexual orientation—place socially constructed groups, and the individuals and families assigned to those groups, in different social locations (Baca Zinn and Eitzen 1999:135–136). Placement in these hierarchies determines to what extent one will have or not have the rewards and resources of society. These are also systems of power and domination, as those from dominant race, class, gender, and sexuality groups play a part in and benefit from the oppression of subordinates.

These stratification hierarchies are interrelated. People of color and women, for example, have fewer occupational choices than do White males. People of color and women typically earn less income for the work they do, resulting in advantage for White males. Thus, these systems of inequality intersect to form a **matrix of domination** in which each of us exists (Collins 1990). These intersections of oppression have important implications.

> *First, people experience race, class, gender, and sexuality differently depending on their social location in these structures of inequality. For example, people of the same race will experience race differently depending on their location in the class structure as poor, working class, professional/managerial class, or unemployed and their location in the gender structure as male or female and in the sexuality system as heterosexual or homosexual.*
>
> *Second, class, race, and gender are components of both social structure and social interaction. As a result, individuals because of their social locations experience different forms of privilege and subordination. In short, these intersecting forms of inequality produce both oppression and opportunity.*
>
> *A third implication of the inequality matrix has to do with the relational nature of dominance and subordination. Power is embedded in each system of stratification,*

> *determining whether one is dominant or subordinate. The intersectional nature of hierarchies means that power differentials are linked in systematic ways, reinforcing power differentials across hierarchies. (Eitzen and Baca Zinn 2001:238–239; see also Baca Zinn and Dill 1996)*

An important insight from this matrix of domination approach is that discrimination is more than additive. To be an African American lesbian with a disability, for example, is to be marginalized and discriminated against in simultaneous and multiple ways. As one woman put it, "As a black disabled woman, I cannot compartmentalize or separate aspects of my identity in this way. The collective experience of my race, disability and gender are what shape and inform my life" (Hill 1994:7). Or put another way,

> *The very nature of simultaneous oppression means that as Black disabled men and women, and Black disabled lesbians and gay men, we cannot identify a single source of oppression to reflect the reality of our lives. No meaningful analysis of multiple oppression can take place without an acknowledgment that Black disabled people are subject to simultaneous oppression and as a consequence of this we cannot simply prioritize one aspect of our oppression to the exclusion of others. (Begum 1994:35)*
> *Thus, we cannot study classism, racism, sexism, homophobia, ableism, or any other oppression in isolation from each other (Oliver 1996b:37; Block, Balcazar, and Keys 2001).*

Discrimination

By definition, minority group members experience discrimination. They are the last to be hired and the first to be fired (e.g., the unemployment rate for African Americans is typically twice that for Whites). Racial minorities experience problems involving fairness in the criminal justice system, in obtaining loans, in housing, in schools, and in other institutions. So, too, do people with disabilities find discrimination throughout their lives. Some examples follow (from Russell 1998, 2000):

- Forty-seven percent of applicants genetically screened for insurance are denied health insurance because of "defects."
- Thirty-four percent of adults with disabilities live in households with an annual income of less than $15,000, compared to 12 percent of those without disabilities.
- Seventy percent of working-age disabled people are unemployed, and 79 percent report that they want a job. In addition, for those who are employed, many are underemployed in low-level, low-paying jobs.
- On average, workers with a disability make 85 percent (for men) and 70 percent (for women) of what their coworkers without disabilities earn. When people who are disabled are also Latino, African American, or Native American, there is an increased chance for unemployment and, for those who are employed, an even greater difference in wages than for their nondisabled co-workers (Kendall 2001).

The discrimination that people with disabilities experience is related to how they are perceived by the rest of society. If society is convinced that disabled people cannot have good lives, then there is no reason to invest in equal education, equal access, and equal opportunity for them (see the Voices panel, "Your Burden, My Realities").

VOICES

YOUR FEARS, MY REALITIES

Most of us are morally certain that we're not prejudiced against people with disabilities. Don't we root for Christopher Reeve and Jerry's Kids with our hearts and minds and checkbooks? (Many disabled people think we shouldn't, but that's another matter.)

Didn't we cheer for Jeannie VanVelkinburgh when she was shot and paralyzed by Nathan Thill? Aren't we genuine admirers of Stephen Hawking and Muhammad Ali? How could we discriminate?

To understand disability discrimination, look close to home. Its most transparent feature is that it is caused by fear. We are the living proof that minds and bodies can go haywire and that it can happen to anyone at any time. Some people aren't ready for that news, so they react to us with overt anxiety or hostility.

But it's more subtle forms of discrimination that harm us the most. To cite one ubiquitous example, every family newspaper in the country runs occasional profiles of people with disabilities. They're usually found in the Living section, and they're usually fawning.

They marvel that we can keep our faith in the face of adversity, graduate from college, raise kids or maintain a generous attitude. If we appear to overcome our disabilities—something that's not really feasible for most of us—so much the better. Then we're brave, we're true, we inspire.

The trouble with these feel-good stories is that they become archetypal. By celebrating a single achiever as newsworthy and remarkable, they confirm society's low expectations for all other people with disabilities. Doesn't the exception prove the rule? And aren't we brave because we live lives that readers think they couldn't or wouldn't live themselves? Don't we inspire because we make them feel grateful that they're not like us?

The reading public loves our imagined triumphs of mind over matter, but not our real issues.

It loves us when we're docile, asexual, and childlike, but not when we vent our anger that the deck is stacked against us. It loved VanVelkinburgh's courage at the crime scene and her readiness to move on with her life, but loved her less after a court appearance when she proved herself to be a real, mercurial person rather than patience on a monument. Real people are harder to deal with than idealized fictions.

After my injury in 1968, my business partner told me he would have killed himself under similar circumstances. Even my mother briefly toyed with the idea that I might be better off dead than disabled. "If I were paralyzed," people still tell me, "I couldn't handle it."

"Nonsense," I say, "you'd cope with it fine." But you seldom believe me. You think I'm still being brave, painting a happy face on the unspeakable. Disability discrimination is about your fears, not my realities.

Discrimination deepens when an entire nation takes this view of disability. If society is convinced that we can't have good lives, it's slow to invest in equal education, equal access, and equal opportunity. And even though most people know at heart that sooner or later they're likely to become disabled themselves, they're slow to act on readily achievable solutions because they're scared to death of disability's stigma. This is disability discrimination, and it's largely unconscious.

The result of this attitude—as successive Harris polls since the early 1980s have consistently shown—is that people with disabilities are the poorest minority in America. We have less money, less employment, less education, less transportation, less recreation, less of almost anything you can think of. We're the have-nots of this country.

It's not because people hate us. It's because they assume that our lives are so terrible that any effort to level the playing field is futile. And it's not because disability is so tough. It's because our cultural bias perpetuates the inequities.

Source: Barry Corbet. 2000. "Your Fears, My Realities." *Denver Post* (August 23):11B.

ISSUES OF GENDER, SEXUAL BEHAVIOR, AND FERTILITY

Although people with disabilities deal with a number of social barriers, our discussion here is limited to sexual relationships and related issues. We focus on sexuality because it demonstrates so clearly how social factors often negatively affect people with disabilities.

Gender Stereotyping

The foregoing section showed that people with disabilities are marginalized and stigmatized in U.S. society. This occurs, in part, because women and men with disabilities do not measure up to the cultural beliefs for each gender (Gerschick and Miller 2001). For the physically disabled, their bodies are perceived as unattractive. The bodies of physically disabled men do not allow them to demonstrate the socially valuable characteristics of toughness, competitiveness, and ability (Messner 1992). Anthropologist Robert Murphy writes of his own experiences with disability: "Paralytic disability constitutes emasculation of a more direct and total nature. For the male, the weakening and atrophy of the body threaten all the cultural values of masculinity: strength, activeness, speed, virility, stamina, and fortitude" (Murphy 1990:94). **Hegemonic** (of the dominant belief system) masculinity privileges men who are strong, aggressive, independent, and self-reliant. But men who are physically disabled are perceived to have polar opposite traits; they are treated as weak, passive, pitiful, and dependent. Men with physical disabilities may cope with the fundamental incongruity by constructing their own sense of masculinity (Gerschick and Miller 2001). They may do all they can to meet society's definition of masculinity by becoming as athletic and competitive as possible (e.g., lifting weights, playing wheelchair basketball, participating in the paralympics). Others may redefine masculinity to fit their own unique characteristics (e.g., achieving a sense of independence by controlling those around them; redefining gender in terms of emotional relations rather than the emphasis on the physical). Still others may reject society's standards by either denying masculinity's importance in their life or by creating alternative masculine identities and subcultures that provide them with a supportive environment. For example, a man who no longer can be sexually active might reject the importance of fathering through sexual intercourse. Consider this rationale by an informant:

> *There's no reason why we (his fiancée and himself) couldn't use artificial insemination or adoption. Parenting doesn't necessarily involve being the male sire. It involves being a good parent. . . . Parenting doesn't mean that it's your physical child. It involves responsibility and an emotional role as well. I don't think the link between parenthood is the primary link with sexuality. (quoted in Gerschick and Miller 2001:323–324)*

As difficult as dealing with disability is for men, it is as burdensome if not more so for women. Women with physical disabilities, similar to men, do not measure up to the cultural ideals of what it is to be a woman. Consequently, many think of themselves as asexual or unattractive. Many of these women feel undermined by a society that defines a woman's sexual attractiveness in terms of physical fitness and physical beauty, characteristics that are impossible for many of them to reach. Nancy Mairs writes about her physicality in this light:

> *My shoulders droop and my pelvis thrusts forward as I try to balance myself upright, throwing my frame into a bony S. As a result of contractures, one shoulder is higher than the other and I carry one arm bent in front of me, the fingers curled into a claw.*

> *My left arm and leg have wasted into pipe stems, and I try always to keep them covered. When I think about how my body must look to others, especially to men, to whom I have been trained to display myself, I feel ludicrous, even loathsome. (Mairs 1992:63)*

Women with disabilities are disadvantaged over men with impairments when it comes to occupying traditional roles. Men with disabilities are more likely to be employed than women with disabilities, even filling socially powerful male roles, as did President Franklin D. Roosevelt (who used a wheelchair and crutches because of polio) or Representative James Langevin of Rhode Island, who in 2000 became the first quadriplegic elected to Congress, or former Senator Max Cleland of Georgia, who is missing both legs and an arm. Disabled women, on the other hand, are often even denied access to traditional female roles, as ableist and sexist stereotypes combine in much of the public, making it difficult even for the friends and relatives of disabled women to envision them as functional wives and mothers (Hanna and Rogovsky 1991).

In heterosexual relationships, men with disabilities are more likely to maintain their relationships, whereas women with disabilities are more likely to be abandoned (Shakespeare 1996:202). At least one-fourth "of all married women who become disabled eventually are separated or divorced, nearly twice the rate for similarly situated nondisabled women and for disabled men" (Silvers 1998:37).

Sexual Relationships

Increasingly, people with disabilities have positive and fulfilled sexual lives. Many form strong and happy relationships with other people with disabilities or with nondisabled partners. The growing disability rights movement (a topic discussed further later in this chapter), with its emphases on removing social barriers and social oppression, is important in this regard because it has helped provide people with disabilities a positive identity by working together to achieve common goals. The resulting activism has opened many possibilities as disabled people end their isolation, engage in political acts, and make friends with others in the movement. But sexual problems remain, not because of individual incapacity but because of prejudice, discrimination, and structural barriers (this section is taken primarily from Shakespeare 1996:192–209).

- **Assumptions about People with Disabilities: Asexual, Unlovely, and Undesirable.** Among the beliefs of nondisabled people about people with disabilities are a number that center on sexual difference:

> That we are asexual, or at best inadequate.
> That we cannot ovulate, menstruate, conceive or give birth; have orgasms, erections, [or] ejaculations; or impregnate.
> That if we are not married or in a long-term relationship, it is because no one wants us and not through our personal choice to remain single or live alone.
> That if we do not have a child, it must be the cause of abject sorrow to us and likewise never through choice.
> That any able-bodied person who marries us must have done so for one of the following suspicious motives and never through love: desire to hide his/her own inadequacies in the disabled partner's obvious ones; an altruistic and saintly desire to sacrifice their lives to our care; neurosis of some sort; or plain old-fashioned fortune-hunting.

> That if we have a partner who is also disabled, we chose each other for no other reason, and not for any other qualities we might possess. When we choose "our own kind" in this way, the able-bodied world feels relieved, until of course we wish to have children; then we're seen as irresponsible. (Morris 1991:20ff)

Add to this list the assumptions discussed earlier that disabled people do not meet the societal standards for beauty and physical attractiveness. Also, "just as public displays of same-sex love are strongly discouraged, so two disabled people being intimate in public will experience social disapproval" (Shakespeare 1996:193).

- **Denial of Sex.** People with disabilities are often not welcome in nightclubs and other social venues where sex is on the agenda. They may not be admitted to a gay or straight facility because they are defined as "not sexy" and are believed to detract from the sexuality of the scene (i.e., their impairment was alienating to other patrons). Clubs designed for sexual interaction are often not designed for the disabled. They may be basements or other inaccessible buildings with steps, narrow hallways, flashing lights, and loud noise, which act as barriers for the disabled. Some lesbians with disabilities may find it difficult to meet with other lesbians because they often meet in inaccessible outdoor or sporting activities.

  People who live in day centers, group homes, adult foster care homes, or other residential environments for people with disabilities may encounter policies and staff members who often deny their patients the right to form emotional or sexual relationships.

- **Difficulty in Finding Partners.** People with disabilities often face barriers to access the environments where nondisabled people make contacts that lead to sexual encounters or romantic relationships. They may be blocked by inaccessible public transport, inadequate income, and inaccessible pubs and clubs, making it difficult to interact with potential partners. The workplace is a likely place for such encounters, but many disabled people lack access to paid employment. People with disabilities may also find churches, another common place for meeting potential partners, inaccessible because of physical or attitudinal barriers.

  Computer chat rooms or advertisements in lonely hearts newspaper columns provide an option to those with physical mobility difficulties. But these options are not usually accessible to people with visual impairments (the exception is software that "talks"). Moreover, the language used in these venues emphasizes one's physical attractiveness, thus disqualifying people with disabilities if they are honest about their impairments. This problem is minimized in the personal advertisements section of disability-related publications, where honesty is expected and the chances for rejection, so common in nondisabled settings, are reduced significantly.

  People who become disabled later in life often find that impairment interrupts their social networks and personal relationships, leaving them isolated. This is more true for women with disabilities than for men with disabilities.

Physical and Sexual Abuse

The evidence is clear that people with disabilities, both children and adults, are more likely to be abused physically and sexually than those without disabilities (Mitchell and Buchele-Ash 2000). Because of the social context and the social opportunity, people with disabilities may experience quantitatively more abuse than the nondisabled (Shakespeare 1996:203).

> *There are the ones who are chosen because they cannot speak of the horror. There are the ones who are chosen because they cannot run away, and there is nowhere to run. There are the ones who are chosen because their very lives depend on not fighting back. There are the ones who are chosen because there is no one for them to tell. There are the ones who are chosen because no one has even taught them the words. There are the ones who are chosen because society chooses to believe that, after all, they don't really have any sexuality, so it can't hurt them.* (Cross 1994:165)

Those most vulnerable to physical and sexual abuse are deaf people who cannot speak and people with learning difficulties who may be lured into situations without understanding the consequences (for a chilling account of sexual assault of a girl with learning difficulties by athletes from her high school, see Lefkowitz 1998). The abuse may occur in institutional settings where staff members or other patients may take advantage of the vulnerable. In these settings, patients lack communication with the outside world, and the youngest or the most impaired are the most likely victims of those who have institutional power or personal power over them. Abuse can take other forms in institutions that are more like warehouses than welcoming environments. In such instances, the goal of profit surpasses patient care, resulting in savings through such activities as the overuse of drugs to control patients, inadequate health care, thermostats set too low in the winter and too high in the summer, cheap food, and other forms of neglect (Press and Washburn 2000; K. Thomas 2001).

Abortion Issue

The primary rationale for prenatal testing is to determine whether the fetus is "normal" or will result in a child with a disability. When the test affirms that possibility, the prospective parents have the choice and the legal right to terminate the pregnancy if they wish. For example, when a test reveals that a fetus has an extra twenty-first chromosome—the hallmark of Down syndrome—an estimated 90 percent of parents choose to terminate the pregnancy (Carmichael 2008). For a poignant argument against aborting a fetus with the extra chromosome, see the essay by columnist George F. Will about his son, Jon, who has Down syndrome (Will 2007:72).

This issue is a thorny one for those who favor a woman's right to choose (and we are among them) if we examine the ramifications of aborting "disabled" fetuses from the perspective of people with disabilities (these arguments are primarily from Hershey 2000).

Foremost, when a woman chooses to abort a fetus rather than to give birth to a disabled child, she accepts society's negative views about people with disabilities:

> *She is making a statement about the desirability or the relative worth of such a child. Abortion based on disability results from, and in turn strengthens, certain beliefs: children with disabilities (and by implication adults with disabilities) are a burden to family and society; life with a disability is scarcely worth living; preventing the birth is an act of kindness; women who bear disabled children have failed.* (Hershey 2000:558)

In short, the choice to abort a disabled fetus is a rejection of children and adults who have disabilities.

Second, most people with disabilities, despite the manifold medical and social difficulties associated with their conditions, affirm that their lives are meaningful and worthwhile. Laura Hershey, for example, has a rare neuromuscular condition. She must rely on a motorized wheelchair for mobility, a voice-activated computer for writing, and the assistance of Medicaid-funded attendants for daily needs such as dressing, bathing, eating, and going to the bathroom. She also has a house, a career, a partner, and a community of friends with and without disabilities. She says,

> *My life of disability has not been easy or carefree. But in measuring the quality of my life, other factors—education, friends, and meaningful work, for example—have been decisive. If I were asked for an opinion on whether to bring a child into the world, knowing she would have the same limitations and opportunities I have had, I would not hesitate to say, "Yes." I know that many women do not have the resources my parents had. Many lack education, are poor, or are without the support of friends and family. The problems created by these circumstances are intensified with a child who is disabled. No woman should have a child she can't handle or doesn't want. Having said that, I must also say that all kinds of women raise healthy, self-respecting children with disabilities, without unduly compromising their own lives. (Hershey 2000:559)*

A similar defense for life is given by Harriet McBryde Johnson:

> *Are we "worse off"? I don't think so. Not in any meaningful sense. There are too many variables. For those of us with congenital conditions, disability shapes all we are. Those disabled later in life adapt. We take constraints that no one would choose and build rich and satisfying lives within them. We enjoy pleasures other people enjoy, and pleasures peculiarly our own. We have something the world needs. (Johnson 2003:53)*

Third, in addition to traditional genetic testing, the Human Genome Project, which maps DNA, can predict hundreds, perhaps thousands, of disorders before birth and, in doing so, has the potential to eliminate hereditary diseases in a generation. It also presents a danger. Many in the disabled community fear that the widespread use of these genetic tools and abortion for the purpose of eliminating disability could inaugurate a new eugenics movement. Two examples from the twentieth century show how governments have viewed the lives of people with disabilities to have little value and indicated they should be extinguished (Silvers 1998):

- A 1939 German decree authorized physicians to put to death impaired persons who could not be cured. In the next two years, about 200,000 physically and mentally impaired children and adults were killed because they were judged to have "lives unworthy of life."
- As late as the 1930s, over half of the states in the United States had laws encouraging sterilization of people with disabilities, typically those with developmental disabilities, epilepsy, the blind, and the deaf.

Abortion, then, presents a major quandary for feminists who defend the right for women to choose, a right that can conflict with efforts to promote acceptance, equality, and respect for people with disabilities. Such is the dilemma of Laura Hershey, cited earlier, a prochoice feminist who is also disabled. She offers this solution to a highly complex issue:

> *I wouldn't deny any woman the right to choose abortion. But I would issue a challenge to all women making a decision whether to give birth to a child who may have disabilities. The challenge is this: consider all the relevant information, not just the medical facts. More important than a particular diagnosis are the conditions awaiting a child—community acceptance, access to buildings and transportation, civil rights*

protection, and opportunities for education and employment. Where these things are lacking or inadequate, consider joining the movement to change them. In many communities, adults with disabilities and parents of disabled children have developed powerful advocacy coalitions. I recognize that, having weighed all the factors, some will decide they cannot give birth to a child with disabilities. It pains me, but I acknowledge their right and their choice. (Hershey 2000:563)

AGENCY

People with disabilities have always had to acclimate to environments and social settings that were designed for the able bodied. As we have seen, they experience discrimination in housing, education, and work. Equal access is frequently denied because of transportation and architectural barriers in streets and buildings. Added to these structural barriers to equality are the stings of widespread stereotypes that demean them as inferior, unattractive, asexual, and pitiful. Their frustration with unequal access and discrimination has led many people with disabilities to become active in the disability rights movement. In joining with others, their feelings of isolation became feelings of a common bond and empowerment. This section focuses on their collective efforts and the results.

Disability Rights Movement

A **social movement** is a group that develops an organization and tactics to promote or resist social change. Its members share a belief system that defines common grievances and goals and group identity. The disability rights movement comprises a wide variety of individuals as well as local and national organizations with a common goal—equal rights for people who are disabled. It is a loose structure of organizations because many focus exclusively on people with particular disabilities (e.g., the National Federation of the Blind, the Disabled American Veterans, the National Association of the Deaf). But this network, although seemingly lacking unity, is united by the overarching objectives of empowerment and collective rights—human, civil, and legal—for people with disabilities.

The civil rights struggles by African Americans in the 1950s and 1960s and, to some extent, the antiwar protests of the 1960s and the student movement served as catalysts for oppressed groups such as women, gays/lesbians, and people with disabilities. Social movements capture the imagination of potential adherents when social conditions are right. "A disability rights movement was much more likely to occur at a historical moment when protests were legitimate, widespread, and focused not only along lines of established economic conflicts but also around issues of identity and social roles" (Scotch 1989:386). People who once were resigned to living their lives in isolation came to believe that in joining with others they could make a difference as they saw protests and heard leaders argue that disability was not their fault but rather the failure of the political system to acknowledge their rights as human beings and to be equal in society.

The disability rights movement began in the late 1960s with local organizing by Ed Roberts at the University of California at Berkeley and Judy Heumann in

People with disabilities have organized protests to make their case to the public and to policy makers.

New York City, both of whom were postpolio quadriplegics. Roberts was instrumental in getting the Berkeley campus to provide students with disabilities peer counseling and support to gain access to university programs and housing (for a history of the fight for disabled rights, see Switzer 2003). By 1972, Roberts and others founded the Berkeley Center for Independent Living, in an apartment, which was the forerunner to the independent living movement and its unofficial newspaper for the disability rights movement—the *Disability Rag* (now called *Ragged Edge*). Meanwhile, Judy Heumann filed a lawsuit when she was denied teaching certification because of her disability. Beginning with this action, others joined to form an organization called Disabled in Action (DIA), which had the goal to break down barriers to full societal participation of people with disabilities. In 1972, DIA, with 1,500 members, organized protests targeted at inaccessible public buildings, the Jerry Lewis telethon (which they believed perpetuated demeaning stereotypes of people with disabilities), and media organizations that either neglected or provided prejudicial coverage of disability issues. This group also blocked traffic in front of Richard Nixon's 1972 New York campaign headquarters to protest his veto of the Rehabilitation Act.

Congruent with the politics of the times (e.g., the war on poverty, passage of the voting rights act), policy makers became more receptive to the civil rights of people with disabilities. Congress, for example, passed the Rehabilitation Act of 1973, which prohibited government agencies and contractors from discriminating against people with disabilities. In 1975, Congress passed the Education for All Handicapped Children Act (legislation that Judy Heumann had worked on as a legislative intern), which required a free and appropriate public education and related services to all children with disabilities. Also, the Developmental Disabilities Amendments of 1975 expanded services for people with such impairments as mental retardation and cerebral palsy and mandated a network of state protection agencies to monitor and protect their rights. In 1977, the Department of Health and Human Services (HHS) issued regulations that required all recipients of HHS funds to provide equal access (through ramps and elevators) to employment or services or lose their subsidies. It is crucial to note that HHS

made these progressive changes only after sit-ins occurred in federal offices across the United States to protest the inaction by HHS on these issues.

Following the election of Ronald Reagan in 1980, the political climate changed for disability rights activists. The 1980s were characterized, in general, by weakened federal requirements, reduced budgets, deregulation, and judicial decisions that threatened previously established guarantees for the disabled. There were occasional victories such as success in organizing opposition to the Reagan administration's attempts to weaken several previously passed laws, including the Education for All Handicapped Children Act. They were defeated, however, when Reagan rescinded a Carter administration requirement that all new transit systems and newly acquired buses be wheelchair accessible. An organization within the disability rights movement, American Disabled for Accessible Public Transit (ADAPT), organized demonstrations in a number of cities to publicize the lack of access for many people with disabilities, but with only limited success during the chilly, politically conservative climate of the 1980s. Despite these setbacks, major progressive legislation was about to be enacted: the Americans with Disabilities Act of 1990.

Americans with Disabilities Act

When President George H. W. Bush signed the Americans with Disabilities Act of 1990 (ADA), it was called by some the most far-reaching civil rights legislation since the Civil Rights Act of 1964. The ADA was intended to eradicate discrimination against people with disabilities:

- The ADA prohibits discrimination in employment against qualified individuals. This means that people with disabilities can participate with equal opportunity in the application process, have an equal chance to perform essential functions, be provided with reasonable accommodations because of disability, and have equal benefits and privileges of employment. This law applies to all employers with fifteen or more employees.
- The ADA prohibits discrimination in programs run by public entities such as state and local governments, including public transportation.

- The ADA mandates that private businesses open to the public must make sure that all buildings, new and existing, are accessible to individuals with disabilities.
- The ADA requires telephone companies to make relay services available for hearing- and speech-impaired people.

Put more simply, because of this landmark legislation, accessibility is now commonplace: parking lots reserve parking spaces for people with disabilities, bathrooms are equipped for wheelchair access, ramps and elevators provide access to public buildings, and elevators feature Braille floor numbers or audio assistance. In short, "the Americans with Disabilities Act promised those forced to live with severe physical impairments the possibility of legal if not functional equality" (Kriegel 2002:32).

These major changes represented in the provisions of the ADA did not occur because it was the right thing to do. The battle was won despite the opposition of the National Association of Manufacturers, the U.S. Chamber of Commerce, and the National Federation of Businesses. Despite the resistance of big business, the progressive legislation was passed because people with disabilities and their compatriots had organized rallies to publicize their grievances and used tactics of civil disobedience, such as disrupting public transportation and blocking access to city hall, to make their lack of civil rights more visible. Some policy makers were persuaded by the message and logic of the protesters, others by the potential political power of people, realizing that about one-fifth of Americans have disabilities. There were also the growing ranks of people with disabilities, including the aged, who, growing in numbers, are disproportionately affected by disabilities, and the increasing proportion of the population with HIV/AIDS. To the degree that people with disabilities act as a cohesive group, they have considerable political clout. Their growing sense of shared grievances and a common identity have made their voting as a bloc on certain issues more likely than ever. The result of this social movement has been legislation guaranteeing their civil rights and greater opportunities.

Despite the significant victories of the disabled people's movement, the battle for full rights for the disabled is far from over. The provisions of ADA have been altered to narrow and weaken some of the provisions (the following is from Russell 1998:108–124). For example, only newly purchased buses are required to have lifts, and companies such as Greyhound are allowed to defer compliance indefinitely. Similarly, only new buildings or those undergoing renovation must be made accessible, and the original act exempted small business employers from compliance and provided a loophole allowing exemption from "undue hardship." Thus, any business could claim that the provisions were too expensive or too difficult to accomplish, permitting them to evade the regulations. Moreover, the government has been lax in enforcing compliance with ADA provisions because the monitoring effort is underfunded. A major consequence of the legislation's weak design is that:

> *Disabled individuals are the ones who must file complaints to see the law enforced. This places the onus on us to make private business and local governments conform to the law, which insidiously undermines our social standing. Disabled people will continue to be viewed as costly to society because government opted out of taking financial responsibility for removing barriers in a directed and planned manner.* (Russell 1998:117)

There have been other political setbacks as well:

- The media tend to treat the ADA as mainly a regulatory issue affecting private businesses rather than as a human rights issue facing society as a whole. Typically, the theme of their stories is the complaint that the ADA "goes too far" in forcing businesses to provide access and jobs (Jackson 2000).
- Among the provisions of the Fair Housing Act is the requirement that new multifamily housing with more units be accessible to people with disabilities. This regulation, according to Barry Corbet, an activist in the disability rights movement, is the most widely ignored law since Prohibition (Corbet 2000b:9b).
- In addition to providing medical benefits to those 65 and over, Medicare also benefits the severely disabled. The beneficiaries who are disabled before age 65, however, must wait 2 years before becoming eligible. This means, for example, that people with amyotrophic lateral sclerosis (known as Lou Gehrig's disease), a neurological disorder that progressively deteriorates the spinal cord and the brain causing loss of muscle control and, typically, death in 3 years, must pay for their expensive care, drawing down their families' resources, requiring them in some cases to raid their children's college funds or sell their homes.
- In 1999, the U.S. Supreme Court narrowed the ADA, ruling that people with physical impairments that can be treated with medication or devices such as eyeglasses or hearing aids are not protected.
- In 2001, by a five to four majority, the U.S. Supreme Court held that state employees could not collect damages from their states for offenses under the federal ADA (Rosenbaum 2001). An organizer in the Denver disabled community, Joe Ehman, said of this ruling: "That basically says that if you're a state employee, you have no rights. Once again, we're second-class citizens, according to the Supreme Court" (quoted in Kirksey 2001:49A).
- The Individuals with Disabilities Education Improvement Act mandated equal educational opportunities for disabled students. In 2005, the Supreme Court ruled that parents have the burden of proving that the school system does not provide a free, appropriate education for the special needs of their child. This ruling protects school districts from challenges, making equity more difficult to obtain.

Most significant, more than a decade after the passage of the ADA and other legislation favorable to people with disabilities, the evidence is that the disabled unemployment and poverty rates remain the highest for any minority group (Russell 2000). A survey by the National Organization on Disability in 2003 found that in a sample of 2,000 people with disabilities, 64 percent stated the ADA had not made a difference in their lives (up from 58 percent in 2000; cited in Gillum 2004).

Despite legislative and judicial setbacks, the disabilities movement perseveres and continues to make a difference. In 2000, for example, a class-action suit, the first of its kind in the United States, was filed against Kaiser Permanente, a health maintenance organization (HMO), on behalf of all its California members with disabilities. The lawsuit argued that Kaiser discriminated against disabled patients by having inaccessible medical equipment (e.g., mammography machines that cannot be used by people in wheelchairs). The next year (2001), Kaiser agreed to

SOCIAL POLICY

REFORMS TO INCLUDE DISABLED PERSONS IN THE WORKFORCE

The ADA has not "leveled the playing field"—the goal of most civil rights legislation—by eliminating economic discrimination. In liberal capitalist economies, redistributionist laws (which, if enforced, will cost business) are necessarily in tension with business interests, which resist additional costs. So far, most employers have resisted providing reasonable accommodations, and the business-biased courts have consistently ruled on behalf of employers, not workers with impairments. If capitalists benefit by not having to employ or retain a worker with an impairment, then many disabled workers are, and will continue to be, eliminated from mainstream economic activity. So the question becomes, Is it possible to reform business practices so that disabled persons are not excluded from the workforce?

- *Remove Discriminatory Insurance Language:* William Robb, an advocate from South Carolina, points out that "employers see disabled workers as a liability rather than as an asset, and this needs to be turned around." Robb proposes government remove the insurance language from ADA Title V, which allows the insurance industry to write up a disabled employee as a risk for private insurance. Robb's logic is persuasive: "If they [disabled people] are already at risk prior to their first guaranteed interview, who will hire them?" But will the insurance industry revolutionize their liability and risk underwriting practices to boost the disabled employment rate?
- *Reduce Risk to Employers:* Government could offer subsidies to offset business costs to level the playing field. It has recently passed one such reform, the Work Incentives Improvement Act of 1999 (WIIA), a subsidy that will allow disabled workers to retain their public health care by permitting them to buy into Medicare and Medicaid. But typical of most reforms, this measure falls way short. For example, it is not mandatory that states adopt WIIA; rather, the Act allows states to "experiment" with such an approach, so WIIA does not guarantee any improvement. Much will depend on how effective advocates can be in implementing good plans in their states.
- *Facilitate Part-Time Work:* Further, WIIA may be a modest first step toward disconnecting health benefits from indigency for those who can hold down a traditional full-time job, but it will do nothing to alleviate the more complicated set of Supplemental Security Income (SSI) and Social Security Disability Insurance (SSDI) pitfalls for the self-employed and those who must rely on part-time and sporadic work to survive. These individuals would need to have

a far-reaching settlement that included not only installing accessible medical equipment but also removing architectural barriers and instituting training programs, handbooks, and a complaint system to meet the needs of the disabled. Sid Wolinksy of Disability Rights Advocates said, "We believe this will be revolutionary in terms of its impact on health care for people with disabilities. The agreement with Kaiser provides a comprehensive blueprint that . . . we intend to use as a template . . . for other major health-care providers" (quoted in Lewin 2001:2).

In 2004, the Supreme Court ruled five to four in *Tennessee v. Lane* that courthouses must provide access to people with disabilities. This was a civil rights landmark case, according to Harriet McBryde Johnson, a lawyer in a power wheelchair:

> *For many decades, long flights of stairs made statements about the grandeur and power of the law. They reflected prevailing assumptions about the abilities of the people who would be participating in public life. By design, they were humbling, even disempowering. Ramps, elevators and appropriate use of government spaces have the*

their personal assistance services, SSI/SSDI, and Medicaid share of cost recalculated every month they earn income, something these systems are not efficient enough to do without delays and shortfalls for the recipient. Los Angeles activist Nancy Becker Kennedy, says, "It would be inadvisable for any disabled individual to work at part-time or sporadic employment because they run the highly probable risk of throwing these very sluggish benefit systems into confusion." Experience shows that this often results in individuals losing their health care, living allowance, and money to pay their attendant costs for months or even years while Social Security Administration and other agencies sort it out (and hopefully get it right when they do).

- *Enforce Minimum Wage Standards:* Other dubious subsidies already exist. Section 504 of the Rehabilitation Act of 1973 provides that federally financed institutions are required to pay a "fair" or "commensurate" wage to disabled workers, but they are not required to meet even minimum wage standards. The traditional sheltered workshop is the prototype for justifying below-minimum wages for disabled people, based on the theory that such workers are not able to keep up with the average widget sorter. Any nonprofit employer is allowed to pay subminimum wage to disabled employees under federal law if the employer can show that the disabled worker has "reduced productive capacity." About 6,300 such U.S. workshops employ more than 391,000 disabled workers, some paying 20 to 30 percent of the minimum wage; others paying as little as $11 per week (*Washington Post*, Dec. 12, 1999). In reality, workers with disabilities in these workshops know that they are sometimes paid less not because they lack productive capacity but because of the nature of segregated employment.
- *Subsidize Accommodations:* Government could pay for disabled workers' reasonable accommodations. Perhaps that would remove the added cost from the employer's bottom line and stop some employers from fighting disabled employees' much needed accommodations in court.
- *Mandate Affirmative Action for Disabled Workers:* Unlike the Civil Rights Act of 1964, the ADA was not followed up with an affirmative action program. While the Labor Department can mandate affirmative action for women and minorities, it only urges employers to hire disabled workers.

Source: Marta Russell. 2000. "The Political Economy of Disablement." *Dollars & Sense,* No. 231(September/October): 15, 48.

opposite effect. For people with disabilities, it is impossible to conceptualize equal protection of the law without them. (Johnson 2004:12)

The Americans with Disabilities Act Amendments Act of 2008 became effective on January 1, 2009 (U.S. Equal Employment Opportunity Commission 2009). The act met objections of the disability advocacy community that the original act was too narrowly defined. Specifically, the original was amended to emphasize that the definition of disability be construed in favor of broad coverage of individuals to the maximum extent permitted by the terms of the ADA. The effect of this change was to make it easier for an individual seeking protection under the ADA to establish that he or she has a disability within the meaning of the ADA.

To provide equal rights and opportunities for people with disabilities requires long-term solutions such as universal health care and a living wage. Some more readily achievable short-term goals, such as government actions to strengthen the ADA and other federal laws, will help the cause immeasurably. (See the Social Policy panel for a suggested list of such reforms.)

CONCLUSION

A fundamental progressive goal for society is social justice. The chapters in this inequality section show vividly that we are far from achieving that goal for racial/ethnic minorities, women, gays, and people with disabilities. In the words of Gail Schoettler, former lieutenant governor and treasurer of Colorado:

> *The Civil Rights Movement made great strides. Yet as long as any person in America is denied a job or housing or simple courtesy because of her or his personal characteristics, whether they be disabilities or skin color or beliefs or sexuality, we have not affirmed the basic equal opportunity promised by our Constitution. (Schoettler 2000:2L)*

■ CHAPTER REVIEW

1. About 20 percent of the U.S. population has some form of impairment. Approximately 15 percent of people with disabilities were born with the condition; 85 percent will experience a disabling condition in the course of their lives.
2. The individual approach (the medical model) defines disability in physiological terms, a physical or mental condition caused by the genes, accident, or disease. The goal is to return people with disabilities to "normal," and if this is not possible, to get them to adapt to their environment.
3. The social model, while acknowledging the biological basis of disability, focuses on the ways that social factors "disable" those with impairments. Some of these social factors are barriers to physical access, limited access to resources, and negative stereotypes.
4. People with disabilities constitute a minority group. Their marginality in society occurs because (a) they are defined as different; (b) the names given to them by society demean, diminish, trivialize, and deprecate; (c) the fact of disability establishes a master status by which people are categorized; (d) they are stigmatized; (e) they are excluded; (f) disability combines with other stratification hierarchies to form a matrix of oppression; and (g) they experience discrimination.
5. People with disabilities face a number of social barriers in the related areas of gender and sexuality. Women and men who are physically disabled are perceived as unattractive, asexual, and undesirable. Although both sexes are disadvantaged by the cultural expectations for what it takes to be feminine or masculine, women are more disadvantaged than men.
6. People with disabilities, both children and adults, are more likely to be abused physically and sexually than those without disabilities. Deaf people who cannot speak and people with learning disabilities are the most vulnerable to both types of abuse.
7. To counter their secondary status in society, many people with disabilities have taken an active part in the disability rights movement, a social movement with the goal of achieving empowerment and collective human, civil, and legal rights. Through the use of demonstrations and protest, this movement has succeeded, in part, to achieve favoring legislation that attempts to eliminate discrimination in housing, schooling, and the workplace, as well as the removal of architectural and other barriers to access to buildings and transportation. Most significant was the passage of the Americans with Disabilities Act of 1990, which, although flawed in its details and in its enforcement, advanced the cause of equality for people with disabilities.

KEY TERMS

Individual model of disability (also known as the medical model). Disability is defined in terms of some physiological impairment because of genetics, accident, or disease.

Social model of disability. The real problem with physical and mental impairment is not physical but social—the way people with able bodies view people with disabilities and the institutionalization of these views in limited physical access and other social barriers that interfere with the potential of people with disabilities.

Impairment. The state of being mentally or physically challenged.

Disability. Reduced ability to perform tasks one would normally do at a given stage of life that is exacerbated by the individual and institutional discrimination encountered.

Ontological truth. Universal and undeniable reality.

Master status. Status that has exceptional importance for social identity, overshadowing other statuses. Being defined as a member of a minority group is a master status.

Stigma. Attribute that is socially devalued and disgraced.

Ableism. Set of often contradictory stereotypes about people with disabilities that act as a barrier to keep them from achieving their full potential.

Matrix of domination. Intersections of the hierarchies of class, race, gender, sexuality, and disability in which each of us exists.

Hegemonic. Of the dominant belief system, which privileges the group in power.

Social movement. Group that develops an organization and tactics to promote or resist social change in society.

SUCCEED WITH PEARSON mysoclab www.mysoclab.com

Experience, Discover, Observe, Evaluate

MySocLab is designed just for you. Each chapter features a pre-test and post-test to help you learn and review key concepts and terms.

Experience sociology in action with dynamic visual activities, videos, and readings to enhance your learning experience. Complete the following activities at www.mysoclab.com.

Social Explorer is an interactive application that allows you to explore Census data through interactive maps.

- Explore the Social Explorer Map: *Social Explorer Report: Disability in the U.S.*

The Core Concepts in Sociology video clips offer a real-world perspective on sociological concepts.

- Watch *ABC Primetime: Returning Vets*

MySocLibrary includes primary source readings from classic and contemporary sociologists.

- Read Jaeger & Bowman, *Disability Discrimination and the Evolution of Civil Rights in Democratic Societies*; Berger, *Hoops and Wheels*; Shuttleworth, *Disabled Masculinity: Expanding the Masculine Repertoire*

CHAPTER 12 Crime and Justice

With so many of our citizens in prison ... there are only two possibilities. Either we are home to the most evil people on earth or we are doing something vastly counterproductive.

—U.S. Senator James Webb

This chapter examines the nature of crime and how society reacts to criminal behavior in the processing of criminals. These topics are important because they help us understand the role of the powerful in regulating social behavior and the bias of the system against the powerless.

CRIME IN SOCIETY

The people of society are concerned with crime for two obvious reasons: if left unchecked, crime destroys the stability necessary for the maintenance of an orderly society, and the people are the potential victims of criminal activities.

Although legitimate, these concerns direct attention away from the deviance that results from the orderly working of society and from crimes that are much more costly than street crimes (which we tend to think are overwhelmingly the greatest criminal danger). These ironies will become apparent as we examine four aspects of crime: its definition, the incidence of crime, the kinds of people arrested, and the various types of criminal behavior.

What Is Crime?

Groups and individuals within society differ in their definition of crime. Some people equate crime with all antisocial behavior. Others argue that crimes are acts such as racism, sexism, and imperialism that violate basic human rights. Similarly, some people use moral rather than legal criteria to define what is or is not a crime. For example, Martin Luther King, Jr., and his followers believed that the laws enforcing racial segregation were morally wrong, so to violate them was not a crime but a virtue. Antiabortion activists believe that abortion is a crime regardless of what the formal law decrees.

Although there is no universally accepted definition of **crime**, the most common one—the breaking of a law—officially labels people and separates society into criminal and noncriminal categories. In other words, criminality is a social status that is determined by how an individual is perceived, evaluated, and treated by legal authorities. Generally, the law designates as criminal any behaviors that violate the strongly held norms of society. There is common agreement in the United States, for example, that the law should protect property from theft and vandalism. There is also universal agreement that society must protect its citizens from bodily harm (rape, assault, and murder). But although there may be consensus in society on certain laws, the political nature of the lawmaking and enforcement process has important negative implications for the individuals caught up in them.

Consider, for example, how local and federal authorities treated antiwar protesters during the late 1960s and early 1970s. Their behavior was considered criminal because it threatened the power structure. What the powerful consider criminal depends, in fact, on what they perceive to be the intent of the individuals they observe. In the United States, society does not always forbid or condemn some acts of force that injure people or destroy property. Property damage during the celebration of sports victories, Halloween, or Mardi Gras is often overlooked or trivialized. Even 10,000 beer-drinking, noisy, and sometimes destructive college students on the beaches of Florida during spring break are allowed to go on such a binge because "kids will be kids." But if the same 10,000 college students were to destroy the same amount of property in a demonstration whose goal was to change the system, the acts would be defined as criminal and the police called to restore order by force if necessary. Thus, violence is condoned or condemned through political pressures and decisions. The basic criterion is whether the act supports or threatens existing social and political arrangements. If they are not supportive, then by definition the acts are to be condemned and punished.

A related implication of the political nature of crime is that the design of laws is influenced by a class bias. "The law and the legal order especially favor the very wealthy, but they favor enough of the rest of the population to appear to be equal. Yet the law clearly has never done a good job supporting the most marginalized sectors of the population: the poor in general, and African Americans, and other minorities" (Shelden 2001:15). That is also the interpretation by notable historian of law and criminal justice Lawrence Friedman:

> *Law is a fabric of norms and practices in a particular society; the norms and practices are social judgments made concrete: the living, breathing embodiment of society's attitudes, prejudices, and values. Inevitably, and invariably, these are slanted in favor of the haves; the top riders, the comfortable, respectable, well-to-do people. After all, articulate, powerful people make the laws; and even with the best will in the world, they do not feel moved to give themselves disadvantage.*
>
> *Rules thus tend to favor people who own property, entrepreneurs, people with good position in society. The lash of criminal justice, conversely, tends to fall on the poor, the badly dressed, the maladroit, the deviant, the misunderstood, the shiftless, the unpopular. (Friedman 1993:101)*

This view pervades the criminal justice system, as discussed later in this chapter.

Because the law defines crime, then what is a crime depends on the current law. As society changes and as new interest groups become powerful, the laws and interpretations of the laws regarding criminal behavior may also change. Many behaviors once considered criminal no longer are, such as marrying someone of another race, harboring a runaway slave, or selling liquor.

Finally, because crime is defined by the powerful in society, the organization and priorities of society are never regarded as harmful to human life (and therefore a moral crime). Yet the order of society itself can be very destructive to some categories of people, as Carmichael and Hamilton showed in their classic 1967 book, *Black Power*. They noted that when White terrorists bombed a Black church in Birmingham, Alabama, and killed five children, the act was deplored by most elements of U.S. society. But when hundreds of Black babies die each year in Birmingham because of the effects of racism, no one in the power structure gets upset and calls this violence. Although high infant mortality and rates of preventable disease, which are perpetuated through discrimination, take many more lives than civil disorder or street crimes, the term *violence* is not applied to these crimes (Carmichael and Hamilton 1967:4). Forty years later, the infant mortality rate is *still* twice as high for Blacks as it is for Whites (*Washington Post* 2007), but this is not labeled a moral crime by the dominant society.

Crime Rates

The innately political nature of crime is clearly evident when one examines the official crime rates, which emphasize certain types of crimes (those of the powerless) while minimizing or ignoring others. These discrepancies have profound implications because they mean, in effect, that some categories of people are disproportionately labeled criminals.

There are two basic sources of crime statistics in the United States. The first is the *Uniform Crime Reports* (UCR), published yearly by the FBI (U.S. Department of Justice, Federal Bureau of Investigation 2009). The *UCR* statistics are based on the arrest figures and reports supplied by 17,000 law enforcement agencies. This means that there is the potential to underreport the actual extent of crime because they list only crimes reported to the police.

Official crime rates from the *UCR* are also misleading because they imply that the amount of crime varies a good deal from year to year or from region to region. These changes may occur, but the official statistics make real variations difficult to determine. In some cases, the actual incidence of crime may not change, but the accuracy of reports may be in question. For example, in a recent survey of retired police officers in New York City, the officers said that the intense pressure to produce annual reductions in crime led some supervisors and precinct commanders to manipulate crime statistics (Rashbaum 2010). Other police departments in Atlanta, Dallas, New Orleans, Washington, and Baltimore have also been accused of tampering with crime data.

Another problem with these statistics is that they focus on traditional crimes and omit white-collar crimes, corporate crime, organized crime, and political crimes. The FBI statistics (called index crimes) emphasize violent crimes (murder, forcible rape, robbery, and aggravated assault) and property crimes (burglary, larceny, motor vehicle theft, and arson). This focus has the effect of directing public attention almost exclusively to crimes involving violence and property, in which the poor and minorities are thought to be the major perpetrators, and away from the crimes of the affluent.

The second major source of crime statistics comes from the National Crime Victimization Survey (NCVS), conducted annually by the Bureau of Justice Statistics (BJS) department. Instead of gathering crime data from police departments, these crime statistics come from a nationally representative survey of households. The benefit of using these statistics to gauge the amount of crime in society is that they include crimes whether or not they were reported to the police. According to the NCVS, only 47 percent of all violent victimizations and 40 percent of all property crimes were reported to the police in 2008 (Rand 2009).

- **Violent Crimes and Property Crimes.** According to NCVS data, violent and property crime rates in 2008 were at or near their lowest levels in over three decades. Overall, U.S. residents experienced 4.9 million violent crimes and 16.3 million property crimes (Rand 2009). This represents a 41 percent decrease in violent crime rates and a 32 percent decrease in property crimes since 1999 (see Table 12.1).

TABLE 12.1

Rates of Criminal Victimization and Percent Change, by Type of Crime, 1999 and 2008

	*Victimization Rate**		
Type of Crime	*1999*	*2008*	*Percent Change 1999–2008***
VIOLENT CRIMES	32.8	19.3	–41.2%
Rape/sexual assault	1.7	0.8	–52.6%
Robbery	3.6	2.2	–39.4%
Assault	27.4	16.3	–40.8%
PERSONAL THEFT	0.9	0.5	–41.4%
PROPERTY CRIMES	198.0	134.7	–32.0%
Household burglary	34.1	26.3	–22.8%
Motor vehicle theft	10.0	6.6	–34.1%
Theft	153.9	101.8	–33.9%

*Victimization rates are per 1,000 persons age 12 or older for violent crime and per 1,000 households for property crime.

**Differences between the annual rates do not take into account changes that may have occurred during interim years.

Source: Rand, Michael R. (2009). *National Crime Victimization Survey, 2008*. Bureau of Justice Statistics, U.S. Department of Justice. (September 2009).

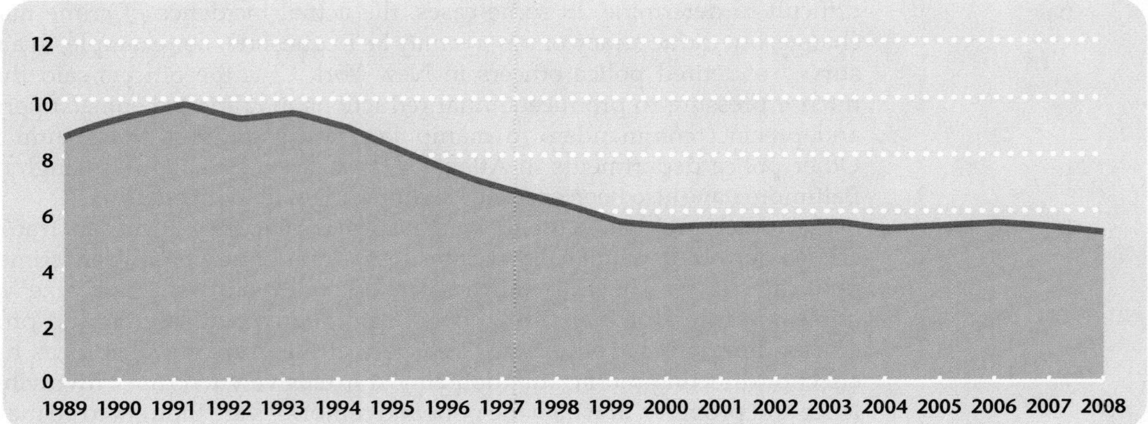

FIGURE 12.1

United States Murder Rate, 1989–2008

*Murder Rate per 100,000 Inhabitants

**The murder and nonnegligent homicides that occurred as a result of the events of September 11, 2001 are not included.

Source: U.S. Department of Justice, Federal Bureau of Investigation (2009). 2008: Crime in the United States. *Uniform Crime Reporting Program.*

- **Murder and Nonnegligent Manslaughter.** According to the *Uniform Crime Report* data, 16,272 people were murdered nationwide in 2008. This represents a significant decrease from 1989 (see Figure 12.1). Looking closely at the 2008 figures, two things are apparent: (1) The majority of murder victims and murder offenders are male (78 percent of victims; 64.9 percent of offenders); and (2) given their numbers in the general population, Blacks are overrepresented among both victims and offenders (48 percent of victims and 36.5 percent of offenders). We will explore further the issues of sex, race, and crime in the next section.

Looking more generally at crime rates over time, crime rates for all types of crimes appeared to rise in the 1990s with a trend toward decreasing rates since 2000. At the same time:

- Expenditures increased 420 percent for police departments, 660 percent for the Department of Corrections, and 503 percent for the Judicial Branch from 1982 to 2006 (Bureau of Justice Statistics [BJS] 2010).
- The prison population increased from 319,598 in 1980 to 1,518,559 in 2008. Currently there are 7,308,200 people in jail, prison, on parole, or on probation (BJS 2010).

Let us examine what kinds of people are arrested and labeled for criminal behavior in U.S. society.

Demographic Characteristics of People Arrested for Crimes

The data from official sources clearly indicate that people from certain social categories are more likely than others to be arrested for criminal activities. We examine these categories of sex, age, social class, and race.

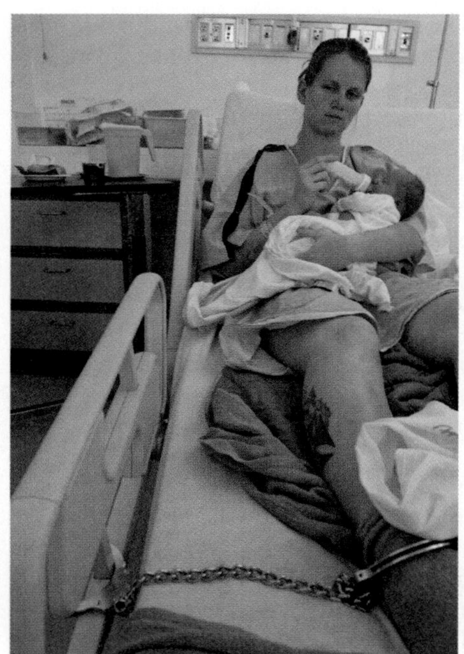

Forty-eight states allow the shackling of female inmates while they are giving birth.

- **Sex.** Overall, men are more likely to be both the offender and the victim in a crime. Although this has remained fairly consistent over the years, women's crime rate is increasing. In terms of arrests, in 2008 men accounted for 75.4 percent of individuals arrested, but this represents a 3.1 percent decrease in their crime rate from 1999, whereas women's crime rate increased 11.6 percent over that same period. *Uniform Crime Report* data show some interesting arrest trends by sex from 1999 to 2008. In the twenty-nine different crimes reported, women's rate increased in fifteen categories while men's rate increased in seven. Women experienced the largest increase in arrests for robbery, stolen property, embezzlement, and driving under the influence.

  The incarceration rate for women was 62 per 100,000 in 2008 (with 114,852 women in prison). This rate is at least three times more than that of any other nation. In fact, the United States incarcerates over 60,000 more women than the countries with the next highest rates (Russia, Thailand, India, Ukraine, and Brazil) combined (Hartney 2006). Even so, women, who make up more than half the general population, constituted only 7.1 percent of the nation's total prison population in 2008. The differences by sex raise two questions: (1) Why is there such an apparent difference in criminal behavior by gender? (2) Why are women committing more property crimes now?

- **Explaining the Gender Gap.** Although both males and females can be physically and verbally aggressive and engage in risky behaviors, gender socialization typically results in differences in behavior. Boys are taught to be aggressive and risk takers, whereas girls are not. Sons are given more freedom by parents, and daughters are typically subject to greater social control.

  Another explanation for gender differences in criminal behavior involves structural barriers that limit the possibilities for lawlessness by women. Women, for example, have fewer opportunities than men in employment to embezzle from their employers or to swindle customers. Also, patriarchy among criminals gives women few opportunities in organized crime, neighborhood gangs, and narcotics networks.

- **Explaining the Rise in Female Criminality.** The number of women arrested and incarcerated is growing faster than that for men. One possible reason for this is that the women's movement for social, political, and economic equality has not only increased gender role equality of women in legitimate ways but has also opened up new opportunities, traditionally reserved for criminal males, in illegitimate and illegal activities. Others argue that the impact of the women's movement on female crime, though real, is less direct. Perhaps, for example, law enforcement agencies have paid more attention to women in general and their criminal activities in particular since the advent of the women's movement. Or possibly, because the present increase in female crime is primarily property crime, their increased participation in the labor force has moved many women closer to opportunities to commit certain crimes. More significant, though, is the link between female criminality and their greater economic marginality.

Many criminal justice scholars attribute the rise in female crime rates more to the growing poverty among young, unattached mothers and the new ways society treats women than to the wider opportunities they have. More men are abandoning their families, leaving women with the burdens of children and with the temptations to commit crimes to care for them.

- **Age.** According to the *Uniform Crime Reports,* young people commit a disproportionate amount of street crime in the United States, with those under 25 accounting for about 46 percent of all violent crime arrests and 56 percent of all property crime arrests. Those aged 50 and over, on the other hand, are responsible for only 6.8 percent of the violent crime arrests in the United States. Why are young people more likely than adults to engage in street crimes? There are several plausible explanations for this tendency. First, young people are increasingly disengaged from their parents and more greatly influenced by their peers. Youths also want to impress their peers, and this is sometimes done by acts of daring, some of which may involve breaking the laws. Related to this reason, adolescents (in groups) may seek pleasure, experiment with drugs and alcohol, and engage in reckless behaviors. Second, adolescents often feel they need more money to provide for their desired lifestyle. Third, adolescence is a time of rebellion, a time of challenging authority. Contrast this with adulthood when individuals acquire full-time jobs, marry, and have children. Adults are much more likely than adolescents to feel tied to and have a stake in the community. This "maturation leads to less crime" phenomenon occurs across White, African American, and Latino populations.

- **Social Class.** The bulk of the people processed by the criminal justice system for committing street crimes are the undereducated, the poor, the unemployed, or those working at low-level, alienating jobs. There are several explanations for this relationship. First, the kinds of crimes listed by the FBI are those of the lower classes (white-collar and corporate crimes, e.g., are omitted). Second, the police and others in the criminal justice system assume that lower-class people are more likely to be criminals. Thus, they place more personnel in lower-class neighborhoods, which ensures that they will find more criminal activity. Third, economic deprivation may induce people to turn to crime to ease their situations. The evidence is clear that direct interpersonal types of crime (robbery, larceny, assault) are committed disproportionately by members of the poor.

  In terms of the victims, the lower a person's income, the more likely he or she is to be at risk of household burglary. Similarly for violent crimes, those with the lowest incomes experience the highest rate of violence (Albanese 2005:92).

  Social class is also significant for crimes in the upper strata of the stratification system. Those in lofty occupational and political roles commit white-collar crimes. Embezzlement, computer crimes, fraud, bribery, manipulation of the stock market, land swindles, and the like involve people at the other end of the social hierarchy from those most likely to engage in street crimes. The irony is that although white-collar, political, and corporate crimes do much more harm to society than do the crimes by the poor, crimes by the poor are seen as the crime problem.

- **Race.** People labeled as criminals in the United States are disproportionately people of color—African Americans, Latinos, and Native Americans. For example, although Blacks are 12.3 percent of the U.S. population, they constitute 39.4 percent of those arrested for violent crimes and 30.1 percent of those arrested for property crimes.

  Although racial minorities have more contact with the criminal justice system than Whites do, this statistic does not mean that race causes crime. Racial minorities commit many crimes on the street because the social conditions of unemployment, poverty, and racism fall more heavily on them. Especially in urban centers, more and more African Americans are living in poverty, jobless, and in conditions conducive to high rates of violence and crime. Moreover, we should remember that the official statistics reflect arrest rates and are not necessarily a true indication of actual rates. The bias of the system against the poor, and especially poor minorities, makes the likelihood of their arrest and conviction greater than for well-to-do Whites, as shown in the section on the criminal justice system.

Categories of Crime

The *Uniform Crime Reports* of the FBI focus on traditional types of crime, which tend to be concentrated among the young and the poor. The focus on traditional crime ignores other types that may actually be more costly to society in terms of lives and property—organized, white-collar, corporate, and political crime. Another type of crime—moral order crime—is significant in enforcement costs but not necessarily in human costs.

- **Traditional Street Crimes.** These are the crimes emphasized by the police, the government, and the media. They are the FBI's index crimes of burglary, larceny, auto theft, robbery, rape, assault, and murder. These are serious crimes against property or **violence** against people that many people consider to be the

TV programs tend to focus on street crime, thereby fostering the stereotype that the crime problem is exclusively street crime.

SOCIAL POLICY

COMPARATIVE CRIME RATES: WE ARE NUMBER ONE IN VIOLENT CRIMES

International comparisons of crime data, although inexact, do provide rough approximations of how crime is patterned geographically. What is accepted is that among the industrialized nations there is not too much difference in burglaries, bicycle thefts, and other property crimes. What is striking, however, is that among these nations, the United States has much higher rates of violent crimes (robberies, assaults, murders, and rapes), although a number of European nations are catching up. To support this assertion, consider the following representative facts:

- Holland's murder rate is one-sixth the U.S. rate. The U.S. national homicide rate ranges from about three to four to more than twenty times that of other industrialized nations. If the United States brought its homicide rate down to the level of Germany or France, it would save more than 15,000 lives every year.
- The rate of burglary was 1,309 per 100,000 people in the United States, compared to 93 in Norway. (Ironically, Denmark had the highest rate of 2,412.)
- The 2005 murder rate was 8.4 per 100,000 people in the United States, compared to .7 in Finland.
- The 2005 rape rate was 37.2 per 100,000 people in the United States, compared to 7.87 in Norway and 1.20 in Portugal.
- Compared to the British, Americans are far more likely to commit robbery, more likely to use a gun in the course of a robbery, and more likely to inflict deadly force on their victim, whether or not they use a gun.

Criminologists are in general agreement that the extraordinarily high rate of violent crime in the United States is the result of the confluence of at least four major forces. First, countries where there is a wide gap between rich and poor have the highest levels of violent crime (for example, South Africa currently has extremely high levels of violent crime). The United States has the greatest inequality gap between the affluent and the poor of the industrialized nations.

Second, the greater the proportion of the population living in poverty, the higher the rate of violent crime. The United States differs from the other industrialized nations "in having an underclass that is not merely poor, but has few chances of escaping poverty" (Rubenstein 1995:20). Currie says, "[We] know that the links between

whole of crime. People accused of these crimes are ones who typically clog the courts and prisons.

The perpetrators of these types of crimes are disproportionately people on the economic margins of society—the poor, the uneducated, the unemployed, the homeless, and racial minorities (see the "Social Policy" panel titled "Comparative Crime Rates").

In evaluating this type of crime, we need to consider two types of offenders. One type is a habitual offender, who, for whatever reason, continues their criminal patterns. For all seven major traditional crime categories, the majority of those arrested are repeaters. Obviously, the career criminal must be converted to a new way of life, to a legitimate career that offers all the gratifications received through criminality, if rehabilitation is to be successful.

The other type is a one-time-only criminal (accidental or incidental criminals). Progressives maintain that such people should not be punished harshly, for that would be counterproductive. For example, locking up a one-time offender might have the unintended consequence of hindering a person's employment prospects and perhaps creating a career criminal.

Conservatives, on the other hand, argue for swift and severe punishment to deter the person from a life of crime and to reinforce the notion in the rest of disadvantage and violence are strongest for the poorest and the most neglected of the poor. . . . [The] people locked into the most permanent forms of economic marginality in the most impoverished and disrupted communities [have] the highest concentrations of serious violent crime" (Currie 1998:127).

Third, violent crime is worse in those societies with weak "safety nets" for the poor. The United States provides few if any social supports (health care, education, child care, and other forms of welfare) for those in the lower social classes. As Elliott Currie has put it, "[The United States,] though generally quite wealthy, is also far more unequal and far less committed to including the vulnerable into a common level of social life than any other developed nation" (Currie 1998:120). In fact, the current trend in the United States is to reduce the meager benefits to the poor even more. The other industrialized nations are also reducing social spending, but their social budgets are still high compared to the United States.

Finally, the greater the availability of guns in a society, the higher the level of violent crime. Without question, the United States has more guns per capita than in any other industrialized nation—an estimated 235 million guns in a population of 300 million. The 1995 rate of gun ownership per capita in Great Britain is 0.006, compared to 0.853 in the United States. This huge arsenal makes gun access relatively easy in the United States, resulting in crimes of rage using guns rather than fists or knives or thrown objects. As Harwood has said, "Eliminating handguns would not eliminate rage or conflict but certainly would lower the life-threatening consequences of these encounters" (Harwood 1997:27).

Thus, by examining crime rates and social policies in other industrialized nations, we have a good sociological handle on what fosters violent crimes. If this understanding guided social policy—that is, if the inequality gap and poverty were reduced by increasing taxes on the affluent while providing greater social supports, more employment opportunities, and better wages to the economically disadvantaged, plus strict controls on handguns and automatic/semiautomatic weapons—then violent crime and the human and social costs accompanying violent crime would be reduced significantly.

Sources: Elliott Currie. 1998. *Crime and Punishment in America*. New York: Metropolitan Books, pp. 15, 24–25, 116–126, 148–160; Stryker McGuire. 1996. The Dunblane Effect. *Newsweek* (October 28):46; Richard Harwood. 1997. America's Unchecked Epidemic. *Washington Post National Weekly Edition* (December 8):27; Ed Rubenstein. 1995. The Economics of Crime. *Vital Speeches of the Day* (October 15):19–21.

society that crime does not pay. The criminal justice system in the United States has mainly approached criminality from this conservative perspective.

> *This growth in punitiveness was accompanied by a shift in thinking about the basic purpose of criminal justice. In the 1970s, the sociologist David Garland argues, the corrections system was commonly seen as a way to prepare offenders to rejoin society. Since then, the focus has shifted from rehabilitation to punishment and stayed there. Felons are no longer* persons *to be supported, but* risks *to be dealt with. And the way to deal with the risks is to keep them locked up. (Loury 2007:2)*

With the 2007 to 2009 economic recession, we may begin to see a change in this philosophy. Because it costs states a large amount to put offenders in prison, cash-strapped states are increasingly turning to alternative sentencing methods and streamlined probation and parole for low-level offenders. It costs approximately $79 a day to keep an inmate in prison but $3.50 a day to monitor the same person on probation or parole (Richburg 2009). Texas, known for its hard sentencing laws and conservative judges, implemented new rules in 2007, including shortened probation (from ten years to five), increasing the rate of offenders receiving parole, and more drug and DWI (driving while intoxicated) courts. They have consequently seen a significant decrease in their prison population

(Richburg 2009). As states see their budgets dwindling, many are considering these cheaper alternatives to prison.

- **Crimes against the Moral Order.** To enforce the morality of the majority, legislation defines certain acts as criminal if they are deemed offensive. Violations of these laws are **moral order crimes**. Examples of this type of crime are gambling, recreational drug use, and prostitution. Sometimes these acts that violate the moral order are called **victimless crimes** because even though they may offend the majority, they do not harm other people. The argument for such laws is that the state has a right to preserve the morals of its citizens in the interest of promoting social stability and consensus.

  Should an individual have the right to choose among alternative forms of behavior without fear of social sanction if that behavior does not harm other people? The answer to this question is not as unqualified as it may seem; many so-called victimless crimes in fact hurt other people, at least indirectly. The family members of an alcoholic, drug addict, or compulsive gambler are affected both materially and emotionally by his or her habit. Overindulgence in alcohol or a drug increases the probability of automobile accidents. Prostitution is a victimless crime, except that some people are unwillingly forced to become prostitutes and to live in servitude to a pimp or organized crime.

  A fundamental problem with legislating morality, aside from putting limitations on individual freedoms, is that it labels people as "criminals" on the basis of the tastes of those in power. Thus, **secondary deviance** (deviant behavior that is a consequence of the self-fulfilling prophecy of a negative label) may result not because someone harmed another but because his or her act was presumed by powerful others to be harmful to them.

  The detection, arrest, and prosecution of victimless criminals is an enormous and expensive task. More than half the arrests and roughly 80 percent of the police work in the United States are related to the regulation of private morals (alcohol abuse, pornography, juvenile runaways, drug use, prostitution, and gambling). About half of the jail and prison populations are there for drug offenses. If these private acts were legalized, then the police, the courts, and the prisons would be free for other, more important duties. Formerly illicit activities could become legitimate businesses providing tax revenues to local and state governments. Most important, organized crime, which now acquires most of its income from providing illegal goods and services, would no longer be able to hide its investments and profits. Thus, laws against victimless crimes are indirectly responsible for maintaining organized crime.

  Moral order crimes also contribute to the corruption of the police and courts. Although many police officers are unwilling to accept bribes from murderers and thieves, they may accept them from the perpetrators of victimless crimes, using the justification that they believe these crimes are harmless and impossible to control anyway. This rationale opens the way for people involved in organized crime to buy protection for their illicit activities.

- **Organized Crime.** **Organized crime** is a business syndicate that seeks profit by supplying illegal goods and services such as drugs, prostitution, pornography, gambling, loan sharking, sale of stolen goods, money laundering, and even disposal of hazardous wastes. In short, people can and do organize to provide what others want, even if it is illegal. In fact, the illegality of what people want ensures that someone will supply the goods or service because the profits are so high.

Several characteristics of organized crime serve to perpetuate it. First, organized crime supplies illegal goods and services that are in great demand. So, one reason for the continued existence of organized crime is that it fills a need of supply and demand. If moral order crimes were decriminalized, organized crime would be left with products and services that could be easily and cheaply supplied by legitimate sources, and its profits and existence might be eliminated.

A second characteristic of organized crime is that it depends on the corruption of police and government officials for survival and continued profitability. Bribery, campaign contributions, delivery of votes, and other favors are used to influence police personnel, government attorneys, judges, media personnel, city council members, and legislators.

Another characteristic of organized crime is its use of violence to enforce conformity with the organization. There are strict rules for conduct and means of enforcing those rules. Individuals who cheat or fail to meet their obligations are disciplined severely. Violence is also used to eliminate competition. When rival organizations vie for the monopoly of a geographic territory or the distribution of a particular service or product, the struggle is often extremely violent.

Finally, organized crime is structured to ensure efficiency. This organization is not composed just of members of a criminal society. There are criminals, of course, but many of these people are linked with legitimate members of society as well. Together, the criminal and legitimate elements combine to form networks within cities, regions, and even nations.

These crime networks that we know as organized crime are often controlled by a racial or ethnic group. The stereotype is that Italians dominate them. The President's Commission on Organized Crime found, however, that various crime networks were controlled by Chinese, African Americans, Mexicans, Italians, Vietnamese, Japanese, Cubans, Colombians, Irish, Russians, Canadians, and a variety of others (Beirne and Messerschmidt 1995:261).

- **White-Collar Crime.** The public, influenced by the media and the FBI reports, focuses its fears on traditional street crimes such as assault and robbery. Even though these are legitimate concerns, crime of the street variety (typically by the young, poor minority person) is much less significant in cost and social disruption than are **white-collar crimes**—those committed by middle-class and upper-middle-class people in their business and social activities (such as theft of company goods; embezzlement; bankruptcy fraud; swindles; tax evasion; forgery; theft of property by computer; passing bad checks; illicit copying of computer software, movies, and music; and fraudulent use of credit cards, automatic teller machines, and telephones). Some examples of the magnitude of white-collar crimes follow:

    - Telephone marketing swindlers cheat U.S. consumers out of an estimated $40 billion annually.
    - Time theft by employees (e.g., faked illness, excessive breaks, and long lunches) costs U.S. businesses as much as $200 billion annually.
    - Seven percent of college students who take out student loans fail to repay them (Nakashima 2000).
    - Surveys by the Internal Revenue Service consistently find that three of ten people cheat on their income taxes. The IRS estimated that Americans underpaid their taxes by $400 billion in 2006 (*Time* 2006). This does not

include the monies received from the selling of goods and services for cash and tips received that go unreported to the government (that if reported would generate an estimated $345 billion in taxes annually).

- Otherwise law-abiding citizens routinely copy or purchase pirate computer software, videos, and music. Many also engage in cable TV theft. Others photocopy copyrighted materials, even though these activities are against the law.
- A poll of workers found that they had seen 37 percent of their co-workers take office supplies or shoplift, 25 percent steal product or cash, and 18 percent claim falsely that they had worked extra hours (*Business Week* 2002).
- A survey by the Federal Trade Commission found that between May 2002 and June 2003, nearly 25 million Americans were the victims of fraud (Maltin 2004).
- Executives at major corporations such as Enron, Global Crossing, and WorldCom, knowing that their companies were soon to lose much of their value, sold stock for personal gain worth about $5 billion from 1999 to 2005.
- In what has been called the largest securities fraud in history, Wall Street financier Bernard Madoff used what is called a **Ponzi scheme** to con investors out of approximately $65 billion. He was sentenced to 150 years in prison in 2009.

Although we know that white-collar crimes are expensive and extensive, we do not know by how much. The statistics just noted understate the actual amount because many of them are so difficult to detect. Moreover, the victims are often embarrassed at their naivete in having been bilked. Whatever the numbers, the losses are huge. Suffice it to say that the criminal activities of the relatively well-to-do are widespread and expensive. What is remarkable, however, is how lenient U.S. society is to such wrongdoers when they are caught. Moreover, for the relatively few who are sentenced to prison (compared to street criminals), they serve relatively light sentences.

Wall Street financier Bernard Madoff conned investors out of approximately $65 billion.

- **Corporate Crime.** Business enterprises can also be guilty of crimes, which are known as **corporate crimes**. The list of illegal acts committed in the name of corporate good includes fraudulent advertising, unfair labor practices, noncompliance with government regulations regarding employee safety and pollution controls, price-fixing agreements, stock manipulation, copyright infringement, theft of industrial secrets, marketing of adulterated or mislabeled food or drugs, bribery, swindles, selling faulty merchandise, and overstating earnings to increase the value of company stock. The magnitude of such crimes far surpasses the human and economic costs from other types of crime manyfold. Some recent examples follow:
  - The National Highway and Traffic Safety Administration has recorded 203 deaths and more than 700 injuries, amid thousands of complaints, involving rollover-prone Ford Explorers that crashed following sudden tread separation on factory-installed Firestone tires. Internal corporate memos at the two corporations reveal that Ford and Firestone "willfully and knowingly kept unsafe products on the market" (Milchen and Power 2001:9).
  - In 2000, the world's largest auction houses, Sotheby's and Christie's, agreed to pay $512 million to settle claims that they cheated buyers and sellers in a price-fixing scheme dating back to 1992.
  - Bayer sold a blood-clotting medicine for hemophiliacs, a medicine that carried a high risk of transmitting AIDS, to Asia and Latin America while selling a new, safer product in the West (Bogdanich and Koli 2003).
  - In 2004, Schering-Plough settled with the government for $345 million because it charged private insurers much lower prices on Claritin than it charged the government programs of Medicare and Medicaid (Schmit 2004).
  - In recent years Exxon, International Paper, United Technologies, Weyerhaeuser, Pillsbury, Ashland Oil, Texaco, Nabisco, and Ralston-Purina have been convicted of environmental crimes.
  - Cosco did not tell the Consumer Product Safety Commission of the more than 200 children who had been injured by its tandem stroller and did not recall the stroller until more than a year after it began receiving what turned out to be 3,000 complaints. "This is a pervasive problem in a wide range of products used by children. . . . Product manufacturers frequently conduct internal investigations but remain publicly silent as complaints about alleged defects pile up. In the past three years, 75 percent of the most dangerous problems that led to recalls were never voluntarily reported to the government" (O'Donnell 2000:1B).
  - Archer Daniels Midland (ADM) pled guilty and was fined $100 million (the company had revenues of $13.6 billion) for its role in conspiracies to fix prices and eliminate competition and allocate sales in the lysine and citric acid markets worldwide. In return for its guilty plea, ADM was granted immunity against charges of price fixing on other products.
  - ConAgra executives knowingly resold 80 tons of meat in 2000 that South Korea customs agents had quarantined because they said it contained a potentially lethal bacteria. Rather than destroy the meat or cook it to kill the pathogens, the meat was sold to other countries with lower standards than South Korea's (Migoya 2002).
  - Costain Coal pled guilty to twenty-nine counts and no contest to three counts of misconduct at a Kentucky mine shaft site where an explosion

killed ten workers. These counts included violations of the Mine Safety Act's mandatory health and safety standards and false statements on records filed by the company.

- Halliburton has been found guilty repeatedly of overcharging the government for fuel, services (food and housing of troops), and construction during and following the first and second Iraqi wars. Moreover, contrary to federal laws prohibiting companies from doing business with countries supporting terror—Iraq, Iran, and Libya—Halliburton circumvented these restrictions by setting up subsidiaries in foreign countries (Herbert 2003a).
- Several newspapers—the *Dallas Morning News*, *Newsday*, and the *Chicago Sun-Times*—admitted that they had overstated weekday circulation (the greater these figures, the more the newspapers can charge for advertising) (McCarthy 2004).

These examples make three points. First, the goal of profit is so central to capitalistic enterprises that many corporate decisions are made without consideration for the consequences to their customers and employees. But not only are entrepreneurs indifferent to people; society is also essentially indifferent to certain offenders. The punishments meted out to individual white-collar criminals, and especially to corporate officials, are incommensurate with their misdeeds. Moreover, criminal corporations are treated much more gently than criminal individuals. For instance, states commonly have "three strikes and you're out" laws (i.e., if found guilty of three felonies, you go to prison for life), but these do not apply to corporations. Consider the case for General Electric Corporation (GE), which from 1990 to 2001 had a rap sheet involving forty-two situations in which the company was fined or ordered by the federal government to make restitution for crimes involving environmental violations, defense contracting fraud, consumer fraud, workplace safety, and employment discrimination (*Multinational Monitor* 2001).

Second, the companies that are criminally prosecuted represent only a fraction of corporate wrongdoing:

> *For every company convicted of health care fraud, there are hundreds of others who get away with ripping off Medicare and Medicaid, or face only mild slap-on-the-wrist fines and civil penalties when caught.*
>
> *For every company convicted of polluting the nation's waterways, there are many others who are not prosecuted because their corporate defense lawyers are able to offer up a low-level employee to go to jail in exchange for a promise from prosecutors not to touch the company or high-level executives.*
>
> *For every corporation convicted of bribery or of giving money directly to a public official in violation of federal law, there are thousands who launder money legally through political action committees to candidates and political parties [see Chapter 2]. They profit from a system that effectively has legalized bribery. (Mokhiber and Weissman 1999:20)*

And third, the costs of corporate crimes far outweigh the costs of street crimes.

> *The General Accounting Office, the investigative arm of Congress, estimates that health care fraud alone costs up to $100 billion each year. Another estimate suggests that the annual cost of antitrust or trade violations is at least $250 billion. By comparison, the FBI estimated that in 2002, the nation's total loss from robbery, burglary, larceny-theft, motor vehicle theft and arson was almost $18 billion. That's less than a third of the estimated $60 billion Enron alone cost investors, pensioners, and employees. (Drutman 2003:2)*

- **Political Crime.** Typically, a **political crime** is seen as any illegal act intended to influence the political system. The operant word in this definition is illegal. Is it illegal to disobey unjust laws such as laws supporting racial segregation? Is it illegal to oppose tyranny? If the answer to these questions is yes, then Martin Luther King, Jr., and George Washington must be considered political criminals. The definition given here assumes that the political system is always right and that any attempt to change it is wrong. Though antithetical to the heritage of the early American colonists and the Declaration of Independence, such thinking is typical of how those in power interpret any attempt to change the existing political system.

  Another way to conceive of political crime is to concentrate on the deviance of the people in power. One example of this type of political crime is the imprisonment or harassment by the powerful of those who act against established authority. Such acts include the jailing of Martin Luther King, Jr., the FBI's infiltration of dissident groups, the Internal Revenue Service's intimidation of people on President Nixon's "enemies list," and the punishment of people involved in providing housing, transportation, and jobs to refugees escaping political repression in Guatemala and El Salvador (the Sanctuary Movement).

  Government itself can be engaged in illicit activities. Some examples are the involvement in covert actions to overthrow legitimate governments, such as the Reagan administration's policy to aid the contra effort in Nicaragua, the U.S. attack on Panama to capture its leader, Manuel Noriega; the suppression of popular revolts in countries favorable to the United States; the use of secrecy, lying, and deceit; the use of people as unwilling and unknowing guinea pigs in medical experiments; and war crimes.

  - The government revealed in 1995 that the Department of Energy conducted 435 human radiation experiments involving 16,000 people during the Cold War. Included among these experiments was one in which eighteen people were injected with plutonium without their knowledge or consent (Eisler 2000).
  - From 1932 to 1972, the U.S. Public Health Service followed 400 African American men with syphilis without treating them. The purpose of the research was to determine the natural course of syphilis. In 1947, when penicillin was found to be an effective treatment for syphilis, it too was withheld from the men and their families (Washington 2006).

We have seen that there are a number of different types of crimes and criminals. However, the laws and their enforcement apparatus selectively focus on traditional street crimes. The social reaction to these crimes is the subject of the remainder of this chapter.

UNJUST SYSTEM OF JUSTICE

Justice refers to the use of authority to uphold what is lawful in a completely impartial and fair manner. Even though fairness is the goal of the U.S. system of justice, it is far from realized. The law itself, the administration of the law by the police and judges, and the prisons all express bias against certain categories of people. To document this assertion, we examine the criminal justice system from three directions.

1. The laws. To assess the fairness of a judicial system, we must know whether its rules are fair. Most important is the question, to what extent do powerful interest groups impose their will in the creation of the laws?

2. The negative reactions (the stigma and segregation) directed at those who break the laws. In a number of studies, researchers have determined that many people at various times are involved in serious acts of deviance, yet only a relatively small proportion are labeled deviant. In other words, something other than the commission of the deviant act must differentiate the deviant(s) and those who consistently work to disadvantage certain categories of people. Or is the process impersonal?

3. The treatment and formal processing of deviants. Here, the focus is on the public and private agencies that process the wayward—the courts, prisons, and mental hospitals. With reference to those accused of criminal behavior, we need to determine how attorneys are assigned, bail set, juries selected, sentences imposed, and parole granted. Is there a bias at each of these levels that works to the disadvantage of certain types of people? What are the consequences of being legally processed as a criminal? Does the process itself promote the deviance it is created to suppress?

This section, then, examines all phases of the system of criminal justice. Are all people accorded equal treatment under the law? Are the police fair? Are the procedures commonly used in the courts free of bias? As a nation, the United States has always pledged equal and therefore fair treatment to all its residents. This section documents that the reality is far removed from the ideal. There is a systematic bias in the criminal justice system that disproportionately labels the powerless as deviants.

Laws

Of all the requirements for a just system, the most fundamental is a body of nondiscriminatory laws. Many criminal laws are the result of public consensus on what kinds of behaviors are a menace and should be punished (such as murder, rape, and theft). The laws devised to make these acts illegal and to specify the extent of punishment for violators are nondiscriminatory because they do not single out a particular social category as the target. Although these laws in themselves are not discriminatory, the remainder of this chapter demonstrates that the administration of them often is.

Other laws, however, do discriminate because they result from the exertions of special interests to translate their objectives into public policy. In contrast, some segments of society (such as the poor, minorities, youth, renters, and debtors) rarely have access to the lawmaking process and therefore often find the laws unfairly aimed at them. Vagrancy, for example, is really a crime that only the poor can commit.

One example of this interest group approach to the law is the pre–Civil War and Jim Crow legislation in the South. The majority created laws to keep the races separate and unequal. Here are a few specific examples of the historical bias of the law against Blacks:

- The law played a critical role in defining and sanctioning slavery. For instance, the law made slavery hereditary and a lifetime condition.
- The slave codes denied Blacks the rights to bring lawsuits or to testify against a White person.

- The slave codes denied Blacks the rights to marriage.
- Jim Crow laws codified the customs and uses of segregation.
- After Reconstruction, the grandfather clause, the literacy test, and the poll tax were legal devices designed to keep Blacks from voting.
- In the nineteenth century, the law allowed only White men to sit on juries.

Not only is the formation of the law political; so, too, is its administration. At every stage in the processing of criminals, authorities make choices based on personal bias, pressures from the powerful, and the constraints of the status quo. Examples of the political character of law administration include attempts by the powerful to coerce other people to their view of morality, resulting in laws against pornography, drug use, and gambling; pressure exerted by the powerful on the authorities to crack down on certain kinds of violators, especially individuals and groups who are disruptive (protesters); pressure exerted to keep certain crimes from public view (embezzlement, stock fraud, the Iran-Contra scandal); pressure to protect the party in power, elected officials, and even the police department; and any effort to protect and preserve the status quo.

Police

Formal law enforcement policy begins with the police. They decide whether a law has been broken. They interpret and judge what behavior is "disorderly," how much noise constitutes a "public nuisance," when a quarrel becomes a "criminal assault," when protest becomes illegitimate, and what constitutes "public drunkenness." Their authority to interpret these questions suggests that the police have great decisional latitude. Unlike other agencies in the criminal justice process, the police in their work often deal with their clients in isolation.

Given the great discretionary powers of the individual police, one must determine whether police officers as a group tend to hold particular biases that affect their perceptions and actions. Several characteristics of the job and the types of people attracted to it suggest that certain biases may prevail among this occupational category.

The job itself causes police personnel to develop a distinctive way of perceiving the world. Foremost is that they are given the authority to enforce the law. They have power, even the ultimate power of legitimate force, at their disposal to uphold the law. As authorities sworn to uphold the law, police support the status quo. Naturally, then, they find people who defile the flag or otherwise protest against the system abhorrent.

Second, the danger inherent in their occupation promotes a particular worldview among the police. The element of danger tends to make them suspicious of behavior that is nonconforming or otherwise unusual. In the interests of self-defense, they tend to assume the worst of people they believe to be dangerous (minorities, protesters, drug users).

The police also tend to be socially isolated. Because they have actual power over other citizens, police personnel are the objects of hostility for many, but especially for minority group members. This hostility is manifested in epithets ("pigs"), abusive language, spitting, and other forms of harassment. The result, of course, is that the police, even those relatively free of prejudice toward minorities, tend to become hostile toward members of certain social categories over time. The harassment directed toward the police also increases the threat of danger to them. The result is a self-fulfilling prophecy: the police, harassed by victimized categories in societies, in turn harass their tormentors, which leads to charges of police brutality and the justification to be hostile toward them.

This characterization presupposes that the police are relatively free of prejudice, at least at the beginning of their career. This assumption, however, is not always true. The evidence is clear that suspects who are poor, minority, and male are more likely to be formally arrested than suspects who are white, affluent, and female. **Racial profiling** (the practice of targeting citizens for police encounters on the basis of race) is common. DWB (driving while Black or Brown), or more recently, DWM (driving while Muslim; Ackerman 2006) or FWM (flying while Muslim) is not a crime, but because of racial profiling by the police, there is the assumption of criminal behavior. For example, over 80 percent of the automobile searches by the New Jersey state police on the New Jersey Turnpike during the 1990s were conducted on vehicles driven by African Americans and Latinos (Kocieniewski and Hanley 2000). A report of Missouri police found that they stop Black motorists at a rate 30 percent higher than White drivers and search them 70 percent more often (Associated Press 2001). This targeting of racial minorities by the police is based on the assumption that racial minorities are more likely than Whites to commit crime (Lichtenberg 2006).

A 2008 report by the American Civil Liberties Union in Arizona found that black and Latino drivers were 2.5 times more likely than white drivers to be searched, and Native American drivers were 3.25 times more likely than whites to be searched, despite the fact that they were *less* likely than Whites to be found with contraband (ACLU 2009). The ACLU concludes,

> *The disproportionate rates at which minorities are stopped and searched, in addition to the often high concentrations of law enforcement in minority communities, continue to have a tremendous impact on the over-representation of minorities (and especially members of African American, Latino, and Native American communities) in the American criminal justice system. (2009:12–13)*

The police engage in racial profiling also in ways other than in traffic encounters. For example, the police are much more likely to engage in a crackdown on the use of crack than on the use of drugs on a middle-class college campus, even though the level of drug use may be higher on campus. The result is that a greater proportion of African Americans are arrested for drug charges than middle-class Whites, thereby reinforcing the stereotypes and the rationale for further use of racial profiling (Kalet 2000).

Judicial Process

How fair is the process by which lawbreakers are prosecuted, tried, convicted, and sentenced? Given that the courts deal only with those whom the police arrest, clearly the process begins with a bias. The question is, Do the courts increase the degree of unfairness or not? A related question involves the operation of the principle that individuals brought before the courts are presumed to be innocent: How great is the gap between principle and practice?

To answer these questions, let us examine the formal procedures of the justice system for the commission of a serious crime. The police arrest the probable offender and bring him or her before a magistrate. The magistrate examines the evidence and decides whether to allow the alleged offender to be free on bail. The case is then turned over to a prosecuting attorney, who formally charges the defendant. This charge is subject to review by a judge at a preliminary hearing or by a grand jury. If the defendant pleads not guilty, then he or she comes to trial, where the facts of the case are argued by the prosecuting and defense attorneys before a judge and jury. If the jury finds the defendant guilty, he or she is sentenced by the judge to a term in prison or to a term of probation.

- **Magistrate and the Setting of Bail.** The primary functions of the magistrate are to inform defendants of their right to counsel, to assign them counsel if so requested, to set a date for a preliminary hearing, and to set bail. In the last procedure, the magistrate exercises considerable discretion.

Bail is the posting of money by the accused to guarantee that he or she will be present at the time of trial. The Constitution provides the right to bail in noncapital cases. Bail allows accused people to stay out of jail, thereby retaining their family, community, and work responsibilities; most important, it allows them a chance to investigate and prepare their cases.

Several practices in setting bail, however, undermine the principle of treating all people fairly. The primary problem is that the amount of bail to be posted is left to the discretion of the magistrate, who may set high bail to "teach the accused a lesson" or to "protect the community." Magistrates have often taken such an approach when the defendants have been political protesters and minority group members. This practice violates the Eighth Amendment, which specifically forbids the setting of excessive bail; moreover, the concept of preventive detention contradicts the presumption of innocence that is supposed to be at the heart of the judicial process.

The setting of bail is also unfair because magistrates tend to determine the amount of bail by the type of crime alleged instead of by the accused's ability to pay. Moreover, the accused or their families typically obtain bail money from professional bondspersons, who receive 5 to 10 percent of the total as their fee. If the bail were set at $10,000 for everyone accused of a felony and the accused had to pay a bondsperson a fee of $1,000, clearly the accused who were poor would suffer the greatest hardship.

The obvious result of the system of setting bail is that the poor remain in jail and the wealthy are released, either because the latter have their own money or bail or because bail bondspersons consider them less risky. This result highlights another problem: the power of bail bondspersons to decide whom they will bond and whom they will not. Of course, the poor are considered more risky. Moreover, bondspersons may refuse to grant bail as a "favor" to the police.

Thus, the biggest problem with the bail-setting practice as it now operates is that it tends to imprison the poor. Time spent in jail before trial varies by locality and by the backlog of pending cases. In some jurisdictions, defendants who cannot make bail spend as long as 18 months in jail awaiting trial. Clearly, this situation violates the principle that the accused person is presumed innocent until proven guilty, for it provides punishment before conviction. And the difference between those who languish in jail before their trial and those who are free is money.

- **Plea Bargaining.** Fewer than 10 percent of the people charged with crimes ever go to trial. The thousands of cases that bypass the trial process do so because either the charges are dropped or the people accused plead guilty to the original or lesser charges. The latter event is called **plea bargaining** because the defendants bargain away their right to a trial in return for their guilty plea and a more lenient punishment than if they were found guilty of the original charge.

Plea bargaining has become the rule, not the exception, in the disposition of criminal cases in the United States.

There are many pressures on defendants, lawyers, prosecutors, and judges to encourage plea bargaining. Foremost is the overwhelming caseload facing police, prosecutors, and judges. Without guilty pleas to speed defendants through the system, the criminal justice process could not function because of impossibly crowded courts. One obvious solution is for judges to encourage guilty pleas by implementing the agreements negotiated by prosecutors and defense counsel. Similarly, prosecutors encourage plea bargaining because of their large caseloads. In addition, prosecutors must have a high conviction rate, and plea bargaining achieves this goal at relatively little expense.

Defendants are pressured in several ways to plea bargain. People who are assigned as defense counsel typically encourage their clients to "cop a plea." One reason they encourage plea bargaining is that assigned counsel receive little compensation, and they would rather return quickly to their more lucrative private practice. Counsel may also feel that plea bargaining is in the best interests of the client because it will reduce time spent in jail awaiting trial. District attorneys often force plea bargaining on defendants by charging them with more serious crimes (carrying heavier penalties). Compelling defendants to plea bargain has the effect of reducing caseloads. A defendant who refuses to bargain faces the possibility of serving a longer sentence and for a more serious offense. Public defenders also encourage plea bargaining to reduce the burden of their large caseloads on their small investigative staffs. They would rather concentrate their efforts on capital crimes.

There are special pressures on defendants who are poor or of moderate means to plead guilty. They will be unable to bear the expense of a lengthy trial. Moreover, those unable to make bail must await trial in jail. These factors deter poor defendants from insisting on their rights. Although overcrowding in the courts may make it a necessity, plea bargaining subverts the basic foundations of the system of criminal justice. Contrary to the Bill of Rights, the practice operates on an implicit assumption of guilt. It fails to distinguish between the innocent and the guilty, thus penalizing the innocent and rewarding the guilty. Moreover, because it reduces sentences, plea bargaining erodes the elements of deterrence on which criminal sanctions are based. The procedure especially discriminates against the poor. The poor defendant, already in jail, is pressured by court-appointed counsel to bargain from a position of weakness. In a plea-bargaining situation, the need for competent and conscientious counsel outweighs all other factors. Yet it is inevitable that a lawyer receiving a handsome fee for his or her services will be more interested in a client's welfare than will an overburdened and undercompensated court-appointed one.

In sum, "When we shine a light on the outcome of justice in the United States, we see that the reality of plea bargaining is not consistent with the American ideal of the criminal trial, which is mentioned in the Declaration of Independence, three amendments to the U.S. Constitution, and scores of Supreme Court cases" (Robinson 2002:249).

- **Adversary System.** An intrinsic feature of the U.S. criminal justice system is the concept of adversary roles. In the **adversary system**, the state and the accused engage in a public battle to argue and provide evidence before an impartial judge or jury. For this principle to work, the adversaries must be relatively equal in ability, incentive, and resources. But this is not usually the case. The state has enormous resources (police, crime labs, detectives) with which to build its case. The accused, if wealthy, can match the resources and expertise of the state. In the famous O. J. Simpson case, for example, the defendant spent between $5 million and $6 million for a team of lawyers, jury selection experts, DNA authorities, and other specialists. In what would have been a speedy trial and probably an open-and-shut case of guilt for a poor defendant, the Simpson team was able to contest every piece of evidence by the prosecution, present countertheories, and raise a reasonable doubt among the jurors:

> *The Simpson case has demonstrated perhaps more starkly than ever before that in the American justice system, as in so much else in this country,* ***money changes everything—and huge amounts of money change things almost beyond recognition.*** *(Gleick 1995:41; emphasis added)*

But the Simpson case was an anomaly. Of all felony defendants in the United States, 80 to 90 percent are too poor to hire their own lawyer and are represented by court-appointed attorneys. These poor defendants are especially disadvantaged by the adversary system. Obviously, they cannot pay for detective work, hire expert witnesses, and do the other things necessary to build their case. States vary in the resources they commit to such cases. In Alabama, for example, the state will pay no more than $1,000 for out-of-court fees for defending a death-penalty case, whereas Indiana averages $53,000 on capital cases. The caseload for public defenders is huge, typically resulting in "assembly-line justice that often is not justice at all" (Gleick 1995:44).

- **Trial by Jury.** Fundamental to a fair system of criminal justice is the right to a trial by a jury consisting of a representative body of citizens. In practice, however, certain categories of people are underrepresented on juries: minorities, people not registered to vote, students, and low-prestige occupational groups. The result is that the poor, especially the poor from minority groups, are typically not judged by a jury of their peers (see A Closer Look Panel, "Jena Six").

The failure of juries to reflect communities is significant because the people least represented are those most likely to challenge community norms. This situation puts a special burden on defendants accused of political crimes (such as antiwar and civil rights protest).

In selecting a jury, the attorneys for the state and the accused attempt to choose jurors who are likely to favor their particular side. The selection process tends to be unfair, however. The state, with enormous investigatory and financial resources at its disposal, may use the police and the FBI to investigate minute details about each prospective juror. Unless the accused is very wealthy, the defense usually decides on the bases of intuition and superficial information.

Trial outcomes are also affected to some extent by whether the case is heard by a jury or a trial judge. The research suggests that juries tend to be more lenient than are judges. This points to another inequity of the judicial system: Because jury trials increase the probability of acquittal for defendants, they should be equally available to all people.

African Americans do not fare as well as Whites in civil trials. Verdicts go against African Americans more often than against Whites, both as plaintiffs and defendants. Not only do Blacks lose more often than Whites, but also when Blacks do win, they win smaller awards than do White plaintiffs.

A CLOSER LOOK

JENA SIX

In high schools across the country teachers and administrators must deal with school fights on a regular basis. Most of the time, the students are punished or suspended, and the public never hears about them. This was not the case, however, for the infamous "Jena Six." In December 2006, racial tensions were mounting at Jena High School in central Louisiana. One particular day, a black student sat under a tree that was known to students as the "white tree" where only white students could sit. The next day, three nooses were hanging from the tree.

The principal expelled the white students responsible, but the school board and superintendent overruled him, reducing the punishment to in-school suspensions. As tensions mounted, there was a fight in which a white student suffered a concussion and multiple bruises. Six black students were arrested and faced felony charges of attempted murder with potential fines of more than $90,000 and potential sentences of up to 20 years. They became known as the "Jena Six."

A judge reduced the charges against five of the six boys and only one of the Jena six went to trial. Mychal Bell (16 years old) was initially tried as an adult for aggravated assault and conspiracy.

> He was tried before a white judge and an all-white jury. He had only a court-appointed counsel who called no witnesses. The prosecutor argued that the gym shoes on his feet constituted a "deadly weapon." He was convicted, jailed with prohibitive bond and faced 20 years in prison. (Jackson 2007:1)

The severity of the charges caught the attention of civil rights groups across the country, and protests mounted. An online civil rights group raised more than $275,000 for legal defense for the Jena Six, and in September 2007 more than 40,000 demonstrators went to Jena to protest unequal justice for the students. In December 2007, Mychal Bell pleaded guilty to second-degree battery and was sentenced to eighteen months in jail.

In 2009, the case was resolved when the other five students pleaded no contest to simple battery and agreed to fines and seven days of probation. The civil rights group (ColorofChange.org) that raised the money for their defense said in a press statement:

> Today's plea deal shows that the original charges in the case were unfair and vastly overblown. The story of the Jena six was an extreme example of what can happen when a justice system biased against black boys operates unchecked. But it's also an example of what can happen when hundreds of thousands of people across the country stand up to challenge unequal justice. (quoted in Facing South 2009:1)

- **Judicial Sentencing.** Until the 1970s, judges were given considerable latitude in determining the exact punishment for convicted criminals. The discretion of the judges was almost without limits, and sometimes the results were very inconsistent from judge to judge and even by a particular judge. This discretionary sentencing permitted individualized justice. In other words, the judge could take into account the peculiar factors of the case in the sentencing decision. Although this ideal is a worthy one, the procedure resulted in a kind of courtroom roulette, depending on the law in the jurisdiction, the ideology of the judge, media attention, and other factors. Most telling among these other factors were the social class and racial characteristics of the defendants, with a strong tendency for middle- and upper-class Whites to receive lighter sentences than lower-class Whites and non-Whites.

  Beginning in the 1970s, there was a movement to curb the discretionary power of judges with the passage of mandatory and determinate sentencing laws. **Mandatory sentencing** forced judges to incarcerate violent and habitual criminals. **Determinate sentencing** means that for a given offense, the judge must impose a sentence (sometimes a fixed sentence and sometimes a range, depending on the state), within the guidelines of the law, depending on the crime and the offender's past record. Typically, a sentencing commission would be appointed in a state to determine these penalties.

  The leading example of mandatory sentencing is the "three strikes and you're out" law passed by the federal government (1994) and many state legislatures. The essence of this law is that someone found guilty of three serious crimes would be locked up for life with no hope for parole (serious is defined differently by the various states, with some accepting only violent crimes in this category, whereas others may include low-level property crimes and drug offenses). This provision is popular because it is punitive on so-called habitual criminals and thus will lower the crime rate. There are several problems with this get-tough policy, however. First, despite having the highest imprisonment rates, the United States still has the highest crime rates.

  Second, this mandatory provision increases the demand on limited prison space. This has two negative implications: increased cost to build and maintain prisons (up to $100,000 to build a cell and $22,000 annually to house a prisoner) and overcrowded prisons that will force the early release of other violent prisoners to make room.

  Third, the prisons are increasingly populated by lower-level offenders (small-time thieves, repeat property criminals, and drug offenders). The percentage of inmates in federal prisons convicted of violent crimes, for example, has decreased while the proportion there for drug offenses has increased to over 50 percent of all federal prisoners (see Figure 12.2).

  As mentioned previously, the rising prison population coupled with the tough economic times has caused some states to ease their mandatory sentencing regulations and seek cheaper alternatives to imprisonment. In 2003, Delaware and Washington, for example, reduced prison terms for nonviolent drug offenders, thus saving millions and reducing prison overcrowding. The trend appears to be in this direction, away from the get-tough sentencing policies of the 1980s.

- **Consequences of a Biased Judicial Process.** The facts make the case that the judicial system is biased against racial minorities:

  - African Americans are three times more likely than Whites to be arrested but seven times more likely to end up in jail (Kalet 2000).

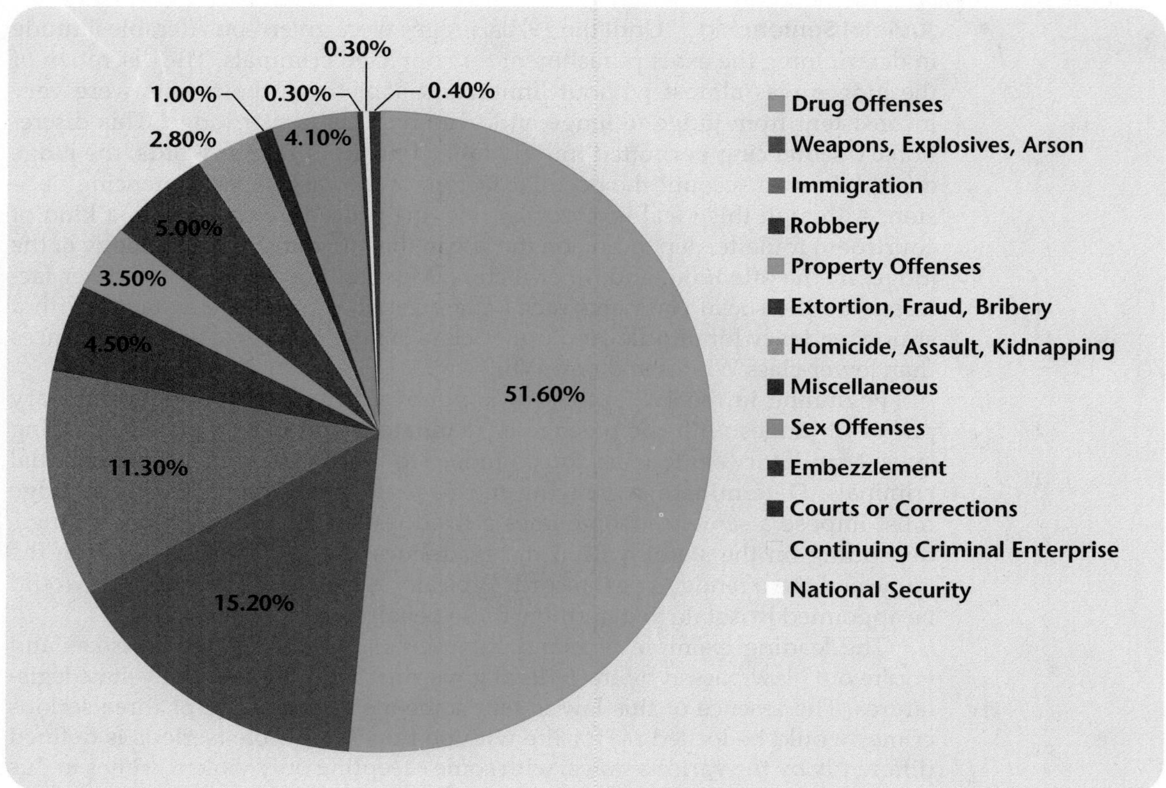

FIGURE 12.2

Types of Offenders in Federal Prison, 2010

Source: Federal Bureau of Prisons, U.S. Department of Justice. Prisoner population as of February 27, 2010.

- Of Black males born in the United States, 28.5 percent go to state or federal prison for a sentence of more than one year. The corresponding chance for Latino males was 16 percent and for White males, 4.4 percent (Stone 1999).
- A study by the U.S. Department of Justice concluded that minority youths, particularly African Americans, are treated significantly worse than Whites at every stage of the judicial process: "They are more likely to be locked up prior to trial, more likely to be tried as adults, more likely to be given hard time and less likely, at any step, to be given a break" (cited in Cose 2000:17A).
- Federal prison sentences overall are almost 50 percent longer for African Americans than for Whites (*Population Today* 2000).
- Although 12 percent of the U.S. population is African American, and 13 percent of drug users are African American, they represent 35 percent of those arrested, 54 percent of those convicted, and 74 percent of those incarcerated for drug-related crimes (Sturr 2006).

Criminologist Randall Shelden summarizes the situation:

> *Our modern system of justice takes place within a society that is highly stratified by race, class, and gender. It is my contention that equal justice cannot be achieved in an unequal society. The justice system in America merely reinforces these inequalities. . . .*

> *One result of social inequality is vast differences in the probabilities of having one's behaviors labeled "criminal." Evidence for this is found throughout the social science literature during the last half century or more. Therefore, the legal system responds accordingly and, more often than not, tends to focus its attention on those from the less privileged sectors of society: the poor, racial, and ethnic minorities and [especially] women of color, who more often than not are also poor. (Shelden 2001:3,18)*

Correctional System

U.S. citizens constitute less than 5 percent of the world's population, yet the number of U.S. prison inmates amount to 23 percent of the world's prisoners, with a higher proportion of its citizens jailed than in any other country in history (Hartney 2006). "The United States has a crime victimization (21 percent) comparable to those of Finland (19 percent), France (21 percent), and Canada (24 percent), even though the incarceration rate here is more than six times as high" (Sturr 2006a). See Figure 12.3.

Not only does the United States have a very high rate of incarceration, but the prison population is also unrepresentative of the general population, being disproportionately racial and ethnic minorities, the poor, and the uneducated. Because of the inequality represented in the prison system, criminologists Randall Shelden and William Brown have called the prison system the New American Apartheid.

> *Modern prisoners occupy the lowest rungs on the social class ladder, and they always have. The modern prison system (along with local jails) is a collection of ghettos or poorhouses reserved primarily for the unskilled, the uneducated, and the powerless. In increasing numbers this system is being reserved for racial minorities, especially blacks, which is why we are calling it the New American Apartheid. (Shelden and Brown 2004, para 1)*

The facts support the thesis of this chapter: that the criminal justice system in the United States is biased against the powerless (the following are from various annual reports by the Bureau of Justice Statistics):

- At the end of 2008, over 7.3 million Americans were under some form of correctional supervision (probation, prison, jail, or parole).
- From 1990 to 2005, the rate of incarceration in prison (federal and state) and jail (local) increased from 1 in every 218 residents to 1 in every 136. Two states—Louisiana and Georgia—had more than 1 percent of the populations incarcerated (*Dollars & Sense* 2006).
- There were 110 female inmates per 100,000 women in the United States, compared to 1,297 male inmates per 100,000 men. A Department of Justice report stated, "The incarceration rate for Black non-Hispanic females was 347 per 100,000—almost two and a half times higher than the rate for Hispanic females (144 per 100,000) and four times higher than the rate for white females (cited in Sturr 2006b:5).
- About 10 percent of all African American men between 25 and 29 were incarcerated in 2005, compared with 1.2 percent of White men and 2.4 percent of Latino men. African American men in their early thirties are imprisoned at seven times the rate of Whites in the same age group (DeParle 2007a). The chances of a Black man going to prison in his lifetime are one in three. Put another way, African American men are more likely to end up in prison than to earn a bachelor's degree (Talvi 2004).

FIGURE 12.3

The U.S. Incarcerates the Largest Number of People in the World

Source: Christopher Hartney, 2006. "U.S. Rates of incarceration, a global perspective," *National Council on Crime and Delinquency Fact Sheet*. (November): 2.

- In 2010 32.8 percent of those incarcerated were Hispanic. They are the fastest-growing segment of the U.S. prison population, with Latino men almost four times as likely as white men to be sentenced to prison during their lifetimes (Coyle 2003).
- In the United States, 1.5 million children have a parent in prison. Among those born in 1990, one in four Black children, compared with one in 25 White children, had a father in prison by age 14 (Eckholm 2009). These children are at risk: estimates are that they are as much as five times more likely to end up in prison themselves as children whose parents are not in prison. These children of the imprisoned most likely come from disadvantaged circumstances. The stings of stigma, family disruption, and living in poverty put these children at increased risk for doing badly in school as well as for early pregnancy, drug abuse, and delinquency.
- The median income for both male and female inmates did not exceed the government's poverty level during the year before arrest or during the year arrested.
- The highest incarceration rate among males age 16 to 64 was among those who were unemployed prior to arrest. Of those inmates who were working prior to arrest, 30 percent were employed outside what they considered their normal occupation. This suggests, very likely, that they were **underemployed** (i.e., employed at a level below that for which they had been trained).
- The proportion of blue-collar workers in prison was more than double that found in the U.S. population. The reverse was true of white-collar workers, who constituted less than one-third of their proportion in the population.
- Over 40 percent of all jail and prison inmates were high school dropouts, compared to 11 percent of the U.S. population of males age 20 to 29. This has been referred to as the "school to prison pipeline," where disadvantaged youth are being pushed out of school and into the criminal justice system.

There are three main reasons for the link between race and class incarceration. First, the crimes defined by official sources as the most important (the FBI's *Uniform Crime Index*) are the ones most likely to be committed by members of the lower classes. As discussed earlier, these official data on crimes are biased, and they bias the public, police, juries, and the courts. Because of the official emphasis, people view these crimes as the most threatening, yet in reality the crimes by the powerful (the well-to-do, the corporations, and organized crime) do more harm to people and their property. Second, as we have seen, the criminal justice system is not just. Economic resources make a crucial difference at every stage, leaving prisons and jails, for the most part, inhabited by the lower social classes. And finally, society continues to be racist. Institutional discrimination works to keep racial minorities disproportionately poor and unemployed. Institutional discrimination has also kept the minorities disproportionately underrepresented among police, lawyers, judges, and juries.

Not only are the more well-to-do less likely to receive a prison sentence, but also white-collar and wealthy criminals who are imprisoned receive advantages over the lower-class and minority inmates. The most extreme example of this privilege can be found by examining what type of person actually receives the death penalty—**capital punishment**. At year end 2008, thirty-six states and the federal prison system held 3,207 prisoners under sentence of death. Of these inmates, 98.2 percent are male, and *50 percent have less than a high school education*. Racial minorities are disproportionately found on death row (e.g., Blacks are 12.3 percent of the population, but they made up 42 percent of those awaiting execution in 2008).

> *Discrimination in the application of the death penalty can be seen most vividly by focusing on the race of the victim. Prosecutors nationwide—more than nine out of ten of whom are white—tend to seek the death penalty more often if the victim is white. To take one typical example, Georgia prosecutors sought the death penalty in 70 percent of the cases where the perpetrator was African-American and the victim was White. When there was a White killer and an African-American victim, the same prosecutors sought the death penalty in only 15 percent of the cases. (Donziger 1996:114)*

Social class also plays an inappropriate role in the determination of who receives the death penalty. First, the higher the social status of the victim, the greater the likelihood that the death penalty will be imposed on the perpetrator. Second, the vast majority of those given the death penalty and executed are poor and undereducated.

The geographical location of a capital crime is also crucial. One study in Nebraska found that judges in rural areas are more likely to impose the death penalty than judges in urban counties (Belluck 2001). Studies consistently show that judges and juries in southern states are much more likely to impose the death penalty than judges and juries in other regions. And, the state in which the capital crime is committed is crucial.

> *Among the 36 states that have capital punishment, Texas is far and away the modern-day leader in implementing it. Although it has 7.6 percent of the nation's total population, Texas carried out 35 percent of the nation's executions between 1976 and June 2004—putting to death 321 of 909 condemned prisoners. . . . Virginia was a distant second with 91 executions. (Rosenbloom 2004:A11)*

Who gets parole is another indicator of a bias in the system. **Parole** is a conditional release from prison that allows a prisoner to return to his or her community

Public opinion surveys show a growing number of Americans are against capital punishment.

under the supervision of a parole officer before completion of the maximum sentence. Typically, a board established for each correctional institution or for the state grants parole. Often, the parole board members are political appointees without training or experience in criminal justice issues. The parole board reviews the prisoner's social history, past offenses, and behavior in prison and makes a judgment about release. The board's decision is rarely subject to review and can be arbitrary or discriminatory.

The bias that disadvantages minorities and the poor throughout the system of justice continues as parole board members, corrections officers, and others make judgments that often reflect stereotyped notions. What type of prisoner represents the safest risk, a non-White or a White? An uneducated or educated person? A white-collar worker or a chronically unemployed, unskilled worker? Research shows, consistently, that decision makers in these situations typically give preferential treatment to people with the social characteristics more valued in society.

That the members of the disadvantaged in society (the poor and the minorities) are disproportionately represented in the prison population reinforces negative stereotypes already prevalent among the majority of the population. The large number of African Americans and the poor in prison is taken as proof that those groups have criminal tendencies. Moreover, the high **recidivism rate** (the return to crime by ex-prisoners; 70 percent of inmates in U.S. prisons or jails are not there for the first time) is viewed as further proof of the criminality of the poor, the uneducated, and minority groups.

Criminologist Jeffrey Reiman states, "Prison produces more criminals than it cures" (Reiman 2007:32). At least four factors related to prison experiences operate to fulfill the expectation that the poor and African Americans will be prone to criminal behavior—and a high recidivism rate. The first is that the disadvantaged view the entire criminal justice system as unjust. There is a growing belief among prisoners that because the system is biased against them, all prisoners are in fact political. This perception increases their bitterness and anger.

A second reason for the high rate of crime among the people processed through the system of criminal justice is the accepted fact that prison is a brutal, degrading, and altogether dehumanizing experience. Mistreatment by guards, sexual assaults by fellow prisoners, overcrowding, and unsanitary conditions are commonplace in U.S. prisons. Prisoners cannot escape humiliation, anger, and frustration. Combined with the knowledge that the entire system of justice is unjustly directed at certain categories of people, these feelings create a desire for revenge in many ex-convicts.

A third factor is that prisons provide learning experiences in the art of crime. Through interaction with other inmates, individuals learn the techniques of crime from experts and develop contacts that can be used later.

Finally, ex-convicts face the problems of adjusting to life without regimentation. More important, because well-paying jobs are difficult for anyone to find, particularly in times of economic recession, ex-convicts, who are automatically assumed to be untrustworthy, must choose between unemployment and jobs nobody else will take.

Nonacceptance by society causes many ex-convicts to return to crime. On the average, previous offenders are arrested for crime within 6 weeks of leaving prison. This fact, of course, justifies the beliefs of police, judges, parole boards, and other authorities that certain categories of people should receive punishment but others should not.

THE CRIMINAL LABEL

The evidence presented in this chapter strongly suggests that the powerless in society (the poor and the minorities) are disadvantaged throughout the criminal justice process. Although the bulk of research has been limited to the poor and African Americans, similar results are found for treatment of Latinos, Native Americans, and other minority groups in the criminal justice system.

That there is a bias is beyond dispute because the studies compare defendants by socioeconomic status or race, controlling for type of crime, number of previous arrests, and type of counsel. These studies, however, do not answer the question so often asked: *Are the poor and minorities more prone toward crime, as the differential arrest rates and composition of the prison population appear to indicate?*

This question is difficult to answer definitively because the crime rate is a function of police activities and does not reflect unreported crimes or activities that are overlooked by the authorities. The actual amount of crime is unknown and probably unknowable. We do know, however, that criminal behavior is found throughout the social structure—by rich and poor, by Whites and non-Whites, by ruralites, urbanites, and suburbanites. Studies that ask respondents to report, under the assurance of anonymity, the type and frequency of their criminal acts show that (1) a huge proportion of crimes go undetected, (2) adults and juveniles, regardless of social class, tend to have committed numerous acts for which they could have been adjudicated and imprisoned if caught, and (3) there is no substantial difference in the amount of criminal behavior of middle-class and lower-class respondents.

If criminal activities are common throughout the social structure, then how do certain groups of people avoid the criminal label while others do not? The data show that the administration of criminal law consistently works to the disadvantage of the poor, minority groups, and others who are powerless. That the system operates with this bias, however, is not proof that there is a conscious attempt to control and punish just certain segments of the population. A number of factors help to explain the bias. There is the widespread assumption that the poor and powerless are less trustworthy than the more well-to-do. Thus, their behavior is subject to greater scrutiny, and there is a greater presumption of guilt for them than for the more advantaged in society. This assumption is based on the predominance of the economically deprived in the official crime statistics and in the composition of prison populations and on their high recidivism rate. Thus, the bias of the system creates a self-fulfilling prophecy and a rationale for citizens, police personnel, judges, jurors, and corrections officers to assume the worst about certain groups of people.

"Proof" that these people are more crime prone is also found in the greater likelihood of their making crime a career. This tendency is the result of crime being a realistic means for a poor person to achieve material success because attainment through conventional means is virtually impossible for many. Just as important a factor is secondary deviance, the criminal behavior that results from being labeled a criminal. Upon release, the ex-convict returns to a community that is apprehensive and distrustful. Jobs are unavailable or, if available, degrading and low wage.

Thus, if the powerless of society are disproportionately singled out for the criminal label, the subsequent stigmatization and segregation they face results in a tendency toward further deviance—thereby justifying society's original negative response to them.

STOPPING THE CRADLE TO PRISON PIPELINE

As this chapter has shown, the United States has the highest crime rate in the industrialized world. We spend billions of dollars each year to imprison more of our citizens than any other country, and our system of justice does not treat all groups of people equally. The president of the Children's Defense Fund, Marion Wright Edelman, wrote,

> *Nationally, one in three Black boys and one in six Latino boys born in 2001 are at risk of going to prison during their lifetimes. Although boys are more than five times as likely to be incarcerated as girls, the number of girls in the juvenile justice system is significant and growing. This shamefully high incarceration rate of Black youths is endangering our children at younger and younger ages and poses a huge threat to our nation's future. America's cradle to prison pipeline is putting thousands of young people on a trajectory that leads to marginalized lives, imprisonment, and often premature death. (2009:1)*

The Children's Defense Fund has started a "Cradle to Prison Pipeline Crusade," aimed at preventing children from entering the pipeline and helping the children already trapped there. A number of states are working on plans to break the pipeline. The Children's Defense Fund points to Missouri as a model for the rest of the country.

> *The state of Missouri used a rehabilitative and therapeutic approach to overhaul its juvenile justice system that has been hailed as a national model for juvenile justice reform. The philosophy behind Missouri's program is to treat youths as potentially productive members of society instead of lost causes in a prison cage. The results are clear. Missouri's juvenile recidivism rate has only eight percent of those incarcerated coming back into juvenile custody and eight percent going into Missouri's prisons. It is one of the best success stories in the country. (Edelman 2009:1)*

The pipeline to prison is connected to many of the topics in this book, especially racial inequality, poverty, and education. High school dropouts are almost three times as likely to be incarcerated as high school graduates, and, as we have seen, half the prison population awaiting execution does not have a high school diploma. Thus, the Children's Defense Fund points to early childhood intervention programs (such as Head Start) and education reform as key components in stopping the pipeline for at-risk youth. The challenge for states is to make the commitment and invest in *prevention,* rather than continue to spend a disproportionate amount of funds and resources on corrections and punishment.

CHAPTER REVIEW

1. Criminality is a social status determined by how an individual is perceived, evaluated, and treated by legal authorities. What is a crime depends on the law, which is created by the powerful. Crime, then, is innately political.
2. There are two basic sources of crime statistics in the U.S. The FBI's *Uniform Crime Reports* is based on reports gathered from law enforcement agencies across the country. These statistics focus on street crimes against people and property. They omit white-collar crimes, corporate crimes, political crime, and organized crime.
3. The second major source of crime statistics is the National Crime Victimization Survey. These statistics come from surveys of households, thus they also include crimes *not* reported to the police.
4. The rates of violent crimes (including homicide) and property crimes are lower now than in 1999.

At the same time, expenditures for police departments and courts have increased over time, and the prison population is at an all-time high.

5. According to the official crime statistics, (a) more males than females commit crimes, (b) juveniles and young adults have the highest street crime rates, and (c) the poor, undereducated, unemployed, and racial minorities are more likely to be arrested and labeled as criminals.
6. Victimless crimes are private acts designated as criminal by powerful interest groups that are able to legislate morality. Making these acts criminal creates several problems: (a) they are costly to enforce, and, if legal, they would bring in significant tax revenues; (b) they make organized crime profitable; and (c) they contribute to the corruption of the police and courts. Moreover, so-called victimless crimes are rarely victimless—they do harm people.
7. Organized crime is a business syndicate that supplies illegal goods and services. Organized crime thrives because of (a) the demand for illegal goods and services is high, (b) corruption among the police and government officials, (c) violence and intimidation, and (d) its well-organized operation at all levels—locally, regionally, nationally, and internationally.
8. Losses resulting from individual white-collar crime amount to many times the monetary loss from street crimes. Yet official agencies do not devote as much attention to white-collar crimes, and the few criminals that are apprehended often receive relatively light sentences.
9. Corporate crimes are the most dangerous and expensive to society because they involve unsafe working conditions, pollution of the environment, unsafe products, and fraud.
10. Political crimes are of two types: (a) acts that threaten the power structure and (b) illegal acts by those in power.
11. The system of justice is fundamentally unjust. The laws favor the powerful. The Crime Index channels police activities toward certain criminal acts (street crimes) and away from others (white collar). The poor are disadvantaged at every stage of the judicial process because lawyers, bail, and an adequate defense are costly. Thus, for similar offenses, the powerless are more likely than the powerful to be found guilty, to be sentenced far more harshly, to wait longer for parole, and if sentenced, to die—actually to be executed.
12. The "cradle to prison pipeline" is the idea that some children in American society are at great risk to end up in the American correctional system. Solutions to the crime problem must veer away from the current ideology of punishment to focus on prevention and breaking this pipeline.

■ KEY TERMS

Crime. An act that breaks the law.

Violence. An act of force perceived by the powerful as threatening to the status quo.

Moral order crimes. Acts that violate laws that enforce the morality of the majority.

Victimless crimes. Acts that violate moral order crimes; they may offend the majority, but they do not harm other people.

Secondary deviance. Deviant behavior that is a consequence of the self-fulfilling prophecy of a negative label.

Organized crime. A business operation that seeks profit by supplying illegal goods and services.

White-collar crimes. Illicit acts committed by middle-class and upper-middle-class people in their business and social activities.

Ponzi scheme. An investment fraud that involves the payment of purported returns to existing investors from funds contributed by new investors (rather than from any legitimate investment activity).

Corporate crimes. Illegal acts by business enterprises.

Political crimes. Illegal acts intended to influence the political system. Also, the abuse of authority by those in power. Finally, actions by governments that are illegal or immoral.

Racial profiling. The practice of targeting citizens for police encounters on the basis of race.

Bail. Posting of money by the accused to guarantee that he or she will be present at the trial.

Plea bargaining. Arrangement between the prosecution and the accused whereby the latter pleads guilty in return for a reduced charge.

Adversary system. The U.S. system of justice, whereby the state and the accused engage in a public battle to argue and provide evidence before an impartial judge or jury.

Mandatory sentencing. By law, judges must incarcerate certain types of criminals.

Determinate sentencing. For a given offense, a judge must impose a sentence that is within the guidelines of the law.

Underemployed. Employed at a level below that for which one has been trained.

Capital punishment. Killing of a criminal by the state.

Parole. Conditional release from prison in which the former prisoner remains under the supervision of a parole office.

Recidivism rate. Percentage of offenders who, after their treatment or punishment has ended, are arrested and convicted of new offenses.

■ SUCCEED WITH PEARSON mysoclab www.mysoclab.com

Experience, Discover, Observe, Evaluate

MySocLab is designed just for you. Each chapter features a pre-test and post-test to help you learn and review key concepts and terms.

Experience sociology in action with dynamic visual activities, videos, and readings to enhance your learning experience. Complete the following activities at www.mysoclab.com.

Social Explorer is an interactive application that allows you to explore Census data through interactive maps.

- Explore the Social Explorer Map: *The Population in Prisons: San Quentin Penitentiary*

The Core Concepts in Sociology video clips offer a real-world perspective on sociological concepts.

- Watch *ABC Primetime: Juvenile Corrections*

MySocLibrary includes primary source readings from classic and contemporary sociologists.

- Read Sampson, *Rethinking Crime and Immigration*; Schaffner, *Injury, Gender, and Trouble*; Reiman, *... And the Poor Get Prison*

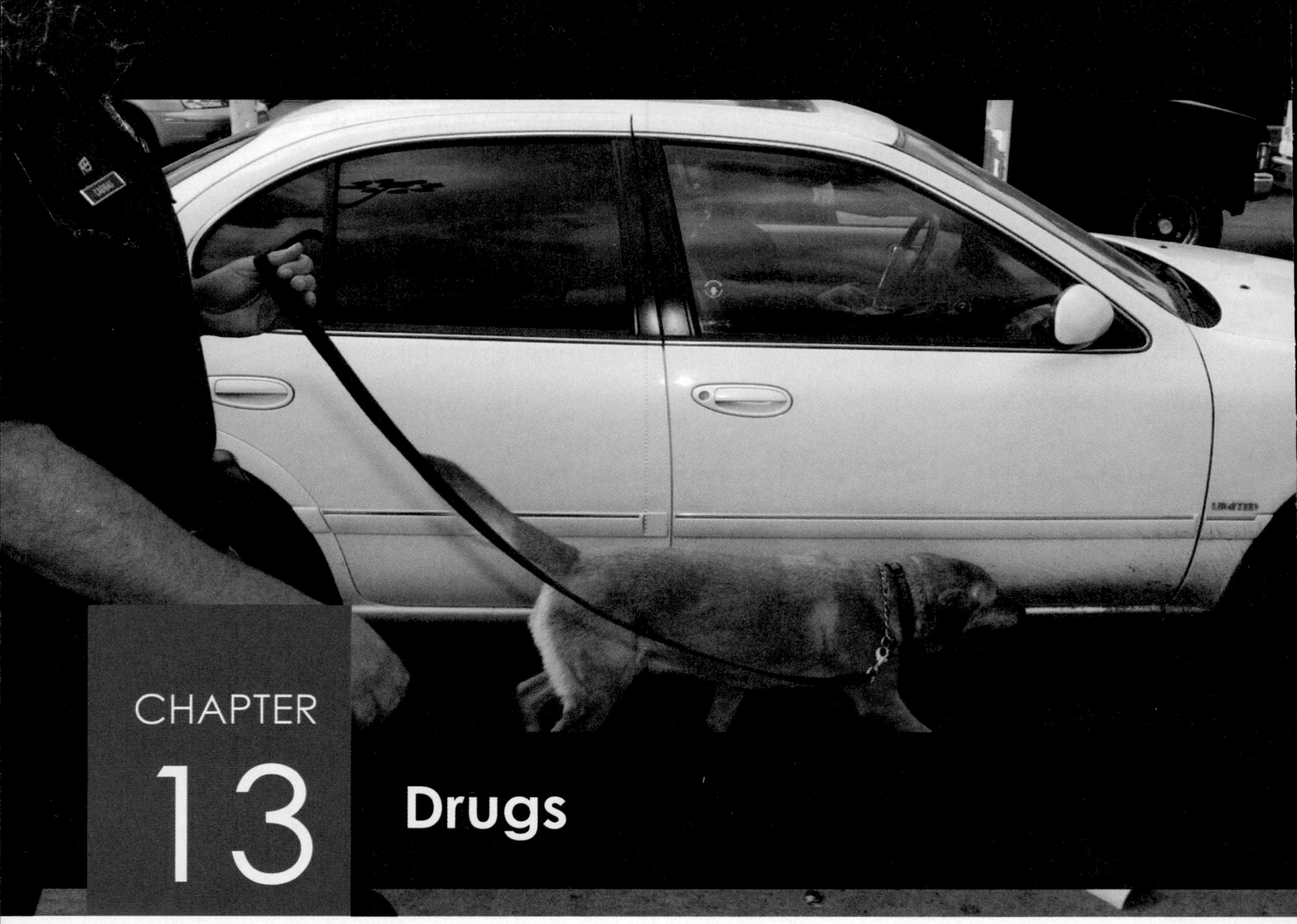

CHAPTER 13 Drugs

Nothing so needs reforming as other people's habits.

—Mark Twain

Throughout history, people have sought to alter their consciousness through the use of both legal and illegal substances. A **drug** is any substance that affects the structure or function of the body when ingested. This broad definition includes such substances as aspirin, caffeine, nicotine, heroin, and alcohol. Every society accepts some drugs as appropriate and regards others as unacceptable. Some drugs are considered dangerous, and others are harmless. But the definitions vary from society to society, and within U.S. society, they are inconsistent and often ambiguous.

Many people in the United States are concerned about the drug problem. But what is meant by "the drug problem"? Is drug use equated with abuse? Why are alcohol and tobacco legal drugs when they are addictive, physically harmful, and socially disruptive? Put another way, why is the use of alcohol accepted by U.S. society, whereas the use of marijuana is not? Is drug use a medical or a criminal problem?

> *In considering issues related to drug use and drug policies in the United States, it is useful to begin by noting some rather strange paradoxes. To take just one example, it is estimated that several million Americans use the antidepressant drug Prozac, and several million more use other antidepressants. These drugs are widely advertised and marketed, and the individuals who consume them experience no legal penalties for their consumption of these substances. At the same time, over half a million individuals, the majority of whom are members of minority groups, languish in American jails and prisons for possession and trafficking in consciousness-altering substances that the United States has deemed to be illegal. In fact, the increasing stringency of drug laws has been one of the primary factors associated with unprecedented levels of incarceration in the United States over the past 25 years. (Mosher and Akins 2007:x)*

Three points should be made at the outset of this discussion. First, definitions concerning drugs and drug-related behaviors are socially constructed. That is, definitions about drugs are not based on some universal standard but rather on meanings that people in groups have imputed to certain substances and behaviors. Second, as is true with all social problems, members of different societies or groups (e.g., religious and political) within societies often differ in their beliefs about this phenomenon. Third, the definition of drugs by the most powerful interest groups in a society will become part of the law and be enforced on others. Thus, the labeling of some drugs as licit and others as illicit involves politics. Therefore, in examining such topics as the history of drug laws, the extent of drug use and abuse, types of drugs, and the consequences of official drug policies, this chapter continually refers to the **politics of drugs**.

THE POLITICS OF DRUGS

Drugs are a social problem in U.S. society. Yet not all drugs are considered problems, nor are all people who take drugs. Some drugs are legal, and others are not. Some drugs caused problems once but are now considered safe; some that were not considered problems now are. Some drug use is labeled "abuse," whereas other use is not. Ironically, the drugs most objected to and most strictly controlled are not those most dangerous to users and society. Marijuana and heroin, though illegal, are less dangerous than are barbiturates, alcohol, and nicotine, which can be legally obtained and used indiscriminately. To explain such irrationality, we must understand how drugs and their use came to be considered safe or illicit.

Historical Legality of Drugs

The definition of drug use and abuse is complicated in U.S. society because different patterns of use are acceptable for different people. Some religious groups forbid the use of any drugs, even for medicinal purposes. Others accept medicines but reject all forms of drugs, including caffeine, for recreational use. At the other extreme are groups that may use drugs in their religious rituals to expand the mind. Time also changes interpretation. Early in the twentieth century, for example, it was socially acceptable for men to smoke tobacco, but not for women to do so. Then around 1950 or so, it became socially acceptable for women to smoke tobacco, and smoking was regularly seen in movies and on television. Now, increasingly, smokers of both sexes find their smoking unacceptable in public places.

Not only is there variance from group to group within society and from time to time, but there has also been virtually no consistency concerning the legality of drugs historically. The history of the acceptance or rejection of opiates (such as opium, morphine, and heroin) in the United States affords a useful example, for it parallels what happened to public attitudes toward other drugs.

Opiates were legal in the nineteenth-century United States and were widely used as painkillers in the Civil War, with many soldiers becoming addicted. Morphine was legally manufactured from imported opium, and opium poppies were legally grown in the United States. Opium was widely dispensed in countless pharmaceutical preparations.

The only nineteenth-century context in which opiates were declared illegal was one created by anti-Chinese sentiment. The Chinese, who were imported to the West Coast to provide cheap labor to build the railroads, brought opium with them. At first, their opium dens were tolerated. But as the cheap Chinese labor began to threaten the White labor market, there was agitation to punish the Chinese for their "evil" ways. San Francisco and several other West Coast cities passed ordinances around 1875 prohibiting opium dens. These laws were, as some analysts have noted, aimed at the Chinese, not the drug.

The early 1900s were characterized as a period of reform. A number of individuals and groups wanted to legislate morals; the Eighteenth Amendment, which prohibited the sale and use of alcohol, was passed in 1919 as a result of pressure from these reform forces. These groups rallied against **psychoactive drugs** because they believed them to be sinful. They fought against "demon rum" and "demon weed," as well as other moral evils such as gambling and prostitution. They believed that they were doing God's will and that, if successful, they would provide a better way of life for everyone. Therefore, they lobbied vigorously to achieve appropriate legislation and enforcement of the laws to rid the country of these immoral influences.

As a result of these reform efforts, Congress passed the Harrison Narcotics Act of 1914. This act was basically a tax law requiring people who dispensed opium products to pay a fee and keep records. The law was relatively mild. It did not prohibit the use of opium in patent medicines or even control its use. It did, however, establish a Narcotics Division in the Treasury Department (which eventually became the Bureau of Narcotics). This department assumed the task (which was not specified in the formal law) of eliminating drug addiction. Treasury agents harassed users, physicians, and pharmacists. The bureau launched a propaganda campaign to convince the public that there was a link between drug use and crime. Finally, the bureau took a number of carefully selected cases to court to broaden its powers. In all these endeavors, the bureau was successful. The net result was that a medical problem became a legal problem.

This point cannot be overemphasized: Prior to the Harrison Act, drug addicts were thought (by the public and government officials) to be sick and in need of individual help. They were believed to be enslaved and in need of being salvaged through the humanitarian efforts of others. But with various government actions (laws, court decisions, and propaganda) and the efforts of reformers, this image of addicts changed from a "medical" to a "criminal" problem. Once defined as a criminal problem, the solution became incarceration.

Factors Influencing Drug Laws and Enforcement

The previous section shows how differently a drug can be viewed over time. Clearly, current policies regarding opium (most common in the form of heroin) are repressive, but alcohol and tobacco continue to be socially acceptable drugs. These differences, especially because the laws do not reflect the drugs' relative dangers to users, demonstrate that official drug policies are arbitrary and problematic. What, then, are the factors that affect the focus of our drug laws? We examine two factors: cultural reasons and interest groups.

- **Cultural Reasons.** Drug laws and policies tend to reflect how people typically perceive drug use. Certain drugs have negative stereotypes, and others do not. Government may have orchestrated these stereotypes or they may be the result of faulty research, propaganda of reformers, negative portrayals in the media, religious ideology, and so on. In the 1940s, for example, most people in the United States shared the assumption that marijuana smokers were "dope fiends." They believed that marijuana users were criminals, immoral, violent, and out of control. Until about 1965, public consensus supported the strict enforcement of marijuana laws. Marijuana was believed to be a dangerous drug associated with other forms of deviance, such as sexual promiscuity and crime. Even college students were virtually unanimous in their condemnation of marijuana smokers as deviants of the worst sort. But the social upheavals of the 1960s included experimentation with drugs and the questioning of society's mores. Rapid changes in attitudes and behavior occurred, especially among the young and college educated. Most significantly, the use of marijuana skyrocketed. In 1965, 18,815 people were arrested for violations of state and local marijuana laws, and these numbers continue to increase each year. Between 1980 and 2002, several million people were arrested for marijuana offenses in the United States (Mosher and Akins 2007).

  Public opinion polls reveal that Americans are divided over the legalization of marijuana. A 2009 Gallup poll found that 44 percent of Americans were in favor of legalizing marijuana, and 54 percent were opposed (Saad 2009). Those opposed believe that marijuana is physically addictive and that its use leads to the use of hard drugs (in other words, they believe it is a "**gateway drug**"). Research has shown both notions to be false. Marijuana is not physically addictive; it does not cause people to use heroin or other harder drugs. Despite the facts, however, the public generally accepts the negative stereotypes and thus fears the drug and supports strict enforcement.

  Some drug use has been interpreted as a symbolic rejection of mainstream values, and in this situation those supporting the status quo condemn the drug. Drugs such as alcohol and nicotine do not have this connotation. Because marijuana use was closely associated with the youth protest of the 1960s, many construed it as a symbol of an alternative lifestyle, a rejection of the traditional values of hard work, success through competition, initiative, and materialism and as support for socialism, unpatriotic behavior, sexual promiscuity, and rejection of authority. As long as this view prevailed, punitive measures against marijuana users seemed justified to many if not most citizens.

- **Interest Groups.** The approaches for controlling drug use have more to do with the power and social class structure of society than with the inherent characteristics of the substance being controlled. Just as the early anti-opium laws were aimed at Chinese workers, not at opium itself, so the reform movements aimed at prohibition of alcohol represented retaliation by the old middle class—rural, Protestant, native born—against the largely Catholic urban workers and immigrants who threatened their privileged status. Jenkins examines the relationship between power and drug laws and finds,

> *Historical examples are not hard to find. Joseph Gusfield's book* Symbolic Crusade *explained the temperance movement in nineteenth-century America in terms of underlying conflicts between old-established elite groups, who were mainly Anglo-Saxon and Protestant, and newer Catholic populations, who were German and Irish. As Catholics viewed alcohol consumption more tolerantly than did Protestants, temperance laws became a symbolic means of reasserting WASP power and values. Other writers have suggested ethnic agendas for the campaigns to prohibit opium in the 1880s (as part of an anti-Chinese movement) and marijuana in the 1930s (which stigmatized a drug associated with African Americans and Mexicans). Repeatedly, African Americans have been the primary targets of such movements, whether the drug in question was cocaine in the progressive era, heroin in mid-century, or crack in the 1980s. During the drug war launched by Presidents Reagan and Bush, for example, the crack cocaine favored by black users attracted savage penalties in the form of severe mandatory sentences for dealing and possession, while lesser sanctions were inflicted upon the mainly white users of cocaine in its powdered form. (Jenkins 1999:13)*

A final example of the relation between social class use and drug policy can be found in the current drive to liberalize marijuana laws. When marijuana was used primarily by the lower working class (such as Mexican Americans), the law against its use was extremely punitive. In the 1960s, this changed when middle-class, White, affluent college youth became the primary users. However much parents may have disagreed with their children's use of marijuana, they did not want them treated as criminals and stigmatized as drug users. The ludicrousness of the gap between the punishments for marijuana use and for alcohol use became readily apparent to the educated. As a result, White, affluent, and powerful people in most communities and states mounted a push to liberalize the laws.

Mosher and Akins (2007) argued that by demonizing certain drugs and not others, the government, the criminal justice system, and the media all serve their own interests. For example, a significant part of U.S. agriculture and consumer industry is engaged (with government support) in the production and marketing of nicotine and alcohol products. Even though it is well known that tobacco is harmful to users, the government will not ban its use because of the probable outcry from farmers, the states where tobacco is a major crop, and the tobacco manufacturers, wholesalers, retailers, transporters, and advertisers. Marijuana, on the other hand, is merchandised and sold illegally, so there is no legitimate economic interest pushing for its legalization.

Similarly, the pharmaceutical industry works diligently to dissuade Congress from further restricting amphetamines and other pills. In 1970, pushed by President Nixon, Congress passed the Comprehensive Drug Abuse Prevention and Control Act. Some forces tried to include amphetamines in the dangerous-drug category in that bill, but without success. The law declared marijuana possession a serious crime but did not do the same for amphetamines, despite irrefutable evidence that they are more dangerous to the user.

The illegal status of some drugs enables illicit economic interests to flourish. Underworld suppliers of drugs oppose changes in the law because legalization would seriously reduce their profits. They therefore promote restrictive legislation. The result is often a strange alliance between underworld economic interests and religious/moral interests seeking the same end—prohibition of the drug—but for opposite reasons. Thus, a member of Congress could safely satisfy religious zealots and organized crime alike by voting for stricter drug laws.

The law enforcement profession is another interest group that may use its influence to affect drug policy. If drugs and drug users are considered threats, then budgets to seize them will be increased. More arrests will be made, proving the necessity of enforcement and, not incidentally, the need for higher pay and more officers. Perhaps the best example of this syndrome is provided by the activity of the Narcotics Bureau, created by the Harrison Act of 1914. As mentioned earlier, the bureau was instrumental in changing the definition of opiate use from a "medical" activity to a "criminal" one. The bureau used a number of tactics to "prove" that its existence was necessary: It won court cases favorable to its antidrug stance; it vigorously used the media to propagate the "dope fiend" mythology; and it used statistics to incite the public or to prove its own effectiveness.

In effect, the Narcotics Bureau created a **moral panic**. Moral panics occur when a social problem is defined as a threat to societal values and interests. Moral panics often involve the exaggeration of social phenomena and can result in changes in social policy. Some examples include the media's portrayal of crack cocaine and "crack babies" in the 1980s; the "dope fiend" mythology promoted by the United States government in the early 1900s and again in the 1960s; and more recently, the media portrayal of methamphetamine, "meth babies," and methamphetamine-related crime. Robinson and Scherlen notes,

> *The danger of moral panics is that they often lead to unnecessary changes in existing public policies or entirely new policies that are based on exaggerated threats. Misguided drug policies result from at least three factors: political opportunism; media profit maximization; and desire among criminal justice professionals to increase their spheres of influence. Following this logic, politicians create concern about drug use in order to gain personally from such claims in the form of election and reelection; they achieve this largely by using the media as their own mouthpiece. After media coverage of drugs increases, so does public concern. Indeed, research shows that public concern about drugs increases after drug threats have been hyped in the mass media. Finally, criminal justice professionals and government institutions . . . agree to fight the war not only because they see drug-related behaviors (such as use, possession, manufacturing, sales) as crimes but also because it assures them continued resources, clients, and thus bureaucratic survival. (2007:11)*

Although *all* drugs are associated with certain harms to individuals and to society, the current drug laws are illogical. They reflect successful political lobbying by a variety of powerful interest groups, with the less powerful suffering the consequences. Despite the drug laws and shifting definitions of certain drugs, an examination of the extent of drug use in U.S. society demonstrates the prevalence of this social problem among all social groups.

DRUG USE IN U.S. SOCIETY

Drugs are used worldwide for pleasure and medicinal purposes. The average U.S. family has about thirty different drugs in its medicine cabinet and numerous alcoholic beverages in its liquor cabinet. Approximately 90 percent of the people in the United States are daily caffeine users, and roughly 59.8 million

Americans currently smoke cigarettes. One of the most comprehensive studies on drug use is the annual National Household Survey on Drug Use and Health conducted by SAMHSA (Substance Abuse and Mental Health Services Administration 2009). According to the most recent reports for 2008, 51.6 percent of the population over age 12 (~129 million people) reported being a current user of alcohol, 28.4 percent (70.9 million people) used tobacco in the past month, and 8.0 percent (20.1 million people) used an illicit drug in the past month (see Figure 13.1). A 2009 University of Michigan survey (Monitoring the Future) found that 36.5 percent of twelfth-graders had used some illicit drug and 66.2 percent had used alcohol in the last year (Johnston et al., 2009). In 2007, there were over 1.8 million state and local arrests for drug abuse violations (Bureau of Justice Statistics 2010). In short, psychoactive drugs, both legal and illegal, are important to a significant portion of Americans.

Commonly Abused Illegal Drugs

- **Marijuana.** Very much like alcohol, marijuana is a social drug. Marijuana comes from the hemp plant *Cannabis sativa,* a plant cultivated for at least 5,000 years and found throughout the world. It is the world's fourth most widely used psychoactive drug (following caffeine, nicotine, and alcohol) and, by far, the most widely used illicit drug in the United States. In 2008, the federal government seized over 1.4 million pounds of marijuana (Drug Enforcement Administration [DEA] 2009). In 2008, approximately 15.2 million Americans used marijuana at least once in the month prior to being surveyed, and an estimated 3.9 million Americans use marijuana on a daily or almost daily basis (SAMHSA 2009). Although it is often thought that marijuana is a relatively harmless drug, in 2006, marijuana was a factor in 290,563 hospital emergency room visits in the United States (SAMHSA 2008).

The main active chemical in marijuana is tetrahydrocannabinol (THC), which stimulates the brain cells to release the chemical dopamine. Dopamine

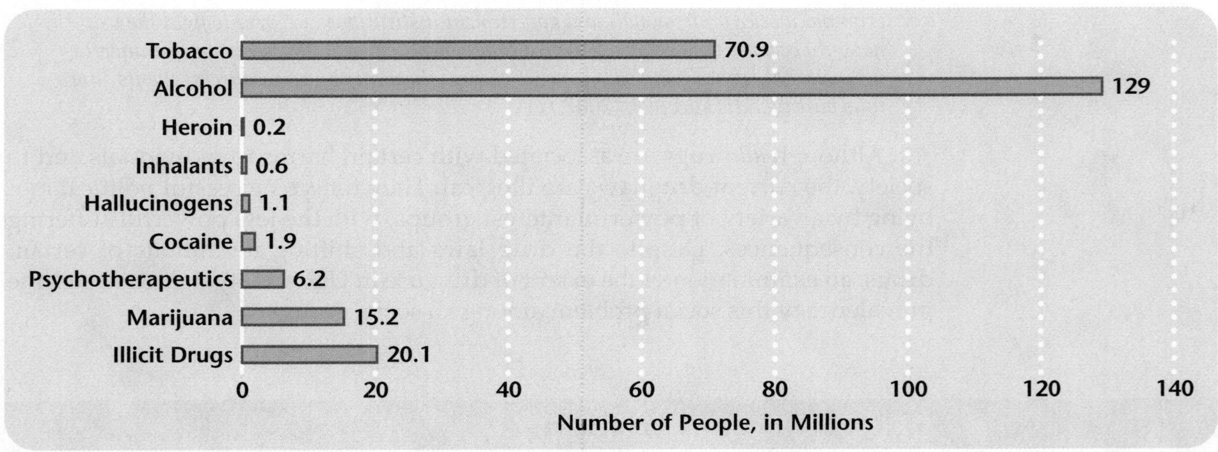

FIGURE 13.1

Past Month Drug Use among Persons Aged 12 and Older: 2008

Source: SAMHSA, Substance Abuse and Mental Health Services Administration. (2009). Results from the 2008 National Survey on Drug Use and Health: National Findings (Office of Applied Studies, NSDUH Series H-36, HHS Publication No. SMA 09-4434). Rockville, MO.

produces a relaxing effect, increases the intensity of sense impressions, and provides a "high" akin to one produced by alcohol.

Marijuana is a widely misunderstood drug. Under the Controlled Substances Act, the Drug Enforcement Administration classifies marijuana as a Schedule 1 drug. That is, it has high potential for abuse and no currently accepted medical use in treatment in the United States. Many consider marijuana addictive, asserting that it creates psychological dependence. Some researchers have argued that it causes lower levels of sex hormones to be produced in males and breaks up chromosomes, causing genetic problems for future generations. The current data on marijuana are inconsistent, however, on these and other alleged problems. For example, five research studies done in the 1970s reported that marijuana caused a loss of motivation and the ability to think straight; another five studies reported no such effect.

Although much remains to be learned about the effects of marijuana, some dangers are evident. Marijuana has a negative effect on the lungs (smokers get about four times as much tar in their lungs per puff as tobacco smokers). As a result, smoking marijuana increases the likelihood of developing cancer of the neck or head, as well as increasing the risk of chronic cough, bronchitis, and emphysema. Its use also increases dangers for people with damaged hearts. A 2001 study indicated that a user's risk of heart attack more than quadruples in the first hour after smoking marijuana (Mittleman et al., 2001). According to the National Institute on Drug Abuse, heavy marijuana use is also associated with depression, anxiety, job-related problems and higher job turnover, lower high school graduation rates, and lower grades (2004). A final danger is arrest and a criminal record, the consequence of its use being officially defined as criminal. On the positive side, we know that marijuana is not physiologically addictive; there is no evidence of a lethal dose; and it has been found to have positive effects for certain medical problems, such as migraine headaches, muscle spasms associated with epilepsy and multiple sclerosis, glaucoma, and asthma. Of special note is the successful use of marijuana to reduce or eliminate the nausea that accompanies chemotherapy treatments for cancer. It can also stimulate appetite in the chronically ill. Currently, Alaska, California, Colorado, Washington, D.C., Hawaii, Maine, Maryland, Michigan, Montana, Nevada, New Jersey, New Mexico, Oregon, Rhode Island, Vermont, and Washington have laws that remove the state-level criminal penalties for growing or possessing medical marijuana, something that the U.S. Drug Enforcement Administration is openly against (DEA 2007). In these states, individuals who use marijuana for medical purposes are not exempt from the federal laws, however.

- **Hallucinogens.** Also called psychedelics, hallucinogens produce sensory experiences that represent a different reality to the user. The person may react to trivial everyday objects as if they had great meaning. Emotions may be greatly intensified. Among the perceptual phenomena experienced by some is the feeling that one is looking at oneself from the outside. Hallucinogens occur naturally in the peyote cactus, some mushrooms, and certain fungi and other plants. Bad experiences with psychedelics include panic associated with loss of control, the common hallucination that spiders are crawling over the body, paranoia and delusions, and occasionally suicide. The psychedelic drug phencyclidine (PCP), also known as angel dust, is perhaps the most dangerous. This drug, which is relatively easy to manufacture, can cause psychotic reactions (hallucinations, combative or self-destructive impulses), loss of bowel and bladder control, slurred speech, and inability to walk. Taken in large quantities, it can induce seizures, coma, and death. There is no evidence that physical dependence develops for any of the hallucinogenic drugs. For some people, though, psychological dependence occurs. In 2008, 1.1 million people reported using a hallucinogen in the previous month (SAMHSA 2009).

The drug ecstasy is a synthetic drug with stimulant and hallucinogenic effects. Users say that ecstasy produces a high for up to 6 hours with feelings of euphoria, empathy, and heightened senses. Ecstasy is one of several popular drugs known as "club drugs," used by youth at all-night dance parties, dance clubs, and bars. In 2008, 555,000 Americans reported using ecstasy in the previous month (SAMHSA 2009). According to research by the University of Michigan, ecstasy use has declined among eighth, tenth, and twelfth graders since it peaked in 2001, but rates are currently holding steady. Researchers are concerned that this may change, however, as the proportion of young people who see "great risk" associated with trying ecstasy has fallen appreciably and steadily since 2004 (Johnston et al., 2009). Regular use can produce blurred vision, confusion, sleeplessness, depression, muscle cramping, fever, chills, hallucinations, and anxiety. Used in combination with alcohol, the effects can be dangerous. The most serious effect of ecstasy is that the drug interferes with the body's ability to regulate temperature. The sharp increase in body temperature can result in severe dehydration, or, on the opposite extreme, an individual will drink too much water and can suffer from water poisoning of their bloodstream.

- **GHB (Gamma Hydroxybutyrate).** GHB is a central nervous system depressant. It is a colorless, odorless liquid that is mixed with alcoholic drinks or fruit juices. It relaxes or sedates the body, slowing breathing and the heart rate. Users feel euphoric, then sleepy. Overdose results in nausea, vomiting, drowsiness, and headache and can escalate to loss of consciousness, seizures, and a comatose state. GHB has two qualities that make it a favorite date-rape drug: (1) it knocks out users and their short-term memory, and (2) it clears quickly from the body, so laboratory tests might not detect it (Leinwand 2001). Hospital emergency room episodes involving GHB rose from 55 in 1994 to a peak of 3,340 in 2001 but decreased to 1,861 in 2005 (Drug Abuse Warning Network [DAWN] 2005).

- **Narcotics (Opiates).** Narcotics are powerful depressants that have a pronounced effect on the respiratory and central nervous systems. Medically, they are used very effectively to relieve pain, treat diarrhea (paregoric), and stop coughing (codeine). These drugs, which include opium and its derivatives, morphine and heroin, also produce a feeling of euphoria. Many users describe the first "rush" as similar to sexual orgasm, followed by feelings of warmth, peacefulness, and increased self-esteem.

  Opiates are highly addictive. Prolonged users experience severe withdrawal symptoms. It is dangerous for four reasons—each a result of the drug's illegal status, not of the drug itself. First, because the drug is not regulated, it can include harmful impurities and be of varying potency. As a result, between 3,000 and 4,000 users die annually of heroin overdoses. In 2006, 189,780 emergency room visits involved heroin abuse (SAMSHA 2006). Second, the sharing of needles is a major cause of hepatitis and, in recent years, HIV infection (the precursor of AIDS). Efforts to supply clean needles to the addict population are resisted by government officials because that would appear to condone, even promote, an illegal activity. The third danger associated with heroin is the high cost of purchasing the illegal drug (maintaining a heroin addiction can cost hundreds of dollars per day). The users must spend much of their time finding funds to supply their habit. For men, finding funds to purchase heroin typically means theft, and for women, shoplifting or prostitution—all hazardous occupations. Fourth, possession of heroin is a criminal offense, leading to incarceration. Taken together, then, the criminal activities an addict turns to plus the complications of poor-quality drugs and infection lead to a relatively high rate of deaths.

The annual prevalence of heroin use has remained fairly constant among teenagers, fluctuating between .7 percent and .9 percent from 2005 to 2008 (Johnston et al., 2009). More disturbing are trends for other opiate-based painkillers such as Vicodin and OxyContin. The potential for addiction to painkillers and other prescription drugs was made public when Rush Limbaugh, a well-known conservative radio host, admitted to being addicted to prescription painkillers in 2003, as well as the drug-related deaths of popular stars Anna Nicole Smith, Brittany Murphy, and Michael Jackson. The authors of the Monitoring the Future study note that "these prescription-type drugs have become more important in the nation's larger drug abuse problem, reflecting their gradual increase in popularity over an extended period of time while the use of a number of illegal drugs (e.g., LSD, ecstasy, and heroin) has receded considerably" (Johnston et al., 2007:14). According to the Centers for Disease Control and Prevention (CDC 2010), prescription drugs have now surpassed heroin and cocaine as the leading cause of fatal overdoses.

- **Cocaine.** Cocaine is a strong central nervous system stimulant. It stimulates an area in the brain that regulates the sensation of pleasure, intensifying sexual highs and producing euphoria, alertness, and feelings of confidence. Two studies conducted in 2004 used rats to demonstrate the addictive nature of cocaine. In a French study, rats were given cocaine for three months, and then the scientists cut the rats' drug supply. They found that a certain percentage of the rats were very persistent in trying to get their cocaine, even if it meant getting shocked electrically. In the British study, they also found that rats were willing to experience shocks on their feet to get their fix of cocaine, but only those rats that had been taking cocaine for a long time. The rats that had been taking cocaine for only a short time gave up after their first electric shock (reported in *Medical News Today* 2004).

In 2008, there were 1.9 million current cocaine users (SAMHSA 2009). Repeated use of cocaine can produce paranoia, hallucinations, sleeplessness, tremors, weight loss, and depression. Snorting cocaine (the typical procedure) draws the cocaine powder through the nasal passages, leading to permanent damage to the mucous membranes and serious breathing difficulties. Moreover, snorting allows the cocaine to be absorbed rapidly into the bloodstream and subsequently the brain. If the user desires a more potent dosage, cocaine can be injected in solution directly into the veins or chemically converted and smoked in the process called *freebasing*. Another variation is to mix cocaine with heroin, which combines a powerful stimulant with a potent depressant.

Crack is a smokable form of cocaine, created by mixing cocaine, baking soda, and water and heating them. This potent drug provides an almost instant rush, reaching the brain within eight seconds, with peak effects within a few minutes. Because crack's effects are more short-lived and more intense than powder cocaine, there is a greater urge toward repeated use. Crack, compared with powder cocaine, is cheaper and provides a quicker high.

- **Methamphetamine.** Also known as speed, crystal, crank, chalk, or ice, methamphetamine is part of a subclass of amphetamines. It is a powerful addictive stimulant that affects the central nervous system. It can be injected, smoked, snorted, and ingested orally or anally. Methamphetamine use decreases appetite, heightens energy levels, enables people to be physically active for long periods, and provides a sense of euphoria similar to that of cocaine (Covey 2007).

  Methamphetamine use is associated with a number of negative effects, both short- and long-term. Short-term effects include higher pulse rate, higher blood pressure, increased body temperature, convulsions, irritability, and nervousness. During the coming-down period, the user may become agitated and potentially violent (Covey 2007). Long-term effects include severe psychological and physical dependence, violent behavior and paranoia, chronic fatigue, depression, open sores and infections on the skin from picking and scratching at imaginary bugs, tooth decay and dental deterioration, and severe weight loss. Methamphetamine acts as a corrosive on the gums and teeth and softens the teeth so that they literally melt away.

  Methamphetamine use and addiction has become a frequent topic in the mass media. Much as it did during the "crack epidemic" of the 1980s and 1990s, the media is again using the word *epidemic* to describe the problem. The government has turned its attention to methamphetamine as well. Congress passed the Comprehensive Methamphetamine Control Act of 1996, the Methamphetamine Anti-Proliferation Act of 2000, and the Combat Methamphetamine Epidemic Act (CMEA) of 2005. The first of these acts doubled the maximum penalties for possession of the drug and possession of equipment used to manufacture the drug from four to ten years. All three acts also focus on limiting the sale of ingredients that can be used to manufacture methamphetamine. The CMEA of 2005 regulates the retail over-the-counter sales of ephedrine, pseudoephedrine, and phenylpropanolamine, which are common ingredients in cough, cold, and allergy products. Those drugs are now placed out of customer reach, customers must show identification and sign a log book, and customers are limited to no more than 9 grams of ephedrine per month. In March 2007, the first arrest was made in New York when log books showed that a customer had purchased over 29 grams of ephedrine from several pharmacies in a one-month period (DEA 2007).

Regular methamphetamine use can cause dramatic physiological damage both inside and outside the body.

  Studies on the amount of methamphetamine use are mixed. Many substance abuse authorities believe that use and distribution are on the rise, thus resulting in an "epidemic" (for a review of these studies, see Covey 2007). On the other hand, the U.S. DEA claims that the number of meth labs has decreased as a result of the Combat Methamphetamine Epidemic Act, and prominent research studies show a decline in use. The Monitoring the Future study indicates that methamphetamine use is low among youth and is declining. In 1999, 4.7 percent of high school seniors had used methamphetamine in the past year compared to 1.2 percent in 2008 (Johnston et al.,

2009). Similarly, the National Survey on Drug Use and Health shows that numbers of past-month users have declined from 731,000 in 2006 to 314,000 in 2008 (SAMHSA 2009). Despite these declining numbers, the spread of methamphetamine use has been "likened to an epidemic moving from the West and Southwest to the rest of the country" (Covey 2007:23).

Legal but Dangerous Drugs

At the beginning of this chapter, we pointed out that the definitions concerning drugs and drug-related behaviors are socially constructed; that is, these definitions shift and change over time. Nothing illustrates this more poignantly than looking at the legality of certain drugs and the age at which the consumption of such drugs becomes *defined* as legal. For example, in 1992, Congress directed all states to establish 18 as the minimum age to purchase and smoke cigarettes. In Alaska, the minimum age is 19. That a person can simply step over a state line and their behavior will be defined as criminal or not demonstrates this social construction.

Nicotine. Nicotine is the active ingredient of tobacco. Because the vast majority of smokers smoke fifteen or more cigarettes a day, they are averaging at least one cigarette for each hour they are awake. Cigarette smoking remains the leading preventable cause of death in the United States—accounting for one of every five deaths (443,000 people) each year (CDC 2010). Nicotine is a stimulant that raises blood pressure, increases the heart rate, dulls the appetite, and provides the user with a sense of alertness. As a stimulant, nicotine is responsible for a relatively high probability of heart disease and strokes among cigarette smokers. In addition to the nicotine, smokers inhale various coal tars, nitrogen dioxide, formaldehyde, and other ingredients that increase the chances of contracting lung cancer, throat cancer, emphysema, and bronchitis. Former Surgeon General Richard Carmona has reported that smoking causes no fewer than twenty-six diseases, including cancers of the stomach, uterus, cervix, pancreas, and kidneys (*Arizona Daily Star* 2004). Moreover, inhaling secondary tobacco smoke contributes to respiratory infections in babies, triggers new cases of asthma in previously unaffected children, and exacerbates symptoms in asthmatic children. Because of all the health problems associated with smoking, the CDC estimates that the cost of smoking to the nation for the years 2000 to 2004 was approximately $193 billion in medical costs and lost worker productivity (CDC 2010).

Current estimates indicate that approximately 59.8 million Americans smoke cigarettes. Looking at patterns of smoking behavior, several points are clear (SAMHSA 2009): (1) more adult men smoke than women (34.5 percent versus 22.5 percent); (2) smoking and education are inversely related. That is, as education level goes up, the incidence of smoking goes down (see Figure 13.2); and (3) cigarette smoking is more common among unemployed adults than among adults who work full or part time (43.0 percent versus 27.2 and 23.8 percent, respectively). Thus, the poor and uneducated are more likely to smoke.

Although the tobacco industry is enormous, it is faced with declining sales due to public smoking bans, increased tobacco taxes, and public antismoking campaigns. The tobacco companies have responded in three ways. First, the tobacco companies have invested heavily in the federal, state, and local campaigns of politicians in the hope of favorable legislation (regarding such issues

FIGURE 13.2

Past Month Tobacco Use among Adults Aged 18 and Over, by Education: 2008

Source: SAMHSA, Substance Abuse and Mental Health Services Administration. (2009). Results from the 2008 National Survey on Drug Use and Health: National Findings (Office of Applied Studies, NSDUH Series H-36, HHS Publication No. SMA 09-4434). Rockville, MO.

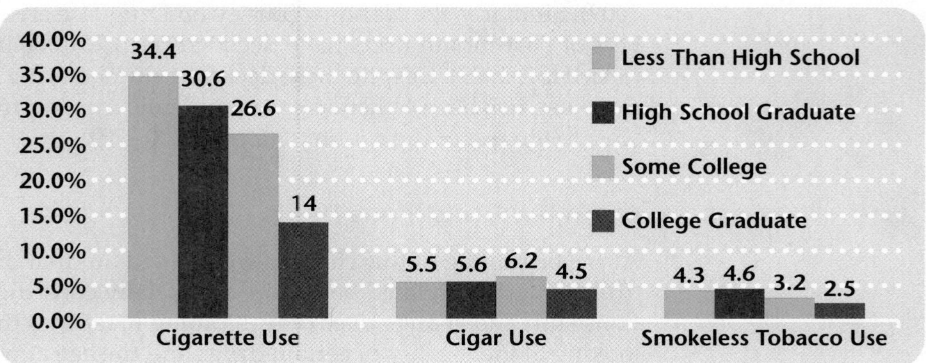

as public smoking, selling through vending machines, reining in the Federal Drug Administration, and the extent of liability in impending lawsuits). The tobacco industry gave more than $2 million in contributions to federal candidates, political parties, and other political action committees in the 2007 to 2008 election cycle (Common Cause and Tobacco-Free Kids Action Fund 2010).

The second strategy of the tobacco companies is to increase their advertising in the United States and attempt to hook new users. According to the CDC (2007b), in 2005, tobacco companies spent $13.1 billion on advertisements and promotions. This amounts to $36 million per day, or annually more than $45 for every person in the United States and more than $290 for each adult U.S. smoker. This advertising is aimed primarily at minorities, women, and youth. Consider the following:

- Studies have found a high density of tobacco billboards in racial and ethnic minority communities. A study by the University of Pittsburgh School of Medicine found that there are 2.6 times as many ads per person in predominantly black neighborhoods as there are in predominantly white neighborhoods (Toland 2007).
- In 2007, R.J. Reynolds unveiled a new product called "Camel No. 9," a cigarette with a decorative pink band, a tiny pink camel, and an ebony box with hot-pink and teal accents. With the slogan "light and luscious," it is clearly a product targeting women and young girls (Quindlen 2007).
- Smoking is featured in many video games targeting youth. For example, the game "The Chronicles of Riddick: Escape from Butcher Bay" has players win packs of cigarettes, and the game makes fun of the warning labels on the packs (Perry 2010).
- In 2007, a report by the Harvard School of Public Health showed that cigarette companies increased the amount of nicotine in their cigarettes by an average of 11 percent from 1998 to 2005 (reported in Siegel 2007). Although tobacco companies deny claims of a deliberate increase in nicotine, antismoking groups argue that this was a calculated move to hook new smokers on their product.

A third strategy of the tobacco companies is to increase advertising and sales overseas to compensate for declining domestic sales. According to Kluger (2009),

> *This year tobacco companies will produce more than 5 trillion cigarettes—or about 830 for every person on the planet. In China, 350 million people are currently hooked on*

tobacco, which means the country has more smokers than the U.S. has people. (Kluger 2009: 50)

In 2007 a federal judge ruled that tobacco companies are prohibited from marketing their cigarettes overseas as "low tar" and "light" and otherwise giving the impression that their cigarettes are less dangerous.

- **Alcohol.** Alcohol is a relatively safe drug when used in moderation but one of the most dangerous when abused. According to the National Household Survey on Drug Use and Health, 51.6 percent of the population over age 12 consumed alcohol in the past month (SAMHSA 2009). Although alcohol is not legal for those under age 21, the University of Michigan found that 43 percent of twelfth graders, 29 percent of tenth graders, and 16 percent of eighth graders had consumed alcohol in the past month (Johnston et al., 2009). Alcohol is a depressant that directly affects the central nervous system, slowing brain activity and muscle reactions. Thus, it is a leading cause of accidents:

    - Approximately 12.4 percent of persons drove while under the influence of alcohol in 2008 (SAMHSA 2009).
    - In 2003, 40 percent of all fatalities from car accidents were alcohol related (National Highway Traffic Safety Administration 2004). Automobile accidents involving intoxicated drivers are a leading cause of death among teenagers.
    - Approximately seven out of ten drowning victims had been drinking prior to their deaths.

    Alcohol consumption is related to other problems as well:

    - Underage drinking costs Americans $62 billion per year in injuries, deaths, and lost work time (reported in Portillo 2006).
    - There are intangible and unmeasurable expenses due to disrupted families, spouse and child abuse, desertion, and countless emotional problems that arise from drinking. Most significant, two-thirds of victims who suffered violence from an intimate (a current or former spouse, boyfriend, or girlfriend) reported that alcohol had been a factor (Bureau of Justice Statistics 2007).
    - Among youth (high school and college), excessive drinking is related to risky sexual behavior, vandalism, racist acts, homophobic violence, and sexual assault.
    - One of the strongest risk factors for attempted suicide in both adults and youth is alcohol use.

    Continued use of large quantities of alcohol can result in indigestion, ulcers, degeneration of the brain, and cirrhosis of the liver; over 20,000 Americans die of cirrhosis of the liver each year. Malnutrition is often associated with prolonged use of alcohol; a pint of whiskey provides about half of a person's daily calorie requirements but without the necessary nutrients. Heavy consumption also reduces the production of white blood cells, so alcoholics have a low resistance to bacteria. Alcoholics, in addition, run the danger of permanent destruction of brain cells, resulting in memory loss and sometimes psychotic behavior. Chronic use also results in physiological addiction. Withdrawal can be very dangerous, with the individual experiencing convulsions and delirium. The conclusion is inescapable, then, that alcohol is the most dangerous legal drug physically for the individual and socially for society.

Drug Use Patterns by Class, Race, and Gender

Drug use and abuse is most often discussed as an individual's choice, an individual's behavior, and an individual's problem. However, examining drug use from a sociological standpoint reveals interesting patterns by class, race, and gender. These patterns demonstrate that a person's place in the social structure can increase or decrease the odds that he or she will use drugs and alcohol. Drug use is not uniform throughout society. For example, men of all ages and races are more likely than women to use illicit drugs. Even marital status matters—married women are less likely to use tobacco, engage in binge alcohol use, or use an illicit drug compared to divorced, separated, never married, or cohabitating women. In terms of social class, intravenous drug users continue to be found predominantly among the inner-city poor. This practice places them at great risk of exposure to the AIDS virus from the sharing of needles. The CDC estimates that 36 percent of the women who are living with AIDS in the United States contracted the disease through intravenous drug use, compared to 23 percent of the men with the disease (2004).

The disproportionate use of drugs by the poor is not limited to illicit drugs. As indicated previously in Figure 13.2, cigarette smoking is inversely related to education level. The lower the education level, the greater the incidence of cigarette smoking. The CDC estimates that nearly 31.5 percent of people living below the poverty line smoke. Statistics also reveal interesting differences by race/ethnicity and smoking. Native Americans have the highest rates of smoking (48.7 percent), and Asians have the lowest rates of smoking (13.9 percent; SAMHSA 2009).

Alcohol use also varies greatly by race, social class, and age. Whites are more likely to report current use (defined as consuming any alcohol in the past month) than any other racial group (56.2 percent compared to 41.9 percent for Blacks and 37 percent for Asians). Youth in general are more likely to report binge and heavy use, with the highest prevalence among 18- to 25-year-olds. Gender, too, is relevant, as Black women are much more likely than White women to be abstainers. Recall that the incidence of smoking decreases with higher levels of education. The opposite is true for drinking. The rates of current alcohol use increase with increasing levels of education. A study by the CDC found this pattern to hold true for women who drink during pregnancy. The study found that women who were White, older, more educated, and had higher income were more likely to drink during their pregnancy than women in other demographic categories (Fong 2004).

To examine further the relationship between social class and alcohol use, consider drinking by college students. College students, mostly from relatively privileged backgrounds, often are heavy binge drinkers during their college years. In fact, research indicates that around 61 percent of college students drink alcohol, and 40.5 percent binge drink (defined as five or more drinks in a row; SAMHSA 2009). At many colleges and universities, there is a very significant drinking subculture. At the University of Virginia, one of the finest public universities in the United States, there is a tradition for seniors to consume a fifth of liquor at the last home football game (a practice known as the "fourth-year fifth"). This tradition resulted in the deaths of eighteen students between 1990 and 1999.

Although Whites report a higher incidence of current alcohol use, illicit drug use reveals a different pattern. Individuals of two or more races report the highest rates of illicit drug use, followed by Native Americans (see Figure 13.3). Illicit drug use is also higher in large metro areas than in nonmetro areas (SAMHSA 2009).

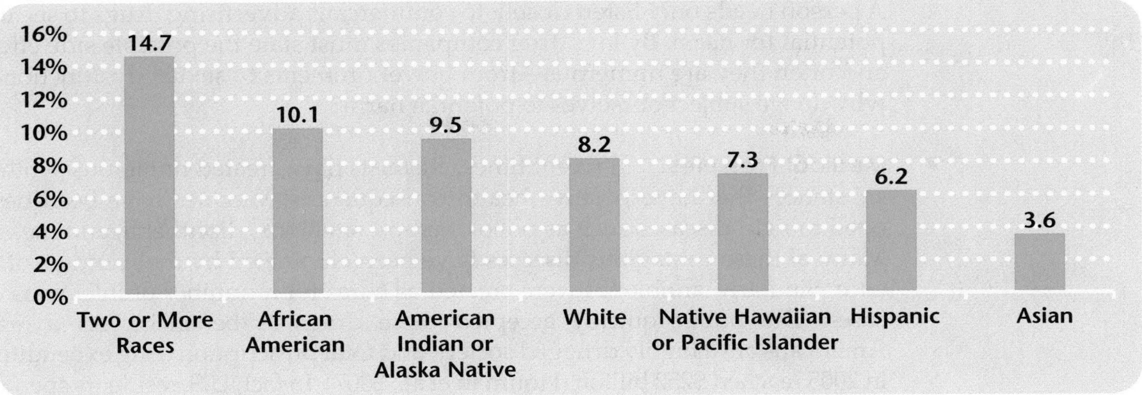

FIGURE 13.3

Past Month Illicit Drug Use among Persons Aged 12 or Older, by Race/Ethnicity: 2008

Source: SAMHSA, Substance Abuse and Mental Health Services Administration. (2009). Results from the 2008 National Survey on Drug Use and Health: National Findings (Office of Applied Studies, NSDUH Series H-36, HHS Publication No. SMA 09-4434). Rockville, MO.

In general terms, the poor are more inclined than the rich to use illicit harmful substances. Why? One possibility is the irrelevance of the antidrug campaigns, which are implicitly based on the premise that a young person has a lot to lose by using drugs. The young poor who live in situations where jobs and other opportunities for advancement are scarce or nonexistent have nothing to lose by using drugs—they have already lost. The threat of drug-screening programs now increasingly used by employers may constrain people with a chance for a job, but it has no hold on the hopeless. Some observers have theorized that the urban poor are prone to take drugs as an escape from a harsh and painful reality.

Others argue that tobacco and alcohol companies target minority neighborhoods. They sponsor sports tournaments and music festivals in predominantly Black neighborhoods and purchase considerable advertising in Black publications. In 2004, cigarette companies came out with a new line of flavored cigarettes that antismoking activists claim specifically targets minority teens. The packaging features graffiti artists and other hip-hop imagery that appeals to minority youth (Associated Press 2004).

In looking at the statistics, it is clear that drug use cuts across all class, racial, and gender lines. It is how the drugs (and the persons using those drugs) are defined that determines drug treatment and handling by the authorities. For example, in 2008 an estimated 4.7 million persons used pain relievers nonmedically, and they are often middle- and upper-class Whites (1.8 million used tranquilizers, 904,000 used stimulants, and 234,000 used sedatives; SAMHSA 2009). Unlike the poor—who tend to use illicit drugs and therefore are hassled by the authorities and treated in prisons and public hospitals—the more affluent tend to use legal and prescription drugs and are treated by private physicians. Thus, their addiction is typically protected and hidden from public awareness.

Why Use Drugs?

It is clear that *all* drugs have the potential for harm, even those drugs that seem completely risk free. Aspirin, for example, may seem like a drug with few side effects, but taken in large doses, it can result in ulcers and stomach bleeding.

A person needs only listen closely to commercials advertising drugs to see their potential for harm. By law, drug companies must state the possible side effects, and often they are numerous—from bowel problems to sexual dysfunction. So why do we subject ourselves to potential harm?

- **Medical Pressures.** In recent times, chemists have created numerous synthetic substances that have positive health consequences. Vaccines have been developed to fight diseases such as polio, mumps, smallpox, diphtheria, and measles. Many of these contagious diseases have been eliminated by the wonders of science. Similarly, antibiotics were created as cures for a number of infectious diseases. The public quickly accepted these drugs as beneficial. As a result, Americans are a highly drugged society, and total prescription drug expenditures in 2005 reached $252 billion (Hoffman et al., 2007). In fact, U.S. residents spend far more on prescription drugs than do people in other developed countries, and rising costs have even driven some to smuggle prescriptions from other countries.

- **Cultural Pressures.** The United States has become a "quick-fix" society, with individuals seeking instant results and striving to meet cultural ideals about perfection. In seeking mental perfection, physical perfection, and improved physical performance, Americans have increasingly turned to artificial substances and enhancements to meet those ideals. In the early 1950s, chemists made a breakthrough in drugs that treated mental disorders such as depression, insomnia, aggression, hyperactivity, and tension. These drugs (tranquilizers, barbiturates, and stimulants) have since been widely prescribed by doctors for these problems.

  Psychopharmacology, the science of drugs that affect the mind, is on the verge of developing pills that will enrich memory, heighten concentration, enhance intelligence, and eliminate shyness or bad moods:

  > *We have become so muddle-headed by constant marketing to take these drugs for every emotional malady that we now live in a ridiculous world where we have signs that say "This is a Drug-Free Zone" on the front of a school that is handing out psychotropics*

© Peter C. Vey/The New Yorker Collection/www.cartoonbank.com.

to the children for depression, hyperactivity, anxiety, etc. Psychiatric drugs have become a first resort. That is the real nightmare that the FDA should confront. Doctors no longer look for causes of depression, such as thyroid problems, lack of exercise, a bad diet, a guilty conscience, medical problems, allergies—the likely culprits could be many. By using drugs to treat the symptoms, they not only expose patients to the effects of the drugs but they let the real causes go untreated. (Stradford 2004:2)

Recently, there has been much controversy over the use of so-called behavior drugs for children. The CDC estimates that in 2006 ADHD (attention deficit/hyperactivity disorder) diagnoses in children rose to 4.5 million (CDC 2010). From 2001 to 2004, there was a 49 percent rise in the use of ADHD drugs by children under the age of 5 and an astonishing 369 percent increase in spending on such drugs. In fact, this spending exceeded the spending for antibiotics and asthma medication for children (Johnson 2004). The symptoms for ADHD are inattentiveness, fidgeting, not listening, being easily distracted, making careless mistakes, and excessive talking. Stimulants such as Ritalin, Adderall, Concerta, and Dexedrine are prescribed to have the paradoxical effect of calming and focusing children who are chronically inattentive and hyperactive. These drugs stimulate the central nervous system, with many of the same pharmacological effects of cocaine. They affect the brain by enhancing the chemical dopamine, the neurotransmitter that plays a major role in cognition, attention, and inhibition. Their side effects are nervousness, insomnia, and loss of appetite. Although these stimulants for children are often successful, their widespread use raises some important questions:

- The United States consumes 80 percent of the world's methylphenidate (the generic name for Ritalin). "Are American youngsters indeed suffering more behavioral illnesses, or have we as a society become less tolerant of disruptive behavior?" (Shute, Locy, and Pasternak 2000:47).
- Is hyperactivity the inevitable by-product of a societywide addiction to speed—to cellular phones, faxes, e-mail, overnight mail, ever-faster computers? How are children affected by the high-stimulus activities that saturate their lives—video games, interactive television, hundreds of cable channels, and fast-action movies with vivid violence?
- According to the CDC (2010), in 2006, 9.5 percent of boys received a diagnosis of ADHD compared to 5.9 percent of girls. Is the preponderance of boys diagnosed as hyperactive because adults find that boys are more difficult to control than girls?
- What is the role of the pharmaceutical companies in the rapid growth of medications for ADHD? This is a billion-dollar sector of the pharmaceutical market. Brand-name ads for ADHD drugs appear in women's magazines and on cable TV, breaking a longstanding agreement between nations and the pharmaceutical industry not to market controlled substances that have high potential for abuse (K. Thomas 2001).
- What is the role of managed-care companies and insurers in promoting the medication of children for ADHD? These organizations are concerned with costs (see Chapter 17), and it is much cheaper to prescribe pills, thus avoiding referring children to more expensive mental health specialists (Bloom 2000; Shute, Locy, and Pasternak 2000).
- Ritalin and other stimulants prescribed for ADHD work on the brain much like cocaine does. Children using this drug are "wired" every day, raising concern over its long-term effects. This is not the only way that children are

wired. Companies promote energy drinks (high in caffeine) targeting youth by using names like RockStar, Monster, Red Bull, and Venom. Are we creating an entire generation (called by some the "Rx generation") with a "sweet tooth for cocaine"?

The widespread use of these stimulants leads to their abuse by adolescents and adults seeking pharmacological highs. Taken in larger amounts than prescribed and crushed and snorted, these drugs produce euphoria, greater energyand productivity, increased sexual appetite, and an overall feeling of being a lot smarter (K. Thomas 2000b). As a result, the DEA says that drugs to treat ADHD rank among today's most stolen prescriptions and most abused drugs (K. Thomas 2001). The Monitoring the Future study found that in 2006, 4.4 percent of high school seniors, 3.6 percent of tenth graders, and 2.6 percent of eighth graders had abused Ritalin in the previous year (Johnston et al., 2007).

Not only has U.S. society become increasingly concerned with mental perfection, but also the cultural ideals of physical perfection are overwhelming. Drugs can offer a way to meet these ideals. Consider the following:

- The largest area of growth in plastic surgery is in Botox injections (2,557,068 procedures in 2009). The injected toxin blocks the nerve impulses, temporarily paralyzing the muscles that cause wrinkles (American Society for Aesthetic Plastic Surgery 2010).
- In 2003, the FDA approved Humatrope, a brand of human growth hormone, for healthy children with short stature (defined as height more than 2 standard deviations below the mean for their age and sex).
- Ephedra, found in products to aid weight loss, enhance sports performance, and increase energy, was banned in 2004 after it was linked to deaths and reports of serious health problems.

Mental perfection and physical perfection pave the way for other performance pressures as well. The pressure to succeed in competitive situations may also encourage some people to take drugs. Individuals who want to be especially alert or calm to do well may take a drug to accomplish their goal. Sports present an excellent example of drug use to enhance performance. Athletes use two types of drugs: **restorative drugs** (to heal a traumatized part of the body) and **additive drugs** (to improve performance). Amphetamines, human growth hormones, hormones such as androstenedione (the favorite of home-run king Mark McGwire) and Creatine, and anabolic steroids are the additive drugs commonly used by athletes. Amphetamines increase alertness, respiration rate, blood pressure, muscle tension, heart rate, and blood sugar. The user is literally "psyched up" by amphetamines. Moreover, these drugs have the capacity to abolish a sense of fatigue. Growth hormones increase body size and strength. Anabolic steroids are male hormones that aid in adding weight and muscle. If an athlete wants to be a world-class weightlifter, shot putter, or discus thrower, the pressures are great to use anabolic steroids: they make the user stronger, and many competitors use such drugs to get the edge on the competition. Prior to the 2010 Winter Olympics, thirty athletes were banned from competition for testing positive for performance-enhancing drugs. Football players, even in high school, also use these drugs to gain weight and strength to be a "star." In 2008, approximately 3.2 percent of high school seniors reported using androstenedione or anabolic steroids in the previous year, and 16 percent of boys reported using Creatine (Johnston et al., 2009).

Performance pressures have also extended into the bedroom, with drugs like Viagra, Cialis, and Levitra available to aid with sexual performance. Viagra, approved by the FDA in 1998, is a $2 billion-per-year seller for Pfizer, Inc.

The pressures to use drugs are unrelenting. They come from doctors, coaches, parents, teachers, peers, and advertising. People may learn to drink in families where social drinking is an integral part of meals, celebrations, and everyday relaxation. In situations such as cocktail parties, guests are expected to drink alcoholic beverages as part of the social ritual. Peer groups are also important for the entry of the individual into the world of illicit drug use. The person learns from others how to use the drug and how to interpret the drug's effects positively. Similarly, the pressures to meet society's ideals of mental and physical perfection and performance can be overwhelming, with drugs offering a "quick-fix" solution.

U.S. OFFICIAL POLICY: A WAR ON DRUGS

The U.S. drug war is fought on two fronts: stopping the flow of drugs into the United States and using the criminal justice system to punish those who sell and use illegal drugs within the United States. The cost of this program is roughly $1 billion per week (Zeese 2006). In fact, the drug war has cost taxpayers more than $1 trillion since 1970 (Cole 2007).

Stopping the supply of drugs into the country (**interdiction**) involves the use of customs agents at the borders inspecting the baggage of passengers and cargo from planes, trucks, and ships. It involves working with other countries (especially Colombia, Peru, Ecuador, Bolivia, and Mexico) to destroy the places

SOCIAL PROBLEMS IN GLOBAL PERSPECTIVE

MEXICO'S DRUG WAR

There is a war going on in Mexico. In 2006, Mexican President Felipe Calderón declared war on the country's drug cartels. Putting 45,000 army troops on the streets, he pledged to arrest the cartel leaders, confiscate their drugs, and seize the large amounts of cash that they need to operate. Since then, over 10,000 people have died in drug-related violence. The drug cartels have conducted kidnappings, executions, and assaults. In early 2009, the police chief in Ciudad Juarez resigned after drug traffickers began to make good on their promise to kill police officers in the city until the chief stepped down (Navarrette 2009). The gangs have dumped severed heads in front of town halls and have essentially terrorized the Mexican people to put pressure on the government to back down.

The United States has a large stake in Mexico's war, as it is estimated that 90 percent of all the cocaine flowing into the United States comes from Mexico, and 90 percent of the guns seized in drug-related violence in Mexico come from the United States (Navarrette 2009). In addition, the Mexican drug cartels have established a presence in approximately 230 U.S. cities (see Figure 13.4). The United States has stepped in and pledged funds (part of the $1.4 billion Merída Initiative) to help combat the war on drugs in Mexico and Central America. In addition, they have added officers and announced new security measures at the border. But according to some experts, the American demand for illegal drugs plays the most important role in fueling Mexico's drug war. "No matter how much law enforcement or financial help the U.S. government provides Mexico, the basics of supply and demand prevent it from doing much good" (Crary 2009:1).

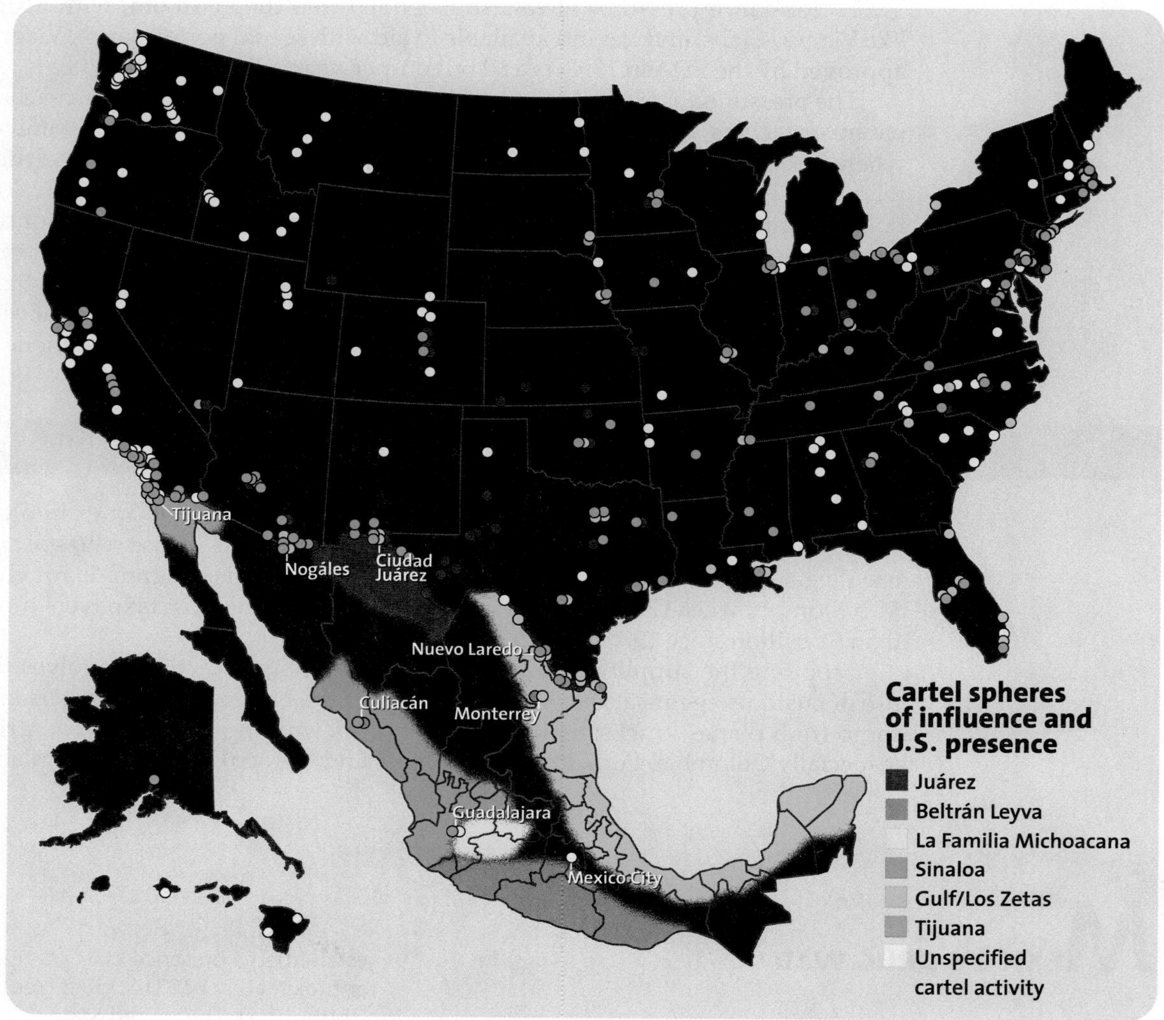

FIGURE 13.4

There are six dominant drug cartels in Mexico with influence spreading into the United States

where drugs are grown, manufactured, and processed and to destroy the transportation networks to the United States (by sea and air, and by land through Mexico). These efforts involve the State Department, the Treasury Department, the Coast Guard, various branches of the military, and the Central Intelligence Agency (CIA). These agencies train local soldiers and supply them with equipment (helicopters, radar, and surveillance aircraft) and supplies (herbicides, guns, munitions). This means, of course, that the United States is involved in destroying the crops (opium poppy and coca) of local farmers. It means the involvement of the United States (through the CIA) in local politics, siding with pro-U.S. factions against anti-U.S. factions, or involvement in civil wars, where rebels finance their operations with drugs in the fight against the established governments. It encourages violence, threats, and bribery as drug cartels use any means to keep their lucrative businesses flourishing (see the "Social Problems in Global Perspective" panel on the drug war in Mexico).

The policy of interdiction clearly is a failure. Drugs are found by the U.S. Customs, sometimes in large amounts. But massive amounts of drugs cross U.S. borders and enter an intricate distribution system within this country. Despite all our efforts, we have not stopped the supply; we have only dented it and made the drugs that enter the United States more expensive. The drug policy of interdiction also fails because it has led to strained relations with drug-producing nations in South America. By fighting our battles on their soil, the United States is often viewed as the villain.

The second front in the war on drugs occurs within the United States. Beginning in the 1970s, the courts became more punitive toward people selling or possessing illegal drugs. In New York State, for example, a law was passed in 1973 requiring a minimum sentence of 15 years to life for a first-time offender caught selling as little as 2 ounces or possessing 4 ounces of cocaine or heroin. The police, too, became more active in ferreting out buyers and sellers through the use of undercover agents, wiretaps, and sting operations. As a result, the number of adults arrested for drug offenses grew from about 500,000 in 1980 to approximately 1.7 million in 2007 (Bureau of Justice Statistics 2010; see Figure 13.5). In fact, the United States imprisons a larger fraction of its population for drug offenses than European nations do for all crimes. This has led to tremendous overcrowding of both the courts and the prisons, resulting in a huge and costly growth in the number and size of prisons (each new cell built costs about $80,000, and each new prisoner added costs about $25,000 annually).

Consequences of Official Drug Policies

The drug laws in the United States are irrational, and they do not achieve their intended goals of deterring crime by severely punishing the seller and user. There are three reasons this approach does not work to deter crime. First, by making drugs illegal and therefore dangerous to produce, transport, and sell,

FIGURE 13.5

Drug Arrests by Age, 1970–2007

This chart can be found on the Bureau of Justice Website, Key Facts at a Glance, on the following page: http://bjs.ojp.usdoj.gov/content/glance/drug.cfm

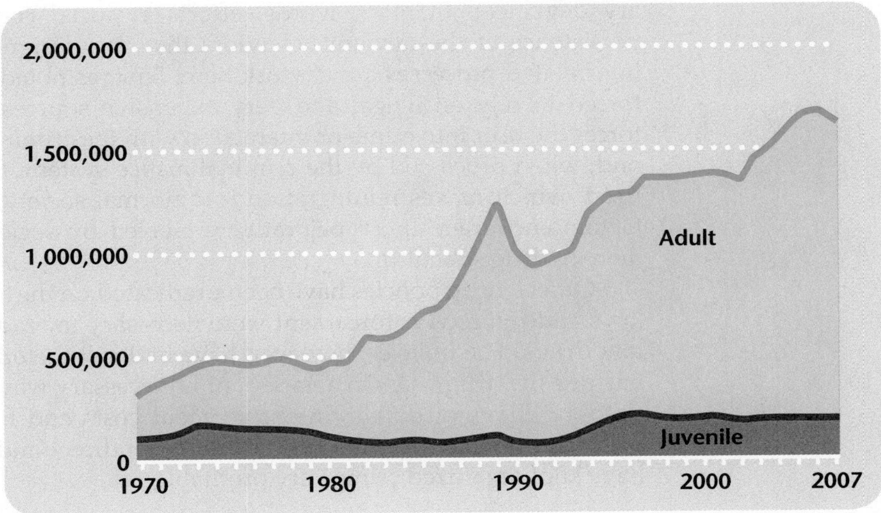

society pushes the cost to many times what it would be if they were legally available. Thus, heroin users, for example, are often forced into crime to sustain a high-cost habit. Crimes committed to produce money for drugs are typically nonviolent (pimping, prostitution, shoplifting, selling drugs, and burglary), but their cost is enormous. Suppose, for example, that there are 100,000 addicts in New York City with habits each costing $50 daily. If they each steal $300 worth of goods daily to get the $50 (a 6-to-1 ratio is about the way fencing works), the amount stolen in the city would be $30 million daily, or $10.68 billion a year!

The second reason that punitive drug laws encourage crime is that someone has to supply the illicit goods. Legislation does not dry up demand, as was vividly shown during Prohibition. Organized crime thrives in this climate. Illegal drugs are, for the most part, imported, processed, and distributed by organized crime groups. Drug laws, then, have the indirect effect of providing organized crime with its most lucrative source of income.

A third source of crime caused by drug laws is police corruption. Black market activities by organized crime or other entrepreneurs are difficult without the cooperation of police officials or drug enforcement agents, so their assistance is often bought.

The end result of police corruption and the realization that drug laws are arbitrary (such as the fact that marijuana is illegal but alcohol is legal) causes widespread disrespect for the law and the judicial system. As Garrison Keillor has said, "A marijuana grower can land in prison for life without parole while a murderer might be in for eight years. No rational person can defend this . . ." (2005:26). A final source of irreverence toward the law is the overzealousness of narcotics agents. In their efforts to capture drug law violators, agents have sometimes violated the constitutional rights of individuals (wiretapping, search and seizure without a warrant, entrapment, use of informants who are themselves addicts, and so on). All these abuses have contributed to an attitude of insolence on the part of many people toward agents of the law.

Criminal laws create crime and criminals. If there were no law regulating a behavior, then there would be no criminal. So it is with drug laws. Prior to 1914, heroin users were not criminals, nor were marijuana users before 1937. The drug laws, then, have created large numbers of criminals. By labeling and treating these people as criminals, the justice system creates further crime (secondary deviance). In other words, efforts at social control actually cause the persistence of the deviant behaviors they are designed to eliminate. Several interrelated processes are at work here. First, as noted earlier, the drug user is forced to rely on illegal and very expensive sources. This reliance typically forces the user into crime or interaction with the criminal fringes of society. Second, when processed by the criminal justice system, the individual is stigmatized, which makes reintegration into normal society very difficult. All these factors encourage those pejoratively labeled by society to join together in a deviant drug subculture.

Official drug policies have been predicated on the assumption that punitive laws and rigorous enforcement were necessary to eradicate the menace of certain drugs. The policies, however, have had just the opposite effect. They have harmed the drug users in a variety of unnecessary ways; they have cost society untold billions of dollars in enforcement costs and have clogged courts and prisons; they have resulted in additional indirect and direct crime; and they have kept organized crime very profitable.

Is the Drug War Racist?

The official policy of the federal government is to punish the sellers and users of illicit drugs. The problem is that the laws and the punishment for their violation are unfair to African Americans and other racial minorities. Four facts buttress this allegation. First, recall that the data on past month illicit drug use by race reveals a rate of 10.1 percent for African Americans, and 8.2 percent for Whites. Given their numbers in the general population, this means that overall there are more Whites using illicit drugs than Blacks, yet the data show consistently that *African Americans are more likely to be imprisoned for drug offenses.*

- In every year from 1980 to 2007, Blacks were arrested nationwide on drug charges at rates relative to the population that were 2.8 to 5.5 times higher than White arrest rates (see Figure 13.6). In some states, Blacks were arrested at rates up to 11.3 times greater than the rate for Whites (Human Rights Watch 2009).
- Of White drug felons, 32 percent are given probation or nonincarceration sentences in state courts, compared to 25 percent of Blacks (U.S. Department of Justice 2000).
- Human Rights Watch reported that Blacks and Latinos are far more likely to be arrested, prosecuted, and given long sentences for drug offenses. Nationally, Latinos comprise almost one-half of those arrested for marijuana offenses (reported by the Drug Policy Alliance 2003).
- Taken together, approximately 22 percent of monthly drug users are Black or Latino, but 80 percent of people in prison for drug offenses are Black or Latino (Glasser 2006).

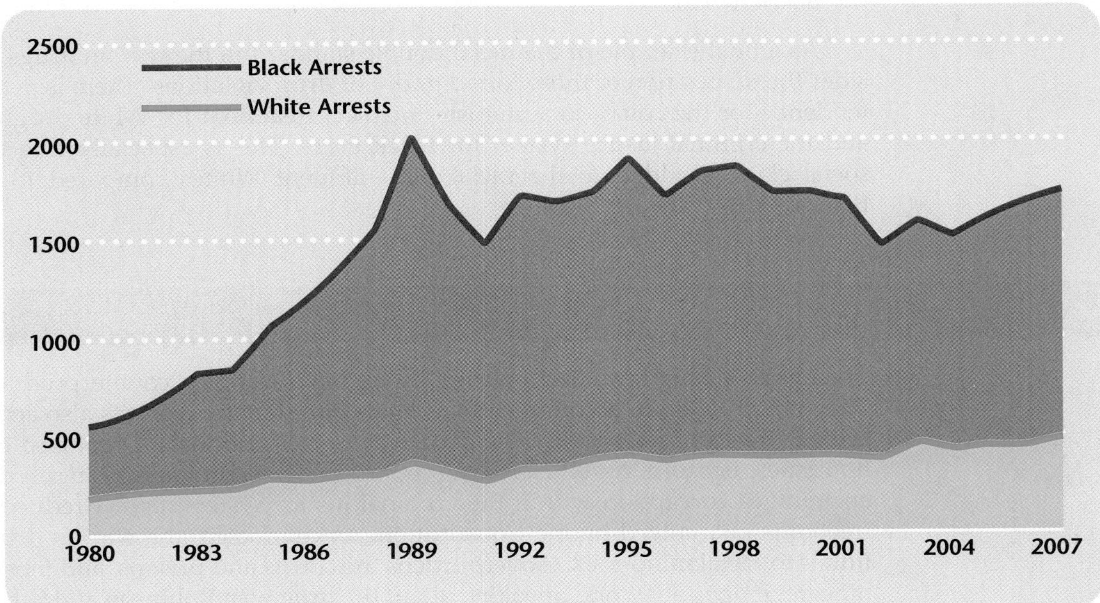

FIGURE 13.6

U.S. Rates of Adult Drug Arrests by Race, 1980–2007

Source: "Decades of Disparity: Drug Arrests and Race in the United States," March 2009. Human Rights Watch: (Figure 1, page 6).

Second, federal drug enforcement has waged its war against crack cocaine almost exclusively in minority neighborhoods. According to SAMHSA (2003), Whites are more likely than African Americans or Hispanics to report lifetime use of cocaine but are much less likely to be arrested for cocaine use. The issue is one of targeting—studies show that Blacks are more likely to be stopped while driving and searched. As Glasser notes,

> *In Florida blacks were seventy-five times more likely than whites to be stopped and searched for drugs while driving. And it turned out that these racially targeted stops were the explicit result of a Drug Enforcement Administration program begun in 1986, called Operation Pipeline, that "trained" 27,000 state troopers in forty-eight states to spot cars that might contain drugs. Most of the cars spotted were driven by blacks. And this happened even though three-quarters of monthly drug users are white! (2006:25)*

Third, the laws differ in the severity of punishment if violated. Although powder cocaine and crack cocaine are the same drugs, federal law treats them quite differently. For example, possession of 5 grams of crack (a teaspoon) gets a mandatory 5-year sentence, while it takes 100 times that amount of powder cocaine to get a comparable sentence. This unfair 100-to-1 ratio is racist because the defendants in crack cocaine cases are almost always Black.

> *A common illustration of the racial bias in drug laws is crack cocaine. . . . In fiscal year 2001, of all of those sentenced to federal prison for crack cocaine, 83 percent were black, compared to only 7 percent for whites and 9 percent for Latinos. For powder cocaine, the discrepancies are not nearly so stark: half of those sentenced for this drug were Latinos, while only 31 percent were black and 18 percent were white. Put somewhat differently, of all blacks sentenced to federal prison for drugs, 59 percent were convicted for crack cocaine; only 5.5 percent of whites were sentenced for this drug. (Shelden and Brown 2004:3)*

As a final example of the racial double standard in the war on drugs, consider the disposition of those found guilty of drug violations. There is a strong tendency for the courts to administer medical treatment for White drug users and the criminal justice system for Black users. This is especially true when social class is added to the racial mix—affluent Whites compared to poor Blacks.

ALTERNATIVES

The nation's drug laws and policies, as we have seen, are counterproductive. They not only fail to accomplish their goals but in many respects also actually achieve the opposite results. The drug war creates criminals. Organized crime flourishes because of official drug policies. The criminalization of drugs encourages corruption within the criminal justice system, and it reduces the freedoms guaranteed by the Constitution. As conducted, the war on drugs is unfair to racial minorities. It overburdens the courts and prisons, and most significant, it does not work. Speaking about the drug war, Robinson and Scherlen concludes,

> *Taken together, all the findings suggest the Office of National Drug Control Policy (ONDCP) failed from 1989 to 1998 to achieve its goals of reducing drug use, healing drug users, disrupting drug markets, and reducing health and social costs to the*

> *public. Yet, during this same time period, funding for the drug war grew tremendously and costs of the drug war expanded as well. Further, despite its manifest failure, ONDCP was reauthorized in 1994, 1998, and 2003. (2007:198)*

The United States has alternatives concerning drug policy: (1) to continue to wage the war on drugs by enacting and enforcing criminal laws, (2) to legalize drugs and regulate them through licensing and taxation, (3) to take a public health approach, with an emphasis on decriminalization, and (4) to address the social causes of drug use. We have already considered the first option—the criminalization of drug use—so we concentrate here on the other alternatives.

Regulation of Trade or Use through Licensing and Taxation

Legalizing a drug but regulating its use, as is now the case with alcohol, tobacco, and prescription drugs has some obvious benefits:

- It ensures the products' conformity to standards of purity and safety.
- It dries up the need for vast criminal networks that distribute drugs.
- It provides the government with revenues.
- Prison space and police activities would be reserved for the truly dangerous.

Most important, prohibition has not worked:

> *Law enforcement can't reduce supply or demand. As a Baltimore police officer, I arrested drug dealers. Others took their place. I locked them up, too. Thanks to the drug war, we imprison more people than any other country. And America still leads the world in illegal drug use. We can't arrest and jail our way to a drug-free America. (Moskos 2008:8)*

Opponents argue that government regulation would actually condone the use of drugs. This apparent approval, together with the easy availability and relatively low prices, would promote experimentation and use of the drug, perhaps increasing the number of users. Politically, such a policy would be difficult if not impossible to implement. Opinion polls show that the public strongly opposes legalization, and politicians do not want to seem "soft on drugs."

Under this regulation option, the biggest population to deal with would be the heroin addicts. These users are a special problem to themselves and society. Their habits are the most expensive, so of all drug users, they are most likely to turn to crime. Their habit also requires almost full-time diligence in securing the drug; and being "strung out," they do not function normally in society. How, then, should the government deal with them? Hard-liners argue that they should be classified as criminals and incarcerated. Other people suggest that addicts could remain in society and be relatively productive if drugs were supplied to them cheaply, under government regulation and medical supervision.

This can be accomplished through **heroin maintenance**, which treats addicts as medical problems rather than criminal problems. Methadone or buprenorphine are medications that can be taken orally for the treatment of narcotic withdrawal and dependence. Taken once per day, methadone suppresses withdrawal symptoms for 24 to 36 hours. The drug does not make the user drowsy, it does not impair cognitive functions, and it does not interfere with

SOCIAL POLICY

DUTCH MARIJUANA POLICY

A wave of marijuana law reform is now occurring today in Latin America, Europe and Australia. Paving the way for this reform was the Netherlands in the 1970s. Following the recommendations of two national commissions, the Dutch Parliament decriminalized cannabis possession and retail sale in 1976. Even before this date, the police seldom made arrests for possession or small-volume sales. Although it does not officially legalize marijuana, the 1976 law allowed the Dutch government to create a set of guidelines under which coffee shops could sell marijuana and hashish without fear of criminal prosecution.

Guidelines for the coffee shops have changed somewhat over time and vary slightly from community to community. The basic rules in place today include a ban on advertising, a minimum purchase age of 18, and a 5-gram limit on individual transactions. The sale of any other illicit drug on the premises is strictly prohibited and is grounds for immediate closure. Local government officials may limit the number of coffee shops concentrated in one area, and they can close an establishment if it creates a public nuisance. In the Netherlands, there are over 700 coffee shops where adults can purchase marijuana and hashish to be used there or carried away for use later.

The decision of Dutch legislators to permit the regulated sale and use of cannabis was based on a number of practical considerations. By allowing marijuana to be sold indoors rather than on the streets, the Dutch sought to improve public order. By separating the retail market for marijuana from the retail market for "hard drugs," they sought to reduce the likelihood of marijuana users being exposed to heroin and cocaine. By providing a nondeviant environment in which cannabis could be consumed, they sought to diminish the drug's utility as a symbol of youthful rebellion. Dutch officials have little faith in the capacity of the criminal law to stop people from using marijuana. They fear that arresting and punishing marijuana users—particularly youthful marijuana users—will alienate them from society's mainstream institutions and values.

These principles of normalization also guide the Dutch approach to drug education and prevention. Programs are specifically designed to be low key and minimalist, to avoid provoking young people's interest in drugs. There are no mass media campaigns against drugs, and school-based programs do not use scare tactics or moralistic "just say no" messages. Instead, in the context of general health education, young people in the Netherlands are given information about drugs and cautionary warnings about their potential dangers. In leaflets distributed through the coffee shops, current users of cannabis are advised to be "sensible and responsible."

Starting in the 1990s, the governments of Switzerland, Germany, Spain, Austria, Belgium,

driving a car or operating machinery. Although it is also addictive, the net effect is that a methadone user can continue to be a productive member of society without having to steal for his or her habit.

About 20 percent of the nation's heroin addicts are on **methadone maintenance** (Office of National Drug Control Policy 2000). Most states control and closely monitor the distribution of the drug. A benefit to this close monitoring is that there is no sharing of needles, a common problem among heroin users. Thus, it helps to control the spread of HIV infection.

In addition, methadone costs about $13 per day, a cheaper alternative to incarceration where the average cost in state prison is approximately $67 per day. Through the methadone maintenance program, addicts are not labeled as criminals. They are considered to have a medical, not a moral, problem. Equally important is that addicts remain participating members of the community.

Luxembourg, and Italy all shifted their laws toward decriminalization of marijuana. In 2001 Portugal decriminalized the use and possession of all drugs, including heroin and cocaine. At the same time, the United States government has moved in the opposite direction toward harsher penalties and increasing arrests for marijuana use and possession (Reinarman and Cohen 2007). Since 1996, in the United States, the number of arrests involving marijuana exceeds arrests for other types of drugs, reaching over 750,000 arrests in 2005 (Bureau of Justice Statistics 2007).

Researchers have found no evidence that the decriminalization of marijuana has led to increased drug use. In fact, a recent study comparing drug use in Amsterdam to drug use in San Francisco found similarities in patterns of marijuana use. The mean age at onset of use was 16.95 years in Amsterdam and 16.43 years in San Francisco (Reinarman and Cohen 2007). A 2010 study found that in comparing 16-year-old boys and girls in the United States and the Netherlands, adolescents in the United States had a *higher* rate of marijuana use (Simons-Morton et al., 2010).

One argument against the decriminalization of marijuana is that it is a "gateway drug," leading to other illicit drug use. Again comparing Amsterdam and San Francisco, Reinarman and Cohen found that Amsterdam respondents reported significantly lower lifetime use of other illicit drugs than respondents in San Francisco (2007). As shown in the following table, marijuana prevalence rates are actually higher in the United States than in the Netherlands, despite high arrest rates for marijuana offenses.

Sources: Simons-Morton, Bruce, William Pickett, Will Boyce, Tom F. M. ter Bogt, and Wilma Vollebergh. (2010). "Cross-National Comparison of Adolescent Drinking and Cannabis Use in the United States, Canada, and the Netherlands," *International Journal of Drug Policy* 21:64–69.

Craig Reinarman and Peter Cohen. 2007. "Law, Culture, and Cannabis: Comparing Use Patterns in Amsterdam and San Francisco." In Mitch Earleywine (Ed.), *Pot Politics: Marijuana and the Costs of Prohibition*. New York: Oxford University Press, pp. 113–137.

Drug Use (Age 12+)	*United States (2002)*	*Netherlands (2001)*
Lifetime marijuana use	40.4%	17.0%
Past month marijuana use	6.2%	3.0%
Lifetime heroin use	1.6%	0.4%
Past month heroin use	0.1%	0.1%
Lifetime cocaine use	14.4%	2.9%
Past month cocaine use	0.9%	0.4%

Sources: SAMHSA, Office of Applied Studies, National Survey on Drug Use and Health. 2002.

National Drug Monitor, Trimbos Institute. Report to the EMCDDA by the Reitox National Focal Point. "The Netherlands: Drug Situation 2002."

Critics of methadone maintenance argue that such programs encourage wider use of hard drugs. They also assert that these plans will not be acceptable to most citizens, who will continue to label addicts as criminals and sinful. Liberals, although likely to approve of either plan over the current criminal model, foresee a danger in government control over an addict population dependent on it for drugs. Also, such programs attack the problem at the individual level (blaming the victim) and ignore the social and cultural sources of drug use.

Noninterference

Libertarians argue that it is none of the government's business what drugs people put into their bodies. There should be no governmental interference in this private act. This view, however, does not excuse drug users from their behavior. Former Seattle police officer Norm Stampler says,

> *If I choose to inject, inhale, sniff, snort, or for that matter, put a bullet in my brain, that's a choice I should have as an adult. Where the line is drawn for society is if I choose to be irresponsible in committing those acts. Then I need to be held accountable for my behavior. For instance, if I furnish a kid with drugs, or if I abuse a spouse, then I need to be held accountable for my criminal actions. The hypocrisy of keeping the prohibition on these substances going, yet making no moves to ban alcohol as a choice for adults, is staggering. We know there are far greater problems associated with alcohol abuse. Just as with alcohol, though, I think it should be viewed as a basic civil liberty for people to be able to use whatever drugs they want, and second, to treat the abuse of drugs as a medical problem, which is what it is. It is a public health issue, not an issue for the law to deal with. (Quoted in Talvi 2005:27)*

Proponents of total **decriminalization of drugs** argue that all societies throughout known history have had psychoactive drugs. Legislation and strict enforcement will not curb the tendency among many people to want to alter their consciousness artificially. Such acts should be neither penalized nor encouraged because it is none of the government's business what individuals do to themselves. The United States could follow the example of Latin American countries such as Brazil, Uruguay, Portugal, and Mexico, who have all changed their laws to eliminate jail time for people carrying small amounts of drugs for personal use. (For the way that the Dutch handle marijuana, see the Social Policy panel titled "Dutch Marijuana Policy.")

Critics suggest that decriminalization will encourage the spread of drug use. Drug use will spread because drugs will be readily available and because commercial interests will see potential profits in these formerly illicit drugs and will produce them and promote their use. Finally, and perhaps most significant, some argue that drug use is not an isolated act that affects only the user. In short, although many people believe that drug use is a "victimless vice," there is always a victim. To those who would argue that at the very least, marijuana should be put in the same category as alcohol and tobacco, Sabet argues,

> *Alcohol and tobacco are a favorite reference point for those who wish to legalize drugs. Since those two killers are legal—indeed alcohol contributes to more violent crime than crack cocaine—why not just legalize other dangerous substances (or at least one more) and regulate their sale? Why the difference between alcohol and tobacco on one hand and marijuana on the other, especially when we know that alcohol use has a much greater association with violence than marijuana use?*
>
> *Even a cursory glance at the status of our two legal drugs shows us that to add a third drug to this list would exacerbate an already difficult public health problem. Tobacco kills half a million people every year. Alcohol is worse—not only is it responsible for negative health effects on the drinker but on people around them. If we are to look at these two legal drugs as indicators of behavior associated with legal drug use, we see a pattern: legal drugs are by definition easy to obtain; commercialization glamorizes their use and furthers their social acceptance, their price is low, and high profits make promotion worthwhile for sellers. Subsequently—inevitably—more users occur, more addicts, and the increased use results in more social and health damage, increased deaths, and greater economic burden. When sellers rely on addiction for profit, there is not a strong case that drugs—even just marijuana—should be sold alongside alcohol and tobacco. (Sabet 2007:341)*

What, then, is the answer to drug use? Probably some combination of these alternatives makes the most sense. Clearly, the arguments about the solution will continue to incite passion. There will be those who are concerned with the use of certain drugs and who feel that society must control such deviance. They insist on imposing their morals on others. At the other extreme are those who are more concerned with how the laws and their rigorous enforcement cause social problems. As the various segments of society continue the debate, legislation will be proposed and eventually passed. The astute observer should note the role of interest groups in what is decided and also who benefits and who loses by the decision reached.

Address the Social Causes of Drug Use

When one looks at drug use across the United States, it is clear that drugs are correlated with poverty, education, gender, social location, and race/ethnicity. Elliott Currie, who has written perceptively about drugs in the United States, writes:

> *If we are to solve the drug problem, we must attack the conditions that breed it. It is not accidental that the United States has both the developed world's worst drug problem and its worst violence, poverty, and social exclusion, together with its least adequate provision of health care, income support, and social services. Taking on the drug problem in an enduring way means tackling those social deficits head-on.* (Currie 1993:280–281)

The United States has spent billions of dollars tackling the supply side of drugs through regulating its borders and other social control efforts, yet an effective drug policy must also focus on reducing the demand for drugs. Addressing social problems such as poverty, violence, and racial-ethnic inequality is a necessary first step in lowering drug use rates in America.

CHAPTER REVIEW

1. Whether drugs in U.S. society are defined as legal or illegal is based not on their potential for harm to the users or society but on politics—the exercise of power by interest groups and the majority to legislate their views on others.
2. The acceptability of certain drugs such as marijuana or heroin has varied historically. Opiates, once legal in the United States, became illegal for two reasons: (a) members of the White working class on the West Coast felt threatened by cheap Chinese labor and sought coercive measures against those Chinese; and (b) religious groups interpreting opiate use as a moral evil mounted successful pressure. The result was the Harrison Narcotics Act of 1914, which established a Narcotics Division of the Treasury Department whose goal was to eliminate drug addiction. Behavior once considered a medical problem became a criminal problem.
3. Laws defining which drugs are legal and which are not reflect negative stereotypes held by the general public and efforts for control by interest groups (such as religious groups, the pharmaceutical industry, and organized crime) and law enforcement professionals. The result is that current drug laws are illogical. They are not related to the danger of the drugs but reflect the political interests of the powerful.
4. Most people in the United States take some drug on a regular basis. Those drugs considered legal are caffeine, alcohol, nicotine, tranquilizers, amphetamines, and barbiturates. Illegal drugs

used by millions in U.S. society are marijuana, cocaine, methamphetamine, inhalants, psychedelics, and heroin.

5. The prevailing culture, group norms, and social pressures strongly affect the patterns of drug use and their behavioral effects. Drug use varies by age, education level, race, gender, and social class. Men of all ages are more likely than women to use illegal drugs.
6. The pressure to use drugs may come from doctors, coaches, pharmaceutical firms, tobacco and alcohol companies, and one's friends and associates. Drugs are used increasingly to meet cultural standards of mental and physical perfection.
7. The U.S. war on drugs costs approximately $1 billion per week. It entails stopping drugs from coming into the country and punishing those who use and sell drugs. In large part, this war has not succeeded.
8. Drug laws promote crime in at least three ways: (a) users often engage in criminal activity because the drugs, being illegal, are so expensive; (b) punitive drug laws encourage organized crime by making importation, processing, and distribution of illegal drugs extremely lucrative; and (c) people selling illicit drugs often corrupt the police.
9. The drug war appears to be racist because of four patterns in the criminal justice system: (a) Blacks and Latinos are overrepresented in the prison population for drug offenses given their numbers in the population and their drug usage statistics; (b) drug enforcement of crack cocaine occurs almost exclusively in minority neighborhoods; (c) although crack cocaine and powder cocaine are basically the same, the government punishes the (primarily Black) users and sellers of crack much more severely; and (d) the courts tend to administer medical treatment for White drug users and the criminal justice system for Black users.
10. Government can adopt alternative policies toward drug use: (a) prohibition of trade and use through enforcement of criminal penalties (the current policy); (b) regulation through licensing and taxation; (c) noninterference (ignoring drugs because what people do to themselves is not the government's business); and (d) address the underlying social causes of drug use to reduce the demand for drugs.

■ KEY TERMS

Drug. Any substance that affects the structure or function of the body when ingested.

Politics of drugs. The labeling of some drugs as licit and others as illicit depends on the definition of drugs by the most powerful interest groups, which are able to get their definitions incorporated into the law.

Psychoactive drug. Chemical that alters the perceptions and/or moods of people who take it.

Gateway drug. The belief that the use of a drug will lead to the use of other hard drugs like heroin and cocaine.

Moral panic. Moral panics occur when a social problem is defined as a threat to societal values and interests. Moral panics typically involve the exaggeration of a social problem; the public response to it is also exaggerated.

Psychopharmacology. Science of drugs that affect the mind.

Restorative drug. Chemical that heals a traumatized part of the body.

Additive drug. Chemical that improves performance.

Interdiction. Public policy of stopping the flow of drugs into the United States by guarding the borders and by curtailing the creation, processing, and distributing of drugs in other countries.

Heroin maintenance. British approach to heroin addiction that treats addicts as sick rather than as criminal; thus, addicts are placed under the jurisdiction of physicians who administer drugs to their patients.

Methadone maintenance. Used for heroin maintenance, this treatment provides a heroin substitute (methadone) to addicts under medical supervision.

Decriminalization of drugs. Legalization of drugs.

■ SUCCEED WITH PEARSON mysoclab www.mysoclab.com

Experience, Discover, Observe, Evaluate
MySocLab is designed just for you. Each chapter features a pre-test and post-test to help you learn and review key concepts and terms.

Experience sociology in action with dynamic visual activities, videos, and readings to enhance your learning experience. Complete the following activities at www.mysoclab.com.

Social Explorer is an interactive application that allows you to explore Census data through interactive maps.

- Explore the Social Explorer Map: *Increases in Prison Populations*

The Core Concepts in Sociology video clips offer a real-world perspective on sociological concepts.

- Watch *Opium Addiction*

MySocLibrary includes primary source readings from classic and contemporary sociologists.

- Read Leo, *American Preschoolers on Ritalin;* Gelles & Cavanaugh, *Association Is Not Causation: Alcohol and Other Drugs Do Not Cause Violence;* MacCoun & Reuter, *Does Europe Do It Better? Lessons from Holland, Britain, and Switzerland*

PART 5 Institutional Problems

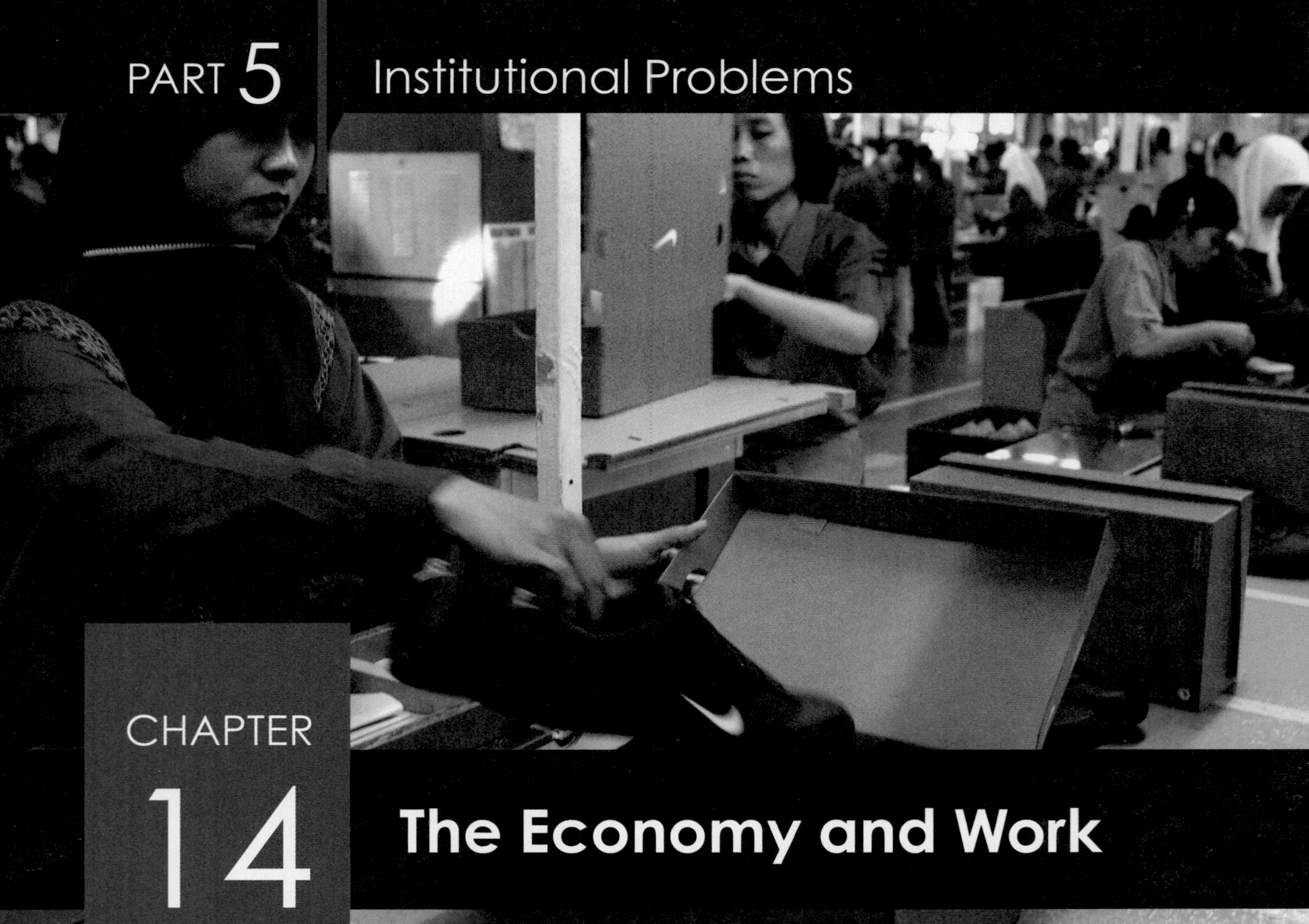

CHAPTER 14 The Economy and Work

Some have jobs with no future. Others have a future without jobs.

—Holly Sklar

This chapter is divided into three parts. The first part describes the two polar types of economic systems: capitalism and socialism and the social problems associated with each: The second examines the great economic trends of our time: the transformation of the economy, globalization, and the Great Recession. Each of these major trends is the source of many social problems. The final section is devoted to the problems of work.

CAPITALISM AND SOCIALISM

Industrialized societies organize their economic activities according to one of two fundamental forms: capitalism or socialism. Although no society has a purely capitalist or socialist economy, the ideal types provide opposite extremes on a scale that helps us measure the U.S. economy more accurately.

Capitalism

Four conditions must be present for pure capitalism to exist—private ownership of property, personal profit, competition, and a government policy of laissez-faire. These necessary conditions constitute the underlying principles of a pure capitalist system. The first is private ownership of property. Individuals are encouraged to own not only private possessions but, most important, also the capital necessary to produce and distribute goods and services. In a purely capitalist society, there would be no public ownership of any potentially profitable activity.

The pursuit of maximum profit, the second essential principle, implies that individuals are free to maximize their personal gains. Most important, the proponents of capitalism (see the insert on Adam Smith) argue that profit seeking by individuals has positive consequences for society. Thus, seeking individual gain through personal profit is considered morally acceptable and socially desirable.

Competition, the third ingredient, is the mechanism for determining what is produced and at what price. The market forces of supply and demand ensure that capitalists produce the goods and services wanted by the public, that the goods and services are high in quality, and that they are sold at the lowest possible price. Moreover, competition is the mechanism that keeps individual profit seeking in check. Potential abuses such as fraud, faulty products, and exorbitant prices are negated by the existence of competitors who soon take business away from those who violate good business judgment. So, too, economic inefficiency is minimized as market forces cause the inept to fail and the efficient to succeed.

These three principles—private property, personal profit, and competition—require a fourth condition if true capitalism is to work: a government policy of

Adam Smith

Adam Smith (1723–1790), a Scottish economist, is the godfather of laissez-faire capitalism. His *Inquiry into the Nature and Causes of the Wealth of Nations,* written in 1776, presented a logical vision of how society was bound inextricably by the private decisions of entrepreneurs and consumers alike.

Of the many issues that Smith addressed, one is paramount for our concerns: How does society hang together when everyone is pursuing his or her own self-interest? For Smith the answer is in the laws of the marketplace: The needs of society and its citizens are met by each person producing what will bring a profit. According to Smith, someone will provide whatever is needed because demand increases the likelihood of profit. But if all entrepreneurs are profit hungry, what will prevent them from taking unfair advantage of their consumers? The answer, simply, is competition. The existence of competition will keep prices fair and product quality high.

The market also regulates the incomes of those who produce the goods. If wages are too high in one kind of work, other workers will rush to that type of job, bringing down the exorbitant wages. Similarly, if wages are too low, then workers will change to better-paying jobs. The marketplace also reduces the possibility of surpluses because entrepreneurs, foreseeing the problem, will move to more profitable arenas where the demand and profits are high. Thus, the laws of the marketplace provide an "invisible hand" that regulates the economy without government intervention. The government is not needed to fix prices, to set minimum wages, or to protect against consumer fraud. All that is needed is a free and competitive marketplace. The question, of course, is whether the nature of the marketplace in a world of huge multinational corporations, multimillion-member labor unions, and conglomerates is the same as it was in the eighteenth century.

laissez-faire, allowing the marketplace to operate unhindered. Capitalists argue that any government intervention in the marketplace distorts the economy by negatively affecting incentives and freedom of individual choice. If left unhindered by government, the profit motive, private ownership, and competition will achieve the greatest good for the greatest number in the form of individual self-fulfillment and the general material progress of society.

Critics argue that capitalism promotes inequality and a host of social problems because the object is profit, not enhancing the human condition. Consider this critique by Jesse Jackson:

> *The operation of free markets is a wondrous and mighty thing. To allocate goods and services, to adjust supply with demand, the market has no equal. But the market sets the price—not the value—of things. It counts consumers, not citizens. . . . The market has no opinion on the distribution of income, wealth, and opportunity in society. . . . The market does not care if kids in Appalachia or Brooklyn go to school in buildings that are dangerous to their health. The market has no opinion on whether opportunity is open to the many or limited to the few. The market does not care that [46] million Americans go to bed every night without health insurance. . . . The market does not care if the economy is swimming in speculative capital, but large segments of the country are effectively redlined [a banking practice of not loaning money within certain boundaries, most typically where the poor and racial minorities are located] as banks merge. The market does not care if the shows our children watch on television are filled with sex, violence, and racial stereotyping. The market measures TV shows by the price of their advertising. On the values they impart, the market has no opinion. (Jackson 1998b:19)*

As the late Molly Ivins observed, "Capitalism . . . is a dandy system for creating wealth, but it doesn't do squat for social justice. No reason to expect it to—that's not its job" (Ivins 2000:22).

The economy of the United States is not purely capitalistic. Taxes are levied on the population to raise monies for the common good, such as the federal interstate highway system, the air traffic control system and the subsidizing of airports, flood control projects, the defense establishment, the postal system, and disaster relief. In many ways, the government interferes with the market by monitoring the safety of food and drugs, prohibiting the sale of certain products, regulating the environment, insisting on health and safety regulations in workplaces, issuing licenses, protecting the civil rights of women and minorities, taxing income, subsidizing certain business activities, overseeing the banking and insurance industries, and raising or lowering interest rates.

Moreover, although U.S. social programs are less generous than those found in the social welfare states, there is nonetheless minimal help for victims of natural disasters, preschool training for children of the poor, low-interest student loans, Medicare, and Medicaid.

Socialism

Socialism is an economic system in which the means of production are owned by the people for their collective benefit. The five principles of socialism are democratism, egalitarianism, community, public ownership of the means of production, and planning for common purposes. True socialism must be democratic. Representatives of a socialist state must be answerable and responsive to the wishes of the public they serve. Nations that claim to be socialist but are totalitarian violate this fundamental aspect of socialism. The key to differentiating between authentic and spurious socialism is to determine who is making the decisions and whose interests are being served. Thus, it is a fallacy to equate true socialism with the politicoeconomic systems found in Cuba or the People's Republic of China. These societies are socialistic in some respects; that is, their material benefits are more evenly distributed than those in the United States. But their economies and governments are controlled by a single political party in an inflexible and authoritarian manner. Although these countries claim to have democratic elections, in fact the citizens have no electoral choice but to rubber-stamp the candidates of the ruling party. The people are denied civil liberties and freedoms that should be the hallmark of a socialist society. In a pure socialist society, democratic relations must operate throughout the social structure: in government, at work, at school, and in the community.

The second principle of socialism is egalitarianism: equality of opportunity for the self-fulfillment of all, equality rather than hierarchy in decision making, and equality in sharing the benefits of society. For some socialists, the goal is absolute equality. For most, though, equality means a limit to inequality, with some acceptable disparities in living standards. This more realistic goal of socialism requires a fundamental commitment to achieving a rough parity by evening out gross inequities in income, property, and opportunities. The key is a leveling of advantages so that all citizens receive the necessities (food, clothing, medical care, living wages, sick pay, retirement benefits, and shelter).

The third feature of socialism is community, which is the "idea that social relations should be characterized by cooperation and a sense of collective belonging rather than by conflict and competition" (Miller 1991:406). This sense of the collective is evidenced by a relatively high taxation rate to provide for the common good—such as universal health care, paid maternity leave, subsidized child care, universal preschool programs, and a generous retirement program (see the panel on Social Policy, which provides the example of the Swedish Welfare State).

The fourth characteristic of socialism is the public ownership of the means of production. The people own the basic industries, financial institutions, utilities, transportation, and communications companies. The goal is serving the public, not making profit.

The fifth principle of socialism is planning. The society must direct social activities to meet common goals. This means that socialists oppose the heart of capitalism, which is to let individuals acting in their own interests in the marketplace determine overall outcomes. For socialists, these uncoordinated activities invite chaos, and although they possibly help some people in the society, they do damage to others. Thus, a purely socialist government requires societal planning to provide, at the least possible individual and collective cost, the best conditions to meet the material needs of its citizens. Planning also aims to achieve societal goals such as protecting the environment, combating pollution, saving natural resources, and developing new technologies. Public policy is decided through the rational assessment of the needs of society and how the economy might best be organized to achieve them. In this situation, the economy must be regulated by the government, which acts as the agent of the people. The government sets prices and wages; important industries are run at a loss if necessary. Dislocations such as surpluses or shortages or unemployment are minimized by central planning. The goal is to run the economy for the good of the society.

Critics of democratic socialism argue that "the nanny state" minimizes individual freedom and choice. Government monopoly is inefficient because of a

SOCIAL POLICY

THE SWEDISH WELFARE STATE

Sweden, although a capitalist economy for the most part, is socialist in its generous welfare provisions that level the extremes in wealth and poverty. The Swedish system is based on the principle that the government is responsible to provide basic services for the entire population. In broad outline, the present welfare system includes the following provisions:

- A national health insurance program. Patients choose their own physicians, and health services are subsidized for all residents of Sweden. The fees charged to patients in 2005 U.S. dollars were $11.21 per day for hospital stays, $21.02 for consultation with a doctor. Once a patient has paid $126, he or she is entitled to free medical care for the remainder of the year. Pharmaceutical costs are paid by the individual until the total reaches $252 in a calendar year, after which they are free for the rest of the year.
- A family support program for parents and children. Prenatal care, delivery, and postnatal care are free. All children under the age of 20 receive free medical and dental care. Working parents may take a leave from work to care for their infant for a total for both parents of 480 days (divided as they choose) while being compensated at 80 percent of their wages. Either parent may take time off for the care of a sick child (60 days a year per child), with compensation for lost earnings. All children ages 4 and 5 are provided three hours of free preschooling a day.
- Care of the elderly. Everyone who has lived in Sweden for at least 3 years is entitled to at least a minimum pension. Full pension is for those who have lived in Sweden for 40 years. The elderly receive a housing subsidy. Institutionalized care is provided when needed, but the preference is for the elderly to receive nursing care in their homes, which is subsidized, whenever possible.
- Subsidized housing. The government provides nonprofit municipal housing, establishes rent ceilings, subsidizes financing, and provides housing allowances. These provisions allow lower-income families to afford decent housing.

To provide these many and expensive services of the welfare state, Swedish taxes are relatively high. Direct taxes include an income tax on employment, income from capital, business income, a national property tax on real estate, and an inheritance tax. Directly, there are a state sales tax and consumption taxes to curb the use of energy (oil and gas, electrical power, and motor vehicles), tobacco, gaming, and alcohol. As a result, the total tax revenue for Sweden as a percentage of gross domestic product in 2000 was 54.2 percent (compared to 29.6 percent for the United States, 37.9 percent in Germany, 37.4 percent in the United Kingdom, and 35.8 percent for Canada).

Source: Excerpted from D. Stanley Eitzen. 2007. "The Swedish Welfare State." In D. Stanley Eitzen (ed.), *Solutions to Social Problems: Lessons from Other Societies,* 5th ed. (Boston: Allyn & Bacon, 2010).

centralized bureaucracy making "one-size-fits-all" decisions. Taxes are high to pay for the social programs, robbing individuals of their earned income. And, the argument goes, the "cradle-to-grave" social programs for individuals and families reduce their motivation to succeed, an attitude that, when held by many, limits creativity, economic productivity, and growth.

MEGA ECONOMIC TRENDS

The structure of contemporary society shapes families and individuals within them. Three interrelated trends of great magnitude especially affect our jobs, incomes, and our futures—the structural transformation of the economy, globalization, and the Great Recession (this section is taken largely from Baca Zinn, Eitzen, and Wells, 2011: Chapter 4).

The Structural Transformation of the Economy

The Industrial Revolution, which began in Great Britain in the 1780s, was a major turning point in human history. With the application of steam power and, later, oil and electricity as energy sources for industry, mining, manufacturing, and transportation, fundamental changes came to the economy, the relationship of people and work, family organization, and a transition from rural to urban life. In effect, societies are transformed with each surge in invention and technological growth. Peter F. Drucker describes the historical import of such transformations:

> *Every few hundred years in Western history there occurs a sharp transformation. We cross . . . a "divide." Within a few short decades, society rearranges itself—its worldview; its basic values; its social and political structure; its arts; its key institutions. Fifty years later, there is a new world. And the people born then cannot even imagine the world in which their grandparents lived and into which their own parents were born. We are currently living through just such a transformation.* (Drucker 1993:1)

For example, the U.S. economy was once dominated by agriculture, but in the twentieth century, while agricultural productivity increased, the number employed in an agrarian economy declined precipitously, replaced by manufacturing. But the manufacturing economy has now shifted to an economy characterized by service occupations and the collection, storage, and dissemination of information. Each of these dramatic turns in the economy involves a **structural transformation of the economy.**

The United States is now in the midst of a new transformation. Reflecting this shift, the United States has lost more than one-fifth of its factory jobs since 2000 to about 11.7 million workers in late 2009 (McCormack 2010:A2). The number of people working in manufacturing accounts for only 8.7 percent of jobs (Hindery and Gerard 2009), down from about 30 percent in 1959. Some other indicators of this shift away from manufacturing (McCormack 2010):

- Total manufacturing gross domestic product in 2008 represented 11.5 percent of U.S. economic output, down from 17 percent in 1999 and 28 percent in 1959.
- The furniture industry lost 60 percent of its production capacity in the United States from 2000 to 2008.
- The manufacture of printed circuit boards (PCB) in the United States accounted for only 8 percent of global production in 2008, down from 26 percent in 2000.

Every new era poses new problems of adjustment, but this one differs from the agricultural and industrial eras. The earlier transformations were gradual enough for adaptation to take place over several decades, but conditions are significantly different now. The rate of change now is phenomenal and unprecedented.

- **The Changing Nature of Jobs.** Joseph Schumpeter (1950) described a process inherent to capitalism that he called "creative destruction." By this he meant that as the economic structure of capitalism mutates, some sectors will lose out while others gain. For example, in 1917, the largest U.S. corporation, with three times the assets of its nearest competitor, was U.S. Steel, which employed 268,000 workers. Today U.S. Steel is worth about one-fifth what it was in 1917 and employs only 26,840 workers. Replacing U.S. Steel at the apex of the nation's corporate elite are companies such as Microsoft, Intel, and Merck. Today the largest employer in the United States is Wal-Mart. These facts illustrate how manufacturing, the backbone of the U.S. economy in the twentieth century, is no longer dominant. It has been replaced by the service sector and knowledge-based companies. Whereas in the past people mostly worked at producing goods, now they tend to do work in offices, banking, insurance, retailing, health care, education, custodial work, restaurant work, security, and transportation.

The shift away from manufacturing to services and information/knowledge means that some sectors of the economy fade in importance or will even die out completely. These sectors are known as **sunset industries** (e.g., steel, tires, shoes, toys, and textiles). Over 1,500 plants in these industries have closed permanently since 1975. And literally millions of blue-collar jobs, most of which were unionized with good pay and benefits, were lost and not replaced.

Many blue-collar jobs have also been lost to automation. Robots, since the 1960s, have replaced humans doing routine work such as picking fruit, welding, assembling, painting, and scanning products for defects. Now robots can see, feel, move, and work together. Similarly, many white-collar jobs are being lost because of new technologies. The Internet, for example, allows people to make their own travel arrangements, reducing or eliminating the need for travel agents, or to buy and sell stocks, making stockbrokers unnecessary. Also, software is available that helps people do their tax returns without the need of a tax specialist. Within firms, computer programs take care of payrolls, inventory control, and delivery schedules, reducing the need for accountants. Primarily because of voice mail, laser printers, and word processors, hundreds of thousands of secretarial and clerical jobs have been eliminated.

The employer/employee relationship is also being reshaped. The Internet is revolutionizing how business is transacted. More than 30 million American workers work in temporary, contracted, self-employed, leased, part-time, and other "nonstandard" arrangements. These workers under **contingent employment** (i.e., employees who work part time, in temporary jobs, or as independent contractors) typically lack an explicit contract for ongoing employment and thus receive sporadic wages. They earn less than their counterparts who do the same work, and they have fewer benefits such as health insurance, family leave, and retirement, thus costing their employers up to 30 percent less than regular employees (Davidson 2009).

One version of contingent employment is that of temporary workers ("temps"). This trend represents a dramatic change in work. Businesses argue that they need this arrangement for flexibility in a rapidly changing competitive economy. These growing numbers of temporary workers are not tied to an employer, which makes them free to choose from available work options. There is a downside to this trend, however: About 60 percent of these nonstandard jobs are low quality, paying less than regular full-time jobs held by similar workers. Temps earn on average 40 percent less per hour than full-time workers. In short, this trend has meant the proliferation of marginal jobs, with employers now shifting the burden of fringe benefits to individual workers and their families.

Another type of contigent work is **homesharing** or **homesourcing** in which independent contractors work from their homes. Home-based work includes word processing, editing, accounting, and telemarketing. Employers contract women to do home-based work because money is saved—the employers pay only for work delivered, they avoid unions, and they do not pay benefits such as health insurance, paid leaves, and pensions.

A generation or so ago, workers tended to work for one or two employers during their working years. Employers were loyal to their workers ("If you do your job, you'll have a job") and workers were loyal to their employers. But the nature of work has changed dramatically. Now many workers are not allied with an employer, working, as we have seen, as contingent workers. Millions of workers are dismissed as their employers modernize the plants or move them elsewhere. Still other workers find their skills not keeping up with technological changes. Others leave jobs for other jobs. Sociologist Richard Sennett has calculated that young workers today with at least two years of college can expect to change jobs at least eleven times before retirement (reported in Schwartz 2004).

- **The New Jobs Pay Less.** But while jobs have shrunk by the millions in the last two decades, many millions more have been created in **sunrise industries** (those industries characterized by increased output and employment). Such jobs are involved in the production of high-tech products (computers, software, medical instruments, bioengineering, robotics). Also, lower-end service jobs such as sales clerks, janitors, and security guards are plentiful (and have the advantage of being immune to outsourcing). The important point for workers is that these new industries pay less than the old ones. The Economic Policy Institute found that from late 2001 through late 2003, sunset (contracting) industries paid, on average, $61,983 in annual compensation (wages and benefits), whereas sunrise (expanding) industries paid $35,546 in compensation (42.7 percent less; Mishel, Bernstein, and Allegretto 2004).

Globalization

Among other changes, the new technologies have, most significantly, magnified the connections among all peoples across the globe (the following is dependent in part on Eitzen, Baca Zinn, and Smith, 2010, Chapter 8, and Eitzen and Baca Zinn, 2009). The Internet makes worldwide communications instantaneous. Money moves across political boundaries with a few keystrokes. Low wages in one country affect wages elsewhere. A drought in one part of the world drives up prices for commodities everywhere, and overproduction of a product in one region brings down the prices of that product elsewhere. A collapse in the stock market of one nation has ramifications for financial markets around the world. Movies, television, and advertising from one society affect the tastes, interests, and styles in other places. Polluted air and water cross national borders. Deforestation in the developing nations has a major effect on climate change everywhere. Global warming, caused by the burning of fossil fuels, changes climates, generates megastorms, and increases the spread of tropical diseases around the world. A disease such as HIV/AIDS left Africa some fifty years ago and now infects 33 million people worldwide and 1.2 million in North America. H1N1 became a pandemic (worldwide health danger) within a few months. There has been a dramatic increase in migration flows, especially from poorer to richer nations. With sophisticated weapons systems, no nation is immune from assault from other nations or terrorist acts by revolutionary groups.

Each of these examples of **globalization** involves the processes by which everyone on Earth becomes increasingly interconnected economically, politically, culturally, and environmentally. Connections among peoples outside their tribes or political units are not new, but the linkages now are increasing geometrically, with few, if any, groups unaffected. We concentrate here on economic globalization.

Although trade between and among nations is not new, global trade entered a new phase after World War II. What has evolved is a global trade network, the integration of peoples and nations, and a global economy, with a common ideology: capitalism. Former colonies have established local industries and sell their raw materials, products, and labor on the global market. The United States emerged as the strongest economic and military power in the world, with U.S. corporations vitally interested in expanding their operations to other societies for profit. The shift to a global economy has been accelerated by the tearing down of tariff barriers. The North American Free Trade Agreement (NAFTA) and the General Agreement on Tariffs and Trade (GATT), both passed in 1994, are two examples of agreements that increased the flow of goods (and jobs) across national boundaries. In 2005 President Bush signed the Central American Free Trade Agreement (CAFTA), which institutes a Western Hemisphere-wide version of NAFTA.

The globalization of the economy is not a neutral process. Decisions are based on what will maximize profits, thus serving the owners of capital and not necessarily workers or the communities where U.S. operations are located. In this regard, private businesses, in their search for profit, make crucial investment decisions that change the dynamics in families and communities. Most significant are the corporate decisions regarding the movement of corporate money from one investment to another (called **capital flight**). This shift of capital takes several forms: investment in plants located in other nations, plant relocation within the United States, and mergers. Although these investment decisions may be positive for corporations, they also take away investment (disinvestment) from others (workers and their families, communities, and suppliers).

As noted earlier, the United States has shifted to an economy based on ideas rather than manufacturing. Most of the manufacturing by U.S. transnational corporations is now done in low-wage economies. Manufacturers have moved offshore because profits are greater and because giant retailers (e.g., Wal-Mart) have compelled manufacturers to move offshore in search of lower prices for consumers and higher profits for themselves (Meyerson 2010:A16-A17). This migration of jobs takes two forms, both related to capital flight: offshoring and outsourcing (Friedman 2005). **Offshoring** is when a company moves its production to another country, producing the same products in the same way, but with cheaper labor, lower taxes, and lower benefits to workers. **Outsourcing** refers to taking some specific task that a company was doing in-house—such as research, call centers, accounting, or transcribing—and transferring it to an overseas company to save money and reintegrating that work back into the overall operation. Even airplane maintenance is being outsourced.

> *An explosion of new technologies—including e-mail, digitization, the Internet, broadband technology, scanners, communication satellites, undersea fiber-optic cables, and videoconferencing—has made it convenient for business to move white-collar jobs overseas. . . . Now, radiologists in India are analyzing X-rays for Massachusetts*

Container ships enter U.S. ports with goods produced elsewhere to be sold here. The merchandise is cheaper, but there is a high cost—lost jobs for U.S. workers.

General and other hospitals. Five hundred engineers in Moscow are helping Boeing design and build aircraft, as Boeing lays off engineers in the United States. The Bank of America moved 1,000 technical and back-office jobs to India while cutting 3,700 jobs in the United States. (Greenhouse 2009:203)

This move to low-wage economies has three negative effects on U.S. workers. First, many have lost their jobs. Second, the wages of those production workers who have not lost their jobs remain relatively low because if they seek higher wages, their employers threaten to move the jobs elsewhere. And, third, workers' unions have been weakened because they, too, have lost clout. When workers had strong unions, the wages and benefits were enough for a middle-class lifestyle.

This phenomenon of outsourcing has three roots. First, there is the worldwide communications revolution spawned by the Internet. Second, there is a supply of qualified workers in English-speaking countries, most notably India but also the Philippines, Barbados, Jamaica, Singapore, and Ireland. And, third, these workers are willing to work for one-fifth or less the salary of comparable U.S. workers. The kinds of jobs affected by outsourcing are software engineers, accountants, architects, engineers, art designers, x-ray technicians, and airplane maintenance. In this latter instance, airlines such as JetBlue and U.S. Airways tune up their planes in El Salvador, where mechanics make $4,500 to $15,000 a year, compared to the average in the U.S. of $52,000 annually (*Business Week*, 2008). Also negatively affected are lower-level white-collar jobs such as customer service representatives, telemarketers, record transcribers, and those who make airline and hotel reservations.

The Great Recession (2007–2010 and Beyond)

The transformation and the economy and the effects of globalization have created considerable economic havoc in the past few decades. Adding to the dislocations brought about by these epochal changes is the Great Recession, which began in 2007 and continues.

- **Prelude to the Economic Crisis.** As the economy shifted away from manufacturing to services and information/knowledge, some sectors (sunset industries) of the economy faded in importance or even died. Tens of millions of jobs were lost permanently, mostly unionized jobs with good pay and benefits creating **displaced workers**. Moreover, weak unions plus the competition from low-wage economies led many U.S. corporations to reduce or eliminate their benefits (health insurance, retirement) to workers. Wages were also negatively affected.

  Thus, the transformation of the economy, at least in the short run, marginalized millions, increased unemployment, drove social mobility downward, and made many millions insecure about their jobs, health care, and retirement. To cope with these problems, employees worked more hours a week, putting in 350 more hours a year than the average European, more women worked in the labor force (70 percent, almost double the percentage in 1970), and families went deeper into debt with credit cards, car loans, college loans, and home equity loans. Families were also buying homes because home values had risen for half a century, most steeply from 1997 to 2006, when they rose by an inflation-adjusted 85 percent (Zuckerman, 2008). This price appreciation tempted many to speculate, "flipping" recently purchased houses for a quick profit. Others took advantage of easy credit to refinance by taking out second mortgages to remodel their homes or to purchase "big ticket" items such as automobiles and boats.

> *Homeowners, armed with easy credit, snapped up properties as if they were playing Monopoly. As prices soared, buyers were able to afford ever-larger properties only by taking out risky mortgages that lenders were happily approving with little documentation or money down. (Gandel and Lim 2008:90)*

Mortgage market lenders encouraged this housing "bubble." About 20 percent of home loans in 2005 were "subprime"—that is, loans sold to people with questionable credit records. These loans went disproportionately to African Americans and Latinos, many buying homes for the first time. They were offered no-money-down loans, with what appeared to be low interest rates. The "low" rates were for the first two years but then the loans increased substantially when the "variable rate" clause (found in the fine print of the loan contract) was enforced.

Add to this mix the reckless and irresponsible deal making on Wall Street, which involved an intricate, intertwined system of loan brokers, mortgage lenders, Wall Street trusts, hedge funds, offshore tax havens, and other predators (Hightower 2007; see also Moyers and Winship 2009). For example, subprime loans were bundled and sold to third parties. These "derivatives" were financial contracts between a buyer and a seller that derive value from an underlying asset, such as a mortgage or a stock. This allowed banks and insurance firms to leverage their assets by as much as 40 times the value of the underlying asset. In the case of subprime mortgages, this was "financial alchemy that turned low-quality mortgages into trillions of dollars of high-priced derivatives" (Karabell 2009:35). The government stood by without interfering with the market when it indulged in these reckless ventures. There were five financial agencies at the federal level that could have regulated these practices but did not because they assumed in accordance with a basic premise of capitalism that the financial players would police themselves (Hightower 2007).

- **The Ensuing Economic Crisis.** These forces converged in 2007, creating a "perfect storm" of economic devastation. It began when subprime borrowers began defaulting on their mortgages. That sent housing prices tumbling, unleashing a domino effect on mortgage-backed securities (Gandel and Lim 2008). Banks and brokerages that had borrowed money to increase their leverage had to raise capital quickly. Some, like Merrill Lynch and Bear Stearns, were forced to sell their assets to other banks at bargain rates (Bear Sterns was sold to JPMorgan for $236 million, down from its value of $20 billion a year earlier). Others, like Lehman Brothers, failed. The stock market dropped precipitously. Credit dried up. Business slowed, causing companies to lay off workers by the hundreds of thousands. What was happening in the United States affected markets elsewhere, causing a worldwide recession and a further slowing of business activity here and abroad. The result was the worst economic downturn in the United States since the Great Depression of the 1930s. Let's consider the contours of the crisis, beginning with unemployment. [This chapter was revised in January 2010 in the middle of the Great Recession. Thus, the reader is warned that the numbers and their magnitude will change and that what appears to be a trend may weaken in time while others strengthen.]

  Unemployment. Since the 1970s, retaining a job has become more precarious (Kalleberg 2009). This trend accelerated in the recent recession as some 7.2 million American workers lost their jobs from late 2007 to December 2009. The official government's unemployment rate jumped from 4.6 percent in mid-2007 to 10.0 percent through January 1, 2010. The rate of 10.0 percent represents 14 million people, but this underreports the actual number of unemployed, as we will see later in this chapter.

Some areas of the country experienced serious declines in housing values during the Great Recession, resulting in distress sales, foreclosures, and owners walking away from their mortgages.

Housing Woes. The value of homes grew rapidly in the new millennium, reaching a peak in 2006. By this time many homeowners were on the financial edge as they purchased overvalued houses, assuming their value would increase even more. But the housing bubble burst, causing values to decline precipitously, losing $4 trillion in value from 2005 to the end of 2008. The newly unemployed found they could not meet their monthly payments. Those who purchased subprime mortgages were especially vulnerable. By 2009 some 1.5 million homes owned mostly by African Americans were lost through subprime foreclosures. Many either walked away from their now unaffordable mortgages, or after missing payments, their mortgages were foreclosed by lenders. Many owners, who were strapped by unaffordable mortgages, now owed more on their mortgages than what their homes were worth. About 12 million mortgage holders (20 percent) owed more on their properties than what they are worth. This created a downward spiral, decreasing home values further. There were 2.8 million foreclosure filings in 2009, touching one of every 45 homes (Armour 2010). In early 2009 nearly 1 in 8 mortgage holders were either delinquent in their payments or in foreclosure. Looking forward from 2009, an estimated 6 million families could lose their homes by the end of 2012 (Mooney 2009).

Renters are not immune from the nation's housing crisis. This occurs in several ways (Armour 2008). First, when owners of apartments are foreclosed on, their renters are evicted, even though they have been paying their rents. According to the National Low Income Housing Coalition, renters make up an estimated 40 percent of families facing eviction because of foreclosure (Fireside 2009). Those who are evicted usually lose their security deposits and any prepaid rent. Second, homeowners forced into foreclosure are becoming tenants, which drives up rents. Third, the cost of renting in many areas of the country is high, as demand exceeds the supply. The median monthly rent in 2008 for 12 metropolitan areas was $1,368. Approximately one in four renters pays more than half their income on rent (rents exceeding 30 percent are considered by the government to be unaffordable). Similarly, 37 percent of homeowners with mortgages are spending 30 percent or more of their before-tax income on housing.

Financial Decline. Consider just the financial losses that occurred in 2008 (Marquart and Shinkle 2009):

- Stock market value declined by $7.3 trillion.
- The Standard & Poor's 500 lost 38.5 percent, its worst fall since 1937.
- Average loss by mutual funds: 38 percent.
- Household wealth dropped $11.1 trillion (18 percent; Bajaj 2009).
- Americans lost over $1 trillion in their 401(k)s (retirement savings). Individuals who had contributed to 401(k)s for 20 years or more lost an average of 20 percent of value, even after counting the money they had added through the years (Ridgeway 2009).
- Over an 18-month period, the investments of public pension plans—the retirement security for 22 million police officers, fire fighters, teachers, and their survivors—lost a combined $1.3 trillion (Byrnes and Palmeri 2009).
- From the start of the Great Recession to May 2009, 2.4 million workers lost health insurance they were getting through their jobs.

In sum, surveys reveal that more than 24 million Americans shifted in 2008 from lives that were "thriving" to ones that were "struggling" (Page 2009).

Personal Bankruptcies. The current economic crisis with rising unemployment, plummeting home values, staggering stock market losses, and increased indebtedness have added to these usual reasons for bankruptcy (medical catastrophe, financial missteps, and divorce). In 2007 there were 801,269 bankruptcies; in 2008 there were 1,042,806, and in 2009 there were 1,402,816 (Baker 2009; Brown 2010). In 2009 a record number of consumers (4.2 percent) were falling delinquent or into default on their loans, meaning that they were only a step or two away from bankruptcy.

A major source of bankruptcy is the inability to pay for catastrophic health care needs. Employers have increasingly cut back on their contribution to health insurance, either dropping coverage altogether, or by decreasing their obligation to provide health insurance, including introducing high-deductible health insurance. Of course, those who lose jobs also lose their health insurance. Because the cost of health care is so expensive (e.g., a heart by-pass costs $200,000; a premature baby close to $1 million), the uninsured are just a catastrophic illness or accident away from economic ruin. The Public Broadcasting System reported that 700,000 go bankrupt each year because of medical bills (PBS, *Frontline* 2009).

Downward Social Mobility. The "American dream," is the belief that in this land of opportunity anyone can succeed with hard work (McNamee and Miller 2009). Through the 1950s and 1960s, this dream was realized by increasingly more Americans as average real wages (i.e., wages adjusted for inflation) and family incomes expanded and the economy created new jobs and opportunities. The result was that many Americans after World War II were able to move up into a growing and vibrant middle class. This trend peaked in 1973, and since then families have tended to either stagnate or decline in their level of affluence. The transformation of the economy, fueled by globalization, had the effect of shrinking the middle class as the gap between the "haves" and the "have-nots" increased. This trend downward accelerated with "The Great Recession," which began in 2007, with unemployment rates climbing dramatically, personal debt rising, and the housing bubble bursting. All this while the costs for health care, college, consumer goods, and transportation continued to rise. The result: many middle-class families plunged in income and resources, thus moving down in social class. Some declared bankruptcy. Some were forced from their homes and had to relocate. Some families became poor, hungry, and even homeless.

Hunger. The poorest among us are suffering the harshest effects of the economic decline. Already on the economic margins, they have been pushed down even further. The welfare "safety net," which has eroded since 1980, was cut further by the welfare reform of 1996, which ended the idea of welfare as an entitlement.

> *Despite soaring unemployment and the worst economic crisis in decades, 18 states cut their welfare rolls last year, and nationally the number of people receiving cash assistance remained at or near the lowest in more than 40 years. (DeParle 2009:para 1)*

Some facts about hunger amid the economic crisis:

- From July 2008 to July 2009, the number of people receiving food stamps increased from 29.2 million to 35.9 million (U.S. Department of Agriculture, reported in *USA Today* 2009).

- One in eight Americans (37.0 million, including 14 million children) received emergency food assistance in 2009. This was an increase of 46 percent over 2006.
- The demand at food banks across the country increased by 30 percent in 2008 from the previous year (Bosman 2009).
- By early 2009 some 16.5 million children received free school lunches, up 6.5 percent from the previous year. Another 3.2 million students received reduced-priced lunches.

This surge in the hungry in the United States indicates the struggle by the new poor to cope with their desperate situations.

> *The message is simple. Ever more Americans need food they can't afford. As tough economic times take their toll, increasing numbers of Americans are on tightened budgets and, in some cases, facing outright hunger. As a result, they may be learning a lot more about food banks and soup kitchens than most of them ever wanted to know. . . . Families who just months ago didn't even know what a food bank was and would never have considered visiting a food pantry now have far more intimate knowledge of both. . . . Other formerly middle class Americans who have never dealt with, or even thought about, food insecurity before simply don't know whom to call or where to turn. (Turse 2009: para 1, 4)*

The New Homeless. The extent of homelessness is difficult to know because those without a permanent home may be doubling up with relatives, sleeping in vehicles, and the like, not just in shelters. Thus the numbers of the homeless understate the actual count. Given that caveat, the official number of homeless prior to the Great Recession was about 1 in 400 Americans (750,000) without a home on any given night, and about 1.6 million experienced homelessness at some point in a given year. Around 40 percent of the homeless population was families, typically a single mother and her children.

During the Great Recession millions more Americans were at greater risk of becoming homeless. Some 9.6 million families were spending more than half their income on housing. Foreclosures brought evictions, even for renters when their apartment buildings were foreclosed. The newly unemployed could not make their mortgage payments or their rents. Costly medical care put some in bankruptcy. As a result, according to the National Alliance to End Homelessness, as many as 3.4 million Americans were assumed to be homeless in 2009—a 35 percent increase since the recession started in December 2007 (Vestal 2009). Unlike the traditional homeless composed mostly of the long-time poor and near poor, the new homeless included the "working poor, who were among the hardest hit by the collapse in subprime mortgages. But others are middle-class families who scarcely expected to find themselves unable to afford homes" (Armour 2008:2B).

WORK AND SOCIAL PROBLEMS

Work is central to the human experience. People everywhere engage in physical and mental activities that enhance the physical and social survival of themselves and others. Societies are organized to allocate work to produce the goods and services needed by the society and its members for sustenance, clothing, shelter, security, and even luxury. Work provides individuals and their families with their social identity, economic resources, and social location. Work dominates their time and is a primary source of life's meaning because it constitutes their contributions to other people.

The world of work also has a dark side, however. The structure of work is a major source of social problems. Work is alienating for many people. The organization of work sometimes exploits, does harm to workers, and often dehumanizes them. The distribution of work and how it is rewarded are major sources of inequality in society. This section focuses on these social problems generated by the social organization of work.

Control of Workers

With the advent of the Industrial Revolution, more and more families left agrarian life, moved to cities, and worked in factories. Work in these factories was sometimes difficult, sometimes dangerous, often tedious, and usually boring. There was always the threat of lowered productivity and worker unrest under these adverse conditions. The factory owners and their managers used several tactics to counteract these potential problems and especially to maintain high productivity—scientific management, hierarchical control, technical control, and extortion.

Scientific management (also called *Taylorization,* after its founder, Frederick Taylor) came to the fore in U.S. industry around 1900. The emphasis was on breaking down work into very specialized tasks, the standardization of tools and procedures, and the speeding up of repetitive work. These efforts to increase worker efficiency and therefore to increase profits meant that workers developed a very limited range of skills. Instead of a wide knowledge of building cars or furniture, their knowledge was severely curtailed. This specialization had the effect of making the workers highly susceptible to automation and to being easily replaced by cheaper workers. But this scientific management approach also had a contradictory effect. In its attempt to increase efficiency by having workers do ever more compartmentalized tasks, it increased the repetition, boredom, and meaninglessness of work—hence, the strong tendency for workers to become alienated and restless. Consider the description by George Ritzer:

> *[The assembly line clearly] offers a dehumanizing setting in which to work. Human beings, equipped with a wide array of skills and abilities, are asked to perform a limited number of highly simplified tasks over and over. Instead of expressing their human abilities on the job, people are forced to deny their humanity and act like robots. (Ritzer 2000:32)*

Closely related to scientific management is the use of bureaucracy to control workers. Work settings, whether in factories, universities, offices, or corporations, are organized into bureaucratized hierarchies. In this hierarchy of authority (chain of command), each position in the chain gives orders to those below, taking responsibility for their actions and following orders from above. The hierarchical arrangement controls workers by holding out the possibility of advancement, with more prestigious job titles, higher wages, and greater benefits as one moves up the ladder. Those who hope to be upwardly mobile in the organization must become obedient rule followers who do not question authority.

Similarly, "the assembly line is also a nonhuman technology that permits maximum control over workers. It is immediately obvious when a worker fails to perform the required tasks" (Ritzer 2000:31).

Workers are also controlled by management's use of technology to monitor and supervise them. Some businesses use lie detectors to assess worker loyalty. Psychological tests and drug tests (80 percent of major companies require employees to undergo urine tests for drugs) are used to screen applicants for work. E-mail and use of the Internet are monitored. Telephone taps have been used to determine whether workers use company time for personal use. Closed-circuit television, two-way mirrors, and other devices have been used by management to determine whether workers are using their time most productively. The most common contemporary technology for worker control is the computer. The computer can count keystrokes, time phone calls, monitor frequency of errors, assess overall employee performance, and even issue warnings when the employee falls short of the ideal.

A final management tool to control workers is extortion. If workers become too militant in their demands for higher wages, safe working conditions, or benefits, management can threaten them with reprisals. In the past, owners threatened to hire cheaper labor (new immigrants, for example) or to use force to end a strike. Today, the most common and successful management tool is the threat to move the plant to a nonunion state or even outside the United States if the union does not reduce its demands or to replace the workers with robots or other forms of automation.

Alienation

Alienation is the separation of human beings from each other, from themselves, and from the products they create. In capitalism, according to Karl Marx, worker alienation occurs because the workers do not have any control over their labor, because they are manipulated by managers, because they tend to work in large, impersonal settings, and because they work at specialized tasks. Martin Nicolaus, in his foreward to Karl Marx's *Grundrisisse*, summarizes Marx on alienation: "With the advance of the division of labor and the growing scale of capitalist production, the role of the worker in the industrial process has a tendency to be transformed from active to passive, from master to cog, and even from participant to observer, as the system of machinery becomes more automatic" (Nicolaus 1973:51). Under these circumstances, workers use only a fraction of their talents and have no pride in their own creativity and in the final product. Thus, we see that worker alienation is linked with unfulfilled personal satisfaction. As Blauner has described it,

> *Alienation exists when workers are unable to control their immediate work processes, to develop a sense of purpose and function which connects their jobs to the overall organization of production, to belong to integrated industrial communities, and when they fail to become involved in the activity of work as a mode of personal self-expression. (Blauner 1964:5)*

Put another way, this time by philosopher Albert Camus, "Without work all life goes rotten. But when work is soulless, life stifles and dies" (quoted in Levitan and Johnson 1982:63).

In the absence of satisfaction and personal fulfillment, work becomes meaningless. When this meaninglessness is coupled with management's efforts to control workers, the repetitious nature of the work, and the requirement of punching a time clock, many workers feel a profound resentment. This resentment may lead workers to join together in a union or other collective group to improve their working conditions. For many workers, though, the alienation remains at a personal level and is manifested by higher worker dissatisfaction, absenteeism, disruption in the workplace, and alcohol or other drug abuse on the job.

Alienation is not limited to manual workers. The work of white-collar workers such as sales clerks, secretaries, file clerks, bank tellers, and data entry clerks is mostly routine, repetitive, boring, and unchallenging. These workers, like assembly line workers, follow orders, do limited tasks, and have little sense of accomplishment.

Studs Terkel, in introducing his book *Working*, summarizes the personal impact of alienating work:

> *This book, being about work, is, by its very nature, about violence—to the spirit as well as to the body. It is about ulcers as well as accidents, about shouting matches as well as fistfights, about nervous breakdowns as well as kicking the dog around. It is, above all (or beneath all), about daily humiliations. To survive the day is triumph enough for the walking wounded among the great many of us.*
>
> *It is about a search, too, for daily meaning as well as daily bread, for recognition as well as for cash, for astonishment rather than torpor; in short, for a sort of life rather than a Monday through Friday sort of dying. Perhaps immortality, too, is part of the quest. To be remembered was the wish, spoken and unspoken, of the heroes and heroines of this book.*
>
> *For the many, there is a hardly concealed discontent. The blue-collar blues is no more bitterly sung than the white-collar moan. "I'm a machine," says the spotwelder. "I'm caged," says the steelworker. "A monkey can do what I do," says the receptionist. "I'm less than a farm implement," says the migrant worker. "I'm an object," says the high-fashion model. Blue collar and white call upon the identical phrase: "I'm a robot." (Terkel 1975:xiii–xiv)*

Dangerous Working Conditions

In a capitalist economy, workers represent a cost to profit-seeking corporations. The lower management can keep labor costs down, the greater its profits. Historically, low labor costs meant that workers received low wages, had inferior or nonexistent fringe benefits such as health care and pensions, and worked in unhealthy conditions. Mines and factories were often extremely unsafe. The labor movement early in the 1900s gathered momentum because of the abuse experienced by workers.

After a long and sometimes violent struggle, the unions were successful in raising wages for workers, adding fringe benefits, and making the conditions of work safer. But the owners were slow to change; and worker safety was, and continues to be, one of the most difficult areas. Many owners of mills, mines, and factories continue to consider the safety of their workers a low-priority item, presumably because of the high cost.

About 30 years ago, the federal government instituted the Occupational Safety and Health Administration (OSHA) to make the workplace safer. However, OSHA's resources are inadequate to meet the challenge of ensuring safe working conditions for workers.

> *There is currently one OSHA inspector for every 66,258 workers, according to [a report by the AFL-CIO]. At these staffing and inspection levels it would take federal OSHA 137 years to inspect each workplace under its jurisdiction just once. . . . (Wedekind 2009:7)*

Around 6,000 workers are killed every year on the job, and 4.5 million are injured.

> *Another 10,000 die later on from job injuries and 50,000 from occupational diseases caused by things as chemicals, asbestos, pesticides, and solvents. Some 50,000 to 60,000 sustain permanent disability, and millions more suffer from work-related illnesses. (Parenti 2008:99)*

Minorities, especially Latinos, have the highest work-related death rates. From 1992 to 2007, the number of Latino worker deaths increased by 76 percent (Jervis 2009). The reason for the higher Latino rate is the influx of Latino immigrants who took the dangerous and hard-to-fill jobs in construction, meatpacking plants, and as farm laborers. Undocumented workers often are exploited because if they complain they will be deported. They usually do not join unions, which help protect workers, and they do not protest when conditions are dangerous. See Figure 14.1 for Latino fatal work injuries and the "A Closer Look" panel on the dangers in meatpacking factories, where recent immigrants are overrepresented.

Significant occupational dangers continue to plague workers, especially those in certain jobs, such as loggers, fishers, structural iron and steel workers, refuse collectors, roofers, electrical power line installers and repairers, miners, and farmers. In addition to falls, fires and explosions, cave-ins, violent weather,

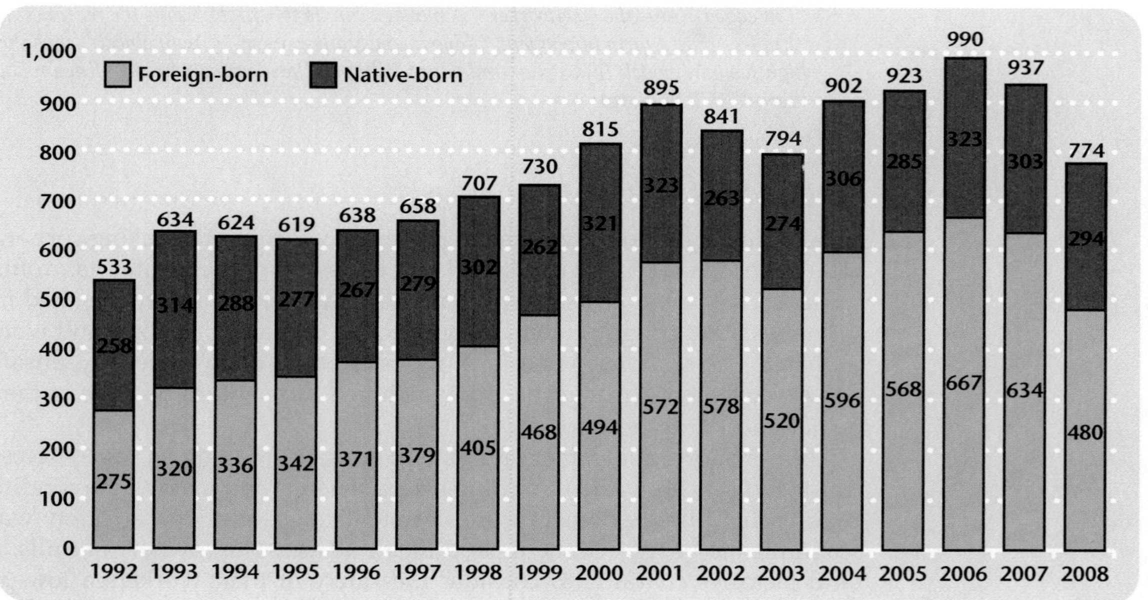

FIGURE 14.1

Number of Fatal Work Injuries Involving Hispanic or Latino Workers, 1992–2008*

Fatal work injuries involving Hispanic or Latino workers continues to decrease in 2008 after reaching a series high in 2006. About three-fifths of fatally injured Hispanic or Latino workers in 2008 were born outside the United States.

*Data for 2008 are preliminary. Data for prior years are revised and final.

Note: Data from 2001 exclude fatalities resulting from the September 11 terrorist attacks.

Source: U.S. Bureau of Labor Statistics, Census of Fatal Occupational Injuries, U.S. Department of Labor, 2009.

A CLOSER LOOK

THE MOST DANGEROUS JOB IN THE UNITED STATES

In 1906, Upton Sinclair published *The Jungle,* an exposé of the meatpacking industry in the United States. In addition to the widespread contamination of meat, Sinclair noted the mistreatment of meatpacking workers, mostly Eastern European immigrants, employed at dangerous, dirty, low-wage jobs. In time, the industry was unionized, and by the 1950s, meatpacking workers had one of the highest-paid manufacturing jobs. But by the 1970s, the industry had changed. Big companies bought out smaller ones. The plants moved from urban areas such as Chicago and Kansas City, where unions were strong, to rural areas such as Arkansas, North Carolina, Texas, Colorado, Kansas, Nebraska, and Iowa, where unions were weak. Employees were mostly recent immigrants from Mexico.

> In some American slaughterhouses, more than three-quarters of the workers are not native English speakers; many can't read any language, and many are illegal immigrants. . . . A wage of $9.50 an hour seems incredible to men and women who come from rural areas in Mexico where the wages are $7 a day. These manual laborers, long accustomed to toiling in the fields, are good workers. They're also unlikely to complain or challenge authority, to file lawsuits, organize unions, fight for their legal rights. They tend to be poor, vulnerable, and fearful. From the industry's point of view, they are ideal workers: cheap, largely interchangeable, and disposable. (Schlosser 2001: para 9)

Just as Sinclair noted a century ago, the workers in the slaughterhouse once again had one of the lowest-paid manufacturing jobs and one of the most dangerous (Schlosser 2006).

According to data from the U.S. Department of Labor, nearly one in three slaughterhouse workers suffers from illness or injury every year, compared to one in ten workers in other manufacturing jobs. The rate of repetitive motion injury (carpal tunnel syndrome) for slaughterhouse employees is thirty-five times higher than it is for those with other manufacturing jobs (Schlosser 2001). Typical injuries are falling on slippery floors, being cut, and asphyxiation from fumes (Human Rights Watch report, cited in Greenhouse 2005).

> Many cows and pigs are still completely conscious when they are hung up by their hind legs and their throats are slit, and they kick, thrash, defecate, and vomit as they die. Killing animals who do not want to die is inherently dangerous work, but the ever-increasing line speeds, repetitive motions, filthy working conditions, and other hazards mean that employees are putting their lives on the line every time they clock into work. (GoVeg.com, n.d.)

Moreover, the meatpacking companies violated human and labor rights by suppressing their employees' efforts to organize a union. In this regard, the U.S. Court of Appeals in 2006 upheld a ruling by the National Labor Relations Board that the Smithfield Packing Company, between 1992 and 1998, had violated a number of labor laws and created an atmosphere of intimidation and coercion to prevent workers from joining the United Food and Commercial Workers (UFCW) union (Scholosser 2006).

and equipment malfunctions, there are also dangers from invisible contaminants such as nuclear radiation, chemical compounds, coal tars, dust, and asbestos fibers in the air. These dangers from invisible contaminants are increasing because the production of synthetic chemicals has increased so dramatically.

This discussion raises some critical questions: Should profits supersede human life? Are owners guilty of murder if their decisions to minimize plant safety result in industrial deaths? Who is a greater threat, the thug in the streets or the executives in the suites? Jeffrey Reiman answers these questions:

> *Is a person who kills another in a bar brawl a greater threat to society than a business executive who refuses to cut into his profits to make his plant a safe place to work? By*

any measure of death and suffering, the latter is by far a greater danger than the former. Because he wishes his workers no harm, because he is only indirectly responsible for death and disability while pursuing legitimate economic goals, his acts are not called "crimes." Once we free our imagination from the blinders of the one-on-one model of crime, can there be any doubt that the criminal justice system does not protect us from the gravest threats to life and limb? It seeks to protect us when danger comes from a young lower-class male in the inner city. When a threat comes from an upper-class business executive in an office, the criminal justice system looks the other way. This is in the face of growing evidence that for every two American citizens murdered by thugs, more than three American workers are killed by the recklessness of their bosses and the indifference of their government. (Reiman 2007:87)

Sweatshops

A **sweatshop** is a substandard work environment where workers are paid less than the minimum wage and are not paid overtime premiums, and where other labor laws are violated. Although sweatshops occur in various types of manufacturing, domestically they occur most frequently in the garment industry. Garment sweatshops are common in New York City, San Francisco, Los Angeles, El Paso, and Seattle. The workers in these places make clothes for such brands as Levi Strauss, Esprit, Casual Corner, the Limited, and the Gap and for such merchandisers as J. C. Penney, Sears, and Wal-Mart. The workers, mostly Latina and Asian immigrant women, are paid much less than the minimum wage, receive no benefits, and work in crowded, unsafe, and stifling conditions.

Modern day slavery exists in the United States. The Central Intelligence Agency estimates that "50,000 people are trafficked into or transited through the United States annually as sex slaves, domestic servants, garment slaves and agricultural laborers" (quoted in Kralis 2006, para 2).

U.S. corporations also sell products produced by workers, many of whom are children, working in sweatshop conditions in other countries. "Every time you buy an imported handmade carpet, an embroidered pair of jeans, a beaded purse, a decorated box or a soccer ball there's a good chance you're acquiring something fashioned by a child" (Bahree 2008:75). Mattel makes tens of millions of Barbies a year in China. Many of Disney's products are made in Sri Lanka and Haiti, countries notorious for the lack of labor and human rights regulations. Nike, Reebok, and other shoe and apparel manufacturers have exploited workers in many Asian countries.

Unions and Their Decline

Historically, labor unions have been extremely important in changing management–labor relations. Joining together, workers challenged owners to increase wages, add benefits, provide worker security, and promote safety in the workplace. Through the use of strikes, work slowdowns, public relations, and political lobbying, working conditions improved, and union members, for the most part, prospered. In wages and benefits, union workers earn about more than nonunion workers. Consider the following differences between union workers and unorganized workers in comparable jobs:

- The median earnings of full-time wage and salary workers in 2009 were $908 per week for union workers, compared with $710 for employees not represented by unions (Bureau of Labor Statistics, reported in Hananel 2010).

- Union members are 59 percent more likely to have employer-provided health insurance than their nonunion counterparts (Reich 2009).
- Women union members earn 33 percent more than women nonunion workers.
- African American union members earn 35 percent more than African American nonunion workers.
- Latino union members earn 51 percent more than Latino nonunion workers (A. Levin 2004).

But unions have lost their power since about 1980, as membership declined from a high of about 35 percent of wage and salary workers in the mid-1950s to 12.3 percent in 2009. With such small and dwindling numbers, labor unions are in danger of becoming irrelevant. The reasons for the decline in union membership (and clout) are several. First, there was a direct assault against unions by Republican presidents Reagan, George H. W. Bush, and George W. Bush. Each of these administrations was unsympathetic with strikes and sometimes used federal leverage to weaken them. Similarly, their appointees to the post of Secretary of Labor and the National Labor Relations Board (NLRB) were probusiness rather than prolabor.

Second, public opinion has turned against unions because some of them are undemocratic, scandal ridden, and too zealous in their demands. Public opinion has also turned against organized labor because of a probusiness, procapitalist bias that increased during the era of supply-side economics that dominated the Reagan and the George H. W. Bush administrations and much of Congress during that time. That bias, although muted a bit, continued during the Clinton administration but was resurrected during George W. Bush's administration.

Third, businesses do all they can to block unions. Typically, companies are required to have a union vote if 30 percent of workers sign a petition. When such an election does occur, companies have won more than half the time, versus 28 percent in the early 1950s. The antiunion vote by workers is the result usually of an all-out assault by the company, including information arguing that unionization may lead to downsizing or even closing plants, "worker appreciation" days with free barbecues or pizza, the selective firing of workers who are union activists (an illegal activity, but it happens in about one-fourth of the union drives, according to a commission study established by President Clinton), and other forms of intimidation. Wal-Mart, for example, "has been formally cited more than 40 times in the past five years for using illegal tactics to deny its workers the right to join a union" (Hightower 2003a:1). The 2010 Supreme Court decision to allow corporations to spend unlimited amounts for or against a political candidate likely will have disastrous consequences for unions because business is so anti-union. Corporations will support anti-union candidates while working to defeat pro-union candidates. After a few election cycles, very few pro-union legislators at the state and federal levels will remain in office.

A major reason for the decline of union strength is the transformation of the economy. Manufacturing jobs, which are in decline, have historically been pro-union, whereas service jobs, which are increasing, have been typically nonunionized. Similarly, the advent of computers, modems, and fax machines has increased the number of people who work at home as temporary and part-time workers. These workers are the least likely to join unions.

And, finally, some corporations have moved their operations to nonunion states. Automobile manufacturers, for example, have bypassed the industrial (and heavily unionized) North and have opened assembly plants in the South, where there is an anti-union climate. Nissan became the first foreign car maker in the South (in Tennessee and later in Mississippi), followed by Toyota (Kentucky, Texas, and Alabama), Honda, Mercedes-Benz, and Hyundai (Alabama), and BMW (South Carolina). Now the aircraft industry is involved in a similar migration with Boeing building an assembly line in South Carolina for its 787 Dreamliner jet.

These forces have given the strong advantage to management. This trend has several negative consequences. First, faced with the threat of plants closing or moving to nonunion localities or to low-wage nations, unions have chosen, typically, to give back many of the gains they made during the 1960s and 1970s. Thus, workers have lost real wages and benefits. A second consequence of union decline is that the workplace may be less safe: some of the most injury-prone industries, like cattle, pig, chicken, turkey, and catfish processing and textiles, have clustered in right-to-work (i.e., nonunion) states across the South.

A major consequence of union decline is the further dwindling of the middle class. In the words of the late Albert Shanker, president of the American Federation of Teachers,

> *[T]he union movement took a lot of workers who were relatively unskilled and turned them into middle-class people who educated their children and supported the United States economy. Now, we've got businesses turning their employees into third-world workers. (Shanker 1992b:E9)*

Implied in this statement is a related consequence: If businesses turn their employees into third-world workers, then they will not be able to purchase enough goods and services to encourage economic growth and societywide prosperity.

Those nations with strong unionized labor (e.g., Canada, Germany, and Sweden) have a social democratic conception of society, which means universal health care, progressive income taxes, and more equitable government programs.

Discrimination in the Workplace: Perpetuation of Inequality

Women and minorities have long been the objects of discrimination in U.S. industry. Currently (and we have progressed mightily), approximately 50,000 charges of discrimination by organizations are filed annually with the Equal Employment Opportunity Commission. The charges now and in the past have centered on hiring policies, seniority rights, restricted job placement, limited opportunities for advancement, and lower pay for equal work. A number of court suits (and those settled out of court) illustrate that discriminatory policies have been common among such major corporations as AT&T, General Motors, and Northwest Airlines and in such industries as banking and steel.

Two mechanisms operating in the U.S. economy perpetuate inequalities in the job market by social class, race, and gender—the segmented labor market and male dominance.

- **Segmented Labor Market.** The capitalist economy is divided into two separate sectors that have different characteristics, different roles, and different rewards for laborers within each. This organization of the economy is called the **segmented labor market**, or the **dual labor market**. The primary sector is composed of large, bureaucratic organizations with relatively stable production and sales. Jobs within this sector require developed skills, are relatively well paid, occur in good working conditions, and are stable. Within this sector there are two types of jobs. The first type, those in the upper tier, are high-status professional and managerial jobs. The pay is very good for the highly educated people in these jobs. They have a high degree of personal autonomy, and the jobs offer variety, creativity, and initiative. Upward mobility is likely for those who are successful. The second type, the lower-tier jobs within the primary sector, are held by working-class people. The jobs are either white-collar clerical or blue-collar skilled and semiskilled. The jobs are repetitive, and mobility is limited. The jobs are relatively secure because of unionization, although they are much more vulnerable than those in the upper tier. When times are difficult, these workers tend to be laid off rather than terminated.

The secondary economic sector is composed of marginal firms in which product demand is unstable. Jobs within this sector are characterized by poor working conditions, low wages, few opportunities for advancement, and little job security. Little education or skill is required to perform these tasks. Workers beginning in the secondary sector tend to get locked in because they lack the skills required in the primary sector, and they usually have unstable work histories. A common interpretation of this problem is that secondary-sector workers are in these dead-end jobs because of their pathology—poor work history, lack of skills, and lack of motivation. Such an explanation, however, blames the victim. Poor work histories tend to be the result of unemployment caused by the production of marginal products and the lack of job security. Similarly, these workers have few, if any, incentives to learn new skills or to stay for long periods with an employer because of the structural barriers to upward mobility. And unlike workers in the primary sector, workers in the secondary sector are more likely to experience harsh and capricious work discipline from supervisors, primarily because there are no unions.

The significance of this dual labor market is threefold. First, placement in one of these segments corresponds with social class, which tends to be perpetuated from generation to generation. Second, employment in the secondary sector is often so inadequately paid that many full-time workers live in poverty, as noted in Chapter 7. And third, the existence of a dual labor market reinforces racial, ethnic, and gender divisions in the labor force. White males, although found in both segments, are overrepresented in the upper tier of the primary sector. White females and White ethnics tend to be clerks in the lower tier of the primary sector. Males and females of color are found disproportionately in the secondary sector. These findings explain why unemployment rates for African Americans and Latinos are consistently much higher than the rate for Whites (usually at least double). They explain the persistent wage differences found by race and gender. That is why there is a vast overrepresentation of people of color and women living in poverty. These facts are especially relevant as the workforce is increasingly composed of racial and ethnic minorities, most notably Latinos.

- **Male Dominance at Work.** Closely tied to segmented labor markets is the dominance of men in work-related roles. This dominance is reflected in two ways—males tend to make the rules and enforce them, and males receive unequal (i.e., greater) rewards.

Current gender inequality results from a long history of patriarchal social relations in which men have consciously kept women in subordinate roles at work and in the home. Men as workers consistently have acted in their own interests to retain power and to keep women either out of their occupations or in subordinate and poorly paid work roles. Historically, through their unions, males insisted that the higher-status and better-paying jobs be exclusively male. They lobbied legislatures to pass legislation supportive of male exclusiveness in occupations and in opposition to such equalization measures as minimum wages for women. Also, the male unions prevented women from gaining the skills that would lead them to equal-paying jobs. The National Typographical Union in 1854, for example, insisted not only that women be refused jobs as compositors but also that they not be taught the skills necessary to be a compositor (Hartmann 1976).

Throughout U.S. history, business owners have used gender inequality in the workplace to their advantage. Women were hired because they would work for less money than men, which made men all the more fearful of women in the workplace. Capitalists even used the threat of hiring lower-paid women to take the place of higher-paid men to keep the wages of both sexes down and to lessen labor militancy.

In contemporary U.S. society, men and women, with some exceptions, are accorded different, and unequal, positions in religious, government, school, work, and family activities. Looking only at work, women and men do different work both in the family and in the labor force. This division of labor between the sexes preserves the differential power, privilege, and prestige of men (see Chapter 9). Men are overrepresented in administrative and supervisory roles. Women are found disproportionately in jobs where they follow orders. Women are found, as just noted, more often than men in the secondary job market, where jobs are menial, poorly paid, and with little or no benefits. Take the pay differential, for example. Women's pay lags behind men's in virtually every sector of the economy. In 2008, full-time female workers made 77 cents for every dollar earned by their male counterparts.

Job Insecurity

A generation ago, workers had realistic hope of lifetime employment with the same employer. That is no longer the case. Corporate America has been downsizing for over 30 years, replacing workers with automation or with workers outside the United States. Mergers have brought more downsizing. When SBC merged with AT&T in 2005, for example, 13,000 jobs were eliminated. Those who kept their jobs found that their wages had stagnated and that their employers often had reduced their benefits. Downsized workers, if they find work, will more than likely work for lower wages than previously (Bureau of Labor Statistics, reported in Renteman 2004).

The Bureau of Labor Statistics supplies the official unemployment statistics. The official unemployment rate in the United States since 2000 has ranged from a low of 3.9 percent in October 2000 to a high of 10.2 percent in late 2009. Early in 2010 the rate was 10 percent (15.4 million unemployed people). The official unemployment rate is misleading, however, because it understates, dramatically, the actual magnitude of unemployment. The unemployment rate does not include those discouraged persons who have stopped looking for jobs, within the past 4 weeks. If these **discouraged workers** were added to the official unemployment rate of 10 percent, it would add 2.3 million people. The official rate also does not include those part-time workers who would prefer to work full time,

Used with permission of Grimmy, Inc. and the Cartoonist Group.

adding another 9.2 million. If both of these categories are included, the actual rate of unemployment/underemployment would be 17.2 percent (Rugaber 2009). The official data of the government, by undercounting joblessness, diminish the perceived severity of unemployment and therefore reduce the zeal to do anything about the problem.

Unemployment is commonly believed to be functional (i.e., have positive consequences) for society by reducing inflationary pressures. It is also kept relatively high by capitalists because high unemployment deflates wages and therefore increases profits. When there are unemployed people willing to work, workers will not make inordinate demands for higher wages for fear that they will be replaced by cheaper labor. Thus, even unionized labor becomes relatively docile when unemployment is high. Fred Magdoff and Harry Magdoff summarize the capitalist argument:

> *One of the central features of capitalism is the oversupply of labor, a large mass of people that enter and leave the labor force according to the needs of capital. During an upswing in the business cycle, additional labor is necessary to utilize a business's full capacity. As sales slacken during a recession, workers no longer needed are then dismissed. The reserve army of labor—with brief and very unusual exceptions—is always present. . . .*
>
> *When considering the surplus of workers in the reserve army of labor, it is important constantly to keep in mind two points. First, there is not an absolute surplus population, but rather a surplus in the context of a society ruled by the profit motive and the golden rule of accumulation for the sake of accumulation. Second, there would be no surplus of labor if everyone had enough to eat, a decent place to live, health care, and education, and workers had shorter work hours and longer vacations so they could have more leisure and creative time. (Magdoff and Magdoff 2004:20–21)*

Unemployment affects some groups more than others. This **reserve army of the unemployed** (unemployed people who want to work) is disproportionately composed of people of color (Latinos, African Americans, Native Americans), teenagers, and residents in declining cities. Typically, the official unemployment rate for African Americans is at least twice as high as the rate for Whites. These proportions by race tend to be relatively constant, whether the overall unemployment rate is high or low, whether the economy is in a boom or a slump. Thus, the labor market assigns people of color disproportionately not only to the low-paying jobs but also to jobs that are the most unstable, precisely the situation of the secondary sector in the segmented labor market.

An important consequence of the reserve army of the unemployed being composed primarily of racial minorities is that it inflames racial antipathies against them by people who hold unstable jobs. These job holders perceive their

© Harley Schwardron.

enemy as the people below them (commonly, recent immigrants), who will work for lower wages, rather than as the capitalists who oppose full employment and adequate wages for all people.

There are clear demographic reasons for the shortage of jobs now and for the near future. In the past 30 years or so, an unusually large number of women entered the labor force, motivated by the necessity of supplementing family income and the need for self-fulfillment in nontraditional roles. About seven in ten married women with children work outside the home. The other demographic force behind unemployment pressures was the very large numbers of young people entering the job market during the 1970s. The baby-boom generation—those 10 million more babies born between 1946 and 1956 than in the previous 10 years—reached the job-seeking stage in the 1970s. These baby boomers increased the pressure for jobs and depressed the wages of people with jobs. The immense burden they put on jobs, wages, and promotions will affect jobs not only for those preceding them but also most notably for those following them. In the 1970s, an astonishing 21 million new jobs were created. But because of the unprecedented number of women and young people entering the job market, the labor force grew by more than 24 million, leaving a shortfall of 3 million jobs.

But as important as these demographic trends are in explaining the unemployment problem, they are relatively minor when compared with the effects of the structural transformation and globalization that are occurring in the U.S. economy.

Benefits Insecurity

With relatively weak unions and competition from low-wage economies, U.S. corporations have been reducing their benefits to workers. Some corporations have even declared bankruptcy to renege on benefits promised to their workers (e.g., United Airlines, Delta Airlines, Northwest Airlines, and Delphi Corporation, the largest U.S. auto parts maker). The following examples are from Barlett and Steele 2005; Gosselin 2005; and Krim and Witte 2005:

- From 1988 to 2004, the share of employers with 200 or more workers offering retiree health insurance dropped from 66 percent to 36 percent.

- The number of defined-benefit pension plans (those guaranteeing a fixed income for life) from employees plunged from 112,200 in 1985 to 29,700 in 2004.
- There were 5 million fewer jobs providing health insurance in 2004 than there were in 2001.
- Those companies that do provide health insurance are requiring their employees to pay a bigger proportion of it. Employee contributions for family coverage were 49 percent higher in 2004 than they were in 2001, and contributions for individual coverage were 57 percent higher.

In effect, then, corporations are shifting the risks of old age and ill health off the corporate ledger and onto the worker (Hacker 2006).

Increased Workload

Americans work more hours per week than in any other country in the advanced industrialized world. In 2004, Americans worked 1,824 hours annually, over 300 to 500 hours more than Western Europeans (Mishel, Bernstein, and Allegretto 2007). The trend for working more is up: "The average American worker has added 199 hours to a year's work since 1973" (Dobbs 2003:58). Following are some additional facts:

- Forty percent of workers work more than 50 hours a week (Robinson 2006).
- Five percent (7.5 million) of the working population have more than one job.
- One-fourth of U.S. workers do not take vacations (Ames 2006).

There are several possible reasons for U.S. workers increasing their workload. First, as noted in Chapter 2, the gap between the haves and the have-nots is widening, and this disparity creates incentives for employees to work harder. Second, the widening inequality gap results in relatively lower wages and net worth for the less-than-affluent, which, with the increased cost of housing and automobiles, makes working more a necessity. The third reason for the increased workload, and one articulated by labor unions, is that many businesses require their workers to work more to reduce the costs of adding more workers and their benefits.

Worker Compensation

Average wages, taking into account inflation, have not caught up with the level reached in 1973. Economist Paul Krugman puts it this way:

> *The stagnation of real wages—wages adjusted for inflation—actually goes back more than 30 years. The real wage of nonsupervisory workers reached a peak in the early 1970s, at the end of the postwar boom. Since then workers have sometimes gained ground, sometimes lost, but they have never earned as much per hour as they did in 1973. (Krugman, 2006a: para 3)*

More specifically "The income of a man in his 30s is now 12 percent below that of a man his age three decades ago" (Reich 2008, para 6). Moreover, in this time of stagnant or declining wages, the cost for health care and college tuition have skyrocketed.

Ironically, wages declined during this prolonged period while worker productivity (i.e., output per hour worked) actually rose. This lag is a consequence,

FIGURE 14.2
Manufacturing Increases and Employment Decreases: Output and Profits Between 2000 and 2005 in Constant 2000 Dollars*

*Data from U.S. Census Bureau, *Statistical Abstract of the United States: 2007* (126th Edition), Washington, DC, 2006. Reprinted from Goldstein 2008:99.

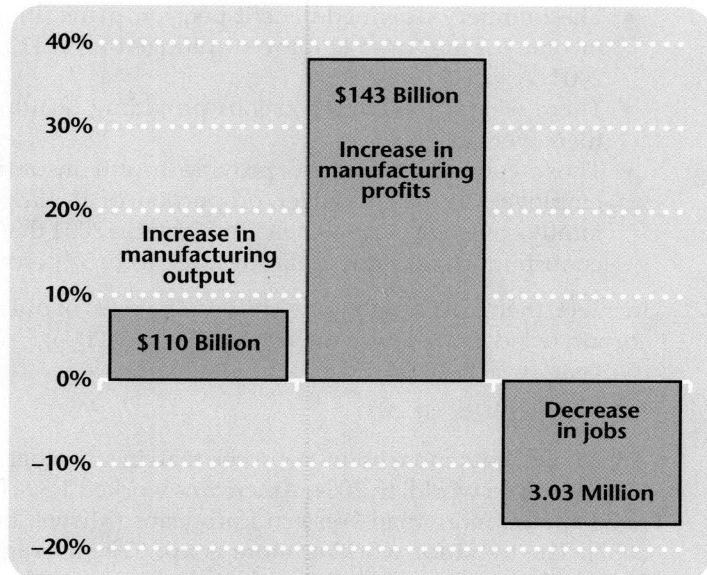

as shown throughout this chapter, of technology (computers, robots), efficiency of production, workers fearing that they will be laid off if they do not produce, and fewer workers working more. See Figure 14.2, which shows increases in manufacturing output and profits, while jobs decreased.

Several factors depress the wages of workers. First, union membership has declined. Second, competition from low-wage countries depresses wages in the United States. As John Cassidy has put it, "More and more American workers will be forced to compete with poorly paid labor in the developing world, and the downward pressure on American wages could become irresistible" (Cassidy 2004:30). For example, Delphi Corporation in 2005, unable to compete with low-wage economies, slashed its wages for production workers from $27 an hour to $10 (decreasing a full-time worker's annual income from about $56,000 to $20,800). Third, corporations, if not moving overseas, have moved to the largely nonunion South, the less-unionized West, and to rural areas where wages are lower. Fourth, corporate management has systematically replaced workers with machines as well as contingent workers—independent contractors, temporary workers, part-time workers, and home-based workers. The salient features of contingent workers are that they are disproportionately women, their wages are relatively low, and they are typically without traditional benefits. Finally, low wages result from a minimum wage (raised to $7.25 in 2009) that is not a living wage (which should be at least $10 an hour).

The higher one looks at the wage distribution, the wider the gap in compensation. As noted in Chapter 2, the gap between those at the top (corporate executives) and the workers who produce the products or services is huge. At the bottom, about 30 million workers earn less than $10 an hour, typically without health insurance and other benefits. They are disproportionately African American, Latino, and female.

Consequently, many Americans are not making it financially. In 2008, some 39.8 million were living below the poverty line, and 46.3 million Americans were without health insurance. Racial and ethnic minorities were disproportionately

© Matt Wuerker/Politico.

disadvantaged. Black households had only 65 percent of the median income of Whites, and Latinos had but 72 percent of the median income of Whites in 2008. Full-time, year-round women workers made only 77 cents for every dollar earned by full-time men workers. Thus, the U.S. economy does not work for everyone. The roots of the problems found in the U.S. economy are found in the changes associated with globalization and its structural transformation.

The Problem: Workers or Jobs?

The argument is advanced often in the business community that there is a jobs/skills mismatch. That is, if graduating students were better prepared, the jobs would be there for them. But this conventional argument misses the point. The problem is not a lack of education but a lack of jobs. Wanda Katz-Fishman makes this point forcefully:

> *Today the factory system of production with machine technology, that was the basis of the expansion of educational opportunities for the working class during the 20th century, no longer exists. The revolution in technology has transformed the production process. Human labor is being displaced permanently by electronically based automated production. Production line workers are being replaced by robots. Secretaries are being replaced by word processors. Technical designers and programmers are being replaced by software packages. Sales clerks are being replaced by uniform pricing code scanners. Low wage workers are being replaced by lower wage workers in the neocolonies. The largest number of jobs being created are those at minimum wage. Full-time jobs with benefits are being split into part-time jobs with no benefits. . . . As the masses of workers, i.e., "human capital," are replaced by forms of automated production, the capitalist system no longer needs to educate them. It should thus be clear that the reason more and more working class youth are not getting good jobs with decent wages is not because they do not have a college degree. Rather, the*

Speaking to Students Panel

The Employment Outlook for Young Adults

A major *Demos* study entitled "The Economic State of Young America," begins with this: "Today's 20-somethings are likely to be the first generation to not be better off than their parents" (Draut 2008:1). Today's young adults have the unfortunate luck to come of age and start careers while facing strong headwinds from the powerful forces discussed in this chapter. They will begin their careers in the steepest economic downturn since the Great Depression. In an article entitled "The Lost Generation," Peter Coy of *Business Week* stated, "Young people are the biggest victims of the current economic slump" (Coy 2009:34). Because of this recession the job market is caught in a vicious circle. With high unemployment and fewer available jobs, U.S. consumers will likely spend less, causing more businesses to release workers (Raum 2009). The shift from a manufacturing economy to one based on services will cause employers to continue lowering wages and benefits for their workers. Jobs are being created and destroyed in this dynamic economy, fueled by the economic transformation, with more jobs destroyed than created resulting in a disconnect between the demand for labor and the supply (Benson 2009). Because they are new to the job market, young adults will be the last to be hired and the first to be fired. Unions no longer have the power to ameliorate the vicissitudes of work. Future job growth will be concentrated in the lower-wage sector of the economy. The jobs squeeze is heightened further by the baby boom generation reaching retirement age but with an increasing number not retiring because of a decline in their investments incurred during the Great Recession (Kotz 2010). For example, from 2000 to 2007 the number of 55- to 64-year-olds working in the retail industry rose by 553,000. At the same time, the number of teens who worked in those stores fell by 419,000 (Gandel 2010). The fierce competition for jobs means that "adults twice their age with college degrees and decades of experience are now applying for entry-level positions" (Ratner 2009:21).

In short, the American economy is not providing enough jobs, "and nowhere near enough good jobs, to maintain the standard of living that most Americans have come to expect" (Herbert 2009: para 4).

How does one cope with this insecure work world? Some young people will succeed, but most will find the job world harsh. The forces that converge to make finding good jobs troublesome will not be going away soon. Here are a few ideas to ponder as you face a difficult economic environment.

- Jobs are migrating away from the industrial heartland to the South and Southwest. The states with the highest job growth are (in order) Texas, New Mexico, Florida, and Georgia.
- Choose a career that cannot be outsourced (e.g., teaching, nursing, law enforcement, food preparation).
- Ride the wave of an information/knowledge economy. "The U.S. Department of Labor spotlights network systems and data communications as well as computer-software engineering among the occupations projected to grow most explosively by 2016. Over the next seven years, the number of jobs in the information-technology sector is expected to swell 24%—a figure more than twice the overall job-growth rate" (Altman 2009:42).
- Choose an occupation that is favored by demographic change. For example, the baby boomers are approaching old age. Moreover, the old are living longer. This increases the need for doctors, nurses, pharmacists, nursing aides, home health aides, recreational therapists, and for people to plan and construct retirement homes and gerontology clinics.
- Choose an occupation that will solve social problems endorsed by the public. For example: The world faces a dangerous overheating of the environment. Green jobs, such as producing solar panels or wind turbines, weatherizing homes, and engineering clean energy projects will add an estimated 2.5 million jobs in the United States by 2018 (Walsh 2009).

reason they cannot get a college education is precisely because there are not enough good jobs that pay decent wages in our society to warrant the college education of the majority of the working class. (Katz-Fishman 1990:23)

In summary, the problems associated with work in U.S. society are structural in origin. The source is not in unmotivated or unwilling or undereducated workers. To understand the work setting in our society, we must understand globalization and the nature of capitalism, where profit—not the human consequences—guides managerial decisions. And in looking at unemployment, we must recognize that the economy fails to produce enough jobs with living wages and adequate benefits for the workers to maintain a middle-class lifestyle. Finally, in examining this labor market, we must understand that the economy is undergoing a profound transformation. The next few generations will be caught in the nexus between one stage and another, and many will suffer because of the dislocations. (See the Speaking to Students panel.) So, too, will a society that refuses to plan, but, rather, lets the marketplace dictate the choices of economic firms.

CHAPTER REVIEW

1. There are two fundamental ways in which society can organize its economic activities: capitalism and socialism.
2. Capitalism in its pure form involves (a) private ownership of property, (b) the pursuit of personal profit, (c) competition, and (d) a government policy of allowing the marketplace to function unhindered.
3. Socialism in its pure form involves (a) democracy throughout the social structure, (b) equality of opportunity, equality rather than hierarchy in decision making, and equality in sharing the benefits of society, (c) public ownership of the means of production, (d) community, and (e) planning for common purposes.
4. The economy of the United States is in the midst of a major structural transformation. This fundamental shift is the consequence of several powerful converging forces: (a) technological change, (b) the globalization of the economy, (c) capital flight, and (d) the shift from an industrial economy to a service/information economy.
5. These forces combine to create considerable discontinuity and disequilibrium in society. The trend toward robotics and other forms of super-automation reduces the jobs for the unskilled and semiskilled. This high-tech society, however, creates a need for workers skilled in communication, reasoning, mathematics, and computer programming. The proportion of workers traditionally found in these jobs (White males) is declining, while the proportion of new workers is increasingly non-White. Because non-Whites are disadvantaged economically and educationally, there is a skills mismatch. This skills gap offers the disadvantaged the potential of upward mobility if they, governments, schools, and businesses, meet the challenge. If not, the gap between the advantaged and the disadvantaged will continue to widen.
6. Deindustrialization and the shift to a service economy have reduced the number of jobs providing a middle-class standard of living and have expanded the number of lower standard-of-living jobs. The result is a bifurcation of the labor force into the haves and the have-nots.
7. Societies are organized to allocate work to produce the goods and services required for survival. The way work is organized generates important social problems.
8. Owners and managers of firms and factories control workers in several ways: (a) through scientific management, (b) through bureaucracy, (c) by monitoring worker behavior, and (d) through extortion.
9. Blue-collar and white-collar workers in bureaucracies and factories are susceptible to alienation, which is the separation of human beings from each other, from themselves, and from the products they create. Specialized work in impersonal settings leads to dissatisfaction and meaninglessness.
10. A primary goal of business firms in a capitalist society is to reduce costs and thus increase profits. One way to reduce costs is not to provide adequately for worker safety.

11. Labor unions have declined in numbers and power. This decline has resulted in lower real wages and benefits, less-safe work conditions, and a declining middle class.
12. Another work-related problem is discrimination, in which women and minorities have long received unfair treatment in jobs, pay, and opportunities for advancement. Two features of the U.S. economy promote these inequities: (a) the segmented labor market and (b) capitalist patriarchy.
13. The official government data on unemployment hide the actual amount by undercounting the unemployed in two ways: (a) people not actively seeking work (discouraged workers) are not counted; and (b) people who work at part-time jobs are counted as fully employed.
14. Unemployment has positive consequences for some people. Having a certain portion unemployed tends to keep inflation in check, according to some economists. Also, unemployment benefits capitalists by keeping wages down.

■ KEY TERMS

Capitalism. The economic system based on private ownership of property, guided by the seeking of maximum profits.

Socialism. The economic system in which the means of production are owned by the people for their collective benefit.

Globalization. The processes by which the earth's peoples are increasingly interconnected economically, politically, culturally, and environmentally.

Capital flight. Investment choices that involve the movement of corporate monies from one investment to another (investment overseas, plant relocation, and mergers).

Structural transformation of the economy. Fundamental change of the economy resulting from several powerful contemporary forces: technological breakthroughs in microelectronics, the globalization of the economy, capital flight, and the shift from a manufacturing economy to one based on information and services.

Offshoring. When a company moves its production to another country, producing the same products but with cheaper labor, lower taxes, and lower benefits to workers.

Outsourcing. The process of transferring a specific task (such as accounting or transcribing) to a foreign firm to save money and reintegrating that work back into the overall operation.

Sunset industries. Industries declining in output and employment.

Sunrise industries. Industries characterized by increased output and employment.

Contingent employment. Employment arrangement whereby employees work as temporaries or independent contractors, freeing employers from paying fringe benefits.

Homeshoring (homesourcing). The process of employing home-based independent contractors.

Displaced workers. Unemployed workers who face never being employed at comparably paying jobs because their training and skills have become obsolete.

Scientific management. Efforts to increase worker efficiency by breaking down work into very specialized tasks, the standardization of tools and procedures, and the speeding up of repetitive work.

Alienation. Separation of human beings from each other, from themselves, and from the products they create.

Sweatshop. Substandard working environment where labor laws are violated.

Segmented labor market (dual labor market). Capitalist economy is divided into two distinct sectors—one in which production and working conditions are relatively stable and secure, the other composed of marginal firms in which working conditions, wages, and job security are low.

Discouraged workers. People who have not actively sought work for 4 weeks. These people are not counted as unemployed by the Bureau of Labor Statistics.

Reserve army of the unemployed. Unemployed people who want to work. Their presence tends to depress the wages of workers and keeps those workers from making demands on employers for fear of being replaced.

■ SUCCEED WITH PEARSON mysoclab www.mysoclab.com

Experience, Discover, Observe, Evaluate

MySocLab is designed just for you. Each chapter features a pre-test and post-test to help you learn and review key concepts and terms.

Experience sociology in action with dynamic visual activities, videos, and readings to enhance your learning experience. Complete the following activities at www.mysoclab.com.

Social Explorer is an interactive application that allows you to explore Census data through interactive maps.

- Explore the Social Explorer Map: *Unemployment Rates Between 1980 and 2000*

The Core Concepts in Sociology video clips offer a real-world perspective on sociological concepts.

- Watch *Diminishing Opportunity*

MySocLibrary includes primary source readings from classic and contemporary sociologists.

- Read Carruthers, *A Sociology of Bubbles;* Ehrenreich, *Maid to Order: The Politics of Other Women's Work;* Weber, *Asceticism and the Spirit of Capitalism*

CHAPTER 15 Families

Although it may seem overwhelming to see family problems as only one symptom of a much larger social crisis, it is in some ways encouraging. It means, for example, that people have not suddenly and inexplicably "gone bad." They are struggling with serious dilemmas and, though many make poor choices or cannot carry out their highest ideals, are generally trying to do their best. There is evidence that we can help families do better and that we can do so now.

—Stephanie Coontz

Family changes occurring in the last few decades have led some social analysts to conclude that the family is in serious trouble, that we have lost our **family values,** and that the "breakdown of the family" causes social problems. The **family** is an easy target for those who blame social problems on bad people doing bad things. They assume that when the family fails, the rest of society fails. This view of the world is flawed in two fundamental respects. First, it reverses the relationship between family and society by treating families as the building blocks of society rather than as *a product of social conditions.* Second, it ignores the structural reasons for family breakdown and the profound changes occurring throughout the world. Even in very different societies, families and households are undergoing similar shifts as a result of global economic changes.

Some social problems have their locus in family settings. Although many of these problems are rooted in conditions outside the family, they become family problems that affect growing numbers of children and adults. This chapter examines the family as a social institution and the social problems that have their locus in family life. The chapter is divided into five parts. The first section shows the gap between common images of the family and family life as it is actually experienced in this society. The remaining four sections examine representative family-based social problems: the economic disadvantages for some families and current changes in the larger economy that are producing new problems for families, problems in balancing work and family without social supports, divorce, and domestic violence. The theme of this chapter is that family life and family problems are intertwined with social forces.

THE MYTHICAL FAMILY IN THE UNITED STATES

There are a number of myths about families. These beliefs are bound up with nostalgia and cultural values concerning what is typical and true about families. The following myths, based on folk wisdom and common beliefs, are rarely challenged except by social scientists and family scholars.

1. *The myth of a stable and harmonious family of the past.* Most people think that families of the past were better than families of the present. They are believed to have been more stable, better adjusted, and happier. However, family historians have found that there is no golden age of the family. Many children were raised by single parents or stepparents, just as now. Divorce rates were lower because of strong religious prohibitions and community norms against divorce, but this does not mean that love was stronger in the past. Many "empty" marriages continued without love and happiness to bind them.

Historian Stephanie Coontz has reexamined our assumptions about family history. Her book, *The Way We Never Were* (1992), exploded the myth that the family has recently "gone bad." In her more recent book, *Marriage: A History* (Coontz 2005), she shows how marriage changed from an economic and political institution to a voluntary love relationship. This change, not the loss of family values, is what makes marriage more fragile today. Family life of the past was quite different from the stereotype. Desertion by spouses, the presence of illegitimate children, and other conditions that are considered modern problems existed in the past. Part of the family nostalgia holds that there were three generations living under one roof or in close proximity. This image of the three-generational family is also false. Few examples of this "classical family of western nostalgia" (Goode 1983:43) have been found by family historians.

2. *The myth of separate worlds.* This is the positive image of the family as a place of love and trust, where individuals escape from the outside world. It makes a distinction between "public" and "private" realms with the family as a "haven in a heartless world." Here, social relations are thought to be different from those in the world at large. Of course, love, intimacy, and trust are the glue for many families, but this glorification of private life tends to mask the dark side of some families, where emotional and physical aggression are commonplace and where competition between spouses and among children sometimes destroys relationships. This myth ignores the harsh effects of economic conditions such as globalization and the Great Recession (e.g., poverty or near poverty, unemployment and underemployment, **downward mobility** or the threat of downward mobility). It ignores the social inequalities (racism, sexism, ageism, homophobia) that prevent many people from experiencing the good things in life. And the idealized family view masks the inevitable problems that arise in intimate settings (tensions, anger, and even violence in some instances).

3. *The myth of the monolithic family form.* We all know what a family is *supposed* to look like. It should resemble the Ozzie and Harriet form. We get this image from our ministers and priests, from our politicians, from children's literature, and from television. This image is of a White, middle-class, heterosexual father as breadwinner, mother as homemaker, and children at home, living in a one-family house. This model, however, represents a small proportion of U.S. households. Less than 10 percent of households consist of married couples with children in which only the husband works. Today, it makes more sense to talk about "types of families" (Mabry et al., 2004:93). Contemporary family types represent a multitude of family forms, including single-parent households, stepparent families, extended multigenerational households, gay and straight cohabiting couples, child-free couples, transnational families, lone householders with ties to various families, and many other kinds of families.

4. *The myth of a unified family experience.* We assume that all family members experience family life in the same way. This image hides the diversity within families. The family is a gendered institution. Women and men experience marriage differently. There are gender differences in decision making, in household division of labor, and in forms of intimacy and sexuality. Similarly, divorce affects them differently. Remarriage patterns differ by gender, as well. Girls and boys experience their childhoods differently, as there are different expectations, different rules, and different punishments according to gender.

5. *The myth of family decline as the cause of social problems.* Partly because of the myths about the past, and partly because the family has changed so much in the past few decades, many conclude that the breakdown of the family is responsible for today's social ills. Fatherless families and women working outside the home are said to be the reasons for poverty, violence, drug addiction, and crime. Divorced or unwed mothers, in this view, are damaging children, destroying families, and tearing apart the fabric of society.

U.S. FAMILIES IN HISTORICAL PERSPECTIVE: THE FAMILY IN CAPITALISM

Family forms in the United States are closely related to economic development. Industrialization moved the center of production from the domestic family unit to the workplace. Families became private domestic retreats set off from the rest of society. Men went off to earn a wage in factories and offices, while women remained in the home to nurture their children. From the rise of the industrial economy until World War II, capitalism operated within a simple framework. Employers assumed that most families included one main breadwinner—

The "breadwinner–homemaker" pattern does not apply to people who lack the opportunities to earn a family wage.

a male—and one adult working at home directing domestic work—a female; in short, jobs with wives. As a result, many men received the income intended to support a family.

The private family with a breadwinner father and a homemaker mother was an important historical development, but economic conditions precluded this pattern for many families. With industrialization, wave after wave of immigrants filled the industrial labor force. Through their labor, entire families became an integral part of society. Immigrant families did not separate themselves into private units. Instead, they used extended family ties to adjust in the new society. Family members helped their newly arrived kin and other members of their ethnic groups to adapt to the new society.

Many immigrants came to the United States in family groupings, or they sent for families once they were established in cities. Kin assisted in locating jobs and housing, and they provided other forms of support. Contrary to the typical portrayal of immigrants, their transplanted kinship and ethnic bonds did not disintegrate but rather were rebuilt in the new society (Early 1983; Vecoli 1964).

The developing capitalist economy did not provide equal opportunities for all people. Racial-ethnic people did not have the opportunity to become part of the industrial labor force. Instead, they labored in nonindustrial sectors of the economy, which often required family arrangements that were different from those in the dominant society. The breadwinner–homemaker pattern never applied to immigrants and racial minorities because they were denied the opportunities to earn a family wage. So, many married women took jobs to make ends meet. Some women took in boarders or did piecework; some worked as maids in middle-class and upper-class homes; and some became wage workers in sweatshops, department stores, and offices. For these families, the support of the community and extended family members was crucial (Albelda 1992:7).

Families have always varied with the social conditions surrounding them. From the original settlement of the American colonies through the mid-twentieth century, families of European descent often received economic and social supports to establish and maintain families. Following World War II, the GI Bill, the National Defense Education Act, the expansion of the Federal Housing Authority and Veterans Administration loan subsidy programs, and government funding of new highways provided the means through which middle-class Whites were able to achieve the stable suburban family lives that became the ideal against which other families were judged (Coontz 1992). These kinds of supports have rarely been available for people of color and, until quite recently, were actively denied them through various forms of housing and job discrimination. Family history makes it clear that social forces have always created many different family types.

What we think of as "the family" is an ideal. It implies a private retreat set apart from society. This image masks the real relationship between families and the larger society. A better way of understanding how families are related to social institutions is to distinguish between families and households. **Family** refers to a set of social relationships, whereas **household** refers to residence or living arrangements (Rapp 1982; Jarrett and Burton 1999). To put it another way, a household is a residence group that carries out domestic functions, whereas a family is a kinship group (Holstein and Gubrium 1999:31). A good example of the importance of distinguishing between family and household is the restructuring of family obligations and household composition after divorce (Ferree 1991:107).

STRATIFICATION AND FAMILY LIFE: UNEQUAL LIFE CHANCES

In previous chapters, we examined growing inequalities in the distribution of resources and rewards. These stratification hierarchies—class, race, and gender—are changing and reshuffling families and individuals. In this section, we examine the effects of social class on families in the United States. Of course, the social patterning of inequality occurs along many other dimensions, including age, family characteristics, and place of residence (see Table 15.1).

Families are embedded in a class hierarchy that is "pulling apart" to shrink the middle class while more families join the growing ranks of the rich or the poor (Usdansky 1992). This movement creates great differences in family living and no longer guarantees that children's placement in the class system will follow that of their parents. Still, a family's location in the class system is the single most important determinant of family life.

Social and economic forces produce different family configurations. In a stratified society, family structures differ because households vary systematically in their ability to acquire, accumulate, and transmit wealth, wages, or welfare (Rapp 1982). Households in different parts of the class structure have different ways of acquiring the necessities of life. Inheritance, salaries, wages, welfare, or various involvements with the hidden economy, the illegal economy, or the irregular economy provide different connections with society's opportunity structures. The social networks or relationships outside the family—at work, school, church, and voluntary associations—are the social forces that shape class and racial differences in family life.

The middle-class family form is idealized in our society. This form, a self-reliant unit composed of a breadwinning father, a homemaker mother, and their

TABLE 15.1

People and Families in Poverty by Selected Characteristics: 2009.

Characteristics	*Below Poverty Percent*	*Characteristics*	*Below Poverty Percent*
People		**Nativity**	
Total	14.3	Native born	13.7
Family Status		Foreign born	19.0
In families	12.5	Naturalized citizen	10.8
Householder	11.1	Not a citizen	25.1
Related children under 18	20.1	**Region**	
Related children under 6	23.8	Northeast	12.2
In unrelated subfamilies	51.1	Midwest	13.3
Reference person	48.7	South	15.7
Children under 18	56.6	West	14.8
Unrelated individuals	22.0	**Families**	
Male	20.0	Total	11.1
Female	24.0	**Type of Family**	
Race		Married couple	5.8
White	12.3	Female household, no husband present	29.9
White, non-Hispanic	9.4		
Black	25.8	Male household, no wife present	16.9
Asian Pacific Islander	12.5		
Hispanic origin	25.3		
Age			
Under 18 years	20.7		
18–64 years	12.9		
65 years and older	8.9		

Source: Carmen DeNavas-Walt, Bernadette D. Proctor, and Jessica C. Smith. U.S. Census Bureau, Current Population Reports, *Income, Poverty, and Health Insurance Coverage in the United States: 2009,* U.S. Government Printing Office, Washington, D.C., 2010, p. 15, Table 4.

children, has long been most characteristic of middle-class and upper-middle-class families. Middle-class families of the twenty-first century are quite different from television's stereotyped family of the 1950s. Today, many families can sustain their class status only through the economic contributions of employed wives. Such families must find ways to provide care for their children. How families in different class locations provide child care in the twenty-first century is the subject of a recent study by sociologist Karen Hansen. Her research challenges the myth that middle-class families are self-sufficient and disconnected from kin. Even if they are middle class, families with two breadwinners must build social networks to help them care for children. In today's world, they have increased their reliance on kin. Hansen concluded that structural changes have given rise to middle-class families that are "not-so-nuclear" (Hansen 2005).

Although middle-class families *appear* to be self-sufficient, they are supported by conditions in the larger society. When exceptional economic resources are called for, nonfamilial institutions usually are available in the form of better medical coverage, expense accounts, and credit at banks (Rapp 1982:181).

These links with nonfamilial institutions are precisely the ones that distinguish life in middle-class families from life in families of other economic groups.

The strongest links are with the occupations of middle-class family members, especially those of the husband–father. Occupational roles greatly affect family roles and the quality of family life (Schneider and Smith 1973). Occupations are part of the larger opportunity structure of society. Occupations that are highly valued and carry high income rewards are unevenly distributed. The amount of the paycheck determines how well a given household can acquire needed resources.

In the working class, material resources depend on wages acquired in exchange for labor. When such hourly wages are insufficient or unstable, individuals in households must pool their resources with other people in the larger family network. The pooling of resources may involve exchanging babysitting, sharing meals, or lending money. Pooling is a way of coping with the tenuous nature of connections between household and opportunity structures of society. It requires that the boundaries of "the family" be expanded. This is one reason that the idealized nuclear family is impossible for many people to sustain. At the lower levels of the class hierarchy, people lack the material resources to form autonomous households.

The fluid boundaries of these families do not make them unstable. Instead, this family flexibility is a way of sustaining the limited resources that result from their place in the class hierarchy. Minority single-parent families, which are criticized as being disorganized, are often embedded in a network of sharing and support. Variation in family organization is often a way of adapting to society.

Middle-class families with husbands (and perhaps wives) in careers have both economic resources and built-in ties with supportive institutions such as banks, credit unions, medical facilities, and voluntary associations. These ties are intrinsic to some occupations and to middle-class neighborhoods. They are structurally determined. Such institutional linkages strengthen the autonomy of middle-class families. But the middle class is shrinking, and many middle-class families are without middle-class incomes because of changes in the larger economy. Changes in family structure have also contributed to the lowering of family income. High divorce rates, for example, create many more family units with lower incomes.

Turning to the upper class, we find that family boundaries are more open than are those of the middle class, even though class boundaries are quite closed. Among the wealthy, "the family" includes not only the nuclear family but also the extended family. The elite have multiple households (Rapp 1982:182). Their day-to-day life exists within the larger context of a network of relatives (Dyer 1979:209).

Wealthy families are nationally connected by a web of institutions they control. In this social class, families throughout the country are linked by private schools, exclusive colleges, exclusive clubs, and fashionable vacation resorts. In this way, the elite remains intact and the marriage market is restricted to a small (but national) market (Blumberg and Paul 1975:69). Marriage legally clarifies the lines of inheritance in a way that is less important to those without property (Hansen 2005:69). Family life of the elite is privileged in every sense, as Stein, Richman, and Hannon (1977:22) reported: "Wealthy families can afford an elaborate support structure to take care of the details of everyday life. Persons can be hired to cook and prepare meals and do laundry and to care for the children." The vast economic holdings of these families allow them to have a high degree of control over the rewards and resources of society. They enjoy freedoms and choices not available to other families in society. These families maintain privileged access to **life chances** and lifestyles.

Kinship ties, obligations, and interests are more extended in classes at the two extremes than they are in the middle (McKinley 1964:22). In the upper extreme and toward the lower end of the class structure, kinship networks serve decisively different functions. At both extremes, they are institutions of resource management. The kin-based family form of the elite serves to preserve inherited wealth. It is intricately tied to other national institutions that control the wealth of society. The kin-based family form of the working and lower classes is a primary institution through which individuals participate in social life as they pool and exchange their limited resources to ensure survival. It is influenced by society's institutions, but it remains separate from them.

CHANGING FAMILIES IN A CHANGING WORLD

Economic Transformation and Family Life

Family life is intertwined with other social institutions. (The following is adapted from Baca Zinn, Eitzen, and Wells 2010:92–132.) In Chapter 14, we discussed the powerful forces that are transforming the U.S. economy: (1) globalization, (2) technological change, (3) capital flight, and (4) the shift from an industrial economy to a service economy. These forces combine to affect families both directly and indirectly. They have reduced the number of jobs providing a middle-class standard of living and have expanded the number of lower-standard-of-living jobs. This results in increased job and benefit insecurity, a shrinking middle class, and downward social mobility for many.

The Great Recession (also detailed in Chapter 14) has magnified these difficulties and created considerable discontinuity for family life. For example, wages for the employed have stagnated, and their benefits have been reduced or eliminated. Unemployment has risen sharply. Investments in stocks and home buying have declined precipitously, causing high rates of foreclosures and bankruptcies. The economic decline has increased the numbers of individuals and families who are "food insecure" and homeless. Tough economic conditions have caused couples to delay marriage and if married to delay childbearing. Financial woes are a major source of financial discord. The bond for some couples may be strengthened as the partners work together to find solutions. Many others find their bonds weakened or severed by difficult economic times. See the Closer Look box, "Layoffs Can Stress Family Ties."

The economic transformation and the Great Recession have had dire consequences for many in the middle class. Katherine Newman describes the experience of the downwardly mobile middle class:

> *They once "had it made" in American society, filling slots from affluent blue collar jobs to professional and managerial occupations. They have job skills, education, and decades of steady work experience. Many are, or were, home owners. Their marriages were (at least initially) intact. As a group they savored the American dream. They found a place higher up the ladder in this society and then, inexplicably, found their grip loosening and their status sliding. Some downwardly mobile middle-class families end up in poverty, but many do not. Usually they come to rest at a standard of living above the poverty level but far below the affluence they enjoyed in the past. They must, therefore, contend not only with financial hardship but with the psychological, social,*

A CLOSER LOOK

LAYOFFS CAN STRESS FAMILY TIES

The gloomy economy is affecting more than the unemployment lines. It's also having a dramatic impact on many families nationwide.

Unemployed professionals are suddenly becoming stay-at-home parents. Pink slips are triggering marital woes. College students have dropped out, taken jobs, or moved home because their parents can't foot their tuition bills. Some young couples are postponing having children because of job problems.

After earning a six-figure salary and almost all his family's income, Ed Simon was laid off in March from his sales and marketing management job at a consumer products firm. His family is still reeling.

His wife, Lori, used to work a half day so she could be home with the kids. Now she's working more, and Simon is Mr. Mom to Ari, 13, and Daniel, 7. Instead of taking business trips and managing a department, he spends his days clipping coupons and attending parent-teacher conferences.

"It's provided a whole lot of conflict. Now I'm telling my wife she has to spend more time with the kids," says Simon, 43, of Princeton, NJ. "It's a complete role reversal, and it's very tough. My wife comes home, and I'm at the kitchen sink saying, 'You have no idea how hard this is.'"

Mounting research suggests there's a strong connection between economic swings and family stability. These are some of the major trends:

Family Time Is Affected

Research indicates that a failing economy forces many working parents to put in longer hours on the job, leaving them with less time for their children. That's because layoffs have intensified job pressures by leaving fewer employees to shoulder the workload. As a result of longer hours, 7 of 10 Americans feel they don't have a healthy balance between work and life, according to a May survey by Expedia.com.

But while the work day may be longer for those with jobs, a growing number of parents are experiencing the opposite extreme—they've been laid off, and that means they're staying home.

Long-term unemployment has been spreading fastest in families with young children, according to a study by the Children's Defense Fund in Washington, DC.

The proportion of families with an unemployed parent jumped by nearly a percentage point to 6.6 percent from 2000 to 2001 because of the economic slump that began early in 2001, according to the Department of Labor. In an average week in 2001, 4.8 million families had at least one member who was unemployed—a rise of 665,000 families from 2000.

They're fathers like Rich Miller, 48, who found himself out of work in May 2002, when the New York office of his advertising agency closed. Miller started his own media placement company, Smarter Media, and tends bar on the weekends to help make ends meet.

It's been tough on his marriage. Says Miller, "The financial issues add an additional strain and magnify other problems. It's changed our life."

But he can also work from home, which means more time with his 8-year-old son, Joshua. "He does appreciate the time we have together," says Miller of Hamilton Square, NJ.

Parental involvement can be shaped by economic trends. A U.S. Census Bureau report found that fathers had more time to spend with their preschool-age children during the recession in 1990 and 1991. But as the economy picked up and job opportunities became more abundant, dads were less likely to provide care.

Working Parents Feel Stressed

While the quantity of family time in some cases increases, the quality often suffers. Unemployment leaves jobless people

and practical consequences of "falling from grace," of "losing their proper place" in the world. (Newman 1988:8)

Thus, individual self-esteem and family honor are bruised. Moreover, this ordeal impairs the chances of the children, as children and later as adults, to enjoy economic security and a comfortable lifestyle.

worrying about money and finding work, while those in the labor force wrestle with job insecurities.

That tension spills into the home. Working women with young children are most likely to say they have little time to relax, according to a 2002 *USA Today*/CNN/Gallup poll.

"People are working under double anxiety," says Niels Nielsen, author of *Princeton Management Consultants Guide to Your New Job*. He founded an unemployment support group, JobSeekers, and started a human resources and general management firm, Princeton Management Consultants. "They're working longer hours and dealing with the prospect of being laid off. The family feels the strain. It's a double whammy."

Relationships Have More Pressures

Job relocations, unemployment, and financial concerns are testing many marriages. More than 70 percent of unemployed workers say family stress has increased since they lost their jobs, according to a poll by the National Employment Law Project.

Financial worries also take a toll. Calls about financial matters to counselors at ComPsych, a Chicago-based employee assistance provider, were up 58 percent in 2002. The majority of calls were for problems such as debt and bankruptcy instead of the typical calls they get for subjects such as money management advice.

Jim Holmes, 42, and his wife, Susan Smith, 40, were both unemployed for about two months last year. Shortly after they relocated from Los Angeles to Seattle for his wife's job, she was laid off, and he was still looking for work.

Today, Holmes is a planner with the city, and his wife is teaching and doing research at the University of Washington. While the stretch without an income gave them extra time with their children, Max, 11, and Sabrina, 6, it also was a time of worry.

"We had a good time together," says Holmes, of Issaquah, WA. "But it was stressful at the same time. . . . You'd worry about how it affects [the children's] lives."

While tensions may mount, research suggests a difficult economy actually tends to depress divorce rates. The reason: Couples have fewer financial resources, making it more cost-efficient to stay together. The divorce rate (which is shaped by numerous factors, including the economy) dipped from 4 percent in 2000 to 3.9 percent in 2002, according to the National Center for Health Statistics.

"It usually takes another job for a spouse to leave," says Carl Steidtmann, chief global economist at Deloitte Research in New York. "Divorce is an expensive proposition for a lot of people, and in a down economy you wait for a better time."

Many are new to unemployment

Many of the families affected by the economy are college-educated professionals with years of career experience. About 35 percent of workers unemployed for six months or longer in 2002 were over 45 years old, according to an analysis by the Economic Policy Institute (EPI) in Washington. About 18 percent of the long-term unemployed had college degrees, and 20 percent were executive, professional, and managerial workers.

"These are people who aren't accustomed to being unemployed," says economist Jeffrey Wenger. "What kind of coping strategies do they come up with? Because you've had such a stable environment for a long time, it's possible to have family friction."

There are other spillover effects of a downturn. One-third of unemployed workers have had to interrupt their own or a family member's education, according to a recent National Employment Law Project study of laid-off workers. And one in four has moved in with a family member or into other housing. . . .

Source: Armour, Stephanie (2003). "Layoffs Can Stress Family Ties." *USA Today* (June 27): B1–B2.

Downward mobility also occurs within the stable working class, whose link with resource-granting opportunity structures has always been tenuous. Many downwardly mobile families find successful coping strategies to deal with their adverse situations. Some families develop a tighter bond to meet their common problems. Others find support from families in similar situations or from their kin networks. But for many families, downward mobility adds tensions that make family life especially difficult. Family members experience stress, marital tension, and depression. Newman suggests that these conditions are normal given the persistent tensions generated by downward mobility. Many families experience some degree of these pathologies and yet somehow endure. But some families disintegrate under these pressures, with serious problems of physical brutality, incapacitating alcoholism, desertion, and even suicide (Newman 1988:134–140).

Although families throughout the social structure are changing as a result of macroeconomic forces, the changes are most profound among the working class. Blue- collar workers have been hardest hit by the economic transformation. Their jobs have been eliminated by the millions because of the new technologies and competition from other lower-wage (much lower) economies. They have been disproportionately fired or periodically laid off. Sometimes their places of work have shut down entirely and moved to other societies. Their unions have lost strength (in numbers and clout). And their wages have declined.

Because family life is intertwined with social forces, we should not be surprised that economic transformations are producing changes that make family life difficult for many. In 1950, some 60 percent of U.S. households fit the intact nuclear households form—a household composed of a male breadwinner, his full-time wife, and their dependent children. Although this family form was dominant in society, its prevalence varied by social class. The pattern clearly prevailed in working-class households, for example, but was much less likely among the poor, where women have always had to work outside the home to supplement family income.

This model for the family, which sociologist Judith Stacey (1990, 1991) calls the **modern family**, was disrupted by the destabilizing effects of globalization on jobs in the United States and by the challenges women face in maintaining traditional ways. Stacey found that working-class families, especially the women in them, created innovative ways to cope with economic uncertainty and domestic upheavals. In effect, these women were and are the pioneers of emergent family forms. Stacey calls these new family forms **postmodern families** because they do not fit the criteria for a modern family. Now there are divorce-extended families that include ex-spouses and their lovers, children, and friends. Households now expand and contract as adult children leave and then return home only to leave again. The vast majority of these postmodern families have dual earners. Many now involve husbands in greater child care and domestic work than in earlier times. Kin networks have expanded to meet economic pressures. Parents now deal with their children's cohabitation, single and unwed parenthood, and divorce. The result is that fewer than 10 percent of households now conform to the modern family form. According to Stacey,

> *No longer is there a single culturally dominant family pattern, like the modern one, to which the majority of Americans conform and most of the rest aspire. Instead, Americans today have crafted a multiplicity of family and household arrangements that we inhabit uneasily and reconstitute frequently in response to changing personal and occupational circumstances. (Stacey 1991:19)*

These postmodern family forms are new to working-class and middle-class families as they adjust to globalization and deindustrialization, *but they are not new to the poor*. The economic deprivation faced by the poor has always forced them to adapt in similar ways: single-parent families, relying on kin networks, sharing household costs, and multiple wage earners among family members.

Economic difficulties produced by the Great Recession have moved family life even further in the direction of postmodern family forms. For example, housing woes and unemployment have led many young people or even middle-aged couples to move back in with their parents, other relatives, or friends for extended periods (doubling up). With economic downturn, more and more children are being raised by their grandparents. In 2007, there were 4.7 million children living in households headed by a grandparent (up from 3 percent in 1970; Lagnado 2009). These grandparents provide a safety net for their children's children when their children cannot provide for them. But these grandparents typically are struggling during the Great Recession with the loss of retirement savings because of the stock market crash and the resulting loss of 401(k)s and IRAs. The added load of dependent grandchildren coupled with much less retirement income has severely eroded their "golden years." Another family form emerging from the economic crisis is the married couple that lives in the same house even though the individuals no longer want to live together. They continue to live together because it is too costly to maintain two homes. So they build walls, real and imaginary, to create separate spaces for each in the same larger space—still married, still living together, but living apart emotionally.

The Great Recession has disproportionately laid off men. Of every five jobs lost, men have lost four of them during this economic crisis (Reed 2009). In Chapter 9, we saw that growing proportions of women are entering the workforce in downturn-resistant sectors like education and health care. This has significant ramifications for family dynamics as women become primary breadwinners "while also retaining their household responsibilities. Meanwhile, husbands must reconstruct their definition of contributing to the family enterprise, often swapping a paycheck for a broom" (della Cava 2009:D2).

More and more children are being raised by grandparents.

Today's Diverse Family Forms

Families are constantly changing through their interactions with other social institutions. Among the most prominent changes are those in family form and composition. To understand current trends in family life, we must return to the distinction between households and families discussed earlier in this chapter. (The following is based on Ahlburg and De Vita, 1992 Bianchi and Casper 2000:8; and Lichter and Qian 2004.) The U.S. Bureau of the Census defines a *household* as all persons living in a housing unit. A **household** may consist of one person who lives alone or of several people who share a dwelling. A *family*, on the other hand, includes household members who are related by blood, marriage, or adoption and who reside together. All families comprise households, but not all households are families under the Census Bureau's definition. Family households include families in which a family member is the householder—the person who owns or rents the residence. These households can also include nonfamily members such as a boarder or friend. A **nonfamily household** includes the householders who live alone or share a residence with individuals unrelated to the householder, such as college friends sharing an apartment.

Some nonfamily households substitute for families and serve many of the same functions. Same-sex couples are one example (Lichter and Qian 2004:2). The growth of the nonfamily household (that is, persons who live alone or with unrelated individuals) is one of the most dramatic changes to occur during the past four decades, as shown in Figure 15.1.

In 1970, 81 percent of households were family households; by 2008, just 67 percent were family households. At the same time, nonfamily households, which consist primarily of people who live alone or who share a residence with roommates or with a partner, have been on the rise. The fastest growth has been among persons living alone. The proportion of households with just one person increased 16 percent between 1970 and 2009 (Fields 2004; U.S. Census Bureau, 2005–2009 American Community Survey). Nonfamily households are a diverse group. They may consist of elderly individuals who live alone, college-age youths who share an apartment, cohabiting couples, individuals who delay or forgo marriage, or those who are "between marriages" (Ahlburg and De Vita 1992:5; Rawlings 1995:22).

Another dramatic shift in household composition has been the decline in the percentage of households with children. Two-parent households with children dropped from 40 to 30.3 percent of all households between 1970 and 2009 (Fields 2004; U.S. Census Bureau, Current Population Survey, 2010 Annual Social and Economic Supplement). This downward trend reflects the postponement of marriage and children and the shift toward smaller families. However, household composition varies considerably among different segments of the population. Minorities are more likely than Whites to live in households that include children. In 2009, 53 percent of African American households and 61 percent of Latino households had at least one child under age 18, compared with 44 percent of White households (U.S. Census Bureau, *America's Families and Living Arrangements*, Current Population Reports, P20-553 and earlier reports; "Families and Living Arrangements," and unpublished data. See also <http://www.census.gov/population/www/socdemo/hh-fam.html>.). This difference arises primarily because minority populations tend to have a younger age structure than the White population (that is, a greater share of minorities are in the prime childbearing ages), and minorities tend to have higher fertility rates than Whites (De Vita 1996:34). In the next decade, the overall composition of households is

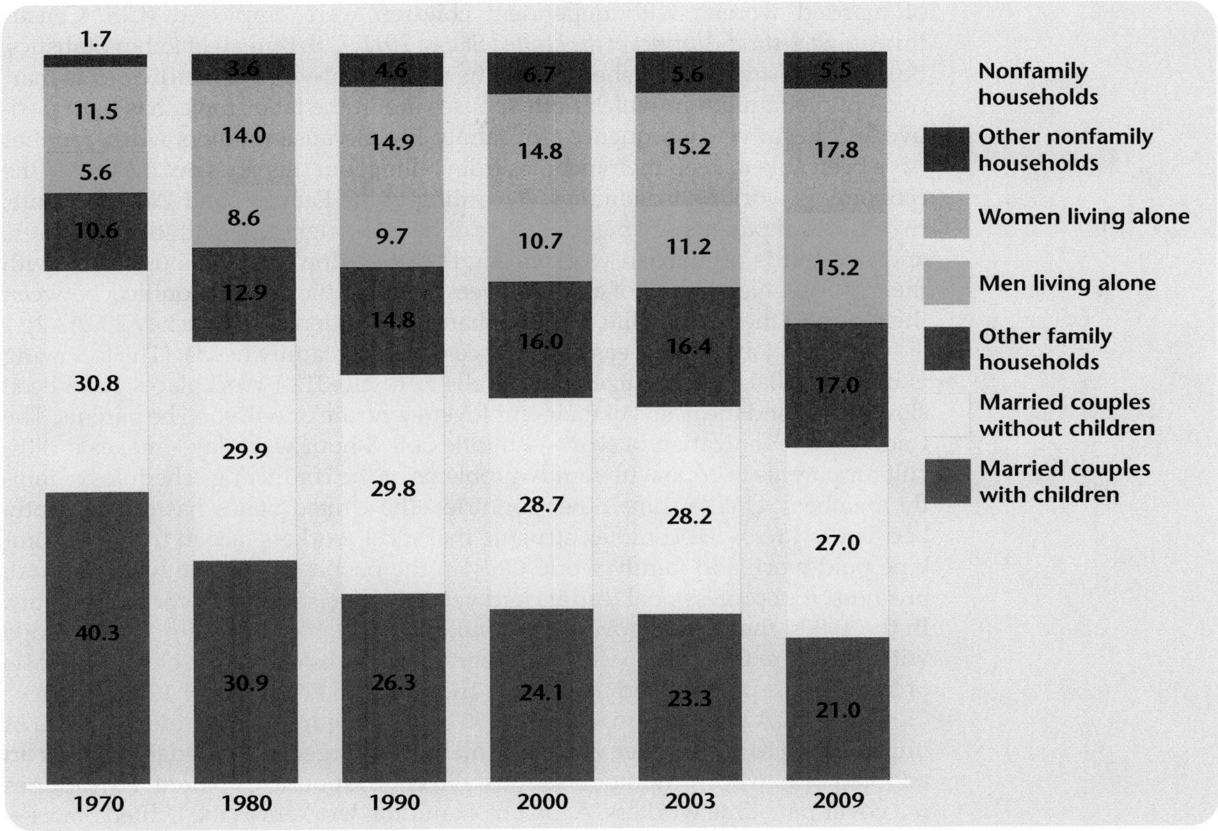

FIGURE 15.1

Households by Type: 1970–2008 (percent distribution)

Sources: Fields, Jason (2004). "America's Families and Living Arrangements: 2003." Current Population Reports, P20-553. Washington, DC: Social Explorer Tables: ACS 2005 to 2009 (5-Year Estimates) (SE), ACS 2005–2009 (5-Year Estimates), Social Explorer; U.S. Census Bureau.

projected to continue to shift, with a decreasing proportion of family households and continued growth of nonfamily households.

Macrolevel changes produce a wide range of family structures, including one-parent families, cohabiting couples (both gay and straight) with children, dual-worker families, and many varieties of extended families such as divorce-extended families and multigenerational families. Still, married couples with children continue to be a prominent family pattern. Parents and children now live in increasingly diverse settings, including intact biological families, stepfamilies and blended families, and single-parent families. Structural changes have made families more diverse and altered family experiences.

Balancing Work and Family with Few Social Supports

Regardless of their form, families now face new challenges. One of the greatest changes in the past few decades has been the increased participation of women in the labor force. Since 1960, the rise of women's participation in the labor force has been dramatic (see Chapter 9). In 1970, 40 percent of married women with dependent children (birth through age 17) were in the workforce. By 2009, 69.8 percent of married women with dependent children were employed (U.S. Census Bureau. *Statistical Abstract of the United States: 2011*, U.S. Bureau of Labor Statistics, Bulletin 2307 and unpublished data). The rise in **dual-worker families**, or in married-couple families in which both spouses are in the labor force, has both positive and negative consequences for family life. Because mothers work, families have been able to keep their incomes from falling, but this does not mean that the economy is working for families. According to the Families and Work Institute, two-thirds of parents say that they do not have enough time with their children, and two-thirds of married workers say that they don't have enough time with their spouse. Nearly half of all employees with families report conflicts between their job and their family life, more so than a generation ago (Boushey 2007:A2).

Very few jobs make it easy to balance work and family needs. (The following is based on Baca Zinn, Eitzen, and Wells 2010:210-212.) Workplaces have been slow to respond the needs of their employees who are or will soon be parents. The traditional organization of work—an inflexible 8-hour workday—makes it difficult for parents to cope with family problems or the conflicting schedules of family members. Unlike some other countries, the United States has only recently become aware of the complex struggle that most workers face in trying to combine paid work and family work. Only in the past decade or so have political, business, and professional leaders had very much to say about work and family. In the 1990s, the federal government made modest efforts to help families cope with child care through tax credits, programs for subsidizing the child-care costs of low-income parents, and the **Family and Medical Leave Act of 1993 (FMLA).**

The FMLA requires employers of 50 or more people to provide 12 weeks of unpaid leave to any worker who has a medical emergency or needs to care for an adopted or newborn child or a seriously ill child, spouse, or parent. FMLA does not cover part-time workers. A total of 41 million workers in the United States—nearly half of the private workers—are ineligible for family leave under this law. The FMLA of 1993 remain unchanged until 2009, when several points of clarification were added to the original legislation. The 2009 bill also expands military family leave entitlements, permitting eligible employees to take up to 26 weeks of leave to care for a service member with a series injury or illness (U.S. Department of Labor 2009a).

Availability of quality day care is often the biggest problem facing working parents.

See the box comparing U.S. government support for working families with other nations around the globe.

More than two-thirds of all children under the age of 5 are in a child-care arrangement on a regular basis by someone other than a parent. Many of these children are young because 75 percent of women go back to work by a child's ninth month. The children may attend day-care centers or nursery schools, go to the home of a provider, or be cared for by a relative, neighbor, or babysitter (Zaslow and Tout 2002).

The United States has no comprehensive child-care system. This lack of a system differentiates us from the other industrialized nations. Currently the federal government is involved modestly in providing for child care through two programs. First, it permits the deduction of child-care payments on income tax returns. This amounts to about a $4 billion tax credit, which is considerable. The problem, however, is that by being tied to taxes, it benefits the most affluent families and has negligible effects on the poor because they do not earn enough to take advantage of it. Second, the welfare legislation of 1996 included approximately $4 billion in new child-care funds over six years. "But the new law forces so many parents into the work force that this increase falls far short of what is needed to meet the new demand for child care generated by the law, much less to ensure that vulnerable children receive good care" (Children's Defense Fund 1997:38).

The government's less-than-adequate child-care programs are fundamentally flawed in at least two respects. Foremost, they are underfunded. The amounts the federal government promised simply do not meet child-care needs. The other problem is that they rely on the states to implement the programs and to match the federal grants if they are to receive monies. The states, through their governors, legislatures, and social service bureaucracies, vary greatly in their enthusiasm for child care, their licensing and monitoring of child-care programs, and the standards they set to ensure quality in child care. If history is a guide, then it is likely that many states will not commit the greater resources needed to receive the federal funds.

Single Parents and Their Children

About one-fourth of all U.S. children lived with just one parent, up from 12 percent in 1970. The disproportionate number of single-parent families headed by a woman is a consequence, first, of the relatively high divorce rate and the very strong tendency for divorced and separated women to have custody of the children. Second, there is the relatively high rate of never-married mothers (in 1960, 5 percent of U.S. babies were born to unmarried mothers; in 2007, 40 percent were). To counter the common myths, the facts indicate that more than three-fourths of out-of-wedlock births are to women age 20 and older. Moreover, although the *unwed birthrate* for African Americans and Latinos is higher than for Whites, there are *more unwed births* among Whites than among African Americans and Latinos.

The important question to answer concerning this trend is, What are the effects on children of living in mother-only families? Research has shown consistently that children from single-parent homes are more likely than children from intact families to have behavioral problems. McLanahan and Booth's (1991) review of the research on children from mother-only families, compared to children from two-parent families, shows the following:

- They have poorer academic achievement. This relationship is even more negative for boys than for girls.
- They are more likely to have higher absentee rates at school.
- They are more likely to drop out of school.
- They are more likely to marry early and to have children early, both in and out of marriage.
- If they marry, they are more likely to divorce.
- They are more likely to commit delinquent acts and to engage in drug and alcohol use.

Because 85 percent of one-parent families are headed by women, the common explanation for the disproportionate pathologies found among the children of single parents has been that the absence of a male adult is detrimental to their development. The presence of both mothers and fathers contributes to the healthy development of the child (Marsiglio et al., 2001). Also, the absence of a spouse makes coping with parenting more difficult. Coping is difficult for any single parent—female or male—because of three common sources of strain: (1) responsibility overload, in which single parents make all the decisions and

SOCIAL POLICY

HOW EUROPE SUPPORTS WORKING PARENTS AND THEIR CHILDREN

Many rich countries do a far better job than the United States does of supporting workers who are balancing the competing demands of employment and parenthood. Several European countries, especially in northern and western Europe, provide extensive work/family reconciliation policies—including paid family leave, public early-childhood education and care, and working-time measures that raise the quality and availability of reduced-hour work. The European Union puts a common floor under several of these national standards.

Parents in much of Europe have access to multiple forms of paid family leave, for both mothers and fathers. Equally important, these programs provide wage replacement, usually financed by social insurance, in order to spread the costs between women and men, across generations, and among enterprises. Social-insurance financing also minimizes employers' resistance to hiring young workers, especially women, who they anticipate will be leave-takers.

The Nordic countries—including Denmark, Finland, Norway, and Sweden—provide especially generous family leave rights and benefits. Most new parents have the right to take approximately one year of leave, and they receive about two-thirds or more of their pay. Family leave policies in the Nordic countries also offer parents substantial flexibility. Denmark and Sweden allow parents to take their allotted leaves in increments until their children are eight years old. Norway and Sweden allow parents to combine pro-rated leaves with part-time employment, and Finland and Norway permit parents to use portions of their leave benefits to purchase private child care instead. Recent reforms add incentives for fathers to take leaves, to encourage more gender-egalitarian usage.

Across Europe, publicly supported child care serves a large proportion of infants and toddlers while their parents are working for pay. In Denmark, for example, three-quarters of one- and two-year-olds are now served in publicly financed child-care settings; half of the children in this age range are in public care in Sweden and more than a third in Norway. In many European countries—including Belgium, France, and Italy—nearly all children from age three to the start of primary school are enrolled in full-day preschools. Throughout Europe, public policy measures assure that early childhood education and care are affordable. Parents typically pay income-scaled fees for infant and toddler care, while educationally oriented preschools (for children age three and older) are usually free for all families.

Parents are further aided by a package of working-time measures, some of which are required by the European Union. European countries set their

provide for all their family's needs; (2) task overload, in which the demands of work, housekeeping, and parenting can be overwhelming for one person; and (3) emotional overload, in which single parents must always be on call to provide the necessary emotional support. Clearly, when two people share these parental strains, it is more likely that the needs of the children will be met.

Although the factors just described help to explain the behavioral differences between children from one-parent and two-parent homes, they sidestep the major reason—a fundamental difference in economic resources. As Andrew Cherlin has argued, "It seems likely that the most detrimental aspect of the absence of fathers from one-parent families headed by women is not the lack of a male presence *but a lack of a male income*" (Cherlin 1981:81; emphasis added). There is a strong likelihood that women raising children alone will be financially troubled. In 2007, for example, 28 percent of children living in single-parent families headed by a woman were poor, compared with 5 percent of children in two-parent families (De Navas-Walt et al., 2008).

standard weekly work hours individually and, across western and northern Europe today, full-time work is generally defined as between 35 and 39 weekly hours. All EU-member countries are required to grant workers a minimum of four weeks of paid time off each year. Furthermore, EU law requires that all member countries ensure part-time workers pro-rated pay and benefits comparable to what full-time workers receive, in order to make shorter-hour work more economically feasible. In addition, since 2000, several countries—including Germany, the Netherlands, and the United Kingdom—have granted workers new rights to request work-schedule changes; employers may refuse, but their refusals are subject to public review.

These work/family measures are provided alongside universal health insurance, which adds crucial economic support for families, and gives workers flexibility when seeking employment that best meets their families' needs. All told, the comprehensive work/family policy packages operating in several European countries offer parents considerable latitude in allocating their time between paid work and care, and indemnify them against substantial fluctuations in disposable income.

Generous work/family policies are good for parents, children, and worker productivity, and especially benefit lower-income workers who tend to have less bargaining power and cannot afford to pay for help privately. Public systems equalize access and affordability, across family types and throughout the income spectrum, leading to outcomes that are more equitable than what market-based systems produce.

Moreover, expansive work/family policies are compatible with good economic outcomes. Consider GDP-per-hour-worked, a powerful indicator of productivity. The six top-ranked countries in the world are European countries with comprehensive work/family policies, including France, the Netherlands, Belgium, and Norway. Furthermore, the World Economic Forum's Competitiveness Index includes, among the top five countries globally, Denmark, Sweden, and Finland—three countries with extensive work/family policies.

In recent decades, many European countries have restructured their social policies to trim costs and improve economic outcomes. However, programs that support workers with family responsibilities—including paid leave, child care, and rights to high-quality reduced-hour work—were singled out for protection and growth rather than cutbacks, both by the EU and in many individual countries. Clearly, high-income industrialized countries can perform productively and competitively while granting workers rights and benefits that recognize the realities of family life.

Source: Reprinted with permission from Janet Gornick, "Atlantic Passages," *The American Prospect*, Volume 18, Number 3: March 01, 2007. The American Prospect, 2000 L Street NW, Suite 717, Washington DC 20036.

The reasons for a disproportionate number of mother-headed families that are poor are obvious. First, many single mothers are young and never married. They may have little education, so if they work, they have poorly paid jobs. Second, many divorced or separated women have not been employed for years and find it difficult to re-enter the job market. Third, and more crucial, jobs for women, centered as they are in the bottom tier of the segmented job market, are poorly paid (women, we must underscore again, presently earn about 78.2 cents for every dollar earned by men; see Chapter 9). Fourth, half the men who owe child support do not pay all they owe, and a quarter of them do not pay anything; women who do receive child support find that the amount covers less than half the actual cost of raising a child.

The economic plight of single-parent families is much worse for families of color. Women of color who head households have the same economic problems as White women who are in the same situation, plus the added burdens of institutional racism. In addition, they are less likely to be receiving child support (their husbands, unlike White husbands, are much more likely to be poor and unemployed), and they are more likely to have been high-school dropouts, further reducing their potential for earning a decent income. The financial difficulties of women heads of households are sometimes alleviated in part by support from a kinship network. Relatives may provide child care, material goods, money, and emotional support. The kin network is an especially important source of emergency help for African Americans and Latinos. But for many, kin may not be near or helpful.

In summary, the behavioral social costs attributed to the children of single mothers are, in large part, the result of living in poverty. Lack of income has negative effects on intellectual development and physical health (Guo and Harris 2000). Living in poverty translates into huge negatives for single mothers and their children—differences in health care, diet, housing, neighborhood safety, and quality of schools, as well as economic disadvantages, leading to a greater probability of experiencing low self-esteem, hopelessness, and despair.

Societal Response to Disadvantaged Children

As a nation, the United States has taken deliberate actions to reduce poverty among the elderly while simultaneously allowing childhood poverty to increase. (The following is adapted from Baca Zinn, Eitzen, and Wells 2010:477–480.) In 1970, the proportion of elderly in poverty was double the national average, yet by 2007, the poverty rate among the elderly was below the national average (9.7 percent compared to the national rate of 12.5 percent). The poverty rate for children under age 18 in 1970 was more than one-third lower than that for the elderly. By 2008, this situation had changed, with 19.0 percent of children under age 18 living in poverty (DeNavas-Walt et al., 2009; see Figure 15.2).

During the last 20 years, federal benefits to the elderly have risen from one-sixth of the federal budget to 30 percent (to about $300 billion annually). This increase occurred because federal policy makers created programs such as Medicare and Medicaid and because Social Security benefits were indexed to offset inflation. Conversely, however, these same decision makers did not provide adequately for needy families with children. The government actually reduced the programs targeted to benefit children (e.g., the children's share of Medicaid, Aid to Families with Dependent Children [AFDC], Head Start, food stamps, child nutrition, and federal aid to education).

Childhood poverty is especially acute for racial minorities. The bias against children in federal programs is heightened for minority children. The late senator Daniel Patrick Moynihan pointed out that there are two ways the federal government provides benefits to children in single-parent families. The first is Aid to Families with Dependent Children. The majority of the children receiving this type of aid are Black or Hispanic. Since 1970, the government has decreased the real benefits by 13 percent. The other form of assistance is Survivors Insurance (SI), which is part of Social Security. The majority of children receiving SI benefits are White, and these benefits have increased by 53 percent since 1970 (adjusted for inflation). Moynihan, writing eight years before the 1996 welfare legislation, said,

> *To those who say we don't care about children in our country, may I note that the average provision for children under SI has been rising five times as fast as average family income since 1970. We do care about some children—majority children. It is minority children—not only but mostly—who are left behind. (Moynihan 1988:5)*

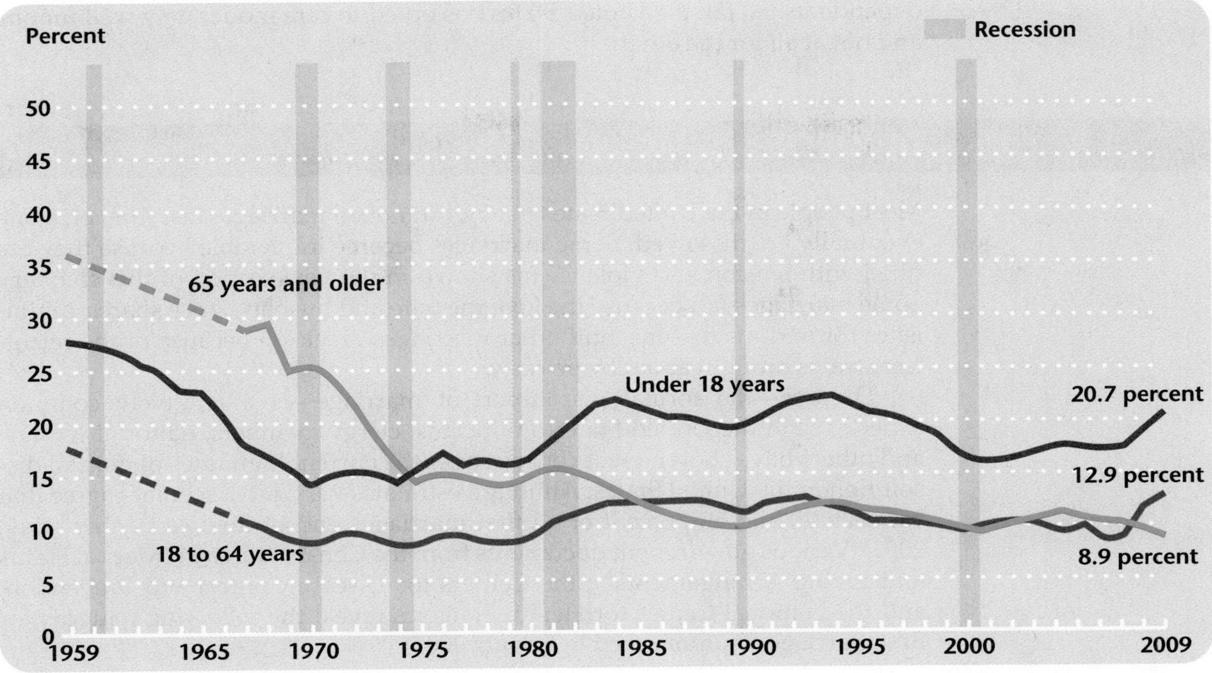

FIGURE 15.2

Poverty Rates by Age: 1959–2007

Note: The data points are placed at the midpoints of the respective years. Data for people 18 to 64 and 65 and older are not available from 1960 to 1965.

Source: DeNavas-Walt, Carmen, Bernadette D. Proctor, and Jessica C. Smith (2008). "Income, Poverty, and Health Insurance Coverage in the United States: 2007." In *Current Population Reports,* P60-235. Washington, DC: U.S. Census Bureau.

Another telling illustration is that although Congress in 1996 eliminated AFDC and severely cut food stamps and school nutrition programs for the poor, it did not cut cash and food programs for poor senior citizens.

The decisions to disproportionately help the elderly reflect the electoral power that the elderly have compared to the young. The elderly are organized, with several national organizations dedicated to political action that will benefit their interests. The American Association of Retired Persons (AARP), for example, is the nation's largest special-interest organization, with more than 40 million members. With the elderly making up 16 percent of the voting public (and much more in states such as Florida and Arizona, which have high concentrations of elderly people), politicians tend to pay attention to their special needs.

Children, on the other hand, have no electoral power and few advocates (an exception is the Children's Defense Fund). Their parents, especially those who are poor, are not organized. So, in a time of fiscal austerity, the needs of children—prenatal care for poor women, nutritional and health care, day care, and better schools—are underfunded. The irony is that the political right wing, which claims to be profamily, limits its political agenda to antiabortion legislation and court cases and ignores or fights governmental assistance to needy children and their struggling parents.

The argument is not that the elderly and the young should compete for scarce resources and that one or the other should win. Rather, both age groups are dependents and are in need. The test of a civilization is the condition of its dependents. So far, the United States has opted to care moderately well for one and not at all for the other.

DIVORCE

Most people in the United States marry, but not all marriages last forever; some eventually are dissolved. Some marriages become intolerable because they are filled with tension and violence (as shown in the next section of this chapter). Some marriages fail because the love the wife and husband once shared diminishes for various reasons. Still other marriages break up because of the relentless strains brought about by poverty.

Divorce—the formal dissolution of marriage—is a relatively common experience in the United States. Politicians, clergy members, editorial writers, and others have shown great concern over the current high rates of marital dissolution in the United States. Although estimates vary, most scholars agree that between 40 and 50 percent of all first marriages end in divorce (Visher et al., 2003). Various government documents from the Census Bureau ("Marital Status and Living Arrangements"), the Centers for Disease Control and Prevention, and the National Center for Health Statistics reveal the following patterns for first marriages (summarized in Coontz 2007):

- One in five marriages ends in divorce or separation within 5 years.
- Couples who separate do so, on average, after seven years and divorce after eight years.
- One in three marriages dissolves within 10 years.
- Divorce patterns for African Americans differ from those of Latinos and Whites. Latinos have divorce rates that are about the same as those of Whites, but African Americans are more likely to experience economic hardships that lead to marital disruption and divorce rates that are twice as high as Whites.

Some of the many reasons for the increased divorce rate include increased independence (social and financial) of women, economic restructuring that eliminates many jobs for men and makes women's employment necessary, women's inequality, greater tolerance of divorce by religious groups, and reform of divorce laws, especially the adoption of no-fault divorce in many states (i.e., one spouse no longer has to prove that the other was at fault to obtain a divorce). An important reason is the striking change in public attitudes toward divorce. Divorce is a difficult step and one that commands sympathy for the partners and children. But it is no longer considered a moral violation. Instead, divorce is generally accepted today as a possible solution for marital difficulties.

Consequences of Divorce

Divorce is an intensely personal event, and this intensity makes the breakup a painful experience, even when both parties want the marriage to end. In this section, we review the personal side of divorce—the consequences for ex-wives and ex-husbands and for their children. (This section is adapted from Baca Zinn, Eitzen, and Wells 2010:385–389.)

- **"His" and "Her" Divorce.** Both partners in a divorce are victims. Each is affected, in the typical case, by feelings of loneliness, anger, remorse, guilt, low self-esteem, depression, and failure. Although ex-spouses tend to share these negative feelings, the divorce experience differs for husbands and wives in significant ways because of the structure of society and gender inequality.

- **"His" Divorce.** Ex-husbands have some major advantages and a few disadvantages over their ex-wives. Men have the advantage of being better off financially than their former wives. Typically, they were the major income producers for their families, and after the separation their incomes stay disproportionately with them.

  Another benefit that men have over women after divorce is greater freedom. If there are children, they usually live with the mother (about 85 percent), so most men are free from the constraints not only of marriage but also of child care. Thus, they are freer than ex-wives to date, travel, go to school, take up a hobby, or work at a second job. Especially significant is sexual freedom because males tend to have more money and leisure time.

  The experience of ex-husbands on some counts, however, is more negative than that of ex-wives. Many divorced men, especially those from traditional marriages, experience initial difficulty in maintaining a household routine. They are more likely to eat erratically, sleep less, and have difficulty with shopping, cooking, laundry, and cleaning. And because ex-wives usually have legal custody of the children, ex-husbands are able to see their children only relatively rarely and at prescribed times. Thus, they may experience great loneliness because they have lost both wife and children.

  The image of liberated ex-husbands as swinging bachelors does not fit many men. Some find dating difficult. They find that women in general have changed or that they themselves have changed. Many men withdraw from relationships because of their fear of rejection. They may also be wary over concerns about AIDS or other sexually transmitted diseases.

- **"Her" Divorce.** Contrary to common belief, about two-thirds of divorces are initiated by women (Sweeney 2002). The only exception is that older wives in long-term unions are less likely than their husbands to file for divorce (Hacker 2003:27). This is an interesting anomaly because women benefit less from divorce than men. To be sure, many ex-wives are relieved to have ended an onerous relationship, and some are even freed from a physically abusive one. Some are now liberated from a situation that stifled their educational and career goals. Of course, divorce also frees spouses to seek new and perhaps more fulfilling relationships.

  For women, the negatives of divorce clearly outweigh the positives. Women oriented toward traditional gender roles tend to feel helpless and experience a loss of identity associated with their husbands' statuses. Divorced mothers who retain sole custody of their children often feel overwhelmed by the demands of full-time parenting and economic survival. The emotional and schedule overloads that usually accompany solo parenting leave little time for personal pursuits. The result is that divorced women often experience personal and social isolation, especially the feeling of being locked into a child's world. White women cope less well with divorce than do African American women. Presumably, this is because Black women have better social supports (extended family networks, friendship and church support networks) than do White women (Fine et al., 2005).

Both ex-husbands and ex-wives tend to lose old friends. For the first 2 months or so after the divorce, married friends are supportive and spend time with each of the former mates. But these contacts soon decline because, as individuals, divorced people no longer fit into couple-oriented activities. This disassociation from marital friends is especially acute for women because their child-raising responsibilities tend to isolate them from adult interactions.

On the positive side, women tend to have stronger family and friendship networks than men. These networks provide support, explaining, in part, why women fare better emotionally than men after divorce (Faust and McKibben 1999). Moreover, because most women receive custody of their children after divorce, they are more connected to their children than noncustodial fathers.

The biggest problem facing almost all divorced women is a dramatic decline in economic resources. Paul Amato, after examining the relevant research, concludes that "overall, mothers' postseparation standard of living [is] only about one half that of fathers" (Amato 2001:1277). As Lenore Weitzman argued, for most women and children,

> *[Divorce] means precipitous downward mobility—both economically and socially. The reduction in income brings residential moves and inferior housing, drastically diminished or nonexistent funds for recreation and leisure and intense pressures due to inadequate time and money. Financial hardships in turn cause social dislocation and a loss of familiar networks for emotional support and social services, and intensify the psychological stress for women and children alike. On a societal level, divorce increases female and child poverty and creates an ever-widening gap between the economic well-being of divorced men on the one hand, and their children and former wives on the other. (Weitzman 1985:323)*

Divorce has drastic social and economic effects on women and their children. It is a major social problem created by institutions that perpetuate gender discrimination and by divorced fathers who do not contribute to the support of their children (Arendell 1990).

Children of Divorce

Approximately 65 percent of divorcing couples have minor children, meaning that about 1 million children are involved in new divorces annually. This means that about two-fifths of children—one in three White children and two in three African American children—by age 16 will experience the permanent disruption of their parents' marriage. Most of them will remain with their mothers and live in a fatherless home for at least 5 years. Most significant, many children of divorce effectively *lose* their fathers (Amato and Booth 1996). "Ten years after a divorce, fathers will be entirely absent from the lives of almost two-thirds of these children" (Weissbourd 1994:68). Some are twice cursed by the broken relationships of their parents. About one-third of White children and one-half of Black children whose mothers remarry will experience a second divorce before the children reach adulthood.

The crucial question is, What are the consequences of divorce for children? There is clearly the possibility of emotional scars from the period of family conflict and uncertainty prior to the breakup. Children will be affected by the permanency of divorce and the enforced separation from one of the parents. Most commonly, this is separation from their father.

There are the possible negative effects of being raised by a single parent who is overburdened by the demands of children, job, economics, and household maintenance. And there are the negative consequences that may result from the sharp decline in resources available to the family when the parents separate. The data are consistent: Female-headed single-parent families, compared to two-parent families and to male-headed single-parent families, have much lower incomes. This severe decline in family resources for female-headed single-parent families produces a number of challenges for children's adjustment, often including moving to a different home and school, eliminating or greatly reducing the probability of a college education, and other alterations in lifestyles. As a result of all of these possible outcomes of divorce, children may experience behavioral problems, decline in school performance, and other manifestations of maladjustment.

Summaries of the research on the consequences of divorce on children (Wallerstein 2003; Amato 2001, 2004; Fine et al., 2005) reveal that children with divorced parents score lower than children with continuously married parents on measures of academic success, conduct, psychological adjustment, self-concept, and social competence. Although the differences between children from divorced and two-parent families are small, they are consistent. Research also finds that children are better off on a variety of outcomes if parents in high-conflict marriages divorced than if they remained married. But because only some divorces are preceded by a high level of conflict, "divorce probably helps fewer children than it hurts" (Amato 2001:1278).

We must note that the long-term effects of divorce are difficult to measure. Does divorce actually cause the problems displayed by divorced children? Could it be that these troubled children are being raised by troubled parents who eventually divorce (Cherlin 1999)? Heatherington points out that many of the adjustment problems of children are the result of inept parenting and destructive family relations that were present *before* divorce and not the consequences of divorce (Heatherington 2002:63). We simply cannot know, for example, how the children from a particular family would have fared if the parents had stayed together in a tension-filled household. Reviews of the studies on the effects of divorce on children find that "the 'large majority' of children of divorce . . . do not experience severe or long-term problems: most do not drop out of school, get arrested, abuse drugs, or suffer long-term emotional distress" (Coontz 1997:100; Amato and Cheadle 2005).

VIOLENCE IN U.S. FAMILIES

The family has two faces. It can be a haven from an uncaring, impersonal world, a place where love and security prevail. The family members love each other, care for each other, and are accepting of each other. But there is also a dark side of the family. The family is a common context for violence in society. "People are more likely to be killed, physically assaulted, sexually victimized, hit, beat up, slapped, or spanked in their own homes by other family members than anywhere else in our society" (Gelles 1995:450). The intensity that characterizes intimate relationships can give way to conflict. Some families resolve the inevitable tensions that arise in the course of daily living, but in other families conflict gives way to violence.

Violence and the Social Organization of the Family

Although the family is based on love among its members, the way it is organized encourages conflict. First, the family, like all other social organizations, is a power system; that is, power is unequally distributed between parents and children and between spouses, with the male typically dominant. As we saw in Chapter 9, male dominance has been perpetuated by the legal system and religious teaching. Threats to male dominance are often resisted through violence. Parents have authority over their children. They feel they have the right to punish children to shape them in ways the parents consider important.

Unlike most organizations, in which activities and interests are relatively narrow, the family encompasses almost everything. Thus, there are more "events" over which a dispute can develop. Closely related to this phenomenon is the vast amount of time in each day that family members spend interacting. This lengthy interaction increases the probability of disagreements, irritations, violations of privacy, and the like, which increase the risk of violence. Family privacy is another characteristic that enhances the likelihood of violence. The rule in our society that the home is private has two negative consequences. First, it insulates the family members from the protection that society could provide if a family member becomes too abusive. Second, the rule of privacy often prevents the victims of abuse from seeking outside help.

Intimate Partner Violence

Violence between husbands and wives, cohabiting partners, and dating couples in the form of beating, slapping, kicking, and rape is relatively common in U.S. society as well as in countries around the world. That such violence occurs between persons who supposedly joined together because of their mutual love is puzzling indeed. (This section is adapted from Baca Zinn, Eitzen, and Wells 2010:343–353.)

Intimate partner violence is difficult to define. Researchers cannot agree on a common definition. As a result, the estimations of this phenomenon vary. The estimates of the incidence of intimate partner violence provided here use the definition in the National Violence Against Women (NVAW) Survey. This survey, undertaken by the National Institute of Justice and the Centers for Disease Control and Prevention (CDC), is the most recent national study of intimate partner violence. The NVAW Survey defines **intimate partner violence** to include rape, physical assaults, and stalking perpetrated by current and former spouses, cohabiting partners, and dating partners (Tjaden and Thoennes 2000:5).

- **Incidence of Intimate Partner Abuse.** Conclusions about the incidence of violence among intimate partners vary according to who is included within the category of intimate partners and what actions are defined as abusive. Some studies continue to focus only on married couples, while others exclude dating couples. Some include same-sex partners, and others do not. Some researchers define domestic violence to include emotional abuse in addition to physical harm. This variation makes it difficult to obtain data on the extent of intimate partner abuse. Nonetheless, research consistently shows that it is a pervasive problem in the United States and a serious public health concern. The findings of the NVAW Survey allow for the following estimates of the scope of the problem:

  - Approximately 33 million Americans have been victims of intimate partner violence at some point in their lifetime.

- Every year, around 1.3 million women and more than 800,000 men are physically assaulted by an intimate partner; many of these individuals are victimized repeatedly.
- In comparing the experience of abused women and abused men, we find that abused women are assaulted more frequently and are more likely to be injured than are men.
- Injuries inflicted by intimate partners are frequently severe enough to require medical care; approximately 550,000 female victims and 125,000 male victims require medical treatment every year (Tjaden and Thoennes 2000).

Both women and men are victims of intimate partner violence; nonetheless, ample evidence—including the most recent report from the U.S. Department of Justice—documents that most victims of domestic violence are women. This report, titled *Intimate Partner Violence in the United States,* finds that more than 80 percent of the victims of intimate partner violence are women (Catelano 2007).

Within the limitations of the data, the following are some estimates of the extent of the abuse of women by their partners:

- Approximately 22 percent of women report that they have been physically assaulted by an intimate partner at some time over their lifetime (Tjaden and Thoennes 2000).
- Women are the victims in 8 of 10 spousal homicides (Durose et al., 2005).
- Every year, more than 1 million women are stalked by intimate partners.

Class, Race, and Intimate Violence. Although the statistics on intimate violence are somewhat unreliable, we do have a more precise understanding about the conditions under which this phenomenon occurs. Foremost, the connection to social class is clear. Although battered women are found in all social strata, they tend to be found primarily in families threatened by economic hardships. This relationship is generally viewed as the outcome of the stresses of poverty or the lack of resources. Managing family life in a context that may include, for example, crowded and substandard housing, unstable work, unreliable transportation, and neighborhood crime is difficult. In such situations, domestic violence against women would be viewed as the outcome of the "pileup of stressors" associated with inadequate resources (Fox et al., 2002:749).

Men's unemployment puts their partners at increased risk for abuse (Tjaden and Thoennes 2000). Unemployment increases economic strains as bills accumulate and debt rises. In addition, unemployment can be devastating for men who believe it is their responsibility to be the primary provider (Gelles and Cornell 1990:75).

Poverty also limits women's range of responses to abuse (Coker 2005:370). Sufficient material resources are key to escaping an abusive situation; inadequate material resources is the primary reason women do not separate from abusive partners.

An individual's vulnerability to abuse is shaped not only by her gender and class but also by her race (Sokoloff and Dupont 2005:02). The NVAW Survey (Tjaden and Thoennes 2000) found that 25 percent of White women reported having been victimized by an intimate partner. For African Americans, the figure was 29 percent; for Hispanics, it was 23 percent; for Native Americans, it was 31 percent; and for Asian Americans, it was 15 percent. These data show that except for Asian Americans, people of color are more susceptible to domestic violence than Whites. There may be some basis for this generalization. Chapter 8 revealed that minority individuals experience disadvantages related to being a member of a minority group, such as a relatively high probability of joblessness, low wages for doing society's "dirty work," substandard housing, inferior schools, high-crime neighborhoods, and police harassment. Minorities have high rates of poverty and must contend with the stresses that accompany poverty.

We must view the apparent overrepresentation of people of color among the abusers and abused with caution. When demographic and socioeconomic factors are controlled, minorities are no more likely to be violent. In other words, racial differences in domestic abuse have less to do with racial patterns than they do with social class (Johnson and Ferraro 2000).

Child Abuse and Neglect

Gelles and Straus have concluded that "with the exception of the police and the military, the family is perhaps the most violent social group and the home the most violent social setting in our society" (Gelles and Straus 1979a:15). "Adult family members who abuse each other also tend to abuse their children" (Mignon et al., 2002:15). "A small child has more chance of being killed or severely injured by its parents than by anyone else. For children, the home is often the most dangerous place to be" (Collins and Coltrane 1995:476–477). Child abuse is even more prevalent than intimate partner violence. Every week, child protective services (CPS) agencies receive nearly 60,000 referrals alleging child abuse or neglect: CPS agencies investigated the family environments of 3.5 million children in 2007 (U.S. Department of Health and Human Services 2009). This problem is reviewed here, focusing on the definition, incidence, causes, and consequences of child abuse. (The following discussion is adapted from Baca Zinn, Eitzen, and Wells 2010:356–362.)

- **Definition.** What is child abuse? The extreme cases of torture, scalding, beatings, and imprisonment are easy to place in this category. But there are problems in determining whether many other actions are abusive. For example, one definition of child abuse is violence "carried out with the intention of, or perceived as having the intention of, physically hurting the child" (Gelles and Straus 1979b:336). This definition includes everything from spanking to murder. The problem is that spanking is used by nine in ten parents and is considered legitimate and acceptable behavior. At what point does appropriate punishment become excessive? This is an important question for counselors, social workers, health practitioners, and the courts to address because the consequences for children and parents are enormous. To have a definition that is too lax imperils the health and safety of children, and to have one that is too stringent jeopardizes parents who might incorrectly receive the label of "child abuser," have their children taken from them, and even be imprisoned.

The Child Abuse Protection and Treatment Act provides minimum federal guidelines that states must use in defining child maltreatment. These guidelines provide four categories of child maltreatment: neglect, physical abuse, sexual abuse, and emotional abuse. Most states include terminology that defines physical abuse as "physical injury due to punching, beating, kicking, biting, burning, or otherwise harming a child" (USDHHS 2008). This type of abuse involves a range of behaviors, including the inadequate feeding of a child or lack of provision of sanitary living conditions. These forms of neglect may be just as damaging to children, physically and mentally, as physical aggression. This type of problem is complicated, too, because the neglect may or may not be willful on the part of parents.

We have chosen an all-inclusive definition of **child abuse**: "the distinctive acts of violence and nonviolence and acts of omission and commission that place children at risk" (Gelles 1976:136). This is consistent with the government's definition in the Child Abuse Prevention and Treatment Act of 1996: "[child abuse is, at a minimum, any act or failure to act] resulting in imminent risk of serious harm, death, serious physical or emotional harm, sexual abuse, or exploitation" (cited in Mignon, Larson, and Holmes 2002:19). We should not be misled, in using this broad definition, into thinking that all forms of child abuse and neglect are essentially alike, caused by the same sources, and subject to a uniform treatment (Gelles 1976). We generalize about this problem, but the reader is warned that child abuse is, like all social problems, very complex.

- **Incidence.** The precise extent of child abuse and neglect is impossible to know, for two reasons. First, studies of the phenomena have not used uniform definitions; and second, the issue is extremely sensitive to the people involved. To be the perpetrator or victim of child abuse is generally something for which people are stigmatized. Acts of violence and neglect are hidden from society because they occur in private. When asked by a survey researcher if they have ever physically abused their children, abusing parents will most likely deny such an act. Thus, many statistics are taken from police, teachers, social workers, and medical personnel who must assume that the children were victims of abuse. Obviously, such subjective observations are subject to error. As one illustration of the problem of subjectivity, we can note that the parents and children of the middle and upper classes are commonly viewed quite differently by authorities than are those from the lower classes. Trained personnel are more likely to assess a poor child with a black eye as a victim of child abuse than a child from a rich family. Also, of course, many cases of abuse and neglect are never seen by authorities. Official statistics, then, always underreport the actual incidence.

Although there are problems with defining and determining the exact incidence of child abuse, the government provides annual statistics. In 2007, the Department of Health and Human Services (DHHS) reported 794,000 substantiated cases of child abuse and neglect, including the deaths of 1,760 children. The rate of child abuse and neglect in 2007 was 10.6 cases per 1,000 children. This represents a decline from a rate of 12.5 in 2001 (U.S. DHHS 2009).

- **Contexts.** The reasons for the abuse and neglect of children by parents are complex and varied, involving personal, social, and cultural factors. The most commonly assumed cause for abusive behavior toward children is that the perpetrators are mentally ill. This assumption, however, is a myth that hinders the understanding of child abuse (Gelles 1976:138). In the view of experts, only about 10 percent of maltreating parents have severe personality disorders or psychoses. This is not to say that personal factors are unimportant. Obviously, abusive parents let their aggressive feelings go too far. There are several possible reasons that they do. One important reason is that abused children have a higher probability of becoming abusive parents than do nonabused children. In short, violence tends to beget violence. Some caution is advised concerning this relationship, however. The evidence is that about 30 percent of physically abused children grow up to be abusive adults. Although this is much higher than the overall societal rate of between 2 and 3 percent, we must not ignore the fact that seven in ten abused children *do not* become abusive adults (Gelles 1993:15).

A relatively common trait of abusing parents is chronic substance abuse. This activity reduces the normal restraints inhibiting aggression in the individual. Parents' alcoholism has long been associated with child abuse. Recent years have seen an increase in reports of child abuse in households in which parents used methamphetamines (Children's Defense Fund 2005). Substance abuse is also associated with a number of other factors that produce strain and disruption in stable family patterns: greater unemployment, poor health, low self-esteem, isolation, and preoccupation with self.

Finally, a caution from Gelles and Strauss: "When our explanations focus on 'kinds of people'—mentally disturbed, poor alcoholics, drug abusers, etc.—we blind ourselves to the structural properties of the family as a social institution that makes it our most violent institution with the exception of the military in time of war" (Gelles and Strauss, 1988:51).

The Children's Defense Fund states the relationship between social class and child abuse starkly: "Poverty is the single best predictor of child abuse and neglect. Children who live in families with annual incomes of less than $15,000 are 22 times more likely to be abused or neglected than those with annual incomes of $30,000 or more" (2005:113).

In fact, rising and falling rates of child maltreatment are closely tied to changes in the poverty rate. Figure 15.3 captures this relationship in recent years. Most poor children are not abused or neglected. In 2003, nearly 13 million children were poor, but fewer than 1 million U.S. children (representing all social classes) were confirmed as abused or neglected (Children's Defense Fund 2005:115).

Unemployment is another condition associated with child abuse. It may lead to poverty, low self-esteem (because of being a failure in a success-oriented society), and depression. The unemployed are also homebound, increasing their interaction with children.

- **Consequences.** Many consequences of child abuse are obvious. More than 1,700 children die annually from abuse. Emergency rooms, clinics, and therapists treat hundreds of thousands more. Less obvious are the long-term consequences of child abuse and neglect. Hundreds of studies have provided evidence on the health outcomes, cognitive behavior, and social behavior outcomes. The following is drawn from the summary of this body of literature provided by Chalk, Gibbons, and Scarupa (2002):

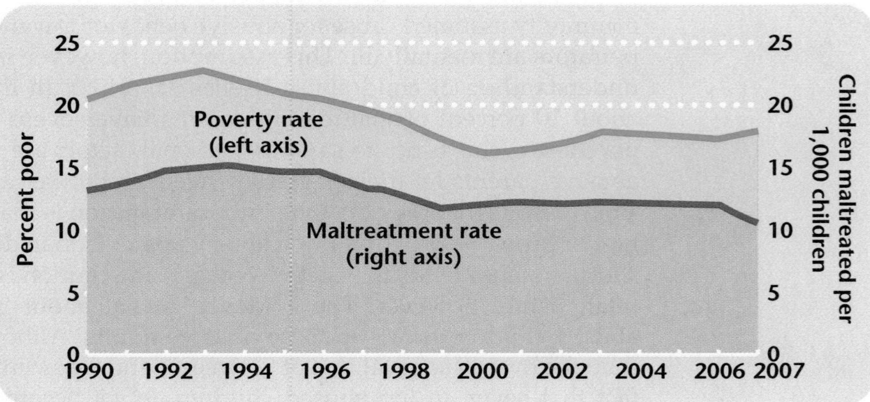

FIGURE 15.3

Poverty and Child Maltreatment Rates, 1990–2007

Sources: Children Defense Fund, *The State of American Children 2005*, p. 115, 2008, p. 19. Online: http://www.childrensdefense.org; U.S. Department of Health and Human Services, *Child Maltreatment 2007*, p. 38. Online: http://www.acf.hhs.gov

Health Outcomes

- Various types of brain injuries are associated with childhood maltreatment, particularly when physical abuse and neglect occur in the first three years of life.
- Abuse and neglect may be associated with physical defects, growth and mental retardation, and speech problems.
- Maltreated children tend to have heightened levels of depression and low self-esteem.

Cognitive and Educational Outcomes

- Some studies find associations between abuse and neglect and language deficits, reduced cognitive functioning, and attention deficit disorders.
- Both neglected and physically abused children tend to do poorly in school, as evidenced by low grades, low standardized test scores, and frequent retention in the same grade.

Social and Behavioral Outcomes

- Antisocial behavior and physical aggression are two of the most consistent outcomes, along with fear and anger, of physical child abuse.
- Maltreatment can have a negative impact on children's emotional stability and self-regulation, problem-solving skills, and the ability to cope with or adapt to new or stressful situations.
- Maltreated children are at risk of getting into trouble with the law and running away from home.
- Several studies have suggested a link between childhood victimization and substance abuse in later life.

Violence in the family presents the ultimate paradox—the physical abuse of loved ones in the most intimate of social relationships. The bonds between wife and husband, parent and child, and adult child and parent are based on love, yet for many people these bonds represent a trap in which they are victims of unspeakable abuses.

Although it is impossible to know the extent of battering that takes place in families, the problem these forms of violence represents is not trivial. The threat of violence in intimate relationships exists for all couples and for all parents and children. Violence in the family, however, is not only a problem at the microlevel of family units. It also represents an indictment of the macrolevel—society, its institutions, and the cultural norms that support violence.

All forms of intimate violence occur within a social context. This social context of intimate violence includes a patriarchal ideology that condones and maintains the power of men over women. The social context includes a media barrage with the consistent message that violence solves social problems. The social contexts include an economy in which poverty, unemployment, and corporate downsizing jeopardize millions of families. The social context includes institutional sexism, institutional racism, and institutional heterosexuality, which make life more difficult for certain categories of people, especially limiting the possibilities for women, people of color, and lesbians and gays. In short, these social forces create the conditions that foster abuse in intimate relationships.

Although the existence of family violence is strongly affected by social forces, individuals acting singly, or with others, can and do shape, resist, and challenge the forces affecting their lives. Concerned citizens—abused women, feminists, and others—have worked through organizations to change the societal forces that encourage abuse. They have also worked to change laws and procedures to protect the victims of abuse.

CHAPTER REVIEW

1. The family is one of the most idealized of all of society's institutions. There are disparities between the common images of the family and real patterns of family life. New sociological research has given us a better understanding of the U.S. family in past and present.
2. Families are closely connected with conditions in the larger society. Their location in class and race hierarchies gives them different resources for family life and creates variation in family form.
3. Changes in the U.S. economy have created discontinuity in family life. Globalization and other transformations have reduced the number of jobs. As the need for skilled labor has diminished, many blue-collar families have experienced unemployment or underemployment. Jobs providing a middle-class standard of living have also disappeared and produced downward mobility for families across the country. These difficulties have been magnified by the Great Recession, which has produced high rates of unemployment and changed the shapes of families in many ways.
4. A major demographic trend since World War II has been the sharp rise in mothers with young children who work outside the home. Few jobs make it easy to balance work and family. Thus, a critical need has emerged in society for accessible and acceptable child care. In general, U.S. society has been unresponsive to this need.
5. More than one-fourth of all households with children are single-parent families, and most are headed by single parents. Single-parent families have a number of unique problems, the most prominent being a lack of economic resources.
6. Nineteen percent of all children in the United States live in poverty.
7. The economic situation of children has worsened relative to the elderly.
8. The divorce rate in U.S. society is the highest in the world. The reasons for this high rate are the increased social and financial independence of women, increased affluence, greater tolerance of divorce by religious groups, no-fault divorce laws, and a more lenient public attitude toward divorce.
9. There are several important consequences of divorce: (a) males and females experience divorce differently, with males having more advantages than females; (b) the economic resources (life chances) for children are reduced; and (c) the trauma for children is heightened for young children, for boys, for large families, and for children whose mother goes to work for the first time after divorce.
10. Researchers on family violence have concluded that the family is among the most violent social groups and that the home is among the most violent settings in U.S. society. The way that families are organized in the United States—the unequal distribution of power, patterns of male dominance, the intensity of interaction, and privacy—encourages conflict.
11. Although family violence occurs across the socioeconomic spectrum, both intimate partner violence and child abuse are correlated with socioeconomic hardship.

KEY TERMS

Family values. Conservative phrase supporting the two-parent family. The implication is that all other family arrangements are the source of social problems.

Family. Social arrangements whereby people related by ancestry, marriage, or cohabitation live together, form an economic unit, and often raise children.

Household. Residential unit in which members share resources. These units vary in membership and composition. A household is not always a family (parents and children), and a family is not always a household (because it may be separate geographically).

Life chances. Opportunities throughout one's life cycle to live and to experience the good things in society.

Downward mobility. Movement to a lower social class.

Modern family. Nuclear family that emerged in response to the requirements of an urban, industrial society. It consisted of an intact nuclear household unit with a male breadwinner, full-time homemaker wife, and their dependent children.

Postmodern families. Multiple family forms and household arrangements that have emerged as a result of a number of social factors, such as women in the labor force, divorce, remarriage, and cohabitation arrangements.

Nonfamily household. Persons who live alone or with unrelated individuals.

Dual-worker family. Family in which both spouses are in the labor force.

Family and Medical Leave Act of 1993. Federal law providing workers in establishments with more than fifty workers the right to unpaid job-protected leave for meeting family health needs.

Divorce. The formal dissolution of a marriage.

Intimate partner violence. Use of force, including rape, physical assaults, and stalking, perpetrated by current and former spouses, cohabiting partners, and dating partners.

Child abuse. Distinctive acts of violence and nonviolence and acts of omission and commission that place children at risk.

■ SUCCEED WITH PEARSON mysoclab www.mysoclab.com

Experience, Discover, Observe, Evaluate

MySocLab is designed just for you. Each chapter features a pre-test and post-test to help you learn and review key concepts and terms.

Experience sociology in action with dynamic visual activities, videos, and readings to enhance your learning experience. Complete the following activities at www.mysoclab.com.

Social Explorer is an interactive application that allows you to explore Census data through interactive maps.

- Explore the Social Explorer Map: *The Increase of Single Women with Children*

The Core Concepts in Sociology video clips offer a real-world perspective on sociological concepts.

- Watch *ABC 20/20: Working Moms*

MySocLibrary includes primary source readings from classic and contemporary sociologists.

- Read Hochschild, *When Work Becomes Home and Home Becomes Work;* Douglas & Michaels, *The Mommy Myth;* Coontz, *The Way We Weren't: The Myth and Reality of the "Traditional" Family*

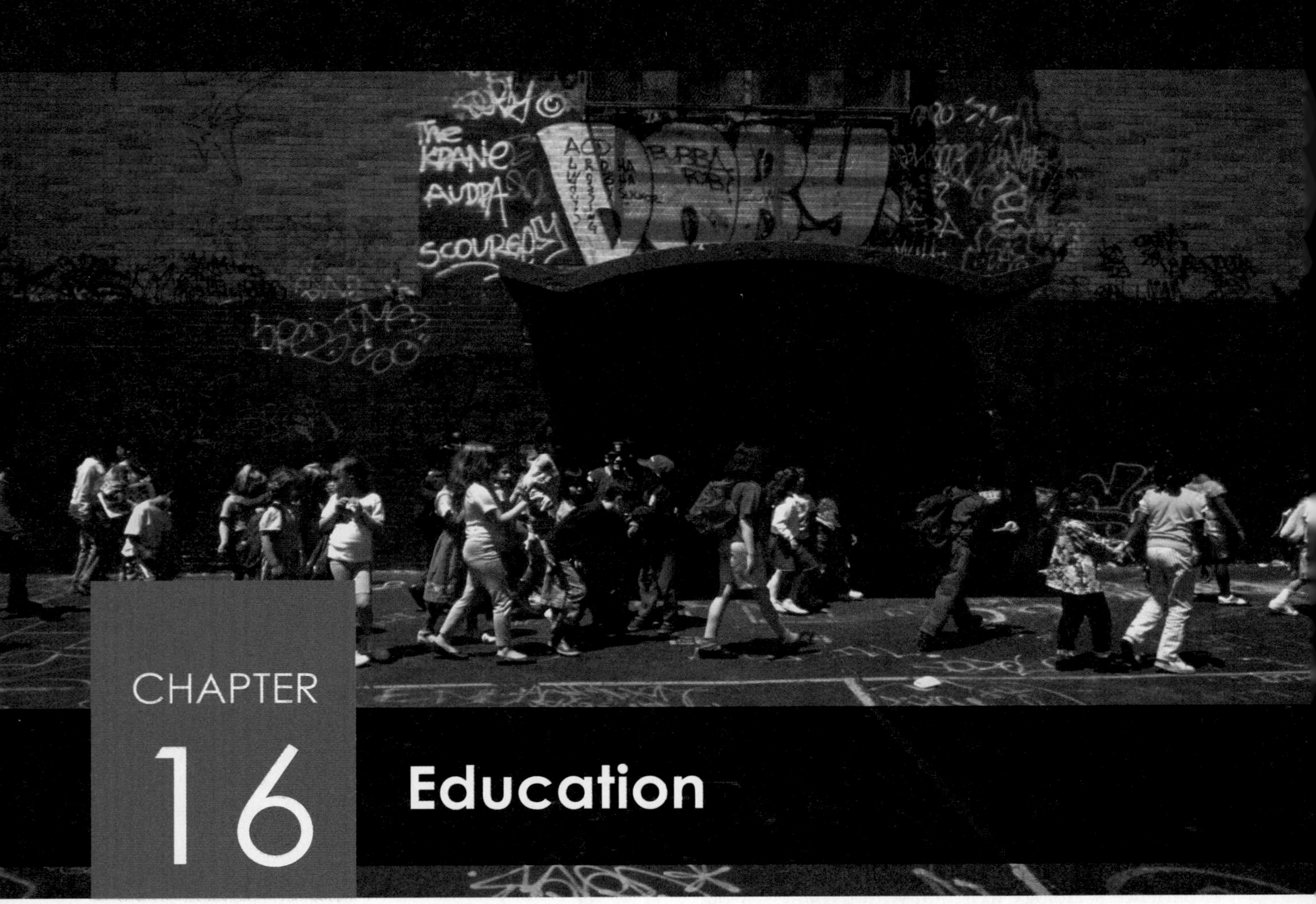

CHAPTER 16 Education

If you look at the history of public education in our country, it's supposed to be the great equalizer. The dividing line in our country, between the have and have nots, is often around educational opportunity. You can come from real poverty, but if you have a great early childhood program, a great K to 12 education and you have access to college, you'll do great. Yet in far too many places in this country, educational opportunity is tied to race, neighborhood, and zip code. There's something wrong with that picture.

—United States Education Secretary Arne Duncan, 2010

This chapter examines one of society's basic institutions—education. The organization of education in society is both a source of and a potential solution to some of our most vexing social problems. The chapter is divided into three main sections. The first describes the characteristics of U.S. education. The second section describes the current role of education in perpetuating inequality in society. The concluding section describes alternatives to eliminate the race and class biases in education.

CHARACTERISTICS OF EDUCATION IN THE UNITED STATES

Education as a Conserving Force

The formal system of education in U.S. society (and in all societies) is conservative because the avowed function of the schools is to teach newcomers the attitudes, values, roles, specialties, information, skills, and training necessary for the maintenance of society. In other words, the special task of the schools is to preserve the culture, not to transform it. Thus, the schools indoctrinate their pupils in the culturally prescribed ways. Children are taught to be patriotic. They learn the myths of the superiority of their nation's heritage; they learn who the heroes are and who the villains are. As Terry Everton notes,

> *Compulsory schooling defines good citizens as those who play by the rules, stay in line, and do as they're told. Learning is defined by how well we memorize and regurgitate what someone else has deemed we need to know. Creativity is permitted within the parameters of the guidance of licensed professionals whose duty it is to make sure we don't get too wacky with our ideas or stray very far from the boundaries of normalcy.* (2004:55)

There is always an explicit or implicit assumption in U.S. schools that the American way is the only really right way. When this assumption is violated on the primary and secondary school level by the rare teacher who asks students to consider the viability of world government or who proposes a class on the teachings of Karl Marx or about world religions, then strong enough pressures usually occur from within the school (administrators, school board) or from without (parents, the American Legion, Daughters of the American Revolution, the Christian right) to quell the disturbance. As a consequence, creativity and a questioning attitude are often curtailed in school.

Mass Education

People in the United States have a basic faith in education. This faith is based on the assumption that a democratic society requires an educated citizenry so that

Children are taught to be patriotic as part of their cultural indoctrination.

individuals can participate in the decisions of public policy. For this reason they not only provide education for all citizens but also compel children to remain in school at least until the eighth grade or until age 16 (although the law varies somewhat from state to state).

Who can quarrel with the belief that all children should be compelled to attend school because it should be for their own good? After all, the greater the educational attainment, the greater the likelihood of larger economic rewards and upward social mobility. However, to compel a child to attend school for 6 hours a day, 5 days a week, 40 weeks a year, for at least 10 years, is quite a demand. The result is that many students are in school for the wrong reason. The motivation is compulsion, not interest in acquiring skills or curiosity about their world. This involuntary feature of U.S. schools is unfortunate because so many school problems are related to the lack of student interest. It is no surprise that despite two decades of intense educational reform, approximately 30 percent of public high school students will drop out before graduation (Thornburgh 2006a).

On the positive side, as a result of the goal of and commitment to mass education, an increasing proportion of people have received a formal education. Between 2005 and 2009, 84.6 percent of Americans over the age of 25 were high school graduates, and another 27.5 percent had a bachelor's degree or higher (Social Explorer Tables: ACS 2005 to 2009 (5-Year Estimates) (SE), ACS 2005–2009 (5-Year Estimates), Social Explorer; U.S. Census Bureau).

Preoccupation with Order and Control

Most administrators and teachers share a fundamental assumption that school is a collective experience requiring subordination of individual needs to those of the school. U.S. schools are characterized, then, by constraints on individual freedom. The school day is regimented by the dictates of the clock. Activities begin and cease on a timetable, not in accordance with the degree of interest shown or whether students have mastered the subject. Another indicator of order is the preoccupation with discipline (i.e., absence of unwarranted noise and movement and concern with the following of orders).

In their quest for order, some schools also demand conformity in clothing and hairstyles. Dress codes are constraints on the freedom to dress as one pleases. School athletic teams also restrict freedom, and the school authorities condone these restrictions. Conformity is also demanded in what to read and how to give the answers the teacher wants.

The many rules and regulations found in schools meet a number of expressed and implicit goals, but many of those goals may be outdated. Zuckerman writes:

> *We are on the threshold of the most radical change in American education in over a century as schools leave the industrial age to join the information age. For most of the past century, our schools were designed to prepare children for jobs on factory lines. Kids lived by the bell, moved through schools as if on conveyor belts, and learned to follow instructions. But today many of these factories are overseas, leaving behind a factory-based school system for an information age. (2005a:68)*

A Fragmented Education System

Certain trends indicate that the educational system in the United States is moving toward greater fragmentation rather than less. According to the National Center for Education Statistics (2009), more and more parents are opting to send their children to private schools (about 11 percent in 2007) or to school them at home (about 2.9 percent). The number of children homeschooled, for example, increased 29 percent from 1999 to 2003. In 2007, roughly 1.5 million children were homeschooled.

Taxpayer-funded charter schools are also growing rapidly. These schools are based on a hybrid "free-market" system in which educators, students, and parents choose a curriculum and educational philosophy free from the dictates of school boards and educational bureaucracies but are financed publicly. In 2006, there were some 3,500 charter schools with more than 1 million students.

Vouchers are another plan that splinters the educational system. This plan gives parents a stipulated amount of money per child that can be used to finance that child's education in any school, public or private. This plan sets up an educational "free market" in which schools have to compete for students. This competition will, theoretically, improve schools because they must provide what parents want for their children, whether that be better discipline, emphasis on learning the fundamentals, religious instruction, focus on the arts, vocational training, or college preparation.

Each of these educational reforms that are underway has strengths and weaknesses. Most important, they represent a trend that is rapidly dividing and subdividing the educational system. For many, this is viewed as a strength, representing the core American values of individualism and competition. Others see this trend as fragmenting further an already disaggregated educational system. Moreover, they see private schools, charter schools, and voucher systems as working against inclusiveness through segregation. For example, 70 percent of Black charter students attend schools where at least 90 percent of students are minorities (Blume 2010). This segregation serves to increase the gap between racial-ethnic groups and social classes in U.S. society.

Local Control of Education

Although the state and federal governments finance and control education in part, the bulk of the money and control for education comes from local communities. There is a general fear of centralization of education under federal control. Local school boards (and the communities themselves) jealously guard their autonomy. Because, as is commonly argued, local people know best the special needs of their children, local boards control allocation of monies, curricular content, and the rules for running the schools, as well as the hiring and firing of personnel.

There are several problems with this emphasis on local control. First, tax money from the local area traditionally finances the schools. Whether the tax base is strong or weak has a pronounced effect on the quality of education received (a point we return to later in this chapter).

Second, local taxes are almost the only outlet for a taxpayers' revolt. Dissatisfaction with high taxes (federal, state, and local) on income, property, and purchases is often expressed at the local level in defeated school bonds and school tax levies. A current population trend—families with school-age children declining while the number of elderly Americans is rising—increases the ever-greater likelihood of the defeat of school issues.

Third, because the democratic ideal requires that schools be locally controlled, the ruling body (school board) should represent all segments of that community. Typically, however, the composition of school boards has overrepresented the business and professional sectors and overwhelmingly underrepresented blue-collar workers, the poor, and various minority groups. The result is a governing body that is typically conservative in outlook and unresponsive to the wishes of people unlike themselves.

Fourth, local control of education may mean that the religious views of the majority (or, at least, the majority of the school board) may intrude in public education. An explicit goal of the Christian Coalition, a conservative religious organization founded by Pat Robertson, is to win control of local school boards. Its agenda opposes globalism, restricts sex education to abstinence from sexual intercourse, promotes school prayer and the teaching of biblical creationism in science classes, and censors books that denigrate Christian values (favorite targets are, for example, *Catcher in the Rye* by J. D. Salinger and John Steinbeck's *The Grapes of Wrath*).

The following are some examples of attempts by states and cities to install religious values in schools:

- In 2002, the Cobb County Board of Education in Georgia voted to insert a sticker in school biology textbooks that reads: "This textbook contains material on evolution. Evolution is a theory, not a fact, regarding the origin of living things. The material should be approached with an open mind, studied carefully, and critically considered" (Slevin 2005). Eleven parents filed suit against the school board, challenging the constitutionality of the textbook warning sticker. On December 19, 2006, a settlement was announced

Some groups have protested the Pledge of Allegiance in schools because of the phrase "one nation under God." Here, students show their support for reciting the pledge in their schools.

in which the school board agreed not to restore the warning sticker or take any actions that would prevent or hinder the teaching of evolution (National Center for Science Education 2006).

- In 2005, the Kansas State Board of Education adopted standards of teaching science whereby evolution was to be represented as scientifically controversial. In February 2007, the board overturned that decision, ruling that evolution should be treated in a scientifically appropriate and responsible way (National Center for Science Education 2007).
- Although the U.S. Supreme Court outlawed the posting of the Ten Commandments in public schools, numerous local school boards believe they can survive legal challenges if the commandments are posted in a display with other historical documents, such as the Magna Carta and the Declaration of Independence (Johnson 2000).
- In 2002, the Texas Board of Education objected to a sixth-grade social studies book that read, "Glaciers formed the Great Lakes millions of years ago," because this statement was counter to the creation timeline of religious conservatives. The book was changed to read, "Glaciers formed the Great Lakes in the distant past" (Russell 2003).

As illustrated by these and a number of other lawsuits in recent years, the separation of church and state remains a volatile subject in the United States.

A Lack of Curriculum Standardization

The local control of education results in another much-debated characteristic of U.S. education—the lack of curriculum standardization across more than 14,000 school districts and fifty states. Arguing for a common curriculum, the late Albert Shanker, then president of the American Federation of Teachers, stated,

> *A common curriculum means that there is agreement about what students ought to know and be able to do and, often, about the age and grade at which they should be able to accomplish these goals. . . . In most countries with a common curriculum, linkage of curriculum, assessment and teacher education is tight. . . . In the U.S., we have no*

such agreement about curriculum—and there is little connection between what students are supposed to learn, the knowledge on which they are assessed, and what we expect our teachers to know. (Shanker 1991:E7)

Since Shanker wrote this in 1991, there has been a national push for education based on common standards while at the same time preserving local control. This idea is embodied in the 2001 **No Child Left Behind Act.** Signed by George W. Bush in 2002, the goal of this legislation was to close the gaps that plague education in the United States and make schools accountable for success or failure. For example, according to National Assessment of Educational Progress data, only 29 percent of the nation's eighth graders are proficient in mathematics and just 32 percent read at their level (reported in Symonds 2004). Compared with other industrialized nations, which have prescribed national curricula or highly specified national standards, U.S. students rank near the bottom in achievement. To improve performance, this legislation required states to develop academic standards in reading, math, and science. States, districts, and schools would then be responsible to ensure that all children achieve these state standards by 2013–2014. Adequate yearly progress is measured by a single, statewide assessment system given annually to all students from third to eighth grade. On the basis of these tests, schools are given a grade of "passing" or "failing." In the 2004 to 2005 school year, 24,470 public schools (over one-quarter of the national total) were labeled as "failing to make adequate yearly progress." In 2007, more than 1,000 of California's 9,500 schools were branded as "chronic failures," and state officials predict that all 6,063 public schools serving poor students will be declared in need of restructuring by 2014 (Schemo 2007). Despite these statistics, the U.S. Department of Education argues that No Child Left Behind is working. They argue that multiple studies show that student achievement in reading and math is rising across the nation and that those schools that have been identified as failing are receiving extra help and resources in order to improve (2006).

Although this legislation has been heralded as the most ambitious federal overhaul of public schools since the 1960s, there are a number of problems. First and foremost, instead of one system, we have fifty. Each state was permitted to set its own proficiency benchmarks, with some setting a high and others setting a low standard. Because the federal government rewards those who meet the standards, the ones with high standards are punished, while the ones with low standards are unfairly rewarded. In their 2007 report "The Proficiency Illusion" (Cronin et al., 2007), researchers from the Thomas B. Fordham Institute examine No Child Left Behind in detail. In their comprehensive review, they found:

- State tests vary greatly in their difficulty, with Colorado, Wisconsin, and Michigan having the lowest proficiency standards in reading and math.
- Improvements in the passing rates on state tests can largely be explained by declines in the difficulty on those tests, rather than true growth in student learning.
- The tests in eighth grade are consistently and dramatically more difficult than those in earlier grades. Many states set the bar much lower in elementary school, giving false impressions to parents and teachers that students are doing well.

Critics of No Child Left Behind argue that there is no attempt to address the funding inequities among rich and poor districts within a state that help perpetuate the achievement gaps, the chronic underfunding of poorer schools, or child poverty itself (Metcalf 2002). To rectify this, in March 2010 President Obama announced that an allocation of $900 million in grants would be awarded to help turn around the nation's lowest-performing schools. Unfortunately, the 2007 to 2009 economic recession has left states in fiscal crisis, and budget cuts to education are rampant, resulting in teacher layoffs and the reduction in school programs and supplies. It remains to be seen what effect this will have on state standards and educational outcomes.

In sum, the lack of a common national curriculum has several negative consequences. First, there is a wide variation in the preparation of students, as

Mathematics (2006)		
Rank		*Score*
1	Finland	548
2	Korea	547
3	Netherlands	531
4	Switzerland	530
5	Canada	527
6	Japan	523
7	New Zealand	522
8	Belgium	520
9	Australia	520
10	Denmark	513
11	Czech Republic	510
12	Iceland	506
13	Austria	506
14	Germany	504
15	Sweden	502
16	Ireland	501
17	France	496
18	United Kingdom	495
19	Poland	495
20	Slovak Republic	492
21	Hungary	491
22	Luxembourg	490
23	Norway	490
24	Spain	480
25	United States	474
26	Portugal	466
27	Italy	462
28	Greece	459
29	Turkey	424
30	Mexico	406
OECD average		498

Science (2006)		
Rank		*Score*
1	Finland	563
2	Canada	534
3	Japan	531
4	New Zealand	530
5	Australia	527
6	Netherlands	525
7	Korea	522
8	Germany	516
9	United Kingdom	515
10	Czech Republic	513
11	Switzerland	512
12	Austria	511
13	Belgium	510
14	Ireland	508
15	Hungary	504
16	Sweden	503
17	Poland	498
18	Denmark	496
19	France	495
20	Iceland	491
21	United States	489
22	Slovak Republic	488
23	Spain	488
24	Norway	487
25	Luxembourg	486
26	Italy	475
27	Portugal	474
28	Greece	473
29	Turkey	424
30	Mexico	410
OECD average		500

Reading (2003)		
Rank		*Score*
1	Finland	543
2	Korea	534
3	Canada	528
4	Australia	525
5	New Zealand	522
6	Ireland	515
7	Sweden	514
8	Netherlands	513
9	Belgium	507
10	Norway	500
11	Switzerland	499
12	Japan	498
13	Poland	497
14	France	496
15	United States	495
16	Denmark	492
17	Iceland	492
18	Germany	491
19	Austria	491
20	Czech Republic	489
21	Hungary	482
22	Spain	481
23	Luxembourg	479
24	Portugal	478
25	Italy	476
26	Greece	472
27	Slovak Republic	469
28	Turkey	441
29	Mexico	400
OECD average		494

Problem Solving (2003)		
Rank		*Score*
1	Korea	550
2	Finland	548
3	Japan	547
4	New Zealand	533
5	Australia	530
6	Canada	529
7	Belgium	525
8	Switzerland	521
9	Netherlands	520
10	France	519
11	Denmark	517
12	Czech Republic	516
13	Germany	513
14	Sweden	509
15	Austria	506
16	Iceland	505
17	Hungary	501
18	Ireland	498
19	Luxembourg	494
20	Slovak Republic	492
21	Norway	490
22	Poland	487
23	Spain	482
24	United States	477
25	Portugal	470
26	Italy	469
27	Greece	448
28	Turkey	408
29	Mexico	384
OECD average		500

FIGURE 16.1

U.S. 15-Year-Old Performance Compared with Other Countries

This figure can be found at: http://www.corestandardards.org. Report: "Benchmarking for Success: Ensuring U.S. Students Receive a World-Class Education," p. 13, Figure 1.

states have the ability to raise or lower their standards. Second, because families move on the average of once every 5 years (and the rate is probably higher for families with school-age children), there are large numbers of children each year who find the requirements of their new schools different, sometimes very different, from their previous schools. Finally, not only are many American students graduating without the skills necessary to compete in an information economy, but they also appear to be ill poised to compete in a *global* economy (see Figure 16.1).

In a push for a common national curriculum, the National Governors Association Center for Best Practices has joined with others to form the Common Core State Standards Initiative, an initiative to develop international benchmarks for all states so that all students are prepared to be competitive in a globalized market. Hoping to push the initiative forward in 2010, they write,

> *The United States is falling behind other countries in the resource that matters most in the new global economy: human capital. American 15-year-olds ranked 25th in math and 21st in science achievement on the most recent international assessment conducted in 2006. At the same time, the U.S. ranked high in inequity, with the third largest gap in science scores between students from different socioeconomic groups. (2008:5)*

"Sifting" and "Sorting" Function of Schools

Schools play a considerable part in choosing the youth who come to occupy the higher-status positions in society. School performance also sorts out those who will occupy the lower rungs in the occupational-prestige ladder. Education is, therefore, a selection process. The sorting is done with respect to two different criteria: a child's ability and his or her social class background. Although the goal of education is to select on ability alone, ascribed social status (the prestige and socioeconomic status of one's family, race, and religion) has a pronounced effect on the degree of success in the educational system. The school is analogous to a conveyor belt, with people of all social classes getting on at the same time but leaving the belt in accordance with social class—the lower the class, the shorter the ride.

EDUCATION AND INEQUALITY

Education is presumed by many people to be the great equalizer in U.S. society—the process by which the disadvantaged get their chance to be upwardly mobile. The data in Figure 16.2 show, for example, that the higher the educational attainment, the higher the income. But these data do not in any way demonstrate equality of opportunity through education. They show clearly that African Americans and Latinos with the same educational attainment as Whites receive lower economic rewards at every educational level. These differences reflect discrimination in society, not just in schools. This section examines the ways that the schools help to perpetuate class and race inequities.

The evidence that educational performance is linked to socioeconomic background is clear and irrefutable (we include race/ethnicity along with economic status since they are highly correlated).

- Children in the poorest families are six times as likely as children in more affluent families to drop out of school (Children's Defense Fund 2004a:88).

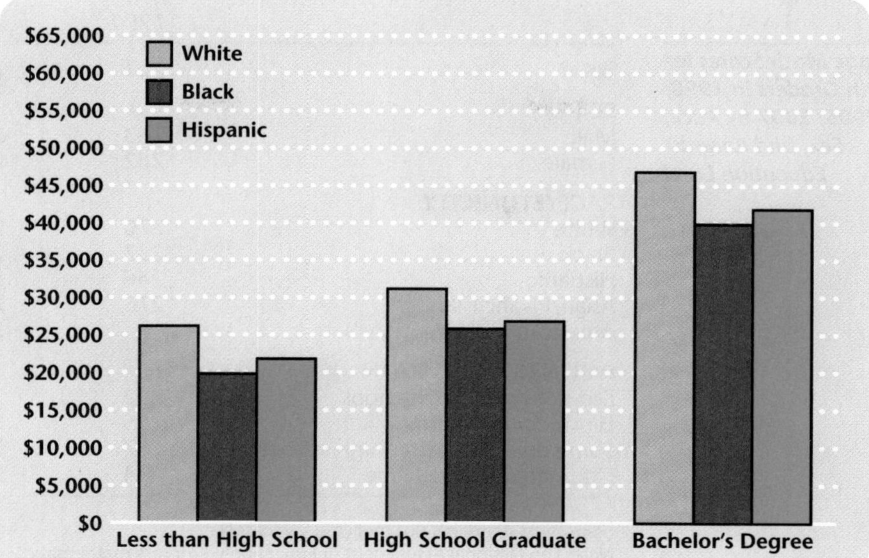

FIGURE 16.2
Median Annual Earnings of Full-Time Salary Workers Ages 25–34 by Educational Attainment and Race/Ethnicity, 2008
Source: U.S. Department of Commerce, Census Bureau, Current Population Survey (CPS), March and Annual Social and Economic Supplement, selected years, 1981–2009.

- Researchers at Cornell University have found that the longer children live in poverty, the lower they tend to score on working-memory tests. In fact, those who spent their entire childhood in poverty scored about 20 percent lower on working memory than those who were never poor. They conclude that the chronic stress of poverty impairs the cognitive development of children (Stein 2009).
- In 2005, fourth-grade students in the highest poverty public schools had an average math assessment score of 221, compared with an average score of 255 for students in the lowest poverty schools (National Center for Education Statistics 2010).
- Achievement gaps in reading, writing, and mathematics persist between minority and White students. In the 2009 Condition of Education, researchers note that in reading, gaps between White and minority students remain relatively unchanged since 1992 (National Center for Education Statistics 2010). Table 16.1 shows the difference in average math scores of eighth graders in 1990, 2005, and 2007. With the exception of Asian students (who scored higher than all other groups), the average score for White students was higher than the scores for Black, Hispanic, and Native American/Alaska Native students in all three years.
- African American, Latino, and Native American students lag behind their White peers in graduation rates and most other measures of student performance. In 2003, the graduation rate from public high school was 78 percent for White students, 72 percent for Asian students, 55 percent for African American students, and 53 percent for Hispanic students (Greene and Winters 2006). A recent study by UCLA indicates that, in the twelve states studied, less than half of American Indian and Alaska Native students graduate from high school each year (Faircloth and Tippeconnie 2010). It is important to note that graduation rates in all racial-ethnic groups also vary greatly by gender. For a closer look at gender and education, see the panel, "Leaving Boys Behind?"
- The high dropout rate for Hispanics and African Americans translates into a lifetime of poor outcomes. According to Thornburgh, "Dropping out of high school today is to your societal health what smoking is to your

TABLE 16.1

Average Math Scores for 8th Graders in 1990, 2005, 2007 by Race, Sex, and Parents' Education Level

	1990	*2005*	*2007*
Total	263	279	281
SEX			
Male	263	280	282
Female	262	278	280
RACE/ETHNICITY			
White	270	289	291
Black	237	255	260
Hispanic	246	262	265
Asian/Pacific Islander	275	295	297
American Indian/Alaska Native	*	264	264
PARENTS' EDUCATION			
Did not finish high school	242	259	263
High school graduate	255	267	270
Some education after high school	267	280	283
Graduated from college	274	290	292

*Reporting standards not met (too few cases).
Note: The National Assessment of Educational Progress mathematics scale ranges from 0 to 500.
Source: U.S. Department of Education, National Center for Education Statistics, National Assessment of Educational Progress (NAEP), 1990–2007 Mathematics Assessments, NAEP Data Explorer.

physical health, an indicator of a host of poor outcomes to follow, from low lifetime earnings to high incarceration rates to a high likelihood that your children will drop out of high school and start the cycle anew" (2006a:32).
- Black, Latino, and Native American students are suspended or expelled in numbers disproportionate to those of Whites. Data from the 2004 to 2005 school year indicate that in every state but Idaho, Black students are being suspended in numbers greater than would be expected from their proportion of the student population. In fact, in twenty-one states the percentage of Black suspensions is more than double their percentage of the student body (Witt 2007).

These social class and racial gaps in academic achievement are found in almost every school and district in the United States. On the surface, these patterns reinforce the social Darwinist assumptions that the affluent are successful because they are intelligent, and, conversely, the poor and minorities are at society's bottom because they do not have the requisite abilities to be successful. Similarly, dysfunctional families, unmotivated students, and the culture of poverty are believed by some to explain the academic achievement gap. We argue, to the contrary, that structural factors explain why the poor and minorities are disadvantaged in our supposedly meritocratic educational system. In effect, the educational system is stacked in favor of middle- and upper-class children and against children from the lowest classes.* Many interrelated factors explain

*We have phrased the sentence to focus on the system, not the victims. This focus is contrary to the typical response, which is to focus on the **cultural deprivation** of the poor. That approach attacks the home and culture of poor people and assumes that poor people perform inadequately because they are handicapped by their culture. Observers cannot, however, make the value judgment that a culture is deprived. They can note only that their milieu does not prepare children to perform in schools geared for the middle class. In other words, children of the poor and/or minority groups are not nonverbal; they are very verbal, but not in the language of the middle class.

A CLOSER LOOK

LEAVING BOYS BEHIND?

In the 1990s, researchers and popular writers started writing about the "girl crisis" in America. According to books like *Reviving Ophelia: Saving the Selves of Adolescent Girls* (Pipher 1994) and *Failing at Fairness: How Our Schools Cheat Girls* (Sadker and Sadker 1994), girls were believed to be suffering when they hit adolescence. In 1992, the American Association of University Women (AAUW) published "How Schools Shortchange Girls," a study conducted by the Wellesley College Center for Research on Women. The report claimed that girls across the country were victims of a pervasive bias in schools. Teachers paid more attention to male students, gave them more time and feedback on their work, and did not encourage girls, especially in the areas of math and science. As a result, millions of dollars in grants were awarded to study the plight of girls in education (Sommers 2000).

More recently, writers have been focusing on a different crisis in education, that of boys, not girls. Christina Hoff Sommers writes,

> The research commonly cited to support the claims of male privilege and sinfulness is riddled with errors. Almost none of it has been published in peer-reviewed journals. Some of the data are mysteriously missing. Yet the false picture remains and is dutifully passed along in schools of education, in "gender equity" workshops, and increasingly to children themselves. . . . A review of the facts shows boys, not girls, on the weak side of an educational gender gap. (2000:14)

According to Garibaldi, boys are increasingly disengaged in the "feminized" classroom (2006). Through movies, television, and rap music, pop culture teaches young boys it is not "cool" to like or do well in school and that to be masculine is to be disengaged and anti-authority (Wenzl 2007). Those who propose that it is boys who are in crisis offer the following arguments:

- Boys are less likely to graduate from high school (65 percent versus 72 percent of girls; Greene and Winters 2006).
- Boys are, on average, a year and a half behind girls in reading and writing (Sommers 2000).
- Each year women receive more bachelor's and master's degrees than men (Mead 2006).
- Boys are more likely to be held back a grade, drop out, and be suspended from school (Sommers 2000).
- Girls continue to score higher on the Scholastic Aptitude test in the area of writing. On the newly revamped SAT in 2006, girls scored an average of 11 points higher in writing (College Board 2006).

So what is the truth concerning the gender gap in education? In a 2006 report by the Education Sector, Mead argued that "the real story is not bad news about boys doing worse; it's good news about girls doing better" (2006:1). In the report, using data from the National Assessment of Education Progress, Mead argued that American boys are scoring higher and achieving more than they have in the past, but girls have improved their performance on some measures even faster, which makes it appear as though boys are doing "worse." The data seem to indicate that younger boys are doing quite well, but older boys are starting to slip when they reach twelfth grade. Mead argued that twelfth-grade girls are sliding as well. She argued, "The fact that achievement for older students is stagnant or declining for both boys and girls, to about the same degree, points to another important element of the boy crisis. The problem is most likely not that high schools need to be fixed to meet the needs of boys but rather that they need to be fixed to meet the needs of *all* students, male and female" (2006:4).

In the battle over who is in crisis and more disadvantaged, two very important ideas seem to get left out. First of all, regardless of the statistics that more boys are dropping out of school and are less likely to go to college, women still, on average, earn less than men at every level of education. Furthermore, women continue to attain a small percentage of high-level jobs in corporations, politics, and other occupations, and they continue to be responsible for the majority of domestic work. In her criticism of the "boy crisis" literature, Douglas writes,

> In 1999, one year before Sommers' book came out, the top five jobs for women did not include attorney, surgeon, or CEO. They were, in order, secretaries, retail and personal

(Cont.)

sales workers (including cashiers), managers and administrators, elementary school teachers and registered nurses. In 2007, when presumably some of the privileged, pampered girls whose advantages over boys Sommers had kvetched about had entered the workforce, the top five jobs for women were, still secretaries in first place, followed by registered nurses, elementary and middle school teachers, cashiers, and retail salespersons.

Farther down the line? Maids, child care workers, office clerks and hairdressers. Not a CEO or hedge fund manager in sight. And, in the end, no president or vice president in 2008. But what about all those career-driven girls going to college and leaving the guys in the dust? A year out of college, they earn 80 percent of what men make. And 10 years out? A staggering 69 percent. (2010:1–2)

Second, for every statistic that indicates a gender gap, there is an even larger gap by social class and race. Mead argues that "the gaps between students of different races and classes are much larger than those for students of different genders—anywhere from two to five times as big, depending on the grade. . . . Overall, poor, Black, and Hispanic boys would benefit far more from closing racial and economic achievement gaps than they would from closing gender gaps" (2006:5).

why the education system tends to reinforce the socioeconomic and racial differences in the United States. We examine a few of these in the following sections.

Financing Public Education

Schools in the United States reflect the economic divide that exists in society:

> *In America, the type of education provided, the way it's funded and the content of the curriculum are local matters directed by local authorities. The result is easy to see. Across America one sees the extremes: from schools that resemble shining mansions on a hill to ramshackle, dilapidated structures.* (Kamau 2001:81)

Approximately 50 million U.S. children attend public schools (6 million attend private schools and about 1.5 million are homeschooled). These schools receive funds from three governmental sources—about 9 percent from the federal government; about 47 percent from the state, depending on the allocation within each state; and 44 percent from local taxes in each district within the state Villano 2009). The result of this distribution is that schools are funded unequally in the United States, with public schools being more successful in educating children in middle-class communities but often failing children in poor neighborhoods.

Equal opportunity in education (at least as measured by equal finances) has not been accomplished nationwide because wealthier states are able to pay much more per pupil than are poorer states. The top-spending states, for example, invest more than double the amount per pupil than those states spending the least. Because the federal government provides only about 9 percent of the money for public schools, equalization from state to state is impossible as long as education is funded primarily by state and local governments because both entities vary in wealth and commitment to public education.

The disparities in per-pupil expenditures within a given state are also great, largely because of the tradition of funding public schools through local property taxes. This procedure is discriminatory because rich school districts can spend more money than poor ones on each student—and at a lower taxing rate. Thus, suburban students are more advantaged than are students from the inner city; districts with business enterprises are favored over agricultural districts; and districts with natural resources are better able to provide for their children than are districts with few resources. In some states, the disparity in spending for each pupil may be as much as three times more in affluent districts than in poor areas. Some examples:

- In Illinois, the children of all-Black East St. Louis receive an education worth $8,000 yearly, while the children of Lake Forest, a predominantly White suburb of Chicago, receive one worth $18,000 (Kozol 2004).
- Including all the costs of operating a public school, a third-grade class of twenty-five children in the schools of Great Neck, New York, receives at least $200,000 more per year than does a class the same size in Mott Haven, New York, where 99.8 percent of children are Black or Latino (Kozol 2002).
- In the Los Angeles area, the students in McKittrick School in the Central Valley receive $17,000 each, more than twice as much as Laguna Beach schools (*Los Angeles Times* 2003).

Data from the U.S. Census Bureau show that in 2008, per-pupil spending ranged from a high of $17,173 in New York to a low of $5,765 in Utah (see Figure 16.3). This gap is even greater when one considers the monies raised in each district from fundraisers, soda machine contracts, and foundation contributions.

There have been a number of court challenges to unequal funding within states, and systems in several states have been judged unconstitutional. Various schemes have been proposed to meet the objections of the courts, but inequities remain even in the more progressive states. Progressive plans to address financial inequities are fought by the affluent districts and their constituents because, they argue, their taxes should be spent on their children, not the children of others.

Overall, research shows that poor students and the schools serving them have fewer computers and other supplies; have teachers who are underpaid and have less teaching experience; are more likely to attend schools in need of repairs, renovations, and modernization (Filardo et al., 2006); and have higher pupil–teacher ratios. See the Speaking to Students panel, "In-School Marketing," for a look at what some schools are doing to generate more funds.

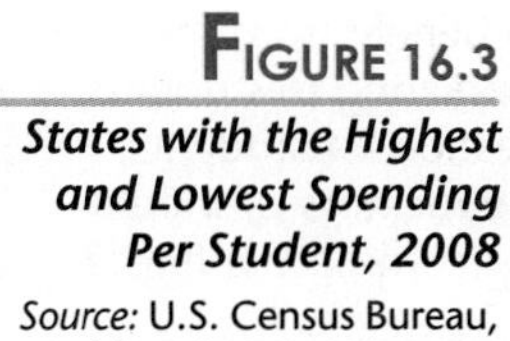

FIGURE 16.3

States with the Highest and Lowest Spending Per Student, 2008

Source: U.S. Census Bureau, Public Education Finances 2008.

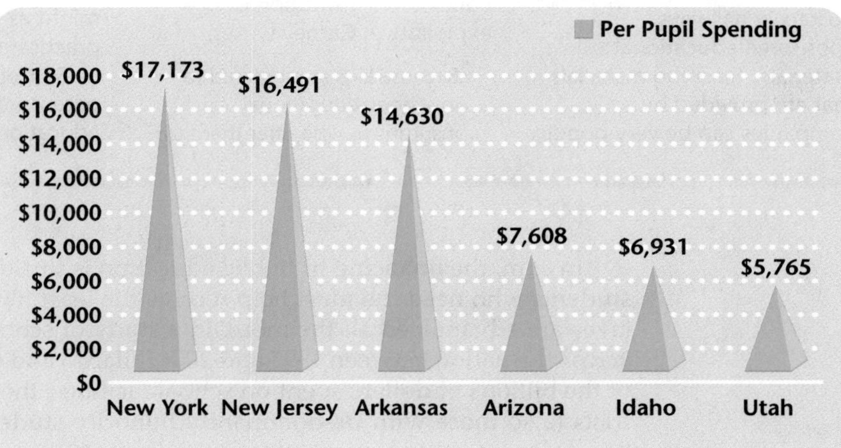

Speaking to Students

In-School Marketing

We live in an advertising age. Through television, radio, billboards, movies, and the Internet, Americans are bombarded with advertisements. Research shows that the average American is exposed to 61 minutes of on-screen ads and promotions per day (Stelter 2009), and the average American living in a big city sees up to 5,000 advertisements per day (Story 2007).

In an effort to make up for declining school revenues, many school districts allow companies to market their products within the school environment in exchange for cash or computers and other supplies. Teenagers provide a target audience for marketers who want to catch consumers early and create brand loyalty. Smart companies understand that teenagers have enormous spending power, and they are ready and willing to capitalize on this through in-school marketing. In elementary, middle, and high schools direct advertising can be found on:

- Book covers and educational posters in hallways.
- Sponsored educational materials. Teaching materials that are provided by companies can be very popular with teachers. "The problem is that the primary goal of the creators is to sell their product; not to educate kids. Content can easily be altered to fit the 'message' that the company wants kids to receive" (Carney, 2007:1).
- Channel One (a division of Alloy Media and Marketing) broadcasts daily to nearly six million teens in approximately 8,000 schools.
- School buses: Some school districts have sold advertising space on the side of their buses, and others broadcast radio programs with advertisements.
- Vending machines: Schools can have exclusive product sponsorships, and can even receive bonuses if certain sales quotas are met (Carney 2007).
- Athletics fields, scoreboards, and gymnasium walls.
- Fundraising items such as cookie dough, magazines, and other branded products.

Critics of this arrangement argue that advertising within an educational institution is exploitative. Carney writes,

> Because kids are required to be in school, educational institutions who offer them to advertisers in exchange for money or other incentives are essentially providing companies with a captive audience. In addition, because the products are being presented in a school environment, kids are more likely to believe the advertising promises and take messages at face value. (2007:2)

In this way, marketing to students is dangerous because it seems as though the school endorses the product. A superintendent in Manassas Park says, "To me, it kind of cheapens the education mission, and it takes a captive audience and shoves advertising down their throats" (quoted in Birnbaum 2009:1).

Others argue that in tight economic times schools are forced to do whatever it takes to bring in resources. Furthermore, in a culture saturated with advertising, students will be exposed to ads whether they are presented within the school environment or presented outside of school. Because this is the case, schools might as well benefit from the practice of marketing to students.

So the question for students, parents, and educators is, should education be "commercial-free"?

In sum, the financing of public education is upside down. The schools and students who need the most help receive the least, whereas those with advantages are advantaged all the more. In a study of school construction spending across the nation between 1995 and 2004, Filardo and colleagues found that out of the billions of dollars spent on school facilities, the least-affluent school districts (also those with predominantly minority student enrollment) made the lowest investment per student, and the most affluent districts made the highest investment (2006). Further, the money spent on schools serving low-income students was more likely used to fund basic repairs, but schools in more affluent districts were more likely to add science labs, technology, or other new programs. As stated by President Barack Obama, "For low-income students, the schools are made less decrepit; for wealthier students, they are made more enriching. . . . For all students to achieve, all must be provided adequate resources: effective teachers, inspiring school leaders, and enriching classroom environments" (2006:1).

Family Economic Resources

The average SAT (Scholastic Aptitude Test) scores for youth from families whose annual income was $200,000 or more was 381 points higher than for youth from families whose income is $20,000 or less (1702 versus 1321). By race, Whites scored about 300 points higher than African Americans on average (Marklein 2009). How are we to explain these differences on the SATs by income and race? One factor highly correlated with income is parents' education level. For SAT takers in the class of 2004, scores were approximately 50 points higher than the national average for those whose parents had a graduate degree and 39 points lower than the national average if their parents had only a high school diploma (Carnahan and Coletti 2006).

Many benefits come from economic privilege. Poor parents (disproportionately people of color), most without health insurance, are unable to afford prenatal care, which increases the risk of babies being born at low birth weight, a condition that may lead to learning disabilities. As these poor children age, they are less likely to receive adequate nutrition, decent medical care, and a safe and secure environment. These deficiencies increase the probability of their being less alert, less curious, and less able to interact effectively with their environment than are healthy children.

Poor children are more likely than the children of the affluent to attend schools with poor resources, which, as we have seen, means that they are less likely to receive an enriched educational experience. In their analysis of a nationally representative sample of kindergarten children, Lee and Burkam argues,

> *Low-SES [socioeconomic status] children begin school in kindergarten in systematically lower-quality elementary schools than their more advantaged counterparts. However school quality is defined—in terms of higher student achievement, more school resources, more qualified teachers, more positive teacher attitudes, better neighborhood or school conditions, private vs. public schools—the least advantaged U.S. children begin their formal schooling in consistently lower-quality schools. This reinforces the inequalities that develop even before children reach school age.* (2002:3)

Similarly, most poor young people live in communities that have few opportunities to apply academic skills and build new ones because such opportunities are either not available or not accessible (libraries, planetariums, summer camps, zoos, nature preserves, museums). The lack of community resources is especially destructive during the summer months, the time when children doing least well in school (a group that is disproportionately poor) slide backward the furthest.

Children from poor families cannot afford private early development programs, which prepare children for school. They can be in Head Start, but these government programs have funding for only about 60 percent of those eligible. As Jonathan Kozol notes,

> *The most exclusive of the private preschools in New York, which are known to those who can afford them as "Baby Ivies," cost as much as $24,000 for a full-day program. Competition for admission to these pre-K schools is so extreme that private counselors are frequently retained, at fees as high as $300 an hour, to guide the parents through the application process. At the opposite extreme along the economic spectrum in New York are the thousands of children who receive no preschool opportunity at all. (2005:46)*

The level of affluence also affects how long children will stay in school because schools, even public schools, are costly. There are school fees (many school districts, e.g., charge fees for participation in music, athletics, and drama), supplies, meals, transportation, and other costs of education. These financial demands pressure youngsters from poorer families to drop out of school prematurely to go to work. The children from the middle and upper classes, not constrained by financial difficulties, tend to stay in school longer, which means better jobs and pay in the long run.

The affluent also give their children educational advantages such as home computers; travel experiences abroad and throughout the United States; visits to zoos, libraries, and various cultural activities; and summer camps to hone their skills and enrich their experiences in such activities as sports, music, writing, and computers. Another advantage available to the affluent is the hiring of tutors to help children having difficulty in school or to transform good students into outstanding ones.

The well-to-do often send their children to private schools (about 11 percent of U.S. children attend these schools). Parents offer several rationales for sending their children to private schools. Some do so for religious reasons. Another reason is that private schools, unlike public schools, are selective in whom they accept. Thus, parents can ensure that their children will interact with children similar to

America's elite prep schools have a distinguished list of alumni, from former presidents to U.S. ambassadors.

theirs in race (some private schools were expressly created so that White children could avoid attending integrated public schools) and social class. Similarly, private schools are much more likely than public schools to get rid of troublesome students (e.g., behavioral problems and low achievers), thereby providing an educational environment more conducive to learning and achievement. A final reason for attending private schools is that the most elite of them provide a demanding education and entry to the most elite universities, which, in turn, lead to placement in top positions in the professional and corporate occupational worlds.

The preceding arguments show that a family's economic resources are correlated to their child's educational success. From test scores to dropout rates, some students are more advantaged than others.

Higher Education and Stratification

As noted earlier, obtaining a college degree is an important avenue to later success. Because the payoff in jobs and pay is directly related to the prestige of the college or university attended, colleges play an important role in maintaining the stratified structure of society. From those who receive no college education to those who attend private, elite universities, each tier in the hierarchy results in different life chances.

On the lowest tier of the hierarchy are those who cannot afford to attend college. Although economic success is possible without a college degree, for most individuals, no college education translates into a lifetime of lower earnings and low-mobility jobs. Throughout the 1980s and 1990s, the cost of college rose at a rate more than twice the inflation rate. In 2009–2010, on average, the total annual expenses to attend a four-year private school as a resident were $26,273 compared to $7,020 for a four-year public school for in-state students and $11,528 for out-of-state students (College Board 2010). The cost of room, board, fees, and tuition at the nation's most exclusive schools is $35,000 or more for a single school year. The high costs, coupled with declining scholarship monies, prohibit college attendance not only for the able poor but also increasingly for children of the working and lower middle classes. A comparison of students from different income groups shows that 14 percent of those from the lowest income group will enroll in college, compared to 64 percent of those from the highest income group (Symonds 2006).

Because racial minorities are much more likely than Whites to be poor or near poor, they are underrepresented in colleges and among college graduates. The percentages of all racial groups who have completed a bachelor's degree or higher have increased since 1971, but the gaps between Whites and Blacks and Whites and Hispanics remain (U.S. Department of Education, National Center for Education Statistics 2006; see Table 16.2). The disproportionately low number of college degrees earned by minorities is reflected in the relatively low number of students who attend and graduate from graduate school. This, of course, results in a low proportion of minorities in the various professions in the near future. Of special significance is the low minority representation among full-time faculty in higher education now and projected for the future.

For students who do attend college, money stratifies. The poorest, even those who are talented, are most likely to attend community colleges, which are the least expensive; these schools emphasize technical careers and are therefore limiting in terms of later success (around 44 percent of the nation's college students attend community colleges).

Students with greater resources are likely to attend public universities. State schools are subsidized by their legislators according to their level of prestige. Similar to the funding of public education from kindergarten through high school, the funding of public higher education benefits the already advantaged and neglects the already neglected. In Colorado, for instance, Colorado State University in 2002 received from the state $5,394 for each student enrolled, compared to the $2,582 that the Community College of Aurora received per student (Greenberg 2002). This means, in effect, that all taxpayers, including those of modest means, support this elitist system.

Finally, on the highest tier of the hierarchy are the students with the greatest financial backing who are the most likely to attend elite and prestigious private institutions. The most prestigious schools have the most resources, which means they can hire the most prestigious professors, maintain the most complete libraries and research facilities, and equip state-of-the-art classrooms. Despite falling endowments due to the economic recession, in 2009 Harvard had an endowment valued at $36.5 billion, Yale had an endowment worth $16.3 billion, and Stanford had an endowment worth $12.6 billion (National Association of College and University Business Officers [NACUBO] 2010).

Although talent is an important variable, it is money—not ability—that places college students in this stratified system. For example, admission committees at elite universities give students from upper-class families favorable ratings if they are children of alumni or children of big contributors to the university's fundraising campaigns (this is a reverse form of affirmative action, benefiting the children of the affluent, the most notable example being George W. Bush's acceptance into Yale). Reporter Daniel Golden argued that these children of celebrities, politicians, and wealthy executives, called "development cases," are often admitted to elite colleges with SAT scores sometimes 300 or 400 points lower than those of some rejected applicants (Golden 2006). Peter Schmidt writes:

> *Conservatives often complain that because of affirmative action, colleges are no longer meritocracies. But the reality is that it's not lesser-qualified black and Hispanic*

TABLE 16.2

Educational Attainment by Race/Ethnicity for U.S. Population 25 Years and Older, 2006–2009

Highest Level Reached	*All Races*	*Asian American/ Pacific Islander*	*White*	*Black*	*Hispanic/ Latino*	*American Indian/ Alaskan Native*
Some High School	15.4%	14.7%	13.1%	20.0%	39.6%	24.0%
High School Graduate	29.3%	16.0%	29.7%	32.9%	27.0%	32.1%
Some College or Associate's Degree	27.7%	19.6%	28.2%	30.0%	20.9%	31.2%
Bachelor's Degree	17.4%	29.7%	18.3%	11.4%	8.7%	8.5%
Graduate or Professional Degree	10.1%	19.7%	10.7%	5.9%	4.0%	4.3%

Source: Social Explorer Tables: ACS 2005 to 2009 (5-Year Estimates) (SE), ACS 2005–2009 (5-Year Estimates), Social Explorer; U.S. Census Bureau; American Community Survey Tables: 2005–2009 (5-Year Estimates) (ACS09_5yr), ACS 2005–2009 (5-Year Estimates), U.S. Census Bureau.

> *students who elbow most of the worthier applicants aside. It's rich white kids with cash and connections. A five-year study of 146 top colleges by the Educational Testing Service found that white students with subpar qualifications were nearly twice as prevalent on such campuses as black and Hispanic students who received an admissions break based on their ethnicity or race. Some of those white students were jocks, recruited to win ballgames. But most had connections to people the institution wanted to keep happy, such as alumni, donors, and politicians.* (2007:14)

A degree from a prestigious school opens doors of opportunity rarely available to graduates of the less-prestigious schools, yet entry goes disproportionately to the already advantaged. A study of the most selective universities found that "just 3 percent of the students admitted were from families of modest social and economic backgrounds. Fully 74 percent of the students came from the top quarter of the nation's social and economic strata" (reported in Sacks 2003:B7).

Segregation

Schools in the United States tend to be segregated by social class and race, both by neighborhood and, within schools, by ability grouping. Schools are based in neighborhoods that tend to be relatively homogeneous by socioeconomic status. Racial and economic segregation is especially prevalent at the elementary school level, carrying over to a lesser degree in the secondary schools. Colleges and universities, as we have seen, are peopled by a middle- and upper-class clientele. Thus, at every level, children tend to attend a school with children like themselves in socioeconomic status and race. A study by Harvard University found that public schools are highly segregated and becoming more so: "Although minority enrollment now approaches 40 percent nationwide, the average White student attends a public school that is 80 percent White. At the same time, one-sixth of Black students—the figure is one-quarter in the Northeast and Midwest—attend schools that are nearly 100 percent non-White" (reported in the *New York Times* 2003a:1). According to Fuentes (2007), Latinos living in New York attend schools that are 80 percent non-White. These figures are the same in the West, which has seen a swell in the Latino population overall. In short, the progress toward desegregation peaked in the late 1980s and has retreated because of racially segregated neighborhoods and school districts across the country challenging integration policies.

Two recent cases illustrate this challenge to integration: Louisville and Seattle. In both cases, officials have worked to ensure that the student bodies of their public schools reflect their city's ethnic composition. Based on the belief that students learn best in a diverse environment, students are assigned by race to some kindergarten to twelfth-grade public schools. White parents have challenged these policies in court, and the Bush administration came forward in siding with these opponents, saying that race-conscious admissions policies violate the Constitution (Lane 2006).

At the college level, some universities have also addressed the issue of segregation through the use of race-conscious admissions. At the University of Michigan, for example, the admissions committee uses a point scale whereby students need 100 points to be accepted to the university. Prior to 2003, underrepresented ethnic minorities received an automatic 20-point bonus toward admission. A 2003 Supreme Court decision (*Gratz v. Bollinger*) found this system to be unconstitutional and too close to a quota system. At the same time, however, another

Supreme Court decision (*Grutter v. Bollinger*) upheld that race could still be considered in the admission process, but minorities could not be awarded a fixed quantity of extra points. This decision has come under fire from the public. In 2006, Michigan residents voted overwhelmingly in favor of barring the state from granting preferences based on skin color or gender in public contracting, employment, and education (Brown 2006).

Tracking and Teachers' Expectations

In 1954, the Supreme Court declared segregated schools unconstitutional. As we have seen, many schools remain at least partially segregated by social class and race because schools draw students from residential areas that are more or less homogeneous by class and race. Segregation is reinforced further by the tracking system within the schools. **Tracking** (also known as ability grouping) sorts students into different groups or classes according to their perceived intellectual ability and performance. The decision is based on grades and teachers' judgments but primarily through standardized tests. The result is that children from poor families and from ethnic minorities are overrepresented in the slow track, whereas children from advantaged backgrounds are disproportionately in the middle and upper tracks. The rationale for tracking is that it provides a better fit between the needs and capabilities of the student and the demands and opportunities of the curriculum. Slower students do not retard the progress of brighter ones, but teachers can adapt their teaching more efficiently to the level of the class if the students are relatively homogeneous in ability. The special problems of the different ability groups, from gifted to challenged, can be dealt with more easily when groups of students share the same or similar problems. The arguments are persuasive.

Although these benefits may be real, tracking is open to serious criticisms. First, students in lower tracks are given low-level work that increases the gap between them and students in the higher tracks, thereby reinforcing the U.S. stratification system. As noted by McLaren and Farahmandpur,

> *As the standardized curriculum and standardized testing widen the achievement gap between poor and wealthy school districts, working class students and students of color continue to be tracked into vocational programs and classes that teach life-skills or offer basic training that prepares them for jobs in the retail and service industry. Even more disturbing perhaps is the placement of high school female students in sewing and cosmetology classes. As we know by now, these classes do little for students who must compete with advanced placement and college-tracked students. It is painfully ironic that just as we are witnessing the factory model of schooling returning with a vengeance, the factories of yesteryear in which working-class students traditionally sought employment after graduation are moving out of the country, escaping the unions and depriving workers of medical benefits. (2006:97)*

Thus the tracking system is closely linked to the stratification system—that is, students from low-income families are disproportionately placed in the lowest track, resulting in a reinforcement of the social class structure.

Second, students in the upper track develop feelings of superiority, while those in the lower track tend to define themselves as inferior. As early as the second grade, students know where they stand on the smart-to-dumb continuum, and this knowledge profoundly affects their self-esteem. These psychological wounds can have devastating effects.

Third, the low-track students are tracked to fail. The negative labels, low teacher expectations, poor education resources (e.g., the highest track is much more likely to have access to computers and to have the most talented teachers), and reluctance of teachers to teach these classes (there is a subtle labeling among teachers regarding who gets to teach what level) all lead to a high probability of failure among students assigned to the lowest track. Given all these negatives, it is not surprising that students who are discipline problems or who eventually drop out come disproportionately from the low track. To summarize, Datnow and Cooper argues,

> *Because of tracking practices, educational institutions, like the communities in which they are embedded, sort individuals by race, social class, language, and ability. Tracking serves as the major vehicle to sort and institutionalize the division between the "haves" and "have-nots," resulting in racially identifiable groups of students, with African American, Latino, and low-income students receiving an unequal distribution of educational access and opportunity. (2002:690)*

The tracking system is powerful in its negative effects. There are four principal reasons this system stunts the success of students who are negatively labeled: stigma, self-fulfilling prophesies, beliefs about future payoffs to education, and the creation of negative student subcultures.

- **Stigma.** Assignment to a lower track carries a strong **stigma** (a label of social disgrace). Such students are labeled as intellectual inferiors. Their self-esteem wanes as they see how other people perceive them and behave toward them. Thus, individuals assigned to a track other than college prep perceive themselves as second class, unworthy, stupid, and in the way. Clearly, assignment to a low track is destructive to a student's self-concept.

- **Self-Fulfilling Prophecy.** A self-fulfilling prophecy (see Chapter 7) is an event that occurs because it is predicted, and people alter their behavior to conform to the prediction. This effect is closely related to stigma. If placed in the college-prep track, students are likely to receive better instruction, have access to better facilities, and be pushed more nearly to their capacity than are students assigned to other tracks. The reason is clear: teachers and administrators expect great things from the one group and lesser things from the other. Moreover, these expectations are fulfilled. Students in the higher track do better, and those in the lower track do not. These behaviors justify the greater expenditures of time, faculties, and experimental curricula for those in the higher track.

  An example comes from a classic controversial study by Rosenthal and Jacobson (1968). Although this study has been criticized for a number of methodological shortcomings, the findings are consistent with theories of interpersonal influence and with the labeling view of deviant behavior. In the spring of 1964, all students in an elementary school in San Francisco were given an IQ test. The following fall, the teachers were given the names of children identified by the test as potential academic spurters, and five of these children were assigned to each classroom. The spurters were chosen by means of a table of random numbers. The only difference between the experimental group (those labeled as spurters) and the control group (the rest of the class) was in the imaginations of the teachers. At the end of the year, all the children were again tested, and the children from whom the teachers expected greater intellectual gains showed such gains (in IQ scores and grades). Moreover, they were rated by their teachers as being more curious, interesting, happy, and more likely to succeed than were the children in the control group.

The implications of this example are clear. Teachers' expectations have a profound effect on students' performance. When students are overrated, they tend to overproduce; when they are underrated, they underachieve. The tracking system is a labeling process that affects the expectations of teachers (and fellow students and parents). The limits of these expectations are crucial in the educational process. Yet the self-fulfilling prophecy can work in a positive direction if teachers have an unshakable conviction that their students can learn. Concomitant with this belief, teachers should hold themselves, not the students, accountable if the latter should fail. Used in this manner, the self-fulfilling prophecy can work to the benefit of all students.

- **Future Payoff.** School is perceived as relevant for students going to college. Grades are a means of qualifying for college. For the non-college-bound student, however, school and grades are much less important for entry into a job. At most, students need a high school diploma, and grades really do not matter as long as one does not flunk out. Thus, non-college-bound students often develop negative attitudes toward school, grades, and teachers. This is reflected in the statistic that students from the lowest income quarter are more than six times as likely to drop out of high school as students from the highest income quarter (U.S. Department of Education, National Center for Educational Statistics 2006).

  As we have seen, being on the lower track has negative consequences. Lower-track students are more rebellious, both in school and out, and do not participate as much in school activities. Finally, what is being taught is often not relevant to their world. Thus, we are led to conclude that many of these students tend to feel that they are not only second-class citizens but perhaps also even pariahs. What other interpretation is plausible in a system that disadvantages them, shuns them, and makes demands of them that are irrelevant?

- **Student Subculture.** The reasons given previously suggest that a natural reaction of people in the lower track would be to band together in a **student subculture** that is antagonistic toward school. This subculture would quite naturally develop its own system of rewards because those of the school are inaccessible.

  These factors (stigma, negative self-fulfilling prophecy, low future payoff, and a contrary student subculture) show how the tracking system is at least partly responsible for the fact that students in the lower tracks tend to be low achievers, unmotivated, uninvolved in school activities, and more prone to break school rules and drop out of school. To segregate students either by ability or by future plans is detrimental to the students labeled as inferior. It is an elitist system that for the most part takes the children of the elite and educates them to take the elite positions in society. Conversely, children of the nonelite are trained to recapitulate the experiences of their parents.

  The conclusion is inescapable: Inequality in the educational system causes many people to fail in U.S. schools. This phenomenon is the fault of the schools, not of the children who fail. To focus on these victims is to divert attention from the real problem—the inadequacies of the school system.

POSSIBILITIES FOR PROMOTING EQUALITY OF OPPORTUNITY

A fundamental tenet of U.S. society is that each individual, regardless of sex, race, ethnicity, religion, sexuality, age, and social class, has the opportunity to be equal on her or his own merits. In other words, the system must not impede individuals from reaching their potential and from gaining the unequal rewards of an unequal society. The data presented in this chapter show that U.S. schools tend to block the chances of minority and poor children in their quest to be successful in society. This section outlines several programs that schools and society could adopt to promote equality of opportunity for all children.

We must realize at the start that if the situation for poor and minority children is difficult now, it will worsen significantly if changes are not made. This assertion is based on three societal trends. The first, documented throughout this book, is that the gap between the affluent and the poor is widening. Also, as the demographic mix of the nation continues to change, increasing numbers of children of color from relatively poor families will attend schools. Today about 22 percent of schoolchildren have a foreign-born parent (mostly Latino and Asian), a proportion that will likely increase. The poor and children of immigrants are disproportionately found in inner cities in increasingly segregated neighborhoods. With the poor and people of color clustered in cities, these local governments, faced with a declining tax base, will be less and less able to provide the services required of their citizens, including education. Similarly, certain regions—the Pacific Coast, the Southwest, and Florida—are especially affected by immigration, placing an extraordinary financial burden on those states and localities.

The second trend that will negatively affect the educational opportunities of minorities unless changes are made is that the number of minority students is increasing and will in the next decades make Whites the numerical minority (as they are today in many school districts). Moreover, racial and ethnic minorities are concentrated in poor states (the South and Southwest), in poor geographical regions (Appalachia, the Ozarks, along the Rio Grande, and in the Mississippi delta), and in poor sections of cities. This is significant because racial/ethnic minorities have higher rates of poverty, more unemployment, and lower educational attainment than do the more fortunate majority. In effect, under current policies, children from minorities are disadvantaged economically and are at greater risk of educational failure. So, wherever these children are overrepresented, there will be disproportionately less local money to meet their educational needs (because of the lower tax base). Ironically, the poor require more money than the affluent to catch up, such as enriched preschool, after-school programs, summer reading programs, and small classes, yet the richest school districts spend more per student.

In addition to the rise in the proportion of racial minority students, several demographic trends make reform difficult. One demographic trend negatively affecting education is the aging of society (see Chapter 5). As a greater proportion of the population no longer has children in school, there will be a greater reluctance on their part to vote for tax increases directed at education. Another population trend is for increased enrollments from the baby boom echo—that is, the children of children of the disproportionately large baby boom generation are in school or soon will be, swelling the numbers significantly. This means that more classrooms and teachers are needed at a time when many states are making cuts to education due to the economic recession.

All the previously mentioned demographic changes point to a society that is at risk for increasing the gap between rich and poor students. The next sections discuss several programs that schools and society could adopt to promote equality of opportunity for all children.

Provide Universal Preschool Programs

The most important variable affecting school performance is not race but socioeconomic status. Regardless of race, children from poor families tend to do less well in school than do children from families who are better off. Long-term studies are beginning to show that the United States needs to invest in preschool-age children from disadvantaged families to counter some of these poor outcomes. In fact, the earlier the investment, the better. For example, in a 40-year study of 123 low-income children, intensive preschool attention resulted in higher academic achievement, higher earnings, and lower rates of criminal activity compared to a control group (reported in Farrell 2006). Although the program was expensive ($10,600 investment per pupil), researchers estimated that the benefit-to-cost ratio comes to $17 for every $1 invested. The Economic Policy Institute argues,

> *Our failure to invest in the healthy development of young children leads to enormous problems and enormous costs to society. Poor children overwhelmingly suffer from society's neglect as they go through school, and then enter the workforce (or, too often, the criminal justice system) unprepared to be productive workers and citizens. And the costs to taxpayers and society are enormous because funds not spent on early childhood programs are spent later on remedial and special education, criminal justice programs and welfare benefits. (Reported in Hickey 2004:12)*

Compensatory programs such as Head Start and Follow Through are predicated on the assumption that if children from lower-class homes are to succeed in middle-class schools, they must have special help to equalize their chances. The Bill and Melinda Gates Foundation plans to invest up to $90 million on early intervention programs and is currently backing several experiments to find out what works (Farrell 2006).

Offer Free Education

Beginning with preschool, there must be a commitment to a free education for all students. Presumably, public education at the elementary and secondary levels is free, but this assumption is a fallacy, as discussed earlier. Although circumstances vary by district, typically children must pay for their supplies, textbooks, laboratory fees, locker rental, admission to plays and athletic events, meals, and participation in extracurricular activities. Some districts waive these costs for poor families. But waivers do not occur uniformly across school districts, and the procedures for granting these waivers are often degrading (i.e., done in such a way that other people know who receives the handouts). These costs are regressive because they take a larger proportion of the poor family's budget, thereby increasing the pressure to withdraw the child from school, where he or she drains the family resources.

By making education absolutely free to all children, communities could reduce dropout rates among the poor. A program of greater scope would also provide a living allowance for each child from a poor family who stayed in school beyond the eighth grade. This program would be analogous to the GI Bill, which provided similar benefits to soldiers returning after World War II. Special care must be given to provide these benefits, as did the GI Bill, without making their acceptance degrading.

An important way to produce equal opportunity is to provide a free college education to all students who qualify. This means the elimination of tuition and fees and an allowance for books for everyone, plus grants and loans for students in need to pay for living expenses while attending college. Students could then "give back" through community service or working on campus.

Set National Education Standards

The government should provide national education standards, a national curriculum, and national tests. As noted before, the No Child Left Behind Act is a step in this direction, but it allows each of the fifty states to set its own standards. There are more than 14,000 school districts and 83,000 schools in the United States. We must require that each school district and school, rather than acting on its own, meet specific standards for school achievement agreed to by a national consensus among educational leaders. The minimum result of this requirement would be that students, whether growing up in Nebraska or New York, would learn the same basic materials at about the same time. It would also mean that as students move with their families from one locality to another, they would not be at a disadvantage because of the esoteric schooling they had received.

Reduce Funding Disparities across States and Districts

Another reform at the federal level would be to spend the federal monies unequally to equalize differences among the states. In effect, the federal government must take the money it receives in taxes, taking disproportionately from the wealthy states, and redistribute it to the poor states. Otherwise, the gap between the rich and poor states will be maintained.

Nationwide, the traditional property tax system of raising money for education locally is under assault. The supreme courts in various states are ruling in case after case that the states are failing the children in the poorer districts. States should be encouraged to distribute their funds to eliminate or minimize disparities between rich and poor districts. This could be done by the federal government's withholding funds from states with discrepancies between their poor and rich districts that exceed federal guidelines. In such cases, the federal government could channel its monies directly to the poorer districts within the offending states.

Reduce Class and School Size

Schools can be restructured to better meet the needs of students. A beginning would be to reduce class size. A Tennessee study (Project Star) found that students in smaller classes tended to achieve higher grades, had better high school graduation rates, and were more likely to attend college, and the gap between Black–White academic achievement narrowed by 38 percent (Herbert 2001b). Not only small classes but smaller schools are also beneficial, generating higher graduation rates, more participation, less alienation, and less violence. Results from the National Longitudinal Study of Adolescent Health, a federally funded survey of 72,000 junior high and high school students, found that when the number of students in a school exceeded 1,200, students became more isolated from one another. Isolation contributes to the greater likelihood of engaging in risky behavior such as drug use, violence, and early sexual activity (reported in Fletcher 2002). Smaller schools and smaller classes create an intimacy that can improve performance. A study of Chicago's experiment with small schools in some of its poorest neighborhoods found that student attendance rose and dropout rates fell with reduced class sizes (reported in Symonds 2001).

Attract and Retain Excellent Teachers

Schools need to attract and retain excellent teachers. This means higher salaries, mentoring of new teachers, and paying teachers a bonus for teaching in difficult school situations. This is especially challenging when states are inclined to make large cuts to education as they attempt to balance their budgets. In 2009, President Obama announced a national grant competition entitled "Race to the Top." State governors will apply for $4.35 billion in grants to improve educational quality and results in their state. In their application they must include a plan to recruit, develop, reward, and retain effective teachers and principals.

Extend the School Day and Year

The United States devotes the shortest amount of time to teaching its children of any advanced nation (see Figure 16.4). The 6-hour day and the 9-month calendar instituted to accommodate farm life have not changed since the nineteenth century. Pushing for an extended school year, President Obama said,

> *We can no longer afford an academic calendar designed when America was a nation of farmers who needed their children at home plowing the land at the end of the day. That calendar may have once made sense, but today, it puts us at a competitive disadvantage. Our children spend over a month less in school than children in South Korea. That is no way to prepare them for a 21st century economy. (quoted in Thomma 2009:1)*

FIGURE 16.4

Average Number of School Days in Global Perspective

Country	Days of School
Japan	243
South Korea	220
Israel	216
Luxembourg	216
The Netherlands	200
Scotland	200
Thailand	200
Hong Kong	195
England	192
Hungary	192
Swaziland	191
Finland	190
New Zealand	190
Nigeria	190
France	185
United States	180

Hold Educators Accountable

Virtually every state has instituted statewide examinations in the past decade, linking the results to such things as grade promotion, high school graduation, and teacher and principal salaries. The cornerstone of the No Child Left Behind legislation is to have nationwide testing, mandating annual tests in grades 3 through 8, plus one in high school, with penalties for those schools that fail. There are difficulties with this assessment of schools, as noted earlier. Do you punish schools from economically disadvantaged districts with children who are more proficient in a language other than English? When a school fails, do you punish, or do you invest in more resources (tutoring, after-school programs, summer school, smaller class size, modern-schools wired for the future)?

The pressure on teachers and administrators that their schools score well may lead to cheating or to manipulating their rankings by exempting special education students and slow learners from taking the tests, or through the subtle encouragement of slow learners to drop out of school.

A final criticism of high-stakes testing is that research at the state level finds that tests attached to grade promotion and high school graduation lead to increased dropout rates, especially for minority students (Orfield and Wald 2000).

These criticisms are valid and important, but to criticize them does not invalidate the need for standards and evaluation. The key is to heavily invest in poor children, beginning in preschool, and to enrich their school with meaningful experiences and talented, caring teachers. With such a commitment, over time all children can be held to the same standards and their schools held accountable.

Reform the Educational Philosophy of Schools

The reforms listed earlier do not question the structure and philosophy of the educational system, which opponents argue stifles children in attaining their potential. In the view of the critics, the system itself is wrong and the generator of many profound problems. These critics want to reconstruct the entire educational enterprise along very different lines. This demand for change is based on three related assumptions. The first is that the school is a microcosm of the larger society. Because society is too competitive, repressive, inhumane, materialistic, racist, and imperialist, so, too, are the schools. Changing society entails changing the schools.

The second assumption of the radical critics of education is that the process of public education as it currently exists damages, thwarts, and stifles children. The schools somehow manage to suppress the natural curiosity of children. They begin with inquisitive children and mold them into acquisitive children with little desire to learn.

Third, the educational system is a product of society and hence shapes its products to meet the requirements of society. The present system is predicated on the needs of an industrial society in which citizens must follow orders, do assigned tasks in the appropriate order and time span, and not challenge the status quo. According to Everton, "This is why school sucks. Rather than do what it pretends to—educate, foster curiosity, expand our intellects, and promote diversity—compulsory schooling segregates people on the basis of how well they're willing to do what they're told. . . . Compulsory schooling is at its best when diluting intellects in preparation for lifetimes of subservience to corporate masters" (2004:55).

The demands of the 21st century require students to work cooperatively, to be knowledgeable about technology, and to think outside the box.

But these behaviors will not be appropriate for life in the twenty-first century. The future will likely require people who can cope with rapid turnover—changes in occupations, human relationships, and community ties. Moreover, the citizens of the future must be able to cope with myriad choices. Does an educational system built on order, a rigid time schedule, and the lecture method adequately prepare youngsters for life as it is and will be? The proponents of these and other alternatives are critical of U.S. education. They conclude that schools are failing not only children from the ghettos of large cities but also suburban and small-town youngsters. Wallis and Steptoe write,

> *For the past five years, the national conversation on education has focused on reading scores, math tests and closing the "achievement gap" between social classes. This is not a story about that conversation. This is a story about the big public conversation the nation is not having about education, the one that will ultimately determine not merely whether some fraction of our children get "left behind" but also whether an entire generation of kids will fail to make the grade in the global economy because they can't think their way through abstract problems, work in teams, distinguish good information from bad or speak a language other than English. (2006:52)*

Today's economy demands that schools rethink their educational philosophy and focus more on twenty-first-century skills. Those skills include (1) knowing more about the world as global citizens, (2) thinking outside the box, (3) becoming smarter about new sources of information, and (4) developing good people skills (Wallis and Steptoe 2006).

Restructure Society

The approaches to equality described previously focus on changing either individual students or the schools. But if equality of opportunity is truly the goal, education cannot accomplish it alone. Closing the achievement gap between advantaged and disadvantaged students cannot be accomplished without a societywide assault on racism and poverty. Poverty can be eliminated only through fundamental revisions in the economic and familial institutions. This is not to say that reform of the schools should be ignored. Efforts to improve our schools should parallel attempts to restructure the other institutions of society.

■ CHAPTER REVIEW

1. The system of education in the United States is characterized by (a) conservatism—the preservation of culture, roles, values, and training necessary for the maintenance of society; (b) a belief in compulsory mass education; (c) a preoccupation with order and control; (d) fragmentation; (e) local control, which results in (f) a lack of curriculum standardization across the country; and (g) reinforcement of the stratification system through the sifting and sorting of students.
2. The belief that our society is a meritocracy, with the most intelligent and talented at the top, is a myth. Education, instead of being the great equalizer, reinforces social inequality.
3. Educational outcomes are strongly linked to social class, race, and ethnicity.
4. The schools are structured to aid in the perpetuation of social and economic differences in several ways: (a) by being financed principally through property taxes so that rich school districts spend more per student; (b) by offering private schools that the poor cannot afford; (c) by increasing the cost of attending college; (d) by segregating students by race and social class; and (e) by tracking according to presumed level of ability.
5. The tracking system is closely correlated with social class; students from low-income families are disproportionately placed in the lowest track. Tracking thwarts the equality of educational opportunity for the poor by generating four effects: (a) a stigma, which lowers self-esteem; (b) the self-fulfilling prophecy; (c) a perception of school as having no future payoff; and (d) a negative student subculture.
6. Demographic changes such as the increasing number of minority students and students with a foreign-born parent are widening the gap between poor and rich students.
7. The government needs to invest in preschool programs to improve the life chances of disadvantaged youth.
8. Beginning with preschool and continuing through college, there must be a societal commitment to free education.
9. The federal government could promote equality of opportunity by providing national educational standards, a national curriculum, and national tests.
10. The federal government must level the playing field by distributing money unequally to the states according to need and encouraging states to minimize economic disparities among their school districts.
11. Promoting equality of opportunity and excellence in the public schools requires (a) reducing class and school size; (b) attracting and retaining excellent teachers; (c) extending the school year; (d) holding educators responsible for their students' outcomes; and (e) changing the philosophy of schools to meet the needs of the twenty-first century and global economy.
12. The restructuring of schools will not meet the goal of equality of educational opportunity, radical critics argue, unless the society is also restructured. This change requires a societywide assault on racism and poverty and a redistribution of wealth to reduce the inequalities that result from economic advantage.

■ KEY TERMS

Cultural deprivation. Erroneous assumption that some groups (e.g., the poor) are handicapped by a so-called inferior culture.

No Child Left Behind Act. Federal legislation requiring states to develop academic standards in reading, math, and science. All children must reach these standards by 2013–2014.

Tracking. Ability grouping in schools.

Stigma. Powerful negative social label that affects a person's social identity and self-concept.

Student subculture. Members of the disadvantaged band together in a group with values and behaviors antagonistic toward school.

■ SUCCEED WITH PEARSON mysoclab www.mysoclab.com

Experience, Discover, Observe, Evaluate

MySocLab is designed just for you. Each chapter features a pre-test and post-test to help you learn and review key concepts and terms.

Experience sociology in action with dynamic visual activities, videos, and readings to enhance your learning experience. Complete the following activities at www.mysoclab.com.

Social Explorer is an interactive application that allows you to explore Census data through interactive maps.

- Explore the Social Explorer Map: *Patterns of Privilege in Public and Private Schools*

The Core Concepts in Sociology video clips offer a real-world perspective on sociological concepts.

- Watch *ABC Nightline: Recipe for Success*

MySocLibrary includes primary source readings from classic and contemporary sociologists.

- Read Bersani & Chapple, *School Failure as an Adolescent Turning Point;* Rosser, *Too Many Women in College?;* Kozol, *Savage Inequalities: Children in America's Schools*

CHAPTER 17 The Health Care System

In industry, finance, music, science, arts, academics, athletics, Americans can match or surpass any other country. Why can't we do that when it comes to health care?

—T. R. Reid

This chapter is devoted to analyzing the system of health care in the United States. How does the current system work? Who benefits and who does not from the current system? Is reform needed? What reforms, if any, emerged from the Obama and Democratic Party initiatives? To answer these questions the chapter is divided into six parts: (1) a description of the contours of the health crises; (2) the social organization of the health care system; (3) the unequal access to health care; (4) models of national health care: lessons from other developed nations (5) the politics of health care reform; and (6) the Obama Health Care Reform of 2010.

THE CRISES IN HEALTH CARE: COST, COVERAGE, AND CONSEQUENCES

Rising Health Care Costs

In 2009 Americans spent $2.5 trillion on health care. The United States has experienced a steep growth rate in medical expenses. In 2009 health care costs were 17.3 percent of its GDP on health care, up from 5 percent in 1960 and 13.6 percent in 2000. This is much more, both in amount spent per capita and percentage of gross domestic product, than any other advanced modern nation. France and Switzerland spend 11 percent of their gross domestic product, Germany and Canada spend 10 percent, France 9 percent, and Great Britain and Japan about 8 percent each.

There are several reasons health care in the United States is so expensive compared to other countries. Most significant, profit drives the U.S. system: private hospitals, insurance companies, and medical equipment manufacturers seek greater returns on their investments. A report by Health and Human Services stated that in 2009 the largest insurance companies—WellPoint, United Health, Cigna, Aetna, and Humana—combined for $12.1 billion in profits, a 56 percent increase from 2008. Most significant, profits for the 10 largest insurance companies increased 10 times faster than inflation over the last decade (cited in Jackson 2010).

Second, the system is inefficient. Especially costly is the paperwork involved in insurance claims from hundreds of different insurance firms. Physicians and hospitals have to hire additional personnel to deal with the layers of paperwork. According to research published in the *New England Journal of Medicine*, 31 percent of the money spent on health care goes for paperwork and administration (reported in Bennett 2010).

> *An estimated 15 cents of each private U.S. health care dollar goes simply to shuffling the paperwork. The administrative costs for our patched-together system of HMOs, insurance companies, pharmaceutical manufacturers, hospitals, and government programs are nearly double those for single-payer Canada. (van Gelder and Pibel 2006:3)*

Third, many physicians practice **defensive medicine**—tests and procedures doctors perform primarily to protect themselves from lawsuits. The practice of defensive medicine means, in effect, that much of the health care that is delivered—as much as one-third, according to a Dartmouth study—is unnecessary (cited in Saporito 2005).

Fourth, lawsuits alleging malpractice on the part of physicians, pharmaceutical companies, and hospitals account for about 4 percent of total health care costs (Weitz 2004:235).

Fifth, science keeps inventing costly new tests, new drugs, and new treatments. Because health insurers pay doctors and clinical facilities most of what they charge, there are financial incentives to use the new and expensive technologies. Related to this, many physicians, to increase their incomes, install expensive equipment in their offices (ultrasound, magnetic resonance imaging, etc.). Research shows that self-referring doctors order tests for their machines far more frequently than doctors who refer patients to radiologists and other specialists (Levin 2004).

Another source of the high cost of health care in the United States is the shortage of primary-care physicians and the overuse of specialists. The income of general practitioners (primary-care physicians) is less than half, on average, of what specialists make. Thus, the financial incentive is for medical students to choose the specialty route. The services of specialists are costly, and they are more prone than primary-care physicians to rely on expensive technical procedures for their livelihood. Because there is a shortage of general practitioners, fewer patients go to them on a regular basis, which means they are less likely to receive preventive care. One estimate is that if everyone went to a general practitioner regularly, health care costs would go down by $67 billion a year (Carmichael 2010).

A final reason for the costly health care system is the wide use of prescription drugs, the greatest part of the health care bill of Americans. The cost in 2008 was $291 billion for prescription drugs, and the cost is expected to rise to at least $325 billion by 2013 (prescription drugs have been rising by more than double the inflation rate). Drug costs are an especially heavy burden on the elderly, who take an average of four prescription drugs.

The U.S. pharmaceutical industry is comprised of profit-seeking companies that conduct research, manufacture, advertise, and sell their products. The United States is the only developed nation that allows direct-to-consumer marketing. Significantly, the pharmaceutical companies spend more on advertising than on research and development (*Science Daily* 2008a).

The profit margin for pharmaceutical firms averages 17 percent, much more than found in other industries. Drug prices in the United States compared to the cost in other industrialized countries are 35 percent to 55 percent higher. Prices in Canada, for example, are one-half to one-fourth the prices in the United States (Wright 2009). As long as drug companies hold the patent to a drug, the prices rise from year to year. In 2008 the price for brand-name drugs rose 8.7 percent, more than double the inflation rate (Werner 2009). When the patent expires, the price drops immediately as generic copies are sold. When several drug manufacturers produce a similar generic, the price drops further due to the competition (Barry 2008).

To summarize, the U.S. health care is system is comprised of various commercial enterprises seeking profits. Indicative of the commercialization of the health care system is that

> *investors own about 20 percent of non-public general hospitals, almost all specialty hospitals, and most freestanding facilities for ambulatory patients, such as walk-in clinics, imaging centers, and ambulatory surgical centers. These medical care businesses, like other businesses, need profits to satisfy their investors, and for this purpose they use marketing and advertising, directed at physicians and the general public (Relman 2009: para 6).*

Consider the emphasis on profit by the health insurance firms. The money paid by the insurance industry to physicians, hospitals, and pharmacies for treating insured patients is referred to as "medical loss."

> *That is, when health insurance actually pays for somebody's health care, the industry considers it a loss. . . . Insurance executives, securities analysts, and the business media carefully watch each company's medical loss ratio to make sure that the actual medical payments don't eat too deeply into administrative costs and profits. According to their filings with the Securities and Exchange Commission, most for-profit insurance companies maintain a medical loss ratio of about 80 percent,* which is to

> say that 20 cents of every dollar people pay in premiums for health insurance doesn't buy any health care *(emphasis added). (Reid 2009:37)*

Does the High Cost of Health Care Translate into Good Health Consequences?

With the United States spending 50 percent more per capita on health care than any other country, it seems reasonable to expect that Americans would be the healthiest people on Earth, yet Americans do not fare as well as those in Western Europe, Scandinavia, Canada, and Japan. Consider the following rankings (taken from Reid 2009: 30–34; 241–244):

- The World Health Organization rated the national health care systems of 191 countries in terms of "fairness" and the United States ranked fifty-fourth.
- The Commonwealth Fund concluded that the United States is the worst of the developed countries on "avoidable mortality." That is, deaths before age 75 from conditions that are at least partially modifiable with effective medical care. Some of these conditions are asthma, diabetes, and kidney transplants.
- The United States ranks forty-seventh in average life expectancy.
- According to the Commonwealth Fund, the United States tied for last among twenty-three nations in healthy life expectancy at age sixty. This predicts not only how long a sixty-year-old will live but also how that person can expect to live before the onset of predictable ailments of the elderly.
- The United States ranks last among twenty-three wealthy countries in keeping newborns alive. Its **infant mortality rate** (babies who die within one year of birth) is more than twice as high as the rate in the top-ranked countries (Sweden and Japan).

Christopher Murray, a physician and health economist at Harvard, summarized the meaning of these last three rankings: "Basically you die earlier and spend more time disabled if you're an American rather than a member of most other advanced societies" (quoted in Reid, 2009:244).

THE HEALTH CARE SYSTEM IN THE UNITED STATES PRIOR TO 2010 REFORM

The health care system in the United States has four unique characteristics. First, there are separate health systems for different categories of people. Second, the system relies heavily on for-profit private insurance to pay the bills and for-profit hospitals to care for the sick. And, third, the system is dominated by privately owned managed care.

Different Plans for Different Categories

Each of the advanced nations has one health program for its people. The United States, in sharp contrast maintains separate systems for different categories of people (this section depends on Reid 2009:16–21).

- **The Plan for Workers.** For most working people under age sixty-five, health insurance is linked to employment. That is, the worker and the employer share the premiums for a health insurance policy (in 2009 the cost for a family plan amounted to a premium of $3,515 for the worker and $9,860 for the employer). But there are problems with this employer-based insurance coverage. Foremost, employers are not required to provide health insurance for their employees. Indeed, the proportion of employers including a health care package declined from 80 percent of all companies in 1991 to 60 percent in 2006. If not dropping health insurance coverage, employers may require employees to pay a larger proportion of the premiums or pay higher deductibles for coverage. A survey by the Kaiser Family Foundation found that 21 percent of employers reduced benefits or increased employee cost-sharing due to the Great Recession (reported in Pugh 2009). Employers have also reduced their health costs by employing more part-time workers and independent contractors because they do not receive any benefits. Finally, basing insurance on employment means that when one becomes unemployed or leaves an employer to work for another, they lose the coverage previously held.

- **The Plan for Native Americans, Military Personnel, and Veterans.** For certain categories health care is provided and financed by the federal government. Native Americans receive free care in government clinics. Those in the active military are cared for as needed. The Department of Veterans Affairs owns and operates clinics and hospitals for military veterans. Health practitioners in these settings are government employees. The cost of health care for these selected categories is free for those who qualify.

- **The Plan for Those 65 and Over.** The government has a near universal health plan for the elderly—**Medicare**. This system covers about 45 million elderly and people with disabilities of any age. Workers pay a payroll tax for Medicare, and when they become eligible most of their health expenses are paid for by the government.

- **The Plan for the Uninsured.** The uninsured have access to medical care if they can pay the bills out-of-pocket at the time of treatment. The other alternative is to go to the emergency room in a public hospital. Public hospitals are required to attend to the medical needs of the indigent.

Private Insurance

The health care system for most Americans depends on the health insurance industry. Health insurance is a necessity. However, 46.3 million people—15.4 percent of the population—were uninsured in 2008, which means that they were essentially left outside the health care system (see Table 17.1 for the characteristics of the uninsured). The Congressional Budget Office projects 54 million uninsured people in 2019 (reported in *New York Times* 2010b).

Because the health insurance firms are for-profit entities, they use various techniques to enhance their profits. Raising rates is the most common one. In 2009, for example, when WellPoint's profit was $2.9 billion, its branch in California raised premiums by as much as 39 percent (Lingeman 2010). Other profit-enhancing tactics are (Reid 2009:38–40, 230):

- They hire armies of adjusters and investigators to examine claims looking for reasons to deny payment.
- They employ "rescission," which is the legal term for "We're canceling your coverage." This occurs, typically, when an insured person, because of injury

TABLE 17.1
The Medically Uninsured, 2008

Characteristics	*Percent Who Are Uninsured*
Total	46.3 million (15.4%)
Age	
Under 18	9.9
18–24	28.6
25–34	26.5
35–44	19.4
45–64	14.4
65 and older	1.7
Race/Ethnicity	
Whites	10.8
Asian Americans	17.6
African Americans	19.1
Latinos	30.7
Nativity	
Native	12.9
Foreign born	33.5
Household Income	
$75,000 or more	8.2
Less than $25,000	24.5
Work experience	
Worked full time	17.2
Worked part time	25.4
Did not work	26.0

Source: Carmen DeNavas, Bernadette D. Proctor, and Jessica C. Smith. 2009. "Income Poverty and Health Insurance Coverage in the U.S.: 2008." *Current Population Reports,* P60-236 (September), p. 21.

or disease, requires long-term expensive care. The justification for cancellation may be that the individual's health problem is the result of being overweight, having a risky lifestyle, or not following doctor's orders.

- They do not insure people with a "preexisting condition." In other words, they refuse to insure the very people who need their services the most.

Despite these considerable shortcomings, health insurance is crucial. Individuals cannot go it alone; they need health insurance either from the government or private insurance companies. Without health insurance, bad things happen. Some examples: A Harvard study found that uninsured patients with traumatic injuries were almost twice as likely to die in the hospital as similarly injured patients with health insurance (Gawande et al., 2009). Lack of health insurance kills 45,000 adults a year, according to a study by the *American Journal of Public Health*. "More Americans die of lack of health insurance than terrorism, homicide, drunk driving and HIV combined" (Sklar 2009:15). And, according to the *American Journal of Medicine,* 78 percent of those filing for bankruptcy in 2007 cited illness and medical bills as having contributed to their financial failure.

Many Americans have inadequate insurance coverage. These underinsured are often left with medical bills they cannot afford to pay, spending more than 10 percent of their income yearly on health care costs and risking bankruptcy if they have a major illness. The problems of the underinsured stem from required deductibles and copayments; long waiting periods before insurance covers preexisting conditions; caps on insurance reimbursement per treatment, per year, or per lifetime; and lack of insurance for certain costs, such as nursing home care and prescriptions (Weitz 2004:243).

Significantly, the uninsured and underinsured are less likely than the insured to receive preventive care. They are more likely to avoid the high costs of doctors, medical tests, and hospitals, putting them at a much higher risk for chronic disease, disability, and premature death.

For-Profit Hospitals

Traditionally, hospitals in the United States have been nonprofit organizations run by churches, universities, and municipalities. Since the mid-1960s, however, private profit-oriented hospitals and hospital chains have emerged, and they have grown rapidly through mergers and acquisitions. These transactions, plus the explosive growth of outpatient centers, have resulted in a reduction of available hospital beds and the number of hospitals.

Also, after a merger or acquisition, the new company can purge its rolls of costly customers or, at a minimum, force them to pay steep premium hikes. This corporate strategy, which is detrimental to many patients, is, however, in compliance with the insurance laws in most states.

In addition to downsizing in the hospital industry, there has been a simultaneous process of concentration of ownership. For example, Columbia/HCA Healthcare Corporation, the world's largest for-profit hospital chain, owned, at the end of 2006, some 173 hospitals, 107 outpatient diagnostic and surgery centers, and hundreds of nursing homes, home care units, blood centers, and psychiatric facilities. It was purchased by Kohlberg Kravis Roberts and Bain Capital for $31.6 billion. Columbia's strategy has been to purchase nonprofit hospitals, creating quasi-monopolies. They then slash basic services and increase the price of services to boost profits. Richard E. Rainwater, a cofounder of Columbia, calls this strategy for hospital empire building "the Wal-Mart approach to health care" (Weiss 1997:68).

For-profit hospitals are established to maximize profits. A number of strategies are employed by the for-profit hospitals to optimize profits. They avoid low-income areas by locating in states and neighborhoods with well-insured populations. Often they build hospitals without emergency departments, neonatal intensive units, or burn units because such facilities often lose money. For-profit hospitals have a special interest in minimizing their care for emergency patients because emergency facilities attract Medicaid and charity cases, and federal law requires that hospitals must care for all emergencies, even if the patients have no insurance. Thus, hospitals without emergency departments or with inadequate emergency facilities can

> *dump tens of thousands of patients a year on the doorsteps of public hospitals. That is, they may minimally "stabilize" poor patients who show up at the ER, but as soon as possible they transport them to a public hospital to avoid having to provide more extensive treatment for little or no reimbursement. (Weiss 1997:72)*

Private hospitals treat people who can afford their services, often leaving aside those who cannot. This practice is called **patient dumping**. These practices help the hospital's bottom line, but they do not help the poor who need specialized care. Also, patient dumping decreases the quality of care at public hospitals because it increases overcrowding and increases the demand on the limited resources of public hospitals. The practice of patient dumping also indirectly increases the profits of private hospitals by increasing the desire of many of the affluent to choose them over public hospitals.

Another strategy to increase profits is to purchase all the nonprofit hospitals in an area, creating a monopoly—and with a monopoly comes higher prices for services. Still other organizations purchase hospitals that are nonunion, which allows them to keep salaries and wages relatively low. They can also skimp on the quality of supplies, the level of cleanliness, and the level of staffing. Thus, as hospitals have become increasingly owned by private profit- seeking interests, the cost of medical care has increased.

To summarize, consider this quote from Carl Ginsburg, which criticizes the shift to for-profit hospitals but is applicable to what has occurred throughout the health care industry as well:

> *Making fat profits on hospitals at the expense of the poor and the sick may not be a prison offense in this country. What is a crime is the galloping privatization of the nation's health resources and the rise of a competitive health care system that has less and less to do with health and access to care and* everything to do with money. *(Ginsburg 1996:22; italics added)*

Managed Care Networks

Doctors used to practice alone or in a small group of doctors, treating patients, setting fees, and billing patients. Now 93 percent of medical school graduates will become employees of large clinics, managed care companies, or hospital systems (the following depends on Glasser 2009). We focus here on the surge to managed care systems that began in the 1970s. This shift to physicians as employees has important implications for the doctor–patient relationship. The relationship has become depersonalized. In the past the focus was on knowing one's patients and in a small practice, knowing one another's patients. Patients in managed care, in contrast, often do not see the same physician. The human relationship between doctor and patient has evaporated.

> *The care you get—and how long you get it—is only the care your health plan will reimburse your doctor for. . . . Personal knowledge and concern have evaporated in the world of employee–physicians, replaced by cookie-cutter best-practice guidelines and rules on prescribing drugs, acceptable lengths of hospital stays and the number of clinic patients a doctor must see per hour.*
>
> *And why not? Everyone in medicine knows that these are no longer the physician's patients. They belong to the insurance companies, the health plans, the hospitals. With that understanding comes personal indifference and professional exhaustion. (Glasser 2009:24).*

The implication is that managed care has taken management of patients' health away from physicians and put it in the hands of ancillary personnel in corporate headquarters. Thus, physicians in managed care networks no longer have the freedom to practice what they believe is the best medicine for their patients.

Managed care networks, as in other profit-oriented medical entities, seek to enhance the bottom line by maximizing the number of healthy and insured patients while restrict the number who are sick. In other words, the sickest patient is a cost center to be avoided. This is accomplished by **medlining** (the practice in health care of avoiding the sick, similar to the practice of redlining, the practice in lending and insurance of avoiding deteriorating neighborhoods or racial minority neighborhoods). One medlining strategy is to not have physicians who treat severe conditions (e.g., cardiologists) in the network. Similarly, when building clinics or recruiting doctors, the managed care network can limit exposure to the chronically sick by seeking those in affluent locales, where the incidence of AIDS and tuberculosis, for example, is low.

UNEQUAL ACCESS TO HEALTH CARE

In examining the structure of a society and any of its institutions, the analyst of social problems asks, Who benefits and who suffers from the way it is organized? When health care delivery is the focus, the answer to this question is clear: Glaring inequities result in some categories of people being less healthy than others. Our examination of this structural inequity focuses on the three fundamental structures of inequality—class, race, and gender—which are key determinants of health (i.e., the distribution of health and disease) and health care delivery (i.e., the distribution of treatment). These structures of inequality make a difference, not surprisingly, with the already advantaged being advantaged even more and the already disadvantaged being disadvantaged further.

> *Whether or not you are healthy, or can be healthy, depends on lots of factors beyond your control. Do you have access to nutritious food and good medical care? That depends on whether you can afford them. Are you able to minimize your stress level? That depends on your working conditions. Is your neighborhood free of environmental hazards? That depends on the color of your skin. In other words, your health depends on where you fit into the larger society, and how your society—or any society—fits into the global, economic scheme.* (Dollars & Sense *2001:2)*

Social Class

Economic disadvantage is closely associated with health disadvantages. Put another way, "How people live, get sick, and die depends not only on their race and gender but primarily on the class to which they belong" (Navarro 1991:2). The poor are more likely than the affluent to suffer from certain forms of cancer (cancers of the lung, cervix, and esophagus), hypertension, low birth weight, hearing loss, diabetes, and infectious diseases (especially influenza and tuberculosis). For example, 13.9 percent with family incomes under $20,000 were diagnosed with diabetes, whereas 6.5 percent those with incomes over $80,000 had diabetes (Painter 2008). Using education as an indicator of social class, men with less than 12 years of education are more than twice as likely to die of heart disease and more than three times as likely to die as a result of injury, compared to those with 13 or more years of education (Reuss 2001).

The physical health of poor people is more likely to be impaired than is the health of the more well-to-do because of differences in diet, sanitation, shelter, exposure to environmental hazards (e.g., air pollution, lead, untreated water), unsafe work conditions, medical treatment, and lifestyle. Regarding lifestyle, for instance, the lower a person's social class, the more likely he or she uses tobacco. Child health, as another example, varies by family income. Table 17.2 compares the health outcomes for poor and nonpoor children.

TABLE 17.2
Poverty Matters

Health Outcomes	*Low-Income Children's Higher Risk*
Death in infancy	1.6 times as likely
Premature birth (under 37 weeks)	1.8 times as likely
Low birth weight	1.9 times as likely
No regular source of health care	2.7 times as likely
Inadequate prenatal care	2.8 times as likely
Family had too little food sometime in the last 4 months	8 times as likely

Source: Reprinted by permission from Children's Defense Fund. *The State of America's Children 2004.* Washington, DC: Children's Defense Fund.

An obvious health advantage of the affluent is access to health-promoting and health-protecting resources and, when needed, access to medical services, typically paid for, at least in part, with health insurance. The lower the prestige and the lower the wages in the job, the less likely the pay will include a health benefits package provided by an employer.

The uninsured, of course, cannot afford the costs for physicians, dentists, and hospitals, so they often do without. Poor pregnant women (26 percent of women of childbearing age have no maternity coverage), as a result, often do not receive prenatal and postnatal health care. The consequences are a relatively high maternal death rate (typically from hemorrhage and infection) and a relatively high infant mortality rate. Ironically, when the uninsured go to a doctor, they pay more for services than the more well-to-do insured patients. The reason is that health insurance companies insist on discounts. The result is that a doctor may charge $25 for a routine exam insured by a group insurance plan but charge $175 for the same exam for a person without insurance.

> *"It's horribly ironic," said Paul Menzel, a professor of philosophy at Pacific Lutheran University in Tacoma, Washington. The care of the poor once was supported by the wealthy and the insured, but now the opposite is happening, he said. "It is the people who are most provided for, not the people who are least provided for, who get the benefit of cost-shifting," Professor Menzel said. (Kolata 2001:1–2)*

Medicaid is the government health program for the very poor. It is funded jointly by the federal government and each state. Each state administers its version of Medicaid with few federal guidelines. Thus, Medicaid varies among states in quality, eligibility of patients, coverage, and the adequacy of fees for the services of physicians and hospitals. The consequence of this policy makes obtaining Medicaid services a function of the state in which one lives, rather than level of poverty or need. Also, when states are short of funds, Medicaid is a likely target for budget cuts, as happened during the Great Recession. Because Medicaid is a partnership between the state and federal governments, state cuts bring a matching loss of federal money as well.

Millions of poor people in the United States are treated under Medicaid, but there are serious problems with this program. Many physicians refuse to treat Medicaid patients (because the government does not reimburse them enough for their services), resulting in delayed medical attention, and then typically in hospital emergency departments, where such patients cannot be turned away. This overburdens hospitals and postpones treatment, as patients often must wait many hours before being seen by a physician. Often the examination is superficial and the treatment careless because the attending physicians are overwhelmed by the numbers of patients.

Even when the poor do go to physicians, hospitals, and clinics, they are more likely than the more affluent to receive inferior services. The poor are more likely to receive care in inadequate (in number of staff and quality of equipment) health care facilities. Without medical insurance, they are relegated to crowded emergency departments staffed by overworked nurses and physicians. Poor communities have fewer hospitals, and the quality of those hospitals is lower than in more affluent communities. Research shows, for example, that the best-performing hospitals are concentrated in higher-income counties. Consequently, heart patients in wealthier communities have a better chance of getting recommended treatments at their local hospitals than do patients in lower-income areas. As the leader of the team that writes the federal government's National Healthcare Disparities Report put it, "Hospitals serving poor populations have very limited resources, and they simply cannot provide the high-quality care delivered in mainstream hospitals" (cited in *USA Today* 2006:8D).

The common belief is that the poor are accountable for their health deficiencies. The poor, from this perspective, have cultural norms that differ from the majority. Their lifestyle is less likely than the lifestyle of the more affluent to include proper exercise for a healthy heart. Their diets are more likely to contain relatively high amounts of fat. They are more likely to smoke cigarettes and to abuse drugs. The children of the poor, for instance, are more likely than the children of the affluent to be born addicted to crack and to be victims of fetal alcohol syndrome.

The essence of this argument is that the problems of ill health that beset the poor disproportionately are a consequence of their different lifestyle. This line of reasoning blames the poor for their failure to follow healthier lifestyles.

This approach, however, ignores the fundamental realities of social class. Williams (1990), in his comprehensive review of the social science literature on socioeconomic status and health, argued that privilege in the social stratification system translates both directly and indirectly into better health in several major ways. First, the privileged live in home, neighborhood, and work environments that are less stressful. The economically disadvantaged, on the other hand, are more subject to the stresses (and resulting ill health) from rates of street crime, financial insecurity, marital instability, death of loved ones, exposure to unhealthy work conditions where they are exposed to hazardous risks and toxic substances, and exposure to pollution and toxic wastes in their neighborhoods. Poor workers are more likely than the nonpoor to be in jobs with low job security. The poor have more stress and hypertension (high blood pressure) because of living in crowded conditions and worrying about having enough resources for food, utilities, and rent. The poor also may not have adequate heat, ventilation, and sanitation, which means that they are more susceptible to infectious and parasitic diseases.

Second, the privileged have more knowledge of positive health habits (adequate sleep, refraining from smoking, drinking moderately, good nutrition, maintaining normal weight, physical exercise, and monitoring cholesterol and blood pressure levels) and the resources to implement them.

Third, the children of privilege have healthier environments in the crucial first five years of life. Many adults from disadvantaged backgrounds suffer

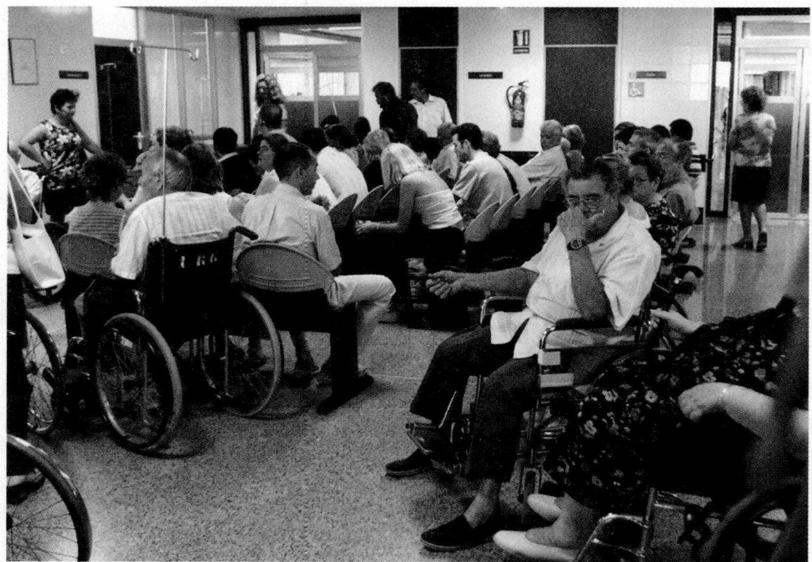

Those without health insurance are relegated to crowded emergency departments staffed by overworked nurses and physicians.

throughout their lives because of an unhealthy environment in their formative years.

Fourth, the privileged have better access to and make better use of the health care system (the primary subject of this chapter). Early intervention at the onset of a disease and medical management of a chronic illness affect both the survival rates and the quality of life. The fewer the economic resources, the less likely a person will receive preventive care and early treatment. This is because medicine in U.S. society is a market commodity and thus is dispensed unequally to the people who can afford it.

As strong as the case is for providing equal access to medical care to all people, it is not the most fruitful approach to correcting the differences in health by socioeconomic class. The answer, most fundamentally, is to reduce the inequalities of class (and race and gender) that perpetuate poor health among the disadvantaged. According to Williams,

> *[T]he available evidence suggests . . . that equality in the health care delivery system [while a legitimate and desired goal] will not eliminate inequality in health status . . . if the inequalities remain in the fundamental reward structures of society. The point here is neither that changes in health care delivery will make no difference nor that the determinants of inequality are static. What is implied is that inequality will persist in a variety of social indicators as long as the basic reward structures remain unequal. (Williams 1990:95)*

Race/Ethnicity

To examine health outcomes by race implies that there are biological differences among the races. But, as David Williams and James Lardner point out,

> *Genetics can't explain much of anything to do about race, which is a socially constructed rather than a biologically based concept to begin with. The fact that you and I know what race we belong to tells us more about the society we live in than about our physical makeup. Some white people are more similar genetically to black people*

> *than they are to other white people.* Race is truly a pigment of our imagination. *(Williams and Lardner 2005:107; emphasis added)*

Therefore, the differences in health outcomes by race are, almost entirely, a consequence of disproportionate poverty and discriminatory treatment.

Non-White people in the United States are disproportionately poor (e.g., about one in four Latinos and African Americans are below the poverty line). This fact combined with racial discrimination leads to unfavorable patterns of health and health care delivery for them. Let us examine some of these health differences by race.

- **Life Expectancy.** Perhaps the best illustration of the difference that race makes on health is in life expectancy. The life expectancy for African American males is 6 years less than for White males, and for Black females it is 4 years less than for White females. The discrepancy is even wider for Native Americans, who have the poorest health of any racial category in the United States, with a life expectancy 10 years below that of the nation as a whole.

- **Infant Mortality.** The rate of infant mortality in the United States reveals striking differences by race. According to the Centers for Disease Control and Prevention (CDC 2007a), the Black infant mortality rate in 2006 (13.3 per 1,000 live births) is almost 2.5 times the White rate (5.6 per 1,000). Among Latinos, the rate for Puerto Ricans (7.8) was more than 50 percent higher than for infants of Cuban origin (4.55), a difference explained in large part by social class differences. The same relationship is found among Asians, with rates for Filipinos almost double that for infants of Chinese origin.

- **Maternal Mortality.** Statistics reveal that the death rate of African American women due to complications during birth is more than triple the rate for White mothers. The main reason for this racial disparity is that Black women are less likely to receive prenatal care.

- **Prenatal Care.** There is a substantial racial disparity in early prenatal care, with about nine of ten White mothers receiving it, compared to about three of four Latino and African American mothers.

- **Low Birth Weight.** Low birth weight is closely related to two factors: mothers not receiving adequate prenatal care and prospective mothers smoking during pregnancy. African Americans are twice as likely to be born with a low birth weight than are White children. This differential by race has remained about the same since 1960.

- **Heart Disease.** Heart disease in all its forms is the nation's leading cause of death. The evidence is that Black men are twice as likely as White men to die from heart disease before the age of 65. Overall, the national death rate for African American men is 841 per 100,000 compared to 666 White men. A study of a national sample of 237,000 Medicare patients from 1999 through 2005 found that Black patients are less likely to receive implantable heart devices than White patients (reported in Rubin 2007).

- **Cancer.** The death rate from cancer is about three and one-half times greater for Black males than for White males. The rate for Black women is also higher than it is for White women. The problem, generally, is that African Americans (and Latinos) are more likely to be diagnosed with cancer in its later stages, making survival less likely. This, of course, is not because of race per se but because of the greater likelihood that African Americans and Latinos are poor and uninsured.

The cancer rate is higher for African Americans than Whites for all cancers except stomach cancer and breast cancer. The latter anomaly may be explained by the apparent fact that the younger a mother is at the birth of her first child, the lower the breast cancer risk, and Black women tend to have children at younger ages. Once cancer is detected in both Blacks and Whites, Whites have a much higher survival rate. Latinos have the lowest incidence of breast cancer, but their chances of survival are not as good as Whites. Overall, Asian American women are much less likely than White or Black women to develop breast cancer, and their five-year survival rate is the best. However, for cervical cancer, the rate for Vietnamese Americans is higher than for Whites. The apparent reason for this higher rate for Vietnamese Americans is their very low early screening rates; because most of them are recent immigrants, they may be unfamiliar with the concept of preventive care or they are too poor to visit a doctor. Related to this last point, the 1996 welfare reform passed by Congress barred recent immigrants from receiving federally funded Medicaid until they had been in the country for five years (Scher 2001), and, as stated, many Vietnamese Americans are recent immigrants.

- **Dementia.** According to the Alzheimer's Association, African Americans are almost twice as likely as Whites to have Alzheimer's and other forms of dementia, and Latinos are about one and a half times more likely to be affected (cited in Marcus 2010). The various forms of dementia are associated with high rates of diabetes and heart disease, both of which are disproportionately high among Blacks and Latinos.

- **Vision Problems.** More than 9 million people in the United States have visual impairment, caused usually by glaucoma, diabetes, and retinal diseases. African American adults are nearly twice as likely as Whites to be legally blind or vision impaired. Latinos are more likely than Whites to be blind, primarily because of complications from diabetes, a disease they are three times more likely than Whites to have.

- **Communicable Diseases.** The diseases especially found among the poor (e.g., influenza, pneumonia, and tuberculosis) are disproportionately found among non-Whites because they are disproportionately poor. Tuberculosis occurs fourteen times more frequently among African Americans than Whites, and it is four times more likely to occur among Hispanics than Whites. Native Americans are four times more likely to die from tuberculosis and dysentery than are non–Native Americans.

  Cultural or lifestyle differences offer some explanations. This blaming-the-victim approach argues that racial minorities do not take proper care of themselves. Their diets tend to be high in fat, sugar, and salt. They are more likely to smoke (a fact not lost on the tobacco companies, as they target their products and advertising to African Americans and Latinos). They are less likely than members of the majority to exercise. Thus, Blacks, for example, have a high incidence of obesity, hypertension, and heart disease.

But even though lifestyle differences among the races account for some variations in health, other factors are more important. Economic factors explain much of the variation. Minority racial and ethnic groups are disproportionately poor. This means that many of them must live in rat-infested neighborhoods, where they are exposed to diseases carried by these vermin. Their neighborhoods also have high concentrations of lead (in the paint and plumbing), which exposes their children to many health dangers, including brain damage. Living in poverty also means living in inadequate shelter, where exposure to the cold leads to complications such as bronchitis and pneumonia. Living in overcrowded situations leads to the spread of communicable diseases. A low income means reliance on a diet of cheap, fattening, nonnutritious food.

Living in poverty also results in the disruption of social networks and in heightened fears and anxieties caused by arson, drug abuse, and violent crime. Regarding this last point, Blacks are nearly six times more likely than Whites to be murdered, are almost twice as likely to be robbed, and are raped at a rate nearly double that of Whites.

The poor also are less likely to receive adequate medical attention. Many, as noted earlier, do not have medical insurance, and being poor they cannot afford medical care on a regular, preventive basis. The absence of insurance coverage is related to race, with Latinos and African Americans much less likely to have medical insurance than Whites. As stated earlier, recent immigrants are denied Medicaid until they have been in this country for five years. Thus, they delay going to the physician, dentist, or hospital until the health problem is too serious to ignore. This may mean that the problem is too advanced for a cure.

But even when African Americans and Latinos seek medical attention, they often are given less attention than Whites. For example, according to a study of 7,000 patients, Black men were 25 to 30 percent less likely to get standard tests to detect a heart attack than were White men (Fischman 2007).

The poor in general, and African Americans and other racial minorities in particular, are much more likely than Whites to rely on emergency and hospital outpatient departments than on a family physician. The two most important reasons for this are that they cannot afford a family physician and, even if they can afford one, physicians are in short supply where the poor live. Most of the uninsured live in areas that have inadequate medical care, including a shortage of primary-care physicians.

There are four negative outcomes from this for racial minorities. First, they do not meet regularly with a physician who is familiar with their health history. Second, the number of hospitals in the poor sections of cities and where rural poverty is prevalent is declining. Third, federal cutbacks since the 1980s have resulted in decreased medical attention for the poor. And fourth, even when health services are accessible, racial minorities may face racial discrimination in attempting to obtain care.

Thus, a major reason for the high death rate of African Americans from cancer is because they often do not have access to quality health care. But the link may be stronger than that—when African Americans (and other racial minorities) have access to good medical care, they do not receive the same treatment as do Whites, a consequence of economics, and possibly of discrimination. Racial minorities (and women), for example, wait longer than White men for liver transplants and are less likely to undergo bypass surgery or angioplasty, resulting in their reduced heart disease survival.

Poverty and its attendant problems are exacerbated by the social inequalities associated with race. To be African American, Latino, or Native American means, for many people, to be considered inferior, even to be despised. Thus, hierarchy and its attendant discrimination creates tensions and stresses. African Americans have higher blood pressure than do Whites. Is the reason genetic or social in origin? African Americans, especially those with low income, have higher hypertension (high blood pressure) rates than the more well-to-do. This is partially the result of a poor diet. But it also is reasonable to assume that the stress associated with hypertension results from blocked social mobility, anger over perceived and real injustices, fear of crime, and being treated as a social inferior.

Gender

The health of women and the health care they receive reflect primarily their status in society and only secondarily their physiological differences from men. Women do have significant health advantages over men; for example, their life expectancy exceeds that of males by about 7 years. These advantages begin in the womb, where female fetuses have a 10 percent higher survival rate than do male fetuses. These advantages continue after birth and throughout the life cycle, as male death rates exceed female death rates at all ages. Women are less likely than men to die from the leading causes of death, including heart disease, cancer, accidents, suicide, and homicide (the only exceptions are death from diabetes and Alzheimer's).

There are both biological and social reasons for some of the health advantages that women have over men. During early childhood, girls have biological benefits over boys, as exhibited by their greater resistance to infectious and chronic diseases. As adults, women in the past were more protected than were men, at least until menopause, especially from heart disease and hypertension, because of the hormone estrogen.

More important, though, than the biological differences between the sexes are the significant social differences that also account for gender differences in health. The adolescent and young adult male gender role includes being assertive and daring. This accounts for the greater likelihood of males being in automobile accidents (five out of seven victims of traffic accidents are men), driving while drunk, and using more alcohol (men are three times as likely to be alcoholics), illegal drugs, and cigarettes (recently, however, the number of women who smoke is increasing, so the difference between men and women is converging). Males also are more likely than females to work at risky jobs (including military combat).

The female gender role is more conducive to good health in several ways. Women are expected to be more knowledgeable about health matters and thus to be more aware of changes in their bodies than are men. Women are also more likely to see a physician or be admitted into a hospital than are men (traditional men tend to see this behavior in males as a sign of weakness).

Women on average are less likely than men to have medical insurance. This is because they are more likely than men to work at part-time jobs or doing contingent work, thus not qualifying for employer-supplied health insurance. This disadvantage is strongest for women between ages 45 and 64 (before they qualify for Medicare) and especially for African American and Latina women in this age category (about 35 percent of women compared with two-thirds of men).

This is because women are more often employed in part-time work, work at low-wage jobs, and work for small businesses. Also, insurance coverage for women stops under their husbands' policies when they are widowed or divorced. As a result, millions of women are too poor to buy health insurance but earn too much to get public aid.

Whether one has health insurance or not is literally a matter of life and death. Using the example of breast cancer, researchers have found that uninsured women are less likely to receive cancer-screening services than are women with private insurance, less likely to have their breast cancer adequately evaluated, less likely to get regular mammograms, and less likely to have their breast cancer aggressively treated (Jackson 2006).

Women face two major health risks. One is childbearing, which can be unhealthy, even deadly, for mothers. The other health risk is a consequence of traditional gender roles. Because women in U.S. society are evaluated by their physical appearance, they are much more likely than men to suffer from anorexia nervosa and bulimia (conditions that result when individuals take extraordinary measures to lose weight). Women are also much more likely than men to risk surgery for cosmetic reasons (tummy tucks, liposuction, breast implants or reduction, and face-lifts), which may have negative health effects.

The advantage women have over men in mortality rates is overshadowed by the advantages men receive from the medical profession. First, the medical schools and the medical profession are dominated by males. Women in medicine are vastly overrepresented in the nurturant, supportive, underpaid, and relatively powerless roles of nurse and aide, or if they are physicians, they are most likely to be in general practice or specialize in pediatrics.

Second, until 1990, when the government confirmed that women had been intentionally left out of federally funded medical research, much medical research has excluded women as subjects. For example, the major study on whether taking daily doses of aspirin can reduce the risk of a heart attack used 22,071 subjects—all men. In most cases, a drug proved effective in men is also effective for women. But the differences in hormone proportions and the menstrual cycle can be important. In the aspirin study, it would have been useful to determine whether taking aspirin prevents heart attacks in premenopausal women, in only postmenopausal women, or not in any women. Another study used 12,866 male subjects to explore the links between heart disease and high cholesterol, lack of exercise, and smoking. By excluding women from the study, the medical profession has no clear scientific proof whether the linkages among these variables found for men also occur for women.

The National Women's Health Resource Center has noted that other major health studies have overlooked women. As in the aspirin and heart disease studies, research using only male subjects has studied diet, exercise, and cholesterol; Type A behavior and heart disease; and alcohol and blood pressure. Since 1990, the representation of women in research studies has increased but only slightly. A review of studies published from 1991 to 2000 found women were 25 percent of the subjects in heart-related research, up from 20 percent in research from 1966 to 1990 (reported in Tanner 2001).

Third, research appears to put women's health priorities second to men's. For example, the National Institutes of Health has spent much less of its research budget on women's health care issues than on men's issues. Perhaps this explains why medical research has yet to come up with an acceptable, safe, and effective male contraceptive. This deficiency has meant that women have had to bear the responsibilities and health risks of contraception. This oversight in medical research is gradually being rectified. Recent research has uncovered genes linked to hereditary breast cancer, made advances in the prevention of osteoporosis, and created drugs to fight ovarian cancer.

Fourth, female patients interacting with male physicians encounter a number of sexist practices. These include paternalistic attitudes; insensitivity toward the special problems of women surrounding the menstrual cycle, childbirth (see the "Voices" panel), and menopause; siding with husbands who were leery of vasectomies and performing, rather, tubal ligations on wives, even though the cost and medical risk were much greater; and requiring more specific tests for men than for women during diagnostic examinations. Another example of male physicians' insensitivity to women often occurs during an unwanted pregnancy. Many male physicians often consider women's interests secondary to fetal survival.

Fifth, women are discriminated against in the treatment they receive or do not receive. For example, a study found that women with cardiac complaints were about 50 percent more likely than men to experience delays by emergency medical services (Boyles, 2009). Moreover, women are less likely than men to receive implantable heart devices (Rubin 2007).

HIV/AIDS: The Intersection of Class, Race, and Gender

Since the killer HIV/AIDS (acquired immunodeficiency syndrome) epidemic began in 1981, the worldwide death toll is 25 million people, with 475,000 Americans dying from the disease. According to the World Health Organization, over 33 million were infected in 2009 worldwide, with 2.7 million new infections and 2 million deaths annually (reported in Henry J. Kaiser Family Foundation 2009). The global epidemic appears to have peaked in 1996, and that the disease is stable in most regions, except for Africa. AIDS it is the world's leading cause of death among both women and men ages 15 to 59 (Annan 2006).

In 1996, for the first time since the epidemic began in the United States, the number of people diagnosed with AIDS declined from the previous year's numbers. This decline was a direct result of these new drugs halting HIV from becoming AIDS. But because the new drugs go only to those who can afford them, and to a fortunate few who are poor but live in states with generous assistance, the drop in AIDS was not across the board but rather benefited those with class and racial privilege. Especially hard hit are minority men and women (see Figure 17.1). Consider the following facts for the United States (CDC 2009):

- Although Blacks make up about 13 percent of the population, they account for about half of all people in the United States who live with HIV.
- HIV/AIDS is the leading cause of death for Blacks 25 to 44 years of age (the fifth leading cause of death for Whites and the fourth leading cause for Latinos).
- The number of AIDS cases per 100,000 population is 7.2 for Whites, 26.8 for Latinos, and 75.2 for African Americans.
- Two-thirds of new infections among women occur in Black women. In 2007, the rate of new AIDS cases for Black women was twenty-two times that of White women and five times greater than the infection rate for Latinas. The rate of AIDS for Black men was almost 8 times the rate for White men.

Those most susceptible to HIV/AIDS are men who have sex with other men (71 percent) and intravenous drug users who share needles. For women,

VOICES

DOES THE DOCTOR'S GENDER MATTER?

[A] female OB or a female nurse can sympathize a little more with what you are going through than a male. . . . [Male attendants] could possibly watch their wives go through it, but they don't know what it's like exactly.

—Tricia, White mother of two

I wanted to be sure to be heard, and I know with medicine, being a child of a physician, I just [know] at times that women's concerns can be seen as overreactive, exaggerating, unfounded concerns.

—Tonya, African American mother of one

You know, when I said to her, "Gee, this really hurts over here," she could relate to it. With a guy, it was kind of like, "It's all just in your mind." She really could relate to everything. And her personality was wonderful, and she had a great bedside manner. She listened to your questions.

—Jill, White mother of two

These women's comments exemplify many others' feelings about women as doctors.* A 1996 study of women's childbirth experiences in a mid-Atlantic state found that the gender of the doctor did affect many women's reproductive experiences. Eight (or 42 percent) of nineteen interviewees specifically chose female doctors. Some explained that they had had prior bad experiences with male OB-GYNs or intimates and thus had switched to female doctors at some point. Other women specifically wanted a doctor who should be "more caring," hinting that feelings and emotions during pregnancy and childbirth were important. Others explained that they wanted to be on more "equal footing" with their attendant.

Vicki, a mother of two from England, recounted her experience with a male OB-GYN:

> Yeah, he basically gave me no information. When I asked him about birth courses, you know, . . . he told me to go to the birthing course at the hospital. And [the class] was mostly on drugs, it was very strange. And he patted me on the head and said, "I'll handle it, don't you worry about a thing." And I didn't like that, and I didn't want any part of it [the second time].

The authoritative medical knowledge that this doctor held supposedly gave him the right to withhold certain types of information from Vicki, leaving her with little knowledge of what would happen during birth. He assumed that Vicki would be comfortable simply allowing him to "handle it." The desire to be heard and informed is also evident in this next woman's response:

> Just from the different experiences I've had, [female doctors will] sit down and listen to you more, they'll understand your concerns, or they'll answer questions you might not have thought of that they've known. . . . Just in general, they seem more, not more caring or sympathetic, just open to other ideas, instead of being a leader person. (Heidi, White mother of three)

The fact that female doctors often have had their own birthing experiences was an additional reason to choose them, for experience was equated with greater competency, knowledge, and understanding of the birth process. Thus, female doctors brought comfort for many women on many levels. Stephanie, a White mother of two, stated: "You have a lot going on, you know, they're prodding and poking you and I just felt—because I'm a modest person—I just knew that I would be more comfortable with a female [doctor]." Rachel, a White mother of one, stated that she "would be more comfortable [asking a] myriad of questions with a woman. I felt that I could get a little bit more of an insight especially because [my doctor] had had children as well." And Natasha, another White mother of one, suggested that she was not comfortable "talking about this kind of stuff to begin with, so I have a hard time talking about this stuff even with a woman. I probably would have been red in the face the whole time talking to a man."

In contrast to the situations explained here, women who received prenatal care from male doctors did not necessarily "choose" the gender of their doctor. Of those who had male doctors, only three out of eleven (approximately 25 percent) stated that the gender of their doctor mattered to them. Thus, we can assume that the rest of the women interviewed simply followed a preestablished model for birth (perhaps going to doctors whom relatives or friends recommended), which included birth in a hospital setting with a male doctor in charge. If gender did matter to a woman, then she was more likely to seek out a female doctor.

Source: Heather E. Dillaway. 2000. Michigan State University, Department of Sociology. This essay was written expressly for *Social Problems.*

* All names of women have been changed to ensure confidentiality.

FIGURE 17.1

Race/Ethnicity of Persons (including children) with HIV/AIDS Diagnosed During 2007

Source: Centers for Disease Control. 2009. "HIV/AIDS among African Americans." (August 2009).

Note: Based on data from 34 states with long-term, confidential name-based HIV reporting.

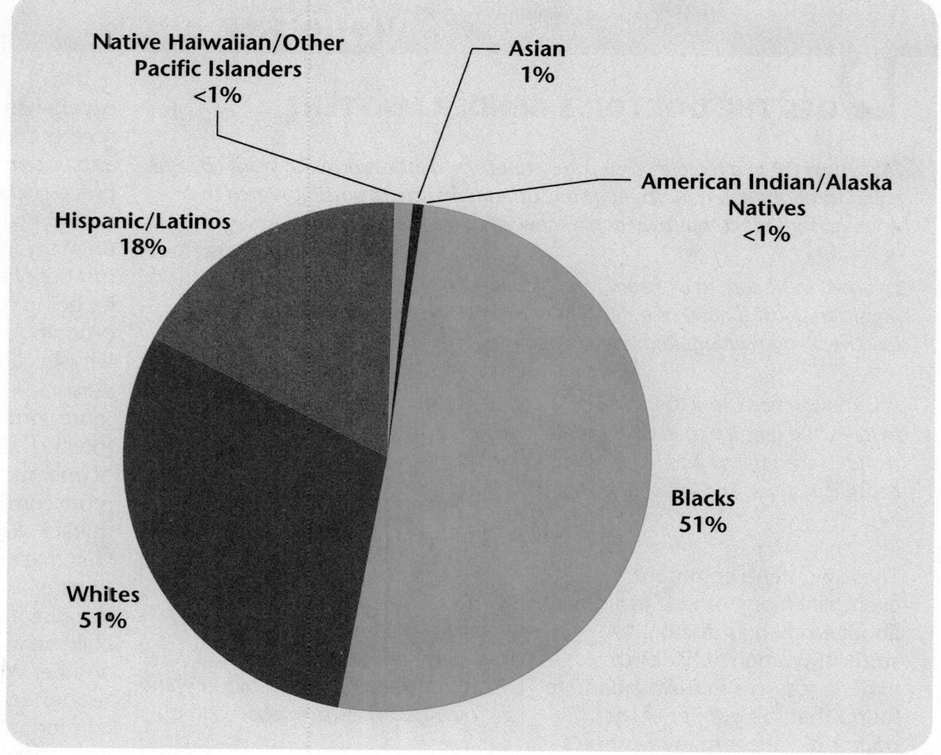

75 percent received the virus from heterosexual contact and 23 percent from drug injections. Young Black gay men are the most vulnerable. According to the CDC,

> *The AIDS virus continues to spread widely among African Americans, who represent just 14% of Americans ages 13–29 but account for half of new infections in that group. . . . Young black gay and bisexual men account for 55% of infections among African Americans in that age group. . . .* (cited in Sternberg 2010:7D)

MODELS FOR NATIONAL HEALTH CARE: LESSONS FROM OTHER SOCIETIES

The United States, as we have stated, spends much more for health care, both in total dollars and as a percentage of its gross national product, than any other nation. Yet, all major indicators of national health show that other nations are getting more for their health dollars than does the United States. Almost 50 million Americans do not have health insurance, and millions more are underinsured. The system is fragmented, inefficient, and wasteful. Most important, the for-profit system that prevails in the United States lacks a social mission; it is more responsive to Wall Street than to Main Street. Economist Robert Kuttner says this:

> *The only way to cut through this mess is, of course, to have universal health insurance. All insurance is a kind of cross-subsidy. The young, who on average need little care, subsidize the old. The well subsidize the sick.*

With a universal system, there is no private insurance industry spending billions of dollars trying to target the well and avoid the sick, because everyone is in the same system. There is no worry about "portability" when you change jobs, because everyone is in the same system. And there are no problems choosing your preferred doctor or hospital, because everyone is in the same system. (Kuttner 1998:27)

Given this gloomy health climate, are there reforms that would improve the health care system in the United States? Other advanced societies have found ways that fit their history, politics, economy, and national values. The general patterns fit into three basic arrangements (the following depends on Reid 2009:17–20).

The Bismarck Model

Named after Otto von Bismarck, who invented the welfare state in Germany in the nineteenth century, this system is found today in Germany, Japan, France, Belgium, and Switzerland. Like the U.S. system, it uses private health insurance plans, usually financed by both employers and employees. Unlike the United States, though, Bismarck-type plans cover everyone, and the insurance companies do not make a profit. There is tight government regulation of medical services and fees to contain cost.

The Beveridge Model

This system, named after a British reformer, is found in Great Britain, Italy, Spain, Cuba, and most of Scandinavia. Health care is provided and financed by the government. There are no medical bills. "Medical treatment is a public service, like the fire department or the public library" (Reid 2009:18). Most hospitals and clinics are owned by the government, and many doctors are government employees. There are private doctors who are reimbursed by the government for their services. There are low costs because the government controls what physicians can do and what they can charge. Ironically,

The two purest examples of the Beveridge Model—or "socialized medicine"—are both found in the Western Hemisphere: Cuba and the U.S. Department of Veterans Affairs. In both of those systems, all the health care professionals work for the government in government-owned facilities, and patients receive no bills. (Reid 2009:18)

The National Health Insurance Model

This system, found in Canada, Taiwan, and South Korea, includes elements of both Bismarck and Beveridge models. Health care providers are private, but the payer is a government-run insurance program. This is known as a **single-payer plan**. The government insurance plan (either a federal or a provincial plan) collects monthly premiums from every citizen and pays the medical bills.

Since there's no need for marketing, no expensive underwriting offices to deny claims, and no profit, these universal insurance programs tend to be cheaper and much simpler administratively than American-style private insurance. As a single-payer covering everybody, the national insurance plan tends to have considerable market power to negotiate for lower prices [for lower pharmaceutical costs, for example]. (Reid 2009:18–19)

Most advocates of universal health insurance argue that the United States should adopt a single-payer plan similar to the Canadian plan. This plan would

Figure 17.2

Health Outcomes: United States vs. Canada

Source: Reprinted from "Health Care For All," the Fall 2006 *YES!* Magazine, PO Box 10818, Bainbridge Island, WA 98110.

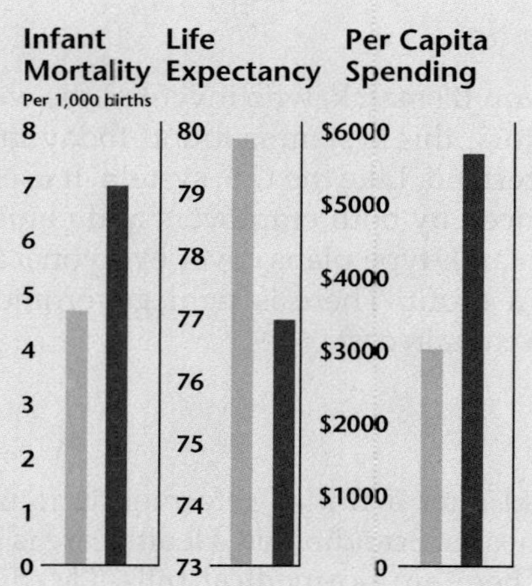

serve all citizens at lower cost; Canada spends 10 percent of its gross domestic product (GDP) on health care, compared to 17 percent in the United States, yet it has better health outcomes (see Figure 17.2). It would be more efficient not only in serving everyone but also in reducing bureaucracy and paperwork; health administration costs in the United States are double the costs in Canada. David Himmelstein and Steffie Woolhandler, cofounders of Physicians for a National Health Care Program, argued that if the United States cut its medical bureaucratic costs to Canadian levels, it would save nearly $400 billion annually (cited in The Hastings Center 2009: para 5). (See the Social Policy panel for an analysis of the Canadian and U.S. health care systems, written by a Canadian physician.)

REFORMING THE HEALTH CARE SYSTEM OF THE UNITED STATES

The United States is the only developed nation without some form of universal health care. There have been attempts to reform the U.S. health care system going back to 1912, but they have all failed. Teddy Roosevelt campaigned for a national health care plan in 1912, but he was defeated by Woodrow Wilson. In 1915 Congress debated a bill providing for universal medical coverage, but when the United States declared war with Germany in 1917, the issue died. In 1935 President Franklin D. Roosevelt passed the Social Security Act. This legislation originally included health care reform but it was dropped because it

SOCIAL POLICY

A CANADIAN DOCTOR DIAGNOSES U.S. HEALTH CARE

Michael M. Rachlis

Universal health insurance is on the American policy agenda for the fifth time since World War II. In the 1960s, the United States. chose public coverage for only the elderly and the very poor, while Canada opted for a universal program for hospitals and physicians' services. As a policy analyst, I know there are lessons to be learned from studying the effect of different approaches in similar jurisdictions. But, as a Canadian with lots of American friends and relatives, I am saddened that Americans seem incapable of learning them.

Our countries are joined at the hip. We peacefully share a continent, a British heritage of representative government and now ownership of GM. And, until 50 years ago, we had similar health systems, health care costs and vital statistics.

The United States' and Canada's different health insurance decisions make up the world's largest health policy experiment. And the results?

On coverage, all Canadians have insurance for hospital and physician services. There are no deductibles or co-pays. Most provinces also provide coverage for programs for home care, long-term care, pharmaceuticals and durable medical equipment, although there are co-pays.

On the United States side, 46 million people have no insurance, millions are underinsured and healthcare bills bankrupt more than 1 million Americans every year.

Lesson No. 1: A single-payer system would eliminate most U.S. coverage problems.

On costs, Canada spends 10% of its economy on health care; the United States spends 16%. The extra 6% of GDP amounts to more than $800 billion per year. The spending gap between the two nations is almost entirely because of higher overhead. Canadians don't need thousands of actuaries to set premiums or thousands of lawyers to deny care. Even the U.S. Medicare program has 80% to 90% lower administrative costs than private Medicare Advantage policies. And providers and suppliers can't charge as much when they have to deal with a single payer.

Lessons No. 2 and 3: Single-payer systems reduce duplicative administrative costs and can negotiate lower prices.

Because most of the difference in spending is for non-patient care, Canadians actually get more of most services. We see the doctor more often and take more drugs. We even have more lung transplant surgery. We do get less heart surgery, but not so much less that we are any more likely to die of heart attacks. And we now live nearly three years longer, and our infant mortality is 20% lower.

Lesson No. 4: Single-payer plans can deliver the goods because their funding goes to services, not overhead.

The Canadian system does have its problems, and these also provide important lessons. Notwithstanding a few well-publicized and misleading cases, Canadians needing urgent care get immediate treatment. But we do wait too long for much elective care, including appointments with family doctors and specialists and selected surgical procedures. We also do a poor job managing chronic disease.

However, according to the New York-based Commonwealth Fund, *both* the American and the Canadian systems fare badly in these areas. In fact, an April U.S. Government Accountability Office report noted that U.S. emergency room wait times have increased, and patients who should be seen immediately are now waiting an average of 28 minutes. The GAO has also raised concerns about two- to four-month waiting times for mammograms.

On closer examination, most of these problems have little to do with public insurance or even overall resources. Despite the delays, the GAO said there is enough mammogram capacity.

These problems are largely caused by our shared politico-cultural barriers to quality of care. In 19th century North America, doctors waged a campaign against quacks and snake oil salesmen and attained a legislative monopoly on medical practice. In return, they promised to set and enforce standards of practice. By and large, it didn't happen. And perverse incentives like fee-for-service make things even worse.

Using techniques like those championed by the Boston-based Institute for Healthcare Improvement, providers can eliminate most delays. In Hamilton, Ontario, 17 psychiatrists have linked up with 100 family doctors and 80 social workers to offer some of the world's best access to mental health services. And in Toronto, simple process improvements

(Cont.)

mean you can now get your hip assessed in one week and get a new one, if you need it, within a month.

Lesson No. 5: Canadian health care delivery problems have nothing to do with our single-payer system and can be fixed by re-engineering for quality.

U.S. health policy would be miles ahead if policymakers could learn these lessons. But they seem less interested in Canada's or any other nation's, experience than ever. Why?

American democracy runs on money. Pharmaceutical and insurance companies have the fuel. Analysts see hundreds of billions of premiums wasted on overhead that could fund care for the uninsured. But industry executives and shareholders see bonuses and dividends.

Compounding the confusion is traditional American ignorance of what happens north of the border, which makes it easy to mislead people. Boilerplate anti-government rhetoric does the same. The U.S. media, legislators and even presidents have claimed that our "socialized" system doesn't let us choose our own doctors. In fact, Canadians have free choice of physicians. It's Americans these days who are restricted to "in-plan" doctors.

Unfortunately, many Americans won't get to hear the straight goods because vested interests are promoting a caricature of the Canadian experience.

Source: Michael M. Rachlis. 2009, "A Canadian Doctor Diagnoses U.S. Healthcare." *Los Angeles Times* (August 3), online: http://www.latimes.com/news/opinion/la-oe-nachlis3-2009aug03,0,538126.story

was considered too divisive. In 1943 Congress considered a bill to establish a national medical care and hospitalization fund, but it failed to pass. In 1949 President Harry Truman called for the creation of a national health insurance plan, but when war broke out with North Korea, it was abandoned. In 1965 President Lyndon Johnson sought to enact universal health care. He dropped the universal aspect of it but was able to establish Medicare and Medicaid. In the early 1970s President Richard Nixon proposed a version of national health care similar to the Obama proposal of 2009, but it did not survive. (At the same Canada adopted its single-payer plan.) President Bill Clinton in 1993 presented a national health care plan to Congress, but it failed to pass. Then in 2009 President Obama, faced with a dysfunctional system, made the overhaul of the health care system his primary goal.

The Politics of Health Reform

During 2009 and 2010 the members of Congress engaged in heated debate over health reform. The sides coalesced into two contentious factions—Democrats generally favoring change and Republicans blocking reform measures with unanimous opposition. Undergirding the arguments was a basic philosophical issue—Is the organization of health care a concern of government (the Democratic position), or should it be left to the marketplace (the Republican position)? At a practical level, roughly $2.5 trillion, the amount spent on health care annually, was at stake. The division of that money was at the center of the debate. Insurance and pharmaceutical companies feared losing their profits. Doctors, hospitals, and managed care networks were concerned about their futures. Individuals and families worried about how changing the system would affect their pocketbooks as well as the quality of health care they would receive. In short, there were interest groups with a huge stake in the status quo. The result was a bitter struggle, with a variety of tactics employed by the forces for and against changing the health care system. We focus here on the efforts opposing reform.

- **Influencing the Public.** Interest groups on all sides of the debate spent more than $210 million on television advocacy advertising in 2009 (Seelye 2010). For example, the U.S. Chamber of Commerce engaged in a multimillion-dollar ad campaign. One of its commercials showed a red balloon (the choice of red was likely intentional because it symbolizes communism) that enlarges as the narrator warns that an overhaul of the health care system would increase deficits, taxes, and government control. Eventually, the balloon pops.

> *"Say no to government-run health care," a narrator says in the advertisement, produced by a conservative group. . . . The spot is part of a cascade of health-related advertising swamping the airwaves across the country as the health care fight has become a full-blown national political campaign, replete with battleground states, polling, leafleting, fractious town-hall-style meetings, op-ed articles, talking points, viral e-mail messages, and videos. (Seelye 2009:1)*
>
> *An orchestrated campaign was also waged by conservative commentators such as Glenn Beck and Rush Limbaugh and media outlets such as Fox News to persuade the public that Obama and Democrats were leading the country down a wrong and dangerous path. These attacks were typical of what happens when a reform president takes on the status quo. Franklin Roosevelt, for example, confronted ferocious, well-organized, reactionary opposition. He was called a socialist and a fascist by the American Liberty League and by demagogues such as Father Coughlin. Similarly, President Obama faced right-wing groups comparing him to Hitler and health-care reform to socialism* (Nation *2009A:3). Consider the following quotes from various opposition politicians that raised fears about health reform (Begley 2009; Lepore 2009):*

- Senate Minority Leader Mitch McConnell accused President Obama and his allies of "an audacious effort to Europeanize the country."
- House Minority Leader John Boehner wrote, "Health care reform will require Americans to subsidize abortion with their hard-earned tax dollars."
- Republican senator Tom Coburn said, "All the health care in this country is eventually going to be run by the government."
- Republican senator Charles Grassley stated, "We should not have a government program that determines if you're going to pull the plug on Grandma."
- Former candidate for vice-president Sarah Palin posted this on Facebook: "People will have to stand in front of Obama's 'death panel' so his bureaucrats can decide, based on a subjective judgement of their 'level of productivity to society' whether they are worthy of health care."

The efforts by those opposed to health care reform were successful in turning public opinion against reform and in turning some people such as Tea Partiers into rabid opponents. The signs at their rallies showed Obama as Hitler, displayed communist symbols such as the hammer and sickle, and stated that: "Obamacare was: Socialized Medicine," "Obama Lies and Granny Dies," "No Socialism—No Death Panels!" "Obama Care: Goodbye to Old People!" and "Congress Ain't My Doctor."

- **Influencing Congress.** In 2009 there were 3,098 health-sector lobbyists in Washington—nearly six for each member of Congress. Their efforts were

Former vice presidential candidate Sarah Palin spoke against health care reform, saying that there would be "death panels" to decide the fate of the elderly.

intended to either block reform legislation or to shape the resulting legislation to maintain their advantage (Sklar 2009). The nonpartisan Center for Responsive Politics found that the federal lobbying by health and health insurance industries amounted to $648 million in 2009, the most money ever by a business sector for federal lobbying (cited in Seelye 2010). One interested industry, the pharmaceutical and health products industry, spent $266.8 million on lobbying in 2009, an all-time record for a single industry (Jackson 2010).

Another tactic to influence the final composition of health care legislation was to funnel money to key legislators. Nearly 60 percent of the health care industry's campaign contributions to members of Congress went to lawmakers sitting on five powerful committees where the health reform legislation was crafted. The hope behind these contributions was that the influential legislators would form the legislation to their advantage. Max Baucus, for example, chair of the Senate Finance Committee, was the leading recipient of Senate campaign contributions from the hospitals, insurers, and other medical interest groups, receiving $1.5 million in 2007 and 2008 (and $3 million from 2003 to 2009; Eggen 2009b).

- **Legislative Blockage by the Minority.** The Republicans, as the minority party in both houses of Congress, agreed on a strategy of total opposition to health reform. For example, when the Senate voted on a crucial health care bill on Christmas Eve 2009, not a single Republican voted in favor. In the 435-seat House, only one Republican broke ranks. There were two roots to this negativism. For some, opposition was based on principle, that it was wrongheaded to go with a government plan rather than let the marketplace determine health care. For others, their extreme partisanship was political. Commentator Joe Klein characterized this position:

> *The party's real goal has been to stop any and all legislation for political reasons—to deny Obama a major victory. To that end, Republicans have purposely mischaracterized the Democratic plan from the start—as socialism, a government "takeover" of health care. (Klein 2010:21)*

Thus, if the Democrats are unsuccessful in achieving health reform, the Republicans will have a better chance to win back the majorities in Congress.

Also, the Republicans in the Senate used the rules of that body to block health reform legislation (see Chapter 2). The rules require 60 votes to stop a filibuster by the minority party.

> *This is not what democracy looks like. When Americans vote, by overwhelming majorities, to place control of the executive and legislative branches in the hands of a party that has promised fundamental change, they are supposed to get that change. They are not supposed to watch as a handful of self-interested and special-interested senators prevent progress by exploiting the arcane rules of the less representative of our two legislative chambers—rules requiring that not a majority but a supermajority be attained in order even to discuss necessary reforms, and that a similar supermajority be in place to thwart a filibuster.* (Nation 2009:3)

The Obama Plan

Because the Democrats controlled both houses of Congress, different bills reforming health care passed in the House and in the Senate. The final bill that emerged from a conference committee did not provide universal health insurance through a single payer plan, which dismayed liberals. It did increase the role of government in the health care system, which upset conservatives.

What emerged in the struggle for passage was legislation with these changes to the status quo.

- There is a mandate that everyone take out health insurance, just as drivers are legally required to have car insurance, or pay a fine. The government will subsidize people with low incomes, covering their premiums through expanded Medicaid coverage or tax credits.
- Individuals may keep their existing insurance plans if they choose.

- Exchanges will be created on which small businesses and people who buy their own coverage directly from insurers could choose from an array of private plans that would compete for their business.
- A Medicare oversight board was created with authority over reimbursement rates.
- There is security for those who get laid off or change employers, or switch to employers that do not offer insurance—they are guaranteed coverage. Moreover, individuals cannot be denied coverage for a preexisting medical condition or because their medical bills are too expensive.
- Young adults will be covered by their parents' policy until age 26.
- Approximately 31 million previously uninsured will become insured.

- **What the Plan is Not.** Obamacare is not socialism. If it were, the government would provide the health insurance, own the hospitals, and hire health professionals as employees. The government will regulate and subsidize health insurance, but it is not a takeover of the American health care system. Although considered in the legislative process, a public option was not included in the final bill. This would have allowed the government to compete with private insurance, thus providing more competition, lower rates, and more government intrusion in the marketplace. In short, the plan keeps health care as a mostly private system.

  The plan does not hurt the commercial health insurers. Although constrained by no longer being able to turn away costly patients, health insurers benefit by an increased number of insured people because everyone is required to have insurance, and they do not have to compete with government insurance.

- **What the Plan Is.** Obamacare is not perfect. It infuriates liberals who feel that it does not go for enough to provide universal health care. It angers conservatives who agree with House Minority Leader John Boehner, who asked: Why change a system that is the greatest health care system in the world? And, it causes anxiety among the public, who are unsure of such a major change—an overhaul of one-sixth of the economy—and how the change will affect their lives.

  Imperfect as it is, it is a historic achievement. Obama and the Democrats have succeeded in a major reform of the health care system, where many previous attempts have failed during the past hundred years.

  Imperfect as it is, Obamacare will fix a health care system that has been "broken for far too many Americans" (*New York Times* 2010b: para 28). In particular, the plan will "make a huge difference to the less fortunate among us . . ." (Krugman 2010: para 13).

■ CHAPTER REVIEW

1. The U.S. health care system is the most expensive among advanced nations. The reasons: (a) profit drives the system; (b) inefficiency; (c) defensive medicine to ward off expensive lawsuits; (d) overuse of specialists; (e) the wide use of prescription drugs; and (e) investor-owned enterprises.
2. The high cost of health care does *not* translate into better health outcomes compared with other advanced nations.
3. The U.S. health care system has unique characteristics: (a) different plans for different categories of people; (b) private insurance; (c) for-profit hospitals; and (d) managed care networks.

4. Economic disadvantage is closely related to health disadvantages. The poor are much more likely than the affluent to die in infancy, to suffer from certain diseases, and as adults to die sooner. They are less likely to receive medical attention because of being uninsured (46 million) or underinsured (50 million), and when they do receive medical care, to receive inferior service.
5. The most commonly held explanation for the strong relationship between social class and health is that the poor are responsible for their disproportionate ill health because of ignorance or neglect. This approach blames the victim because it ignores the primary role that privilege plays in good health and the lack of privilege in poor health. The fundamental solution for reducing socioeconomic differences in health is to reduce the inequalities in society that perpetuate poor health among the disadvantaged.
6. Race is also related to health, with non-Whites disadvantaged by a combination of economic disadvantage and racial discrimination.
7. Health and ill health are also related to gender differences. Women have health advantages over men because of their physical differences and differing gender expectations. Women are placed at risk, however, by childbearing, the greater likelihood of unnecessary surgery such as hysterectomies, the relative lack of medical research using women as subjects, and the still-common sexist practices by physicians, who are predominantly male.
8. AIDS, once a death sentence, can now be controlled for the most part by combinations of very expensive drugs. Those with HIV (the precursor to AIDS) who are most likely to die from AIDS are the poor in the developing nations and the poor in the United States who live in states that do not subsidize the expensive treatments. Although the number of new cases of AIDS has dropped appreciably among Whites in the United States, it has remained high among young Black gay men, Black users of intravenous drugs, and Black heterosexual women.
9. There are three major systems of universal health care employed by other advanced societies: the Bismarck model, the Beveridge model, and the national health insurance model (single-payer plan). The United States does not have a universal health care plan.
10. During 2009 and 2010 Congress engaged in heated debate over health care reform. Efforts by opponents of reform included influencing the public through advertising, commentary by conservative media outlets and political leaders, influencing Congress through lobbying and funneling money to key legislators, and by block maneuvers in Congress, especially the Senate.
11. Included in the reform bill that passed were these provisions: (a) mandates for everyone to have medical insurance; (b) an oversight board; (c) guarantees that insurance companies cannot deny coverage; and (d) coverage of young adults through their parents' policy until age 26.
12. Obamacare is not socialism. It is not a government takeover of the health care system. The plan keeps health care in a mostly private system.

■ KEY TERMS

Defensive medicine. The practice of requiring extra diagnostic tests and medical procedures to protect the physician from liability.

Infant mortality rate. Number of deaths before age 1 per 1,000 live births.

Medicare. Government program that provides partial coverage of medical costs primarily for people age 65 and older.

Patient dumping. Practice by physicians and private hospitals of treating only patients who can afford their services.

Medlining. Practice of managed care organizations of limiting the number of patients with health problems while maximizing the number of healthy patients.

Medicaid. Government health program for the poor.

Single-payer plan. Tax-supported health program in which the government is the sole insurer.

■ SUCCEED WITH PEARSON mysoclab www.mysoclab.com

Experience, Discover, Observe, Evaluate

MySocLab is designed just for you. Each chapter features a pre-test and post-test to help you learn and review key concepts and terms.

Experience sociology in action with dynamic visual activities, videos, and readings to enhance your learning experience. Complete the following activities at www.mysoclab.com.

Social Explorer is an interactive application that allows you to explore Census data through interactive maps.

- Explore the Social Explorer Map: *Lifespan Differences Between Men and Women*

The Core Concepts in Sociology video clips offer a real-world perspective on sociological concepts.

- Watch *PBS FRONTLINE: Sick Around America*

MySocLibrary includes primary source readings from classic and contemporary sociologists.

- Read Daniels, *Men at War: Vietnam and Agent Orange;* DeLorey, *Health Care Reform—A Woman's Issue;* Silverstein, *Millions for Viagra, Pennies for Diseases of the Poor*

CHAPTER 18 National Security in the Twenty-First Century

By inspiring legions of anti-American terrorists where there were few, by straining the U.S. military to its breaking point, by alienating traditional and potential allies abroad, by frightening other states into acquiring new weapons and by provoking popular revulsion around the world, the [Iraq] war has undermined our real national security. . . .

—Stephen F. Cohen

The mission of the Department of Defense is to protect the American people and advance the nation's interests (U.S. Department of Defense 2010). Every four years the Pentagon reviews the mission of the military in the light of changes in international and domestic environments. The *2010 Quadrennial Review* provides the current state of U.S. national security: "The United States faces a complex and uncertain security landscape in which the pace of change continues to accelerate" (p. iii). Among the challenges for defending the nation's interests are (U.S. Department of Defense 2010:iii–iv):

- The rise of China and India will continue to shape an international system that is no longer easily defined.

- Globalization has transformed the process of technological innovation while lowering the entry barriers for a wider range of actors to acquire advanced technologies.
- Nonstate actors (i.e., terrorist groups) will continue to gain influence.
- The proliferation of weapons of mass destruction (WMDs) continues to undermine global security. The instability or collapse of a WMD-armed state is among the most troubling concerns.
- Several powerful trends such as demographic pressures, the increasingly limited resources (e.g., arable land, water, oil), the effects of climate change, the emergence of new strains of disease, and rapid urbanization may exacerbate future conflicts.

Reflecting the new realities, the Defense Department states,

> *The U.S. military must prepare for a combination of humanitarian missions, untraditional threats such as cyberattacks, environmental disasters, terrorist groups seeking weapons of mass destruction and as many as two major conflicts.* (The Quadrennial Defense Review, *reported in Youssef 2010:1A)*

These sections of this chapter describe (1) the magnitude of the military establishment, (2) the threat of nuclear weapons, (3) the threat of domestic terrorism, and (4) the threat of international terrorism.

THE U.S. MILITARY ESTABLISHMENT

Nation-states organize to defend their **national security** by protecting borders, guarding their national interests, and shielding their citizens and businesses abroad with armies, military bases, intelligence networks, embassies, and consulates. National security in the United States is a responsibility of the president and the cabinet members who run the departments of State, Justice, Defense, and Homeland Security.

The Size of the U.S. Military

The size of the U.S. military establishment is enormous. Here are the facts:

- In 2009 there were 1,454,515 active military personnel. This is an all-volunteer military (see the "Speaking to Students" panel). Conscription can be enacted by request of the president and approval of Congress.
- In 2009 there were 848,000 members of the guard and reserve. These are people who can be "called up" by the Defense Department to carry out a number of activities ranging from patrol of our airports to support missions, like guarding prison detainees, and who back up the troops in combat areas such as Afghanistan and Iraq.
- There were 678,025 civilians on the military payroll in 2009. Most of them do clerical work, report writing, and technical jobs.
- The military operates 865 military bases and other facilities in 135 nations located on every continent. About 451,000 of the Defense Department's personnel are overseas or afloat. The United States spends approximately

Speaking to Students

Recruiting an All-Volunteer Military

The Pentagon in 2009 had a $5 billion recruiting budget. In that year the U.S. military met its annual recruiting goals for the first time in thirty-five years. This shift occurred because of three factors. The first was unplanned. That is, the economic downturn (the Great Recession) and rising joblessness led more youths to enlist (Tyson 2009). Pentagon research shows that a 10 percent increase in the national unemployment rate generally translates into a 4 to 6 percent improvement in recruiting (reported in the *Progressive* 2009).

A second reason for the rise in volunteer recruits in 2009 was that recruits were enticed by an average signing bonus of $14,000 compared to $12,000 in 2008.

Third, military recruiters were armed with information on each potential recruit, giving them an edge in gaining rapport and softening them up to the decision to join up.

> In the past few years, the military has mounted a virtual invasion into the lives of young Americans. Using data mining, stealth websites, career tests, and sophisticated marketing software, the Pentagon is harvesting and analyzing information on everything from high school students' GPAs and SAT scores to which video games they play. *Before an Army recruiter even picks up the phone to call a prospect, the soldier may know more about the kid's habits than do his own parents* (emphasis added). . . .
>
> To put all of its data to use, the military has enlisted the help of Nielsen Claritas, a research and marketing firm whose clients include BMW, AOL, and Starbucks. Last year, it rolled out a "custom segmentation" program that allows a recruiter armed with address, age, race, and gender of a potential "lead" to call up a wealth of information about young people in the immediate area, including recreation and consumption patterns. The program even suggests pitches that might work while cold-calling teenagers. "It's just a foot in the door for a recruiter to start a relevant conversation with a young person," says Donna Dorminey of the U.S. Army Center for Accessions Research. (Goodman 2009:21–22)

$250 billion annually to maintain troops, equipment, fleets, and bases overseas (Danes 2009).

- The headquarters of the Department of Defense is the Pentagon in Washington, D.C. It is one of the world's largest office buildings, with 17.5 miles of corridors.
- The military has a worldwide satellite network providing constant intelligence, surveillance, and communication.
- The United States has the world's largest navy and air force and the most sophisticated weapons.
- The carbon footprint of the military is huge (e.g., the U.S. armed forces consume about 14 million gallons of oil per day; Johansen 2009).
- The government outsources some military operations to private firms. There are more of these nonmilitary personnel (53 percent) in Iraq and Afghanistan than military personnel. For example, there were more than 218,000 private U.S. contractors in Iraq and Afghanistan in 2009 (Schwartz 2009). The largest of these security companies is Blackwater, which provides security, conducts clandestine raids against suspected insurgents, and transports detainees. These contractors deploy "private forces in a war zone

free of public scrutiny, with the deaths, injuries and crimes of those forces shrouded in secrecy. [They] are shielded from accountability, oversight and legal constraints" (Scahill 2007:13; see also, Scahill 2009).

- In 2008 there were 23.2 million military veterans. Of these veterans, 2.9 million received compensation for service-connected disabilities for a total compensation of $36.2 billion.

The Cost of Maintaining U.S. Military Superiority

Military might has been the typical security strategy of nations. Since World War II, the United States, for example, has spent more than $20 trillion (adjusted for inflation) on military defense. The **defense budget**, which represents the government's spending plan for the military for fiscal 2011 (which begins on October 1, 2010) was $741 billion. The military budget includes an operating budget of $549 billion, plus funding for the Iraq and Afghanistan wars at $192 billion, including an extra $33 billion for expanding the war in Afghanistan (*Sojourners* 2010). Significantly, for the first time the cost of the war in Afghanistan will exceed the cost in Iraq. Not included in the military budget are the indirect costs of war: veterans benefits, including health care and disability costs, federal debt payments due to military expenditures, covert intelligence operations, federal research on military and space programs, and at least half the budget for the Energy Department (Parenti 2008:78). Taken together, actual military spending for fiscal 2011 will exceed $1 trillion.

The United States with a formal military budget of $741 billion ($2.2 billion a day) outspends all other nations on national security. In fact, the United States spends more than 40 percent of the combined total of worldwide military expenditures. The "military outlay by the U.S. plus its NATO allies accounts for about 70 percent of world military spending. Add in America's other allies and friends, such as South Korea, and the total share of global military outlay hits 80 percent" (Bandow 2010: para 12). Not counting the costs of the Iraq and Afghanistan wars, the U.S. outspends China by five times and ten times that of Russia, and twenty-nine times the combined spending of the six "rogue" states (Cuba, Iran, Libya, North Korea, Sudan, and Syria; Greenwald 2010a).

There are at least four reasons why U.S. defense spending is so high and continues to grow. First, there is the ongoing fear of nuclear weapons. Russia has a huge nuclear arsenal. Russia and other nations of the former Soviet Union, although much less a threat than before 1990, remain a potential threat to U.S. security. Rogue states such as North Korea and Iran pose a significant threat as they join the nuclear club.

Second, the world, even without the Soviet threat, is an unsafe place, where terrorism and aggression occur and must be confronted and contained. Several nations, including regimes with expansionist agendas and hated enemies, have nuclear weapons or soon will have them. They also have chemical and biological weapons. Several nations are suspected of supporting terror and working to develop **weapons of mass destruction** (nuclear, biological, or chemical weapons capable of large-scale deaths and destruction). Iran, in particular, is a special worry in the tense Middle East, especially for Israel.

Third, defense expenditures bring profits to corporations, create jobs, and generate growth in the economy. For example, many corporations benefited from the wars in Afghanistan and Iraq as Defense Department contracts more than doubled from 2000 to 2005. The five largest contractors in 2009 were Lockheed

Martin ($14.9 billion), Boeing ($10.8 billion), Northrup Grumman ($9.9 billion), General Dynamics ($6.1 billion), and Ratheon ($5.9 billion; *Washington Technology* 2010). (See the Closer Look panel on Lockheed Martin.) With huge contracts available, these corporations spend millions on lobbying. For example, the ten largest defense contractors spent more than $27 million lobbying the federal government in the *last quarter* of 2009, an increase of $7.2 million from the last quarter of 2008 (Hattern 2010). Corporate military contractors are eager for more contracts, for the following reasons (Parenti 2008:80):

- There are few risks. Unlike manufacturers who must worry about selling the goods they produce, defense corporations have a guaranteed contract.
- Almost all contracts are awarded without competitive bidding and at whatever price the corporation sets. If the cost exceeds the bid (cost overruns) then the government picks up the tab.
- The Pentagon directly subsidizes defense contractors with free research and development, public lands, buildings, and renovations.
- Defense spending does not compete with the consumer market. Moreover, the market is virtually limitless, as there are always more advanced weapons systems to develop and obsolete weaponry to replace.

Members of Congress are eager to support an expansive military machine for two reasons. First, no politician would campaign to reduce the military for fear of being labelled unpatriotic and thereby risk defeat in the next election. Second, politicians gain support from their constituents if they bring military money to their corporations, communities, and state. Lawmakers even team up with defense contractors to fight for certain targeted programs even when the Pentagon says that it does not need the weaponry in question.

> *The C-17 Globemaster offers one illustration of successful opposition to the Obama-Gates [Secretary of Defense] push for control of weapons spending. C-17s are large cargo planes produced by Boeing that cost $250 million apiece. They have been used heavily since 1993 to transport troops, tanks, and supplies. Every year since 2006, the Pentagon has said that it has enough C-17s. And every year, Congress overrules the military and authorizes funds for additional planes. In October the Senate approved $2.5 billion in the 2010 budget for 10 more C-17s, which would bring the fleet to 215. (Elgin and Epstein 2009:47)*

The 2011 Obama budget proposal excluded funds for additional C-17s.

In 2009, California led the way with defense contract expenditures in that state totaling $27.9 billion, followed by Virginia ($23.4 billion) and Texas ($21.1 billion; *StateMaster* n.d.). As an example, consider the consequences for military spending in Massachusetts, which received $8.3 billion in 2006, almost $1,300 for every person living in that state. The money was spread among twenty-seven communities and was the fifth-largest source of jobs in the state (Belkin 2006). Even a small state such as Kansas has three major bases, has 40,000 members in the military, and receives a military boost to the economy of $7.7 billion (Milburn 2009). In sum, business, labor, the states, Congress, and academia combine to present a unified voice supporting massive and increasing military expenditures. Opposing this behemoth are only faint voices from individuals and groups seeking to reduce the huge costs of the military-industrial complex.

Finally, the disproportionate amount that the United States appropriates for war is based on the assumption that by having the world's costliest military force and being so far ahead of other nations in military strength and technology,

A CLOSER LOOK

LOCKHEED MARTIN

- Government contracts 2009: $14,983,515,367 (*Washington Technology* 2010)
- Total lobbying expenditures in 2009: $13,533.782 (Schouten 2010)
- Campaign contributions to federal candidates through PACs in 2008: $1,623,944 (*SourceWatch* 2009)

Lockheed Martin was formed in 1995 with the merger of two of the world's premier technology companies—Lockheed Corporation and Martin Marietta Corporation. The company employs about 140,000 people worldwide.

It has 1,000 facilities in 500 cities, 46 states, and in 75 nations and territories. Lockheed Martin is the world's number one military contractor, as well as the world's largest arms exporter. It dominates the fighter aircraft sector and is heavily involved in transport aircraft, missiles, and space systems.

In addition to lobbying and campaign contributions, Lockheed Martin has links with the government and the Pentagon that make it easier to obtain government contracts. For example, its board of directors includes a number of former high-ranking government officials: the former head of the U.S. Strategic Command, former vice president of the Joint Chiefs of Staff, former deputy Secretary of Homeland Security, former Secretary of Commerce, and a former Secretary of Defense (Derysh 2009). One of the above, former Secretary of Defense Pete Aldridge, in the month before he left the Pentagon to join Lockheed's board, approved a $3 billion contract to build 20 Lockheed planes. Furthermore, while on Lockheed's Board of Directors, Aldridge was appointed by President George W. Bush, to chair the president's commission on space exploration—a possible conflict of interest (*SourceWatch* 2008).

Lockheed has also been able to exercise its influence in a larger way—in support of the invasion of Iraq. The company's former vice president, Bruce Jackson, chaired the Coalition for the Liberation of Iraq, a bipartisan group formed to promote Bush's plan for war in Iraq. Jackson was also involved in corralling the support for the war from Eastern European countries, going so far as helping to write their letter of endorsement for military intervention. Not surprisingly, Lockheed also has business relations with these countries.

In the last few years, the SEC has investigated Lockheed for insider trading and falsifying its accounts. Lockheed Martin leads all defense contractors with 50 instances of misconduct from 1995 to 2008 (American Project on Government Oversight [POGO] 2009). These instances include age, race, and sex discrimination, contract fraud, unfair business practices, contractor kickbacks, federal election law violation, environmental violations, improper charges, nuclear safety violations, pricing irregularities, and overcharges. In 2010, the Secretary of Defense, Robert Gates, fined the military officer overseeing the Pentagon's new F-35 stealth-fighter-jet program for cost overruns and technical failures and punished Lockheed Martin by withholding $615 million in fees. Despite the ongoing cases of misconduct (a serious example of corporate recidivism), Lockheed Martin continues to be the number one supplier of military goods to the government.

no one would dare challenge us militarily. Although other nations may have more people (China and India), they do not have the United States' sophisticated weaponry, weapons delivery systems, and nuclear stockpile. The United States chooses to retain this superiority because its leaders believe there is "peace through strength."

This strategy succeeded for the most part during the Cold War years, as the United States and the Soviet Union engaged in an expensive arms race to strike first if necessary and to scare the other side into not attacking first. The attacks on the World Trade Center and the Pentagon showed that this rationale does not hold for the terrorism that we confront in the twenty-first century.

"Oh, that's good, sir, that's very good—'What if they gave a war and nobody profited.'"

> *It [the U.S. military machine] is probably the most effective conventional-war fighting force in history. But the basic assumptions, the culture, of the military-intelligence complex seem suddenly anachronistic. The nexus of national defense and intelligence agencies may be as unsuited for a long-term offensive anti-terrorist campaign as they were to defend New York and Washington against the aerial attacks of September 11th. (Klein 2001:44)*

THE THREAT OF NUCLEAR WEAPONS

Nuclear weapons involve the most destructive technology on Earth. During the **Cold War** (the intense tension and arms race between the United States and the Soviet Union that lasted from the end of World War II until 1990), the two superpowers had most of the nuclear weapons. The United States and Russia in 2009 possessed 96 percent of the world's nuclear warheads. Other nuclear power holders were France, Britain, China, Israel, Pakistan, India, and North Korea (*Guardian* 2009). The year 1998 was a turning point, as the world entered a new nuclear era when India tested five bombs, followed two weeks later by its rival neighbor, Pakistan.

> *The second nuclear era, unlike the dawn of the first nuclear age in 1945, is characterized by a world of porous national borders, rapid communications that facilitate the spread of technical knowledge, and expanded commerce in potentially dangerous dual-use technologies and materials. (*Bulletin of the Atomic Scientists *2007:67)*

Thus, in this globalized world, we face a threatening situation in which as many as forty countries have the capacity to develop nuclear weapons in a very short time span. Two nations, designated by President George W. Bush as part of the "axis of evil," are in this group: North Korea tested a bomb in 2006, and Iran is believed to be close to developing nuclear weapons.

What we have now is not a tight club of nuclear powers with interlocking interests and an appreciation for the brutal doctrine of "mutually assured destruction" but an unpredictable host of potential Bomb throwers: a Stalinist Bomb out of unstable North Korea; a Shiite Bomb out of Iran; a Sunni Bomb out of Pakistan; and, down the road, possibly out of Egypt and Saudi Arabia as well; and, of course, an al-Qaeda Bomb out of nowhere. (Powell 2006:32)

The newcomers to the nuclear club, unlike the charter members, are not governed by elaborate rules and sophisticated technology designed to prevent accidents and firing in haste. Instead, they are dealing with the savagery of ethnic strife, intense religious differences, and insecure nations. Moreover, there is the danger of nuclear weapons or weapons-grade materials falling into the hands of terrorists—"the one enemy we know would probably not hesitate to use them" (Keller 2003:51).

Nuclear technology is expected to accelerate as nations turn to atomic power for their domestic energy requirements. This technology gives them the ability to make reactor fuel, or with the same equipment and a little more effort, bomb fuel (Broad and Sanger 2006). Thus, the tension and the threat will continue to accelerate.

THE TERRORIST THREAT

Terrorism is a major national security threat, as the United States experienced with the ramming of hijacked planes into the World Trade Center and the Pentagon on September 11, 2001. **Terrorism** is any act intended to cause death or serious injury to civilians or noncombatants to intimidate a population and weaken their will or draw attention to the perpetrator's cause. Thus, terrorist acts are political acts. In the case of the September 11 terrorist attack, al-Qaeda, Osama bin Laden's organization, sought to show the vulnerability of the United States and to rally other extremist Islamists in a war against—in their words—"the Great Satan." So, too, was the bombing of the federal building in Oklahoma City by ex-soldier Timothy McVeigh, who had grievances with the U.S. government. Also, when Joseph Stack flew an airplane into a building housing Internal Revenue Service offices in Austin, Texas, to advance his political grievances, it was an act of terrorism (Greenwald 2010b). Similarly, the killing of abortion doctors and the bombing of abortion clinics are terrorist acts, making a political statement.

Terrorism is "not an enemy; it is a methodology of using violence to gain political objectives" (Greider 2004:11). It is a tactic used historically by groups against governments and organizations viewed as unjust and oppressive. Terrorists believe that they are legitimate combatants, fighting for a just cause, by whatever means possible. The warfare is asymmetric—that is, terrorism is the method of less well-armed and less powerful opponents. Because, typically, they do not have sophisticated weapons, terrorists use what is cheap and available. Instead of guided missiles, they use suicide bombers—"the poor man's air force" (Davis 2006). Because they do not have weapons of mass destruction, they use "weapons of mass disruption" such as arson, infecting computers with viruses (cyberterrorism), and disrupting mass transit. They instill fear through kidnapping, raping, and torturing victims and even showing the beheading of these victims on television. Note that terrorism as a method of asymmetric warfare is not exclusively a Muslim or al-Qaeda method but also a method used, for example, by the American revolutionaries, the Irish Republican Army, the Viet Cong, and antidictatorial forces in Latin America.

Terrorism is a social construction (Turk 2004). That is, what is defined as terrorism and who is labeled a terrorist are matters of interpretation of events and their presumed causes. Consider the different meanings for these words: terrorist/freedom fighter or suicide bomber/martyr.

> *The powerful conflict parties, especially governments, generally succeed in labeling their more threatening (i.e., violent) opponents as terrorists, whereas attempts by opponents to label officially sanctioned violence as "state terrorism" have little chance of success unless supported by powerful third parties (e.g., the United Nations). (Turk 2004:272)*

Most of the remainder of this chapter is devoted to international terrorism, but let us begin with a brief account of the internal terrorist threat: attacks by Americans on Americans.

DOMESTIC TERRORISM

Typically, we typically think of terrorism as deadly acts committed by foreigners, usually Islamic fundamentalists from the Middle East. Thus, when a bomb destroyed the federal building in Oklahoma City in 1995, killing 168, the immediate suspects were Muslim extremists. But Timothy McVeigh and Terry Nichols, two American ex-military men, were convicted of that crime. (McVeigh received the death penalty for detonating the bomb and was executed in 2001; Nichols was sentenced to life imprisonment for his involvement in planning the attack.) As extreme as the Oklahoma City bombing was, the act of an American detonating a bomb to harm other Americans is not unusual because there are about 2,000 illegal bombings annually within the United States (National Academies 1998).

Foreigners acting alone or as agents of their organization or government killing Americans is relatively easy to understand, but Americans killing Americans is more difficult to comprehend. The history of the United States, however, is full of examples of various dissident groups that have used violence against their neighbors to achieve their aims (Hewitt 2003). Colonists, farmers, settlers, Native Americans, immigrants, slaves, slaveholders, laborers, strike breakers, anarchists, vigilantes, the Ku Klux Klan and other White supremacist organizations, antiwar protesters, radical environmentalists, and prolife extremists have acted outside the law to accomplish their ends.* Just in recent years antiabortion terrorists have bombed abortion clinics and murdered abortion doctors. One of those doctors, George Tiller, was wounded in 1993, his clinic was bombed and vandalized, and then in 2009 he was killed by an antiabortion zealot. Also, various extremists have bombed African American churches,

*It is important to note that the law can be a friend or an enemy. The agents of government (e.g., police, FBI, military, national guard, and the courts) defend the law even with force but what if a group considers the law immoral, as do prolife supporters or Martin Luther King, Jr., who led protests against the Jim Crow laws in the South? Is it appropriate for them to use unlawful acts to overturn what they consider a bad law?

By Mike Smith. *Las Vegas Sun*. United Features Syndicate.

Jewish synagogues, and Islamic mosques throughout the United States, U.S. Bureau of Land Management and Forest Service offices, and the 1996 Olympic games in Atlanta. In addition to bombings, there have been acts of arson, beatings, killings, and letters/packages with bombs or anthrax addressed to political targets.

Extreme actions by the government have persuaded some individuals to become part of extremist groups. The government's actions in conducting the Vietnam War and its reactions to protesters (e.g., the killing of Kent State students by the National Guard) led some groups such as the "Weathermen" to use violence to further their cause. Two events in the 1990s energized the Patriot movement. In 1992 the Bureau of Alcohol, Tobacco, and Firearms (ATF) attacked Randy Weaver, a White supremacist in Idaho, for gun violations. In the process Weaver's wife and son were killed by ATF snipers. The second event was the 1993 assault by ATF on David Koresh and the Branch Davidians near Waco, Texas. This siege, again over guns violations, ended with the deaths of 86 men, women, and children. Those in the Patriot movement interpreted these acts as government run amok, using its power to take away the liberties that individuals are granted by the Constitution. Thus, the membership in this movement, "far from thinking itself outside the law, believes it is the critical force making for a restoration of the Constitution" (Wills 1995:52). See the "Voices" panel for a letter from Timothy McVeigh, airing his grievances with the U.S. government.

The Patriot movement faded somewhat in the late 1990s, although pockets remained. But ten years later the momentum was revived. In 2009 the number of hate groups rose to 932, up 54 percent since 2000. In 2009 another 50 new right-wing militia groups emerged (Southern Poverty Law Center, reported in D'Oro 2009). The U.S. Department of Homeland Security issued a report warning that current political and economic conditions resembled those of the early 1990s, when there was an upsurge in right-wing extremism that culminated in the Oklahoma City bombing (Blow 2009; Krugman 2009a).

VOICES

A LETTER FROM TIMOTHY McVEIGH

Three years before he ignited a bomb that destroyed the federal building in Oklahoma City, killing 168 people, Timothy McVeigh wrote a letter to his hometown newspaper, the Lockport (N.Y.) *Union-Sun & Journal,* listing his concerns about the government.

> Crime is out of control. Criminals have no fear of punishment. Prisons are overcrowded so they know they will not be imprisoned long. . . .
>
> Taxes are a joke. Regardless of what a political candidate "promises," they will increase taxes. More taxes are always the answer to government mismanagement. . . .
>
> The "American Dream" of the middle class has all but disappeared, substituted with people struggling just to buy next week's groceries. Heaven forbid the car breaks down! . . .
>
> Politicians are out of control. Their yearly salaries are more than an average person will see in a lifetime. They have been entrusted with the power to regulate their own salaries, and have grossly violated that trust to live in their own luxury. . . .
>
> Who is to blame for the mess? At a point when the world has seen communism falter as an imperfect system to manage people, democracy seems to be headed down the same road. No one is seeing the "big" picture. . . .
>
> What is it going to take to open up the eyes of our elected officials? AMERICA IS IN SERIOUS DECLINE.
>
> We have no proverbial tea to dump; should we instead sink a ship full of Japanese imports? Is a Civil War imminent? Do we have to shed blood to reform the current system? I hope it doesn't come to that. But it might.

There was a resurgence of populist anger, coinciding with the Great Recession, that emerged in 2009. Leading the charge was the Tea Party movement (there is some dispute over the name's origin: was it taken from the 1773 tax revolt, or is it an acronym for "taxed enough already"?). This movement is a platform for conservative populist discontent. It embodies a brand of politics historically associated with libertarians, populists, and those on the fringe: militia groups, hate groups, and anti-immigration advocates. Tea Party activists, although divided on a number of issues, agree that "government is too big. Spending is out of control. Individual freedom is at risk. And President Barack Obama's policies are making it all worse" (Associated Press 2010: para 1). The catalyst was the election of Barack Hussein Obama, the first African American president. This raised two fears for some in the movement: that he was African American and that he was a Muslim. There is more than a hint of racism here. "For some white Americans of a certain age and background, the sight of a black man in the Oval Office, even one who went to Harvard Law School and conducts himself in the manner of an aloof WASP aristocrat, is an affront" (Cassidy 2010: para 2). Also, there is an anti-Islam strain among some in the movement. Fanning these flames, the *Washington Times* ran an article declaring that President Obama "not only identifies with Muslims, but actually may be one himself" (quoted in Krugman 2009a: para 8). One segment of the movement—the Birthers—questioned the legitimacy of Obama to be president because, they argued, his birth certificate was bogus and his father was an African. These fears were fomented by conservative talk show hosts on radio and cable television, who "have gone out of their way to provide a platform for conspiracy theories and apocalyptic rhetoric" (Krugman 2009a: para 5). Most significant, under Obama and the Democrats, broad federal programs were initiated, such as attempted national health care; bailouts of Wall Street banks (actually begun

The Tea Party Movement is a platform for conservative populist discontent. They are enraged by an expanding federal government and liberal government programs and policies.

by President Bush), General Motors, and Chrysler; the $787 billion stimulus (TARP); and an immense and rapidly growing national debt. These were interpreted as moving the nation toward a totalitarian socialist state, with subsequent loss of freedoms, again fueled by talk show rhetoric. Fox News's Glenn Beck, for example, warned viewers that the Federal Emergency Management Agency (FEMA) "might be building concentration camps as part of the Obama administration's 'totalitarian' agenda" (Krugman 2009a: para 7). Obama, by the way, receives on average of 30 death threats a day (a 400 percent increase from the number received by President George W. Bush; Harnden 2009).

Obama's government programs were not only perceived as centralizing authority (an orchestrated "power grab") but also that they benefit the wealthy and educated elites but not average people (see the Closer Look panel airing the grievances of the Texas Suicide Flyer). And many of these average people were suffering in the bad economy. They were worried about their jobs, their retirement incomes, and their mortgages and paying for their children's education. Some were concerned that Whites were losing their numerical majority to non-Whites. For them, immigration, especially illegal immigration, has to be stopped. As Bill O'Reilly of Fox News complained to Senator John McCain about the number of undocumented Latino immigrants:

> *"Do you understand what the* New York Times *wants, and the far-left want? They want to break down the white, Christian, male power structure, of which you're a part and so am I. They hate America, and they hate it because it's run primarily by white, Christian men. They want to bring in millions of foreign nationals to basically break down the structure that we have." (quoted in Benjamin 2009: para 5)*

The Tea Party movement is difficult to define because there is no single Tea Party. "This is an amorphous, factionalized uprising with no clear leadership and no central structure" (Barstow 2010: para 15). Comprised within the movement are a number of local groups, often focusing on different issues. Some followers are gun rights activists, some rally against taxes, some want state sovereignty, some are White Supremacists, whereas others are concerned about

A CLOSER LOOK

THE TEXAS SUICIDE FLYER'S SUICIDE MANIFESTO

Reminiscent of the 9/11 attack, on February 18, 2010, Joseph Stack flew his single-engine plane into an Austin, Texas, office building that housed the Internal Revenue Service, killing two and injuring thirteen. He left behind a manifesto listing his grievances against Big Government and Big Business. Specifically, he railed against (Benjamin 2010):

- A crippled economy dominated by political and corporate potentates
- A campaign and election system rotted by special interests and money
- Government bailouts of corporate and banking interests, paid for with taxes from the "little guy"
- Excessively complicated tax laws that baffle small business owners and individuals

Stack's manifesto calls for a citizen's movement to change this foul system, and to change it through violence:

> I know I'm hardly the first one to decide I have had all I can stand. It has always been a myth that people have stopped dying for their freedom in this country, and it isn't limited to the blacks, and poor immigrants. I know there have been countless before me and there are sure to be as many after. But I also know that by not adding my body to the count, I insure nothing will change. I choose to not keep looking over my shoulder at "big brother" while he strips my carcass. I choose not to ignore what is going on all round me. I choose not to pretend that business as usual won't continue. I have just had enough.
>
> I can only hope that the numbers quickly get too big to be whitewashed and ignored that the American zombies wake up and revolt; it will take nothing less. I would only hope that by striking a nerve that stimulates the inevitable double standard, knee-jerk government reaction that results in more stupid draconian restrictions people wake up and begin to see the pompous political thugs and their mindless minions for what they are. Sadly, though I spent my entire life trying to believe it wasn't so, *but violence not only is the answer, it is the only answer.* (emphasis added; Stack 2010: para. 32–33)

Rich Benjamin argues that Stach's complaints echo the issues raised by the Tea Party movement and should be taken seriously because they resonate with the protestations of so many.

> Deplorable though he might be. Stack is not quite a "random bad apple." His act might be uncommon, but his jumbled populism is not. His crime is in no way excusable, but it spotlights a larger problem that both political and corporate elites like to caricature or dismiss: visceral populist anger. Stack may have suffered from mental illness, but he is also an acute symptom of this nation's neglected wounds. (Benjamin 2010: para. 16)

the federal government's interference in their freedoms. Connecting the disparate issues that preoccupy many Tea Party supporters is the strong feeling of impending governmental tyranny. This theme permeates the far right's commentary, the Tea Party websites, Facebook pages, Twitter feeds, and YouTube videos (Barstow 2010). Although many of these are relatively benign, some are not. In fact, the Simon Wiesenthal Center (Jewish human rights organization) noted that there was a 25 percent rise from 2008 to 2009 in the number of "problematic" social networking groups on the Internet. The report found that there are over 10,000 networking groups, portals, blogs, chat rooms, and videos on the Internet that promote racial violence, anti-Semitism, homophobia, hate music, and terrorism (cited in Parsons 2009).

This movement represents a passionate rebellion that has the potential to change the political landscape. It is important to note, that although most Tea

Partiers are nonviolent, there is a violent edge to the movement, fueled by frustration, anxiety, fear, and anger. Research shows that in difficult economic times, extremist groups emerge and flourish—groups such as Skinheads, neo-Nazis, militias, White Supremacists, and "Sovereign citizens," who believe that they do not have to pay taxes or obey most other laws, such as having a driver's license. (When Scott Roeder, the convicted killer of abortionist Dr. George Tiller, was arrested, sheriff deputies stopped his car because it had no license plate. Instead there was a tag declaring him a "sovereign" and immune from state law.) During hard times membership in these extremist groups increases, and the number of hate crimes (against gays, Muslims, recent immigrants, and people of color) rises dramatically.

At Tea Party rallies there are occasional placards that incite violence. There are pictures of Obama, redrawn as Hitler, the use of Nazi symbols such as swastikas, and signs reading "Death to Obama" and "Death to Michelle and her two stupid kids."

To reiterate: not all Tea Partiers are violent. They are angry and upset; they feel threatened. The movement represents a genuine backlash against current trends (Berlet 2010). And for some this backlash includes the seeds for violence by some individuals and groups.

INTERNATIONAL TERRORISM

The context for terrorist activity in today's world varies. The terrorists may be seeking separation from the dominant group by establishing an independent state, which is the goal of the Basques in Spain, the Chechnyans in Russia, and Northern Ireland, which seeks independence from Great Britain. They may be rival religious groups such as the Protestants and Catholics in Northern Ireland or Sunnis and Shiites, warring Muslim sects in the Middle East. Ethnic/religious groups in the former Yugoslavia—Serbs (Eastern Orthodox), Croatians (Catholics), and Bosnians (Muslims)—have fought each other with brutal tactics for centuries. Palestinian terrorists attack the Israeli government that keeps them in secondary status. Israeli extremists attack the Israeli government (e.g., the assassination of a moderate leader) when they believe that it will compromise with the Palestinians, as do Palestinian extremists who fear their leaders are not being militant enough with Israel. Various African countries have warring tribes seeking control through ethnic cleansing, and governments such as in Sudan use ethnic militias to terrorize through killings, rapes, and destruction of villages and farms to quell rebellious groups.

Globalization has quickened the pace, scale, and fear of terrorism. As nations become all the more connected, they are increasingly vulnerable to terrorist attacks. The United States, in particular, is relatively unprotected from terrorist attacks because it is a mobile, open society with porous borders that are difficult to police. Every day, over a million people enter the country legally (and many others illegally), as do almost 3,000 aircraft and over 16,000 containers on 600 ships. Satellite communications give the world an instant look at the consequences of terrorist acts. This capability heightens the motivation of terrorists, who seek to dramatize their grievances to a wide audience. Modern societies provide a huge array of possible targets for terrorists. The United States, for example, has 60,000 chemical plants and 103 nuclear plants that could be sabotaged. So, too, could hydroelectric dams, power grids, oil refineries, oil and natural gas pipelines, water treatment plants, and factories. Transportation systems (planes, trains, cargo ships) can be easily disrupted with explosions or computer glitches.

Clearly, humankind lives in an increasingly dangerous world—the context in which nations must seek national security. This section broadly outlines the challenges to the United States by the new terrorism; the U.S. response to terrorism, using the wars in Afghanistan and Iraq as the case study; and the consequences of this response for these nations, the United States, and the world.

U.S. NATIONAL SECURITY AND THE WAR ON TERROR

The U.S. attacks on Afghanistan and Iraq were the result of a number of historical events that converged to bring about the response of war.

Precursors to the 9/11 Attacks

Horrible and incomprehensible as the 9/11 attacks were, terrorism by Islamic radicals against the United States and its citizens was not born on that day. A chronology of terrorist acts directed at the United States by Islamic groups before 9/11 includes the following:

- In 1983, Shiite Muslim suicide bombers destroyed U.S. Marine and French paratrooper barracks in Lebanon, killing 299, including 241 Americans.
- In 1988, terrorists linked to Libya bombed a Pan Am 747 headed for the United States over Lockerbie, Scotland, killing 270 passengers and residents of the town.
- In 1993, a truck bomb was detonated in the garage of the World Trade Center, killing 6 and injuring more than 1,000.
- In 1995, the Army training headquarters in Riyadh, Saudi Arabia, was bombed, killing 5 Americans and wounding 31.
- In 1996, 19 U.S. soldiers were killed and 372 Americans injured by an attack on military housing in Dhahran, Saudi Arabia.
- In 1998, car bombs, organized by al-Qaeda, exploded outside U.S. embassies in Tanzania and Kenya, killing 224 people, including 12 Americans.
- In 2000, the USS *Cole* was attacked in a Yemen harbor by al-Qaeda suicide bombers in a small boat, killing 17 sailors and injuring 39.
- On September 10, 2001, the National Security Agency intercepted messages that said, "The match is about to begin" and "Tomorrow is zero hour." These messages were not translated until September 12 (Dickinson and Stein 2006).

The history of U.S. involvement in the Middle East, Afghanistan, and Iraq in the twentieth century helps to explain why the United States initiated wars after 9/11 and why it is having difficulty winning those wars.

• **A Brief History of U.S. Involvement in the Middle East.** Before World War II, the United States had only a very limited role in the Middle East. Following that war, three factors prompted U.S. involvement there—the great reserves of oil in the Middle East, the Cold War, and Israel. Because of the need for Middle East oil, the United States sought relationships with the leadership, especially in Saudi Arabia, Kuwait, and Iran, which often has meant siding with antidemocratic despots. In the case of Iran, the CIA backed the coup that overthrew Mossadegh in 1953 and installed the Shah of Iran. Under the Shah's despotic rule, the United States was actively involved in Iran. However, the Shah was forced to flee his nation in 1979 and was replaced by Ayatollah Ruhollah Khomeini, a very anti-American and highly revered spiritual leader. Also in that year, Islamic militants seized the U.S. embassy in Tehran and took sixty-six diplomats hostage.

This region was deemed strategic in the Cold War, as evidenced by the Eisenhower Doctrine, which declared that the United States would use economic and military aid and armed forces to stop the spread of communism in the Middle East. Under President Nixon, this doctrine was reinforced when the United States saw Israel as an anti-Soviet asset, made a military alliance with it, and supported it with massive military aid. Previously, in 1967, the United States backed Israel in its defeat of Egypt and Syria in the Six Day War, and Israel gained control of the West Bank, Gaza, and East Jerusalem. Since then, the Palestinians have lived under Israeli occupation. The rest of the Middle East sided with Palestine, bitterly opposing the Israeli occupation, thus sowing the seeds for the bitter feelings against the United States in the region today. Although the Cold War is over, the U.S. policy toward Israel remains totally pro-Israel, which inflames anti-U.S. actions in the Middle East.

- **A Brief History of Modern Afghanistan.** Afghanistan is a rural, mountainous country, with warlord-led tribal groups controlling various regions. The population is primarily Sunni Muslim. In 1979, the Soviet Union invaded and set up a local government (the following chronology is from BBC News n.d.). The Soviets were resisted by the mujahedin (Afghan freedom fighters), who were supplied with money, supplies, and arms by the United States, Pakistan, China, Iran, and Saudi Arabia. Beginning in 1986, the United States supplied the mujahedin with Stinger missiles (over 1,000 in a three-year period), enabling them to shoot down Soviet helicopters. Among the mujahedin leaders was a Saudi exile, Osama bin Laden. The Stinger missiles and bin Laden's organization—al-Qaeda—were later used against the United States. This is an example of **blowback** (the unintended consequences of a government's policies, whereby supplies and support given to a presumed ally are later used by the recipient against the benefactor, in this case, the United States; Johnson 2000).

  In 1989, the last Soviet troops left Afghanistan, but civil war continued as rival militias competed for influence and control. Eventually, a government was formed, but in 1996, the Taliban seized control, introducing and enforcing an extreme fundamentalist version of Islam. In 1997, the Taliban was recognized as legitimate by Pakistan and Saudi Arabia. In 1998, the United States launched missile strikes at suspected bases of Osama bin Laden because of al-Qaeda's bombing of embassies in Africa. Beginning in 1999, the United Nations imposed an embargo and financial sanctions in an effort to force Afghanistan to hand over bin Laden for trial. In October 2001, the United States and Britain launched air strikes against Afghanistan after the Taliban refused to give up bin Laden, who was held responsible for the September 11, 2001 attacks on the United States.

- **A Brief History of Modern Iraq.** When Iraq was created in 1920, yet under British control, the boundaries were made without taking into account the different ethnic and religious groups within the territory. Thus, three major divisions currently plague Iraq: The Kurds are fiercely independent Sunnis residing in the north, where much of the oil is located (Iraq has the second or third greatest oil reserves in the world); the Shiites are mainly in the southeast; and the

Sunnis occupy the rest. These differences in ethnicity and religion are not trivial. Although the Shiites and Sunnis share the same Koran, they fundamentally differ in who they believe was the legitimate successor to the prophet Muhammad, who died in 632. This disagreement is a serious schism that divides the Muslim world, often resulting in violence (Ghosh 2007). Complicating these divisions today in Iraq is that although the Shiites are a majority, the Sunnis have historically had the power. Their power began when the British supported Sunni leadership, a tradition later followed by Saddam Hussein. So, although the Sunnis are a numerical minority, they have kept the Shiites in a relatively powerless position since 1932. This balance changed in postwar Iraq with the election of a Shiite-controlled government.

The British mandate ended in 1932, giving independence to Iraq. Iraq was ruled by King Faisal from 1935 to 1958. In 1961, Kuwait gained independence from Britain, and Iraq claimed sovereignty over Kuwait. Britain objected and sent troops to deter Iraq's territorial expansionist claims. Iraq backed down. In 1979, Iraq's president resigned, and his chosen successor was Saddam Hussein. Saddam ruled Iraq with an iron hand, suppressing dissidents through torture and death, even engaging in mass killings of alleged rivals. Under Saddam's leadership, Iraq engaged in a war with Shiite-dominated Iran (1980–1988). This effort was supported by the United States with arms shipments (another instance of blowback, as Iraq later used these weapons against the United States).

In 1990, Iraq again invaded Kuwait. The United Nations condemned the Iraqi invasion and imposed an economic embargo on Iraq. Later it authorized member states to use military action against Iraqi forces occupying Kuwait. In 1991, allied troops from twenty-eight countries, led by the United States, launched an aerial bombardment on Baghdad. The war, Operation Desert Storm, lasted only 6 weeks and ended in the defeat of Iraq. Significantly, President George H. W. Bush chose to limit the war to freeing Kuwait, to not invade Baghdad, and to leave Saddam in power. Some of the president's advisors felt that without removing Saddam and occupying the country, the war was incomplete. Some of these advisors joined Bush's son's administration when he became president.

In 1993, there was an alleged assassination attempt on former President George H. W. Bush by Iraqi agents. President Clinton responded by targeting Iraqi intelligence headquarters in Baghdad with Tomahawk cruise missiles.

The sanctions imposed by the United Nations continued through the 1990s because it was unclear whether Iraq had removed its weapons of mass destruction.

The Precipitating Event

On the morning of September 11, 2001, four commercial planes left East Coast airports loaded with passengers and fuel for cross-country flights. These flights were taken over by hijackers who piloted the planes to new destinations, and the course of history was changed. The first plane left Boston for Los Angeles but headed instead for New York City, where it rammed into the World Trade Center's north tower, setting its upper floors ablaze. Fifteen minutes later, a second plane, scheduled for a Boston to Los Angeles flight, steered into the south tower of the World Trade Center. Within the next hour, both towers, each 110 stories high, melted from the intense heat and collapsed. A third plane departed from Washington, D.C., for Los Angeles, but turned around and plunged into the Pentagon. The fourth plane left Newark for San Francisco, changed direction, but, possibly because of heroic passengers attacking the hijackers, failed in its mission, presumably to dive into the White House or Capitol Hill, crashing instead in rural Pennsylvania. Thus, within about 2 hours, these four planes, commandeered by terrorists in synchronized suicide missions, had attacked two symbols of the United States—the World Trade Center, the hub of U.S. capitalism, and the Pentagon, the headquarters of the world's greatest military—killing nearly 3,000 people, about the same number of Americans who died at Pearl Harbor. "Not since the Civil War have we seen as much bloodshed on our soil. Never in our history did so many innocents perish on a single day" (Gergen 2001:60).

A Rush to War

Responding to the acts of terrorism against the United States that took place on September 11, 2001, President Bush, just nine days later, declared the war on terror. The president could have declared the 9/11 events a criminal act, limiting the response to capturing the criminals and bringing them to justice. The decision, however, was to declare a war. Moves against al-Qaeda—the terrorist group that carried out the 9/11 attacks—would begin the war, he said, but the war would not end "until every terrorist group of global reach has been found, stopped, and defeated." The president advised Americans to expect "a lengthy campaign, unlike any other we have ever seen." He explained,

> *We will starve terrorists of funding, turn them one against another, drive them from place to place, until there is no refuge or no rest. And we will pursue nations that provide aid or safe haven to terrorism. Every nation, in every region, now has a decision to make. Either you are with us, or you are with the terrorists. From this day forward, any nation that continues to harbor or support terrorism will be regarded by the United States as a hostile regime. (Bush 2001a:3)*

- **A War Like No Other.** This "war on terror" was to be a war like no other. In the twentieth century, wars were fought by nations over land, resources, and ideology. But the terrorists of 9/11 did not represent a nation, and they were not intent on occupying territories. Terrorists do not have battleships and airfields to be targeted. Instead of an organized army, they are loosely organized through small groups with embedded "cells" to carry out terrorist activities. Containment, the strategy of the Cold War, was no longer possible when there are, as the U.S. State Department noted, thirty-seven foreign terrorist organizations with bases in at least twenty-five nations and the Palestinian territories. These terrorists located around the globe do not wear uniforms but rather live in their host countries as students or workers, just as other residents. If the leaders are identified and killed, others will take their place. Combat includes the use of conventional force as well as car bombs and suicide bombers (the "guided missiles" of the poor). In this new warfare, the combatants will not know victory. "There's no land to seize, no government to topple, no surrender that will bring closure" (Parrish 2001:2). Finally, in this new kind of warfare, great advantages in military technology, as demonstrated by the successful attacks on the World Trade Center and Pentagon, do not make a nation safe.

- **The War in Afghanistan.** With broad international support, Operation Enduring Freedom launched the war on October 7, 2001, as President Bush had promised, against the Taliban of Afghanistan, which supported al-Qaeda. The immediate war offensive moved rapidly so that control of all the major cities of Afghanistan had been wrested from Taliban control within 2 months of the beginning of combat. A year after starting the operation, the U.S. government claimed that "al-Qaeda went on the run . . . losing their power, their safe havens and much of their leadership. . . . They are fragmented and their leaders are missing, captured, killed or on the run" (The White House 2002a:1).

This optimistic view proved to be wrong. At the beginning of 2007, more than five years after the war began, the Taliban terrorists had not been defeated. Actually, beginning in mid-2006, there has been a resurgence of the Taliban and violence in Afghanistan. Meanwhile, bin Laden and the al-Qaeda leadership had not been found. Incidentally, the main agricultural crop in Afghanistan continues to be poppies, which provides the world with as much as 90 percent of its heroin supply.

- **The Bush Doctrine.** Believing in the rightness of their cause and the evil of the terrorists, the Bush administration developed guidelines for U.S. military actions in the war on terror and the longer-range plan for national security in the twenty-first century. This policy, known as the **Bush Doctrine**, has its roots in a particular vision about America's role in the world.

> *The great struggles of the twentieth century between liberty and totalitarianism ended with a decisive victory for the forces of freedom—and a single sustainable model for national success: freedom, democracy, and free enterprise. . . . These values of freedom are right and true for every person, in every society—and the duty of protecting these values against their enemies is the common calling of freedom-loving people across the globe and across the ages. . . . Today, the United States enjoys a position of unparalleled military strength and great economic and political influence. We seek . . . to create a balance of power that favors human freedom: conditions in which all nations and all societies can choose for themselves the rewards and challenges of political and economic liberty. (The White House 2002b:i)*

From this vision flow the strategic principles that guide U.S. military actions in the war on terror.

The Line in the Sand. Addressing the nation on the day of 9/11, President Bush said, "We will make no distinction between the terrorists who committed these acts and those who harbor them" (Bush 2001b:1). He clarified later that the United States was drawing a line in the sand, and that all world nations had a "decision to make." "Either you are with us, or you are with the terrorists," the president proclaimed (Bush 2001a:3). Later, that binary principle of "us versus them" led the president to his now famous designation of Iraq, Iran, and North Korea as an "axis of evil" and his denunciation of our allies such as France and Germany when they chose not to join in the Iraq war.

Unbounded U.S. Military Superiority. A second principle of the Bush Doctrine calls for building a military "beyond challenge" and for "experimentation with new approaches to warfare" to give the United States the "capability to defeat any attempt by any enemy" and "dissuade potential adversaries . . . with hopes of surpassing, or equaling, the power of the United States" (The White House 2002b:29–30). In a separate classified policy statement, the Bush Doctrine policy makers even declared that the United States reserves the right to respond to danger with overwhelming force—including potentially nuclear weapons—if necessary (*Washington Times* 2003).

Unilateral Preventive War and Regime Change. The Bush administration asserted the right of the United States to carry out preventive wars unilaterally to remove governments (regime change) that it deems to be engaged in long-range plans to develop weapons of mass destruction (WMDs) and to support terrorism. This pillar of the Bush Doctrine, an astonishing departure from U.S. practice and tradition, was first conveyed by the president in a graduation speech to West Point cadets. "We must take the battle to the enemy, disrupt his plans, and confront the worst threats before they emerge. If we wait for threats to fully materialize, we will have waited too long" (quoted in Ricks 2006:38). "We cannot let our enemies strike first. The overlap between states that sponsor terror and those that pursue WMD compels us to action. . . . To forestall or prevent such hostile acts by our adversaries, the United States will, if necessary act preemptively" (quoted in Ricks 2006:62).

The Bush Doctrine includes the assertion that the United States can engage in a **preventive war** as well as a **preemptive war**. The late historian Arthur Schlesinger notes the differences in these two principles.

> *The distinction between "pre-emptive" and "preventive" is well worth preserving. It is the distinction between legality and illegality. "Pre-emptive" war refers to a direct, immediate, specific threat that must be crushed at once; in the words of the Department of Defense manual, "an attack initiated on the basis of incontrovertible evidence that an enemy attack is imminent." "Preventive" war refers to potential, future, therefore speculative threats. (quoted in Singh 2006:18–19)*

Using this distinction, Robert Singh said, "The Iraq war was as clear an instance of preventive war—illegal under the U.N. Charter—as possible" (Singh 2006:19).

The Bush Doctrine does not require imminent threat for the United States to swing into full offensive military force; it requires only distant threat as determined by U.S. leaders. This is the "One Percent Solution," as enunciated by Vice President Cheney (hence, also known as the "Cheney Doctrine"): "If there was even a one percent chance of terrorists getting a weapon of mass destruction . . . the United States must now act as if it were a certainty" (quoted in Suskind 2006:62). In March 2003, Operation Iraqi Freedom became the first proof of U.S. commitment to this principle for national security in the war on terror.

The Spread of Democracy. The assumption is that the national interests of the United States are best pursued by spreading democratic forms of governance. As President Bush said in his 2004 speech at West Point,

> *"Some who call themselves 'realists' question whether the spread of democracy in the Middle East should be any concern of ours. But the realists in this case have lost contact with a fundamental reality. America has always been less secure when freedom is in retreat. America is always more secure when freedom is on the march" (quoted in Singh 2006:20).*

The War in Iraq

With the early defeat of the Taliban in Afghanistan, the Bush administration's attention turned to Iraq. The Bush administration justified a preventive war against Iraq because its leader, Saddam Hussein, was guilty of mass murder against his own people, but also because, it was alleged, he was amassing weapons of mass destruction (nuclear, chemical, and biological), and there was a strong connection between Saddam Hussein and al-Qaeda's terrorism. A debate rages as to whether these last two charges are factual, as claimed by the Bush administration. An editorial in the *Los Angeles Times* asked: "Did President Bush and his aides completely trump up the case for war and then set out to discredit anyone who called them on it? Did they instead allow themselves to be convinced too easily by evidence that tended to show them what they wanted to see? Or was the president acting reasonably on information that appeared solid at the time?" (quoted in *USA Today* 2007b:13A). Historians will eventually provide a definitive answer to this crucial debate that during the war and postwar years was so highly politicized.

Operation Iraqi Freedom began in March 2003 without a clear United Nations mandate. As in the war in Afghanistan, the initial offensive moved swiftly. Some 340,000 U.S. military personnel were deployed in the Persian Gulf region, along with more than 47,000 British troops and smaller numbers from a few other nations, to carry out the initial invasion of Iraq. After just 25 days, the United States and coalition forces were in some degree of control of all major Iraqi cities. President Bush declared an end to major combat operations on May 1, 2003. No weapons of mass destruction were found, and the rationale for the war shifted to bring democracy to Iraq, which would serve as a model for democracy for other nations in the Middle East to adopt.

Although military victory was achieved, the aftermath of the war proved more complicated and very costly for the United States. Coalition military forces faced significant problems of restoring civil order and the infrastructure and providing basic services because they were challenged by a persistent Iraqi resistance movement. Most significant, sectarian violence between the Shiite majority, which, for the first time since 1932, controlled the new government and the Sunni minority erupted. This had all the earmarks of a civil war with the United States in the middle.

The Iraq War—an Evaluation

The political objectives of the United States in its war with Iraq were bold and ambitious, as summarized by Michael R. Gordon and General Bernard E. Trainor:

> *The military operation was intended to strike a blow at terrorism by ousting a long-standing adversary, eliminating Iraq's weapons of mass destruction, and implanting a moderate and pro-American state in the heart of the Arab world. It was also to be a powerful demonstration of American power and an object lesson—for Iran, Syria, and other would-be foes—of the potential consequences of supporting terrorist groups and pursuing nuclear, biological, and chemical arms. The United States would not just defeat a dictator. It would transform a region and send the message that the American intervention in Afghanistan was not the end but just the beginning of Washington's "global war on terror."* (Gordon and Trainor 2006:497)

The Bush Doctrine was the first attempt at a grand strategy since the end of the Cold War. But did it work? Did it eliminate the threat from terrorist networks and rogue states? Did it spread democracy to the Middle East?

Ultimately these goals may be achieved, but as this is written in early 2010 (at the seven-year anniversary of the invasion of Iraq), the U.S. mission did not succeed. Supporters of the war argued that Saddam Hussein had been captured, tried, and executed as were his sons. The Shia became the majority. A semblance of democracy was established. Opponents argued that the war was not a success. The United States remained the power "behind the throne," and civil unrest was rampant.

A number of errors promoted division and civil war in Iraq, actually increased the numbers of terrorists in Iraq, and led to ever greater anti-U.S. sentiments among the population. Foremost, there was a failure to understand the seriousness of Iraq's ethnic and sectarian differences and a failure to anticipate the threat of insurgency (Cordesman 2006:xxi–xxii). As a result, the United States has been ineffective as Sunni and Shiite militias continuously attack each other's neighborhoods and holy places. Both sides in this struggle use car bombs, suicide bombers, roadside bombs, and guerrilla-style ambushes. The U.S. forces have been caught in the middle of this civil war.

> *Neither the United States nor the Shiite militias can defeat the Sunni forces in their home areas, and the Sunnis cannot hope to defeat the majority Shiites, but horrific ethnic cleansing is underway in mixed areas—a grinding and bloody stalemate, with U.S. troops in the middle. (Dreyfuss and Gilson 2007:61)*

U.S. interests were undermined when the soldiers finally tried to enforce order, as they engaged in house-to-house raids that terrified and embittered the Iraqi citizens. A government survey found that 10 percent of U.S. troops in Iraq reported that they had mistreated civilians in Iraq, such as kicking them or needlessly damaging their possessions (reported in Ricks and Tyson 2007:33). Adding to the bitterness were the occasional incidents of rapes by American soldiers, the deliberate killing of innocents, and U.S. accidents that killed civilians (Bacevich 2006). Furthermore, the United States did not realize "the disastrous symbolic potential of detaining thousands of suspects at the same Abu Ghraib prison that had been Saddam Hussein's torture center, and through either negligence or intention letting it become a site of abuse and torture again" (Fallows 2006:220).

The war had destroyed much of Iraq's infrastructure (e.g., roads, bridges, buildings, private homes, and the means for providing essential services such as electricity and water). The United States was held responsible for this destruction, which was compounded by the slow rebuilding of the infrastructure because of terrorist acts, bureaucratic mismanagement, scandal, profiteering, and insufficient of funds. All these factors resulted in the quick erosion of U.S. prestige.

Amid the chaos and because of the porous borders, extremists infiltrated from neighboring countries, most notably Iran and Syria, to engage in terrorist activities aimed at exploiting the sectarian divide and to increase anti-American fervor. Moreover, the sectarian schism has led Shiite Muslims in Iran to lend support to Shiites in Iraq and Sunni Muslims in Saudi Arabia to aid Sunnis in Iraq. Ironically, then, Iraq, which initially was not part of the terrorist network, became part of the network *because* of the U.S. "war on terror."

In time there was an election, and Iraqis were trained to eventually take the place of the U.S. military. A drawdown of U.S. troops was completed by the summer of 2010, with a contingent left to back up the Iraqi troops. Meanwhile, almost daily bombs exploded in marketplaces, on transportation, and elsewhere. The Iraqi government was ineffective in bringing the country together.

As troops were withdrawn from Iraq, President Obama ordered an increase in the U.S. military in Afghanistan, which will rise to 98,000. President Obama's plan is to start drawing down troops in July 2011, handing over security responsibilities to Afghan soldiers and police, which are currently under U.S. tutelage.

CONSEQUENCES OF THE U.S. RESPONSES TO 9/11

The United States chose to respond to the 9/11 terrorist attacks by invading Afghanistan and later Iraq. This response has had enormous consequences for the United States, for the people of Afghanistan and Iraq, for the Middle East, and for international relations. Recognizing that the U.S. involvement in the Middle East continues and the end results are unknown, this section outlines the immediate costs of the wars and speculates on the long-term legacy of U.S. actions.

The Costs of the Iraq and Afghanistan Wars

- **Loss of Human Life.** As of June 2009, the deaths from both wars surpassed 5,000 U.S. soldiers (see the "Voices" panel).

  In addition to the deaths of U.S. military personnel, there were deaths of other coalition soldiers, Iraqi and Afghani soldiers/police, U.S. defense contractors, journalists, and civilians. The number of civilian deaths in Iraq is unknown, with estimates varying from 100,000 to 600,000 deaths.

  As for the deaths of Afghans, the numbers rise with the acceleration of the war. According to the United Nations, bombs killed over 2,000 civilians in 2008,

VOICES

ARMY MAJ. DAVID G. TAYLOR, JR., AUG. 9, BAGHDAD

(Journal for His Newborn Son)

It occurred to me again that I don't know how old you'll be when you read this. It wouldn't do to write things an 18-year-old might understand if you read this when you're five. I think I'll assume you're young when you read this. Anything you don't understand, we can talk about when you're older.

That was on my mind the other night when I was sitting in my HMMWV [Humvee] on a street in Baghdad, waiting for one of our companies to raid a suspected militia warehouse. It's a bad part of town. It was 0300, I was tired, and I started thinking of some of the more complicated aspects of this fight here.

[. . .] We were raiding a place reputed to be where one of the Shia militias stores rockets, IEDs, and small-arms weapons. We were the Shia's saviors when we arrived in 2003. Back then, only disgruntled Sunnis who were loyal to Saddam attacked us. Now it's kind of the other way around.

Shia militias kill Sunnis. Sunni militias kill Shia. Foreign terrorists kill them both to incite more Shia/Sunni violence, hoping for a civil war. All of them target U.S. forces, but the Shia and Sunni aren't bold enough yet to admit they do it. [. . .] It's annoyingly complicated [. . .]

So what does all this have to do with you? Well, in my sleep-deprived frame of mind the other night, not knowing if we were about to get into a fight, I thought it was going to be very important for your mom and me to help you through the moral and ethical ambiguities in the world. Everything seems to be more complicated as time goes by. It's probably hard for some people to not just throw up their hands and go with whatever "everyone" else thinks on a complicated moral question. It's our job to arm you to know the right thing to [do], in all situations [. . .]

But how do you live those things in a place like this? Being gentle gets you killed here. [. . .]

Major Taylor was killed by an improvised explosive device (IED) on October 22, 2006.

Source: "Voices of the Fallen." 2007. *Newsweek* (April 2): 50–51.

up 40 percent from 2007. From 2004 to 2007 the bomb tonnage dropped in Afghanistan rose dramatically from 163 tons to 1,956 tons (reported in DeGennaro 2009). In April 2009 alone the U.S. military dropped 438 bombs in Afghanistan. With the military surge beginning in 2010, the killing of Afghans will continue to accelerate.

- **The Injured.** For every U.S. service member killed in Iraq, fifteen more have been wounded, injured, or contracted a serious illness. More than 80,000 were injured or wounded, and another 300,000 required medical treatment. Taking care of these veterans is going to cost at least $59 billion (Bilmes and Stiglitz 2009). Because of better protective equipment and improvements in medical trauma care, more injured troops are surviving the war in Iraq than in any previous war. Although this is good news, the downside is that because of the terrible force of explosions the combat soldiers experience, more are surviving with brain injuries (Bazell 2006).

  In addition, the trauma of war is haunting many soldiers when they return home. More than 17 percent of returning soldiers suffer from posttraumatic stress disorder, with symptoms of flashbacks, nightmares, feelings of detachment, irritability, trouble concentrating, and sleeplessness. Those who have been deployed more than once have a 50 percent increase in acute combat stress over those who have been deployed only once (Thompson 2007).

  Indicative of the higher stress levels felt by wartime troops, in 2007 five U.S. soldiers tried to kill themselves every day, up from one attempt a day before the Iraq war began (CNN 2009).

  Often overlooked in the injuries of war are the consequences of long separations and psychological trauma on the intimate lives of soldiers and their spouses, resulting in a rising divorce rate. Their divorce rate for fiscal 2009 was 3.6 percent, up from 3.4 percent a year earlier, and a full percentage point above the 2.6 percent in 2001, when the United States began sending troops to Afghanistan (Jelinek 2009). The incidence of spouse abuse within military couples has also increased as the war progressed.

More than 80,000 troops were injured or wounded in the Iraq War.

Many Iraqis, who fear bombs, raids, and death, suffer various forms of trauma. A study of Iraqi children by the Iraqi Ministry of Health found that around 70 percent of primary school students suffered symptoms of trauma-related stress such as bed-wetting, stuttering, voluntary muteness, and increased aggressive behavior (Palmer 2007).

- **The Displaced.** Of Iraq's total population of about 28 million, 4.5 million are displaced, with more than half of them having fled the country (*Nation* 2009).

- **The Monetary Costs of the Iraq and Afghanistan Wars.** Before the invasion of Iraq, the Bush administration estimated that combat operations there would cost about $50 billion. Seven years later (at the beginning of 2010) the amount allocated to both wars was $1.05 trillion, not including the funds to support the "surge" of 30,000 additional troops to Afghanistan (likely an additional cost of $30 billion; National Priorities Project 2010). Nobel laureate Joseph Stiglitz and former chair of the Council of Economic Advisors Linda Bilmes states that in addition to the more than $1 trillion spent on military operations

> *It will cost perhaps $2 trillion more to repay the war debt, replenish military equipment and provide care and treatment for U.S. veterans back home. Many of the wounded will require indefinite care for brain and spinal injuries. Disability payments are ramping up and will grow higher for decades. (Stiglitz and Bilmes 2009: para. 4).*

New York Times columnist Bob Herbert interviewed Professor Stiglitz, asking how that money might have been better spent. Stiglitz replied,

> *About $560 billion, which is a little more than half of the study's conservative estimate of the cost of the war, would have been enough to "fix" Social Security for the next 75 years. If one were thinking in terms of promoting democracy in the Middle East, the money being spent on the war would have been enough to finance a mega-mega-mega-Marshall Plan, which would have been so much more effective than the invasion of Iraq. (quoted in Herbert 2006, para. 12)*

The Social Policy panel, "What $1.2 Trillion Can Buy," provides some further suggestions for social spending rather than military spending, using a middle estimate of $1.2 trillion for the cost of the war.

- **Who Makes the Sacrifice to Conduct the War?** The Bush administration decided to conduct the war with a volunteer military instead of a draft. The volunteers tend to come from economically struggling areas, mostly rural, with few job opportunities. For example, the death rate for rural soldiers is 24 per million adults, a rate 60 percent higher than the death rate for soldiers from cities and suburbs (15 deaths per million; Engelhardt 2007). Because the military offers educational opportunities and financial inducements, youth from poor and working-class families are overrepresented. For example, 75 percent of those killed came from U.S. towns where the per capita income was below the national average (*Newsweek* 2007). As a result, most Americans do not have family members in the fight. They are not really in the war emotionally.

Typically, during wartime the government reevaluates tax and spending policies to add revenue and to shift resources from less vital pursuits to pay the additional costs of conducting and winning the war. Not so in this war, as the president and Congress, for the first time in modern history, went into a major war by *reducing the tax burden on the wealthy* (Borosage 2003). Moreover,

SOCIAL POLICY

WHAT $1.2 TRILLION CAN BUY

The human mind isn't very well equipped to make sense of a figure like $1.2 trillion. We don't deal with a trillion of anything in our daily lives, and so when we come across such a big number, it is hard to distinguish it from any other big number. Millions, billions, a trillion—they all start to sound the same.

The way to come to grips with $1.2 trillion is to forget about the number itself and think instead about what you could buy with the money. When you do that, a trillion stops sounding anything like millions or billions.

For starters, $1.2 trillion would pay for an unprecedented public health campaign—a doubling of cancer research funding, treatment for every American whose diabetes or heart disease is now going unmanaged, and a global immunization campaign to save millions of children's lives.

Combined, the cost of running those programs for a decade wouldn't use up even half our money pot. So we could then turn to poverty and education, starting with universal preschool for every 3- and 4-year-old child across the country. The city of New Orleans could also receive a huge increase in reconstruction funds.

The final big chunk of the money could go to national security. The recommendations of the 9/11 Commission that have not been put in place—better baggage and cargo screening, stronger measures against nuclear proliferation—could be enacted. Financing for the war in Afghanistan could be increased to beat back the Taliban's recent gains, and a peacekeeping force could put a stop to the genocide in Darfur.

All that would be one way to spend $1.2 trillion. Here would be another: The war in Iraq.

Source: David Leonhardt, "What $1.2 trillion Can Buy." *New York Times* (January 17, 2007).

the poor were unequally disadvantaged because programs to help them (e.g., food stamps, subsidized housing) have been cut to aid the war effort. In the long run, the cost of the war will be a burden for this and succeeding generations. If the war costs $2 trillion, then that comes to $18,000 per household (Dorrien 2006).

The Legacy of the War

The long-term consequences of the U.S. military interventions in Afghanistan and Iraq appear to be serious and far reaching. We do not know the full extent of the ramifications, but we have some clues. We begin with the successful scenario, followed by a number of negative possibilities.

- **The Effort Is Successful.** Vice President Cheney gave this optimistic prediction:

> *Ten years from now, we'll look back on this period of time and see that liberating 50 million people in Afghanistan and Iraq really did represent a major, fundamental shift, obviously, in U.S. policy in terms of how we dealt with the emerging terrorist threat—and that we'll have fundamentally changed circumstances in that part of the world (quoted in Nye, 2006, paragraph 2).*

Cheney is correct on two counts. First, the U.S. effort freed Iraq from the tyranny of Saddam Hussein. But are the Iraqis better off? Will democracy get a foothold there and spread across the Middle East as apologists for the war believe? Seven years after the war in Iraq began, the answers to these questions are negative. Long term, these are questions for historians to answer. And, second, Cheney asserted that the Middle East will be fundamentally changed by

U.S. efforts. He was correct, but will the U.S. war on terror bring about beneficial changes for that region? Or will they be overwhelmingly detrimental?

- **Iraqis and Afghans Turn against the United States.** The United States did liberate Iraq from the oppressive Saddam Hussein regime, but in the process, much of Iraq was destroyed, rebuilding has been slow and ineffective, and violence is rampant. As the *New York Times* editorialized,

> *Washington's disgraceful failure to deliver on its promises to restore electricity, water and oil distribution, and to rebuild education and health facilities, turned millions of once sympathetic Iraqis against the American presence. Their discovery that the world's richest, most technologically advanced country could not restore basic services to minimum prewar levels left an impression of American weakness and worse, of indifference to the well-being of ordinary Iraqis. That further poisoned a situation already soured by White House intelligence breakdowns, military misjudgments and political blunders.* (New York Times *2006: para. 2)*

The war and the ensuing violence have propelled an estimated 2.3 million Iraqis to flee to neighboring countries, mostly to Syria and Jordan. In addition, more than 2 million are displaced within Iraq. Clearly, Iraq is not safe, and the blame is no longer on Saddam Hussein but on the occupying force of the United States, which cannot keep order.

- **The Civil War in Iraq Is Polarizing the Sunni–Shiite Schism Worldwide.** Ethnic and regional political divisions in Iraq have been exacerbated by the war, and these resulting sectarian schisms are increasing tensions in the Muslim world. Iraqi Sunni militias bomb Shiite neighborhoods and their holy places. Shiites retaliate by lobbing mortars into Sunni districts and kidnapping Sunni men. These actions are viewed by Arabs on regional television across the region, inflaming sectarian passions and resulting in similar clashes between Sunnis and Shiites in Egypt, Pakistan, Saudi Arabia, and elsewhere. Even in Muslim neighborhoods in the United States, these tensions are felt as, for example, when Shiite shopkeepers were victims of arson, presumably perpetrated by Sunnis, in Dearborn, Michigan.

Of the world's 1.3 billion Muslims, 85 percent are Sunni. Shiites are a majority in five countries, most notably Iran and Iraq. These Shiite nations form a crescent from Iran to Lebanon. The Sunnis fear the growing power influence of Iran and the new Shiite government in Iraq brought to power by the war. Ironically, the United States finds itself favoring the Shiite government in Iraq but favors Sunni leaders everywhere else, which angers both sides (Feldman 2007).

Shiite leaders sense that the United States incites sectarianism as a way of blunting Iran's influence:

> *The growing Sunni–Shiite divide is roiling an Arab world as unsettled as at any time in a generation. Fought in speeches, newspaper columns, rumors swirling through cafes and the Internet, and occasional bursts of strife, the conflict is predominantly shaped by politics: a disintegrating Iraq, an ascendant Iran, a sense of Arab powerlessness and a persistent suspicion of American intentions. (Shadid 2007:6)*

- **Loss of U.S. Image and Credibility in the Arab World.** A goal of the Iraq war was to install a pro-U.S. democracy there with the intention that this model would eventually spread democracy and freedom throughout the Arab world. The war and the occupation, however, turned more and more people in that region against the United States. Gallup polls comparing results from 2002 and

2006 found that the percentage holding "an unfavorable view" of the United States had risen from

- 64 percent to 79 percent in Saudi Arabia
- 33 percent to 62 percent in Turkey
- 41 percent to 49 percent in Morocco.

Another polling organization—Zogby International—found in a 2005 survey of six basically U.S.-friendly Muslim countries (Egypt, Jordan, Lebanon, Morocco, Saudi Arabia, and the United Arab Emirates) that only 12 percent of those surveyed expressed favorable attitudes toward the United States. In addition, the respondents believed that the war in Iraq had created more, not fewer, terrorists, and 86 percent believed that there has been "less peace" in the region since the removal of Saddam Hussein (reported in Regan 2007; see also the BBC World Service poll, reported in *Time* 2007a).

Indicative of the shifting Arab attitude against the United States, in 2007, King Abdullah of Saudi Arabia, a staunch ally and close friend of the Bush family, characterized U.S. troops in Iraq as an "illegitimate foreign occupation" before the Arab summit (quoted in Associated Press 2007a).

Among the reasons Muslims have less regard for the United States since the Iraq war are the preventive attack on Iraq, the subsequent chaos in Iraq, the assumption that the United States is involved because of oil and to weaken the Muslim world, the secret prisons, and the torture of Muslims (per the images of prisoners at Abu Ghraib and Guantanamo Bay, Cuba; Sweig 2006).

- **Inhumane Treatment of Suspected Terrorists Aids the Cause of the Terrorists.** The Geneva Conventions are international agreements on humane treatment of combatants and civilians by opposing governments and military forces during times of war. The first of these treaties dates back to 1864, and since then, the agreements evolved so that nearly every nation (188 of them) was a signatory to the Geneva Conventions at the beginning of the war on terror. Although the Bush administration never suggested that the United States withdraw from these core provisions of international law, there has been a pattern of circumventing them. The pattern began after the 2001 military campaign in Afghanistan, which netted thousands of captive Taliban supporters and suspected al-Qaeda operatives, many of whom were imprisoned and subjected to sometimes barbaric treatment in "defiance of American and international law" (Conason 2007:12). This practice continued with the war in Iraq, as suspects were kidnapped and taken to prisons around the world for months and years at a time. Under American law, these acts were illegal.

In 2006, Congress passed the Military Commissions Act. When President Bush signed this act, he announced: "In memory of the victims of September 11, it is my honor to sign [this Act] into law" (quoted in Sussman 2007:7). This act (Herman 2006):

- Significantly broadens the definition of "enemy combatant" and makes it a matter of presidential discretion. An "enemy combatant" is defined as a person who is designated by the commander-in-chief as someone who has engaged in hostilities against the United States.
- Removes habeas corpus rights of noncitizens. **Habeas corpus**, a human right considered fundamental to the western world since the Magna Carta (ce. 1215), prevents the police from arresting and holding someone without

"The terrorist barriers seem to be working."

cause. In other words, enemy combatants are denied the right to challenge their detentions in civil courts.

- Permits aggressive interrogations in secret prisons. The act does not list acceptable and unacceptable "methods of interrogation." The legislation keeps methods open-ended and subject to the president's interpretation of the Geneva Conventions.
- Suspension of normal rules of evidence and due process. The act, unlike the procedures in U.S. courts, permits the use of hearsay and coerced evidence and evidence obtained in warrantless searches, and it fails to allow prisoners on trial ensured access to the evidence against them.

The Military Commissions Act may eventually be declared unconstitutional by the Supreme Court because it violates our judicial heritage (e.g., the Bill of Rights). But in the meantime, the U.S. reaction to terrorism was a "five-year transformation from beacon of freedom to autocratic torture state" (Rall 2006:19).

- **The Erosion of Civil Liberties at Home.** Faced with the threat of terrorism, the president sought, and Congress passed, the USA Patriot Act of 2001 (Uniting and Strengthening America by Providing Appropriate Tools Required to Intercept and Obstruct Terrorism). This act was hailed by supporters as a crucial piece of legislation giving the nation's law enforcement and intelligence-gathering personnel the "tools they need" to catch terrorists and stop another 9/11. The provisions of the USA Patriot Act:

  - Expanded the ability of law enforcement personnel to conduct secret searches and conduct phone and Internet surveillance and to access a wide range of personal financial, medical, mental health, and student records. Government monitoring of communication between federal detainees and their lawyers is allowed. Judicial oversight of these investigation activities is reduced by the act.
  - Expanded the legal definition of terrorism beyond previous laws in a manner that subjects ordinary political and religious organizations to surveillance, wiretapping, and criminal action without any evidence of wrongdoing.

- Allowed FBI agents to investigate any American citizen without probable cause of crime if they say it is for "intelligence purposes." As a result, some American citizens, mostly of Arab and South Asian origin, have been held in secret federal custody for weeks or months, many without any charges filed against them and without access to lawyers.
- Allowed noncitizens to be jailed based on suspicion, even without evidence. Suspects can be detained indefinitely without judicial review, and hundreds have been detained. Immigration hearings for post-9/11 noncitizen detainees are conducted in secret.

Some argue that ordinary law-abiding folks have nothing to fear from laws like the USA Patriot Act unless they are involved in some kind of clandestine activity. But this reaction misses the point according to critics. The USA Patriot Act is only one of hundreds of laws and legal regulations rewritten by the Bush administration to create barriers to the possibility of terrorists penetrating U.S. borders. More than any other legal change, it points out the uncanny contradiction of the war on terror policies. Under the Bush Doctrine, the United States has conducted aggressive military campaigns to liberate Afghans and Iraqis and bring democracy to "the greater Middle East." Yet, the actions of the government have restricted civil liberties that are the foundation of the U.S. Constitution and democracy. How can we expand democracy in the wider world when we do not practice it in fortress America?

Senator Russ Feingold from Wisconsin was the only senator to vote against the Patriot Act. His rationale delivered to his colleagues was,

> *There is no doubt that if we lived in a police state, it would be easier to catch terrorists. If we lived in a country where the police were allowed to search your home at any time for any reason; if we lived in a country where the government was entitled to open your mail, eavesdrop on your phone conversations, or intercept your e-mail communications; if we lived in a country where people could be held in jail indefinitely based on what they write or think, or based on mere suspicion that they were up to no good, the government would probably discover and arrest more terrorists, or would-be terrorists, just as it would find more lawbreakers generally. But that would not be a country in which we would want to live, and it would not be a country for which we could, in good conscience, ask our young people to fight and die. In short, that country would not be America. (Feingold 2001:2)*

To conduct the war on terror, domestic surveillance programs have been conducted by the FBI, the Defense Department, Homeland Security, and the National Security Agency (all of which are justified as inherent in the "wartime" powers of the president). Here are some examples of domestic spying:

- Surveillance by the FBI and local police of domestic activist organizations (e.g., American Friends Service Committee, Greenpeace, and United for Peace and Justice; Dunn 2006).
- The departments of Justice, State, and Homeland Security buy commercial databases that track Americans' finances, phone numbers, and biographical information (Woellert and Kopecki 2006).
- Using a "national security letter," the FBI can demand that an Internet provider, bank, or phone company turn over records of who you call and e-mail; where you work, fly, and vacation; and the like. No judge has to approve the demand. Moreover, the individual under surveillance is unaware of what is happening because it is classified (*USA Today* 2005).
- The Department of Homeland Security recruited utility and telephone workers, cable TV installers, postal workers, delivery drivers, and others

who regularly enter private homes to become federal informants, informing of suspicious persons, activities, and items that they observed (Conason 2007:194).

- To qualify for federal homeland security grants, states must assemble lists of "potential threat elements"—individuals or groups suspected of possible terrorist activity (Kaplan 2006).
- The Justice Department funded a private contractor, Matrix (Multistate Anti-Terrorism Information Exchange), which used "data mining" technology to search public records and matched them with police files to identify some 120,000 "suspects" with "high terrorist factor" scores.

Proponents argue that the dangers are serious, and these and other security measures are needed to make the nation secure by making it easier to identify, prevent, and punish terrorists.

Critics, on the other hand, argue that these measures go too far in expanding the government's abilities to intrude on citizens' lives, thereby weakening individual rights. Citizens have guarantees from the Constitution that protect them from government surveillance, reading the mail, and listening to phone conversations of its citizens—in short, Americans have the right to privacy and freedom from unreasonable search and seizure. Moreover, there is a high probability that the invasion of privacy will not be randomly distributed but more likely will be directed to noncitizens, Muslims, and people who look "Middle Eastern."

There is a fine line between what is needed for security and protecting the freedoms that characterize the United States. If we stray too far toward restricted freedoms, we end up, ironically, terrorizing ourselves. Another irony is that President Bush declared on the night of the assault on the World Trade Center and Pentagon that "America is the brightest beacon for freedom in the world and no one will keep that light from shining," yet the domestic antiterrorism actions taken by the government "darken that very beacon of freedom by making a new attack on our own people's already-endangered civil liberties" (Hightower 2001:1).

STRATEGIES TO COMBAT THE NEW TERRORISM

The strategies employed to achieve national security in the post-9/11 world do not resemble those used during the Cold War. Unmatched military might is not answer. Nor is a missile shield or other military technology the answer. The enemy is not a nation or alliance of nations. This time it is different. How, then, do we address the problem of terrorism by a relatively small, militarily weak, shadowy network of people and groups willing to blow up themselves and innocent others for a cause greater than themselves? Although terrorism is possible from many sources, we concentrate here on ways to neutralize the current and future threat from Islamic extremists. What follows are some ideas from which to develop strategies organized around lessons that we know.

Lesson 1: Military Might Alone Does Not Make a Nation Secure

Overwhelming military and economic superiority did not protect the United States from nineteen men who hijacked four planes with plastic knives, turning them into guided missiles. Moreover, the immense firepower of the United

States and its worldwide network of military bases appears to others as evidence of imperialist goals.

Lesson 2: Vengeance Is Self-Defeating

Responding to attacks with similar attacks ("an eye for an eye and a tooth for a tooth") may make the combatants feel better, but it fuels existing hatreds that extend from generation to generation in a never-ending cycle of violence. As proof, consider the history of the Sunni–Shiite atrocities or the Israeli–Palestinian conflict. The response to attacks must be limited to seeking justice, not revenge.

Vengeance is also self-defeating because it plays into the hands of the terrorists. A noted military scholar, Sir Michael Howard of Oxford University, traced examples of terrorism over the last 130 years and concluded that one of the principal aims of terrorists has always been to provoke savage acts of retaliation to win sympathy for their cause (cited in B. Lewis 2001). If the United States wreaks a holocaust in Arab countries such as Afghanistan or Iraq, or Iran, or Syria, then bin Laden or whomever replaces him will have accomplished his goal of bringing most of the world's 1.3 billion Muslims into a *jihad* against the West.

Lesson 3: The Solution to Terrorism Is to Address Its Root Causes

The United States should take seriously the grievances of the Muslim people in the Middle East. First, the Israeli–Palestinian conflict must be resolved equitably. While ensuring security for Israel, a Palestinian state must be established, with a multinational peacekeeping force placed between the two nations. Further, this Palestinian homeland must be provided with ample aid to bolster its economy, provide jobs for its people, and provide the necessary infrastructure (e.g., housing, schools, irrigation systems, roads, and sewage treatment). As it is, the Muslim world only sees the United States bolstering Israel militarily and economically while the Palestinians languish in refugee camps or as second-class citizens.

Second, U.S. troops and bases must be removed from Saudi Arabia, Egypt, Oman, and other Arab states in the region, thus eliminating the U.S. military, the symbol of domination, from the cradle of Islam.

Third, most societies in the Middle East, for example, have a few very rich people, a small middle class, and a huge population of very poor people. The vast majority suffer from hunger, disease, and hopelessness. This poverty extends across many countries to form the setting where the seeds of terrorism flourish. If the affluent West were to provide investment, aid, technical assistance, and technology to these countries, then their people would thrive, and the attractiveness of the terrorist cause would diminish. The safety of the world can be enhanced appreciably. The United States must adapt to a shrinking world, where all nations are increasingly interdependent. This means that unless the United States and the developed nations find ways to help those left behind in the developing nations, they will be in serious trouble.

Lesson 4: In Planning for War, the Question Guiding the Plan Must Be, How Does the Conflict End?

Implied in this is another question: What will be the definition of success? The generally accepted appraisal is that the United States did not enter the Iraq war with answers to these crucial questions raised by the *Washington Post*: "How

Iraq will be secured and governed after a war that removes Saddam Hussein, and what the U.S. commitment to that effort will be. . . . Who will rule Iraq, and how? Who will provide security? How long will U.S. troops remain?" (*Washington Post* 2007a:24). These questions were not answered inside the administration before the war, but eventually, after considerable meandering, they were. President Obama, in contrast, has laid down a specific plan for concluding the war in Afghanistan. The United States will start drawing down troops in July 2011, handing over more and more security responsibilities to Afghan soldiers until they are in control.

Lesson 5: The U.S. Goal of Spreading Democracy in the Middle East Will Likely Fail

The nations of the Middle East have no history of democracy. Iraq and Afghanistan may, in time, develop democratic institutions, but surely this will not happen because an occupying power imposes them. Some of the countries in the Middle East, including some U.S. allies, are governed by tyrants. It is hypocritical, then, for the United States to depose one despot (Saddam Hussein) while allowing others in Saudi Arabia and Kuwait, for example, to be untouched by us because they are our allies (and, not so incidentally, they supply the United States with oil). Spreading our way of life is also viewed by others as a form of imperialism.

Most important, the United States will fail to plant the seeds of democracy if it is not itself democratic. The conduct of the Iraq war reveals a fundamental contradiction: The Bush administration's goal was to export democracy, yet policies have systematically undermined civil liberties at home by using a variety of tactics to invade the privacy of citizens, by rounding up thousands of American Muslims without evidence and incarcerating hundreds of them without charges, by restricting habeas corpus, and by asserting the power to ignore hundreds of duly enacted laws—all because of an open-ended "war on terror" (Green 2007:20–21). To elaborate, in response to the terrorist threat, the United States has been restructured in undemocratic ways. The presidency, using its war powers, took more and more power from Congress, thereby removing the checks and balances between the executive and the legislative branches. For example, the Constitution requires the president to "take care that the laws are faithfully executed." If a president does not like a bill, he is supposed to veto it. A way around this is through signing statements, whereby the president lists exceptions, allowing him to eviscerate the legislation. President Bush did this to over 750 statutes. "Through signing statements, the president has repeatedly signaled his contempt for Congress and his intention to flout the law on matters ranging from torture to the protection of executive branch whistle-blowers" (Brooks 2006: para. 9).

Moreover, the executive branch engaged in secrecy, claiming national security would be breached if documents were made public. Thus, the public's right to know was thwarted by a government bent on keeping secret the existence of CIA prisons, that it conducted illegal wiretaps, and the like (*USA Today* 2007c).

Lesson 6: The Path to the Moral High Ground Goes through International Organizations and International Law

The United States undermined the possibility of success in its war on terror when, in violation of the U.N. Charter, it invoked preventive war, condoned torture, and denied basic rights to prisoners. To right these wrongs, the United States must revoke these actions and must join the nations of the world in seeking peaceful solutions to such vexing problems as the Palestinian–Israeli conflict; the trouble between India and Pakistan; the threats of Iran, Syria, and North Korea; genocide in Africa; and a variety of unstable political situations in Latin American nations such as Colombia and Peru. In the long run, rather than seeking unbounded military supremacy, the United States should be promoting greater democracy in world bodies such as the United Nations, the World Bank, the International Monetary Fund, the World Trade Organization, and others. Presently, only the votes of a few nations in these and other global venues count, and the U.S. vote is foremost. Reforming the United Nations and other multilateral organizations to allow more equal participation and influence by other nations, especially the poor and developing countries, is not against American interests. It is a matter of promoting democracy and freedom in a globalized world.

If we do not solve national security problems, then the other social problems discussed in this text are immaterial. These global social problems, although seemingly far away and removed from everyday life, hold the ultimate consequences to our individual and collective security.

■ CHAPTER REVIEW

1. Military might, to be second to none in power, is the principle guiding national security in the United States. The U.S. military is the largest and most expensive in the world. Military spending is high because (a) of the fear of nuclear weapons held by others; (b) there are nations with expansionist agendas; (c) defense spending benefits business, labor, the states, the members of Congress, and academia; and (d) outspending others is said to give the United States "peace through strength."
2. Nuclear weapons are the most destructive weapons on earth. The United States and Russia possess 96 percent of the world's nuclear warheads. As many as forty countries have the capacity to develop nuclear weapons.
3. Terrorism is a strategy of using violence to gain political advantage. It is a social construction. That is, what is defined as terrorism and who is labeled a terrorist are matters of interpretation.
4. Domestic terrorism (Americans killing Americans) has occurred throughout U.S. history. The current threats come from individuals and groups focusing on particular issues such as abortion or gun control or a more generalized fear of government overreach and government mistakes, as well as feeling powerless against not only by big government but also big banks and big Wall Street. The Tea Party movement embodies these fears and is a source of unrest. Most movement followers are not violent, but the seeds of violence are.
5. The war on international terror is like no other war because terrorists do not represent a nation but are loosely organized and are willing to use tactics such as suicide bombers.
6. The Bush Doctrine that emerged to guide national security in response to the September 11, 2001, attacks included the following principles: (a) the right of the United States to engage unilaterally in preventive wars and to change governments it deems to be dangerous; (b) the spread of democracy; (c) the building of a military beyond challenge; and (d) dividing nations into those who are with us and those who are against us.
7. The war on terror has been very costly in human life, injury, and treasure. The costs to the United States in conducting this war are not evenly distributed. The soldiers come disproportionately from minorities, the working and lower classes, and rural areas.
8. The possible long-term negative consequences of these wars include (a) the loss of Iraqi and Afghani support; (b) the polarizing of the Sunni– Shiite schism worldwide; (c) the loss of U.S. image and credibility in the Arab world; (d) unintended support for the cause of the terrorists through U.S. actions against suspected terrorists; and (e) the loss of civil liberties in the United States.
9. There are lessons to be learned from conducting this new kind of war: (a) military might does not bring security; (b) vengeance is self-defeating; (c) occupiers rarely succeed in imposing their

way of life on the locals—in this case the United States will likely fail in its efforts to plant democracy; (d) the planning for war must include an endgame; (e) if terrorism is to be diminished, its root causes must be addressed; and (f) the United States will not succeed unless it acts within the framework of international organizations and international law.

KEY TERMS

National security. The ways nations organize to protect borders, guard their national interests, and shield their citizens and businesses abroad with armies, military bases, intelligence networks, embassies, and consulates.

Defense budget. The government's spending plan for maintaining and upgrading the military defenses of the United States.

Weapons of mass destruction (WMDs). Nuclear, biological, and chemical weapons capable of large-scale death and destruction.

Cold War. The tension and arms race between the United States and the Soviet Union from World War II until 1990.

Terrorism. A methodology of using violence to gain political objectives.

Blowback. The unintended consequences of policies whereby supplies and support given to a presumed ally are later used by that entity against the original benefactor.

Bush Doctrine. The policy guiding U.S. military actions in the "war on terror" and the long-range plan for national security in the twenty-first century.

Preventive war. A war in response to a presumed future threat.

Preemptive war. A war in response to a direct, immediate, and specific threat.

Habeas corpus. A basic human right in the Western world that prevents the police (or government) from arresting and holding someone without cause.

SUCCEED WITH PEARSON mysoclab www.mysoclab.com

Experience, Discover, Observe, Evaluate
MySocLab is designed just for you. Each chapter features a pre-test and post-test to help you learn and review key concepts and terms.

Experience sociology in action with dynamic visual activities, videos, and readings to enhance your learning experience. Complete the following activities at www.mysoclab.com.

Social Explorer is an interactive application that allows you to explore Census data through interactive maps.

- Explore the Social Explorer Map: *The Population in the Military*

The Core Concepts in Sociology video clips offer a real-world perspective on sociological concepts.

- Watch *PBS American Experience: The Living Weapon*

MySocLibrary includes primary source readings from classic and contemporary sociologists.

- Read Derber, *The Wilding of America: Iraq and the War Against Terrorism;* Nguyen, *We Are All Suspects Now: Untold Stories from Immigrant Communities after 9/11;* Hoffman, *Why Don't They Like Us*

PART 6 Solutions

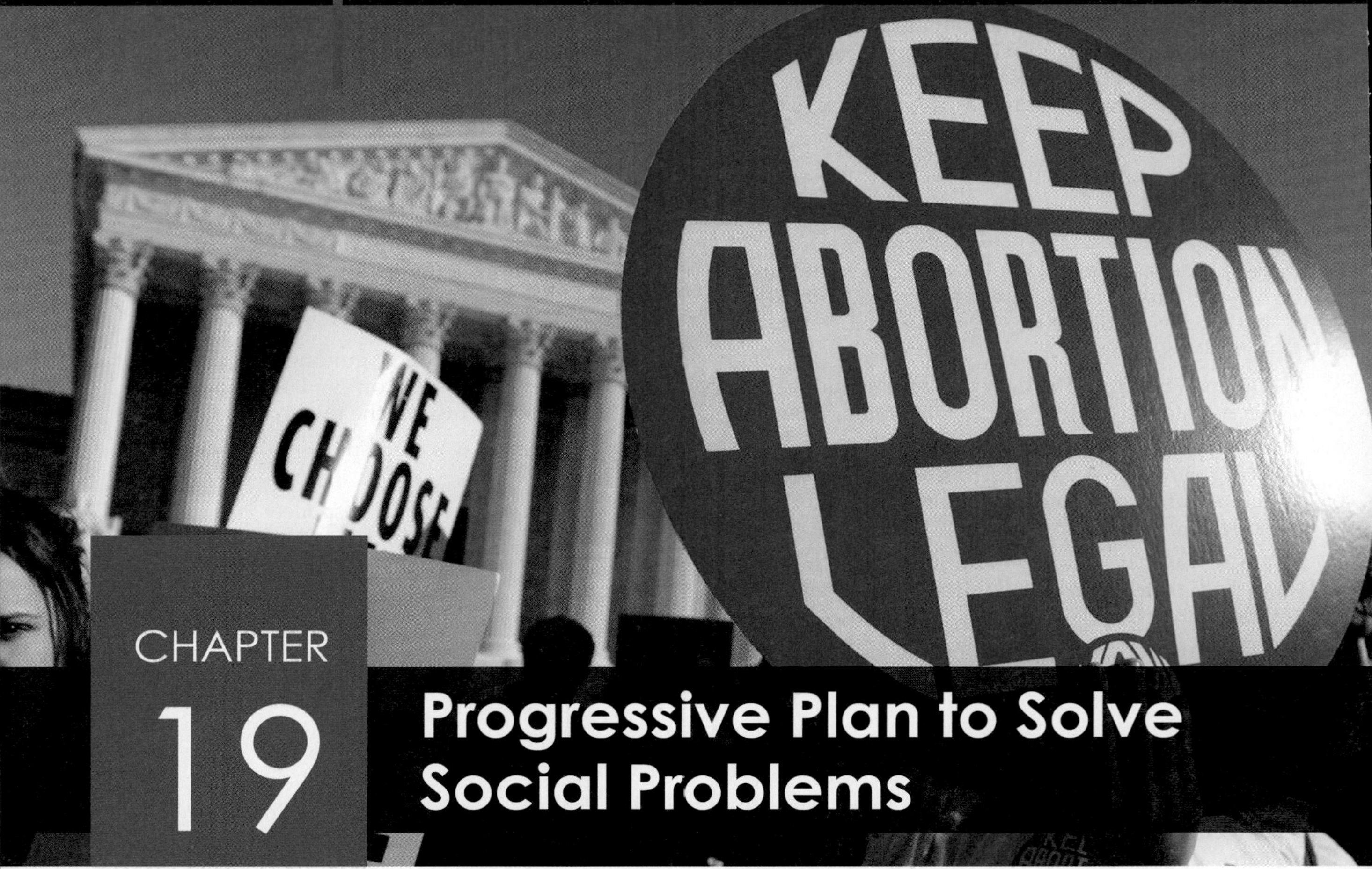

CHAPTER 19 Progressive Plan to Solve Social Problems

Society has a moral obligation, which includes taking government action when necessary, to meet basic human needs and pursue justice in economic life.
—National Conference of Catholic Bishops

Social problems are social. That is, they are human arrangements, created and sustained by people. The politicoeconomic system of a society, from which social problems emanate, does not simply evolve from random events and aimless choices. The powerful in societies craft policies to accomplish certain ends within the context of historical events, budgetary constraints, and the like. Addressing the issue of inequality, Claude S. Fischer and his colleagues say,

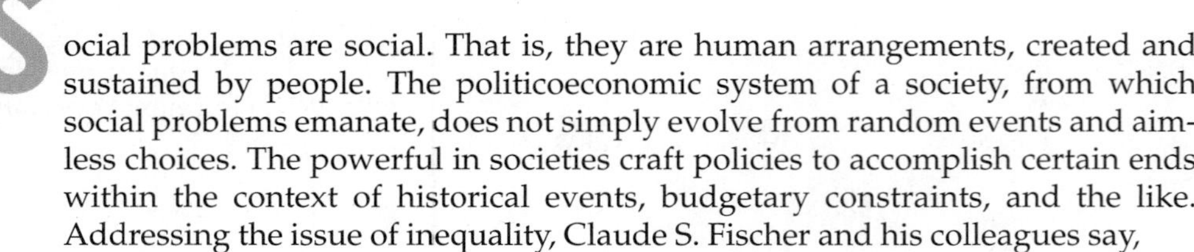

> *The answer to the question of why societies vary in their structure of rewards is . . . political. . . . By loosening markets or regulating them, by providing services to all citizens or rationing them according to income, by subsidizing some groups more than others, societies, through their politics, build their ladders [the height and breadth of*

the rungs of the stratification system]. To be sure, historical and external constraints deny full freedom of action, but a substantial freedom of action remains. . . . In a democracy, this means that the inequality that Americans have is, in significant measure, the historical result of policy choices Americans—or, at least, Americans' representatives—have made. In the United States, the result is a society that is distinctly unequal. Our ladder is, by the standards of affluent democracies and even by the standards of recent American history, unusually extended and narrow—and becoming more so. (Fischer et al., 1996:8)

In other words, America's level of inequality, which is greater than found in any of the Western democracies, is by design (Fischer et al., 1996:125).

Social policy is about design, about setting goals and determining the means to achieve them. Do we want to regulate and protect more, as the well-developed welfare states do, or should we do less? Should we create and invest in policies and programs that protect citizens from poverty, unemployment, and medical inattention, or should the market economy sort people into winners, players, and losers according to their abilities, efforts, and the luck or misfortune of the families into which they were born and raised? In the past two decades, decision makers in the United States have opted to reduce drastically the welfare system (e.g., elimination of Aid to Families with Dependent Children [AFDC], reduced monies for food stamps) while the taxes on the affluent have been reduced significantly and subsidies such as the tax exemption on the interest and taxes paid on housing have been retained. Congress and state legislatures have rejected subsidies to low-income families for child care, medical care, and job training. Similarly, the boards of corporations, faced with major profit gains and increased productivity, have rewarded their executives with ever more generous salaries and stock options. Meanwhile, these same corporations have downsized their workforces, reduced entry-level wages, hired more temporary and contingent workers, and reduced health and other benefits to employees (Hacker 2006). Thus, the combined acts of federal and state governments and corporations have increased the gap between the top one-fifth ("the fortunate fifth") and those in the bottom one-fifth of the income/wealth distribution. The resulting inequality gap is a major source of social problems.

The important sociological point is that if societies are designed, and some of the arrangements result in social problems, they can be changed to reduce or eliminate those problems. In other words, the design can be changed.

Such change is not easy, though. Social arrangements can be tradition bound and often imbued with religious approval, which impedes efforts at change. The status quo is defined as natural, and those who challenge it are seen as "impractical, ridiculous, crazy, dangerous and/or immoral. By definition, the conventional wisdom of the day is widely accepted, continually reiterated and regarded not as ideology but as reality itself" (Willis 1998:19). But change is possible. In the words of the late progressive Senator Paul Wellstone,

It's the power that won the eight-hour day, women's right to choose, civil rights laws, and the end of the Vietnam War. Grassroots movements brought about these and most great changes that have advanced the people of this country. People organized, protested, educated one another, kept up the pressure, and held their ideals high. [In doing so] the collected voices of concerned and committed Americans spoke clearly and loudly enough to be heard over those who resisted change. (Wellstone 1998b:1)

SOCIOLOGY, SOCIAL PROBLEMS, AND SOCIAL CHANGE

This textbook is a sociological introduction to the understanding of social problems, their sources, and their consequences. Let us look more closely at the discipline of sociology and make explicit what has been implicit throughout this book.

The Sociological Imagination and Social Problems

Among the components of the sociological imagination (see Chapter 1) is that it involves moving away from thinking in terms of the individual and her or his problem and focusing rather on the social, economic, and historical circumstances that produce the problem for many. In other words, when seeking solutions to social problems, we focus on changing the social structure rather than on changing problem people.

Changing attitudes to reduce or eliminate racism, although important, does not solve the underlying problem of institutional racism in U.S. society. Changing the structure of society to ensure equality of opportunity for jobs, income, education, housing, and health care is the solution.

Sociological Paradox: Structure and Agency

Throughout the discussions in this book, we have emphasized the power of social context and the social forces that so strongly affect human behavior (the following is from Eitzen, Baca Zinn, and Smith 2010:521–522). As sociologist Peter Berger says,

> *Society not only controls our movements, but shapes our identity, our thoughts and our emotions. The structures of society become the structures of our own consciousness. Society does not stop at the surface of our skins. Society penetrates us as much as it envelops us. (Berger 1963:121)*

This **deterministic view** is too strong, however. Although society constrains what we do, it does not determine what we do (Giddens 1991:863). Although society and its structures are powerful, the members of society are not totally controlled. We are not passive members. We can take control of the conditions of our own lives. Human beings cope with, adapt to, and change social structures to meet their needs. Individuals, acting alone or with others, can shape, resist, challenge, and sometimes change the social organizations and social institutions that impinge on them. These actions constitute human agency.

The paradox of sociology—the power of society over its members versus the power of social actors to change society—has several important meanings and implications. Foremost, society is not a rigid, static entity composed of robots. People in interaction are the architects of society in an ongoing project. That is, society is created, sustained, and changed by people.

Second, the social forms that people create often take on a sacred quality—the sanctity of tradition—that constrains behavior in socially prescribed ways. The sociological insight is, to restate the previous point, that what many consider sacred and unchangeable is a social construction and can therefore be reconstructed.

A third implication is that because social structures are created and sustained by people, they are imperfect. There are both positive and negative consequences of the way people have organized. Many are content with the status quo because they benefit from it. Others accept it even though they are disadvantaged by it. But some also seek change to improve the social structure or, perhaps, to transform it into something completely different. They are the agents of change.

In sum, the essence of agency is that individuals, through collective action, are capable of changing the structure of society and even the course of history. But although agency is important, we should not forget the power of the structures that subordinate people, making change difficult or, at times, impossible.

A Sociological Dilemma: Recognition and Rejection

Sociologists wish to be taken seriously by those in power. We are experts on social life. We have answers, not all by any means, but many, nonetheless, based on empirical research (see any issue of the sociological journal *Contexts*). But society's governmental and corporate leaders rarely seek sociological expertise in tackling social problems. Repeatedly, for example, sociologists have pointed out to political deaf ears that it "costs less to educate people than to leave them untrained. It costs less to provide prenatal care than to care for underweight babies. It costs less to house people than to build prisons to warehouse them" (Jackson 1998a:20). It costs less and is more effective to deal with children before they get into trouble than to ignore them and put them in the criminal justice system after they have become disheartened, alienated, and angry because they have no hope of conventional success. But this understanding goes unheeded as budgets for Head Start–type programs dry up and budgets for prisons escalate.

Sociologists Barbara Risman and Donald Tomaskovic-Devey conveyed this dilemma of having helpful knowledge but being marginal in our effectiveness as public intellectuals:

> *One of the wonderful things about being sociologists is knowing that collectively we have something powerful to contribute to the understanding of most, probably all, problems faced by society. One of the most frustrating things about being sociologists is how rarely we see sociological knowledge guiding the social choices and strategies of others. This happens at all levels, from the construction of global warming policy, to campaign finance reform, to affirmative action in our own universities, to couples struggling to create egalitarian relationships. (1998:vii)*

Why is this the case? Why are sociologists rejected by those in power? Several related reasons combine to make sociologists marginal (the following is from Risman and Tomaskovic-Devey 1998; and Eitzen and Baca Zinn 1998b:8–9). Foremost, the sociological perspective is subversive. That is, sociology undermines everything because it questions all social arrangements, whether religious, political, economic, or familial. Such an approach is threatening to those in power. As Risman and Tomaskovic-Devey say, "Our insights, regardless of how intellectually and empirically powerful they might be, are not always welcomed by the privileged" (1998:vii). But it is not just the powerful elites who are threatened; it is those who are powerful because they are in the majority by virtue of their social class position, their race/ethnicity, their gender, or their sexual orientation. Sociology unmasks the institutional classism, racism, sexism, and homophobia that is present in the "normal" and "accepted" ways that social structures work to discriminate against the powerless and keep them "in their place."

The message of sociologists is rejected by many because it challenges the core of society's dominant ideology. The economy of the United States is capitalism.

This system has its strengths, but it also leads to many social problems, as has been amply shown throughout this book.

Related to capitalism is the emphasis in U.S. society on individualism. Unlike Canada, the Scandinavian countries, and the nations of Western Europe, the United States focuses more on individual achievement and competition, letting the losers fend mostly for themselves. In essence, we say for the most part, you are on your own; get an education; get a job; take care of yourself and your family; and you are not obligated to take care of others. Thus, government programs to help the economically disadvantaged are minimal. The governments of the other Western democracies have a different philosophy. They are much more inclined to provide for the common good (e.g., generous welfare programs to lift people out of poverty; universal health insurance; more public resources for parks, orchestras, and mass transit). Sociologists are quick to point out the difference between the United States and its peers, noting that although the United States is the wealthiest country, among its peers (other modern industrialized nations) it has the highest proportion of people living in poverty, the highest proportion of children growing up in poverty, and the most unequal income and wealth distributions. Thus, the individualism that pervades U.S. society has a severe downside, leading to serious social problems. But because the individualist ideology is a core belief of most Americans, any criticism of it is viewed with alarm, as being un-American. Thus, when sociologists examine and report what they see as the consequences of public policy, which has as its foundation the emphasis on individualism, they are moved to the margins of public discourse about social problems.

We are confident that many of the readers of this book have found the sociological examination of social problems uncomfortable. Perhaps you have found it subversive because it questions underlying assumptions about U.S. society. Even though this critical approach may be uncomfortable to many people, it is necessary to understand human social arrangements and find solutions to social problems. Thus, we ask that you think sociologically: (1) to view social arrangements critically, and (2) to view social problems as emanating from social structure, not bad people. In essence, we ask that you overcome the societal bias against sociology by adopting the sociological imagination as you consider what society should do about its social problems.

PROGRESSIVE PRINCIPLES TO GUIDE PUBLIC POLICY

This book has focused on the structural basis for social problems. These problems are formidable, but not insolvable. We can do something about them. This effort to change problematic social arrangements is the essence of **human agency**.

What, then, do we do to solve social problems? The first step must be to determine the facts. We must challenge the myths that often guide public opinion and policy makers. Providing the facts and demythologizing social life have been major goals of this book.

The second step is to establish, as a society, the principles that will guide public policy to accomplish the common good. This, we realize, is politically impossible at the moment for at least three related reasons. Foremost, underlying many of the problems in the United States is the power of money over the decision-making process, a problem that was magnified by the 2010 Supreme Court ruling giving corporations and other organizations the right to give unlimited amounts of money to affect the political process. The problem, of course, is that the powerful use money to retain and expand their power, and the relatively powerless (e.g., single mothers, the homeless, renters, children, the working poor, recent immigrants, and contingent workers) are left with no effective political voice. This is not democracy; it is a **plutocracy** (a government where the wealthy class rules).

Until campaign finance is straightened out, no significant change is possible (Lessig 2010; Moyers and Winship 2010). As it is, politics is guided by the "golden rule": *Those who have the gold will make the rules*. Donald Kaul, writing about the Supreme Court decision, provides this dire assessment:

> *The decision,* Citizens United vs. Federal Election Commission, *ended limits on the money corporations and unions can spend on influencing elections, thus writing a finish to the experiment in democracy we've been conducting for 220 years.*
>
> *We'll still have elections and rallies and arguments and tea parties. So what? It's all a show, the political equivalent of professional wrestling. (Kaul 2010:23)*

If money rules, we do not have a democracy. The public must demand campaign finance reform and accept nothing less.

The second stumbling block to change is that politicians (at both state and federal levels) are "incapable of tackling long-term social and economic challenges, whether the solutions come from the left or the right" (Harwood 2010: para. 5). The reason: One rarely gets elected to public office by asking citizens to sacrifice by paying higher taxes to pay for problems with long-term positive consequences for society. Consider infrastructure: The American Society of Civil Engineers prepares a "report card" on the state of the infrastructure—roads, bridges, dams, levees, ports, water systems, sewage systems, the electric grid, etc. The most recent grade was "D," and the cost of bringing all systems up to adequacy was estimated at $2.2 trillion over five years (cited in Fallows 2010). Is there a politician who would run on a platform to remedy this serious (and very costly) problem now and with higher taxes? Added to this is the political component: Many (e.g., about 20 percent of adult Americans identified with the Tea Party movement in 2010) view government as the problem, not the solution. Hence, for them, the government has no role in solving national problems. What, then, is the solution to the crumbling infrastructure? But not only the physical infrastructure but the social infrastructure as well needs fixing. Do we not need public investment in health care, education, child care, and nutrition programs? Or are these problems to be left to local decisions or the marketplace? The problem is not only weak legislators who vote on the safe side to get reelected. "The fault lies everywhere. The president, the Congress, the news media and the public are to blame. Shared sacrifice is not part of anyone's program" (Herbert 2010: para. 12). Significant in their culpability are the people who favor candidates who, for example, pledge to never vote for higher taxes. This unwillingness of lawmakers to sacrifice for the public good is the dark side of democracy.

The third obstruction to solving social problems is gridlock among decision makers at the state and federal levels (Beinart 2010). We concentrate here on Congress. To begin, as noted in Chapter 2, the filibuster in the Senate has made it virtually impossible to enact important legislation. This has worsened as Congress

Politicians seem unable to raise taxes to improve the infrastructure because they fear that they will be defeated in the next election

has become more divided in the last twenty years or so. In the late 1960s, for example, senators filibustered less than 10 percent of major legislation, but in 2009 Senate Republicans filibustered 80 percent of important legislation. Behind this is the polarization of Congress. Winners in primary elections, where only members of a party can vote, tend to side with their party's base, which has unyielding beliefs about civil rights, abortion rights, climate change, the wars in Iraq and Afghanistan, the role of the federal government, and the free market system. The result is fewer moderates becoming candidates in the general election and less compromise with the opposition when elected. This is exacerbated by the practice of **gerrymandering**, the carving up of districts by the party in power to maintain their favorable balance of power. The politicians favored in this arrangement have no incentive to compromise.

Richard Stengel puts it this way:

> *The United States faces enormous problems for the foreseeable future: the national debt; the rising costs of Social Security, Medicare and Medicaid; the wars in Afghanistan and Iraq. The ability to solve these problems means asking people to make a sacrifice, which requires a spirit of compromise and bipartisanship. (Stengel, 2010:2).*

Compromise and bipartisanship are rare qualities in today's politicians and political bodies. These are further complicated by the dysfunctional political structure of Congress.

Assuming that the bias of money in politics, the short-term outlook of politicians, and the gridlock in our political bodies can be overcome—dubious assumptions at best—let us propose some principles that we believe ought to guide public policy to reduce or eliminate major social problems that plague U.S. society. We realize, of course, that this is a controversial exercise, but we ask you to ponder these proposals and improve on them.

1. *A call for policies and behaviors that enhance our moral obligation to our neighbors (broadly defined) and their children, to those unlike us as well as those similar to us,* *and to future generations.* This principle runs counter to our societal celebration of individualism. But, we argue, the emphasis on individualism over community leads to exacerbated inequality; the tolerance of inferior housing, schools, and services for "others"; and public policies that are punitive to the economically disadvantaged. Moreover, exaggerated individualism is the antithesis of cooperation and solidarity—the requirements of community.

What happens when the gap between the rich and the poor widens? This phenomenon of income inequality has implications for democracy, crime, and civil unrest. As economist Lester Thurow has asked,

> *How much inequality can a democracy take? The income gap is eroding the social contract. If the promise of a higher standard of living is limited to a few at the top, the rest of the citizenry, as history shows, is likely to grow disaffected, or worse. (Thurow 1995b:78)*

Similarly, sociologist Todd Gitlin's reading of history leads him to conclude that "[g]rowing inequality erodes social solidarity" (Gitlin 1995:225).

The welfare states of Canada, Europe, and Scandinavia have comprehensive social supports for their peoples. They provide universal health care insurance systems. They have a much more ample minimum wage than does the United States. They provide generous pensions and nursing home care for the elderly. They have paid maternity (and in some cases paternity) leave. Education is free through college. These benefits are costly, with income, inheritance, and sales taxes considerably higher than in the United States. The trade-off is that poverty is rare, and the population feels relatively safe from crime and from the insecurities over income, illness, and old age. Most important, there is a large middle class with a much stronger feeling of community and social solidarity than is found in the United States. And, the people are better off. As Robert Borosage stated:

> *"On every social indicator—health, longevity, education, social cohesion, crime, generosity—more equitable societies fare better than richer, less equitable ones like our own" (Borosage 2010:12).*

In sharp contrast, the United States has the highest poverty rate by far among the industrialized countries, a withering bond among those of different social classes, a growing racial divide, and an alarming move toward a two-tiered society. Should we move further toward an extreme bipolar society, the following is likely to occur:

> *If you had a million dollars, where would you want to live, Switzerland or the Philippines? Think about all the extra costs, monetary and otherwise, if you chose a vastly unequal country like the Philippines. Maybe you'd pay less in taxes, but you'd wind up shuttling between little fenced-in enclaves. You'd have private security guards. You'd socialize only in private clubs. You'd visit only private parks and beaches. Your kids would go to private schools. They'd study in private libraries. (James Fallows, quoted in Carville 1996:87)*

The United States is not the Philippines, but we are already seeing a dramatic rise in private schooling and homeschooling and in the number of walled and gated affluent neighborhood enclaves on the one hand and ever greater segregation of the poor and especially poor racial minorities in deteriorating neighborhoods and inferior schools on the other. Personal safety is more and more problematic as violent crime rates increase among the young and disaffected.

Finally, democracy is on the wane as more and more people opt out of the electoral process, presumably because, among other things, they are alienated and their choice among politicians is limited to those whose interests favor the wealthy, not the economically disadvantaged.

There is a flaw in the individualistic credo. We cannot go it alone entirely—our fate depends on others. Thus, it is in our individual interest to have a collective interest. As sociologist Alan Wolfe, discussing the Scandinavian countries, has put it,

> *The strength of the welfare state—indeed, the accomplishment that makes the welfare state the great success story of modern liberal democracy—is the recognition that the living conditions of people who are strangers to us are nonetheless our business. (Wolfe 1989:133)*

2. Acceptance of the first principle leads to the second: *A call for government programs that provide for people who cannot provide for themselves.* This is a call to bring all members of society up to a minimum standard of dignity. At a minimum, this includes universal health insurance, jobs, a living wage that places workers above the poverty line, and guaranteed and adequate pensions.

This position is opposite the direction of current policy makers in Congress and the state legislatures, whose stance is to reduce rather than expand the already constricted U.S. welfare safety net. The ideological consensus among the Republicans, the Blue Dog (conservative) Democrats, and various pressure groups has two related propositions. First, government subsidies exacerbate social problems rather than solve them. Second, individuals who fail are to blame for their failure. Ironically, these propositions are assumed by the powerful to hold for individuals but not for corporations.

Since the 1930s, the United States has had a social safety net of AFDC, food stamps, Head Start, subsidized housing, and the like to help those in need. Conservatives see this safety net as the problem because they believe that it destroys incentives to work and encourages poor single mothers to have children. They argue, then, that welfare is the problem and that social problems will get worse if we are more generous to the poor. By this logic, if we spend less on welfare, we save money, government is reduced, and the lot of the poor improves. Thus, since about 1970, the federal government has gradually reduced or eliminated welfare programs. Has this dismantling of a relatively meager welfare program helped the poor? Has it made society safer?

From the progressive position, the poor have fared badly "because of an erosion of their labor market opportunities, not because of an erosion of their work ethic" (Danziger and Gottschalk 1995:4).

3. Acceptance of these principles leads to a third: *A special commitment to children, all children, and to implement this commitment with viable, universal programs.* In sociologist Jay Belsky's words,

> *The time has come for this nation to regard child care as an infrastructure issue and make the same kind of investment in it that we talk about making in our bridges and roads and that we initially made in these vital transportation systems. We need to recognize that, in the same way that the massive capital investment in transportation and communication systems resulted in huge capital gains that we continue even to this day to realize, investment in child care can bring with it comparable long-term benefits. To gain insight into the costs, specifically foregone opportunity costs of not endeavoring to improve child care and increase options for families, imagine for a moment an America with the automobile but without paved roads. (Belsky 1990:11)*

Such a commitment to children involves providing prenatal and postnatal medical care, childhood immunization, protection from exposure to toxic chemicals, adequate nutrition, the elimination of child poverty, access to preschool and after-school programs, safe neighborhoods, and equitably financed schools.

Jonathan Kozol, the longtime children's advocate, speaking on behalf of these children, said this:

> *"Conservatives," [Kozol] said, "now demand that poor children prove their worthiness before aid can be considered while liberals wring their hands and capitulate to the ethos of our time." In New York's South Bronx, as many as 25 percent of children are born HIV-positive while the nation's richest neighborhoods in Manhattan, a 12-minute bus ride away, look on and do nothing. Across the country, the story is the same everywhere.*
>
> *[Kozol] noted that the nation balks at spending $6,000 a year to educate poor children while it unhesitatingly spends $60,000 a year to incarcerate them when their hopelessness leads to crime. "What honorable Judeo-Christian society would pay 10 times as much to punish a child as to educate him? The neglect of America's children," argued Kozol, "is nothing less than collective sin." (quoted in Judson 1997:2A)*

Kozol's term "collective sin" is important for our consideration because the neglect of children is not just a matter of the neglect of individual parents, as it sometimes is, but much more important, it is a matter of society's neglect. As a society, the United States could eliminate poverty, provide universal health insurance, and ensure that all children receive preschool training. But as a society, we continue to look the other way (see the "Looking toward the Future" panel, which insightfully describes an imaginary society that collectively provides for all children).

4. *A call to redistribute societal resources to lift those urban and rural areas that are economically disadvantaged. Some areas of the nation are especially at risk.* There are many pockets of rural poverty, such as Appalachia, the Mississippi Delta,

LOOKING TOWARD THE FUTURE

THE CHILDSWAP SOCIETY: A FABLE

Sandra Feldman, president of the American Federation of Teachers, wrote of a pretend society in which a national child lottery was held every four years:

Every child's name was put in—there were no exceptions—and children were randomly redistributed to new parents, who raised them for the next four years. Babies were not part of this lottery. Parents got to keep their newborn children until the next lottery, but then they became part of the national childswap. The cycle was broken every third swap, and kids were sent back to their original parents until the next lottery. So by the time you were considered an adult, at age 26, the most time you could have spent with your birth parents was 10 years. The other 16 were simply a matter of chance.

Maybe one of your new parents would be the head of a gigantic multinational company and the most powerful person in the country or the president of a famous university. Or you might find yourself the child of a family living in a public housing project or migrant labor camp. . . . People in the childswap society took the lottery for granted. They didn't try to hide their children or send them away to other countries; childswapping was simply a part of their culture. And one thing the lottery did was to make the whole society very conscientious about how things were arranged for kids. After all, you never knew where your own child would end up after the next lottery, so in a very real sense, everyone's child was—or could be—yours. As a result, children growing up under this system got everything they needed to thrive, both physically and intellectually, and the society itself was harmonious.

What if someone wrote a story about what American society in the [early twenty-first] century takes for granted in the arrangements for its children? We might not want to admit it, but don't we take for granted that some kids are going to have much better lives than others? Of course. We take for granted that some will get the best medical treatment, and others will be able to get little or none. We take for granted that some kids will go to beautiful, well-cared-for schools with top-notch curriculums, excellent libraries, and computers for every child, and others will go to schools where there are not enough desks and textbooks to go around—wretched places where even the toilets don't work.

We take for granted that teachers in wealthy suburban schools will be better paid and better trained than those in inner-city or rural schools. We take for granted, in so many ways, that the children whom the lottery of birth has made the most needy will get the least. "After all," we say to ourselves, "it's up to each family to look after its own. If some parents can't give their children what they need to thrive, that's their problem."

Obviously, I'm not suggesting that the United States adopt a childswap system. The idea makes me cringe, and, anyway, it's just a fable. But I like to imagine what would happen if we did. We'd start with political figures and their children and grandchildren, with governors and mayors and other leaders. What do you suppose would happen when they saw that their children would have the same chance as the sons and daughters of poor people—no more and no less? What would happen to our schools and health care system—and our shameful national indifference to children who are not ours? I bet we'd quickly find a way to set things straight and make sure all children had an equal chance to thrive.

Source: From Sandra Feldman, "The Child-Swap Society." Reprinted by permission of the American Federation of Teachers, AFL-CIO. http://www.aft.org/presscenter/speechescolumns/wws/1998/0198.htm.

and the Rio Grande Valley in Texas, where jobs are few and poorly paid and poverty rates are many times higher than the national average. These areas need federal assistance for schools, job training, and infrastructure. They need government subsidies through tax rebates to encourage businesses to locate there and hire local workers (the subsidies to be received when company performance conditions—jobs, pay, benefits to workers—are met).

There are extraordinary numbers of recent immigrants in California, Texas, and Florida who are poor and have special needs such as job training. Those people need jobs, shelter, food, and services such as education and health care. Those states especially affected by immigration need help from the federal government to supply assistance to the immigrants. At present, immigration is a federal policy, but the states are left with the financial responsibility (as mentioned in Chapter 5). This overburden results in either the immigrants not receiving the necessary assistance or the states stretching their welfare budgets too thin for the immigrant and nonimmigrant poor. Clearly, these states need federal assistance to meet the special needs of recent immigrants.

The other important area of neglect is the declining central cities. As noted in Chapter 6, the central cities have been abandoned by the middle classes, who have moved to the suburbs, and by corporations that have moved their businesses (and jobs) to the suburbs, to other parts of the country, or out of the country. The tax base in the cities has eroded, leaving declining transit systems, parks, and services, most notably schools. This erosion contributes to cutbacks in services and more flight to the suburbs. The high unemployment and continued job flight leads to despair, hopelessness, drug and alcohol abuse, and crime, further justifying the decisions of businesses and families to leave.

Policies of the federal government are partly responsible for urban decay:

> *We have spent trillions building non-metro roads, but nowhere near that on metro ones or mass transit. Federal annual funding for mass transit has never been more than a fifth of highway funding, and state ratios are even more unbalanced. The overwhelming share of federal and state economic development funding also goes to non-metro sites—more highways, sprawl—supporting infrastructure, exurban tax credits and low-interest loans for new development. Similarly, the deliberate siting of military bases and other government facilities outside cities or more developed regions remains a deliberate national policy. (Rogers 1998:14)*

The federal government can reverse these antiurban policies, thus helping to revitalize the cities. To date, there is no political will to do so. These politicians choose to ignore the human and economic costs of this neglect.

5. *Although some social policies should be made and administered at the local level, others must be largely financed, organized, and administered by the federal government.* This principle is based on the assumption that some issues are national in scope and require uniform standards (e.g., nutrition guidelines, immunization timetables, preschool, elementary through high school goals, the certification of teachers, and health care guarantees). Other policies, such as reducing poverty, require the massive infusion of money and compensatory programs, coupled with centralized planning.

While dismantling the welfare system, the strategy has been to cut funds and move the programs from the federal level to the states (called **devolution**). This devolution trend has the effect of making benefits very uneven, as some states are relatively generous while others are much less so. The distinguished historian, the late Arthur Schlesinger, Jr., has said this about the role of the federal government vis-à-vis the state governments:

> *It is a delusion to say that, because state government is closer to the people, it is more responsive to their needs and concerns. Historically it is national government that has served as the protector of the powerless. It is national government that affirmed the Bill of Rights against local vigilantism and preserved natural resources against local greed. The national government has civilized industry, secured the rights of labor organizations, improved income for the farmer, and provided a decent living for the old.*

> *Above all, the national government has vindicated racial justice against local bigotry. Had the states' rights creed prevailed, the U.S. would still have slavery. And historically the national government has been more honest and efficient than state and local governments. . . . As for bureaucracy, duplication, and waste, will there be more or less if a single federal agency is to be replaced by fifty separate state agencies? (quoted in Shanker 1995:E7)*

IS A PROGRESSIVE SOCIAL POLICY POSSIBLE?

Three questions remain: (1) Why should we adopt a progressive social agenda? (2) How do we pay for these programs? (3) Is there any hope to enact progressive solutions to social problems?

Should a Progressive Plan Be Adopted by U.S. Society?

Why should the United States adopt a progressive plan to deal with its social problems? Foremost, these are serious problems, and market solutions will not alleviate them. Reliance on the bottom line (profits) means, for example, that companies will move their operations wherever labor is cheapest. It means lobbying to remove government oversight of their operations. Market-based strategies result in winners and losers and, moreover, it means opposition to social programs to help these "losers." We are convinced that public policy based on abandoning the powerless exacerbates social problems.

A second reason to favor progressive solutions has to do with domestic security. We ignore the problems of poverty, wealth inequality, and a rationed health care system at our own peril. If we continue on the present path of ignoring these problems or reducing or eliminating programs to deal with them, we will be less secure, and we will have more problem people who require greater control—and at an ever greater social and economic cost.

The final argument for a progressive attack on social problems is an ethical one. We need, in our view, to have a moral obligation to others. We need to restore a moral commitment to the safety net. We should take the moral high ground, as Jonathan Kozol has argued: "There is something ethically embarrassing about resting a national agenda on the basis of sheer greed. It's more important in the long run, more true to the American character at its best, to lodge the argument in terms of simple justice" (quoted in Nore 1991:36).

Or consider this moral warning from an unlikely source, the very conservative British Chancellor of the Exchequer Kenneth Clarke, who explained his resistance to calls for a minimalist state: "This is a modern state. It is not the fifties . . . not southeast Asia. I believe in North American free-market economics, but I do not wish to see [here in Great Britain] the dereliction and decay of American cities and the absolute poverty of the American poor" (*The Nation* 1996:5).

Financing the Progressive Agenda

There are several sources of additional funds. The first is to reduce defense spending. We are the world's mightiest nation by far, and although there no longer is a Soviet threat, there is the threat of terrorism. The United States maintains a global network of bases, many of which are not needed. Similarly, there are expensive forms of military equipment are no longer required. The U.S. defense budget is enormous—$740 billion for fiscal year 2011—a sum that exceeds the amount spent by all of our allies combined. If the United States reduced annual military spending by $200 billion, it would still outspend everyone else.

A second source of funds would be to reduce or eliminate corporate welfare and subsidies to the wealthy. At the moment, corporations receive much more than $100 billion in direct subsidies and tax breaks. The wealthiest Americans pay lower tax rates and have more tax loopholes than found in any other modern nation. Annually, we have about $400 billion in "tax expenditures" (i.e., money that is legally allowed to escape taxation). The economically advantaged receive most of these tax advantages.

A third source of funds is to increase the taxes on the wealthy, the opposite position of the Bush administration and the Republican-controlled Congress. Congress, with the urging of President Bush, provided tax cuts in 2001, 2002, and 2003, totaling $1.7 trillion over 10 years. Imagine if the government took that money ($170 billion a year) to help pay for various aspects of the physical infrastructure (repairing or replacing aging bridges and water systems, providing better transportation systems, replacing crumbling school buildings), and social infrastructure (e.g., universal health care, adequate pensions, a living wage, free education through college, and subsidized day care).

Finally, we should increase tax revenues. Totaling federal, state, and local taxes equals 30 percent of the gross domestic product. This is the lowest rate of any industrialized nation. In comparison, the English pay 36 percent, Germans and Canadians pay 37 percent, the French pay 44 percent, and at the high end the Swedes pay 56 percent. In addition, we should enact a truly progressive income tax.

Is There Any Hope of Instituting a Social Agenda Based on Progressive Principles?

The final issue—and, of course, the crucial issue—is: Is there any hope of mounting a successful progressive program? At first, the negative side seems overwhelming. We have already mentioned several formidable obstacles: (1) the widely held belief in individualism as the core of American ideology, (2) the current anger by the Tea Partiers and others at the federal government that appears more beholden to Wall Street than to Main Street; this level of anger and angst is the highest in two decades, and (3) the two major parties and political candidates are financed by Big Money, and Big Money favors the status quo. Big Money opposes public investment in health care, education, and various social supports.

There are at least three other barriers to progressive change. The first is the massive multitrillion-dollar debt ($12 trillion in 2010, and growing an average of $3.87 billion each day; Connolly, Hirsh, and Kosova 2010), which is viewed by politicians of both parties as a giant weight on government that makes it difficult to fund existing programs, let alone institute new ones. The momentum is to cut programs. Adding to this impetus toward reduced government is the overall low tax rates, which limit revenues to the federal government.

Another major obstacle is the present weakness of the union movement in the United States. Each of the generous welfare states of Canada, Scandinavia, and Western Europe has a heavily unionized workforce. Unions use their collective power to work for pensions, universal health care, worker safety, a strong minimum wage, and other benefits to workers and their families. This condition is not present in the United States.

The final barrier to progressive change is that those who will benefit most from progressive social policies (the poor, the working poor, racial minorities, inhabitants of the inner cities, and the rural poor) are the least likely to vote, and they do not have the money to fund lobbyists and politicians sympathetic to their needs. So their speech (which the Supreme Court has defined as spending money to support political causes) is limited, whereas the speech of the advantaged is not. The disaffected do not vote because neither political party speaks to their needs. Is it because there is little difference between Republicans and Democrats, both of whom direct their attention to the White, affluent suburban voters?

The Tea Party movement, which is opposed to progressive reforms, steps into this vacuum to speak to the needs of the politically alienated. There is a question, though, as to whether the Tea Party movement is a passing fad, reflecting a transient political mood, or one with a lasting impact (Schmitt 2010).

Given these obstacles to progressive change, is there a possibility that the progressives might eventually prevail? We are in the midst of societal upheaval. The Great Recession has ravaged the middle class. Employment is difficult to obtain and keep. Wages are stagnant yet the big banks and corporations, bailed out by the government when they were on the brink of disaster, are reaping large benefits. This leads to two possible scenarios. One is that the Tea Party movement gains momentum and is successful in reducing government significantly by lowering taxes and by reducing government programs. This dooms progressive social policies at least in the near term. But there is an alternative scenario.

Looking at lessons from history (Dionne 1996; Weisberg 1996), more than 100 years ago, the Progressive movement began as a reaction to unchecked capitalism, the robber barons, economic exploitation, and political corruption. Out of the Progressive era came an activist government that addressed problems of the workplace by instituting workplace safety regulations, prohibiting child labor, mandating the eight-hour workday, and providing disability compensation. The government broke up business monopolies, established a national parks system, and gave women the vote.

During the depths of the Great Depression, President Roosevelt and Congress passed sweeping social programs including Social Security, unemployment insurance, AFDC, and massive public building projects that provided jobs, wages, and physical infrastructure (bridges, dams, roads, parks, schools, gymnasiums, libraries, rural electrification, and water conservation).

Following World War II and lasting for about three decades, society became more inclusive with the racial integration of the armed forces, sports, and workplaces. Despite significant opposition, civil rights protections, including the right of all citizens to vote, were mandated by the law. After World War II, Congress opened up college education to all social classes by passing the GI Bill, which made a college education a reality for millions of returning veterans of all class and racial backgrounds.

In short, there are times in U.S. history when progressive steps were taken. Former secretary of labor Robert Reich summarized,

> *Nations are not passive victims of economic forces. Citizens can, if they so choose, assert their mutual obligations to extend beyond their economic usefulness to one another and act accordingly. Throughout our history the United States has periodically asserted the public's interest when market outcomes threatened social peace—curbing the power of great trusts, establishing pure food and drug laws,*

implementing a progressive federal income tax, imposing a forty-hour workweek, barring child labor, creating a system of social security, expanding public schooling and access to higher education, extending health care to the elderly and so forth. We effected part of this explicitly through laws, regulations, and court rulings, and partly through social norms and expectations about how we wanted our people to live and work productively together. In short, this nation developed and refined a strong social compact that gave force to the simple proposition that prosperity could include almost everyone. The puzzle is why we seem to have stopped. (Reich 1998:12)

The choices are there for legislators and the public. Small government or big government. A society of individuals on their own or a society working for the common good. In our view, if we take the individualistic view, then there will be a further unraveling of social solidarity, and our society will be less secure. And, a hopeful note, that may lead to a search for new answers—perhaps a new progressive era, just as it did 110 years ago.

Two necessary conditions for progressive social policies to prevail are a strong union movement and a class-based labor party or Social Democratic party. Although the labor movement has been moribund for two decades or so in the United States, there is, under the right conditions, the resurgence of labor with a shift toward more organizing and more ambitious and aggressive approaches against hostile employers and unfriendly laws. Should that occur, then there is hope not only for a labor renaissance but also for an organized push for progressive social policies.

A new progressive era will work only if a class-based party emerges. In particular, progressive leaders need to articulate a vision, a sense of direction, that builds a sense of community. Our future, we must recognize, depends on the welfare of all in the community in which we live and the society of which we are a part, not just on our own accumulated wealth.

The alternative vision that we have proposed may seem very radical. We do not think so. Most of the suggestions are found in one form or another in each of the Western social democracies except the United States. Can we learn from them? Should we learn from them? Can we afford massive policy changes? Can we afford not to make them?

HUMAN AGENCY: SOCIAL CHANGE FROM THE BOTTOM UP

Sociologists know that social problems emanate from social structure. That is why the progressive agenda, which aims at changing social structure, makes sense. The progressive agenda that we propose is aimed at societal changes, at macrosolutions. But what can we do as individuals in families, at work, in our churches, and in our communities, to bring about changes to solve social problems? What can we do to make a difference—to be agents of social change?

We begin with the premise, already stated, that individuals can make a difference through collective action. Individuals need to join with others who share their goals to have any hope of success. Sociologists Kenneth Kammeyer, George Ritzer, and Norman Yetman show the importance of collective actions for individuals to be effective agents of change:

As individuals, we are limited in our ability to make the societal changes we would like. There are massive social forces that make change difficult; these forces include the government, large and powerful organizations, and the prevailing values, norms, and attitudes. As individuals protesting to officials, we have minimal power. As individuals standing against the tide of public opinion, we have little hope of exerting influence. As individuals confronting a corporate structure, we are doomed to frustration and failure. But if we combine with others who share our convictions, organize ourselves, and map out a course of actions, we may be able to bring about numerous and significant changes in the social order. Through participation in a social movement, we can break through the social constraints that overwhelm us as individuals. (Kammeyer, Ritzer, and Yetman 1997:632–633)

Individuals Protesting and Organizing for Change

Throughout U.S. history, individuals have organized to change elements of society that they deemed unethical, unjust, racist, sexist, or oppressive. Harlan Cleveland puts it this way:

> *The tidal waves of social change of our lifetimes—environmental sensitivity, civil rights for all races, the enhanced status of women, recognition of the rights of consumers and small investors—were not generated by the established leaders in government, business, labor, religion, or higher education. They boiled up from people (and new leaders) who had not previously been heard from. (Cleveland 1992:16)*

Let us examine briefly two representative movements.

- **Racial Minorities.** Although collective efforts by African Americans for freedom and justice have occurred throughout their history in the United States, a major shift to bring justice to Blacks occurred in 1955. Before then, racial segregation in the South was as entrenched as was apartheid in South Africa. But in 1955 an African American woman, Rosa Parks, was jailed in Montgomery, Alabama, for not giving her seat on a bus to a White man, as was the custom fortified by the law. As a result of this courageous act, the Black community

Under the leadership of Martin Luther King, Jr., African Americans and other civil rights supporters mobilized to desegregate public facilities in the South.

in Montgomery mobilized to bring down the segregated public busing system (Eitzen and Stewart 2007:1–3). A leader emerged, a young local minister, Martin Luther King, Jr., who inspired Blacks to use nonviolent resistance to overthrow their oppressors and their unfair laws and practices. The Blacks boycotted the transportation system for 381 days, walking to work or using a car-pooling network. The city eventually abolished segregation in public transportation—a clear case of agency, as the powerless successfully changed an unfair system through their collective power.

Under the leadership of Reverend King, African Americans and White sympathizers mobilized to desegregate other public facilities in the South. There were sit-ins in restaurants, waiting rooms, and churches, and wade-ins at public beaches. Economic boycotts were organized. Court cases were initiated. Brave students became the first African Americans to attend integrated schools. And there were protest marches to publicize grievances. These efforts were violently resisted by Whites. King and others were jailed. Demonstrators were abused verbally and physically. There were lynchings, bombings, drive-by shootings, and other forms of intimidation to keep Blacks "in their place," especially to keep them from registering to vote. The Blacks persisted, however. Their cause was to change the laws and the political establishment that kept them second class. In the words of the late historian Howard Zinn:

> *So black people in the South decided they had to do something by themselves. They boycotted and sat in and picketed and demonstrated, and were beaten and jailed, and some were killed, but their cries for freedom were soon heard all over the nation and around the world, and the President and Congress finally did what they had previously failed to do—enforce the 14th and 15th Amendments to the Constitution. Many people had said: The South will never change. But it did change. It changed because ordinary people organized and took risks and challenged the system and would not give up. That's when democracy came alive. (Zinn 2005: para. 7)*

King's movement was bent on tearing down the segregationist norms and practices and substituting new ones. To a limited but nonetheless significant extent, the movement succeeded. Schools were desegregated with the help of federal troops. The 1964 Civil Rights Bill banned discrimination in public facilities, education, employment, and any organization receiving government funds. The 1965 Voting Rights Act prohibited the use of literacy and similar tests to screen voting applicants and allowed federal examiners to monitor elections.

But although civil rights battles have been won, the war for racial equality is still being fought in legislatures, in the courts, in school districts, in the workplace, and in neighborhoods. These are the facts from 2008 of the ongoing structural legacy of racism (Rivera et al., 2009; DeNavas-Walt, Proctor, and Smith 2009):

- Black households earned $34,218 a year, compared to $52,312 for White households.
- The Black poverty rate was 24.7 percent, compared to 11.2 percent for Whites.
  - Among young Black males aged 16–19, the unemployment rate was 32.8 percent, while their White counterparts were at 18.3 percent.
  - On *average*, people of color have 18 cents for every dollar of White wealth.
- Life expectancy for Black men was 6 years shorter than for White men.

So the war for racial equality is far from over. Individuals and groups need to continue to take agency seriously, working to change institutional racism in all its forms.

- **Workers.** Early in the nineteenth century, U.S. workers were nonunionized. As a result, work conditions were often unsafe, work was poorly paid, and child labor was commonplace. Eventually, despite the aggressive opposition of business owners, workers formed unions. With unionization, workers were no longer alone in their bargaining with management. Collectively, workers had power to demand and receive higher wages and benefits and safer working conditions or they would strike or boycott the products of the company. Their unions were engaged politically, lobbying for social legislation and working for the election of candidates sympathetic to the cause of workers. Unquestionably, unions have improved the conditions for U.S. workers.

By the 1990s, unions had lost much of their power. Union membership has declined significantly. The result has been a worsening of conditions for workers—declining wages and benefits, increasing job insecurity, and the tendency of management to hire temporary workers. In this climate, the Teamsters in 1997 conducted a strike against United Parcel Service (UPS, a company that at the time employed 340,000 workers worldwide and delivered 80 percent of all packages shipped by ground in the United States; the following is from Brecher 1998). Although better working conditions and wages were part of the Teamsters' demands, the major point of contention was that UPS hired too many part-time workers who were paid much less than full-time workers. The Teamsters wanted UPS to make many of the part-timers into full-time positions. Because this issue was an important one for labor, the AFL-CIO supported the Teamsters with loans of $10 million a week and promoted solidarity rallies in a number of cities. Faced with this opposition and the loss of $30 million a day in profits because of the strike, UPS accepted a settlement that created 10,000 new full-time jobs, promoted a minimum of 10,000 part-timers to full-time status, and granted full-timers a raise of 15 percent over 5 years and part-timers a raise of 37 percent, to reduce the wage differential. "It's a big win not only for the union but for labor," said Robert Ridley, a 44-year-old UPS driver in Austin, Texas. "This was labor against corporate America" (Brecher 1998:27). And labor, composed of individual working women and men with power gained collectively, won.

In sum, society's structural arrangements are not inevitable. Individuals converging across lines of race, ethnicity, gender, and sexual orientation can work at the grassroots level organizing opposition, educating the public, demonstrating to promote a cause, electing allied candidates, using the courts, or employing other tactics to transform society. Human beings are the agents of change if they choose to be. The choice is ours.

Frances Fox Piven, the eminent social scientist, in writing about the need for social change to solve our current social problems, said,

> *No one has ever successfully predicted the movements when ordinary people find their footing, discover new capacities for solidarity and power and new visions of the possible. Still, the development of American democracy depended on the perennial emergence of popular revolt in the past, and it does once again. (Piven 1996:67)*

CHAPTER REVIEW

1. The politicoeconomic system of a society, from which social problems emanate, is the result of historical events and conscious choices by political elites.
2. Social policy is about the way society should be designed—setting goals and determining the means to achieve them. If societies are designed, and some of the arrangements result in social problems, they can be changed to reduce or eliminate those problems.
3. The sociological paradox involves two opposing forces affecting human behavior. On the one hand, social forces constrain what we do. But although societies and their structures are powerful, people are not totally controlled. They shape, resist, challenge, and sometimes change the social organizations and social institutions that impinge on them. These actions constitute human agency.
4. Sociologists, as the experts on social life, have answers to many social problems based on empirical research, but society's governmental and corporate leaders rarely seek their advice. Sociologists tend to be rejected by those in power because their perspective is subversive, and they challenge the core of society's dominant ideology.
5. We propose five progressive principles to guide public policy: (a) policies and behaviors that enhance our moral obligation to others; (b) government provision of benefits to people who cannot provide for themselves; (c) a special commitment to all children to ensure health, safety, preparation for school, and equal funding for schools; (d) a redistribution of jobs and resources to economically troubled rural and urban locations; and (e) addressing many problems with federal money, standards, and administration.
6. A progressive agenda is needed because (a) it would reverse the current trend toward greater inequality; (b) it would make society more secure; and (c) it would promote social justice.
7. A progressive agenda, although expensive, could be financed by reducing the military budget, eliminating corporate welfare and subsidies to the wealthy, using the budget surplus for social programs, and increasing tax revenues.
8. Despite many obstacles, there are several possibilities for progressive change. The conservatives who control government could go too far with their market-based strategies, thereby alienating many who would resist. Historically, there have been progressive periods (the progressive era of the 1890s, the Great Depression, the 30 years following World War II) when social programs were instituted, corporate power thwarted, and inclusive policies implemented.
9. Social change can occur from the bottom up—from individuals acting collectively with a plan and mobilizing for action. Throughout U.S. history, individuals sharing a vision have organized to change elements of society. Case studies of successful changes were presented using racial minorities and workers.

KEY TERMS

Deterministic view. Belief that some variable controls social life.

Human agency. Individuals acting alone or with others shape, resist, challenge, and sometimes change the social organizations and the social institutions that impinge on them.

Plutocracy. Government in which the wealthy class rules.

Gerrymander. The practice by the political party in power to carve up voting districts in a manner that keeps them in power.

Devolution. Process of shifting federal programs to the states.

■ SUCCEED WITH PEARSON mysoclab www.mysoclab.com

Experience, Discover, Observe, Evaluate

MySocLab is designed just for you. Each chapter features a pre-test and post-test to help you learn and review key concepts and terms.

Experience sociology in action with dynamic visual activities, videos, and readings to enhance your learning experience. Complete the following activities at www.mysoclab.com.

Social Explorer is an interactive application that allows you to explore Census data through interactive maps.

- Explore the Social Explorer Map: *Slavery and Early Racial Segregation*

The Core Concepts in Sociology video clips offer a real-world perspective on sociological concepts.

- Watch *Grievances, Anger, and Hope*

MySocLibrary includes primary source readings from classic and contemporary sociologists.

- Read Etzioni, *Community Building: Steps Toward a Good Society;* Johnson, Haenfler, & Jones, *Creating a More Just and Sustainable World;* Shehzad, *The Living Wage Movement and the Economics of Morality: Frames, Ideology and the Discursive Field*

Bibliography

All highlighted entries are new to the twelfth edition.

Abbott, Greg. 2009. "Colonias Prevention." (October 8). Online: http://www.oag.state.tx.us/consumer/border/colonias.shtml.

Acker, Joan. 1990. "Hierarchies, Jobs, Bodies: A Theory of Gendered Organizations." *Gender and Society* 4:139–158.

Acker, Joan. 1992. "Gendered Institutions: From Sex Roles to Gendered Institutions." *Contemporary Sociology* 21 (September):565–568.

Ackerman, Spencer. 2006. "Driving While Muslim." Nation (October 9): Online. Available: www.the Nation.com/doc/20061009/ackerman.

Adamson, Rebecca. 2009. "Foreword to Dedrick Muhammad," *Challenges to Native American Advancement*. New York: Institute for Policy Studies.

Adamuti–Trache, Maria, and Lesley Andres. 2008. "Embarking on and Persisting in Scientific Fields of Study: Cultural Capital, Gender, and Curriculum along the Science Pipeline." *International Journal of Science Education* 30(12): 1557–1584.

Adeola, Francis O. 2005. "Racial and Class Divergence in Public Attitudes and Perceptions about Poverty in U.S.A.: An Empirical Study." *Race, Gender, and Class* 12(2):53–80.

Ahlburg, Dennis A., and Carol J. De Vita. 1992. "New Realities of the American Family." *Population Bulletin* 47 (August): entire issue.

Alan Guttmacher Institute. 1999. "Teen Sex and Pregnancy: Facts in Brief." Online. Available: http://www.agi–usa.org/pubs/fb_teen_sex.html.

Albanese, Jay S. 2005. *Criminal Justice*, 3rd ed. Boston: Allyn & Bacon.

Albelda, Randy. 1992. "Whose Values, Which Families?" *Dollars & Sense*, No. 182 (December):6–9.

Albelda, Randy, and Chris Tilly. 1997. *Glass Ceilings and Bottomless Pits: Women's Work, Women's Poverty*. Boston: South End Press.

Alderman, Leslie. 2009. "Uptick in Vasectomies Seen as Sign of Recession." New York Times (April 11). Online: http://www.nytimes.com/2009/04/11/health/11patient.html.

Allegretto, Sylvia. 2006. "Economic Snapshots." Economic Policy Institute (August 23). Online: http://www.epi.org/content.cfm/wefeatures_snapshots_20060823.

Allen, Mike. 2002. "As the Victims Would Have Wanted It." *Washington Post National Weekly Edition* (July 14):31.

Allen, Walter R., and Angie Y. Chung. 2000. "Your Blues Ain't Like My Blues: Race, Ethnicity and Social Inequality in America." *Contemporary Sociology* 29 (November): 796–805.

Alliance Defense Fund. 2006. DOMA Watch. Online. Available: http://www.domawatch.org/amendments/amendmentsummary.html.

Alter, Jonathan. 2007. "The Other America: An Enduring Shame." In D. Stanley Eitzen and Janis E. Johnston (Eds.), *Inequality: Social Class and Its Consequences*. Boulder, CO: Paradigm Publishers, pp. 35–42.

Alter, Jonathan. 2010. "High–Court Hypocrisy." *Newsweek* (February):15.

Altman, Alex. 2009. "High Tech, High Touch, High Growth." *Time* (May 25):42.

Amato, Paul R. 2001. "The Consequences of Divorce for Adults and Children." In Robert M. Milardo (Ed.), *Understanding Families into the New Millennium: A Decade in Review*. Minneapolis: National Council on Family Relations, pp. 1269–1287.

Amato, Paul R., and Alan Booth. 1996. "A Prospective Study of Divorce and Parent–Child Relationships." *Journal of Marriage and the Family* 58 (May): 356–365.

Amato, Paul R., and Jacob Cheadle. 2005. "The Long Reach of Divorce: Tracking Marital Dissolution and Child Well-Being across Three Generations." *Journal of Marriage and Family* 67:191–206.

American Academy of Actuaries. 2007. "Women and Social Security." Washington, DC. (June).

American Association of University Women (AAUW). 1992. "How Schools Shortchange Girls." Executive Summary. AAUW Report. Washington, DC: American Association of University Women Educational Foundation.

American Association of University Women (AAUW). 1999. *Gender Gaps: Where Schools Still Fail Our Children*. New York: Marlowe & Company.

American Civil Liberties Union (ACLU). 2002. "ACLU Sues on Behalf of CA 8th Grader Barred From Gym Class Because of Sexual Orientation." (December 17). Online: Available: http://www.aclu.org/lgbt/youth/12027prs20021217.html.

American Civil Liberties Union (ACLU). 2003. "ACLU Warns Arkansas School to Stop Persecuting Gay Student." (March 13). Online: Available: http://www.aclu.org/lgbt/youth/12051prs20030313.html.

American Civil Liberties Union (ACLU). 2007. "Rights of Lesbian and Gay Parents after Heterosexual Divorce." Online: Available: http://www.aclu.org/getequal/par/divorce.html.

American Civil Liberties Union (ACLU). 2009. "The Persistence of Racial and Ethnic Profiling in the United States: A Follow- Up Report to the U.N. Committee on the Elimination of Racial Discrimination." Available online: http://www.aclu.org/files/pdfs/humanrights/cerd_final report.pdf#page=13.

American Council on Education. 2000. "ACE Study Shows Gains in Number of Women College Presidents, Smaller Gains for Minority CEOs." Available online: http://www.acent.edu/news/pres–release.

American Project on Government Oversight. 2009. "POGO Updates Contractor Misconduct Database." (April 22). Online: http://www.contractormisconduct.org.

American Psychiatric Association. 2007. Gay, Lesbian, and Bisexual Issues. Online: Available: http://healthyminds.org/glbissues.cfm.

American Society for Aesthetic Plastic Surgery. 2010. Available online: http://www.surgery. org.

American Sociological Association. 2003. The Importance of Collecting Data and Doing Scientific Research on Race. Washington, DC: American Sociological Association.

Ames, Mark. 2006. "For U.S. Workers, Vacation Is Vanishing." AlterNet (September 8). Online: http://www.AlterNet.org/story 141404/.

Amott, Teresa. 1993. *Caught in the Crisis: Women and the U.S. Economy Today.* New York: Monthly Review Press.

Andersen, Margaret L. 2009. *Thinking about Women*, 8th ed. Boston: Allyn & Bacon.

Andersen, Margaret L., and Howard F. Taylor. 2000. *Sociology: Understanding a Diverse Society*. Belmont, CA: Wadsworth.

Angier, Natalie. 1993. "Bias against Gay People: Hatred of a Special Kind." *New York Times* (December 26):4E.

Angier, Natalie. 2000. "Scientists: DNA Shows Humans Are All One Race." *Denver Post* (August 22):2A, 5A.

Annan, Kofi A. 2006. "How the World Can Conquer AIDS." *USA Today* (November 29): 13A.

Arellano, Kristi. 2000. "Minority Group Finds Disparities in Mortgage Lending." *Denver Post* (September 29):2C.

Arendell, Terry. 1990. "Divorce: A Woman's Issue." In Christopher Carlson (Ed.), *Perspectives on the Family: History, Class, and Feminism*. Belmont, CA: Wadsworth, pp. 460–478.

Arizona Daily Star. 2004. "Carmona Cites Smoking as a Culprit in 26 Diseases." (May 28).

Armour, Stephanie. 2008. "Renters Can't Escape Housing Crisis." *USA Today* (April 2): 1B–2B.

Armour, Stephanie. 2004. "Gay Marriage Debate Moves into Workplace." *USA Today* (April 14): B1.

Armour, Stephanie. 2009. "2008 Foreclosure Filings Set Record." *USA Today* (January 15). Available online: http://www.usatoday.com/money/economy/housing/2009-01-14-foreclosure-record-filings_N.htm.

Armour, Stephanie. 2010. "Foreclosure Filings Increase in December after Months of Decline." *USA Today* (January 4):3b.

Associated Press. 1999. "Priest, Nun Told to End Ministry to Gays." (July 14).

Associated Press. 2001. "Report: Blacks Searched More Often." (June 1).

Associated Press. 2004a. "Ads for Flavored Smokes Decried as Minority-Targeted." (August 19).

Associated Press. 2004b. "Data: Renting Tough on Minimum Wage." (December 21).

Associated Press. 2005a. "Gay-Clergy Measure Defeated at Gathering of U.S. Lutherans." (August 13).

Associated Press. 2005b. "Study: Gays' Response to Sex Chemical Differs." (May 10).

Associated Press. 2006b. "Catholic Bishops' Document Calls for Reaching Out to Gays." (October 29).

Associated Press. 2007a. "Saudi King's Remarks Prompt U.S. Retort." (March 30).

Associated Press. 2007b. "Nation's Homeless Numbered 754,000 in '05, HUD Reports." (February 28).

Associated Press. 2009. "Therapy to Turn Gays Straight is Repudiated." (August 6).

Associated Press, 2010. " 'Tea Party' Movement Faces Uncertain Future." (February 5).

Avert. 2009. "Worldwide HIV and AIDS Statistics." (September 2). Online: http://www.avert.org/worldstats.htm.

Baca Zinn, Maxine, and Bonnie Thornton Dill. 1994. "Difference and Domination." In Maxine Baca Zinn and Bonnie Thornton Dill (Eds.), *Women of Color in U.S. Society*. Philadelphia: Temple University Press, pp. 3–12.

Baca Zinn, Maxine, and Bonnie Thornton Dill. 1996. "Theorizing Difference from Multicultural Feminism." *Feminist Studies* 22 (Summer):1–11.

Baca Zinn, Maxine, and D. Stanley Eitzen. 1999. *Diversity in Families*, 5th ed. New York: Longman.

Baca Zinn, Maxine, D. Stanley Eitzen, and Barbara Wells, 2011. *Diversity in Families*, 9th ed. Boston: Allyn and Bacon.

Baca Zinn, Maxine, Pierrette Hondagneu-Sotelo, and Michael A. Messner. 2005. *Gender through the Prism of Difference*, 3rd ed. New York: Oxford University Press.

Bacevich, Andrew J. 2006. "The Costs of War." *Washington Post National Weekly Edition* (July 17):21.

Bach, P. B. 2004. "Primary Care Physicians Who Treat Blacks and Whites." *New England Journal of Medicine* 351, no. 6: 515–584.

Bahree, Migha. 2008. "Child Labor." *Forbes* (February 25):73–79.

Baicker, K. 2004. "Who You Are and Where You Live: How Race and Geography Affect the Treatment of Medicare Beneficiaries." *Health Affairs* 47 (October):48–59.

Bajaj, Vikas. 2009. "Household Wealth Falls by Trillions." New York Times (March 13). Online: http://www.nytimes.com/2009/03/13/ bbusiness/economy/13wealth.html.

Baker, Mike. 2009. "Bankruptcies Surge in Spite of Law." Associated Press (April 19).

Baldor, Lolita. 2006. "Pentagon Alters Homosexuality Guidelines." *Washington Post* (November 16). Online. Available: http://www.washingtonpost.com/wp-dyn/content/article/2006/11/16/AR2006111601088.html.

Bales, Kevin. 1999. *Disposable People: New Slavery in the Global Economy*. Berkeley: University of California Press.

Bales, Kevin. 2000. *New Slavery: A Reference Book*. Santa Barbara, CA: ABC-CLIO.

Balswick, Jack, with James Lincoln Collier. 1976. "Why Husbands Can't Say 'I Love You.'" In Deborah S. David and Robert Brannon (Eds.), *The Forty-Nine Percent Majority*. Reading, MA: Addison-Wesley, pp. 58–59.

Balswick, Jack, and Charles Peck. 1971. "The Inexpressive Male: A Tragedy of American Society." *Family Coordinator* 20:363–368.

Bamshad, Michael J., and Steve E. Olson. 2003. "Does Race Exist?" *Scientific American* (December):78–85.

Bandow, Doug. 2010. "Military Spending—for What?" The Japan Times (January 19). Online: http://search.japanTimess.co.jp/cgi-bin/en201000119db.html.

Banfield, Edward C. 1977. *The Unheavenly City Revisited*. Boston: Little, Brown.

Barlett, Donald L., and James B. Steele. 2005. "The Broken Promise." *Time* (October 31): 33–38.

Barlow, Maude. 2008. "Where Has All the Water Gone?" *The American Prospect* (June).

Barna, George. 2001. "Born Again Adults Remain Firm in Opposition to Abortion and Gay Marriage." *The Barna Update*. (July 23). Online: Available: http://www.barna.org.

Barnes, Colin, and Geof Mercer. 2003. *Disability*. Malden, MA: Blackwell.

Barnes, Colin, Geof Mercer, and Tom Shakespeare. 1999. *Exploring Disability: A Sociological Introduction*. Malden, MA: Blackwell.

Barnett, Rosalind, and Caryl Rivers. 2004. *Same Difference*. New York: Basic Books.

Barry, Patricia. 2008. "Generic Drug Prices Go Down Sharply." AARP Bulletin (May 15). Online: http://www.bulletin.aarp.org/yourhealth9Medications) articles/aarp_report_generic_ drugs.

Barsamian, David. 1997. "Howard Zinn." *The Progressive* 61 (July):37–40.

Barstow, David. 2010 "Tea Party Movement Lights Fuse for Rebellion on Right." *New York Times* (February 16). Online: http://www.nytimes.com/2010/02/16/politics/16teaparty.html?

Bartlett, D. L., and J. B. Steele. 2000. "How the Little Guy Gets Crunched." *Time* (February7):40–43.

Barton, Len. 1996. "Sociology and Disability: Some Emerging Issues." In Len Barton (Ed.), *Disability and Society: Emerging Issues and Insights*. London: Longman, pp. 3–17.

Basow, Susan. 1996. "Gender Stereotypes and Roles." In Karen E. Rosenblum and Toni-Michelle Travis (Eds.), *The Meaning of Difference*. New York: McGraw-Hill, pp. 81–96.

Bauer, Karlin S. 2000. "Promoting Gender Equality in Schools." *Contemporary Education* 71 (2):22–25.

Bauerlein, Monika, and Clara Jeffery. 2008. "Editor's Note." *Mother Jones* 33, no. 3 (May/June):4.

Bazell, Robert. 2006. "Brain Injuries Common for Iraq War Vets." MSNBC.com (April 26): Online: http://www.msnbc.msn.com/id/12482733/.

Bean, Frank D., Jennifer Lee, Jeanne Batalova, and Mark Leach. 2004. *Immigration and Fading Color Lines in America*. New York: Russell Sage Foundation and Population Reference Bureau.

Beck, Joan. 1995. "Preschool Can Help Close the Poverty Gap." *Denver Post* (January 19):7B.

Beck, Melinda. 1990. "The Goal: A Nurse in Each Nursing Home." *Newsweek* (October 8): 77–78.

Becker, Howard S. 1967. "Whose Side Are We On?" *Social Problems* 14 (Winter):239–247.

Begley, Sharon. 2009. "Attack! The Truth about Obamacare." *Newsweek* (August 24): 40–43.

Begum, Nasa. 1994. "Mirror, Mirror on the Wall." In Nasa Begum, M. Hill, and A. Stevens (Eds.), *Reflections: Views of Black Disabled People on Their Lives and Community Care*. Washington, DC: Central Council for Education and Training in Social Work.

Beinart, Peter. 2010. "Why Washington's Tied Up in Knots." *Time* (March 1):20–24.

Beirne, Piers, and James Messerschmidt. 1995. *Criminology*, 2nd ed. Orlando, FL: Harcourt Brace.

Belkin, Douglas. 2006. "The Defense Dollars Flow." *Boston Globe* (November 19). Online: http://www.boston.com/news/local/articles/2006/11/19/the_defense_dollars_flow/.

Belluck, Pam. 2001. "Nebraska Is Said to Use Death Penalty Unequally." *New York Times* (August 2). Online: http://www.nytimes.com/2001/08/02National/02NEBR.html/.

Belsie, Lourent. 2009. "Why Do Firms Lobby?" *Christian Science Monitor* (April 10). Online: www.law.KU-edu/media/inthenews/2009/2009/April/10/lobbying.shtml.

Belsky, Jay. 1990. "Infant Day Care, Child Development, and Family Policy." *Society* (July/August):10–12.

Bender, William, and Margaret Smith. 1997. "Population, Food, and Nutrition." *Population Bulletin* 51 (February): entire issue.

Benedetto, Richard. 2001. "President Asks Mayors to Back Faith-Based Plan." *USA Today* (June 26):11A.

Bengston, V. L., C. Rosenthal, and L. Burton. 1990. "Families and Aging: Diversity and Heterogeneity." In R. H. Binstock and L. K. George (Eds.), *Handbook of Aging and Social Sciences*, 3rd ed. San Diego, CA: Academic Press, pp. 263–287.

Benjamin, Rich. 2009. "Pockets of White America Are in the Throes of an Existential Crisis." *AlterNet* (December 19). Online: http://www.AlterNet.orgg/module/printversion/144672.

Benjamin, Rich. 2010. "Texas Suicide Flyer Had Real Populist Grievances." *AlterNet* (February 20). Online: http://www.AlterNet.org/rights/145745.

Bennett, Amanda. 2010. "Lessons of a $618,616 Death." *Business Week* (March 15):32–40.

Benokraitis, Nijole, and Joe R. Feagin. 1995. *Modern Sexism*, 2nd ed. Upper Saddle River, NJ: Prentice Hall.

Benson, Clea. 2009. "Uncreative Destruction." *Congressional Quarterly* (October 26):2444–2450.

Berger, Peter. 1963. *Invitation to Sociology: A Humanistic Perspective.* Garden City, NY: Doubleday Anchor Books.

Bergman, Jake, and Julia Reynolds. 2002. "The Guns of Opa-Locka: How U.S. Dealers Arm the World." *Nation* (December 2):19–22.

Berlet, Chip. 2010. "Taking Tea Partiers Seriously." *The Progressive* 74 (February): 24–27.

Bernard, Tara Siegel, and Ron Lieber. 2009. "The High Price of Being a Gay Couple." The New York Times (October 3). Available online: http://www.nytimes.com/2009/10/03/your-money/03money.html.

Bernstein, Aaron. 2004. "Women's Pay: Why the Gap Remains a Chasm." *Business Week* (June 14):58–59.

Berube, Michael. 1998. "Pressing the Claim." In S. Linton (Ed.), *Claiming Disability: Knowledge and Identity*. New York: New York University Press, pp. viii–xi.

Bianchi, Suzanne. 1995. "Changing Economic Roles of Women and Men." In Reynolds Farley (Ed.), *State of the Union: America in the 1990s*, Vol. 1. New York: Russell Sage Foundation, pp. 107–154.

Bianchi, Suzanne M., and Lynn M. Casper. 2000. "American Families." *Population Bulletin* 55 (December): entire issue.

Bilmes, Linda, and Joseph Stiglitz. 2009. "The $10 Trillion Hangover." *Harper's* 318 (January):31–35.

Birnbaum, Michael. 2009. "Money-Hungry Schools Getting Down to Business." Commercial Alert. org (March 13). Available online: http://www.commercialalert.org/news/archive/2009/03/money-hungry-schools-getting-down-to-business.

Blauner, Robert. 1964. *Alienation and Freedom.* Chicago: University of Chicago Press.

Blauner, Robert. 2001. *Still the Big News: Racial Oppression in America.* Philadelphia: Temple University Press.

Block, Fred, Anna Korteweg, Kerry Woodward, Zach Schiller, and Imrul Mazid. 2006. "The Compassion Gap in American Poverty Policy." *Contexts* 5(2):14–20.

Block, Pamela, Fabricio Balcazar, and Christopher Keys. 2001. "From Pathology to Power: Rethinking Race, Poverty, and Disability." *Journal of Disability Policy Studies* 12 (Summer): 18–27, 39.

Block, Sandra. 2006. "Boomer Inheritances Shrink as Parents Live Longer, Health Costs Rise." *USA Today* (June 27):3B.

Bloom, Amy. 2000. "Generation Rx." *New York Times* (March 12). Online. Available: http://www.nytimes.com.library/library/magazine/home/2000/03/12 mag-kidsdrugs.html.

Blow, Charles M. 2009. "The Enemies Within." *New York Times* (April 18). Online: http://www. nytimes.com/2009/04/18/opinion/18blow. html?

Blumberg, Paul M., and P. W. Paul. 1975. "Continuities and Discontinuities in Upper-Class Marriage." *Journal of Marriage and the Family* 37 (February):63–78.

Blume, Howard. 2010. "Charter Schools' Growth Promoting Segregation, Studies Say." *Los Angeles Times* (February 5). Available online: http://latimes.com/news/local/la-me-charters5-2010feb05,0, 3300930.story.

Bobo, Lawrence D. 2009. "The Color Line, The Dilemma, and the Dream." In *Race and Ethnicity in Society*, Elizabeth Higginbotham and Margaret L. Anderson (eds.). Belmont, CA: Wadsworth Cengage Learning.

Bogdanich, Walt, and Eric Koli. 2003. "2 Paths of Bayer Drug in 80's: Riskier Type Went Overseas." *New York Times* (May 22). Online: http://www.nytimes.com/2003/05/22/business/22BLOO.html.

Bok, Derek. 1993. *The Cost of Talent: How Executives and Professionals Are Paid and How It Affects America*. New York: Free Press.

Bonacich, Edna. 1992. "Inequality in America: The Failure of the American System for People of Color." In Margaret L. Andersen and Patricia Hill Collins (Eds.), *Race, Class, and Gender*. Belmont, CA: Wadsworth, pp. 96–109.

Bonilla-Silva, Eduardo. 2009. "Racism Without Racists." In *The Matrix Reader,* Aby Ferber, Andrea O'Reilly Herrera, Christine M. Jimenez, and Dena R. Samuels (eds.). New York: McGraw-Hill.

Bonilla-Silva, Eduardo. 2003. *Racism without Racists.* Lanham, MA: Rowman & Littlefield.

Booher-Jennings, Jennifer. 2008. "Learning to Label: Socialization, Gender, and the Hidden Curriculum of High-Stakes Testing." *British Journal of Society and Education* 29, No. 2 (March):149–160.

Borosage, Robert L. 2001. "Forked-Tongue Budget." *Nation* (April 30):4–5.

Borosage, Robert L. 2003. "Sacrifice Is for Suckers." *Nation* (April 28):4–5.

Borosage, Robert L. 2010. "Common Sense on Budgets." *Progressive Populist* (March 1):12.

Bosman, Julie (2009). "Newly Poor Swell Lines at Food Banks." New York Times (February 20). Online: http://www.nytimes.com/2009.92/20/nyregion/20food.html.

Boushey, Heather. 2007. "Values Begin at Home, But Who's Home?" *American Prospect* 18 (March):A2–A4.

Bowe, John. 2007. *Nobodies: Modern American Slave Labor and the Dark Side of the New Global Economy*. New York: Random House.

Boyle, D. Ellen, Nancy L. Marshall, and Wendy W. Robeson. 2003. "Gender at Play: Fourth-Grade Girls and Boys on the Playground." *The American Behavioral Scientist* 46 (10): 1326–1345.

Boyles, Saivnn (2009). WebMD Health News (January 13). Online: www.americanheart.org/presenter.jhtml?identifier=3003499.

Bradbury, Danny. 2009. "EPA Proposes Permits for Large Polluters." *Business Green* (October 5). Available online: http://www.businessgreen. com/business-green/news/2250552/epaproposes-permits-large.

Braile, Robert. 2000. "Report: Earth's in Bad Shape." *Denver Post* (January 16):16A.

Brault, Matthew W. 2008. "Americans with Disabilities: 2005." *Current Population Reports* P70–117 (December).

Brecher, Jeremy. 1998. "American Labor on the Eve of the Millennium: The Implications of the UPS Strike." *Z Magazine* 11 (October):25–28.

Brecher, Jeremy, Tim Costello, and Brendan Smith. 2000. *Globalization from Below: The Power of Solidarity*. Cambridge, MA: South End Press.

Bremer, Jason, Carl Houb, Marlene Lea, Mark Mather, and Eric Zuehlke. 2009. "World Population Highlights." *Population Bulletin* 64 (September).

Brezosky, Lynn. 2002. "Shantytown Near Border Is Poorest Community." Associated Press (June 7).

Briggs, Xavier de Souza (Ed.). 2005. *The Geography of Opportunity: Race and Housing Choice in Metropolitan America*. Washington, DC: Brookings Institution Press.

Briscoe, D. 1999. "Faltering Pledge Leaves 275M Kids Uneducated." Associated Press (March 27).

Brisenden, S. 1986. "Independent Living and the Medical Model of Disability." *Disability, Handicap and Society* 1(2):173–178.

Broad, William J., and David E. Sanger. 2006. "Restraints Fray and Risks Grow as Nuclear Club Gains Members." *New York Times* (October 15). Online: http://www.nytimes.com/2006/10/15/world/asia/15nuke.html?ei=5094&en=2be24775f27.

Brodkin, Karen. 2009. "How Did Jews Become White Folks." In Elizabeth Higginbotham and Margaret L. Andersen (Eds.), *Race and Ethnicity in Society* . Belmont, CA: Wadsworth Cengage Learning.

Brooks, Rosa. 2006. "Washington's Abuser in Chief." *Los Angeles Times* (May 5). Online: http://www. latimes.com/news/opinion/commentary/la-oebrooksk5may05,0,4579950,print.

Brown, Jim. 2006. "Universities Continue Race-Based Admissions Despite Law." OneNewsNow.com. (December 22). Online: Available: http://www.onenewsnow.com/2006/12/universities_continue_racebase.php.

Brown, Lester R. 2001. "Eradicating Hunger: A Growing Challenge." In Lester R. Brown et al. (Eds.), *State of the World 2001*. New York: W. W. Norton, pp. 43–62.

Brown, Michael, and David Wellman. 2005. "Embedding the Color Line." *DuBois Review* 2:2:187–207.

Brown, Rachael. 2010. "The State of the Union Is . . ." *The Atlantic* (January/February):56–57.

Broyles, William, Jr. 2004. "A War for Us, Fought by Them." *New York Times* (May 4): A25.

Bruck, Connie. 2006. "Millions for Millions." *The New Yorker* (October 30):62–73.

Bullard, Robert D. 2000. *Dumping in Dixie: Race, Class, and Environmental Quality*, 3rd ed. Boulder, CO: Westview Press.

Bullard, Robert D. 2007. "Poverty and Pollution in the United States." In D. Stanley Eitzen and Janis E. Johnston (Eds.), *Inequality: Social Class and Its Consequences*. Boulder, CO: Paradigm Publishers, pp. 186–194.

Bullard, Robert D., and Beverly Wright. 2009. "The Color of Toxic Debris." *The American Prospect* 20 (March):A9–A11.

Bureau of Justice Statistics. 2003. U.S. Department of Justice. Online. Available: http://www.ojp.usdoj.gov/bjs/dcf/.

Bureau of Justice Statistics. 2007. "Drugs and Crime Facts: Enforcement." Online. Available: http://www.ojp.usdoj.gov/bjs/dcf/enforce.htm.

Bureau of Justice Statistics (BJS). 2010. Available online: http//bjs.ojp.usdoj.gov.

Bureau of Labor Statistics. 2006. "Women in the Labor Force: A Databook," Table 11. Online: http://www.bls.gov/cps/wlf-databook-2006.pdf.

Bureau of Labor Statistics. 2009a. "Employment Situation Summary." Online: http://www.bbls.gov/news.release/empsit.toc.htm.

Bureau of Labor Statistics. 2009b. "Women in the Labor Force: A Databook," Table 11. Online: www.bls.goov/cps/tables.htm.

Bureau of Labor Statistics. 2010. Available online: http://www.bls.gov.

Buriel, Raymond, and Terri De Ment. 1997. "Immigration and Sociocultural Change in Mexican, Chinese, and Vietnamese American Families." In Alan Booth, Ann C. Crouter, and Nancy Landale (Eds.), *Immigration and the Family*. Mahwah, NJ: Erlbaum, pp. 165–200.

Burt, Keith B., and Jacqueline Scott. 2002. "Parent and Adolescent Gender Role Attitudes in 1990s Great Britain." *Sex Roles* 46 (7/8):239–245.

Bush, George W. 2001a. "Address to a Joint Session of Congress and the American People." Office of the Press Secretary, The White House (September 20). Online. Available: http://www.whitehouse.gov/news/releases/2001/09/20010920-8.html.

Bush, George W. 2001b. "Address to the Nation." Office of the Press Secretary, The White House (September 11). Online. Available: http://www.whitehouse.gov/news/releases/2001/09/20010911-16.html.

Business Week. 2001. "The 21st Century Corporation." (August 28):278.

Business Week. 2002. "Crime Spree." (September 9):8.

Business Week. 2007. "Profile of Union Workers." (December 3):11.

Business Week. 2008. "Flying in for a Tune-Up Overseas." (April 21):26–27.

Butz, William P., and Barbara Boyle Torrey. 2006. "Some Frontiers in Social Science." *Science* 12 (June): 1898–1899.

Bybee, Roger. 2010. "Which Side Are You On?" *In These Times* 34 (March):11.

Byne, William M. 1999. "Why We Cannot Conclude That Sexual Orientation Is Primarily a Biological Phenomenon." *Journal of Homosexuality* 34(1):73–80.

Byrnes, Nanette, and Louis Lavelle. 2003. "The Corporate Tax Game." *Business Week* (March 31):79–87.

Byrnes, Nanette, and Christopher Palmeri. 2009. "Pensions Wade into Toxic Assets." *Business Week* (April 27):22.

Cain, Sean. 2004. "The Political Economy of Hunger." *Z Magazine* 17 (December):10–12.

Campbell, Frances A., Craig T. Ramey, E. P. Pungello, J. Sparling, and S. Miller-Johnson. 2002. "Early Childhood Education: Young Adult Outcomes from the Abecedarian Project." *Applied Developmental Science* (6):42–57.

Campenni, C. Estelle. 1999. "Gender Stereotyping of Children's Toys: A Comparison of Parents and Nonparents." *Sex Roles* 40 (1/2):121–138.

Carman, Diane. 2001. "Gay Teens Need Our Support." *Denver Post* (March 22):1B.

Carmichael, Mary 2008. "New Era, New Worry." *Newsweek* (December 15):60.

Carmichael, Mary 2010. "The Data Won't See You Now." *Newsweek* (March 8):46–47.

Carmichael, Stokely, and Charles V. Hamilton. 1967. *Black Power: The Politics of Liberation in America*. New York: Random House.

Carnahan, Kristin and Chiara Coletti. 2006. "SAT Scores Hold Steady for College-Bound Seniors." *College Board*. Online: Available: http://www.collegeboard.com/prod_downloads/about/news_info/cbsenior/yr2004/CBS2004Report.pdf.

Carney, Susan. 2007. "Advertising in Schools." Suite 101.com. (August 24). Available online: http://youthdevelopment.suite101.com/article.cfm/advertising_in_ schools.

Carter, Michael J., and Susan Boslego Carter. 1981. "Women Get a Ticket to Ride after the Gravy Train Has Left the Station." *Feminist Studies* 7:477–504.

Carville, James. 1996. *We're Right, They're Wrong: A Handbook for Spirited Progressives*. New York: Random House.

Cary, Nathaniel. 2010. "Andre Bauer Equates 'Stray Animals' to People on Government Aid." Greenville Online.com. (January 25). Available Online: http://greenvilleonline.com.

Catalano, Shannan. 2007. *Intimate Partner Violence in the United States*. U.S. Department of Justice, Bureau of Justice Statistics. Online: http://www.ojp.usdoj.gov/bjs/intimate/ipv.htm

Catholic.com. 2004. "Homosexuality." Available online: http://www.catholic.com/library/homosexuality.asp.

Cassidy, John. 1997. "The Melting Pot Myth." *The New Yorker* (July 14):40–43.

Cassidy, John. 2004. "Winners and Losers: The Truth about Free Trade." *The New Yorker* (August 2): 26–30.

Cassidy, John. 2010. "The Tea Party U.S.A.: It's Still the Economy Stupid!" *The New Yorker* (February 19). Online: http://www.commondreams.org/print/52997.

Cauchon, Dennis. 2009. "Women Gain in Historic Job Shift." *USA Today* (September 9):1A.

Cawthorne, Alexandra, and Stephanie Gross. 2008. "Equal Benefits for Women." Center for American Progress (December 9). Online: http://www.americanprogress.org/issues/2008/12/equal_benefits.html.

Center for American Women and Politics. 2009. "Women in Elective Office 2009." Online: http://www.cawp.rutgers.edu/fastfacts/index.php.

Center on Social Welfare and Law. 1996. "Welfare Myths: Fact or Fiction?" Washington, DC: Author.

Centers for Disease Control, National Center for Health Statistics. 2004. *Health, United States, 2004*. Online. Available: http://www.cdc.gov/nchs/fastats/drugs.htm.

Chafel, Judith A. 1997. "Societal Images of Poverty." *Youth and Society* 28 (June):432–463.

Chafetz, Janet Saltzman. 1997. "Feminist Theory and Sociology: Underutilized Contributions for Mainstream Theory." *Annual Review of Sociology* 23:97–120.

Chalk, Rosemary, Alison Gibbons, and Harriet J. Scarupa. 2002. "The Multiple Dimensions of Child Abuse and Neglect." Child Trends Research Brief. Online: http://www.child trends. org/files/ChildAbuseRB.pdf.

Chapin, Laura. 2010. "Supreme Court Ruling Empowers Corporations More Than Labor Unions." *U.S. News & World Report* (January 22). Online: http://www.usnews.com/blogs/laura-chapin/2010/01/22.

Cherlin, Andrew. 1981. *Marriage, Divorce, Remarriage*. Cambridge, MA: Harvard University Press.

Cherlin, Andrew. 1999. "Going to Extremes: Family Structure, Children's Well-Being and Social Science." *Demography* 36 (November):421–428.

Chideya, Farai. 1999. "A Nation of Minorities: America in 2050." *Civil Rights Digest* 4 (Fall):35–41.

Children's Defense Fund. 1997. *The State of America's Children: Yearbook 1997*. Washington, DC: Children's Defense Fund.

Children's Defense Fund. 2004a. *The State of America's Children 2004*. Washington, DC: Children's Defense Fund.

Children's Defense Fund. 2005. *The State of America's Children 2005*. Online: http://www.childrensdefense.org/site/PageServer.

Children's Defense Fund. 2008. *The State of America's Children 2008*. Washington, DC.

Chronicle of Higher Education. 1998. "Note Book." (January 9): A55.

Chronicle of Higher Education. 1999. "A 'Gay Gene'? Perhaps Not." (April 30):A21.

Chronicle of Higher Education. 2004. "Average College Costs, 2003–4." (August 27):33.

Clarren, Rebecca. 2003. "Fields of Poison." *Nation* (December 29):23–25.

Cleveland, Harlan. 1992. "The Age of People Power." *Futurist* 26 (January/February):14–18.

Cloud, John. 2005. "The Battle over Gay Teens." *Time* (October 10): 43–51.

Cloud, John. 2007. "Yep, They're Gay." *Time* (February 5):54.

CNN. 2009. "Concern Mounts over Rising Troop Suicides." (January 30). Online: http://www.cnn.com/2009/us/02/01/military.suicides/index.html.

Cockburn, Andrew. 2009. "21st Century Slaves." In D. Stanley Eitzen and Maxine Baca Zinn (Eds.), *Globalization: The Transformation of Social Worlds*, 2nd ed. Belmont, CA: Wadsworth Cengage Learning.

Cody, Paul. 2002. "Suicide and Gay, Lesbian, Bisexual and Transgender Youth." University of New Hampshire Counseling Center. Online: Available: http://www.unhcc.unh.edu/resources/glbt/glbtsuicide.html.

Coker, Donna. 2005. "Shifting Power for Battered Woman Law, Material Resources and Poor Women of Color." In Natalie J. Sokoloff (Ed.), *Domestic Violence at the Margins: Readings on Race, Class, Gender, and Culture*. New Brunswick, NJ: Rutgers University Press, pp. 369–388.

Cole, David. 1994. "Five Myths about Immigration." *Nation* (October 17):410–412.

Cole, Jack. 2007. "War on Drugs Has Been a Whopper of a Failure." *Wichita Eagle* (January 23):7A.

Cole, Wendy, and Christine Gorman. 1993. "The Shrinking Ten Percent." *Time* (April 26):27–29.

College Board. 2006. "College Board Announces Scores for New S.A.T. with Writing Section." Press Release (August 29). Online: Available: http://www.collegeboard.com/press/releases/150054.html.

College Board. 2010. Available online: http://www.collegeboard.com.

Collins, Chuck, Betsy Leondar-Wright, and Holly Sklar. 1999. *Shifting Fortunes: The Perils of the Growing American Wealth Gap*. Boston: United for a Fair Economy.

Collins, Patricia Hill. 1990. *Black Feminist Thought*. Cambridge, MA: Unwin Hyman.

Collins, Randall, and Scott Coltrane. 1995. *Sociology of Marriage and the Family*, 4th ed. Chicago: Nelson-Hall.

Colvin, Roddrick. 2004. "The Extent of Sexual Orientation Discrimination in Topeka, KS." Equal Justice Coalition and the National Gay and Lesbian Task Force Policy Institute. Online: Available: http://www.thetaskforce.org/down loads/reports/reports/TopekaDiscrimination.pdf.

Common Cause and Tobacco-Free Kids Action Fund. 2010. Available online: http://tobaccofree action.org/contributions.

Conason, Joe. 2007. *It Can Happen Here: Authoritarian Peril in the Age of Bush*. New York: Thomas Dunne Books.

Conlin, Michelle, and Aaron Bernstein. 2004. "Working and Poor." *Business Week* (May 31): 57–68.

Connell, Robert W. 1992. "A Very Straight Gay: Masculinity, Homosexual Experience, and the Dynamics of Gender." *American Sociological Review* 57:735–751.

Connell, Robert W. 1998. "Masculinities and Globalization." *Men and Masculinities* 1 (July):3–23.

Connolly, Katie, Michael Hirsh, and Weston Kosova. 2010. "How the GOP Sees It." *Newsweek* (March 1):27–31.

Constable, Pamela. 1999. "India's Clock Just Keeps on Ticking." *Washington Post National Weekly Edition* (August 30):16.

Consumer Reports. 2004. "A Victory in Fight against Insurance Redlining." (August):61.

Contemporary Sociology. 1995. "Symposium: The Bell Curve." 24 (March):149–161.

Cook, Christopher D. 2002. "Drilling for Water." *The Progressive* 66 (October):19–23.

Coontz, Stephanie. 1992. *The Way We Never Were*. New York: Basic Books.

Coontz, Stephanie. 2004. *Marriage: A History*. New York: Viking.

Coontz, Stephanie. 2007. "New Census Report on Marriage." Council on Contemporary Families List Serve (September 18). Online: http://www.census.gov/population/www/socdemo/marr-div.html.

Copeland, Larry. 2005. "Traffic Jams." *USA Today* (May 10):3A.

Corbet, Barry. 2000a. "Your Fears, My Realities." *Denver Post* (August 13):11B.

Corbet, Barry. 2000. "Disabled Could Be King-Makers." *Denver Post* (September 27):9B.

Cordesman, Anthony H. 2006. *Iraqi Security Forces: A Strategy for Success.* Westport, CT: Praeger Security International.

Cose, Ellis. 2000. "Facts Support Inequity Beliefs." *USA Today* (May 4):17A.

Cousineau, Michael R. 2006. "Dumping the Homeless in Hospitals." *Los Angeles Times* (December 31). Online: http://www.latimes.com/news/opinion/la-op-cousineau31dec31,0,4874183,print.story?col.

Covey, Herbert C. 2007. *The Methamphetamine Crisis: Strategies to Save Addicts, Families, and Communities.* Westport, CT: Praeger Publishers.

Cox, Stan. 2006. "Cooling the Mall, Heating the Planet." *Progressive Populist* (September 1):6.

Coy, Peter. 2009. "The Lost Generation." *Business Week* (October 19): 33–35.

Coyle, Michael J. 2003. "Latinos and the Texas Criminal Justice System." National Conference of La Raza (July).

Crabb, Peter, and Dawn Bielawski. 1994. "The Social Representation of Material Culture and Gender in Children's Books." *Sex Roles* 30 (1/2):69–79.

Crary, David. 2009. "American Market Fuels Drug Violence." The Associated Press (May 27).

Cronin, John, Michael Daklin, Deborah Adkins, and G. Gage Kingsbury. 2007. "The Proficiency Illusion." Thomas Fordham Institute. (October). Available online: http://www.edexcellence.net/doc/The_Proficiency_Illusion.pdf.

Crooks, Robert, and Karla Baur. 1987. *Our Sexuality,* 3rd ed. Menlo Park, CA: Benjamin Cummings.

Cross, Merry. 1994. "Abuse." In L. Keith (Ed.), *Mustn't Grumble*. London: Women's Press.

Crowley, Sheila. 2002. "The National Low Income Housing Coalition." *Poverty and Race* 11 (January/February):24–26.

Cullen, Lisa, and Daren Fonda. 2006. "What It Means for Your Wallet." *Time* (April 10):43.

Curran, Daniel J., and Claire M. Renzetti. 2000. *Social Problems: Society in Crisis,* 5th ed. Boston: Allyn & Bacon.

Currie, Elliott. 1993. *Reckoning: Drugs, the Cities, and the American Future.* New York: Hill & Wang.

Currie, Elliott. 1998. *Crime and Punishment in America: Why the Solutions to America's Most Stubborn Social Crisis Have Not Worked—and What Will*. New York: Metropolitan Books.

Curtin, Dave. 2001. "Report Blasts Teacher Prep." *Denver Post* (February 3):1B.

Curtis, Emory. 2000. "The Poor Pay More." *Exodus* (March 30). Online. Available: http://www. exodusnews.com/editorials/editorial-065.htm.

Danes, Anita. 2009. "The Cost of the Global U.S. Military Presence." *Policy Report,* Institute for Policy Studies, (July 3).

Danziger, Sheldon, and Peter Gottschalk. 1995. *America Unequal*. New York: Russell Sage Foundation.

Datnow, Amanda and Robert Cooper. 2002. "Tracking," In David L. Levinson, Peter W. Cookson, Jr., and Alan R. Sadovnik (Eds.). *Education and Sociology: An Encyclopedia*. New York: Routledge Falmer, pp. 687–692.

David, Deborah S., and Robert Brannon. 1980. "The Male Sex Role." In Arlene S. Skolnick and Jerome H. Skolnick (Eds.), *Family in Transition,* 3rd ed. Boston: Little, Brown.

Davidson, Kay. 2005. "Harvard President under Microscope: Female Scientists Debate Comments on Gender, Science." *San Francisco Chronicle* (January 31):4A.

Davidson, Nicholas. 1990. "Life Without Father: America's Greatest Social Catastrophe." *Policy Review* 51 (Winter):40–44.

Davidson, Paul. 2009. "Contract Workers Swelling Ranks." *USA Today* (December 7):1B.

Davis, Mike. 2006. "The Poor Man's Air Force." *Harper's Magazine* 313 (October):15–20.

Davis-Delano, Laurel R. 2000. Personal communication.

Davis-Delano, Laurel R. 2009. Personal communication.

DAWN: Drug Abuse Warning Network, 2005. "National Estimates of Drug-Related Emergency Department Visits." U.S. Department of Health and Human Services, Substance Abuse and Mental Health Services Administration. Online: Available: http://dawninfo. samhsa. gov.

DeGennaro, Patricia. 2009. "Afghanistan: Casualties of War—Is It Worth It? *Huffington Post* (May 12). Online: http://www.huffingtonpost.com/patricia-degenaro/the-surreal-value-of-war.

DeGraw, David. 2010. "The Richest 1% Have Captured America's Wealth—What's It Going to Take to Get It Back?" *Alternet.org* (February 17). Online: http://www.alternet.org/economy/145705.

della Cava, Marco R. 2009. "Women Step Up as Men Lose Jobs." *USA Today* (March 19):D1-D2.

del Pinal, Jorge, and Audrey Singer. 1997. "Generations of Diversity: Latinos in the United States." *Population Bulletin* 52 (October): entire issue.

DeNavas-Walt, Carmen, Robert W. Cleveland, and Bruce H. Webster, Jr. "Income in the United States: 2002." *Current Population Reports,* P60–221, U.S. Census Bureau, Washington, DC: U.S. Government Printing Office.

DeNavas-Walt, Carmen, Bernadette D. Proctor, and Jessica C. Smith. 2008. "Income, Poverty, and Health Insurance Coverage in the United States: 2007. U.S. Census Bureau, *Current Population Reports*, P60–235.

DeNavas-Walt, Carmen, Bernadette D. Proctor, and Jessica C. Smith. 2009. "Income, Poverty, and Health Insurance Coverage in the United States: 2008." U.S. Census Bureau, *Current Population Reports*, P60–236.

DeNavas-Walt, Carmen, Bernadette D. Proctor, and Jessica C. Smith. U.S. Census Bureau, Current Population Reports, *Income, Poverty, and Health Insurance Coverage in the United States, 2009*. U.S. Government Printing Office.

Denizet-Lewis, Benoit. 2009. "Coming Out in Middle School." *The New York Times Magazine* (September 27).

Denver Post. 1994. "Blacks Less Apt to Drink in College." (September 14):18A.

Denver Post. 2001. "The Haves and the Have-Nots." (June 17): 6D.

Denver Post. 2002. "Smokers Costly to Society." (April 12).

DeParle, Jason (2009). "Welfare Aid Isn't Growing as Economy Drops Off.." New York Times (February 2). Online: http://www.nytimes.com/2009/02/02/us/02welfare.html.

DeParle, Jason. 2007. "The American Prison Nightmare." *New York Review of Books* (April 12). Online: http://www.nybooks.com/articles/20056.

Dervarics, Charles. 2000. "Health Experts Make Case for Environmental Justice." *Population Today* 28 (May/June):1,4.

Derysh, Igor. 2009. "Ties Between Government, Defense Contractors too Strong." *Congress Examiner* (June 8). Online: http://www.examiner.com/CP/CleanPrintProxy.aspx?1265473212400.

De Souza, Roge, John S. Williams, and Frederick A. B. Meyerson. 2003. "Critical Links: Population, Health, and the Environment." *Population Bulletin* 58 (September): entire issue.

De Vita, Carol J. 1996. "The United States at Mid-Decade." *Population Bulletin* 50 (March): entire issue.

Dickinson, Tim, and Jonathan Stein. 2006. "Chronicle of a War Foretold." *Mother Jones* 31 (September/October):61–69.

di Leonardo, Micaela. 1992. "Boyz in the Hood." *Nation* (August 17/24):178–186.

Dionne, E. J., Jr. 1996. *They Only Look Dead: Why Progressives Will Dominate the Next Political Era*. New York: Simon & Schuster.

Dobbs, Lon. 2003. "The Perils of Productivity." *U.S. News & World Report* (November 10):58.

Dollars & Sense. 2001. "Here's to Our Health." No. 235 (May/June):2.

Dollars & Sense. 2006. "Mass Incarceration Continues Apace." No. 266 (July/August):4.

Domhoff, G. William. 1978. *The Powers That Be: Processes of Ruling Class Domination in America*. New York: Random House.

D'Oro, Rachel. 2009. "More Militia Groups Springing Up in U.S." *Wichita Eagle* (November 22):9A.

Donziger, Steven R. (Ed.). 1996. *The Real War on Crime: The Report of the National Criminal Justice Commission*. New York: Harper Perennial.

Dorrien, Gary. 2006. "Grand Illusion: Costs of War and Empire." *Christian Century* (December 26):26–29.

Douglas, Susan J. 2010. "Enlightened Sexism: 'Women's Success' Means It's Fine to Resurrect— Even Celebrate—Sexist Stereotypes." *In These Times* (March 1). Available online: http://www. AlterNet.org/story/145843.

Doyle, Jack, and Paul T. Schindler. 1974. "The Incoherent Society." Paper presented at the American Sociological Association, Montreal, Canada, August 25–29.

Draut, Tamara. 2008. "Economic State of Young America." *Demos* (Spring).

Dreier, Peter. 2000. "Sprawl's Invisible Hand." *Nation* (February 21):6–7.

Dreyfuss, Robert, and Dave Gilson. 2007. "Sunni, Shiite? Anyone? Anyone?" *Mother Jones* 32 (March/April):57–65.

Drucker, Jesse. 2008. "Income Up for Richest Americans; Tax Rate Fell." *Wall Street Journal* (July 24).

Drucker, Peter F. 1993. *Post-Capitalist Society*. New York: HarperCollins.

Drucker, Peter. 2001. "The Next Society." *The Economist* (November 3):3–8.

Drug Enforcement Administration. 2007. Online: Available: http://www.usdoj.gov/dea/index/htm.

Drug Enforcement Administration. 2009. Available online: http://www.justice.gov/dea.

Drug Policy Alliance. 2003. Online. Available: http://www.drugpolicy/org.

Drutman, Lee. 2003. "Corporate Crime Acts Like a Thief in the Night." *Los AngelesTimes* (November 4). Online. Available: http://www.latimes.com/news/opinion/commentary/la-oe-drutman4no.

Dubeck, Paula J., and Dana Dunn (Eds.). 2002. *Workplace/Women's Place: An Anthology*. Los Angeles: Roxbury.

Dunayer, Joan. 1995. "Sexist Words, Speciest Roots." In Carol J. Adams and Josephine Donovan (Eds.), *Animals and Women: Feminist Theoretical Exploration*. Durham, NC: Duke University Press, pp. 11–31.

Duncan, Cynthia M. 1999. *World Apart: Why Poverty Persists in Rural America*. New Haven: Yale University Press.

Duncan, Margaret Carlisle. 2001. "The Sociology of Ability and Disability in Physical Activity." *Sociology of Sport Journal* 18(1):1–4.

Dunn, Andy. 2006. "The Other Domestic Spying." *Z Magazine* 19 (March):47–52.

Dunn, Dana. 1996. "Gender and Earnings." In Paula J. Dubeck and Kathryn Borman (Eds.), *Women and Work: A Handbook*. New York: Garland, pp. 61–63.

Durose, Matthew R., Caroline Wolf Harlow, Patrick A. Langan, Mark Motivans, Romona R. Rantala, and Erica L. Smith. 2005. *Family Violence Statistics*. Washington, DC: U.S. Department of Justice.

Dwyer, Jim. 2009. "Without Health Care, and Just a Hamburger from Financial Ruin." *New York Times* (September 13):37.

Dwyer, Paula. 2004. "The New Fat Cats." *Business Week* (April 12):32–35.

Dybas, Cheryl Lyn. 2005. "Growing Fast and Tall." *Washington Post National Weekly Edition* (November 28):35.

Dyer, Everett. 1979. *The American Family: Variety and Change*. New York: McGraw-Hill.

Earle, Sylvia A. 2003. "Oceans Are in a World of Trouble." *Los Angeles Times* (May 20). Online. Available: http://www.latimes.com/news/opinion/commentary/la-oe-earle20.may20,1,361387.story?coll=.

Early, Frances H. 1983. "The French-Canadian Family Economy and Standard of Living in Lowell, Massachusetts, 1870." In Michael Gordon (Ed.), *The American Family in Social Historical Perspective*, 3rd ed. New York: St. Martin's Press, pp. 482–503.

Easterbrook, Gregg. 1999. "Overpopulation Is No Problem—in the Long Run." *New Republic* (October 11):22–28.

Eaton, Leslie. 2007. "In Mississippi, the Poor Lag in Hurricane Aid." *New York Times* (November 16). Online: http://www.nytimes.com/2007/n/16/us/16mississippi.html?

Eckholm, Erik. 2009. "In Prisoners' Wake, a Tide of Troubled Kids." *The New York Times* (July 5).

Economic Policy Institute. 2001. "Staying Poor in America." Available online: http://www.epi.org/economic_snapshots/entry/webfeatures_snapshots_archive_01102001.

Economic Policy Institute. 2004. Online. Available: http://www.epinet.org.

Edelman, Marion Wright. 2009. "Promising Models for Reforming Juvenile Justice Systems." Children's Defense Fund (September 5). Available online: http://www.childrensdefense.org/child-research-data-publications/data/marian-wright-edelman-child-watch-column/promising-models-for-reforming.html.

Edelman, Peter. 2001. "The Question Now Isn't Just Poverty. For Many, It Is Survival." *Washington Spectator* 27 (August 1):1–3.

Edwards, Renee, and Mark A. Hamilton. 2004. "You Need to Understand My Gender Role: An Empirical Test of Tannen's Model of Gender and Communication." *Sex Roles* 50(7/8):491–504.

Edwards, Richard C., Michael Reich, and Thomas E. Weisskopf. 1978. "Sexism." In R. C. Edwards, M. Reich, and T. E. Weisskopf (Eds.), *The Capitalist System*, 2nd ed. Upper Saddle River, NJ: Prentice Hall, pp. 331–341.

Eggen, Dan. 2009a. "The Downturn Reaches K Street." *Washington Post National Weekly Edition* (September 14):13.

Eggen, Dan. 2009b. "The Health Care Industry Operation." *Washington Post National Weekly Edition* (July 27):18.

Ehrenreich, Barbara. 2004. "Gouging the Poor." *Progressive* (68):12–13.

Ehrenreich, Barbara. 2006. "The High Cost of Being Poor." *AlterNet* (July 25). Online: Available: http://www.AlterNet.org/story/39273.

Ehrenreich, Barbara, and Dedrick Muhammad. 2009. "The Recession's Racial Divide." *New York Times* (September 13):17.

Ehrlich, Paul R., and Anne H. Ehrlich. 1972. *Population/Resources/Environment: Issues in Human Ecology*, 2nd ed. San Francisco: Freeman.

Ehrlich, Paul, and Anne Ehrlich. 2008. "The Problem is Simple: Too Many People, Too Much Stuff." *AlterNet* (August 7). Available online: http://www.AlterNet.org/story/94268.

Eilperin, Juliet. 2005. "Flooded Toxic Waste Sites Are Potential Health Threat." *Washington Post* (September 10):A15.

Eisenstein, Zillah. 1979. "Developing a Theory of Capitalist Patriarchy and Socialist Feminism." In Zillah Eisenstein (Ed.), *Capitalist Patriarchy and the Case for Socialist Feminism*. New York: Monthly Review Press, pp. 5–40.

Eisler, Peter. 2000. "Toxic Exposure Kept Secret." *USA Today* (September 6):1A–2A, 15A–18A.

Eisler, Peter. 2002. "Fallout Likely Caused 15,000 Deaths." *USA Today* (February 28):1A.

Eitzen, D. Stanley. 1984. "Teaching Social Problems: Implications of the Objectivist–Subjectivist Debate." *Society for the Study of Social Problems Newsletter* 16 (Fall):10–12.

Eitzen, D. Stanley. 2004. "The Atrophy of Social Life." *Society* 41 (September/October).

Eitzen, D. Stanley. 2007. *Solutions to Social Problems: Lessons from Other Societies*, 4th ed. Boston: Allyn & Bacon.

Eitzen, D. Stanley, and Maxine Baca Zinn. 1989. "The De-Athleticization of Women: The Naming and Gender Marking of Collegiate Sport Teams." *Sociology of Sport Journal* 6:362–370.

Eitzen, D. Stanley, and Maxine Baca Zinn. 1998. "The Shrinking Welfare State: The New Welfare Legislation and Families." Paper presented at the annual meeting of the American Sociological Association, San Francisco, California, August 21–25.

Eitzen, D. Stanley, and Maxine Baca Zinn. 2001. *In Conflict and Order: Understanding Society*, 9th ed. Boston: Allyn & Bacon.

Eitzen, D. Stanley, and Maxine Baca Zinn (2009). *Globalization: The Transformation of Social Worlds*, 2nd ed. Belmont, CA: Wadsworth Cengage Learning.

Eitzen, D. Stanley, Maxine Baca Zinn, and Kelly Eitzen Smith. 2010. *In Conflict and Order,* 12th ed. Boston: Allyn and Bacon.

Eitzen, D. Stanley, and Kelly Eitzen Smith (Eds.). 2003. *Experiencing Poverty: Voices from the Bottom*. Belmont, CA: Wadsworth.

Eitzen, D. Stanley, and George H. Sage (Eds.). 2007. *Solutions to Social Problems from the Top Down: The Role of Government*. Boston: Allyn & Bacon.

Eitzen, D. Stanley, and George H. Sage. 2010. *Sociology of North American Sport,* 8th ed. Boulder, CO: Paradigm Publishers.

Eitzen, D. Stanley, and Kenneth L. Stewart (Eds.). 2007. *Solutions to Social Problems from the Bottom Up: Successful Social Movements*. Boston: Allyn & Bacon.

Elgin, Ben, and Keith Epstein. 2009. "It's a Bird, It's a Plane, It's Pork." *Business Week* (November 9): 46–48.

Elliot, James R., and Jeremy Pais. 2006. "Race, Class, and Hurricane Katrina: Social Differences in Human Responses to Disaster." *Social Science Research* 35: 295–321.

El Nasser, Haya. 2001. "Census Analysis Shows Birth of 'Boomburgs.'" *USA Today* (June 22): 1A,11A.

El Nasser, Haya. 2008a. "Reinventing America's Suburbs." *USA Today* (July 29):1A–2A.

El Nasser, Haya. 2008b. "Suburbs Get Urban Makeover." *USA Today* (July 16):3A.

El Nasser, Haya. 2010. "Multiracial No Longer Boxed in by the Census." *USA Today* (March 3): 1A.

El Nasser, Haya, and Lorrie Grant. 2005. "Immigration Causes Age, Race Split." *USA Today* (June 9):1A.

Engelhardt, Tom. 2007. "Rural America Pays the Price for War in Iraq." *AlterNet* (January 27). Online: http://www.AlterNet.org/waroniraq/47235.

Epstein, Cynthia Fuchs. 1970. *Woman's Place*. Berkeley, CA: University of California Press.

Equal Employment Opportunity Commission. 2007. "Occupational Employment in Private Industry by Race/Ethnic Group/Sex and by Industry, United States, 2005." Online: http://www.ecoc.gov/stats/jobpat/2005/National. html.

Espiritu, Yen Le. 1996. "Asian American Panethnicity." In Karen E. Rosenblum and Toni-Michelle Travis (Eds.), *The Meaning of Difference*. New York: McGraw-Hill, pp. 51–61.

Everton, Terry. 2004. "Why School Sucks." *Z Magazine* (November):54–56.

Facing South. 2009. "Jena Six Case Comes to an End; Shone Light on Racism in Criminal Justice System." *The Institute for Southern Studies*. (June 30). Available online: http://www.southern studies.org/2009/06/post-34.html.

Fackelmann, Kathleen. 1999. "Does Unequal Treatment Really Have Roots in Racism?" *USA Today* (September 16):10D.

Fackelmann, Kathleen. 2002. "Moving Slowly on Sludge." *USA Today* (September 30):5D.

Fahim, Kareem. 2003. "The Moving Target." *Amnesty Now* 29 (4) (Winter):6–9.

Faircloth, Susan C., and John W. Tippeconnie III. 2010. "The Dropout/Graduation Rate Crisis Among American Indian and Alaska Native Students: Failure to Respond Places the Future of Native Peoples at Risk." *The Civil Rights Project/Proyecto Derechos Civiles at UCLA*. Los Angeles, CA. Available online: http://www.civilrightsproject.ucla.edu.

Falk, Erika. 2008. "Cutting Women Out." *In These Times* (March):20–23.

Fallows, James. 2006. *Blind into Baghdad: America's War in Iraq*. New York: Vintage Books.

Fallows, James. 2010. "How America Can Rise Again." *Atlantic* 305 (January/February):38–55.

Faludi, Susan. 1991. *Backlash: The Undeclared War against Women*. New York: Crown.

Farley, John E., and Gregory D. Squires. 2009. "Fences and Neighbors: Segregation in 21st Century America." In Elizabeth Higginbotham and Margaret L. Andersen (Eds.), *Race and Ethnicity in Society*. Belmont, CA: Wadsworth Cengage, pp. 360–368.

Farrell, Christopher. 2006. "Going Beyond Head Start." *Business Week* (October 23):108–110.

Faust, Kimberly A., and Jerome N. McKibben. 1999. In Marvin Sussman, Suzanne K. Steinmetz, and Gary W. Peterson (Eds.), *Handbook of Marriage and the Family,* 2nd ed. New York: Plenum Press, pp. 475–499.

Fausto-Sterling, Anne. 1992. *Myths of Gender: Biological Theories about Women and Men*. New York: Basic Books.

Feagin, Joe R. 2000. *Racist America*. New York: Routledge.

Feagin, Joe R. 2006. *Systemic Racism: A Theory of Oppression*. New York: Routledge.

Feagin, Joe R., Clairece Booher Feagin, and David V. Baker. 2006. *Social Problems: A Critical Power-Conflict Perspective,* 6th ed. Upper Saddle River, NJ: Prentice Hall.

Feagin, Joe, and Melvin P. Sikes. 1994. *Living with Racism: The Black Middle-Class Experience*. Boston: Beacon Press.

Federal Bureau of Investigation (FBI). 2008. "2008 Hate Crime Statistics." Online: http://www.fbi.gov/ucr/hc2008/locationtype.html.

Feingold, Russ. 2001. "At the Debate of the Anti-Terrorism Bill, From the Senate Floor." (October 11). Online. http://feingold.senate.gov/~feingold/speeches/01/10/101101at.html.

Feldman, Noah. 2007. "Choosing a Sect." *New York Times* (March 4). Online: http://www.nytimes.com/2007/03/04/magazine/04wwInlede.t.html?ref=magazine&pagewanted.

Ferree, Myra Marx. 1991. "Feminism and Family Research." In Alan Booth (Ed.), *Contemporary Families: Looking Forward, Looking Back*. Minneapolis, MN: National Council on Family Relations, pp. 103–121.

Fields, Jason. 2004. "America's Families and Living Arrangements." *Current Population Reports*, P20–553. Washington, DC: U.S. Bureau of the Census.

Filardo, Mary W., Jeffrey M. Vincent, Ping Sung, and Travis Stein. 2006. "Growth and Disparity: A Decade of U.S. Public School Construction." Building Educational Success Together (BEST). Online: Available: http://www.21csf.org/csf-home/publications/BEST-Growth-Disparity-2006.pdf.

Fine, Mark A., Lawrence H. Ganong, and David H. Demo. 2005. "Divorce as a Family Stressor." In Patrick C. McKenry and Sharon J. Price (Eds.), *Families and Change: Coping with Stressful Events and Transitions*, 3rd ed., Thousand Oaks, CA: Sage, pp. 227–252.

Fineman, Howard. 2009. "On a Downtown Train." *Newsweek* (February 2):29.

Fireside, Daniel (2009). "Not Just Homeowners, But Renters Are Really Getting Screwed." *Dollars & Sense* (March 19). Online: http://www.alternet.org/story/131384.

Fischer, Claude S., Michael Hout, Martin Sanchez Jankowski, Samuel R. Lucas, Ann Swidler, and Kim Voss. 1996. *Inequality by Design: Cracking the Bell Curve Myth*. Princeton, NJ: Princeton University Press.

Fischman, Josh. 2007. "Unequal Treatment in the ER." *U.S. News & World Report* (February 12):82.

Fletcher, Michael A. 2002. "When It Comes to Schools, Size Counts." *Washington Post National Weekly Edition* (April 22): 34.

Flora, Cornelia Butler, Jan L. Flora, Jacqueline D. Spears, and Louis E. Swanson. 1992. *Rural Communities: Legacy and Change*. Boulder, CO: Westview Press.

Folbre, Nancy. 1985. "The Pauperization of Motherhood: Patriarchy and Social Policy in the U.S." *Review of Radical Political Economics* 16(4).

Folbre, Nancy, James Heintz, and the Center for Popular Economics. 2000. *The Ultimate Field Guide to the U.S. Economy*. New York: New Press.

Fong, Tillie. 2004. "10% of State's Moms-to-Be Imbibe." *Rocky Mountain News* (July 2):32A.

Forbes. 2006. "*Forbes* Global 2000: The Biggest Companies in the World." (April 17).

Forbes. 2009a. "The Best Companies in the World: The Top 50 in Sales." (April 27):130–131.

Forbes. 2009b. "The *Forbes* 400: The Richest People in America." (October 19).

Forrest, Christopher B., and Ellen-Marie Whelan. 2000. "Primary Care Safety-Net Delivery Sites in the United States: A Comparison of Community Health Centers, Hospital Outpatient Departments, and Physicians Offices." *JAMA*, 284, No. 16 (October 25):2077–2083.

Fost, Dan. 1991. "American Indians in the Nineties." *American Demographics* 13 (December):26–34.

Fox, Greer Litton, Michael L. Benson, Alfred A. De Maris, and Judy Van Wyk. 2002. "Economic Distress and Intimate Violence: Testing Family Status and Resource Theories." *Journal of Marriage and Family* 64 (August):793–807.

Francis, David R. 2009. "Can Obama's Family-Planning Policies Help the Economy?" *Christian Science Monitor* (January 26).

Frank, Robert H. 2001. "Traffic and Tax Cuts." *New York Times* (May 11). Available online: http://www.nytimes.com/2001/05/11/opinion/11FRAN. html.

Frank, Thomas. 2004. *What's the Matter with Kansas? How Conservatives Won the Heart of America*. New York: Metropolitan Books.

Freeman, Jo. 1979. "The Women's Liberation Movement: Its Origins, Organizations, Activities, and Ideas." In J. Freeman (Ed.), *Women: A Feminist Perspective*, 2nd ed. Palo Alto, CA: Mayfield, pp. 557–574.

Freiberg, Peter. 1987. "The March on Washington." *Advocate* (November 10):11–22.

Frey, William H. 2002. "Multilingual America." *American Demographics* 24 (July/August):20–23.

Friedman, Lawrence. 1993. *Crime and Punishment in American History*. New York: Basic Books.

Friedman, Thomas L. 2005. *The World Is Flat*. New York: Farrar, Straus, and Giroux.

Friedman, Thomas L. 2008. *Hot, Flat, and Crowded*. New York: Farrar, Straus, and Giroux.

Fuentes, Annette. 2007. "Segregation Is Back in Class." *USA Today* (March 14):11A.

Gais, Thomas, Lucy Dadayan, and Suho Bae. 2009. "The Decline of States in Financing the U.S. Safety Net: Retrenchment in State and Local Social Welfare Spending, 1977–2007." The Nelson A. Rockefeller Institute of Government. Available online: http://www.rockinst.org/pdf/workforce_welfare_and_social_services/2009-11-social_welfare_spending.pdf.

Gallagher, Charles A. 2010. "Color Blind Privilege: The Social and Political Functions of Erasing the Color Line in Post Race America." In Margaret L. Andersen and Patricia Hill Collins (Eds.), *Race, Class, and Gender*, 7th ed. Belmont, CA: Wadsworth Cengage, pp. 95–97.

Gallup. 2009. "Majority of Americans Continues to Oppose Gay Marriage." Gallup.com. (May 27). Available online: http://www.gallup.com/poll/118378/majority-americans-continue-oppose-gay-marriage.aspx.

Gandel, Stephen. 2010. "The Teen Job Chop." *Time* (January 18):38–42.

Gandel, Stephen, and Paul J. Lim. 2008. "What Do I Do Now?" *Money* (November):89–91.

Gans, Herbert J. 1990. "Second Generation Decline." *Ethnic Racial Studies* 15:173–192.

Gardner, David. 2009. "There's No Reason Only Poor People Should Get Malaria: The Moment Bill Gates Released a Jar of Mosquitos at Packed Conference." *Daily Mail* (February). Online: http://www.dailymail.co.uk/news/worldnews/article-1136463.

Gardner, Gary, Erik Assadourian, and Radhika Sarin. 2004. "The State of Consumption Today." In Linda Starker (Ed.), *State of the World 2004*. New York: W.W. Norton, pp. 3–21.

Gardner, Gary, and Brian Halweil. 2000. "Escaping Hunger, Escaping Excess." *World Watch* 13 (July/August): 25–35.

Garibaldi, Gerry. 2006. "How the Schools Shortchange Boys." *City Journal* (Summer). Online: Available: http://www.city-journal.org/print able.php?id=2041.

Garrahy, Deborah A. 2001. "Three Third-Grade Teachers' Gender-Related Beliefs and Behavior." *The Elementary School Journal* 102(1):81–94.

Gates, Bill and Melinda, Foundation. n.d. "Our approach: Malaria." Online: http://www.gatesfoundation.org/topics/pages/malaria.aspx.

Gates, Gary J. 2009. "Same-Sex Spouses and Unmarried Partners in the American Community Survey, 2008." The Williams Institute. Available online: http://www.law.ucla.edu/williamsinstitute/pdf/ACS2008_Final(2).pdf.

Gates, Gary J. (2010). "Lesbian, Gay, and Bisexual Men and Women in the U.S. Military: Updated Estimates," *The Williams Institute* (May 2010). Available Online: http://www.law.ucla.edu/williamsinstitute/pdf/GLBmilitaryUpdate(2).pdf

Gates, Gary, M.V. Lee Badgett, Jennifer Ehrle Macomber, and Kate Chambers. 2007. "Adoption and Foster Care by Gay and Lesbian Parents in the United States." The Williams Institute.(March). Available online: http://www.law.ucla.edu/williamsinstitute/publications/FinalAdoptionReport.pdf.

Gates, Gary J., and Jason Ost. 2004. *The Gay and Lesbian Atlas*. Washington, DC: The Urban Institute Press.

Gawande, Atul, E. S. Fisher, J. Gruber, and M. B. Rosenthal. 2009. "Downwardly Mobile. The Accidental Case of Being Uninsured." *Archives of Surgery* 144(11):1006–1012.

Gavzer, Bernard. 1999. "Take Out the Trash, and Put It . . . Where?" *Parade Magazine* (June 13): 4–6.

Gay and Lesbian Leadership Institute. 2010. "Openly LGBT Appointed and Elected Officials." Available online: http://www.glli.org/out_officials.

Gay, Lesbian, and Straight Education Network. 2008. "2007 National School Climate Survey." (October 18). Available online: http://www.glsen.org.

Geiger, H. Jack. 1990. "Generation of Poison and Lies." *New York Times* (August 5):E19.

Gelles, Richard J. 1976. "Demythologizing Child Abuse." *Family Coordinator* 25 (April).

Gelles, Richard J. 1993. "Family Violence." In Robert L. Hampton, Thomas P. Gullota, Gerald R. Adams, Earl H. Potter, and Roger P. Weissberg (Eds.), *Family Violence: Prevention and Treatment*. Newbury Park, CA: Sage.

Gelles, Richard J. 1995. *Contemporary Families: A Sociological View*. Thousand Oaks, CA: Sage.

Gelles, Richard J., and Claire Pedrick Cornell. 1990. *Intimate Violence in Families,* 2nd ed. Newbury Park, CA: Sage.

Gelles, Richard J., and Murray A. Straus. 1979a. "Determinants of Violence in the Family." In Wesley R. Burr, Reuben Hill, F. Ivan Nye, and Ira L. Reiss (Eds.), *Contemporary Theories about the Family,* Vol. 1. New York: Free Press, pp. 549–581.

Gelles, Richard J., and Murray A. Straus. 1979b. "Domestic Violence and Sexual Abuse of Children." In Alan Booth (Ed.), *Contemporary Families: Looking Forward, Looking Back*. Minneapolis, MN: National Council on Family Relations, pp. 327–340.

Gelles, Richard J., and Murray A. Straus. 1988. *Intimate Violence*. New York: Simon & Schuster.

Gergen, David. 2001. "It's Not Can We, But Will We?" *U.S. News & World Report* (September 24):60.

Gerschick, Thomas J., and Adam Stephen Miller. 2001. "Coming to Terms: Masculinity and Physical Disability." In Michael S. Kimmel and Michael A. Messner (Eds.), *Men's Lives,* 5th ed. Boston: Allyn & Bacon, pp. 313–326.

Ghosh, Bobby. 2007. "Why They Hate Each Other." *Time* (March 5):29–40.

Giddens, Anthony. 1991. *Introduction to Sociology*. New York: W. W. Norton.

Giele, Janet Z. 1988. "Gender and Sex Roles." In Neil J. Smelser (Ed.), *Handbook of Sociology*. Newbury Park, CA: Sage, pp. 291–323.

Gillespie, Ed. 2003. "The Embedded Lobbyist." *Public Citizen* (June 16). Online. Available: http://www.citizen.org/comgress/welfare/index.ifm.

Gillum, Jack. 2004. "Disabled are Losing Optimism." *USA Today* (June 28):6D.

Gilman, Richard. 1971. "Where Did It All Go Wrong?" *Life* (August 13):40–55.

Gilson, Stephen French, and Elizabeth Depoy. 2000. "Multiculturalism and Disability: A Critical Perspective." *Disability and Society* 15 (March):207–218.

Ginsburg, Carl. 1996. "The Patient as Profit Center: Hospital Inc. Comes to Town." *Nation* (November 18):18–22.

Gitlin, Todd. 1995. *The Twilight of Common Dreams*. New York: Henry Holt.

Glasser, Ira. 2006. "Drug Busts = Jim Crow." *The Nation* (July 10):24–26.

Glasser, Ronald J. 2009. "'He Who Has the Gold Sets the Rules': How Managed Care Has Created an Unsustainable System for Doctors, Patients and Our Society." *Washington Post National Weekly Edition* (June 8):24.

Glassman, James K. 1997. "Corporate Welfare in the Sky." *U.S. News & World Report* (July 28):49.

Gleick, Elizabeth. 1995. "Rich Justice, Poor Justice." *Time* (June 19):40–47.

Goffman, Irving. 1963. *Stigma: Notes on the Management of Spoiled Identity.* Englewood Cliffs, NJ: Prentice Hall.

Golden, Daniel. 2006. *The Price of Admission: How America's Ruling Class Buys Its Way into Elite Colleges and Who Gets Left Outside the Gates.* New York: Crown Publishing/Random House, Inc.

Gonzalez, Antonio, and Stephanie Moore. 2003. "Wealthy Campaign Donors Stifle Minority Voices." *USA Today* (December 11):23A.

Goode, William J. 1983. "World Devolution in Family Patterns." In Arlene Skolnick and Jerome Skolnick (Eds.), *Family in Transition*, 4th ed. Boston: Little, Brown, pp. 43–52.

Goodgame, Dan. 1993. "Welfare for the Well-Off." *Time* (February 22):36–38.

Goodman, David. 2009. "Data Minefield." *Mother Jones* 34 (September/October): 21–22.

Goozner, Merrill. 2000. "The Price Isn't Right." *American Prospect* (September 11):25–29.

Gordon, Beth Omansky, and Karen E. Rosenblum. 2001. "Bring Disability into the Sociological Frame: A Comparison of Disability with Race, Sex, and Sexual Orientation Statuses." *Disability and Society* 16 (January):5–19.

Gordon, Michael R., and Bernard E. Trainor. 2006. *Cobra II: The Inside Story of the Invasion and Occupation of Iraq.* New York: Pantheon Books.

Gore, Al. 2006. *An Inconvenient Truth.* New York: Rodale.

Gorman, Anna. 2007. "Immigrant Children Grow Fluent in English, Study Says." *Los Angeles Times* (November 30). Online: http://www.latimes.com/news/local/la-me-english30nov30, 0,1163558.story?

Gorman, Christine. 2006. "An African Miracle." *Time* (December 4):96–97.

Gosselin, Peter G. 2005. "Corporate America Pulling Back Pension Safety Net." *Los Angeles Times* (May 15). Online: http://www.latimes.com/business/specials/lall-na-risk151505,1,6671136.print.story?coll.

Gould, Stephen J. 1998. "The Sharp-Eyed Lynx, Outfoxed by Nature." *Natural History* (May):16–21, 70–72.

Gouldner, Alvin. 1962. "Anti-Minotaur: The Myth of Value-Free Sociology." *Social Problems* 9 (Winter).

Gould, Stephen Jay. 1994. "Curveball." *New Yorker* (November 28): 139–149.

GoVeg.com. n.d. "The Most Dangerous Job in America." Online: http://www.goveg.com/workerRights_dangerous.asp.

Green, Mark. 2002. *Selling Out: How Big Corporate Money Buys Elections, Rams Through Legislation, and Betrays Our Democracy.* New York: Regan Books.

Green, Mark. 2006. *Losing Our Democracy.* Naperville, IL: Sourcebooks, Inc.

Green, Mark. 2007. "How to Fix Our Democracy." *Nation* (March 12):20–23.

Greenberg, David Ethan. 2002. "Higher Education." *Denver Post* (June 16):1E, 4E.

Greene, Jay P., and Marcus A. Winters. 2006. "Leaving Boys Behind: Public High School Graduation Rates." *Civic Report* (April)(48). The Manhattan Institute for Policy Research. Online: Available: http://www.manhattan-institute.org/html/cr_48.htm.

Greenhouse, Linda. 2003. "Ruling on Texas Sodomy Law Affirms Gays' Privacy." *Denver Post* (June 27):4A.

Greenhouse, Steven. 2005. "U.S. Meat Packing Industry Criticized on Human Rights Grounds." *New York Times* (January 25). Online: http://www.corpwatch.org/article.phpd=11806.

Greenhouse, Steven. 2009. *The Big Squeeze: Tough times for the American Worker.* New York: Anchor Books.

Greenwald, Glenn. 2010a. "The Sanctity of Military Spending." *Salon.com* (January 26). Online: http://www.commondreams.org/print/52079.

Greenwald, Glenn. 2010b. "Terrorism: The Most Meaningless and Manipulated Word." *Salon. com.* (February 19). Online: http://www.common dreams.org/print/529991.

Greider, William. 2004. "Under the Banner of the 'War' on Terror." *Nation* (June 21);11–14,18.

Greim, Lisa. 1998. "Working Women Protest Pay Gap." *Rocky Mountain News* (April 4):1B.

Grossman, Cathy Lynn. 2001. "Protestants Face Annual Sexual Divide." *USA Today* (June 6): D1–D2.

Grow, Brian. 2005. "Embracing Illegals." *Business Week* (July 18): 56–64.

Guardian. 2009. "Nuclear Weapons: How Many Are There in 2009, and Who Has Them?" (September 6): Online: http://www.gguardian.co.uk/news/dataablog/2009/sep/06/nuclear- weapons.

Guastello, Denise D., and Stephen J. Guastello. 2003. "Androgyny, Gender Role Behavior, and Emotional Intelligence among College Students and Their Parents." *Sex Roles* 49 (1/2):663–673.

Gunther, Marc. 2006. "Queer Inc. How Corporate America Fell in Love with Gays and Lesbians. It's a Movement." *Fortune* (November 30). Online: Available: http://money.cnn.com/magazines/fortune/fortune_archive/2006/12/11/8395465.

Guo, Guang, and Kathleen Mullan Harris, 2000. "The Mechanisms Mediating the Effects of Poverty on Children's Intellectual Development." *Demography* 37 (November):431–447.

Hacker, Andrew. 2003. *Mismatch: The Growing Gulf Between Women and Men*. New York: Scribners.

Hacker, Jacob S. 2006. *The Great Risk Shift*. New York: Oxford University Press.

Hagan, Frank E. 1994. *Introduction to Criminology*, 3rd ed. Chicago: Nelson-Hall.

Hagan, John. 1994. *Crime and Disrepute*. Thousand Oaks, CA: Pine Forge Press.

Hagedorn, John. 1998. *People and Folks: Gangs, Crime and the Underclass in a Rustbelt City*, 2nd ed. Chicago: Lake View Press.

Hahn, Harlan. 1986. "Public Support for Rehabilitation Programs: The Analysis of U.S. Disability Policy." *Handicap and Society* 1 (2):121–138.

Hahn, Harlan. 1988. "The Politics of Physical Difference: Disability and Discrimination." *Journal of Social Issues* 44:39–47.

Hall, M. Ann. 1985. "Knowledge and Gender: Epistemological Questions in the Social Analysis of Sport." *Sociology of Sport Journal* 2:25–42.

Hamer, Dean, and Michael Rosbash. 2010. "Genetics and Proposition 8." LATimes.com. (February 23). Available online: http://latimes. com/news/opinion/commentary/la-or-rosbash 23-2010fed23, 0,2291603.story.

Hampson, Rick. 2009. "The 2000s: A World Forever Changed." *USA Today* (December 22):1A–2A.

Hananel, Sam. 2010. "Layoffs Affect Union Ranks." Associated Press (January 23).

Hanna, William J., and Elizabeth Rogovsky. 1991. "Women with Disabilities: Two Handicaps Plus." *Disability, Handicap and Society* 6 (1):55–56.

Hannon, Lance, and Donna Shai. 2003. "The Truly Disadvantaged and the Structural Covariates of Fire Death Rates." *The Social Science Journal* 40:129–136.

Hansen, Karen V. 2005. *Not-So-Nuclear Families: Class, Gender, and Networks of Care*. New Brunswick, NJ: Rutgers University Press.

Harden, Blaine. 2006. "America's Population Set to Top 300 Million." *Washington Post* (October 12): A1.

Harnden, Toby. 2009. "Barack Obama Faces 30 Death Threats a Day, Stretching U.S. Secret Service." Telegraph (August 3). Online: http://www.telegraph.co.uk/news/worldnews/northamerica/usa/barak obama_faces_deaththreats.html.

Hardy, Quentin. 2004. "Hitting Slavery Where it Hurts." *Forbes* (January 12):76–78.

Harjo, Susan Shown. 1996. "Now and Then: Native Peoples in the United States." *Dissent* 43 (Summer):58–60.

Harper's Magazine. 2001. "*Harper's* Index." Vol. 302 (April):7.

Harrington, Michael. 1963. *The Other America: Poverty in the United States*. Baltimore: Penguin Books.

Harrington, Michael. 1979. "Social Retreat and Economic Stagnation." *Dissent* 26 (Spring):131–134.

Harrington, Michael. 1985. *Taking Sides*. New York: Holt, Rinehart & Winston.

Harris, Kathleen Mullan. 1996. "The Reforms Will Hurt, Not Help, Poor Women and Children." *Chronicle of Higher Education* (October 4):B7.

Harris, Roderick J., and Claudette Bennett. 1995. "Racial and Ethnic Diversity." In Reynolds Farley (Ed.), *The State of the Union: America in the 1990s*, Vol. 2. New York: Russell Sage, pp. 141–210.

Hartmann, Heidi I. 1976. "Capitalism, Patriarchy, and Job Segregation by Sex." *Signs* 1 (Spring):137–169.

Hartney, Christopher. 2006. "The U.S. Rates of Incarceration: A Global Perspective." *Council on Crime and Delinquency Fact Sheet* (November).

Harwood, John. 2010. "Does Washington Need Fixing?" *New York Times* (February 19). Online: http://www/nytimes.com/2010/02/2/weekinreview/21Harwood.html?

Harwood, Richard. 1997. "America's Unchecked Epidemic." *Washington Post National Weekly Edition* (December 8):27.

Hastings Center. 2009. "A Conversation with David Himmelstein and Stiffie Woolhandler." *Health Care Cost Monitor* (August 27).

Hattern, Julian. 2010. "Top Defense Contractors spent $27 Million Lobbying at Time of Afghan Surge Announcement." *Huffington Post* (January 21). Online: http://www.huffingtonpost.com/2010/01/21/top-defense-contractors-s-n.

Haynes, V. Dion. 2009. "Young, Willing and Able—but Jobless." *Washington Post National Weekly Edition* (December 7):22.

Hazelden Foundation. 2003. "Rural America Rivals Big Cities in Drug Abuse" (June 2). Online. Available: http://www.hazelden.org/servlet/hazelden/cma/ptt/hazl_alive_and_free.

Heatherington, E. Mavis. 2002. "Marriage and Divorce American Style." *American Prospect* (April 8):62–63.

Heckman, James J. 2006. "Skill Formation and the Economics of Investing in Disadvantaged Children." *Science* 312 (June):1900–1902.

Henderson, Nell. 2006. "Winners and Losers in the Short Run." *Washington Post National Weekly Edition* (April 24):21.

Henig, Jess. 2009. "Climategate." Factcheck.org. (December 10). Available online: http://www.factcheck.org.

Henry J. Kaiser Family Foundation. 2009. "Over 33 Million People Worldwide Living with HIV/AIDS." (November 24). Online: http://www.thebodypro.com/content/world/art/54563.html.

Herbert, Bob. 2001. "Fewer Students, Greater Gains." *New York Times* (March 12). Online. Available: http://www.nytimes.com/2001/03/12/opinion/12HERB.html.

Herbert, Bob. 2003a. "Dancing with the Devil." *New York Times* (May 22). Online. Available: http://www.nytimes.com/2003/05/22/opinion/22HERB.html.

Herbert, Bob. 2003b. "Locked Out at a Young Age." *New York Times* (October 20) Online. Available: http://www.nytimes.com/ 2003/10/20/opinion/20HERB.html.

Herbert, Bob. 2006. "George Bush's Trillion-Dollar War." *New York Times* (March 23). Online: http://select.nytimes.com/2006/03/23/opinion23herbert.html?pagewanted-print.

Herbert, Bob. 2009. "A Scary Reality." *New York Times* (August 8). Online: http://www.nytimes.com/2009/08/11opinion/11herbert.html.

Herbert, Bob. 2010. "An Uneasy Feeling." *New York Times* (January 5). Online: http://www.commondreams.org/print/51238.

Herman, Edward S. 1994. "The New Racist Onslaught." *Z Magazine* 7 (December):24–26.

Herman, Edward S. 2006. "Torture, Moral Values, and Leadership of the Free World." *Z Magazine* 19 (November): 27–30.

Hernandez, Raymond, and David W. Chen. 2008. "Keeping Lawmakers Happy Through Gifts to Pet Charities." *New York Times* (October 19):1A, 19A.

Herrnstein, Richard. 1971. "I.Q." *Atlantic* 228 (September):43–64.

Herrnstein, Richard J. 1973. *I.Q. in the Meritocracy*. Boston: Little, Brown.

Herrnstein, Richard J., and Charles Murray. 1994. *The Bell Curve: Intelligence and Class Structure in American Life*. New York: Free Press.

Hershey, Laura. 2000. "Choosing Disability." In Estelle Disch (Ed.), *Reconstructing Gender: A Multicultural* Anthology, 2nd ed. Mountain View, CA: Mayfield, pp. 556–563.

Hewitt, Christopher. 2003. *Understanding Terrorism in America from the Klan to Al Queda*. New York: Routledge.

Hickey, Roger. 2004. "Kids Are a High Yield Investment." *Progressive Populist*. (November 15):12.

Higginbotham, Elizabeth. 1994. "Black Professional Women: Job Ceilings and Employment Sectors." In Maxine Baca Zinn and Bonnie Thornton Dill (Eds.), *Women of Color in U.S. Society*. Philadelphia: Temple University Press, pp. 113–131.

Higginbotham, Elizabeth, and Margaret L. Andersen. 2009. "Introduction, Race: Why It Matters." In Elizabeth Higginbotham and Margaret L. Andersen (Eds.), *Race and Ethnicity in Society*. Belmont, CA: Wadsworth Cengage Learning.

Hightower, Jim. 2001. "Stand Up for your Democracy." *AlterNet* (September 19). Online: www.alternet.org/story.html?StoryID=11537.

Hightower, Jim. 2002a. "Looting the Treasury under Cover of the Flag." *The Hightower Lowdown* 4 (February):1–4.

Hightower, Jim. 2002b. "Stop the Corporate Takeover of Our Water." *The Hightower Lowdown* 4 (June):1–4.

Hightower, Jim. 2003. "Wal-Mart Rides Again." *The Hightower Lowdown* 5 (November):1–2.

Hightower, Jim. 2007. "Subprine Loans = Primetime for Vampire Lenders." *Hightower Lowdown* (August 22).

Hill, M. 1994. "Getting Things Right." *Community Care Inside* 31 (March):7.

Hill, Shirley A., and Joey Sprague. 1999. "Parenting in Black and White Families: The Interaction of Gender with Race and Class." *Gender & Society* 13 (4):480–502.

Hindery, Leo, Jr., and Leo W. Gerard. 2009. "Out Jobless Recovery." *The Nation* (July 13):22–24.

Hockstader, Lee. 2002. "Dreams among the Poorest of the Poor." *Washington Post National Weekly Edition* (September 2–8):29.

Hoffman, James M., Nilay D. Shah, Lee C. Vermeulen, Glen T. Schumock, Penny Grim, Robert J. Hunkler, and Karrie M. Hontz. 2007. "Projecting Future Drug Expenditures, 2007." *American Journal of Health-System Pharmacy* 64(3):298–314.

Hole, Judith, and Ellen Levine. 1979. "The First Feminists." In Jo Freeman (Ed.), *Women: A Feminist Perspective*. Palo Alto, CA: Mayfield.

Holstein, James A., and Jay Gubrium. 1999. "What Is Family? Further Thoughts on a Social Constructionist Approach." *Marriage and Family Review* 28 (3/4):3–20.

Holzer, Harry J., Diane Whitmore Schanzenbach, Greg Duncan, and Jens Ludwig. 2007. "The Economic Costs of Poverty in the United States: Subsequent Effects of Children Growing Up Poor." *Center for American Progress*. Online: Available: http://www.americanprogress.org/issues/2007/01/pdf/poverty_report.pdf.

Housing Assistance Council. 2004. Online. Available: http://www.ruralhome.org.

Human Rights Campaign. 2007. Online: Available: http://www.hrc.org.

Human Rights Campaign. 2009. Available online: http://www.hrc.org/sites/passendanow/index.asp.

Human Rights Watch. 2009. "Decades of Disparity: Drug Arrests and Race in the U.S." (March). Available online: http://www. hrw.org.

Huntington, Samuel P. 2004. *Who Are We? The Challenges to America's National Identity.* New York: Simon & Schuster.

Hutchins, Robert M. 1976. "Is Democracy Possible?" *Center Magazine* 9 (January/February):2–6.

Hutchinson News. 2007. "Oil Company Misinforms Public on Global Warming, Scientists Claim." (January 4):B4.

Hyman, Rebecca. 2008. "America's Frightening Alzheimer's Epidemic." *AlterNet* (May 16). Online: http://www.alternet.org/story/85532.

Idle, Tracey, Eileen Wood, and Serge Desmarias. 1993. "Gender Role Socialization in Toy Play Situations: Mothers and Fathers with Their Sons and Daughters." *Sex Roles* 28 (11/12):679–691.

Intelligence Report. 2001. "Reevaluating the Net." *The Southern Poverty Law Center* 102 (Summer):54–55.

ISR Newsletter. 1982. "Why Do Women Earn Less?" Ann Arbor, MI: University of Michigan, Institute for Social Research, Spring/Summer.

Ivins, Molly. 2000. "Capitalism Gets a Really Bad Name." *Progressive Populist* (May 15):22–23.

Ivins, Molly. 2003. "Bush Tax-Cut Plan Wrong in Oh So Very Many Ways." *Rocky Mountain News* (January 9):39A.

Jackson, Derrick Z. 2010. "No More Concessions on Health Reform." *Boston Globe* (March 2). Online: http://www.commondreams.org/print/53345.

Jackson, Janine. 2000. "A Right, Not a Favor: Coverage of Disability Act Misses Historical Shift." Online. Available: http://www.fair.org/extra-0011/ada.html.

Jackson, Jesse. 1998a. "The Coming Collision." *Progressive Populist* 4 (August):19–20.

Jackson, Jesse. 1998b. "Leave No One Behind: A Call to Action in Appalachia." *Liberal Opinion Week* (September 28):3.

Jackson, Jesse. 2001. "Talking the Talk about the Poor." *Progressive Populist* (July 1):19.

Jackson, Jesse. 2006. "Healthcare Scandal Has Real Victims." *Progressive Populist* (November 15): 14.

Jackson, Jesse. 2007. "Racially Biased Justice Still Infects American Courtrooms." *The Chicago Sun-Times* (September 18). Available online: http://www.commondreams.org/archive/2007/09/18/3911.

Jarrett, Robin, and Linda Burton. 1999. "Dynamic Dimensions of Family Structure in Low-Income African American Families." *Journal of Comparative Family Studies* 30 (Spring):177–187.

Jeffries, Sheila. 2008. "Keeping Women Down and Out: The Strip Club Boom and the Reinforcement of Male Dominance." *Signs: Journal of Women in Culture and Society* 34:151–173.

Jeffery, Clara. 2006. "Poor Losers: How the Poor Get Dinged At Every Turn." *Mother Jones* (July/August):20–21.

Jelinkek, Pauline. 2009. "Military Divorce Rate Edges Higher." Associated Press (November 27).

Jenkins, Philip. 1999. *Synthetic Panics: The Symbolic Politics of Designer Drugs.* New York: New York University Press.

Jensen, Arthur R. 1969. "How Much Can We Boost IQ and Scholastic Achievement?" *Harvard Educational Review* 39 (Winter): 1–123.

Jensen, Arthur R. 1980. *Bias in Mental Testing*. New York: Free Press.

Jensen, Leif, Diane K. McLaughlin, and Tim Slack. 2003. "Rural Poverty: The Persisting Challenge." In David L. Brown and Louis E. Swanson (Eds.), *Challenge for Rural America in the Twenty-First Century*. University Park: Pennsylvania State University Press, pp. 118–131.

Jervis, Rick. 2009. "Hispanic Workers Deaths up 76%." *USA Today* (July 20):1A.

Johansen, Bruce E. 2009. "The Carbon Footprint of War." *Progressive* 73 (October):27–28.

Johnson, Chalmers. 2000. *Blowback: The Costs and Consequences of American Empire*. New York: Metropolitan Books.

Johnson, Dirk. 2000. "Commandments Find Way into Schools." *Rocky Mountain News* (February 27): 68A.

Johnson, Dirk. 2004. "Policing a Rural Plague." *Newsweek* (March 8):41.

Johnson, Dirk, and Vince Kuppig. 2004. "The Smell of Success." *Newsweek* (July 12):40.

Johnson, Harriet McBryde. 2003. "Should I Have Been Killed at Birth?" *New York Times Magazine* (February 16):50–55, 74, 78.

Johnson, Harriet McBryde. 2004. "Stairway to Justice." *New York Times Magazine* (May 30):11–12.

Johnson, Kevin. 2006. "Center Ties Hate Crimes to Border Debate." *USA Today* (May 17):3A.

Johnson, Linda A. 2004. "Behavior Drugs Top Kids' Prescriptions." *Denver Post* (May 17).

Johnson, Mark. 2009. "Inconvenient Truth: Reducing CO2 Emissions Will NOT Save the Planet." Global Warming Hoax.com (January 20). Available online: http://www.globalwarminghoax. com/comment.php?comment.news.102.

Johnson, Michael P., and Kathleen J. Ferraro. 2000. "Research on Domestic Violence in the 1990s: Making Distinctions." *Journal of Marriage and Family* 60 (November):948–963.

Johnston, L. D., P. M. O'Malley, J. G. Bachman, and J. E. Schulenberg. 2009. "Monitoring the Future: National Survey Results on Drug Use, 1975–2008. Volume 1: Secondary School Students." National Institute on Drug Abuse. NIH Publication No. 09-7402. Bethesda, MD.

Johnston, L. D., P. M. O'Malley, J. G. Bachman, and J. E. Schulenberg. 2007. "Monitoring the Future, National Results on Adolescent Drug Use: Overview of Key

Findings, 2006." NIH Publication No. 07-6202. Bethesda, MD: National Institute on Drug Abuse. Online: Available: http://www.monitoringthefuture.org/pubs/monographs/overview2006.pdf.

Judson, David. 1997. "Neglect of Kids 'No Less than Collective Sin.'" Gannett News Service (June).

Kaiser Family Foundation. 2004. Online at http://www.kkf.org.

Kaiser Family Foundation. 2005. "Poverty Rate by Age, States (2004-2005), U.S. (2005)." Online: Available: http://www.statehealthfacts.org.

Kalet, Hank. 2000. "Unequal Justice." *Progressive Populist* (June 1):14.

Kalof, Linda, Amy Fitzgerald, and Lori Baralt. Forthcoming. "Animals, Women and Weapons: Blurred Sexual Boundaries in the Discourse of Sport Hunting." *Society and Animals*.

Kamau, Pius. 2001. "Education Funding Unfair." *Denver Post* (April 8):8I.

Kammeyer, Kenneth C. W., George Ritzer, and Norman R. Yetman. 1997. *Sociology*, 7th ed. Boston: Allyn & Bacon.

Kalleberg, Arne L. 2009. "Precarious Work, Insecure Workers: Employment Relations in Transition." *American Sociological Review* 74 (February):1l–22.

Kanter, Rosabeth Moss. 1977. *Men and Women of the Corporation*. New York: Basic Books.

Kaplan, David E. 2006. "Spies Among Us." *U.S. News & World Report* (May 8):40–49.

Karabell, Zachary. 2009. "The Case for Derivatives." *Newsweek* (February 2):35–36.

Katz, Bruce, and Jennifer Bradley. 1999. "Divided We Sprawl." *Atlantic Monthly* (December):26–42.

Katz-Fishman, Walda. 1990. "Higher Education in Crisis: The American Dream Denied." *Society for the Study of Social Problems Newsletter* 21 (Fall):22–23.

Kaul, Donald. 2010. "Next We'll Sell Senate Seats to Exxon Mobil and AT&T." *Progressive Populist* (March 1):23.

Kay, Jane Holtz. 1997. *Asphalt Nation: How the Automobile Took Over America and How We Can Take It Back*. New York: Crown.

Kay, Jane Holtz. 2002. "Why 'Friendly' Skies?" *Progressive Populist* (October 1):18.

Kay, Jane Holtz. 2004. "Our Culture's Excess Rolls toward Oblivion." *Los Angeles Times* (May 31). Online. Available: http://www.latimes.com/news/opinion/commentary/la-oe-kay3/may 31.

Kehrl, Brain H. 2004. "Don't Breathe Easy." *In These Times* (June 21):6–7.

Keillor, Garrison. 2005. "A Foul Tragedy: Democrats Fled in the Face of Danger." *In These Times* (November 21):26–27.

Keller, Bill. 2003. "The Thinkable." *New York Times Magazine* (May 5):48–53, 93–94.

Kelly, Erin. 2004. "Earth Day Has Seen Great Gains, But Earth Can Do Better." *USA Today* (April 20):8D.

Kendall, Diana. 2001. *Sociology*, 3rd ed. Belmont, CA: Wadsworth.

Kennedy, David. 1996. "Can We Still Afford to Be a Nation of Immigrants?" *Atlantic Monthly* (November):51–80.

Kennickell, Arthur B. 2009. "Ponds and Streams: Wealth and Income in the U.S. 1989 to 2007." Federal Reserve Board Working Paper (January 7).

Kent, Mary M., Kelvin M. Pollard, John Haaga, and Mark Mather. 2001. "First Glimpses from the 2000 U.S. Census." *Population Bulletin* 56 (June): entire issue.

Kibria, Nazli. 1997. "The Concept of 'Bicultural Families' and Its Implications for Research on Immigrant and Ethnic Families." In Alan Booth, Ann C. Crouter, and Nancy Landale (Eds.), *Immigration and the Family*. Mahwah, NJ: Erlbaum, pp. 205–210.

Kimmel, Michael. 1992. "Reading Men, Masculinity, and Publishing." *Contemporary Sociology* 21 (March): 162–171.

Kimmel, Michael S. 2004. *The Gendered Society*, 2nd ed. New York: Oxford University Press.

Kimmel, Michael S., and Michael A. Messner (Eds.). 2007. *Men's Lives*, 7th ed. Boston: Allyn & Bacon.

King, Ledyard. 2000. "A Fight to Die without Poverty." *USA Today* (October 19):12D.

Kirchhoff, Sue. 2005. "Minorities Depend on Subprime Loans." *USA Today* (March 17):4B.

Kirksey, Jim. 2001. "Activist Decries Impact on Disabled." *Denver Post* (February 22):49A.

Klein, Joe. 2001. "Closework: Why We Couldn't See What Was Right in Front of Us." *New Yorker* (October 1):44–53.

Klein, Joe. 2010. "Their Own Worst Enemy." *Time* (March 15):21.

Klinenberg, Eric. 2004. "Bourgeois Dystopias." *Nation* (June 28): 40–44.

Kluger, Jeffrey. 2009. "Big Tobacco's New Targets." *Time*. (July 27):50–51.

Knickerbocker, Brad. 2006. "The Environmental Load of 300 Million: How Heavy?" *Christian Science Monitor* (September 26). Online: http://www.csmonitor.com/2006/0926/p01s01-usssc.htm.

Knickerbocker, Brad, and Patrik Jonsson. 2006. "As U.S. Nears Milestone, A Rising Mix of Immigrants." *Christian Science Monitor* (September 19). Online: http://www.csmonitor.com/2006/0919/p01s03-ussc.htm.

Koch, Wendy. 2006. "Homelessness Catches Families Even Amid Affluence." *USA Today* (December 22):1A–2A.

Kocieniewski, David, and Robert Hanley. 2000. "Racial Profiling Routine, New Jersey Finds." *New York Times* (November 28). Online. Available: http://www.nytimes.com/2001/11/28/nyregion/28TROOMet. html.

Kolata, Gina. 2001. "Medical Fees Are Often Higher for Patients without Insurance." *New York Times* (April 2). Online. Available: http://www.nytimes.com/2001/04/02/national/02INSU.html.

Kolbert, Elizabeth. 2006. "Butterfly Lessons: Insects and the Toads Respond to Global Warming." *The New Yorker* (January 9):32–39.

Koretz, Gene. 1998. "Wanted: Black Entrepreneurs." *Business Week* (December 14):26.

Koretz, Gene. 2002. "The Web's Role as Equalizer." *Business Week* (May 13):32.

Kosberg, Jordan I. 1976. "Differences in Proprietary Institutions Caring for Affluent and Nonaffluent Elderly." In Cary S. Hart and Barbara B. Manard (Eds.), *Aging in America*. Port Washington, NY: Alfred.

Kotz, Deborah. 2010. "Get Ready for the Age Wave." *U.S. News & World Report* (February):19–22.

Kozol, Jonathan. 2002. "Malign Neglect." *Nation* (June 10):20–23.

Kozol, Jonathan. 2004. "Jonathan Kozol." *Nation* (May 3):23–24.

Kozol, Jonathan. 2005. "Still Separate, Still Unequal: America's Educational Apartheid." *Harper's Magazine* (September):41–54.

Kralis, Barbara. 2006. Modern Day Slavery Flourishes." *Renew America* (July 19). Online: http://www.renewamerica.us/column/kralis/060719)

Krannich, Richard S., and Peggy Petrazelka. 2003. "Tourism and Natural Amenity Development." In David L. Brown and Louis E. Swanson (Eds.), *Challenges for Rural America in the Twenty-First Century*. University Park: Pennsylvania State University Press, pp. 190–213.

Kriegel, Leonard. 2002. "Handicapping the Crippled." *Nation* (August 19/26): 32–35.

Krim, Jonathan, and Griff Witte. 2005. "Middle Class No More." *Washington Post National Weekly Edition* (January 10):20–21.

Kristof, Nicholas D. 2003. "Gay at Birth?" *New York Times* (October 25):A19.

Kristof, Nicholas D. 2008. "Raising the World's IQ." *New York Times* (December 4). Online: http://www.nytimes.com/2008/12/04/opinion/04kristof.html.

Kroeger, Brook. 1994. "The Road Less Rewarded." *Working Woman* (July):50–55.

Kroll, Andy. 2009. "Lobbyists Still Run Washington." *Progressive Populist* (October 15):8–9.

Krugman, Paul. 2004. "The Death of Horatio Alger." *Nation* (January 5):16–17.

Krugman, Paul. 2006. "The Big Disconnect." *New York Times* (September 1): Online: http://select.nytimes.com/2006/09/02/opinion/01/krugman.html?pagewanted-printed.

Krugman, Paul. 2008. "Grains Gone Wild." *New York Times* (April 7). Online: http://www.ny times.com/2008/04/07/opinion/107krugman. html.

Krugman, Paul. 2009a. "The Big Hate." *New York Times* (June 12). Online: http://www.nytimes.com/2009/06/12/opinion/12krugman.html.

Krugman, Paul. 2009b. "A Dangerous Dysfunction." *New York Times* (December 21). Online: http://www.nytimes.com/2009/12/21/opinion/21krugman.html.

Krugman, Paul. 2010. "Health Reform Myths." *New York Times* (March 12). Online: http://www.nytimes.com/2010/03/12/opinion/12krugman.html.

Kulik, Liat. 2002. "Like-Sex versus Opposite-Sex Effects in Transmissions of Gender Role Ideology from Parents of Adolescents in Israel." *Journal of Youth and Adolescence* 31 (6):451–457.

Kurdek, Lawrence A. 2001. "Differences between Heterosexual-Nonparent Couples and Gay, Lesbian, and Heterosexual-Parent Couples." *Journal of Family Issues* 22(6):728–755.

Kurdek, Lawrence A. 2003. "Differences between Gay and Lesbian Cohabiting Couples." *Journal of Social and Personal Relationships* 20(4):411–436.

Kuttner, Robert. 1998. "Toward Universal Coverage." *Washington Post National Weekly Edition* (July 20):27.

Ladner, Joyce A. 1971. *Tomorrow's Tomorrow*. New York: Doubleday.

Lagnado, Lucette. 2009. "Grandfamilies' come Under Pressure." *Wall Street Journal* (April 4). Online: http://online.wsj.com/article/SB1238807041/19588951.html.

Lakoff, Robin. 2003. "Language, Gender, and Politics: Putting 'Women' and 'Power' in the Same Sentence." In Janet Holmes and Miriam Meyerhoff (Eds.), *The Handbook of Language and Gender*. Malden, MA: Blackwell, pp. 161–178.

Lane, Charles. 2006. "White House Fights Race-Based Admissions Policies." *Washingtonpost.com* (September 4): 17A. Online: Available: http://www.washingtonpost.com/wp-dyn/conten1t/article/2006/09/03/AR2006090300767-pf.html.

Lapham, Lewis. 2004. "Notebook: Straw Votes." *Harper's Magazine* 309 (November):7–9.

Lappe, Frances Moore, and Joseph Collins. 1979. *Food First: The Myth of Scarcity*. New York: Ballantine Books.

Lappe, Frances Moore, and Joseph Collins. 1986. *World Hunger: Twelve Myths*. New York: Grove Press.

Lauer, Nancy Cook. 2002. "Studies Show Women's Role in Media Shrinking." Online: Available: http://www.equality2020.org/media.htm.

Laumann, Edward O., John H. Gagnon, and Stuart Michaels. 1994. *The Social Organization of Sexuality: Sexual Practices in the United States*. Chicago: University of Chicago Press.

Laurance, Jeremy. 2006. "Chemical Pollution 'Harms Children's Brains.'" *The Independent* (November 8). Online: http://news.independent. co.uk/uk/health_medical/article1962438.ece.

Lazare, Daniel. 2001. *America's Undeclared War: What's Killing Our Cities and How We Can Stop It*. New York: Harcourt.

Lee, Sharon M. 1998. "Asian Americans: Diverse and Growing." *Population Bulletin* 53 (June): entire issue.

Lee, Valerie E. and David T. Burkam. 2002. *Inequality at the Starting Gate*. Economic Policy Institute. Washington, DC. Online: Available: http://www.epinet.org/books/starting_gate.html.

Lefkowitz, Bernard. 1998. *Our Guys*. New York: Random House Vintage.

Leinwand, Donna. 1999. "Debate Rages on Remedies for Women's Pay Gap." *Denver Post* (October 11):15A.

Leinwand, Donna. 2001. "The Lowdown on the Hippest Highs." *USA Today* (August 28):6D–7D.

Lekachman, Robert. 1979. "The Specter of Full Employment." In Jerome H. Skolnick and Elliott Currie (Eds.), *Crisis in American Institutions*, 4th ed. Boston: Little, Brown, pp. 50–58.

Lemann, Nicholas. 1986. "The Origins of the Underclass." Parts 1 and 2. *Atlantic Monthly* (June):31–55; (July):54–68.

Leonard, Arthur S. 1990. "Gay/Lesbian Rights: Report from the Legal Front." *Nation* (July 2): 12–15.

Leondar-Wright, Betsy, Meizhu Lui, Gloribell Mota, Dedrick Mohammad, and Mara Voukydis. 2005. *State of the Dream 2005: Disowned in the Ownership Society*. Boston: United for a Fair Economy.

Leopold, Les. 2009. "Wall Street's Gall." *The Progressive* 73 (September):26–28.

Lepore, Jill. 2009. "Preexisting Condition." *New Yorker* (December 7):29–30.

Leslie, Jacques. 2000. "Running Dry: What Happens When the World No Longer Has Enough Fresh Water?" *Harper's Magazine* 301 (July):37–52.

Lessig, Lawrence. 2010. "How to Get Our Democracy Back." *The Nation* (February 22):12–19.

Lever, Janet. 1976. "Sex Differences in the Games Children Play." *Social Problems* 23 (April):478–487.

Levin, Andy. 2004. "Speech." C-Span (September 6), AFL-CIO.

Levin, David C. 2004. "Me and My M.R.I." *New York Times* (July 6): Online. Available: http://www.nytimes.com/2004/07/06/opinion/06LEVI.html.

Levitan, Sar A., and Clifford M. Johnson. 1982. *Second Thoughts on Work*. Kalamazoo, MI: W. E. Upjohn Institute for Employment Research.

Lewin, Tamar. 2001. "Disabled Patients Win Sweeping Changes from H.M.O." *New York Times* (April 13). Online. Available: http://www.nytimes.com/2001/04/13/national/13DISA.html.

Lewis, Amanda E., Maria Kryson, Sharon M. Collins, Korie Edwards, and Geoff Ward. 2004. "Institutional Patterns and Transformations: Race and Ethnicity in Housing, Education, Labor Markets, Religion, and Criminal Justice." In Maria Kryson and Amanda E. Lewis (Eds.), *The Changing Terrain of Race and Ethnicity*. New York: Russell Sage, pp. 67–122.

Lewis, Amanda E., Maria Kryson, and Nakisha Harris. 2004. "Introduction: Assessing Changes in the Meaning and Significance of Race and Ethnicity." In *The Changing Terrain of Race and Ethnicity,* Maria Krysan and Amanda Lewis (eds.). New York: Russell Sage Foundation, pp. 1–24.

Lewis, Bernard. 2001. "Understanding bin Laden." *Rocky Mountain News* (September 22):4B–5B.

Lewis, Sunny. 2004. "Latino Fives, Health at Risk." *AlterNet* (June 30). Online. Available: http://alternet.org/module/printversion/19108.

Lewis, Tyler. 2006. "Race Categories to Change on 2010 Census Form." Leadership Conference on Civil Rights. Online: http://www.civilrights.org/census/about/race-categories-to-change-on-2010l-census-form.html.

Liazos, Alexander. 1972. "The Poverty of the Sociology of Deviance: Nuts, Sluts, and Preverts." *Social Problems* 20 (Summer): 103–120.

Liazos, Alexander. 1982. *People First: An Introduction to Social Problems*. Boston: Allyn & Bacon.

Lichtenberg, Illya. 2006. "Examining Race as a Tool in the War on Drugs." *Police Practice and Research* 7 (March):49–60.

Lichtenberg, Judith. 1992. "Racism in the Head, Racism in the World." Report from the Institute for Philosophy and Public Policy. University of Maryland, Vol. 12 (Spring/Summer):3–5.

Lichter, Daniel T., and Zhenchao Qian. 2004. *Marriage and Family in a Multiracial Society*. Washington, DC: Russell Sage Foundation.

Linden, Eugene. 2000. "Condition Critical." *Time* (April 30): 18–24.

Lindsey, Rebecca. 2007. "Tropical Deforestation." Earth Observatory at NASA. Available online: http://earthobservatory.nasa.gov/features/deforestation/deforestation_ update.php.

Lingeman, Richard. 2010. "Noted." *Nation* (March 15):5.

Linton, Simi. 1998. *Claiming Disability: Knowledge and Identity*. New York: New York University Press.

Llanos, Miguel. 2009. "U.S. Poverty at 40 Million—or 47 Million?" MSNBC.com. (October 20). Available online: http://www.msnbc.msn.com/id/33395012/ns/us_news_life.

Llewellyn, A., and K. Hogan. 2000. "The Use and Abuse of Modes of Disability." *Disability and Society* 15 (January): 157–165.

Lockheed, Marlaine. 1985. "Sex Equity in the Classroom Organization and Climate." In Susan S. Klein (Ed.), *Handbook for Achieving Sex Equity through Education*. Baltimore: Johns Hopkins University Press, pp. 189–217.

Longman, Phillip J. 2001. "American Gridlock." *U.S. News & World Report* (May 28):16–22.

Lopiano, Donna. 2008. "Pay Inequity in Athletics." Women's Sports Foundation. Online: http://www.womenssports-foundation.org/cgi-bin/iowa/issues/disc/article.html?record=118.

Lorber, Judith. 1994. *Paradoxes of Gender*. New Haven, CT: Yale University Press.

Lorber, Judith. 2005. *Gender Inequality: Feminist Theories and Politics*. Los Angeles: Roxbury.

Los Angeles Times. 2003. "A Formula for Inequity." (December 13). Online. Available: http://www.latimes.com/news/opinion/editorials/la-ed-schoolfund13d.

Los Angeles Times. 2004. "Twisted Population Priority." (June 24). Online. Available: http://www.latimes.com/news/opinion/editorials/la-ed-population24jre.

Los Angeles Times (2009). "Medical Bills Led to Two-thirds of Bankruptcies in 2007, Study Finds." (June 4).

Los Angeles Times. 2009. "Medical Bills Led to Two-Thirds of Bankruptcies in 2007, Study Finds." (June 4). Online: http://latimesblog.latimes.com/bbooster_shots/2009/06/medical-bills-led-to-two-thirds-of-bankruptcies.

Lott, Juanita Tamayo, and Judy C. Felt. 1991. "Studying the Pan Asian Community." *Population Today* 19 (April 1):6–8.

Loury, Glenn C. 2007. "Why Are So Many Americans in Prison?" *Boston Review*. (September 1). Available online: http://bostonreview.net/BR32.4/article_loury.php.

Love, Alice Ann. 1998. "Gender Wage Gap Shrinks Slightly." *USA Today* (June 10):1A.

Lowenstein, Roger. 2006. "Who Need the Mortgage-Interest Deduction?" *New York Times* (March 5). Online: Available: http://www.nytimes.com.

Lucal, Betsy. 1996. "Oppression and Privilege: Toward a Relational Conceptualization of Race." *Teaching Sociology* 24 (July):245–255.

Luker, Kristin. 1991. "Dubious Conceptions: The Controversy over Teen Pregnancy." *American Prospect* 5 (Spring):73–83.

Lydersen, Kari. 2002. "Banking on Poverty: Predatory Lenders Take Advantage of the Poor." *In These Times* (October 14):19.

Mabry, J. Beth, Roseann Giarrusso, and Vern L. Bengston. 2004. "Generations, the Life Course, and Family Change." In Jacqueline Scott, Judith Treas, and Martin Richards (Eds.), *The Blackwell Companion to the Sociology of Families*. Malden, MA: Blackwell, pp. 87–108.

MacEwan, Arthur. 2001. "Ask Dr. Dollar." *Dollars & Sense*, No. 233 (January/February):40.

MacGillis, Alec. 2009. "The Gang on the Hill." *Washington Post National Weekly Edition* (August 17):26–27.

Mach, Henry Jay. 1987. "Shrink, Shrank, Shrunk: The Stormy Relationship between Gays and Mental Health Experts." *Advocate* (October 13):43–49.

Magdoff, Fred, and Harry Magdoff. 2004. "Disposable Workers: Today's Reserve Army of Labor." *Monthly Review* 55 (April):18–35.

Mairs, Nancy. 1992. "On Being a Cripple." In L. McDowell and R. Pringle (Eds.), *Defining Women*. Cambridge: Polity.

Males, Mike. 1996. *The Scapegoat Generation: America's War on Adolescents*. Monroe, ME: Common Courage Press.

Malveaux, Julianne. 2003. "'Banking While Black' Hurts Homeowners." *USA Today* (December 12):13A.

Mann, Coramae Rickey, Leon Pittiway, and Ralph Weisheit. (n.d.). "Drugs and the Rural Community." Online. Available: http://www.asc41.com/task reports/drugs&community.txt.

Marcus, Mary Brophy. 2010. "Minorities More Likely to Develop Alzheimer's." *USA Today* (March 9):4D.

Markham, Victoria. 2006. "America's Supersized Footprint." *Business Week* (October 30):132.

Marklein, Mary Beth. 2009. "SAT Scores Show Disparities by Race, Gender, Family Income." *USAToday.com*. (August 26). Available online: http://www.usatoday.com/news/education/2009-08-25-SAT-scores_N.htm.

Marshall, Stephen. 2003. "Prime Time Payola." *In These Times* (May 5):23–24.

Marsiglio, William, Paul Amato, Ronald D. Day, and Michael E. Lamb. 2001. "Scholarship on Fatherhood in the 1990s and Beyond." In Robert M. Milardo (Ed.), *Understanding Families into the New Millennium: A Decade in Review*. Minneapolis: National Council on Family Relations, pp. 392–410.

Martin, Karen A. 2005. "William Wants a Doll: Can He Have One?" *Gender & Society* 19 (August):456–479.

Martin, Patricia Yancey. 2003. "Said and Done Versus Saying and Doing: Gendering Practices, Practicing Gender at Work." *Gender & Society* 17 (June):342–366.

Martin, Philip, and Elizabeth Midgley. 1999. "Immigration to the United States." *Population Bulletin* 54 (June): entire issue.

Martin, Philip, and Elizabeth Midgley. 2006. "Immigration: Shaping and Reshaping America," revised and updated 2nd ed. *Population Bulletin* 61 (December): entire issue.

Marquardt, Katy, and Kirk Shinkle (2009). "Terrible Tale of the Tape." U S. News & World Report (March):54.

Maslow, Abraham H. 1954. *Motivation and Personality*. New York: Harper & Row.

Research: An Agenda for the 1990s." *Items*, Social Science Research Council, 47 (March):7–11.

Massey, Douglas S. 1996. "Concentrating Poverty Breeds Violence." *Population Today* 24 (June/July):5.

Massey, Douglas S. 2006. "The Wall That Keeps Illegal Workers In." *New York Times* (April 4). Online: http://www.nytimes.com/2006/04/04/opinion/04massey.html.

Massey, Douglas S., and Nancy Denton. 1993. *American Apartheid: Segregation and the Making of the Underclass*. Cambridge, MA: Harvard University Press.

Mather, Mark. 2008. "Population Losses Mount in U.S. Rural Areas." *Population Reference Bureau* (March).

Matthews, Jay. 2006. "Study Casts Doubt on the 'Boy Crisis.'" *Washington Post* (June 26):A1.

McAdoo, John. 1988. "Changing Perspectives on the Role of the Black Father." In P. Bronstein and C. P. Cowan (Eds.), *Fatherhood Today, Men's Changing Role in the Family*. New York: Wiley, pp. 79–92.

McCarthy, Michael. 2004. "Circulation Scandals Cast Shadow on Newspaper." *USA Today* (August 9):5B.

McClam, Erin. 2000. "Less Teens Smoked in '99, CDC Says." Associated Press (August 25).

McCormack, Richard. 2010. "The Plight of American Manufacturing." *American Prospect* 21 (January/February):A2–A5.

McGinn, Daniel. 2009. "The Greenest Companies in America." *Newsweek* (September 28).

McGranahan, David A. 2003. "How People Make a Living in Rural America." In David L. Brown and Louis E. Swanson (Eds.), *Challenge for Rural America in the Twenty-First Century*. University Park: Pennsylvania State University Press, pp. 135–151.

McIntosh, Pegg. 1992. "White Privilege and Male Privilege." In Margaret L. Andersen and Patricia Hill Collins (Eds.), *Race, Class, and Gender*. Belmont, CA: Wadsworth, pp. 70–81.

McKinley, Donald Gilbert. 1964. *Social Class and Family Life*. Glencoe, IL: Free Press.

McLanahan, Sara, and Karen Booth. 1991. "Mother Only Families." In Alan Booth (Ed.), *Contemporary Families: Looking Forward, Looking Back*. Minneapolis: National Council of Family Relations, pp. 405–428.

McLaren, Peter and Ramin Farahmandpur. 2006. "The Pedagogy of Oppression: A Brief Look at 'No Child Left Behind.'" *Monthly Review* (July/August):94–99.

McNamee, Stephen J., and Robert K. Miller, Jr. 2009. *The Meritocracy Myth*, 2nd ed. Lanham, MD: Rowman & Littlefield.

Mead, Sara. 2006. "The Truth About Boys and Girls." Education Sector Report (June 27). Online: Available: http://www.educationsector.org/analysis_show.htm?doc_id=378705.

Means, Marianne. 1996. "Blatant Bigotry in Name of Christ." *Rocky Mountain News* (June 15):56A.

Media Report to Women. 2007. "Industry Statistics." Online: www.mediareporttowomen.com/statistics.htm.

Medical News Today. 2004. "Addicted Rats Have Same Compulsive Drive for Cocaine as Humans Do." (August 13). Online: Available: http://www.medicalnewstoday.com/medicalnews.php?newsid=12032.

Memmott, Mark. 2001. "Report: Poor Nations Need Help with Debts." *USA Today* (April 30):3B.

Messner, Michael A. 1992. *Power at Play: Sports and the Problem of Masculinity*. Boston: Beacon.

Messner, Michael A. 1996. "Studying Up on Sex." *Sociology of Sport Journal* 13:221–237.

Metcalf, Stephen. 2002. "Reading between the Lines." *Nation* (January 28):18–22.

Meyerson, Harold. 2009. "America's Decade of Decline." *Washington Post National Weekly Edition* (December 21):30.

Meyerson, Harold. 2010. "The Politics of Industrial Renaissance." *American Prospect* 21 (January/February):A16–A18.

Mignon, Sylvia I., Calvin J. Larson, and William M. Holmes. 2002. *Family Abuse: Consequences, Theories, and Responses*. Boston: Allyn & Bacon. Available online: http://www.feminist.com/fairpay.

Migoya, David. 2002. "Rejected Meat Resold by ConAgra." *Denver Post* (July 28):1A,11A.

Milburn, John. 2009. "State's Relationship with Military Means Big Bucks." *Hutchinson News* (December 7):A3.

Milchen, Jeff, and Jonathan Power. 2001. "Why Is Killing for Capital Not a Capital Crime?" *Progressive Populist* (July 15): 9.

Miles, Rosalind. 1988. *A Women's History of the World*. London: Joseph.

Miller, Casey, and Kate Swift. 1980. *The Handbook of Nonsexist Writing*. New York: Lippincott & Crowell.

Miller, David. 1991. "A Vision of Market Socialism." *Dissent* 38 (Summer):406–414.

Miller, Kathleen K., and Bruce A. Weber. 2004. "How Do Persistent Poverty Dynamics and Demographics Vary across the Rural–Urban Continuum?" *Measuring Diversity* 1(1):1–7. Online. Available: http://sdrc.msstate.edu/measuring/series/miller-weber.pdf.

Miller, Lisa. 2008. "Our Mutual Joy." *Newsweek*. (December 15).

Mills, C. Wright. 1962. "The Big City: Private Troubles and Public Issues." In Irving Louis Horowitz (Ed.), *Power, Politics, and People: The Collected Essays of C. Wright Mills*. New York: Ballantine Books, pp. 395–402.

Mishel, Lawrence, Jared Bernstein, and Sylvia Allegretto. 2004. *The State of Working America 2004/2005*. Washington, DC: The Economic Policy Institute.

Mishel, Lawrence, Jared Bernstein, and Sylvia Allegretto. 2007. *The State of Working America 2006/2007*. Ithaca, NY: Cornell University Press.

Mitchell, Linda M., and Amy Buchele-Ash. 2000. "Abuse and Neglect of Individuals with Disabilities." *Journal of Disability Policy Studies* 10(2):225–243.

Mittleman, Murray, Rebecca A. Lewis, Malcolm Maclure, Jane Sherwood, and James Muller. 2001. "Triggering Myocardial Infarction by Marijuana." *Circulation* 103:2805–2809.

Moberg, David. 2001. "Bush's Energy Deficiency." *In These Times* (June 11):14–15.

Mohan, Geoffrey, and Ann M. Simmons. 2004. "Diversity Spoken in 39 Languages." *Los Angeles Times* (June 16). Online. Available: http://www.latimes.com/news/locak/la-me-multilingual16jun16,1,157.

Mokhiber, Russell. 2010. "The Monopolization of America." *Corporate Crime Reporter* (February 13). Online: http://www.commondreas.org/view/2010/02/13–1.

Mokhiber, Russell, and Robert Weissmann. 1999. "The 100 Corporate Criminals." *Progressive Populist* 5 (October):20.

Montgomery, Mark R. 2009. "Urban Poverty and Health in Developing Countries." *Population Bulletin* 64 (June).

Mooney, Chris. 2006. "Some Like It Hot." *Mother Jones* (May/June):36–49.

Mooney, Nan (2009). "Foreclosure Crisis Hits Warp Speed." AlterNet (March 30). Online: http://www.alternet.org/module/module/printversion/134003.

Moore, Joan W., and Raquel Pinderhughes (Eds.). 1994. *In the Barrios: Latinos and the Underclass Debate*. New York: Russell Sage Foundation.

Moore, Martha. 2006. "Episcopal Church Torn by Gay Issue as More Parishes Leave U.S. Branch." *USA Today* (March 3):1A.

Morin, Richard. 2009. "Black-White Conflict Isn't Society's Largest." *Pew Social and Demographic Trends.*" Online: http://persocialtrends.org/pubs/44/social-divisionso-black-white-conflict-not-society-largest.

Morris, Jenny. 1991. *Pride against Prejudice*. London: Women's Press.

Morton, Lois Wright. 2003. "Rural Health Policy." In David L. Brown and Louis E. Swanson (Eds.), *Challenges for Rural America in the Twenty-First Century*. University Park: The Pennsylvania State University Press, pp. 290–302.

Mosher, Clayton J. and Scott Akins. 2007. *Drugs and Drug Policy: The Control of Consciousness Alteration*. Thousand Oaks, CA: Sage.

Moskos, Peter. 2008. "Too Dangerous Not to Regulate." *U.S. News and World Report*. (August 11):8.

Mouawad, Jad, and Simon Romero. 2005. "Unmentioned Energy Fix: A 55 M.P.H. Speed Limit." *New York Times* (May 1):24xt.

Moyers, Bill. 2006. "Saving Our Democracy." *AlterNet* (February 27). Online: http://www.alternet.org/story/32750.

Moyers, Bill, and Michael Winship. 2009. "Changing the Rules of the Blame Game." *Common Dreams.Org*. (April 8). Online: http://www. commondreams.org/print/40559.

Moyers, Bill, and Michael Winship. 2010. "What Are We Bid for American Justice?" *Common Dreams.Org* (February 20). Online: http://www.commondreams.org/print/53016.

Moynihan, Daniel P. 1988. "Our Poorest Citizens—Children." *Focus* 11 (Spring):5–6.

Muhammad, Dedrick. 2009. *Challenges to Native American Advancement: The Recession and Native America*. New York: Institute for Policy Studies.

Mukhopadhyay, Carol, and Rosemary C. Henze. 2003. "How Real Is Race? Using Anthropology to Make Sense of Human Diversity." *Phi Delta Kappan* (May):669–678.

Multinational Monitor. 1997. "The Great Digital Giveaway." 18 (May):5.

Multinational Monitor. 2001. "The Case against GE." 22 (July/August): entire issue.

Murdoch, William M. 1980. *The Poverty of Nations: The Political Economy of Hunger and Population*. Baltimore: Johns Hopkins University Press.

Murphy, Robert F. 1990. *The Body Silent*. New York: W.W. Norton.

Murphy, Robert F. 1995. "Encounters: The Body Silent in America." In B. Instad and S. Reynolds White (Eds.), *Disability and Culture*. Berkeley, CA: University of California Press, pp. 140–157.

Murray, Charles. 1984. *Losing Ground*. New York: Basic Books.

Muwakkil, Salim. 1994. "Dangerous Curve." *In These Times* (November 28):22–24.

Muwakkil, Salim. 1998a. "Movin' on Apart." *In These Times* (March 22):11–12.

Muwakkil, Salim. 1998b. "Real Minority, Media Majority: TV News Needs to Root Out Stereotypes about Blacks and Crime." *In These Times* (June 28):18–19.

Myrdal, Gunnar. 1944. *An American Dilemma*. New York: Pantheon Books.

NAACP. 2009. "End Campus Racism Campaign, 2009." Available online: http://www.naacp.org/youth/college/endcampusracism/index.htm

NACUBO. 2010. National Association of College and University Business Officers. Available online: http://www.nacubo. org.

Nader, Ralph. 2001. "Corporate Welfare Spoils." *Nation* (May 7):7, 26.

Nader, Ralph. 2010. "Time to Rein in Out-of- Control Corporate Influence on Our Democracy." *CommonDreams.org* (January 23). Online: http://www.commondreams.org/print/51993.

Nakashima, Ellen. 2000. "Student Loan Default Rate Plummets to 6.9 Percent." *Denver Post* (October 2):12A.

Naples, Nancy A. 1998. "Women's Community Activism and Feminist Action Research." In Nancy A. Naples (Ed.), *Community Activism and Feminist Politics*. New York: Routledge, pp. 1–27.

Nation. 1996. "In Fact. . . ." (January 1):5.

Nation. 2006. "The *Nation*al Entertainment State." (July 3):23–26.

Nation 2009a. "Bush's War Totals." (February 16):6.

Nation. 2009b. "Filibustering the Public." (December 14):3.

National Academies. 1998. *Containing the Threat from Illegal Bombings*. Washington, DC: National Academy Press.

National Center for Education Statistics. 2008. "Digest of Education Statistics: 2008," Tables 243, 249. Online: http://nces.ed.gov/programs/digest/d08/tables/dt08_243.asp?referrer=list.

National Center for Education Statistics. 2009. "The Condition of Education 2009." U.S. Department of Education. Available online: http://nces.ed. gov.pubsearch/pubsinfo.asp?pubid=2009081.

National Center for Education Statistics. 2010. Available online: http://nces.ed.gov.

National Center for Science Education. 2006. "Defending the Teaching of Evolution in the Public Schools." Online: Available: http://www.ncseweb.org.

National Center for Science Education. 2007. "Evolution Returns to Kansas." (February 14). Online: Available: http://www.ncseweb.org/resources/news/2007/KS/286_evolution_returns_to_Kansas_2_14_2007.asp.

National Center on Elder Abuse. 1998. *National Elder Abuse Incidence Study*. Washington, DC: American Public Health Services Association.

National Committee on Pay Equity. 2007. "Current Legislation." Online: http://www.pay-equity.org/info-leg.html.

National Committee on Pay Equity. 2009. "Ledbetter Bill Becomes Law." Online: http://www.pay-equity.org/

National Conference of State Legislators. 2009. "Disparities in Health." (August) Available online: http://www.ncsl.org/?tabid+14494#Life *Expectancy Orenstein, Peggy. 2008/"Girls Will Be Girls." New York Times (February 28). Available online:* http://www.nytimes.com/2008/02/10/magazine/10ww/n-1ede-t.html.

National Council of La Raza. 1999. "The Mainstreaming of Hate: A Report on Latinos and Harassment, Hate Violence, and Law Enforcement Abuse in the '90s." (July). Washington, DC.

National Governors Association Center for Best Practices. 2008. "Benchmarking for Success: Ensuring U.S. Students Receive a World-Class Education." The National Governors Association, the Council of Chief State School Officers, and Achieve, Inc. Available online: http://www.corestandards.org.

National Highway Traffic Safety Administration. 2004. Online. Available: http://www.nhtsa.dot.gov.

National Institute on Drug Abuse. 2004. National Institute of Health/US Department of Health and Human Services. Online. Available: http://www.nida.nih.gov.

National Organization for Women. 2002. *Watch Out, Listen Up!* 2002 Feminist Primetime Report. Washington, DC: National Organization for Women.

National Organization for Women. 2005. *Facts about Pay Equity*. Online: http://www.now.org/issues/economic/factsheet. html.

National Organization for Women. 2010. "Celebrating 37 Years of *Roe v. Wade*, NOW Asserts that Abortion Care is a Human Right." Online: http://www.now.org/press/01-10/01-22.html.

National Priorities Project. 2010. "Cost of War to Your Community." (January 1). Online: http://www.nationalpriorities.org/costofwar_home.

NationMaster. 2010. "Energy Statistics: Oil Consumption by Country." Nationmaster.com. Available online: http://www.nationmaster.com.

Native American Aid. 2006. "Living Conditions." A Program of National Relief Charities. Online: Available: http://www.nrcprograms.org/site/pageserver?pagename=naa_livingconditions.

Navarrette, Ruben. 2009. "What Mexico's Drug War Means for U.S." CNN.com. (February 27). Available online: http://www.cnn.com/2009/politics/02/27/navarette.mexico/index.html.

Navarro, Vicente. 1991. "Class and Race: Life and Death Situations." *Monthly Review* 43 (September):1–13.

Neilson, Joyce McCarl. 1990. *Sex and Gender in Society*, 2nd ed. Prospect Heights, IL: Waveland Press.

New York Times. 2000. "A Fix for the Broadcast Giveaway." (October 11). Online. Available: http://nytimes.com/2000/10/11/opinion/11WED2.html.

New York Times. 2002. "The Population Slowdown." (March 28). Online. Available: http://www.nytimes.com/2002/03/28/opinion/_28THU2.html.

New York Times. 2003a. "Fighting School Resegregation." (January 27). Online. Available: http://www.nytimes.com/2003/01/27/opinion/27MON1.html.

New York Times. 2003b. "Suburban Sprawl Adds Health Concerns, Studies Say." (August 31):15.

New York Times. 2006. "Money Down the Drain in Iraq." (October 26): Online: http://www.ny times. com/2006/10/26/opinion/26thr1.html?pagewanted=print.

New York Times. 2008. "An Even Poorer World." (September 2). Online: http://www.nytimes.com/2008/09/02/opinion/02tue3. html.

New York Times. 2010a. "The Court's Blow to Democracy." (January 22). Online: http://www. nytimes.com/2010/01/22/opinion/22fri1.html.

New York Times. 2010b. "If Reform Fails." (March 7). Online: http://www.nytimes.com/2010/03/07/opinion/07sun1.html.

Newman, Katherine S. 1988. *Falling from Grace: The Experience of Downward Mobility in the American Middle Class*. New York: Free Press.

Newsweek. 2007. "The Human Cost of War." (April 2): 42–43.

Nichols, Michelle. 2006. "Conservative Jews OK Gay Rabbis." Reuters (December 6). Online: Available: http://today.reuters.com/news/articles news.aspx?type=domesticNews&storyID=2006-12-06T2116492_01.

Nicolaus, Matin. 1973. Foreword to Karl Marx, *Grundrisse: Foundations of the Critique of Political Economy*. New York: Vintage Books. First published in 1939.

Nilges, Lynda M., and Albert F. Spencer. 2002. "The Pictorial Representation in Notable Children's Picture Books: 1995–1999." *Sex Roles* 45 (1/2):89–101.

Nore, Gordon W. E. 1991. "An Interview with Jonathan Kozol." *Progressive* 55 (December):34–36.

Nye, Joseph S. Jr. (2006). "Transformation is Hard" Time (July 9). Online: Time.com/time/magazine/article/0,9171,1211591,00.html.

Obama, Barack. 2006. "Growth and Disparity: A Decade of U.S. Public School Construction." Statement by Senator Barack Obama. Online: Available: http://www.21csf.org/csf-home/publications/Obama statement.pdf.

Obama, Barack. 2009. "Obama's Speech on Climate Change." *The New York Times* (September 22). Available online: http://www.nytimes.com/2009/09/23/us/politics/23obama.text.html.

O'Brien, Rebecca Davis. 2008. "Who Gets U.S. Foreign Aid." *Parade* (December 14). Online: http://www.parade.com/news/intelligence-report/archive/who-gets/us-foreign-aid.

O'Brien, Timothy L., and Stephanie Saul. 2006. "Buffett to Give Bulk of His Fortune to Gates Charity." *New York Times* (June 26). Online: http://www.nytimes.com/2006/06/26/business/26buffett.html.

O'Donnell, Jayne. 2000. "Suffering in Silence." *USA Today* (April 3):1B–2B.

Office of National Drug Control Policy. 2000. "Methadone." Online. Available: http://www.whitehousedrugpolicy.gov/publications/factsht/methadone.

O'Hare, William P. 1992. "America's Minorities: The Demographics of Diversity." *Population Bulletin* 47 (December): entire issue.

O'Hare, William P. 1996. "A New Look at Poverty in America." *Population Bulletin* 51 (September): entire issue.

O'Kelly, Charlotte. 1980. *Women and Men in Society*. New York: Van Nostrand.

Olinger, David, and Gwen Florio. 2002. "Fiery Debate Rages as Immigrants Pour In." *Denver Post* (October 17):1A, 26A.

Oliver, Melvin L., and Thomas M. Shapiro. 1995. *Black Wealth/White Wealth: A New Perspective on Racial Equality*. New York: Routledge.

Oliver, Mike. 1996. "A Sociology of Disability or a Disablist Sociology?" In Len Barton (Ed.), *Disability and Society: Emerging Issues and Insights*. New York: Longman, pp. 18–42.

Oliver, Rachel. 2008. "Rich, Poor, and Climate Change." CNN.com.(February 17). Available online: http://edition.cnn.com/2008/business/02/17/eco.class.

Olson, Laura R., Wendy Cadge, and James Harrison. 2006. "Religion and Public Opinion about Same-Sex Marriage." *Social Science Quarterly* 87(2):340–357.

Omi, Michael, and Howard Winant. 1986. *Racial Formation in the United States*. London: Routledge & Kegan Paul.

Omi, Michael, and Howard Winant. 1994. *Racial Formation in the United States*, 2nd ed. New York: Routledge & Kegan Paul.

Ong, Paul. 2004. "Auto Insurance Redlining in the Inner City." *Access*, No. 25 (Fall): 40–41.

Oppenheim, Jerrold, and Theo MacGregor. 2006. "The Economics of Poverty: How Investments to Eliminate Poverty Benefit All Americans." *Entergy Corporation* (June). Online: Available: http://www.democracyandregulation.com/detail.cfm?artid=99.

Ore, Tracy. 2009. "Constructing Differences." In *The Social Construction of Difference and Inequality*, Tracy Ore (ed.). New York: McGraw-Hill.

Orenstein, J. B. 2001. "America's Hospital Emergency." *Washington Post National Weekly Edition* (April 30):21.

Orfield, Gary, and Johanna Wald. 2000. "Testing, Testing." *Nation* (June 5):38–40.

Orfield, Gavy. 2009. "Reviving the Goal of an Integrated Society: A 21st Century Challenge." Los Angeles, CA: The Civil Rights Project/Projecto Derechos Civilies at UCLA.

Orlando, Laura. 2001. "Sustainable Sanitation." *Dollars & Sense*, No. 235 (May–June): 28–31.

Ortner, Sherry B. 1974. "Is Female to Male as Nature Is to Culture?" In Michelle Zimbalist Rosaldo and Louise Lamphere (Eds.), *Woman, Culture, and Society*. Stanford, CA: Stanford University Press, pp. 66–88.

Oskamp, Stuart, Karen Kaufman, and Lianna Atchison Wolterbeek. 1996. "Gender Role Portrayal in Preschool Books." *Journal of Social Behavior and Personality* 11(5):27–39.

Pace, David. 2005. "Blacks, Poor More Likely to Breathe Most Unhealthy Air." Associated Press (December 14).

Page, Susan (2009). "In One Year, 24 Million Slide from 'Thriving' to "'Struggling.'" *USA Today* (March 10):1A–2A.

Painter, Kim. 2008. "Can Wealth Affect Health?" *USA Today* (March 24):4D.

Palmer, James. 2007. "Trauma Severe for Iraqi Children." *USA Today* (April 16):1A.

Parenti, Michael. 1978. *Power and the Powerless*, 2nd ed. New York: St. Martin's Press.

Parenti, Michael. 1980. *Democracy for the Few,* 3rd ed. New York: St. Martin's Press.

Parenti, Michael. 1988. *Democracy for the Few,* 5th ed. New York: St. Martin's Press.

Parenti, Michael. 1995. *Democracy for the Few,* 6th ed. New York: St. Martin's Press.

Parenti, Michael. 2008. *Democracy for the Few,* 8th ed. Boston: Thomson Higher Education.

Parrish, Geov. 2001. "Fanning the Flames of Terrorism." *AlterNet* (September 20). Online: www.alternet.org/story.html?StoryID=11547.

Pascual, Cathy. 2000. "Cervical Cancer's Ethnic Tie." *Denver Post* (October 14):33A.

Parsons, Claudia. 2009. "Hate Goes Viral on Social Network Sites." Reuters (May 13). Online: http://www.reuters.com/assets/print?aid=USTRE54C4KW20090513.

Patterson, Orlando. 2007. "The Root of the Problem." *Time* (May 7):58.

Paulson, Michael. 2000. "More Women Embracing the Study of Jewish Faith." *Boston Globe* (March 13):1B, 5B.

Paulson, Tom. 2008. "The Lowdown on Topsoil: It's Disappearing." *Seattle PI* (January 22). Available online: http://www.seattlepi.com/local/348200_dirt22.html.

PBS. 2010. "What Are Ecosystems?" Bill Moyers Reports, Earth on Edge. Available online: http://www.pbs.org/earthonedge/ecosystems/index.html.

Pear, Robert. 2002. "9 of 10 Nursing Homes Lack Adequate Stuff, Study Finds." *New York Times* (February 18). Online. Available: http://www.nytimes.com/2002/02/18/national/18NURS.html.

Pear, Robert. 2004. "Selling to the Poor, Stoves Bill U.S. for Top Prices." *New York Times* (June 6):1.

Pearce, Diana. 1978. "The Feminization of Poverty: Women, Work, and Welfare." *Urban Change Review* 2 (February): 24–36.

Pelka, Fred. 1997. *The Disability Rights Movement*. Santa Barbara, CA: ABC-CLIO.

Pellow, David N. 2000. "Environmental Inequality Formation." *American Behavioral Scientist* 43 (January):581–601.

Penalver, Eduardo M. 2008. "The End of Sprawl?" *Washington Post National Weekly Edition*" (January 7):31.

Peplau, Letitia Anne, Rosemary C. Veniegas, and Susan Miller Campbell. 2004. "Gay and Lesbian Relationships." In Michael S. Kimmel and Rebecca F. Plante (Eds.), *Sexualities: Identities, Behaviors, and Society*. New York: Oxford University Press, pp. 200–215.

Perry, Susan. 2010. "Tobacco Industry Constantly Re-invents its Marketing Efforts, a Minnesota Report Points Out." MinnesotaPost.com (February 11). Available online: http://www.minnpost.com/healthblog/2010/02/11/15845/tobacco_industry_constantly_reinvents_its_marketing_efforts_report_points_out.

Peters, Peter J. 1992. *Intolerance of Discrimination against, and the Death Penalty for Homosexuals as Prescribed in the Bible*. LaPorte, CO: Scriptures for America.

Peterson, Linda, and Elaine Enarson. 1974. "Blaming the Victim in the Sociology of Women: On the Misuse of the Concept of Socialization." Paper presented at the Pacific Sociological Association, San Jose, California, March.

Peterson, Peter. 1999. "The Global Aging Crisis." *Denver Post* (February 7):1J–2J.

Pew Research Center. 2009. "Majority Continues to Support Civil Unions." (October 9). Available online: http://people-press.org/report/553/same-sex-marriage.

Peyser, Marc. 1999. "Home of the Gray." *Newsweek* (March 1): 50–53.

Phillips, Kevin. 2002. *Wealth and Democracy: A Political History of the American Rich*. New York: Broadway Books.

Pierre, Robert E. 2004. "Pockets of the Poor." *Washington Post National Weekly Edition* (July 26/August 1):30.

Pike, Jennifer J., and Nancy A. Jennings. 2005. "The Effects of Commercials on Children's Perceptions of Gender Appropriate Toy Use." *Sex Roles* 52 (1/2): 83–91.

Pillard, Richard C. and J. Michael Bailey. 1998. "Human Sexual Orientation Has a Heritable Component." *Human Biology* 70, no. 2 (April):347–365.

Pillemer, Karl A. 1993. "Abuse Is Caused by the Deviance and Dependence of Abusive Caregivers." In Richard J. Gelles and Donileen R. Loseke (Eds.), *Current Controversies on Family Violence*. Newbury Park, CA: Sage, pp. 237–249.

Pinello, Daniel. 2009. "Location, Location, Location: Same-Sex Relationship Rights by State." *Law Trends and News*. 6(1). Available online: http://www.abanet.org/genpractice/newsletter/lawtrends/09_fall/bl-feat5.html.

Pipher, Mary. 1994. *Reviving Ophelia: Saving the Selves of Adolescent Girls*. New York: Ballantine Books.

Piven, Frances Fox. 1996. "Welfare and the Transformation of Electoral Politics." *Dissent* 43 (Fall):61–67.

Piven, Frances Fox, and Richard A. Cloward. 1971. *Regulating the Poor*. New York: Random House.

Pollard, Kelvin M., and William P. O'Hare. 1999. "America's Racial and Ethnic Minorities." *Population Bulletin,* 54, No. 3 (September). Washington, DC: Population Reference Bureau.

Pollitt, Katha. 2001. "Childcare Scare." *Nation* (May 14):10.

Pollitt, Katha. 2010. "The Decade For Women: Forward, Backward, Sideways?" *The Nation* (January 15):10.

Population Reference Bureau. 2009. "2009 World Population Data Sheet." Washington, DC.

Population Today. 2000. "Unequal Justice in U.S. Courts, Prisons." 28 (July):5.

Portes, Alejandro, and Min Zhou. 1993. "The New Second Generation: Segmented Assimilation and Its Variants." *Annals of the American Academy of Political and Social Science* 530:74–96.

Portillo, Ely. 2006. "Costs of Teen Drinking Add Up to $62 Billion." *Wichita Eagle* (June 30):4A.

Powell, Bill. 2006. "When Outlaws Get the Bomb." *Time* (October 23):32–37.

Powers, Kristen A. 2007. "Immigrants Become Target for All of Society's Ills." *USA Today* (August 29):13A.

Press, Eyal, and Jennifer Washburn. 2000. "Neglect for Sale." *American Prospect* (May 8):22–29.

Prewitt, Kenneth. 2003. *Politics and Science in Census Taking*. New York: Russell Sage Foundation.

Progressive. 2009. "Job Loss Is Pentagon's Gain." Vol. 73 (December):5.

Public Broadcasting System. 2009. "Frontline: The Failure and Future of the Private Insurance Industry." (March 31).

Public Citizen. 2003. "The Other Drug War." (June 23). Online. Available: http://www.citizen.org/pressroom/release.cfm?ID=1469.

Pugh, Tony. 2009. "Health Premiums Soar." *Wichita Eagle*. (September 15):1A, 3A.

Purdum, Todd S. 2000. "Shift in the Mix Alters the Face of California." *New York Times* (July 4) Online. Available: http://www.nytimes.com/library/national/070400calatin.html.

Pyke, Karen. 2004. "Immigrant Families in the U.S." In *The Blackwell Companion to the Sociology of Families*. Malden, MA: Blackwell, pp. 253–269.

Pyke, Karen. 2008. "Immigrant Families in the U.S." In Stephanie Coontz (ed.), *American Families: A Multicultural Reader*, 2nd ed. New York: Routledge, pp. 210–221.

Quindlen, Anna. 2007. "Killing the Consumer." *Newsweek* (October 1).

Quinney, Richard. 1970. *The Social Reality of Crime*. Boston: Little, Brown.

Rall, Ted. 2006. "End of the U.S. as a Civilized Nation." *Progressive Populist* (November 15):19.

Rampell, Catherine. 2009. "The Mancession." Economix. Available online: http://economix.blogs.nytimes.com/2009/08/10/themancession/

Rand, Michael R. 2009. "Criminal Victimization, 2008." *Bureau of Justice Statistics, National Crime Victimization Survey*. Available online: http://bjs.ojp.usdoj.gov/content/pub/cv08.pdf.

Rapp, Rayna. 1982. "Family and Class in Contemporary America." In Barrie Thorne and Marilyn Yalom (Eds.), *Rethinking the Family: Some Feminist Questions*. New York: Longman, pp. 168–187.

Rashbaum, William K. 2010. "New York Police Manipulated Crime Data, Retired Officials Say." *New York Times*. (February 7):20.

Raum, Tom. 2009. "Higher Jobless Rates Could Be a 'New Normal.'" Associated Press (October 20).

Rawlings, Steve. 1995. "Households and Families: Population Profile of the United States: 1995." *Current Population Reports*, Series P23–189. Washington, DC: U.S. Government Printing Office.

Re, Richard. 2002. "A Persisting Evil." *Harvard International Review* 23 (Winter):32–35.

Reed, Adolph, Jr. 1990. "The Underclass as Myth and Symbol: The Poverty of Discourse about Poverty." *Radical America* 24 (January/March):21–40.

Reed, Adolph, Jr. 1994. "Looking Backward." *Nation* (November 28):654–662.

Reed, Betsy. 2009. "Unemployment Is Hitting Men Particularly Hard—and Both Sexes are Losing Out." *AlterNet* (April 8). Online: http://www.alternet.org/story/135521.

Regan, Tom. 2007. "Polls Show Anti-American Feelings at All-Time High in Muslim Countries." *Christian Science Monitor* (February 22). Online: http://www.csmonitor.com/2007/0222/p99s01-duts.htm.

Reich, Robert B. 1989. "Yes: Blame Election Funds." *New York Times* (October 12):A29.

Reich, Robert B. 1998. "Broken Faith: Why We Need to Renew the Social Compact." *Nation* (February 16):11–17.

Reich, Robert B. 2000. "What's the Difference?" *American Prospect* (August 28):64.

Reich, Robert B. 2008. "Totally Spent." *New York Times* (February 13). Online: http://www. nytimes.com/2008/02/13/opinion/13reich.html.

Reich, Robert B. 2009. "The Union Way Up." *Los Angeles Times* (January 26). Online: http://www.latimes.com/news/opinion/la-oe-reich26-2009gav26,0,38.

Reid, T. R. 2009. *The Healing of America*. New York: Penguin Press.

Reiman, Jeffrey. 2004. *The Rich Get Richer and the Poor Get Prison: Ideology, Class, and Criminal Justice*, 7th ed. Boston, MA: Allyn and Bacon.

Reiman, Jeffrey H. 2007. *The Rich Get Richer and the Poor Get Prison: Ideology, Class, and Criminal Justice*, 8th ed. Boston: Allyn & Bacon.

Reinarman, Craig, and Peter Cohen. 2007. "Law, Culture, and Cannabis: Comparing Use Patterns in Amsterdam and San Francisco." In Mitch E. Earleywine (Ed.). *Pot Politics: Marijuana and the Costs of Prohibition*. New York: Oxford University Press, pp. 113–137.

ReligiousTolerance.org. 2009. "Judeo-Christianity and Homosexuality." Available online: http://www.religioustolerance.org/hom_bibl.htm.

Relman, Arnold. 2009. "The Health Reform We Need and Are Not Getting." *New York Review of Books* 56 (July 2). Online: http://www. nybooks.com/articles/22798.

Renteman, Rob. 2004. "Sobering Statistics to Ponder over Labor Day." *Rocky Mountain News* (Sept 4):2C.

Renzetti, Claire M., and Daniel J. Curran. 2003. *Women, Men, and Society*, 5th ed. Boston: Allyn & Bacon.

Reskin, Barbara F. 1999. "Occupational Segregation by Race and Ethnicity among Women Workers." In Irene Brown (Ed.), *Latinas and African American Women at Work: Race, Gender, and Economic Inequality*. New York: Russell Sage.

Reskin, Barbara F., and Patricia A. Roos. 1990. *Job Queues, Gender Queues*. Philadelphia: Temple University Press.

Reuss, Alejandro. 2001. "Cause of Death: Inequality." *Dollars & Sense*, No. 235 (May/June):10–12.

Revkin, Andrew C. 2009. "Global Warming." *New York Times* (December 8). Available online: http://topics.nytimes.com/top/news/science/topics/global warming/index.html

Richburg, Keith B. 2004. "A Smorgasbord of Cultures." *Washington Post National Weekly Edition* (November 107):17.

Richburg, Keith B. 2009. "When Locking 'Em Up Costs Too Much," *Washington Post National Weekly* (July 20–26): 33.

Richmond-Abbott, Marie. 1992. *Masculine and Feminine: Sex Roles over the Life Cycle*, 2nd ed. New York: McGraw-Hill.

Ricks, Thomas E. 2006. *Fiasco: The American Military Adventure in Iraq*. New York: Penguin.

Ricks, Thomas E., and Ann Scott Tyson. 2007. "Unseen Casualties." *Washington Post National Weekly Edition* (May 14):33.

Ridgeway, Cecilia L. 1997. "Interaction and the Conservation of Gender Inequality: Considering Employment." *American Sociological Review* 62 (April):218–235.

Ridgeway, Cecilia L., and Lynn Smith-Lovin. 1999. "The Gender System and Interaction." *Annual Review of Sociology* 25: 191–216.

Ridgeway, James. 2009. "Who Shredded Our Safety Net?" Mother Jones 34 (May/June):28–33, 81–82.

Risman, Barbara J. 1998. *Gender Vertigo*. New Haven, CT: Yale University Press.

Risman, Barbara J., and Donald Tomaskovic-Devey. 1998. "Editors Note." *Contemporary Sociology* 27 (March):vii–viii.

Ritzer, George. 2000. *The McDonaldization of Society: New Century Edition*. Thousand Oaks, CA: Pine Forge Press.

Rivera, Amaced, Jeannette Hullga, Christina Kasica, and Dedrick Muhammad. 2009. "*The Silent Depression: State of the Dream 2009*." Boston: United for a Fair Economy.

Roberts, Sam. 2005. "More Africans Enter U.S. than in Days of Slavery." *New York Times* (February 21):A1.

Roberts, Sam. 2008. "In a Generation, Minorities May Be the U.S. Majority." *New York Times* (August 14). Online: http://www.nytimes.com/2008/08/14/washington/14census.html.

Robinson, Eugene. 2007. "Pulling over for Prejudice." *Washington Post National Weekly Edition* (May 7):31.

Robinson, Joe. 2006. "Bring Back the 40-Hour Workweek—and Let Us Take a Long Vacation." *Los Angeles Times* (January 1). Online: http://www.latimes.com/news/opinion/commentary/lal-op-robinson 1Jan01,0,6642632,print.st.

Robinson, Matthew B. 2002. *Justice Blind: Ideals and Realities of American Criminal Justice*. Upper Saddle River, NJ: Prentice Hall.

Robinson, Matthew B. and Renee G. Scherlen. 2007. *Lies, Damned Lies, and Drug War Statistics: A Critical Analysis of Claims Made by the Office of National Drug Control Policy*. Albany: State of University of New York Press.

Rodgers, Harrell R. 2006. *American Poverty in a New Era of Reform*, 2nd ed. Armonk, New York: M.E. Sharpe.

Rogers, Heather. 2005. *Gone Tomorrow: The Hidden Life of Garbage*. New York: The New Press.

Rogers, Joel. 1998. "Turning to the Cities: A Metropolitan Agenda." *In These Times* (October 18):14–17.

Rogers, Susan Carol. 1978. "Women's Place: A Critical Review of Anthropological Theory." *Comparative Studies in Society and History* 20 (1):123–162.

Romaine, Suzanne. 1999. *Communicating Gender*. Mahwah, NJ: Erlbaum.

Romero, Adam P., Amanda K. Baumie, M. V. Lee Badgett, Gary J. Gates. 2007. "Census Snapshot." The Williams Institute. Available online: http://www.law.ucla.edu/williamsinstitute/publications/USCensus Snapshot.pdf.

Ronai, Carol Rambo, Barbara A. Zsembik, and Joe R. Feagin. 1997. "Introduction." In Carol Rambo Ronai, Barbara A. Zsembik, and Joe R. Feagin (Eds.), *Everyday Sexism in the Third Millennium*. New York: Routledge, pp. 1–11.

Rosaldo, Michelle Zimbalist. 1974. "Women, Culture, and Society: A Theoretical Overview." In Michelle Zimbalist Rosaldo and L. Lamphere (Eds.), *Woman, Culture, and Society*. Stanford, CA: Stanford University Press, pp. 17–42.

Rosaldo, Michelle Zimbalist. 1980. "The Use and Abuse of Anthropology." *Signs* 5 (Spring):389–417.

Rosenbaum, David E. 2001. "Ruling on Disability Rights Is a Blow, Advocates Say." *New York Times* (February 22). Online. Available: http://www.nytimes.com/2001/02/22/national/22REAC.html.

Rosenberg, Debra. 2006. "A Renewed War Over 'Don't Ask, Don't Tell.'" *Newsweek* (November 27):8.

Rosenbloom, Joseph. 2004. "The Unique Brutality of Texas." *American Prospect* (July): A11–A13.

Rosenthal, Elisabeth. 2008. "China Tops U.S. to Become World's Top Carbon Emitter." *Wichita Eagle* (June 14):5A.

Rosenthal, Robert, and Lenore Jacobson. 1968. *Pygmalion in the Classroom: Teacher Expectations and Pupils' Intellectual Development*. New York: Holt, Rinehart & Winston.

Rothschild, Scott. 2003. "Aquifer's Depletion Brings Warning." *Lawrence Journal-World* (February 7).

Rothstein, Richard. 2007. "A Wider Lens on the Black–White Achievement Gap." In D. Stanley Eitzen and Janis E. Johnston (Eds.), *Inequality: Social Class and Its Consequences*. Boulder, CO: Paradigm Publishers, pp. 120–128.

Roughgarden, Joan. 2004. *Evolution's Rainbow: Diversity, Gender, and Sexuality in Nature and People*. Ewing, NJ: University of California Press.

RTNDA (Radio-Television News Directors Association. 2008. "Cover Story: 2008 Women and Minorities Survey." Available online: http://www.rtdna.org/pages/mediaitems/the-face-of-the-workforce 1472.php

Rubenstein, Ed. 1995. "The Economics of Crime." *Vital Speeches of the Day* 62 (October 15):19–21.

Rubin, Lillian B. 2006. "What Am I Going to Do with the Rest of My Life?" *Dissent* (Fall):88–94.

Rubin, Rita. 2007. "Study: Women, Blacks Less Likely to Get Implantable Heart Devices." *USA Today* (October 3):6D.

Rugaber, Christopher S. 2009. "Number of Long-Term Jobless Grows." Associated Press (December 5).

Rupp, Leila J. 2007. "Everyone's Queer." In Susan J. Bunting (Ed.) *Annual Editions: Human Sexuality*, 30th ed. Dubuque, IA: McGraw-Hill., pp. 55–58.

Russell, Jan Jarboe. 2003. "Religious Right 'Monkeying with Our Kids' Textbooks Again." *San Antonio Express-News* (September 14):1H.

Russell, Marta. 1998. *Beyond Ramps: Disability at the End of the Social Contract*. Monroe, ME: Common Courage Press.

Russell, Marta. 2000. "The Political Economy of Disablement." *Dollars & Sense*, No. 231 (September/October):13–15, 48–49.

Ryan, William. 1976. *Blaming the Victim*, rev. ed. New York: Random House (Vintage).

Saad, Lydia. 2009. "U.S. Support for Legalizing Marijuana Reaches New High." Gallup.com (October 19). Available online: http://www.gallup.com/poll/123728/u.s.-support-legalizing-marijuana-reaches-new-high.aspx.

Sabet, Kevin A. 2007. "The (Often Unheard) Case Against Marijuana Leniency." In Mitch Earleywine (Ed.) *Pot Politics: Marijuana and the Costs of Prohibition*. New York: Oxford University Press.

Sacks, Karen. 1974. "Engels Revisited: Women, the Organization of Production, and Private Property." In Michelle Zimbalist Rosaldo and Louise Lamphere (Eds.), *Woman, Culture, and Society*. Stanford, CA: Stanford University Press, pp. 207–222.

Sacks, Peter. 2003. "Class Rules: The Fiction of Egalitarian Higher Education." *Chronicle of Higher Education* (July 25):B7–B10.

Sadker, David. 2002. "An Educator's Primer on the Gender War." *Phi Delta Kappan* 84(3):235–244.

Sadker, Myra, and David Sadker. 1994. *Failing at Fairness. How America's Schools Cheat Girls*. New York: Scribner.

Saenz, Rogelio. 2004. *Latinos and the Changing Face of America*. New York: Russell Sage Foundation and the Population Reference Bureau.

Saenz, Rogelio. 2005. "The Social and Economic Isolation of Urban African Americans." *Population Reference Bureau*. Online: http://www.prb.org/Articles/2005/TheSocialandEconomicIsolationofUrbanAfricanAmericans.aspx.

Samuels, Jocelyn. 2009. "Equal Pay Day! Women Catch Up with Men on 2008 Wages." *AlterNet* (April 28). Online: http://www.alternet.org/story/138594/

Samuelson, Robert J. 2005. "The Dawn of a New Oil Era?" *Newsweek* (April 4):37.

Samuelson, Robert J. 2006. "300 Million Reasons to Worry?" *Washington Post* (October 4):A25.

Sanders, Bernard. 1994. "Whither American Democracy." *Los Angeles Times* (January 16):B1.

Sanders, Bernard. 2004. "We Are the Majority." *The Progressive* 68 (February):26–28.

Sandler, Lauren. 2009. "Code Pink." *Mother Jones* 34 (September/October):73–75.

Sapiro, Virginia. 1999. *Women in American Society*, 4th ed. Mountain View, CA: Mayfield.

Saporito, Bill. 2005. "The e-Health Revolution." *Time* (June 27):55–57.

Sarasohn, David. 1997. "Hunger on Main St." *Nation* (December 8):13–18.

Sawin, Janet L. 2004. "Making Better Energy Choices." In Linda Stark (Ed.), *State of the World 2004*. New York: W.W. Norton, pp. 24–43.

Scahill, Jeremy. 2007. "Bush's Shadow Army." *Nation* (April 2): 11–19.

Scahill, Jeremy. 2009. "283 Bases, 170,000 Pieces of Equipment, 140,000 Troops, and an Army of Mercenaries: The Logistical Nightmare in Iraq." *AlterNet* (March 30). Online: http://www.alternet.orgg/module/printversion/133676

Scheer, Robert. 2002. "Playing Population-Explosion Politics." *Los Angeles Times* (November 5): Online. Available: http://www.latimes.com/news/opinion/commentary/laoe-scheer5nov05,0,5557144.column?cnl.

Schemo, Diana. 2007. "Failing Schools Strain to Meet U.S. Standard." *New York Times* (October 16). Available online: http://www.nytimes.com/2007/10/16/education/16child.html.

Schepp, David. 2004. "Corporate America Swings Open Its Doors to Gay Workers." *The Coloradoan* (April 19):A3.

Scher, Abby. 2000. "Corporate Welfare: Pork for All." *Dollars & Sense,* No. 229 (May/June):11.

Scher, Abby. 2001. "Access Denied: Immigrants and Health Care." *Dollars & Sense,* No. 235 (May/June):8.

Schlosser, Eric. 2001. "The Chain Never Stops." *Mother Jones* (July/August). Online: http://www.motherjones.com/news/feature/2006/07/meatpacking.html.

Schlosser, Eric. 2006. "Hog Hell." *Nation* (September 11):28–31.

Schmidt, Peter. 2007. "How to Get Into Yale With a 'B' Average." *The Week* (October 19): 14.

Schmid, Randolph E. 2006. "Study: Having Brothers Raises Chance of Being Gay." *Arizona Daily Star* (June 27):3A.

Schmit, Julie. 2004. "Drug Companies Dodge Ban from Medicare, Medicaid." *USA Today* (August 16):1D.

Schmitt, Christopher H. 2002. "The New Myth of Old Age." *U.S. News & World Report* (September 30):66–74.

Schmitt, Mark. 2010. "The End of the Tea Party." *American Prospect* (February 22). Online: http://prospect.org/cs/articles?article=the-end-of-the-tea-party.

Schneider, David M., and Raymond T. Smith. 1973. *Class Differences and Sex Roles in American Family and Kinship Structure*. Upper Saddle River, NJ: Prentice Hall.

Schoettler, Gail. 2000. "You Can't Buy Human Decency." *Denver Post* (October 1):2L.

Schouten, Fredreka. 2008. "Donors Pick Up Parties Expenses." *USA Today* (August 15):1A.

Schouten, Fredreka. 2010. "Lobbying Industry Booms in Recession." *USA Today* (February 2). Online: http://www.usatoday.com/news/washington/2010-02-04-lobbying-N.htm.

Schouten, Fredreka, and Patrick O'Driscoll. 2007. "Conventions Welcome Corporate Cash." *USA Today* (July 27):1A.

Schouten, Fredreka, and Paul Overberg. 2009. "Lobbyists Unlimited in Honoring Lawmakers." *USA Today* (June 8):1A, 5A.

Schrag, Peter. 2007. "As California Goes . . ." *Nation* (April 9):18–21.

Schumpeter, Joseph. 1950. *Capitalism, Socialism, and Democracy,* 3rd ed. New York: Harpers.

Schur, Edwin. 1971. *Labeling Deviant Behavior: Its Sociological Implications*. New York: Harper & Row.

Schwartz, John. 2004. "Always on the Job, Employees Pay with Health." *New York Times* (September 5):1, 23.

Schwartz, Moshe. 2009. "Department of Defense Contractors in Iraq and Afghanistan." *Congressional Research Service,* R40764 (December 14).

Schwartz, Pepper. 2007. "The Social Construction of Heterosexuality." In Michael S. Kimmel (Ed.), *The Sexual Self: The Construction of Sexual Scripts*. Nashville, TN: Vanderbilt University Press, pp. 80–92.

Science Daily. 2008a. "Big Pharma Spends More on Advertising Than Research and Development." (January 7). Online: http://www.sciencedaily.com/releasess/2008/01/080105140107.htm.

Science Daily. 2008b. "Symmetry of Homosexual Brain Resembles that of Opposite Sex, Swedish Study Finds." Available online: http://www.sciencedaily.com/releases/2008/06/080617151845.htm.

Scorecard. 2010. "The Pollution Information Site." Available online: http://scorecard.org.

Scotch, Richard K. 1989. "Politics and Policy in the History of the Disability Rights Movement." *Millbank Quarterly* 67, Suppl. 2, Pt. 2:380–400.

Seabrook, John. 2002. "The Slow Lane." *The New Yorker* (September 2):120–129.

Seelye, Katharine Q. 2009. "Competing Ads on Health Plan Swamp Airwaves." *New York Times* (August 16):1, 8.

Seelye, Katharine Q. 2010. "Pro or Con, Lobbying Thrived." *New York Times* (January 31):20.

S.E.I.U. Service Employees International Union, AFL-CIO, CLC. 2005. Online. Available: http://www.seiu.org.

Sen, Amartya. 1999. *Development as Freedom*. New York: Knopf.

Sen, Amartya. 2000. "Population and Gender Equity." *Nation* (July 24):16–18.

Sengupta, Kim, and Patrick Cockburn. 2007. "The War on Terror Is the Leading Cause of Terrorism." *AlterNet* (March 1). Online: http://www.alternet.org/module/printversion/48620.

Servicemembers Legal Defense Network. 2006. "Executive Summary: 10th Annual Report on 'Don't Ask, Don't Tell.'" Online: Available: http://www.sldn.org/templates/press/record.html?section= 3&record=1450.

Servicemembers Legal Defense Network. 2009. "About Don't Ask, Don't Tell." Available online: http://www.sldn.org/pages/about-dadt.

Serwer, Andy. 2009. "The Decade from Hell." *Time* (December 7):30–38.

Shadid, Anthony. 2007. "A Widening Rift: Sunni–Shiite Tension Is Spreading Across the Arab World." *Washington Post National Weekly Edition* (February 19):6–7.

Shah, Anup. 2008. "Consumption and Consumerism." *Global Issues* (September 3). Available online:

http://www.globalissues.org/issue/235/consumption-and-consumerism.

Shah, Anup. 2009. "U.S. and Foreign Aid Assistance." *Global Issues.Org*. (April 13). Online: http://www.globallissues.orgg/article35/usa-and-foreignaid-assistance#M.

Shakespeare, Tom. 1996. "Power and Prejudice: Issues of Gender, Sexuality, and Disability." In Len Barton (Ed.), *Disability and Society: Emerging Issues and Insights*. New York: Longman, pp. 191–214.

Shakespeare, Tom. 2006. *Disability Rights and Wrongs*. London: Routledge.

Shanker, Albert. 1991. "Dumbing Down America." *New York Times* (January 27):E7.

Shanker, Albert. 1992a. "Children in Crisis." *New York Times* (February 16):E9.

Shanker, Albert. 1992b. "How Far Have We Come?" *New York Times* (August 16):E9.

Shanker, Albert. 1995. "In Defense of Government." *New York Times* (November 5):E7.

Shanker, Thom. 2009. "Despite Slump, U.S. Role as Top Arms Supplier Grows." *New York Times* (September 7). Online: http://www.nytimes.com/2009/09/07/world/07weapons.html.

Shapiro, Judith. 1981. "Anthropology and the Study of Gender." In Elizabeth Langland and Walter Gove (Eds.), *A Feminist Perspective in the Academy*. Chicago: University of Chicago Press, pp. 110–129.

Shapiro, Thomas M. 2004. *Houses Dividend: The Hidden Cost of Being African American*. New York: Oxford University Press.

Shaw-Taylor, Yoku. 2009. "The Changing Face of Black America." *Contexts* 8 (Fall):62–63.

Shelden, Randall G. 2001. *Controlling the Dangerous Classes: A Critical Introduction to the History of Criminal Justice*. Boston: Allyn & Bacon.

Shelden, Randall G., and William B. Brown. 2002. "Crime Rate Stagnant: Where Did the Money Go?" *Progressive Populist* (July 1):8.

Shelden, Randall G., and William B. Brown. 2004. "The New American Apartheid." *ZNet* (June 22). Online: http://www.zmag.org/content/print_article.cfm?itemID=5758§ion.

Shepard, Judy. 2003. "Five Years Later, Progress Against Gay Hatred Lags." *USA Today* (October 13):15A.

Shipler, David K. 2004. *The Working Poor: Invisible In America*. New York: Alfred A. Knopf.

Shorris, Earl. 2004. "Ignoble Liars." *Harper's Magazine* (June): 65–71.

Shreve, Anita. 1984. "The Working Mother as Role Model." *New York Times Magazine* (September 9):43.

Shuit, Douglas P. 1995. "Filling the Void." *Los Angeles Times* (July 27):B2.

Shulman, Beth. 2007. "America's Low Wage Workers." In D. Stanley Eitzen and Janis E. Johnston (Eds.), *Inequality: Social Class and Its Consequences*. Boulder, CO: Paradigm Publishers, pp. 97–102.

Shute, Nancy, Toni Locy, and Douglas Pasternak. 2000. "The Perils of Pills." *U.S. News & World Report* (March 6):45–50.

Sidel, Ruth. 1994. *Battling Bias*. New York: Penguin Books.

Siegel, Michael. 2007. "Unsafe at Any Level." *New York Times* (January 28). Online: Available: http://www.nytimes.com/2007/01/28/opinion/28Siegel.html.

Silvers, Anita. 1998. "Formal Justice." In Anita Silvers, David Wasserman, and Mary B. Mahowald (Eds.), *Disability, Difference, Discrimination*. Lanham, MD: Rowman & Littlefield, pp. 13–145.

Simons-Morton, Bruce, William Pickett, Will Boyce, Tom F. M. ter Bogt, and Wilma Vollebergh. 2010. "Cross-National Comparison of Adolescent Drinking and Cannabis Use in the United States, Canada, and the Netherlands." *International Journal of Drug Policy* 21:64–69.

Singer, Matt. 2006. "Overpaying for Jobs." *Progressive Populist* (August 1):6.

Singh, Robert. 2006. "The Bush Doctrine." In Mary Buckley and Robert Singh (Eds.), *The Bush Doctrine and the War on Terrorism*. London: Routledge, pp. 12–31.

Sklar, Holly. 1993. "The Upperclass and Mothers and the Hood." *Z Magazine* 6 (March):22–36.

Sklar, Holly. 2004a. "Don't Get Duped Out of Your Social Security." Knight Ridder/Tribune News Service (March 8).

Sklar, Holly. 2004b. "Break That Glass Ceiling." *Progressive Populist* (June 15):16.

Sklar, Holly. 2009. "Medicare for All: Yes We Can." *Progressive Populist* (November 1):15.

Skolnick, Jerome, and Elliott Currie. 1973. "Introduction: Approaches to Social Problems." In Jerome Skolnick and Elliott Currie (Eds.), *Crisis in American Institutions*, 2nd ed. Boston: Little, Brown, pp. 1–17.

Slevin, Peter. 2005. "The Anti-Evolution Revolution." *The Washington Post National Weekly Edition* (March 21–27):6.

SmartMoney.com. 2008. "Long-Term Care" (September).

Smith, Maureen. 2001. "An Exploration of African American Preschool-Aged Children's Behavioral Regulation in Emotionally Arousing Situations." *Child Study Journal* 31(1):13–45.

Smith, Michael D., and Richard S. Krannich. 2000. "'Culture Clash' Revisited: Newcomer and Longer-Term Residents' Attitudes toward Land Use, Development, and Environmental Issues in Rural Communities in the Rocky Mountain West." *Rural Sociology* 65(3):396–421.

Snipp, Matthew. 1996. "The First Americans: American Indians." In Silvia Pedraza and Ruben G. Rumbaut

(Eds.), *Origins and Destinies: Immigration, Race, and Ethnicity in America*. Belmont, CA: Wadsworth, pp. 390–403.

Sojourners. 2010. "Cut the Deficit—Cut Military Spending." (February 4).

Sokoloff, Natalie J., and Ida Dupont. 2005. "Domestic Violence: Examining the Intersection of Race, Class, and Gender: An Introduction." In Natalie J. Sokoloff (Ed.), *Domestic Violence at the Margins: Readings on Race, Class, Gender, and Culture*. New Brunswick, NJ: Rutgers University Press, pp. 1–13.

Solomon, Sondra E., Esther D. Rothblum, and Kimberly F. Balsam. 2005. "Money, Housework, Sex, and Conflict: Same-Sex Couples in Civil Unions, Those Not in Civil Unions, and Heterosexual Married Siblings," *Sex Roles* 52(9/10):561–575.

Sommers, Christina Hoff. 2000. *The War Against Boys: How Misguided Feminism Is Harming Our Young Men*. New York: Simon and Schuster.

SourceWatch. 2008. "Government-Industry Revolving Door." (July 23). Online: http://www.sourcewatch.org/index.php?title-Government-industry-revolving.

SourceWatch. 2009. "Lockheed Martin." (December 14). Online: http://www.sourcewatch.org/index.php?title=Lockheed-Martin.

Southern Poverty Law Center (SPLC). 2006. "Immigration Fervor Fuels Racist Extremism." *SPLC Report* 36 (June):1.

Southern Poverty Law Center (SPLC). 2007. "Hate Group Numbers Continue to Increase." *SPLC Report* 37 (Spring):1.

Southern Poverty Law Center. 2008. "Nativist Rage Fuels Hate Group Growth." *SPLC Report* 38 (Spring):1.

Southern Poverty Law Center. 2009a. "N. Y. County is Microcosm of Anti-Immigrant Violence." *Southern Poverty Law Center Report* 39 (Summer):5.

Southern Poverty Law Center. 2009b. "Militia Movement Resurgent, Infused with Racism." *Southern Poverty Law Center Report* 39 (Fall):1.

South Texas Colonia Initiative. 2010. "Who We Are." (January 9). Online: http://www.southtexascolonia.org.

Spector, Malcolm, and John I. Kitsuse. 1987. *Constructing Social Problems*. Hawthorne, NY: Aldine de Gruyter.

Spencer, Porche, and E. Toleman. 2003. "We've Come a Long Way—Maybe: New Challenges for Gender Equity in Education." *Teachers College Record* 105(9): 1774–1807.

Squires, Gregory D. 2005. "Predatory Lending: Redlining in Reverse." National Institute of House, Shelterforce Online, Issue #139 (January/February). Online: http://www.nhi.org/online/issues/139/redlining.html.

Stacey, Judith. 1990. *Brave New Families: Stories of Domestic Upheaval in Late Twentieth-Century America*. New York: Basic Books.

Stacey, Judith. 1991. "Backward toward the Postmodern Family: Reflections on Gender, Kinship, and Class in the Silicon Valley." In Alan Wolfe (Ed.), *America at Century's End*. Berkeley: University of California Press, pp. 17–34.

Stack, Carol B. 1990. "Different Voices, Different Visions: Gender, Culture, and Moral Reasoning." In Faye Ginsburg and Anna Lowenhaupt Tsing (Eds.), *Uncertain Terms: Negotiating Gender in American Culture*. Boston: Beacon Press, pp. 19–27.

Stack, Joseph. 2010. "Joseph Stack Manifesto." *Fox News* (February 18). Online: http://www.foxnews.com/printer-friendly-story/0,3566,586627,00.html.

StateMaster. n.d. "Defense Contracts: Expenditures by State. Online: http://www.statemaster.com/graph/mil_def_con_exp-military-defense-contracts-expenditures.

Stein, Peter J., Judith Richman, and Natalie Hannon. 1977. *The Family: Functions, Conflicts, and Symbols*. Reading, MA: Addison-Wesley.

Stein, Rob. 2009. "Poor Memory: Researchers Say Chronic Stress Impairs the Thinking of Children Raised in Poverty." *The Washington Post National Weekly Edition* (April 13-19):37.

Steinberg, Jacques. 2001. "Gains Found for the Poor in Rigorous Preschool." *New York Times* (May 9). Online. Available: http://www.nytimes.com/2001/05/09/national/09SCHO.html.

Steinmetz, Suzanne K. 1978. "Battered Parents." *Society* 15 (July/August):54–55.

Stelter, Brian. 2009. "8 Hours a Day Spent on Screens, Study Finds." *The New York Times* (March 26). Available online: http://www.nytimes.com/2009/03/27/business/media/27adco.html.

Stengel, Richard. 2006. "Tracking America's Journey." *Time* (October 30):8.

Stengel, Richard. 2010. "Our Broken Government." *Time* (March 1):2.

Sternberg, Steve. 2002. "AIDS Will Claim 68 Million More in 20 Years." *USA Today* (July 3):10D.

Sternberg, Steve. 2010. "'I Know' How to Rally Young Blacks." *USA Today* (March 4):7D.

Stiglitz, Joseph, and Linda Bilmes. 2009. "Adding Up the True Costs of Two Wars." *The Capital Times* (July 7). Online: http://www.commondreams.org/print/44291.

Stolberg, Sheryl Gay. 2002. "Minorities Got Inferior Care, Even If Insured, Study Finds." *New York Times* (March 21).

Stone, Christopher. 1999. "Race, Crime, and the Administration of Justice." National Institute of Justice (April): 26–32.

Story, Louise. 2007. "Anywhere the Eye Can See, It's Likely to See An Ad." *New York Times* (January 15). Available online: http://www.nytimes.com/2007/01/15/business/media/15everywhere.html?_r=1.

Stradford, Dan. 2004. "For Every Little Problem, A Pharmaceutical Answer." *Los Angeles Times*.com (April 3). Online: Available: http://www.latimes.com/news/opinion/commentary/la-vo-stradford3a.

Streitland, David. 2006. "Illegal—But Essential." *Los Angeles Times* (October 1). Online: http://www.latimes.com/business/la-fi-immigecon1oct01,0,2804532,print.story?coll-la-ho.

Stretesky, Paul B., Janis E. Johnston, and Jeremy Arney. 2003. "'Environmental Inequity' An Analysis of Large-Scale Hog Operations in 17 States, 1982–1997." *Rural Sociology* 68 (June):231–252.

Sturr, Chris. 2006a. "The Political Economy of the Prison Crisis." *Dollars & Sense,* No. 263 (January/February):8–9.

Sturr, Chris. 2006b. "More Women in Prison." *Dollars & Sense,* No. 267 (September/October):5.

Suarez-Orozco, Marcelo M., and Mariela M. Paez. 2002. "Introduction: The Research Agenda." In Marcelo M. Suarez-Orozco and Mariela M. Paez (Eds.), *Latinos: Remaking America*. Berkeley: University of California Press.

Substance Abuse and Mental Health Services Administration (SAMHSA). 2003. "Results from the 2002 National Survey on Drug Use and Health: National Findings." Office of Applied Studies, NHSDA Series H-22, DH HS Publication No. SMA 03-3836. Rockville, MD.

Substance Abuse and Mental Health Services Administration (SAMHSA). 2008. "National Estimates of Drug-Related Emergency Department Visits, 2006." Office of Applied Studies, Drug Abuse Warning Network. Series D-30, DHHS Publication NO. (SMA) 08-4339. Rockville, MD.

Substance Abuse and Mental Health Services Administration (SAMHSA). 2009. "Results from the 2008 National Survey on Drug Use and Health: National Findings." Office of Applied Studies. NSDUH Series H-36, HHS Publication NO. (SMA) 09-4434. Rockville, MD.

Surowiecki, James. 2008. "What Microloans Miss." *The New Yorker* (March 17):35.

Suskind, Ron. 2006. *The One Percent Solution*. New York: Simon & Schuster.

Sussman, Aaron. 2007. "The Military Commissions Act." *Z Magazine* 20 (January):7–9.

Swain, John, Sally French, and Colin Cameron. 2003. *Controversial Issues in a Disabling Society*. Buckingham, UK: Open University Press.

Sweeney, Megan. 2002. "Remarriage and the Nature of Divorce. *Journal of Family Issues* 23:410–440.

Sweig, Julia E. 2006. "Why They Hate Us." *Los Angeles Times* (August 15). Online: http://www.latimes.com/news/opinion/commentary/la-oe-sweig15aug15,0,1068539.

Switzer, Jacqueline Vaughn. 2003. *Disabled Rights: American Disability Policy and the Fight for Equality*. Baltimore, MD: Georgetown University Press.

Symonds, William C. 2001. "How to Fix America's Schools." *Business Week* (March 19):67–80.

Symonds, William C. 2004. "No Child: Can It Make the Grade?" *Business Week* (March 8):78–80.

Symonds, William C. 2006. "Campus Revolutionary." *Business Week* (February 27):65–70.

Szasz, Thomas S. 1970. *The Manufacture of Madness*. New York: Delta Books.

Takaki, Ronald. 1993. *A Different Mirror: A History of Multicultural America*. Boston: Little, Brown.

Talvi, Silja J. A. 2004. "Prison in the Cards." *In These Times* (August 30):8–9.

Talvi, Silja J. A. 2005. "Breaking Rank: Former Seattle Police Chief Norm Stamper Takes on the Drug War." *In These Times* (November 21): 27–28.

Tanner, Lindsey. 2001. "Cardiac Studies Not Representative." *USA Today* (August 8):7D.

Taub, Diane E., and Patricia L. Fanflick. 2000. "The Inclusion of Disability in Introductory Sociology Textbooks." *Teaching Sociology* 28 (January): 12–23.

Taylor, Howard F. 2009. "Defining Race." In Elizabeth Higginbotham and Margaret L. Andersen (Eds.), *Race and Ethnicity in Society*. Belmont, CA: Wadsworth Cengage Learning.

Taylor, Sunny. 2004. "The Right Not to Work: Power and Disability." *Monthly Review* 55 (March):30–44.

Teller-Elsberg, Jonathan, Nancy Folbre, James Heintz, and the Center for Popular Economics. 2006. *Field Guide to the U.S. Economy,* revised and updated. New York: New Press.

Tepperman, Jonathan. 2004. "Our Oil Policy Isn't Immoral." *Los Angeles Times* (April 29). Online. Available: http://www.latimes.com/news/opinion/commentary/la-oe-tepperman2.

Terkel, Studs. 1975. *Working: People Talk about What They Do All Day and How They Feel about What They Do*. New York: Avon Books.

Texas Health and Human Services Commission. 2003. "Colonias Initiative" (August). Online: http://www.hhsc.state.tax.us/hhst_projects/colonias/colonia_home.html.

Thomas, Karen. 2000. "Stealing, Dealing and Ritalin." *USA Today* (November 27):1D–2D.

Thomas, Karen. 2001. "Back to School for ADHD Drugs." *USA Today* (August 28):1D–2D.

Thomas, Oliver. 2007. "Having Faith in Women." *USA Today* (April 9):13A.

Thomma, Steven. 2009. "Obama Urges Longer School Hours, Extended School Year." McClatchy Newspapers (March 10). Available online: http://www.mcclatchydc.com/2009/03/10/63663/obama-urges-longer-school-hours.html.

Thompson, Larry. 1995. "Search for a Gay Gene." *Time* (June 12):61–62.

Thompson, Mark. 2007. "Broken Down." *Time* (April 16): 28–35.

Thornburgh, Nathan. 2006. "Dropout Nation." *Time* (April 17): 29–40.

Thorne, Barrie. 1993. *Gender Play: Girls and Boys in School*. New Brunswick, NJ: Rutgers University Press.

Thornton, Russell. 1996. "North American Indians and the Demography of Contact." In Silvia Pedraza and Ruben Rumbaut (Eds.), *Origins and Destinies: Immigration, Race, and Ethnicity in America*. Belmont, CA: Wadsworth, pp. 43–50.

Thurow, Lester C. 1995. "Why Their World Might Crumble." *New York Times Magazine* (November 19):78–79.

Tienda, Marta, and Susan Simonelli. 2001. "Hispanic Students Are Missing from Diversity Debates." *Chronicle of Higher Education* (June 1): A16.

Time. 2006. "Numbers." (March 13):17.

Time. 2007a. "Hearts and Minds." (March 26): 16–17.

Time. 2007b. "Mortality." (May 7):22.

Timmer, Doug A., and D. Stanley Eitzen. (forthcoming). *Home Sweet Home: Why Many in American Cities Can't Find It and Keep It*. Boulder, CO: Paradigm Publishers.

Timmer, Doug A., D. Stanley Eitzen, and Kathryn D. Talley. 1994. *Paths to Homelessness: Extreme Poverty and the Urban Housing Crisis*. Boulder, CO: Westview Press.

Tingus, Steven. 2000. "Telethon Broadcasts the Wrong Message." *Denver Post* (September 4):10B.

Tivnan, Edward. 1987. "Homosexuals and the Churches." *New York Times Magazine* (October 11): 84–91.

Tjaden, P., and N. Thoennes. 2000. *Extent, Nature, and Consequences of Intimate Partner Violence*. Washington, DC: National Institute of Justice/ Center for Disease Control and Prevention.

Toland, Bill. 2007. "Pitt Study Says Black Americans Exposed to More Tobacco Advertising." *Pittsburgh Post-Gazette*. (August 21). Available online: http://www.post-gazette.com/pg/07233/810904-114.stm.

Townsend, Johnny. 1996. "Murder Is a Family Value." *Z Magazine* 9 (June):11–12.

Traub, James. 2003. "City Slights." *New York Times Magazine* (May 4):17–18.

Trent, Charles, Richard Caputo, and Chris Baker. 2004. "Poverty as a Social Problem: A Call for Action." In Robert Perrucci, Kathleen Ferrero, JoAnn Miller, and Paula C. Rodriguez Rust (Eds.). *Agenda for Social Justice: 2004*. Knoxville, TN: Society for the Study of Social Problems.

Tritch, Teresa. 2006. "The Rise of the Super-Rich." *New York Times* (July 19). Online: http://select.nytimes.com/2006/07/19/opinion/19talkingpoints.html?pagewanted=print.

Tullock, S. (Ed.). 1993. *The Reader's Digest Oxford Wordfinder*. Oxford: Clarendon Press.

Turk, Austin T. 2004. "Sociology of Terrorism." *Annual Review of Sociology* 30:271–286.

Turse, Nick. 2009. "Younger and Hungrier in America." TomDispatch.com (March 9). Online: http://www.commondreams.org/print/39230.

Tyson, Ann Scott. 2009. "The U.S. Military Easily Meets Its Recruiting Goals." *Washington Post National Weekly Edition* (October 19):35.

Union of the Physically Impaired against Segregation (UPIAS). 1976. *Fundamental Principles of Disability*. London: UPIAS.

United Nations. 2003. Human Development Reports. Online. Available: http://hdr.undp. org.

United Nations. 2004. Online. Available: http://www.un.org/esa/index.html.

Unnithan, N. Prabha. 1994. "The Processing of Homicide Cases with Child Victims: Systemic and Situational Contingencies." *Journal of Criminal Justice* 22(1):41–50.

Urban Institute. 2002. Online. Available: http://www.urban.org.

U.S. Bureau of the Census. 2008a. *Current Population Survey, Annual Social and Economic Supplement*. "The Hispanic Population of the United States" Online: http://www.census.gov/poppulation/www/ssocdemo/hispaanic/cps2008.html.

U.S. Bureau of the Census. 2008b. "Fact Sheet: United States." American Community Survey, 2006-2008. Available online: http://factfinder.census.gov/servlet/ACSSAFFFacts?_submenuld=factsheet_1&_sse=on.

U.S. Bureau of the Census. 2008c. *Statistical Abstract of the United States: 2009,* 128th ed. Washington, DC.: U.S. Government Printing Office.

U.S. Bureau of the Census. 2009a. American Community Survey. "School Enrollment by Level of School for the Population 3 Years and Over." Online: http://factfinder.census.gov.

U.S. Bureau of the Census. 2009b. *America's Families and Living Arrangements: 2008*. Online: http://www.census.goov/population/www/socdemo/hh-fam/cps2008.html.

U.S. Bureau of the Census. 2009c. "2008 American Community Survey." Online: http://factfinder.census.gov.

U.S. Census Bureau, 2010 Census Redistricting Data (Public Law 97-171) Summary File, Table P1.

U.S. Census Bureau. *Statistical Abstract of the United States: 2011*, U.S. Bureau of Labor Statistics, Bulletin 2307 and unpublished data.

U.S. Conference of Mayors. 2009. "Hunger and Homelessness at Record Levels in U.S. Cities." (December 24). Available online: http://www.citymayors.com/features/uscity_poverty.html.

U.S. Department of Agriculture. 2006a. "Rural America at a Glance: 2006 Edition." *Economic Information Bulletin*, No. 18 (August).

U.S. Department of Agriculture. 2006b. "Rural Employment at a Glance." *Economic Information Bulletin*, No. 21 (December).

U.S. Department of Agriculture. 2009. "State Fact Sheets: United States." *Economic Research Service* (December 9).

U.S. Department of Defense. 2010. *Quadrennial Defense Review Report* (February). Washington, DC.

U.S. Department of Education, National Center for Education Statistics. 2009. *Digest of Education Statistics, 2008*. (NCES 2009-020).

U.S. Department of Education. 2006. "No Child Left Behind Act Is Working." (December). Online: Available: http:// www.ed.gov/nclb/overview/importance/nclbworking.html.

U.S. Department of Education, National Center for Education Statistics. 2006. *Digest of Education Statistics*. (NCES 2006-030). Online: Available: http://nces.ed.gov.

U.S. Department of Health and Human Services. 2004. "Health Gap." Available online: http://www.healthgap.omhrc.gov/cancer.htm. Retrieved on July 12, 2004.

U.S. Department of Health and Human Services. 2008. "What is Child Abuse and Neglect?" Child Welfare Information Gateway. Online: http://www.childwelfare.gov/pubs/factsheets/whatiscan.pdf.

U.S. Department of Health and Human Services. 2009a. *Child Maltreatment 2007*. Washington, DC: U.S. Government Printing Office.

U.S. Department of Health and Human Services. 2009b. "HIV/AIDS Data Statistics. Online: http://minorityhealth.hhs.gov/templates/browse.aspx?lvll=3&lvlio.

U.S. Department of Justice. 2000. "State Court Sentencing of Convicted Felons." *Bureau of Justice Statistics Bulletin* (March).

U.S. Department of Justice, Federal Bureau of Investigation. 2009. "2008: Crime in the United States." *Uniform Crime Reporting Program*. Available online: http://www.fbi.gov/ucr/cius 2008/index.html.

U.S. Department of Labor. 1965. *The Negro Family: The Case for National Action*. Washington, DC: U.S. Government Printing Office.

U.S. Department of Labor. 2008. "20 Leading Occupations of Employed Women." Online: http://www.dol.gov/wb/factsheets/20lead 2008.htm.

U.S. Department of Labor. 2009. "Employment Situation: February 2009." Online: http://www.bls.gov/news.release/archives/empsit_03062009.pdf.

U.S. Department of Labor. 2010. "Metropolitan Area Employment and Unemployment—November 2009." *Bureau of Labor Statistics Economic News Release* (January 5).

U.S. Equal Employment Opportunity Commission. 2009. "Notice Concerning the Americans with Disabilities Act Amendments Act of 2008." Online: http://www.eeoc.gov/laws/statutes/adaa-notice.cfm.

USA Today. 2002a. "Much Toxic Computer Waste Lands in Third World." (February 25). Online: http://www.usatoday.com/tech/news/2002/02/25/computer-waste.htm.

USA Today. 2002b. "Rigged Voting Districts Rob Public of Choice" (August 28):13A.

USA Today. 2005. "FBI May Be Checking On You, But You Have No Way of Knowing" (November 9):14A.

USA Today. 2006. "Heart Care is Better in High-Income Areas" (September 28):8D.

USA Today. 2007a. "Everyone Looks Bad in Libby Trial" (March 9):13A.

USA Today. 2007b. "Secrecy Rises: Washington Gives Public Less and Less" (March 12):8A.

USA Today. 2008. "Latino Numbers" (January 28):7A.

USA Today. 2009. "People Receiving Food Stamps" (October 20):1A.

Usdansky, Margaret L. 1992. "Middle Class 'Pulling Apart' to Rich, Poor." *USA Today* (February 20):A1.

Valian, Virginia. 1998. "Running in Place." *Sciences* 38 (January/February):18–23.

Van Biema. David. 2004. "Rising above the Stained-Glass Ceiling." *Time* (June 28):59–61.

van Gelder, Sarah, and Doug Pibel. 2006. "If America's So Great, Where's Our Health Care?" *AlterNet* (September 23). Online: http://www.alternet.org/module/printversion/42011.

Vasey, S. 1992. "A Response to Liz Crow." *Coalition* (September): 42–44.

Vecoli, Rudolph J. 1964. "Contadini in Chicago: A Critique of the Uprooted." *Journal of American History* 51:405–417.

Vestal, Christine. 2009. "States Coping with Rising Homelessness." Stateline.org (March 18). Online: http://www.stateline.org/live/details/story?ContentId=385137.

Villano, Matt. 2009. "Reading, Writing, and Recession." *Time* (February 23):54–55.

Visher, Emily B., John S. Visher, and Kay Pasley. 2003. "Remarriage, Families, and Stepparenting." In

Froma Walsh (Ed.), *Normal Family Processes: Growing Diversity and Complexity*, 3rd ed. New York: Guilford Press, pp. 153–175.

Vogel, Jennifer. 1994. "A Poor Excuse: If You Don't Have Money, It's Your Own Damn Fault." *Utne Reader* 62 (March/April):30–32.

Von Drehle, David. 2007. "The Boys Are All Right." *Time* (August 6):40–42.

Wage Gap. 2003. Available online: http://www.infoplease.com/ipa10/7/6/1/7/a076317.phtml.

Wagner, Peter and Susan Edwards. 2007. "New Orleans by the Numbers," In D. Stanley Eitzen and Janis Johnston (Eds.) *Inequality: Social Class and Its Consequences*. Boulder, CO: Paradigm Publishers.

Walby, Sylvia. 2000. "Gender, Globalization, and Democracy." *Gender and Development* 8 (March): 20–28.

Wali, Alakka. 1992. "Multiculturalism: An Anthropological Perspective." *Report from the Institute for Philosophy and Public Policy*. University of Maryland, 23 (Spring/Summer):6–8.

Wallerstein, Judith S. 2003. "Children of Divorce: A Society in Search of Policy." In Mary Ann Mason, Arlene Skolnick, and Stephen D. Sugarman (Eds.), *All Our Families*, 2nd ed. New York: Oxford University Press, pp. 66–95.

Wallis, Claudia and Sonja Steptoe. 2006. "How to Bring Our Schools out of the 20th Century." *Time* (December 18):50–56.

Walter, Norbert. 2001. "Gobbling Energy and Wasting It, Too." *New York Times* (June 13). Online. Available: http://www.nytimes.com/2001/06/13/opinion/13WALT.html.

Walsh, Bryan. 2009. "It Will Pay to Save the Planet." *Time* (May 25):47.

Wardrip, Keith E. 2009. "Out of Reach 2009." *National Low Income Housing Coalition* (April).

Warren, Patricia, Donald Tomosakovic-Devey, William Smith, Matthew Zingraff, and Marcinda Mason. 2006. "Driving While Black: Bias Processes and Racial Disparity in Police Stops." *Criminology* 44, no. 3:709–738.

Washington, Harriet A. 2006. *Medical Apartheid: The Dark History of Medical Experimentation on Black Americans from Colonial Times to the Present.* New York: Doubleday.

Washington Post. 2004. "An Insulting Waste." (April 5): A24.

Washington Post. 2007a. "Lessons of War." *Washington Post National Weekly Edition* (March 26):24.

Washington Post. 2007b. "U.S. Infant Mortality Rate Twice as High for Blacks." (May 2). Available online: http://www.washingtonpost. com/wp-dyn/content/article/2007/05/02/AR2007050201436.html.

Washington Technology. 2010. "2009 Top 100." Online: http://washingtontechnology.com/toplists/top-100-lists/2009.aspx.

Washington Times. 2003. "Bush Signs Paper Allowing Nuclear Response." (January 31). Online. Available: http://www.washtimes.com/archive/20030131111255020010.html.

Wasow, Bernard. 2004. "Rags to Riches? The American Dream Is Less Common in the United States than Elsewhere." *The Century Foundation*. Online. Available: http://www.tcf.org.

Weatherall, Ann. 2002. *Gender, Language, and Discourse*. New York: Routledge.

Weber, Lynn. 2010. *Understanding Race, Class, Gender, and Sexuality*, 2nd ed. New York: Oxford University Press.

Webster's New World Dictionary of American English, 3rd ed. 1991. Victoria Neufeldt and David B. Guralnik (Eds.). Cleveland, NY: Simon & Schuster.

Wedekind, Jennifer. 2009. "Dying for Work." *Multinational Monitor* 30 (May/June):7–8.

Weisberg, Jacob. 1996. *In Defense of Government*. New York: Scribner.

Weise, Elizabeth. 2005. "As Suburbs Grow, So Do Environmental Fears." *USA Today* (December 28):9D.

Weiss, Lawrence D. 1997. *Private Medicine and Public Health: Profit, Politics, and Prejudice in the American Health Care Enterprise*. Boulder, CO: Westview Press.

Weissbourd, Richard. 1994. "Divided Families, Whole Children." *American Prospect* 18 (Summer):66–72.

Weissman, Robert. 2009. "$5 Billion in Lobbying for 12 Corrupt Deals Caused the Multi-Trillion Dollar Financial Meltdown." *Multinational Monitor* (March 9). Online: http://www.alternet.org/story/130683.

Weitz, Rose. 2004. *The Sociology of Health, Illness, and Health Care*, 3rd ed. Belmont, CA: Wadsworth.

Weitzman, Lenore J. 1985. *The Divorce Revolution: The Unexpected Social and Economic Consequences for Women and Children in America*. New York: Free Press.

Weitzman, Lenore J., Deborah Eifler, Elizabeth Hokada, and Catherine Ross. 1972. "Sex-Role Socialization in Picture Books for Preschool Children." *American Journal of Sociology* 77 (May):1125–1150.

Welfare Rights Organizing Coalition. 2000. Online. Available: http://www.wroc.org.

Wellman, David T. 1977. *Portraits of White Racism*, 2nd ed. Cambridge: Cambridge University Press.

Wellstone, Paul. 1998a. "The People's Trust Fund." *Nation* (July 27/August 3):4–5.

Wellstone, Paul. 1998b. "A Time for Change." *On the Road with Paul Wellstone. Newsletter* (Summer):1–2.

Wenzl, Roy. 2007. "Are We Losing Our Boys?" The *Wichita Eagle* (February 25):1A.

Werner, Erica. 2009. "AARP: Prescription Drug Prices Up." *Health News*. Online: http://www.myfoxla.com/dpp/health/dpg-AARP-Prescription-Drug-Prices-Up.

West, Candace, and Don Zimmerman. 1987. "Doing Gender." *Gender & Society* 1:125–151.

Wharton, Tony. 1998. "Expect Hurricanes Because of Gays, Pat Robertson Says." *Denver Post* (June 10):14A.

Wheatcroft, Geoffrey. 2007. "Who Made Her Queen." *Washington Post National Weekly Edition* (October 15):27.

Wheeler, David L. 1992. "Studies Tying Homosexuality to Genes Draw Criticism from Researchers." *Chronicle of Higher Education* (February 5):A1–A2, A9.

Wildmon, Donald E. 2007. "Ford Helps Sponsor Explicit, Sickening Homosexual Scene." American Family Association. (January 23). Online: Available: http://www.afa.net/aa012307.asp.

Will, George. 2007. "Golly, What Did Jon Do?" *Newsweek* (January 29):72.

Williams, Christine. 1992. "The Class Escalator: Hidden Advantages for Men in the 'Female' Professions." *Social Problems* 39 (August):253–267.

Williams, Christine. 1995. *Still a Man's World: Men Who Do Women's Work*. Berkeley: University of California Press.

Williams, David R. 1990. "Socioeconomic Differentials in Health: A Review and Redirection." *Social Psychology Quarterly* 53 (June):81–99.

Williams, David R., and Pamela Braboy Jackson. 2005. "Social Sources of Racial Disparities in Health." *Health Affairs* 24, No. 2:325–334.

Williams, David R., and James Lardner. 2005. "Cold Truths about Class, Race, and Health." In James Lardner and David A. Smith (Eds.), *Inequality Matters*. New York: Free Press, pp. 102–114.

Williams, Juan. 2007. "The Legacy of Little Rock." *Time* (October 1):61.

Williamson, Theresa. 2000. "Minorities Pay Higher Interest, Group Says." *Chicago Sun-Times* (November 1):71, 74.

Willis, Ellen. 1998. "We Need a Radical Left." *Nation* (June 29):18–21.

Wills, Garry. 1995. "The New Revolutionaries." *New York Review* (August 10):50–55.

Wilson, E. O. 2000. "Vanishing before Our Eyes." *Time* (April/May):29–34.

Wilson, William J. 1987. *The Truly Disadvantaged: The Inner City, the Underclass, and Public Policy*. Chicago. University of Chicago Press.

Wilson, William J. 1996. *When Work Disappears: The World of the New Urban Poor*. New York: Knopf.

Winant, Howard. 1994. *Racial Conditions: Politics, Theory, Comparisons*. Minneapolis, MN: University of Minnesota Press.

Winant, Howard. 2009. "Just Do It: Notes on Politics and Race at the Dawn of the Obama Presidency." *DuBois Review* 6 (1):49–70.

Witt, Howard. 2007. "Report: Schools Still Unequal in Discipline." *The Wichita Eagle* (September 25):5A.

Witt, Susan. 1997. "Parental Influence on Children's Socialization to Gender Roles." *Adolescence* 32 (126): 253–259.

Woellert, Lorraine, and Dawn Kopecke. 2006. "The Snooping Goes Beyond Phone Calls." *Business Week* (May 29):38.

Wolf, Rosalie S. 2000. "The Nature and Scope of Elder Abuse." *Generations* 24 (Summer):6–12.

Wolfe, Alan. 1989. *Whose Keeper? Social Science and Moral Obligation*. Berkeley: University of California Press.

Worldwatch Institute. n.d. "Good Stuff?—Computers." Online: http://www.worldwatch.org/node/1487.

Wright, D. Brad. 2009. "The Price of Prescription Drugs Around the World." *Huffington Post* (March 2). Online: http://www.huffingtonpost.com/d-brad-wright/the-price-of-prescription-drugs.

Yardley, Jonathan. 2002. "A Disaster from More than Just Heat." *Washington Post National Weekly Edition* (August 19–25):32.

Yen, Hope. 2009. "Minority Kids in Majority by 2023." Associated Press (March 5).

Youssef, Nancy A. 2010. "Pentagon Redefines Military's Mission." *The Wichita Eagle* (February 2):1A, 5A.

Z, Mickey. 2006. "Read This Before You Vote." *Z Magazine* 19 (November):6–7.

Zaslow, Martha J., and Kathryn Tout. 2002. "Child-Care Quality Matters." *American Prospect* (April 8), p. 49.

Zeese, Kevin. 2006. "The Futility of Drug Prohibition." *AlterNet* (December 13). Online: Available: http://www.alternet.org/story/45010.

Zeitlin, Maurice, Kenneth G. Lutterman, and James W. Russell. 1977. "Death in Vietnam: Class, Poverty, and the Risks of War." In Maurice Zeitlin (Ed.), *American Society, Inc.*, 2nd ed. Chicago: Rand McNally, pp. 143–155.

Zelizer, Gerald L. 2004. "Time to Break the Stained Glass Ceiling." *USA Today* (September 16):1A.

Zepezauer, Mark, and Arthur Naiman. 1996. *Take the Rich Off Welfare*. Tucson, AZ: Odonian Press.

Zepezauer, Mark. 2004. *Take the Rich off Welfare*, new, expanded edition. Cambridge, MA: South End Press.

Zeskind, Leonard. 2005. "The New Nativism." *American Prospect* 16 (November):A15–A18.

Zhou, Min. 1997. "Growing Up American: The Challenge Confronting Immigrant Children and Children of Immigrants." *Annual Review of Sociology* 23:63–95.

Zimmerman, Jonathan. 2008. "Poverty, Not Sex Ed, Key Factor in Teen Pregnancy." SFGate.com (September 4). Available online: http://articles.sfgate.com/2008-09-04.

Zinn, Howard. 2005. "Against Discouragement." Commencement Address, Spelman College (May 15).

Zuckerman, Mortimer B. 2000. "A Bit of Straight Talk." *U.S. News & World Report* (October 2):76.

Zuckerman, Mortimer. 2005a. "Classroom Revolution." *U.S. News and World Report* (October 10):68.

Zuckerman, Mortimer B. 2005b. "Our Energy Conundrum." *U.S. News & World Report* (April 25):72.

Zuckerman, Mortimer B. 2006a. "Getting Serious about Oil." *U.S. News & World Report* (August 7):68.

Zuckerman, Mortimer B. 2006b. "A Little Sanity, Please." *U.S. News & World Report* (April 17):74.

Zuckerman, Mortimer B. 2008. "The Haunted Housing Market." *U.S. News & World Report* (February 25):64.

Index

C

D

H

M

N

Q

R

S

V

W

Y

Z

Credits

Chapter 1

page 2 and page v: UPI Photo/Landov
page 4: Reuters/Jeff Topping/Landov
page 14: © Jim Richardson/Corbis

Chapter 2

page 30 and page v: Reuters/Jim Young/Landov
page 35: AP Images/Peter Cosgrove
page 47: UPI/Gary Fabiano/Pool/Landov

Chapter 3

page 60 and page vi: © Firoz Ahmed/Drik/Majority World/The Image Works
page 65: John Javellana/Reuters/Corbis
page 73: Reuters/Andrew Biraj/Landov

Chapter 4

page 82 and page vi: Justin Stumberg/U.S. Navy/U.S. Department of Defense/Sipa Press (Released)/1005071839 via Newscom
page 87: photo by Spencer Tirey/ZUMA Press, © copyright 2001 by Spencer Tirey, via Newscom
page 93: © Dan Lamont/Corbis
page 95: © Glow Images/Alamy
page 97: © Chad Ehlers/Alamy
page 106: Newscom

Chapter 5

page 114 and page vi: Xinhua/Landov
page 125: Dave Gatley/MAI/Landov
page 130: Owen Franken/Corbis

Chapter 6

page 145 and page vii: © Larry Mulvehill/Corbis
page 148: Ethan Miller/Getty Images
page 151: The Plain Dealer/Landov

Chapter 7

page 176 and page vii: Axiom/Newscom
page 184: UPI Photo/Landov
page 196: Richard B. Levine/Newscom
page 202: © Rick Friedman/Corbis

Chapter 8

page 208 and page vii: Yuri Gripsas/AFP/Getty Images
page 216: © Melanie Stetson Freeman/The Christian Science Monitor/Getty Images
page 231: © Steve Rubin/The Image Works
page 233: © Orjan F. Ellingvag/Corbis

Chapter 9

page 239 and page viii: © Steve Skjold/PhotoEdit
page 250: © Mary Kate Denny/PhotoEdit
page 258: AP Images/Dennis Cook
page 270: UPI Photo/Landov

Chapter 10

page 273 and page viii: ©Marilyn Humphries/The Image Works
page 276: (top), Reuters/Win McNamee/Landov; (bottom), AP Images//Matt Sayles
page 284 and page 292: © Marilyn Humphries/The Image Works
page 297: The Kobal Collection/ABC-TV/Bob D'Amico

Chapter 11

page 300 and page ix: WENN.com via Newscom
page 302: Newscom
page 318: Karen Bleier/AFP/Getty Images via Newscom

Chapter 12

page 326 and page ix: AP Images/Stephen Morton
page 331: Mark Allen Johnson/2005 via Newscom
page 333: © Bob Daemmrich/PhotoEdit
page 338: Reuters/Shannon Stapleton/Landov
page 348: © Vernon Bryant/Dallas Morning News/Corbis
page 354: © Jana Birchum/The Image Works

Chapter 13

page 360 and page ix: David McNew/Getty Images
page 370: Reuters/HO/Landov

Chapter 14

page 392 and page x: Reuters/Crack Palinggi/Landov
page 401: Newscom
page 403: © Jim West/The Image Works

Chapter 15

page 426 and page x: Lambert/Getty Images
page 429: © Halfdark/fstop/Corbis
page 437 and page 440: © Lawrence Migdale/PIX

Chapter 16

page 458 and page x: Ted Thai/Time Life Pictures/Getty Images
page 459: © Michael Ventura/PhotoEdit
page 464: Newscom
page 474: © Susan Van Etten/PhotoEdit
page 481: AP Images/Garden City Telegram, Brad Nading

Chapter 17

page 489 and page xi: Krista Kennell/Sipa Press./bluecrossprotest.032/0910152322 via Newscom
page 500: AFP Photo/J. F. Moreno via Newscom
page 514: Robyn Beck/AFP/Getty Images via Newscom

Chapter 18

page 519 and page xi: Joel Saget/AFP/Getty Images via Newscom
page 529: © Jim West/The Image Works
page 542: Brooks Kraft/Corbis

Chapter 19

page 554 and page xii: UPI Photo/Kevin Dietsch via Newscom
page 560: © Ken Cedeno/Corbis
page 570: AP Images

The Demographics of U.S. Poverty

People and Families in Poverty by Selected Characteristics: 2009

Characteristics	*Below Poverty Percent*
People	
Total	14.3
Family Status	
In families	10.5
Householder	10.3
Related children under 18	18.5
Related children under 6	21.3
In unrelated sub families	46.0
Reference person	45.7
Children under 18	47.8
Unrelated individuals	20.8
Male	18.9
Female	22.6
Race	
White	11.7
White, non-Hispanic	10.0
Black	25.8
Asian and Pacific Islander	11.4
Hispanic origin	23.5
Age	
Under 18 years	19.6
18–64 years	13.1
65 years and older	6.1

Characteristics	*Below Poverty Percent*
Nativity	
Native	12.6
Foreign born	17.8
Naturalized citizen	10.2
Not a citizen	23.3
Region	
Northeast	11.6
Midwest	12.4
South	14.3
West	13.5
Families	
Total	10.3
Type of Family	
Married couple	12.7
Female household, no husband present	42.5
Male household, no wife present	21.5

Source: Carmen DeNavas-Walt, Bernadette D. Proctor, and Jessica C. Smith (2009). "Income, Poverty, and Health Insurance Coverage in the U.S.: 2009" *U.S. Census Bureau, Current Population Reports,* P.60–236, Washington, D.C., U.S. Government Printing Office, P. 14. From American Community Survey 2009 Reports.

Demographics of the Poverty Population, 1980, 2000, 2009

		Percentage of the Poor		
		1980	*2000*	*2009*
	All People	13.0%	11.3%	13.2%
Race/Ethnicity	White	9.1	7.4	8.6
	African American	32.5	22.5	25.8
	Latino	25.7	21.5	23.5
	Asian/Pacific Islander	17.2	9.9	11.4
Nativity	Native	*	10.8	13.8
	Foreign born	*	15.4	17.3
Family Structure	In all families	11.5	9.6	11.5
	In families, female householder, no spouse present	36.7	28.5	31.4
Age	Children under 18	18.3	16.2	20.0
	Adults age 65 and older	15.7	9.9	9.5
Residence	Central cities	17.2	16.3	18.7
	Suburbs	8.2	7.8	11.0
	Outside metropolitan areas	15.4	13.4	16.6

Sources: U.S. Bureau of the Census. 2009. Historical Poverty Tables. Current Population Survey, Annual Social and Economic Supplements. From American Community Survey 2009 Reports. From Census 2010 table POV41.